C0-AVK-801

Nineteenth-Century Literature Criticism

Guide to Thomson Gale Literary Criticism Series

For criticism on	Consult these Thomson Gale series
Authors now living or who died after December 31, 1999	*CONTEMPORARY LITERARY CRITICISM (CLC)*
Authors who died between 1900 and 1999	*TWENTIETH-CENTURY LITERARY CRITICISM (TCLC)*
Authors who died between 1800 and 1899	*NINETEENTH-CENTURY LITERATURE CRITICISM (NCLC)*
Authors who died between 1400 and 1799	*LITERATURE CRITICISM FROM 1400 TO 1800 (LC)* *SHAKESPEAREAN CRITICISM (SC)*
Authors who died before 1400	*CLASSICAL AND MEDIEVAL LITERATURE CRITICISM (CMLC)*
Authors of books for children and young adults	*CHILDREN'S LITERATURE REVIEW (CLR)*
Dramatists	*DRAMA CRITICISM (DC)*
Poets	*POETRY CRITICISM (PC)*
Short story writers	*SHORT STORY CRITICISM (SSC)*
Literary topics and movements	*HARLEM RENAISSANCE: A GALE CRITICAL COMPANION (HR)* *THE BEAT GENERATION: A GALE CRITICAL COMPANION (BG)* *FEMINISM IN LITERATURE: A GALE CRITICAL COMPANION (FL)* *GOTHIC LITERATURE: A GALE CRITICAL COMPANION (GL)*
Asian American writers of the last two hundred years	*ASIAN AMERICAN LITERATURE (AAL)*
Black writers of the past two hundred years	*BLACK LITERATURE CRITICISM (BLC)* *BLACK LITERATURE CRITICISM SUPPLEMENT (BLCS)*
Hispanic writers of the late nineteenth and twentieth centuries	*HISPANIC LITERATURE CRITICISM (HLC)* *HISPANIC LITERATURE CRITICISM SUPPLEMENT (HLCS)*
Native North American writers and orators of the eighteenth, nineteenth, and twentieth centuries	*NATIVE NORTH AMERICAN LITERATURE (NNAL)*
Major authors from the Renaissance to the present	*WORLD LITERATURE CRITICISM, 1500 TO THE PRESENT (WLC)* *WORLD LITERATURE CRITICISM SUPPLEMENT (WLCS)*

ISSN 0732-1864

Volume 186

Nineteenth-Century Literature Criticism

Criticism of the
Works of Novelists, Philosophers, and Other
Creative Writers Who Died between 1800
and 1899, from the First Published Critical
Appraisals to Current Evaluations

Kathy D. Darrow
Russel Whitaker
Project Editors

WITHDRAWN
FAIRFIELD UNIVERSITY
LIBRARY

THOMSON
_____*_____ ™
GALE

Detroit • New York • San Francisco • New Haven, Conn. • Waterville, Maine • London

Nineteenth-Century Literature Criticism, Vol. 186

Project Editors
Kathy Darrow and Russel Whitaker

Editorial
Dana Barnes, Thomas Burns, Elizabeth Cranston, Kristen Dorsch, Mandi Rose Hall, Jeffrey W. Hunter, Jelena O. Krstović, Michelle Lee, Thomas J. Schoenberg, Noah Schusterbauer, Catherine Shubert, Lawrence J. Trudeau

Data Capture
Frances Monroe, Gwen Tucker

Indexing Services
Factiva, Inc.

Rights and Acquisitions
Margaret Abendroth, Jackie Jones, Timothy Sisler

Composition and Electronic Capture
Amy Darga

Manufacturing
Cynde Bishop

Associate Product Manager
Marc Cormier

© 2008 Thomson Gale, a part of The Thomson Corporation. Thomson and Star Logo are trademarks and Gale is a registered trademark used herein under license.

For more information, contact
Thomson Gale
27500 Drake Rd.
Farmington Hills, MI 48331-3535
Or you can visit our internet site at
http://www.gale.com

ALL RIGHTS RESERVED
No part of this work covered by the copyright herein may be reproduced or used in any form or by any means—graphic, electronic, or mechanical, including photocopying, recording, taping, Web distribution, or information storage retrieval systems—without the written permission of the publisher.

This publication is a creative work fully protected by all applicable copyright laws, as well as by misappropriation, trade secret, unfair competition, and other applicable laws. The authors and editors of this work have added value to the underlying factual material herein through one or more of the following: unique and original selection, coordination, expression, arrangement, and classification of the information.

For permission to use material from the product, submit your request via the Web at http://www.gale-edit.com/permissions, or you may download our Permissions Request form and submit your request by fax or mail to:

Permissions Department
Thomson Gale
27500 Drake Rd.
Farmington Hills, MI 48331-3535
Permissions Hotline:
248-699-8006 or 800-877-4253, ext. 8006
Fax 248-699-8074 or 800-762-4058

Since this page cannot legibly accommodate all copyright notices, the acknowledgments constitute an extension of the copyright notice.

While every effort has been made to secure permission to reprint material and to ensure the reliability of the information presented in this publication, Thomson Gale neither guarantees the accuracy of the data contained herein nor assumes any responsibility for errors, omissions or discrepancies. Thomson Gale accepts no payment for listing; and inclusion in the publication of any organization, agency, institution, publication, service, or individual does not imply endorsement of the editors or publisher. Errors brought to the attention of the publisher and verified to the satisfaction of the publisher will be corrected in future editions.

LIBRARY OF CONGRESS CATALOG CARD NUMBER 84-643008

ISBN-13: 978-0-7876-9857-7
ISBN-10: 0-7876-9857-1
ISSN 0732-1864

Printed in the United States of America
10 9 8 7 6 5 4 3 2 1

Contents

Preface vii

Acknowledgments xi

Literary Criticism Series Advisory Board xiii

Preface

Since its inception in 1981, *Nineteenth-Century Literature Criticism* (*NCLC*) has been a valuable resource for students and librarians seeking critical commentary on writers of this transitional period in world history. Designated an "Outstanding Reference Source" by the American Library Association with the publication of is first volume, *NCLC* has since been purchased by over 6,000 school, public, and university libraries. The series has covered more than 500 authors representing 38 nationalities and over 28,000 titles. No other reference source has surveyed the critical reaction to nineteenth-century authors and literature as thoroughly as *NCLC*.

Scope of the Series

NCLC is designed to introduce students and advanced readers to the authors of the nineteenth century and to the most significant interpretations of these authors' works. The great poets, novelists, short story writers, playwrights, and philosophers of this period are frequently studied in high school and college literature courses. By organizing and reprinting commentary written on these authors, *NCLC* helps students develop valuable insight into literary history, promotes a better understanding of the texts, and sparks ideas for papers and assignments. Each entry in *NCLC* presents a comprehensive survey of an author's career or an individual work of literature and provides the user with a multiplicity of interpretations and assessments. Such variety allows students to pursue their own interests; furthermore, it fosters an awareness that literature is dynamic and responsive to many different opinions.

Every fourth volume of *NCLC* is devoted to literary topics that cannot be covered under the author approach used in the rest of the series. Such topics include literary movements, prominent themes in nineteenth-century literature, literary reaction to political and historical events, significant eras in literary history, prominent literary anniversaries, and the literatures of cultures that are often overlooked by English-speaking readers.

NCLC continues the survey of criticism of world literature begun by Thomson Gale's *Contemporary Literary Criticism* (*CLC*) and *Twentieth-Century Literary Criticism* (*TCLC*).

Organization of the Book

An *NCLC* entry consists of the following elements:

- The **Author Heading** cites the name under which the author most commonly wrote, followed by birth and death dates. Also located here are any name variations under which an author wrote, including transliterated forms for authors whose native languages use nonroman alphabets. If the author wrote consistently under a pseudonym, the pseudonym will be listed in the author heading and the author's actual name given in parenthesis on the first line of the biographical and critical information. Uncertain birth or death dates are indicated by question marks. Single-work entries are preceded by a heading that consists of the most common form of the title in English translation (if applicable) and the original date of composition.

- The **Introduction** contains background information that introduces the reader to the author, work, or topic that is the subject of the entry.

- The list of **Principal Works** is ordered chronologically by date of first publication and lists the most important works by the author. The genre and publication date of each work is given. In the case of foreign authors whose works have been translated into English, the list will focus primarily on twentieth-century translations, selecting those works most commonly considered the best by critics. Unless otherwise indicated, dramas are dated by first performance, not first publication. Lists of **Representative Works** by different authors appear with topic entries.

- Reprinted **Criticism** is arranged chronologically in each entry to provide a useful perspective on changes in critical evaluation over time. The critic's name and the date of composition or publication of the critical work are given at the beginning of each piece of criticism. Unsigned criticism is preceded by the title of the source in which it appeared. All titles by the author featured in the text are printed in boldface type. Footnotes are reprinted at the end of each essay or excerpt. In the case of excerpted criticism, only those footnotes that pertain to the excerpted texts are included. Criticism in topic entries is arranged chronologically under a variety of subheadings to facilitate the study of different aspects of the topic.

- A complete **Bibliographical Citation** of the original essay or book precedes each piece of criticism.

- Critical essays are prefaced by brief **Annotations** explicating each piece.

- An annotated bibliography of **Further Reading** appears at the end of each entry and suggests resources for additional study. In some cases, significant essays for which the editors could not obtain reprint rights are included here. Boxed material following the further reading list provides references to other biographical and critical sources on the author in series published by Thomson Gale.

Indexes

Each volume of *NCLC* contains a **Cumulative Author Index** listing all authors who have appeared in a wide variety of reference sources published by Thomson Gale, including *NCLC*. A complete list of these sources is found facing the first page of the Author Index. The index also includes birth and death dates and cross references between pseudonyms and actual names.

A **Cumulative Nationality Index** lists all authors featured in *NCLC* by nationality, followed by the number of the *NCLC* volume in which their entry appears.

A **Cumulative Topic Index** lists the literary themes and topics treated in the series as well as in *Classical and Medieval Literature Criticism, Literature Criticism from 1400 to 1800, Twentieth-Century Literary Criticism,* and the *Contemporary Literary Criticism* Yearbook, which was discontinued in 1998.

An alphabetical **Title Index** accompanies each volume of *NCLC*, with the exception of the Topics volumes. Listings of titles by authors covered in the given volume are followed by the author's name and the corresponding page numbers where the titles are discussed. English translations of foreign titles and variations of titles are cross-referenced to the title under which a work was originally published. Titles of novels, dramas, nonfiction books, and poetry, short story, or essay collections are printed in italics, while individual poems, short stories, and essays are printed in roman type within quotation marks.

In response to numerous suggestions from librarians, Thomson Gale also produces an annual paperbound edition of the *NCLC* cumulative title index. This annual cumulation, which alphabetically lists all titles reviewed in the series, is available to all customers. Additional copies of this index are available upon request. Librarians and patrons will welcome this separate index; it saves shelf space, is easy to use, and is recyclable upon receipt of the next edition.

Citing *Nineteenth-Century Literature Criticism*

When citing criticism reprinted in the Literary Criticism Series, students should provide complete bibliographic information so that the cited essay can be located in the original print or electronic source. Students who quote directly from reprinted criticism may use any accepted bibliographic format, such as University of Chicago Press style or Modern Language Association style.

The examples below follow recommendations for preparing a bibliography set forth in *The Chicago Manual of Style,* 14th ed. (Chicago: The University of Chicago Press, 1993); the first example pertains to material drawn from periodicals, the second to material reprinted from books:

Franklin, J. Jeffrey. "The Victorian Discourse of Gambling: Speculations on *Middlemarch* and *The Duke's Children*." *ELH* 61, no. 4 (winter 1994): 899-921. Reprinted in *Nineteenth-Century Literature Criticism*. Vol. 168, edited by Jessica Bomarito and Russel Whitaker, 39-51. Detroit: Thomson Gale, 2006.

Frank, Joseph. "*The Gambler*: A Study in Ethnopsychology." In *Freedom and Responsibility in Russian Literature: Essays in Honor of Robert Louis Jackson,* edited by Elizabeth Cheresh Allen and Gary Saul Morson, 69-85. Evanston, Ill.: Northwestern University Press, 1995. Reprinted in *Nineteenth-Century Literature Criticism*. Vol. 168, edited by Jessica Bomarito and Russel Whitaker, 75-84. Detroit: Thomson Gale, 2006.

The examples below follow recommendations for preparing a works cited list set forth in the *MLA Handbook for Writers of Research Papers,* 6th ed. (New York: The Modern Language Association of America, 2003); the first example pertains to material drawn from periodicals, the second to material reprinted from books:

Franklin, J. Jeffrey. "The Victorian Discourse of Gambling: Speculations on *Middlemarch* and *The Duke's Children*." *ELH* 61.4 (Winter 1994): 899-921. Reprinted in *Nineteenth-Century Literature Criticism*. Eds. Jessica Bomarito and Russel Whitaker. Vol. 168. Detroit: Thomson Gale, 2006. 39-51.

Frank, Joseph. "*The Gambler*: A Study in Ethnopsychology." *Freedom and Responsibility in Russian Literature: Essays in Honor of Robert Louis Jackson.* Eds. Elizabeth Cheresh Allen and Gary Saul Morson. Evanston, Ill.: Northwestern University Press, 1995. 69-85. Reprinted in *Nineteenth-Century Literature Criticism*. Eds. Jessica Bomarito and Russel Whitaker. Vol. 168. Detroit: Thomson Gale, 2006. 75-84.

Suggestions are Welcome

Readers who wish to suggest new features, topics, or authors to appear in future volumes, or who have other suggestions or comments are cordially invited to call, write, or fax the Associate Product Manager:

Associate Product Manager, Literary Criticism Series
Thomson Gale
27500 Drake Road
Farmington Hills, MI 48331-3535
1-800-347-4253 (GALE)
Fax: 248-699-8054

Acknowledgments

The editors wish to thank the copyright holders of the criticism included in this volume and the permissions managers of many book and magazine publishing companies for assisting us in securing reproduction rights. Following is a list of the copyright holders who have granted us permission to reproduce material in this volume of *NCLC*. Every effort has been made to trace copyright, but if omissions have been made, please let us know.

COPYRIGHTED MATERIAL IN *NCLC*, VOLUME 186, WAS REPRODUCED FROM THE FOLLOWING PERIODICALS:

Bucknell Review, v. 28, 1983. Copyright © 1983 by Rosemont Publishing & Printing Corp. All rights reserved. Reproduced by permission.—*Civil War History,* v. 41, June, 1995. Copyright © 1995 by The Kent State University Press. Reproduced by permission.—*Classical and Modern Literature,* v. 12, winter, 1992. Copyright © 1992 by CML, Inc.. Reproduced by permission.—*Deutsche Vierteljahrsschrift fur Literaturwissenschaft und Geistesgeschichte,* vol. 66, March, 1992, p. 31-47, for "*Geschichtsbewußtsein* and Public Thinking: Rousseau and Herder" by Frederick M. Barnard. Copyright © 1992 J. B. Metzlersche Verlagsbuchhandlung und Carl Ernst Poeschel Verlag GmbH in Stuttgart. Reproduced by permission of the author.—*Folklore Forum,* v. 24, 1991. Copyright © 1991 Folklore Publications Group, Inc. Reproduced by permission.—*Jahrbuch für Amerikastudien,* v. 13, 1968. Copyright © 1968 Carl Winter Universitatsverlag. Reproduced by permission.—*Journal of Unitarian Universalist History,* v. 26, 1999. Copyright © 1999 The Unitarian Universalist Historical Society. Reproduced by permission.—*North Dakota Quarterly,* v. 57, summer, 1989. Copyright © 1989 North Dakota Quarterly Press. Reproduced by permission.—*Studies in Eighteenth-Century Culture,* v. 23, 1994. Copyright © 1994 American Society for Eighteenth-Century Studies. All rights reserved. The Johns Hopkins University Press. Reproduced by permission.—*Victorian Newsletter,* v. 97, spring, 2000; v. 103, spring, 2003. All reproduced by permission of the publisher and author.—*Victorian Poetry,* vol. 35, spring, 1997 for "Christian Allegory and Subversive Poetics: Christina Rossetti's Prince's Progress Reexamined" by Dawn Henwood. Copyright © West Virginia University, 1997. Reproduced by permission of the author.—*Victorians Institute Journal,* v. 25, 1997. Copyright © 1997 *Victorians Institute Journal.* Reproduced by permission.—*Women's Writing,* v. 5, 1998 for "A Career of One's Own: Christina Rossetti, Literary Success and Love" by Emma Parker; v. 12, March, 2005 for "A Chink in the Armour: Christina Rossetti's 'The Prince's Progress,' 'A Royal Princess,' and Victorian Medievalism" by Noelle Bowles. All reproduced by permission of the publisher and the respective authors.

COPYRIGHTED MATERIAL IN *NCLC*, VOLUME 186, WAS REPRODUCED FROM THE FOLLOWING BOOKS:

Albrecht, Robert C. From *Theodore Parker.* Twayne, 1971. Copyright © 1971 by Twayne Publishers, Inc. Reproduced by permission of the author.—Baum, Manfred. From "Herder's 'Essay on Being,'" in *Herder Today: Contributions from the International Herder Conference Nov. 5-8 1987 Stanford California.* Edited by Kurt Mueller-Vollmer. Walter de Gruyter, 1990. Copyright © 1990 by Walter de Gruyter & Co., D-10785 Berlin. All rights reserved. Reproduced by permission.—Collison, Gary L. From "Toward Democratic Vistas: Theodore Parker, Friendship, and Transcendentalism," in *Emersonian Circles.* Edited by Wesley T. Mott and Robert E. Burkholder. University of Rochester Press, 1997. Copyright © 1997 Contributors. Reproduced by permission.—Cumberland, Debra. From "Ritual and Performance in Christina Rossetti's 'Goblin Market,'" in *Things of the Spirit: Women Writers Constructing Spirituality.* Edited by Kristina K. Groover. University of Notre Dame Press, 2004. Copyright © 2004 University of Notre Dame Press. Reproduced by permission.—D'Amico, Diane. From *Christina Rossetti: Faith Gender and Time.* Louisiana State University Press, 1999. Copyright © 1999 by Louisiana State University Press. All rights reserved. Reproduced by permission.—Garlick, Barbara. From "Defacing the Self: Christina Rossetti's *The Face of the Deep* as Absolution," in *Tradition and the Poetics of Self in Nineteenth-Century Women's Poetry.* Edited by Barbara Garlick. Rodopi, 2002. Copyright © 2002 Editions Rodopi B. V. Reproduced by permission.—Hassett, Constance W. From *Christina Rossetti: The Patience of Style.* University of Virginia Press, 2005. Copyright © 2005 by the Rector and Visitors of the University of Virginia. Reproduced with permission of the University of Virginia Press.—Hutchison, William R. From *The Transcendentalist Ministers: Church Reform in the New England Renaissance.* Yale University Press, 1959. Copyright © 1959 by Yale University. Copyright renewed 1987 by William R. Hutchison. All rights reserved. Reproduced by permission.—Koepke, Wulf. From "Herder and the Sturm und Drang," in

Literature of the Sturm und Drang. Edited by David Hill. Camden House, 2003. Copyright © 2003 by the Editor and Contributors. All rights reserved. Reproduced by permission.—Montfrans, Manet van. From "An Orange on a Pine Tree: French Thought in Herder's Linguistic Theory," in *Yearbook of European Studies 7/Annuaire d'Etudes Européennes.* Edited by Joep Leerssen and Menno Spiering. Rodopi, 1994. Copyright © 1994 Editions Rodopi B. V. Reproduced by permission.—Norton, Robert E. From *Herder's Aesthetics and the European Enlightenment.* Cornell University Press, 1991. Copyright © 1991 by Cornell University. Used by permission of the publisher, Cornell University Press.—Psomiades, Kathy Alexis. From "Whose Body? Christina Rossetti and Aestheticist Femininity," in *Women and British Aestheticism.* Edited by Talia Schaffer and Kathy Alexis Psomiades. University Press of Virginia, 1999. Copyright © 1999 by the Rector and Visitors of the University of Virginia. Reproduced with permission of the University of Virginia Press.—Saine, Thomas P. From "Johann Gottfried Herder: The Weimar Classic Back of the (City)Church," in *The Camden House History of German Literature Volume 7: The Literature of Weimar Classicism.* Edited by Simon Richter. Camden House, 2005. Copyright © 2005 by the Editor and Contributors. Reproduced by permission.—Smulders, Sharon. From *Christina Rossetti Revisited.* Twayne, 1996. Copyright © 1996 by Twayne Publishers. Reproduced by permission of the author.—Tantillo, Astrida Orle. From "Herder and National Culture: A Case Study of Latvia," in *Eighteenth-Century Research: Universal Reason and National Culture during the Enlightenment.* Edited by David A. Bell, Ludmila Pimenova, and Stéphane Pujol. Honore Champion Editeur, 1999. Copyright © 1999 Editions Champion, Paris. Reproduced by permission.—Van Der Laan, James M. From "Herder's Essayistic Style," in *Johann Gottfried Herder: Language History and the Enlightenment.* Edited by Wulf Koepke. Camden House, 1990. Copyright © 1990 by Camden House, Inc.. Reproduced by permission.—Wilmer, S. E. From "Herder and European Theatre," in *Staging Nationalism: Essays on Theatre and National Identity.* Edited by Kiki Gounaridou. McFarland, 2005. Copyright © 2005 Kiki Gounaridou. All rights reserved. Reproduced by permission of McFarland & Company, Inc., Box 611, Jefferson NC 28640. www.mcfarlandpub.com.

Thomson Gale Literature Product Advisory Board

The members of the Thomson Gale Literature Product Advisory Board—reference librarians from public and academic library systems—represent a cross-section of our customer base and offer a variety of informed perspectives on both the presentation and content of our literature products. Advisory board members assess and define such quality issues as the relevance, currency, and usefulness of the author coverage, critical content, and literary topics included in our series; evaluate the layout, presentation, and general quality of our printed volumes; provide feedback on the criteria used for selecting authors and topics covered in our series; provide suggestions for potential enhancements to our series; identify any gaps in our coverage of authors or literary topics, recommending authors or topics for inclusion; analyze the appropriateness of our content and presentation for various user audiences, such as high school students, undergraduates, graduate students, librarians, and educators; and offer feedback on any proposed changes/enhancements to our series. We wish to thank the following advisors for their advice throughout the year.

Barbara M. Bibel
Librarian
Oakland Public Library
Oakland, California

Dr. Toby Burrows
Principal Librarian
The Scholars' Centre
University of Western Australia Library
Nedlands, Western Australia

Celia C. Daniel
Associate Reference Librarian
Howard University Libraries
Washington, D.C.

David M. Durant
Reference Librarian
Joyner Library
East Carolina University
Greenville, North Carolina

Nancy T. Guidry
Librarian
Bakersfield Community College
Bakersfield, California

Heather Martin
Arts & Humanities Librarian
University of Alabama at Birmingham, Sterne Library
Birmingham, Alabama

Susan Mikula
Librarian
Indiana Free Library
Indiana, Pennsylvania

Thomas Nixon
Humanities Reference Librarian
University of North Carolina at Chapel Hill, Davis
 Library
Chapel Hill, North Carolina

Mark Schumacher
Jackson Library
University of North Carolina at Greensboro
Greensboro, North Carolina

Gwen Scott-Miller
Assistant Director
Sno-Isle Regional Library System
Marysville, Washington

Johann Gottfried von Herder
1744-1803

German critic, essayist, translator, editor, poet, and playwright.

The following entry provides critical commentary on Herder's works from 1987 to 2005. For further information on Herder's life and works, see *NCLC,* Volume 8.

INTRODUCTION

One of the most prominent and influential critics in literary history, Johann Gottfried von Herder is also well known as a primary theoretician of the *Sturm und Drang* (Storm and Stress) and Romantic movements in Germany. His essays on various topics, including religion, history, and the development of language and literature, are considered important to later studies on evolution and the development of the social sciences. Although his works are often faulted for their lack of organization, critics nevertheless praise Herder for his intellectual diversity and erudition.

BIOGRAPHICAL INFORMATION

Herder was born in Mohrungen, East Prussia, into a family of limited means. His father, a cantor, sexton, and schoolmaster, reared his three children in the Protestant faith and emphasized gentle discipline and manners. He encouraged his son to complete his education at the town school where the youth also mastered Latin and Greek studies. Following his graduation, Herder worked as a secretary to a manufacturer of religious pamphlets. He then entered the University of Königsberg where he studied medicine and theology. Herder remained at Königsberg until 1764, when he accepted a post as both master and minister at the Cathedral School of Riga. Although Herder did not begin writing seriously until after his move to Riga, his later works reflect two major forces in his life at Königsberg—the influence of his professor, the philosopher Immanuel Kant, and his friendship with the religious writer Johann G. Hamann, who challenged the eighteenth-century school of rationalism. In 1769, Herder left Riga and sailed to Brittany and Nantes, France, where he met the prince of Holstein. Although he agreed to become the prince's tutor and accompany him on a grand tour of Italy, Herder remained with him for only a short time before a painful eye infection forced him to seek corrective surgery. During his recuperation Herder met Johann Wolfgang von Goethe and formed an influential and fortuitous friendship. He urged the young Goethe to study and value his German cultural heritage. By this time, Herder had come to be regarded as the leader and initiator of the *Sturm und Drang* movement, which is characterized by emotional intensity and which often derived its inspiration from folk legend. He also promoted the study and emulation of "natural" poets such as Homer and Shakespeare instead of the "artificial" poets of French Neoclassicism. Under the recommendation of Goethe, Herder became the general superintendent at Weimar Court in 1776, but felt disassociated from Goethe's literary and cultural circles and was unhappy. The ideas presented in Herder's *Ideen zur Philosophie der Geschichte der Menschheit* (1784-91; *Outlines of a Philosophy on the History of Man*) met with considerable disapproval from his colleagues, particularly from Goethe and the followers of Kant. Although Goethe later insisted that he and Herder had remained on amicable terms, Herder considered the breach between them to be irreparable. Herder further isolated himself by challenging the doctrines of Kant's *Critique of Pure Reason,* a study in transcendental philosophy. He never reconciled with his former colleagues and in 1803 died in isolation at Weimar.

MAJOR WORKS

The significant influence of Kant and Hamann is perhaps most evident in his *Über die neuere deutsche Litteratur* (1767), a three-part essay in which Herder responds to Gotthold Ephraim Lessing's collection of literary letters, *Litteraturbriefe*. In his work, Herder defines his concept of literary historicism, stating that the current character of every nation is the culmination of an evolutionary process which can be traced through the development of that culture's literature and language. Herder further maintains that literature must be judged in light of this history and not by the standards represented by French Neoclassical literature or the Latin and Greek classics. Thus, with this work, Herder joined the movement against Neoclassicism. Herder's literary theories were also evident in the emerging German Romantic movement. His essay *Abhandlung über den Ursprung der Sprache, walche den von der Königl* (1772; *Treatise upon the Origin of Language*) outlines Herder's concept of language, which he considers a natural development of every culture. Herder's continued interest in folklore, folksongs, and German sagas is further evidenced in his edition of *Volkslieder* (1778), a collection of folk songs, some of which Herder translated into German. *Vom Geist der ebräischen Poesie* (1782-83; *The Spirit of Hebrew Poetry*) is another historical and cultural study. In this essay Herder discusses the development of Hebrew literature and cites it as a primary example of the natural historical maturation of folklore. As in his other works, Herder's theories in this essay are informed by his love of primitive poetry. In 1784, Herder published the first part of *Outlines of a Philosophy on the History of Man*, perhaps his most influential treatise. In the essay, Herder expanded his ideas from *Über die neuere deutsche Litteratur* and *Treatise upon the Origin of Language* and added a scientific component on organic evolution.

CRITICAL RECEPTION

Critics have often observed that Herder's works lack both the style and structure that distinguish the creative efforts of his fellow German Romantics, and he has been unfavorably compared with Friedrich von Schiller, Goethe, and Lessing. Herder's genius, according to commentators, rests in his ability to recognize in the folklore and myths of Germany and other cultures a literary heritage previously unstudied and unrecognized. Although Herder's methods of analysis are now considered somewhat dated, modern commentators generally agree that his importance lies in his influence rather than in the literary value of his works. Herder remains important for his contributions to both the *Sturm und Drang* and Romantic movements, as well as for his recognition of the importance of German folklore and literature. While his works of literature will undoubtedly remain less important than those of succeeding German writers, his ideas remain central to German literature today.

PRINCIPAL WORKS

Über die neuere deutsche Litteratur. Fragmente (essays) 1767

Kritische Wälder (essays) 1769

Abhandlung über den Ursprung der Sprache, walche den von der Königl [*Treatise upon the Origin of Language*] (essay) 1772

"Shakespear" (essay) 1773

Volkslieder [editor] (folk songs) 1778; also published as *Stimmen der Völker in Liedern*, 1807

Vom Geist der ebräischen Poesie. 2 vols. [*The Spirit of Hebrew Poetry*] (essay) 1782-83

Ideen zur Philosophie der Geschichte der Menschheit. 4 vols. [*Outlines of a Philosophy of the History of Man*] (essays) 1784-91

Gott! Ein Gespräch [*God: Some Conversations*] (essay) 1787

Briefe zu Beförderung der Humanität. 10 vols. (epistles) 1793-97

Adrastea. 6 vols. (plays and poetry) 1800-04

Der Cid [translator, from the ancient Spanish epic poem *Cantàr de mio Cid*] (poetry) 1805

J. G. Herders sämmtliche Werke. 45 vols. (poetry, essays, criticism, and folk songs) 1805-20

Journal meiner Reise im Jahr (journal) 1846

Herders sämmtliche Werke. 33 vols. (poetry, essays, criticism, and folk songs) 1877-1913

CRITICISM

Manfred Baum (essay date 1987)

SOURCE: Baum, Manfred. "Herder's 'Essay on Being,'" In *Herder Today: Contributions from the International Herder Conference, Nov. 5-8, 1987, Stanford, California,* edited by Kurt Mueller-Vollmer, pp. 126-37. Berlin and New York: Walter de Gruyter, 1990.

[*In the following essay, first delivered at a conference in 1987, Baum places Herder's* Essay on Being *within the context of eighteenth-century philosophical debate to demonstrate how the author's innovative approach is informed by other thinkers of his era.*]

1. FROM IDEALISM TO SPINOZISM AND BACK AGAIN

Herder's "metaphysical exercise" (metaphysisches Exercitium: 9)[1] on Being is introduced by the "Prolegomena" and is concluded by a "final observation" (Schlußbetrachtung: 20). These sections contain epistemological reflections on the formation of concepts in human and divine thought. In the introductory part of his [*Essay on Being*] Herder first deals with the empiricist thesis that all our concepts are derived from the senses. In its Lockean form this thesis amounts to the denial of inborn truths (angeborene Wahrheiten).[2] If Locke's distinction of inner sense from outer senses is also accepted, the empiricist claim could be stated more precisely in the following manner: there is no other way to consciousness or inner sense than through the outer senses. That all our concepts are sensible would then mean that the content of these concepts is provided by the outer senses and that their function as concepts is due to the reflection of this content in inner sense. In this theory of concept formation it is presupposed that there are objects outside the mind which affect the outer senses and thereby make possible concepts of the inner sense which could not be produced in any other way.

Although this empiricist theory seems to be well-founded by facts of experience, it has a metaphysical implication that is not obviously true, viz., that there are objects outside the mind which are the causes of its concepts. This metaphysical claim cannot itself be established by empirical knowledge since what is at issue here is not one or another experience, but the explanation of the possibility of experience in general in terms of the relation of things to the mind. This relation can and must be called into question. For the empiricist account of experience takes for granted what the idealist doubts, viz., that there are objects whose activity produces concepts in the mind such that experience of these objects is possible. It follows that there cannot be an empirical refutation of idealism since experience itself could have more than one cause.[3]

Other than being generated by objects of the outer senses, there is another possibility that must be considered, namely, that experience is the product of an inner principle of the human mind, viz., that of imagination. If idealism becomes dogmatic, it flatly denies the existence of outer objects; it does so on the strength of the indemonstrability of the existence of such objects by empirical arguments which already presuppose a realistic ontology. There is, then, an alternative to the empiricist theory of concept formation, namely, a theory that explains the possibility of concepts by their being products of the powers of the knowing mind alone. This would mean that (at least some) concepts would not merely reside in inner sense, but would also be the effects of spiritual powers within the thinking mind.

A refutation of this idealism presupposes certain insights concerning the relation of our faculty of representation to consciousness or inner sense. If the latter would indicate a spontaneity of the thinking self that went beyond the mere awareness of the representations of the outer senses, such a refutation would become difficult if not impossible. What, then, is consciousness or inner sense?

Comparison with other animals shows that they think or have concepts derived from outer senses without being conscious of them. Consciousness is the mark which distinguishes human thought from that of other animals. To be aware of one's thought is to see the pictures provided by the senses as one's own pictures. But is this faculty of consciousness as inner sense restricted to impressions of the outer senses such that there could not be an inner sense if there were no outer senses (as assumed by the realists)? If inner sense is not defined as the faculty of becoming conscious of the outer representations, but merely as a faculty of distinct represen-

tations (or of concepts in general), no realistic ontology is presupposed. For human beings concepts are only the result of abstraction and reflection exercised on the representations of outer things which we—like all other animals—get through the senses. Yet this does not preclude the possibility that such ideas of outer things were not derived from outer senses but are the products of a spiritual power of the mind. These ideas of the outer senses, and the outer senses themselves in their relation to the universe could both be mere ideas of a thinking self. This thinking self would be conscious of these ideas as its own and of the fact that they originate only from within its very self. In this case idealism would be driven to the extreme of solipsism. Whereas idealism takes only thinking beings as real, solipsism (or 'egoism') goes so far as to deny the existence of any beings outside the one thinking self having representations of bodies and persons. Solipsism amounts to the denial of the existence of the objects of thought (be they material or spiritual objects) outside of the thinking self itself. For the allowance of such beings would only be justified if there were an unambiguous way of inferring from a representation to an object as its cause. Since this is at least a doubtful mode of inference, any refutation of idealism or solipsism would require the proof that our concepts cannot be the products of our own mind's spiritual powers. As long as such a proof has not been provided, egoism remains a real possibility in metaphysics.

An egoistic world of thought (*mundus egoisticus*)[4] consisting only of concepts generated by the thinking self is not only a possibility but a metaphysical fact. There is one *mundus egoisticus* of thought, namely God, or rather the God of the philosophers, which has no exterior objects related to it through outer senses. God is conceived of as free of all sensible impression or as Herder would put it, without any *given* concepts.[5] This thinking being is a spiritual principle of thoughts endowed with consciousness of its thoughts and with self-consciousness or an image of itself. The divine consciousness is not conditioned by representations of outer senses and therefore its inner sense cannot be a mere awareness of such outer representations. The faculty of self-consciousness can be expressed by God's saying "I" to himself and, as Herder adds, God is perhaps the only being that can truly say "I" to itself, because all there is in it is a product of itself. The divine self-consciousness is not only denoted by the self-ascription of the "I", but by an expression of its absolute independence in thinking: "I think through myself" (ich denke durch mich: 11). Everything other than itself is only thought through it and is thereby immanent in it or is its thought. 'Being' means either God's being or being a thought of God in God. This divine egoism is not only a conception which can serve as a means of contrasting the human dependent mode of thinking with God's self-sufficient thought. For if it is true that everything other than God is thought by God, his all-embracing thought is the sole principle of being. And this means that all other thinking beings, and all human beings are only the thoughts of God. God as "one egoistic world of thought" (eine egoistische Gedankenwelt: 11) is the one Being of a Spinozistic monism in terms of Wolffian metaphysics. Herder's presentation of divine egoism reveals a Spinozism *avant la lettre* (independent of Spinoza's actual writings) that can be construed from elements of sensualistic idealism.

This is confirmed by a remark that Herder makes in his concluding reflections after he has expounded his doctrine of being and its knowledge. There he notes in passing the "childish inference" (auf kindische Art geschlossen: 21) that God to whom no concept is given from outside has a concept of his own being as unanalyzable to him as our concept of being is to us. Since such an unanalyzable concept derived from the consciousness of his own being must also be called a sensible concept, his relation to himself must be that of inner sense. This yields a sensible impression or idea which would, as such, have the obscurity and yet certainty that is characteristic of the unique concept of being. But since all his other concepts are not given to him, but are products of his own thought, his own being would be the only thing that remained opaque to him.

This connection of metaphysical egoism as an extreme form of idealism with Spinozistic monism is not Herder's own invention. In Kant's *Reflexionen* on Baumgarten's *Metaphysica,* stemming from the years 1764-66, that is from about the time that Herder heard Kant, we find the remark: "Omnis spinozista est egoista. Quaeritur, utrum omnis egoista necessario sit spinozista".[6] The latter question which addresses Herder's way of understanding egoism as a metaphysical monism is answered in Kant's later lectures on metaphysics: "Dogmatic egoism is a hidden Spinozism." (Der Dogmatische Egoismus ist ein versteckter Spinozismus.)[7]

Now this identification of solipsism with Spinozism was to have a great career in the future of German Idealism. Jacobi in his *Letters on Spinoza* reports of his conversations with Lessing shortly before his death. There we read: "One time Lessing said with a half smile: he himself might be the supreme being, and presently in the state of the utmost contraction.—I—says Jacobi—asked for my existence".[8] This Lessingian joke can only be understood if we assume that he was combining solipsism with Spinozism. If I can be certain only of my own existence, and if there is only one existing thing, these two existences must be one and the same thing. This means that I myself am the supreme being or Spinoza's unique substance. Jacobi mentions another occasion on which he had a conversation with Lessing: "When we sat at Gleim's table in Halberstadt,

suddenly a rain came and Gleim regretted this because he wanted us to go into his garden after the meal, Lessing, who sat beside me, said to me: 'Jacobi, you know, perhaps *I* do that [namely, let it rain].' I responded: 'Or *I*'".[9]

These playful allusions to solipsistic Spinozism are only the occasional reflections of the ways in which metaphysical monism made its way through this epoch of German philosophy. It was Herder who gives us another account of Lessing's Spinozism in his letter to Jacobi (February 6, 1784). On the wallpaper in Gleim's house he found a formula from Lessing's hand: "Hen ego Kai pan" (I am one and all) in which Spinoza's monism is expressed in terms of a metaphysical egoism. This was a memento of Lessing's visit to Halberstadt and his jocular conversations with Jacobi.

When Fichte published his *Science of Knowledge* (1794/95), he compared his transcendental idealism with Spinoza's metaphysical system and found an important agreement between the theoretical part of his philosophy and Spinoza's monism: "The theoretical portion of our Science of Knowledge . . . is in fact . . . Spinozism made systematic; save only that any given self is itself the one ultimate substance".[10] Instead of Herder's divine egoist, we have here "any given self" (eines jeden Ich) as the idealistic principle which is in certain respects the same as Spinoza's unique substance. Herder's youthful construction of an egoistic world of thought has now become a doctrine of the self's being all reality. By that time Lessing's joke had been taken seriously.

2. The Concept of Being and the Limits of Philosophy

Herder arrives at the concept of Being by a meditation on the human condition, i. e. on the sensibility of all our ideas and concepts. Being is introduced as the most sensible (der allersinnlichste: 12) and, therefore, the most unanalyzable concept, which is yet a most certain (höchst gewiss: ibid.) concept, but one that is entirely indemonstrable. For human beings it is therefore true that their conviction of Being, of the existence of the objects of their senses, is at once most certain and most obscure.

The sensualist doctrine that all my representations are sensible is accepted by Herder simultaneously with the Wolffian doctrine that the sensibility and obscurity of a representation (or concept) are synonymous. A good reference for this doctrine is Baumgarten's *Metaphysica* § 520 f: to know something *"obscure confuseque seu indistincte"* depends on the faculty called *"facultas cognoscitiva inferior"*, and the representation which is *"non distincta"* is called *"representatio sensitiva"*. Since all analysis of sensible representations has a limit in the first origin of our concepts in sensibility, the unanalyz-able remnant of sensibility and indistinctness is in principle undisposable.

But the expectation that a lack of analyzability is equivalent to a lack of certainty is only a prejudice of the philosopher. This opposition of the philosopher and the common man, or of the philosopher and the plebeian (Pöbel) is one of the traces of Herder's study of Hume's *Inquiry*.[11] (The presence of the plebeian in Hume's text indicates his indebtedness to Cicero on this account.) The most unanalyzable concept would be the most uncertain concept for the philosopher, but not for man. Whereas for man sensible concepts are certain in the sense that they have a convincing power, the analyzed concepts of the philosopher owe their certainty to their power of demonstration. Demonstration as well as all logical truth rests on the analysis of concepts. This Leibniz-Wolffian theory of judgement and inference, also present in Kant's *Falsche Spitzfindigkeit* (1762) and in his lectures on metaphysics as reported by Herder,[12] complements the sensualist theory of concept-formation (as far as man is concerned). Here again we find the mixture of British empiricism and Wolffian rationalism which was characteristic of Kant at that time and which is Herder's Kantian heritage lasting the rest of his life.

This Herderian syncretism is manifest when he exclaims: "Take here the two extreme thoughts of our hybrid humanity. . . ." (11). Man is as such a hybrid of animality and rationality, and within mankind this double character is represented by the opposition of the philosopher to the plebeian. Both of them stand for a one-sided preponderance of the rational or sensible powers of man who is as such neither a philosopher nor a plebeian. The same thought is more drastically expressed in Kant's lecture on metaphysics; this we know from Herder's lecture notes: man is "half an angel, half an animal: a centaur".[13]

But what are the two extreme thoughts of our hybrid humanity, which pair of concepts is alluded to? It must be the concept of something (Etwas) and the concept of Being (Sein). Being is the most sensible concept that underlies all other concepts insofar as they are concepts of beings. As such, Being also appears to be the most general concept, the most abstract concept. But this is implicitly denied by calling it the most sensible concept. The most abstract concept is taken from Baumgarten's ontology: something. It is only the most general of all the concepts that presuppose the concept of Being. But Herder says nothing of the logical status of this most sensible concept, whether it is a concrete or a singular concept. And since there is no distinction between concepts, thoughts, images, sensations, impressions etc., the notion of concept means just the same as representation or distinct representation. Clearly Herder inists

on its sensibility. Taken literally this would mean that the concept lost its universality and thereby its logical character as *notio communis*. Thus Being would not only be undefinable (since it is logically insoluable), but also not a concept at all. If, however, we take its sensibility only as a synonym for unanalyzability, then the concept of Being becomes describable in terms of its logical development in the human mind. Here, and on several other occasions of Herder's *Essay*, its indebtedness to Crusius' logic and metaphysics becomes obvious.[14] For Being is thought to be at the top of a hierarchy of unanalyzable concepts, and it is followed by the concepts *juxta, post* and *per*, i. e., space, time and force. By this order of abstractness of unanalyzable concepts, the concept of Being becomes the most abstract and the common content of space (place) and time.

"Being" and "Something" are related to one another as "real Being" (Realsein) to "logical Being", or as the natural impression (Eindruck der Natur) of Being to its copy in thought. This manner of disposition clearly shows Herder's attempt to reconcile Baumgarten's ontology with Hume's doctrine of the origin of ideas. The unanalyzability and indefinability of real Being is an indication of the greatest possible certainty despite its logical unaccessibility. Such a certainty derives from mother nature, or from a "theoretical instinct" (12) of man, and not from the human understanding as excercised in philosophy. Idealism on the other hand can be seen as an attempt to deny Being with the intention of pointing out to philosophers the "end of philosophy" (13) as a demonstrative and rational undertaking.[15]

Herder's criticism of Baumgarten's attempt to define his logical Being or *aliquid*[16] largely proceeds on Kantian lines. His arguments are taken from Kant's *Versuch den Begriff der negativen Grössen in die Weltweisheit einzuführen* (1763) and his *Einzig möglicher Beweisgrund* (1763). When Baumgarten defines *aliquid* as *non-nihil*, he ignores that the nothing from which he proceeds must be the absolute cancellation of real Being, and not the logical nothing that is the result of a contradiction, or something impossible. But if real Being is absolutely cancelled, there can be no logical contradiction. For any such logical impossibility presupposes something that is posited and cancelled at the same time. Such a formal relation of contradiction can only arise if there is already something posited as material, and this is excluded *ex hypothesi*. But without any matter or material, the formal relation of contradiction is itself impossible, or rather, without some material, impossibility is impossible. Thus Baumgarten's attempt to define *aliquid* as *non-nihil* or the logical opposite of the impossible fails insofar as his *nihil* already presupposes something and therefore Being. Being is to be considered as the basis (Grundlage) and element of all thinking, of all contradiction, and of all logic.

But even if the attempted definition of Being does not proceed from nothing, but from possibility (Wolff's *existentia* or *actualitas* as *complementum possibilitatis*) it can be shown with Crusius that the concept of Being (actuality) is prior to the concept of possibility, and that real possibility is earlier than logical possibility. Herder elucidates the subjective priority of real possibility by a reflection on the discovery of causality and the concept of force by early mankind. The explanation of the actual as a consequence of the possible presupposes the concept of force, and thereby the concept of something existing that has this force. Such forces and the substances in which they reside are only empirically knowable. Being as allegedly derived from real possibility therefore proves to be an entirely empirical concept. And since logical possibility cannot be understood without real possibility and force, which can only be empirically known, all logical attempts to define Being in an original way have failed.

But Baumgarten's and Wolff's definition of Being can also be rejected with the empiricist argument that any concepts of Being are only concepts which—as such—must be abstracted from their objects. They remain themselves untouched and unaltered by such abstraction. Logical possibility as the possibility of thoughts and real possibility thus both presuppose real Being.

Only in passing Herder criticizes Kant's definition of Being as absolute positing. The two arguments he adduces are: (1) positing is synonymous with Being and can therefore not define it. (2) If Being could be defined as absolute positing, one could also speak of God's Being as his absolute positing which is not an adequate way of talking about God.

After Herder's proof of the undefinability of the concept of Being, he analyzes existential propositions in order to prove the indemonstrability of every such proposition, that is, of Being.

According to Herder existential propositions have no logical predicate. The way Herder tries to prove this assertion is rather curious. For Herder every logical predicate must be contained as a partial concept in its subject. This is Leibniz's doctrine that every true judgement asserts the inherence of a predicate in a subject, which in its Wolffian form says that every true judgement is an analytic judgement (to use Kant's later terminology). In the time of Herder's sojourn at Königsberg, Kant was still an adherent of this doctrine. Now Herder's argument makes a particular use of this doctrine based on his conception of concepts. Since concepts are only logical creatures of our mind, every subject-concept of a proposition must be a logically possible combination of all (possible) predicate-concepts that can be asserted of it in a true and therefore analytic judgement. But since Being has not to be taken as a logical concept, it

cannot be a partial concept of the subject-concept that is combined with other possible predicate-concepts according to the rule of logical possibility, i. e., to the rule of non-contradiction. Therefore Being should and could not be a possible predicate of any subject. (In Kant's later terminology: existential propositions are not analytic, but synthetic propositions. But this implies that Being is a logical predicate.) Now Herder does not say that Being is not a possible predicate of *any* subject, but he says that "this" subject of the proposition "God is existent" is only a logical creature, a relation of concepts according to logical possibility. The subject-concept of this particular proposition is "God," or the "*ens realissimum*" whose determinations are thought as united in him without contradiction. The logical possibility of the *ens realissimum* does not imply its existence since Being as a real concept (*Realbegriff*) cannot be asserted of God on the strength of an analysis of the logically possible concept of the *ens realissimum*. Thus Being cannot be deduced from possibility by way of an analysis of concepts which would have to be the case if there should be a proof of existential propositions. This is true of every existential proposition since Herder thinks (with the Kant of that period) that proof of a proposition can only be established by means of concept-analysis. On the basis of the theory of true judgements as analytic judgements, every proof requires the establishment of a partial identity of the predicate and the subject in the conclusion by means of a middle term. The general result of this argument is that every existential proposition is indemonstrable since Being is a real concept and as such not contained in any logical subject-concept. This argumentation relies heavily on Kant's *Einzig Möglicher Beweisgrund*, but it makes no use of Kant's definition of Being as absolute positing. Instead Herder employs the unclear notion of a "real concept" which, according to him, is an exclusively empirical concept and which cannot be predicated *a priori*. Herder's argument against the ontological proof thus consists of a combination of Kantian and Humean insights. It amounts to the claim that every existential proposition is indemonstrable *because* it is exclusively empirical.

The same is true of Herder's argument against a demonstration of the reverse proposition: "something existing is God" (etwas existiert: ist Gott: 17).[17] This reversal of an existential proposition is taken from Kant's *Einzig Möglicher Beweisgrund*, but the argument that such a proposition cannot be proved by an analysis of its concepts rests entirely on the claim that the subject-concept of existence is not a logical concept in which the concept of God is contained. This is true because the subject-concept is an empirical concept. Herder's empiricism precludes any proof of existence because it opposes the *a priori* connection of this concept with any logical concept, be it subject or predicate of a proposition. And Herder appeals to mere common sense when he says: "You do not try to prove *a priori* any empirical concept" (17).[18]

Finally Herder criticizes Kant's new proof of God's existence which rests on the concept of an absolutely necessary being. Herder argues that Kant made an unjustified move when he proceeded from the lack of an inner possibility (in the absence of a material for thought) to the absolute impossibility of anything (under the same condition). For from there not being a possibility of something there follows no absolute impossibility of something. As Kant himself had shown in his *Einzig Möglicher Beweisgrund,* a denial of a possibility for lack of the material of possibility is not the same as impossibility, since the latter is only a result of a logical conflict or a contradiction. This formal relation within the impossible presupposes two materials that stand in conflict and cancel each other out.[19] Now just this material is denied being if all inner possibility is sublated and therefore there is no way of thinking an impossibility as a result of the lack of inner possibility.

This argument that turns Kant's doctrines against their author ignores the core of Kant's new conception of an absolute impossibility as a consequence of the lack of any inner possibility. For Kant's argument only rests on the consideration that it is contradictory (impossible) to think of something as possible when at the same time nothing exists that provides the matter for the formal relation of possibility. Thus it is absolutely impossible that something be possible without the existence of the necessary condition of any possibility, i. e., the existence of a Being that is thereby known to be an absolutely necessary Being.

In his concluding section Herder draws together all the consequences of his investigation: Being is indemonstrable, therefore God's existence is indemonstrable. And since the existence of something outside the mind is equally indemonstrable, a refutation of idealism is impossible. This seems to lead to the skeptical consequence that certainty concerning the existence of states of affairs and objects or demonstrable knowledge of matters of fact is impossible, since all existential propositions are indemonstrable. If our knowledge of facts rests on the proof of existential propositions, there is no knowledge proper in this greatest part of human cognition. All that could be known with certainty would be Hume's relations of ideas that are expressed in analytic propositions. Herder refers to these analytic relations of ideas in his remark: "All propositions that are now demonstrable in the best way [i. e. analytically] are nothing without Being: mere relations" (19).

But this way of drawing consequences from the preceding investigation would be precipitous. It is not true that all Being is uncertain. The certainty of Being is obvious and it does not rest on demonstration. In fact there is no need for a demonstration of Being as far as empirical Being is concerned since nobody has ever denied it. Thus it is not the case that the proof of existing things is an uncertain proof, but there is no proof whatsoever for Being. And there need not be a proof since the certainty of Being as the first and entirely sensible concept is even the model for all other certainty in demonstration and science. The reason for this certainty is to be sought in the nature of man. Certainty of Being is an inborn certainty. Nature herself convinces man of Being and it is only philosophy that invented an unnatural skeptical doubt in it. As a result of such an artificial skepticism concerning the existence of an external world, philosophers ventured to give a proof for it. But this was only possible as long as the nature of Being was not understood, and its relation to knowledge, to concepts and propositions, was not made perspicuous.

In Herder's ***Essay*** such an investigation is undertaken and systematically brought to completeness. Thereby the limits of philosophy are made clear. Since Being is the common principle for all beings in the sensible world and in the world of reason, philosophy has a supreme subject matter, and this—as has been shown—cannot be known by demonstration. However, the limits of philosophy as a demonstrable science are not at the same time the limits of human nature. The most essential concerns of human knowledge lie outside the realm of philosophy, taken as a science. Nature is the teacher of mankind and provides it with all the certainty it can reasonably claim to have. Thus Rousseau's trust in nature neatly combines with Hume's doctrine of the irrationality of our knowledge of Being.

Notes

1. Quotations are from: J. G. Herder, *Werke,* Band 1, ed. U. Gaier, Frankfurt am Main 1985. Page numbers following the quotations refer to this editon, translations are my own.

2. From a deleted passage printed in: *Herder als Schüler Kants,* ed. G. Martin, Kant-Studien 41 (1936), p. 296.

3. Cf. Hume's *Inquiry Concerning Human Understanding,* ed. L. A. Selby-Bigge, Oxford 1966, p. 152 f.

4. This is the term used in Baumgarten's *Metaphysica,* 4th ed., Halle/Magdeburg 1757, §§ 392, 438.

5. We thus have a system of thoughts or representations of the outer and inner senses in the following table:

animals	outer senses	—
humans	outer senses	inner sense
God	—	inner sense

6. Kant's *Gesammelte Schriften,* ed. Königlich Preußische Akademie der Wissenschaften, Band 17, Berlin/New York 1966, Reflexion 3803.

7. *ibid.*

8. *Die Hauptschriften zum Pantheismusstreit,* H. Scholz, ed., Berlin 1916, p. 92 (my translation).

9. *ibid.,* p. 95.

10. J. G. Fichte, *Science of Knowledge,* ed. and trans. by P. Heath and J. Lachs, Cambridge 1982, p. 119.

11. Hume, *op. cit.,* pp. 9, 7 and H. D. Irmscher, *Der handschriftliche Nachlaß Herders und seine Neuordnung,* in: *Herder-Studien,* ed. W. Wiora, Würzburg 1960, p. 9.

12. Kant, *op. cit.,* Band 28, Berlin/New York 1968/70, pp. 9 f, 158, 868 f.

13. *ibid.,* p. 895.

14. Cf. Chr. A. Crusius, *Weg zur Gewißheit und Zuverlässigkeit der menschlichen Erkenntnis,* 2nd ed., Leipzig 1762, §§ 172, 175, 364 and *id., Entwurf der nothwendigen Vernunft-Wahrheiten,* 2nd ed., Leipzig 1753, §§ 29, 56, 57, 444.

15. This reliance on an instinct and the absurdity and yet irrefutability of idealism again remind us of Hume's *Inquiry.*

16. Baumgarten, *op. cit.,* §§ 7, 54, 62.

17. U. Gaier's addition of *Wenn* is misleading. The sense of the sentence is:‚etwas Existierendes ist Gott'(something existing is God).

18. Herder's empiricism makes him not only insist on the dependence of the concept of Being or existence on sensation, but also precludes all *a priori* assertion of this empirical concept of any subject whatsoever.

19. See above, p. 93.

Samson B. Knoll (essay date summer 1989)

SOURCE: Knoll, Samson B. "Beyond the Black Legend: The Anticolonialism of Johann Gottfried Herder." *North Dakota Quarterly* 57, no. 3 (summer 1989): 55-64.

[*In the following essay, Knoll offers a detailed analysis of Herder's arguments against colonialism.*]

In the view of Fernand Braudel, the discovery of the New World meant that Europeans recreated slavery in colonial America seeking to meet the economic problems of the new world periphery with practices no longer adequate for its European center. For, "moving from one zone [of the world economy] to another meant for several centuries passing synchronically from wage labor to serfdom and slavery."[1]

Similarly, Eric Williams (later to become Prime Minister of Trinidad and Tobago) postulated in his incisive *Capitalism and Slavery* that in historical perspective slavery "forms a part of the general picture of the harsh treatment of the underprivileged classes . . . and [of] the indifference with which the rising capitalist class was 'beginning to reckon prosperity in terms of pound sterling, and . . . becoming used to the idea of sacrificing human life to the deity of increased production.'"[2] In the seventeenth and eighteenth centuries, which Williams characterizes as "the centuries of trade"[3]—a perception anticipated, as we shall see, by Herder—the attitude he describes was pervasive in secular as well as in religious thought.

Thus, Edmund Burke, champion of the liberties of the American colonies, in 1772 opposed in the House of Commons a bill which would admit to control of the African Committee members who were not slave traders. He argued not against the slave trade but, on the contrary, that such an act would legally treat like a monopoly "what was intended for a free trade."[4] And when England by the Treaty of Utrecht (1713) was conceded the *Asiento* (control of the slave trade from Africa to the colonies in America), one of the British plenipotentiaries at the negotiations, Bishop Robinson of Bristol—then an important slave trade center—was promoted to the See of London. Decades later, in the 1790s, when George Wilberforce's motion for abolition was defeated in Parliament, church bells rang in Bristol, and as late as 1833, Anglican bishops sided with the Duke of Wellington in his opposition to the Emancipation Act.

Paradoxically, it was through the religious revival led by "Anglican evangelists under the leadership of [William] Wilberforce with the backing of Nonconformist sects, [that from] 1787 on there was a new spirit of religion in active political protest, and its most enduring expression was found in the Anti-Slavery crusade."[5] The prominent role of religious groups in the British Anti-Slavery movement clearly distinguishes it from the more secular movement in France. Yet, in the two leading colonial powers of Europe, not coincidentally, opposition to colonialism generally was not directed against the system itself, but only against its flagrant abuses. What Edith F. Hurtwitz says of England can be applied equally to France: "Abolitionists did not wish to do away with the existing order."[6]

This is clearly illustrated by the fact that, although the end of slavery was formally decreed by Revolutionary France, economic considerations led to its reinstatement in the French colonies; final abolition did not come to the French empire until 1848. In England, too, colonial slavery was not abolished until well into the nineteenth century, after years of the Abolitionist crusade culminated in passage of the Reform Bill of 1832 and the Emancipation Act of 1833 (which was, however, not fully implemented until 1838). In sum, anti-colonial agitation in eighteenth-century European thought was expressed most vociferously through the antislavery, above all, the antislave trade movements which, in the course of the century, gained increasing momentum in France and England.

The widespread opposition to slavery and the slave trade must be viewed as a function of the political philosophy of the Enlightenment, especially its libertarian concepts of the dignity—and thus the essential freedom—of human beings, everywhere. Fanned by stories of the cruelty and bigotry of the conquerors of Spanish and Portuguese America and the (mostly Jesuit) missionaries who accompanied them—the Black Legend—this opposition was also informed by the decided anticlericalism which, especially in France, characterized Enlightened thought.

To the *philosophes,* slavery was inconsistent with the teachings of Christianity. As Montesquieu noted in his *Persian Letters* (No. LXXV):

> A long time ago, Christian princes freed all their slaves from servitude because, they said, Christianity makes all men equal . . . Subsequently, they made conquests in countries where they saw it was to their advantage to have slaves; they allowed the buying and selling of them, oblivious of the principles of their religion.[7]

Some two decades later, in *The Spirit of Laws* (first published in 1748), he argued (Book XV, ch. 2): "Slavery is [no] less opposite to the civil law than to that of nature."[8] At the same time he sharpened his attack on the role which religion had played in the institutionalization of slavery:

> The notion [that religion gives its professors the right to enslave those who dissent from it] encouraged the ravagers of America in their iniquity. Under the influence of this idea, they founded their right of enslaving so many nations; for these robbers, who would absolutely be both robbers and Christians, were superlatively devout.[9]

Almost fifty years later (1794), in his grandly optimistic *Sketch for a Historical Picture of the Progress of the Human Mind,* Condorcet praised the philosophers of his age who "raised an outcry in Europe against the crimes of greed that sullied the shores of America, Africa and Asia. English and French philosophers considered themselves honoured to be called the *friends* of the black races whom foolish tyrants disdained to consider as members of the human race."[10] Even in the Tenth Stage

of progress, the final stage where he sketches so promising a future for humankind, Condorcet felt the need to denounce what Europeans had wrought with their penetration of the colonial world:

> Survey the history of our settlements in Africa or in Asia, and you will see how our trade monopolies, our treachery, our murderous contempt for men of another colour or creed, the insolence of our usurpations, the intrigues and proselytic zeal of our priests, have destroyed the respect and goodwill . . . first won for us in the eyes of the inhabitants.[11]

In No. CXXI of his *Persian Letters* Montesquieu had questioned the economic importance of colonies for the motherland; Adam Smith in his *Wealth of Nations* similarly questioned the profitability of slave over free labor. With the inclusion of trade monopolies in his catalog of grievances against colonial practices, Condorcet had turned from questioning to censure.

This nascent condemnation of the economic system upon which colonialism was founded became central to the anticolonialism of Johann Gottfried Herder, the most seminal German thinker of the eighteenth century. Herder's work and influence embraced a wide range of scholarly disciplines: history, theology, linguistics as well as literature and literary criticism. In addition, being himself a poet, he was one of the earliest collectors and editors of the folk poetry of the world's peoples. His prodigious readings in history and the anthropological and travel literature of his time afforded him an unexcelled grasp of both European and non-European cultures. Thus, where Montesquieu and Condorcet drew their arguments chiefly from Enlightened moral and legal philosophy, Herder's anticolonialism, in addition, received persuasive authority from a universalistic conception of history, the discipline which integrated all his scholarly endeavors. As a result, his anticolonial writings were more than outpourings of a humanitarian mind; they were essential elements of a word view based upon the lessons drawn from a lifelong study of history.

In Herder's perception, history was the social and cultural evolution of all humankind in which each society is representative of all humanity and yet, simultaneously, a reflection *sui generis* of that humanity. The first thesis in Book 7 of Herder's *magnum opus,* his ***Ideas for a Philosophy of the History of Humankind*** (which he began publishing in 1784), states: "In whatever form the human race appears on earth, everywhere it is one and the same."[12] Accordingly, all human societies have an equal potential for cultural growth. Herder asserts (in Book 9): "the chain of culture and enlightenment stretches to the end of the globe. . . . The difference between enlightened and unenlightened, between civilized and uncivilized peoples is therefore not specific but only one of degree."[13] What is true of societies is also true of individuals: "The cannibal in New Zealand and Fénélon, the wretched savage from Tierra del Fuego and Newton, all are creatures of one and the same species."[14] Herder therefore rejected introducing racial theories into the study of history: "Neither four nor five races nor exclusive varieties exist on earth. Colors combine, physical characteristics serve genetic functions. In the total picture, however, all are but hues on one and the same broad canvas stretched across all spaces and all ages of the earth."[15] It is this commonality of origin and potentials which prescribes the standards for the conduct of human beings toward one another: "Therefore, oh man, honor thyself! Neither the pongo nor the *longimanus* [ape] is your brother; but the American [Indian] or the Negro is. Hence thou shalt neither oppress him nor murder him nor rob him, for he is a human being like yourself."[16]

From this perspective Herder was bound to view European domination of the then known world with decided skepticism and deep concern. The misgivings and anguish aroused by his examination of the colonial world are reflected not only in his scholarly writings but also in the poetry which, since adolescence, had been an essential part of his creative efforts. Herder did not achieve greatness as a poet; his didactic intent too often interfered. But his poems bear witness to the depth of his commitment to the world view which his study of history had helped to mold. Central to this view was an appreciation of all the world's cultures and the conviction that they must be allowed to develop to the fullest in dignity and freedom.

Confronted with the historical realities, Herder could not but react with conflicting emotions to the course of events since the discovery of the New World. Much as he appreciated what that discovery had meant for broadening the geographical and intellectual horizons of civilized Europe, he was gravely concerned about its impact upon the many peoples who had fallen under European military as well as cultural domination. His doubts are evident in an epigrammatic poem, **"Columbus,"** written in 1772:

> Lo, Colon Creator! Lo! thou hast expanded by one-fourth
> Our world with lands, with peoples and with silver treasure,
> With jewels, with adornments—
> And with knowledge!
>
> Alas, Colon Assassin! thou hast as well destroyed
> With poison our world and all its beauties,
> Its charms, its customs and, alas,
> Its life and youthful vigor![17]

Many of the poems and prose fragments in which Herder bares his feelings about the happenings in the colonial world reflect the image of the Noble Savage, the symbol of cultural alienation in eighteenth-century Europe. How important these writings were to Herder is indicated by the vehicle he chose for their publication: a significant number of them were included in the ***Letters for the Advancement of HUMANITÄT*** which Herder began to publish in 1793 at a time when the outbreak of the French Revolution had decisively heightened his social consciousness and social conscience. In the "Tenth Collection" of the ***Letters,*** published in 1797, Herder vehemently denounced the Europeans' enslavement of the world:

> What can be said of the civilization which Spaniards, Portuguese, Englishmen and Dutchmen have brought to the East and West Indies, to the Negroes of Africa, to the peaceful islands of the southern world? Do not all these countries more or less cry out for revenge? For revenge all the more since, for an unpredictable future, they have been cast into ever greater ruination? All these stories have been brought to light in the reports of travelers; they have partially been revealed in the outcry over the slave trade. Books have been written . . . about Spanish atrocities, British avarice, the cold insolence of the Dutch . . .
>
> If the genius of Europe existed anywhere but in books, we should stand disgraced before all the nations on earth, convicted of the crime of offending humanity. Name the land where Europeans have come without sinning, perhaps for all eternity, against defenseless, trusting humanity with prejudices, unjust wars, avarice, deceit, disease and harmful gifts! Our continent should not be known as the wise, but as the arrogant, meddlesome, profiteering part of the globe; it did not civilize; on the contrary, wherever and however possible, it destroyed the seeds of an indigenous national culture.[18]

This indictment is followed (in **"Letter 114"**) by a group of poems under the heading "Negro Idylls," in which acts of inhumanity and treachery perpetrated by Europeans against natives are contrasted with acts of nobility and loyalty with which natives—even slaves—responded to their European masters. Frequently Herder documents in footnotes the stories that were his inspiration.

A number of these poems and tales reveal Herder's interest in colonial America and, after independence, the young United States. The important commentary on the Abbé Saint Pierre's famous essay, "Perpetual Peace," for instance, is woven around an account of the peace treaty which the League of the Iroquois had concluded with the Delaware Indians. It is pointedly captioned "Eternal Peace. An Iroquois Scheme."[19] An example of the care with which Herder selected his sources is provided by the poem which concludes this group. Entitled **"The Birthday,"** it eulogizes a Quaker "on the Delaware" who freed his slaves on their twenty-first birthdays. The poem was inspired by the actions of Warner (in Herder's poem *Walter*) Mifflin, a Quaker of Camden, Delaware, and cousin of the famous Governor of Pennsylvania, who between 1774 and 1775 freed his slaves in the manner described by Herder.[20]

In the responding **"Letter"** a significant argument enters the discussion: the right of self-defense against exploitation and deception. It is to the respondent the most powerful of "the passions motivating all that lives," exercised by "all nations called savages, whether they defend themselves against foreign intruders with cunning or with violence, [for] was not the land theirs?"[21] Here Herder echoed thoughts he had expressed with even greater passion more than a decade earlier in Book 7 of the *Ideas for a Philosophy of the History of Humankind*. In a spirited defense of the revolts which conquest, slavery, and slave trade had triggered in the colonial world, he queried: "And by what right did you monsters approach the land of these unfortunates, let alone seize it from them, and them from it, by theft, cunning and violence?"[22] The savage uprisings were the results of the oppression and cruelty perpetrated against aboriginal peoples:

> Cruel, indeed, are the wars of the savages for their land and for its sons, their kidnapped, dishonored and tortured brothers. . . . To us they appear atrocious, as no doubt they are. However, it was the Europeans who first drove them to such outrage: for why did they come into their land? Why did they conduct themselves there like exacting, brutal, all powerful despots?[23]

Herder concluded (in an unpublished fragment for Book 9): "Europeans have been the most violent destroyers of the true, though modest, happiness of simple and natural human societies."[24]

Earlier, in *One More Philosophy of the History of Humankind* (1774), Herder's indictment had been even more impassioned when, in the mood—and style—of Storm and Stress, he had derisively blasted the myth of the superiority of European civilization over the cultures of the non-European peoples:

> Where in the world do we not establish European colonies and will continue to do so? Everywhere those savages will become ripe for conversion by us, particularly as they learn to love our firewater and our affluence! Everywhere our brandy and luxury will help them catch up with our civilized ways—and soon, God help us! they will be humans like ourselves! Such good, strong, happy human beings![25]

It is indicative of Herder's bent towards a historical view of human societies (which anticipated the modern concept of cultural relativity) that he dwells most on the devastating impact which colonialism had on the free development of the native populations and their cultures. Despite his outspoken opposition to tyranny and slavery in any form, he was not an activist in the growing debate on slavery and the slave trade. His attitudes are expressed within the conceptual framework of his historical, philosophical, and theological writings, as well as in his literary and poetic efforts. But rarely, if ever, are they aired in the context of his observations on the living world around him. Thus, during his prolonged stay in Nantes on his famous voyage to France, in 1769 (his first experience with the living French culture), his comments on life in that city are devoid of any awareness that Nantes was the principal slave trade port in France. This may at least in part be due to the fact that eighteenth-century Germany was not a colonial power; slave trade and slavery thus were not of immediate moral or political concern to German thinkers.

Paradoxically, this may also be a reason why Herder's indictments of the colonial system were more than outbursts of the Rousseauan alienation which had informed his Storm and Stress youth. As his study of history broadened and his understanding of human cultures grew, his opposition to colonialism matured. It was strengthened by a growing awareness, not common in his days, of the economic roots of the colonizing urge. His anticolonialism became, in fact, an attack upon the commercial capitalism of the age and its tragic impact upon the peoples whose welfare it pretended to promote. Herder attacks this pretension in an especially interesting essay of the group, "Attitudes toward Peace," which forms part of the comments on the Abbé Saint Pierre in the *Letters for the Advancement of HUMANITÄT* (Tenth Collection). Significantly, it is the one negative among the positive attitudes he outlines. Its title is **"Pretensions of Commerce"** (*Handelsanmassungen*).

Commerce, Herder asserts, "even though not from the noblest of motives," should be an instrument of peace; it "should unite humanity, not divide it." But the reality is such that "human feeling must rebel against the arrogant pretensions of commerce as soon as innocent, toiling nations are victimized for a profit in which they are not even allowed to share."[26]

This denunciation of the commercial system recurs repeatedly in Herder's historical writings and thus attests to the importance which he attached to it. It appeared first and in its most passionate form in *One More Philosophy of the History of Humankind*:

> "Our System of Commerce!" Can anyone imagine the refinement of this all-pervasive science? . . . In Europe slavery has been abolished—because we have calculated how much more these slaves cost, and how much less they bring in, than freedmen. Only one thing have we reserved for ourselves: To exploit and barter away as slaves three continents and to abandon them in silver mines and sugar mills—but then, they are not Europeans, not Christians. So we trade them for silver and precious stones, for spice, sugar and—secret disease: in other words, for the sake of commerce, [that] instrument of mutual aid and of the community of nations!

> "System of Commerce!" The grandeur and uniqueness of that scheme is evident! Three continents by us devastated and policed, and we by them depopulated and

unmanned, choking in luxury, exploitation, and death: That is what they call trading richly and happily! . . . Some day, when the whole cloud bursts in a hundred storms—Great God Mammon, whom now we serve, help us![27]

Herder here closely echoes the sentiments concerning America voiced by the physiocrat and finance minister to Louis XVI, Turgot:

Oh America! You vast regions! Have you been discovered for us only to be the sad victims of our ambitions and our greed? By what scenes of horror and cruelty have we become known to you? Entire nations vanishing from the land or buried in mines, annihilated by the harshness of torture or by the perpetual torture of a slavery more cruel than death, under masters who refuse to ease its brutality even though long-term profit could be the return?[28]

But where Turgot castigates colonial exploitation as inhuman as well as shortsighted, Herder directs his attacks against the roots of colonialism itself, its economic drive. In Book 7 of the *Ideas* Herder places the blame for the increasing death rate and lower death age of aboriginal populations squarely on the Europeans' "arrogant and stubborn greed for profit."[29] And he concludes (in Book 14): "We Europeans roam through the entire world as traders, or rather as robbers; and for that we often neglect what is ours . . . Our bodies politic have become behemoths which insatiably devour what foreigners have to offer: good or bad, spice or poison, coffee or tea, silver and gold."[30]

Much as Herder's persistent denunciation of commercial capitalism and expansionism sets him apart from many, if not most, of his contemporaries, it receives a convincing validity from his premonition of the ultimate repercussions of the colonial system. Here Herder's concept of Nemesis in history comes into play. He had developed it under the impact of the French Revolution, and in the *Adrastea,* a magazine he began to edit in 1801, he made it the *leitmotif* of his own contributions. Nemesis is the eternal Law of Retribution which in the historic future retaliates for the errors and wrongs committed in the past. In the "Tenth Collection" of the *Letters for the Advancement of HUMANITÄT* Herder evokes that law:

The law of fairness is not alien to any nation: all, and each in its own way, have had to atone for its transgression . . . Who can guarantee to Europeans that, in several corners of the earth, what happened to Abyssinia, China or Japan might not—and will not—happen to them? . . . Intellectual and brute forces can combine in ways which now we can barely surmise. Who can look into a future whose seeds, perhaps, have already been planted? Civilized states can arise where now we believe them hardly possible; civilized states which we believed immortal may wither away . . .

Certain fevers and follies of humankind must vanish with the passage of centuries and of ages. Europe must repair the wrongs it has done, make good the crimes it has committed.[31]

Here, with inspired perceptiveness, Herder anticipated a central issue in the continuing controversy which, since the end of the Second World War, has clouded relations between the industrialized nations and the Third World. No further proof is needed of the modernity and relevance of Herder's anticolonial thought.

Notes

1. Fernand Braudel, *The Perspective of the World* (New York: Harper & Row, 1984), p. 62.

2. Eric Williams, *Capitalism and Slavery* (New York: G. P. Putnam's Sons, 1966), p. 5. (The quote refers to M. James, *Social Problems and Policy During the Puritan Revolution* [London, 1930], p. 111.)

3. *Ibid.,* p. 51.

4. *Ibid.,* p. 41.

5. Edith F. Hurwitz, *Politics and the Public Conscience: Slave Emancipation and the Abolitionist Movement in Britain* (London: George Allen & Unwin, Ltd., 1973), p. 18.

6. *Ibid.*

7. Quoted in *The Enlightenment,* ed. Peter Gay (New York: Simon & Schuster, 1973), p. 128.

8. Montesquieu, *The Spirit of Laws,* ed. David Wallace Carrithers (Berkeley: University of California Press, 1977), p. 260.

9. *Ibid.,* p. 261.

10. Condorcet, *Sketch for a Historical Picture of the Progress of the Human Mind,* tr. June Barraclaugh (New York: The Noonday Press, 1955), p. 141.

11. *Ibid.,* pp. 175-76.

12. *Herders Sämmtliche Werke,* ed. Bernhard Suphan (hereafter cited as *SW*), 33 vols. (Berlin: Weidmannsche Buchhandlung, 1877-1913), XIII, p. 252. (All quotations from Herder are given in the author's translation.)

13. *Ibid.,* p. 348.

14. *Ibid.,* p. 147.

15. *Ibid.,* pp. 257-58.

16. *Ibid.*

17. *SW* XXIX, p. 426.

18. *SW* XVIII, p. 222-23.

19. *Ibid.,* pp. 262ff.

20. *Ibid.,* pp. 233-34.

21. *Ibid.,* p. 236.

22. *SW* XIII, p. 263.

23. *Ibid.,* pp. 263-64.

24. *Ibid,* p. 451.

25. *SW* V, p. 546.

26. *SW* XVIII, p. 272.

27. *SW* V, p. 550.

28. Quoted in Hermann Ley, *Geschichte der Aufklärung und des Atheismus* (Berlin: VEB Deutscher Verlag der Wissenschaften, 1986), vol. 5, Part 1, p. 611, footnote 143. (This is the author's translation from the original French.)

29. *SW* XIII, p. 288.

30. *SW* XIV, p. 37.

31. *SW* XVIII, pp. 288-89.

James M. Van Der Laan (essay date 1990)

SOURCE: Van Der Laan, James M. "Herder's Essayistic Style." In *Johann Gottfried Herder: Language, History, and the Enlightenment,* edited by Wulf Koepke, pp. 108-23. Columbia, S.C.: Camden House, 1990.

[*In the following essay, Van Der Laan examines the importance of Herder's distinctly essayistic style in his prose writings.*]

Johann Gottfried Herder figures prominently in the history and development of the German essay. He is a preeminent and masterful exponent of the genre and may well be the exemplary essayist of his age. His famous essays on Shakespeare and Ossian, for instance, are now classics and stand out as prototypical and representative models of the form. Ludwig Rohner even included the former in the first volume of his anthology, *Deutsche Essays: Prosa aus zwei Jahrhunderten.*[1]

Herder's essayistic oeuvre is extensive. He wrote and published a profusion of short prose expositions. His *Zerstreute Blätter* alone comprise six collections of such shorter compositions. Also a prolific journalist, he contributed sundry book reviews, critical articles, encomia, and other similar pieces to a number of different periodicals.[2] Short expository prose—the essayistic mode of expression—constitutes a large part of his vast literary output. In fact, it seems to be his preferred medium.

Herder's essayistic production is not limited to essays proper nor to short prose expositions, however. On the contrary, such works as the *Fragmente, Humanitätsbriefe* and *Ideen* also have a decidedly essayistic character. To be sure, they consist of numerous short segments within longer, large-scale works, but more important, they have a particularly essayistic texture and tone. Herder's prose output in general is essentially essayistic.

While form or structure is important, there are no special formal markers to identify the essay. After all, formal considerations count for little where the essay is concerned. According to Michael Hamburger, the essay is not so much a specific form as it is a specific style.[3] Similarly, the essayistic character of Herder's literary legacy does not so much derive from a mass of short prose compositions as from his style. Indeed, a distinctly essayistic style informs virtually all his prose writing. In consequence, both his essays proper and those works not ordinarily regarded as such are essayistic, for the same essayistic style—though with slight variations—pervades Herder's prose opus. Whether **"Shakespear"** or *Plastik,* **"Briefwechsel über Ossian"** or *Ursprung der Sprache, Fragmente* or *Ideen, Alteste Urkunde,* or *Humanitätsbriefe*—all are intrinsically essayistic.

Here it might be useful to call to mind and enumerate some of the more distinctive features typically associated with the essay and essayistic writing. In his book, *Deutsche Stilistik,* Richard Meyer writes of the essay as follows:

> To its origin, it owes its monologic character which differentiates it from the treatise that is much more closely adapted to communication needs: it also wants only to stimulate, not to communicate set views or information; it wants to be a kernel with as little shell as possible. It therefore also tends to paradoxes, to pointed expressions, and it loves to evoke the paradoxes and pointed expressions of others—therefore the frequency of quotations in essays. It has also its dilemma, like the aphorism, diary, letter: while artistically rounded it is supposed to be "unfinished," as it reaches its true conclusion only in the continuing reflexions based on it.

> [Von seinem Ursprung her hat er das Monologische, das ihn von der viel stärker dem Mitteilungsbedürfnis angepaßten Abhandlung unterscheidet: auch er will nur anregen, nicht wirkliche Anschauungen oder Kenntnisse fertig mitteilen; auch er will ein Kern sein mit möglichst wenig Schale. Auch er neight deshalb zur Paradoxie, zum pointierten Ausdruck, und liebt anderer Paradoxien und Pointen anzurufen—daher die Häufigkeit des Zitats im Essay. Auch er hat, wie Aphorismus, Tagebuch, Brief, sein Dilemma: daß er nämlich bei künstlerischer Abrundung doch "unfertig" sein soll, insofern als er erst in dem an ihn geknüpften weiterführenden Nachdenken seinen wahren Abschluß erreicht.][4]

According to Ludwig Rohner, author of *Der deutsche Essay*—the most extensive and elaborate treatment of the subject to date—the essay is:

> . . . a shorter, self-contained, relatively loosely composed piece of reflexive prose which in an aesthetically demanding form elucidates one single incommensu-

rable topic through a critical interpretation, preferably with a synthetic, associating, imagistic method; with sophistication it entertains the fictional partner in an intellectual conversation and activates his educational background, his combinatory thinking, his imagination in an experimental manner.

[. . . ein kürzeres, geschlossenes, verhältnismäßig locker komponiertes Stück betrachtsamer Prosa, das in ästhetisch anspruchsvoller Form einen einzigen, inkommensurablen Gegenstand meist kritisch deutend umspielt, dabei am liebsten synthetisch, assoziativ, anschauungsbildend verfährt, den fiktiven Partner im geistigen Gespräch virtuos unterhält und dessen Bildung, kombinatorisches Denken, Phantasie erlebnishaft einsetzt.][5]

Additional traits he lists include such attributes as "subjective, aesthetic, carpet-like woven, direct, associative and inductive, circle, does not draw conslusions, dialogic character, . . . disjointed." [subjektiv, ästhetisch, teppichartig, unvermittelt, assoziativ und induktiv, Kreis, verzichtet auf Konklusionen, Gesprächscharakter, . . . sprunghaft.][6] The *Reallexikon der deutschen Literaturgeschichte, Sachwörterbuch der Literatur,* and *Deutsche Philologie im Aufriß* provide similar definitions and descriptions.[7]

In summary, the essay is loosely structured with no overriding principle of organization. Exposition of the theme typically occurs unsystematically, erratically, even elliptically. The essay presents ideas in a free-flowing, desultory, and rhapsodic manner. While essayistic is by name experimental, it is also typically dialogic, that is, conversational in tone and so evokes a special sense of conviviality. It seeks participation from the reader and accordingly engages, addresses, and appeals to him or her directly. The essay is, moreover, characteristically fragmentary, consequently inexhaustive and incomplete. At the same time, it supplies a number of different points of view, since no single perspective tells the whole truth. On the contrary, several may be valid. Tentative and indefinite, the essay asks more than answers. Equivocal and undogmatic, it represents an inductive and stochastic approach to each issue or subject under investigation. Precisely these essayistic traits distinguish Herder's prose.

Herder understood the nature of his own prose style and himself offers some accurate assessments of it. In the foreword to his *Zerstreute Blätter* (5. Slg.), for instance, he mentions his encomium for Hutten and describes it as an "a somewhat wild growth" [etwas wildes Gewächs.][8] Similarly, he compares *Ueber Thomas Abbts Schriften* to "a badly organized mixture" [ein übel zusammen geordnetes Gemisch] (II, 265). *Vom Erkennen und Empfinden der menschlichen Seele* he refers to as "jotted-down traits" [hingeworfne Züge] (VIII, 225), and with that comment alludes again to the unsystematic, disconnected, and preliminary character of his works. He likewise characterizes the *Kritische Wälder*

as free-flowing and loosely structured. By his own account and as the title is to indicate, the work consists in "collected materials without plan or order" [gesammelten Materien ohne Plan und Ordnung] (III, 188). His own remarks attest to the unsystematic and irregular, that is, essayistic aspect of his style.

As the word *essayistic* suggests, Herder's style is characteristically experimental. He experimented with grammar, diction, and syntax, in other words, with style and its manifold possibilities. He took liberties with prose style and as a result repeatedly came into conflict with his contemporaries. Hamann and Nicolai, for example, took him to task again and again for his heterodox and irregular style of writing. According to Hamann, "the alcibiadic misuses of the article, the monstrous word combinations, the dithyrambic syntax and all other poetic licences . . . betray such a spasmodic way of thinking" [. . . die alcibiadischen Verhunzungen des Artikels, die monstrosen Wort-Kuppeleyen, der dithyrambische Syntax und alle übrige *licentiae poeticae* . . . verrathen eine so spasmodische Denkungsart.][9] Despite his disapproval, Hamann has accurately identified several features of an experimental, namely, essayistic style. Experimentation gave rise to Herder's neologisms, his new, unusual, and bold metaphors, as well as a range of (often unconventional) grammatical forms and sentence structures.

Throughout his life, Herder struggled to break the bonds and burst the bounds of established literary theory and practice. Already in the *Fragmente* (3. Slg., Nr. 2), he expressed his dissatisfaction with the rigid and restrictive Latin period and *Kanzleistil.* In his opinion, the Latin, scholastic tradition left a legacy of "eternal barbarism in the German language" [ewige Barbarey in der [deutschen] Sprache] (I, 365). Similarly, he blamed "scholastische Wortkrämerei" (I, 372) for the dismal state of the language. He even held "die lateinische Form" per se responsible for the "state of scholarship, the foundation and institution of the academies, and the conventional laws of literature" [Zuschnitt der Gelehrsamkeit, die Stiftung und Einrichtung der Akademien, [und] die Zunftgesetze der Litteratur] (I, 371-2)—all of which he heartily despised. At the same time, he inveighed against contemporary writers, the "prosaic-poetic stumblers, erudite wise men, edifying orators" [Prosaisch-Poetische Stolperer, gelehrte Weisen, . . . erbauliche Redner] who with their "adacemic periodic style" [akademischen Paragraphenstil] and "bureaucratic style" [Kanzleistil] corrupted both German language and literature (I, 373). His image of German "in academic and homilectic chains" [unter Akademischen oder Homiletischen Fesseln] (I, 373) summarizes his view of the language.

Herder continued to crusade against a blighted and debased style in his tribute to Thomas Abbt:

What do indeed our complicated sermon periods help us? Our plodding style in paragraphs? The language of the Weeklies without flexibility and force? The inflated presentation of our schoolish translations and school orators? The slow pace of our historians? The polite delicatesse of our beaux esprits?

[Was helfen uns doch unsre verkettete Predigtperioden? Unser schleppender Paragraphenstil? Die Hüft- und Marklose Sprache der Wochenblätter? Der aufgeblähte Vortrag unsrer Schulübersetzungen und Schulredner? Der langsame Trab unsrer Geschichtsschreiber? Der artige Anstand unsrer schönen Geister?]

(II, 274-5)

His criticism leaves almost no one unscathed and shows how pervasive the problem is.

Herder constantly opposed that *Kanzlei-* and *Paragraphenstil* and its embodiment the *gelehrte Abhandlung.* He rejected its stodgy, impersonal, lifeless character as well as its systematic method and teleological orientation. Likewise, he challenged its claims for objectivity, logic, and completion. According to Eric A. Blackall, there was in Herder "an instinctive dislike of cold, reasoned exposition."[10] Nor could Herder write to fit such a mold. On the contrary, he broke free of such constraints and with his writing sought to give new life and direction to his native language and literature.

Unlike that of the learned treatise, Herder's style is unorthodox and ebullient, conversational and idiosyncratic. He disregarded syntactical, grammatical, and stylistic rules and conventions. "I may say it to these people," he asserts in *Thomas Abbts Schriften,* "that I did not want to write according to academic rules, but according to my own manner." [Diesen darf ich sagen, daß ich nicht nach Akademischen Regeln, sondern nach meiner Art habe schreiben wollen.] (II, 267) Instead of carefully proportioned periods, he crafted uneven and disjointed sentences. He abandoned standard and accepted procedures and patterns of writing for a freer and more experimental mode of expression. That same experimentation and independence resulted in his own individual, highly irregular and unsystematic, essayistic style. Consider a few examples representative of his writing. They epitomize his prose style. The first excerpt below—taken from the *Kritische Wälder*—exemplifies Herder's typically uneven, unsystematic, and experimental idiom.

Then, therefore, then there flowed, when death, when ill fate separated those whom life could not separate, such noble tears of heroes, as Achilles the hero shed for his Patroclus, as Pylades for his Orestes, as David the hero for his Jonathan.

[Da also, da flossen, wenn der Tod, wenn ein Unglück die trennete, die das Leben nicht trennen konnte, so edle Heldenthränen, wie der Held Achilles um seinen Patroklus, wie ein Pylades um seinen Orestes, wie der Held David um seinen Jonathan weinten.]

(III, 33)

The sentence components seem fragmented and disjunct. Repitition (*da, wenn, wie*) interrupts the flow and evokes a tentativeness, while the ensuing restatement reflects a search for the right word, phrase, or image.

A passage from *Vom Erkennen und Empfinden der menschlichen Seele* similarly features certain stylistic patterns characteristic of Herder's prose and essayistic writing.

If the true historian of self would then pursue this self-portrait through all consequences, would show that no weakness and no force remains in one place, but continues its effects, and that the soul continues unexpectedly to go on according to such given patterns: would show that each wrongness and coldness, each false combination and missing emotion occurs again and again by necessity, and that in each effect one has to supply the imprint of the entire ego with its force and weakness—what instructive examples descriptions of such a kind would be!

[Verfolgte der treue Geschichtsschreiber sein selbst dies sich selbst zeichnen sodenn durch alle Folgen, zeigte, daß kein Mangel und keine Kraft an Einem Ort bleibe, sondern fortwürke, und daß die Seele nach solchen gegebnen Formeln unvermuthet fortschließe: zeigte, wie jede Schiefheit und Kälte, jede falsche Kombination und fehlende Regung nothwendig immer vorkommen und in jeder Würkung man den Abdruck seines ganzen Ich mit Kraft und Mangel liefern müsse—welche lehrende Exempel wären Beschreibungen von der Art!]

(VIII, 181)

Herder proceeds in a desultory and elliptical (circular) fashion. The string of clauses parallels his thoughts as he jumps back and forth from one to another. He sets out in one direction (*verfolgte*), but as soon interrupts himself (*zeigte*) and takes another course. A moment later, he interrupts himself again, not once (*und daß*), but twice (a second *zeigte*), returns to a previous point in the sentence, and there begins once more.

The following quotation from *Auch eine Philosophie der Geschichte zur Bildung der Menschheit* especially recommends itself as a paradigm of Herder's prose style.

The most cowardly evil-doer without doubt has still a distant potential and possibility to be the most generous hero—but between it and "the entire feeling of being, the existence in such a character"—chasm! Even if you needed only time, opportunity to transform your potential to be an Oriental, a Greek, a Roman into real skills and solid drives—chasm! We speak only of drives and skills. The whole nature of the soul, which pervades everything which patterns all other inclinations and powers of the soul after itself, which colors even the most negligible actions—in order to empathize with this, do not go by the words, but enter into the age, the geographical region, the entire history, try to gain a feeling for this all—only now are you on the way to understanding the word; only now even the thought will disappear, "as if that, taken individually or together, would be you!" You, everything together? Quintessence of all times and peoples? that already shows how foolish this it!

[Der feigste Bösewicht hat ohne Zweifel zum großmüthigsten Helden noch immer entfernte Anlage und Möglichkeit—aber zwischen dieser und "dem ganzen Gefühl des Seyns, der Exsistenz in solchem Charakter"—Kluft! Fehlte es dir also auch an nichts, als an Zeit, an Gelegenheit, deine Anlagen zum Morgenländer, zum Griechen, zum Römer in Fertigkeiten und gediegne Triebe zu verwandeln—Kluft! nur von Trieben und Fertigkeiten ist die Rede. Ganze Natur der Seele, die durch alles herrscht, die alle übrigen Neigungen und Seelenkräfte nach sich modelt, noch auch die gleichgültigsten Handlungen färbet—um diese mitzufühlen, antworte nicht aus dem Worte, sondern gehe in das Zeitalter, in die Himmelsgegend, die ganze Geschichte, fühle dich in alles hinein—nun allein bist du auf dem Wege, das Wort zu verstehen; nun allein aber wird dir auch der Gedanke schwinden, "als ob alles das einzeln oder zusammengenommen auch du seyst:" Du alles zusammengenommen? Quinteßenz aller Zeiten und Völker? das zeigt schon die Thorheit!]

(V, 502-3)

Herder's essayistic style comes to full expression in the paragraph above. He experiments with punctuation, sentence types, and word-order. His punctuation, for example, (commas, dashes, question and quotation marks, exclamation points) is typically heavy and idiosyncratic. Basic declarative sentences alternate with questions and exclamations, interjections and interruptions. He opposes long, complex, run-on sentences with short, incomplete fragments. Inversions further distinguish his prose and let him explore the possibilities of syntax and diction in yet another way. The dialogic or conversational character of his style also manifests itself here. Herder addresses the reader directly and draws him or her into the discussion with second person singular pronouns (*dir, deine, dich, du*) not to mention imperatives (*antworte, gehe, fühle*) and interrogatives. Such features as those outlined and present in the examples given here are typical of Herder's style. What is more, they are typical of essayistic prose per se.

The fragmentary and fragmented character of Herder's writing likewise belongs to an essayistic style. His predilection for the fragmentary is readily evident. After all, he is the author of the famed *Fragmente* as well as many other pieces entitled *Fragment*.[11] Even a work like the *Ideen* can be considered fragmentary, however. The chapters of Book 20 (XIV, 448ff.), for example, consist of several separate segments. Asterisks mark the end and beginning of each section, in effect, break the text down into discrete parts. As Rudolf Haym so poignantly notes, Herder's entire literary output bears the stamp of fragmentation: "As he began with fragments, he also concluded with fragments. And everything that lies in between is more or less fragment in more than one sense." [Wie er mit Fragmenten anfing, so hat er mit Fragmenten aufgehört; Fragment in mehr als Einem Sinne ist mehr oder weniger alles Dazwischenliegende.][12]

Of particular interest is a pervasive fragmentation common to his prose, even to the sentence unit. Herder himself testifies to the fragmentation in his writing. In the **"Auszug aus einem Briefwechsel über Ossian und die Lieder alter Völker,"** for instance, the reference to "abgebrochene Materie" (V, 196) is by no means casual or incidental. After all, the entire essay consists in broken-off segments of letters. He describes the piece devoted to Thomas Abbt in much the same way. In his words, it is nothing but "a mutilated torso" [ein verstümmelter Torso] (II, 262).

Herder's sentences are typically partial and incomplete. Sentence fragments—phrases, interjections, and exclamations—characterize and punctuate his compositions. The ellipses and dashes he so regularly uses likewise break and interrupt his periods. In other words, they add further to the splintering and segmentation of both sentence and paragraph.

Such fragmentation typifies Herder's prose. In a passage from *Plastik,* for example, Herder interrupts himself in midsentence. "And it was," he declares, "as if I had a sense to feel anxiously from afar the nature of beauty where—but I talk too soon and too much." [Und es war, als ob mir ein Sinn würde, die Natur des Schönen da furchtsam von ferne zu ahnden, wo—doch ich plaudre zu frühe und zu viel.] (VIII, 15) One need only open "Ossian" for further evidence of fragmentation. The very first paragraph begins and ends with an ellipsis (V, 158). In fact, ellipses seem to be the governing principle for the whole composition. In the following quotation from *Kritische Wälder,* Herder not only interrupts himself (twice) with his idiosyncratic dashes, but then also breaks the sentence off—precisely where one would expect more.

> The aching sound comes closer, it becomes a whining, a deep, miserable "Agh"—now it is really audible! You are not mistaken: Philoctet has to come, and alas! the shepherd comes with a tone of the shawm, and Philoctet with a tone of misery—he appears! or rather he sneaks up, in order—
>
> [Das Ach kommt näher, es wird ein Wimmern, ein tiefes, klägliches Ach—nun ists erst vernehmlich! Sie haben sich nicht geirrt: Philoktet muß kommen, und ach! der Hirt kommt mit einem Tone der Schalmei, und Philoktet mit einem Tone des Jammers—er tritt auf! oder vielmehr er schleicht sich hinan, um—]

(III, 42)

So the paragraph ends, sentence unconcluded, even without a final period. Herder simply suspends the discussion. Sometimes he breaks off with a dash, sometimes he trails off in an ellipsis, or he may just as inconclusively end a composition with a question mark, as he does **"Von Ähnlichkeit der mittlern englischen und deutschen Dichtkunst."** (IX, 534)

Essayistic writing is fragmentary in yet another way, for it is characteristically inexhaustive. Similarly, a sense of incompleteness pervades Herder's prose works and manifests itself both in sentence structure as well as in exposition of a theme or topic. As Rudolf Haym observes, "never really completed, the same idea returns in more than one place; . . . it migrates more or less unchanged, from one essay to another, from one work to the next." [niemals rein abgeschlossen, kehrt dieselbe Idee an mehr als Einem Orte wieder; . . . sie wandert, mehr oder weniger unverändert, aus einem Aufsatz in den anderen, aus einem Werk in das andere.][13]

Herder makes no pretense to finality. He typically offers only a partial account of the issue or subject under investigation. Certain formulations appear again and again in his writing and subtly convey the unfinished and incomplete nature of his investigations and observations. In his tribute to Lessing, for example, he remarks at one point: "—perhaps at another time more of this." [—vielleicht zu einer andern Zeit hievon ein Mehreres.] (XV, 492) In other words, one simply cannot supply all the details, no matter how pertinent they might seem.

Even in the thoroughgoing *Abhandlung über den Ursprung der Sprache,* he must leave some questions unanswered, some depths unplumbed. "It was the breath of God," he notes, "blowing air which the ear caught, and the dead letters which painted it there, were only the corpse which had to be animated with vital power while reading." [Es war Othem Gottes, wehende Luft, die das Ohr aufhaschete, und die todten Buchstaben, die sie hinmaleten, waren nur der Leichnam, der lesend mit Lebensgeist beseelet werden muste.] He goes on to say, however, "what enormous influence that had for the understanding of the Greek language cannot be described in this place." [was das für einen gewaltigen Einfluß auf das Verständniß ihrer [der Griechen] Sprache hat, ist hier nicht der Ort zu sagen.] (V, 14) The same type of comment turns up throughout his works, as, for instance, in **"Ossian,"** "but I will not make a book out of my letter." [doch aus meinem Brief soll kein Buch werden.] (V, 174); in **"Ähnlichkeit der mittlern englischen und deutschen Dichtkunst:"** "there is neither time nor place for it here;" [hier ist dazu weder Ort noch Zeit;] (IX, 526): and in *Vom Erkennen und Empfinden*: "Yet, I would not succeed in tracing the course of this grandiose phenomenon of action and rest, of contraction and expansion through all its ways." [Doch, ich würde nicht fertig werden, dies große Phänomen von Würkung und Ruhe, Zusammenziehung und Ausbreitung durch alle seine Wege zu verfolgen.] (VIII, 174) Even in the monumental and comprehensive *Ideen,* Herder makes exception: "But I cannot indulge here in such explanations: even the investigation of a point so important for our history, as is the shortening of the human lifespan and the beforementioned great flood itself, has to wait for another occasion." [Doch dergleichen Erläuterungen darf ich mich hier nicht überlassen: ja selbst die Untersuchung eines für unsre Geschichte so wichtigen Punkts, als die Verkürzung der menschlichen Lebensjahre und die genannte große Ueberschwemmung selbst ist, muß einen andern Ort erwarten.] (XIII, 438)

Such remarks are typical both of Herder and of the essayist per se. With them, Herder (essayist) expresses the incompleteness and inconclusiveness of his observations and researches. In characteristic essay fashion, Herder provides only the impulse, the point of departure, of which Meyer and Rohner speak in their definitions. Herder articulates that very notion in the foreword to his *Ideen,* where he writes:

> The author imagined himself in the circle of those who are really interested in what he wrote and whose participating, whose better thoughts he wanted to elicit. This is the highest value of writing, and a well-meaning human being will be much happier with the response he evoked than with what he said.
>
> [Der Verfasser dachte sich in den Kreis derer, die wirklich ein Interesse daran finden, worüber er schrieb und bei denen er also ihre theilnehmenden, ihre bessern Gedanken hervorlocken wollte. Dies ist der schönste Werth der Schriftstellerei und ein gutgesinneter Mensch wird sich viel mehr über das freuen, was er erweckte, als was er sagte.]
>
> (XIII, 5-6)

Herder's pieces come to true and final conclusion only in the minds of the readers as they afterward reflect on and contemplate the issues he raised.

Time and again, Herder gives voice to the catalytic function his writing is to have. Indeed, the essayistic concept of the literary work as impetus runs like a red thread through his writings. In the *Kritische Wälder,* for example, he remarks: "I would only wish that my readers might survive the somewhat dry and closed paths of this first part in order to reach freer perspectives behind them." [Ich wünschte nur, daß meine Leser die etwas trocknen und verschlossenen Pfade dieses ersten Theils überstehen möchten, um hinter denselben zu freiern Aussichten zu gelangen.] (III, 188) As he here indicates, he intends his words as a stimulus to further thought. It is outside and beyond the composition that the reader is to come to answers and insight.

Probably the clearest and most succinct formulation of such essayistic thinking comes in the second part of *Vom Erkennen und Empfinden der menschlichen Seele.* "I would wish nothing," he states, "except that these jotted-down traits find readers who do not enthusiastically declare them as truth, but who empathize before and after reading with a gently beating heart." [Ich wünschte nichts, als daß diese hingeworfne Züge Leser finden, die ihnen Wahrheit nicht zujauchzen, sondern mit sanftklopfendem Herzen nach- und vorempfinden.] (VIII, 225) Herder does not claim to speak the authoritative word, nor to give a definitive and conclusive analysis. Rather, he presents a few disconnected strokes of the pen and leaves the reader to form his or her own opinion, to draw his or her own inferences, so to bring the investigation to a close. Because they are essentially inexhaustive and inconclusive, Herder's works ultimately remain fragments.

Essayistic writing is not only experimental and fragmentary, but also dialogic. Like experimentation and fragmentation, dialogue informs Herder's style. His predilection for the dialogue is particularly apparent as the external form a number of his publications take. Among others, *Gott,* "Verstand und Herz," "Die heilige Cäcilia," "Ueber die Seelenwandrung," "Einige vaterländische Gespräche," and *Vom Geist der Ebräischen Poesie* are all *Gespräche.* As epistolary works, "Ossian," "Briefe über Tempelherrn, Freimäurer und Rosenkreuzer," "Litterarischer Briefwechsel," and the *Humanitätsbriefe,* to name only a few, should also be mentioned, for they too represent a type of dialogue between author and his understood correspondent.

Herder's dialogic tendency extends beyond any external or outward form, however. It is fundamental to his literary idiom. For him, all speech and communication derive from dialogue. As he remarks in the *Abhandlung über den Ursprung der Sprache,* "I cannot think the first human thought, not line up the first judgement of reflexion, without dialoguing in my soul or trying to dialogue. The first human thought, therefore, by its nature, prepares one to be able to enter into a dialogue with others!" [Ich kann nicht den ersten Menschlichen Gedanken denken, nicht das Erste besonnene Urtheil reihen, ohne daß ich in meiner Seele dialogire oder zu dialogiren strebe; der erste Menschliche Gedanke bereitet also seinem Wesen nach, mit andern dialogiren zu können!] (V, 47). That very thought underlies his entire prose production.

Indeed, almost all Herder's writing possesses a certain dialogic quality. Whenever he writes, he seems to have a reader in mind. He typically addresses and appeals to the reader, often directly. Consider the following salutations: "Leser! laß die Geschichte reden," (*Fragmente* I, 363); "denke dir, mein Leser," (*Kritische Wälder,* III, 75); "gehe hin, mein Leser, und fühle" (*Auch eine Philosophie,* V, 486); "lies weiter, Leser: und du wirst sehen!" (*Älteste Urkunde,* VI, 196). Interrogatives, imperatives, and (for lack of a better word) vocatives appear with great frequency. Sometimes Herder poses

questions: "Siehst du nicht?" (*Auch eine Philosophie,* V, 485) or "und was denken Sie?" ("Ossian," V, 165). Sometimes he challenges the reader with a command: "Jetzt denke weiter!" (*Fragmente,* I, 366) or "wer diese Länder kennet, und Deutschland kennet, antworte." (*Humanitätsbriefe,* XVII, 309) In each case, he creates a sense of give and take between author and reader. With his questions and exhortations, he draws the reader into the discussion, engages him or her in conversation as it were.

Herder employs the pronoun *wir* to the same ends. With the first person plural, he opens up the discussion to include the reader and to make him or her a complete partner in the investigation. He treats the reader, moreover, as an active participant. In *Vom Erkennen und Empfinden,* for example, he writes: "Now all steps which we have completed so far show that the Godhead provided us with all this through ways and channels which always receive, clarify, carry away, unify, make more similar to the soul what apart from it was so dissimilar." [Nun aber zeigen alle Tritte, die wir bisher zurückgelegt haben, daß die Gottheit uns dies Alles durch Wege und Kanäle schaffte, die immer empfangen, läutern, fortschwemmen, mehr einigen, der Seele ähnlicher machen, was ferne ihr noch so unähnlich war.] (VIII, 193) Herder does not speak of the steps he has gone through and laid out before an audience. On the contrary, he speaks of work he and the reader have done together. The same regard for the reader comes to expression in the *Ideen.* In the *Vorrede,* he voices the hope that "the more experienced reader will think with him and bring the imperfect closer to perfection." [der erfahrnere Leser mit ihm denke und sein Unvollkommenes der Vollkommenheit näher führe.] (XIII, 6) He constantly promotes that desired reader involvement and so uses the inclusive *we* throughout the work. The section "Was ist Klima?" (XIII, 265-273) may serve as one of many illustrations, since it is particularly rich in such constructions. Herder's *Ursachen des gesunkenen Geschmacks* provides another sample of essayistic author/reader cooperation. After some explanation, he declares: "Finally this way of presentation provides the richest and deepest application: let us therefore try it!" [Endlich gibt dieser Weg der Betrachtung auch die reichste und tiefste Anwendung: wir versuchen ihn also!] (V, 613). Herder introduces another avenue of inquiry, but before entering it summons the reader's participation.

Herder similarly solicits reader participation and involvement with "let us" formulations. Once again, examples abound: "Lasset uns also ein Volk setzen" ("Shakespear," V, 217): "Lasset uns Sophokles aufschlagen, lasset uns lesen," (*Kritische Wälder* III, 13); "lasset uns . . . die Philosophie vom Wolkenhimmel auf die Erde rufen" (*Erkennen und Empfinden,* VIII, 207); "lasset uns noch einige Meisterzüge betrachten."

(*Ideen,* XIII, 423) Such language is inviting and inclusive. With it, Herder makes the undertaking a joint and cooperative effort. Even where such dialogic elements are absent, a dialogic moment nonetheless remains, for one then finds Herder in conference with himself. After all, monologue is also a form of conversation-discourse with oneself.

A study of Herder's prose reveals yet another distinctly essayistic trait—what John A. McCarthy calls "polyperspectivity."[14] This term describes the essayistic approach, for the essayist looks at and attempts to illuminate an issue or topic from various, different sides. The essayist in fact tries to take as many different perspectives as possible into account. The same is true of Herder. He never tired of writing and rewriting, for instance, and was ever taking a new approach to his topics and themes. The *Fragmente* are a prime example, for he constantly revised and amended them and eventually published a completely reworked second edition. The *Kritische Wälder, Humanitätsbriefe,* and *Ideen* similarly reach such great length, because Herder always found some other modification or variation he had yet to communicate. With each revision and addition, he sought to bring some new dimension or different aspect of his topic to light.

The *Humanitätsbriefe* illustrate that need to offer another and still another perspective. Number 41 in the fourth collection bears the title **"Grundsätze seiner [Realis de Viennas] Prüfung des Europäischen Verstandes und seine Velledenblätter."** The next letter, number 42, then furnishes a perspective on number 41: **"Eine Meinung über die vorige Meinung."** (XVII, 205-213) Herder's essayistic and polyperspective approach is even more striking in numbers 67-69 of the sixth collection. While the first letter deals with "Verschiedener Gebrauch und Untersuchung der Mythologie in verschiedener Absicht," the next supplies "Einwendungen dagegen," and the last yet another point of view, "Beantwortung derselben." (XVII, 359-367)

The patterns of Herder's prose themselves convey a certain polyperspectivity. Herder relies heavily on amplification, that is, repitition of nouns, verbs, adverbs, and adjectives—generally in groups of three. Each restatement gives another perspective on the matter in question. Consider an example from *Auch eine Philosophie der Geschichte zur Bildung der Menschheit*:

> If I succeeded in connecting the most disparate scenes without confusing them—to show how they relate to each other, grow out of each other, lose themselves in each other, all of this only details by themselves, but means to an end through continuity alone—what a sight! what a noble application of human history! which motivation to hope, to act, to believe.
>
> [Wenns mir gelänge, die disparatsten Scenen zu binden, ohne sie zu verwirren—zu zeigen, wie sie sich auf einander beziehen, aus einander erwachsen, sich in ein-

ander verlieren, alle im Einzelnen nur Momente, durch den Fortgang allein Mittel zu Zwecken—welch ein Anblick: welch edle Anwendung der Menschlichen Geschichte: welche Aufmunterung zu hoffen, zu handeln, zu glauben.]

(V, 513)

With each new noun (*Anblick, Anwendung, Aufmunterung*) and with each new verb (*hoffen, handeln, glauben*), he adds another nuance of meaning.

The pattern asserts itself throughout Herder's prose works. An excerpt from *Plastik* beautifully illustrates his amplificational style. One brief passage contains three different word clusters—nouns, adverbs, and verbs.

> Words and instructions cannot give it to him; but experience, trial attempts. In a few moments he [the child] learns more and everything more vividly, more truly, more strongly, than all gaping and explanation of words would teach him in ten thousand years. Here, by combining sight and touch incessantly, examining, expanding, lifting, reinforcing one through the other—he forms his first judgement.
>
> [Worte und Lehren können sie ihm nicht geben; aber Erfahrung, Versuch, Proben. In wenigen Augenblicken lernt er [das Kind] da mehr und alles lebendiger, wahrer, stärker, als ihm in zehntausend Jahren alles Angaffen und Worterklären beibringen würde. Hier, indem er Gesicht und Gefühl unaufhörlich verbindet, eins durchs andre untersucht, erweitert, hebt, stärket—formt er sein erstes Urtheil.]

(VIII, 7-8)

Here form and content converge, for Herder both describes and employs a polyperspective, essayistic approach to knowledge. He not only gives voice to the same idea in the *Humanitätsbriefe,* but in the same form as well. "But to collect, to order, to direct, to use ideas; this is the great unending advantage of [human nature] throughout all ages." [Aber Gedanken zu sammlen, zu ordnen, zu lenken, zu gebrauchen; dies ist ihr [der menschlichen Natur], für alle Zeiten hinaus, unabsehlicher großer Vortheil.] (XVII, 27) With each subsequent word, he expands the view as it were and adds another dimension to his statement and our understanding.

Close examination of Herder's writing also reveals extensive use of "entweder/oder," "einerseits/andererseits," and "je/desto" constructions. They let him compare and contrast, advance and retract various opinions and ideas. Likewise, Herder tends often to use such qualifiers as "vielleicht" and "wahrscheinlich," as well as expressions like "mich dünkt," "wie ich glaube," and "meiner Meinung nach."[15] They too enhance the perspectivity of his writing, since they allow for error and for different, even opposing, points of view. What is more, they convey the tentativeness and equivocation so characteristic of essayistic writing. In typical essay fashion, Herder qualifies and tempers his assertions.

The essayist tends to avoid unequivocal, absolute statements, since others may be equally valid. Indeed, he takes an inductive and stochastic approach to the subjects and issues under consideration. Herder subscribes to the same way of thinking—and writing. He himself asserts the undogmatic and undoctrinaire stance of the essayist. In *Ueber Thomas Abbts Schriften,* for example, he writes:

> I want to generate thoughts for the other: evoke images in him: create ideas in him: stimulate sensations in him—but not just tell him my thoughts, show my images, give an allusion of my sensations. I want to awaken geniuses, to teach readers, not to satisfy critics.
>
> [Erzeugen will ich dem andern Gedanken: aufruffen in ihm Bilder: in ihm Ideen schaffen: in ihm Empfindungen aufregen—nicht aber ihm meine Gedanken blos erzählen, meine Bilder vorkramen, meine Empfindungen hingaukeln. Genies will ich wecken, Leser lehren, nicht Kunstrichter gnügen!]
>
> (II, 280)

As he here explains, he does not advance his ideas as the ultimate truth or as absolute authority. His goal, moreover, parallels that of every essayist, for he encourages independent thought. According to Ralph-Rainer Wuthenow, such *Selbstdenken* characterizes the essay.[16]

Herder does not supply definitive and dogmatic answers. He elucidates the same notion again in *Vom Erkennen und Empfinden der menschlichen Seele.* "We want more to sense than to know," he observes, "would rather find out for ourselves, possibly too much, than to have everything slowly told to us." [Wir wollen lieber empfinden, als wissen, lieber selbst und vielleicht zu viel errathen als langsam hergezählt erhalten.] (VIII, 209) The essayist refrains from authoritative pronouncements. Instead he acknowledges his own limitations, even fallibility. He does not impose his views on others and allows himself the luxury of error. One need only think of the many occasions where Herder contradicts himself. For him, as for the essayist per se, the process is more important than the outcome, discussion more important than the conclusion. To paraphrase him, better to sense than to know, even better to guess and be wrong than to learn through tedious dictation.

As an essay about essayistic writing, the present study offers but a few illustrations of and an incomplete and inexhaustive commentary on Herder's style. Some of his works are more essayistic (*Auch eine Philosophie der Geschichte,* "Ossian," the *Fragmente,* and *Humanitätsbriefe,* to name but a few), others less so (as, for example, the *Abhandlung über den Ursprung der Sprache* and the *Ideen*), yet all bear the stamp of a distinctly essayistic style. Indeed, in view of his style, Herder is first and foremost essayist.

One of Herder's most famous and oft quoted statements concerns the style of another great essayist—Gotthold Ephraim Lessing.

> Lessing's way of writing is the style of a poet, that is, a writer who has not already made, but is making, who does not say he has already thought it out, but who thinks before us; we see how his work comes into being, like Achilles's shield in Homer. He seems to present to us the reason for each reflection, to show its parts, to put it back together again; now the spring works, the wheel is turning, one idea, one inference leads to the next, the conclusion approaches, there is the product of the contemplation. Each section something thought-out, the *tetagmenon* of a concluded thought: his book a continuing poem, with digressions and episodes, but always in movement, always working, in progress, in the process of becoming . . . his book an entertaining dialogue for our mind.
>
> [Leßings Schreibart ist der Styl eines Poeten, d.i. eines Schriftstellers, nicht der gemacht hat, sondern der da machet, nicht der gedacht haben will, sondern uns vordenket, wir sehen sein Werk werdend, wie das Schild Achilles bei Homer. Er scheint uns die Veranlassung jeder Reflexion gleichsam vor Augen zu führen, Stückweise zu zerlegen, zusammen zu setzen; nun springt die Triebfeder, das Rad läuft, ein Gedanke, ein Schluß giebt den andern, der Folgesatz kommt näher, da ist das Produkt der Betrachtung. Jeder Abschnitt ein Ausgedachtes, das *tetagmenon* eines vollendeten Gedanken: sein Buch ein fortlaufendes Poem, mit Einsprüngen und Episoden, aber immer unstät, immer in Arbeit, im Fortschritt, im Werden . . . sein Buch ein unterhaltender Dialog für unsern Geist.]
>
> (*Kritische Wälder,* III, 12)

With those words, Herder provides at once both a poignant explication and illustration of his own essayistic style.

Notes

1. Johann Gottfried Herder, "Shakespeare," in *Deutsche Essays: Prosa aus zwei Jahrhunderten* ed. Ludwig Rohner (Neuwied und Berlin: Luchterhand, 1968), I, pp. 185-207.

2. The editor of the Suphan collection of Herder's works lists 24 different periodicals for which Herder wrote. Of those, I cite a few of the better known: *Königsbergsche gelehrte Zeitungen,* Nicolai's *Allgemeine Deutsche Bibliothek, Vossische Zeitung, Wandsbecker Bote, Frankfurter Gelehrte Anzeigen, Teutscher Merkur, Deutsches Museum, Die Horen, Göttinger Musenalmanach,* Schiller's *Musenalmanach,* and *Der Neue Teutsche Merkur.* See Herders *Sämmtliche Werke,* ed. Bernhard Suphan, (Berlin: Weidmannsche Buchhandlung, 1913), XXXIII, 198-199.

3. Michael Hamburger, "Essay über den Essay," *Akzente,* 12, Heft 4 (1965), 291.

4. Richard M. Meyer, *Deutsche Stilistik,* 3rd ed., *Handbuch des deutschen Unterrichts an höheren Schulen,* ed. Adolf Matthias, Vol. 3, Part 1 (München: C. H. Beck'sche Verlagsbuchhandlung, 1930), p. 168.

5. Ludwig Rohner, *Der deutsche Essay: Materialien zur Geschichte und Ästhetik einer literarischen Gattung* (Neuwied: Luchterhand, 1966), p. 672.

6. Rohner, *Der deutsche Essay,* p. 511.

7. Fritz Martini, "Essay," in *Reallexikon der deutschen Literaturgeschichte,* ed. Werner Kohlschmidt and Wolfgang Mohr (Berlin: Walter de Gruyter & Co., 1958), I, pp. 408-410; Gero von Wilpert, "Essay," in *Sachwörterbuch der Literatur,* 5th ed., Kröners Taschenausgabe, Vol. 231 (Stuttgart: Alfred Kröner Verlag, 1969), pp. 235-237; Klaus Günther Just, "Essay," in *Deutsche Philologie im Aufriß,* ed. Wolfgang Stammler, 2nd ed., (Berlin: Erich Schmidt Verlag, 1960), II, cols. 1897-1948.

8. Johann Gottfried Herder, "Vorrede," *Zerstreute Blätter,* 5. Slg., in *Herders Sämmtliche Werke,* ed. Bernhard Suphan, XVI (Berlin: Weidmannsche Buchhandlung, 1887), p. 133. All further references to Herder's works appear parenthetically in the text. Roman numerals indicate the volume, arabic numbers the page. Translations are my own.

9. Johann Georg Hamann, as quoted by Eric A. Blackall, in *The Emergence of German as a Literary Language 1700-1775,* 2nd ed. (Ithaca/London: Cornell University Press, 1978), p. 459.

10. Blackall, p. 459.

11. Besides his *Fragmente* and his contributions to Lavater's *Physiognomische Fragmente,* Herder published several other so-called fragments, among them: "Das Land der Seelen. Ein Fragment;" "Fragment eines Gesprächs des Lords Shaftesburi;" nine "Fragmente" in the 7. and 8. Sammlungen of the *Humanitätsbriefe;* and "Fragment über die beste Leitung eines jungen Genies zu den Schätzen der Dichtkunst."

12. Rudolf Haym, *Herder: Nach seinem Leben und seinen Werken dargestellt,* ed. Wolfgang Harich (Berlin: Aufbau-Verlag, 1954), I, p. 146.

13. Haym, I, p. 148.

14. John A. McCarthy, "The Poet as Journalist and Essayist: Ch. M. Wieland. Part II. Wieland as Essayist: The Cultivation of an Audience," *Jahrbuch für Internationale Germanistik,* 13, Heft 1 (1981), 121.

15. The *Ideen* contain a wealth of such constructions and formulations, and they too are a rich source of essayistic passages.

16. Ralph-Rainer Wuthenow, "Literaturkritik, Essayistik und Aphoristik," in *Zwischen Absolutismus und Aufklärung: Rationalismus, Empfindsamkeit, Sturm und Drang 1740-1786,* ed. Ralph-Rainer Wuthenow, Vol. IV of *Deutsche Literatur: Eine Sozialgeschichte,* ed. Horst Albert Glaser (Reinbek bei Hamburg: Rowohlt Taschenbuch Verlag, 1980), pp. 136-137.

Lael Weissman (essay date 1991)

SOURCE: Weissman, Lael. "Herder, Folklore, and Modern Humanism." *Folklore Forum* 24, no. 1 (1991): 51-65.

[*In the following essay, Weissman maintains that Herder's emphasis upon the morality and spirituality of humanity impacts his philosophy and treatment of nationalistic issues.*]

William Wilson's article "Herder, Folklore and Romantic Nationalism" presents the dominant view in folklore that the roots of our discipline are tied to nationalistic motives:

> [Serious folklore studies] were from the beginning intimately associated with emergent romantic nationalistic movements in which zealous scholar-patriots searched the folklore record of the past not just to see how people lived in by-gone days—the principal interest of the antiquarians—but primarily to discover "historical" models on which to reshape the present and build the future.
>
> (1973:819)

Certainly it is true that these romantics were trying to effect change in their political climate by reformulating the past, but ideology governed this reformulation. Wilson simplifies romantic nationalism as "the wistful dream of scholars and poets who endeavored through constant education and propaganda to rekindle the spark of national consciousness in the hearts of their fellow countrymen" (1973:820).

In Germany, this dream of romantic nationalism was born out of a new world conception, a mythology if you will; and, as mythos it was comprised of both immediate and ultimate concerns. To ignore the mythological aspect of the origin of our own field is to pretend in effect that we are myth-free. We must apply to our own history the realizations we have gleaned from the study of others.

Nationalism was part of a larger movement, loosely called *modern humanism* (Schütze 1920). Modern humanism contains as an essential characteristic a conflict between the ideal and the actual: romantic nationalism, as product of these ideas, contains the same tensions. This movement strove to manifest the ideal nation in the actual world; thus folklore began as a reformist endeavor. Herder's philosophy was essentially a critique of his times, and his concept of nationalism emerged out of that critique. "Herder's attack on his own century can no longer be of so great interest as his revolutionary idea of the autonomy of each individual culture. In the eyes of its author, however, the idea was probably a by-product" (Clark 1955:196).

An examination of the historical currents of the eighteenth century helps to create a contextual backdrop for evaluating Herder's work. German intellectual life was more advanced than the country's social and political development. The Holy Roman Empire of the German Nation, a loose confederation of small states, was still in existence, and aside from one or two exceptions, Germany had no statesmen who could act to change this fragmentation. Constant comparison occurred between countries on the Continent, a situation which may be difficult for Americans to imagine. At this time cultural relativism was being invented and its implications thought through. Modern humanistic ideology is largely responsible for our ability to conceive of different conditions in each country as historical and cultural rather than as more or less advanced; that is, it may be this line of thought that moved us beyond notions of evolution.

Germany had suffered the disruptions of the Reformation, the Counter-Reformation, and the Thirty Years War all during the seventeenth-century; it was divided into 1,800 different territories with an equal number of rulers. Among the elite, foreign influences dominated; in fact, most elites spoke languages different from those in lower classes, making communication impossible. Aristocrats imitated the court life at Versailles, and these French habits were filtering through to the middle classes. German writers not only used French as their medium of expression but also adopted French and classical models to shape form and content. Similarly, the language of the intellectuals was Latin, used exclusively in the schools: during this period, Kant, in a revolutionary act, lectured in German for the first time.

Through modern humanism, a shift in understanding had been accomplished. Until that time, foreign influences were not seen as demeaning but as uplifting what some saw as a backward culture. Germans did not consider themselves as an autonomous culture, but instead the upper and middle classes evaluated themselves in relation to other cultures which they considered superior. Through modern humanism, Germans began to conceive of themselves as having an independent and valuable cultural heritage. Clearly, this shift occurring in the intellectual class was related to the Enlightenment in France and Britain.

There was much intellectual and artistic exchange between these countries. With the Enlightenment had come another set of abstract ideals by which knowledge was measured, and what was not rational according to this measurement was considered irrational and thus false. Herder revolted against the Enlightenment and its emphasis on reason and argued for the importance of the emotions, which united feeling with reason. Clark sums up Herder's aim as being "the destruction of what may be called the caste system in eighteenth century philosophic anthropology" (1955:249). Great changes were occurring in the the intellectual and the political worlds. The French and American revolutions helped to characterize the period as a time of action: the *Sturm und Drang* movement has been termed by Ergang, "the German form of the French revolution" (1966:192).

Many view Herder's work and involvement in intellectual movements in a cursory way, emphasizing his association with great philosophers and literary figures of his day, and overlook his profession as a preacher. Born in East Prussia in 1744 to a poor family, he was able to develop a good hand for calligraphy and came to work for his teacher, Trecho. Herder began to satiate his desire for knowledge in Trecho's library. Through Trecho, he met an officer who offered to support his medical training, but Herder could not stand the sight of blood and so enrolled as a theology student; legend has it that he was so poor that he survived on no money and lived for some time on only bread and water.

Herder worked as preacher but his orthodoxy was often challenged, despite his strong commitment to leading his congregation to spiritual regeneration. He felt called to restore harmony between the world and the will of God; he considered the absence of this harmony to be the origin of spiritual degeneration of his day (Gillies 1945:58). And though his peasant congregation did not always understand him and often wanted a more orthodox approach, Herder delivered brilliant sermons (Gillies 1945:58). Chronicler Alexander Gillies summarizes their content:

> The existence of a divine purpose in the world, which is inscrutable and cannot be fully revealed until the end; the activity of God throughout all nature; the demand that life should obey the divine laws of nature, and fulfill the powers that have been given to it; the condemnation of sins, unnaturalness, or a falling-away from God's purpose; a Peagian assumption of the innate purity in man; the assertion that the one central factor in all human effort is religion and that religion is founded upon revelation and faith—all these are themes that Herder is constantly expanding and stressing.
>
> (1945:62)

This message was not exclusively religious for Herder but penetrated each subject he took up; he read widely and attempted to rebuild various areas of study by giving them new spiritual and philosophical foundations.

All of Herder's vast work bore the same sub-structure: an examination of humans as moral and spiritual beings. Herder assumed that people evolve spiritually; he termed the ultimate end of this evolution *Humanität* (humanity). "Humanity," he wrote, "is the character of our race . . . we do not bring it ready-made into the world. But in the world it must be the goal of our strivings, the sum of our exercises, our guiding value" (Herder quoted in Wilson 1973:823). With this assumption, he proceeded with his reinterpretation and formulated a dissertation which consciously included the idea of humans having both purpose and destiny.

His conception of nature illustrated his assumptions; it was based on the unification of different forms of knowledge. He saw, for example, no reason why purely scientific investigation should embarrass religion, which he considered the palladium of truth (Clark 1955:275). He saw nature as "a universe filled with the spirit of God, progressively revealing Himself and completing His work through nature and man" (Herder in Gillies 1945:54). Awareness of matter resulted from the recognition of this omnipresence of divinity. "Through the similarity of the effects of this 'energy' or 'force' in nature to its effects in us we become aware, according to Herder's psychology of 1778, of what we call matter" (Clark 1955:223). God speaks to people through nature by analogy—that is, in understandable terms. Herder conceived of nature as an artist and therefore brought the natural sciences more closely together with aesthetics, bridging the already-established dichotomy between science and art.

> Nature, the greatest artist of all, economically re-uses its protoforms as the human artist re-uses the fundamental structures of all art, and the over-all effect is that of an ascending series culminating in man, who is thus akin to all creation but not derived from it by any process of physical transformation.
>
> (Herder in Clark 1955:306)

Herder conceptualized evolution as symbolic rather than temporal.

Just as in nature, Herder saw artistic genius in poetry, which was to him the mechanism of the universe.

> [For Herder] Shakespeare was more than divinely inspired; that he was god-like, a creator in miniature, whose work followed and illustrated the same process of Creation itself. . . . The poet's function is to make known God's purpose; to interpret nature or the universe, of which he is a part, by making it live again, by reconstructing and reproducing its modes of operation, by re-creating it, as it were, before the eyes and ears of his fellow-men, so that they may perceive and comprehend its workings.
>
> (Gillies 1945:49-50)

Herder similarly considered philosophical systems as poetry (*Dichtung*) unless they could be applied (Clark 1955:178).

He linked poetry with revelation in several ways. Herder suggested that "poetry was originally theology," but he later inverted this notion when he conceptualized theology as poetry. "The oldest and most venerable heathen poets, lawgivers, fathers and educators of mankind, Orpheus and Epimenodes and all the fabulous names of early time, sang of the gods and gave rapture to the world" (Gillies 1945:55). The Old Testament was for him a kind of poetic folk song. "One can see," he wrote, "that I am not here using poetry to mean falsehood; for in the realm of understanding the significance of the poetically composed symbol is truth" (Herder in Clark 1955:297). Neither does he deny the possibility of the role of history in shaping the quality and content of the poetry. The universe, for him, was permeated by God: "history and revelation were thus identical" (Gillies 1945:54).

Clearly, there is difficulty in discussing one topic in isolation when considering Herder's work. He made connections with disparate realms of thought and aspects of man's nature that had not been central foci of the Enlightenment. The superiority of reason over sensibility was challenged by the new unity of being and purpose which Herder proclaimed. Herder's arguments were persuasively shaped by his revolt against the Enlightenment, for in a significant way its narrow-mindedness inspired him to articulate a more comprehensive philosophy.

One of the best examples of his confrontation with a rationalistic perspective is his criticism of Kant. Kant held that humans were animals who needed a master; Herder posited, to the contrary, that "man is an animal as long as he needs a master to rule over him; as soon as he attains the status of a human being he no longer needs a master in any real sense" (Herder in Barnard 1969:323). In this juxtaposition one can see Herder's main counter-argument to Enlightenment thinking. Whereas the Enlightenment had placed human beings at the peak of history—the dawn of a new age, Herder reinstated the continuity of human life and joined together what could not fit under the umbrella of pure reason—sensibility and will. Thus, he automatically identified not only areas for action—the arts, for example—but also a directive for the will, and an ultimate goal; he preached the possibility that these three aspects of human experience could become unified.

Unification is a central impulse in Herder's work and one of the goals of modern humanism. Several authors have noted Herder's remarkable similarity to Faust and suggested that Goethe must have based this character in part on Herder; Goethe, in fact, did directly quote him. According to Gillies, "Herder shows at this time more than a little affinity with Faust. The desire to grasp the whole of the universe and to set forth its meaning so as 'To help or convert a fellow creature [Faust]' is certain"

(1945:61). "His chief aim," writes historian Robert Ergang, "[is] to understand the purpose and destiny of man as an inhabitant of this earth" (1966:82). To that end, Herder began by looking at mankind, placing him at the center, in order to come to a new understanding.

In his early work Herder posited a new conception of the difference between the human and the animal: the two were distinguished by the fact that humans can speak. Language, for him, was the outward manifestation of *Bessonenheit* (reflection), while reason was its internal function. "Language is the real external, as reason is the real internal character essential factor to our species" (Herder in Schütze 1925:528). He did not consider reason as a distinct faculty of mind, but indicated that reason could be employed to different degrees: "But does thinking rationally mean the same as thinking with fully developed reason? Does it mean that an infant thinks reflectively or uses logic like a sophist at his desk? It is clear that such an objection does not touch the mental power as such but only different degrees of use" (Herder in Schütze 1925:529). Through the development of reason, people become creators and acquire a kind of freedom within nature. "By virtue of 'Bessonenheit' every idea ceases to be an immediate work of nature and becomes man's own work. No longer an infallible machine of nature, man creates the motives and purposes of his own constructive efforts" (Herder in Schütze 1925:529). Again, Herder extended the Enlightenment tenet of the human being as a perfected machine of nature to include a will: "Knowledge without will is false and incomplete knowledge. . . . Impulse is the mainspring of being" (Herder in Schütze 1925:536).

In his system Herder offered a primary unity of thought, will, and feeling and so synthesized science and philosophy, two polar modes of thought—rationalism which understood existence to be governed by nerve processes, and vitalistic naturalism which defined being as governed by impulse. He described sensibility, will, and thought as acting reciprocally and argued that each always be interpreted in relation to the other two. "Isolation of genetic conditions, of technique, subject matter, inherent mental, moral, and aesthetic character, is contrary to the unity which functions integrally throughout the activities of the living individual" (Herder in Schütze 1925:541). For Herder, sensibility led to knowledge rather than threatened it: "We must conclude that the strongest passions and impulse properly ordered, are merely the sensible outline of strong reason within them" (Herder in Schütze 1925:547).

Establishing the primacy of human aspects more directly associated with feeling, Herder stated that the arts should not be based on clearly defined models established by the reasoning self; that is, one need not comply with classical rules. Indeed, he challenged the

very heart of Enlightenment thinking by suggesting that there are other sources of knowledge beyond that of pure thought, ways of knowing which precede reason.

> This is therefore the principal law according to which nature has regulated both faculties; namely, that feeling operates where perception cannot yet be; that it introduces a great deal at once into the soul obscurely, so that this latter may clarify it to some extent and discover thereby what its own existence can achieve; that this takes place in the easiest and pleasantest possible way so that the greatest possible amount may be perceived in the shortest possible time, and the soul may be gently led forth outside itself in its operations, as if it were operating in isolation and concerned only with itself. . . . In every minute part of the infinite prevails the truth, wisdom and goodness of the whole; in every perception, as in every feeling is reflected the image of God, there with the rays or the brilliance of white light, here into which the sunbeam is divided. . . . Honour therefore, the genius of mankind and seek to serve it as purely as you can.
>
> (Herder in Gillies 1945:71)

Similarly, Herder conceived of reason not as distinct from feeling but "nothing more than something formed by experience, an acquired knowledge of the propositions and directions of ideas and faculties, to which man is fashioned by his organization and mode of life" (Herder in Barnard 1969:264). Rather than viewing reason as an *a priori* faculty, Herder saw it "as the accumulation or product of the impressions that are received, the examples that are followed, and the internal power and energy with which they are assimilated within the individual mind" (Herder in Barnard 1969:264-265).

Herder's philosophy of history was in effect an epistemological inquiry. His process of reexamination hinges on two central principles: that a people's knowledge is shaped by the environment, and—more difficult to identify—that there is a divine will manifested through the process of Creation, which has its end in Humanity. "Man considered as an animal is the child of the earth and is attached to it as his habitation; but considered as a human being, as a creature of Humanität, he has the seeds of immortality within him and these require planting in other soil" (Herder in Barnard 1969:280). For Herder, people are at once animalistic and human, and they strive to emphasize their humanity. Their mission is what Herder calls "paligenesis [which] means . . . a purification and regeneration of our whole life in this world as a means of winning a higher than earthly life" (Herder in Gillies 1945:99).

Understanding the notion of *continuity* in Herder's work is vital to comprehending his philosophies of history and nationalism. Edgar Schick (1971) reads Herder's work as poetry, identifies the primary images of organicism, and finds a continuity of thought and execution. Herder described the nature of thought, feeling, and will as being one and articulated a system which united these impulses. Schick further illustrates Herder's consistency of feeling and thought, but more interestingly demonstrates the relationship between these two and the will. We have seen how Herder found unity in every subject he approached, recasting each according to his own longing and faith.

Summarizing Herder's understanding of the relationship between mind, sensibility, and will, Schütze draws the following conclusions: 1) Mind and sensibility are one and can only be separated in words; 2) pure reason is a delusion because it originates and remains in the sensibility and stays there; 3) ridding oneself of the sensibility does not liberate reason; 4) people cannot demonstrate their own immortality; and 5) absolute being, or immortality, is an article of faith, but faith generates its own truth from sensibility rather than reason (1925:550). Faith is not excluded from Herder's thought: it is instead the goal of human will. Thus, we can understand the nature of his pedagogy and his concept of Humanität, which he claimed as the foundation of his work.

Herder's thoughts on history and nationalism have a tendency to overshadow their foundation in modern humanism. His main impulse was to synthesize disparate aspects of human knowledge and redefine knowing as involving various facets of the personality and as being shaped by the environment and the genetic force of Divine Nature. This process could be called "creative analogy," beyond mere analogy because it entails more than the breaking down of boundaries between preformulated logical systems. Infusing faith, longing, and will, Herder created a new relationship between different aspects of thought, between preestablished dualisms. Frederick Smith in *Studies of Religion under German Masters* characterizes Herder as "the great master who led his way back into this ancient time" as captured in the folk poetry he studied (Smith 1880:131). "Herder penetrated the recesses of that time when sense and spirit were one, because this was the secret of his own inward life. . . . All his labours, as philosopher, theologian, critic, historian, and scientific inquirer, have this as their aim, to bring man back to the point, whence he started as a child, of harmony within himself and between himself and the universe around him" (Smith 1880:131-132). But Herder could not be called a primitive thinker, for we tend to conceive the primitive as not choosing harmony consciously over other forms of thought.

According to Gillies, Herder's own desire became problematic. The harmony he consciously sought through his pedagogy did not correspond with his own environment:

> The trouble arose from Herder's strong pedagogic sense, from the desire to criticize and to improve his own age, and ultimately, therefore, from his own personal dissatisfaction. This clearly conflicted with his historical outlook, as it had done before. Herder was always seeking deficiencies and striving to eliminate them, always seeking and never finding harmony between himself and the world. . . . Humanität was now Herder's consolation in the face of contemporary shortcomings; he clung to it with great—but not unshaken—optimism, and into it projected the qualities he missed so much around him—peace, religion, sympathy, equity, reason, truth. He proclaimed his doctrine, which rested on personal longing, as if it were the law of nature.
>
> (Gillies 1945:93)

The nature of Herder's pedagogy was two-fold, critiquing the existing social, political, intellectual, and spiritual situation as well as illustrating the ideal process with which people need to establish contact. Inseparable from these two tendencies, Herder suggested how to realize this pedagogy, nowhere more frequently than in his discussions of the nation.

Herder's conceptions of nationalism and ideal culture were strongly influenced by his reading of Giambattista Vico's *Scienza Nuova*. From Vico he borrowed two significant ideas. He focused on the existence of different historic ages, which evolve from one another in the continuity of history. He also embraced the notion that each historical epoch forms an independent cultural entity whose various parts are integrally related to form an organic whole. Similarly, Herder borrowed from Montesquieu the idea that cultural types are primarily determined by the physical environment in which the nations are located. From these ideas emerged his philosophy of history which assumes that history is "a stream that flows unceasingly toward the ocean of humanity" (Herder in Ergang 1966:220). While Aristotle had placed the city-state at the end of history, and Vico the idealized civilization, Herder envisioned "Humanity" as the ultimate goal of the historical process.

For Herder, history takes place in terms of organic entities of culture: "Each age, each nation possesses an individuality, with temporal or local characteristics, never to be repeated; it cannot be other than imperfect. It cannot be judged by any standards other than its own, since they are equally imperfect; it carries its own criterion within itself" (Herder in Gillies 1945:65). History is then "an account of ethnic groups or nationalities considered as historical, genetic, organic entities. In each national group there is an active power which, influenced by environment and tradition, effects an orderly development or historical continuity" (Herder in Ergang 1966:220). One is not to study individuals or political events, but "all that the nationalities did and thought" (Herder in Ergang 1966:220). The study is to be undertaken by means of sympathy rather than abstract reasoning; the subject must be regarded "in the spirit of the age (*Zeitgeist*)" (Herder in Ergang 1966:216).

This ideal motion of the nation as an organic unit proved particularly challenging in the practical world. Other aspects of Herder's conception of nationalism must be considered in close relation to his period. Again, Germany had been exposed to many foreign influences. As Gillies states, "The loss of Charles the Great's folksong collection, the Latin domination of German culture in the Middle Ages, followed by the Renaissance and Wars of Religion—had cheated German literature of its due, so weakened it as to make it subservient to French literature, and made an irreparable breach between the present and its own national past" (1945:51). Meanwhile, contemporary thinkers considered nationality as an obstruction to humanity. In all cases, Herder used *nation* to denote a cultural rather than political distinction. Thus, the nation becomes the central factor in human development but still not an end in itself. Opposing the shallow individualism of his time, Herder clearly articulated how individual needs, selves, and knowledge related to those of the group (Ergang 1966:248). "For no one of us is by himself alone. The whole structure of man's humanity is connected by a spiritual genesis—education—with his parents, teachers and friends, with all the circumstances of life, and hence with his countrymen and forefathers. Indeed, in the last analysis, he is connected with the whole chain of the human species, since some links of this chain inevitably come into contact with, and thus act upon, the development of mental powers" (Herder in Barnard 1969:312-313).

With Herder's thinking about nationality he began to apply his whole abstract epistemology to the concrete world: on this subject he united his most idealistic thoughts and his criticism of contemporary trends. Between these conflicting projects, he proposed techniques for bridging this gap between the ideal and the practical. Even within his work he recognized, and struggled over, the presence of conflicting impulses. In his early travel journal, he showed himself torn between becoming "a man of action" or pursuing his intellectual insights (Barnard 1969). Accordingly, he later voiced concern about the effect and influence of his work—that is, whether it had a substantial *Wirkung*—and wrote "complete truth is always and exclusively *action*" (Clark 1955:230). Ultimately, both his activism and his thought concentrated on the nation.

This activism could not have happened apart from his focus on culture; Ergang outlines three main reasons for a lack of political interest at that time. Government was monopolized by rulers; absolutism was common. Conditions were poor, and minds were turned away: "Political resignation seems to have been widespread." Writings were still censored at this time (Ergang 1966:240). Intellectually, Herder challenged the Enlightenment view that negated the cultural lines which he believed nature had drawn; "the members of nationality and state

are joined together by inner spiritual bonds" (Ergang 1966:101). Herder proclaimed that these differences were decreed by God and must be emphasized rather than ignored or erased (Ergang 1966:92). "In contrast to the division of the German people and the drab political affairs of his time, he [Herder] continually reminded the German people of their common part and of the heritage which must be preserved if German culture was to continue to exist" (Ergang 1966:231-32). Preaching a doctrine of self-realization (at the level of nation), he sought to "eliminate the boundaries between classes by stimulating the national feeling, national consciousness" (Herder in Ergang 1966:52).

A nation's consciousness, thought Herder, should naturally produce its own expressive forms; so the absence of a unique and explicitly German literature troubled him. He explained Germany's lack of literature as a lack of connection to its essential character and happiness:

> Thus, from ancient times we have absolutely no living poetic literature upon which our modern poetry might grow, as a branch upon a national stem; whereas other nations have progressed with the centuries, and have shaped themselves upon their soil, from native products, upon the belief and taste of the people, from the remains of the past. In that way their language and literature have become national, the voice of the people has been used and cherished, they have secured more of a public in these matters than we Germans have. We poor Germans were destined from the start never to remain ourselves; ever to be the lawgivers and servants of foreign nationalities, the directors of the fate and their battered, bleeding, exhausted slaves.

> (Herder in Gillies 1945:52)

Ergang points out that Herder was the first to explain to the German people, "in a way both large and impressive, the idea that literature is the evolutionary product of national conditions" (Ergang 1966:190). Thus, he not only identified the causes for the absence of literature but also, and more importantly, hastened the advent of a cure. Herder states that "there is no absolute poison in nature which might not on the whole be also a medicament and a balm" (Ergang 1966:198). Herder diagnosed the illness (the lack of literature) as a result of Germany's breaking away from her own cultural foundation; only a reconnection to this essential identity could cure the nation.

To connect with this source of culture, people would have to identify the most recent time in German history when the spiritual connection was still present: the Middle Ages. Herder thus recreated the idea of the *volk*; no longer were they the rabble of the streets, but "the body of the nationality." This group, which had remained on its national foundations, was most in harmony with the national soul (Ergang 1966:195). Folklore was the instrument of his social program; through this medium, one could work to change the present situation. According to Ergang, Herder suggested "that they go back to the sources of their own language and literature and liberate the former power and noble spirit which, unrecognized up to now, lie dormant in the documents of the national past" (Ergang 1966:235). He described the native language as being "filled with the life and blood of our forefathers" and thought that folklore was a treasure to be unlocked to release its spirit and heal his nation (Ergang 1966:253).

> The persistence of vestigal elements in culture is balanced by eternal rebirth through 'evolutions' rather than revolutions, through orderly cyclic progressions rather than through violent upheavals. It is the nature of culture that institutions, long since outlived, manage to perpetuate themselves long after loss of their functional value, while from the very embrace of senility arises the promise of a new day.
>
> (Herder quoted in Clark 1955:363)

Here again, Herder observed the real workings of culture and contrasts this reality with his ideal.

This contrast is even clearer in his thinking about relationships within and between nations.

> It is nature which educates families: the most natural state is therefore, one nation, an extended family with one national character. . . . Nothing, therefore, is more manifestly contrary to the purpose of political government that the unnatural enlargement of states, the wild mixing of various races and nationalities under one sceptre.
>
> (Herder quoted in Barnard 1965:324)

Although this statement easily could be read as foreshadowing a racist love of "purity," Herder was in fact referring exclusively to the "unnatural enlargement of states" taken up by government. His emphasis on the importance of remaining on one's cultural foundation conflicted with his goal of not becoming self-contained on the other. "It was not his goal," writes Ergang, "to make the German nationality self-contained. . . . Although he was vehemently opposed to imitation of other nationalities, he wished his countrymen to learn from the example of others, to emulate their great achievements" (Ergang 1966:265). The borrowing, then, would represent an improvement, a deeper understanding: Germans would not just take on the ways of others but find their roots in humanity.

> I walk through strange gardens merely to get flowers for my language, the betrothed of my mode of thought. I see strange customs so that I may bring mine, like fruits ripened by a foreign sun, as an offering to the genius of my fatherland.
>
> (Herder in Ergang 1966:160)

Here Herder advocated a method for social action: he did not meditate on the nature of Germany's penchant for imitation, but instead tried to conquer it with his strict focus on the commitment to one's nation. Still the foundation of his nationalism "was human brotherhood . . . he was driven by the desire of . . . having them fulfill their mission to mankind" (Ergang 1966:263). However, he could only suggest preliminary steps to transform his ideal into reality.

Schütze suggests that Herder's basic purpose was to force people to recognize the centrality of personality, of individuality; this individual is not the shallow, isolated subject of the Enlightenment, but rather one formed by cultural diversity and the depth of history. Herder's work strove to bring this individuality into awareness; he encouraged his contemporaries to offer up the richness of their culture simply because it belonged to them, and not because it passed the test of some abstract and celebrated measurement. So, his work focused on the nation, and he urgently identified ways in which the individual consciousness could be reawakened in terms of a cultural heritage. In addition to the possibility of changing culture, Herder recognized the importance of the individual.

It was during this period that the individual was first being recognized as an entity. Psychology was just beginning as a science, and there is evidence that Herder read widely in this area, expecting great things from it (Clark 1955:93). So Herder emphasized change at both the national and individual levels:

> It is possible to overcome egoism, whether this be innate or acquired from one's environment, to free oneself from the irregularities of too singular a condition, and, ultimately released from the peculiarities of the national, temporal, personal taste, to grasp beauty wherever found, in all times and all kinds of taste. . . . He is initiated into the Mysteries of the Muses and of all times and memories and works. The sphere of taste is unlimited as the history of mankind. Its periphery lies through all the centuries and their works; its center is he.
>
> (Schütze 1925:521)

Herder's focus extends beyond culture: "The deepest foundation of our being both in sensibility and in thought is individual" (Schütze 1925:542-43). Since the content of his sermons is not available to us, it is difficult to say to what degree he tried to change individuals. But there is evidence that he preached on the importance of a well-balanced life as a prerequisite to work in the arts and sciences, so that a reform of life must precede a reform of the arts (Gillies 1945:73). "The highest knowledge is undoubtedly the art of living; and how many men have been robbed by their fine arts of this one thing, this divine art" (Gillies 1945:73). Schütze's brand of modern humanism involves four necessary components: genetic history, biological growth, the social character of man, and the unity of these three in the individual personality (Schütze 1925:549).

Herder came to his conceptualization of humanism by trying to correct the narrow thinking of the Enlightenment and to effect change in his time. He conceived of a holistic universe by applying the precepts of Leibniz and Spinoza, creating a system which releases cultures from domination; thus he unified these different forms of knowledge. In validating the experiences of each culture, he also accommodated intuition, sensibility, and intentionality.

Herder's vast but unifying thought has been taken in bits and pieces; some have said his greatest contribution was the inspiration he gave to Goethe, the Grimm brothers, and other contemporaries. Because German romanticists took Herder's nationalism and adopted it for their own purposes, our understanding of him is filtered through their perceptions (Clark 1955:418). As we consider our own history as a discipline, we must examine the entirety of our roots; we resist the inclination to isolate a single application of a historical work and examine it out of context. The impulse which preceded the "wedding with nationalism," as Wilson calls it, is most profoundly the pursuit of freedom—not in the American sense of civil rights, not political per se—but cultural and individual, especially in the sense of the inner life. For Herder, freedom could always be discovered in culture, as there is only *freedom within law*: "The first germ of freedom is to perceive that one is not free, and to know the bonds by which one is held" (Schütze 1925:539).

To find freedom in our culture, we need to re-examine our intellectual heritage, criticize the ways in which our predecessors applied their insights, as well as understand the fullness and complexity of their inspiration. To learn from Herder's difficulties, we must identify and acknowledge the aspirations which guide our own work today. Three centuries have not bridged the gap between the ideal and the practical.

References Cited

Andress, James Mace. 1916. *Johann Gottfried Herder as an Educator.* New York: G. E. Stechert.

Barnard, F. M., ed. 1969. *J. G. Herder on Social and Political Culture.* Cambridge: Cambridge University Press.

———. ed. 1965. *Herder on Social and Political Thought from Enlightenment to Nationalism.* Oxford: Clarendon Press.

Clark, Robert T. Jr. 1955. *Herder: His Life and Thought.* Berkeley: University of California Press.

Ergang, Robert Rienhold. 1966. *Herder and the Foundations of German Nationalism.* New York: Columbia University Press.

Gillies, Alexander. 1945. *Herder.* Oxford: B. Blackwell.

Schick, Edgar B. 1971. *Metaphorical Organicism in Herder's Early Works: A Study of the Relation of Herder's Literary Idiom to his World-view.* The Hague: Mouton.

Schütze, Martin. 1920. Fundamental Ideas in Herder's Thought. *Modern Philology* 18 (1920):65-78, 289-302. 19 (1921-22):113-130, 361-382. 21 (1923): 29-48, 113-132.

———. 1925. Herder's Psychology. *The Monist* 35:507-554.

Smith, John Frederick. 1880. *Studies in Religion under German Masters.* London and Edinburgh: Williams & Norgate.

Wilson, William A. 1973. Herder, Folklore and Romantic Nationalism. *Journal of Popular Culture* 6:819-835.

Robert E. Norton (essay date 1991)

SOURCE: Norton, Robert E. "The Ideal of a Philosophical History of Aesthetics: The Diverse Unity of Nature." In *Herder's Aesthetics and the European Enlightenment*, pp. 51-81. Ithaca, N.Y. and London: Cornell University Press, 1991.

[*In the following essay, Norton surveys Herder's philosophical and analytical approach to history.*]

> I believe this is the historical Age and this the historical Nation.
>
> David Hume

In a review in 1771 of Johann Georg Sulzer's encyclopedic work, the *Allgemeine Theorie der schönen Künste* (*General Theory of the Beautiful Arts*), Herder warmly praised the author for his ability to illuminate the "dark" and "confused" psychological moments of the aesthetic experience. Although Sulzer was considerably indebted to the Leibniz-Wolffian school for the framework of his thought, Herder still admired what he took to be the clarity and accuracy of Sulzer's presentation. Yet Herder's general enthusiasm for Sulzer was not wholly unqualified, and on one account in particular Herder reprimanded the academician rather severely. Sulzer seemed to treat the concepts of art as if they could be arbitrarily determined in a fashion similar to the way in which mathematical or logical definitions were derived. Herder objected strongly to this, insisting that a theory of aesthetics demanded a method that could account for the independent development and naturally occurring diversity of the objects and concepts of art it is by definition intended to explain:

> It is simply impossible for there to be a philosophical theory of the beautiful in all arts and sciences *without history*. . . . Why? Never, or rarely, are there ideas here that are definite in themselves, let alone arbitrarily given ones, as in mathematics or in the most general metaphysics; rather, its concepts have arisen from a great variety of 'concretis,' concepts that appear in numerous kinds of phenomena, concepts, therefore, in which 'genesis' is everything.
>
> (*SW* [*Sämmtliche Werke*] V, 380)

In addition to or beyond their basic ontological character, Herder deeply understood that works of art are subject to and reflect the external forces of time and environment that give them their unique appearance. He felt that history, in other words, in all of its complexity, must be an integral part of any philosophy of aesthetics worthy of the name.

Perhaps more than any other single aspect of his entire oeuvre, Herder's contribution to the philosophy of history has ensured him the reputation of having played a substantial role in the development of modern thought.[1] As one of the most recent interpretations of Herder's "historical sense" states, "Herder's philosophical significance doubtlessly has to do with the fact that he shifted history into the center of philosophical thinking."[2] And yet it is equally true that there are few other facets of Herder's work that have been subject to more misunderstanding and distortion.[3] According to the traditional account, Herder introduced the notion of historical relativism into an era that until then had judged the past as an imperfect prelude to the superiority exemplified by its own "Age of Reason."[4] Herder's "historicism" was thus presented as his unique creation, as the fulfillment of his critique and supersession of a fundamentally unhistorical Enlightenment. But both the assertion of his singular achievement in establishing our modern conception of history and the thinly veiled discredit of all previous philosophies of history have prevented us from seeing Herder within a broad and complex tradition of thought and in this way have directed our attention away from the actual aims of his reflections on the problem of history.

Given his predilection for pursuing the origin of a matter as the key to its understanding, it would seem reasonable that Herder would have also wanted simply to analyze aesthetic issues according to their historical beginning and gradual development. And this was indeed an essential part of his program. But it must also be seen within a larger theoretical context. Herder's philosophy of history, and in particular the application of the sort of genetic method to questions of aesthetics that he demanded with reference to Sulzer, was an im-

mediate outgrowth of his confrontation with the subjects and methods of Enlightenment philosophy as a whole. Herder's insights concerning the philosophy of history arose in conjunction with his adoption of the general method of analysis that he, along with his contemporaries, had chosen as the ideal of philosophical procedure. For Herder—but not only for Herder—history was a supremely philosophical discipline, and as such it was to be conducted by observing the most strict philosophical method available. This, and not the advocacy of an absolute cultural relativism, is the authentic aspect of Herder's historical thought that lived on to influence scholars of the nineteenth and twentieth centuries, as the following comment by Ernst Robert Curtius vividly demonstrates:

> A narrative and enumerative history never yields anything but a cataloguelike knowledge of facts. The material itself it leaves in whatever form it found it. But historical investigation has to unravel it and penetrate it. It has to develop analytical methods, that is, methods which will "decompose" the material (after the fashion of chemistry with its reagents) and make its structures visible. The necessary point of view can only be gained from a comparative persual of literatures, that is, can only be discovered empirically. Only a literary discipline which proceeds historically and philologically can do justice to the task.[5]

Curtius's description of the aims and method of literary history can be traced directly to its origin in the Enlightenment, and the terms in which it is formulated have more than a coincidental resemblance to the words and intentions of Herder himself. In the following I will show, by examining not Herder's philosophy of history per se, but only that part of it which contributed directly to his developing aesthetic theory, that his "historical sense" was in fact the result of his attempt to harness the greatest diversity of empirical data within a single theoretical model.

In general, as Hume's self-assured claim that his was the "historical age" would attest, thinkers of the Enlightenment not only were fascinated with the problems of history, they conceived of themselves as eminently historically minded as well. But it was a particular *kind* of historical thinking that began to emerge during the second quarter of the eighteenth century, a new way of approaching the facts that had been meticulously gathered and compiled by the antiquarians of the two preceding centuries. The great erudition of what Arnaldo Momigliano has termed the "traditional school of learned historians," which was represented by such scholars as Bayle, Le Clerc, Montfaucon, Mabillon, Spanheim, and Muratori, was being challenged by the "new school" of philosophical history embodied in the writings of Voltaire, Montesquieu, Condorcet, and Hume himself.[6] We therefore find d'Alembert advising that his contemporaries "gratefully make use of the work of these industrious men," but at the same time somewhat patronizingly suggesting that "erudition" was "necessary to lead us to belles-lettres."[7] While the antiquarians compiled great masses of facts and catalogued the events and figures of the past, the "philosophes" saw themselves as trying to understand the greater forces that shaped and governed culture in the broadest sense.[8] It fell to the heirs of these two main currents of eighteenth-century historical thought, among whom Herder occupies a prominent position, to unify the concerns of exact scholarship and detailed research with a philosophical elaboration of the actual causes for historical change and development.

It is indicative of the age that was equally fascinated with the theory of art that the resultant emergence of a distinctly new way of approaching the historical record coincided with, or perhaps even resulted from, a reorientation of perspectives within contemporary poetic theories.[9] Whether the two facts are intrinsically related or not, it is remarkable that, as Alfred Baeumler observed, "the rise of the historical view of life in the eighteenth century is inextricably connected with the genesis of modern aesthetics."[10] Near the end of the seventeenth century, the dawning realization that one could not simply ignore the inalterable effects of history took place alongside the growing dissatisfaction and eventual abandonment of "normative" or classicist poetics. In the well-known "doctrine classique" of seventeenth-century France, history, understood as an inevitable process of fundamental change, was vigorously or very deliberately disregarded.[11] The poetic theory of Nicolas Boileau, whose *Art poétique* of 1674 stood as the authoritative expression of the principles of this "doctrine" for nearly one hundred years, essentially relied on the rationalistic view that human beings are endowed with certain invariable, innate capacities of reason that, when allowed to flourish, would uniformly govern human habits and thoughts.[12] According to this basic assumption, that which is manifestly true, good, and beautiful at the present moment possessed—or should have possessed—the same value at every other time in human history. Similarly, the things that the people of past eras had valued most highly when human reason was not obscured by ignorance and superstition must logically have equal validity and legitimacy for us as well. And, for the classicist, the supreme model of such a perfectly rational past was, of course, the culture of ancient Greece and Rome. Johann Christoph Gottsched, who in 1730 gave these ideas their German stamp in his *Versuch einer Critischen Dichtkunst* (*Essay on a Critical Poetics*), was therefore able to cite Aristotle as an absolute authority not only on the drama of Sophocles, but on the poetry of Gottsched's own day as well. Not only is Aristotle the most trenchant critic ever to have lived, Gottsched thus wrote, but the rules he set forth were also eternally valid: "He most profoundly understood the essence of eloquence and poetry, and all

of the rules he prescribes are based both on the unchanging nature of humanity and on sound reason."[13]

The consequences of this highly abstract and intentionally static view of human nature for a theory of artistic production were obvious enough. In order to create a beautiful work of art, one had to abide by the rules that had been established as inhering within the great works of the classical past. Gottsched was also very explicit in this regard: "The universal approbation of a nation is thus not a valid judgment of the talent of a master in the liberal arts until the good taste of that nation has been demonstrated. And this occurs when one shows that this taste corresponds to the rules of art which have been derived from reason and nature."[14]

But Gottsched mentioned that the rules governing a work of art were derived from both reason *and* nature. In the appeal to this last source of authority we find the common element that reappears, always somewhat varied in its meaning, in every eighteenth-century theory of aesthetics.[15] In classicistic poetics, nature, which was understood less as the physical reality of "rocks and valleys" than as the embodiment of certain functions and laws, was always regarded as the ultimate guarantor of truth and artistic beauty.[16] Within this dictum there is contained the theoretical justification for the principle of the "imitatio naturae" as the foremost criterion for artistic creation. Since the concept of antiquity as an inviolable model and the concept of nature were not obviously distinguished from one another in the mind of the classicist, Gottsched also maintained without apparent contradiction that the poet "has this as one of his main qualities: that he imitates nature and lets her be his only model in all of his descriptions, fables and ideas."[17] The laws of nature and the rules of ancient poetry were thus virtually synonymous in the "doctrine classique."[18] Poets were therefore advised to imitate nature as closely as possible, for in so doing they would inevitably receive direct instruction from that natural source of authority which had guided the hands of the artists who produced the acknowledged masterpieces of antiquity.

There was simply no interest in the question of significant historical change or cultural progress in the classical doctrine. If the issue of historical variations did arise in conjunction with works of poetry, these were treated as aberrations from the one valid standard represented by nature or—what was virtually the same thing—the theory and works of classical antiquity. Historical documents were thus primarily employed as a source of examples against which the superiority of the ancients could be more easily and clearly demonstrated.

As it often happens when popular ideas are transplanted from one cultural context into another, the precepts that Gottsched introduced to the German-speaking public in

1730 had by then already lost much of their authority in the country from which they issued. The first sign of rupture arose from Charles Perrault, whose *Parallèle des Anciens et des Modernes en ce qui regarde les Arts et les Sciences* (*Comparison of the Ancients and Moderns in All That Regards the Arts and the Sciences*) appeared in four volumes from 1688 to 1697. Perrault's practice of favorably comparing the moderns to the ancients enraged Boileau, against whom it was primarily aimed. Encouraged and emboldened by Boileau's loss of inviolability, others soon followed Perrault's example. In 1719 the French Abbé Jean-Baptiste Du Bos, who was a correspondent and personal acquaintance of Locke, then subjected the principles of normative poetics to an even more persuasive critique in his *Réflexions critiques sur la poésie et sur la peinture* (*Critical Reflections on Poetry and Painting*).[19] Under the general influence of Locke's philosophy, the *Réflexions critiques* represent perhaps the first work that attempted to provide an objective explanation of the "original" of historical diversity, of the reason why cultures differed from one another, rather than to condemn them for not resembling the Greeks or Romans.[20] A significant part of Du Bos's theory, which found an enthusiastic reception both within and outside of France, rested on his belief that, in addition to the so-called moral sphere, the immediate physical environment in which the members of a culture find themselves had a direct and powerful impact on the formation of their national identity. The sum of the various influences that constituted this physical environment, for which Du Bos used the broad, though convenient, designation of "climate" or "air" was thus manifested in the collective character of the people who are immediately affected by it.[21] Du Bos confidently concluded that "the difference of the character of nations is attributed to the different qualities of the air of their respective countries; in like manner the changes which happen in the manners and genius of the inhabitants of a particular country, must be imputed to the alterations of the qualities of the air of that same country."[22] Obviously, these characteristics would never be precisely identical for any cultural group, and the manner of self-expression of the inhabitants of certain "climates" would likewise differ according to their respective habitat. The individuality of artistic expression was therefore, in Du Bos's view, a necessary and unavoidable product of geographical and temporal differences.

The critical intent of Du Bos's *Réflexions critiques* was immediately apparent: rather than judge works of art according to their resemblance—or their lack of it—to Greek and Roman models, he proposed that one ought to understand and explain them as products of their given milieu. Criticism should consist, he suggested, in determining the individual circumstances that prevailed when a work of poetry was created, for he thought that in these circumstances lay the first causes for its particular appearance.[23] The traditional critic's role of exhorting poets to imitate nature and of fixing the rules by which they should do so was thereby rendered defunct and replaced by something approaching a model of scientific descriptive analysis.[24] Du Bos's appeal for a dispassionate investigation into the original causes of artistic difference marked in this way a first step away from the classicist ideals embodied in prescriptive poetics and toward the kind of impartial historical analysis that Herder later also espoused.

Significantly, however, the regulative concept of nature, in the guise of the multiform "climate," still found a prominent place in Du Bos's critical work. Even though he no longer cast it in the form of the "imitatio naturae" that stood as the governing precept in classicist prescriptive poetics, Du Bos's description of the relationship between nature and art reveals his retention of the belief that nature followed the basic laws of cause and effect, that it exhibited uniformity, simplicity, regularity, and symmetry—in short, that nature conformed to rational paradigms. The underlying assumption sustaining Du Bos's *Réflexions critiques* is that, although the external accidents manifested by nature will vary from region to region, the laws it embodies and imposes on humanity remain forever the same. Du Bos's conception of nature implies, then, an abstraction and an idealization of both nature and artistic production that was not unrelated to the more overtly rationalistic doctrines of his predecessors. Although the concept of nature had certainly been a central component in poetic theories since Aristotle, during the Enlightenment nature became through Du Bos's example, in addition, increasingly intimately associated with the concept of history.[25] Nature, or that infinitely complex bundle of external circumstances into which each person was born, came to be seen as a central cause of cultural diversity and even of historical change itself. Abstracted to an even finer degree of pure functionality, this concept of nature would thus also leave its evident traces in Herder's own literary-historical writings.

This theory of the formative effects of climate on the character and fortunes of humankind, of which Du Bos was only one of its most influential exponents, found its way into almost every historical work of the century. The concept of climate plays a considerable role, to name only the most conspicuous examples, in Montesquieu's *De l'esprit des lois* (*The Spirit of the Laws*) of 1748, Winckelmann's *Geschichte der Kunst des Altertums* (*History of the Art of Antiquity*) of 1764, and in Gibbon's *History of the Decline and Fall of the Roman Empire,* the first volume of which appeared in 1776. None was satisfied, however, that the climate was the only agent responsible for all the apparent differences between cultures. Thomas Blackwell's *Enquiry into the Life and Writings of Homer,* which was published in 1735 and greatly impressed and influenced Herder, was one of the first attempts to apply this nascent historical sensibility to an extended study of particular works of ancient poetry.[26] Although he adopted Du Bos's theory of climate, Blackwell also compensated for its relative narrowness by enumerating still other "Circumstances" that he claimed served to shape the character of a people. These included what he called the "Manners," the "Constitution civil and religious," "Education," and a host of other sociopolitical influences that were effective on both the individual and communal levels.[27] Remarkable in Blackwell's account, however, is his concentrated effort to explain the more abstract idea of historical development, to give an account of the phenomenon of the progression of time as it is manifested in the alteration of those "manners" he mentions. In his introduction Blackwell wrote:

> There is . . . a thing, which, tho' it has happened in all Ages and Nations, is yet very hard to describe. Few People are capable of observing it, and therefore Terms have not been contrived to express a Perception that is taken from the widest Views of Human Affairs. It may be called a *Progression of Manners*; and depends for the most part upon our Fortunes: as they flourish or decline, so we live and are affected; and the greatest Revolutions in them produce the most conspicuous Alterations in the other: For the Manners of a People seldom stand still, but are either polishing or spoiling.[28]

This "thing" that Blackwell found so difficult to explain is of course the actual process of historical change itself. Yet Blackwell did not merely describe a single, straight, and continuous march of progress, stretching from the beginning of time to culminate in the munificent perfection of the Kingdom of Great Britain. Rather, he isolated a predictable, regular sequence that he claims necessarily occurs in every cultural formation. That is, depending on its current state, he thought that each culture will "flourish or decline," and will be found to be either "polishing or spoiling." Although Blackwell did not use the traditional analogy of the stages of life ("Lebensalter") that Herder later favored to describe the nature of the historical process, the implications of his historical scheme are nevertheless readily apparent.[29] Just as an organism cannot return to a previous state of its existence, but must follow the course of its growth and decay, so is a culture determined to pass without fail through its own proper stages until it reaches the inevitable end of exhaustion and, finally, death.[30] In order to conform to the biological analogy, this kind of teleology forces one to assume that at the beginning of a particular development lies all the freshness and vitality we associate with the innocence of unspent youth. In speaking of early Greece, therefore, Blackwell contrasted the natural simplicity he perceived in Greek "manners" with the "refined but double Characters" of modern people in terms that remind one of the elegiac opening words of Schiller's great essay, *Über naive und sentimentalische Dichtung* (*On Naive and Sentimental Poetry*). Blackwell extolled

the Pleasure which we receive from a Representation of *natural* and *simple Manners*: It is irresistible and inchanting; they best shew human Wants and Feelings; they give us back the Emotions of an *artless* Mind, and the plain Methods we fall upon to indulge them: Goodness and Honesty have their share in the Delight; for we begin to like Men, and wou'd rather have to do with them, than with more refined but *double Characters*. . . . Innocence, we say, is beautiful; and the Sketches of it, wherever they are truly hit off, never fail to charm.[31]

Implied in Blackwell's praise of the "Emotions of the artless Mind" is that "art" is the forced and feeble version of what was at first effortlessly or naturally accomplished. "Artful" is the attribute of those who are somehow alienated from nature, and through the temporal process of polishing and increasing refinement, this division between nature and art can grow more acute. The antagonistic opposition of art and nature was thus a direct result of Blackwell's particular deterministic conception of history, and it found its corollary in his notion of artistic production. Poets can portray most easily and naturally that which is most familiar to them, Blackwell maintained. The poetry that we esteem the most will thus not be an artful dissimulation or pretense, but of the kind that delivers an accurate reflection of "Nature," by which Blackwell meant the totality of the poet's individual cultural and physical environment. Once again, the idea of nature, now given only the unity of an abstract conception of an organic whole made manifest by the change of appearances, provides the backbone of the theory: "So true it is, *That every* kind of Writing, but especially the Poetick, depends upon the Manners of the Age in which it is produced. The best *Poets* copy from *Nature,* and give it such as they find it. When once they lose Sight of this, they write false, be their natural Talents ever so great."[32]

Yet neither is this a restatement of the principle of "imitatio naturae," nor is it simply a superficial refinement of Du Bos's theory. Despite the element of deterministic necessity contained within his biological notion of historical change, Blackwell, unlike Du Bos, recognized that individual poets may not in fact be rigidly and absolutely determined by the immediate effect of their respective "natural climate." Poets, that is, may indeed try to write about matters outside of their natural sphere. Because of this possible "cultural infidelity," as it were, Blackwell suggested that poets must consciously resolve to devote themselves to their own time and surroundings. Obliquely—for he wanted to avoid pronouncing dogma—Blackwell thus recommended to contemporary poets that they also represent what is familiar from their own experience and cease trying to imitate distant or foreign manners. Thus, in making what appears to be a purely descriptive comment on historical fact, he was simultaneously formulating a general postulate for modern poetry as well. It seems a fitting expression of the irony of an age that was only just becoming aware of the practical disadvantages of a fawning adoration of antiquity that Blackwell should have made his affirmation of modernity within the pages of a study of Homer.

Simply noting that the ideas of historical development, of cultural progress and deterioration, and of the inimitable individuality of every civilization were being energetically discussed long before Herder was born would be trivial in itself. But this observation gains greater significance when coupled with the realization that these very ideas constitute a part of that preeminently critical tradition which represents the Enlightenment he would inherit. My insistence that Herder was not the first to discern the importance of these notions does not—or should not—in any way diminish his stature. On the contrary, the ways in which he implemented them are perhaps even more deserving of our admiration than the originality of invention that has been claimed for him. For it was here, in Herder's application of Enlightenment philosophical conceptions of history to the study of aesthetic questions, that he exhibited a complex understanding of their implications even as he raised them to a greater level of abstraction and generality.

We have seen that, in every case, the concept of nature occupies a place of special significance in the new approach that writers of the Enlightenment took toward poetry and its creation. The relinquishment of the doctrine of "imitatio naturae," which coincided with the effort to understand the past according to criteria not arbitrarily externally imposed, had not, therefore, exorcised the central importance of nature and its functional, indeed normative, status. The introduction of a historical consciousness had not really suppressed the conception of nature as a distinct system of regular laws and rules; it had merely clothed these laws in a greater variety and abundance of attire. In 1765 Herder made his debut in the Enlightenment debate concerning the relationship between poetics, history, and nature in a short work that, like his earlier essay on Kant, constitutes a critical assessment of the thought of a close acquaintance. This time he turned to the work of Johann Georg Hamann.[33] Herder's essay, titled ***Dithyrambische Rhapsodie über die Rhapsodie Kabbalistischer Prose*** (***Dithyrambic Rhapsody on the Rhapsody of Cabalistic Prose***), contains an explicit and occasionally vehement rejection of most of the basic tenets Hamann had espoused in his *Aesthetica in nuce,* which had appeared three years earlier, in 1762, in the famous collection titled *Kreuzzüge des Philologen* (*Crusades of the Philologist*).

Hamann, not unlike the many eighteenth-century French and especially English philosophers (including Blackwell) whom he admired, believed that earlier, more "primitive" peoples enjoyed a more immediate and authentic relationship with nature. They were not fettered, he believed, by the "unnatural" constraints imposed by reason, which were seen as afflicting more advanced civilizations. Hamann, however, deriving inspiration from the mystical writings of Böhme and Swedenborg, admixed to this eighteenth-century anthropological platitude an idiosyncratic religious vision. Central to Hamann's religious primitivism was his belief that the original, unspoiled relationship with nature that was supposedly indicative of uncivilized peoples was fundamentally linguistic in character.[34] Hamann characteristically portrayed the world as the physical manifestation of God's creative word. As the famous lines of the *Aesthetica in nuce* tell us: "Speak so that I may see You!—This wish was fulfilled by Creation, which is a discourse addressed to the Created by the Created."[35] By understanding the ancient metaphor of the "book of nature" in this eminently literal fashion, Hamann conceived of the people of earlier cultures as having had the ability to comprehend and commune with this "language of nature." And by thus conversing both with and in nature, these first people had been afforded the linguistic paradise of an uninhibited and constant access to God.[36] Nature, always a cipher of the Divine in Hamann's writings, could thus acquire vital significance only for those who had not, through the overcultivation of their rational faculties, destroyed their ability to understand it. Aimed at just such people, the *Aesthetica in nuce* therefore amounts to an extended indictment of the linguistic, which is to say moral depravity Hamann perceived in modern humanity: "We have nothing left in nature for our use other than disordered verses and the 'disiecti membra poetae.' It is the modest task of the scholar to collect them; the philosopher's to interpret them, and to imitate—or, more boldly!—to bring them into play is the role of the poet" (N II, 198-99). As these short quotations sufficiently show, Hamann's style itself served as part of his argument against the linear logic of conventional rationality. Indeed, his writing is so dense and metaphorically allusive that no one less than Hegel, in his review of Hamann's works, accused him of deliberately obscuring his meaning and fostering "unintelligibility" in his writings.[37]

Like almost everyone else who wrote on the subject during the eighteenth century, Hamann thought that poetry chronologically preceded prose as the natural form of human expression. Hamann's celebrated remark that "Poetry is the mother tongue of the human race" (N II, 197), was in fact a commonplace in the works of many Enlightenment thinkers.[38] Nevertheless, this notion acquired a distinct meaning in Hamann's pseudomystical writings. He seemed to believe that through a Rousseau-like return to the kind of ecstatic language that he thought characterized the poetic tongues of primitive peoples, a partial—if not complete—return to this original state of linguistic innocence might be possible: "We must become children if we are to receive the spirit of truth" (N II, 202). Thus a step toward earthly redemption could be taken by casting aside the linguistic trammels laid on by reason and culture in order to receive once again an intimation of the Divine through the immediate apprehension of God's "Word-become-Nature." Hamann's express wish, therefore, was "to resurrect the extinct language of nature from the dead" (N II, 211). Until this occurred, however, Hamann saw the activity of the modern poet, scholar, and philosopher as a very privative and even damnable undertaking.

One of the most deeply held beliefs of scholarship devoted to Herder's thought maintains that he was decisively, indeed predominantly, influenced by Hamann. Herder met the "Magus of the North"[39] when he went to Königsberg, and he quickly became his friend and admirer. But this personal sympathy has been seen as having had great consequences for Herder's writing as well. While it has usually been allowed that Herder may have added depth and clarity to Hamann's obscurantist ideas, the implication is that Herder remained essentially true to his friend's antirational aims.[40] In actuality, Herder's *Dithyrambische Rhapsodie* shows him distancing himself as early as 1765 from Hamann and offers evidence that his ideas played a relatively minor role in the formation of Herder's conceptual universe. In fact, there is (to my mind) convincing confirmation that Herder had criticized Hamann, and specifically his *Aesthetica in nuce,* even before he wrote the *Dithyrambische Rhapsodie,* namely in the *Versuch über das Sein* of 1763. In an oblique allusion to "a nut" (*in nuce* means "in a nut") that is worthy of Hamann himself, Herder accused Hamann of simply rebelling against philosophical systems without submitting himself to the necessary labor of mastering them on their own terms and thus criticizing them without personal familiarity. Failing to do this, Herder wrote, one just makes oneself "ridiculous":

> A few fine minds who perceived the *end* of philosophy and the *endless* efforts of the philosophers threw them a nut to show them their finiteness: they disavowed the Being which Mother Nature had convinced them of long ago; see how they prove our orthodox writers— become ridiculous—and revile them with venom in their mouths; instead of showing them the impossibility of analyzing this concept, which would fulfill the purpose of their problem—.

(*W* [*Werke*]13)[41]

As we discover from his footnotes to the *Dithyrambische Rhapsodie,* Herder had by 1765 already read and assimilated at the very least the historical notions of Winckelmann, Condillac, Blackwell and Du Bos, whose *Réflexions critiques* is extensively quoted in Condillac's *Essay.*[42] The most important lesson that Herder's predecessors taught him, though, was that no one of those external manifestations of history's flow, nei-

ther the "moral" nor the "physical causes" of change, could be legitimately used as an absolute rule of measurement in determining the intrinsic worth of any other moment in history. The truth of history lay rather in observing the more deeply submerged but omnipresent laws that gave this natural diversity its intelligible form.

In comparison with the incandescence of Hamann's patchwork of furious tirades against a Godless age, one breathes the cool air of detached reflection in Herder's *Dithyrambische Rhapsodie.* What strikes one immediately is Herder's calm acceptance and resolute affirmation of precisely those aspects of the modern situation which Hamann had so severely criticized. Throughout his essay, Herder opposed a tranquil recognition of the historical necessity of our present condition against Hamann's paroxysms of impotent rage. Herder accepted the thesis that poetry was the original human language. He rejoined, however, that the antithesis was no less true: "If poetry is the mother tongue: then ours is prose—" (*W* 31). Herder insisted that we live in an age when prose is spoken naturally, not verse, and whether one thinks this state is welcome or lamentable, it is a historically necessary circumstance that cannot be blithely dismissed. Convinced of the basic correctness of the sort of organic determinism he found within the works of Du Bos, Blackwell, Montesquieu, and many others, Herder never entertained Hamann's illusory and unhistorical hopes that a return to a previous stage of cultural development would ever be possible. Moreover, not only did Herder deny that human beings could escape their historical determination, but he also willingly embraced what he perceived to be the proper mission of the eighteenth century: to write philosophy and history, and to leave all yearning for primitive poetry behind. Herder thus wrote, referring to the just-quoted passage from Hamann: "And why do we want to rebuild poetically dismembered bodies; let us collect them as scholars and interpret them as philosophers in order to write a history from them: since poetry became prose, painting became writing, song became recitation, dancing became measured stride; thus we stop making poetry, painting, singing, dancing, and behold! Lessing's swallow, which could not sing, learned to build!" (*W* 33).

Herder thus clearly dissociated himself from Hamann's unhistorical demand for a return to a kind of poetry that Herder believed his era was no longer capable of producing. In its place, Herder advocated the ideal of a scholarly and philosophical history of the arts, with this explicit end: "let us . . . at least secure our aesthetics: for our poetic tongue is bewildered!!!" (*W* 37). Herder was already too imbued with the historical spirit of the Enlightenment to have made the self-contradictory claim that anything like the poetry of primitive peoples would have been conceivable or even desirable in eighteenth-century Germany. The European states had already passed through their own tumultuous "child-hood" and "adolescence" and had laboriously achieved a sober, dignified, and philosophical maturity. This is not to say, as Herder emphasized, that poetry per se was no longer feasible. A few years later, in the second edition of the **Fragmente** of 1768, when this conclusion seemed to be raised as an objection to his thesis, he asked with rhetorical incredulity: "I thus say that I deny poets to this manly age? I am dismayed! For I would be denying something contrary to all history, contrary to the entire nature of language, contrary to all reason!" (*SW* II, 79). Poetry will indeed continue to be written, but we must understand, he insisted, that modern poetry can in no way be commensurable with the ecstatic songs of ancient or uncivilized peoples. For at that advanced stage of Europe's development, it would have been highly anachronistic and even somewhat foolish to expect that poetry could be a natural means of immediate, individual expression. Modern Europeans speak an entirely different language, the prose suited to discursive thought. And this language itself is responsible for what Herder called an "immense chasm" between our own origins in the poetic age and the late, prosaic present. Hamann's hope that we could recapture and not merely attempt to understand that age was no more than an idle self-deception.

> Prose is the only natural language for us, and this has been the case from time immemorial, and our po-etry—it may otherwise be whatever it wants—is in any case not the *singing Nature* it was, and had to be, when it was close to its origin. It has so little of *singing Nature* that we can hardly cross over into the Poetic Age, we can hardly traverse such an immense chasm to understand and appropriately feel it. And precisely the astonishment that greeted my hypothesis shows how far away we are from this land of the poets; to be sure, it is far away, and too far for us ever to enter it and to be able to view it as our Fatherland; but not too far away to get to know it and use the information we receive from it.
>
> (*SW* II, 76)

Herder's "hypothesis" will no doubt still occasion "astonishment" in the minds of those readers who see him as the "priest in a long black silk coat . . . who, although not yet old, was already in full possession of his mysteries."[43] Precisely because of his secular and unmystical historical standpoint, it was clear to Herder that the "land of the poets" had irretrievably vanished, to appear no more in identical form within his own time and culture. Only four years later, in the *Journal meiner Reise* of 1769, Herder once again wrote fervently about this "great theme," namely "to be what one should be . . . exactly the enlightened, informed, fine, rational, educated, virtuous, joyous human being which God demands at our stage of culture" (*SW* IV, 364-65). Thus Herder was simply unable to accept Hamann's idea of a lost natural immanence that could be recaptured through a return to some original form of

poetic language, and he proposed instead an endeavor more in conformity with his own historical station. If poetry is out of our reach, he wrote, "then our century in Germany is at least a philosophical one. Even if we possess no original geniuses in odes, dramas and epics, and even if none could be hoped for: then one should *explain* this barren poetic strain, one should set forth the entire original trait of every poetic genre and determine its multifarious and often so paradoxical progress in every age. Not *poetry,* but rather *aesthetics* should be the field of us Germans, who—at best—can be original in didactic poems" (*SW* XXXII, 82).[44]

Philosophy, and in particular aesthetics, was thus in Herder's opinion the historically necessary activity for a people who had moved past their own poetic age. This belief gave aesthetics a powerful historical justification and the dignity of being the most appropriate occupation for a modern writer who felt an interest or inclination toward the arts. In particular, the idea of a philosophical literary history, as part of a general aesthetics, is already contained within the sentiment just cited. And, in fact, at the very time when Herder wrote his critique of Hamann, he was exploring the concrete possibilities of these insights in a series of essays, or "fragments," devoted to the history of the ode.

The ode was, to the minds of eighteenth-century writers, the oldest form of poetry of which there was any surviving record, and its consequent proximity to the absolute origins of human culture made it an attractive object of speculation.[45] In Edward Young's *Discourse on Lyric Poetry,* for instance, which first appeared in English in 1728 and was translated into German in 1759, Young enumerated those aspects of the ode that could not fail to excite Herder's imagination as well. Young explained that "the Ode, as it is the eldest kind of poetry, so it is more spiritous, and more remote from prose than any other, in sense, sound, expression, and conduct."[46] But Young did not seem to think that these qualities of the ode were in any way historically bound to a particular level of civilization, and he continued his description with the tone and gesture of prescriptive poetics: "Ode should be peculiar, but not strained; moral, but not flat; natural, but not obvious; . . . thick, but not loaded with numbers, which should be harmonious."[47] Encapsulated within the one word "should" lies all of the difference between Young and Herder. By including the word "should," Young implied that it was still possible, if perhaps difficult, to write this kind of ode if one only fulfilled the necessary requirements he named. Those attributes, which were supposed to characterize only the "oldest kind of poetry," thus undergo in Young's *Discourse* a subtle hypostasis to become the timeless essence of the form, and it was this last step that Herder, with his historical acumen, had no choice but to reject. Herder would also claim in one of his fragments on the ode, "since imitation certainly was not originally the essence of *poetry,* . . . the first *ode,* the second child of nature, certainly remained the most loyal to sensation" (*SW* XXXII, 72). But he meant for this to apply only to the odes of a particular historical moment, not to be understood as an essential characteristic of the ode in general. In words that hark back to his critique of Hamann, Herder also plainly stated his reasons for making such a consistent and precise distinction: "The more the subjects are enlarged and human *intellectual* powers developed, the more the faculties of the sensible animal soul die out. The spread of the sciences constricts the arts, the formation of poetics likewise with poetry; finally we have rules instead of poetic sensations; we borrow remains from the ancients, and poetry is dead!" (*SW* XXXII, 69). It is not just that the generic form of the ode had undergone a profound transformation in the course of its history; the most basic human capacities themselves, which find expression in works of art, have also gradually changed their aspect, making the imitation of odes produced at an earlier time and in a different culture a questionable, indeed impossible, venture.

Nevertheless, Herder never abandoned the notion that there must be a common thread that inconspicuously, but undeniably, linked the poetic works of various epochs and nations and made comparison among them at all possible. For without the existence of some shared resource, he thought, the historian would perceive only the thin shell of surface appearance and never fathom the necessary similarities that allowed one to juxtapose works of a particular genre that had been written in completely different historical circumstances.[48] Herder's efforts to reconcile both of these perspectives—the awareness of the historical specificity of every poetic work and the simultaneous assertion that there must be a shared principle that underlies each unique artistic creation—form the philosophical basis of the *Fragmente einer Abhandlung über die Ode.* This simultaneous consideration of the historical uniqueness and abstract uniformity of the ode is immediately apparent in the following well-known words:

> If any one type of poetry is a Proteus among nations, then it is the ode, which has so changed its spirit and content and features and rhythm in terms of its sensations, its subjects and its language that perhaps only the magic mirror of the aesthetician could recognize the same living thing in so many forms. Nevertheless, there still is a certain universal Unity [*Eins*] of sensation, expression and harmony that enables a comparison between them all.
>
> (*SW* XXXII, 63)

Usually cited as early evidence of Herder's historical "relativism," this passage is most often rendered without the crucial final sentence. For it was toward the discovery of this "certain universal '*Eins*'," which asserted an inner unity among the variegations of factual data,

that his entire aesthetic philosophy ultimately tended. Herder did in fact believe that there were constant, basic forces always present in history that molded the materials of a culture into its unique and individual form. And while it is true that he wished to study these cultures in and of themselves and to isolate the unique ways in which each historical moment expressed itself, he primarily wanted to identify the most elemental modes of the forces and laws of history in general, and to avoid taking the concrete, manifest expression of these qualities to be the "essence" of any cultural artifact. The difficulty resided in trying to combine the acknowledgment of the manifest diversity of the historical past with the desire to discover the most general laws that allowed us to comprehend this apparently infinite variety.

In 1766, one year after Herder's intensive work on the ode, he wrote another relatively short essay titled *Von der Verschiedenheit des Geschmacks und der Denkart unter den Menschen* (*On the Variation of Taste and Mentality among Peoples*). More explicitly than before, Herder stressed here that, while change constituted the primary outward characteristic of history, the task of the philosopher resided in finding the underlying motivating causes of this change and in unifying them in a comprehensive vision:

> The spirit of change is the kernel of history; and whoever does not take this as his main consideration: to distill, as it were, this spirit, to combine the taste and character of every epoch into ideas, and to travel through the various periods of world events with the penetrating gaze of a wanderer hungry for knowledge, he sees, like every blind man, people as trees and dines on history as on a meal consisting of husks devoid of grain, and ruins his stomach
>
> (*SW* XXXII, 27)

In the fourth *Kritisches Wäldchen* of 1769, Herder broadened the terms of this basic approach by no longer limiting his inquiry to specific genres but by extending it to the most general questions concerning beauty and taste. In a turn of thought one might be tempted to call dialectical, Herder argued that the phenomenon that certain causes are always responsible for the universal and inevitable changes of taste is itself proof of some basic unity—the "Eins"—of beauty:

> And is it [i.e., "taste"] not to be explained by the times, customs and people? and does it not thus always have a first principle that has just not been understood well enough, just not felt with the same intensity, just not applied in the correct proportion? and does not even this Proteus of Taste, which changes anew under every stretch of the heavens, in every breath it draws in foreign climes; does it not itself prove by the causes of its transformation that there is only One Beauty [*daß die Schönheit nur Eins sey*], just like Perfection, just like Truth?
>
> (*SW* IV, 40-41)

It is worth emphasizing that Herder conceived of this unity or "Eins" in an extremely abstract fashion. He fixed no specific predicative attributes to it that could in any way be affected by the vicissitudes of time or place. Rather, this unifying principle was deliberately cast very much in terms of a natural law, in that the law was only evident through its effects and not itself available to immediate perception. As we have seen in his critique of Hamann, Herder advocated the biological notion of historical development, which he had gathered from the works of other Enlightenment thinkers, in order to explain the way in which a culture maintained its unique identity through the stretch of time. If we generalize on the implications of his argument concerning the respective stages that poetry and prose represent within the development of a particular culture, then the way in which he conceived of this "Eins" will become more apparent. Herder thought that, as a culture moved through its own organic course of growth and decline, each of its "ages" conformed to a particular paradigm of specific qualities that necessarily excluded all those other possibilities that were not compatible with that immediate stage. Or, to put it in more modern terms, Herder believed that at every point along the diachronic axis of cultural progression each of the successive synchronic possibilities was exhaustively and necessarily determined. This sort of teleological conception obviously gives the historian a very convenient and clearly defined interpretive model. Since the laws are already known, one does not look for the laws that govern historical necessity. Rather, it is the particular way in which they are expressed that becomes the object of interest. In another version of his reflections on the ode, the ***Versuch einer Geschichte der lyrischen Dichtkunst (Essay on the History of Lyric Poetry)***, Herder accordingly stated that his motivating wish was to understand "how these things *could* have arisen according to their similarity to other times and according to the conditions of their own, and whether one could not, while considering certain circumstances, come upon something like a *necessity* of how they *had* to arise" (***SW*** XXXII, 92).

Applied specifically to the understanding of poetry, this approach to the past would thus entail analyzing each complex cluster of intertwined circumstances that contributed to the creation of a particular work so that one might uncover the original and fundamental components of its eventual genesis. From here, it is implied, we would proceed to analyze the works of entire cultures, then whole epochs, until we reached the point at which the most general laws of poetic production would finally stand revealed before us. At this point, then, the connection between Herder's earliest philosophical studies in epistemology and the subsequent formation of his philosophy of history becomes evident. An empirically grounded, historical analysis of art must carefully sort through and separate each complex bundle of given data with the intention of locating the fundamental principles that were responsible for organizing this historical material into its particular form. Such an analytic approach would allow the historian not only to identify the inner laws that organized history, but simultaneously to appreciate for its own sake any cultural diversity as well. If we make a small chronological leap to the beginning of the 1770s and take a glance at Herder's essay on Shakespeare, we can observe how he first set these ideas into effective critical practice.

Herder's famous Shakespeare essay, which appeared in 1773 in what has been called the "manifesto of the Sturm und Drang movement,"[49] titled *Von deutscher Art und Kunst,* has often been thought to exemplify the exhilaration of the young German spirit wresting itself from its supposed inner servitude to rationality.[50] In more sober interpretations of the work, Herder is given credit for being the first to abolish the contemporary practice of applying classicistic poetic criteria to the evaluation of Shakespeare's plays by introducing a completely "new" historical viewpoint.[51] Common to almost every one, however, is the assumption that Herder's primary aim was to prove that Shakespeare and his creations are in every way utterly and irreconcilably different from the character and works of the Greeks.[52]

Herder himself is partly responsible for this confusion. For at the beginning of the Shakespeare essay, he emphasized with great rhetorical flourish the evident differences that distinguish ancient Greek drama from that written in Elizabethan England. This in itself should not surprise us, for the first priority of an analytically guided inquiry was to break down the elements of the chosen field of study into its distinct and individual constituents. But Herder's argument is also further obscured by the performative allure of his rhetoric. A careful examination will show, however, that the reason he so strongly emphasized the disparities between the dramas of Shakespeare and Sophocles was to allow the deeper, hidden similarity to appear with all the more force and persuasive effect. Herder thus began with a reflection that was familiar to his contemporaries:

> Drama arose in Greece in a way that it could not arise in the North. In Greece things were as they cannot be in the North. In the North things thus are and cannot be the way they were in Greece. The drama of Sophocles and Shakespeare are therefore two things that, in a certain respect, hardly even have the same name in common . . . one can observe the genesis of one thing through another, but one simultaneously sees change, so that they no longer remain the same.
>
> (*SW* V, 209-10)

Herder did not intend for these words to criticize those of his contemporaries whom he felt had failed to note the obvious differences between the two dramatic worlds. He delivered them, rather, as a sort of résumé of common and accepted knowledge. The thinkers of the Enlightenment were, of course, not unaware of or insensitive to the gulf separating antiquity from modern Europe. Indeed, we have seen that a number of English and French writers of the first part of the century, beginning with Perrault, had devoted their labors to discerning wherein these differences lay and the causes for their development. If anything, their researches had created an even wider divide between ancient and modern times, leaving the Renaissance tradition of appropriating the culture of antiquity as one's own appear ever less tenable. Herder clearly attended to this sense of growing alienation from the cultures of the past, a sense that resulted from both the insight into the individuality of every culture and a sharper perception of the ineluctable pull of time. This sense of irretrievable loss is eloquently expressed in the closing lines of the essay, in which he spoke of Shakespeare in a manner that is reminiscent of his earlier thoughts on the vanished poetic age:

> The thought is sadder and more important that this great creator of history and world soul is growing older and older! that his words and customs and ages are withering and falling as leaves in autumn, that we are already so far away from the great ruins of this age of chivalry, . . . and soon, perhaps, since everything draws to a close and vanishes so completely, even his drama will no longer be capable of exciting lively representations and will be like the ruins of a colossus or a pyramid which everyone stares at in wonder and no one understands.
>
> (*SW* V, 231)

But here, as always, Herder was far from succumbing to any kind of romantic resignation or despair. He applied himself instead to a rational understanding of the past, which he thought properly befitted an eighteenth-century mind. Unlike Young or Lessing, who had made polemical pleas for Shakespeare in the context of a general reluctance to consider him seriously as a playwright, Herder desired to proffer a more objective evaluation of the English poet. Herder emphasized that he wanted "neither to excuse, nor to defame him, but to explain him" (*SW* V, 208).

Herder had said at the beginning of his essay that the drama of Sophocles and Shakespeare were two things that "in a *certain respect* hardly even have the same name in common." In the first part of the work, he thus contrasted the original natural circumstances that ostensibly gave rise to the drama in Greece with those of Shakespeare's time in order to illustrate how one could think that in a "certain respect" these works were hardly deserving of the same name. The irony of this phrase is that it appears that in every conceivable fashion the plays produced by the two cultures are totally different. To make clear the extent of their disparity, Herder first provided what amounts to a catalog of contemporary notions about the nature of ancient Greece. Like Winck-

elmann and Blackwell before him, Herder stressed the "simplicity" and the "sobriety of the Greeks," and he thought that their art was "not art! It was nature!" (*SW* V, 210-11). That is, Herder believed that Greek drama was not "artful" in Blackwell's sense of the word, but that it was a faithful reflection of life. Against this placid background he then opposed the necessarily different milieu that confronted the English writer: "—and Heavens! how far away this was from Greece! History, tradition, customs, religion, spirit of the times, of the people, of emotion, language—how far away from Greece!" (*SW* V, 218). The gulf between Shakespeare and Sophocles had never seemed any greater. Quite literally everything, the historical circumstances, the manners, customs, religion, and whole "spirit of the time," had changed their entire complexion. It followed, Herder thought, that the works of poetry must necessarily reflect this change in both their substance and their form. The Aristotelian rules of classicist drama thus do not and cannot possibly be expected to apply to Shakespeare for the simple reason that his plays were written under such completely different conditions. Still, there is nothing revolutionary or surprising in Herder's words so far, nor did he intend for there to be. He wanted only to define the extreme boundaries separating the respective objects of his investigation in order to render his conclusion more irresistibly and impressively striking.

Herder worked toward this conclusion by adopting the notion that the artist represents most faithfully what he finds within his own natural sphere. As Blackwell had said: "Here . . . was *Homer's* first Happiness; He took his plain natural images from *Life*: He saw *Warriors,* and *Shepards,* and *Peasants,* such as he drew; and was daily conversant among such People as he intended to represent."[53] Herder extracted the principle contained within this characterization of Homer, which Blackwell had attributed to the ancient poet alone, and applied it to his more modern equivalent: "*Shakespeare* did not find a chorus about him; but he did find the games of states and marionettes—fine! He thus fashioned out of these games, out of such poor material! the magnificent creation that stands and lives before us!" (*SW* V, 218). Shakespeare's plays are different from those of Sophocles because the world he saw was different. Like the Greek, Shakespeare "took his plain natural images from *Life,*" but since this "life" was entirely unlike that which Sophocles had experienced, the English dramatist's "natural images" have no equivalent in the works of the ancients. Yet while Herder elicits nodding agreement from his reader in this regard, he has already intimated the secret affinity, the submerged law of artistic production that would enable one to locate where the parallel may be drawn between the Greek and the Englishman.

The concept of nature, which is the essential component of virtually every Enlightenment theory of poetics, here assumes a central position in Herder's work as well. We saw how, during the first half of the eighteenth century, the idea of nature became at once more variegated and rich in its characteristic attributes, yet at the same time more abstractly refined with respect to its functional status. That is, "nature" came to represent the totality of the world that poets found before them, the concentrated sum of their cultural and physical environment, and it was precisely this natural complexity that served as a stabilizing and unifying agent in the explanation of how poetic works were created. Nature—that is, the manners, the political state, religion, climate, and so on—always changes, and poets always follow it. This is obviously a very abstract principle. But it seemed to eighteenth-century thinkers to be the only one that allowed one to recognize and appreciate the realities of "the varying experiments of time" and simultaneously prevented the historian from losing every point of comparison and orientation.

Herder had made this view his own, and in the Shakespeare essay he triumphantly displayed the one basic modus operandi that united the otherwise apparently so dissimilar playwrights: "*Shakespeare* is thus *Sophocles's* brother even where he apparently seems to be so dissimilar, and is just like him at heart [*im Innern*]. . . . Sophocles remained true to nature because he treated One action of One place and One time: *Shakespeare* could only remain true to nature by having his world events and human fate tumble through all of the places and times where they—well, where they happened" (*SW* V, 225-26).[54] The functional concept of nature and of poets' creative relationship to the nature that surrounds them thus also lie at the center of Herder's work. Herder could allow for the greatest range of artistic freedom, the disparity of style, manner, the broadest dissimilarity of both the content and form of their drama and still assert that, because this very diversity issued from a single source, they could be explained according to the same theoretical principle. The entire Shakespeare essay builds up to this conclusion, and Herder had very carefully shown how Sophocles and Shakespeare were literally worlds apart in every other respect but in their representative fidelity to nature. In a sense, then, the discussion of the individual dramas themselves was incidental to Herder's real objective, which was to find the "certain universal Unity [*Eins*]" he had already theoretically envisioned in the fragments on the ode.[55] The announcement of this single principle was therefore not an error or a slip on Herder's part, but the intended and essential core of his essay.[56]

The essay on Shakespeare is an example of the young Herder's ideal of historical analysis at its practical best. But it was the last time that he would limit his investigation of the problem of history solely to art or aesthetics. Excited by the prospects that opened before him, Herder began to add more concrete detail to his theoretical plans in his next major work, *Auch eine Philosophie der Geschichte zur Bildung der Menschheit* (*Another Philosophy of the History for the Formation of Humanity*) of 1774. This essay also marks the beginning of a new era in Herder's intellectual life, for after its publication he began to devote himself increasingly exclusively to history, a trend that culminated in what many still consider to be his greatest work, the *Ideen zur Philosophie der Geschichte der Menschheit* (*Ideas on the Philosophy of the History of Humanity*), the several volumes of which appeared intermittently between the years 1784 and 1791.

The ideas concerning the historical variation and development of cultural phenomena, coupled with the desire to discover the necessary laws that guided these processes, permeate Herder's writings on all of the subjects that captured his interest. This is especially true of his treatment of language, which he considered to be the most profound historical achievement of human culture and reason.

Notes

1. The literature on Herder's concept and philosophy of history is of course vast, but a great deal of what has been written has tended to concentrate on the issue of the originality or priority of Herder's ideas and his opposition to the Enlightenment. See Robert T. Clark, Jr., *Herder: His Life and Thought* (Berkeley: University of California Press, 1955), p. 179. On Herder's ostensible role in the development of "historicism," see the classic account in Friedrich Meinecke, *Die Entstehung des Historismus* (Munich: R. Oldenbourg Verlag, 1965), pp. 355-410. However, Peter Gay's reservations, in *Enlightenment,* vol. II, p. 657, should always be remembered when reading Meinecke: "to my mind Meinecke . . . gravely underestimates the historical urge of the Enlightenment and equally gravely overestimates the contribution of German Protestantism, and German thought in general, to historical ways of thinking." Cf. also Peter Hanns Reill, *The German Enlightenment and the Rise of Historicism* (Berkeley: University of California Press, 1975); and Rudolf Stadelmann, *Der historische Sinn bei Herder* (Halle: Niemeyer, 1928); and the very thorough Max Rouché, *La philosophie de l'histoire de Herder* (Paris: Société d'Édition Les Belles Lettres, 1940). Concerning the relationship between Vico and Herder see: Isaiah Berlin, *Vico and Herder: Two Studies in the History of Ideas* (London: Hogarth Press, 1976), and the newly published reconsideration of this relationship by Wolfgang Proß, "Herder und Vico: Wissenssoziologische Voraussetzungen des Historischen Denkens," in *Johann Gottfried Herder, 1744-1803,* ed. Gerhard Sauder, pp. 88-113.

2. See Josef Simon, "Herder und Kant: Sprache und 'historischer Sinn'," in *Johann Gottfried Herder, 1744-1803,* ed. Gerhard Sauder, p. 3.

3. For a critique of what has been said about Herder's historicism, or "genetic method," see Nisbet, *Herder and the Philosophy and History of Science,* p. 68. There are a few recent scholarly works that call Herder's historicism into question: Heinz Stolpe, "Die Auffassung des jungen Herder vom Mittelalter," in *Beiträge zur deutschen Klassik,* I Weimar (1958); Otto Mann, "Wandlungen des Herder-Bildes: Eine Kritik seiner Interpretation aus dem Historismus," *Der Deutschunterricht,* X (1958), pp. 27-48; William Robson-Scott, "The Legend of Herder's Medievalism," *Publications of the English Goethe Society,* XXXIII (1963), pp. 99-129; Claus Träger, *Die Herder-Legende des deutschen Historismus,* and Janos Rathmann, "Der gesellschaftliche Fortschritt in Herders Geschichtsphilosophie," in *Bückeburger Gespräche über Johann Gottfried Herder* (Rinteln: C. Bösendahl, 1980), pp. 94-101.

4. See Georg G. Iggers, *The German Conception of History: The National Tradition of Historical Thought from Herder to the Present* (Middletown, Conn.: Wesleyan University Press, 1983), p. 30.

5. Ernst Robert Curtius, *European Literature and the Latin Middle Ages,* trans. Willard R. Trask (New York: Pantheon, 1953), p. 15. See also Jauß, "Geschichte der Kunst und Historie," in *Literaturgeschichte als Provokation,* p. 212. See also Robert S. Mayo, *Herder and the Beginnings of Comparative Literature* (Chapel Hill: University of North Carolina Press, 1969), esp. pp. 104-40.

6. See Arnaldo Momigliano, "Gibbon's Contribution to Historical Method," in *Studies in Historiography* (New York: Harper & Row, 1966), pp. 42-43.

7. D'Alembert, *Preliminary Discourse,* p. 64.

8. See Momigliano, "Gibbon's Contribution," p. 43.

9. See Krauss, *Studien zur deutschen und französischen Aufklärung,* p. 176. Cited from Hans Robert Jauß, "Ästhetische Normen und geschichtliche Reflexion in der 'Querelle des Anciens et des Modernes'," in *Parallèle des Anciens et des Modernes en ce qui regarde les Arts et les Sciences. Par M. Perrault* (Munich: Eidos, 1964), p. 11.

10. Baeumler, *Das Irrationalitätsproblem,* pp. 53-54. Baeumler specifically credits Du Bos for initiating the increase of eighteenth-century historical consciousness. See, however, Jauß, "Ästhetische Normen und geschichtliche Reflexion in der 'Querelle des Anciens et des Modernes'." See also Karl Menges, "Herder and the "Querelle des Anciens et

des Modernes'," in *Eighteenth-Century German Authors and Their Aesthetic Theories: Literature and the Other Arts,* ed. Richard Critchfield (Columbia, S.C.: Camden House, 1988), pp. 147-83.

11. See René Bray, *La formation de la doctrine classique en France* (Paris: Nizet, 1951), especially the "Seconde Partie," pp. 63-190.

12. D'Alembert, *Éloge de Despréaux,* in *Oeuvres,* II, p. 355, called the *Art poétique* "the code of good taste in our language, as that of Horace is in Latin." Cited in the translator's footnote 8 to the *Preliminary Discourse,* p. 67.

13. Johann Christoph Gottsched, *Versuch einer Critischen Dichtkunst* (Darmstadt: Wissenschaftliche Buchgesellschaft, 1962), p. 97.

14. Ibid., p. 95.

15. See Arthur O. Lovejoy, "'Nature' as Aesthetic Norm," in *Essays on the History of Ideas* (Westport, Conn.: Greenwood Press, 1978), pp. 69-77, in which he presents an analytic charting of the senses of the term "nature."

16. See Cassirer, *Philosophy of the Enlightenment,* p. 281. *Das Irrationalitätsproblem,* p. 74, Baeumler points out the continuity of this concept of nature in all eighteenth-century forms of classicism.

17. Gottsched, *Versuch einer Critischen Dichtkunst,* p. 99.

18. On the gradual separation of the two concepts during the eighteenth century, cf. Herbert Dieckmann, "Die Wandlung des Nachahmungsbegriffes in der französischen Ästhetik des 18. Jahrhunderts," in *Nachahmung und Illusion,* ed. Hans Robert Jauß (Munich: Eidos, 1964), pp. 28-59.

19. The standard work on Du Bos is still A. Lombard, *L'Abbé Du Bos: Un initiateur de la pensée moderne (1670-1742)* (Geneva: Slatkine Reprints, 1969), first published in 1913.

20. Ibid., p. 194.

21. Cf. Armin H. Koller, *The Abbé Du Bos—His Advocacy of the Theory of Climate: A Precursor of Johann Gottfried Herder* (Champaign, Ill.: Garrard Press, 1937). See also the essay by Gonthier-Louis Fink, "Von Winckelmann bis Herder: Die deutsche Klimatheorie in europäischer Perspektive," in *Johann Gottfried Herder, 1744-1803,* ed. Gerhard Sauder, pp. 156-76. Krauss, p. 35, however, is of the opinion that the climate theory is among the most often discussed and the most overevaluated intellectual possessions of the early Enlightenment. Cited from Jauß, "Ästhetische Nor-

men und geschichtliche Reflexion," p. 15. I agree with Jauß's counterargument, in which he points out that what is decisive is not whether the climate theory is convincing from our point of view or whether it was "really" gained from immediate empirical observation, but rather the philosophical and historical explanatory power that contemporary thinkers like Du Bos invested in it.

22. Cited from Abbé Jean Baptiste Du Bos, *Critical Reflections on Poetry and Painting,* trans. Thomas Nugent, vol. II (London: Nourse, 1748), p. 224.

23. See Lombard, *L'Abbé Du Bos,* p. 260.

24. Ibid., p. 189. In "Diderot's conception of genius," in *Studien zur europäischen Aufklärung* (Munich: Wilhelm Fink, 1974), first published in the *Journal of the History of Ideas,* II (1941), p. 16, Herbert Dieckmann criticized this aspect of Du Bos's theory, saying that "we are faced with a vague pseudoscientific naturalism which believes that scientific conceptions used in a merely descriptive way are already explanations."

25. See Cassirer, *Philosophy of the Enlightenment,* p. 199.

26. Inexplicably, historians have often made short shrift of Blackwell, as does Meinecke, in *Die Entstehung des Historismus,* who devotes precisely one page to his ideas under the heading of "English Preromanticism."

27. Thomas Blackwell, *An Enquiry into the Life and Writings of Homer* (London: 1735), pp. 11-12.

28. Ibid., pp. 13-14.

29. Herder's "Lebensalter" analogy, which he first uses in the *Fragmente* (*SW* I, 151-53.), has received a great deal of attention and emphasis in the scholarly literature. See Emil Staiger, "Der neue Geist in Herders Frühwerk," in *Stilwandel: Studien zur Vorgeschichte der Goethezeit* (Zurich: Atlantis, 1963), p. 163; and Eugen Kühnemann, *Herder* (Munich: Beck'sche Verlagsbuchhandlung, 1917), p. 52. The clear implication is that Herder was the first to coin the analogy, or at the very least to realize fully its significance. St. Augustine was one of the first to apply it as a sort of heuristic device for the understanding of the whole of humanity. In *European Literature and the Latin Middle Ages,* p. 20, Curtius mentions St. Augustine's "history of philosophy," in which the six days of creation are harmonized with the six stages of life. In the eighteenth century this analogy can be found in the writings of almost every thinker; it was used, among others, by such otherwise incompatible figures as Gottsched, Warburton, Condillac, Diderot, Abbt, and, though not explicitly,

by Blackwell as well. See also Gaier's commentary, pp. 1034-35.

30. See "Herder and the Enlightenment Philosophy of History," in *Essays on the History of Ideas,* p. 181, where Lovejoy maintains that Herder's ideas "stand out sharply" against "these widely current attitudes towards history." One of the thinkers whose ideas are made to represent "these widely current attitudes" is Bolingbroke and his *Letters on the Study and Use of History,* which was published in the same year as Blackwell's book, in 1735.

31. Blackwell, *Enquiry,* p. 24. Blackwell goes on to write: "But on the contrary, when we consider our own customs, we find that our first Business, when we sit down to poetize in the higher strains, is to unlearn our daily way of Life; to forget our manner of Sleeping, Eating and Diversions; We are obliged to adopt a Set of *more natural* Manners, which however are foreign to us; . . . Nay, so far are we from enriching Poetry with *new* Images drawn from Nature, that we find it difficult to understand the *old.*"

32. Ibid., pp. 68-69.

33. Herder's short essay on Hamann shares an additional similarity with the one devoted to Kant in that it, too, was not published in Suphan's edition of Herder's works and has therefore remained all but unknown. It has been included in the new edition of Herder's works edited by Ulrich Gaier, to which I will refer in my text. The essay was first discovered and published by A. Warda, "Ein Aufsatz J. G. Herders aus dem Jahre 1764," *Euphorion,* 8. Ergänzungsheft (1909), pp. 75-82. Albrecht Schöne, "Herder als Hamann-Rezensent: Kommentar zur Dithyrambischen Rhapsodie," *Euphorion,* LIV (1960), pp. 195-201, also reported on the manuscript, which had by then become lost. Cited in Gaier's commentary, p. 877.

34. See James C. O'Flaherty, "Hamanns Begriff vom ganzen Menschen," in *Sturm und Drang,* ed. Manfred Wacker (Darmstadt: Wissenschaftliche Buchgesellschaft, 1985), p. 179.

35. Johann Georg Hamann, "Aesthetica in nuce," in *Sämtliche Werke,* ed. Josef Nadler, vol. II (Vienna: Herder, 1950), p. 198. All further references to Hamann's works will be incorporated into the text within parentheses indicating the editor, volume, and page, for example, (N II, 198).

36. Concerning the history of the metaphor of "the book of nature," see Curtius, "The Book of Nature," appendix to *European Literature and the Latin Middle Ages.* Cf. also Hans Blumenberg, *Die Lesbarkeit der Welt* (Frankfurt a/M: Suhrkamp, 1983).

37. Georg Wilhelm Friedrich Hegel, *Werke*, vol. XVII (Berlin: Duncker und Humblot, 1835), p. 89. See also the helpful essay by Sven-Aage Jörgensen, "Zu Hamanns Stil," in *Johann Georg Hamann*, ed. Reiner Wild (Darmstadt: Wissenschaftliche Buchgesellschaft, 1978).

38. Blackwell, *Enquiry*, for example, pp. 38-39, claimed: "That Poetry was before Prose. The Geographer *Strabo*, a wise Man, and well acquainted with Antiquity, tells us, that *Cadmus, Pherecydes*, and *Hecataeus* first took the Numbers, and the Measure from Speech, and reduced that to Prose which had always been Poetry before." One can find many other examples in the eighteenth century in which Strabo (?63 B.C.-?23 A.D.) is cited as an authority on the issue. For instance, John Brown, *A Dissertation on the Rise, Union, Power, the Progressions, Separations, and Corruptions, of Poetry and Music,* (London: 1763), refers to Strabo, p. 50, but he writes with more caution: "'Their [i.e., the Greeks'] earliest Histories were written in verse.' This Fact is indisputable; but seems not, as yet, to have been resolved into its true Cause."

39. Hamann first received this epithet from Karl Friedrich Moser (1723-98). See James O'Flaherty, *Hamann's "Socratic Memorabilia," A Translation and Commentary* (Baltimore: Johns Hopkins University Press, 1967), p. 4.

40. See, as a kind of compendium of scholarly opinion, Friedrich Wilhelm Kantzenbach, *Johann Gottfried Herder* (Hamburg: Rowohlt, 1970), pp. 22-23.

41. Gaier—mistakenly, I believe—thinks these lines refer only to Pascal and Descartes. See his commentary, p. 859.

42. Condillac cites Du Bos in the *Essay,* I, i, §§ 16-61, et passim.

43. Max Kommerell, *Der Dichter als Führer in der deutschen Klassik: Klopstock, Herder, Goethe, Schiller, Jean Paul* (Berlin: G. Bondi, 1928), p. 63.

44. In "Éléments de la philosophie," in *Oeuvres*, vol. I, p. 122, d'Alembert also wrote: "Every century that thinks well or poorly, provided that it believes that it thinks and that it thinks differently than the century that preceded it, adorns itself with the title of *philosophical*; . . . Our century has consequently called itself supremely the *century of philosophy*."

45. On the importance of the ode to eighteenth-century and particularly German writers, see Karl Viëtor, *Geschichte der deutschen Ode* (Munich: Drei Masken, 1923), p. 142.

46. Edward Young, *Conjectures on Original Composition*, ed. Edith J. Morley (Manchester: Manchester University Press, 1918), appendix B, "On Lyric Poetry," pp. 57-58. See also Viëtor, *Geschichte*, p. 134. He notes that the German translation appeared in the second volume of the *Sammlung vermischter Schriften zur Beförderung der schönen Wissenschaften und der freyen Künste* (Berlin: 1759), p. 210.

47. Young, "On Lyric Poetry," *Conjectures*, p. 60.

48. See the discussion by Klaus R. Scherpe, *Gattungspoetik im 18. Jahrhundert: Historische Entwicklung von Gottsched bis Herder* (Stuttgart: Metzler, 1968), p. 235.

49. This epithet of the "manifesto" was suggested by H. A. Korff, *Geist der Goethezeit*, vol. I (Leipzig: J. J. Weber, 1923), p. 150. Peter Szondi, "Antike und Moderne in der Ästhetik der Goethezeit," in *Poetik und Geschichtsphilosophie*, vol. I (Frankfurt a/M: Suhrkamp, 1974), p. 64, also refers to the Shakespeare essay as a fundamental work of the "Sturm und Drang."

50. See Friedrich Gundolf, *Shakespeare und der deutsche Geist* (Berlin: Georg Bondi, 1923), pp. 198-99. See also Gottfried Weber, *Herder und das Drama: Eine literarhistorische Untersuchung* (Weimar: A. Duncker, 1922), p. 33.

51. See May, *Lessings und Herders Kunsttheoretische Gedanken*, p. 98. Szondi's interpretation, "Antike und Moderne," p. 67, also rests on the assumption that Herder broke with this "prejudice" by choosing a new perspective of evaluation, namely that of history.

52. Thus Gundolf, *Shakespeare und der deutsche Geist*, p. 202; Szondi "Antike und Moderne," p. 67; and Roy Pascal, *The German Sturm and Drang* (Manchester: Manchester University Press, 1953), pp. 256-57. The essay by Mann, "Wandlungen des Herder-bildes," *Deutschunterricht*, X (1958), pp. 27-48, marks an important exception to this general tendency in that the writer refutes all facile portrayals of Herder as a historical relativist. See also Fugate, *Psychological Basis of Herder's Aesthetics*, p. 225.

53. Blackwell, *Enquiry*, p. 34.

54. For the probable source of Herder's assertion that Shakespeare was Sophocles's "brother," see Young, *Conjectures on Original Composition*, p. 34: "*Shakespeare* mingled no water with his wine, lower'd his genius by no vapid imitation. *Shakespeare* gave us a *Shakespeare*, nor could the first in antient fame have given us more! *Shakespeare* is not their son, but brother; their equal, and that, in

spite of all his faults." See also Martin William Steinke, *Edward Young's "Conjectures on Original Composition" in England and Germany* (New York: F. C. Stechert, 1917).

55. One of the most often raised criticisms against Herder's essay is that he does not provide an analysis of Shakespeare's plays themselves. This reproach is prompted by Herder himself, who wrote at the end of the essay: "Now would be the place where the heart of my investigation would begin, what? In what artistic and creative manner could *Shakespeare* have composed such a lively whole from such a sorry romance, novella and fable? What laws of our *historical, philosophical, dramatic art* lie in each of his steps and artistic techniques? What an investigation! How much for our construction of history, philosophy of human souls and drama" (*SW* V, 229). Haym, *Herder nach seinem Leben,* vol. I, p. 439, was the first to find fault with Herder for not delivering what he himself had indicated was not going to appear. Since Haym's work appeared, this reproach has become almost a ritual gesture in the scholarly literature, often accompanied by the suggestion that it was due to some inherent inability that Herder "recoils," as Pascal, in *German Sturm and Drang,* p. 259, says, from providing an analysis of Shakespeare's plays. See further Alexander Gillies, "Herder's Essay on Shakespeare: 'Das Herz der Untersuchung'," *Modern Language Review,* XXXII (1937), pp. 262-80; and Szondi "Antike und Moderne," pp. 78-79.

56. In "Antike und Moderne," p. 53, Szondi argues that Herder's use of the concept of nature links him, in a way he was not conscious of, with the "normative thought of Enlightenment aesthetics." The notion of a single, unified "Enlightenment aesthetics" is a questionable abstraction that, even if it did exist, was certainly not representative of "normative thought." And, as I have tried to demonstrate, Herder did not unconsciously fall back on this conception of nature, but very determinedly guided his argument toward its revelation.

A Note on the Translations

I have, of course, quoted extensively from Herder's works, the majority of which are unavailable in English. Where I have referred to the existing translations, I have indicated their source, but I have modified them where it seemed appropriate to me. All other translations of Herder's writings are my own.

Wherever possible, I have also located translations of the works by the eighteenth-century French and German writers I have discussed. Again, when I was unable to find translations of this material, I translated it into English myself.

Bibliography

Alembert, Jean Le Rond d'. *Oeuvres.* Paris: A. Belin, 1821.

———. *Preliminary Discourse to the Encyclopedia of Diderot.* Trans. and intro. Richard N. Schwab. Indianapolis: Bobbs-Merrill, 1963.

Baeumler, Alfred. *Das Irrationalitätsproblem in der Ästhetik und Logik des 18. Jahrhunderts bis zur Kritik der Urteilskraft.* Darmstadt: Wissenschaftliche Buchgesellschaft, 1981.

Blackwell, Thomas. *An Enquiry into the Life and Writings of Homer.* London, 1735.

Bray, René. *La formation de la doctrine classique en France.* Paris: Nizet, 1951.

Brown, John. *A Dissertation on the Rise, Union, Power, the Progressions Separations, and Corruptions, of Poetry and Music.* London, 1763.

Cassirer, Ernst. *Das Erkenntnisproblem in der Philosophie und Wissenschaft der neueren Zeit.* IV vols. Berlin: Bruno Cassirer, 1911.

———. *Freiheit und Form.* Darmstadt: Wissenschaftliche Buchgesellschaft, 1975.

———. *The Philosophy of the Enlightenment.* Trans. Fritz C. A. Koelln and James P. Pettegrove. Princeton: Princeton University Press, 1951.

Clark, Robert T., Jr. "Hamann's Opinion of Herder's 'Ursachen des gesunkenen Geschmacks'." *MLN,* LXI (1946), 94-99.

———. *Herder: His Life and Thought.* Berkeley: University of California Press, 1955.

———. "Herder's Conception of 'Kraft'." *PMLA,* LVII, 3 (1942), 737-52.

Condillac, Étienne Bonnot de. *An Essay on the Origin of Human Knowledge.* Trans. Thomas Nugent. Gainesville, Fla.: Scholars' Facsimiles & Reprints, 1971. First published London, 1756.

———. *La logique/The Logic.* Trans. and intro. W. R. Albury. New York: Abaris Books, 1980.

———. *Treatise on the Sensations.* Trans. Geraldine Carr. Los Angeles: University of Southern California Press, 1930.

Curtius, Ernst Robert. *European Literature and the Latin Middle Ages.* Trans. Willard R. Trask. New York: Pantheon, 1953.

Du Bos, Abbé Jean-Baptiste. *Critical Reflections on Poetry and Painting.* Trans. Thomas Nugent. III vols. London: Nourse, 1748.

Fugate, Joe K. *The Psychological Basis of Herder's Aesthetics.* The Hague: Mouton, 1966.

Gaier, Ulrich. *Herders Sprachphilosophie und Erkenntniskritik.* Stuttgart-Bad Cannstatt: frommann-holzboog, 1988.

Gay, Peter. *The Enlightenment: An Interpretation.* II vols. New York: Norton, 1977.

Gillies, Alexander. *Herder.* Oxford: Basil Blackwell, 1945.

———. "Herder's Essay on Shakespeare: 'Das Herz der Untersuchung'." *MLR,* XXXII (1937), 262-80.

Gottsched, Johann Christoph. *Versuch einer Critischen Dichtkunst.* Darmstadt: Wissenschaftliche Buchgesellschaft, 1962.

Gundolf, Friedrich. *Shakespeare und der deutsche Geist.* Berlin: Georg Bondi, 1923.

Hamann, Johann Georg. *Sämtliche Werke.* Ed. Josef Nadler. Vienna: Herder, 1949-57. [Abbreviated as *N.*]

Herder, Johann Gottfried. *Abhandlung über den Ursprung der Sprache: Text, Materialien, Kommentar.* Ed. Wolfgang Proß. Munich: Carl Hanser, 1980.

———. *Briefe.* Ed. Wilhelm Dobbek and Günter Arnold. IX vols. Weimar: Hermann Böhlaus Nachfolger, 1977-84.

———. *On the Origin of Language. Jean-Jacques Rousseau: Essay on the Origin of Language. Johann Gottfried Herder: Essay on the Origin of Language.* Trans. John H. Moran and Alexander Gode. New York: Frederick Ungar, 1966.

———. *Sämmtliche Werke.* Ed. Bernhard Suphan. XXXIII vols. Berlin: Weidmannsche Buchhandlung, 1877-1913. [Abbreviated as *SW*]

———. *Sprachphilosophische Schriften.* Ed. Erich Heintel. Hamburg: Felix Meiner, 1960.

———. *Werke.* Ed. Ulrich Gaier. Vol. I. Frankfurt a/M: Deutscher Klassiker Verlag, 1985. [Abbreviated as *W*]

———. *Werke.* Ed. Wolfgang Proß. II vols. Munich: Carl Hanser, 1984-87.

Iggers, Georg G. *The German Conception of History: The National Tradition of Historical Thought from Herder to the Present.* Revised Edition. Middletown, Conn.: Wesleyan University Press, 1983.

Jauß, Hans Robert. "Ästhetische Normen und geschichtliche Reflexion in der 'Querelle des anciens et des modernes'." In *Parallèle des Anciens et des Modernes en ce qui regarde les arts et les sciences.* Par M. Perrault. Munich: Eidos, 1964.

———. *Literaturgeschichte als Provokation.* Frankfurt a/M: Suhrkamp, 1970.

———, ed. *Nachahmung und Illusion.* Munich: Eidos, 1964.

Kantzenbach, Friedrich Wilhelm. *Johann Gottfried Herder.* Hamburg: Rowohlt, 1970.

Koller, Armin H. *The Abbé Du Bos—His Advocacy of the Theory of Climate: A Precursor of Johann Gottfried Herder.* Champaign, Ill.: Garrard Press, 1937.

Kommerell, Max. *Der Dichter als Führer in der deutschen Klassik: Klopstock, Herder, Goethe, Schiller, Jean Paul.* Berlin: Georg Bondi, 1928.

Korff, H. A. *Geist der Goethezeit.* IV vols. Leipzig: J. J. Weber, 1923-53.

Krauss, Werner. *Die französische Aufklärung im Spiegel der deutschen Literatur des 18. Jahrhunderts.* Berlin: Akademie, 1963.

———. "Literaturgeschichte als geschichtlicher Auftrag." *Sinn und Form,* IV (1950), 65-126.

———. *Perspektiven und Probleme: Zur französischen und deutschen Aufklärung und andere Aufsätze.* Berlin: 1965.

———. *Studien zur deutschen und französischen Aufklärung.* Berlin: Rütten & Loening, 1963.

Kühnemann, Eugen. *Herder.* Munich: Beck'sche Verlagsbuchhandlung, 1917.

Lombard, A. *L'Abbé Du Bos: Un initiateur de la pensée moderne (1670-1742).* Geneva: Slatkine Reprints, 1969.

Lovejoy, Arthur O. *Essays on the History of Ideas.* Westport, Conn.: Greenwood Press, 1978.

Mann, Otto. "Wandlungen des Herder-Bildes: Eine Kritik seiner Interpretation aus dem Historismus." *Deutschunterricht,* X (1958), 27-48.

May, Kurt. *Lessings und Herders kunsttheoretische Gedanken in ihrem Zusammenhange.* Berlin: Emil Ebering, 1923.

Mayo, Robert S. *Herder and the Beginnings of Comparative Literature.* Chapel Hill: University of North Carolina Press, 1969.

Meinecke, Friedrich. *Die Entstehung des Historismus.* Munich: R. Oldenbourg, 1965.

Momigliano, Arnaldo. *Studies in Historiography.* New York: Harper & Row, 1966.

Nisbet, Hugh Barr. *Herder and the Philosophy and History of Science.* Cambridge, Eng.: Modern Humanities Research Association, 1970.

O'Flaherty, James C. "Hamanns Begriff vom ganzen Menschen." In *Sturm und Drang.* Ed. Manfred Wacker. Darmstadt: Wissenschaftliche Buchgesellschaft, 1985.

———. *Hamann's "Socratic Memorabilia": A Translation and Commentary.* Baltimore: Johns Hopkins University Press, 1967.

Pascal, Roy. *The German Sturm and Drang.* Manchester: Manchester University Press, 1953.

Rathmann, János. "Der gesellschaftliche Fortschritt in Herders Geschichtsphilosophie." In *Bückeburger Gespräche über Johann Gottfried Herder.* Rinteln: C. Bösendahl, 1980. Pp. 94-101.

———. *Zur Geschichtsphilosophie Johann Gottfried Herders.* Budapest: Akadémiai Kiadó, 1978.

Sauder, Gerhard, ed. *Johann Gottfried Herder, 1744-1803.* Hamburg: Felix Meiner, 1987.

Scherpe, Klaus R. *Gattungspoetik im 18. Jahrhundert: Historische Entwicklung von Gottsched bis Herder.* Stuttgart: Metzler, 1968.

Schöne, Albrecht. "Herder als Hamann-Rezensent. Kommentar zur Dithyrambischen Rhapsodie." *Euphorion,* LIV (1960), 195-201.

Staiger, Emil. "Der neue Geist in Herders Frühwerk." In *Stilwandel: Studien zur Vorgeschichte der Goethezeit.* Zurich: Atlantis, 1963.

Steinke, Martin William. *Edward Young's "Conjectures on Original Composition" in England and Germany.* New York: F. C. Stechert, 1917.

Stolpe, Heinz. "Die Auffassung des jungen Herder vom Mittelalter." *Beiträge zur deutschen Klassik,* I. Weimar (1958), 32-51.

———. "Die Handbibliothek Johann Gottfried Herders—Instrumentarium eines Aufklärers." *Weimarer Beiträge,* XII (1966), 1011-39.

———. "Herder und die Ansätze einer naturgeschichtlichen Entwicklungslehre im 18. Jahrhundert." In *Neue Beiträge zur Literatur der Aufklärung.* Ed. Werner Krauss and Walter Dietze. Berlin: Rütten & Loening, 1964. Pp. 289-316.

Szondi, Peter. "Antike und Moderne in der Ästhetik der Goethezeit." In *Poetik und Geschichtsphilosophie.* Vol. I. Ed. Senta Metz and Hans-Hagen Hildebrandt. Frankfurt a/M: Suhrkamp, 1974. Pp. 11-265.

Träger, Claus. *Die Herder-Legende des deutschen Historismus.* Berlin: Verlag Marxistischer Blätter, 1979.

Viëtor, Karl. *Geschichte der deutschen Ode.* Munich: Drei Masken, 1923.

Warda, A. "Ein Aufsatz J. G. Herders aus dem Jahre 1764." *Euphorion,* 8. Ergänzungsheft (1909), 75-82.

Young, Edward. *Conjectures on Original Composition.* Ed. Edith J. Morley. Manchester: Manchester University Press, 1918.

Edgar C. Reinke (essay date winter 1992)

SOURCE: Reinke, Edgar C. "Johann Gottfried Herder on the Humanity of Homer." *Classical and Modern Literature* 12, no. 2 (winter 1992): 161-67.

[*In the following essay, Reinke studies Homer's "view of life, as it appears in the* Iliad *and as interpreted by Herder."*]

An excellent subject for the study of classical influence on German thinking would be Johann Gottfried Herder (1744-1805), essayist, dramatist, Court Preacher at Sachsen-Weimar and, from first to last, Hellenist of the greatest enthusiasm. The works of this universalist are concerned with religion, society, literature, history, psychology, science, aesthetics, the arts, and education. Yet they all ultimately "crystallize" around the word humanity.[1] J. G. Robertson, in his *Gods of Greece in German Poetry,* declares that "It was Herder, that 'Mehrer des Reiches' of the spirit, as no other German of the eighteenth century, who revealed the meaning of Greece to the modern world."[2]

Of the thirty-three books of Herder's complete works, which contain many passages that have a bearing on his Hellenism, we think particularly of his ***Ideen zur Philosophie der Geschichte der Menschheit.***[3] Here, in three of its several books, Herder gives us a vivid picture of ancient Greece: He surveys the various causes of its greatness, its geographical position, its climatic advantages, its place in the history of the world, and in its poetry, art, and mythology, all uniformly composed in a style so lively as to provide pleasure and profit still today. Though Herder in his humanity did not believe that every use of force is necessarily evil, he, like his contemporary Schiller, deplored war as tragic, even in a just cause. And in his ***Humanitätsbriefe*** he finds Homer's attitude toward war of sympathetic appeal.[4] Though the *Iliad* celebrates the military exploits of mighty warriors, this does not prevent Homer, as Herder stresses, from describing war as rich in tears, man-devouring, cruel and wicked, with accompanying evils that expose its true nature.

The object of this paper accordingly is to present a paraphrased, running account of Homer's view of life, as it appears in the *Iliad* and as interpreted by Herder. Summarizing comments will be offered at the end, followed by a *Nachwort* for those who may be unfamiliar with Herder and his work.

As the *Iliad* opens, we find ourselves in the tenth and final year of the Trojan War and so are not immediately acquainted with the feelings and thoughts that were passing through the minds of the Greeks at the time of their departure for Troy from ties in the homeland. After nine years of fruitless toil, however, with their wooden ships now rotting on the beach and sails moldering,

Ihre Weiber daheim und unerzogene Kinder
Schmachten, sie wiederzusehn.[5]

Furthermore, hardly had Agamemnon in a ruse proposed to the war-weary, dispirited Greek troops that they scale their vessels and set sail for their longed-for fatherland, when

> Der Staub stieg unter den Fußen der Männer
> Wallend empor, und einer ermahnte den andern zur Eile,
> Daß sie die Schiff' erreichten und bald ins Wasser sie zögen.[6]

And only the king's royal sceptre, forcefully wielded by Odysseus, could induce the army to return to the battlefield. For in addition to pining for house and home, natural even after a protracted period of a decade, there had been added to the trials and tribulations of war a pestilential plague, described by Homer at the outset of the *Iliad*:

> . . . Die Völker aus Argos
> Fielen bei Haufen dahin; die scharfen Pfeile des Gottes
> Flogen tödtend umher im ganzen achäischen Kriegsheer,
> Daß man täglich die Leichen, getürmt in Haufen, verbrannte.[7]

Here Homer realizes the dread effects of contagious disease, which, as a concomitant of war, Herder observes, slaughters even more cruelly than the sword of the enemy.

Though, at the instigation of Pallas Athena, desire for battle is again kindled in the Danaans, Homer still seems to wish to avoid an ensuing, bloody melee; for Menelaus and Paris, in the interest of whose personal quarrel countless men are being sacrificed, shall settle the conflict in a duel:

> Ihn hörten mit Freude die Griechen und Trojer
> Hoffend, das Ende zu sehn des Elendbringenden Krieges.[8]

On the failure of this stratagem the two armies, through divine exhortation, are once again driven to move, the one against the other. The Trojans are thereupon stirred up by Ares, whom his father Zeus later denounces severely:

> Wisse, dich haß' ich am meisten von allen Bewohnern des Himmels:
> Denn du findest nur Lust an Zank und Kriegen und Schlachten.
> Ähnlich bist du der Mutter am unerträglichen Starrsinn,
> Der nie weichet und kaum von mir durch Worte gezähmt wird.[9]

Continuing with Herder, the Greeks in turn are further incited by Pallas, which leads Homer to portray the next bloody scene:

> Das *Schrecken*, die *Furcht*, die rastloswütende *Zwietracht*,
> Schwester des Menschenverderbenden Mars und seine Gehülfinn,
> Die erst klein sich immer erhebt, bis endlich ihr Haupt sich
> Hoch in Wolken verbirgt, indem sie die Erde bewandelt:
> Diese durcheilte die Heer' und sä'te zu beider Verderben
> Streitgier unter sie aus, und mehrte der Krieger Getümmel.[10]

These personified spectres, Herder declares, add vividly to the picture of terror that Homer desires to paint: Even if we disregard all artistic purpose, he asserts, how true and how terrible! Out of nothing there arises a dissension which in a short time becomes immeasurable. It emerges perhaps from a chamber and rushes through states, rushes through armies, sows destruction and strife, its head always concealed in lofty, invisible clouds; seldom do the contestants know the reason why they are fighting-but the longer they contend, the more stubbornly they continue, for an insatiable Eris, which with each stride rises ever higher and higher:

> Jetzo trafen sie nah' auf Einem Raume zusammen,
> Schild und Lanzen begegneten sich und Kräfte der starken
> Eisengepanzerten Männer. Es stießen die bäuchigen Schilde
> Wechselnd gegen einander, und ward ein schrecklich Getöse.
> Laut ertönte zugleich das Jammern und Jauchzen der Krieger,
> Schlagender und Erschlagner; es strömte von Blute die Erde.[11]

Here also Herder is deeply impressed by the poet's humanity, which becomes poignant in this scene of butchery. For the dead are never allowed to fall like mere brutes. As a friend of humankind, Homer in a verse or two contemplates the sad fate of the fallen: one will never again return to his kindred, to his helpmate and his offspring; a second left riches, position, a happy repose, which he can no longer enjoy; a third was an artisan, a skilled, handsome, divinely talented man—his art is vanished, his beauty withered, and his divine gifts will be buried with his ashes; a fourth was lured into battle by a false hope, in the guise of a deceitful oracle—death has seized him, and black night has enshrouded his vision. Many of these reflections are so pathetic that, as Herder thoughtfully points out, they would have served as appropriate epitaphs on the tombstones of the slain, had these unfortunates been honored with sepulchre and urn.

Noteworthy in this connection is that it is mainly the Trojans whom the *Iliad* commemorates with such touching detail. According to Herder, Homer is a Greek who wishes to immortalize the fame and glory of Greek heroes, but at the same time an Asiatic, an Ionian, a human being and sympathetic observer of the tragic fate of Troy; far from representing the Trojans as barbarians, Homer mentions their sensitivity, the moderating influence of their mild climate, their devotion to the family, their arts, and their life of ease in time of peace. The ill-starred Trojans are to the poet a herd of sheep attacked by a pack of wolves. Among the men of Troy are their many foreign allies, who share in the lot of the beleaguered royal city purely out of compassion. In order to demonstrate for us the culturally superior inner city, encouraging us to commiserate even further with the oppressed, Homer, at the commencement of the latest struggle, directs the noble Hector to return within the city's walls. There we are shown the palaces of Priam and of his sons, likewise Helen herself in a frankly lowered, though not unworthy state, then the elders of the city and finally Hector's spouse Andromache and the child Astyanax.

In this very moving scene of the *Iliad,* the parting of Hector from wife and child, Andromache speaks for the poet in the name of all Trojan women, for them and for their captive, orphaned children. But, as Herder remarks, by confining his theme to the wrath of Achilles, Homer felicitously avoids the narrative of the atrocities which Hector's sorrowful departure merely foreshadows; and yet the entire *Odyssey* and the disastrous return voyages of the Greeks depend to a great degree on these atrocities. Furthermore, Homer's Muse does not stain herself with the base crime of Ajax, committed before the image of Pallas, or with the foul murder of Priam, or of Polyxena, or of other helpless Trojan victims. In contrast, Hector's last visit within the city is in every respect noble and sublime; the hero desires to reconcile the angry goddess and purify his beloved native town, to this end even challenging Paris, the evildoer, to engage in a *monomachia* with Menelaus on the field of battle.

However, as Herder continues, despite his martial prowess, Hector, like all Homer's heroes, is also but a mortal; his fate is interwoven with the fate of Achilles, Homer's greatest champion and Hector's chief opponent, and the fate of the one sounds the knell of the other. Nevertheless, the champion of Troy is honored no less in death than life: Since he cannot rescue Hector from his implacable foe Hera, Zeus sacrifices his own prized son Sarpedon along with Hector and magnanimously removes the corpse of the Trojan from the bitter enmity of Achilles.

This nice discrimination by Homer Herder further discerns in the burial of the fallen, when King Priam exhorts his people to refrain from tears and lamentation. For at their funerals the Trojans, as Asiatics, were even more than the Greeks accustomed to loud expressions of grief. When about to bury their closest friends and fellow-countrymen before the walls of the city and within sight of their families, the Trojans were consequently more in need of restraint than the harder Greeks, who would be interring their dead far away from their kith and kin. Still the Hellenes do weep violently around the body of Patroclus, especially Achilles' Myrmidons and, most violently, Achilles himself.

But Herder sees the humanity of Homer perhaps most clearly illustrated in the wisdom with which he reflects on the phenomenon of war: All conflicts with their attendant miseries Homer attributes to mistakes, to the mistakes of human beings and to the passions of gods. Old Troy is sacrificed by Zeus to the stubbornness of an irreconcilable wife, prepared to yield a number of her cities provided that her spouse grant her one wish: The most chaste and proud goddess without a blush makes her embrace serve as a snare of deceit; with deep rancor she assumes a loveless love, and with borrowed finery she is converted in the light of day from an honorable helpmate into an ensnaring coquette, solely to see a few more Trojans perish; meantime her bribed chamberlain, Sleep, closes the eyes of the god who holds the scales of destiny. Here, states Herder, is displayed the extreme vengeance of a woman: Two women are arrayed against Troy; for Troy, two men. Who can doubt, Herder asks grimly, which side, if hate shall decide the issue, will ultimately succeed in attaining its goal?

Herder feels that a final tribute must be paid to Homer's treatment of Agamemnon. On the human stage, Herder realizes, the troubles of the Danaans are entirely the fault of the vanity and pride, the hubris, of this son of Atreus, whom none of the counsel-giving princes dare oppose. A false dream is Agamemnon's instructive deity. This false dream Homer calls illusion; but by adopting its deceptive advice Agamemnon destroys a large part of his army. By asserting that the dream has appeared in the form of Nestor, Agamemnon is enabled to win over his wisest counselor; the other princes are either silent, or they foolishly vie for the fame of the sulking Achilles. Hence the entire army is at long last brought to the brink. Too late are words spoken, too late tears wept. And yet in spite of his obtuse stupidity the King of Mycenae, leader of the Greek expeditionary force, remains the most blameless and caring shepherd of his people.

Herder furthermore cherishes Homer as kind in all his forms and aspects. Marshaled then by Herder in order before the reader are Paris and Helen, Castor and Pollux, Menelaus, Odysseus, Ajax, Diomed, Idomeneus, Nestor, and, above all, Achilles; tribute is paid to those to whom tribute is due; crimes are reduced to misdemeanors or aberrations, with merely an exhortation from Vergil: "discite iustitiam moniti et non temnere divos" (*Aen.* 6.620, with *moniti* softened by Herder to *miseri*).

"O Homer," exclaims Herder with much feeling, "so oft ich von neuem Deine Iliade lese, finde ich in ihr neue Züge der ordnenden Weisheit, Klugheit und Menschenliebe, mit der du wilde Verhältnisse eines rohen Zeitalters erzählest. Und keine Lehre, keine Warnung entfließt deinen Lippen, als ob sie die deinige wäre; jedes Laster, jede Thorheit, jede Leidenschaft selbst lehret und warnet."

In his exaltation of the humanity of Homer, Herder as theologian might be expected to have pointed out that in the *Iliad* there is no hint of the ethereal Beatitudes of the Sermon on the Mount, the compassion of the Greeks being strictly limited: "Help your friends, and harm your enemies," was their moral principle. Thus, on the slaying of Patroclus, Achilles' one aim, justified by Herder, is to avenge his friend, and only the spirit of vengeance persuades the sullen hero to emerge from his tent and meet Hector in single combat. A little later, in a scene of great pathos, Achilles and Priam together lament the cruelties of war. Though both break down in tears, neither commiserates with the other: Achilles weeps for his sire Peleus, who resides in isolation far away at his home in Thessaly; Priam's streaming tears flow for the loss of his prized Hector. Similarly, the tears shed by Briseis and the other women are over their own misery, not over Patroclus. Ardent feminists may resent Herder's failure to mention the brave Amazons, volunteer allies of Troy, who were all summarily dispatched by Achilles, *omnes ad unam.*[12]

Yet Herder is to be warmly commended for his ***Briefe zu Beförderung der Humanität.*** The Letters under review, composed in a lucid, literary style, are a refreshing antidote to the hostility of ideologues of the New Age, particularly intellectuals at colleges and universities. Any person who upholds the timeless ideals of the Western Tradition, of Athens and Jerusalem, is certain to come quickly under the contemptuous attacks of these strange nihilists. Herder's reaction to the New Age would undoubtedly have been a complete rejection of its inexplicable, dehumanizing hominism. The criticism of a contemporary, the poetaster Klotz, who faulted Herder for the comic elements in the *Iliad* and *Odyssey,* as in the *Iliad*'s Thersites scene, Herder ascribed to ignorance.[13]

Herder the universalist serves as an ideal example of the lasting attachment to the classics of the person who has been imbued with the classical spirit, especially at an early age. Though he lived through Germany's Period of *Sturm und Drang* (1770-1784), he never wavered in his affection for humane Homer. Herein he is in the tradition of Horace, whose esteem for the incomparable bard is expressed in one of his *Epistles,* "Troiani belli scriptorem . . . . / . . . relegi; / qui quid sit pulchrum, quid turpe, quid utile, quid non, / . . . dicit" (1.2.1-4). Herder moreover regarded the classics as religion's staunchest ally. As Goethe has it, "Die Griechen und immer wieder die Griechen." In his tribute to Hellenism Herder would be more specific: "Der Homer und immer wieder der Homer."[14]

EPILOGUE.

Johann Gottfried Herder was born in Mohrungen, East Prussia, in 1744, of parents in meager circumstances. Following his grammar-school education, he entered Koenigsberg University, where Kant was teaching. Here he studied theology. In 1764 he received an appointment as teacher at the cathedral school in Riga, Latvia, where he became a popular preacher in the cathedral. In 1767 Herder published an excellent review of the literature current in Germany, impressive for its original ideas of a fertile imagination. His ***Kritische Waelder*** (1769) includes a discussion on J. J. Winckelmann's history of the art of antiquity and on the *Laocoon* of G. E. Lessing. In 1769, in his ***Journal meiner Reise,*** he recorded his feelings gained from a trip to France in the same year. In 1773 Herder married Caroline Flachsland (1750-1809), whom he had met in Darmstadt. She was a member of the *Darmstaedter Kreis,* a literary group devoted to the ideas especially of Rousseau. Three years earlier Herder had met Goethe; thereupon he and Goethe became the main contributors to a series of essays published by Herder in the journal ***Art und Kunst.*** In 1771 Herder became the court-preacher at the court of Schaumburg-Lippe in Bueckeburg. This proved to be a stepping-stone to Herder's decisive selection by Elector Karl August as court-preacher at Sachsen-Weimar, an appointment to be credited to Goethe's recommendation.

The first decade of this appointment, which the restless Herder gladly accepted, was the *decennium aureum* of his career (1776-1778). During this period he published his widely acclaimed ***Ideen zur Philosophie der Geschichte der Menschheit.*** Both Herder and his wife actively supported the movement of *Sturm und Drang* (1771-1778), adopting Rousseau's "exaltation of freedom and nature," exemplified by Herder's high estimation of those poets and literary works closest to nature, especially the Old Testament, Homer, Shakespeare, Ossian, and folk-songs. As the literary focus of Germany, Weimar too was the departure point for the Grand Tour; in 1788 Herder himself set out for Italy, but because of developing eye-trouble he abandoned the tour to seek medical attention.

During the next decade his published work was chiefly theological, e.g., ***Von der Auferstehung als Glauben, Geschichte, und Lehre*** (1794-1798). Herder's later years indicated a dimunition of intellectual power, reflected in his ***Adrastea*** (6 vols., 1801-1804), which repeated theories advanced in his earlier years and resulted in a waning influence among his supporters. Also

Herder had become hypersensitive and quick tempered and in fact already after his first decade at Weimar found himself out of harmony with Duke Karl August as well as Goethe. Yet as *Allerweltsfreund* Herder's personality could be delightfully charming and persuasive. His perception of the total perrsonality of the individual replaced the idea of the primacy of reason. Herder's contribution to German literature and historical thought is outstanding.

Notes

1. Wulf Koepke, *Johann Gottfried Herder* (Boston: Twayne, 1987), Preface, 2f. (unnumbered).

2. J. G. Robertson, *The Gods of Greece in German Poetry* (Oxford: Clarendon Pr, 1924), 11.

3. Johann Gottfried Herder, *Sämtliche Werke,* ed. Bernhard Suphan et al., 33 vols. (Berlin: Wiedmann, 1877-1913; rept., Hildescheim: Olm, 1967); vols. 13-14, *Ideen zur [Philosophie der] Geschichte der Menschheit,* ed. Julian Schmidt, 3 vols. (Leipzig: Brockhaus, 1869).

4. *Briefe zu Beförderung der Humanität,* in *Sämtliche Werke,* vols. 17-18. Hereafter *Sämtliche Werke* will be cited as *SW* with the appropriate volume and page numbers.

5. *Il.* 2.136-137/*SW* 17:175 (line numbers are to the Greek text; Herder's lines are unnumbered). Herder's aim was to reproduce the spirit of Homer's text (*Nachdichtung*), not a word for word equivalent (*Übersetzung*). For these essays on the humanity of Homer Herder says that he used an uncompleted manuscript called *Ionien* by the unnamed author, whom Herder chose not to identify. Herder disregarded the translation of the *Iliad* by J. H. Voss (1793) and F. A. Wolf's *Prolegomena ad Homerum* (1776).

6. *Il.* 2.149-152/*SW* 17: 175.

7. *Il.* 1.49-52/*SW* 17: 176.

8. *Il.* 3.111-112/*SW*: 176.

9. *Il.* 5.890-894/*SW* 17: 176.

10. *Il.* 4.440-445/*SW* 17: 176-177.

11. *Il.* 4.446-451/*SW* 17: 177.

12. Because of his unorthodox theological views Herder more than once almost lost his appointment as official preacher at the court of Sachsen-Weimar.

13. C. A. Klotz (1738-1771), Professor at Göttingen and Halle.

14. Herder is believed to represent the *Pastor* in Goethe's *Hermann und Dorothea,* his epyllion in dactylic hexameter.

Frederick M. Barnard (essay date March 1992)

SOURCE: Barnard, Frederick M. "*Geschichtsbewußtsein* and Public Thinking: Rousseau and Herder." *Deutsche Vierteljahrsschrift für Literaturwissenschaft und Geistesgeschichte* 66, no. 1 (March 1992): 31-47.

[*In the following essay, Barnard assesses the ways in which Herder and Jean-Jacques Rousseau, using different approaches, influenced the manner in which individuals viewed themselves in relation to their respective societies and nations.*]

Neither Rousseau nor Herder could accept that humans should act in the dark, not knowing who or what they are, or whither they are going, within the stream of events called history. Like other eighteenth-century thinkers, both men felt that a better understanding of human natůre could vastly improve a person's self-knowledge. Additionally, though, as Vico before them, they insisted that the study of history could eminently further this self-knowledge. Principally, in their view, it could do so in two ways: firstly, it could aid one's reflective self-identification and self-location within time, space, and a context of others; and, secondly, it could bring about one's realization that one is not born to be a merely passive observer, that human capacities fully enable a person to be an active participant within the world in which he or she is placed. For the most part, therefore, "self-understanding" has to do with such questions as who I am, where I fit in, what I can do, what I am to others, and others are to me. Since a consciousness of history is thus viewed as closely related to a person's self-recognition as a doer, it is not surprising that Rousseau and Herder, in one form or another, associate historical consciousness with political consciousness, with an emergent awareness that public life is not beyond the scope of people's own control.

Herder is of course an acknowledged pioneer of *Geschichtsbewußtsein,* of historical consciousness, which for him, as for Wilhelm Dilthey after him, constitutes the presupposition of historical understanding, of what Dilthey specifically meant by *Verstehen.* At the same time, Herder is less known, if at all, as a political thinker. Rousseau, by contrast, has an unquestioned place among the great in political thought, yet is not usually linked with speculations on the meaning or use of history. This essay, in its limited way, seeks to redress the balance; it attempts to show that, notwithstanding important differences, both men, viewing history essentially as an instrumentality, succeeded in bringing about a revolution in public thinking, in the course of which subjects came to understand themselves as citizens and unrelated individuals as kindred members of distinctive nations.

I.

Both Rousseau and Herder might be described as ideological rather than historical in that their interpretation of the past is designed to influence human action in the here and now, and not simply to render it intelligible for its own sake. They go to history not so much to find out what actually had happened as to discern what is to be gained from such excursions, to bring to light the range of human possibilities, for good or for ill. Of the two, in spite or because of his intense philosophical preoccupation with history, Herder seems, surprisingly perhaps, the more ideological, by conferring upon historical change a far more positive quality than Rousseau ever dared to fancy. Seeing his task essentially as a negative task, Rousseau for the most part used history to sound warnings against the ever-present threat of corruption. Herder, though eschewing the belief in linear progress, nonetheless viewed history or "time" as a positive agent of human development, of *Humanität* and *Bildung.* Spurred on by time and its allegedly inherent force of ideas (*Drang der Ideen*), humans are said to actively intervene in translating ideas—what I call purposes *of* history—into their own purposes *in* history. Where Vico only juxtaposed these twofold purposes, invoking Providence as the hidden source of mediation, Herder presented this mediation in ways that are altogether within the grasp of human self-direction.[1]

As is widely known, Herder was urged by Kant, his favourite teacher at Koenigsberg, to read Rousseau. And, though Herder's praise of him is more restrained than that of Kant, there is no dearth of proof that Herder hat indeed read all there was from Rousseau's pen by the 1760s. Rousseau's "great theme," Herder tells us in his diary of those days, "is also very much my own," and there can be little doubt that, despite undeniable divergences, Rousseau was ever far from Herder's mind.[2]

Comparative observations will be made throughout the discussion, but the focus of the first section is primarily on Rousseau's conception of history. While he evidently gave much thought to the evolution of society, Rousseau appears to have shown less interest in history as a subject for philosophical reflection. It is not without moment, therefore, that, when he did turn his attention to this field, his insights are quite remarkable, and not least so because frequently they go against the currents of his own time. Possibly contra Voltaire, Rousseau puts major emphasis on the "valleys" of history, arguing that it is they rather than the "peaks" which are of greatest aid to human self-understandings. The valleys, the broad stretches of happenings, show best that ordinary folk *can* inject themselves into processes of creation and destruction, and, once historians would pay more heed to history's valleys, they could throw much light on humans as doers. Being some distance from the occurences they survey, historians could view human action with circumspection and detachment, seeing "the stage without ever being able to act upon it, as simple spectators, disinterested and without passion," and hence tell us something about our fellow-humans "as their judges, and not as their accomplices or their accusers."[3]

What comes through most tellingly is Rousseau's acute perception of what Marx and Engels were to call false consciousness. Deception of the self, as of others, is for him the most corruptive force in history and society. Rousseau is at once fascinated and repelled by this corroding force. Genuine self-enactment is constantly imperilled by the warping of values, the blurring of truth, and the abuse of reason. By far the most offending source of such corruption Rousseau sees in the use of words. Words deceive, and indeed are intended to deceive, for rhetoric is frequently empty, and spoken truth false truth. Deeds, by contrast, are transparently authentic, in that they truly speak for themselves. Thus, Rousseau argues, in order to know humans, and know them properly, we must "see them act."[4] That is where history comes in. In history, from the vantage point of hindsight, human actions are uncovered, freed from the disguise of words. Even words now appear in a new light. Instead of helping to conceal what people are up to, they serve to disclose the difference between "what they do and what they say," so that one is able to "see both what they are and what they appear to be." Indeed, Rousseau adds, "the more they disguise themselves, the better one knows them."[5]

Opinions, or ideas, in themselves, therefore, are no key to the history of deeds, as Herder at times seems to suggest. On the contrary, deeds alone are a key to the true meaning and importance of opinions, of the ideas and beliefs that men and women profess to cherish. Outcomes, to be sure, need not correspond to what was intended. Rousseau is alive to this possibility, but insists that it is precisely the historian's task to determine how genuine professed intentions are, and to what extent their lack of follow-up truly reflects strivings that had miscarried. Apparently, only the historian is able to uncover the degree of deception or self-deception that beclouds human deeds, and to reveal the excess of falsehoods over truths or the triumph of truth, sincerity, and authenticity over lies, clouded judgments, and sheer ignorance.[6] How the historian is to discern this by riveting attention on deeds actually performed seems at first somewhat perplexing. It transpires, however, that deeds are only historical actions for Rousseau when they contain the generating source of dispositions, motives, or intentions. Clearly, as we shall note below, history is inseparable from psychology for Rousseau; the study of the human past is essentially a study of the human heart. The historian's success, therefore, lies precisely in eliciting the true springs of action; this, and this only, betokens for Rousseau the true measure of historical understanding.

Unfortunately, defects in the historian and shortcomings in his or her methods mar the benefits that the study of history could bestow. One of these defects is the odd if not perverse selectiveness of historians. It inclines them to "paint people's bad sides more than their good ones," since these have a far more dramatic impact on them than the peaceful pursuits of daily life.[7] Revolutions and catastrophes absorb their interest rather than whatever brings forth well-being and serenity of mind. "So long as a people grows and prospers calmly, with a peaceful government, history has nothing to say of it. History begins to speak of a people only when, no longer sufficing unto itself, it gets involved with its neighbour's affairs or lets them get involved in its affairs."[8]

The upshot of this selectiveness is a fatal misreading of reality. What in fact is deterioration is taken for amelioration, and decline is taken for ascent. A people that appears illustrious is in truth on the brink of disaster. Historians begin where they ought to finish; they ought to be silent where they are the most eloquent. Yet, precisely about those items in which human life is at its best and political government at its soundest history keeps mum.[9] Rousseau denies therefore, in opposition to Hobbes, that history, as it is commonly found, lays bare what humans in general are, or that it helps to yield so-called laws of human nature. Focusing almost exclusively on the wicked and famous, on the startling rather than the quietly honourable, historians fail to tell us about those deeds which, for the most part, define the quality of human virtue. Humanity, Rousseau concludes, cannot be judged by the criteria of historical selection and historical recording; history, while pointing to the possible, does not instruct us about the generally necessary or even the commonplace and ordinary. Although we may learn from it, we cannot deduce principles of universal applicability.[10]

Apart from being selective, historical findings are loaded with bias. Facts are not merely selected facts, they are also value-laden, in that bias, known or unknown, enters into the historian's judgment. "The facts described by history," Rousseau states, "are far from being an exact portrayal of the same facts as they happened. They change form in the historian's head; they are moulded according to his interests; they take on the complexion of his prejudices."[11] A historian's bias need not, however, be a purely personal bias. For, like everybody else, the historian cannot escape the prevailing currents of his or her time; they surreptitiously colour the historian's assumptions and fashion the pattern of his or her thinking.[12] While, in his most cynical moods,

Rousseau rates historical findings at their best no higher than being among several lies the ones most resembling the truth, he does recognize that, despite fluidity of the lines that separate facts from their interpretation, historical judgments need not be bereft of values that are genuine values, or of conjectures that are "reasonable conjectures."[13] In other words, Rousseau's admission of historical relativism does not imply a position of anarchic nihilism.

The restrained nature of Rousseau's relativism is borne out also by what he has to say about the mediating role of historical perspectives. Thus, while he is perfectly aware, as we saw, of their proneness to distort facts, he is no less aware that without perspectives of any kind there could be no historical judgment. Somehow a balance has to be struck between having perspectives that are too rigid and having no perspectives at all. Clearly if perspectives are too set and exclusionary, the same object, viewed from different perspectives, could never even remotely be the same. If, among spectators looking at a play, each sees an entirely different play, there is no way of knowing if they indeed watch the same show. Relativism, thus pushed to its extreme, confers upon facts as many faces as there are perspectives of viewing them. Even if nothing had changed, all would appear different, and for no reason other than that the eyes of the spectator had undergone a change.[14]

Finally, there is what might perhaps best be described as the danger of misplaced concreteness. History, in so far as it generally records only "palpable and distinct" facts, facts which can be fixed by names, places, and dates, leaves unknown those occurrences whose causes, being slow and cumulative, cannot similarly be assigned. "One often finds in a battle won or lost," Rousseau declares, "the reason for a revolution which, even before this battle, has become inevitable."[15] Dramatically startling events mislead us to attribute to them a causality they do not truly possess. In Rousseau's own words, "war hardly does anything other than make manifest outcomes already determined by moral causes which historians rarely know how to see."[16] Too interested in fitting causes into preconceived systems, they prefer what they think to what they see. Noticing only the palpable effects, they *impose* causes rather than *discover* them. Furthermore, because they only see the surface of things, they mistake dressed-up reality for true, unadorned reality; they see men in certain selected moments, when they happen to be on parade, dressed up in their parade clothes. As a result, they depict an actor playing his role; they portray his costume rather than his person.[17]

II.

Despite Rousseau's emphasis on accomplished deeds as a basis for historical judgment, his paramount concern is clearly the uncovering of motives and intentions. Just like Montaigne before him, and Herder after him, Rousseau searches for causes working within the human heart. This, we noted, is held to be the primary task of the genuine historian. But, to be a genuine historian, to truly discover human dispositions and human motives, he or she must pursue their subject everywhere, for people frequently hide their real intentions.[18] Only by revealing the hidden, by uncovering the concealed, can the historian hope to lay bare the true nature of human deeds. Interestingly, Rousseau calls attention to the fact that humans acting in concert with others are not motivated in the same manner as they are when acting by themselves. One would, therefore, know the human heart very imperfectly if one did not "examine it also in the multitude."[19] It follows that in order to understand human dispositions and human intentions, we have to do both: we have to study "men or peoples," when they are assembled, in order to judge them individually, and we have to "study man" as an individual, "in order to judge men" acting with others. In either case, however, historians must not be overly concerned with "propriety," for if they are, they will neither see nor want to see what stares them in the face; unadorned reality will totally escape them. They will continue "to put on costumes and pass cords over pulleys," mistake decline for growth, degradation for improvement, and self-destruction for self-perfection.[20] In the end historians, like the rest of us, will no longer see with their own eyes, feel with their own hearts, or judge with their own reason.[21]

But, whether or not historians can be made to do their work as Rousseau would have them do, the passing of time itself is an agonizing problem for him. In sharp contrast to Herder, who looks upon time as being, on the whole, a force making for good, Rousseau sees in the sheer passing of time a likely source of advancing deception and corruption, of unhappiness and loss of innocence. Herder, it is true, has his moments of doubt as well, and talk about the world's ceaseless amelioration certainly leaves him stone-cold;[22] yet in few of Herder's writings will one come across the degree of almost tragic foreboding that Rousseau betrays. Although he agrees with Rousseau that every change carries risks in that the alternatives displaced may involve losses exceeding gains, Herder nonetheless wants to think that a synthesis might be forged between progress and preservation, between the demands of commerce and industry and the demands of *Humanität*.

If Herder, therefore, saw at least a chance for humanity's self-transformation over time, Rousseau could never altogether suppress his anxiety over attempting to make the world over; he could never quite overcome the fear that much that at first promised to yield improvements, would in fact prove detrimental to the lot of humankind. Efforts seeking to provide effective solutions, to make things work, backfire, for they invariably threaten

to injure or destroy what gave them life and inner value. Change always involves tremendous risks, and risks that are not calculable in the way that problems are in geometry. Methods that are eminently applicable to geometry, or to science generally, are therefore not at all appropriate when applied to the realm of human affairs and the philosophy of human history; indeed they may be worthless, and principles that are held in high regard in the former prove absurdities in the latter.[23] Although Rousseau certainly believed that the study of history might enhance human self-knowledge, he at the same time rejected the idea that each century cumulatively added its enlightenment to that of preceding centuries. Human self-understanding, he felt, simply does not work like this, for, inherently, its scope of development is strictly bounded.[24] Political self-understandings, likewise, have their limits, and it is unwise to have buoyant expectations about infinite improvements, as, for example, about the prospect of finding a form of government that would put laws above men. "I frankly confess," Rousseau writes toward the end of his life, "that I believe that it is not to be found."[25]

Unlike Herder, who, as he grew older, displayed an increasing confidence in the future, Rousseau became progressively more sceptical. Whatever, therefore, sustained his belief in reason as a means of averting chaos or total destruction, was a thoroughly chastened belief. The philosophy of reason may reign supreme and command universal lip-service, but the application of reason may serve deception as it may serve enlightenment. It may distort our vision and impair what we see, so that we can no longer believe what we see; rather we see what we believe, what we wish to see.[26] Rousseau's prize essay of 1750 (on the arts and sciences) is one of the most eloquent indictments of naive progressivism as of all that is spurious, glib, and meretricious. As Herder and Tocqueville after him, Rousseau is particularly fearful of projects that use fanciful rhetoric, invoking progress, liberty, and equality, when in truth they are merely trying to conceal tyranny and to adorn the chains that are to bind us, and bind us fare more banefully than the unadorned chains of the most despotic of tyrants.[27]

In spite of undeniable differences, then, particularly as regards the portent of time itself, there are also quite striking similarities. Anyone reading Herder's seminal *Yet Another Philosophy of History* (1784) cannot have the slightest doubt about its (acknowledged) debt to Rousseau's *Discourses*. Although inclined, unlike Rousseau, to acclaim the benefits of trade, science, and technology, Herder, no less than Rousseau, was acutely conscious of the price of these advances. Modern people travel in ships, but how many can *build* a boat? Every change, every advance in techniques, knits a new pattern of thinking and acting; it creates new needs and generates new problems.[28] This is the gist of Herder's pioneering theory of displaced alternatives. While it is not hostile to change *per se,* or bent upon painting a dismal picture of its eventual outcome, in its main thrust it is not a great deal more sanguine about linear progress than Rousseau's own speculations on human advancement. If Herder nonetheless felt that, ultimately, gains outstrip losses, he most likely did so because the ideologue in him managed to subdue the sceptic.

Furthermore, Rousseau's stress on the historical causality of purposive intentions found a remarkable echo in Herder's own speculations on history. Like Rousseau, Herder wants to enter the inner person, trace his or her motives and intentions, in order to penetrate and "feel himself into" the minds of other people and other periods, and discover the purposive drift of history, its inherent continuity. And, again like Rousseau, he seeks historical understanding as a means, not as an end. Historical understanding is to mediate between purposes *in* history—what people in fact strive for in pursuit of their own interests—and purposes *of* history—the kind of ends they ought to strive for within God's providential order.[29] The point of historical understanding, therefore, is not simply to find general explanations of past occurrences, analogously to explanations in science, but rather to evaluate what did happen in the light of what might or should have happened, if purposes in history and purposes of history had coincided. Intentions, moreover, are viewed not as causal antecedents in the mechanical sense of cause, but as suitable criteria for the ascription of praise and blame, that is, as conceptual properties, whose presence is a matter not of physical fact but of evaluative and interpretative comprehension. It is above all this insight which confers upon Herder's ideas on historical understanding their impressive originality and continuing fascination.

Herder's teleological conception of history, despite its perplexing tensions, makes three things clear. One is that to discover meaning is not the same as to discover general laws of causality comparable to those in the physical sciences; to discover purpose is not like discovering gravity. The other is that understanding meaning through *Hineinfühlen,* through historical empathy, is not simply finding out "what is," that is, identifying what is, or has been, going on, but rather an attempt to grasp "what it is like," what it is to undergo a particular experience. *Hineinfühlen* is evidently designed to set apart the intelligibility of an utterance or deed, as such, from the intelligibility of the intentions behind it. The third thing that plainly emerges is that historical understanding can be put to work in shaping the future as in tracing the past. In all three directions there are unmistakable points of contact with Rousseau, although Herder does go some distance beyond him, both in his theory of historical empathy and in his ideas on the didactic or "ideological" uses of history. Indeed, in arguing that because they understand what others have made

and brought about, humans are able to enter into history and partake in its shaping, Herder goes not only beyond Rousseau, but also beyond Vico, who never even attempted to give his "science" of history an ideological twist.[30]

The main assumption underlying Herder's ideological concern, in which he links historical consciousness with the shaping of social life and "political culture" (a term Herder invented), is the belief that human nature is not an inexorable given, through and through, but is something capable of being cultivated, if not altogether implanted. Like Rousseau, Herder firmly presumes that true reform involves the nurture of appropriate dispositions, and, as in Rousseau's scheme, such nurturing demands a matrix of suitable institutions.[31] But with Herder, as with Rousseau, it is not at all clear how, if the cultivation of individual *Bildung*—the process of human self-development—is to *follow* the creation of an institutional matrix, the latter is to come about in the first place. This problem oppressed Rousseau, but Herder thought he could surmount it by means of "interplay," his idea of continuous interaction between *Bildung* and *Tradition,* between forces pressing for change and forces pressing for preservation. It is precisely this internal dynamic that characterizes Herder's hermeneutics of history and culture. In this hermeneutics we can never hope to understand the meaning of change or continuity by exploring *Bildung* in total isolation from *Tradition,* in that tradition is the guide development and not its jailer. Conversely, if tradition is isolated from development, traditional norms may fail to disclose the true spirit of the times, the way men and women authentically feel about traditional justifying concepts that they are wont to invoke. It follows, therefore, that, even though norms could formally remain the same, their perceived meaning and practical significance would not be the same. Each norm, each belief, each human creation and institution, can, accordingly, be grasped only within a decidedly complex interplay of *Bildung* and *Tradition,* of goals pointing toward the future and of forms of life recalling the past, each acting upon the other.[32]

Reform, on this view, involves a delicate balance of continuity and change. At the same time, change, development, individual and collective *Bildung,* have, in Herder's use, predominantly positive overtones, whereas for Rousseau they have essentially negative and by no means recognizably liberal meanings: warding off corruption need not exclude *coercing* people to be free. Time itself, which for Herder is an inherently beneficial agent in the service of reform, is for Rousseau the potential harbinger of evil, an ever-threatening seducer, whose corrosive work can at best only be halted. Unlike Herder, therefore, who appears willing enough to put his faith into the ever-spreading gospel of *Humanität,* Rousseau is torn by doubt, little given to hopeful optimism. It is this basic difference in viewing "time" and "self-development" (*Bildung*) which most revealingly marks off Herder's "ideological" commitment from that of Rousseau.

III.

Herder's approach to history and culture, in particular his insistence on viewing each period and people (*Volk*) as uniquely distinctive, contained a message which nationalists of the subsequent century were not slow to notice. If Rousseau launched upon the world the belief that once a people gained consciousness of itself as a people it could raise itself by its own boot-straps in and through an act of will, Herder may be said to have both detracted from and enlarged upon this belief, by putting less weight on sheer will and proportionately more weight on the force of culture. In view of this contrasting emphasis, Rousseau is frequently opposed to Herder as a *political* nationalist, whereas Herder is seen as an essentially *cultural* nationalist, whose sole concern is the distinctiveness of ethnic characteristics. Elsewhere I have shown why I believe this opposition between political and cultural nationalism to be overdrawn.[33] There are undoubtedly important differences between Rousseau and Herder, but these do not derive from one being non-culturally political and the other non-politically cultural. Instead, as I see it, the two approaches represent two variants of legitimating national self-government, with Rousseau putting major accent on the act of *creation,* assisted by the founding aid of a superhuman lawgiver, and with Herder putting major accent on the *emergence* of national self-government, viewing it as a spontaneous and autonomous process of natural unfolding.

This variation stems, I believe, from their contrasting historical presuppositions. For Herder there never was nor could have been any human life outside the life of families, and even the nation was but an extension of the natural family. He sees therefore no point whatsoever in Rousseau's solitary man of nature, not even as a hypothetical construct. The natural origin of human existence is for him of necessity a "contextual" origin. A human being, to be at all human, needs a context of others, and that context is primarily the nuclear and extended family. No state, not even the nation-state, can ever wholly displace humanity's original context. The nation, therefore, does not displace families, clans, tribes, and other primeval groups, but is continuous with them, and, in this literal sense, their extension, as natural a growth as the family itself. For Herder, accordingly, who presumably follows here the thinking of medieval Aristotelianism, membership in a state is not direct but mediated, in sharp contrast to Rousseau's understanding of citizenship. Thus, while for Rousseau a citizen owes an undivided loyalty to the state, in Herder's's political vision citizenship is perfectly compatible with plural loyalties, with a diversity of allegiances; the nation is no monolithic rock, but a composite ensemble; not a single organism, but a complex of organisms, which, diverse though they are, still have a purpose in acting together, in *Zusammenwirken.*[34]

The other consideration underlying Herder's differing position consists in his insistence that bonds which link members of a nation are not, as with Rousseau, artifacts generated through a separate and ahistorical act of will, but are instead the outcome or "fruit" of historical growth; something which only awaits the ripening through time, and hence has no need of being created. That "something" takes the form of shared meanings, of common understandings, that are deeply rooted in a people's psyche, in its collective soul. No law-giver, no social contract, is required for converting a nation in itself into a nation for itself.[35] Becoming conscious of oneself as a German, Russian, or American, is an integral part of history. Personal growth and national self-consciousness is in principle one and the same process of historical unfolding.

Consistent with this doctrine, the envisioned political transformation from hereditary tutelage to democratic self-government is viewed as an essentially historical process of evolvement, which, for Herder, is analogous to nature: decay from above and growth from below. It is only during the aftermath of the French Revolution that Herder painfully discovers that historical change is not at all like natural change; that decay from above need not ensure growth from below. Some form of political intervention is now called upon to prepare the "soil" and "sow the seed." Herder expects these political gardeners to be men of the people—he calls them aristo-democrats—who are to emerge by virtue of their exceptional political wisdom and patriotic dedication to the nation. How, precisely, they are to emerge, Herder fails to disclose. Their appearance, therefore, seems almost as mysterious as the appearance of Rousseau's lawgiver. Only Herder does wish to believe that basically aristo-democracy is a matter not of collective will but of history and culture. Will no doubt is a component, but the real driving force is the ripening process of national *Bildung,* of the "political culture" of a people. The aristo-democrats merely help to accelerate this process, they are not meant to embody its culmination. Their intervention is a matter of passing moment; its purpose is not a regime of paternalist rulers or guardians. Rather it is to become dispensable: as soon as the Volk has learned to walk by itself, aristo-democracy is to make way for democracy proper, for true self-government.[36]

The decisive impulse in Herder's historical-political thinking is the conviction that the ordinary folk who hitherto have been thought of as an inarticulate mob, are no mob at all, but are in truth, apart from being the most numerous, the most precious part of the nation. This qualitative assessment, rather than a strictly majoritarian principle, seems uppermost in Herder's vision of democracy and rightful association. And it is in essence this qualitative assessment of "the people" which subsequently provided the ideological fuel for the agitation in support of the idea of national self-determination, an idea that effectively telescopes the argument for cultural self-expression with the argument for "democracy" and political self-government.

The political self-understandings, then, which a consciousness of history was to mediate, and toward which Rousseau and Herder directed their thought, have this in common: they both carry the conviction that it is the ordinary people, and not dynastic rulers, who are the source of a nation's rightful existence; and that it is therefore their will and their culture which matter and which sanction what is to be done in the name of the common good. In this demand for self-government Rousseau and Herder are at one. What they differ about is the meaning that history is assumed to have in bringing forth the legitimate state. For Rousseau the creation of the rightful state is essentially a matter of ahistorical willing in the form of a consensual determination to found an association, whereas for Herder it is essentially a matter of an historical process comparable to natural unfolding (*Entwicklung*) over time. Not surprisingly, therefore, Rousseau, in keeping with the idea of instant creation through making, favours mechanical images, viewing the state as a machine, while Herder favours organic metaphors, and the idea of growth and gradual maturation.[37] And where for Herder the whole is not separate from or superior to its parts, it is for Rousseau inherently different and ethically superior, just as the general will differs from and qualitatively transcends the will of all.[38]

IV.

It is not hard to account for these divergences in doctrinal emphasis. Although Rousseau is by no means unaware of the role of history in the formation of society, he virtually abandons historical evolvement when it comes to founding the legitimate state. Herder, on the other hand, attempts to maintain a strictly historical stance, by linking the emergence of self-government with a people's historical self-awakening. And, as we saw earlier, Herder, unlike Rousseau, ascribes to history, as to the sheer passing of time, an ultimately positive function. Humans, on this assumption, *can* put their faith into the future. Rousseau, by contrast, is in no position to preach such a faith. While the study of history is recommended as a means of acquiring greater self-knowledge, history by itself, or the passing of time, contains for him no promise of rightful self-enactment, individually and collectively. Similarly, historical cultures, though important for Rousseau, are no substitute

for rational willing. Culture refers to the soil and its cultivation; it does not determine the product. There is for the political Rousseau a cut-off point at which making takes over from growing, and at which the machine replaces the plant.

These (by no means negligible) differences apart, politics for both is infused with an understanding of the self as a doer, as a potentially active participant in history and the public realm. This understanding in turn is traced to a certain reflexive knowledge said to be attainable through a grasp of the past, through a consciousness of history. In effect, therefore, historical consciousness is intimately linked with political consciousness, and it is this inner fusion that injected a powerful spur into the kind of nationalism which came to assume prominence in Europe and the rest of the world.

But if the merging did have this momentous global impact, it also helped to bring about two sharply contrasting results. On the one hand it heralded an enormous historical upsurge of individual self-assurance and, with it, the shift from command to contract, from concession to right, and from subject to citizen. Collectively it emboldened those who hitherto counted for little—be they the despised within a nationality or a despised nationality altogether—to feel that they did matter, that they indeed had a right to be heard. And it was this collective self-discovery which forged the transition from the state-nation (as Meinecke put it) to the nation-state, from the domain of dynastic rulers to the self-authenticated commonwealth. On the other hand, the merging involved a radical switch from ideological individualism to ideological holism. Henceforth a person could be fully human only as part of a national "whole." Conversely, for a state to be a proper state, its inhabitants had to be—and had to feel themselves to be—integral components of a distinctive associative culture, of a collective self all of its own.

Parallel, therefore, with the marriage of historical and political consciousness, there emerges a degree of collective and individual oneness, which, while it conceivably points to the resolution of the problem of two moralities that Machiavelli so acutely brought to the attention of the preceding age, at the same time poses the troubling question whether oneness may not have to be purchased at too high a price.

To say this is not to imply that Rousseau, let alone Herder, was a collectivist or nationalist in the sense in which either word is commonly understood today. Herder, no less than Rousseau, was intensely alive to the baffling predicament of social existence, of at once needing others and being at the mercy of others who may harm and abuse us. Forming an association such as the state, therefore, may humanize us, but it may also corrupt us, and make us dependent on each other in onerous ways. It is this predicament which, for both, raises the question whether a person can attain personhood without injury to others. And it is this question which, at heart, forms the crux of morality in society and politics.

In attempting to come to grips with this question, Rousseau and Herder, if they cannot be called collectivists in any recognizably contemporary sense, neither can they be thought of as traditional individualists. For both of them, in one way of another, had serious doubts whether the problem of rightful association was resolvable in terms of purely individual strivings and purely individual ends. And the "more," we found, consists in the creation of institutions capable of generating in people's minds symbols of a new reality, the reality of social wholes that are other than mere aggregations of individuals. In particular, the envisaged transformation, calling for the symbiosis of context and source, of public structures and personal understandings, is designed to make one profoundly conscious that one's own individual good is inseparable from the good of one's fellows.

It is above all this symbiosis which lends Rousseau's and Herder's search for rightful association its distinctive character as well as its problematic causality. Distinctive because it departs at once from individualism *and* universalism. Problematic, because, as Rousseau himself remarked, the effect would need to become the cause.[39] This problematic causality, together with the implied narrowing down of who "one's fellow" tangibly is, somewhat bedevils the desired fusion of right and law and of rulers and ruled.

That both men did not feel altogether daunted by the peculiar causality nor unduly disturbed by the implied threat to universal solidarity can, I believe, be attributed to mainly three reasons: their extraordinary sensitivity to contemporary history, their ideas of optimum size, and their deep distrust of cosmopolitanism. Rousseau made no secret of his historical hunches. He bluntly declared the end of the great monarchies of Europe in face of revolutions and recurrent crises of legitimacy. Herder, likewise, made no attempt to conceal his sympathies for the French Revolution, whose importance he was one of the first to publicly recognize.[40] With respect to size, neither thought of existing states, let alone of multi-national empires, while the belief in universal citizenship seemed to both an utter chimera, totally beyond the grasp of ordinary minds. If Rousseau throughout his life kept his eyes on Geneva, Herder regarded the Baltic port of Riga as the most appropriate state for civic *Zusammenwirken.*[41] Geneva, as is well-known, yielded and sustained Rousseau's hope that a public self could be a legitimate self, in that, by its size, it could provide the chance for civic solidarity and a sense of civic belonging.[42] Riga and Geneva, therefore, paradigmatically served as approximations to the attainable, as symbols of potentiality.

To be sure, whatever expectations Rousseau and Herder entertained in this direction were no more than an inkling of what was possible, for neither underrated the hindrances impeding the translation of vision into reality. Even so, each felt that the possible needed stating to make it at all thinkable.

V.

Although, unlike Rousseau, Herder is usually not thought of as a political philosopher, I tried to suggest that by his blending of historical consciousness and civic culture he managed to complement Rousseau's own doctrine of political association, according to which nation and *patrie,* sovereign and citizen, the socially useful and the politically rightful, were to form one seamless whole. To trace one's roots, to make the past of one's people the source and inspiration of one's own self-understanding, and, thereby, attain the utmost sense of cultural, communal, and civic belonging: this was Herder's idea of bringing about human self-insertion into a given political culture as also into the process of history itself.

Herder's historical vision of political regeneration, together with Rousseau's less historical but politically more systematic speculations, set in motion, I argued, individual and collective self-understandings, in the light of which nothing in society and politics was ever the same again. While neither was prepared to entirely turn his back on things treasured by the European Enlightenment, each, in his own way, fostered a collective ethos which could not but impair traditional notions of both individualism and universalism. By matching historical consciousness with political consciousness, political consciousness with individual enactment, and individual enactment with the enactment of the self-determining nation, Herder, similarly to Rousseau, succeeded in giving birth to modes of justificatory discourse, without which present-day variants of political legitimation would be hard to grasp and even harder to account for.

Notes

1. In his search for order and meaning in history, Herder puts forward a theory of "ideas" which anticipates somewhat Hegel's "cunning of reason," in that ideas—which, for Herder, include ends, values, and purposes—are objectified as an independent force, having, so to speak, a life of their own. They are said to press on humans rather than that humans give rise to them. The phrase "pressure" or "impulse" of ideas is used in the *Ideen* (Herder's best-known work on the philosophy of history), *Werke,* ed. B. Suphan, 33 vols. (1877-

1913), XIII, 186. For a comparative discussion of Herder and Vico, see I. Berlin, *Vico and Herder: Two Studies in the History of Ideas* (1976), and my "Natural Growth and Purposive Development: Vico and Herder," *History and Theory*, 18 (1979), 16-36.

2. J. G. Herder, *Werke*, XXXII, 41.

3. J.-J. Rousseau, *Emile*, ed. A. Bloom (1979), p. 237 (*Œuvres Complètes*, ed. Pleiade [1959-69], IV, 525-26. References to this edition are subsequently cited by volume and page after the translated source). Isaiah Berlin concedes that Voltaire's interest in history embraced social and economic activities, but nonetheless maintains, rightly, I think, that it was the "peaks, not the valleys, of the achievements of mankind" on which his historical inquiry was riveted. *The Crooked Timber of Humanity: Chapters in the History of Ideas,* ed. Henry Hardy (1990), pp. 51f.; see also pp. 49-59, for a masterly succinct overwiew of types of historical writing.

4. *Emile,* p. 237 (IV, 525-26).

5. *Emile,* p. 237 (IV, 525-26).

6. For Rousseau most existing states were fraudulent contraptions, designed to fool the many for the benefit of the few. The historian is to detect such false claims and thereby puncture public lies. See his *Discourse on the Origin of Inequality,* ed. G. D. H. Cole, *Social Contract and Discourses* (1946), pp. 204f. Henceforth cited as *Inequality* (*Œuvres,* III, 176-77). Herder, similarly, views history as a sort of world-court, in which (as, subsequently, in Schiller's conception of history) historians are called upon to act as judges, to distinguish true claims from false claims, and to decide which, on balance, do prevail, or should have prevailed.

7. *Emile,* p. 237 (*Œuvres,* IV, 525-26).

8. *Emile,* p. 238 (IV, 526f.).

9. *Emile,* p. 238 (IV, 526f.).

10. *Emile,* p. 238 (IV, 526f.).

11. *Emile,* p. 238 (IV, 526f.).

12. *Emile,* p. 238 (IV, 526f.).

13. *Emile,* p. 238 (IV, 526f.); see also *Inequality,* pp. 172, 190f. (III, 142-45, 161-63).

14. *Emile,* p. 238 (IV, 527).

15. *Emile,* pp. 239-40 (IV, 529-30).

16. *Emile,* p. 240 (IV, 530).

17. *Emile,* p. 240 (IV, 530f.).

18. *Emile,* p. 240 (IV, 530f.).

19. *Emile,* p. 240 (IV, 530f.).

20. *Emile,* pp. 240-2; see also Rousseau's *Discourse on the Arts and Sciences,* ed. Cole, pp. 129-32, 140-2. Henceforth cited as *Arts and Sciences* (*Œuvres,* IV, 529-34; III, 15-20, 27-30).

21. *Emile,* pp. 244-55 (IV, 535-52).

22. For a more extensive discussion of this point, see my *Self-Direction and Political Legitimacy: Rousseau and Herder* (1988), ch. 10.

23. *Emile,* pp. 268-75 (IV, 567-79). See also Rousseau's letter to Deschamps of May, 1761. *Correspondance Complète,* ed. R. A. Leigh (1965-86), VIII, 320f.

24. See Rousseau's letter to Mirabeau, in C. E. Vaughan, *Rousseau's Political Writings* (1915), II, 159.

25. *Political Writings,* II, 160-1.

26. This is the main thrust of Rousseau's argument in *Arts and Sciences.*

27. *Arts and Sciences,* 120-21 (*Œuvres,* III, 6-8).

28. Herder, *Werke,* XIII, 371.

29. More extensive comments on the problem of historical empathy may be found in my "Accounting for Actions: Causality and Teleology," *History and Theory,* 20 (1981), 291-312, and in *Self-Direction and Political Legitimacy,* pp. 133-4, 196-206.

30. Herder wants humans to be their "own gods upon earth" (*Werke,* VI, 64; XIV, 210), and hence, unlike Vico, searches for a secular link between purposes in and purposes of history. "Historical consciousness" is to provide this link. Only those possessed of historical consciousness perceive change as something humans themselves have brought about in the past and, therefore, can also bring about in the future. Herder's treatment of historical consciousness bears remarkable affinities with contemporary (anthropological) approaches to ideology, which view it in a neutral rather than a pejorative sense.

31. It might not be wrong to speak of "contextual individualism." While for Rousseau it comes into being only in civil society, it is for Herder a natural, indeed a defining, characteristic of being human. For a most explicit statement of human contextualism, see Herder's chapters on the human condition in the *Ideen, Werke,* XIII and XIV; see also XXI, 152: "As everything around us, man, too, is to himself a given; he *finds* himself in a

universe into which he did not place himself" (Herder's emphasis). On Herder's use of the term "political culture," see *Werke*, XIV, 67. For Herder's intriguing observations on diverse political cultures, see his *Travel Diary* (the originally unpublished *Journal meiner Reise im Jahre 1769*), *Werke*, IV, 354-64, 401-45.

32. Herder, *Werke*, V, 28-30, 93, 113-4, 134-5, 542-5; XXIII, 321.

33. "National Culture and Political Legitimacy: Herder and Rousseau," *Journal of the History of Ideas*, 44 (1983), 231-53.

34. XIII, 347; *Wirken* and *Zusammenwirken* are key notions in Herder's philosophy of history in *Yet Another Philosophy of History* and the *Ideen*. Unfortunately, neither word is precisely translatable.

35. I make use here of Hegelian terminology in order to point up the difference between the unreflective existence of collectivities and their self-conscious existence. Only the latter, apparently, can be pressed into service to ground political self-understandings.

36. Herder, *Werke*, XXXII, 56; XVIII, 33; XIII, 149; IV, 454. See also R. Haym, *Herder nach seinem Leben und seinen Werken* (1877-85), II, 529-34.

37. Rousseau, *Social Contract*, bk. 1, ch. 7 (*Œuvres*, III, 362-64). Herder loves to imagine the world as a garden in which nations grow like flowers, blossom, and bear fruit in their utmost variety (*Werke*, XIV, 84). The "garden" is at once the symbol of human creativity and human interconnectedness with nature. See also *Werke*, XIII, 341, 384; and IX, 375: "Republics are like plants which are grown from seed."

38. Rousseau, *Social Contract*, bk. 2, ch. 3 (*Œuvres*, III, 371-72).

39. Rousseau, *Social Contract*, bk. 2, ch. 7 (III, 381-84).

40. Rousseau, *Emile*, p. 194 (*Œuvres*, IV, 468-69). "These events," Herder writes, "certainly open one's mouth and overwhelm one's soul"; and, on another occasion, he adds: "Speaking for myself, I cannot deny that, of all the remarkable events of our Age, the French Revolution has appeared to me by far the most important." In a letter to Jacoby of 11 November, 1792 (H. Düntzer, *Aus Herders Nachlaß*, 3 vols. [1856], II, 298-301); and *Werke*, XVIII, 314.

41. Herder, who had lived in Riga after completing his studies at Koenigsberg, never ceased to admire the civic spirit of this "free city," in which "well merited" meant so much more than "well born." Herder, *Werke*, XVII, 391, 413.

42. Rousseau refers to Geneva as "a State, in which all the individuals being well known to one another, neither the secret machinations of vice, nor the modesty of virtue should be able to escape the notice and judgment of the public; and in which the pleasant custom of seeing and knowing one another should make the love of country rather a love of the citizens than of its soil" (*Inequality*, p. 144) (*Œuvres*, III, 112). The "Dedication to the Republic of Geneva" with which Rousseau starts his *Discourse on Inequality*, is possibly the most eloquent declaration in support of smallness of size (Cole, 144-53) (III, 111-121). The immense importance Rousseau attached to it is borne out also in his essays on *Corsica* and *Poland*, and in his *Letters from the Mountain*.

Hans Adler (essay date 1994)

SOURCE: Adler, Hans. "Johann Gottfried Herder's Concept of Humanity." *Studies in Eighteenth-Century Culture* 23 (1994): 55-74.

[*In the following essay, Adler examines Herder's humanism and historical analysis within the context of Enlightenment thought.*]

1. HERDER—AN IRRATIONALIST?

For one hundred fifty years Johann Gottfried Herder (1744-1803) was perceived as the great "stimulator" of German literary and intellectual history: "father" of Storm and Stress (together with Johann Georg Hamann), renewer of German literary criticism and of folk poetry, precursor of historicism (of the *old* historicism), precursor of Romanticism, philosopher of humanity.

The presumed positive aspects of these roles as father, stimulator, and precursor, however, seemed confounded by apparent contradictions in his work. As is often the case, if the interpreter of a work does not have the means to explain contradictions *within it,* then he tends to transfer these contradictions to the extratextual reality—in our case to the *person of the author.* It is not a matter of creating meaningful relationships between text and context, for example by embedding ideas in the historical context in the broadest sense or by connecting them to traditions, but rather of a shaky "explanation" of a text based on the "character" of its author. Thus older scholarship often characterized Herder as a "rhapsodist," as an eternal "fragmentist," or as a stubborn moralist who did not have the strength either to bring his work to a systematic conclusion or to follow the new developments of his time. Psychological-biographical speculation easily replaced the critical investigation of prerequisites for an original analysis; or, stated in more modern terms, the peculiar characteristics of the object of investigation were adjusted to the paradigm bias of the one doing the analysis and thus were at least partially obliterated.

Those who are concerned with Johann Gottfried Herder do not get far without a profound knowledge of the German and European Enlightenment. This sounds self-evident when contemplating an author with the encyclopedic knowledge of a Herder. However, it is by no means self-evident, because the term "enlightenment" itself was not and is not self-evident, if one does not want to reduce it (for the German-language realm) to the poles of rationalism and transcendental philosophy, as was long done and is still done. According to this concept of "enlightenment," whoever does not submit to the paradigms of rationalism (in the general fashion of the Wolffian school) and of transcendental philosophy (above all, of course, of the Kantian mold), is a daydreamer, an irrationalist, a person permanently of the past, or even a pathological case. From the end of the eighteenth until the middle of the twentieth century Herder was classified in just this way. The one who provided the cues for this interpretation was no less a figure than Herder's teacher from 1762 until 1764, Immanuel Kant. In his review of the first two volumes of Herder's great philosophy of history, *Ideen zur Philosophie der Geschichte der Menschheit,* Kant turned Herder into a daydreamer, an irrationalist, a person permanently of the past, and finally a pathological case. When the celebrated founder of transcendental philosophy crushed the "poetic philosopher" Herder with the force of his authority, there was no place left for him in the guild of philosophers who are to be taken seriously.[1] But more; Kant denied him any reliability, stating as late as 1799 that "intentional deception [was] Herder's hallmark."[2] The history of philosophy has clearly shown that Kant was the winner. No one will seriously want to deny that his *Critiques* were epoch-making or that they had a lasting influence even beyond German philosophy. Undoubtedly Herder, who stepped forth as an opponent of Wolffian rationalism as well as of Kantian criticism, was the loser. But who says that the loser is wrong?

History consists of *data* (from the Latin: "datum"—that which is given), which in historical discourse become *facts* (from the Latin: "factum"—that which is made). And both "history" and historical discourse are subject to historical change. Decisive movement does not necessarily come into the humanities when new data are found, but rather when the discourse of history changes its perspectives, its method, and/or its intention. Thomas Kuhn's concept of paradigm shift still seems to me well suited for understanding these phenomena of the discontinuity of the history. It is certainly no accident that within the context of the recent discussion of the "postmodern," Herder scholarship has received a new

and very strong impetus. The last two chapters of Jean François Lyotard's book *La Condition Postmoderne: Rapport sur le savoir,*[3] published in 1979, bear the titles, "La science postmoderne comme recherche des instabilités" and "La légitimation par la paralogie." The text closes with the auspicious statement: "Une politique se dessine dans laquelle seront également respectés le désir de justice et celui d'inconnu."

The essential result of the postmodern discussion seems to me to be the regaining and enhancing of our sensibility for the non-dominant; attention to that which is important for humanity as a whole, without having been recognized by the majority; a plea for the permanent birth of the avant-garde; a sensitivity for the "counterrational," the peripheral, at a moment when innovation still seems to be mere deviation, if not simply "wrong." This position includes necessarily a plea for an anti-total approach—with at least one exception. Prerequisite for the postmodern claim is an assumption which may separate me from many postmodern combatants: I cannot see how the history of humanity can be imagined and shaped without the basic assumption that each human being is allowed to develop his capabilities (ἐντελέχεια). There *is* a "master narrative"; it is humanity's own. Even if proclaimed "humanity" may turn out de facto to be deeply scornful of mankind—which politician, which philosopher would want to obligate himself to a model of "inhumanity"? But "humanity" is not obligated to a linear progression. It is rather an explosion of capabilities into skills which determine culture, politics, science, economics, and ecology.

The fact that Herder scholarship has taken a considerable upswing in the context of the postmodern, does not mean that it presents itself explicitly as "postmodern." Rather I see a connection between the postmodern trend and Herder scholarship in their common sensibility for the non-dominating which is recognized from a new angle as important. The "loser" Herder is reevaluated as an advocate of ἐντελέχεια of the human. One could briefly characterize the new efforts in Herder's behalf as examinations of his work from a non-Kantian and non-orthodoxrationalistic perspective to determine its coherence, validity, and historical meaning. It is understood that I am not speaking of the admirers of Herder's "irrationalism," but rather of those who understand Herder's "irrationalism" from a new perspective as a *type* of rationalism which is to be taken seriously; which fell sacrifice to a historical, scientific-political constellation, but did not simply succumb because of its argumentative invalidity. Together with other recent Herder scholars, I claim that this new view of Johann Gottfried Herder and the Enlightenment is worth some effort.

In the last thirty years carefully and thoroughly annotated new editions of Herder's work have appeared in German and in English.[4] To be sure they cannot replace

Bernhard Suphan's standard edition,[5] but they considerably facilitate access to Herder's work. What is lacking is a new historical-critical edition which also takes into account the still unpublished material.[6] This desideratum has been around for a long time, but it is easier to state it than to do it.

The formulation of a new image of Herder is also attributed to the cooperative efforts of scholars. Since 1971 the "Bückeburger Gespräche über Johann Gottfried Herder" have taken place at irregular intervals. They are supported by the Evangelical-Lutheran State Church of Schaumburg-Lippe under the professional organizational leadership of Hans Dietrich Irmscher who is currently, together with Ulrich Gaier, one of the most influential Herder scholars. In 1978, on the occasion of the 175th anniversary of Herder's death, a Herder conference took place in Weimar and in 1984 the first international West-German Herder conference met in Saarbrücken.[7] In particular the latter, which was organized by the *Deutsche Gesellschaft für die Erforschung des achtzehnten Jahrhunderts* (DGE18J), the German equivalent of ASECS, gave new impulse to the most recent Herder scholarship because of the high level of the contributions.

Two years *before* the conference in Saarbrücken a volume appeared containing contributions by American and Canadian scholars which was the result of their loose association through a common interest in Herder. In 1985 the first Herder symposium took place in Monterey, where it was resolved to establish the first *International Herder Society* (IHS). This new society turned out to be very fruitful. Conferences of the IHS at Stanford in 1987 and in Charlottesville in 1990,[8] demonstrated the great interest in this author and made it apparent that leaving behind the image of the "contradictory" Herder and developing new perspectives was no dream. Rather a productive, integrative access to Herder was made possible. The conference in Bochum, Germany in 1992 likewise showed promising steps in this direction.

Recent monographs by Eva Knodt, Ulrich Gaier, Christoph Fasel, Gebhard Fürst, Michael Morton, Robert Norton, Marion Heinz, and Hans Adler, together with a considerable number of essays concerning Herder,[9] confirm the impression that there is increasing interest in this figure who was a contemporary of the Enlightenment, Storm and Stress, classicism, and early Romanticism. A comprehensive overview which could replace those of Rudolf Haym, Robert Clark, and Emil Adler is still lacking.[10] But in 1992 a *Herder Yearbook* was initiated.[11]

The more or less expressed common interest of recent Herder scholarship can probably best be formulated in two questions.

FIRST

If Herder's "irrationality" is understood as a polemic attribute which was ascribed to him by a group of "rationalists" historically defined as superior (including Kant), then this "irrationality" is first of all nothing other than a historical counter-position to a certain "rationality" that is also an historical construct. The first question therefore reads: Is there a rationality to Herder's "irrationality"? Or, formulated more pragmatically: What did Herder's irrationality achieve that could not be achieved by the dominating "rationality"? Behind this stands not the understanding of an epoch which equates "rationality" with "enlightenment," but rather the insight that the "rational" has its own history and is indebted to group-constitutive paradigms.[12] Stated differently: in the course of history, *types* of rationality compete with each other, are immunized against an argumentative debate with one another and therefore polemize against each other by means of non-argumentative mechanisms. Kant's chapter concerning transcendental methodology in his *Critique of Pure Reason* is very revealing in this connection.[13]

SECOND

It is known that Herder wrote "unsystematically" and "fragmentarily," that he liked to rework rather than to "complete," and that he walked the borderline between philosophical and literary discourse. Here lie the roots for Herder's exploitation as a "stimulator." If by a systematic statement we understand the kind of statement which, on the basis of an epistemological decision with a limited number of well defined concepts and rules concerning their connection (syntax), is capable of describing a set of circumstances exhaustively, then such a text can claim consistency for itself. For a receiver this means that he cannot transfer arbitrarily parts from the text into other contexts, since the elements connote the system in which they were valid. The second question therefore reads: What does writing which is "fragmentary," "unsystematic," and discourse-bridging mean in the case of Herder? This question can only be answered if the appropriateness of the epistemological choice and the method of presentation is also considered. The criterium of appropriateness, however, refers to the basic epistemological option as well as to the relationship between that which is signifying and that which is signified. Herder does not write "systematically," etc., for the reason that he takes as his point of departure the unavoidable ontological basic assumption of being, which is accessible only to mute experience, that is, is not presentable, although it must be presupposed. He does not start out, like Kant, from assumptions which precede all experience, and he does not start out, like the rationalistic metaphysicians, from the speculative generating of being from the negation of nothing as something which is impossible.[14] Formulated in a Shakespearean apparent paradox: the unsystematic seems with Herder to have a system. Consequently, even with a traditional understanding of "systematic," Herder would no longer be at our disposal for the arbitrary appropriation of quotations for every occasion. That said, I am not excluding the possibility of contradictions in Herder's work, even if with new investigations much that seemed to be "contradictory" has already been resolved.

2. THE "GENETIC" CLARIFICATION OF "HUMANITY"

As is well known, the most elaborate sources for Herder's concept of "humanity" ("Humanität") are his Weimar philosophy of history, ***Ideen zur Philosophie der Geschichte der Menschheit,*** and his ***Briefe zu Beförderung der Humanität.***[15] Herder has been praised from nearly all sides as the philosopher of humanity in the German history of ideas. The question is whether Herder's concept is what one means when employing the term "humanity," or whether one is only making use of the reputation of both—of the concept itself and of Herder as the philosopher behind the concept—in order to pursue interests which serve other goals. When asking this, one is not necessarily insinuating a conscious manipulation of the source. The complaint about the obscure and self-contradictory Herder is, after all, a topos which has accompanied Herder studies so stubbornly that one wonders at times why there is any esteem for this author. With these questions the dilemma is not in the "nuts and bolts," but rather in the general; for selective reception subsists on the fading out of the general, thus tending to become a fake. This fake comes into being when the concept "humanity" is reduced to only one of its aspects, although it exhibits a number of aspects and levels with Herder. My thesis is that Herder's concept of humanity is multi-layered but not imprecise. That means that the concept "humanity" designates sets of circumstances which lie on various levels, whereby these levels stand in a certain, describable relationship of substantiation to each other. This relationship of substantiation is specific for Herder's "genetic" procedure—a procedure which always assumes knowledge to be *historical* knowledge, and tries to understand the process of history instead of classifying historical "cases" or explaining history by deducing it from generic categories. Herder's procedure embraces four steps:

(1) What "humanity" is can consequently be described from the multitude of things which were formed and which have been caused by human beings in history (induction). (2) From the things which have happened in history Herder then concludes with Leibniz that there is a *power* which lies back of that which can be experienced. (3) Rules can be set up which describe the connection between this power and the phenomena which

emanate from it. (4) If a rule can be given, then a basis is also given for speculations or doctrines concerning that which is not yet history—the future—and that which is and will be appropriate for the person who has part in this "power"—a regulative.

The first three steps can be understood completely as procedures which are known from the empirical natural sciences. Thus in the ***Ideen*** Herder also does not tire of stressing that his procedure in the philosophy of history is analogous to the natural sciences. For Herder understands creation to be a totality whose manifested multiplicity in all realms can be described as order—as in nature, so also in history. In the preface to the ***Ideen*** Herder expresses it as follows:

> The God who arranged everything in nature according to measure, number, and weight, who accordingly established the essence of things, their form and connection, their course and their preservation, so that from the great universe to the particle of dust, from the force which supports the earths and the suns to the thread of a spider web, only *one* wisdom, goodness, and power rules, He, who also in the human body and in the faculties of the human soul considered everything in such a wonderful and godly way that when we merely dare from afar to follow the thought of the only wise one, we lose ourselves in an abyss of his thoughts; how, I said to myself, should this God refrain from his wisdom and grace in the determination and establishment of our human race as a whole and here have no plan?
>
> (***Ideen,*** *SWS,* 13: 7)

And at the beginning of the 15th book he states:

> If there is . . . a God in nature: then He is also in history: for the human being is also a part of the creation and must in his wildest aberrations and passions follow laws which are not less beautiful and excellent than those according to which all celestial and terrestrial bodies move. However, since I am convinced that what man must know he both can and may know: therefore I also go forth from the turmoil of the scenes . . . with confidence and freely toward the great and beautiful laws of nature, which they also follow.
>
> (***Ideen,*** *SWS,* 14:207)

What Herder describes here as the way up is the path from the "turmoil of the scenes" to history's "laws of nature." In the epistemological terminology of the eighteenth century, it is the path from the *cognitio historica* to the *cognitio philosophica.* The former—the *cognitio historica*—is the lowest level of human knowledge, but it is the essential prerequisite for further levels. The content here is taking note of that "which is and occurs."[16] The latter—the *cognitio philosophica*—is the next higher level of human knowledge. The content meant is the knowledge of the "reasons for that which is or occurs."[17] If Herder therefore is engaging in *philosophy* of history, a discipline, by the way, which, under this name, was scarcely twenty years old, then he does not intend to describe "what was and occurred," but rather he intends to penetrate into "why something was and occurred." Since not every event has its own law, the project of the philosophy of history consists in finding an order in the endless multiplicity of events in human history, that is, a limited number of rules.

What role now does the concept "humanity" play in this connection, and what constitutes it? Decisive is the fact that "humanity" is no predetermined ideal. Nothing is accessible to human beings, according to Herder, *prior* to all experience: "humanity" is no *datum,* "humanity" is always a *factum,* and specifically it is something made by human beings themselves—in a double sense. On the one hand, it is "made" as knowledge of human beings about themselves; for mankind knows about itself and the world only that which is accessible to its abilities and "organs" (from the Greek "organon"—tool, instrument) of cognition. Each piece of knowledge is based on experience and on "human" knowledge, and thus it is conditioned anthropologically. "Angelical truths" ("englische Wahrheiten") are not comprehensible to human beings: This "fact" of humanity concerns its dimension as knowledge of "power" (facultas), and this knowledge lies *after* the experience of phenomena of humanity. This latter is the other aspect of the "fact" of humanity. Humanity is experienced in manifestations, in actions of human beings. Thus the concept of humanity is of necessity open, because the "activity of humanity" is simultaneously that which constitutes it and changes its constitution. Thereby human beings themselves are determined as beings which can "make themselves," namely can constitute themselves as human beings. They are creators of themselves within the framework of their possibilities, the full extent of which they do not know, as long as they have not tested and developed them. The plant is bound to its location; the animal is bound to its drives; mankind, according to Herder, is free—by nature:

> The human being is the first emancipated being of creation [der erste Freigelassene der Schöpfung]; he stands upright. The scale of good and evil, of error and truth resides in him; he can investigate, and he is supposed to choose. Just as nature has given him two free hands as tools and a surveying eye which can direct his path, so also he has within him the power not only to place the weights, but also . . . *to be himself a weight* on the scale.

> (*Ideen, SWS,* 13: 146)

From the form of human beings and, connected with that, their upright walking, their ability to speak, and reason, which is unique to them, Herder derives the notion that "humanity" is the *nature* of human beings whose lives have their purpose in themselves. However, what human beings are, they become through themselves: their "definition" is self-constitution. Therefore, the "nature" of human beings here does not mean determination, but rather the opposite: disposition to freedom.

> The human being has a will, and he is capable of laws; his reason is a law to him. A holy, absolute law, from which he may never escape and from which he should never escape. He is not only a mechanical part of the chain of nature; but rather the spirit which governs nature is in part in him. He should follow the former (that is, reason); he should arrange the things around him, particularly his own actions, in accordance with the general principle of the world. Herein he is not subjected to any compulsion, indeed he is not capable of any compulsion.

> (*Briefe zu Beförderung der Humanität, SWS,* 17:143)

And then follow the two decisive statements: "He constitutes himself; together with others, who are of like mind with him, and according to holy, absolute laws, he constitutes a society." (Ibid.)

Human history is thus an open process which is advanced by its representatives through curiosity and the will to self-creation. Each action, even one which appears ever so absurd, contributes to this process which can be described as an arranged process with an objective intention to which the most divergent subjective intentions all contribute. It is the assumption of this difference between objective and subjective intention which lets Herder become a critic of linear progressive historical models. Nature, the anthropological, and the history of humanity belong together for Herder. Anthropologically conditioned cognition is referred to experiences of humankind, that is, its history. Human history derives its possibilities from what is given anthropologically, which for its part is closely connected with nature, but also is changeable historically or by evolution. As the development of "humanity" is a goal in itself, the process of human history has no end. Herder's optimism does not allow him to conceive seriously of a self-destruction of humanity as a possible goal—not only the end—of the unfolding of humanity.

"Humanity" is first of all an ontological-anthropological concept. On this level the concept of humanity designates the specific being of mankind, but not its existence which consists in the actualization of humanity's potential. Herder's concept of humanity is not identical with that of humanitarianism (Menschenfreundlichkeit), but rather designates the complex of capabilities which differentiates a human being from inanimate things, plants, animals, angels and gods, or rather God. "Humanity" is a *concept of differentiation* which designates that which is unique to human beings alone. This concept as a designation of the "human" potential has no moral dimension because it precedes all that is moral and in this sense is a-moral. This does not mean that it is *capable* of no moral dimension. As a concept of differentiation it defines itself negatively by contrast with that which it is not—humanity is not brutality and it is not the realm of angels. Defined positively, it is a notion which as a formulation of ontological identity turns out to be virtually tautological: "if we observe the human race as we know it, according to the laws inherent in it; then we recognize nothing more sublime than humanity in the human being." (*Ideen, SWS,* 14: 208)

To be sure, the following quotation also makes clear that a definition of the word is not at all important for Herder. The term "humanity" designates a "quality" (the capability specific to human beings) which all human beings have. For Herder the meaning of that which every human being is cannot be enumerated as a limited number of qualities[18] because what constitutes "humanity" is not predetermined, but is developed by human beings in their history through their actions. Repeatedly the concept "humanity" has rightly been pointed to as an energetic concept. The phenomenological variety of the concept "humanity" thus cannot be given exhaustively because its manifestation is the object of historical experience as *manifestation.* Herder states that clearly when he does not determine what "humanity" is, but rather expresses the *desire* that the concept may at least embrace that which has historically become manifest, that is, that which has been actualized: "I would hope that I could embrace in the word 'humanity' all that I have said to this point concerning the human being's noble development to reason and freedom, to finer senses and drives, to the most gentle and strongest health, to the fulfillment and governance of the earth" (*Ideen, SWS,* 13:154). It may now no longer be paradoxical when Herder at this point appends the following phrase: "the human being has no nobler word for his destiny than He himself is" (ibid.). Three things are meant simultaneously by Herder with this reference: the ontological laying of the foundation, the anthropological differentiation, and—of decisive importance for Herder's entire work—experience as basis of all knowledge, a point he repeatedly emphasizes, from his early essay **"Versuch über das Sein,"**[19] right up to his last writings.

Herder is very precise when it is a matter of warding off the sentimental in defining the concept of "humanity." In the first of the **Letters Concerning the Advancement of Humanity** (1793) he programmatically quotes the familiar statement from Terence's *Heautontimoroumenos:* "I am a human being . . . and nothing concerning humankind is alien to me."[20] And in the third collection of his **Humanitätsbriefe** (1794), Herder gives reasons for preferring the word "humanity" (Humanität), which is a foreign word in German, derived from the Latin, to the German terms "Menschlichkeit" or "Menschheit":

We are *human beings* [Menschen] altogether, and in this respect *humanity* [Menschheit] is ours, or we belong to *humanity* [Menschheit]. Unfortunately, in our language a connotation of humbleness, weakness, and false pity has been added to the word *human being* [Mensch]—and even more to the charitable word *humaneness* [Menschlichkeit]—so that we are accustomed to accompany the former merely with a contemptuous look and the latter with a shrug. . . . We . . . want to be on guard against writing letters to promote such a humaneness. . . . Therefore, we want to adhere to the word *humanity* [Humanität].

(***Briefe zu Beförderung der Humanität,***
SWS, 17:137, 138)

"Humanity" or enthusiasm for that which is "common to all human beings," which is so often mentioned in ceremonial speeches or commemorative articles,[21] and with which concrete, historical, and problematic aspects of humanity can so easily be ignored—in short, sentimental humanitarianism (*Humanitätsduselei*) is not Herder's cause: "The beautiful word *philanthropy* [Menschenliebe] has become so trivial that one usually loves humanity in order to love none of the human beings effectively" (***Briefe zu Beförderung der Humanität,*** *SWS,* 17: 138).[22] Let there be no misunderstandings; Herder by no means rejects humanitarianism or Christian mercy. His concern is to keep the two separate: "Humanität" as a basic concept of his philosophy of history and anthropology on the one hand, and the humanitarian as a moral command on the other. More precisely: humanitarianism is a part of actualized "Humanität." Despite this critical distinction, the two concepts are not foreign to each other in Herder's view. In fact, Herder entertains the idea that the history of humanity shows a strong tendency to bring moral and anthropological humanity into agreement.

Herder's "humanity" is what distinguishes human beings from all other living creatures, a specific dowry which equips human beings by nature with a potential for culture. Since the purpose of human nature, as of nature in general, is the unfolding of abundance, that is, the development of the greatest possible variety of individuals, "humanity" must be viewed as the precondition of this variety which comes before every valuation of its creations. Since morality can only unfold if the possibility is given to say no, and the freedom to choose non-reason is a component of the potential of humanity, therefore the way to evil is just as open to human beings who can refuse the dowry of humanity and succumb to brutality.

To this point there has been mention of this only implicitly. To be sure, "humanity" is according to Herder a specification of human beings, but it does not make up the entire human being. When Herder defines "humanity" as the nature of human beings, he does not thereby mean human beings as natural beings. Taking a critical stance toward Moses Mendelssohn's *Phädon*, Herder wrote in 1769: "A soul freed from sensuousness is . . . a deformity. It is a human nature formed in the most disproportionate way; it is according to its destination a monstrosity."[23] This is a central point in Herder's entire work: human beings are soul *and* body, reason *and* body; they think *and* feel.[24] They are a "middle being" ["Mittelgeschöpf"] (*Ideen, SWS,* 13: 65); but this does not mean that they stand in the center of creation. Herder represents an epistemological—not an ontological—anthropocentrism.

According to Herder, the human being is a "middle being" from two points of view. On the one hand, he lives on a planet in a middle position in the solar system (ibid., 13:16); Herder calls the earth itself a "middle being" (ibid.). The middle position of the earth determines what we today call the ecological conditions of life which exclude extremes and thereby determine the constitution of human beings in the size of the mesocosmos. On the other hand, human beings are "middle beings" insofar as they partake in the animal and the godly, just as the whole human being is both body and spirit. Herder—unlike Descartes—has a completely positive attitude toward this human constitution. He accepts body and spirit as given and recognizes the independent value of each and their interrelatedness. To Descartes' "Cogito" he responds with an emphatic "Sentio": "I feel myself! I am!" ["Ich fühle mich! Ich bin!"] (*Zum Sinn des Gefühls, SWS,* 8: 96). He reproaches the rationalistic metaphysicians by stating that they are engaging in a philosophy which is standing literally on its head and is well on its way to a notion of human beings as Cephalopodes. To explicate the animal nature of human beings and their likeness to God, Herder conjectures that "the current condition of human beings . . . is probably that of a connecting middle link between two worlds" ["der jetzige Zustand des Menschen . . . wahrscheinlich das verbindende Mittelglied zweener Welten" sei] (*Ideen, SWS,* 13: 194).

Sensuousness as a condition of human knowledge and action is Herder's steadfast basic assumption. Consequently he not only writes *about* it, but his writings are also characterized *by* it. Intuition and discursive knowledge, metaphor and concept, are modes to which Herder, following this logic, gives equal application in his writings. From this point it is also understandable that Herder hoped for a "*humanity* of the reader" for his *Ideen* (*SWS,* 13:6), a notion which cannot be comprehended only as a topos of modesty. Humanity of the reader and humanity of the author are no charitable designations for the weakness of the person (infirmitas), as we have already seen with Herder's remark about the concept of philanthropy. Rather these dimensions of humanity belong to Herder's program of making philosophy "human." In a draft of his essay **"Wie die Philosophie zum Besten des Volkes allgemeiner und**

nützlicher werden kann" (*FHA,* 1: 101-134), Herder speaks of the "retraction of philosophy to anthropology" ["Einziehung der Philosophie auf Anthropologie"] (ibid., 132)[25] and explains further: "All philosophy which is supposed to be a philosophy of the people must make the people its central point, and if one changes the point of view of philosophy in the way that the Copernican system developed from the Ptolemaic system; what new fruitful developments do not have to emerge, if our entire philosophy becomes anthropology" (ibid., 134). After this "Copernican turn" of 1765 (twenty years *before* Kant, using the analogy for different purposes, made it famous), "humanity" is no longer merely a possible object of philosophy, but rather its essential determinant: "human philosophy" *is* anthropology.[26]

In his 1940 anthropology text Arnold Gehlen asserted: "Philosophical anthropology has not made the slightest progress since Herder. . . . It does not need to progress because this is the truth [i.e., that according to Herder the human being is an imperfect being ("Mängelwesen")]."[27] This statement is as "non-Herder" in the historical sense as Gehlen's neoconservative thesis of "cultural crystallization" in "post-history," namely our present,[28] is wrong. Herder has repeatedly and more correctly been described as stipulating that human beings are charged with themselves.[29] This mandate frees human beings above all from the postulate of imitation.[30] On the one hand, Herder affirms the tradition that human beings are free, analogous to nature, to develop their world, that is, human history. On the other hand, he contends they are freed from the obligation to repeat what went before, or more exactly: human beings *can not* imitate what for them is already past. They can *represent* the past, and only in this way do they become conscious of their humanity. However, they can and should not imitate, because their nature is not aimed at copying but rather at variety.

3. "HUMANITY" AND POIESIS

In her book, *The Tyranny of Greece over Germany*, Eliza M. Butler detects in the Romantic era the first rebellion against this tyranny which is later revitalized. Butler inaccurately and on the basis of a dubious ethnopsychology (which, however, should be understood in the context in which the 1933 book was written) states: "If the Greeks are tyrants, the Germans are predestined slaves. . . . Germany is the supreme example of her triumphant spiritual tyranny."[31] For Herder neither the "tyranny of Greece" nor any other tyranny of another culture is a fundamental problem—unless it contributes to reducing the possibilities of unfolding humanity, as is evident in Herder's critique of the rationalist artificiality of French classicism. In book 13 of his *Ideen* (1787), Herder deals with Greece:

> Greek poetry . . . is perhaps the most perfect of its
> kind, if one considers it in light of its place and

time. . . . Even the most miserable Greek artist is a Greek in his manner: we are able to excel him; but we will never equal the genetic kind of Greek art: the genius of these times is past. . . . Never . . . should the level of ethical development of the Greeks—neither in their public history nor in their orators and dramatic poets—be measured according to the standard of abstract morals, because such a standard does not lie at the basis of any of these cases. History shows how the Greeks at any time were everything they could be in good or evil, according to their conditions.

([*Ideen*] *SWS,* 14: 98, 113, 123)

The "German *Winckelmann*" (***Über die neuere deutsche Literatur II, FHA,*** 1: 310) whom Herder wanted to become, would have as his most important duty the task of disclosing the *alterity* of the past. The solution of this problem consists in recognizing the present, that is in disclosing its *identity*. To "imitate" highly appreciated cultural achievements of the past is a structural term for Herder. He does not mean the imitation of artistic results, but the imitation of the way in which the spatio-temporal conditions of the fine arts were related to the fine arts themselves, namely so that fine arts and poetry correspond to the respective state of human development. Thus, fine arts and poetry are defined as specifically individual—namely historically and topographically determined cultural achievements which cannot be reproduced at other times and places. The "hic" and "nunc" gains profile against the alterity of what is past at other places, and, by comprehending alterity, the observer explores present possibilities for creating works of art and makes these possibilities available in the mode of reflection.

The concept of imitation is thus stripped of an essential element of commitment: reproduction. Neither the past conditions of art and literature, nor the products of art and literature themselves are to be reproduced, but the successful *interrelation* of art and literature and their conditions. However, if both the product and the conditions of production change to the point of incomparability, then the concept of mimesis has become obsolete. Herder's concept of "imitation of ourselves" (***Über die neuere deutsche Literatur II, FHA,*** 1: 311) is a clear proof of this, because it means the aesthetic transformation of the philosophical-historical realization that the purpose of history lies in the process of unfolding qualitative variety. To put it in terms of poetics: poetry must express the respective present and present it to intuition. It is, like every phenomenon, fixed to tradition, but it is only obliged to it inasmuch as poetry may and must choose from the past what is necessary to do justice to the task of the present. Imitative formations [Nachbildungen] of the Greeks are possible for Herder and may even be desirable under certain circumstances. But they are not, as for Winckelmann, the path to lead (back) art (and the development of society) to its pinnacle. The imitative formations should, according to

Herder, "suit our times" (ibid., 323). It may be that Herder, like others of his time, adhered for pragmatic reasons to the term of "imitation," even in its significant variations (such as imitative *formation*). What is meant, however, is the active element of unfolding the present in art and literature—analogous to the force which results in historical events, in articulated phenomena which are presented to intuition.

History is for Herder an irreversible process in which each historical moment is a singularity *sub specie humanitatis*—a singularity, however, which has been produced in a way specific to humanity and thereby according to rules. Human beings imitate themselves, as Herder states in a seemingly paradoxical manner. Cultures of the past may have produced exemplary models—exemplary for posterity's understanding; later generations can see in them how much could be achieved at a certain time and under certain conditions. Viewing that which was produced in the past as a function of humanity is to experience the quality of the species and thereby achieve the self-knowledge which opens the way to the new, to that which has not yet been. Herder's sentence: "I become what I am!" ["Ich werde, was ich bin!"][32] is the precise formulation of the "task" or the "problem" of "humanity": the past bears witness to it, the present postulates it, the future will bring it into being more fully but not completely, "For the nature of human beings is *art*" ("Denn die Natur des Menschen ist *Kunst*" [***Briefe zu Beförderung der Humanität, SWS,*** 17: 117]). Thus, history is creation—poiesis, and the philosophy of history is its poetics; the events of history are, like all perceivable elements of nature, "*disiecti membra poëtae*" (***Ideen, SWS,*** 13: 68)—the universe as a whole is a work of art, and history is humanity's part.

Notes

I would like to thank Cora Lee Nollendorfs (Madison) for the translation into English, and Valters Nollendorfs (Madison) for the technical revision of the paper.

1. Immanuel Kant, review in *Allgemeine Literatur-Zeitung* (Jena and Leipzig), no. 4, supplement (6 January 1785) and no. 271 (15 November 1785). See Hans Adler, "Aesthetic and Anaesthetic Science: Kant's Critique of Herder as a Document of Modern Competition of Paradigms," to be published in *Deutsche Vierteljahrsschrift für Literaturwissenschaft und Geistesgeschichte.* The best documentation of Kant's review and its context can be found in: "Der Aufstieg zur Klassik in der Kritik der Zeit: Die wesentlichen und umstrittenen Rezensionen aus der periodischen Literatur von 1750 bis 1795, begleitet von Stimmen der Umwelt," *Ein Jahrhundert deutscher Literaturkritik. 1750-1850,* ed. Oscar Fambach (Berlin: Akademie-Verlag, 1959), 3:357-97.

2. Immanuel Kant, *Gesammelte Schriften,* ed. Preußische Akademie der Wissenschaften (Berlin: Reimer, 1930) 21:225, quoted in Heinrich Clairmont "'Metaphysik ist Metaphysik.' Aspekte der Herderschen Kant-Kritik," *Idealismus und Aufklärung: Kontinuität und Kritik der Aufklärung in Philosophie und Poesie um 1800,* ed. Christoph Jamme and Gerhard Kurz (Stuttgart: Klett-Cotta, 1988), 200.

3. Jean François Lyotard, *La Condition Postmoderne: Rapport sur le savoir* (Paris: Les Editions de Minuit, 1979), 88, 98ff., 108.

4. J. G. Herder, *Werke,* 3 vols., ed. Wolfgang Pross (München: Hanser; Darmstadt: Wissenschaftliche Buchgesellschaft, 1984ff.): vol. 1, *Herder und der Sturm und Drang: 1764-1774* (1984); vol. 2, *Herder und die Anthropologie der Aufklärung* (1987); vol. 3, *Ideen zur Philosophie der Geschichte der Menschheit* (forthcoming). J. G. Herder: *Werke in zehn Bänden,* ed. Martin Bollacher, Jürgen Brummack, Ulrich Gaier, Gunter E. Grimm, Hans Dietrich Irmscher, Rudolf Smend, Rainer Wisbert, Thomas Zippert, 4 vols. to date (Frankfurt a.M.: Deutscher Klassiker Verlag, 1985ff.): vol. 1, *Frühe Schriften 1764-1772,* ed. Ulrich Gaier (1985); vol. 3, *Volkslieder, Übertragungen, Dichtungen,* ed. Ulrich Gaier (1990); vol. 6, *Ideen zur Philosophie der Geschichte der Menschheit,* ed. Martin Bollacher (1989); vol. 7, *Briefe zu Beförderung der Humanität,* ed. Hans Dietrich Irmscher (1991). (I cite this edition hereafter as *FHA,* giving volume and page numbers.) Among the separate Herder editions the following should be mentioned: *Ideen zur Philosophie der Geschichte der Menschheit,* 2 vols., ed. Heinz Stolpe (Berlin and Weimar: Aufbau-Verlag, 1965); *Briefe zu Beförderung der Humanität.* 2 vols., ed. Heinz Stolpe in cooperation with Hans-Joachim Kruse and Dietrich Simon (Berlin and Weimar: Aufbau-Verlag, 1971); *Über die neuere deutsche Literatur: Fragmente,* ed. Regine Otto (Berlin and Weimar: Aufbau-Verlag, 1985); *Kritische Wälder: Erstes bis Drittes Wäldchen. Paralipomena,* 2 vols., ed. Regine Otto (Berlin and Weimar: Aufbau-Verlag, 1990); three more volumes in this Aufbau-Verlag series are planned. *Briefe: Gesamtausgabe,* 9 vols. to date, ed. Wilhelm Dobbek and Günter Arnold (Weimar: Hermann Böhlaus Nachfolger, 1977ff.); *Abhandlung über den Ursprung der Sprache,* ed. Hans Dietrich Irmscher (Stuttgart: Reclam, 1966). [Herder, Goethe, Frisi, Möser:] *Von deutscher Art und Kunst,* ed. Hans Dietrich Irmscher (Stuttgart: Reclam, 1968). *"Stimmen der Völker in Liedern,"* ed. Heinz Rölleke (Stuttgart: Reclam, 1975). *Journal meiner Reise im Jahr 1769,* Historical-critical edition, ed. Katharina Mommsen in cooperation with Momme Mommsen and Georg Wackerl (Stuttgart: Reclam, 1976). *Auch eine Philosophie der Geschichte zur Bildung der Menschheit,* ed. Hans Dietrich Irmscher (Stuttgart: Reclam, 1990). *Italienische Reise,* ed. Albert Meier and Heide Vollmer (München: Deutscher Taschenbuch Verlag, 1988). Wolfgang Pross, *Johann Gottfried Herder: Abhandlung über den Ursprung der Sprache. Text, Materialien, Kommentar* (München: Hanser, [1978]). Johann Gottfried Herder, *Selected Early Works: 1764-1767. Addresses, Essays, and Drafts; Fragments on Recent German Literature,* ed. Ernest A. Menze and Karl Menges, trans. Ernest A. Menze with Michael Palma (University Park: Pennsylvania State University Press, 1992).

5. Johann Gottfried Herder, *Sämmtliche Werke,* 33 vols., ed. Bernhard Suphan (Berlin: Weidmann, 1877-1913) reprinted as *Sämtliche Werke,* [2nd reprint-edition] (Hildesheim, New York: Olms/Weidmann, 1978-79). I cite this edition hereafter as *SWS,* giving volume and page numbers.

6. Cf. *Der handschriftliche Nachlass Johann Gottfried Herders,* ed. Hans Dietrich Irmscher and Emil Adler, Staatsbibliothek Preussischer Kulturbesitz, Kataloge der Handschriftenabteilung, ed. Thilo Brandis, Zweite Reihe: Nachlässe 1 (Wiesbaden: Harrassowitz, 1979).

7. *Bückeburger Gespräche über Johann Gottfried Herder,* ed. Johann Gottfried Maltusch (Bückeburg: Grimme, 1973; Rinteln: Bösendahl, 1976ff.); *Herder-Kolloquium 1978: Referate und Diskussionsbeiträge,* ed. Walter Dietze in cooperation with Hans-Dietrich Dahnke, Peter Goldammer, Karl Heinz Hahn, and Regine Otto (Weimar: H. Böhlaus Nachfolger, 1980); *Johann Gottfried Herder: 1744-1803,* ed. Gerhard Sauder, Studien zum 18. Jahrhundert 9 (Hamburg: Meiner, 1987).

8. *Johann Gottfried Herder: Innovator Through the Ages,* ed. Wulf Koepke in cooperation with Samson B. Knoll (Bonn: Bouvier, 1982); *Johann Gottfried Herder: Language, History, and the Enlightenment,* ed. Wulf Koepke (Columbia, Camden House, 1990); *Herder Today: Contributions from the International Herder Conference, Nov. 5-8, 1987, Stanford, California,* ed. Kurt Mueller-Vollmer (Berlin: Walter de Gruyter, 1990). The proceedings of the conference in Charlottesville will be edited by Wulf Koepke and Karl Menges.

9. *Johann Gottfried Herder: A Bibliographical Survey 1977-1987,* ed. Tino Markworth (Hürth-Efferen: Gabel Verlag, 1990). The standard bibliography (to 1977) is: *Herder-Bibliographie,* ed. Gottfried Günther, Albina A. Volgina, and Siegfried Seifert (Berlin: Aufbau-Verlag, 1978); Eva M. Knodt, *"Negative Philosophie" und dialo-*

gische Kritik: Zur Struktur poetischer Theorie bei Lessing und Herder (Tübingen: Niemeyer, 1988); Ulrich Gaier, *Herders Sprachphilosophie und Erkenntniskritik* (Stuttgart-Bad Cannstatt: Frommann-Holzboog, 1988); Christoph Fasel, *Herder und das klassische Weimar: Kultur und Gesellschaft 1789-1803* (Frankfurt a.M.: Lang, 1988); Gebhard Fürst, *Sprache als metaphorischer Prozeß. Johann Gottfried Herders hermeneutische Theorie der Sprache* (Mainz: Matthias Grünewald, 1988); Michael Morton, *Herder and the Poetics of Thought: Unity and Diversity in "On Diligence in Several Learned Languages"* (University Park: Pennsylvania State University Press, 1989) and *The Critical Turn: Studies in Kant, Herder, Wittgenstein, and Contemporary Theory* (Detroit: Wayne State University Press, 1993); Robert E. Norton, *Herder's Aesthetics and the European Enlightenment* (Ithaca: Cornell University Press, 1991); Marion Heinz, *Sensualistischer Idealismus: Untersuchungen zur Erkenntnistheorie und Metaphysik des jungen Herder,* habil. diss. University Köln, 1991, Studien zum 18. Jahrhundert (Hamburg: Meiner, forthcoming); Hans Adler, *Die Prägnanz des Dunklen: Gnoseologie—Ästhetik—Geschichtsphilosophie bei J. G. Herder,* Studien zum 18. Jahrhundert 13 (Hamburg: Meiner, 1990). On the average, 44 essays per year have been published between 1977 and 1987.

10. R[udolf] Haym: *Herder nach seinem Leben und seinen Werken dargestellt,* 2 vols. (Berlin: Weidmannsche Buchhandlung, 1880, 1885; Berlin: Aufbau-Verlag, 1958). Robert T. Clark, Jr., *Herder—His Life and Thought* (Berkeley: University of California Press, 1955). Emil Adler, *Herder und die deutsche Aufklärung* ([Warsaw, 1965]; Wien: Europa Verlag, 1968). Two recent monographs do not intend to replace the older ones mentioned above. See Wulf Koepke, *Herder* (Boston: Twayne, 1987) and Günter Arnold, *Johann Gottfried Herder,* 2nd ed. (Leipzig: VEB Bibliographisches Institut, 1988).

11. *Herder Yearbook. Publications of the International Herder Society,* ed. Karl Menges, Wulf Koepke, Wilfried Malsch, vol. 1 (Columbia: Camden House, 1992).

12. I am not including here the discussion concerning evolutionary epistemology because that would go completely beyond the scope of this essay.

13. Immanuel Kant, *Kritik der reinen Vernunft.* Nach der ersten und zweiten Original-Ausgabe herausgegeben von Raymund Schmidt. Mit einer Bibliographie von Heiner Klemme (Hamburg: Meiner, 1990), 651-92, esp. 686-92 (= A 750-A 758).

14. See Alexander Gottlieb Baumgarten, *Metaphysica* (1739; 7th ed., 1779; Hildesheim: Olms, 1963) §

7: *"Nihil . . . est A & non-A."* "Nonnihil est ALIQVID" (§ 8).

15. The *Ideen* were published originally 1784-1791 (*SWS* 13 [1887] and 14 [1909]). The *Briefe* were originally published 1793-1797 (*SWS* 17 [1881] and 18 [1883]).

16. Christian Wolff defined this as follows: *"Cognitio eorum, quae sunt atque fiunt, sive in mundo materiali, sive in substantiis immaterialibus accidant, historica a nobis appellatur." Philosophia rationalis sive Logica,* Pars 1 [1740], Edition critique avec introduction, notes et index par Jean Ecole (Hildesheim: Olms, 1983) § 3.

17. *"Cognitio* rationis eorum, quae sunt, vel fiunt, *philosophica* dicitur." Ibid. § 6.

18. Here, too, might lie one reason for the repeated complaint that "humanity" is a central concept with Herder, but that it is not precisely defined. See Emil Adler, *Herder,* 311. Clark, *Herder,* 314, confronts this problem with an "arbitrary distinction," which he presents very concisely. See also Wilhelm Dobbek, *J. G. Herders Humanitätsidee als Ausdruck seines Weltbildes und seiner Persönlichkeit* (Braunschweig: Westermann, 1949), 44-122. Useless, despite the title, is the partial printing of the Bryn Mawr dissertation of Irmgard Taylor, *Kultur, Aufklärung, Bildung, Humanität und verwandte Begriffe bei Herder,* Gießener Beiträge zur deutschen Philologie, 62 (Gießen: Kindt, 1938). Hans Dietrich Irmscher, "Herders 'Humanitätsbriefe,'" also states in his most recent contribution concerning the concept of humanity that Herder himself had trouble formulating it clearly: "Nicht nur die bisherige Forschung, auch Herder selbst hatte Schwierigkeiten, 'Humanität' eindeutig zu bestimmen" (*FHA,* 7:817).

19. Johann Gottfried Herder, "Versuch über das Sein" [ca. 1763/64], *FHA,* 1: 9-21.

20. *SWS,* 17: 5; emphasized in the text. In its Latin version this sentence had already served in 1785 as a motto for the second part of the *Ideen.*

21. See Paul Hensel, "Herders Humanitätsbegriff in seinem Verhältnis zur Methodenlehre der Geschichte" [1903], *Kleine Schriften und Vorträge,* ed. Ernst Hoffmann and Heinrich Rickert (Tübingen: Mohr [Paul Siebeck], 1930), 41-50. Fritz Ernst, "Herder und die Humanität: Aus einer Antrittsvorlesung [1944] an der E[idgenössischen] T[echnischen] H[ochschule]," *Essais* (Zürich: Fretz & Wasmuth, 1946), 3:287-306.

22. Karl Philipp Moritz's critique of the type of "philanthropic citizen of the world" which was inspired by Basedow is aimed in the same direction. We

read in his *Andreas Hartknopf: Eine Allegorie,* ed. Hans Joachim Schrimpf (1786; Stuttgart: Metzler, 1968), 31f., about the hypocrite Hagebuck who was "converted" to Basedow's philanthropy as follows: "The individual human being meant nothing to him . . . but he was able to embrace with love the whole of humanity—for it his heart beat, as he said, with powerful throbs; for it he sacrificed . . . his powers."

23. Herder to Mendelssohn, Riga, around the beginning of April, 1769. Herder, *Briefe,* 1: 138.

24. See the programmatic essay "Vom Erkennen und Empfinden der menschlichen Seele" [1778], *SWS,* 8: 165-333 (all three versions).

25. See Gaier's commentary, *FHA,* 1: 990.

26. See Hans Dietrich Irmscher, "Die geschichtsphilosophische Kontroverse zwischen Kant und Herder." *Hamann—Kant—Herder. Acta des vierten Internationalen Hamann-Kolloquiums im Herder-Institut zu Marburg/Lahn 1985,* ed. Bernhard Gajek (Frankfurt a.M.: Lang, 1987), 113.

27. Arnold Gehlen, *Der Mensch. Seine Natur und seine Stellung in der Welt* [1940] (Frankfurt a.M.: Athenäum, 7th ed., 1962), 84. Quoted from Regine Otto, "Herders Auffassung vom Menschen und die philosophische Anthropologie," *Wissenschaftliche Zeitschrift [der Friedrich-Schiller-Universität Jena],* Gesellschafts-und Sprachwissenschaftliche Reihe 27 (1978), part 5: 555.

28. Arnold Gehlen, "Über kulturelle Kristallisation" [1963], *Wege aus der Moderne: Schlüsseltexte der Postmoderne-Diskussion,* ed. Wolfgang Welsch (Weinheim: VCH, Acta Humaniora, 1988), 140-41. Gehlen defines "cultural crystallization" as follows: "that condition in any cultural area . . . which sets in when the possibilities laid out therein are all developed in their basic components. One has also discovered and either accepted or shut out the opposite possibilities and antitheses, so that from then on changes in the premises, in the basic views, become improbable . . . Innovations, surprises, genuine productivities are possible, but only within the area already staked out and on the basis of those principles already established; these are no longer abandoned."

29. See Dobbek, *J. G. Herders Humanitätsidee,* 53ff. and Irmscher in his commentary to *FHA,* 7: 818.

30. *"The first holy songs [must] from the very beginning have been more in tune with living action than with dead painting."* Herder, "Versuch einer Geschichte der lyrischen Dichtkunst" (1764), *Werke,* ed., Pross, 1:33.

31. See E.[liza] M. Butler, *The Tyranny of Greece over Germany: A Study of the Influence Exercised* by Greek Art and Poetry over German Writers of the Eighteenth, Nineteenth and Twentieth Centuries (1935; Boston: Beacon Press, 1958), 6.

32. See Herder, *Briefe,* 1:138.

Manet van Montfrans (essay date 1994)

SOURCE: Montfrans, Manet van. "'An Orange on a Pine Tree': French Thought in Herder's Linguistic Theory." In *Yearbook of European Studies 7: German Reflections,* edited by Joep Leerssen and Menno Spiering, pp. 55-76. Amsterdam and Atlanta, Ga.: Rodopi, 1994.

[*In the following essay, Montfrans surveys how Herder's thoughts on linguistics are informed by French Enlightenment scholars.*]

> The mania of the search for 'forerunners' has often falsified the history of philosophy beyond remedy.
>
> (Alexandre Koyré)

In a recent paper entitled *De Boom van Herder* ('Herder's Tree'), the writer and essayist Ian Buruma contrasted two different explanations of the origins of culture.[1] One is held by what Buruma dubs the Herder school, after the eighteenth-century philosopher Johann Gottfried Herder (1744-1803), whose name tends to evoke negative associations with concepts such as nationalism and *Volksgeist.* Buruma styles adherents of the other as the Hobsbawm school, after the British historian who co-edited and contributed to the study *The Invention of Tradition,* published in 1983.[2]

Herder's disciples regard culture as a collection of traditions which has grown organically, which is peculiar to a people and a country, and which determines the individual identity of members of a people. According to Buruma, Herder describes culture as a tree whose roots have grown deep into the national soil, going back to time immemorial. Each people is an organism, with roots as deep as their national tree. Each nation has its own, unique organic culture. Herder resisted the Enlightenment notion of universal values, of a single ideal human being and a single ideal society. He saw everything as growing and flourishing in its own compost, and rejected the notion that ideas could be transferred between nationalities. It was as foolish as tying an orange to a pine tree; transplanted culture could not be made to grow. Herder saw cultural differences not just as inevitable, but as valuable in themselves.[3]

Hobsbawm shows that cultural traditions are by no means invariably 'naturally' determined, but may be artificially introduced. *The Invention of Tradition* demonstrates that various national rituals have often been consciously revived from obscurity or even invented, with a view to justifying the political status quo, or to creating or strengthening a sense of national identity and continuity in times of great upheaval. Examples of such spurious 'traditions'—usually nineteenth-century in origin—include the rituals of the British monarchy, the German cult of Arminius and Barbarossa, and the French adulation of Vercingetorix. A further illustration can be found in the cultivation of anachronistic feudal values and standards by British colonists in Kenya and Rhodesia at the beginning of this century.[4]

It is ironic that the stereotyped contrast between Herder and the Enlightenment indicated by Buruma in itself illustrates Hobsbawm's thesis. The picture of Herder as the fervent opponent of 'superficial' rationalism and the 'bloodless' abstractions which are so readily ascribed to the French philosophers of the Enlightenment—a blind eye being turned to all nuances—is a typical nineteenth-century distortion of reality, an 'invented tradition'. This image originated in a Germany striving for national unity, being born of an increasing desire, especially from 1871 onwards, to define the precise contours of a specific German culture by contrasting it with Latin civilization, notably in its French form. The works of the linguist Wilhelm Scherer (1841-1886) and the literary historian Julian Schmidt (1853-1913) were typical in their desire to provide the newly-formed, independent German state retroactively with a characteristically German, autonomous literature.[5] This led to the postulation of the existence of an eighteenth-century intellectual tradition which supposedly originated in response to the Enlightenment. Herder was seen in this context as the initiator and first representative of the *Sturm und Drang* movement, as the champion of the imagination, intuition and emotion, as the pioneer of German romanticism and national German literature.[6]

Paradoxically, this image worked in the favour not only of the Germans, but also of the French, who after 1871 found in it a useful basis for opposition. Whereas the Enlightenment had on the whole been viewed unfavourably by many French philosophers in the first half of the nineteenth century, by 1870 concepts such as reason and free will were once again seen in a positive light.[7] Ernest Renan, for instance, in a polemic with the German academic Strauss,[8] solemnly countered the latter's linguistic and historical justification of the German annexation of Alsace-Lorraine with a reminder of the existence of universal values, and argued, in his famous *Qu'est-ce qu'une nation* that a nation is a union based on the will of individuals, not an organic totality.[9] In the preface to this latter text, which is presented as his political will and testament, Renan warns of the explosive nature of concepts such as nation, race and nationality:

[*Qu'est-ce qu'une nation*] est ma profession de foi en ce qui touche les choses humaines, et quand la civilisa-

tion moderne aura sombré par suite de l'équivoque funeste de ces mots: *nation, nationalité, race,* je désire qu'on se souvienne de ces vingt pages-là.[10]

AN INVENTED TRADITION REVISITED

In a number of studies published over the last three decades this nineteenth-century simplification, which does justice neither to Herder nor to the French philosophers of the Enlightenment, has been replaced by a much more nuanced approach. There has been a growing realization that the artificial and overly polarizing contrast between *Sturm und Drang* and the Age of Reason constitutes one of the most tenacious topoi of literary history, that Herder was primarily a product of the Enlightenment, and that if his ideas are to be understood, they have to be placed in this context.[11] This reappraisal can be seen in the light of growing interest in the genesis of national identities. The Germans, burdened by the legacy of the past and filled by an urgent need for a 'postnational' identity, have been more in a hurry than, say, the French, to sift the wheat from the chaff in the nineteenth-century body of thought.[12]

One of the areas in which Herder's close contacts with French philosophers is evident—though long obscured by the nineteenth-century 'invented tradition'—is in the field of philosophy of language. I shall attempt to outline the nature and substance of these relationships below, on the basis of various secondary studies and a closer look at two primary texts. It must be emphasized that the scope of this paper only allows for an orientational survey.[13]

ON THE ORIGIN OF LANGUAGE

One of Herder's most famous doctrines is that of the close relationship between *Volksgeist* and language: nations possess a collective soul and a true spiritual unity, which shape their identity. This unity is most evident in language. German is accordingly held to be the exclusively authentic expression of the true German *Volksseele*, while French is seen as the expression *par excellence* of the *esprit français*. This doctrine was formulated by Herder in his 1772 **Abhandlung über den Ursprung der Sprache,** which was long regarded as the starting point of the history of linguistic philosophy.[14] The French Enlightenment philosopher Condillac, however, had already put forward a similar view in his *Essai sur l'origine des connaissances humaines* (1746).[15] In it he claims, for instance, that 'tout confirme donc que chaque langue exprime le caractère du peuple qui la parle' (p. 267), and that

par cette histoire des progrès du langage, chacun peut s'apercevoir que les langues, pour quelqu'un qui les connaîtrait bien seraient une peinture du caractère et du génie de chaque peuple.

(p. 267)

Was Condillac, who still tends to be seen as the prototype of the materialistic Enlightenment philosopher and as the most prominent representative of sensualism, actually a crypto-romantic? Was he less of a universalist than he was commonly thought to be, or is this doctrine perhaps a German pine cone which, through some strange quirk of nature, has grown on a French orange tree? Were Herder's ideas perhaps less original, less typically German than has been supposed? Why is Condillac often overlooked, while Herder is still being quoted?

A European debate

Herder's essay was for a long time one of the best known and most influential works in the history of linguistic philosophy. Less well known is the historical context in which the essay came to be written. Herder wrote his ***Abhandlung*** in response to an essay competition organised by the Berlin Academy; it was one of the last contributions to an international debate on the origin of language which had been going on for over twenty years. It had been initiated by Condillac's *Essai* of 1746. In France, Condillac's ideas were adopted and debated by Voltaire, Rousseau and Diderot, as well as forming the subject matter for a large number of articles in the *Encyclopédie*. Rousseau wrote *Sur l'origine du langage,* part of which appeared in *Le discours sur l'origine et les fondements de l'inégalité* (1755) and which was published in its entirety in 1781, three years after his death.[16] Diderot devoted attention to the question in his *Lettre sur les sourdsmuets à l'usage de ceux qui entendent et parlent* (1751). Condillac's ideas were introduced in Germany by the Frenchman Pierre-Louis Moreau de Maupertuis, who in 1746 was charged by Frederick II with the task of breathing new life into the moribund Royal Academy in Berlin, and who held the post of president of the Academy up to 1759. In Britain, too, there was a response to the debate on the problem of the origin of language, notably from Adam Smith, with his *Considerations Concerning the Origin and the Formation of Languages* (1761) and Lord Monboddo (James Burnett) with *Of the Origin and Process of Language* (1773).

The problem of the origin of language

The search for the origin of the various aspects of human abilities, institutions and products was of course characteristic of the eighteenth-century approach to science. Attempts were made to find the origins of thought and of language, of polity and of social rules, of art and of crafts. The aim was to separate what was natural or inborn from what was artificial or acquired in order to reach a better understanding of the functioning of the human spirit and of human institutions. This was the preoccupation which sparked off hypotheses on the natural state of mankind, and not, as was often errone-

ously supposed in the nineteenth century, a naive need to discover some kind of primitive historical reality in order to describe how things were in the past.[17]

It was hoped that the search for the origin of language would lead to a better understanding of the nature of language and of thought, and of the way in which the human mind functioned, and that it would provide an instrument for the evaluation of knowledge formulated in a given language.[18] In other words, answers were being sought to two closely-related questions: what is the connection between thought and language (which came first: thought or language) and how does knowledge expressed in language relate to reality?

Essai sur l'origine des connaissances humaines

In the original 1746 edition, the full title of Condillac's *Essai* was given as *Essai sur l'origine des connaissances humaines, ouvrage où l'on réduit à un seul principe tout ce qui concerne l'entendement humain.* The first part, *Des matériaux de nos connaissances et particulièrement des opérations de l'âme,* concerns the building blocks of our knowledge, sensory perception, and the intellectual operations associated with the development of understanding and the acquisition of knowledge. The second part, *Du langage et de la méthode,* concerns the crucial role which Condillac accorded to language in this latter process. Language is the principle to which the functioning of the intellectual powers is reduced.

Locke, whose views in *An Essay Concerning Human Understanding* had been adopted as a starting point by Condillac, believed that knowledge was brought about by the combined effect of observation and thought; he did not regard language as playing a significant role in the development of human cognitive faculties, seeing it merely as an instrument which served to express and communicate the existing sum of knowledge. In Locke's universalist view, language and thought are two independent systems: every individual thinks in the same way, and this process is not affected by the differences in the various languages. The role of philosophy here was simply to improve and refine language as an instrument for the transfer of knowledge.[19]

Condillac, too, regards perception and subsequent reflection as elementary cognitive operations, but through analysis of the various intellectual capacities (attention, association, imagination, memory) mobilised in this process he demonstrates that it is impossible to abstract or generalize without recourse to language. According to Condillac, ideas are not gradually formed solely as the result of perception. He sees the development of understanding as resulting from conventional linguistic signs. In the introduction to his *Essai* Condillac puts it in the following words:

Il faut remonter à l'origine de nos idées, en développer la génération, les suivre jusqu'aux limites que la nature leur a prescrites, parlà fixer l'étendue et les bornes de nos connoissances et renouveler tout l'entendement humain [. . .] j'ai ce me semble, trouvé la solution de tous ces problèmes dans la *liaison des idées,* soit avec *les signes,* soit entre elles. [. . .] Les idées se lient avec les signes, et ce n'est que par ce moyen, comme je le prouverai, qu'elles se lient entre elles.

(p. 101)

Condillac thus places language at the heart of the cognitive process by claiming that the linking of ideas by linguistic signs is the most important process connecting the moment of perception to the activity of reflection:

Aussitôt qu'un homme commence à s'attacher à des signes qu'il a lui-même choisis on voit se former en lui la mémoire. Celle-ci acquise il commence à disposer par lui-même de son imagination et à lui donner un nouvel exercice.

(p. 131)

Language is an essential element in the development of an individual's intellectual powers, and not simply an external vehicle designed for the purpose of maintaining social contact. Language and thought are inextricably related, reason has gradually developed in close connection with language.

In the first part of his essay, Condillac thus develops a model of thought which provides not only for a step-by-step account of the development of human knowledge, but also for an indication of the difference between man and beast. In order to demonstrate convincingly the gradual progress of language and thus of thought, Condillac, in the second part of his essay, *Du langage et de la méthode,* gives the hypothetical example of two children who, some time after the Flood, grow up in isolation in the desert, subsequently meet and then establish a primitive form of communication, in which actions, gestures and sounds are symbolic of the situations with which they are normally associated.[20]

The use of these symbols, which always directly link the sign and the referent, would accordingly have served as a basis for the invention of new and this time arbitrary sound symbols as names for objects. *Arbitrary,* in this sense, does not necessarily mean that there is by definition no reasoned connection between symbol and object, but that a language user can make use of symbols at his discretion to conjure up certain concepts. Symbols provide him with a means of divorcing himself from the here-and-now of the concrete world.

Although Condillac views the transition from natural signs (*signes naturels* or *cris et gestes naturels*) to arbitrary sound signs (*signes institués*) as a gradual process, he sees the difference between them as fundamental, and as characteristic of the difference between man and beast:

Voilà où l'on commence à apercevoir la supériorité de notre ame sur celle des bêtes; car d'un côté, il est constant qu'il ne dépend point d'elles d'attacher leurs idées à des signes arbitraires; et de l'autre, il paroît certain que cette impuissance ne vient pas uniquement de l'organisation. Leur corps n'est-il pas aussi propre au langage d'action que le nôtre? Plusieurs d'entre elles n'ont-elles pas tout ce qu'il faut pour l'articulation des sons? Pourquoi donc, si elles étaient capables des mêmes opérations que nous, n'en donneraient-elles pas des preuves?[21]

Condillac thus expressly regards language not as of animal origin, but as a human achievement. However, he does see a need for communication and therefore a form of society as an essential precondition for the linked development of language and of the intellect: 'les hommes ne possèdent le langage qu'autant qu'ils vivent ensemble' (p. 172).

Condillac goes on to demonstrate how language must have developed, from this first language of isolated words and unarticulated expressions (actions, gestures, sounds), via the poetic and musical language which sprang from the imagination of primitive peoples, to the stage which language had reached in his day, and to which he refers as the philosophical stage. If the various languages have developed gradually and separately, they will reflect the circumstances in which they originated. These are the thoughts which prompted Condillac's relativist theory on the relationship between national character and language: people who speak different languages also think and act differently:

Par cette histoire des progrès du langage [. . .] chacun verrait comment l'imagination a combiné les idées d'après les préjugés et les passions: il y verrait se former chez chaque nation un esprit différent à proportion qu'il y aurait moins de commerce entr'elles. Mais si les moeurs ont influencé sur le langage, celui-ci lorsque les écrivains célèbres en eurent fixé les règles, influa à son tour sur les moeurs et conserva longtemps à chaque peuple son caractère.[22]

PRIZE ESSAYS

The questions raised by Condillac's *Essai* sparked off the following debate. In 1757 the Berlin Academy launched its first essay competition with the subject: What is the influence of a people's opinions on language, and what influence does language have on opinions? This question was directly inspired by the above-quoted views of Condillac, and had already been formulated by Maupertuis in his critical response to Condillac's dissertation, *Réflexions sur l'origine des langues et la signification des mots* (1748).

Language is not a reliable source of knowledge of reality, and this is the cause of the numerous difficulties we encounter in our quest for knowledge. If it was possible to discover how the various languages originated, it would also be possible to rid them of their impurities. The author of the winning essay, *Beantwortung der Frage von dem Einflüss der Meinungen in die Sprache und der Sprache in die Meinungen* (1760), the oriëntalist Johann David Michaëlis endorses the view that certain instances of faulty reasoning or certain notions are indeed attributable to the structure of the language in which they are formulated. However, he rejects the solution proposed by Maupertuis to this problem—the creation of a written, universal, ideal language.[23]

The subject of one of the following contributions to the debate sprang not from observation of the shortcomings of the various languages, but rather of their grammatical regularity and complexity. This regularity upsets the theory of a process of gradual growth, with unavoidable mistakes and deviations. The question must then be whether man can have created such a perfect system from nothing? Language is the tool with which we make use of our reason; without language our intellect is worthless: we cannot abstract, we cannot generalize and we cannot reason. If language had been devised by man, he would have to have been equipped with sound intellectual powers before he had access to language. Therefore language cannot be the product of man's brain, but must have been created by God and given to man in all its perfection in the beginning. This was the reasoning put forward by Johann Peter Süssmilch in *Versuch eines Beweises dass die erste Sprache ihren Ursprung nicht vom Menschen, sondern allein vom Schöpfer erhalten habe,* a dissertation which was written in 1756, but only published in 1766.

Another question raised by Condillac's essay concerned the precise moment at which language originated. Could the inner association of ideas (a kind of internal logic) already be classified as language, a specific mental language, or does language only originate in its manifestation as a spoken form? And would man also invent language if deprived of contact with others?

The theme of the essay competition held by the Academy in 1769 gave competitors the chance to review the whole question in the light of the various responses to Condillac's essay: Assuming that human beings are dependent on their natural powers, would they be in a position to create language and how could they successfully do so without outside aid?

Abhandlung über den Ursprung der Sprache

In the subtitles of the two parts of the winning essay, the **Abhandlung** submitted in 1770 by Herder, he repeated these questions: 'Haben die Menschen, ihren Naturfähigkeiten überlassen, sich selbst Sprache erfinden können?' and, 'Auf welchem Wege der Mensch sich am füglichsten hat Sprache erfinden können und müssen?' The first part concerns the relationship between language and thought and the origin of language, the second concerns the evolution of language in its various forms.

Herder commences his dissertation with a provocative claim: 'Schon als Thier, hat der Mensch Sprache'. It will be evident that the provocation lies in the possible denial of the difference between man and animal implicit in the declaration that language—generally regarded as symptomatic of such difference—is inherent to the animal state. Herder is playing here with two possible interpretations of the concept of language: later in the essay he distinguishes between natural language (the inarticulate expression of emotions) and conventional, artificial language. If the concept *Sprache* is understood to mean natural language, Herder endorses the thesis of his opening sentence, but if *Sprache* also refers to conventional language, he rejects this thesis. For, as Herder continues, man is the only creature who from the beginning possessed both reason and the conventional language without which reason cannot function, and thus can be said to differ materially from animals.

Before formulating this material difference, however, Herder dwells at some length on the view to which his provocative opening thesis refers and which he erroneously attributes to Condillac. According to Herder, Condillac had discarded the fundamental difference between man and beast in maintaining that there was no discontinuity between conventional language and the inarticulate expressions of pain, joy, sorrow and high spirits which man shares with animals. Herder in no way denies that man, too, has a natural language, going so far as to describe this language with a lyricism quite alien to Condillac:

> Der auffahrende Sturm einer Leidenschaft; der plötzliche Überfall von Freude oder Frohheit; Schmerz und Jammer, wenn sie tiefe Furchen in die Seele graben; ein übermannendes Gefühl von Rache, Verzweiflung, Wuth, Schrecken, Grausen u.s.w. alle kündigen sich an, und jede nach ihrer Art verschieden an.

> (p. 10)

But, he writes, although traces of these natural sounds can still be found in the various languages, these are not the roots of those languages, solely the sap which flows through the roots. In other words, the spoken language has not developed from these natural expressions, and the philosophers who share such views, imputed to Condillac, deny a real difference between man and beast:

> Aber ich kann nicht meine Verwunderung bergen, dass Philosophen, das ist, Leute, die deutliche Begriffe suchen, je haben auf den Gedanken kommen können, aus diesem Geschrei der Empfindungen den Ursprung Menschlicher Sprache zu erklären: denn ist diese nicht offenbar ganz etwas anders? Alle Thiere bis auf den

stummen Fisch tönen ihre Empfindung; desswegen aber hat doch kein Thier, selbst nicht das Vollkommenste, den geringsten, eigentlichen Anfang zu einer Menschlichen Sprache. [..] Der Abt Condillac ist in dieser Anzahl.

(p. 18)

Herder does not confine his polemic engagements to Condillac, but also takes up the cudgels against Rousseau. Rousseau, who had placed his hypothetical primitive man in an animal state and total isolation, could not think how he could have invented language, and stated, in part one of his *Discours sur l'origine de l'inégalité* that he regarded the problem of the origin of language as insoluble.[24] While Condillac equated animal with man, Rousseau made man into an animal.[25] After having dwelt on the aberrations of those whom he rightly or wrongly considered to be his opponents, Herder goes on to formulate his own ideas—ideas which he shares, without apparently realizing it, with Condillac and nearly all the participants[26] in the Academy debate: human beings are characterized by their powers of reasoning and their freedom of choice, while animals blindly obey their instincts and possess skills suited only to limited number of situations. The difference between man and beast is not gradual but fundamental:

> Der Unterschied ist nicht in Stuffen, oder Zugabe von Kräften sondern in einer ganz verschiedenartigen Richtung und Auswickelung aller Kräfte. Man sei Leibnitzianer oder Lockianer [. . .] Idealist oder Materialist, so muss man bei einem Einverständnis über die Worte, zu Folge des Vorigen, die Sache zugeben, einen eignen Charakter der Menschheit, der hierinn und in nichts anders bestehet.

(p. 27)

And since reason cannot function without language, this fundamental difference lies in possession of a language:

> Der Mensch, in den Zustand von Besonnenheit gesetzt, der ihm eigen ist, und diese Besonnenheit (Reflexion) zum erstenmal frei würkend, hat Sprache erfunden.

(p. 31)

Reason cannot operate without language; it presupposes and requires the existence of language. The origin of reason is identical to that of language:

> Ich habe erwiesen, dass der Gebrauch der Vernunft nicht etwa blos füglich, sondern dass nicht der mindeste Gebrauch der Vernunft, nicht die einfachste, deutliche Anerkennung, nicht das simpelste Urtheil einer menschlichen Besonnenheit ohne Merkmal möglich sei: den der Unterschied von Zween lässt sich nur immer durch ein Drittes erkennen. Eben dies Dritte, dies Merkmal, wird mithin inneres Merkwort: also folgt die Sprache aus dem ersten Aktus der Vernunft ganz natürlich.

(p. 35)

HERDER AND CONDILLAC

Aarsleff ascribes Herder's curious approach in the ***Abhandlung*** to the circumstances under which the essay was written. When Herder wrote his dissertation in December 1770, he was in Strasbourg, and was unable to consult the requisite literary sources. At the time he had only read the second part of Condillac's essay, the part which describes the development of language and which opens with the example of the two children in the desert.[27]

Since he was unfamiliar with Condillac's views on the interrelation of language and intellect, Herder did not know that these remarks on language were made in the broader context of the development of human cognitive powers. He concluded from the part which he had read that Condillac saw language as having animal origins. In his repudiation of these views he develops the same ideas set out by Condillac in the first part of his *Essai*. Herder thus also connects the ability to think and to reason with conventional language, and he answers the question as to whether man could have invented language with only his natural abilities to aid him in the affirmative, thus explicitly rejecting the views of Süssmilch and Rousseau.[28]

While Herder, in part two of his dissertation, sees the development of reason as closely connected to that of spoken language (just as Condillac had), he assumes, in part one of his essay, the existence of a kind of internal language, the precursor of spoken language. According to Herder, man would invent this internal language even if he were alone:

> [. . .] der Wilde, der Einsame im Walde hätte Sprache für sich selbst erfinden müssen; hätte er sie auch nie geredet. Sie war einverständniss seiner Seele mit sich, und ein so nothwendiges Einverständniss als der Mensch Mensch war.

(p. 34)

Not only the savage in the forest, but also the lamentable blind and dumb man whom Herder, in a typical eighteenth-century fantasy, maroons on an uninhabited island, would, by means of what he hears and feels, learn to name the objects around him. The cool breath of the Western wind on his face, the bleating of the sheep whose milk he drinks, the soporific murmur of the brook, the rustling of the tree which feeds him with its fruit: the poor blind man would distinguish between all these sounds by means of his intellect, and would be able to use them as inward signs with which to order and chart the world around him (p. 43). Just as an individual, in an interior dialogue, isolates an element of perception (*Merkmal*) in order to refer to perception, he will, if a need for communication arises, make use of audible signs to refer to such inner abstraction (p. 53).

In the second half of his essay Herder describes how the various spoken languages developed historically, according to four natural laws, from this hypothetical beginning. These views add nothing to the theoretical insight formulated in the first half of the essay, and will not be discussed here.

RISE AND FALL OF AN INVENTED TRADITION

Herder's polemic interpretation of Condillac was accepted unthinkingly throughout the nineteenth century and has lived on for the greater part of the twentieth century. Whereas Rousseau's views on language survive, buoyed up by his literary fame, the *Essai sur l'origine des connaissances humaines*—whose title bears absolutely no reference to language, and which, like other dissertations written by philosophers of the Enlightenment, was anathematized by the strong historical orientation of the nineteenth century—quickly sank from sight. Subsequent dissertations by Condillac, such as the *Traité des sensations* (1754) and *Traité des animaux* (1755), reinforced the misconception that Condillac saw perception as the sole source of knowledge. The revolutionary notion of the interrelation of language and thought, formulated by Condillac in his *Essai* and never subsequently retracted—a notion which sparked off a twenty-year-long debate at the Berlin Academy—was ascribed to Herder's compelling dissertation, along with the resultant romantic ideas concerning the connection between language and national character and the celebration of the specific rather than the universal.[29]

The artificially sharp contrast between Herder and the French Enlightenment has been criticized from various sources and in various ways. In Germany it was the attempt to erase the traces of excessive nationalism in academic and scientific circles which led, in the 1960s, to an about-turn in Herder studies. In Anglo-Saxon countries, criticism (by Aarsleff and others) of Chomsky's linguistic theories, especially his *Cartesian Linguistics: A Chapter in the History of Rationalist Thought* (1966), led to the rediscovery of the eighteenth-century French 'prelinguists'. In France, structuralist and poststructuralist interest in the theory of linguistic signs developed by the nineteenth-century linguist Ferdinand de Saussure gave a fresh boost to research into Enlightenment ideas on language. The rediscovery of this past has given a much-needed historical perspective to linguistic relativism, which, during the 1960s and 1970s, was embraced in a highly dogmatic form by the French humanities, and which, it seems, can be traced back via Wilhelm von Humboldt, not, as has long been supposed, to Herder, but to Condillac.

Notes

1. In *De Volkskrant,* Het Vervolg, 30 October 1993, pp. 7, 8. The Far East expert Ian Buruma (who has published three books on the theme of the search for national identity in Asiatic countries, including *God's Gruis: Een reis door het moderne Azië* (Amsterdam: Arbeiderspers, 1990), original title *God's Dust*), addressed the tendency to seek supposedly unique and essentially cultural explanations for economic or political issues in the Far East, an approach which is less often adopted where neighbouring European countries are concerned. Cultural and historical explanations often conceal a lack of ready knowledge of actual reality: cultural determinism is a dangerous line of reasoning and leads to culture being reduced to a mask, apologetically, in international relations.

2. Eric J. Hobsbawm & Terence Ranger (eds.), *The Invention of Tradition* (Cambridge University Press, 1983).

3. Herder formulated these ideas in various works, including *Auch eine Philosophie der Geschichte zur Bildung der Menschheit* (1774), in: *Herder's Werke* (Berlin: Aufbau Verlag, 1978), III: 41-137. Cf. Alain Finkielkraut's concise summary of this viewpoint: 'Depuis toujours, ou pour être plus précis depuis Platon jusqu'à Voltaire, la diversité humaine avait comparu devant le tribunal des valeurs; Herder vint et fit condamner par le tribunal de la diversité toutes les valeurs universelles', in: *La défaite de la pensée* (Paris: Gallimard, 1973), p. 18. The idea that variety is preferable to uniformity and not simply a manifestation of a human inability to find the one true answer, is a modern one. It was unknown to the thinkers of antiquity or the Middle Ages.

4. See Terence Ranger, 'The Invention of Tradition in Colonial Africa', in *op. cit.,* pp. 211-262.

5. Both academics held chairs at Strasbourg at a time when the Alsace-Lorraine question was highly topical and when much was being made of French-German antagonism (Scherer from 1871-1877, Schmidt from 1877-1880). Cf. 'Herder und Goethe', in Wilhelm Scherer, *Geschichte der deutschen Literatur* (13th ed. Berlin: Weidmannsche Buchhandlung, 1915), pp. 470-501; 'Herder', in Julian Schmidt, *Geschichte der deutschen Literatur von Leibniz bis auf unsere Zeit* (Berlin: Wilhelm Herß, 1886), II: 65-87.

6. See Jörn Stückrath, 'Der junge Herder als Sprach- und Literatur-theoretiker—ein Erbe des französischen Aufklärers Condillac?', in *Sturm und Drang,* ed. W. Hinck (Kronberg: Athenäum, 1978), p. 91.

7. The French traditionalists Joseph de Maistre and Louis de Bonald rejected the idea of a universal man and universal values. De Maistre famously remarked: 'Il n'y a point d'homme dans le monde.

J'ai vu dans ma vie des Français, des Italiens, des Russes. Je sais même grâce à Montesquieu qu'on peut être Persan; mais quant à l'homme, je déclare ne l'avoir rencontré de ma vie; s'il existe, c'est bien à mon insu.' J. de Maistre, *Oeuvres complètes,* I (Lyon: Vitte, 1884), p. 75.

8. Ernest Renan, 'Lettre à M. Strauss' (16 September 1870) and 'Nouvelle Lettre à M. Strauss' (15 September 1871), in *Oeuvres complètes* (ed. H. Psichari, Paris: Calmann-Lévy, 1947), I: 437-462. A comparable polemic took place in 1870 between the historians Fustel de Coulanges and Theodor Mommsen.

9. Ernest Renan, 'Qu'est-ce qu'une nation', *op. cit.,* pp. 887-906.

10. Renan wrote this preface in 1887. Cited by Ph. Forest in *Qu'est-ce qu'une nation, Littérature et Identité nationale de 1871-1914* (Paris: Bordas, 1991), p. 28.

11. Cf. Werner Kraus, 'Zur Periodisierung. Aufklärung, Sturm und Drang, Weimarer Klassik', in *Studien zur deutschen und französischen Aufklärung* (Berlin: Rütten und Loening, 1963), pp. 376-399; Christophe Siegrist, 'Aufklärung und Sturm und Drang: Gegeneinander oder Nebeneinander?', in W. Hinck, *op. cit.,* pp. 1-13.

12. See on this subject, Rudolf von Thadden, 'Aufbau nationaler Identität, Deutschland und Frankreich in Vergleich', in *Nationale und kulturelle Identität,* ed. B. Giesen (Frankfurt /Main: Suhrkamp, 1991), pp. 493-510. According to Von Thadden, more general factors which played a role with respect to this interest in national identity included the fragmentation of the power block policy, the emergence of regional movements and the problem of immigration.

13. The central source of reference for this subject is Hans Aarsleff, 'The Tradition of Condillac: The Problem of the Origin of Language in the Eighteenth Century and the Debate in the Berlin Academy before Herder', an article published in 1974 in *From Locke to Saussure, Essays on the Study of Language and Intellectual History* (London: Athlone Press, 1982), pp. 146-209. Aarsleff's view on the relationship between Condillac and Herder derives from his study of the history of linguistic philosophy. Aarsleff is cited approvingly by almost all the authors of subsequent works on Herder and Condillac. These include: Jörn Stückrath in the article cited above, 1978; Nicolas Rousseau, *Connaissance et langage chez Condillac* (Geneva: Droz, 1986), and Robert E. Norton in *Herder's Aesthetics and the European Enlightenment* (Cornell University Press, 1991).

14. Johann Gottfried Herder, *Abhandlung über den Ursprung der Sprache,* ed. Wolfgang Pross (Munich/Vienna: Carl Hanser, 1978), pp. 9-134. Page references following quotations in the text refer to this edition. This view of the *Abhandlung* is propounded *inter alia* by Hansjörg Salmony, *Die Philosophie des jungen Herder* (Zürich: Vineta, 1949), p. 55; Emil Adler, *Herder und die deutsche Aufklärung* (Vienna: Europa, 1968), p. 129, but also by Hayden White, 'The Irrational and the Problem of Historical Knowledge in the Enlightenment' in his *Tropics of Discourse: Essays in Cultural Criticism* (Johns Hopkins University Press, 1978), p. 146.

15. Etienne Bonnot de Condillac, *Essai sur l'origine des connaissances humaines, ouvrage où l'on réduit à un seul principe tout ce qui concerne l'entendement humain* (Paris: Galilée, 1973), pp. 98-291. Prefaced by an essay by Jacques Derrida, *l'Archéologie du frivole.* Page references following quotations in the text refer to this edition.

16. J.-J. Rousseau, *Discours sur l'origine et les fondements de l'inégalité parmi les hommes* (Paris: Ed. Sociales, 1983); *Essai sur l'origine des langues,* published in *Traités sur la musique* (Geneva, 1781).

17. That eighteenth-century philosophers were aware of the possibility of such an interpretation is apparent from the following utterance of Rousseau's: 'Il ne faut pas prendre les recherches, dans lesquelles on peut entrer à ce sujet, pour les vérités historiques, mais seulement pour des raisonnements hypothétiques et conditionnels, plus propres à éclaircir la nature des choses qu'à en montrer la véritable origine, et semblables à ceux que font tous les jours nos physiciens sur la formation du monde'. J.-J. Rousseau, *op. cit.* (note 16), pp. 85, 86.

18. This problem has long fascinated mankind, for different reasons. Herodotus, for instance, relates the story of the Egyptian king Psammetichus I (seventh century B.C.), who commanded a goatherd to raise two children without speaking to them. Psammetichus thought that the children would spontaneously develop a language, and he hoped in this way to discover which was the oldest language on earth. The story goes that after a period of two years the children said something like 'becos'. Some felt that this echoed the bleating of goats, others said it was typical of the prattling sounds made by all children learning to talk. But once Psammetichus had established that 'becos' was the Phrygian word for bread, he was able to conclude that the Phrygians were older

than the Egyptians. Herodotus, *The Histories,* Book II, 2 (London: Oxford University Press), p. 94.

19. John Locke, *An Essay concerning Human Understanding,* III: 'Of Words' (London: Dent, 1961), II: 9-106. Locke regarded words simply as 'the signs of men's *ideas* and, by that means, the instruments whereby men communicate their conceptions, and express to one another those thoughts and imaginations they have within their own breasts' (p. 14).

20. One of the few documented examples of children who have grown up without language is that of two Indian infants who were literally plucked from a wolf's den by an Indian missionary in 1920 in Bengal. The children were three and six years old. The oldest child survived, but learnt no grammatical constructions, only isolated words. This would seem to confirm the hypothesis that there is a critical period in the acquisition of a native language: if it is not learnt before a certain age it is too late and will never be acquired. See Jean Aitchison, *The Articulate Mammal* (London: Routledge, 1989).

21. p. 131. Numerous other passages can be cited in which Condillac stresses the difference between man and beast, between natural language and conventional language. Cf. *Lettres à Cramer*: 'les signes naturels ne sont point proprement des signes; ce ne sont que des cris qui accompagnent les sentiments de douleur, de joie, etc, et que les hommes alors poussent par instinct et par la seule conformation des organes'. Quoted by N. Rousseau, *op. cit.,* p. 232.

22. p. 267. Condillac's linguistic theory was revived in France in the course of the 1970s, a development due in part to the 'linguistic turn' which had taken place in the humanities, inspired partly by Saussure's theories concerning linguistic signs. Cf. the above-mentioned essay by J. Derrida (note 15); *Condillac et les problèmes du langage,* ed. Jean Sgard (Geneva/Paris: Slatkine, 1982); Nicolas Rousseau, *op.cit.,* pp. 15-23.

23. Further significant contributions to the Berlin Academy debate referred to by Aarsleff are Maupertuis' *Dissertation sur les moyens différents employés par les hommes d'exprimer leurs idées,* and Samuel Formey's *Survey of the principal means that have been employed to discover the origin of human language, ideas and knowledge* (1762). For a summary of their contents see Aarsleff, *op. cit.,* pp. 178-193.

24. Cf. Rousseau 'Quant à moi, effrayé des difficultés qui se multiplient et convaincu de l'impossibilité presque démontrée que les langues aient pu naître et s'établir par des moyens purement humains, je laisse à qui voudra l'entreprendre la discussion de ce difficile problème; lequel a été le plus nécessaire, de la société déjà liée à l'institution des langues, ou des langues déjà inventées à l'établissement de la société', *Essai sur l'origine et les fondements de l'inégalité, op. cit.,* p. 115. A German translation of this *Essai* appeared as early as 1756.

25. Herder: 'Condillac und Rousseau mussten über den Sprachursprung irren, weil sie sich über diesen Unterschied so bekannt und verschieden irrten: da jener die Thiere zu Menschen und dieser die Menschen zu Thieren machte' (p. 22).

26. With the exception of Süssmilch and Formey, who ascribe divine origins to language.

27. In 1763 the Breslau *Vermischte Breitäge zur Philosophie und den schönen Wissenschaften* published a translation of the first eight chapters of the second part of Condillac's essay. It is evident from a postscript to the fragments *Über die neuere Deutsche Literatur* (1766/67) that Herder had at least read these chapters before 1767. 'Der zweite Teil von dem *Essai sur l'origine des connaissances humaines* enthält Betrachtungen, die mein Fragment von den Lebensaltern der Sprache sehr ins Licht setzen'. Since this remark concerning the *Lebensaltern der Sprache* is regarded as the germ of Herder's revolutionary views on language and literature, the reference to Condillac made at this particular point should be taken seriously. See: Norton, *op. cit.,* p. 93, and Stückrath, *op. cit.,* p. 83.

28. pp. 34-36. On the relationship between Herder/Condillac see also N. Rousseau, *op. cit.,* pp. 372-383.

29. Although Herder's misconception was exposed by various authors, it is still encountered in recent publications. The section on the *Abhandlung* in *Kindlers Neue Literaturlexikon,* for instance, alleges that in it Herder rejects the 'Sprachtheorien der französischen Aufklärung, etwa Condillacs, der Sprache aus Nachahmung tierischer Laute entstanden wissen wollte' (Munich: Kindler, 1990), VII: 707-709.

Astrida Orle Tantillo (essay date 1999)

SOURCE: Tantillo, Astrida Orle. "Herder and National Culture: A Case Study of Latvia." In *Eighteenth-Century Research: Universal Reason and National Culture during the Enlightenment,* edited by David A. Bell, Ludmila Pimenova, and Stéphane Pujol, pp. 31-46. Paris: Champion, 1999.

[In the following essay, Tantillo analyzes Herder's early writings in and about Latvia as a means of evaluating the author's relationship to the ideals of the Enlightenment.]

Johann Gottfried Herder (1744-1803) is generally considered an anti-Enlightenment figure because of his "scorn for the idea of unilateral progress"[1], and because of his rejection of universal reason as a standard for criticizing various historical time periods, artistic endeavors, nations, or even laws. He is instead often considered the father of modern historicism, because he, "in contrast to natural law philosophy assumes that all values and all cognitions are historic and individual," and because he also assumed no "universally valid values"[2]. Moreover, his work on folk culture—which inspired a kind of eighteenth-century frenzy to study other cultures—is often considered a further rejection of rational, Enlightenment standards for culture. Many critics today see Herder as a precursor to modern cultural relativism because he presented "a radical critique of the rationalist discourse of cosmopolitan human development advanced by the Enlightenment thinkers of his day" and because he rejected the idea of "rational perfectibility"[3]. Others also claim that Herder is the founder of modern approaches to comparative literature.[4]

Yet, if we look at Herder's discussions on nations, cultures, or *Volk,* we begin to see that he does not simply reject Enlightenment ideals. While stressing the potential of each nation to develop its own great national literature, Herder still felt justified in ranking national literatures. While fiercely arguing for the necessity of keeping indigenous literatures "pure" from admixture, he simultaneously praises some people for adopting certain aspects from the literatures of others and even argues that some cultures should imitate others. At times he embraces Rousseau's claim about the Golden Age of humankind, while at others he rejects Rousseau's condemnation of progress and seems rather to embrace Enlightenment notions of it.

In exploring these issues in Herder's work, this essay will focus on Herder's early work written either in or about Latvia as a kind of case study for his relationship to Enlightenment ideals[5]. I have selected these works for several reasons. First, it was in Riga that Herder developed his theory of nationalism[6]. Second, his experiences with Latvian folk culture served as an impetus to his research on folk culture generally[7]. Third, Herder had political plans and ambitions for this Baltic area. Finally, we can turn to Latvia as a specific example of the influence of Herder's work. His ideas on *Volk,* as well as his statements on nations and culture, played a central role in the "Latvian National Awakening," an indigenous, nineteenth-century, literary and political movement which based its foundations upon Latvian folk culture. I will further argue that some of the same ambiguities which are evident in Herder's early works on culture appeared within this nineteenth-century movement that he inspired.

Herder arrived in Livonia's principal city of Riga in 1764. Although Livonia itself had been part of the Russian Empire since 1710, the governance of the area lay primarily in German hands, as it had for centuries. The Teutonic Knights had conquered the area during the crusades of the thirteenth century, and Germans had maintained day to day control of the area throughout its political fortunes—the area had passed through the hands of the Russians, Poles, and Swedes. German was the official bureaucratic language. Germans controlled the Riga City Council, the local guilds, and nearly all aspects of trade (Riga had been a Hanseatic city.) German architecture characterized the city, and Protestantism, not Russian Orthodoxy, prevailed as the main religion in the area.

Native Latvians were not allowed to belong either to the city council or to the guilds. Indeed, the cleft between the two groups was so large that the Baltic Germans passed city ordinances in 1738 and 1749 which respectively prohibited Latvians from owning property within the city or suburbs and which forbade Latvians from wearing "German," i.e., European, clothes[8]. Nor was German influence confined to the city walls. German landowners controlled most of the land in Livonia, and serfs, who were tied to the land, constituted most of the population. The German noblemen had "reputation for harshness" in Livonia, and during the late eighteenth century "German scholars of the enlightenment who visited the Baltic provinces also accused the barons of cruel and oppressive treatment"[9]. Serfdom, as in the rest of the Russian Empire, still prevailed in Livonia, and conditions actually worsened during the Age of the Enlightenment. The literary historian Andrups cites a 1719 decree that "run-away peasants shall have their noses and ears cut off"[10], while Latvian serfs, even during Herder's day, were sold openly in markets—families often being broken up during such sales[11]. Hupel, a German protestant minister, reported in 1777:

> A man servant can be bought in Livonia for thirty to fifty rubles silver; an artisan, cook or weaver for anything up to one hundred rubles; . . . children can be bought for four rubles each. Agricultural workers and their children are sold or bartered for horses, dogs, pipes, etc.[12]

The local German nobility further saw Catherine the Great's attempts to reform serfdom within the Russian empire in 1783 as "an unwarranted and unnecessary imposition" on their power—a power which the Germans claimed had been guaranteed them by the Russian Empire since 1561[13].

Herder's own reactions to the conditions in Riga were mixed and reflect some of the contradictions in his views on the value of native culture. On the one hand, Herder, who had just escaped from authoritarian Prussia, praised the "republican freedoms" enjoyed by the ruling Baltic German class, and, as F. M. Barnard argues, "Riga became for Herder what the political image of Geneva had been for Rousseau"[14]. On the other hand, Herder also wrote in defense of the political rights of native peoples and their cultures and even wanted one day to implement his own reforms in the area. In order to examine this tension in his thought, I will turn to several of his early works where he discusses issues of language and nationality generally and the specific political positions of Livonia and Kurland. We shall see that even in his defense of the conditions or culture in this Baltic area, he does not strictly employ those ideals of cultural relativism for which he is so well known, but instead employs a more complicated perspective which partly relies upon the principles of Enlightenment reason and progress.

Herder went to Riga in order to be teacher at the Cathedral School (Domschule). Shortly after his arrival at the school, he composed a lecture entitled: **"On Diligence in the Study of Several Learned Languages" ("Über den Fleiß in mehreren gelehrten Sprachen")**. In this lecture he outlines his principles regarding the development of human language, and he discusses the necessity of learning other languages. He identifies as the "golden age" [die Zeit des Glücks] the time in which all people had "one tongue and language" [eine Zunge und Sprache]. He retraces the dispersement of peoples with the development of new languages and cultures: "and a thousand languages were created in tune with the climes and mores of a thousand nations [und es schufen sich tausend Sprachen nach dem Klima und den Sitten von tausend Nationen]"[15]. Herder, using the metaphor of a plant, describes how different soils and climates changed the character of a language and the people who spoke it. National character, especially during the time of a culture's initial development, was closely tied to the natural surroundings of the people. As a result, "nature imposes upon us an obligation only to our mother tongue [so scheint mir die Natur bloß zu meiner Muttersprache eine Verbindlichkeit aufzulegen]"[16].

Modern culture, Herder explains, is now quite different from that earlier time of simplicity. Where the mother tongue represents for Herder the world of nature, foreign language signifies the world of culture. Modern human beings, with their increased dependence on material goods, need to be able to navigate between both worlds. While Herder on the one hand questions the modern emphasis of gold and riches, he recognizes, on the other hand, that with an increase of material trade comes an increase in knowledge as well:

> How little progress would we have made, were each nation to strive for learnedness by itself, confined within the narrow sphere of its language? A Newton of our land would torture himself striving for a discovery that, for the English Newton, long since had been an unsealed secret.
>
> Wie wenig Fortschritte würden wir getan haben, wenn jede Nation in die enge Sphäre ihrer Sprache eingeschlossen, vor die Gelehrsamkeit allein arbeitete? Ein Newton unseres Landes würde sich mit einer Entdeckung quälen, die dem englischen Newton lange ein entsiegeltes Geheimnis war[17].

Foreign languages then are both "an indispensable evil" [ein unentbehrliches Übel] and "almost a genuine good" [beinahe ein wirkliches Glück]. Although nature gives us but one mother-tongue, necessity now requires that we learn other languages. Moreover, the mother tongue becomes a means of learning about other cultures by serving as a kind of sounding board against which other cultures may be compared. The comparisons of each culture will differ depending upon the individual experiences of the judge as well as the particular course of development of each language and culture. Accordingly, Herder rejects Enlightenment universal standards of reason in judging cultures. First, because cultures would differ in so far as climates differ, different standards must be applied to each. Second, each culture, by necessity, would judge others according to its own standards, making universal standards impossible.

Herder, however, is quite specific about how and why one should go about learning foreign languages—whether one is studying modern languages or ancient ones. He warns that one should avoid setting up false hierarchies and standards among the languages, and he admonishes the reader always to keep his or her own native language in a place of primary importance. Greek and Latin authors have influenced Western culture to such an extent, Herder argues, that we must go back and learn these languages—not because they belong to a culture higher than our own—but in order to study how they might have influenced our own mother tongue. He encourages us to learn about other cultures, but advises us "to keep our native language on our tongue" if we are ever to understand other cultures at all ["Wenn wir unsre Muttersprache auf der Zunge behalten: so werden wir tief in die Dunkelheiten des Nationalcharakters jeder Sprache eindringen"][18].

In learning other languages, Herder emphasizes the power of empathy. He "transplants" himself and expands his soul into every climate and culture. He further seeks "to join the thorough English temperament, the wit of the French, and the resplendence of Italy with German diligence [Mit dem deutschen Fleiß suche ich die gründliche englische Laune, den Witz der Franzosen, das Schimmernde Italiens zu verbinden]"[19]. Throughout his journey into the past and into other cultures and languages, he stresses how he uses the love of fatherland and the love of the mother tongue as his guide. It becomes the standard of comparison for all other languages and cultures, not because he considers the German language or culture as higher, but because each individual is only capable of judging according to his or her own experiences. Our thoughts have been formed by our first language, and we must accordingly compare all others to it:

Just as a child compares all images with the first impressions, our mind clandestinely compares all tongues with our mother tongue, and how useful this can be! Thereby, the great diversity of languages is given unity.

Ein Kind vergleichet all Bilder, mit dem ersten, das sich ihm eindruckte, und unser Geist insgeheim alle Mundarten mit unserer Sprache. Sie sehen, wie nützlich dies ist, da es in diese große Mannichfaltigkeit Einheit bringt[20].

In other words, Herder was advocating a kind of relativism in this essay which is similar to some strands of multiculturalism today, where one seeks to learn from other cultures without imposing one's own culture or standards upon others. Herder likens the traveller's task to that of a bee. A bee gathers pollen from abroad in order to return and make "the honey of wisdom" [Honig der Weisheit] back home. The traveller is to enrich his own culture, not that of others—to take what is best in foreign lands in order to improve his own. Significantly, in this essay, Herder does not discuss exporting his own culture to others. Rather, the student's task is to empathize and not to criticize—to compare and not to judge—all in order to enrich his or her own culture. As we turn to some of Herder's other works, however, it will become clear that not all languages or peoples are equal and that some cultures need outside influence in order "properly" to "develop" or even to be "original."

In an essay which Herder wrote one year after **"On Diligence,"** relativism, on the surface, seems to extend even into his very definition of nationalism. In 1765, upon the occasion of the opening of a new courthouse in Riga, Herder wrote an essay reflecting upon the topic of the fatherland: **"Do We Still Have the Public and Fatherland of Yore?"** [**"Haben wir noch jetzt das Publikum und Vaterland der Alten?"**] This essay begins with panegyric praise for the principles of justice espoused in the new courthouse: a place which Herder sees a refuge for the poor and oppressed. In this essay, which Herder admits came about under official suggestion, he praises the city of Riga as a prime example of freedom in the fatherland. As in **"On Diligence,"** Herder goes back to Greek and Roman roots in order to compare the past with the present, and once again emphasizes how we must have a new beginning: governments and people have changed too much in order to follow the models of the Greeks and Romans. The "public" has been replaced by the "state" and the "orator" by the "author." The central point of comparison for the latter half of the essay becomes the question: "Do we no longer have a fatherland in regard to *honor, usefulness, freedom, courage,* and *religion*? [Haben wir kein Vaterland mehr in Ansehung der *Ehre,* des *Nutzens,* der *Freiheit,* der *Tapferkeit,* und *Religion*?]"[21] He then goes through the list in reverse order comparing Riga with Greece and Rome. When he arrives at the topic of freedom, he questions whether we "have a fatherland whose

sweet surname is freedom [haben wir ein Vaterland, dessen süßer Zuname *Freiheit* ist]". He answers that one does indeed still exist:

In our day, all states have settled into a system of balance; whoever cannot protect himself needs a patron, a father; our people no longer are characterized by the *brazen audacity* of the ancients; there prevails, instead, a finer, more modest *freedom,* the freedom of *conscience,* to be an honest man and a Christian, the *freedom* to enjoy in the shadow of the throne one's dwelling and vineyard in peace and quiet, and to possess the fruit of one's labors; the *freedom* to be the shaper of one's happiness and comfort, the friend of one's intimates, and the father and guardian of one's children. That is the *freedom,* the modest *freedom,* that every patriot today desires for himself; it is the jewel that *Riga* has received so splendidly from the hands of its just *Empress* and enjoys most gratefully.

Zu unsern Zeiten sind alle Staaten in ein Gleichgewicht gesunken; was sich nicht selbst Schutz ist, braucht Schutzherren, braucht Väter: der Charakter unseres Volks ist nicht mehr die *dreuste Wildheit* der Alten; sondern eine feinere und mäßigere *Freiheit,* die Freiheit des *Gewissens,* ein ehrlicher Mann und ein Christ sein zu dörfen, die *Freiheit* unter dem Schatten des Thrones, seine Hütte und Weinstock in Ruhe genießen zu können, und die Frucht seines Schweißes zu besitzen; die *Freiheit,* der Schöpfer seines Glückes und seiner Bequemlichkeit, der Freund seiner Vertrauten, und der Vater und Bestimmer seiner Kinder sein zu können, dies ist die *Freiheit,* die gemäßigte *Freiheit,* die sich heut zu Tage jeder Patriot wünschet, sie ist das Kleinod, das *Riga* aus den Händen seiner gerechtesten *Monarchin* so vorzüglich, und mit aller Dankbarkeit genießet.[22]

I have quoted from this passage at length in order to give the full flavor of Herder's prose. While we must grant that he was trying to impress Catherine the Great (who, he hoped, would read this essay), his example of Riga as a model of freedom in the fatherland raises several questions. It is quite noteworthy that Herder speaks of Riga as the fatherland at all. First, it was not his place of birth, and therefore would not satisfy his earlier criterion which linked fatherland to geographical location and climate. Second, although Germans enjoyed many powers in the area, politically it still was part of the Russian Empire, and his praises are directed at a Russian ruler, not a German one. Ergang, in his discussion of this passage, emphasizes that "[a]t no time does his [Herder's] German patriotism seem to have been in jeopardy." He stresses that Herder could feel at home in this highly Germanized town, and that Herder's "Russian patriotism did not prevent him from being, at the same time, a German patriot, for he was a Russian patriot only in the sense that he preferred the atmosphere of freedom in Riga to that of militarism in Prussia"[23].

While it may be true that Herder's "German" patriotism was not compromised by his statements of allegiance to Catherine II, his implicit definition of fatherland in the quote above is different from the more relativistic tone of his earlier essay, **"On Diligence."** In **"On Diligence,"** Herder emphasizes the central importance of one's mother tongue in the shaping of our own standards of judgement. In so arguing, Herder appears to reject Enlightenment standards of reason but embraces instead a relativism based upon individual experiences. In **"Do We Still Have the Public,"** the whole concept of the "fatherland" becomes defined by Enlightenment principles of natural rights: the right to own property, the right to keep the products of one's labors, and the freedom to pursue one's life, liberty, and happiness. In other words, one's nationality, native language, or even the political structure do not determine whether one lives in a fatherland or not, but whether one has certain types of universally definable freedoms available to them.

Herder's discussion of freedom becomes even more problematic when we consider that the majority of the population of Livonia scarcely enjoyed any of the freedoms he lists. Freedom seems pertinent to one class or nationality of people only. What is perhaps most interesting about Herder's prose is not that he justifies the right to power as one based upon political might, but that he specifically rejects the political philosophies of Hobbes and Machiavelli as demeaning to human beings. He postulates instead an ideal ruler who cares for his or her own subjects as a loving parent cares for his or her own children. Herder's rhetoric here once again embraces conservative standards of rule—just as in Aristotle's ideal state where the ruler is like a father, the subject a child, so too does Herder here envision the necessity of a set and imposed hierarchy for successful rule: not everyone is entitled to the same rights. We can further judge how seriously Herder took the notion of paternal governance—and the necessity of imposing standards from without—if we look to his travel journal.

However we might interpret Herder's initial thoughts on German rule in the area, it becomes clear that when he left in 1769, he was quite critical of the situation in Livonia and Kurland. In his *Travel Journal [Journal meiner Reise]*, he openly criticizes the status quo and ruminates on possible solutions for Livonia and Kurland. Where his more theoretical works could be seen to advocate cultural relativism, his practical reflections clearly spell out a belief in Enlightenment progress. Unlike the traveller of his **"On Diligence,"** the task of this traveller—of the travelling Herder—becomes the exportation of culture. Herder muses about what he could accomplish if allowed to import Western European standards of education and culture to the Russian Empire. Within this work, Herder ranks literatures, cultures, and peoples according to standards of progress and development. Where scholars such as Whitton argue that Herder "looks to a world of infinite cultural diversity and his writings represent a celebration of cultural diversity as the source of all that is rich and progressive in human life," Herder's own practical, political plans exhibit somewhat more rigid and conservative tendencies[24].

In 1769, upon leaving Riga, Herder kept a travel diary, in which he reflected upon various issues, including thoughts about his own education and theoretical questions about culture and politics. Within this work, he begins to be more explicit in dividing cultures into groups, according to their stage of "development." Less developed countries must attempt to follow other paths in order to achieve the cultural standards of the Germans or the French. Russians, for example, belong to a "developing nation," and as such, need to become better imitators than they have been in the past. Herder praises what he sees as the Russian proclivity for imitation, but wishes they were better at it:

> All the same, I see in this desire to imitate, in this childlike passion for innovation, nothing but the healthy disposition of a developing nation—a tendency in the right direction. Let it learn, imitate and compile from all sides; let it even remain for a time less than fully developed. But let there also come a time, a monarch, a century which will lead the nation to the stage of fruition. What a great intellectual undertaking we have here for a statesman—to consider how the energies of a youthful, half-savage people can be brought to maturity so that it becomes a genuinely great and original nation.

> Ich sehe, in dieser Nachahmungsbegierde, in dieser kindischen Neuerungssucht nichts als gute Anlage einer Nation, die sich bildet, und auf dem rechten Wege bildet: die überall lernt, nachahmt, sammlet: laß sie sammlen, lernen, unvollkommen bleiben; nur komme auch eine Zeit, ein Monarch, ein Jahrhundert, das sie zur Vollkommenheit führe. Welche große Arbeit des Geistes ist hier für einen Politiker, darüber zu denken, wie die Kräfte einer jungendlichen halbwilden Nation können gereift und zu einem Original Volk gemacht werden![25]

In other words, Russia must follow the example of more "enlightened" nations in order to progress to a position of "originality." And while Herder in the passage above speaks of ripening or maturing, he uses it in the passive form so that the growth does not follow a natural process, but it must be brought about from without. Nor does he here simply compare cultures, but he criticizes Russia's development and postulates that its full potential could only come about if it is led by others—whether the other is an abstract notion (an age or century) or a physical agent (monarch or politician). In concluding this paragraph, Herder praises Peter the Great for his efforts to initiate change in Russia, but states "that the great work of 'civilizing a nation to perfection' [das große Werk 'Kultur einer Nation zur Vollkommenheit']" remains unfinished[26].

Where Herder in his earlier works described the development of language according to organic growth, in his journal he ponders what an outside force, what a philosopher-king—what a Herder—could do in the area of Livonia:

> Livonia, thou province of barbarism and luxury, of ignorance and pretended taste, of freedom and slavery, how much would there be to do in thee! How much to do to destroy the barbarism, to root out ignorance, to spread culture and freedom, to be a second Zwingli, Calvin or Luther to this province! Can I do this? Do I have the disposition, the opportunity, the talents?

> Liefland, du Provinz der Barbarei und des Luxus, der Unwissenheit und eines angemaßten Geschmacks, der Freiheit und der Sklaverei, wie viel wäre in dir zu tun? Zu tun, um die Barbarei zu zerstören, die Unwissenheit auszurotten, die Kultur und Freiheit auszubreiten, ein zweiter Zwinglius, Calvin und Luther, dieser Provinz zu werden! Kann ichs werden? habe ich dazu Anlage, Gelegenheit, Talente?[27]

Herder, within his musings expresses the desire to know every aspect of Livonia so that he will be able to talk persuasively to the world, the nobility and the people [Welt, Adel und Menschen überreden]. In his journal, Herder no longer considers Riga his fatherland. He now considers himself a foreigner, but one with a higher calling: "Livonia is a province given over to foreigners! And many foreigners have enjoyed it in the past, but only in their merchants' way, in order to get rich from it; to me, also a foreigner, it is given for a higher purpose, that I may develop it! [Liefland ist eine Provinz, den Fremden gegeben! Viele Fremde haben es, aber bisher nur auf ihre Kaufmännische Art, zum Reichwerden, genossen; mir, auch einem Fremden, ists zu einem höhern Zwecke gegeben es zu bilden]"[28].

While one may argue that Herder does not mean to include the indigenous population in his reforms—that he wanted, as a Lutheran minister, to reform the Germans only and thought of himself as a foreigner because he was Prussian as opposed to a Baltic German—I would argue that Herder means to include all levels of society in Livonia within his reforms for several reasons. First, it would not be out of the ordinary for a German minister to consider peasant reforms. The parish clergy—even in the outlying villages—were almost exclusively German and several of Herder's clerical forerunners and contemporaries were attempting to implement educational and even political reforms (e.g. Gotthard Friedrich Stender 1714-1796; the Moravian Brethern, i.e. the Herrnhutists). Second, Herder had enough of an interest in the area to learn Latvian. Third, in a later work, *Ideas for a Philosophy of the History of Mankind* [*Ideen zur Philosophie der Geschichte der Menschheit* (1784)], Herder states directly, what I believe is implied in the passages above: that any true reforms in this area required improved conditions for the peasants.

In his *Ideas,* he goes so far as to describe how the Latvians and Lithuanians were displaced [verdrängten], subjugated [unterjochten], and robbed of their land and freedom [ihr Land und ihre Freiheit raubte]. In referring to the German Teutonic Knights and the battles which eventually enslaved these peoples, Herder writes that "Mankind shudders at the blood, which was here spilled in the long, wild wars [Die Menschheit schaudert vor dem Blut, das hier vergossen ward in langen wilden Kriegen]". Herder even suggests that at some future time their freedom and land will be returned out for the sake of humanity[29].

Where Rousseau praised the noble savages and the simple patriarchal life, Herder argues that we have gone beyond these ages and should no longer praise what does not exist. He argues that while other ages and countries had different virtues, God expects a human being of the modern times to be "enlightened, instructed, refined, reasonable, educated, virtuous, and capable of enjoyment" [der aufgeklärte, unterrichtete, feine, vernünftige, gebildete, Tugendhafte, genießende Mensch][30]. Herder believed that he could transform this "land of license and poverty, of freedom and confusion [das Land der Lizenz und der Armut, der Freiheit und der Verwirrung]," with the help of the rational tools of libraries, public learning institutions, and scientific collections[31]. Herder predicts massive changes for Eastern Europe when the "spirit of culture [Geist der Kultur]" will visit it: Ukraine will become a new Greece and further spread its new culture to Hungary, Poland, and Russia. Where in his earlier essay, he likens the development of nations and cultures to that of a plant, which grows naturally according to climates and locations, the peoples of Eastern Europe need the help of an enlightened educator to awaken (aufwecken) their culture: "What seeds lie in the spirit of these people that will give them a mythology, a poetry, a living culture [Was für Samenkörner liegen in dem Geist der dortigen Völker, um ihnen Mythologie, Poesie, lebendige Kultur zu geben?]"[32] It would require, Herder conjectures, a man greater than Francis Bacon, a man who "would have to observe with the spirit of a Montesquieu, write with the fiery pen of a Rousseau and have Voltaire's good fortune in catching the ear of the great [da muß man aber mit dem Geist eines Montesquieu sehen; mit der feurigen Feder Roußeaus schreiben und Voltaires Glück haben, das Ohr der Großen zu finden]." The young Herder wants himself to make an attempt in this direction" [Hier will ich etwas versuchen][33].

It would appear that the theory of cultural relativism—a theory whose main tool according to Herder is empathy—is only applicable once a nation reaches a certain level of "progress." The methods used to attain this level are not those typically associated with Sturm und Drang, but those of the Enlightenment: one learns and achieves culture through education.

One could argue, in response to the above assertions of Herder's allegiance to Enlightenment thinking, that his work on folk songs, *Volkslieder,* attempted a broader understanding of other cultures. Yet, if we further examine the language which Herder uses in his *Volkslieder,* we will see that while he is praising certain aspects of other cultures, he still seems to be comparing them according to certain standards of excellence—of an excellence based upon Enlightenment ideals of progress[34]. And while his **"On Diligence"** explains that one must use one's culture as the basis for comparisons, the language of the *Volkslieder* in discussing Latvian literature goes beyond comparison and enters into the field of critical judgment.

When discussing the folk songs of the Latvians, Herder praises their ability to evoke emotions, yet he also condemns their music for being "rough" and "undeveloped [grob und unausgewickelt]"[35]. He praises Latvian love songs as uncommonly moving but characterizes the music generally as a drone. He further reports his parents' opinions about the Latvians. His mother compares their language to table bells (Tischglöcken)—the German language to church bells (Kirchenglöcken). Despite conjectures to the contrary, his father denies the possibility of Latvian epic verse, claiming that the genius of their language and nation is a that of a shepherd (Schäfergenie). And while Herder declares that certain aspects of ancient Greek poetry became clear to him by studying Latvian folk poetry, he uses the term "un-German folk" (das undeutsche Volk) as an equivalent of "the Latvian folk" (das lettische Volk) when speaking about the people[36].

Whatever one may say about the tone of the work, or even Herder's own intentions, his influence on cross-cultural studies was profound[37]. His philosophy began an era of intense study of other literatures and cultures from anthropological to literary perspectives. Moreover, it also had wide political implications. Herder's social and political thought generally, as Barnard points out, influenced British, French, Italian, Pole, Czech, and Russian political philosophers and reformers[38]. By briefly turning to the individual example of Latvia, we will be able to study both Herder's influence on the nationalist movement there and how many of the contradictions present within his works were evident in this movement as well.

The historian Bilmanis argues that Herder's philosophy had a direct influence on several late eighteenth-century Baltic German reformers, who tried, unsuccessfully, to improve living conditions for the Latvians[39]. Herder's ideas, however, had a larger political impact a generation later with the Latvians themselves. His promotion of folk literature, for example, provided the basis for the "Latvian National Awakening" (Tautas Atmoda Laikmets) in the mid to late nineteenth century, which

eventually led to Latvian independence in the early twentieth century. Literary historian Andrups describes how Herder's "emergence on the historical scene decided the fate of the Latvian folk-songs and, with it, the further development of Latvian literature"[40].

This national awakening centered upon Latvian folk songs and culture[41]. One of the most influential members of this group which advocated Latvian nationalism was Krišjānis Barons. His main contribution to the movement was his efforts to collect and classify Latvian folk poetry. The interest and cultivation in Latvian literature directly coincided with the political movement whose aim was independence. Barons, for example also edited a newspaper which called for political reforms. In 1873, the first National Latvian Singing Festival was organized. For the organizers of this event, its importance was to promote Latvian culture as well as political reform. Dravnieks comments that this folk festival brought the cultural and political movement directly to the people for the first time[42]. A nationalistic song, which later became the independent Latvia's anthem, was first performed here. As Kalve notes: "The conscious aim of the poets in the period of the national awakening was the independence and freedom of the Latvian people"[43].

Until the time of the Latvian National Awakening, Baltic Germans still denied the existence of Latvian culture or nationality. Any Latvian who received a university education was no longer considered a Latvian, but a German[44]. Krišjānis Valdemārs (1825-1891) became the first university educated Latvian to "maintain" his nationality: he refused to be called a German, but insisted upon being called a Latvian[45]. In Valdemārs' attempts at political and educational reform, he often turned to many of Herder's ideas of Volk in order to argue for the legitimacy of Latvian nationality and culture.

As important as Herder's ideas were in the earlier stages of Latvian nationalism, the next generation of authors and reformers abandoned their roots in folk culture. As the movement grew, the emphasis on folk culture diminished, and the model and inspiration for the "national" literature became the more "sophisticated" Greek and German models, based upon "universal" standards of excellence. Imitation became the standard for Latvian authors: they imitated classical authors from Homer to Goethe. Only later did Latvian authors return to the folk culture in order to try to integrate it with their more modern works—a literary movement, which, perhaps not accidentally, coincided with the time of Latvia's independence. Authors such as Jānis Rainis reintegrated folk poetry and myths into their works—in part in order to make political statements. Lieven even argues for the strong influence of Herder's ideas on the Baltic political outlook of today: "His [Herder's] stress on national individuality, and denunciations of internationalism and cosmopolitanism, have become even more popular as a result of opposition to the grim Soviet version of 'internationalism' which threatened to destroy Baltic culture."[46] Yet, as Lieven points out, Latvians have had a difficult time separating out from their literature that which is truly "folk" and that which has been imitated from other cultures and traditions (e.g. late nineteenth-century imitations of epic verse with Latvian folk-themes)[47].

Herder's early works, as we have seen, display a tension in his thought between cultural relativism and Enlightenment ideals. On the one hand, he consciously rejects many of the tenets of the Enlightenment and warns against judging cultures according to one set standard of excellence. On the other hand, Herder's works themselves contain an implicit hierarchical system which in effect ranks cultures according to Enlightenment standards of "development," i.e., education and high culture. In other words, Herder's early works do not unambiguously support historicism or cultural relativism, but rather simultaneously embrace on several different levels some of the ideals and goals of the Enlightenment. Moreover, this same ambiguity of relativism versus natural law principles continued within his sphere of influence. Emerging political nations, such as Latvia, both wanted to base their development upon their own cultures, while simultaneously judging themselves and modeling themselves on more "developed" ones.

Notes

1. Robert T. Clark Jr., *Herder: His Life and Thought,* Berkeley, 1955, p. 188.

2. George G. Iggers, *The German Conception of History,* Middletown, Connecticut, 1983, p. 35.

3. Brian J. Whitton, "Herder's Critique of the Enlightenment: Cultural Community versus Cosmopolitan Rationalism," *History and Theory,* XXVII (1988), p. 146; 150.

4. Robert Reinhold Ergang, *Herder and the Foundations of German Nationalism,* New York, 1966, p. 106; Robert S. Mayo, *Herder and the Beginnings of Comparative Literature,* Chapel Hill, 1969, p. 5-10.

5. Part of this area was known in Herder's time as Kurland and part as Livonia. (Livonia also included part of what today is known as Estonia.) For the historical background of these areas, see David Kirby, *The Baltic World 1772-1993: Europe's Northern Periphery in an Age of Change,* New York, 1995, p. 54-74.

6. Helen Liebel-Weckowicz, "Nations and Peoples: Baltic-Russian History and the Development of Herder's Theory of Culture," *Canadian Journal of History,* XXI (1986), p. 3; Anatol Lieven, *The Baltic Revolution: Estonia, Latvia, Lituania and the Path to Independence,* New Haven, 1993, p. 113.

7. Janis Andrups and Vitants Kalve, *Latvian Literature,* Stockholm, 1954, p. 85.

8. Alfred Bilmanis, *A History of Latvia,* Westport, Connecticut, 1951, p. 221.

9. Lieven, p. 135.

10. Andrups and Kalve, p. 76.

11. Bilmanis, p. 218.

12. Quotes in *ibid.,* p. 218.

13. Kirby, p. 23, 78.

14. F. M. Bernard, *Herder's Social and Political Thought: From Enlightenment to Nationalism,* Oxford, 1965, p. xii.

15. Johann Gottfried Herder, *Selected Early Works, 1764-1767,* ed. Ernest A. Menze and Karl Menges, trans. Ernest A. Menze and Michael Palma, University Park, Pennsylvania, 1992, p. 29. German original in Johann Gottfried Herder, *Werke,* 9 vols., Frankfurt, 1990, vol. I, p. 22.

16. Herder, *Selected,* p. 30; *Werke,* vol. I, p. 23.

17. Herder, *Selected,* p. 31; *Werke,* vol. I, p. 24.

18. Herder, *Selected,* p. 33; *Werke,* vol. I, p. 27.

19. Herder, *Selected,* p. 32; *Werke,* vol. I, p. 26.

20. Herder, *Selected,* p. 32-33; *Werke,* vol. I, p. 27.

21. Herder, *Selected,* p. 59; *Werke,* vol. I, p. 48. Emphasis in original.

22. Herder, *Selected,* p. 61; *Werke,* vol. I, p. 50. Emphasis in original.

23. Ergang, p. 64-65.

24. Whitton, p. 156.

25. Johann Gottfried Herder, *J. G. Herder on Social and Political Thought,* ed. and trans. F. M. Barnard, Cambridge, 1969, p. 87; *Werke,* vol. VII, p. 21.

26. Herder, *J. G. Herder on Social . . . ,* p. 87; *Werke,* vol. VII, p. 21.

27. Herder, *J. G. Herder on Social . . . ,* p. 88; *Werke,* vol. VII, p. 28.

28. Herder, *J. G. Herder on Social . . . ,* p. 89; *Werke,* vol. VII, p. 29.

29. *Werke,* vol. VI, p. 689.

30. *Werke,* vol. VII, p. 30.

31. Herder, *J. G. Herder on Social . . .* , p. 90; *Werke,* vol. VII, p. 67.

32. Herder, *J. G. Herder on Social . . .* , p. 90; *Werke,* vol. VII, p. 68.

33. Herder, *J. G. Herder on Social . . .* , p. 91; *Werke,* vol. VII, p. 68-69.

34. For a defense of Herder's language see Liebel-Weckowicz, p. 12-14.

35. *Werke,* vol. III, p. 295-97.

36. *Werke,* vol. III, p. 217.

37. Some critics, such as Mayo, have postulated that Herder's main purpose in publishing the folk songs of other lands was to "inspire some German writer to gather together the German heritage, and thus to provide a rich source for the development of their national literature" (144). Mayo further argues that in "all of Herder's works which are concerned with comparative literature . . . a nationalistic tone predominates" (144).

38. Barnard, p. 167-177.

39. Bilmanis, p. 222.

40. *Ibid.,* p. 85.

41. Teodors Zeiferts, *Latviešu Rakstniecības Vēsture,* Riga, 1993, p. 246.

42. A. Dravnieks, *Latviešu Literātūras Vēsture,* Grand Haven, Michigan, 1976, p. 148.

43. Andrups and Kalve, p. 101.

44. Dravnieks, p. 143, 147.

45. Zeiferts, p. 278.

46. Lieven, p. 113.

47. *Ibid.,* p. 122-123.

Wulf Koepke (essay date 2003)

SOURCE: Koepke, Wulf. "Herder and the Sturm und Drang." In *Literature of the Sturm und Drang,* edited by David Hill, pp. 69-93. Rochester, N.Y.: Camden House, 2003.

[*In the following essay, Koepke offers a comprehensive, scholarly consideration of Herder's impact on the Sturm und Drang movement.*]

HERDER IN HISTORIES OF LITERATURE

Histories of German literature present Johann Gottfried Herder as one of the intellectual fathers of the Sturm und Drang. The *Brockhaus* encyclopedia of 1957 sum-marized the matter for a general readership by saying that the Sturm und Drang received its theoretical foundation, above all, from Johann Georg Hamann and Herder.[1] "Hamann und Herder" was a typical formula in this context. Four texts by Herder are mentioned: **Journal meiner Reise im Jahre 1769**; **Auch eine Philosophie der Geschichte zur Bildung der Menschheit**; and his two contributions to *Von deutscher Art und Kunst,* the Ossian essay and **"Shakespear."** These should, we are told, be regarded as marking the birth of the Sturm und Drang.

Journal meiner Reise im Jahre 1769, also known as the **Reisejournal,** was not published until much later; *Von deutscher Art und Kunst* appeared in 1773; **Auch eine Philosophie der Geschichte zur Bildung der Menschheit** in 1774; and, while Goethe and Lenz read these texts, their impact on others is in many cases less certain. It is, therefore, only partly true that Herder formulated ideas and beliefs that other writers then received from him. Herder may have articulated what was "in the air" and what corresponded to the aspirations of the younger generation. Nevertheless, two questionable statements seem to perpetuate themselves: that Hamann and Herder share all their fundamental beliefs and that the writers of Goethe's generation were inspired by them. Hamann's writings, cryptic and "private" as they were in an age of clarity in public discourse, were known and read only by a few, although Herder did his best to make Hamann a household word in his circles. Moreover, he differed from Hamann on fundamental points of theology, a difference that became evident when Herder's essay *Über den Ursprung der Sprache,* written in 1770 and published in 1772, opted for a human and not a divine origin of language.

Even though he praised some of Goethe's early writings and Lenz's major plays, Herder never considered himself part of an exclusive movement—let alone the spiritual head of it. During the heyday of the Sturm und Drang, Herder lived in Bückeburg in almost total isolation, far from cultural and economic centers such as Frankfurt am Main, Leipzig, Göttingen, and Hamburg. Herder's tastes were catholic: he admired Klopstock and Klopstock's poetry, he considered Lessing Germany's greatest writer after Klopstock, and he liked some of Wieland's writings. But at that time he did not consider himself primarily a poet and literary critic. He was concerned with the text of the Bible, with theological and homiletic questions, with the training of ministers and the educational system, with the philosophy of history, with the propagation of the writings of the Dutch philosopher François Hemsterhuis (1721-90), and also with the collection, translation, and publication of folk songs. The two works of this period that were closest to his heart were *Älteste Urkunde des Menschengeschlechts* (*The Oldest Document of the Human Race,* 1774) and *Auch eine Philosophie der Geschichte zur*

Bildung der Menschheit. Although *Von deutscher Art und Kunst* has been considered by many a "manifesto" of the new movement for a "German" art and literature, it was, in Herder's eyes, an "occasional" publication without lasting significance—"einige Fliegende Blätter" (a few loose leaves), as the subtitle indicates. Scholars and literary histories have generally considered the ***Älteste Urkunde des Menschengeschlechts*** an embarrassment and have made much of the two Herder essays in *Von deutscher Art und Kunst*; but even if we allow for Herder's habit of downgrading his new works and lowering the expectations of his readers, his own view of his writings of the Bückeburg period of 1771-76 differs fundamentally from that of later critics, especially German critics. Herder's later writings on the Old Testament, however, notably ***Vom Geist der Ebräischen Poesie*** (***On the Spirit of Hebrew Poetry,*** 1782-83), were in a different style and spirit. He never came back to the ***Älteste Urkunde,*** while ***Auch eine Philosophie der Geschichte zur Bildung der Menschheit*** was superseded by his magnum opus, ***Ideen zur Philosophie der Geschichte der Menschheit*** (***Ideas on the Philosophy of the History of Mankind,*** 1784-91).

Critics attribute many fundamental aspects of Sturm und Drang thinking to the impact of Herder: the affirmation of emotionality—and, more generally speaking, irrationality—over abstract thinking and a rationalistic view of life and the universe; the affirmation of the "genius" and of "original" creativity not bound by the rules of a prescriptive aesthetic theory, specifically, the three unities in drama; the advocacy of free-verse poetry and of expressiveness over a beautiful and elegant style; and truth, including naturalistic prose, over beauty. A true work of art is, for Herder, the creation of a genius, not the fulfillment of rules and conventions by a person of talent and erudition.

Herder's models of great literature—Homer and Sophocles in Greek antiquity; Shakespeare; the realistic English novel from Henry Fielding to Oliver Goldsmith, in particular Laurence Sterne; Rousseau; Denis Diderot; Lessing; Klopstock; even folk songs—were neither formless, spontaneous, nor "original." Goethe's *Werther*, too, is forever raving about nature, but he experiences nature with Homer and Ossian in his pocket and with Klopstock's "Die Frühlingsfeier" (Celebration of Spring), and he praises the authenticity of Goldsmith's *The Vicar of Wakefield* (1766). He quotes the Bible abundantly, and his last reading before his suicide is the latest event in German letters in 1772, Lessing's *Emilia Galotti*. Herder and the Sturm und Drang writers lived in the context of the entire European literature, philosophy, and theology of the time.

The prevalent views of the connections between Herder and the Sturm und Drang go back to the lasting impact of Goethe's account in *Dichtung und Wahrheit*. Popular history demands to be personalized. In the cultural tradition of the Germans the Sturm und Drang, the first German youth movement (the first of many), and maybe the *"Deutsche Bewegung"* (German Movement)[2] itself, had its real inception in the encounter of the ailing Herder and the youthful student Goethe in Herder's inn "Zum Geist" in Strasbourg in the fall of 1770, vividly narrated by Goethe in his autobiography. Herder the mentor is associated with the gestation of the *Faust* drama, with Goethe's new tone in poetry, with an iconoclastic circle of friends in Strasbourg around Goethe that may be more *"Dichtung"* than *"Wahrheit,"* more poetry than truth. He is associated with the inspiration of Goethe the genius through a new view of language, with a new understanding of Shakespeare, the Bible, Homer, and all of this led to the evolution of the greatest genius of German letters, Goethe. In this picture of the creation of the genius Herder plays an ambiguous role: he is the inspiring mind, but also the negative critic, sometimes the destructive and sarcastic Mephisto. He is generous with his gifts and insights but equally envious that he does not possess Goethe's creative ability. Thus, the drama unfolds that will be played out over more than three decades until Herder's death in 1803: a drama of attraction and repulsion between these two great men, in which Goethe the classicist will always have the upper hand and the "better press." According to this narrative, Herder, unlike Goethe and Schiller, was unable and unwilling to mature to classicism. Instead, he remained in a posture of futile opposition and envy toward the achievements of the Weimar alliance of Schiller and Goethe and regressed into a sterile Enlightenment attitude.

This was the consensus of the majority of the critics until quite recently, and it followed the views of Schiller himself. This personal drama reaches far beyond the Sturm und Drang, but Goethe's later account of its beginning diagnosed its course from the perspective of Herder's last years. Shoehorned into the myth of Weimar, the place of Herder in literary history is still overshadowed by the tradition of partisan opinions generated by the various cultural and political movements of the nineteenth and twentieth centuries. In order to place Herder in the framework of the Sturm und Drang and to discuss his views on poetry, history, language, and society as a theoretical expression or "foundation" of the philosophy of life espoused by the Sturm und Drang, it is first necessary to analyze both Herder's writings of the earlier 1770s as his own Sturm und Drang and to consider his personal relations with writers of the Sturm und Drang, notably Goethe and Lenz.

HERDER'S STURM UND DRANG

In May 1769 Herder abruptly quit his post as a teacher and preacher in Riga and sailed to France. He spent the first four months in Nantes, ostensibly to gain fluency in French. His subsequent stay in Paris was short and uneventful. Even Diderot, whose writings he respected so much, cannot have made a lasting impression on him as a person. The only real gain from this stay was a firsthand acquaintance with much visual art, primarily sculptures and statues, which helped to clarify the ideas he later developed in his *Plastik* (*Sculpture,* 1778). Herder accepted the position of tutor to the Prince of Holstein-Gottorp on the latter's Grand Tour; he hoped that it would give him the opportunity for an educational journey through Europe, particularly to Italy and England. But after six weeks of traveling Herder resigned his position and went to Strasbourg, where he hoped that the well-known surgeon Lobstein would cure him of an eye ailment. The cure, which included several painful operations, lasted for many months. During this time he met Goethe and finished his essay *Über den Ursprung der Sprache,* which received a prize from the Berlin Academy of Sciences. In May 1771 Herder went to work as a consistorial councilor and court preacher to Graf Wilhelm von Schaumburg-Lippe in Bückeburg. He was lonely and depressed for the first two years, but his mood changed markedly when he married Caroline Flachsland in the spring of 1773. It was in Bückeburg in 1773 and 1774 that Herder published the writings associated with the Sturm und Drang. His publications during his first years in Weimar—for instance, the collections of folk songs of 1778-79—were based on the work done in Bückeburg.

In Nantes, where he had led a rather isolated life, Herder had written down an assessment of his previous years and outlined plans for the future. These plans included the future school curriculum in Riga, to which he still planned to return, but in larger part they concerned future publications and the dream of his own role as a reformer of Russia. This unfinished "diary," the *Reisejournal,* was never meant for publication. Parts of it were published in 1846 by one of Herder's sons, and the entire text did not appear until 1878. It was, therefore, only with Rudolf Haym's seminal biography, which began to appear in 1877,[3] that Herder scholars began to have full access to this crucial text. In Friedrich Wilhelm Kantzenbach's biography we read that the *Reisejournal* is "das lebendigste Selbstbekenntnis, das Herder uns hinterlassen hat. Es geht dabei nicht um eine Reisebeschreibung, sondern um eine Konfession aus vollem Herzen, ohne Rückhalt, ganz im Sinne des Sturm und Drang, dessen prohetischer Botschafter Herder in diesen Aufzeichnungen ist."[4] Considering this description, which is typical of many, we will not be surprised to find very little on the voyage itself, except some often-quoted "philosophical" reflections; but we are surprised to find that the confession takes up so little space. Herder seems to start out in the manner of pietistic autobiographies; but soon and, as it seems, with relief he returns to his book plans and his pedagogical and political visions. Herder faults himself for too much reading and writing and missing out on "real" life, but it seems that for him only reading and writing provide access to life. The *Reisejournal* is an abundant source for the genesis of Herder's ideas and later writings; it shows also a man torn between the needs for action and for writing. At the time of the *Reisejournal* he thought that his field of activities had been too confining; but later, after the experiences of Bückeburg and Weimar, he knew that a self-governing city such as Riga provided much more opportunity for action than the petty principalities of Germany. Herder was an ambitious man. He wanted to be remembered as the reformer of a state or, at least, of its educational system. He compared himself with Martin Luther, and he never abandoned the feeling that he was wasting his time with trivial tasks, especially during the later Weimar years.

The bulk of the text of the *Reisejournal* discusses books he had read, French books in particular, and his own plans for books. In later years Herder wrote about the value of self-observation and autobiography, but the "confession" that Kantzenbach attributed to him was something that he never, in fact, contemplated. And he had no urge to publish the *Reisejournal.* He was always mindful of his position in society: that of a church administrator and pastor who has to be careful about his appearance, who represents an important institution that is under attack and that needs to be defended.

Herder's Sturm und Drang writings proper were typically published anonymously, continuing the game of denial that he had played, much to his regret, with his *Kritische Wälder* (*Critical Groves,* 1769). One of the primary contradictions of this complex person and writer was his penchant for biting criticism and satire, which earned him the nickname "Swift" in the Strasbourg circle, and his extreme sensitivity to counterattacks. This sensitivity began with his feuds with Christian Adolf Klotz in *Kritische Wälder* and culminated in the Bückeburg years in his controversies with August Ludwig Schlözer and Johann Joachim Spalding. Herder later relented and kept his biting wit to himself or his circle of friends, but it still caused frictions, especially with Goethe. In his writings between 1773 and 1776 Herder appeared as one who insists on taking the opposite view to that of the best-known authors of the age: he attacked the Voltairean vein of philosophy of history, especially the notion of "progress"; he challenged the entirety of contemporary theology with a totally new approach to the text of the Bible; and he opposed the ruling notion of literature and literary theory with his view of Shakespeare and his praise of folk songs.

One of the strikingly provocative features of Herder's writings from this period is his style. It is highly rhetorical: there are many question marks and exclamation marks; there are even more dashes, sometimes indicating incomplete phrases; and there are gestures that indicate that here is a writer offering new revelations to an audience that he expects to have a closed mind. His phrases are often teasing; rhetorical questions abound, promising statements that will not come; they always challenge the authorities of the day; they demand a totally new approach and perspective. This could only come across as arrogant, as the voice of one who claimed to know the absolute truth, and common-sense Enlighteners such as Friedrich Nicolai resented it. Nicolai had invited Herder, as the author of the **Kritische Wälder,** to review books for his *Allgemeine Deutsche Bibliothek,* which Herder did for several years; but Nicolai found it hard to tolerate the style Herder adopted in, for example, his reviews of Gerstenberg's *Ugolino,* Klopstock's poetry, and "bardic" lyric poetry. (Herder's reviews have subsequently been praised as the beginning of a new style, examples of an empathetic identification with the text as opposed to coldly critical distance and prescriptive dogmatism.) The Nicolai connection came to a quarrelsome end in 1774 with a sarcastic letter by Nicolai on the style of the **Älteste Urkunde.** In later years Nicolai repeatedly provoked Herder, beginning with his polemical collections of folk songs *Ein feyner kleyner Almanach vol schönerr echterr liblicherr Volkslieder, lustiger Reyen unndt kleglicher Mordgeschichten, gesungenn von B. Gabryell Wunderlich* (1777-78).[5] Nicolai knew Herder's Ossian essay and Gottfried August Bürger's *Herzensausguß über Volkspoesie* (Outpourings of the Heart on Folk Song, 1776), which was inspired by the essay, and he knew that Herder was preparing his own collection of folk songs. After breaking with Nicolai, Herder rushed his two volumes of **Volkslieder (Folk Songs,** 1778-79) into print; the seminal collection later became known as **Stimmen der Völker in Liedern (Voices of the Peoples in Songs)** after it was republished under that title in 1807 by Johannes von Müller. Among those who were not fooled by Herder's rather overblown rhetoric was Lessing, who read Herder's texts carefully and, even in disagreement, considered them stimulating.

In 1773 Herder published a collection of five essays and gave it the title *Von deutscher Art und Kunst.* Hans Dietrich Irmscher describes it as the programmatic statement of the Sturm und Drang but stresses that it owes its origins to chance.[6] Herder and Johann Joachim Bode, the translator of major English novels and also a publisher in Hamburg, wanted to give Herder's Ossian essay, originally destined for a discontinued journal, more weight and context. Herder added his essay **"Shakespear"**; Goethe's "Von Deutscher Baukunst" (On German Architecture), on Erwin von Steinbach and the Strasbourg cathedral; excerpts from "Versuch über die Gothische Baukunst" (Essay on Gothic Architecture, 1766), by Paolo Frisi; and parts of the introduction to the *Osnabrückische Geschichte* (History of Osnabrück), by Justus Möser, which Herder called "Deutsche Geschichte" (German History). Herder mentioned Frisi's

and Möser's names but neither his own nor Goethe's. He placed his own essays first, giving them more weight and intimating that the rest were fillers to give him enough pages for a book.

Herder's and Goethe's contributions have always overshadowed the rest. Herder's inclusion of Möser's text makes good sense, as Möser insisted on the Germanic traditions in German history and, in addition, called for a "universal" history, meaning a history encompassing the interplay of all societal areas—law, religion, political and military events, and culture. Only this interplay would give a true picture of the past and of its significance for the present. Herder's excerpt highlights Möser's emphasis on honor and property and the liberty of the independent landholders as the only sound basis for a well-balanced and truly free society. Möser preferred traditional laws and customs to abstract rules and bureaucracies and local and regional control to a centralized imperial administration. He has been called conservative, but in the context of the absolutism of the eighteenth century the demand for a more participatory government is better described as reformist.

The inclusion of the Frisi essay is surprising, as it is a rather dry dissertation on the advantages and disadvantages of various types of domes and on the architectural problems of the pointed arch. Frisi's understanding is that gothic architecture was the product of the decline of ancient Roman architecture, but that it produced remarkable buildings, sometimes with "mixed" designs— that is, both antique and gothic. His prime example is the cathedral in Milan. One cannot really say that Frisi is hostile to the gothic style, but he clearly prefers Palladio. Remarkably, he claims a German origin for the gothic style, and sees both the gothic and the Moorish architecture of Spain as noteworthy antitheses to the neoclassical "norm." Herder wanted to contrast Goethe's enthusiastic praise of Erwin von Steinbach with an unemotional analysis of such structures, and he was not sure whether such youthful enthusiasm as Goethe's was justified. He himself refused to reject the norm of antiquity in such a flagrant manner. This refusal is indicated by his footnote between the two essays: "Der folgende Aufsatz, der beinahe das Gegentheil und auf die entgegen gesetzteste Weise behauptet, ist beigerückt worden, um vielleicht zu einem dritten mittlern Anlaß zu geben" (**H-SW** [*Herders sämmtliche Werke*], 5: xx).[7] Maybe that third essay would offer an investigation into the real principles of beautiful architecture. Herder did not agree with the legend that the gothic style had a German origin; he liked to trace it back to Moslem Spain.

The word *deutsch* in the title of the collection has been at the center of many controversies and interpretations. It is clear from these texts, as well as from Herder's other writings, that the word did not designate the political entity of the Holy Roman Empire but the entire non-Roman, non-Mediterranean tradition in Northern Europe, Great Britain in particular, including the Scots and Irish. He was concerned about the evolution of a new national literature and its orientation. He emphasized, both with his title and in the texts, an alternative to Roman models and to French norms, and, with the reference to Möser, an affirmation of the indigenous traditions of the Germans in their laws, constitutions, customs, and family structures.

Herder's Ossian essay is the first and by far the longest of the contributions. Although Herder was an enthusiastic believer in the authenticity of the Ossianic epics, this essay does not deal with them as such but only with their recent translation in hexameters by Michael Denis, which appeared in 1768. The Ossian text cannot be translated in the manner of Klopstock's *Messias* (The Messiah), Herder argues, because "Oßians Gedichte *Lieder, Lieder des Volkes, Lieder* eines ungebildeten sinnlichen Volks sind, die sich so lange im Munde der väterlichen Tradition haben fortsingen können" (*H-SW,* 5: 160).[8] Denis's Ossian is, therefore, beautiful; it is well done; but it is not Ossian. As proof, Herder offers comparisons with old songs that appear in Shakespeare or in English collections. He insists that the closer these songs, especially the "Lieder der Wilden" (*H-SW,* 5: 168; songs of savages), are to the oral tradition, the less polished they must be. Herder's examples include the famous "Edward" ballad and songs from Latvia and the Lapps, as well as "Odins Höllenfahrt" (Odin's Descent into Hell). The specimens underscore the Nordic bent of his essay and show the impact of the fashion for things bardic. Subsequently, Herder turns to original German songs from olden times. His examples include Goethe's "Heidenröslein" (Little Heath-Rose), and he insists on counting religious songs among folk songs. To emphasize the poetic dignity of folk poetry he offers a long lament from Greenland as an example of a model elegy. The essay has no real conclusion, and this fact is not changed by the later postscript. But Herder has made his point. Although his views about the authenticity of Ossian are problematic, he had offered a most stimulating description of what ancient folk songs all over the world must have been, had shown that such songs existed in Germany, and had urged that their examples should invigorate the poetry of his own day.

The impact of Herder's ideas on the development of the German *Lied* and the ballad was enormous; but in spite of its suggestive tone, the impact of his essay on Shakespeare is not so easily defined. Herder's purpose was to justify the form and content of Shakespeare's plays through the historical context of the Elizabethan age. Sophocles had written the perfect drama for his time and his stage in Athens, and Shakespeare reached perfection in his own age and on his own stage precisely because he did not imitate the drama of antiquity, as the French did, but did what his society demanded.

Inevitably, Herder's concluding reflection must be: is it right, or is it possible, to "imitate" Shakespeare in our time? Are Shakespeare's texts not also documents of a past age that we have difficulty understanding? Historical empathy has its narrow limits, especially in the case of productive reception, and the Germans should not do with Shakespeare what the French had done with Euripides and Seneca. Shakespeare could, however, he believed, still be revived in an original way, and the proof was Goethe's *Götz von Berlichingen*, which Herder praises in his essay, though without mentioning names. The Germans, Herder argues, had begun to appropriate Shakespeare, but, as the reception of *Hamlet* showed, the translations reflected the age and the beliefs of the translators rather than those of Shakespeare.

Herder was concerned with the text of the Bible throughout his life, and the whole complex of divine revelation through the word, the poetic word in particular, was central to his thinking. Hamann's dictum, "Poesie ist die Muttersprache des Menschengeschlechts,"[9] has to be understood in a religious sense: the language of revelation was poetic. Eighteenth-century theology had tried in various ways to harmonize the words of the Bible with the discoveries of the sciences. A major stumbling block proved to be the story of creation in Genesis, which was contradicted by the multiplying evidence of a long and slow evolution of plants, animals, and the earth itself. Physico-theology, the theology based on the evidence of design in nature, offered various ways of harmonizing the natural sciences with the Bible, but Herder rejected such compromises between revelation and reason or experience. He was convinced that scientific methods could never reach back to the very beginning of humankind and of the world. The text of the Bible was the expression of an early sensuous people and their need for images to understand the invisible God.

Herder made several assumptions that would remain fundamental to his philosophy of history. One was the origin of humankind in one place and from one group—in other words, from Adam and Eve. A second assumption was that geographically the origin of the human race was to be found in the Orient and that it was in Oriental texts, if anywhere, that it would be documented. Herder used the term "*Morgenland*" for the Orient and was attracted by the analogy of the origin of the world with the morning, the rising sun, dawn, the "*Morgenröte.*" For Herder, basing himself on deficient and sometimes misleading information about ancient Oriental texts, the Book of Genesis in the Bible was the oldest, the most original documentation of the origin of the human race. He struggled with an adequate understanding of the biblical text. In spite of Martin Luther's great work, he felt it incumbent on himself to produce his own translation—a work he never accomplished, although he translated poetic texts in *Vom Geist der Ebräischen Poesie* and also translated the Song of Songs. The *Älteste Urkunde* must be considered, on one level, as a new translation of Genesis.

During his Riga years Herder had made extensive studies of what he called the archaeology of the Orient, and in Strasbourg he told Goethe about them. In Bückeburg, Herder returned to the subject, and when he was on leave in Göttingen and buried in books from that library, he wrote to Christian Gottlob Heyne in mid-February, 1772, "daß ich in einem Stücke, das wir alle auswendig wissen, eine Rune gefunden zu haben glaube, die ich für das älteste Symbolgebäude des menschlichen Geschlechtes mit dem Zeugniß des ganzen Alterthums angeben kann;"[10] this "rune" leads to "den Ursprung des Buchstaben, den ersten Schlüssel der Aegyptischen Hieroglyphe, Mythologyie u.s.w." (*H-B* [*Briefe: Gesamtausgabe, 1763-1803*], 2: 134).[11] This was a kind of epiphany or revelation; and, as far as the hieroglyph was concerned, Herder was to remain impervious to all doubts and criticisms.

The story of creation is equally the story of the first instruction of the human race, and what Herder means by the term *hieroglyph* is a symbol predating the separation of writing and picture, through which God instructed the first humans. The origin of the human race, of human language, and of human knowledge is bound together in this one moment of divine presence and impact, in this revelation. Reason is not an antagonist of revelation: it is the outcome of revelation.

Herder's claim was bound to raise questions, especially since he emphasized that after thousands of years of examinations and investigations, he was the first who had the insight that would change the whole of theology. Herder did not pursue this claim after its initial rejection, but it continued to provide the unstated basis for his views on religion and on history. To do justice to this much maligned text, it is fair to consider in greater detail the concept of the rune, which Herder later renamed the "hieroglyph." Herder develops it in steps, after commenting on his version of the Genesis text. The hieroglyph binds together time and space as it represents the pictograph of the seven days of creation: light, earth and water, creatures of the earth and the sky, high and low, and, finally, the Sabbath. Herder's creation story is dominated by the motif from Genesis, "And God said, let there be light: and there was light." In the beginning there was dawn, "*Morgenröte.*" Herder's first concern is, as always, to find the unifying principle in the disparate sequence of events. The unifying point is found in the origins—the origin of language, the origin of the history of the human race. The scientific and scholarly view of the world was, for Herder, characterized by fragmentation, by the lack of a point of view that would bring order, proportions, and harmony into the chaos that scholars had created for themselves.

The theologians of Herder's day and of later times have rejected his speculations and claims. Nevertheless, he inspired others—poets, in particular—who felt that his account of the creation of nature and the human race had a deeper meaning for them as an analogy to the power of poetic creation.[12] Herder was averse to the dominant trends of his age, and, as a fundamental critic of the methods and goals of scholarship, he did not want to add to the growing body of learned information. He wanted to cut through the secondary and tertiary literature and reopen the path to the sources—to reality. In his contribution to historiography, which in his Sturm und Drang years was represented above all by *Auch eine Philosophie,* he opposed, on the one hand, the emerging professional or academic historical research as lacking a unifying point of view, and he also disagreed sharply, on the other hand, with the optimistic narratives of philosophies of history that adhered to the principle of "progress" and that saw the present age as the highest point in the evolution of humankind. Recently Isaak Iselin from Switzerland had found wide acceptance with his *Philosophische Muthmassungen über die Geschichte der Menschheit* (Philosophical Speculations on the History of Humankind, 1764; new edition, 1770). Herder, in his conception of a unified philosophy of human history, thought to replace the principle of progress with that of self-contained epochs. Herder's book, which he later called a pamphlet, bears the subtitle *Beytrag zu vielen Beyträgen des Jahrhunderts* (*Contribution to Many Contributions of the Century*), indicating its critical and polemical nature. The work is celebrated for its exposition of the theory that historical periods correspond to the life stages of the individual human being: childhood, youth, maturity, and old age. Herder pursued this analogy through ancient history, from the childlike stage of the Patriarchs and the Egyptians through the youthful culture of the Greeks to the manhood of Roman civilization. He modified it later by arguing that each civilization reached a certain stage of its development and remained there. For instance, Chinese culture had remained in a childlike stage—a widespread prejudice of Herder's age.

To go beyond the history of the ancient world demands different categories, as the history of Europe was based on the combination of the Roman tradition, the dominance of the Germanic peoples, and Christianity. Encouraged by Möser, Herder's evaluation of the Middle Ages was fairer than that of his Enlightened predecessors; and in spite of his praise of Luther's achievements, Herder was much more balanced in his views of the modern age as he leveled two major criticisms against it: the dominance of absolutist rulers and the pervasiveness of mechanical principles. For Herder, the philosophy, the laws and constitutions, the bureaucracy, and the military all obeyed the mechanical principle. Mechanical thinking favors utilitarian rationalism over all other human faculties and creates states of rulers and puppetlike subjects that are hostile to any individuality and original creativity.

These objections give impetus to Herder's main point that it would be foolish to call the present age the best of all times. In fact, for Herder there is a balance in history: what an age gains on the one hand, it loses on the other. It is impossible to ask which age of human history was or could be the happiest or most perfect: progress means loss, and imperfection is the human condition. The outstanding trait of the present age of "enlightenment" is its arrogance, and this is especially true for Europe. The Europeans are foolish to consider their civilization the yardstick of human accomplishments.

In his laments and his polemics Herder is in danger of seeing human history as a process of degradation and decadence from an original golden age. There is an antidote, however: he retains his faith in divine providence. In spite of all suffering, all senseless violence and human error, there is order behind the seeming chaos that we are unable to see because our perspective cannot encompass the whole of human history. We can only see some fragments and, at best, make some general assumptions, mainly through analogies. There is also a strongly critical attitude toward the state that has been criticized by prominent scholars such as Friedrich Meinecke[13] and that leads to the ideal of a stateless community, which could be called anarchism. For Herder, absolutist rulers and their arbitrary methods of government represented the negative consequences of the mechanical powers of bureaucracies and standing armies.

Auch eine Philosophie contains many elements of historicism, that is, the idea that each historical period and each civilization is an end in itself and has to be judged by its own criteria; and historicism implies a critique of Eurocentrism: the European values of today cannot be the yardstick for an evaluation of other civilizations. Herder maintains the analogy between the course of a civilization or epoch and the development of a living being from birth through maturity, old age, decay, and death. States with an artificial structure resulting from wars and conquests can maintain themselves beyond their "natural" age, but they will eventually die. Herder was looking for more "natural" or organic units of human communities than states. These he called "nations"; each is united by a common history, customs, traditions, and language. At no point, however, does Herder equate linguistic borders with political boundaries. What he has in mind are culturally cohesive, nonaggressive republics with participatory governments. This is scarcely the ideal to which the nationalisms of the nineteenth and twentieth centuries conformed.

HERDER AND OTHER WRITERS OF THE STURM UND DRANG

The connection between Herder and Goethe is a ubiquitous topic in literary histories and in biographies of Goethe and Herder; it has generated studies of various specific problems, but by no means as many as one might expect. Since the relationship lasted from 1770 until Herder's death in 1803, it underwent many changes and phases. The best-known part is the encounter in Strasbourg, when the young student Goethe considered Herder his mentor, and his letters to Herder of 1771-72 testify to the warmth of his attachment, even after a harsh critique by Herder of the first version of *Götz von Berlichingen*. Herder, however, wrote to Caroline Flachsland on March 21, 1772, in a much more detached manner, "Göthe ist wirklich ein guter Mensch, nur äußerst leicht u. viel zu leicht, u. Spazzenmäßig, worüber er meine ewige Vorwürfe gehabt hat . . . auch glaube ich ihm, ohne Lobrednerei, einige gute Eindrücke gegeben haben, die einmal wirksam werden können."[14]

After Goethe settled in Weimar, the opportunity arose to appoint Herder to the position of general superintendent, consistorial councilor, and court preacher—to the relief of Herder, who longed to leave Bückeburg and whose appointment as a professor of theology in Göttingen had just run into insurmountable obstacles. Some correspondence resulted, and it reveals the continuation of Herder's close attachment to Goethe. Herder arrived in Weimar on October 1, 1776, and stayed for the rest of his life. A closer friendship between Herder and Goethe developed in 1783 and lasted for a decade before being overshadowed by political disagreements after the French Revolution. With Goethe's and Schiller's alliance in 1794 and their programmatic journal *Die Horen*, Herder's estrangement from Goethe grew: in addition to various personal conflicts, the later Herder's concept of literature and literary culture was diametrically opposed to that of Weimar Classicism.

Outsiders had good reasons for considering Herder part of the Frankfurt circle of Sturm und Drang writers. He contributed fourteen reviews to the iconoclastic year of 1772 of the *Frankfurter Gelehrten Anzeigen,* edited by Johann Heinrich Merck, Goethe, and Goethe's future brother-in-law Johann Georg Schlosser. Contrary to the typical reviews of the time, especially in the *Allgemeine Deutsche Bibliothek,* which attempted to be objectively informative, Herder made a point of being partisan, of either praising or condemning. He praised François Hemsterhuis, still virtually unknown in Germany, and he condemned J. D. Michaelis (1717-91), a prominent Bible scholar in Göttingen. But his most conspicuous controversy involved the Göttingen historian August Ludwig Schlözer, who published in 1772 an outline and guide for his course on universal history. Herder was not only irked by the arrogance of someone claiming to have his own history but also found no unity or spirit in the compilation. Herder's piece was most provocative and aroused Schlözer's anger, moving him to write an entire book, a sequel that was designed to refute Herder's few pages and punish the impertinent reviewer (by name) as an incompetent amateur. Herder did not respond, but a number of passages in *Auch eine Philosophie* show that he had read the book, and he refuted it in his own way without mentioning Schlözer.

The most conspicuous collaboration of Herder and Goethe during these years was Herder's inclusion of Goethe's "Von Deutscher Baukunst" in *Von deutscher Art und Kunst.* Goethe's enthusiastic piece was a eulogy of Erwin von Steinbach and his greatness, embodied in the greatness of his building, Strasbourg cathedral. Goethe celebrates Erwin as the genius who, like Herder's Shakespeare, was able to unify, to make a whole, out of disparate parts. Goethe recalls how he approached the cathedral with neoclassical prejudices and was overwhelmed by its warmth and unity. He compares the building to a tree reaching to the heavens, contrasting it with the "regular" arcades and pillars of classical monuments. We must, he argues, reject the prejudice against the word "gothic" and accept the work of genius, free from the dictates of one single prescriptive taste. Goethe's polemic turns against French theoreticians and regulatory aesthetics that generate mechanical principles and rules. Goethe did not republish this enthusiastic piece until 1824.

At the end of his **"Shakespear"** essay Herder praised an unnamed friend for his dramatization of the times of the German knights, mentioning Goethe's *Götz von Berlichingen*; but he was even more direct in his praise of other works by Goethe from this period. Somewhat surprisingly, he applauded *Stella* in its first version and recommended the play to others.[15] In 1775-76 he spoke highly of Goethe and his talents; for instance, in a letter to Hamann he referred to Lenz as Goethe's younger brother (*H-B,* 2: 188). Goethe's response to Herder's publications in the early Weimar years seems to have been cool; but during the period of their renewed friendship Goethe was one of the first readers of the *Ideen,* and Herder responded to Goethe's interest in the natural sciences and to the progress of *Wilhelm Meisters Theatralische Sendung* (Wilhelm Meister's Theatrical Mission, written circa 1777-85, published 1911). He was also helpful in the editing of Goethe's collected works, which were published during his time in Italy. While the alliance between Goethe and Schiller has received close scrutiny, based on their correspondence and on Eckermann's reports, the friendship of Herder and Goethe deserves new investigation—especially the lasting impact of Herder's ideas on Goethe beyond their estrangement and beyond Herder's death in 1803.

The connection between Herder and Lenz was short but intense. It fell in the years of Lenz's greatest productivity and prominence, 1775 and 1776. They saw each other once, briefly and under unfavorable circumstances, when Herder arrived in Weimar in October, 1776, and Lenz was about to be banished from the court. In his letter of March 9, 1776, Herder is already trying to give the self-doubting Lenz more confidence: "Und Du, was zitterst Du, wie ein Irrlicht zu erlöschen. In Dir is wahrlich Funke Gottes, der nie verlöscht u. verlöschen muß. Glaube!" (*H-B,* 3: 256).[16] Herder was instrumental in securing the publication of *Die Soldaten,* and he praised *Der Hofmeister* and *Der neue Menoza.* But he was also familiar with Lenz's problems as the son of a stern Lutheran minister trying to find his own way both professionally and in his religion. Herder's writings from the Bückeburg period, particularly those on the Bible, were a new point of orientation for Lenz. For Lenz, Herder could have been a father figure, and he defended Herder's controversial writings both publicly and privately—for instance, against his father, who disapproved of his son's relationship with an unorthodox clergyman who had the reputation among theologians of being a "Socinian." Herder was opposed by the clergy in Bückeburg, in Weimar, and among the professors of theology in Göttingen, who prevented his appointment as university preacher. Herder acknowledged with gratitude Lenz's sympathetic reading of his *Älteste Urkunde* and *Auch eine Philosophie.* Lenz referred to Herder in the prologue to his *Meynungen eines Layen den Geistlichen zugeeignet* (Opinions of a Layman Dedicated to the Clergy, 1775), and Herder repaid the compliment with a footnote on *Der neue Menoza* in the second volume of *Älteste Urkunde.* In Lenz's *Pandämonium Germanicum* Herder appears as someone who thinks positively of Lenz's talents and encourages him. Lenz's essays, such as "Versuch über das erste Principium der Moral" (Essay on the First Principle of Morality, written 1771-72), show his proximity to Herderian views, and their ideas on Shakespeare and tragedy are close. Although Herder appears mostly as the giver, the dialogue with a searching mind such as Lenz's might under other circumstances have developed into the kind of give-and-take relationship on which he thrived.

Johann Caspar Lavater, a minister in Zurich, was known for his *Aussichten in die Ewigkeit* (Prospects of Eternity, 1768-78); for his effusive style in his correspondence with many personalities of his day, including Goethe; and, later, for his monumental *Physiognomische Fragmente,* an extremely controversial demonstration of the way in which faces and skulls express the personality, that sold widely in spite of its high price and grew to four huge volumes. During the period under consideration Lavater enticed Herder into engaging in a regular correspondence. Herder was not a born letter writer,[17] and he hesitated for a long time before he entered into the correspondence with Lavater, who became notorious when he publicly challenged Moses Mendelssohn in 1769 either to refute Bonnet's *Apologie des Christentums* (Apology for Christianity, just translated by Lavater) or to convert. But in his depressing isolation in Bückeburg, Herder wrote a long letter to Lavater, dated October 30, 1772, followed by others in which he wrestled with his major problem: his attempt to find access to revelation through a poetic, divinely inspired language—Klopstock is mentioned again and again. After his marriage in the spring of 1773, Herder's exchange with Lavater becomes more collegial in character and concerns publications and theological ideas. Lavater was repeatedly hurt by Herder's criticisms of his writings; but they were well meaning and constructive, and Herder did his best to restore harmony. In the end, after Herder's move to Weimar and his turn to practical concerns, Lavater came to dislike Herder's **Briefe, das Studium der Theologie betreffend** (**Letters Concerning the Study of Theology,** 1780-81), and their ways parted. In Bückeburg, Herder found in Lavater's *Aussichten in die Ewigkeit* passages that appealed to his needs, and he found a correspondent who gave him the opportunity to express some of his religious strivings. Herder connected the idea of physiognomics with the ideas on sculpture that he formulated in his **Plastik,** but Lavater's *Physiognomische Fragmente* assumed only a modest role in the dialogue between the two men.

Scholarship and the Image of Herder

German scholarship has, for the most part, emphasized Herder's earlier works and has seen his publications after the **Ideen** as products of a mind in decline and one that was unwilling and unable to advance with the changing times. Until at least 1945 the Sturm und Drang was regarded as the first period of a new national German literature that resulted from transcending the Enlightenment; Herder's achievement was seen in this light, and his late works seemed to fall back into Enlightenment patterns that had long been overcome by Goethe and Schiller and the Romantics.

Herder's views were defined as antirationalistic, as a philosophy rooted in feeling; but this strength was also considered his weakness: he never arrived at the clarity and purity of Goethe's classicism. In other words, Herder's achievements were never considered without a comparison with Goethe—a comparison in which he was bound to lose. As scholars noted, he left a work rich in seminal ideas but a work of fragments, of unfinished projects. He never wrote the great work that would crown and unify all his endeavors. The focus on Goethe led to a relative neglect of Herder's religious and theological writings and to a neglect of Herder's own poetic production, except for his translations.

Herder was active in many domains, and research on him has, therefore, been conducted in many areas: linguistics, aesthetics and literary theory, literary history, anthropology, historiography, geography, theology, psychology, and philosophy. For the most part these branches of scholarship have remained separate, without much profiting from each other—which is certainly contrary to Herder's own spirit and procedures. Nevertheless, the overall image of Herder, largely influenced by Goethe's account in *Dichtung und Wahrheit,* is evident everywhere. It has made of Herder a genius of intuition and historical/cultural empathy who felt and thought many things that later research by sober scientists would have to sift through, examine, and reassess. What remains true is that Herder stands at the crossroads between the man of universal knowledge and the professional specialists in the sciences who were developing at the universities. In this respect he resembles Goethe. For the Sturm und Drang period, scholars stress three contributions by Herder: his call for the creation of a new national literature; his initiation of a new historical consciousness and hermeneutics; and his controversial Bible studies and theology, the last passed over by many historians and literary scholars.

Work on editions of Herder's works began soon after his death, initiated by his widow, Caroline. They were supplemented by testimonials and, later, a wealth of information and documents on his life and works. Heinrich Düntzer and other nineteenth-century Germanists worked on the letters, and Herder's **Sämtliche Werke,** edited by Bernhard Suphan and his team of collaborators, appeared in thirty-three volumes between 1877 and 1913 (**H-SW**). During the same period Düntzer and Anton Eduard Wollheim da Fonseca produced a twenty-four-volume edition of Herder's works;[18] they reprinted the first editions, whereas Suphan took Herder's final versions as definitive. Suphan's edition was praised as a model for critical editions, and it provided the basis for Herder scholarship in the late nineteenth and all of the twentieth century; but from today's perspective many problematic editorial decisions are apparent. The recent edition by the Deutscher Klassiker Verlag (1985-2000) contains indispensable new material and important commentaries.[19]

Critical Herder scholarship began with an unsurpassed achievement: the biography by Rudolf Haym published in two volumes, 1877 and 1885, which was able to make use of the first volumes of the Suphan edition and much unpublished material. This monumental work contains a wealth of information and many incisive observations and evaluations. At the same time, it reflects, as it must, the political, cultural, and stylistic prejudices of its author, including his condemnation of **Die Älteste Urkunde** as frighteningly formless, hurried, immature, and unreadable (1: 587).

The scholar who followed Haym in his intention of presenting the "whole" Herder was Eugen Kühnemann.[20] He was less interested in facts and individual analyses of texts than in a unified picture of Herder's personality and creativity. By contrast with Haym's nineteenth-century liberalism, Kühnemann reflects the impact of Friedrich Nietzsche, together with the intense German nationalism of his day. Comparing Herder, once again, with Goethe, he considers Herder's tragedy to be a decisive lack of vitality that prevented him from creating the great work he had in mind. Kühnemann stands at the beginning of the tradition of the history of ideas, which preferred generalities and initiated a tendency to disregard Herder's texts, declaring them vague and contradictory, in favor of a general view of his personality and his philosophy of life.

The hundredth anniversary of Herder's death in 1903 generated a wide-ranging discussion of Herder's idea of "*Humanität*" in which writers of all persuasions, including socialists, participated. In 1907 a rather short section on Herder in Meinecke's *Weltbürgertum und Nationalstaat* defined Herder's political attitude as suitable for a "*Kulturnation*" (cultural nation), a new concept at the time, but argued that this was now an anachronism, since vital and aggressive "*Staatsnationen*" (state nations) were needed. Herder was too soft, too feminine, too weak for such a "manly" view of history. This view of Herder perpetuated itself through the first half of the century. On the other hand, Meinecke credited Herder's *Auch eine Philosophie* with the breakthrough to truly historicist thinking, a mode of thought that views past epochs in their own right and without prejudice.[21] Such a view of history, he argues, does more justice to the history of Germany, especially when it sees, as Herder did, the nation as the core unit of human communities and the moving force in history. Meinecke's and Kühnemann's image of Herder, modified by Josef Nadler in 1924[22] and Max Kommerell in 1928,[23] legitimized Herder as the herald of the nation and of a true conception of history but declared him too soft, too humanistic, to be a direct model to be followed in the present. This characterization was echoed in publications during the period after 1933 by such writers as Gerhard Fricke,[24] Benno von Wiese,[25] and Wolfdietrich Rasch.[26]

Herder's association with the idea of the nation meant that it took a long time after 1945 to liberate him from the liabilities of the past. Scholarship in the German Democratic Republic (GDR) approved his concepts of folk art and history and declared Herder part of the great movement of European Enlightenment, rather than someone who had either opposed or transcended it, and it revalued his later political views in the light of his positive attitude toward the French Revolution. This revaluation called for a reinterpretation of the Bückeburg period as a phase of the Late Enlightenment rather than the onset of a German national revival.

The most comprehensive attempt to see Sturm und Drang as a movement in its own right came from British scholars who were unburdened by the need of German studies in Germany to justify and define German classicism or to see its origins in nationalistic terms. They had a keener eye for the foreign influences on the Sturm und Drang and had the necessary distance to see in it a unity that the Germans were not always able to perceive. Roy Pascal[27] treated the Sturm und Drang as a group movement, including Herder, Merck, Goethe, Lenz, and Klinger, with authors such as Maler Müller, Wagner, and Leisewitz at the periphery and close to groups such as the Göttinger Hainbund and personalities such as Lavater and Friedrich Heinrich Jacobi. "Herder's unhappy temperament gives us perhaps the deepest insight into the psyche of the Sturm und Drang" (12), says Pascal; it "mirrors a cultural crisis, the conflict within his century" (19).

Pascal is highly critical of the political philosophy implied in *Auch eine Philosophie,* although he acknowledges that Herder showed a concern for individual welfare. He agrees that the *Älteste Urkunde* was "the most important statement of Herder's religious views" (95) in this period but sees it also as "a crisis in Herder's thought" (95). It represented an attempt to return to simple faith, accentuated by the intensity of an "all-sided experience" (100). Herder's turn from "thinking" to "feeling" and "doing," which included the immersion in nature—first in the *Reisejournal,* then in many poems and in *Vom Erkennen und Empfinden der menschlichen Seele*—Pascal sees as informing Goethe's early work on *Faust* and his poems. He describes *Auch eine Philosophie* as the "profound expression of the glory and the tragedy of the Sturm und Drang" (232); but the achievement of the Sturm und Drang, for Pascal, lies ultimately in its poetry and dramas.

In his 1952 study of the Sturm und Drang, H. B. Garland[28] downplays Herder's impact on Goethe: "Herder accelerated processes which Goethe would have completed eventually of his own accord" (26). Herder is characterized as "a powerful mind and striking, if unsatisfactory, personality" exemplifying "romantic impatience with reality" (14-15). Herder's response to Shakespeare was purely "emotional"; *Von deutscher Art und Kunst* was "repetitive and elliptical, slipshod and obscure" and may not have had the impact that is often claimed for it, but "its symptomatic and evidential value" is considerable (18-19). Garland argues that the lack of clarity and substance in Herder's ideas diminished their impact, and he relegates Herder to one of the "forerunners" of the movement together with Klopstock and Hamann: all in all, Herder comes across as inferior to Gerstenberg and, of course, Klopstock.

Robert T. Clark published his lifetime study of Herder in 1955[29] and largely determined the image of Herder in the United States for the second half of the twentieth century, especially since the scarcity of English translations makes the secondary literature even more important for all except those few who can read Herder's difficult texts in the original.

A new impetus for Herder scholarship in the Federal Republic of Germany and in the United States developed in the 1970s and manifested itself in conferences and in the foundation in 1985 of the International Johann-Gottfried-Herder Society, which publishes a yearbook that includes a Herder bibliography. One of the features of more recent Herder scholarship is its closer attention to the words of Herder's texts and their meanings. Whereas more attention has been given to the later Herder and to Herder's struggle against Kant's critical philosophy, there have been several publications on philosophical and psychological issues in the work of the earlier Herder, as well, with a clear emphasis on the antecedents, implications, and impact of his theory of language.

Surprisingly, most of the studies of the relationship of Goethe and Herder have dealt primarily with positivistic questions of details of their life and work; Hans Dietrich Irmscher's article on their lifelong attraction and repulsion is a foray into new territory.[30] There has been even less interest in the results of the short but intense correspondence between Herder and Lenz; but at a time when the Sturm und Drang is considered less as a "movement" of a whole generation than as the totality of the affinities of loosely connected small groups of writers, personal exchanges seem to take on greater significance. This emphasis can serve to define more precisely Herder's uniqueness in the group. He was, at the same time, part of other groups: he was on friendly terms with Lessing, Mendelssohn, and Matthias Claudius; he tried to cooperate with Friedrich Nicolai; and he was embroiled in several theological controversies.

An earlier German tradition had seen the Sturm und Drang as a youth movement: the German version of "Pre-Romanticism," a first phase leading to the greater achievements of Weimar Classicism and Romanticism.[31] The opposite view involves the integration of the Sturm und Drang into the European Enlightenment as part of the Late Enlightenment, as Ehrhard Bahr has formulated it.[32] This perspective emphasizes the continuity of historical developments and considers the Sturm und Drang as a final, innovative phase of the Enlightenment, leading into the new epoch of Romanticism. Moreover, the impact of French and English philosophers is emphasized. While it is generally acknowledged that Herder's view of history, together with that of Möser, had great significance for Goethe's generation of writers, it is primarily in Herder's concept of language and its evolution that the most productive energies seem to lie. Furthermore, the Sturm und Drang can be seen as the awakening of a new awareness of the self, a self-reflection and self-consciousness that are

not sufficiently defined by the term "subjectivity." It is evident in the writings of Goethe and Lenz but equally in Herder's poems and in some passages from his *Reisejournal,* and his *Vam Erkennen und Empfinden der menschlichen Seele* (*On the Cognition and Sensation of the Human Soul,* 1778) can serve as a theoretical underpinning of this new awareness of the self.

Literary scholars tend to consider Herder's views and ideas as unchanging, although they generally acknowledge considerable modifications from the Riga to the Bückeburg and then to the Weimar period. The question arises in this context whether it was really the Bückeburg period that made Herder the seminal figure for German letters, as scholars have maintained. During the nineteenth century Herder's most popular work in Germany, by far, was *Der Cid* (1803). Internationally, his reputation rested mainly on his *Ideen,* while Goethe's memories of Herder centered on his personality and on their conversations. To get a clearer picture of Herder's writings and achievements, they have to be disentangled from many prejudices and established clichés.

The Herder scholarship of the last thirty years has shown that many discoveries can be made through a closer reading of Herder's texts. This is true of his Sturm und Drang period as much as for any other period of his life. It has also become evident that a reading of Herder without preordained comparisons, such as "Hamann and Herder," "Goethe and Herder," or "Kant and Herder," is productive and clears the way for a fresh look at these essential relationships. Furthermore, the writings of the Bückeburg period should not be limited by the label "Sturm und Drang." They represent a distinct period in Herder's work, but are also the continuation of previous ideas and trends and not without a continuation in Weimar. The first requirement is, therefore, openness. It needs to be remembered that Herder's poetic writings from the period, his poems and a cantata such as *Brutus* (1774), do not conform to the image of Sturm und Drang poetry, which is primarily determined by Goethe. In investigating the Sturm und Drang connections, critics have been primarily concerned with the style of the prose writings. While the consensus that Herder provided the philosophical underpinnings of the Sturm und Drang seems to be unchanged, it is still not clear exactly how much of an impact his works had on the young writers, especially those beyond his personal acquaintance. The phrase "Herder and the Sturm und Drang" often conceals more than it reveals: each of these three areas of debate—Herder, the Sturm und Drang, and the relationship between Herder and the Sturm und Drang—is considerably more complex than has often been acknowledged.

Notes

1. *Der große Brockhaus* (Wiesbaden: Brockhaus, 1957), 11: 309.

2. The term, which refers to the revival of a German national culture at the end of the eighteenth century, was popularized by Heinz Kindermann in his *Durchbruch der Seele: Literarhistorische Studie über die Anfänge der "Deutschen Bewegung" vom Pietismus zur Romantik,* Danziger Beiträge, 1 (Danzig: Kafemann, 1928).

3. Rudolf Haym, *Herder nach seinem Leben und seinen Werken dargestellt,* 2 vols. (Berlin: Gaertner, 1877-85).

4. "The liveliest confession that Herder has left us. It is not a travelogue but a confession, flowing without restraint from the fullness of his heart, wholly in the spirit of the Sturm und Drang, whose prophet Herder shows himself in these sketches to be." Friedrich Wilhelm Kantzenbach, *Johann Gottfried Herder in Selbstzeugnissen und Bilddokumenten,* Rowohlts Monographien, 164 (Reinbek: Rowohlt, 1979), 39-40.

5. The title, which is in a deliberately old-fashioned German, may be translated "A Splendid Little Almanac Full of Beautiful, Charming and Genuine Folksongs, Jolly Tunes and Pitiful Street Ballads sung by B. Gabryell Wunderlich."

6. Hans Dietrich Irmscher, ed., *Von deutscher Art und Kunst,* Universal-Bibliothek, 7497 (Stuttgart: Reclam, 1968), 163.

7. "The following essay, which makes almost the opposite claims, and does so in the most antithetical way, has been included in order, perhaps, to give rise to a third, lying between these two."

8. "Ossian's poems are *songs, songs of the people, songs* of an uneducated, sensual people, which paternal tradition could sustain as songs."

9. "Poetry is the mother tongue of the human race." From *Aesthetica in nuce,* in Johann Georg Hamann, *Sämtliche Werke: Historisch-kritische Ausgabe,* 6 vols., ed. Josef Nadler (Vienna: Herder, 1949-53), 2: 197.

10. "That I believe I have found in a piece that we all know by heart a rune that, basing myself on the evidence of the whole of antiquity, I can claim to be the oldest symbol structure of the human race."

11. "The origins of the alphabet, the first key to Egyptian hieroglyphs, mythology, etc."

12. The best example is Goethe's letter to Schönborn of June 8, 1774, in which he comments on the *Älteste Urkunde.*

13. Friedrich Meinecke, *Weltbürgertum und Nationalstaat* (1908), rpt. in his *Werke,* vol. 5 (Munich: Oldenbourg, 1969).

14. "Goethe is truly a good man, he is just extremely easy-going, much too easy-going and sparrowlike, which I repeatedly reproached him over . . . and without boasting, I think I can say that I have given him a few good ideas that will play their part in due course." Herder, *Briefe: Gesamtausgabe, 1763-1803,* 10 vols., eds. Karl-Heinz Hahn et al. (Weimar: Böhlau, 1977-96), 2: 154. This edition of Herder's letters will henceforth be abbreviated *H-B.*

15. He wrote, for example, to Johann Georg Zimmermann in a letter of March 23, 1776: "Welch ein Paradiesisch Stück seine Stella!" ("What a heavenly play his *Stella* is!" *H-B,* 2: 260).

16. "And you, why are you anxious about losing your light, like a will-o'-the-wisp? You truly have the spark of God, which never goes out and must never go out. Have faith!"

17. Apart from the letters he wrote on official business and the intense exchange of letters with Caroline, Herder corresponded with Hamann, with Christian Gottlob Heyne in Göttingen, with Gleim, and with his publisher Hartknoch. There were also temporary affinities expressed in letters to Zimmermann and Merck.

18. *Herder's Werke,* 24 vols., eds. Heinrich Düntzer and Anton Eduard Wollheim da Fonseca (Berlin: Hempel, n.d.).

19. Herder, *Werke,* 10 vols., eds. Günter Arnold et al. (Frankfurt am Main: Deutscher Klassiker Verlag, 1985-2000).

20. Eugen Kühnemann, *Herders Leben* (Munich: Beck, 1895), much expanded and modified in the second edition, *Herder* (Munich: Beck, 1912).

21. Friedrich Meinecke, *Die Entstehung des Historismus,* 2 vols. (Munich & Berlin: Oldenbourg, 1936).

22. Josef Nadler, "Herder oder Goethe?" (1924); rpt. in his *deutscher geist/deutscher osten: zehn reden,* Schriften der Corona, 16 (Munich, Berlin, & Zurich: Oldenbourg, 1937), 127-40.

23. Max Kommerell, *Der Dichter als Führer in der deutschen Klassik* (Berlin: Bondi, 1928).

24. Gerhard Fricke, "Das Humanitätsideal der klassischen deutschen Dichtung und die Gegenwart: Herder," *Zeitschrift für Deutschkunde* 48 (1934): 673-90.

25. Benno von Wiese, *Herder: Grundzüge seines Weltbildes* (Leipzig: Bibliographisches Institut, 1939); Wiese, "Der Philosoph auf dem Schiffe, Johann Gottfried Herder," in *Zwischen Utopie und Wirkli-*

chkeit: Studien zur deutschen Literatur (Düsseldorf: Bagel, 1963), 32-60.

26. Wolfdietrich Rasch, *Herder: Sein Leben und Werk im Umriß* (Halle: Niemeyer, 1938).

27. Roy Pascal, *The German Sturm und Drang* (Manchester: Manchester UP, 1953).

28. H. B. Garland, *Storm and Stress* (London: Harrap, 1952).

29. Robert T. Clark, *Herder: His Life and Thought* (Berkeley & Los Angeles: U of California P, 1955).

30. Hans Dietrich Irmscher, "Goethe und Herder im Wechselspiel von Attraktion und Repulsion," *Goethe-Jahrbuch* 106 (1989): 22-52.

31. The classical formulation of this view is to be found in Hermann August Korff, *Geist der Goethezeit,* 5 vols. (Leipzig: Koehler & Ameland, 1954-57). Korff tried to overcome the irksome overlapping of shorter periods in literary history with the broader concept of the "age of Goethe."

32. Ehrhard Bahr, ed., *Geschichte der deutschen Literatur: Kontinuität und Veränderung. Vom Mittelalter bis zur Gegenwart,* vol. 2, *Von der Aufklärung bis zum Vormärz* (Tübingen: Francke, 1988).

Abbreviations

G-CW Goethe's Collected Works, 12 vols., eds. Victor Lange et al. (New York: Suhrkamp, 1983-89).

G-HB Goethe, *Briefe: Hamburger Ausgabe,* 4 vols., eds. Karl Robert Mandelkow and Bodo Morawe (Hamburg: Wegner, 1962-67).

G-MA Goethe, *Sämtliche Werke nach Epochen seines Schaffens: Münchner Ausgabe,* 21 vols., eds. Karl Richter et al. (Munich: Hanser, 1985-99).

H-SW Johann Gottfried Herder, *Herders sämmtliche Werke,* 33 vols., ed. Bernhard Suphan (Berlin: Weidmann, 1877-1913).

Thomas P. Saine (essay date 2005)

SOURCE: Saine, Thomas P. "Johann Gottfried Herder: The Weimar Classic Back of the (City)Church." In *The Literature of Weimar Classicism,* edited by Simon Richter, pp. 113-31. Rochester, N.Y.: Camden House, 2005.

[In the following essay, Saine views Herder's works within the context of Weimar Classicism.]

Anyone who has become familiar with the *loci* of Classical Weimar can place Herder on the city map: the Herderplatz is on the open, visible side of the Stadt-kirche of Saints Peter and Paul—long since, of course, renamed the Herderkirche—just off the city center, where Herder preached and is buried. The plaza is adorned with a statue of the famous man. Overshadowed by the church, on the other side, "back of" it, as Herder often said, is the street where the parsonage is located, where Herder and his growing family lived from his arrival in Weimar in 1776 until his death in 1803. A parsonage is of course a "Dienstwohnung"—the Herders never owned any real property in Weimar, and in spite of his exalted official titles Herder was too often regarded and treated as just one of the help. After all, keeping the people properly religious was (and of course still is) often regarded as a function of the state, not just a personal vocation.

In identifying himself or talking about himself, Herder was likely to place himself "hinter der Kirche" (back of the church) or "hinter der Stadtkirche." This was not simply a geographical location; it was above all an expression of the Herders' resignation to their meager and often uninfluential circumstances (poor and meek of spirit, like the church mice "hinter der Kirche"), but it described their place professionally and socially as well. The irony of the post at the Stadtkirche (instead of a Hofkirche [court church]) is not to be overlooked: Herder was the official court preacher (*Hofprediger*) at a court that rarely took communion or heard him preach (especially not Duke Carl August),[1] so that he mostly preached to the *Stadt,* or at least the more privileged part of the city population. Such service to the bourgeois stratum moreover points to Herder's true socio-economic and political sympathies,[2] which were often in conflict with the needs of his master and had to be toned down, out of loyalty and in order to avoid frictions in his job. His social place was between court and city; he moved in court circles at times, but only officially, and not by right (in contrast to Goethe, who enjoyed free access and could participate fully, especially after his ennoblement in 1782). And finally his position "back of" the church determined both his profile (obscured, hidden by the church) and in many respects his intellectual attitudes: he was first and foremost a churchman and theologian, with a relatively restricted sphere of free self-expression.

Although Herder was hired for Saxe-Weimar on the strong recommendation of Goethe, who had a high opinion of his friend's talents and great expectations for his contributions both to official life and to making his (Goethe's) own social and intellectual life more interesting, the appointment was handled in the end not so much as a gracious exercise of ducal patronage, but rather more like the tailor's seven flies at one blow. Herder was appointed in the main to be church superintendent for Saxe-Weimar, which also entailed supervision of the schools;[3] he had some responsibilities for theological education at the university in Jena and for

examining and certifying newly fledged preachers before they could be put into service; he was a member of
the Weimar consistory with the title *Oberconsistorialrat*
(over-consistorial councilor; after 1788 vice-president
and in his last years even president thereof) and court
preacher entrusted with the Stadtkirche (and thus also
the parsonage). He was to be paid the sum of the bud-
geted allocations for the different parts of his duties, so
that, especially taking account of the free use of the
parsonage, he should have been assured of a comfortable living in exchange for the burdens of his many offices. Because, however, Carl August generally assigned
church and school affairs a low priority to begin with—
probably a good thing as far as tolerance and liberal
thinking were concerned[4]—it was a constant struggle
for Herder to avoid budget cuts and downsizings
(leaving positions unfilled) right and left as Carl August's political ambitions and military play-acting cost
ever more in the 1780s, the *Fürstenbund* (League of
Princes) period (not to speak of the costs and strains of
the French Revolutionary period after 1789). Significant
reforms and improvements in pay scales so as to attract
more qualified preachers and teachers were out of the
question.[5] Furthermore, Herder was faced with significant conservative opposition in both Church and school
affairs and had to be careful not to antagonize all his
colleagues and underlings. Goethe supported him man-
fully and long mediated between Herder, Carl August,
and the rest of the government where he could, but
eventually dropped Herder (and especially Caroline
[1750-1809], as is well known) like hot potatoes in
1795 over Caroline's demands that Carl August fulfill
his promises to provide for the education of the Herder
sons.[6]

Herder was a bargain for the Saxe-Weimar government,
especially since at least until 1788 he was not even paid
all that he had been promised when he moved to Weimar.[7] It is well known that the family was in constant
financial difficulties, though it is not clear that the Herders were spendthrifts or whether an inability to handle
money complicated their situation. In any case, like
many other eighteenth-century intellectuals unable to
survive on official bread alone and forced to sell himself in print, Herder had a busy agenda governed by the
symbiotic relationship with his old friend and publisher
Johann Friedrich Hartknoch in Riga: continuing advances and loans from Hartknoch kept Herder writing
and in debt to Hartknoch's company store. In March
1788, not long before Herder's departure for Italy, he
received a gift of 2000 *Gulden* from an anonymous admirer and a *Gehaltszulage* (bonus) of 300 *Reichstaler*
from Carl August, which, according to Christoph Fasel,
sufficed to pay the family's most pressing debts.[8] Yet by
the time Herder (then in Italy) received a letter from
Christian Gottlob Heyne (dated March 15, 1789), officially offering him a position as professor of theology
and consistorial councilor in Göttingen and inviting him

to name his own salary and terms,[9] the Herders were
back in debt by some 2000 talers. Much of the deliber-
ating in the correspondence between Herder and Caroline before Herder's return to Weimar revolved around
the question of whether it was more realistic to try to
get Göttingen to help pay off the debts in exchange for
his accepting the position, or to pressure Carl August to
help out in order to keep him in Weimar.[10] In the end,
Goethe mediated between Carl August and the church
superintendent (who in reality, when push came to
shove, did not want to become a professor of theology
after all[11]), and Herder stayed in Weimar. But in spite of
all the promises and a temporary improvement in his
situation, in the long run he was no better off, for he
was still in debt, swamped with official duties, and
chained to his writing desk. The churchman had made
one attempt to break out of his confinement back of the
church and live the life of a Goethe when he traveled to
Italy in 1788-89. In this regard, and in most others, the
trip was a failure; in addition, it was a great strain on
his marriage and the family finances. Returning to his
space after the journey, he soon found a lot in Weimar
culture, personal politics, government attitudes, and
other shenanigans to be unhappy with. And in the course
of the 1790s he became more and more isolated from
Goethe and the court, and from the newest trends in
contemporary culture.[12]

Was Herder Classical?

Obviously it would not do to claim that Herder was always classical, just as Goethe, Schiller, and other writers of the age went through various stages or phases in
their development before reaching a "classical" stage;
Schiller died a Classic (final stage) because he died pre-
maturely, while in Goethe's case, Classicism was superseded by other and possibly better phases during the
rest of his long life. Particularly in the case of major
authors such as Herder, Goethe, and Schiller, rethinking
periodization is always in order. In fact these three writers all began in similar enthusiastic and elevated fashion in the mode known as *Sturm und Drang* (Storm and
Stress), of which Herder unfortunately has been tagged
by literary historians as having been the initiator without quite knowing what he was doing (since the *Stürmer
und Dränger* were a gaggle of younger literati with no
better ideas of their own, and whom, with the exception
of Goethe, Herder hardly even knew).[13]

A main tenet of *Sturm und Drang* has been alleged to
be antipathy to the Enlightenment, which it is claimed
was shallow and worn-out by the time Herder and the
Stürmer und Dränger received it, and consequently the
urge to overthrow and transcend it. This entailed as
much verbal violence as sharp-eyed critique. While Goethe and others are allowed to have fulfilled the goal of
getting beyond Enlightenment, Herder is often alleged
to have struggled to overcome it only to relapse into

Enlightenment modes of thought again at some unspecified point instead of going on to become a "classic" like some of his contemporaries. Clearly, Herder was not thinking "classic" or "classicism" in much of his early work; he promoted the indigenous Northern or "German" culture of the English (Shakespeare) and the Norse, while being highly critical of contemporary French classical models such as Voltaire.[14] He damaged his eventual influence and reputation severely with the oracular, often elliptical, and rhetorical effusions that made up so much of his early oeuvre and were so breathlessly imitated by the youngsters of the 1770s. Part of his enthusiasm and exuberance manifested itself in the urge to devour books and express his opinions and ideas about them (for example, the earliest published work, the three-volume **Kritische Wälder** [**Critical Sylvae,** 1769], with which he threw himself upon the literary landscape, aiming to change it instantaneously). An ambitious scholar, he hungered to get close to the sources, as in his *Volkslied* (folk song) collecting and his interpretation of Genesis, the **Älteste Urkunde des Menschengeschlechts** (**Oldest Document of the Human Race,** 1774; followed later by much more favorably received studies such as **Vom Geist der ebräischen Poesie** [**On the Spirit of Hebrew Poetry,** 1782-83]). In much of his early work, for example on the Old Testament, Herder was not "anti" anything and he made grateful use of older and contemporary scholarship, enlightened or otherwise.

To be sure, in his early major treatise on the philosophy of history, **Auch eine Philosophie der Geschichte zur Bildung der Menschheit** (**Also a Philosophy of History for the Education of Mankind**) of 1774, Herder became shrilly polemical and critical of the presumption of so-called enlightenment (not actually of the Enlightenment itself, but of the "enlightened age"). The end of the work features a critique of colonialism that is actually comparable to twenty-first-century anti-globalism:

> Was warens für elende *Spartaner,* die ihre *Heloten* zum Ackerbau brauchten,[15] und für barbarische *Römer,* die ihre Sklaven in die Erdgefängnisse einschlossen! In Europa ist die Sklaverei abgeschafft, weil berechnet ist, wie viel diese Sklaven mehr kosteten und weniger brächten, als freie Leute: Nur Eins haben wir uns noch erlaubt, *drei Weltteile als Sklaven* zu *brauchen,* zu *verhandeln,* in Silbergruben und Zuckermühlen zu *verbannen*—aber das sind nicht *Europäer,* nicht *Christen,* und dafür bekommen wir Silber und Edelgesteine, Gewürze, Zucker und—heimliche Krankheit: also des *Handels* wegen und zur *wechselseitigen Bruderhülfe* und *Gemeinschaft* der Länder . . . *Drei Weltteile* durch uns *verwüstet* und *polizieret,* und wir durch sie *entvölkert, entmannet,* in Üppigkeit, Schinderei und Tod versenkt: das ist reich gehandelt und glücklich . . . Der alte Name, Hirt der Völker, ist in Monopolisten verwandelt—und wenn die ganze Wolke mit hundert Sturmwinden denn bricht—großer Gott Mammon,—dem wir *alle jetzt dienen,* hilf uns!—[16]

> [What kind of miserable people were the *Spartans,* who used their *helots* for tilling the fields, and the barbarian *Romans,* who locked their slaves in dungeons! In Europe slavery is abolished, because it was calculated how much more slaves cost and how much less they bring in than free men: Yet we have permitted ourselves one new thing, namely to *use three whole parts of the world* as our *slaves,* to *deal* in them, and to *put them away* in silver mines and sugar mills—but those aren't *Europeans,* not *Christians,* and by using them we get silver and precious stones, spices, sugar and—a secret illness: so for the sake of *trade* and for the sake of *fraternal assistance* and *community* of the nations . . . *Three quarters of the world laid waste* and *governed* by us, and we are *depopulated, emasculated* by them, debauched in luxury, villainy and death: that is acting richly and happily . . . The old name, shepherd of the peoples, has been turned into monopolist—and if then the whole huge cloud bursts with a hundred storm winds—great God Mammon—whom *we all serve now,* help us!—]

Such passages of historical and social critical engagement could be multiplied from the works of the young Herder almost at will, but he was not yet "classical" and of course could not simply repeat the anger later in classical dress, although he retained most of his critical views.

To raise the question why Herder should be regarded as Classical or as a Classic is not really much different than posing the same question in the case of Goethe, Schiller, and assorted lesser figures of the period; it is essentially a matter of choosing and agreeing on definitions (and readers can agree that "X" is a Classic without agreeing entirely on the reasons). Definitions can begin at the bottom with the narrow "classical Weimar" of the Goethe-Schiller collaboration and friendship. Such a specification of course disregards the fact that Schiller had been in Weimar and Jena for seven years before he managed to focus Goethe's interest on himself and also poses the question whether Goethe's *Iphigenie auf Tauris* and *Torquato Tasso* can really be regarded as classical if Schiller was not involved in their production, while *Egmont,* a decidedly un-classical and Romantic piece, was completed at the same time. One should conclude that Goethe's classicism was post-Italian, but that not all his post-Italian production was classical. From the Goethe-Schiller parameter one can then proceed to the philosophical movement to resurrect the "classical" atmosphere of ancient Greece and Rome by resurrecting the artist as a genius and the work of art as a piece of perfection in itself without reference to externals, along the lines of Karl Philipp Moritz's doctrine of "das in sich selbst Vollendete" (that which is complete in itself) and Immanuel Kant's "interesseloses Wohlgefallen" (disinterested pleasure) which, by way of Schillerian theorizing, also contributed to the rise of Romantic theory. One problematic aspect of this train of thought is that the definitions and prescriptions are much more easily applicable to the visual arts, possibly also to mythology, than to poetry. Another problem is the status of Schiller himself and his Kant-based aesthetic theory within that context, regarding Goethe as the true naïve classic and trying to justify his own existence as a sentimentalist. Under one pretext or another, this involved much imitation of the ancients, à la Laocoön and Winckelmann, and admiration of "edle Einfalt und stille Größe" (noble simplicity and quiet grandeur).[17] Finally, we can choose between the narrow world of Goethe/Schiller and their epigones, or the wide world of a "Classical Age" that takes in major first-rate writers (another dictionary definition of classical, of course, based on the Roman "classicus" tax category), from Lessing and Wieland to young Grillparzer and Heine at the end of the Age of Goethe or, to use Heine's term, the *Kunstperiode* [age of art]).

Under the circumstances, and not least of all because he definitely belongs in a volume that treats Goethe and Schiller, it should not be a large stretch to get Herder under the classical tent. Herder journeyed to Italy shortly after Goethe had returned from there, but found he could not enjoy the milieu and ambience of Italy like Goethe had, because he was not an artist himself, and he was also very much a Christian and not able to let himself go like a sensual pagan, à la Winckelmann. He was not able to finish his course of study in Roman antiquities with Aloys Hirt (1759-1837), the hired *cicerone,* because of the disruptive lack of interest of his traveling companions in such antiquities,[18] and as far as hands-on experience of classical landmarks and remains, it is unlikely that he advanced far beyond the level of Volkmann's tourist guide, the major resource and Bible of most German visitors of the period.

Goethe while in Italy had discovered definitively and gratefully that he was a poet. There was nothing comparable for Herder to discover. He reaped some fond memories and much disillusionment and brought home a diary of sorts.[19] Most of the high-ranking acquaintances he made were thanks to Duchess Anna Amalia and thanks to the fact that he represented Saxe-Weimar as the equivalent of a Lutheran bishop, and while he felt honored to meet Italian nobles and princes of the Church, they were surely of little consequence for his later life. When he invested himself in art and art appreciation, he got into trouble: he praised Angelika Kaufmann and wrote so touchingly of his sentimental appreciation of her that Caroline became quite jealous, and some apologizing had to be done. But Angelika remained safely in Rome when Herder returned to Weimar; what did eventually make the trip to Weimar was Alexander Trippel's (1744-93) bust of Herder, commissioned by Carl August as a counterpart to Trippel's bust of Goethe, to which, however, Herder unfavorably compared his own.[20] Another highly interesting and revealing Roman acquaintanceship was that with the writer Karl Philipp Moritz, which was mediated by Goethe.

Herder met Moritz in Rome shortly before Moritz's own return to Germany and was impressed with his person and with his aesthetic views. In turn, he recommended Moritz to Caroline because Moritz was passing through Weimar on his way back to Berlin. In Weimar, Moritz stayed several weeks with Goethe; he also visited Caroline a number of times and impressed her favorably. Goethe, too, was solicitous of Caroline, all of which Caroline reported back to Herder in her letters (which unfortunately were always two to three weeks in transit, leaving him to nurse his feelings of jealousy). Finally, all this was too much for poor Herder, and he exploded in a fit of pique directed at both Moritz and Goethe:

> So ists auch mit Moriz Philosophie u. Abhandlung [*Über die bildende Nachahmung des Schönen*]. Sie ist ganz Göthisch, aus seiner u. in seine Seele; er ist der Gott von allen Gedanken des guten Moritz . . . mir ist diese ganze Philosophie im feinsten Organ zuwider: sie ist selbstisch, abgöttisch, unteilnehmend u. für mein Herz desolierend. Ich mag die Öde nicht, in der auch ein Gott um sein selbst willen allein existieret.[21]

> [It's the same with Moritz's philosophy and his treatise (On the Creative Imitation of the Beautiful). It is completely Goethean, written from his soul and for his soul; he is the God of all of good Moritz's thoughts . . . I find this whole philosophy abhorrent to the depths of my soul: it is selfish, idolatrous, uncaring and desolating for my heart. I can't stand the desert in which a god too could exist for his own sake.]

It was important for Herder that art had to speak to the heart. He was never engaged in culture abstractly or only from a theoretical point of view, but always from a personal-moral perspective. He was not a deep thinker addicted to systematic philosophical and aesthetic thought, but his was a fertile and suggestive mind. From the 1780s on, as he shed the *Sturm und Drang* mannerisms of his beginnings, he can be regarded as a serious, popular writer in the Lessing-Mendelssohn mold, with an audience for his works: a publisher could count on selling his books. He was genuinely interested in the history and culture of antiquity, and, one might assume, more broadly so than Goethe, Schiller, and others in the Weimar sphere of influence, who had a more limited interest, namely in the imitation and re-creation of ancient art. Herder, for his part, as he began to demonstrate in his ***Ideen zur Philosophie der Geschichte der Menschheit (Ideas towards the Philosophy of the History of Mankind)***, wanted to fit all human endeavor and development, including art and culture, into the grand scheme of universal history.

It is naturally not possible to deal in the space available with all of Herder's works of the 1780s and 1790s; in any case, there is enough redundancy among them that some can be left out without detriment to the whole, including, for example, the ***Zerstreute Blätter (Scattered***

Leaves) of the 1780s, which paralleled his work on the **Ideen,** and the ***Christliche Schriften (Christian Writings***), which Herder wrote in the 1790s at the same time as the ***Briefe zu Beförderung der Humanität*** (***Letters for the Furthering of Humanity,*** 1793-97).[22] It is, however, essential to keep in mind that Herder was a thoroughly religious and Christian person from start to finish, a fact that distinguished him from other Weimar luminaries. He began his career as a preacher and teacher in Riga with a strong sense of his vocation, and throughout his life he held responsible Church positions.[23] From the late 1770s on he was in mental dialogue with Gotthold Ephraim Lessing: with the posthumous fragments of Hermann Samuel Reimarus's deistic critique of the Bible and Gospel history that had been published by Lessing; with the positions argued in the ensuing controversy between Lessing and pastor Johann Melchior Goeze (1717-86), an orthodox cleric who considered drama immoral; and with *Die Erziehung des Menschengeschlechts* (The Education of the Human Race, 1780), in which Lessing had argued that human history's relationship to God was driven by a sequence of divine "primers" made available to mankind, each at exactly the right time to illuminate a "new" and important truth about the nature of God and the immortal destiny of mankind. The possibility put forward by Lessing at the end of the *Erziehung* that every human being might benefit in the attainment of moral perfection by being reborn over and over until that pinnacle is reached (metempsychosis), was categorically denied by the speakers in Herder's ***Über die Seelenwanderung. Drei Gespräche*** (***On Transmigration of Souls: Three Dialogues***) of 1782.[24] Five years later, Herder was moved to formulate his own position in the Spinoza and pantheism controversy that had been unleashed by Goethe's friend Friedrich Heinrich Jacobi (1743-1819) when he published his account and interpretation of conversations with Lessing in 1780, shortly before the latter's death in 1781. Jacobi had made Lessing out to be a Spinozist and therefore a rationalistic atheist.[25] Herder, for his contribution to the debate, set out to reconcile his understanding of Spinoza's thought with Leibnizian monadological philosophy in ***Gott: Einige Gespräche*** (***God: Some Dialogues,*** 1787), attempting in so doing both to pull Lessing out of danger and to salvage Spinoza for polite philosophical company.[26] The view of God and Nature elaborated in these dialogues is similar to what he had already put forward in the first two parts of the **Ideen.**

As a modern thinker who, although admiring Martin Luther for his achievement in reforming the Church in Northern Europe and supposedly liberating religious thought from the Roman yoke,[27] no longer identified with strict Lutheran orthodoxy, Herder distanced himself from the Neologians, the theological innovators of the middle and later eighteenth century. Herder's major work on theological correctness, ***Briefe, das Studium der Theologie betreffend*** (***Letters On the Study of Theology***), first published in 1780, with a second revised edition published in 1784, was contemporaneous with intensive work on the **Ideen.** In the letters, addressed to a beginning theology student, Herder stresses that the student should learn first things first and worry about more complicated or controversial things later. For now he should concentrate on the basics and not waste his time with learned commentaries (aside from dictionaries and other philological helps) or abstruse subjects, such as the investigation of the canon. Most of the books recommended fall in the mainstream of eighteenth-century German Lutheran theology and Church history and include many that Herder himself must have read during his studies in Königsberg. Neologians receive little attention. Not surprisingly, Luther is a favorite source of wisdom (serving the function of an arbiter), for example with regard to the doctrine of justification by faith: "Die Lehre der *Rechtfertigung* ist mit jener vom *Glauben* so nahe verwandt, daß Eine mit der andern stehn und fallen muß; auch bei ihr, dem Eckstein des Luthertums, halten Sie sich vorzüglich an Luthers Schriften"[28] (The doctrine of *justification* is so closely related to that of *belief* that the one must stand and fall with the other; here too, with this cornerstone of Lutheranism, you must orient yourself above all according to Luther's writings). Herder has little sympathy for Pietism and what he calls its "Methodismus," or for enthusiasm (*Schwärmerei*) in general. He abhors the skeptic David Hume (1711-76) and is highly critical of Rousseau, but can find things to praise in Shaftesbury (1621-83) and some of the English deists and Bible scholars. He is no friend of Wolffian theology, which he blames for hopelessly and completely subverting Lutheran dogmatics. By encouraging the student to look to Luther and the Bible itself for his understanding of doctrine, Herder manages to sidestep, or at least to downplay the controversy between orthodox and Enlightenment theologians that so stultified eighteenth-century Lutheran intellectual life.[29]

Before proceeding to discussion of the **Ideen** and **Humanitätsbriefe,** it should be stressed that Herder was not advocating any religious or philosophical program of his own; he was, in fact, quite tolerant, that is, open and receptive to other religions and variant religious practices. In the **Ideen,** he in fact argues a largely secularist point of view; he does not insist on Genesis, for example, as an orthodox Lutheran would have both then and now, as the only credible or true account of the Creation or seek to locate a Middle Eastern Garden of Eden in which mankind might have been innocent before the Fall; in treating the books of Moses as (the most ancient extant) works of inspiration and poetry, he assumes the possible existence of other, equally valid documents of early "history." He is able to note both the good and the not so good in ancient and pre-modern religions and cultures, since he sees them all contributing in one way or another to the establishment and growth of **Humanität.** There is one partial exception to this tolerance, of course: Herder's attitude toward Roman Catholicism was of necessity quite ambivalent because it was not only a historical religion, but also in fact still the majority religion of Europe and the largest Christian confession world-wide. As a Church official in a non-monolithic religious landscape, he had to be accustomed to dealing with counter-parties to a certain extent, both officially and privately. His traveling companion in Italy, Johann Friedrich Hugo von Dalberg (1752-1812), was a canon of the Trier cathedral, while his older brother, Karl Theodor von Dalberg (1744-1817), coadjutor of the Archbishop-Elector of Mainz and governor of Erfurt, was a political and intellectual ally and favorite of the Weimar government and court. In Italy, Herder had the diplomatic status of a bishop and as such was an adornment of Anna Amalia's retinue (he fretted considerably about procuring the attire appropriate to his status and his social obligations). Yet he could be very testy about the "unenlightened" nature of Catholic tradition and practice, as in his remarks about Bamberg and other Catholic territories on his way to Italy.[30] In the **Ideen,** he had to sort through multiple layers of meaning and stances toward the Roman Church in history: appreciative of its indispensable role in nurturing and spreading Christianity, hypercritical of its hegemony of superstition that had led to spiritual tyranny and to the Reformation; appreciative of its role in restoring and preserving order and culture during the turbulent Middle Ages, and bitterly denouncing the Roman hierarchy for usurping wealth and power and subjecting European rulers and societies, including empires and emperors, to its dictates and whims.[31] It was in fact precisely at the point where Humanism, the Renaissance, and the Reformation should have begun, that is, where the Roman church had to become the central topic of the work for a while again in the early modern age, that Herder ultimately broke off the **Ideen.**

IDEEN AND HUMANITÄTSBRIEFE

Of all Herder's works, it is the **Ideen zur Philosophie der Geschichte der Menschheit** and the **Briefe zu Beförderung der Humanität** that are best remembered and most often studied by those who deal with German literature (including history and philosophy of history) and Weimar Classicism. Many of the other works, important as they may be or may have been, are the province of specialists (scholars of Oriental scholarship, for example) or of those with axes to grind. The **Ideen** (especially the first two parts, because of their subject matter) garnered Goethe's full interest and sympathy and rekindled the warm friendship between the two one last time. The work was published in four parts, of five books each, in 1784, 1785, 1787, and 1791. Originally meant to be an expanded and more "scientific" (also more calmly presented) revision of the earlier **Auch**

eine Philosophie der Geschichte zur Bildung der Menschheit, the work never quite measured up to its intention or ambition. The first part is a compilation of the science of the material and physical world relevant to the development of the human race; the second part deals with the various geographical and climatic conditions and the human beings who adapted to them, concluding in book 10 with a series of deliberations regarding the location of the beginnings of culture and traditions of the Creation. Part 3 is a survey of ancient cultures starting with Asia (China and India), moving through the Middle East to the Greek and Roman worlds, and concluding in book 15 with a series of thesis chapters drawing the religio-philosophical conclusions from the preceding history. Part 4 is devoted to the peoples of Northern Europe, the rise of Christianity, the fall of the Roman Empire, the Germanic migrations, and medieval history, including the growth of the influence and power of the Roman church hierarchy, the rise of Islam, and the Arab conquests in Spain and the Middle East. Book 20 contains a serious of concluding chapters devoted to commerce, chivalry, the Crusades (including crusades against heresy within Europe itself and the beginnings of the Inquisition), the culture of reason, and geographical discoveries. There was to have been a fifth part devoted to the Reformation, the rise of modern thought and science, and the Enlightenment, but Herder's plans for this last part were thwarted by the unfavorable political currents of the French revolutionary age. (The repressive atmosphere of political conservatism and censorship in the wake of the outbreak of war with France, in which Carl August played the role of a Prussian general and had to be careful to keep his own subjects under control, was no small factor.) In Herder's original conception, the **Humanitätsbriefe** were meant to be the continuation of the **Ideen** in another form, but they too failed in large part to fill in the historical gap and developmental argument left by the failure to complete the **Ideen.**

Especially in the first two parts of the **Ideen,** Herder is participating in contemporary debates about nature, the place of man on earth and in the universe, the beginnings of the human race, the destiny of man, and so on. The content is unavoidably a mixture of natural science, history, and speculation. For all the effort to keep the discussion on a natural-scientific plane, the subject matter also impinges constantly on religious and theological "certainties" that have to be taken account of in one way or another in the course of the work. There is constant difficulty, for example, in keeping God and nature separate, already in the preface:

> Niemand irre sich . . . daran, daß ich zuweilen den Namen der Natur personifiziert gebrauche. Die Natur ist kein selbstständiges Wesen; *sondern Gott ist Alles in seinen Werken*: indessen wollte ich diesen hochheiligen Namen . . . durch einen öftern Gebrauch, bei dem ich ihm nicht immer Heiligkeit gnug verschaffen konnte,

wenigstens nicht mißbrauchen. Wem der Name 'Natur' durch manche Schriften unsres Zeitalters sinnlos und niedrig geworden ist, der denke sich statt dessen *jene allmächtige Kraft, Güte und Weisheit,* und nenne in seiner Seele das unsichtbare Wesen, das keine Erdensprache zu nennen vermag.[32]

[Let no one be misled by the fact that I sometimes use the name of Nature as though it were a person. Nature is not any kind of independent being, but rather *God is everything in his works*; but I did not want to misuse his most holy name . . . by invoking it so frequently without always being able to give it all the devout respect it deserves. Whoever feels that the name "Nature" has become cheap and meaningless by being used in so many modern-day publications should imagine to himself, instead of "Nature," *that all-powerful might, goodness, and wisdom,* and recognize in his heart the invisible Being that can be properly named in no earthly language.]

Here Herder may recommend a way of dealing with the two concepts, nature and God, but their intermixing causes recurrent difficulties. To be objective and scientific, one would have to explain things solely in terms of natural laws without appealing to the will of God, yet Herder cannot avoid insisting that God is not only present in nature, but also in history as well, as evinced in the argument of book 15, which opens with a rhetorical movement into despair over the evils of the moral-historical world (quite common among those like Rousseau, Moritz, and others who paint the moral world black in order seemingly to deny that there is a divine order in it), a despair which, once evoked, is rhetorically overcome by faith that there is a *telos* in Nature and that God's providence rules all:

Ist indessen ein Gott in der Natur: so ist er auch in der Geschichte: denn auch der Mensch ist ein Teil der Schöpfung und muß in seinen wildesten Ausschweifungen und Leidenschaften Gesetze befolgen, die nicht minder schön und vortrefflich sind, als jene, nach welchen sich alle Himmels und Erdkörper bewegen. Da ich nun überzeugt bin, daß was der Mensch wissen muß, er auch wissen könne und dürfe: so gehe ich aus dem Gewühl der Szenen, die wir bisher durchwandert haben, zuversichtlich und frei den hohen und schönen Naturgesetzen entgegen, denen auch sie folgen.[33]

[If, meanwhile, there is a God in Nature: then he is also in History: for man too is part of the Creation and must, even in his wildest actions and passions, follow laws which are no less beautiful and excellent than those which all heavenly and earthly bodies obey. Since I am convinced that man can and must know what it is he has to know, I proceed confidently and willingly from the chaos of the scenes through which we have passed up to now towards the sublime and beautiful laws of Nature which they too obey.]

Law of nature, law of God, law of history—which actually has the power to explain what the work needs to explain?

Not a natural scientist himself, Herder was largely dependent on Goethe's knowledge and insights and the work of scientist-philosophers such as Bonnet, Haller (1708-77), Linnaeus (1707-78), ethnographers and writers on exploration like Johann Reinhold Forster, and the like. Regarding the place of man and the earth in the system, he actually reverts to ideas put forward by, among others, Immanuel Kant as early as 1755 in his *Allgemeine Naturgeschichte und Theorie des Himmels* (General History of Nature and Theory of the Heavens). In debates about man it was always necessary to emphasize on the one hand that he was the apex of Creation on earth, but to concede on the other hand that he occupied only a middling position in the universe as a whole, so as to make room for creatures both beneath and above him in the great chain of being who might be flourishing or approaching perfection on other planets or in other parts of the universe. Already in the dialogues *Über die Seelenwanderung* Herder had developed an argument about the place of man as a *Mittelgeschöpf* (middling creature) on a middling planet in the solar system situated between Saturn and the Sun.

In much of the first two parts of the *Ideen,* Herder is, in fact, not up to date at all in his science and scholarship, but rather synthesizes the state of knowledge and debate from earlier in the century.[34] His discussion of the place of man in the solar system plays into a common theme of eighteenth-century popular philosophy, inspired as it was by the thought that there were countless other worlds where rational creatures could either be inferior to humans or increase in perfection and surpass humans on their earth. Often it was assumed that humans proceeded to these other worlds to continue the progress of their perfection after their sojourn on earth—death did not necessarily lead straight to Heaven or Hell but to another stage in the transformation or a transposition of the individual. Covering most of the available viewpoints in the debate on immortality and perfectibility, Lessing argued in *Die Erziehung des Menschengeschlechts* for increasing perfection of the individual through metempsychosis; Herder argued vaguely for increasing perfection of the individual first during life and through transformation after death; and Kant, critizing Herder sharply on this point in his blistering review of part 1 of the *Ideen,* argued that it was not the individual, but the species that nature had destined for progress, not through spiritual perfection, but through the development of reason, gifts, and talents sharpened in the egoistic competition of individuals and societies among themselves.[35]

Although personal perfection and immortality may be the transcendent goal of the individual, Herder posits also a developmental goal in history for individuals and societies alike: all history, all culture, all human interactions contribute to furthering *Humanität,* which as an ideal can perhaps best be rendered as "the true nature of humanity and the human race." This has nothing (at least not primarily) to do with religion or religious values alone, although for Herder, of course, Jesus was the most humane person in the history of the world. He devotes considerable space at the end of the third part of the *Ideen* (book 15, after the jeremiad about moral evil in the world) to explaining what he means by it. *Humanität* is the all-encompassing ideal for humans, he claims, because even if we imagine to ourselves angels or gods, we imagine them as ideal humans. The approach to *Humanität* is not continual or without interruption in history; in fact, societies and cultures can remain for centuries on end in their original primitive state without progressing at all, or they can even regress. But in all ages one principal law of nature remains constant: "Der Mensch sei Mensch! er bilde sich seinen Zustand nach dem, was er für das Beste erkennet" (632; Let man be man! may he create his condition according to his best lights). God/Nature created man as a "God on earth," responsible to and for himself, and through the ages people and societies have struggled to be free and to enjoy their freedom according to the "great and beneficent law of human fate":

> . . . daß was ein Volk oder ein gesamtes Menschengeschlecht zu seinem eignen Besten mit Überlegung wolle und mit Kraft ausführe, das sei ihm auch von der Natur vergönnet, die weder Despoten noch Traditionen sondern die beste Form der Humanität ihnen zum Ziel setzte.
>
> (634)

> [. . . that whatever a people or a whole race wants for itself after due consideration, and turns its strength to carrying out, that is granted it by Nature, who sets neither despots nor traditions as their goal, but rather the best form of *Humanität*.]

Humanität, a matter of self-determination and self-fulfillment, cannot depend on the other, nor can the failure to strive and achieve one's share of *Humanität* be blamed on the other:

> Mit nichten gründete sich z. B. der lange Gehorsam unter dem Despotismus auf die Übermacht des Despoten; die gutwillige, zutrauende Schwachheit der Unterjochten, späterhin ihre duldende Trägheit war seine einzige und größeste Stütze. Denn Dulden ist freilich leichter, als mit Nachdruck bessern; daher brauchten so viele Völker des Rechts nicht, das ihnen Gott durch die Göttergabe ihrer Vernunft gegeben.
>
> (635)

> [In no way, for example, was the long obedience under despotism based on the superiority of the despot; the good-natured trusting weakness of the subjugated, and afterward their forbearing patience was its sole and greatest possible support. For forbearance is easier than emphatic improvement; that's the reason so many peoples didn't make use of the right that God gave them through the divine gift of their reason.]

Those were words not only about the medieval age that was the subject of the last part of the *Ideen,* they were words for the age in which Herder was writing. For his own age Herder began the project of the *Briefe zu Beförderung der Humanität.* They took a different form than the *Ideen.* Whereas the *Ideen* was a treatise in twenty books, the *Briefe* were conceived as a correspondence among several participants. The different participants remain anonymous, and in fact, the individual letters are not attributed to specific authors, for, as the editor asks in a note at the end of the first letter, what could initials indicate that the letters themselves don't tell us. Whereas at the outset there is a pretense of variant points of view, the letters very quickly lose the appearance of difference. The work contains a total of 124 letters in ten *Sammlungen* (collections) published in the years from 1793 to 1797.

The years when Herder was publishing the *Humanitätsbriefe* were likewise the years when the French Revolution was having its strongest impact on Germany: the beginning of the wars that were to consume Germany and Europe until the defeat of Napoleon in 1814, the execution of Louis XVI on 21 January 1793, the Reign of Terror, the occupation of much German territory. Herder did not live long enough to experience the worst. He was not free to express his opinion in all respects because of recently sharpened censorship in Prussia and other territories of the Holy Roman Empire, and because Saxe-Weimar was firmly aligned with the Prussian cause against France. Herder's own sentiments were several degrees too liberal for his master, Carl August, for Goethe, and for his Weimar surroundings. The original version of several of the letters in the second collection, in which Herder's correspondents aired their thoughts frankly about the situation in France and the undesirability of intervention by the German powers (Prussia and Austria) to save the throne of Louis XVI, was withdrawn and never published during Herder's lifetime.[36] The most direct effect of this political-intellectual situation was that instead of presenting a frank and freewheeling (and perhaps also thoroughly cohesive and connected) discourse in the letters, Herder resorted to illustrating much of the progress of *Humanität* in various ages, from Greek antiquity to modern times, by excerpting the works of others. In the first three collections alone he excerpts from Benjamin Franklin's (1706-90) autobiography, which had just been translated into German, from recently published (posthumous) works of Frederick II of Prussia (1712-86), materials dealing with Emperor Joseph II (1741-90), poems by Klopstock and others, passages from Martin Luther, part of a dialogue by Lessing, and so on. The writer who in younger years had had nothing good to say about Frederick or Joseph was now able to relate their reigns to some progress in *Humanität* after all—especially when compared to France, which, until the Revolution, had been exceedingly backward.

Both the *Ideen* and the *Humanitätshriefe* were major works by a writer who was intensely engaged in the social and political issues of his time, who lacked nothing to be a significant political writer but the opportunity to express his opinions without fear of censorship or threat of intimidation. He was of course not free to give up or lose his post and his parsonage back of the city church without fear of harm to himself and his family. Consequently, it was not possible for either work to fulfill its original promise. It was for the younger generation to shine as political writers and critics of the affairs of the age in which Herder found himself, in the end, marooned.

Notes

1. In one attempt to better his situation, Herder proposed to take over a vacated chair of theology at the University of Jena while continuing to fulfill his official duties as court preacher; since the court so seldom took communion, it would be no problem for him to commute from Jena to Weimar for the purpose when necessary!

2. In his early years, he dreamed of reforming Russia, or at least Riga and the Baltic provinces, where he had begun his career; and late in life, when he had given up on the chances of reform in Weimar, he idealized his recollections of the "republican" city government of Riga.

3. The small scale of the supervisory function is to be noted: the Saxe-Eisenach portion of Carl August's domain had its own Church/school hierarchy and consistory.

4. This had the effect of an unofficially large scope for freedom of the press (eventually embodied officially, albeit briefly, in the post-Napoleonic constitution of the Grand Duchy).

5. See Christoph Fasel, *Herder und das klassische Weimar: Kultur und Gesellschaft 1789-1803* (New York: Peter Lang, 1988), 57-58: "Noch 1792 gab es mehrere Lehrerstellen, die jährlich weniger als 15 Taler (!) eintrugen, sehr viele, die kaum 50 Taler einbrachten." (As late as 1792 there were some teaching posts that brought in less than 15 talers per annum, and many that barely brought in 50 talers). Fasel's work is highly informative with regard to conditions and circumstances in Weimar during the period.

6. For a succinct treatment of Goethe's relations with the Herders, see Günter Arnold's article on Herder in *Goethe Handbuch* (Stuttgart, Weimar: Verlag J. B. Metzler, 1998), 4.1:481-86.

7. See Fasel, 163: "Hauptgrund für die finanzielle Misere bis zu den neunziger Jahren ist nicht primär die Gastfreundschaft und Größe des Herderschen Haushaltes oder gar ein in ihm betriebener Luxus, sondern die Tatsache, daß die ursprünglich auf 2000 Taler veranschlagte Stelle, die sich ja aus den Einkommen der verschiedensten Ämter zusammensetzte, im Mittel nur 1200 Taler einbrachte." (The main reason for the financial difficulties up until the nineties was not primarily the affability or the size of the Herder's household, much less any luxuries they indulged in, but rather the fact that the originally-promised 2000 taler position, which was put together out of the incomes of the different posts, yielded on average only 1200 talers).

8. Fasel, 77.

9. This was the second time Herder had negotiated with Göttingen. Because of opposition from other professors Heyne had not been able to get through a favorable appointment in the 1770s before Herder went to Weimar.

10. See Herder's *Italienische Reise. Briefe und Tagebuchaufzeichnungen 1788-1789.* Edited and with commentary and afterword by Albert Meier und Heide Hollmer (Munich: Deutscher Taschenbuch Verlag, 1988). This collection of documents, hereinafter referred to simply as *Italienische Reise,* is remarkably short on insightful comments by Herder on his actual experiences during his Italian trip; but it is fascinating to read because of the constantly changing, ambivalent attitudes of Caroline and Herder both toward each other and toward their mutual friends and acquaintances, and their attempts to agree on their situation and the decisions to be taken (the Göttingen offer) at such long distance.

11. Not only did the Herders finally decide he was not really cut out to be a professor of theology, who would have to endure the jealousy and criticism of his more senior and orthodox colleagues, teach several hours each day, and still write a lot as well; they were definitely apprehensive about the influence of student life in a university town on their still impressionable young sons (the nearby bad example of Jena could not be overlooked).

12. Fasel points out, however, that it was not only Herder who was isolated in Weimar; everyone was isolated from everyone else: "Allgemein ist nicht nur die Isolation, verbreitet sind auch die Klagen in Weimar, die in der Forschung häufig als das Monopol Herders erscheinen" (152; Not only was there a general feeling of isolation, complaints were also widespread which are often treated in the scholarly literature as Herder's monopoly).

13. On this whole matter see Wulf Koepke, "Herder and the Sturm und Drang," in *Literature of the Sturm und Drang* (vol. 6 of the Camden House History of German Literature), ed. David Hill (Rochester, NY: Camden House, 2003), 69-93.

14. While appreciative also of the classical Greek dramatic models, for example in his famous Shakespeare essay.

15. This is, it seems to me, actually a rather perceptive view of Greek society. Most contemporary interpretations of Greek culture emphasized "classical" beauty and totally ignored the cruel and unjust foundations of the society that produced such beauty. At the turn of the century Johann Gottfried Seume (1763-1810), like Herder a man of the people, launched a more thoroughgoing critique of ancient slavery.

16. Herder, *Schriften zu Philosophie, Literatur, Kunst und Altertum* 1774-1787, ed. Jürgen Brummack & Martin Bollacher (Frankfurt am Main: Deutscher Klassiker Verlag, 1994), 74.

17. In which Herder, taking a broader view of antiquity and the spread of culture from Asia to Europe in his major works (not just in *Auch eine Geschichte der Philosophie . . .*), was thankfully much less implicated.

18. Johann Friedrich Hugo von Dalberg and his lady friend, Sophie von Seckendorff. See frequent mention of the problem posed by the presence of Frau von Seckendorff in Herder's letters to Caroline in the Meier/Hollmer edition of *Italienische Reise,* as well as extensive discussion in their "Nachwort," 623-45.

19. Published in Meier/Hollmer's *Italienische Reise.*

20. Herder to Trippel from Milan, 15 June 1789, on his way back to Weimar: "Zuerst wünschte ich, daß die Schultern nicht so breit ausfielen: der Kopf bekommt dadurch etwas kolossalisches u. Gigantisches, welches in einer großen Höhe zwar Wirkung machte, aber in einer Höhe, wie unsre Busten meistens gesetzt werden, scheint es mir drückend u. schwer zu werden. Ich weiß nicht, ob Göthe seine. Buste kolossal bestellt hat; meine ist aber selbst größer geworden, als die seine . . . Zweitens auf der Stirn wünschte ich *etwas mehr Haar* . . . Mich dünkt, der Kontrast zwischen mir u. Göthe sei etwas zu stark: er sieht wie ein junger Alexander oder Apollo aus, u. ich gegen ihn wie ein kahler, trockner Alter" (First of all I wish that the shoulders wouldn't turn out so broad: the head gains something colossal and gigantic as a result, which at a great height would, to be sure, have quite an effect, but in the height in which our busts are usually displayed it seems to me to become oppressive and heavy. I don't know whether Goethe ordered his bust colossal, mine however has become even larger than his . . . Second I would wish for more hair on the brow . . . It seems to me the contrast between Goethe and me is somewhat too stark: he looks like a young Alexander or Apollo, and I look like a bald dry old man in comparison; *Italienische Reise,* 501-2).

21. Herder to Caroline, 21 February 1789 (*Italienische Reise,* 350). The passage is often quoted. Herder displays great ambivalence towards Goethe in his Italian correspondence with Caroline, not only here.

22. This title will be referred to as *Humanitätsbriefe.* It is quite impossible to translate *Humanität* as Herder uses it: it could be "Humaneness" as well as "Humanness." It does not mean "Mankind" or simply "Humanity" in any case, although perhaps it could be rendered "Humanity" in the sense of what ideally makes humankind human or humane.

23. His involvement in church affairs was serious and never *pro forma,* as can be seen in the volume edited long ago by Eva Schmidt, *Herder im geistlichen Amt: Untersuchungen/Quellen/Dokumente* (Leipzig: Koehler & Amelang, 1956). The volume deserves to be vastly expanded and re-issued.

24. Herder was motivated not just by Lessing's text, which was a kind of culmination of a discussion that had been going on since mid-century beginning with popular works like Johann Joachim Spalding's *Bestimmung des Menschen* of 1748 and Moses Mendelssohn's *Phädon* of 1767 (both works were reprinted and discussed many times over the years). See the editor's introduction to Herder's *Seelenwanderung* in *Schriften zu Philosophie . . .* (cited above), 1172-78.

25. *Über die Lehre des Spinoza, in Briefen an Herrn Moses Mendelssohn,* 1785. The complete Jacobi-Mendelssohn controversy was published in *Die Hauptschriften zum Pantheismusstreit zwischen Jacobi und Mendelssohn,* ed. Heinrich Scholz (Berlin: Reuther & Reichard, 1916).

26. Goethe, who received a copy of the work while in Italy, was enthusiastic in his praise.

27. See Karl Aner, *Die Theologie der Lessingzeit* (Halle/Saale: Niemeyer, 1929); with respect to Herder, especially, Michael Embach, *Das Lutherbild Johann Gottfried Herders,* Trierer Studien zur Literatur, 14 (Frankfurt am Main: Verlag Peter Lang, 1987).

28. Herder, *Theologische Schriften,* ed. Christoph Bultmann and Thomas Zippert (Frankfurt am Main: Deutscher Klassiker Verlag, 1994), 450.

29. Controversies which, one must add, are still carried on with zest and righteousness by American Lutheran fundamentalists today. There is no space to consider here Herder's actual understanding of the Bible as a book of history whose veracity can

be assumed in all important respects. The Old Testament, for example, including all the reports therein of God's direct intercourse with his chosen people, can safely be read as an authentic history of the Jewish people; similarly, Herder views the Gospels' account of the life, career, and death of Jesus, including the reports of his miracles, his resurrection and ascent into Heaven, as truthful relations of fact. In this he rejects, without explicitly saying so, Reimarus's critique and Lessing's refusal in *Über den Beweis des Geistes und der Kraft* (On the Proof of the Spirit and the Power) to accept the Gospel events as credible history.

30. See the close of his letter to Caroline from Bamberg, 10 August 1788: "Der Katholizism ist ein abscheulich Ding, so fett, wohlbeleibt, etabliert, rund, behäglich, daß einem angst u. bange wird. Bloß hübsche fromme Weiber gibts in ihm. Gestern sah ich eine, die den Augenblick eine Madonna sein konnte. O mir Armen! wie wird mirs das Jahr hin ergehen! Ich glaube, ich sterbe vor Gemälden, Pfaffen u. Katholizismus" (Catholicism is a monstrous thing, so fat, plump, round, selfindulgent, that it is scary. There are only pretty, pious women in it. Yesterday I saw one who could instantly have become a Madonna. O poor me! what kind of a year am I going to have! I believe I'll die of paintings, priests, and Catholicism; *Italienische Reise*).

31. In the *Ideen,* Herder displays no ambivalence at all regarding the Byzantine Empire and the Greek Church; he levels the same criticisms as at the Roman Church hierarchy but without any countervailing positive comments.

32. *Ideen zur Philosophie der Geschichte der Menschheit,* ed. Martin Bollacher (Frankfurt am Main: Deutscher Klassiker Verlag, 1989), 17. I quote from the Frankfurt edition because it is the most recent and most accessible edition with commentary; but I would like to praise the two-volume edition edited by Heinz Stople (Berlin and Weimar: Aufbau Verlag, 1965 [*Ausgewählte Werke in Einzelausgaben*]) for its massive commentary and its role in furthering understanding of the work. The same must be said also of Stolpe's later edition of the *Humanitätsbriefe* (Aufbau Verlag, 1971).

33. *Ideen,* 630.

34. In his review of the second part of the *Ideen,* Kant noted that much had been excerpted from other authors.

35. Kant's other main criticism of Herder's effort had to do with Herder's use of analogical argument: if this is true here in the mineral world, and in the plant and animal worlds, then it must hold for man as well, etc. Kant missed a certain philosophical-logical rigor in Herder's work.

36. Interestingly enough, in the suppressed version of the second collection the various correspondents were in fact identified by initials.

S. E. Wilmer (essay date 2005)

SOURCE: Wilmer, S. E. "Herder and European Theatre." In *Staging Nationalism: Essays on Theatre and National Identity,* edited by Kiki Gounaridou, pp. 63-85. Jefferson, N.C. and London: McFarland, 2005.

[*In the following essay, Wilmer studies the influence of nationalism on European drama and discusses Herder's instrumental role in encouraging this expression of national identity.*]

In the eighteenth century, German intellectuals fostered a Romantic belief in the importance of the cultural traditions of the common people.[1] Influenced by the ideas of Rousseau, Friedrich Klopstock urged Germans to create their own works of art that would compete with, rather than imitate, the values of supposedly superior cultures from abroad (especially France, England, and Italy). Likewise, Johann Gottfried von Herder encouraged German-speaking people to take pride in their own cultural traditions and their native language. He urged them to acknowledge the importance of the German folk poets of the past: "These barbarians are our fathers, their language the source of our language and their unrefined songs the mirror of the ancient German soul."[2] But unlike Klopstock, Herder believed in national distinctiveness and a *Volksgeist* (spirit of the people) and encouraged all nations to express themselves in their own individual ways.

The ideas of Herder impelled intellectuals in countries throughout Europe to search for the unique aspects of cultural expression amongst their own peoples that would testify to separate and distinct identities. In seeking to formulate their own notion of what tied their people together and made them unique, cultural nationalists reinvented the past to some extent, often writing ancient national histories that came to justify the creation of separate nation-states.[3] In this essay, I will examine the development of nationalism and specifically its effect on the national theatres in Europe. Today, the links back to German Romanticism are barely visible in other countries because nationalist ideologies favor the notion that national identity emerges "organically" rather than being subject to rhetorical construction influenced by outside forces. However, one can demonstrate the influence of Herder's ideas by analyzing the similarities in emerging "national" cultural forms, especially in the practices of emerging national theatres. In order to do this, I will examine the emergent national theatres and compare certain common choices regarding language and repertory. It will thereby become evident how dramatists and theatre managers helped formulate a sense of national identity, partly through an emphasis on folk culture and national mythologies. The results were not always successful, nor the reception predictable, because these assertions of a shared mythic "national" identity had to be negotiated with the local audience and critics.

Unlike the solitary reader of a novel or a newspaper who reacts in isolation, the theatre-goer is part of a community of spectators who can express their approval or disapproval to the performers and to each other. As Stephen Greenblatt has shown, theatre "is a collective creation," both as "the product of collective intentions" and also because it "addresses its audience as a collectivity."[4] But theatre is also a place for interaction between performers and audience. In a manner consonant with Renan's notion of the nation as a "daily plebiscite,"[5] the theatre can act as a public forum in which the audience scrutinizes and evaluates political rhetoric and assesses the validity of representations of national identity. The theatre can serve as a microcosm of the national community, passing judgment on images of itself.

In the early days, national theatres, especially in emergent nations, maintained complex and contradictory relationships with the governments in power that were often in opposition to their aims. In Finland and Ireland, for example, operating under the control of the Russian and British empires respectively, both national theatres had to steer a careful path to avoid governmental interference. The Finnish Theatre had to submit all of its plays to the state censor. Likewise, W. B. Yeats and Lady Gregory guided the Abbey Theatre away from plays that were politically sensitive, partly because of an injunction by their English patron Annie Horniman who refused to support political drama. Such theatres, however, pursued what John Hutchinson has termed the politics of cultural nationalism. According to Hutchinson, "Cultural nationalism is a movement quite independent of political nationalism. It has its own distinctive aims—the moral regeneration of the national community rather than the achievement of an autonomous state—and a distinctive politics."[6] In this sense, the national theatres in such areas as Germany, Norway, Bohemia, Finland, and Ireland, in the period prior to becoming separate nation-states, were more cultural than political institutions. Although political nationalists sometimes used them for their own purposes, and although their very existence was predicated on the notion that they represented a distinct nation that could ultimately challenge the dominance of the hegemonic imperial power, the theatres were primarily myth-

making, rather than "rationally" motivated organizations, and arguably fostered self-expression more explicitly than self-determination. As I explain below, the theatres used language, actors, and repertory to help construct a sense of national identity, especially through a reliance on local plays about historical, mythological, and rural characters.

Herder expressed his faith in cultural (rather than political) unity through the *Volk.* Lamenting the disrespect in Germany (by contrast with other countries such as England and Spain) for their own cultural past, and what he saw as the over dependence on foreign traditions that stultified the growth of German literature, he argued:

> From ancient times we have absolutely no living poetry on which our newer poetry might grow like a branch upon the stem. Other nationalities have progressed with the centuries and have built with national products upon the beliefs and tastes of the *Volk.* In that way their literature and language have become national. The voice of the *Volk* is used and cherished, and in these matters they have cultivated a much larger public than we have. We poor Germans were destined from the start never to be ourselves; ever to be the lawgivers and servants of foreign nationalities. [. . .] It will remain eternally true that if we have no *Volk,* we shall have no public, no nationality, no language, no literature of our own which will live and work in us. Unless our literature is founded on our *Volk* we shall write eternally for closet sages and disgusting critics out of whose mouths and stomachs we get back what we have given. [. . .] Our classical literature is like a bird of paradise, showy in plumage, pert in aspects, all flight, all elevation, but without any true footing on German soil.[7]

Herder was much impressed by the recovery in Britain of early folk tales and songs and in particular by the publication in the 1760s of the Scottish epic of Ossian, supposedly a third century Gaelic bard (who later turned out to be an eighteenth-century forger), as well as a collection of English ballads called *Reliques of Ancient English Poetry,* edited by Thomas Percy in 1765. Comparing German unfavorably with British literature, Herder proposed, "How much further we would be [. . .] if we had used these folk ideas and folk tales like the British and had built our entire poetry upon them as Chaucer, Spenser, and Shakespeare built upon them, took from them, and created on the basis of them."[8]

Herder called on Germans to look for the folksongs of the past, such as those from the Middle Ages. To set an example, he began collecting what he called the *Nationallieder* (national songs) of different nations in the 1760s, later encouraging Goethe to help him.[9] He published the first international collection of folk songs in Germany in 1778 and a second volume in 1779 as **Stimmen der Völker in Liedern,** coining the term *Volkslied* (folksong or folk poetry).[10] The collection was ready for publication in 1773, but, due to adverse reaction by various critics to his enthusiasm for folk poetry, Herder withdrew it from the publisher and later resubmitted it when his ideas began to gain more favor.[11] (He planned another collection, to be organized by nationality, period, and language, as well as a volume of folk tales, but did not manage to complete either of these projects.) He also emphasized the importance of folk literature, such as the Ossian tales in his ***Über Ossian und die Lieder alter Völker*** of 1771, referring to folk literature as *Nationalstücke,*[12] and encouraged Germans to make a "complete critical study of the chronicles and legends of the Middle Ages."[13] As a result of his endeavors and his admiration for folk songs and literature, Herder instilled a new respect for the German common people and German folk traditions, thereby helping to undermine the prevailing class distinctions of the day, and developed a persuasive notion of national cultural unity, which influenced other writers.

Influenced by the ideas of Herder, cultural nationalists in nineteenth-century Europe investigated and exploited folklore, myths, legends, and local history, and also romanticized the lives of the rural folk. Likewise, medieval epics such as the *Nibelungenlied* and the Nordic sagas were suddenly regarded as important and used as raw material for creating new works of art. In most European countries, the interest in folk culture did not start from scratch during this period, but had evolved over centuries. However, from the late eighteenth century, folklore and folk culture or ethnography (as well as philology) became important reservoirs for notions of national identity. In Greece in the early nineteenth century, nationalists looked back to ancient Greece and the Homeric epics as their cultural heritage, tracing their roots back more than 2000 years and overlooking the long intervening period of Turkish rule. In some countries nationalist feelings caused over-enthusiastic folklorists to manufacture their own heritage and create their own epics where none existed. In the late eighteenth century in Scotland, the notion of Scottish kilts as being distinctive for individual families was invented by British manufacturers eager to sell tartan clothing to Scots who took pride in what they supposed had been an ancient and suppressed tradition.[14] Similarly, James Macpherson created an international stir by supposedly discovering the epic *Poems of Ossian,* which he had written himself. In Germany, both Herder (as we have seen) and Goethe, not knowing it was fraudulent, used the Ossian epic for their own purposes. Goethe celebrated its sentiments by quoting it at length in his 1774 *Sturm und Drang* novel *The Sorrows of Young Werther,* and, Herder praised it as an especially fine version of Nordic folk poetry.[15] Likewise in Bohemia, where three writers, Josef Dobrovský, Jan Kollár and Pavel Josef Šafařík, were primarily responsible for spreading the ideas of Herder, the Czech nationalist Vá-

clav Hanka supposedly discovered manuscripts of Czech folk poetry from the Middle Ages (1290-1310) that were heralded as early examples of their folk heritage, but were later shown to be forgeries.[16] Similarly in Lapland, a Lutheran priest named Anders Fjellner composed epic songs that he attributed to the Saami cultural tradition.[17]

In the case of the Finnish *Kalevala,* Elias Lönnrot and others collected folksongs for many years and then Lönnrot revised the songs and structured them into narratives about individual heroes, publishing an early edition in 1835 and an expanded version in 1849. Using the Homeric epic tradition as a model, Lönnrot shaped his material so that it would flow chronologically, rhythmically, and poetically. In discussing the 1849 version, he explained that his work was not definitive but somewhat arbitrary, since he was unable to discover an original form for the work.[18] Nevertheless, enthusiastic nationalists testified to the authenticity of the *Kalevala* and proclaimed it as their national epic. Far from viewing the epic as the labor of a single individual, Finnish nationalists proclaimed the *Kalevala* to be the work of the Finnish nation and evidence of the importance of the Finnish language and culture. Furthermore, perhaps because it was more important to their construction of national identity to have ancient heroes than an ancient mythology, nationalists generally regarded the *Kalevala* characters as historical, and the stories as evidence of a long Finnish history that was now at last being written.[19] By 1900, the collection of Finnish folklore (or what Wilson has called "an imagined heroic past") had become a national movement.[20]

In Ireland in the late nineteenth century, a similar cultural movement gave expression to a separate identity for the island of Ireland, which at the time was wholly under the domination of Great Britain. In a pattern similar to the one in Finland, the Irish cultural movement reflected the need to reject the dominant ideology of the British colonial government and replace it with a new national ideology. As in Finland, Irish nationalists, influenced by the German example,[21] had collected folklore tales and published them to give a greater sense of an ancient history and culture in Ireland. Yeats, Lady Gregory, and others assembled folklore and legends in particular about the Red Branch Knights. The *Táin,* like the *Kalevala,* became recognized as an epic saga close in character to other national epics. Through his collection of folklore in *The Celtic Twilight,* Yeats attempted to create a sense of Irish identity as well as literary history. Similarly, Lady Gregory wrote that she wanted to "put together the Irish legends, into a sort of *Morte d'Arthur,* choosing only the most beautiful or striking."[22] Her *Cuchulain of Murithemne,* published in 1902, was an inspiration to Yeats for his plays about the same character.

Again, there was an element of myth making in the assertions about national identity. For example, Richard Warner, archaeologist at the Ulster Museum in Belfast, argued in 1999:

> In round terms, the image of the Irish as a genetically Celtic people, in fact the whole idea of a Celtic ethnicity and of Celtic peoples, Irish, Welsh and all the rest of it, is a load of complete cock and bull. [. . .] The average Irish person probably has more English genes than Celtic. The whole Celtic/Irish thing was invented in order to make the Irish different from the English.[23]

Even Lady Gregory wrote that she "never quite understood the meaning of the 'Celtic Movement' which we were said to belong to. When I was asked about it, I used to say it was a movement meant to persuade the Scotch to begin buying our books, while we continued not to buy theirs."[24]

Theatre was one of the principle and most visible forms of this cultural nationalist movement of "recovery" and mythification in emerging European states. In the late eighteenth century in Germany, while the ideas of the Enlightenment were still very much in vogue, Lessing in his *Hamburg Dramaturgy* advocated the need to avoid French neo-classical influences and to compose plays about humbler domestic characters: "The misfortune of those whose circumstances come closest to our own must naturally invade our souls the deepest."[25] His comedy *Minna von Barnhelm* (1767) indirectly called for German unity by representing the need for reconciliation between the opposing states of Prussia and Saxony during the Seven Years' War. Furthermore, it emphasized the importance of German culture, as was particularly evident in a scene where a German lady, in response to a Frenchman who asks her to speak in French, answers, "Sir, I would seek to speak it in France. But why here?"[26] At about the same time Johann Elias Schlegel's German folk play *Hermann*, about a Germanic hero who defeated the Romans, was first staged. In 1872, Herder's collection of essays *Von deutscher Art und Kunst* (*Concerning German Style and Art*), which included papers by Goethe on architecture and by himself on German folk songs, inspired the early Romantic *Sturm und Drang* literary movement of the 1770s. Under Herder's influence, Goethe dramatized German history in *Götz von Berlichingen* and began work on the German legend *Faust*. Schiller, whose *The Robbers, Don Carlos,* and *Wilhelm Tell* represented a call for freedom, advocated the use of the theatre for nationalist expression: "In the drama the national features must be marked in the most prominent manner." He added, "Let [our drama] be truly historical, drawn from a profound knowledge, and let us transport ourselves wholly back to the great ideas of old. In this glass let the poet enable us to see, though to our deep

shame, what the Germans were in former times, and what they must be again."[27] Christophe Wieland, looking back a decade later, commented on the growing trend:

> German history, German heroes, a German scene, German characters, customs and habits were something completely new on German stages. What could be more natural than that German spectators had to feel the most lively pleasure to see themselves transferred, like through a magic switch, into their own country, into well known cities and areas, amongst their own people and ancestors—amongst people they felt at home with and who showed them, more or less, the features that characterize our nation.[28]

Goethe and Schiller, who broke away from the *Sturm und Drang* approach to develop a more international and neo-classical style of drama at the Court Theatre in Weimar, nevertheless, wrote of the potential of theatre to galvanize the nation.[29] Goethe acknowledged the ability of such work as his *Götz von Berlichingen* to "awaken self-consciousness in a nation."[30] Likewise, Schiller proposed,

> If in all our plays there was one main stream, if our poets reached an agreement and created a firm union for this final purpose—if a strict selection led their work and their brushes dedicated themselves only to national matters—in one word, if we had a national stage, we would also become a nation.[31]

Following the defeat of the Germans by Napoleon at Jena in 1806, Herder's promotion of individual nationalism gained widespread acceptance. Alain Finkielkraut argues that,

> Broken up into a multitude of principalities, Germany regained its sense of unity through the *Volksgeist*. It was the Germans' response to a conquering France. [. . .] The nation found solace from the humiliation it was suffering through the marvelous discovery of its culture. To forget their powerlessness they embraced everything Teutonic with a passion. In the name of German specificity they rejected the universal values of the French used to justify the hegemony of France.[32]

The early nineteenth century saw the rise of new Romantic movements based in Heidelberg, Berlin, and Dresden, which emphasized German history, folk songs and folk poetry as well as philology. Achim von Arnim and Clemens Brentano published an important selection of folk songs, the Brothers Grimm began to collect and publish folk stories, and Johann Gottlieb Fichte published his nationalist philosophical tract, *Reden an die Deutsche Nation* (Address to the German Nation) in 1807. Kleist started the nationalist journal *Abendblätter* (Evening News) in Berlin as well as a society that included Fichte, Brentano, Arnim, and others which stimulated many German historical dramas. Kleist himself wrote *Die Hermannsschlacht* (Hermann's battle), which he dedicated to "my fatherland" to take advantage of the nationalist spirit of the times, and *Prinz Friedrich von Homburg*.[33]

The German Romantic movement of the late eighteenth and nineteenth centuries, as Marvin Carlson has pointed out, significantly influenced dramatic literature and theatre production in Europe, such as the work of Oehlenschläger in Denmark, Victor Hugo in France, Kisfaludy and Katona in Hungary, Pushkin in Russia, Alfieri, Manzoni, and Niccolini in Italy, Kivi in Finland, and Yeats in Ireland.[34] Oehlenschläger, whose *Hakan Jarl* was written under the inspiration of Fichte in Berlin, echoed Herder in commenting that every nation "ought to have its own peculiarly national dramas. The peculiarly national is the finest flower of poetry."[35]

Likewise, opera and symphonic poems proved to be a powerful medium for National Romanticism. In Germany, E. T. A. Hoffman followed the eighteenth-century practice of using folk stories for themes in opera with his *Undine,* followed in 1821 by Carl Maria von Weber's *Der Freischütz.* Weber also flirted with the possibility of an opera based on the legendary character of Tannhäuser, anticipating the work of Richard Wagner. Franz Liszt developed the composition style of the symphonic or tone poem that used another work of art (such as a poem, play, story, or painting) as a source of inspiration and created a musical rendition of it, normally in one movement. Liszt used both German legends, such as Faust, and Greek myths for his source material, and inspired other Romantic nationalist composers such as Smetana and Sibelius to apply the genre to their domestic settings. Franz Schubert composed long song cycles to German Romantic poems, especially those of Wilhelm Müller.

Wagner developed the idea of a *gesamtkunstwerk* (total work of art) that would use folk legends as their subject. Unlike other opera composers, he wrote his own librettos, often exploiting German folklore. He celebrated the traditional poets and singing contests of Germany in *Tannhäuser* and *Die Meistersinger,* as well as employing old legends for *The Flying Dutchman, Parsifal, Lohengrin,* and *Tristan and Isolde.* Famously, he availed of the *Nibelungenlied* (though, perhaps surprisingly, the Nordic rather than the German version[36]) for his four-opera masterpiece *Der Ring des Nibelungen,* in which a strong sense of German geography is evoked with the images of the Rhein countryside in the final opera, *Götterdämmerung.* Wagner wrote in words echoing Herder, "To the operatic poet and composer falls the task of conjuring up the holy spirit of poetry as it comes to us in the sagas and legends of past ages." He also advised that artists focus on pre-Christian myths because Christianity had diluted the original popular spirituality: "Through the adoption of Christianity the folk has lost all true understanding of the original, vital

relations of the *mythos.*"[37] Notorious for his anti-Semitism and notions of racial purity and the superiority of the Aryan race, Wagner took nationalistic feelings (and egotism) to the extreme: "I am the most German of beings. I am the German spirit. Consider the incomparable magic of my works."[38] As a vehicle for his own work, he created the festival theatre in Bayreuth with the help of his admirer and patron King Ludwig II of Bavaria, and he was crowned with a silver laurel wreath after its opening season in 1876.

In Italy, Verdi composed operas with libretti adapted from five of the plays of Schiller, one of which, *Giovanna d'Arco,* contained especially strong nationalistic sentiments to which the audience responded. Moreover, his *Nabucco* in 1842, created a powerful metaphor for Italians wanting to unite Italy and overthrow Austrian rule. The beautiful "*Va, Pensiero*" chorus, in which the Jews sing of freedom from Babylonian captivity, contained the poignant lines: "*o mia patria sì bella e perduta*" (o my country so beautiful and lost). Significantly the hero of this song was the oppressed masses rather than an individual. According to Charles Osborne, "With this one chorus in an opera on a biblical subject, Verdi immediately [. . .] became the composer of the Risorgimento."[39] After working on Shakespearean themes such as *Macbeth* and *King Lear,*[40] Verdi was encouraged to return to nationalistic subjects by the Italian poet Giuseppe Giusti, who wrote to him, urging him to express "the sorrow that now fills the minds of us Italians [. . .], the sorrow of a race that feels the need of a better destiny."[41] Against the background of the 1848 revolution and the Milanese uprising against Austrian rule, Verdi composed *La Battaglia di Legnano* to a libretto by Cammarano about the twelfth-century defeat of the German King Barbarossa by the Italian cities of the Lombard League. Verdi also used libretti adapted from two anti-monarchist plays by Victor Hugo: *Ernani* (based on *Hernani*) and *Rigoletto* (based on *Le Roi s'amuse*). *Le Roi s'amuse,* about a scandalously immoral king, had been banned in France after its first performance in 1832 and Verdi's opera was likewise censored by the Austrian authorities. After a few compromises, the production was allowed to go ahead and proved to be a great success in various Italian theatres, often with a change in title to avoid censorship.

Likewise, in Bohemia, Smetana invoked the folk legend of the origins of the nation in his opera *Libuše,* as well as Czech historical characters in *Dalibor,* and folk characters in *The Bartered Bride.* Although deliberately not quoting from folk songs, Smetana created music that seemed imbued with folk music. In *The Bartered Bride,* according to Harold Schonberg, Smetana exploited "Bohemian polkas and other dance music, though he did not quote directly. He invented all of the melodies. The opera is so spiced with the very spirit of the country that many find this hard to believe, but Smetana was proud of his ability to avoid direct quotation."[42] As well as in these operas, Smetana's nationalism was perhaps best expressed in his cycle of symphonic poems *Má vlast* (My country) which included his ode to the river that runs through Prague, *Vltava* (The Moldau). Following Smetana in a similar spirit, Dvořák used the Undine legend for his opera *Rusalka*. Of him, Schonberg has written, "Nearly all of his best melodies are nationalistic. He was at his best when Bohemia took over; when, un-selfconsciously, he wrote music that expressed his native land and his love for it. He, like Smetana, seldom used actual folk themes, but his nationalism runs just as deep as Smetana's, and perhaps deeper."[43]

In Finland, Siebelius was inspired by Wagner's example of basing operas on national folk legends and tried to write a full-scale opera using Karelian mythology to be called *The Building of the Boat*. However, after a trip to Munich and Bayreuth, where he hoped to gain inspiration from seeing *Parsifal, Lohengrin,* and other Wagnerian operas, Sibelius, it seems, despaired of competing with Wagner's success and abandoned the effort. However, he used much of his material for a series of tone poems based on the *Kalevala* hero Lemminkäinen known as the *Lemminkäinen Suite*. The overture for *The Building of the Boat,* for example, was renamed *The Swan of Tuonela* (echoing perhaps the swan imagery in *Parsifal* and *Lohengrin*.)[44]

In many cases, national theatres were established to further the aims of the cultural nationalist movements.[45] For example, the German National Theatres in Hamburg and in Mannheim (which hired Lessing and Schiller respectively as employees), the Norwegian Theatre in Bergen, the National Theatre in Prague, the Finnish National Theatre in Helsinki, and the Abbey Theatre in Dublin closely interacted with their respective cultural nationalist movements. In territories with emerging nationalist movements as well as in established nation-states, plays and theatre performances became important sites for expressing new approaches to national identity. Marvin Carlson suggests that,

> Few of the emerging national/cultural groups of the post-romantic period neglected to utilize the drama as a powerful tool for awakening a people to a common heritage and, not infrequently, encouraging them through an awareness of this heritage to seek both national identity and national liberty in opposition to the demands of dominant and external political and cultural influences.[46]

In *Imagined Communities,* Benedict Anderson emphasizes this notion of "awakening" as a common trope for nascent nationalism, the sense that the people of the nation are "awakened" to the call of their "natural" national allegiances.[47] In the nationalist drama and the work of many national theatres of the nineteenth and early twentieth centuries, one can see the attempt to "awaken the nation" to what was professed as its natural sense of nationhood and to promote and foster a notion of national identity.

The national theatres played an important role in trying to construct distinctive national identities as well as in asserting the cultural achievements of their nations. Yet they often experienced initial growing pains. The National Theatre in Prague, which was perhaps more politically motivated than others, was imagined as early as the eighteenth century. In 1793 the Czech nationalist Prokop Šedivý, basing his arguments on Schiller's, called for an independent Czech theatre to unify the nation. After the 1848 revolution, a committee headed by Františčk Palacký, published an *Announcement* outlining their intentions to build a national theatre and simultaneously raising hopes for greater political autonomy: "Our national theatre will soon arise as a monument to our constitutional rights and equality."[48] Nevertheless, it took another thirty years to build the theatre, amidst considerable controversy. In Norway, the establishment of the national theatre in Bergen by Ole Bull led some critics to feel that the theatre was misplaced. The dramatist Bjørnstjerne Bjørnson, for example, while praising Bull's efforts, wrote that the national theatre should eventually be located in the nation's capital of Christiania (later Oslo).[49] Wagner, who became involved in the 1848 revolution and the uprising in Dresden against the Prussian King, proposed a national theatre for Dresden that would operate as a democratic institution with the director being elected, but his proposal was rejected.[50] Some countries such as Finland and Ireland had no history of indigenous drama before their nationalist movements began. The first major performance of a Finnish-language drama occurred in 1869, and Irish-language drama only began to be written at the beginning of the twentieth century. Nevertheless, well in advance of national independence, the national theatre companies in these two countries used the stage—even though theatre was an art form more associated with the cultural oppressor—to project notions of national identity in opposition to a dominant foreign culture.

The act of building a national theatre edifice was often a way of spreading the ideas of nationalism from the intellectual few to the masses and celebrating their communal endeavor. In Bohemia and Finland, for example, collections were made around the country for the construction of the theatre, and so the theatre became a commonly owned enterprise (at least in spirit if not in law). The foundation-laying ceremony for the Prague National Theatre took place at a time of patriotic protest as a result of the Czechs' disappointment in failing to gain autonomy on the occasion of the Austrian-Hungarian *ausgleich* (a compromise which gave Hungary special status). When the Prague national theatre was finally constructed twenty years later, the curtain tapestry facing the audience as they awaited the beginning of a performance reminded them of their spiritual ownership of the theatre in its depiction of images from the national collection of money for the new theatre.[51] According to the national theatre literature, the curtain also portrayed "artists and craftsmen" as well as "the coats of arms of the towns which the foundation stones for the National Theatre building came from."[52] The stones originated from "sacred places in the Czech national mythology and into whose mortar the leaders of the Czech people had poured water from the 'miraculous' Hostýn Spring."[53] Significantly, from the proscenium arch hung the slogan "Národ sobě!" (The Nation to Itself), and on the ceiling of the main foyer was painted a triptych of "The Golden Age of Art," "The Decline of Art," and the "Renaissance of Art," in which the national theatre building was shown being presented to the figure of Czechia. (Interestingly the design for another painting for the foyer depicting a Czech deity with a dog's head was rejected because such a pagan image was considered demeaning for the nation.) At the opening of the theatre in 1881 and at its reopening two years later, following a fire and massive renovation, Smetana's nationalistic opera *Libuše* was staged.

In Finland, in response to the Tsar's February 1899 Manifesto that threatened the country with a policy of Russification, nationalists seized the opportunity to assert their cultural independence by building a massive granite temple to their art near the center of Helsinki.[54] A national collection was made and the foundation-laying ceremony in 1900 occurred amidst a three-day singing event organized by the Fennomanic Society of Popular Education. The opening of the new cultural fortress in 1902, on the one-hundredth anniversary of Lönnrot's birth, heightened the sense of Finnish cultural achievement and brought together the new theatre and its ties to ancient Finnish culture and the *Kalevala* in a symbolic event. Because a statue of Lönnrot had failed to arrive in time from France because of poor weather conditions, it was particularly important that the theatre should be completed for Lönnrot's birthday. The workers worked feverishly to finish the building, and despite Russian governmental plans to delay its opening by demanding a sprinkler system, the building was finally declared safe by the inspectors on the evening before the event.

Naturally, the invitation list and the program for the occasion were major issues for the Board. Because of the political situation at the time, Finnish political figures argued that inviting Russian government officials (who in some cases had helped with providing money to complete the building) would be tantamount to treason, and they threatened to demonstrate and shame the Board at the celebration if the officials were invited. Such was the public interest in the event that the Board decided to hold two opening performances on the same evening,

and the celebrations continued for five days. The program included Aleksis Kivi's *Lea* and a new *Kalevala*-based play critical of Russian oppression by J. H. Erkko called *Pohjolan häät* (The Northland Wedding) which the censor almost prevented. The occasion also featured patriotic songs and a piece by Sibelius based on the 47th rune of the *Kalevala* that predicts a new race of Finnish heroes. The Finnish Literary Society (of which Lönnrot had been the first president) declared that,

> In all civilized countries the national theatre is considered the most powerful representative of the national poetry and use of artistic language, and therefore the moving of the Finnish Theatre to its magnificent fortress is to be seen as a very important victory in the same direction as Lönnrot has influenced more effectively than any other.[55]

The linguistic identity of national theatres was often one of their most crucial aspects. In Prague, the theatre staged plays and operas in Czech to overcome the dependence on German culture. In Norway the National Stage in Bergen introduced the Norwegian language to demonstrate its ascendancy over Danish (and Swedish). In the Finnish theatre, although some of the nationalists (such as Topelius) favored two branches of a national theatre, one in Swedish and one in Finnish, this position was rejected by nationalists, who stressed the importance of creating a Finnish language theatre. In Ireland the situation was a bit more complicated. The Irish language, which had been discouraged under British rule and had nearly disappeared, was again a powerful tool in the hands of the Irish nationalists. Plays in Irish including Douglas Hyde's *Casadh an tSúgáin* (The Twisting of the Rope), which was staged by the Irish Literary Theatre in 1901, provided blatant expressions of a distinctive Irish identity and evoked strong nationalist feelings when they were performed. Moreover, in the future company, the Irish actors would be expected to perform both in Irish and in English. However, compared to other countries, fewer of the Irish nationalist leadership managed to master the Irish language, which was spoken by a small minority. In a sense a compromise was proposed in the use of a Hiberno-English language in drama, such as in the work of J. M. Synge, that inserted a mixture of Irish syntax and translated Irish expressions into English and thereby made the language a distinctive cultural hybrid. According to Declan Kiberd, "Synge saw that a deterritorialized Irish might yet deterritorialize English."[56] Moreover, this compromise enabled a wider market for Irish plays and for tours by the Abbey Theatre, not only in Ireland but also abroad and particularly to England and the U.S.A.

Often the building of a national theatre was accompanied by the demand and in some cases the development of an acting school, which would help educate the actors to speak correctly. In countries where the national language (such as Czech, Hungarian, and Finnish) had not yet been securely established as a medium for high culture, the correct use and pronunciation of the language on the national stage was a major issue in creating national theatres and ultimately became an important feature for the audience and a topic on which the critics frequently commented. In Hungary, the Parliament assigned the Academy of Sciences the role of establishing a national theatre as part of its function in "the institutional cultivation of the Hungarian language."[57] In Germany the term *Bühnensprache* (stage language) as a term for correct pronunciation indicates the role of the theatre in helping to standardize the German language.[58]

The repertory of each theatre was of course a major concern to the nationalists. The nationalist canon often included plays about historical or legendary figures engaged in the nation-building or national liberation process or in some way representing certain nationalistic ideals, such as *Wilhelm Tell* in Switzerland (and Germany), *Joan of Arc* in France, *Libuše* in Bohemia, *Boris Godunov* in Russia, and *Cathleen Ni Houlihan* in Ireland. In some cases national figures in one country were borrowed for similar purposes in another. Joan of Arc, for example was serviceable in several countries as a cross-cultural archetype. Schiller's play *Die Jungfrau von Orleans* (The Maid of Orleans) was used as the basis for a libretto for Verdi's opera *Giovanna d'Arco*, and was immediately appreciated in Italy for its nationalistic rhetoric. In a production of the opera in Palermo two years later, the police intervened, necessitating the performance of the music to a different libretto.[59]

As previously mentioned, the repertory also included characters from the local mythological and folkloric tales such as the Norse and Germanic epics in Scandinavia and Germany. More interestingly, the repertory also featured dramas about anti-heroes that sometimes caused controversy when they first appeared in print or on the stage (such as Ibsen's *Peer Gynt,* Synge's *Playboy of the Western World,* and Aleksis Kivi's novel *Seven Brothers,* which was later adapted for the stage). Often these plays about anti-heroes were sanitized in subsequent stage productions, and the characters were accepted as loveable national figures in spite of their roguish or amoral behavior (and, in some cases, the author's implicit attack on society). Sometimes, particular sections of such plays, for instance the fourth act of *Peer Gynt* (which featured an Ibsenian attack on Norwegian nationalists who wished to purify the Norwegian language of foreign influences), were omitted because of their problematic nature.[60]

While national theatre directors were often anxious to include both foreign classics as well as domestic drama in the repertory, they frequently ran the risk of offending nationalists who wished to promote the distinctiveness of the national culture. Echoing the sentiments of

Herder as well as Hans Sachs' aria at the end of Wagner's *Die Meistersinger* that praises "holy German art," several eminent artists in Finland tried to create a sacred Finnish theatre style. Images from the *Kalevala* were deployed in drama, *tableau vivant* theatre performances (several with music composed by Sibelius for the occasion), and concerts, as well as in the celebrated paintings of Akseli Gallen-Kallela. The Finnish dramatist, Kasimir Leino, in an article entitled "Individual art and the Possibility of a Finnish Stage Style," accused the Finnish director Bergbom of imitating a foreign style and urged that theatre art be nationalistic and be created from domestic elements.[61] Likewise, Yeats was accused by nationalists in Ireland of being too influenced by Wagner and by Japanese Noh theatre.

At the turn of the century in the Irish Theatre, the issues of race, historical and mythical memory, religion, and language became critical in the debates over the repertory and the methods for illustrating the collective identity of the Irish people. In 1899, John Eglinton asked where the Irish dramatist should look for "the subject of a national drama. [. . .] Would he look for it in the Irish legends, or in the life of the peasantry and folk-lore, or in Irish history and patriotism, or in life at large as reflected in his own consciousness?" Eglinton recommended the path chosen by the Greeks and the Germans:

> The ancient legends of Ireland undoubtedly contain situations and characters as well suited for drama as most of those used in the Greek tragedies which have come down to us. It is clear that if Celtic traditions are to be an active influence in future Irish literature [. . .] we must go to them rather than expect them to come to us, studying them as closely as possible, and allowing them to influence us as they may. The significance of that interest in folklore and antiquities, which is so strong in this country, can hardly be different from that of the writings of [Johann Gottfried] Herder and others in German literature.[62]

Yeats and others recognized the power of the theatre to influence the nationalist movement, and they looked for appropriate symbols for a new national identity. In a letter to Gilbert Murray (suggesting a version of *Oedipus Rex* for the Abbey), Yeats wrote, "Here one never knows when one may affect the mind of a whole generation. The country is in its first plastic state, and takes the mark of every strong finger."[63] Yeats also indicated his debt to the ideas of German and Norwegian nationalists: "The national movement must learn to found itself, like the national movement of Norway, upon language and history."[64] In founding the Irish Literary Theatre, the organizers asserted that the theatre should project a new image of the Irish character, as opposed to the stereotype of the stage Irish buffoon which had been generated by the English theatre: "We will show that Ireland is not the home of buffoonery and of easy sentiment, as it has been represented, but the home of an ancient idealism. We are confident of the support of all Irish people, who are weary of misrepresentation."[65] At the same time, Yeats was never comfortable with simply presenting nationalist sentiments and often challenged his audience by using nationalist rhetoric for the theatre enterprise but presenting images on the stage that were discordant with that rhetoric.

As a result of German Romanticism, national theatres looked to mythical, historical, and rural characters in order to provide national protagonists who would help to define the character of the "awakened" nation. Cultural nationalists often blurred the border between folklore and history. As we have seen, some nationalists in Finland celebrated the characters in the *Kalevala* as historical. Likewise, Irish nationalists used folklore to create a national mythology about ancient Irish history that helped distinguish themselves from the English colonists. In Bohemia legendary stories about the origins of the Czech royal family became the subject matter of plays and operas. Plays dealing with folkloric heroes helped authenticate the folk culture and construct alternative histories to those that had been imposed by the dominant cultures. The legendary characters and stories that were created became an important source for inculcating notions of national identity. While Wagner exploited the *Nibelungenlied*, Finnish dramatists used the *Kalevala* and Irish playwrights the *Táin*. Yeats wrote a cycle of plays about Cuchulainn including the tragedy *On Baile Strand*. For inspiration, Yeats not only studied Wagner and Ibsen but also the *Kalevala*.[66] In Hutchinson's assessment, Yeats' vision of Irish theatre was attempting through an integration of the arts—poetry, music, stage décor, costume, and lighting—as in Wagner's music-drama, to suggest a higher symbolic reality. For Yeats the Irish theatre would be a national shrine, in which, presenting a unified cycle of plays based on Irish legend, focusing in particular on the warrior hero Cuchulain, he would project the Irish archetype into the national consciousness.[67]

In his play *Cathleen Ni Houlihan* in 1902, Yeats created a nationalist archetype, who was mythical but rooted in history. Yeats, who collaborated with Lady Gregory in writing it, set the play in the context of the 1798 rebellion led by Wolfe Tone, but avoided the obvious strategy of characterizing the male leader. Instead, he created a mythical figure of mother Ireland calling out her sons to fight for their country. As the spirit of a suppressed people longing for independence, she speaks in metaphors to an audience on stage as well as in the audience, urging them to fight for independence. She complains that there are "too many strangers in the house" and that her "four beautiful green fields" (the four provinces of Ireland) have been taken from her. She inevitably persuades a young man about to marry to go off with her to fight for the country as she warns, "They

that have red cheeks will have pale cheeks for my sake, and for all that, they will think they are well paid. They shall be remembered forever. They shall be alive forever. They shall be speaking forever. The people shall hear them forever."[68] This national image conflated the historical with the mythical, historicizing myth and mythologizing history. Maud Gonne helped legitimate the character that she not only played but also simultaneously ghosted since she was not known as an actress but as one of the leading nationalists and one of the most radical opponents of British rule.[69]

As already discussed, European national theatres exploited their folk traditions and folk poetry as suggested by German philosophers such as Herder. In many countries, the early cultural nationalists who exploited these traditions belonged to the elite of society, but as cultural nationalism spread, they had to vie for authority with a second wave of nationalists who represented the middle or lower-middle class and the core community.[70] What often solidified the movements in the different countries was the notion fostered by cultural nationalists of a common identity amongst the various strata of society. As Wachtel has observed of the nationalist movements in the Austro-Hungarian Empire,

> The glue that held these movements together was cultural and linguistic rather than political, and it is the cultural basis for these movements that explains why, even today, those nineteenth century writers, composers, and artists who dipped into the wellsprings of the national folk culture for their inspiration are treated as national heroes throughout Eastern and Central Europe—Petöfi, Mickiewicz, Mácha, Prešeren, Smetana, and Dvořák are the George Washingtons and Thomas Jeffersons of the former subject peoples of the Austro-Hungarian Empire.[71]

To this list of national heroes could be added many others playwrights and theatre directors, including those whose work was initially rejected. Realism in a mythic-heroic world or positive images of rural life suited Romantic notions but too much reality or social criticism was problematic. As the Subaltern Studies Collective has argued, nationalism claims to represent and speak for all the people of the nation, but in reality it is very selective and excludes numerous voices such as the working class and women.[72]

Similarly, the ugly side of nationalism, particularly apparent in the fascist movements of the 1930s, used the symbols of national identity, fostered in the nineteenth century, to exclude dissident, alternative, multicultural, and multiracial elements of the population. It is not surprising that some of those people associated with the earlier national theatre movement became involved with fascist and right-wing organizations, and that Yeats, for example, wrote lyrics for the Irish Blue Shirts in the 1930s.

The notions of national identity remain a product of nineteenth-century myth-making by cultural nationalists who were influenced by the values and ideals of Johann von Herder and German nationalism and Romanticism. Although the social circumstances in the various countries were somewhat different in the late nineteenth century, the process was similar. The national theatres helped construct and promote notions of national identity by putting various types of national protagonist on the stage and trying them out in front of a live audience who could accept or reject them. In this sense, the theatres acted as a "daily plebiscite" in determining, inventing, and assessing national character and images of the nation.[73]

Notes

1. Some parts of this article appeared earlier in my essay "German Romanticism and its Influence on Finnish and Irish Theatre" 15-70.

2. Herder, *Sämmtliche Werke,* vol. 2, 246. Trans. Anna Lohse.

3. For example, Henri Pirenne in his *Histoire de la Belgique* tried to prove the existence of a Belgian people, hence nation, dating back to the Roman period. Benedict Anderson has observed, "If nation-states are widely conceded to be 'new' and 'historical,' the nations to which they give political expression always loom out of an immemorial past." Benedict Anderson, *Imagined Communities* 11. Also, Ernest Gellner argues, "The cultural shreds and patches used by nationalism are often arbitrary historical inventions. Any old shred would have served as well. [. . .] Nationalism is not what it seems. [. . .] The cultures it claims to defend and revive are often its own inventions, or are modified out of all recognition." Ernest Gellner, *Nations and Nationalism* 56. Although the dissemination of such political and cultural ideas throughout Europe was assisted by political events such as the American Revolution in 1775 and the French Revolution in 1789 (both of which promoted the importance of individual human rights), German nationalism stressed the sovereignty of the nation as opposed to the sovereignty of the individual. Rather than the Kantian idea that the common people should be voluntary participants in a state and could equally opt out of it and go somewhere else. Herder's ideas carried a notion of obligation on the part of the people to belong to a particular nation that was their natural place of belonging. This sense of obligation allowed intellectuals and political leaders later on to exert a certain coercive force in imploring the common people to sacrifice themselves for the greater glory of their nation, for their fatherland or motherland.

4. Greenblatt, *Shakespearean Negotiations* 4-5.

5. Renan, "What Is a Nation?" 154.

6. John Hutchinson, *Dynamics of Cultural Nationalism* 9.

7. Herder, *Sämmtliche Werke,* vol. 9, 528-9. Trans. Anna Lohse.

8. Herder, *Sämmtliche Werke,* vol. 9, 525. Trans. Anna Lohse.

9. Goethe collected twelve Alsatian songs on his travels in 1771 for the publication. See Ergang, *Herder and German Nationalism* 210.

10. According to Robert Ergang, Herder also coined the terms *Volkspoesie* and *Volksdichtung.* Ergang, *Herder and German Nationalism* 198, note 3.

11. See Robert Ergang, *Herder and German Nationalism* 203.

12. Ergang, 197.

13. Herder, *Sämmtliche Werke,* vol. 16, 389. Trans. Anna Lohse.

14. See Hugh Trevor-Roper, "The Invention of Tradition" 15-41.

15. See Christa Kamenetsky, "The German Folklore Revival in the Eighteenth Century" 843.

16. David Sayer, *The Coasts of Bohemia* 144-147.

17. Interview with Professor László Keresztes, 8 April 2000.

18. See Wilson, *Folklore and Nationalism* 40.

19. See Wilson, *Folklore and Nationalism* 49-53.

20. Wilson, *Folklore and Nationalism* 206.

21. On reading Douglas Hyde's *Literary History,* Sir Fredrick Burton wrote to Lady Gregory, "Now true light has been let in and Irish history, archaeology, literature, and poetry are the gainers. Let us not grudge to the Germans their [n]eed of honour in having led the way." Augusta Gregory, *Our Irish Theatre* 42.

22. James Pethica, *Lady Gregory's Diaries* 290.

23. Qtd. in *Sunday Times,* Irish ed., 14 November 1999: 3. See also Simon James, *The Atlantic Celts,* which questions the existence of Irish Celts.

24. Gregory, *Our Irish Theatre* 21.

25. Lessing, *Hamburgische Dramaturgie* 14: 76. Trans. Anna Lohse.

26. Lessing, *Minna von Barnhelm* 90. Trans. Anna Lohse.

27. A. W. Schlegel, *A Course of Lectures* I, 30; II, 403.

28. C. M. Wieland, "Briefe an einen jungen Dichter" 3, 478. Trans. Anna Lohse.

29. Goethe, however, drew away from Herder's ideas later in life, arguing for an international rather than a national approach to literature. See Alain Finkielkraut, *The Defeat of the Mind* 37.

30. Goethe, however, considered some of "the martial feelings of defiance" as dangerous. Qtd. in Marvin Carlson, "Nationalism and the Romantic Drama in Europe" 141.

31. Schiller, *Werke in drei Bänden,* vol.1, 728. Trans. Anna Lohse.

32. Alain Finkielkraut, *The Defeat of the Mind,* New York: Columbia University Press, 1995.

33. It was not produced because it failed to please the authorities owing to weaknesses in the character of the Prince.

34. See Marvin Carlson, "Nationalism and the Romantic Drama in Europe" 139-152.

35. Qtd. in Marvin Carlson, "Nationalism and the Romantic Drama in Europe" 142.

36. *The Nibelungenlied* 215-216.

37. Qtd. in Harold C. Schonberg, *The Lives of the Great Composers* 257.

38. Harold C. Schonberg, *The Lives of the Great Composers* 264.

39. Charles Osborne, *The Complete Operas of Verdi* 52.

40. He worked on *King Lear* for many years but never completed it.

41. Qtd. in Charles Osborne, *The Complete Operas of Verdi* 189.

42. Harold C. Schonberg, *The Lives of the Great Composers* 366.

43. Harold C. Schonberg, *The Lives of the Great Composers* 368.

44. *The Swan of Tuonela* soon became recognized as Sibelius's "first incontestable masterpiece" and the series of pieces, known as the *Lemminkäinen Suite,* achieved a more marked success even than *Kullervo* had enjoyed." Rickards, *Jean Sibelius* 58.

45. Writing of the theatres in Northern and Eastern Europe, Laurence Senelick has argued, "Most national theatres arose in reaction to a dominant culture imposed from without; they were a means of protest as well as of preserving what were considered to be salient features of the oppressed group. Theatre was a catalytic factor in the formation of its identity. So, Norwegian theatre struggled to divorce itself from Danish influence, Finnish theatre renounced Swedish [and Russian] elements, Estonian and Latvian theatre tried to extirpate their German antecedents. The Austrian hegemony was opposed in Bohemia, Moravia, Slovenia and Hungary, while Slovakia and Upper Croatia tried to overthrow the yoke of Magyar culture; the Russian hegemony was violently rejected in Poland and Lithuania." Laurence Senelick, "Recovering Repressed Memories: Writing Russian Theatre History" (in *Writing and Rewriting National Theatre Histories,* ed. S.E. Wilmer, Iowa University Press, 2004) 50.

46. Marvin Carlson, "Nationalism and the Romantic Drama" 152.

47. Anderson, *Imagined Communities* 195.

48. Qtd. in Kimball, *Czech Nationalism* 39. See also František Černý, "Idea Národního divadla" 17-25.

49. Laurence Senelick, ed., *National Theatre in Northern and Eastern Europe, 1746-1900* 151.

50. See *New Grove Dictionary of Opera,* vol. IV, 1056.

51. This was in fact the second curtain because the first, with a different design, was destroyed in a fire shortly after the opening of the theatre in 1881.

52. The first curtain tapestry with a neoclassical image designed by Ženíšek was destroyed in the fire, and Hynais was commissioned to produce a new version for the reopening in 1883. The design proved quite controversial with the Committee responsible for the reconstruction. See *Národní Divadlo* 40.

53. *Národní Divadlo* 98.

54. Although the location was somewhat peripheral to Senate Square, it was located next to the central train station and across from the Atheneum art school. The organizers were disappointed that they could not obtain a more central location.

55. Aspelin-Haapkylä, *Suomalaisen teatterin historia* 4: 187.

56. Declan Kiberd, *Inventing Ireland* 174. See also Josephine Lee, "Linguistic Imperialism" 165-181.

57. Laurence Senelick, ed., *National Theatre in Northern and Eastern Europe* 287.

58. See Michael Patterson, *The First German Theatre* 9. For a discussion of the standardization of languages, see Ronald Wardhaugh, *Introduction to Sociolinguistics* 33-37.

59. Osborne, *The Complete Operas of Verdi* 108.

60. See Sarah Bryant-Bertail, *Space and Time in Epic Theatre* 122.

61. Reitala, "Kalevalainen esitysperinne Suomalaisessa teatterissa vuoteen 1912" 75.

62. Eglinton, "What Should be the Subjects of National Drama?" 386-8.

63. Yeats to Gilbert Murray, 24 January 1905, qtd. in D. R. Clark and J. B. McGuire, *W. B. Yeats: The Writing of Sophocles' King Oedipus* 8.

64. Chicago *Daily News,* 16 March 1903, qtd. in R. F. Foster, *W. B. Yeats: A Life,* vol. 1, 291.

65. Qtd. in Hugh Hunt, *The Abbey* 18.

66. Tawastjerna, *Sibelius,* vol. 1, 168.

67. Hutchinson, *Dynamics of Cultural Nationalism* 134.

68. Edward Said in his *Culture and Imperialism* discusses Yeats' poetry at length but fails to mention this play, which would undermine his argument that Yeats never approved of liberation. See, for example, 224.

69. Various actors longed to play the character after Maud Gonne, including Maire Quinn and even Lady Gregory. See Maud Gonne letter to W. B. Yeats, 3 January 1903, *The Gonne-Yeats Letters 1893-1938,* 161, and Mary Lou Kohfeldt, *Lady Gregory* 259.

70. For a discussion of the development of a mass nationalist movement in Finland from 1870 to 1900, see Liikanen, *Fennomania.*

71. Wachtel, *Making a Nation* 21.

72. See Ania Loomba, *Colonialism/Postcolonialism* 197-199.

73. Ernest Renan, "What Is a Nation?" 154.

Works Cited

Anderson, Benedict. *Imagined Communities,* rev. ed. London: Verso, 1995.

Aspelin-Haapkylä, Eliel. *Suomalaisen teatterin historia.* Helsinki: SKS, 1906-1910.

Bryant-Bertail, Sarah. *Space and Time in Epic Theatre: The Brechtian Legacy.* Rochester: Camden House, 2000.

Carlson, Marvin. "Nationalism and the Romantic Drama in Europe." *Romantic Drama.* Ed. Gerald Gillespie. Amsterdam: John Benjamins Publishing Co., 1994.

Černý, František. "Idea Národního divadla." *Divadlo v české kultuře 19.století.* Prague: Národní galerie v Praze, 1985.

Clark, D. R., and J. B. McGuire. *W. B. Yeats: The Writing of Sophocles' King Oedipus.* Philadelphia: American Philosophical Society, 1989.

Eglinton, John. "What Should Be the Subjects of National Drama?" *Modern Irish Drama.* Ed. John Harrington. New York: W.W. Norton, 1991.

Ergang, Robert. *Herder and German Nationalism.* New York: Columbia University Press, 1931.

Finkielkraut, Alain. *The Defeat of the Mind.* New York: Columbia University Press, 1995.

Foster, R. F. *W. B. Yeats: A Life.* Oxford: Oxford University Press, 1997.

Gellner, Ernest. *The Gonne-Yeats Letters 1893-1938.* Eds. White and Jeffares. London: Pimlico, 1993.

———. *Nations and Nationalism.* Oxford: Basil Blackwell, 1983.

Greenblatt, Stephen. *Shakespearean Negotiations.* Berkeley: University of California Press, 1988.

Gregory, Augusta. *Our Irish Theatre.* New York: Capricorn Books, 1965.

Herder, Johann von. *Sämmtliche Werke.* Ed. Bernhard Suphan. Berlin: Weidmannsche Buchhandlung, 1877.

Hunt, Hugh. *The Abbey: Ireland's National Theatre, 1904-1979.* Dublin: Gill and Macmillan, 1979.

Hutchinson, John. *Dynamics of Cultural Nationalism.* London: Allen & Unwin, 1987.

James, Simon. *The Atlantic Celts: Ancient People or Modern Invention?* London: British Museum Press, 1999.

Kamenetsky, Christa. "The German Folklore Revival in the Eighteenth Century: Herder's Theory of *Naturpoesie.*" *Journal of Popular Culture* VI.4 (Spring 1973).

Kiberd, Declan. *Inventing Ireland: The Literature of the Modern Nation.* London: Jonathan Cape, 1995.

Kimball, Stanley Buchholz. *Czech Nationalism: A Study of the National Theatre Movement, 1845-83.* Urbana: Illinois University Press, 1964.

Kohfeldt, Mary Lou. *Lady Gregory.* London: André Deutsch, 1985.

Lee, Josephine. "Linguistic Imperialism, the Early Abbey Theatre, and the *Translations* of Brian Friel." *Imperialism and Theatre: Essays on World Theatre, Drama and Performance.* Ed. J. Ellen Gaynor. London: Routledge, 1995.

Lessing, Gotthold Ephraim. *Hamburgische Dramaturgie. Lessings Werke,* Fünfter Teil. Mit Einleitung von Julius Petersen. Berlin: Deutsches Verlagshaus Bong & Co., 1910.

————. *Minna von Barnhelm.* Eds. W. F. Leopold and C. R. Goedsche. Boston: D. C. Heath and Company, 1937.

Liikanen, Ilkka. *Fennomania ja kansa. Joukkojärjestäytymisen läpimurto ja Suomalaisen puolueen synty.* Jyväskylä: SHS, 1995.

Loomba, Ania. *Colonialism/Postcolonialism.* London: Routledge, 1998.

————. *Národní Divadlo: History and Present Day of the Building.* Prague: Národní Divadlo, 1999.

————. *New Grove Dictionary of Opera.* Ed. Stanley Sadie. New York: Macmillan, 1997.

————. *The Nibelungenlied.* Trans. Helen M. Mustard. *Medieval Epics.* New York: Modern Library, 1963.

Osborne, Charles. *The Complete Operas of Verdi.* New York: Da Capo, 1977.

Patterson, Michael. *The First German Theatre.* London: Routledge, 1990.

Pethica, James. *Lady Gregory's Diaries, 1892-1902.* Gerrards Cross: Colin Smythe, 1996.

Reitala, Heta. "Kalevalainen esitysperinne Suomalaisessa teatterissa vuoteen 1912." Teatteritieteen pääainetutkielma, Helsinki University, 1990.

Renan, Ernest. "What Is a Nation?" *The Nationalism Reader.* Eds. Dahbour and Ishay. Amherst, NY: Humanity Books, 1995.

Rickards, Guy. *Jean Sibelius.* London: Phaidon Press, 1997.

Said, Edward. *Culture and Imperialism.* New York: Vintage, 1994.

Sayer, David. *The Coasts of Bohemia.* Cambridge: Cambridge University Press, 1998.

Schiller, Friedrich. *Werke in drei Bänden.* Munich: Hanser, 1976.

Schlegel, A. W. *A Course of Lectures on Dramatic Art and Literature.* Trans. John Black. London: J. Templeman, J. R. Smith, 1840.

Schonberg, Harold C. *The Lives of the Great Composers.* New York: W.W. Norton, 1970.

Senelick, Laurence, ed. *National Theatre in Northern and Eastern Europe, 1746-1900.* Cambridge: Cambridge University Press, 1991.

————. "Recovering Repressed Memories: Writing Russian Theatre History." *Writing and Rewriting National Theatre Histories.* Ed. S. E. Wilmer. Iowa City: Iowa University Press, 2004.

Tawaststjerna, Erik. *Sibelius.* Trans. Robert Layton. London: Faber and Faber, 1976.

Trevor-Roper, Hugh. "The Invention of Tradition: The Highland Tradition of Scotland." *The Invention of Tradition.* Eds. Eric Hobsbawm and Terence Ranger. Cambridge: Cambridge University Press, 1983.

Wachtel, Andrew B. *Making a Nation, Breaking a Nation: Literature and Cultural Politics in Yugoslavia.* Stanford: Stanford University Press, 1998.

Wardhaugh, Ronald. *An Introduction to Sociolinguistics.* Fourth ed. Oxford: Blackwell, 2002.

Wieland, C. M. "Briefe an einen jungen Dichter." *Brief, Werke.* Munich: Carl Hanser, 1967.

Wilmer, S. E. "German Romanticism and Its Influence on Finnish and Irish Theatre." *Theatre, History, and National Identities.* Ed. Helka Makinen, S. E. Wilmer, and W. B. Worthen. Helsinki: Helsinki University Press, 2001.

Wilson, William A. *Folklore and Nationalism in Modern Finland.* Bloomington: Indiana University Press, 1976.

FURTHER READING

Criticism

Askedal, John Ole. "Johann Gottfried Herder's Conception of the Origin of Language." In *Semiotics around the World: Synthesis in Diversity, I-II. Approaches to Semiotics,* edited by Irmengard Rauch and Gerald F. Carr, pp. 183-86. Berlin, Germany: Mouton de Gruyter, 1997.

> Maintains that "Herder's theory of language is . . . a fairly coherent theory of linguistic sign constitution, where considerable attention is devoted to language evolution and change."

Baildam, John D. *Paradisal Love: Johann Gottfried Herder and the Song of Songs.* Sheffield, England: Sheffield Academic, 1999, 368 p.

> Book-length assessment of how The Song of Songs informs Herder's theories, illustrating the author's "unique interpretation of the work as the voice of pure, paradisal love."

Broce, Gerald. "Herder and Ethnography." *Journal of the History of the Behavioral Sciences* 22, no. 2 (April 1986): 150-70.

> Highlights the importance of the ethnographical content in Herder's works, and asserts that the author's scientific description of cultures is closely related to his views on German nationalism and his experience as a travel writer.

Chase, Bob. "Herder and the Postcolonial Reconfiguring of the Enlightenment." *Bucknell Review* 41, no. 2 (1998): 172-96.

Argues that scholars should re-configure philosophical classifications rather than characterize Herder as part of a "counter-Enlightenment" group of thinkers.

Grossman, Jeffrey. "Herder and the Language of Diaspora Jewry." *Monatshefte* 86, no. 1 (spring 1994): 59-79.

Describes the influence Herder's humanist and linguistic theories had upon "intellectual discourse and the institutions of the Prussian state at the turn-of-the-nineteenth-century" and how this affected Jewish culture and the treatment of Jews.

Koepke, Wulf. "Herder's Craft of Communication." In *The Philosopher as Writer: The Eighteenth Century,* edited by Robert Ginsberg, pp. 94-121. London: Associated University Presses, 1987.

Focuses on how Herder's "system of metaphors" is informed by the author's "views on language, style, and communication."

Menges, Karl. "Herder and the 'Querelle des Anciens et des Modernes.'" In *Eighteenth-Century German Authors and Their Aesthetic Theories: Literature and the Other Arts,* edited by Richard Critchfield and Wulf Koepke, pp. 147-83. Columbia, S.C.: Camden House, 1988.

Consider Herder's treatment of the literary debate, dubbed the "Querelle des Anciens et des Modernes," that began in seventeenth-century France, within the context of various German philosophers' responses to the debate.

———. "Identity as Difference: Herder's 'Great Topic' and the 'Philosophers of Paris.'" *Monatshefte* 87, no. 1 (spring 1995): 6-18.

Investigates Herder's repudiation of French Enlightenment thought despite the author's "life-long dedication to the improvement of the human condition."

Menze, Ernest A. "'Gang Gottes über die Nationen': The Religious Roots of Herder's *Auch eine Philosophie* Revisited." *Monatshefte* 92, no. 1 (spring 2000): 10-19.

Concentrates on the manner in which religion informs Herder's humanist philosophy.

Morton, Michael. "The Infinity of Finitude: Criticism, History, and Herder." *Herder Yearbook* 1 (1992): 23-58.

Delineates how Herder anticipates later scholars' conclusions regarding the nature of reality.

Mücke, Dorothea E. Von. "Pygmalion's Dream in Herder's Aesthetics: Or, Male Narcissism as the Model for *Bildung.*" *Studies in Eighteenth-Century Culture* 19 (1989): 349-65.

Studies the concept of *Bildung* within Herder's treatment of the "soul-shaping impact of an aesthetic object" as well as his notion of "the ideal relation between the subject and the aesthetic object" in his works on sculpture.

Norton, Robert. "Racism, History, and Physiognomy: Herder and the Tradition of Moral Beauty in the Eighteenth Century." In *Ethik und Ästhetik: Werke und Werte in der Literatur vom 18. bis zum 20. Jahrhundert. Forschungen zur Literatur- und Kulturgeschichte. 52,* edited by Richard Fisher, pp. 43-54. Frankfurt: Peter Lang, 1995.

Assesses the intent of Herder's essay "Ist die Schönheit des Körpers ein Bote von der Schönheit der Seele?" as supportive of the racist tenets of physiognomy, which equates morality with physical appearance.

Salmon, Paul. "Herder's *Abhandlung über den Ursprung der Sprache*: Reception and Reputation." In *'Das unsichtbare Band der Sprache': Studies in German Language and Linguistic History in Memory of Leslie Seiffer,* edited by John L. Flood, Paul Salmon, Olive Sayce, and Christopher Wells, pp. 253-77. Stuttgart: Heinz Akademischer, 1993.

Offers a close analysis of Herder's essay, *Abhandlung über den Ursprung der Sprache.*

Additional coverage of Herder's life and career is contained in the following sources published by Thomson Gale: *Dictionary of Literary Biography,* **Vol. 97;** *European Writers,* **Vol. 4;** *Literature Resource Center;* **Nineteenth-Century Literature Criticism, Vol. 8; and** *Twayne's World Authors.*

Theodore Parker
1810-1860

(Also wrote under the pseudonym Levi Blodgett) American preacher, lecturer, essayist, critic, autobiographer, and poet.

INTRODUCTION

Theodore Parker was a controversial figure in America during the period known as the American Literary Renaissance, or New England Renaissance. Although he was an active Unitarian minister and regarded as a prominent theologian, Parker became well-known for his lectures and essays, and in particular for his steadfast support of various reform movements of the time, including women's rights and the abolition of slavery. He famously clashed with church leaders over issues of theology and church doctrine, and as a result he was hailed as a visionary by some and as an infidel by others. Parker was also widely regarded as an abrasive, stubborn man, and he appeared to embrace this image. His visibility as an active member of reform movements distinguish him from other well-known Transcendentalists of this period, such as Ralph Waldo Emerson, who chose to disengage from active debate over reform issues.

BIOGRAPHICAL INFORMATION

Born in Lexington, Massachusetts on August 24, 1810, Parker was the youngest son of eleven children born to John and Hannah Stearns Parker. John Parker was a farmer and the son of Captain John Parker, who led the Lexington minutemen in the famous first battle of the Revolutionary War on the morning of April 19, 1775. Because of his grandfather's legacy, Parker grew up with a strong belief in the active pursuit of liberty and in the virtue of resistance to tyranny and oppression. Parker's mother died when he was eleven, and by the time Parker was twenty-eight, only two of his siblings were still living. Parker spent his youth working on the family farm, and educated himself through extensive reading and obsessive study in an effort to leave the rural life behind. As a young adult he worked as a schoolteacher, and in 1834 he entered Harvard Divinity School to become a minister. Because of his intensive self-education, Parker finished the three-year Harvard program in two years, and was able to read twenty languages when he graduated in 1836. In 1837 Parker was

ordained as a minister, assumed leadership of a congregation in West Roxbury, a village outside of Boston, and married Lydia Cabot. Their marriage was, by all accounts, very unhappy; his wife's family members were reportedly incensed by Parker's defiance of church authority, and this had a tremendously detrimental effect on the couple's relationship. Parker maintained a rigorous schedule of traveling, lecturing, preaching, and writing until 1859, when he developed tuberculosis and his physicians urged him to move to a warm climate and rest. He and his wife traveled to the Virgin Islands, where he compiled his autobiography, *Theodore Parker's Experience as a Minister* (1859). In the summer of 1859 the Parkers left the West Indies and sailed to Europe, where after a period of slightly improved health, Parker succumbed to his disease in Rome on May 10, 1860.

MAJOR WORKS

Parker firmly aligned himself with the Transcendentalist movement after hearing Emerson's Divinity School Address in Cambridge on July 15, 1838. He became actively involved in the controversy over whether the source of religious truth was external (evident in the physical world or in the records of historical events handed down by our ancestors) or internal (a result of human intuition and personal consciousness). Parker argued for the internal locus of religious truth, which reflected the Transcendentalist position on the issue. This position was considered radical at best, and heretical at worst by those members of the church leadership who held that the teachings of Jesus Christ were the external—and sole—source of religious truth, being the means by which God's word was communicated to humankind. In his sermon, *A Discourse on the Transient and Permanent in Christianity* (1841), and in a series of lectures that he delivered in Boston during 1841 and 1842 that were collected in *A Discourse of Matters Pertaining to Religion* (1842), Parker outlined his religious philosophy, defining God as a logical objectification of the universal human apprehension of religious truth, and explaining how this related to Jesus Christ, Christian traditions and doctrine, and to the Bible. Although he offered great praise for and deference to Jesus Christ, unlike some of his fellow Transcendentalists, Parker's theological stance alienated him from some of the members of the Boston Association, the organization of Christian ministers to which he belonged. Parker subsequently became the minister to the independent Twenty-Eighth Congregational Society which was formed by a group of Boston gentlemen. By 1845 Parker had become a popular lecturer in Boston, as well as an active voice in social reform movements, evidenced in such works as *A Sermon of War, Preached at the Melodeon, on Sunday, June 7, 1846* (1846) and *A Letter to the People of the United States Touching the Matter of Slavery*, a pamphlet published in 1848. *Theodore Parker's Experience as a Minister* offers not only a detailed account of Parker's biography and philosophy, but also provides insights into the scholastic atmosphere that surrounded and informed the Transcendentalist and social reform movements in New England during the mid-nineteenth century.

CRITICAL RECEPTION

Parker is regarded by scholars as an influential figure in the literary and social movements during the New England Renaissance. Not only was he well acquainted with such Transcendentalists as Emerson, Thomas Wentworth Higginson, and James Freeman Clarke, he engaged vigorously in the anti-slavery movement, in which he assumed a pivotal role. Because of his overtly contentious and often abrasive manner of speech and behavior, Parker was derided by many of his peers; nevertheless, some of those who found fault with his manner expressed respect and admiration for his scholarship. The precise nature of Parker's often complex theological arguments, as well as his controversial positions on the nature of African Americans and the causes of slavery, which provoked controversy and debate during his lifetime, continue to serve as subjects of scholarly study and debate today.

PRINCIPAL WORKS

The Previous Question between Mr. Andrews Norton and His Alumni, Moved and Handled in a Letter to Those Gentlemen [as Levi Blodgett] (pamphlet) 1840

A Discourse on the Transient and Permanent in Christianity (sermon) 1841; edited by George Willis Cooke and published as *The Transient and Permanent in Christianity,* 1908

A Discourse of Matters Pertaining to Religion (lectures) 1842; revised edition, 1855

Lecture on the Education of the Laboring Classes (sermon) 1842

The Critical and Miscellaneous Writings of Theodore Parker (criticism and essays) 1843

A Sermon of Slavery (sermon) 1843

The Excellence of Goodness. A Sermon Preached in the Church of the Disciples, in Boston, on Sunday, January 26, 1845 (sermon) 1845

A Letter to the Boston Association of Congregational Ministers, Touching Certain Matters of Their Theology (letter) 1845

The Relation of Jesus to His Age and the Ages. A Sermon Preached at the Thursday Lecture in Boston, December 26, 1844 (sermon) 1845

The Idea of a Christian Church. A Discourse at the Installation of Theodore Parker as Minister of the Twenty-Eighth Congregational Church in Boston, January 4, 1846 (lecture) 1846

A Sermon of War, Preached at the Melodeon, on Sunday, June 7, 1846 (sermon) 1846

A Letter to the People of the United States Touching the Matter of Slavery (pamphlet) 1848

Speeches, Addresses, and Occasional Sermons. 2 vols. (lectures and sermons) 1852

A Friendly Letter to the Executive Committee of the American Unitarian Association, Touching Their New Unitarian Creed or General Proclamation of Unitarian Views (pamphlet) 1853

Sermons of Theism, Atheism, and the Popular Theology (sermons) 1853

Ten Sermons of Religion (sermons) 1853

The Nebraska Question. Some Thoughts on the New Assault upon Freedom in America, and The General State of the Country in Relation Thereunto, Set Forth in a Discourse Preached at The Music Hall, in Boston, on Monday, Feb. 12, 1854 (sermon) 1854

The New Crime against Humanity. A Sermon, Preached at the Music Hall, in Boston, on Sunday, June 4, 1854 (sermon) 1854

Additional Speeches, Addresses, and Occasional Sermons. 2 vols. (lectures and sermons) 1855

The Trial of Theodore Parker, for the "Misdemeanor" of a Speech in Faneuil Hall against Kidnapping, before the Circuit Court of the United States, at Boston, April 3, 1855 (pamphlet) 1855

The Effect of Slavery on the American People. a Sermon Preached at the Music Hall, Boston, on Sunday, July 4, 1858 (sermon) 1858

Theodore Parker's Experience as a Minister (autobiography) 1859

Discourses of Politics (lectures) 1863

Discourses of Slavery. 2 vols. (lectures) 1863

Discourses of Theology (lectures) 1863

Discourses of Social Science (lectures) 1864

Miscellaneous Discourses (lectures) 1864

Transcendentalism. A Lecture (lecture) 1876

The American Scholar [edited by George Willis Cooke] (sermon) 1907

The Works of Theodore Parker. 15 vols. (sermons, lectures, autobiography, pamphlets, poetry, and prose) 1907-16

The World of Matter and the Spirit of Man: Latest Discourses of Religion [edited by George Willis Cooke] (lectures) 1907

Sermons of Religion [edited by Samuel A. Eliot] (sermons) 1908

CRITICISM

John White Chadwick (essay date 1900)

SOURCE: Chadwick, John White. "Philosophy and Theology." In *Theodore Parker: Preacher and Reformer,* pp. 170-99. Boston and New York: Houghton, Mifflin, 1900.

[*In the following essay, Chadwick surveys Parker's writings on the relationship between philosophy, science, and theology.*]

By laying violent hands upon itself the Thursday lecture pretty effectually closed the second Unitarian controversy,—that of Theodore Parker with the Boston Unitarians. At least that controversy passed about this time (1845) from an acute into a chronic stage. Henceforth Mr. Parker absented himself from the meetings of the Boston Association, and, with a few exceptions, had no professional fellowship with the neighboring clergy. The parting words on his side were those of a **"Letter to the Boston Association of Congregational Ministers, touching Certain Matters of their Theology."** It reviewed the situation and concluded with a list of four major and twenty-four minor questions. The major questions asked for definitions of the terms Salvation, Miracle, Inspiration, Revelation. The minor questions were amplifications of the major ones. All were intended to bring out the fact that the Association stood for no definite body of belief, but was deeply implicated in the heresies of the brother who plied his Socratic method with such demoralizing ingenuity. The date of this letter was March 20, 1845, and the *Examiner*[1] of the same month contained an article by Dr. Gannett reviewing eight pamphlets contributed to the controversy. One should read this article if he would see the conservative statement putting its best foot forward. It is a model of controversial writing, and Mr. Parker could not have desired a more frank and kindly criticism of his works and ways. His belief of "the Christian truths" was cheerfully conceded; also his Christian character; but he was not "a Christian believer" because he did not accept the truths of Christianity as supernaturally taught: "According to the theory which Mr. Parker advocates the words of Christ derive little authority from the fact of his having spoken them; they are to be believed not because they are his words, but because they are absolute truth." The modern reader will say, Surely here was exaltation and not degradation; but *then* the sensual miracle was more than the spiritual truth.[2] There was some criticism of the way in which Mr. Parker handled sacred matters. Here evidently was a prime source of trouble. Sacred matters had had a vocabulary of their own. Channing and Buckminster had dared to give them literary form. Parker spontaneously translated them into the common speech of men, hoping to make them better understood. The effect was often shocking to his contemporaries, for whom every holy spade must have its euphuistic name. Emerson summed up the state religion of England in five words, "By taste ye are saved." Dr. Bellows said, "Tastes separate more than opinions." And Parker's taste was not infallible. In general his homely secular utterance was a step forward—a stride. But he was sometimes painfully unhappy in his choice of words and illustrations.

Having stated the case, Dr. Gannett asked, "What then shall we do?" and answered that there must be no anger or abuse. The impregnable bulwarks of Christianity must not be defended by covering them with inflammatory placards. But the new doctrines must be shown to be unsound, unscriptural, and mischievous. The conservative mind must have found his doing of this quite satisfactory. His thinking on the subject of intuition was closer than Mr. Parker's own. But what should be done with the heretic?

Shall he be persecuted? No. Calumniated? No. Put down? No; if by this phrase be signified the use of any but fair and gentle means of curtailing his influence. Shall he be silenced, or be tolerated? Not tolerated, for the exercise of toleration implies the right to restrain the expression of opinion by force, but the validity of such a right cannot be admitted in this country and should not be allowed in the Christian church. Nor silenced; unless open argument and fraternal persuasion may reduce him to silence. But on the other hand he should not be encouraged nor assisted in diffusing his opinions by those who differ from him in regard to their correctness.

For such to exchange pulpits with him would be for them to encourage and assist him. Therefore they must not do this. This does not seem unfair.[3] A man's pulpit is his castle, into which he should not lightly welcome any one who he thinks will trifle with the magazine. But the exchange of pulpits was in 1845 the accepted sign of ministerial fellowship. To generally deny it to Mr. Parker was to resort to "the exclusive policy" of the Trinitarians thirty years before. It was to say, "Independence forever! But if you exercise your independence you are to us a heathen man and a publican." Dr. Gannett took issue with those who required "that he be cast out from the professional sympathies of those with whom he had been associated, and that a rebuke be administered to him by some formal act of the denomination." The majority agreed with Dr. Gannett. At the Association meeting which considered Mr. Parker's expulsion, there were but two votes for it. Why sacrifice the jewel of consistency when there had already been discovered a more excellent way?

But it is high time for us to be considering in some more definite manner than heretofore the general scope of Parker's philosophical and theological opinions. These were of less importance to his peculiar work than they have been generally esteemed, while yet they were of very great importance. It was neither as a philosopher nor as a theologian that he was most significant, but there was no schism in his personality, and between his philosophy, his theology, his politics and his religion there was continual ebb and flow. The interaction was habitual and complete. And the action of his philosophical opinions on his theological opinions and religious life and action was extremely vivid and intense. But while we may agree with Mr. Frothingham that "with a different philosophy he would have been a different man," it is quite as true that if he had been a different man he would have had a different philosophy. Mr. Frothingham is persuaded that "his great power as a preacher was due in chief part to the earnestness of his faith in the transcendental philosophy." But that philosophy as he held it took

> the shape,
> With fold on fold, of mountain or of cape,

of his own spiritual topography. The personal equation was the greater part. The doctrine had the features of his mind. We should make a great mistake if we went to Kant or Fichte or Schelling or Hegel for a right view of Transcendentalism and then proceeded to assume that Parker's was the same. We should not go so far astray if we went to Jacobi for the plan of Parker's thought. For Jacobi taught that God, the Soul, and Free Will were intuitive beliefs of the mind and had the same validity as Time, Space, and the External World as postulated by the demands of sensuous perception. Here certainly was a very close resemblance to Parker's transcendental consciousness of God, Immortality, and the Moral Law, but the resemblance was probably much more a matter of coincidence than a matter of sequence. Moreover the positiveness of Jacobi's tone was unique among the German Transcendentalists. Kant said, It is not in me; and Fichte, It is not in me. Schelling passed him by contumeliously on the other side. The essential principle of Transcendentalism—that there are elements in knowledge which transcend experience—this was common to all the members of the group and Parker shared it with them. But, for all their common ground, their differences among themselves were very great, as were Parker's also from each of them, not even Jacobi excepted.

The difference was incalculable between his view and that of Kant—the Moral Law given in consciousness, while God and Immortality are posited as intellectual forms, convenient for its operation, and for the ultimate reward of right doing. Even more repulsive to him must have been Fichte's towering idealism, with no God but his own moral consciousness, while Time and Space and Matter were but projections of the individual mind. Schelling, even in his earlier and more sober stage, must have considered much too curiously for him, so eager was his craving for simplicity. It is strange that Schelling's monism of an Absolute Being phenomenalized in Mind and Matter did not attract him more, and that he preferred thinking of matter as "a datum objective to God," but God himself the giver. Parker cared little for Philosophy except as the handmaid of Religion, and consequently he had little use for Hegel with a Becoming for his God, a God gradually developing and arriving at self-consciousness in man.

There were more points of contact between Parker's philosophy and that of the French Eclectics, Cousin, Constant, and Jouffroy, and the English Germanists, Carlyle and Coleridge, than between it and any German system except Jacobi's; but as compared with these also he was "to his native centre fast." He was not less self-poised as related to his American contemporaries. He has been often characterized as a concreter Emerson, but his Transcendentalism and Emerson's were cast in very different moulds. Emerson's, in fact, was not cast in any. It was a stream of tendency. His intuitions were a more feeble folk than Parker's sturdy affirmations of God, the Moral Law, and Immortality as directly known. His biographer, Mr. Cabot, says: "His reverence for intuitions and his distrust of reasoning were only the preference of truth over past apprehension of the truth." Parker was troubled by his incoherency, but Emerson saw more "in part" than Parker, who lived so "resolvedly in the whole." Parker's genius was not metaphysical. Emerson's was much more so; Alcott's far more; so Ripley's, Hedge's, Brownson's, each in turn. There were men who came after him, Samuel Johnson and David Atwood Wasson, who are to be preferred before him as exponents of the Transcendentalist philosophy. There never was a more English mind than Parker's, and because it was so English, it was not metaphysical. Coleridge flouted the understanding, and Parker inclined to his disparagement, but a capacious understanding was his most characteristic intellectual gift. The ease—if I should not say the inevitableness—with which he lapsed from "the high *priori* road" to the plodding footpath of scientific induction is significant of this. His passion for facts, his stomach for statistics, was fundamental to his mind. Buckle's delight in statistics was not more keen. His journal has great piles of them, ranging all the way from West India rum to the Egyptian dynasties. Not infrequently we find him inductive in the very act of stating his position as a Transcendentalist. For example:—

> Then Transcendentalism uses the other mode, the *a posteriori* . . . [In its argument for God] it finds signs and proofs of him everywhere, and gains evidence of God's existence in the limits of sensational experience. . . . At the ends of my arms are two major

prophets, ten minor prophets, each of them pointing the Transcendental philosopher to the infinite God of which he has consciousness without the logical process of induction.

We have this same Transcendentalism with an inductive attachment in the following expression:

> Transcendentalism has a work to do, to show that physics, politics, ethics, religion, rest on facts of necessity, *and have their witness and confirmation in facts of observation.*

Apart from this confusion, whereby Transcendentalism is set to do the drudgery of Science, Parker never is disdainful of the aid and comfort which is brought by Science to the transcendental intuitions. Variations of Paley's argument from design appear frequently in his discussions, and make up the bulk of them. But Transcendentalism furnished him with an admirable formula of his personal religion, and the formula reacted on the religion in the happiest manner. He would have been shorn of much of his public strength if he could have offered his glorious trinity of God, Immortality, and the Moral Law as merely the data of his own private faith. To offer them as truths of human nature and the human mind, as such, was quite another matter. Professor Dowden, writing of "Julius Cæsar," suggests that Shakespeare means "to signify to us unobtrusively that the philosophical creed which a man professes grows out of his character and circumstances so far as it is really a portion of his own being; and that so far as it is received by the intellect in the calm of life from teachers and schools, such a philosophical creed does not adhere very closely to the soul of a man, and may, upon the pressure of events or passions, be cast aside." It was because Parker's Transcendentalism grew out of his character that it was so vital. But because the soul's form does not always, or often, shape the body of the philosophic creed, his inferences from creed to character were liable to possible mistake.

Were it so sure, as many think, that the pendulum of thought has swung back from intuitionalism to sensationalism in these last years, the intuitionalism of Parker and his contemporaries would not be thereby dishonored. It was a valid protest against the sensationalism of their time, and if the sensationalism of the present time has better standing, it is, in good part, because the transcendental criticism upon it has been taken well to heart. In Parker's time it was generally assumed that materialists could not be idealists in spite of Berkeley's important evidence to the contrary, in his own person, which evidence did not escape Parker's scrutiny. In our own time Science is as idealistic as Metaphysics.[4] "'What is matter?' 'Never mind,'" was formerly a good joke. It is very pointless now, seeing that matter, as we know it, is "mind-stuff" for the most part. Moreover, the pendulum has swung back not a little from the sensational side.

Thomas Hill Green, the two Cairds, Bosanquet, Ritchie, Henry Jones, Bradley, Alexander, Wallace, Watson, Royce, all sitting rather loose to Hegel, but nothing if not metaphysical, have ridden well and brought important news. The persuasion is gathering strength that Science at her best can only write a Book of Exodus; that the Book of Genesis is a book of metaphysics. In the meantime Experientialism has enlarged its borders. Sensationalism does not now exhaust it as it did formerly.[5] Mind is seen to be a fact which also is somewhat, and the attempt to construct a rational conception of the universe from the world below man is felt to be a palpable absurdity.

It was so much Parker's habit to set his special lesson in a frame of general ideas that we have many statements of his philosophical position. With much general resemblance, one notes a certain latitude and looseness of expression. He did not use philosophical language with a nice exactness. His most elaborate statement is contained in **"Transcendentalism,"** a lecture written about 1850, and first published in 1876 by the Free Religious Association. It covers about forty pages, and twenty-five of these are exhausted by an arraignment of the Sensational School. Probably it would not have been accepted as a true bill by any reverent disciple of Locke, and certainly it is not a fair account of Sensationalism in its evolutionary form, which was just beginning to emerge when Parker died. One cannot help wondering whether he would have made any terms with this, if it had come in time for him to reckon with it. Would he have recognized any validity in the claim that certain truths are necessary, not because we *can,* but because we *cannot* transcend experience?—being irresistibly persuaded that the thing which always has been, always will be.

In the tractate, **"Transcendentalism,"** he criticises Sensationalism under the heads of Physics, Politics, Ethics, and Religion; judging the tree by its fruits. This was a favorite way with him. It reflected his personal experience. His philosophical ideas had profound reality for him; they were a constant inspiration to his moral life. He assumed that it was so with others, and so drew out from the sensational philosophy what seemed to be its logical consequences with unsparing hand. Could any good come out of that poor Nazareth? Not much, he thought; but there were individual sensationalists who should have given him pause: Voltaire with his passionate humanity; Franklin with his sturdy sense of political rights and duties and his large benevolence; and many besides these. If he had lived a little longer he would have found Carlyle, the Transcendentalist, blind as a bat to the merits of our American struggle, and John Stuart Mill, the Sensationalist, as clear-eyed to them as Garrison. But Parker had a postern by which to escape from these practical difficulties: The Sensationalists did not know their own minds; they were half Transcendentalists and more, without knowing it.

Coming to the religious application he was fortified by his first-hand knowledge of the Unitarian and other orthodoxy of his time, the alliance of which with the sensational philosophy was palpably in evidence. It was of the very essence of sensational materialism to prefer a physical miracle as the evidence of Christian truth to the truth as its own evidence. In his "Foundations of Belief" Mr. Arthur Balfour has exhibited Christian supernaturalism as one of the grossest forms of Naturalism, that being his word for what Parker called Sensationalism, choosing the better term.

As with Sensationalism, so with Transcendentalism: Parker spends little time on its primary concepts, much on its logical outcome. It is defined as the doctrine

> that man has faculties which transcend the senses; faculties which give him ideas and intuitions that transcend sensational experience; ideas whose origin is not in sensation nor their proof from sensation; that the mind (meaning thereby all that is not sense) is not a smooth tablet on which sensation writes its experience, but is a living principle which of itself originates ideas when the senses present the occasion; that, as there is a body with certain senses, so there is a soul or mind with certain powers which give the man sentiments and ideas. . . . It [the transcendental school] maintains that it is a fact of consciousness that there is in the intellect somewhat that was not first in the senses; and also that they have analyzed consciousness and *by the inductive method* [*sic*] established the conclusion that there is a consciousness that never was sensation, never could be; that our knowledge is in part *a priori*; that we know, 1, certain truths of necessity; 2, certain truths of intuition, or spontaneous consciousness; certain truths of demonstration, a voluntary consciousness; all of these truths not dependent on sensation for cause, origin, or proof.

This summoning of Caliban,—the Understanding, according to Lowell,—to prove his own incompetency, is only one of many helps that Prospero (the Transcendental Reason) gets from him in Parker's scheme. Our evolutionary psychology affects this matter sensibly. Even with Parker the intellect was not a constant, and it was not mind *as mind,* but mind acting under the most favorable conditions, that did all the fine things transcending sense and reflection. But if mind is an evolutionary product, its original capacity must have been slight as compared with the most ordinary modern mind, and we are interested to know when it began to have its transcendental powers. Intellect, as an evolutionary refinement of sense-perception, hints at the possible evolution of the transcendental from the inductive intellect. Assured of this, a radical distinction in the nature of the two would be improbable. In any case there must be Mind involved in the first stage of the ascending series

or there could be none in the last. Evolution of a higher from a lower, except in virtue of an antecedent higher, is not to be conceived.

I shall be less likely to do Parker injustice if I let him speak for himself. He describes Transcendentalism in Physics, Politics, Ethics, and Religion.

> In Physics it starts with the maxim that the senses acquaint us actually with body and therefrom the mind gives us the idea of substance answering to an objective reality. Thus is the certainty of the material world made sure of. Then *a priori* it admits the uniformity of action in nature; and its laws are known to be universal and not general alone.

Evidently the doctrine here has more the concreteness of Parker's mind than the warrant of the German schools. He admits the evils that have come from drawing out a system of Nature from the transcendental "nature of things" and specifies the blunders of Schelling. Those of Hegel were more utterly absurd. The haste with which Parker passes directly from Physics to Politics is eloquent of where his treasure was and his heart also. Transcendental Politics

> does not so much quote precedents, contingent facts of experience, as ideas, necessary facts of consciousness. It only quotes the precedent to illustrate the idea. It appeals to a natural justice, natural right; absolute justice, absolute right. Now the source and original of this justice and right it finds in God—the conscience of God; the channel through which we receive this justice and right is our own moral sense, our conscience; which is our consciousness of the conscience of God.

> In Ethics Transcendentalism affirms that man has moral faculties which lead him to justice and right and by his own nature can find out what is right and just and can know it and be certain of it. Right is to be done come what will come. . . . While experience shows what has been or is, conscience shows what should be or shall. Transcendental ethics looks not to the consequence of virtue in this life or the next to lead men to virtue. That is itself a good, an absolute good, to be loved not for what it brings but is.

Practically the lessons of experience meant much more for Parker than in this depreciation. He used them with tremendous force to marshal men the way that they should go. Coming to Religion, he says:—

> Transcendentalism admits a religious faculty, element, or nature in man [a wide range in the choice of terms] as it admits a moral, intellectual and sensational faculty. . . . Through this we have consciousness of God as through the senses consciousness of matter. . . . The idea of God is a fact given in the consciousness of man: consciousness of the infinite is the condition of a consciousness of the finite; . . . for if I am, and am finite and dependent, then this presupposes the infinite and independent.

In all this we seem to miss the quality which distinguishes the metaphysical as a peculiar type of thought, and see why Martineau and others have not conceded to

Parker metaphysical ability. What his philosophy actually signified was his abounding confidence in the realities of the moral and religious life. The sensational system repelled him because it set the senses higher than the soul and endeavored to recommend spiritual truths to him by physical marvels. He erected into a system of philosophic certainty his inborn and inbred faith in God, Immortality, and Conscience. It had a certain formal resemblance to other transcendental systems of his time, but the personal equation in it was immense and all important. His mother's part in it was much greater than Kant's or Schelling's. Its simplicity constituted for him one of its greatest attractions, so manifestly did that simplicity make it apprehensible to the great majority of people whom Parker wished to influence and impress with his ideas. Few have had his robust capacity for belief in the great things of religion. Hardly could he imagine other men as having less. It taxed his ingenuity to reconcile particular disbelief in God or Immortality with universal consciousness of these. But what a coign of vantage was the persuasion of that consciousness in others and in his own lofty mind! It is not strange that thousands heard him gladly. It is strange that every thousand was not ten. For men could not resist the high contagion of a faith so pure and bold. They could not but believe themselves entitled to his absolute confidence in God and Man and God's Voice in Man's Heart.

The higher ranges of Parker's philosophy and theology run up into one central peak of which we get many different views as we follow him from one book or sermon to another. It is hard to choose out of the many. If we let him decide we shall go for the best statement of his theology to his **"Theism, Atheism, and the Popular Theology"** (1853). He begins by painting-in a sombre background, the commingling gloom of two sermons on Speculative and Practical Atheism and two others on the Speculative and Practical Working of the Popular Theology. He found the amount of real atheism much less than the apparent. Given belief in Nature as the cause of its own existence, the Mind of the Universe and the Providence thereof, and the denial of God is only formal and not real: "The name is of the smallest consequence. All those men that I know, who call themselves atheists, really admit the existence of all the qualities I speak of." "The real Speculative Atheist denies the existence of the qualities of God; denies that there is any Mind in the Universe, any self-conscious Providence, any Providence at all." He then proceeds to work out the subjective effects of this theory as a theory of the world of matter, as a theory of individual life, and as a theory of the life of mankind.

The most orthodox of Parker's contemporaries did not believe in theology more completely than he did, or in the influence which it exerts on human life. Ideas of all kinds were for him the great human forces. He could make the individual exception, but that did not swerve

him from his faith in the general operation of ideas, good and ill, upon the social mass; and he never tired of drawing out the subjective and objective effects of the ideas he revered and those which he abhorred. He drew out with great force the logical results of real atheism upon men's thought of Nature and the individual and social life. Then he turned to **"Practical Atheism, regarded as a Principle of Ethics,"** and showed how a man would act who should translate the terms of a real speculative atheism into the terms of individual and social life. The applications to domestic life and politics were very close indeed. The power of these sermons was in their entire sincerity. The preacher did not endeavor to excite a horror which he did not feel. Atheism, speculative and practical, was for him something so monstrous that his command of language, which was great, was inadequate to express all that he felt. The strong-built sentences stagger under a burden of imaginative misery that is too great for them to bear.

In the popular theology he finds five great truths: "the existence of God, the immortality of man, the moral obligation of man to obey the law of God, the connection between God and man" [inspiration, prayer], and the connection of love between man and man." He says, "These are, I think, by far the most important speculative doctrines known to the human intellect." But he does not dwell on them. He passes to the "great defects" of the system, its finite and imperfect God, selfish and cruel, while the Devil, "the unacknowledged but most effective fourth person in the God-head," is "stronger than God the Father, God the Son, and God the Holy Ghost, all united." "The doctrine concerning Man is no better." The particulars need not be repeated. They are those of every well authenticated exposition of the traditional theology. The doctrines of original sin, total depravity, election, atonement, eternal hell, are painted in colors to which black is rosy red. Summing up, he said,—

> God is not represented as a friend, but as the worst foe to men; existence is a curse to all but one of a hundred thousand; immortality is a curse to ninety-nine out of every hundred thousand on earth; religion is a blessing to only ten in a million; to all the rest a torment on earth, and in hell.

As between no God at all and "a God who is Almighty but omnipotently malignant," and "a universe which is itself an odious and inexorable hell," he did not hesitate to choose. Let it by all means be no God. Those who thought he had done his worst for the popular theology came again the next Sunday to find that he had not. The subject was **"The Popular Theology of Christendom regarded as a principle of Ethics."** The text was, "A corrupt tree bringeth forth evil fruit." His purpose was to set forth the logical effects of such a system and he did it well. He was a master in this kind. He exhibited these effects as corrupting the Feelings, the Intellect, the Practical Life, not only logically but actually. It was an exhibition to make one's whole head sick, one's whole heart faint.

No account of Parker's preaching can be complete that does not make due mention of his terrible denunciations of the popular theology. These fixed his standing in the orthodox imagination of his time. Their proportion to the sum total of his preaching has been much misunderstood. They frequently recurred, but seldom in such mass as in the sermons now under consideration; oftener as incidental strokes. Much oftener he dwelt upon the dignity and glory of that higher faith to which he had attained. It is above all things necessary that, in our estimate of such preaching, we should consider the important theological changes which have taken place within the last half century. We read these awful indictments and we say, "Nobody believes such things now." This is not true, and we are much too apt to impute the liberality of some to all. Moreover they are explicit or implicit in the creeds which the churches stiffly decline to change ever so little. But it is true that there are now hundreds of books written by men snugly ensconced in one orthodox connection or another who repudiate Calvinism as passionately as did Theodore Parker; there are hundreds of preachers standing in orthodox pulpits, with no one to molest or make them afraid, while they make substantially his damning accusations. One of these, Dr. A. W. Momerie, declares, "The orthodox idea of God is the most horrible idea that it is possible for the imagination to conceive;" and Dr. Henry J. Van Dyke, loaded with Presbyterian honors, says of the God once reverenced, "To worship such a God would be to worship an omnipotent devil," "a nightmare horror of monstrosity, infinitely worse than no God at all." Such examples might easily be multiplied a hundredfold. Had orthodoxy been in Parker's time the painted flame which it is now in many pulpits, he would have dealt with it less vehemently, though he might well have demanded a more nice conformity between the accepted creed and the habitual speech. It was because the God of his apprehension was infinite in every possible perfection that he resented with hot indignation the horrible caricatures and slanders of the popular theology. He had given them a fair trial in his young manhood in Lyman Beecher's Hanover Street Church, and he hated them with a perfect hatred for men's sake as much as God's.

He was at little pains, however, to measure orthodoxy by the emphasis that was laid upon its better parts, or by the moral ideals that were involved both in its more popular representations and its more refined interpretations. It is what men love that makes them good or bad, and not many loved the God fashioned in the furnace-heat of Edwards's pitiless imagination, or hewn by Calvin's frozen steel. It is not a theology as a species which is most significant, but its variations that are selected by the common sense and good will of the ma-

jority. If we find scant recognition of this fact in Parker's preaching it is still likely that his means were well adapted to the end he had in view.

Having painted-in his sombre background with remorseless hand, he proceeded to dash in against it five sermons of heroic size, the first **"Speculative Theism regarded as a Theory of the Universe."** He distinguished Theism not only from Atheism and the Popular Theology, but also from Deism, which affirms a moral God, "but still starts from the sensational philosophy, abuts in materialism, and so gets its idea of God solely from external observation and not at all from consciousness, and, accordingly, represents God as finite and imperfect." At this point his readers are referred back to former statements of his fundamental theology. These, as found in the **"Discourse,"** start from *the sense of dependence* which seems to have been Schleiermacher's contribution. This is the *sentiment* of God, of the Infinite, the vague *henotheism* on which Dr. Max Müller has insisted a good deal. Besides this we have the *idea* of God as infinite in power, wisdom, and goodness. This idea is given in consciousness, and is "the logical condition of all other ideas," and yet, inconsistently thinks Martineau, is "afterwards fundamentally and logically established by the *a priori* argument." The conception of God is something less simple than the idea, but as Parker sometimes apparently confounds the sentiment and the idea, so, again, he sometimes apparently confounds the idea and the conception.[6] God as infinite must have all possible perfections,—"the perfection of being, self-existence, eternity of duration, endless and without beginning; of power, all-mightiness; of mind, all-knowingness; of conscience, all-righteousness; of affection, all-lovingness; of soul, all-holiness, absolute fidelity to himself."[7] Being perfect in himself, everything that proceeds from him must be perfect, the universe adequate for its uses; man adequate for his functions. There seems to be no apprehension that in passing out into finiteness the Infinite must deliberately or perforce forego its infinite perfection,—"Life, like a dome of many-colored glass," staining "the white radiance of eternity." But in practice he sufficiently qualified the perfection of all things when he came to Northern dough-faces and Southern kidnappers; to Mr. Facing Both Ways in the pulpit and Mr. Worldly Wiseman in the pew.

Denounced by many as a Pantheist, and warned by Martineau of his Pantheistic tendency, Parker was careful to distinguish his Theism from either material Pantheism, which resolves God into the material universe, or spiritual Pantheism, which resolves the material universe into God. If his doctrine of God everywhere and always immanent in matter and in man has often a Pantheistic fall, it finds its practical correction in a doctrine of God as "our Father and our Mother," which is warmly and tenderly anthropomorphic, and Martineau had little cause to fear that in his conception of God's immanence in man, *as in matter,* the divine inundation would swamp the human will. Perhaps logically it should have done so, but then God's immanence in man was not for Parker quite the same as his immanence in matter. It was the divine possibility conditioned by the organization of the individual and his deliberate faithfulness. This was his doctrine of universal inspiration, to which he recurred more frequently than to any other, and which, of all his theological doctrines, had the most religious and ethical significance.

"Of God as perfect Cause: the Infinite God must create all from a perfect motive, for a perfect purpose, of perfect material, as perfect means."—"Next of God as perfect Providence: Creation and Providence are but modifications of the same function. Creation is momentary providence; Providence, perpetual creation." "In Nature God is the only Cause, the only Providence," but in man there is an element of freedom, yet here also God is perfect Providence. The freedom is not exclusive of the providence. "The quantity of human oscillation with all its consequences must be perfectly known to God before the creation."

> Though human caprice and freedom be a contingent force, yet God knows human caprice when He makes it, knows exactly the amount of that contingent force, all its actions, movements, history, and what it will bring about. And as He is an infinitely wise, just, and loving Cause and Providence, so there can be no absolute evil or imperfection in the world of man more than in the world of matter, or in God himself.

These doubtful matters are developed with great elaboration and much effective illustration in three sermons which conclude the volume on Theism, etc. The subjects are **"Providence," "The Economy of Pain,"** and the **"Economy of Moral Error."** His doctrine of Providence is so inclusive and so optimistic that it baulks at no fact, however ugly, in the natural or human world. Man's partial freedom makes a great difficulty, but it is not too great for him to grapple with and satisfactorily master, himself the judge. A half page goes to the description of an old oak-tree, broken, crooked, gnarled, and yet a microcosmos, serving many uses, sustaining many happy lives. A score of farm-lore recollections went to the growing and the peopling of that tree. He takes it for a symbol of the world, which we judge as the lumberman judges the old oak, merely with reference to our uses.

> How little do we know! A world without an alligator, or a rattlesnake, or a hyena, or a shark, would doubtless be a very imperfect world. The good God has something for each of these to do; a place for them all at His table, and a pillow for every one of them in Nature's bed.

In the discussions of Pain and Moral Error, Parker's method is mainly inductive. God being perfect, there can be no absolute harm in either, but he does not leave the matter here, and for the rest, he writes, as Mr. Frothingham has said, in the manner of a Bridgewater Treatise. Physical and moral pain are justified as warnings and deterrents, saving from worse mishaps.[8] His doctrine of sin was not evangelical,—not enough so even for James Freeman Clarke, who, preaching at the Music Hall, when Parker's preaching was all done, made certain criticisms on his teachings, to which Parker replied:—

> Now a word about *sin.* It is a theological word and commonly pronounced *ngsin-n-n-n!* But I think the thing which ministers mean by *ngsin-n-n-n* has no more existence than *phlogiston,* which was once adopted to explain combustion. I find *sins,* i. e., *conscious violations of natural right,* but no *sin,* i. e., no conscious and intentional preference of wrong (as such) to right (as such); no condition of "enmity against God."

There follows an imaginary conversation with Deacon Wryface of the Hellfire Church, who repudiates all his special *sins,* but clings with desperate conviction to his consciousness of the general *ngsin-n-n-n* of his fallen *natur'.* "Oh, James," he continues, "I think the Christian (?) doctrine of sin is the Devil's own and I hate it—hate it utterly." Whatever he might think of sin in the abstract, no one of his generation had a clearer sense of concrete sins than he, or struck at them more powerfully. It was as if he conserved all the energy that others wasted on "the common ground of evil in human nature" to make his fight with concrete sins more indomitable and effectual.

As he worked out the practical effects of Atheism and the Popular Theology, so he works out the practical effects of Theism; man's perfect confidence in his own nature and destiny "plain as the farmer's road to mill;" the absolute love of God as the Beauty of Truth, Justice, Love, Holiness, and as the total Infinite Beauty; a perfect trust in Him as Cause and Providence; "a real joy in God, the highest joy and the highest delight of the human consciousness;" a Beauty of Soul, "a harmonious whole of well-proportioned spiritual parts," "a continual and constant growth in all the noble qualities of man." With these subjective effects there are others, objective, but not more practical: keeping the Body's law without asceticism or excess; keeping the law of the Spirit, "giving each spiritual faculty its place in the housekeeping of the spirit;" and the true scale of spiritual values, first Intellect; next higher, Conscience; next the affections; highest of all the religious faculty, "the Soul, that seeks the infinite Being, Father and Mother of the Universe, loves Him with perfect love and serves Him with perfect trust." Theism has its domestic form, and that is pictured forth with glowing words, warm from the preacher's heart; it has its social form, which is commercial, political, and ecclesiastical, and, oh, the difference between these and the forms naturally consequent on Atheism or the Popular Theology!

There are parts of Parker's theological system which have not been considered in this survey. They will find their place in connection with other phases of his life and work. Among them are his views of prayer, and immortality. He does not lend himself graciously to condensation or abstraction, and thinking of the pages from which I have drawn out the foregoing statements, as much as possible in his own words, I am painfully aware of their inadequacy, so thin and meagre do they appear in comparison with the abounding flood of his discourse, bearing great argosies of sumptuous illustration on its rushing tide. And yet, it is not Parker speaking as philosopher or theologian who is most at home and speaks in the most friendly voice. His formal statements are his least satisfactory performances. Happily these are frequently invaded by his religious genius and by this invasion made as much more beautiful as is the body's framework by its investiture of gleaming flesh. His theology, almost equally with his philosophy, was an heroic but not quite successful endeavor to render his spontaneous religiousness in such terms of the intellect as would enable him to communicate to others that which was to him so wonderfully sweet. Not that he would have dominion over their faith, but that he would be a helper of their joy.

Notes

1. By the *Examiner* the *Christian Examiner* is meant here and elsewhere. It began its course in 1824 and finished it in 1869. It was a lineal successor of the *Christian Disciple* (1813-24), the *General Repository* (1812-13), and the *Monthly Anthology* (1803-11). Considering the periods covered, the amount of controversial matter in all these magazines was very small: for a section of twenty years less than one article a year.

2. More as recommending the truth as of divine origin and establishing its Christian character.

3. For those differing from him. For those agreeing with him it was different, though these, while agreeing with his matter, might have objected to his manner. Parker, in his demand for perfect liberty of free inquiry and free utterance, was faithful to the most explicit and most prominent emphasis of the older Unitarians; who tacitly assumed that their scheme of supernatural Christianity was wholly rational. But for this assumption the demand from 1815 to 1830 for complete intellectual liberty would not have been so simple and unwavering. There was no injustice or unfairness in making their implicit assumption explicit. They had not meant to follow Free Inquiry so far as to admit that Christianity might be a natural religion. Therefore, says W. C. Gannett, they did right to disclaim Parker. Yes, if, so doing, they had frankly abandoned their principle of free inquiry as one to the exigency of which they were unequal. Yes, if they had frankly confessed that principle to be subordinate to the affirmation of the necessity for miraculous support of Christian truth. But these things they did not do.

4. See Huxley's "Bishop Berkeley on the Metaphysics of Sensation," in *Critiques and Addresses.*

5. In Professor Royce's exposition it includes Metaphysics. See his *The World and the Individual,* p. 259.

6. "He is too ardent to preserve self-consistency throughout the parts of a large abstract scheme; too impetuous for the fine analysis of intricate and evanescent phenomena." Martineau: *Personal and Political Essays,* p. 154.

7. By analysis of the reflective *conception* he found in it substantially what was given in the intuitional *idea.*

8. Professor Royce, *Problems of Good and Evil,* pp. 8, 9, treats this argument with absolute scorn, but, if it does not touch the root of evil, it is very instructive in regard to our behavior towards "the God of things as they are."

Henry Steele Commager (essay date 1936)

SOURCE: Commager, Henry Steele. "Slavery and the Higher Law." In *Theodore Parker,* pp. 197-213. Boston: Little, Brown, 1936.

[*In the following essay, Commager outlines Parker's views on slavery and abolitionism.*]

"Southern Slavery is an institution which is in earnest. Northern Freedom is an institution that is not in earnest." So said Parker, pointing the moral cowardice of the North, its insincerity, its futility, its blundering. Here was the North, with twice the population of the South and twice its wealth, celebrating every year the Declaration of Independence, and knuckling under, just as regularly, to the South. Here was the North, dedicated to freedom by Nature itself, schooled in the politics and the philosophy of freedom, but voting the slaveholders' ticket every time. New England went for slavery, the South choosing for her errand boy the favorite son of the Granite State; Massachusetts went for slavery, her greatest Senator speaking for compromise and fastening the Fugitive Slave Bill on the land; Boston went for slavery, Winthrop, Eliot, and Appleton all toeing the line spun by the fine logic of John Calhoun. Faneuil Hall went for slavery, her walls reverberating to the tumultuous applause of Mr. Webster's new doctrine, "the great object of government is the protection of property." State Street signed for slavery, and fifteen hundred merchants volunteered to send Thomas Sims back to his Georgia master. The Press pled for slavery, the *Post* stating, "In every point of view New England seems to have been made for the South and the South for New England. How could either live and flourish without the other?" while the *Courier* and the *Advertiser* urged the proscription of lawyers who dared to defend fugitive slaves. Society sustained slavery, Sumner and Dana and Palfrey ostracized by the first families of the town. Even the Church preached slavery, Brattle Street and Old South taking for their text the "Southside View," and Andover reconciling "Conscience and the Constitution." Slavery in the State House, slavery in the Court House, slavery on Beacon Hill, the city of Hancock and Adams faithless to her past.

It was a singular infamy that Boston could boast. Look through her history these twenty years, from the day she had mobbed Garrison, dragging him through the streets with a rope around his neck, to the day she had welcomed Mason as he stood on Bunker Hill and called the roll of his slaves. When had her men of property and position failed to do the bidding of the slave power? How many abolition meetings had been broken up, how many speakers howled down! Fugitives were hunted in her streets and sent back to the slave pens of the South, her Court House turned into a barracoon, old Judge Shaw crawling beneath the iron chains that were strung around it. When the Fugitive Slave Bill was passed, Boston greeted it with a salute of a hundred guns, and when Webster came out for compromise, 987 men of "property and position" assured him that "he had convinced the understanding and touched the conscience of a nation." ("There never was an event half so painful occurred in Boston," Emerson wrote.) Charles Follen was dropped from Harvard College for his abolitionism, and when he died the Federal Street Church would not allow its own Doctor Channing to hold services for him. Richard Dana espoused abolition and lost his clients; Doctor Bowditch walked arm in arm with Frederick Douglass and lost his patients; Charles Sumner denounced Webster and lost his friends. Well might James Freeman Clarke say, "When I came back to Boston, it was harder to speak of slavery than it had been in Kentucky." Well might Garrison write that here he had found "contempt more bitter, opposition more active, detraction more relentless, prejudice more stubborn, and apathy more frozen than among slave owners themselves."

Northern Freedom was not in earnest, but Parker was in earnest, terribly, implacably in earnest. He came late to abolition, as to social reform, but he made amends for his tardiness. He came fifteen years after Garrison, a decade after Phillips, but within five years from his first appearance in Faneuil Hall he was one of the triumvirate that led the anti-slavery fight, the newspapers of

Boston calling on the people of the town to repudiate him, his speeches reprinted in Greeley's *Tribune* as the best that the North had to offer and in Daniel's *Examiner* as the worst. He spoke and his voice rolled like thunder over the land; he hammered and Boston complacency cracked under his blows; he fulminated and reputations shriveled in that terrible flame. He preached in Boston and the Music Hall could not hold the thousands who came to hear of the **"New Crime against Humanity"**; he lectured in New York, and the Tabernacle was electric with excitement as he described the **"Great Battle between Slavery and Freedom"**; he carried his message to the people of the country, from the Bay to the Mississippi, and they came to hear him, fifty thousand strong. "I know well," he said that morning when he preached on Anthony Burns—"I know well the responsibility of the place I occupy this morning. To-morrow's sun shall carry my words to all America. They will be read on both sides of the Continent; they will cross the ocean." And it was not boasting or a vain thing that he said.

But these great rugged encyclopædic sermons did not exhaust his passion nor did the pulpit circumscribe his labors. He organized Vigilance Committees and harbored fugitive slaves in his house. He fomented rebellion against wicked laws and offered to lead attacks upon the Court House and the jail. He was indicted for "offending against the peace and dignity of the United States," and so welcomed the indictment that the Judge did not dare let the case go to trial. He helped inspire and finance the Kansas Crusade; he was one of John Brown's secret committee of six, privy to his plans; he incited slaves to insurrection, the disciple of the Prince of Peace counseling violence and bloodshed.

He was a practical man, no non-resistant, but ready for a fight at any time, no anarchist, but willing to use politics and parties to gain his ends. He had no political ambitions, but he was a power in politics all the same, never for a moment to be ignored. He described himself as a humble minister but he spoke with the authority of a Pope. He lashed judges and excoriated Senators and flayed Presidents; he drove Loring off the bench and out of Boston, he gave Curtis a terrible notoriety, he pronounced on Webster the most awful judgment ever read over a great man, and Adams and Dana said that it was just. When Sumner delayed his assault upon the slave power, he explained his delay to Parker; when Chase refused to attack slavery where it already existed, he justified himself to Parker; when Wilson plunged into Know-Nothingism, emerging with political spoils, he apologized to Parker. Seward and Chase and Lincoln, Sumner and Wilson and Hale, read what he wrote and acknowledged his power. "I congratulate you," wrote Seward, "on the awakening of the spirit of Freedom in the Free States. I hope you recognize in this awakening the fruits of your own great and unwearied labors. If you do not, I am sure that I do, and not only I but thousands more acknowledge it."

What was it that Whittier had written, in that dark hour when troops were moving on Mexico and the Whigs stood in Faneuil Hall and voted down Stephen Phillips's anti-slavery resolutions?

> Where's the man for Massachusetts, Where's the voice to speak her free?
>
> Where's the hand to light up bonfires, from her mountains to the sea?
>
> Beats her Pilgrim pulse no longer? Sits she dumb in her despair?
>
> Has she none to break the silence? Has she none to do and dare?
>
> O my God for one right worthy to lift up her rusted shield,
>
> And to plant again the Pine-tree in her banner's tattered field!

Did Parker think that he was the man? That same year he too had stood in Faneuil Hall and lifted his voice on behalf of the slave, Joe, carried back from Boston to New Orleans. "I felt like a Hebrew prophet," he wrote, "I have seldom risen so high as that night; never thundered and lightened into such an atmosphere. I did not think of such words; they *came,* and I thank God for it. I did greater than I could counsel, far greater than I knew. My caprice, my personal taste, stood in the background; and my nature—the nature of mankind—and honest blood spoke in me, through me."

2

For fifteen years Parker spoke and wrote about slavery. Yet what did he know about slavery, after all? To hear him talk you would think that he knew everything about it. He knew the whole history of the institution, from ancient times. He could tell Phillips about slavery in Rome, and Sumner about slavery in Gaul, and when Andrew Dickson White came to New Haven to lecture on Russia, Parker astonished him with his knowledge of slavery under the Tsars. He knew the origin of slavery in the New World, and he could trace its progress in minute detail and enlarge upon its law and custom, its economy and its sociology. He could tell you the statistics of slavery in every State of the Union—he was writing a book on the subject, and the whole Census of 1850 was to go into the book. It went into his sermons instead, and Hinton Helper was anticipated by a decade.

He knew everything about slavery. He had read all the books, had most of them in his own library. He had listened to the narratives of a hundred fugitive slaves and he could tell a thing or two to Mrs. Stowe. He knew all the Negroes of Boston, Lewis Hayden and Roger Morris were his parishioners and Frederick Douglass was his friend. When Moncure Conway came to Boston, looking for the husband of a slave-woman, it was to Parker that he was sent, and Parker took him through the Negro quarters and to the hiding places of the fugitives, and Conway remembered that "every room into which we entered was hushed with reverence as if God had entered." Slaveowners told him their side of the story, Yeadon and Dawson up from Charleston to debate with him; they wrote him long letters of protest, closely written arguments from the Bible and from history, or letters filled with abuse. He subscribed to the Richmond *Examiner* and read *DeBow's Review,* he filled his scrapbook with advertisements for runaway slaves, and convicted the South on its own testimony.

He knew the philosophy of slavery, he had read Calhoun and the Pro-Slavery Argument, and he could say the Biblical sanctions by heart. Did Abraham have "servants bought with his money," did Paul say, "Slaves, obey your masters"? That argument had no terrors for him, he put no stock in the inspiration of the Scriptures. Abraham lived in a barbarous age, Paul was wrong; it was as simple as that. He had only scorn for Mr. Everett, "A Cambridge Professor of Greek, he studied the original tongue of the Bible to learn that the Scripture says slaves where the English Bible says only servants." A poor thing, Everett, "an *electro-gilder,* you carry him to any piece of metal no matter how base, and he covers it over with his thin tinsel."

He knew as much about slavery as any Yankee could, yet what did he really know? Slavery wasn't something you got at through an encyclopædia or through the Census Reports; slavery wasn't something you learned from fragmentary narratives of escaped slaves, as if you should get at the heart of Catholicism through the stories of Lahey, "the monk of La Trappe." Slavery wasn't something simple and single, a question of profit or loss, a question of progress or decay, a question of right or wrong. It wasn't something the South could put off like a coat; it was something that had grown into Southern society, tied to the South with a thousand sensitive nerves. What could Parker know of slavery? Channing had lived in Richmond and Clarke had preached in Louisville, Birney had owned a plantation in the deep south, the Grimké sisters had come from Charleston, but Parker had never been below Mason and Dixon's line. For all of his apparent realism, his crowding array of facts and figures, he dealt with slavery as an abstraction, and his vocabulary was incomprehensible to the South. His logic was plausible enough, but you might as well try to convert a Hard-Shell Baptist to Catholicism by logic; his statistics were impressive, but suppose you could prove that the family was an extravagant institution, community barracks the most efficient way of raising children—what good were statistics for things like that? His criticism was just, and he could substantiate it, item by item; but who ever heard of a society responding to criticism? His moral appeals were irresistible, if you admitted the premises, but the South did not admit the premises.

Curious what came over Parker when he dealt with slavery. He had balance enough in most things, his feet were on the ground. He made no fetish of temperance, he was no doctrinaire pacifist, he took woman's rights in his stride, he never ranted against property, only against its abuse. He saw the wrongs of industrialism, but he would not topple the factories down, he would not even escape to Brook Farm; he knew the corruption of politics, but he never failed to vote. He had studied the history of the institution of slavery, too, and could write his own "Sociology for the South"; he knew well enough that the planter was not to be blamed for the sin of slavery any more than the State Street banker was to be blamed for the evils of industry. He could distinguish, when he wanted to, between the sinner and the sin, and he took no stock in the doctrine of the depravity of man. But all to no purpose; when he got on the subject of slavery Garrison himself was not more uncompromising, Sumner not more doctrinaire.

He pitched into slavery with a two-pronged fork, and slavery slid in between. He announced that slavery was a moral wrong, a crime against Nature and against Man: this was an *a priori* truth, an intuitive fact, a transcendental axiom. He announced that slavery was unprofitable and inefficient, it did not pay dividends, economically or culturally, and his evidence could not be gainsaid. But what was the value of evidence to prove a natural law? Suppose Calhoun's dream of a Greek Democracy had come true in the Palmetto State, suppose Tidewater Virginia were that paradise its planters said it was: would Parker have admitted defeat and abandoned his position? It was not because Alabama lacked railroads, because immigrants avoided Virginia, because illiteracy in South Carolina was high, that Parker was an abolitionist; he was an abolitionist because he hated slavery, and had Alabama been crisscrossed with railroads, had the Irish crowded into the Old Dominion, and every Carolinian read Shakespeare, Parker would have hated slavery none the less. It was the old dilemma that had troubled him in the past, and he never resolved it.

Besides, he missed the point, for all of his massive statistics. There were his sermons, his lectures, his pamphlets, sagging under the weight of evidence. Taken together they constituted a sociological encyclopædia such as was not to be found in the whole literature of the controversy: Helper added little to what Parker had assembled. Here were the comparative statistics, North and South, for industry and commerce and trade, for manufactures and inventions and labor, for population and immigration, for public and private wealth, public debt and expenditures, for literacy and education and religion too; here they were, all pointing to the same conclusion, and Parker thought that he had proved his case. But no such thing. His logic had failed him, his zeal had led him astray. (He was in good company; who was not led astray?) His figures were irrelevant, his conclusions impertinent. All that he had accomplished was to prove that Negro labor was unprofitable, that ignorant labor was unprofitable. No need to go to South Carolina for that. Boston could teach him that.

3

What though his statistics were irrelevant; had they been as relevant as the Commandments and as valid as the axioms of Euclid, they would not have been accepted in the South. Parker's argument was, of necessity, addressed to the North, and his appeal there was to morals, not to expediency. He could not hope to wean the slaveholder from his peculiar institution, but he might hope to arouse the freeman from his apathy. His task was to make Northern Freedom in earnest. It was for him to stir up the people of the Northern States, to fight down the aggressions of the slave power, to impeach the Hunkers and exalt the Free-soilers, to nullify the Fugitive Slave Bill, to expose the perfidy of the Nebraska Act, to win Kansas for freedom.

This was the work of a moral agitator, and Parker was on familiar ground. It was not as an economist that Parker made his special contribution to anti-slavery, nor as an organizer, but as a minister. When he hid Ellen Craft from the kidnappers, it was as a minister taking care of his parishioner. When he demanded the nullification of the Fugitive Slave Bill it was as a minister preaching on the **"Function of Conscience in Relation to the Laws of Men,"** when he advised jurors to ignore their oaths and follow their consciences, it was as a minister comparing the **"Laws of God and the Statutes of Men."** He made abolitionism a religious duty, and gave to nullification the sanction of the Higher Law.

Others invoked the Higher Law, but none so insistently as Parker, none with such cogent logic or such moral fervor. He announced it in his first **"Sermon on Slavery,"** preached in West Roxbury 'way back in 1841. "I know that men urge in argument that the Constitution of the United States is the supreme law of the land," he said, "and that sanctions slavery. There is no supreme law but that made by God; if our laws contradict that, the sooner they end or the sooner they are broken, why, the better." He maintained it in his last formal pronouncement, the letter on John Brown: "The freeman has a Natural Right to help the slaves recover their liberty." He presented it year in and year out, from the pulpit and the lyceum platform, in private letter and in formal argument. He gave it an historical basis, exploring the history of Puritan England and Revolutionary America to prove its validity; he gave it a philosophical basis, justifying it by the logic of idealism and the dialectics of transcendentalism; he gave it a religious basis, finding its sanctions in the injunctions of the Commandments and the Beatitudes.

Parker pointed the way to the nullification of wicked laws, but it was not such nullification as Calhoun prescribed, resting on constitutional metaphysics; he pointed the way to civil disobedience, but it was not such disobedience as Garrison advised, publicly burning the Constitution. It was not revolution that Parker enjoined, for it is not revolutionary to ignore immoral statutes, only to enact them; it was not anarchy that he counseled, for it is not anarchy to conform to natural law, only to flout it. He spoke as the grandson of Captain John Parker and reminded men that their fathers had nullified the Stamp Act and thrown tea into Boston harbor. He spoke as a transcendental idealist and recalled that all men were created equal and endowed by their Creator with certain unalienable rights, life, liberty, and the pursuit of happiness. But it was when he spoke as a minister that he was most effective; even the most orthodox could not find fault with his text: "Thou shalt worship the Lord thy God, and Him only shalt thou serve."

Listen to him as he expounded the **"Function of Conscience in Relation to the Laws of Men"**: "The law of God has eminent domain everywhere, over the private passions of Oliver and Charles, the special interests of Carthage and Rome, over all official business, all precedents, all human statutes, over all the conventional affairs of one man or of mankind. My own conscience is to declare that law to me, yours to you, and is before all private passions or public interests, the decision of majorities and a world full of precedents. You cannot move out of the dominions of God nor escape where conscience has not eminent domain." Hear what he told his parishioners of the Fugitive Slave Act: "When rulers have inverted their function and enacted wickedness into a law which treads down the inalienable rights of man to such a degree as this, then I know no ruler but God, no law but natural Justice. I tear the hateful statute of kidnappers to shivers; I trample it underneath my feet, I do it in the name of all law; in the name of Justice and of Man, in the name of the dear God." When the Ministerial Conference daintily discussed the duty of Ministers toward the law, and clergymen trembled for the Union, Parker reminded them that their loyalty was to God, not man. "O my brothers, I am not afraid of men. I can offend them. I care nothing for their hate or their esteem. But I should not dare to violate the eternal law of God. I should not dare to violate His laws, come what may come—should you? Nay, I can love nothing so well as I love my God."

When Mr. Benjamin Curtis said, "The standard of Morality by which the Courts are to be guided is that which the law prescribes. Your honors are to declare what the Law deems moral or immoral," Parker asked whether it was "moral for the servants of King Pharaoh to drown all newborn Hebrew boys, moral for Herod's butchers to murder the Innocents at Bethlehem." When Justice Peleg Sprague said, "there is no incompatibility between the will of God and the laws of Man," Parker reminded him of the law of King Ahab that the Hebrews should serve Baal, and the law of the Scribes and Pharisees that "if any man knew where Jesus were, he should show it that they might take him," the law which Judas obeyed. When Judge Curtis cried him down for advising jurors to ignore the law, and, standing in Faneuil Hall, asked "the Reverend Gentleman in what capacity he expects to be punished for his *perjury*," Parker rose in the gallery. "Do you want an answer to your question now, Sir?" he shouted. Mr. Curtis did not; but Parker answered him anyway, from his pulpit: "Suppose a man has sworn to keep the Constitution of the United States and the Constitution is found to be wrong in certain particulars, then his oath is not morally binding, for before his oath, by his very existence, he is morally bound to keep the law of God as fast as he learns it. No oath can absolve him from his natural allegiance to God."

He had often been called an Infidel and an Atheist, but here was real infidelity—infidelity to the laws of God; here was practical atheism, the denial of the laws of God. "To say that there is no law higher than what the State can make," he asserted, "is practical atheism. It is not a denial of God in His person; this is only speculative atheism. It is a denial of the functions and attributes of God; that is real atheism. If there is no God to make a law for me, then there is no God for me."

It was something for him to turn the tables on his critics, it was something to show who were the real heretics—Nenemiah Adams taking his "South Side View" and Moses Stuart joining in unholy union "Conscience and the Constitution" ("All Southern men of intelligence and fairness admire your pamphlet," wrote Webster); President Lord of Dartmouth, posting his "Letter of Inquiry on Slavery," and Francis Wayland of Brown, proving "Slavery, a Scriptural Institution"; Orville Dewey of New York, who boasted that he would return his own brother to slavery if the law required it; and Hubbard Winslow, who deplored all agitation of the painful subject. "It seems amazing," said Parker, "that American Christianity of the Puritanic stock, with a philosophy that transcends sensationalism, should prove false to the only principle which at once justifies the conduct of Jesus, of Luther, of the Puritans themselves. For certainly if obedience to the established law be the highest virtue, then the Patriots and Pilgrims of New England, the Reformers of the Church, the glorious company of the Apostles, the goodly fellowship of the prophets, and the noble array of martyrs, nay, Jesus himself, were only criminals and traitors."

The magistrates went for atheism, making an idol of the law and asking people to bow down and worship it. A new philosophy of government was announced (new for America, new for Massachusetts), and it was the philosophy of materialism. "Here is the first maxim," said Parker—"'There is no Higher Law.' That is the proclamation of objective atheism; it is the selfish materialism of Hobbes, De la Mettrie and Helvetius, gone to seed. You have nothing to rely on above the politicians and their statutes; if you suffer, nothing to appeal to but the ballot-box. Here is the next maxim—'Religion has nothing to do with politics.' That is subjective atheism, with a political application. If there be no law inherent in mind and matter above any wicked statute of a tyrant, still the instinctive religious sense of man looks up with reverence, faith and love, and thinks there is a God and a higher law."

But perhaps the orthodox would argue that Parker was not competent to test things by religion: he had abandoned religion. So thought Andrews Norton, for example. "It is lamentable," he said, on the occasion of Parker's first speech in Faneuil Hall, "that what is put forward most prominently is a speech by one disgraced in the eyes of good men as an infidel clergyman." But Parker's argument was based on history, too; and here no one could impugn his credentials. "When a small boy," he wrote, closing his **"Defence"** in the case of The United States *versus* Theodore Parker—"When a small boy my mother lifted me up, one Sunday, and held me while I read the first monumental line I ever saw: SACRED TO LIBERTY AND THE RIGHTS OF MANKIND. Gentlemen, the Spirit of Liberty, the Love of Justice, was early fanned into a flame in my boyish heart. That monument covers the bones of my own kinsfolk; it was their blood which reddened the long green grass at Lexington. It is my own name which stands chiselled on that stone; the tall Captain who marshalled his fellow farmers and mechanics into stern array was my father's father. I learned to read out of his Bible, and with a musket he that day captured from the foe, I learned also another religious lesson, that REBELLION TO TYRANTS IS OBEDIENCE TO GOD."

He was in the American tradition, in the tradition of Otis and Adams and Jefferson. He was at home in Faneuil Hall, he and his doctrine of the Higher Law, more at home than Webster, who advised Massachusetts to "conquer her prejudices" for liberty, more at home than Everett, who invoked the "patriotism of all citizens to abstain from discussion" of slavery, more at home than Curtis, who stood on its platform and encouraged the crowd to howl down the Higher Law. The pretensions of the Government did not impose on him; he knew the history of Stuart England and of the Protectorate—

"That which concerns the mysterie of the Kings Power is not lawful to be disputed," said James I, but Cromwell said, "There is one general grievance, and that is the Law." The presumption of the Courts held no terrors for him; he knew the use that despotic governments made of pliant judges, Judge Kelyng arguing, "If a company of people will go about any public reformation, this is high treason," Chief Justice Finch sustaining the Ship-money, Jeffreys and Scroggs doing the bloody work of James II. He knew the history of independency in Puritan Massachusetts and of the Charter Oak in Connecticut, he was familiar with the philosophy of the Revolution and of the Declaration of Independence and could fling the words of Otis and Adams and Jefferson in the teeth of those who denied the Higher Law.

And how fitting for a transcendentalist to espouse the Higher Law! It was idealism applied to politics, intuition in the realm of social ethics. Parker could take out those sermons and articles on religion and he wouldn't have to change a single idea. He could write "State" where he had said "Church," change "Bible" to "Constitution," and "pharisees" to "politicians," substitute "Higher Law" for "Conscience," and there you were. He had always taught the ultimate authority of the soul, the sufficiency of intuition, the validity of *a priori* truths. He was an old hand at nullification; he had nullified the Scriptures where they were contrary to the teachings of Nature; he had nullified social institutions where they ran counter to the principles of justice. Now he was ready to nullify the laws of slavery because they stultified the Higher Law, and when his friends in Syracuse spirited a slave, Jerry, out of jail, Parker wrote to them: "Injustice mounted on a statute is not the less unjust, only the more formidable. There are some statutes so wicked that it is every man's duty to violate them."

It was an impregnable position that he occupied, as impregnable as the Declaration of Independence; in any argument he was bound to have the best of it. Challenge his facts and he would face you down; slavery was a fact that couldn't be gainsaid, and all qualifying facts were, in the last analysis, irrelevant. Show him the statutes and he would deny that they were binding. Ask for his own authority, and he would refer you to "the law which God wrote ineffaceably in the hearts of mankind."

There was only one way of meeting this argument from the Higher Law: you could charge that, in effect, it led to anarchy. If every man is to judge for himself what is the law, then there is no law, and no authority, and society is back in a state of nature. Jefferson had faced this same problem, and had met it, not with logic, but with common sense: he had appealed to prudence, that laws should not be nullified for light and transient causes, and had called on experience to prove that "mankind are more disposed to suffer than to right themselves by abolishing the forms to which they are accustomed." The Higher Law abolitionist had to meet the same argument, and he did it as best he could. He entered an objection as to facts and another as to logic. "If we do not obey this law (it is said) we shall disobey all laws. It is not so. There is not a country in the world where there is more respect for human laws than in New England, nowhere more than in Massachusetts. Even if a law is unpopular, it is not popular to disobey it. . . . Who is it that oppose the fugitive slave law? Men that have always been on the side of law and order and do not violate the statutes of man for their own advantage. This disobedience to the fugitive slave law is one of the strongest guarantees for the observance of any *just* law. You cannot trust a people who will keep a law *because it is law*; nor need we distrust a people that will only keep a law when it is just."

And by what right did Hunkers charge abolitionists with disrespect for law? The accusation should have palsied their tongues. By what logic did magistrates show so fine a frenzy for the enforcement of the slave law; there were laws enough on the statute books flouted and ignored, if they wished to make a name for themselves. Parker was not one to stand on the defensive; he raided the enemy's camp.

> Are the laws of Massachusetts kept in Boston, then? The usury law says, "Thou shalt not take more than six per cent on thy money." Is that kept? There are thirty-four millions of banking capital in Massachusetts and I think that every dollar of this capital has broken the law within the past twelve months, and yet no complaint has been made. There are three or four hundred brothels in this city of Boston, and ten or twelve hundred shops for the sale of rum. All of them are illegal; some are as well known to the police as is this house, indeed a great deal more frequented by some of them than any house of God. Does anybody disturb them? How many laws of Massachusetts have been violated this very week, in this very city, by the slave-hunters here, by the very officers of the State? What is the meaning of this? Every law which favours the accumulation of money must be kept, but those which prohibit the unjust accumulation of money—by certain classes—they need not be kept.

Tax Parker with disrespect for the law! The only laws he cared to respect were the laws of human nature. Indict him for contempt of court! There was only one Judge whose authority he acknowledged; black-robed judges could not scare him. Confront him with the prohibitions of the Constitution, he pointed to the guarantees. Charge him with inciting rebellion, he would reply that "rebellion to tyrants is obedience to God." To the argument of the Higher Law there was no effective answer; even force was not effective.

Here, then, was Parker's philosophy of freedom and his program of abolition. It was a philosophy which assumed as intuitive truths that freedom was right and

slavery wrong. It judged slavery by its own ideal standards, and found it morally indefensible. It was, at the same time, a pragmatic philosophy which taught that slavery was a failure. It judged slavery by its fruits and found that they were demonstrably rotten. It was inspired by idealism and sustained by faith; it was rooted in experience and bottomed on fact. Its premises were general and timeless; its data were particular and circumstantial. It was no sudden inspiration, no theory hastily concocted to meet an emergency, but it was broad enough to embrace any emergency and realistic enough to cope with any crisis. Its formulation was independent of measures or men, but its application was immediate and opportunistic. So Parker always had his speeches ready; the particular illustrations might change, but the general principles never. So he was always ready to fight; the tactics of each foray differed, but the grand strategy remained the same.

Works Cited

I do not think it necessary to list here even a part of the vast literature on slavery. There is an excellent bibliography of the anti-slavery movement in A. B. Hart's "Slavery and Abolition" (N. Y., 1906). This [essay] is concerned only with Parker's view of the institution and with his philosophy, as distinct from his active attack upon it. Two collections of Parker's anti-slavery sermons and speeches appeared during his lifetime: *Speeches, Addresses and Occasional Sermons*, 3 vols. (Boston, 1852) and *Additional Speeches, Addresses and Occasional Sermons*, 2 vols. (Boston, 1855). Volume 11 of the Centenary Edition, *The Slave Power*, is edited by J. K. Hosmer; Vol. 12, *The Rights of Man in America*, by F. B. Sanborn: these contain the more important speeches on slavery. The same speeches can be found in the Cobbe Edition in Vols. 5, 6, 7, and 8. Volume 2 of Weiss's biography contains a mass of anti-slavery material, so badly arranged that it will baffle even the most patient student. There is no satisfactory study of Parker's contribution to the Higher Law doctrine in American politics: that it was great cannot be doubted.

David Mead (essay date winter 1948-49)

SOURCE: Mead, David. "Theodore Parker in Ohio." *Northwest Ohio Quarterly* 21, no. 1 (winter 1948-49): 18-23.

[*In the following essay, Mead details the content and reception of Parker's public speaking engagements in Ohio during the 1850s.*]

1

The eloquent pastor of Boston's Twenty-Eighth Congregational Society was one of the first of New England's fiery divines to follow the lyceum circuit beyond the Alleghenies.[1] In 1852, the year of his first appearance in Ohio, Parker's reputation as a courageous, outspoken thinker was well known to the Western public. His pronouncements as a minister had often been reprinted in Ohio's newspapers; his opinions on the mediation of Christ, his disbelief in miraculous revelation, and his sermons on temperance, slavery, and woman's rights had made him, to some Western minds, one of the most notorious of New England's free-thinking clergymen.

As the forces for and against slavery slowly gathered themselves during the decade preceding the Civil War, the propriety of an anti-slavery discussion in the pulpit was a topic which aroused nation-wide comment. The question was debated in every lyceum in the land, and anti-slavery sermons delivered by Parker or Henry Ward Beecher were frequently followed by accusations of treason and disunion in the Democratic press. Westerners who knew Parker chiefly through the newspaper accounts of his sermons and his passionate orations in Faneuil Hall against Webster's Seventh of March Speech or the Fugitive Slave Law, and who expected him to repeat his incisive opinions on the platform, were often surprised by the calm, intellectual quality of his lectures.

In announcing **"The Progress of Mankind"** and **"The False and True Idea of a Gentleman,"** the *Cincinnati Gazette* (November 3, 1852) predicted that Parker's lectures not only would "excite a good deal of interest among the literary portion of our citizens" but also would offer sentiments to which "there would be a very general dissent." But as Parker was "undoubtedly a man of great ability," his opinions, however offensive, would be "worthy of consideration."

"The Progress of Mankind" contained no inflammatory statements, Parker choosing to avoid any controversy over his "peculiar views." A correspondent of the *Cleveland Herald* (November 9, 1852) wrote from Cincinnati that Parker's audience, accustomed to hearing lectures read from manuscript, was delighted when he strode to the front of the platform and delivered his discourse "with all the freshness and added interest of extemporaneous speaking." He impressed "a crowded audience of the best intelligence of Cincinnati" as a "man of great directness, remarkable affluence of thought," and "learning of universal variety." In appearance, Parker was "intellectual and scholarly, and his elocution reminds you, in some particulars, of Emerson."

On Sunday, November 7, Parker delivered two sermons to "very crowded audiences" at Moncure Conway's Unitarian Church. The *Gazette* testily branded these discourses "a vigorous attack on the prevailing opinions in regard to the Godhead, to Christ, and upon most other received views on religious topics." Indeed this

correspondent had supposed that, because of Parker's objectionable religious opinions, "Sunday would not have found a Christian church open to him, or professing Christians amongst his hearers." But the "immense audience that thronged the inside and outside of the Unitarian Church" proved that "these are progressive days."

"The False and True Idea of a Gentleman" apparently evoked no comments from Cincinnati's journalists, but when this lecture was delivered before the Cleveland Mercantile Library Association the *Herald* observed that Parker's large audience generously applauded the discourse, "abounding as it did with lofty and noble ideas, interspersed with flashes of humor and satire on the principal follies of the age."[2] The editor of the *True Democrat* (November 11, 1852) withheld his usual political antagonism toward abolitionists when he declared that "this eloquent, finished, truthful Lecture" could never be forgotten by those who heard it. Parker ranked among the great thinkers of the age, and his lecture possessed "a chaste, easy and flowing style, a lurking, pungent, but apparently unsought sarcasm and wit."

Parker occupied Cleveland's Melodeon again on January 12, 1854, when he delivered **"The Progress of Mankind"** to a "crowded house." The *Herald* reported that "He is about as graceful a speaker as Horace Greeley, and yet his peculiarities secured the earnest attention of his audience through a very long lecture."[3] This editor made a further, and more ill-tempered, comment on Parker's lecture on January 25. After hearing William Henry Channing's "Great Men and the Elements of Greatness," given before the Cleveland Library Association on January 24, the reviewer pointed out that "Mr. Channing is not an orator, yet he is eloquent. His lecture was in strong contrast with the rigmarole, disjointed, visionary *'talk'* of the man who is so deeply in love with himself, Theodore Parker."

In October, 1854, the Ohio Mechanics' Institute, in Cincinnati, presented a course of weekly lectures on "American Slavery." The project was a money-making scheme, as the offering of political topics by lecture associations was considered to be in poor taste and detrimental to the true cultural purpose of the lecture system. The speakers announced included Parker, William Lloyd Garrison, Frederick Douglass, and Wendell Phillips, all of whom were calculated to attract large crowds and rich profits to the Mechanics' Institute.

Parker delivered the introductory lecture of the course on October 19. His subject, **"The Condition and Prospects of Slavery in America,"** drew a large and "oddly assorted" audience, "a considerable number of negroes being present, and also a delegation of gentlemen from Covington." According to the *Commercial* (October 20, 1854) the lecture was "principally made up of statistics, by which it was attempted to be shown that the South is the master of the North." Parker dwelt upon the effects of slavery on society, morality, and industry. As a remedy for slavery he proposed that the slaves be "purchased by the general government."

Parker's Ohio journey in 1854 took him also to Toledo, Dayton, and Yellow Springs. A correspondent of the *Toledo Blade* (January 16, 1854) reported that the purpose of **"The False and True Idea of a Gentleman"** was "to trample down the love of wealth and of self, and diffuse a universal kindliness and brotherhood and charity among the human family." At Yellow Springs, Parker visited Horace Mann, president of Antioch College, and lectured before the students on **"The Condition, Character and Prospects of America."**[4] Parker's generosity and his esteem for Mann were illustrated by his returning his forty-dollar lecture fee as a gift to the college.[5]

During these early lecture trips Parker developed small liking for the West. He observed "a certain largeness to everything"—plains, trees, pumpkins, apples, swine, and men. In Ohio he marveled at a huge hog weighing 2150 pounds. But in addition to largeness there was "a certain *courseness of fibre* also noticeable in all things." Here were ugliness and squalor in sharp contrast with the neatness, beauty, and refinement of New England. The climate was raw and unhealthful and seemed to sap the energy of the inhabitants. "The men look sickly, yellow, and flabby," Parker wrote in 1854. "The women are tall and bony, their hair lank, their faces thin and flabby-cheeked." His conclusion was that "the West deteriorates Americans."[6]

2.

Unlike many of the orators who spoke before Western lyceums in the 1850's Parker was more concerned with popular education than with financial profits for himself. "The business of lecturing," he once wrote, "is an original American contrivance for educating the people. The world has nothing like it. In it are combined the best things of the Church, and of the College, with some of the fun of the theatre."[7] The pleasant excitement of lecturing before curious audiences in the West and the assurance that he was spreading truth and knowledge more than compensated for the hardships of his winter journeys and his reluctance to leave his Boston congregation.

In the season of 1855-1856, during one of Parker's most ambitious Western trips, he delivered nine lectures and two sermons in twelve days among the communities of northern Ohio.[8] This tiring schedule illustrates Parker's devotion to the lyceum's aim of "doing good," as none of the lecture fees was more than $25. His first performance was on November 7, 1855, at Hudson, where he spoke to the students of Western Reserve Col-

lege.[9] The next evening he gave **"The Progress of Mankind"** in Ravenna. The *Portage Sentinel* (November 10, 1855) commended Parker as "a model lecturer." "There is no attempt at display, no flourish, no declamation. He is plain, frank and candid."

A "large audience" heard this lecture in Salem. The editor of the *Columbiana County Republican* (November 14, 1855) was pleased because Parker's oratory was "not boisterous." He depended for effect upon "the merits of his subject" and an "argumentative manner" and did not display "any of the spasmodic efforts and exertions of the body, so common among speakers who are compelled, for want of ability, to attract attention by noise."

At Wooster, Parker's declaration that "the progress of mankind" had been hindered by slavery, that "monument of misdirected industry," aroused the ire of the anti-abolitionist editor of the *Wayne County Democrat* (November 15, 1855). This critic wished to "warn democrats and Union men, that it looks like a Massachusetts Abolition Disunion trick to get their abominable and fanatical ideas before the people, under the plea of Moral Lectures." The people should "not be humbugged by any abolition tricks" or "party fanaticism" aimed at "sowing the seeds of disunion broadcast in the land."

The "very crowded" Akron audience which attended **"The False and True Idea of a Gentleman"** expected to hear a fiery orator. "Instead of such an one," reported the *Summit County Beacon* (November 21, 1855), "was a plain and quiet man, plainly clad and not extremely prepossessing; concealing a small keen eye behind a pair of spectacles; making little more use of his hands than was consistent with profound repose of manner, and barely raising his voice above the conversational pitch." His attempt "to gibbet 'cod fish aristocracy'" and "satirise proud ignorance" was entirely successful.

For two hours Parker "enchained his audience" at Toledo "with illustrations of the wonderful strides that mankind had taken in civilization." Parker's power as a lecturer resulted from "the easy composure of his manner, the thoroughness with which his ideas are matured in his own mind, his mastery over forms of expression." Though "pretending to none of the graces of oratory nor mere elegancies of diction," he was "one of the most powerful and instructive speakers" the people of Toledo had ever heard.[10]

Parker's success upon Ohio's lyceum platforms was greatly enhanced by the sincerity and earnestness of his delivery, his manner of talking "like an apostle who has a great mission to fulfil." Here was a man with "a boldness about his speech," a determination to say what he thought "without any unnecessary circumlocution or whipping the devil round a stump." Except where political issues were involved, Parker and the other "eccentric but brilliant" orators from the East were likely to meet with less adverse criticism in the West than they were accustomed to receive in New England. The pioneers' long struggle against the hardships of the frontier had given to the Western mind an independent spirit and a curiosity to hear all sides of a question. The distinction between moral right and wrong was not so clearly marked to Westerners as it was to New Englanders.[11] There were doubtless many Ohio people who were prepared to find offense in Parker's opinions, but the newspaper reviews of the day suggest that among his hearers was a goodly number of independent Western citizens who were inclined to agree that "Mr. Parker speaks, as he believes, the whole truth, caring little where it hits. His fearlessness is grand. He stands up before earth and heaven a true man."[12]

Notes

1. Orestes Brownson lectured in the West in February, 1852, and Henry Ward Beecher visited Ohio in 1854 and 1855. For a general discussion of Parker as a lecturer, see Henry Steele Commager, *Theodore Parker,* Boston, Little, Brown and Company, 1936, pp. 144-150.

2. November 10, 1852. The title of this lecture was usually reported by the press as "The True and False Idea of a Gentleman." In his *MS. Lyceum Diary* (Massachusetts Historical Society) Parker calls the lecture "The False and True Idea of a Gentleman." Parker's *MS. Lyceum Diary* is used with the kind permission of the Massachusetts Historical Society.

3. January 13, 1854. Although Greeley was a notoriously poor speaker, his editorial fame and bold opinions made him a favorite with Ohio's lecture public. In the fall of 1852 he had campaigned strenuously in Cleveland and Cuyahoga County for General Winfield Scott, the Whig presidential nominee who was defeated by the Locofoco candidate, Franklin Pierce.

4. *MS. Lyceum Diary. MS. Diary of Maria L. Moore* (Antioch College Library).

5. According to the *MS. Lyceum Diary,* Parker's fees for individual lectures ranged from $30 at Toledo and Dayton to $50 at Cleveland and Cincinnati. After deducting expenses and gifts, he had net earnings of $310.15 for twelve lectures in the West in 1854. In addition to his Ohio lectures, Parker appeared in Pittsburgh, Indianapolis, and Adrian, Michigan.

6. Commager, p. 147. John Weiss, *Life and Correspondence of Theodore Parker,* 2 vols., New York, Appleton and Company, 1864, I, 327.

7. Commager, p. 144. Weiss, I, 304.

8. Two additional lectures, scheduled at Cleveland, November 6, 1855, and at Sandusky, November 16, 1855, were not given. *MS. Lyceum Diary.* At Cleveland his lecture negotiations apparently were not completed; at Sandusky he disappointed an audience of four hunderd when he failed to arrive in time to lecture.

9. *MS. Minutes of the Phi Delta Literary Society* (Western Reserve University Library).

10. *Daily Toledo Blade,* November 19, 1855. On Sunday, November 18, Parker delivered two sermons in Toledo: "False Rules of Action and False Guides of Conduct" and "Overruling Providence." Both were attended by large audiences.

11. This "moral instability" of the Western mind was disturbing to many Eastern people, and especially to the New England supporters of the Society for the Promotion of Collegiate and Theological Education at the West. ". . . . we want principles of stability," declared a speaker before the Society in 1846; "we want a system of permanent forces; we want deep, strong, and constant influences, that shall take from the changefulness and excitability of the western mind, by giving it the tranquility of depth, and shall protect it from delusive and fitful impulses, by enduing it with a calm, profound, and pure reason." Albert Barnes, "Plea in Behalf of the Western Colleges," *Third Annual Report of the Society for the Promotion of Collegiate and Theological Education at the West,* New York, J. F. Trow, 1847, pp. 12-13.

12. *Daily Toledo Blade,* January 16, 1854.

William R. Hutchison (essay date 1959)

SOURCE: Hutchison, William R. "Theodore Parker and the Confessional Question." In *The Transcendentalist Ministers: Church Reform in the New England Renaissance,* pp. 98-136. New Haven, Conn.: Yale University Press, 1959.

[In the following essay, Hutchison relates Parker's role in the controversy within the Unitarian church over various theological issues during the mid-nineteenth century.]

The phase of controversy which began in 1841 and which centered in the person of Theodore Parker was the great trauma of mid-nineteenth-century Unitarianism. It brought out in bold relief the fundamental issues of supernaturalism, of church "discipline," and of the definition of Christianity which had been involved in the earlier discussion. Parker's ideas of religious reform were similar to those of other Transcendentalists, but his advocacy had a singular impact, first because he refused to allow his opinions or the objections raised against them to separate him from the Unitarian ministry, and secondly because he boldly voiced the denial, always latent in Transcendentalist theology, that Christianity is based on a special revelation of God. The Parkerite attack, unlike the earlier one, forced the denomination to rediscover and define its theological position. Though Unitarianism after the 1850's was still beset by the conflicting demands of free inquiry and Christian confessionalism, that church has never, since the Parker experience, suffered from its early delusion that the two can exist together as absolute principles.

The village preacher whose transcendental heresies brought him into the full glare of public attention in 1841 was then just thirty-one years of age. In physical appearance Parker was not prepossessing. He was short and sturdy, with a large head and a massive forehead that was made more so by a thinness of hair which had become a predominant baldness before he was forty. His rather ordinary facial lineaments were set off in later years by a "more than current" gray beard; but in the 1840's it was the steel-blue eyes, partly obscured by gold-mounted spectacles, that were his most arresting feature. Simple dress and unassuming manner, together with a certain awkwardness of bearing and a lack of musical quality in the voice, suggested to some that a ploughman or schoolmaster, not a priest, was occupying the pulpit. The task of captivating audiences was left almost entirely to his rhetorical abilities, which were more than adequate for that purpose.[1]

One of the youngest members of the Transcendentalist circle when he began attending their meetings in 1837, Parker even then had boasted greater scholarly attainments than most of them, and this in spite of a meager formal education. Born in 1810, the youngest son of a Lexington farmer, he had attended grammar school eleven weeks each winter for a period of ten years, and then had spent less than a year at the Lexington Academy. Home study, however, had enabled him to pass the entrance examinations for Harvard College, and without attending classes he had subsequently fulfilled all except the monetary requirements for the B.A. degree.[2] He had then spent two years (1834-36) in the Divinity School and in June of 1837 had been ordained to the Unitarian pastorate at West Roxbury, Massachusetts.[3]

A competent work of self-education would have been laudable in itself, but Parker's acquirements were prodigious. At age twenty-one he had been able to read in six languages, and four years later he claimed some degree of facility in eleven more. While attending the Divinity School he had been called upon to teach classes in Hebrew, and he had entered the field of biblical criticism as an editor of the *Scriptural Interpreter*. In the year preceding his settlement at West Roxbury he had translated DeWette's *Introduction to the Old Testament*, which he published with his own notes and commentaries in 1843.[4]

Parker had made his anonymous entrance into the Transcendentalist controversy with the **"Levi Blodgett letter of 1840,"** (above, p. 86), but he had shown his allegiance to the New School before that time. He had told a former Divinity School classmate in 1837 that he was preaching "abundant heresies" to his congregation, including "the worst of all things, Transcendentalism . . ." He had greeted Emerson's Divinity School Address with enthusiasm, and had deplored the "illiberality" shown by some members of the Boston Association who debated whether Emerson could be called a Christian.[5]

The philosophical and theological basis of Parker's campaign against orthodox Unitarianism was stated in numerous forms over the period 1841-53, when that campaign was most intense. It is necessary to explain this theoretical structure in some detail, since Parker's was the most complete and important of the more radical Transcendental theologies.

Parker, though he gave various names to his own highly individual formulations, regarded his system as falling within the limits of the "transcendental" philosophy. It was his view that "in metaphysics there are and have long been two schools of philosophers," the "sensationalists" and the "transcendentalists." The principal tenet of the sensationalists, he said, is that "there is nothing in the intellect which was not first in the senses." That of the transcendentalists is the reverse:

> that there is in the intellect (or consciousness), something that never was in the senses, to wit, the intellect (or consciousness) itself; that man has faculties which transcend the senses; faculties which give him ideas and intuitions that transcend sensational experience; ideas whose origin is not from sensation, nor their proof from sensation.[6]

Although such a division of the philosophical world may seem vastly overgeneralized, it must be remembered that an active controversy produces broad alignments which in the abstract would seem quite impossible. To a zealot like Parker, sensationalism and transcendentalism were two great armies in the field of thought. The names emblazoned on their respective banners represented sharply contrasting approaches to contemporary problems, even though the makeup of each contending force was heterogeneous.

Parker saw clear differences between the practical effects of the two philosophies. In physics, he said, sensationalism produces a lack of ultimate assurance about the facts of the universe, while transcendentalism leads to metaphysical certainty. In politics the sensational philosophy leads to a denial of immutable laws, while the transcendental proclaims natural justice. In ethics, the first denies eternal rules of morality and counsels expediency, while the second encourages an ethical system based upon the universal and immutable promptings of intuition. In religion the logical result of the sensational philosophy is either a denial of God or a complete deference to revelation, while transcendentalism affirms the reality of divine things by making a priori belief the basis for all formulations.[7]

Parker had misgivings about some of the foot soldiers in the Transcendental army. He deplored the tendency of some of them to scorn observation and neglect the lessons of the past, and he blamed others for confusing personal whims with universal laws. Some devotees, he thought, were "transcendental-mad" rather than "transcendental-wise."

His own form of the philosophy attempted to avoid such extravagances. His theory of knowledge emphasized induction as well as intuition. Like Cousin among European transcendentalists and Brownson and several others of the American group, Parker warned repeatedly that mere awareness of an intuitive fact of consciousness is insufficient. If deductions from consciousness are to become usable ideas, they must be formulated with the help of empirical observation.[8]

It is possible to argue that this kind of interest in scientific demonstration vitiated the whole intuitionist idea, but Parker, however inconsistently, believed it did not. The reasoning process, he thought, confirms and actualizes intuition, but does not displace it as the basis of the knowing process. His account of the way men attain to a knowledge of God is a striking illustration of this epistemological approach—and also of the Transcendentalist tendency to mix the ingredients of the Kantian critiques into a theological *potpourri*:

> Our belief in God's existence does not depend on the *a posteriori* argument, on considerations drawn from the order, fitness and beauty discovered by observations made in the material world; nor yet on the *a priori* argument, on considerations drawn from the eternal nature of things, and observations made in the spiritual world. It depends primarily on no *argument* whatever, not on reasoning, but *Reason*. The fact is given outright, as it were, and comes to the man, as soon and as naturally, as the belief of his own existence . . . This intuitive perception of God is afterwards fundamentally and logically established by the *a priori* argument, and beautifully confirmed by the *a posteriori* argument; but we are not left without the Idea of God till we become metaphysicians and naturalists and so can discover it by much thinking. It comes spontaneously, by a law of whose actions we are, at first, not conscious. The belief always precedes the proof; intuition gives the thing to

be reasoned about. Unless this intuitive function be performed, it is not possible to attain a knowledge of God.[9]

The passion for "systematic ransacking of the facts of history" which has justly been attributed to Parker,[10] was not an outright rejection of intuitionism. The scholar who ransacks history to put together many instances of human intuitiveness is not constructing a denial of intuition, even though his method has been partly inductive. Until the investigator shifts his fundamental reliance in epistemology to scientific demonstration, the intuited fact remains basic, the inductive demonstration auxiliary. Parker did not reject the Transcendentalist belief in man's religious consciousness. Instead, like Cousin and many others, he sought by an inductive process to bolster the intuitionist argument and make it at least appear scientifically respectable. To the frequent criticism of transcendentalism as too abstruse, he answered that "the transcendental philosophy. . . . does not neglect experience. In human history it finds *confirmations, illustrations,* of the ideas of human nature . . . It *illustrates* religion by facts of observation, facts of testimony."[11]

Parker was far enough from a primary reliance upon the "facts" of history to reject what he termed the "historical method" of theological construction. Theologians using this method, he said, "get the sum of the theological thinking of the human race, and out of this mass construct a system . . ." Such a procedure is useful, he said, for showing "what has been done," but can no more lead to the perfect theology than the eclectic method can lead to a perfect philosophy. "Former researches," he argued, "offer but a narrow and inadequate basis to rest on." The more desirable method, which he called the philosophical, looks to the facts of history and of natural science simply as confirmations of "the primitive gospel God wrote on the heart of his child," and in this way uses "both the reflective and the intuitive faculties of man" in theological construction. The time would come, Parker believed, when men would attain to a true system of Nature and theology "by observation and reasoning"; but that time was still far off, and "meantime . . . the great truths of morality and religion . . . are perceived intuitively, and by instinct . . ."[12]

Parker applied the "philosophical method" in a theological system which he was calling spiritualism in 1842 but was defining as theism a decade later. Its basic tenets were the infinitude and absolute perfection of God, and the immanence of God in man and nature. Parker held that though God is different in kind from both matter and man, he must nonetheless be recognized as immanent in both, since to deny this would be to say there are places where God is not, and thus to deny his infinitude. All that exists or occurs, therefore, is God's doing, and there can be no distinction of supernatural from natural, of clean from unclean, or of "special" revelation from God's constant revelation in the human soul.[13]

In accordance with this fundamental theism, Parker regarded Christ as a human being, though a religious genius and supreme teacher. Jesus taught some errors, said Parker, but he also taught "Absolute Religion." The basic teachings of Absolute Religion are "love of God and love of man"; and the Scriptures or the Church are wrong insofar as they suggest that Christ's teaching was more than this. The Incarnation, he argued, has been misconstrued by the Church, for God is incarnate in the entire human race, not simply in Jesus. Christ did not "redeem" mankind, as the Church teaches, or even live for mankind: "He lived for himself; died for himself; worked out his own salvation . . ."[14] Neither Jesus nor the Scriptures, Parker reasoned, can make any valid claim to infallibility, for the teachings of both are true only insofar as they conform to Absolute Religion.[15]

Parker called himself a Christian because he believed Jesus to have been the only man thus far in human history who actually discerned and taught Absolute Religion. In Parker's detailed rendering of this basically Emersonian theme, the Gospel teachings were reinterpreted to conform to a monistic and naturalistic system. The references of Jesus to human sinfulness, for example, were taken to mean that men are degraded by too low an opinion of their own powers. Though Christ is reported to have called himself the Way, the Truth, and the Life, he must have meant, Parker explained, that his teachings were these things. And when the Scriptures speak of Christ as the Son of God, they are merely asserting that Jesus achieved the communion with God which is possible to all men.[16]

Parker regarded the Church as an institution of entirely human origin. Although Jesus, he said, was the central figure or "model-man" of the institution founded by the Apostles, Jesus himself founded no Church. Even if he had done so, this would not have constituted a transmission of divine authority, since Jesus was no more than human.[17]

In applying these conceptions to the religion of his own time, Parker first of all acknowledged that the "popular theology," even in its Calvinist form, contained "some of the greatest truths of religion which man has attained thus far." And Unitarianism was given credit for having modified the worst features of the Calvinist creed, for attempting "to apply Good Sense to theology, to reconcile Knowledge with Belief, Reason with Revelation, to *humanize* the church."[18]

But Unitarianism, he argued, had not gone far enough. It had refused to "develop the truth it has borne, latent and unconscious in its bosom," and was therefore full of contradictions. Philosophically, Unitarianism was "too rational to go the full length of the supernatural theory," yet "too sensual to embrace the spiritual method." Unitarian theology, he said,

> humanizes the Bible, yet calls it miraculous; believes in man's greatness . . . yet asks for a Mediator . . . admits man can pray for himself . . . yet prays 'in the name of Christ' . . . censures the traditionary sects, yet sits itself among the tombs, and mourns . . . believes the humanity of Christ . . . yet his miraculous birth likewise and miraculous powers . . . stops [men's] ears with texts of the Old Testament, and then asks them to listen to the voice of God in their heart . . .[19]

Parker's remedy for these inconsistencies was a complete rejection of the supernaturalist elements in the popular faith. He made no effort, in his later writings at least, to hide his contempt for supernaturalism, and implicitly for the silliness of those who held to it. He stated a concise *non credo* in a sermon of 1852:

> Of course I do not believe in a devil, eternal torment, nor in a particle of absolute evil in God's world or in God. I do not believe there ever was a miracle, or ever will be . . . I do not believe in the miraculous inspiration of the Old Testament or the New Testament . . . I do not believe in the miraculous origin of the Hebrew Church, or the Buddhist Church, or the Christian Church; nor the miraculous character of Jesus. I take not the Bible for my master, nor yet the Church; nor even Jesus of Nazareth for my master . . . I try all things by the human faculties . . . Has God given us anything better than our nature?[20]

A sermon by Parker in 1841, *The Transient and Permanent in Christianity,* brought these various rejections of traditional belief to public notice. The sermon was delivered on May 19 at the ordination of Charles Shackford in the Hawes Place Church of South Boston.

The public outcry which followed was a protest against the tone of the sermon as well as against its heresies. Parker's affirmation in it that Christian rites and doctrines are mutable expressions of eternal religious truths would in itself have caused little offense. What aroused anger was that he pronounced certain tenets of the common faith as not merely imperfect but vulgar and absurd. He stated that Christian doctrines in general owed more to heathenism, Judaism, and "the caprice of philosophers" than to the teachings of Jesus. Many of these doctrines, he said, are "the refuse of idol temples . . . wood, hay, and stubble, wherewith men have built on the cornerstone Christ laid." The pure stream of Christ's message had, he thought, been "polluted by man with mire and dirt." Men have "piled their own rubbish against the temple of Truth."[21] Whatever the substantive merits of such assertions, this was a kind of invective which had not been heard since Norton's trumpetings in the *Advertiser.*

As for the alleged authority of Jesus, Parker could not see "why the great truths of Christianity rest on the personal authority of Jesus, more than the axioms of geometry rest on the personal authority of Euclid, or Archimedes." The preacher stated his belief that Christ did actually exist, but added, in a phrase which conservatives took as an absolute rejection of Christian faith, that "if it could be proved . . . that Jesus of Nazareth had never lived, still Christianity would stand firm, and fear no evil."[22]

Parker's sermon, like nearly all of his controversial works, also contained positive elements—appreciations of the excellence of Christ and the truths of the Bible, eloquent and lofty appeals to man's spiritual nature. Such affirmations in Parker's writings should not go unrecognized, since they formed the bulk of his noncontroversial preaching and unquestionably accounted for much of his popular influence. Some of Parker's opponents of 1841 can be criticized for ignoring this more constructive side of his doctrine, although the severity of the preacher's negative utterances made it natural that discussion should center in that area.

The first opposition to the *Transient and Permanent* came not from Unitarians but from the Orthodox churches and newspapers. Even Parker's strongest partisans have recognized that the Unitarian press, particularly in the early days of the dispute "did their best . . . to be charitable," and "cultivated a generous spirit."[23] But the non-Unitarian papers almost immediately were filled with such epithets as "infidel," "scorner," and "blasphemer," and the Orthodox began declaring somewhat pompously that the liberal faith had ended in pure naturalism, just as they had always predicted it would.[24] The Unitarian clergy, to be sure, were in no position to join immediately in this general hue and cry; for, like it or not, they bore a degree of responsibility. Parker was one of their number, and Unitarians had given him the opportunity to speak at an official ceremony of ordination.

The invitation to Parker had been issued by a committee of the Hawes Place Church with the approval of their minister-elect. A clerical "Ordaining Council," invited in the same way, included, besides Parker, Chandler Robbins and Samuel K. Lothrop of Boston, Nathaniel Folsom of Haverhill, Dr. John Pierce of Brookline, and five others.[25] It was the members of this Council who came in for the most immediate criticism, since they had allowed the ordination to come to an end without expressing their disapproval of Parker's remarks.

The gage was thrown down in an open letter from three non-Unitarian ministers[26] who had attended the ordination service by special invitation from candidate Shackford. Their brief letter, which appeared in the *New En-gland Puritan* on May 28, stated that they had found Parker's sentiments so contrary to their own religious conceptions that they felt constrained to ask whether the Unitarian clergy, and the Council in particular, considered Parker a preacher of Christianity. They expressed surprise that no member of the Council had asked Shackford to disavow Parker's opinions as a condition to continuation of the ordination service.[27]

The first reply to the Orthodox questions came from Nathaniel Folsom, who denied that any formal disavowal of Parker had been necessary. All of the other participants in the service, he said, had expressed their Christian faith so strongly as to make their position perfectly clear; and Shackford had been preaching "the Gospel of the New Testament" in that very pulpit for the seven months preceding his ordination.[28] But this answer satisfied neither the Orthodox clergyman nor the non-Unitarian press, and the liberal ministers were kept on the defensive. Samuel K. Lothrop, of the Ordaining Council, outlined his position in two extended letters to J. H. Fairchild, one of the Orthodox complainants. He refused to speak for other members of the Council, but declared that for his own part he could no longer consider Parker a Christian minister, or at least could have no "intimate sympathy and fellowship" with him. However, if Mr. Parker thought himself a Christian, Lothrop said, and could find "a people willing to hear him, and ministers willing to exchange with him, that is his affair and their affair."

The "official statement" desired by non-Unitarians apparently was not to be had. "No Unitarian clergyman," as Lothrop explained, "feels himself responsible for his brethren, or authorized to speak for them. We recognize no creed, covenant, or union of any kind, that interferes with individual liberty and independence."[29] Parker was, however, reprimanded publicly in the *Register* for having expounded his heresies on an occasion when he was acting in association with other ministers. The editors, while conceding that the sermon had contained "many good things and many beautiful things, that came home to our hearts," thought that its tone of "sneer and ridicule" had been inexcusable.[30]

Parker's angry reply accused the *Register* of distorting the meaning of his sermon. He did not mind being harshly dealt with, he said—"it is a very small thing that I should be judged of you"—but he wished to be told more precisely what the "sneering" passages had been. He desired, he said, to have "the very head and front of my offending made manifest." And since the *Register* had disclaimed responsibility for his opinions, he wanted its editors to "tell me *for whose sentiments you are responsible*—always excepting your own." The *Register* gave its rebuttal in the same issue, by quoting a number of the passages in the *Transient and Permanent* which seemed to them to be "sneering" denials of the inspiration of Scripture or the authority of Christ, or to throw ridicule on particular beliefs cherished by many Christians.[31]

The *Monthly Miscellany* also took Parker to task. The reviewer (probably Gannett) prefaced his remarks with a hope that Parker would not "consider the open and fair expression of dissent from his opinions an act of injustice to him," as he had apparently done in the case of the *Register*'s review. Parker's irreverent opinions about Christ and the Bible, said the *Miscellany,* had occasioned grief and surprise among Unitarians; but a more fundamental difficulty was that Parker's principles, if adhered to logically, would leave no ground for believing any part of the Christian Gospel, even those parts to which Parker assented. "Here—on the matter of *authority,*" the writer asserted, "is the essential difference between Mr. Parker and others who value the Gospel." It was not necessary, he said, to question Parker's faith "in Christianity, viewed merely in its internal character. But on his principles *we* should have no faith in Christianity."[32]

In September the highly respected *Examiner* came out with the most thorough denunciation of the South Boston sermon that was to be given in the Unitarian press. The writer was A. P. Peabody, the conservative whom Norton had thought too lenient toward the Transcendentalists in 1839. Peabody now atoned for his earlier moderation. His strongly worded article attempted to "follow Mr. Parker, as he passes with his besom among the time-hallowed furniture of the Christian Temple," but professed to find the iconoclast almost too erratic to follow. The basic inconsistency, Peabody thought, was in Parker's wish to give the Christian name to a system of "absolute religion" which admittedly "is so entirely independent of Christ, as to stand equally well without him." It seemed, he said, that the term "Christian" was in danger of becoming "a mere name of courtesy."

Parker had stated the requirements of Absolute Religion as "love to God and man." Its only creed, he had said, is belief in a perfect God, its only "form" a "divine life," its sole rule of morality, that one should do "the best thing, in the best way, from the highest motives." All of this, said Peabody, is very fine, "but why call it *Christianity*? It was all known before Christ; and, as Mr. Parker justly deems, is known independently of Christ. . . . To give it one name rather than another, is a mere matter of fancy."

Peabody discussed in detail Parker's assertion that the traditional forms and doctrines of Christianity had not been initiated by Jesus himself, and adduced scriptural and theological proofs to the contrary. He dealt in the same way with Parker's statement that the scriptural writers never had claimed special inspiration. The reviewer denied that the canonical books had been assembled by "caprice or accident." And he ridiculed Parker's assertion that traditional Christianity had always regarded Jesus as speaking on his own rather than God's authority. He knew of few sects which had ever believed such a thing. The true question, Peabody concluded, was not "whether truth is to be received on the authority of God or on that of Jesus. It is, whether truth is to be taken on any authority higher or other than our own."[33]

During the following winter Parker was given an opportunity to answer such criticisms. In June 1841 he had declined an invitation from "several gentlemen of Boston"[34] to give a course of lectures there late in the same year; but when the invitation was renewed several months later Parker accepted, very probably with the thought of vindicating his position before the Boston public.

The five lectures he delivered at the Old Masonic Temple on Tremont Street were enthusiastically received by the public. The hall (capacity 750) was filled nearly every time. His biographer Weiss later recalled that "all the earnest thinkers" were there; and Gannett's magazine, which could scarcely be accused of predisposition in Parker's favor, reported that his audiences sat through the learned two-hour discourses without showing "the least impatience."[35] The success of the series gave Parker his first definite assurance that he could find a ready audience in Boston if the Unitarian clergy should shut him out of their pulpits, as indeed they were already beginning to do.[36]

The lectures of 1841-42 were published, in expanded and heavily annotated form, as the ***Discourse of Matters Pertaining to Religion.*** The Rev. John H. Morison, of Milton, Mass., reviewing this work for the *Examiner,* found Parker's attitude and modes of expression more dogmatic than the popular theology which Parker so deplored. A more serious charge was that Parker's great show of learning, which might seem to justify his assertiveness, was too full of inaccuracies to merit the reader's trust. Morison cited and documented some of the most flagrant examples of Parker's carelessness, and stated that he had found many more.

As for the cry of "persecution" which was being raised against the conservatives for questioning Parker's standing as a Christian minister, Morison suggested that "the terms bigot, superstitious, fanatic, pharisee, and hypocrite" which Parker was accustomed to apply to those "whose crime consists in differing from himself," were as unpleasant and could be quite as unjust as the epithets of which Parker was complaining.[37]

Another comment on the ***Discourse of Religion*** was written by Samuel Osgood, who still considered himself a Transcendentalist but believed that Parker had gone beyond what any of the other theologians in the New School could accept. "As the Strauss of our American theology," he said, Parker had come to occupy a position "almost alone." There had been some apprehension, Osgood remarked, that the radical preacher would gain a following among the Unitarian clergy; but "not a single voice has been raised by any of our preachers, or pen wielded by any of our writers" in support of the *Discourse of Religion.* It could be said, in fact, that "he is not now in any way identified with the Unitarian body." It was Osgood's position that Parker, having slurred the institutions valued by Unitarians, should not now feel grieved if the clergy "are not disposed to offer him the position of a champion of those institutions" by inviting him to address their congregations. Parker should of course be free to express his opinion, but his opponents must be allowed to exclude non-Christian preaching from their pulpits.[38]

Parker's intense and constant feeling that he was being "persecuted"[39] was based upon genuine inability to believe that his attitudes could cause pain or indignation to others. When close friends warned him about his impulsiveness or his scornful language, he received their criticism gracefully but remained utterly unconvinced. "While I thank you for your frankness," he told Mrs. Caroline Dall on one such occasion, "I by no means admit the justice of what you say. I am by no means conscious of giving utterance to 'an unchristlike sneer or an unkind accusation' in any of my writings, preachings, or prayings."[40] Since this was always his attitude toward his own behavior and motives, one is not surprised to find him expressing ever-greater shock and indignation as the churches of Boston gradually cease to extend the customary invitations to him. The decline in Parker's pulpit exchanges had begun in 1840, and by late 1842 only eight of the local ministers remained on his list of "probables."[41]

A crisis in the development of this exclusion policy was marked by a special meeting of the Boston Association in January 1843. The purpose of the session was to discuss Parker's relation to the Unitarian clergy, which had become strained not only because of the South Boston Sermon and the *Discourse of Religion* but also because of accusations which Parker had brought against some members of the Association for the part they had played in a dispute between the Rev. John Pierpont and his society.

Pierpont, who had been minister of the Hollis Street Church since 1819, had displeased some of his parishioners by his advocacy in the pulpit of prison reform, the peace and temperance movements, and antislavery. Since some of his more influential pew-holders had acquired their wealth in the distilling business, and for some years had stored New England rum in the cellar of the church, Pierpont's sermon against "Rum-making,

Rum-selling, and Rum-drinking" met with particular disfavor, and an attempt was made to force his resignation. Pierpont, however, held his ground, and a "mutual ecclesiastical council" was agreed upon by the contending parties. Under the chairmanship of Dr. Francis Parkman, and with S. K. Lothrop as secretary, the Council eventually, in August of 1841, advised against dismissal of Pierpont. The decision was widely hailed as a triumph for freedom of the pulpit.[42]

An Ecclesiastical Council, however, was something of an anomaly in the liberal church, even if agreed to by both parties, and Parker protested against its having been called in the first place. He was indignant also because the Council, while clearing Pierpont, had reprimanded the Hollis Street pastor for some of his conduct during the dispute. Finally, to Parker's way of thinking the procedures of the Council had been inexcusably dilatory and unsystematic.

Parker's strictures were about as severe as they could have been had the Council decided unfavorably to Pierpont. Writing in the *Dial,* he damned all ecclesiastical tribunals and inquisitions, without leaving any doubt that he considered the Hollis Street Council to be one of the genre. He denounced their report as a "piece of diplomacy worthy of a college of Jesuits."[43] To other Unitarians, who believed that the Council had performed an unpleasant duty conscientiously—and courageously, some said, considering the final stand against the vested interests—this utter disparagement seemed out of order. By stretching the point a bit, Parker's opponents managed to construe his article as an attack upon the Boston Association itself.[44]

The ministerial group determined upon a full-scale discussion of this issue and of the *Discourse of Religion.* But they wished Parker to be present to defend himself, and so sent a carefully worded notice to him particularly urging his attendance on January 23, 1842. When the session was convened in the home of the Rev. Robert C. Waterston,[45] tension and embarrassment were apparent on both sides. It became clear almost immediately that the most influential members of the Association were hoping to persuade Parker that he ought to withdraw voluntarily. Gannett argued that the Hollis Street Council article had compromised and injured Parker's fellow ministers, and Dr. Nathaniel Frothingham, chairman of the meeting, explained that the *Discourse of Religion,* which he called a "vehemently deistical book," had made it impossible for normal ministerial relations with Parker to continue, even though personal and scholarly associations need not cease. Chandler Robbins, putting the question directly, asked Parker whether he did not feel, in view of his lack of sympathy with the opinions of the other members, that it was his duty to withdraw.

Parker answered that, on the contrary, he believed that differences of theological opinion ought to exist and had always existed within the Boston Association; and when Frothingham countered by asserting that in this case the difference was one "between Christianity and no Christianity," Parker desired to know "the precise quiddity" which must be added to his Absolute Religion to make it "Christian."

When Gannett explained that "the miracles" and "the authority of Christ" must be added, the doctrinal line had been drawn, with Parker on one side and the rest of the Association at least nominally on the other. Neither party, however, was willing to regard adherence to this doctrinal standard as an absolute condition of membership. Parker had been asked to withdraw and had refused. In a body committed to free inquiry nothing more could be done unless dissolution of the Association itself were decided upon.[46] The meeting ended in anticlimax when personal tributes to Parker by Gannett, Robbins, and Cyrus Bartol caused the accused man to break into tears and leave the room.[47]

A hiatus of nearly two years followed this indecisive encounter. In the summer of 1843 Parker completed his edition of DeWette's *Introduction to the Old Testament*; in September, exhausted by the work and controversy of the previous three years, he sailed for a year in Europe. Ezra Gannett told readers of the *Examiner* that the Parker controversy was over. Transcendentalism as a philosophical movement, he said, would continue to have its beneficial "spiritualizing" effect upon Unitarian thought, but "as one of the religious vagaries of the times," attacking the authority of Christ and the Gospels, it had ceased to be a danger. Since reaching full expression in Parker's *Discourse of Religion,* the "assailant movement" had lost the support of most of those who at first had thought it consistent with piety.

Gannett continued by attempting a vindication of the Boston Association against those who thought Parker ought to have been expelled. The Unitarian clergy, he said, had taken the strongest stand that was possible or necessary. Under Congregational polity Parker could be "deposed" as a minister only by the West Roxbury congregation which had elected him; and to have expelled him from the Boston Association because his opinions were "not Christian" would have been to beg the very question in dispute.

> All that they could consistently do, was to express to Mr. Parker their individual views, and set before him in free and friendly conversation the inconsistency of his course in continuing to exercise the functions of a Christian minister while he rejected the main facts of the Christian Scriptures. And this they did. They had no authority to depose him from his place or cast him out from their company.[48]

Gannett's announcement that the Parker controversy had ended was, as it turned out, premature. The danger of Parker's obtaining a following among the established Boston clergy may indeed have been past, but it soon became clear that the fight within the denomination had only begun. Parker returned from Europe in September 1844, and the next seven months were full of new incidents. In November the Rev. John Sargent, whose mission chapel on Suffolk Street was supervised by the Benevolent Fraternity of Churches, exchanged with Parker and was thereupon reprimanded so severely by his superiors that he saw no course but to resign. Then, at the end of December, Parker took his turn preaching the traditional "Great and Thursday Lecture" in the First Church of Boston. His discourse on that occasion, **"The Relation of Jesus to His Age and the Ages,"**[49] brought his heresies again into public notice, and the Boston Association moved to exclude him from further participation in the lecture series. In January, James Freeman Clarke also exchanged with Parker and by this action provoked the secession of fifteen leading families from his Church of the Disciples.[50]

All these incidents were brought under a general head of discussion in an open letter which Parker addressed to the Boston Association in March 1845. Parker's most immediate complaint was against the action excluding him from the Thursday Lecture; for, unlike the refusal of pulpit exchanges, this was a concerted move on the part of the Association. It had, moreover, been accomplished by a device which Parker considered underhanded—namely returning the right of invitation to the incumbent at First Church, in whose hands it had originally resided.[51]

The excluded preacher had always suspected that some who were nominally in opposition to him actually shared his heresies and were simply giving way to conformist pressures. The open letter of 1845 was an attempt to implant this same suspicion in the public mind by asking the Association as a body for a detailed statement of belief. "I shall take it for granted," he wrote, "that you have, each and all, thoroughly, carefully, and profoundly examined the matters at issue between us; that you have made up your minds thereon, and are all entirely agreed in your conclusions, and that, on all points . . ." It would not be charitable, Parker said, to suppose that the clergy would undertake to "censure and virtually condemn" one of their number if this were not the case. He then put twenty-eight questions to the Association, asking for their definitions of such terms as "miracle," "salvation," "inspiration," and "revelation," and posing particular questions in the areas of christology and biblical criticism.[52]

Parker's letter, which preserved an entirely cordial tone, was more than a little disingenuous. Its major queries had long since been answered, and no association of Unitarians had ever pretended to agree in detail on points of biblical interpretation. Although no "official" answer was forthcoming, Gannett probably expressed the predominant conservative reaction when he wrote that "though Mr. Parker professes to expect he shall find agreement among the members of the Association, he must know that any half dozen men, who are in the habit of thinking for themselves, would probably differ." It was well known, he said, that Parker's opponents were agreed on the essential point at issue, namely the defining of Christianity as a unique revelation.[53]

After Parker's *Letter to the Boston Association,* Unitarian writers abandoned the amenities of reserved statement and seemed fairly well settled in the conviction that Parker was neither a Unitarian nor a Christian.[54] Gannett, who had objected on principle to excluding Parker from the Boston Association in 1843, had no scruples about the technically different measures which had been taken since Parker's return from Europe. He had no doubt, he said, about the right of a minister to refuse to invite a colleague into his pulpit if he was personally convinced that the other's views were "unscriptural, unsound, and mischievous." To the question whether this was not a recession from ground taken by Unitarians when they themselves had been "excluded" from Boston churches, Gannett answered that possibly it was, but that he himself had never complained about being kept from Trinitarian pulpits, and that he would not invite Unitarians to preach in his church if he were a member of the Orthodox party. The correct policy, whatever might have been done or said in the past, was to withhold exchanges from Parker without trying to prevent his speaking elsewhere.[55]

The Rev. Orville Dewey of New York, addressing the Berry Street Conference in May of 1845, put the case for "exclusion" in even stronger terms. Showing some impatience with his Boston brethren for their constant soul-searchings about free expression, he attempted to set the record straight on the meaning of such terms as "liberality" and "persecution." Freedom of thought, he argued, does not imply an inalienable right to utter, without any risk of censure, what others regard as pernicious untruth. Nor does Christian liberality mean that the opinions of anyone who happens to call himself a "Christian" are *ipso facto* beyond reproach. Parker and his friends, therefore, must get over their tenderness and hurt feelings. "Reformers—as they consider themselves—must somewhat sturdily take their ground. They must not wonder at resistance nor rejection. They must let other people think too, and say what they think."

The real reason for Parker's feeling of persecution, Dewey believed, was his inability to understand how opinions opposite to his own could be held strongly and sincerely. "He has passed into another hemisphere of thought and feeling with regard to Christianity, and he does not know what is thought and felt in ours." The ideal of unlimited ministerial fellowship, he said, is an amiable one; but sometimes, as in the present case, it simply does not work. "We preach an authoritative and miracle-sanctioned Christianity. How can we unite in teaching with him who abjures all this . . . ?"[56]

Opposition to the exclusionist policy, however, had not been entirely stilled. William H. Furness, who had wavered in his support of Transcendentalism during the Ripley-Norton debate, was aroused by the treatment of Parker to print two sermons denouncing the "exclusive principle." William Ware, former editor of the *Examiner,* brought the traditional Unitarian prescription of "righteousness before doctrine" to Parker's defense. And a prominent layman told the Boston ministers that, though their right to exclude Parker from their pulpits was undeniable, it was "un-Christian" of them to exercise it.[57]

Despite such dissenting voices, it was clear by late 1845 that Unitarian clergymen were going to stand by the exclusion policy. It was plain, also, as Gannett had admitted, that the liberal tradition as once expounded by Unitarians had been considerably modified. The tortured attempt to find a middle way had failed, and in order to preserve their doctrinal tradition the conservatives had been forced to adopt measures which bore a painful resemblance to Orthodox maneuvers of thirty years before.

Parker's generally acknowledged right to "speak elsewhere" than in Unitarian pulpits was one which could not have been withheld from him even if his opponents had wished to do so. In February 1845 Parker had accepted an invitation from several Unitarian laymen to preach regularly at the Melodeon Theatre in Washington Street. His first year of preaching in that place had been so successful that in December he was persuaded to leave his pastorate in West Roxbury and give full time to the new group, which had organized itself in November as the Twenty-Eighth Congregational Society.[58]

Both parties to the intense dispute of the early 1840's had thus settled into fairly secure positions. Conservatives had their policy, Parker had his audience, and neither was likely to be moved by further argument. The conflict passed from an acute to a chronic stage, in which, for some seven years, a kind of strained cordiality was the dominant note. The Unitarian press began to refer to Parker as a "lecturer . . . formerly recognized as a Unitarian preacher." His writings and speeches were reviewed in a tone of detached and on the whole not unfriendly interest.[59]

A number of circumstances contributed to bringing this cold war to an end in 1853. The most important was that the security of the conservative position was being undermined by the continuance of Parker's influence within the Unitarian body. Though the older ministers were showing no movement toward Parker's opinions, young and devoted Parkerites were coming up from the Divinity School and being elected to Unitarian pulpits. O. B. Frothingham, a graduate in 1846, was pastor of the North Church in Salem. His classmate Samuel Longfellow was preaching for the Second Unitarian Society in Brooklyn.[60] Samuel Johnson, Thomas Wentworth Higginson, and many others of less note were spreading the gospel of Parkerism. Parker himself was gaining a greater public reputation through his increasing antislavery efforts, and the size of his audiences at the Melodeon had necessitated a move in 1852 to the new Music Hall, whose seating capacity of 2,700 was frequently taxed to the limit.[61] Parker's *Massachusetts Quarterly Review,* a robust journal dealing with all public questions—"the *Dial* with a beard," Parker called it—had appeared in 1847, and had provided him with an additional forum during the three years following.[62] The Unitarian conservatives felt a growing apprehension, therefore, that the *modus vivendi* of the previous several years was becoming unsatisfactory.

In the summer of 1853 occurred the last serious clash between Parker and his opponents. For the first time in the history of their long debate, the immediate provocation came from the conservative side. The Executive Committee of the American Unitarian Association, in the professed belief that the taint of Parkerite radicalism was compromising the liberal party and discouraging public support of their projects, secured the adoption of an elaborate "declaration of opinion" that strongly resembled a creed.[63]

This declaration was significant in showing the uncharacteristically assertive position into which the denomination had been driven. Never before or since have Unitarians in any official statement come so close to creed-making. It is true that the declaration contained no hint of formal excommunication. It implicitly recognized that Parker was still a member of the denomination, since he had not been barred formally from the local ministerial association or barred in any way from the state and national groups.[64] Defenders of the declaration insisted that the document could not be construed as a "creed" or as an act of exclusion. The Association, as they said, was nonrepresentative, and could not make the declaration binding on any but the individuals who approved it.[65] But despite such disclaimers, it was obvious to many that the Unitarians had legislated a "creed" that was as official as any concerted action could be in this denomination. The most nearly representative Unitarian group in the eastern United States was on record as "basing its united action" upon belief in the supernatural origin of Christianity.[66] Leaders of the Association might deny that this was a creed, but they did expect the declaration to reassure Unitarians and influence the general public in their favor; and such hopes, after all, had meaning only if the Association had more actual power to "bind and loose" than it had in theory.

Under the leadership of Dr. Lothrop, who had been president of the Association since 1851, the Executive Committee[67] presented its controversial report on May 24, 1853. The report began with an account of the historical development of Unitarianism, and of the current crisis which the declaration was intended to meet. The slow growth of the liberal church was attributed to five major causes. The first four of these[68] did not involve Parker or radicalism; but the fifth was expressed in such a way as to suggest that it had been the main provocation to the creed-making activity which was being undertaken:

> One of the chief clogs impeding our numerical advance, one of the principal sources of the odium with which we are regarded . . . has been what is considered the excessive radicalism and irreverence of some who have nominally stood within our own circle . . . They have seemed to treat the holy oracles and the endeared forms of our common religion with contempt. They have offensively assailed and denied all traces of the supernatural in the history of Christianity and in the life of its august Founder. In this way, shocking many pious hearts, and alarming many sensitive minds, they have brought an unwarranted and injurious suspicion and prejudice against the men and views that stood in apparent support of them and theirs, and have caused an influential reaction of fear against liberal opinions in theology. It seems to us that the time has arrived when, by a proclamation of our general thought on this matter, we should relieve ourselves from the embarrassments with which we as a body are thus unjustly entangled by the peculiarities of a few . . .[69]

There was no intention, the Report continued, of "dogmatizing" about such people, "their opinions, or their position." The Association ought simply to "state what our own position is, leaving every individual perfectly free to think, decide, and act for himself." It should assert, "in a denominational capacity . . . our profound belief in the Divine origin, the Divine authority, and the Divine sanctions, of the religion of Jesus Christ." The liberal party, "so far as it can be officially represented by the American Unitarian Association," should go on record as believing "that God . . . did raise up Jesus to aid in our redemption from sin, did by him pour a fresh flood of purifying life through the withered veins of humanity and along the corrupted channels of the world, and is, by his religion, for ever sweeping the nations with renovating gales from heaven, and visiting the hearts of men with celestial solicitations."[70]

Such language, it was recognized, would suggest to many a reversion to Orthodox views of human sinfulness. The Committee tried to forestall inferences of this kind by reiterating Unitarian disbelief in Original Sin, as well as in the Deity of Christ and other "current dogmas" of the Calvinist system. And the more affirmative portions of the declaration did contain strong assertions of human ability. There was, nonetheless, an unmistakable emphasis upon the need of a revelation, upon "the existence and influence of hereditary evil," and on man's need of a Redeemer.[71] Such explicit affirmations of traditional beliefs were bound to cause some surprise, even though individual conservatives had been stating similar positions throughout the Transcendentalist Controversy.

The essential meaning of the entire document was expressed in the first of three "resolutions" which were voted upon separately from the Report as a whole. This first resolution stated "that the Divine authority of the Gospel, as founded on a special and miraculous interposition of God for the redemption of mankind, is the basis of the action of this Association."[72] While the full report, with its detailed treatment of theological issues, aroused vigorous discussion and was not passed unanimously, this statement of the essential Unitarian position was agreed to "without a dissenting voice."[73]

In October, Parker took up the challenge with his *Friendly Letter to the Executive Committee of the American Unitarian Association.*[74] He made it clear in this pamphlet that whatever others might think he considered himself still a Unitarian. "As a life-member in long standing in the Association," he said, he felt called upon to ask some clarifications of the recent Report. He wanted to know what persons were referred to as having "nominally stood within" the denomination and having brought disgrace upon it. He asked, further, what the "offensive doctrines" were that had been alluded to, and what the Association proposed to do about those who held them—whether it was planned to expel them from the denomination or just to "give them a bad name, and let them go." He asked precise definitions, as he had in writing to the Boston Association in 1843, of such terms as "supernatural" and "Divine Authority." He desired to know what was meant by "renovating gales from Heaven," "celestial solicitations," and "the withered veins of humanity."[75]

Again, as in 1845, Parker's questions were chiefly rhetorical, and this time they seemed even more so, since most of them had just been answered, in full and rather tiresome detail, in a formally approved public document. Parker could have stopped any intelligent Bostonian in the street and learned whether his antagonists "individually as men, and professionally as the executive committee, believe that the religion of Jesus had a miraculous origin." Anyone who had watched the movement and expressions of conservative opinion knew whether Unitarians believed "that God did raise up Jesus miraculously, in a manner different from that by which he raises up other great and good men"; and whether they believed doctrines are "any more divinely an-

nounced, when taught by Jesus, than when taught by another person of the same purity of character."[76] The Unitarian Association clearly had answered all of these questions in the affirmative.

A number of Parker's questions, such as those which pointed out the unresolved tensions in Unitarian thought between trust and distrust of human nature, or which deflated the Report's sometimes pompous phrasing, were perfectly legitimate. The criticisms they implied were well taken. But Parker unfortunately vitiated the effect of these questions by the general tone of his writing, and opponents were justified in feeling that the *Letter,* having served the polemical purpose for which it was intended, scarcely required an answer. The *Register* remarked that "some of Mr. Parker's inquiries have . . . the appearance of ungenerous and unwarrantable assumptions, that the clergymen and laymen he so extensively catechises, do not really believe, what they deliberately say they do believe." Why, they asked, must Mr. Parker always accuse others of insincerity and false pretenses the moment they disagree with him?[77] No further answer, apparently, was forthcoming.[78]

Parker's *Sermons of Theism, Atheism, and the Popular Theology,* his most thorough indictment of the conservative position since the *Discourse of Religion,* appeared later in the autumn of 1853. The *Examiner's* review, written by Rufus Ellis of the First Church, showed neither the hot resentment nor the chilly cordiality which had characterized the Unitarian reaction at various earlier stages. His article, which probably was an accurate reflection of conservative feeling at this time, was a three-page sigh of weariness—an oblique and somewhat caustic admission that further argument with this man would be futile. Ellis said he had found nothing new in Parker's latest book. "The only wonder is that we have not more repetition. The variety in sermons is an admirable illustration of the doctrine of permutations and combinations." And he added, in the tone of one who had argued for the recent Unitarian declaration and who now considered matters quite settled: "We have read the volume through, every word of it. Whether from prejudice or some better cause, we are still believers in the Gospel of Jesus Christ . . . and we apprehend that Christianity will survive *Theism* as well as Deism."[79]

By late 1853 the great Transcendentalist Controversy had resulted in very much the kind of denominational retrenchment which Norton had demanded so vehemently in the early years. The Unitarian leaders of the 1830's had been timid and recalcitrant, in Norton's opinion, but the work of Gannett, Lothrop, Dewey, and George Ellis in the 1840's must have nearly satisfied him. It is worth remembering, however, that the methods of these later leaders were not those of Norton himself. The conservatives were firm, and from the point of view of anyone who disagrees with their theology they were also reactionary; but they acted on the whole with a fairness and restraint at least equal to that of their antagonist. Hardly an instance of so-called conservative intolerance can be found which was not provoked by intolerance or insult on the part of Parker himself.

It has sometimes been argued, justly enough, that Parker could not have had his immense influence in the enlivening of American religion and the remedying of social evils had he been more sensitive to the feelings of others and more indulgent toward what he found to be their shortcomings. But it should be possible to acknowledge the reformer's contributions without adopting his rather distorted view of the opposition. Though Parker seems to have believed that his opponents were dogmatic and illiberal, the record shows that they were acutely conscious of the liberal tradition in which they had been trained, and that they made a strenuous effort to preserve what they could of it.

But they had to choose, and the choice could not please everyone. As Hedge later observed, "a movement is strong by what it includes, an organism by what it excludes."[80] Unitarians by 1853 had come reluctantly to the decision that some ideals of the Movement must be sacrificed in order to preserve the organic integrity of the Church. They had therefore made their affirmative beliefs explicit, and had declared that whatever the consequences for traditions of "free inquiry," a Christian church must take its stand with the Christian confession.

Notes

1. Roy C. McCall, "Theodore Parker," in William N. Brigance et al., eds., *A History and Criticism of American Public Address* (3 vols. New York, McGraw-Hill, 1943-55), *1*, 259-60; *DAB*; Chadwick, *Parker*, pp. 211-12.

2. Harvard awarded Parker an honorary Master of Arts degree in 1840. Frothingham, *Parker*, p. 27.

3. Ibid., pp. 41-87.

4. Goddard, p. 85; Weiss, *1*, 72; Frothingham, *Parker*, pp. 75-85, 177-78. The *Scriptural Interpreter* was "a small magazine designed for easy family instruction," begun in 1831 by Gannett and ceasing publication in 1836. Ibid. p. 55.

5. J. E. Dirks appears to believe that Parker has generally been considered a thoroughgoing disciple of Emerson (Dirks, *Critical Theology*, p. 136). While superficial studies of Transcendentalism may have sometimes exaggerated the resemblance, biographers of both men have been aware of the differences between them: see Chadwick, *Parker*, p. 177; Commager, *Parker*, p. 141; Rusk, *Life*, p.

386; Cabot, *Memoir*, *2*, 406. And Parker's "discipleship" in the practical area of church reform should not be minimized; he criticized the metaphysics of the Divinity School Address but was strongly in accord with its "picture of the faults of the Church." Weiss, *1*, 113.

6. Parker, *Works*, *6*, 7, 23.

7. Ibid., pp. 7-37.

8. Ibid., pp. 25, 29, 31-36. Dirks, *Critical Theology*, p. 81.

9. Parker, *Discourse of Religion*, pp. 22-23. See also *Works*, *4*, 169; *6*, 32-34.

10. Henry S. Commager, "The Dilemma of Theodore Parker," *New England Quarterly*, *6* (1933), 269.

11. Parker, *Works*, *6*, 32. Italics supplied. Dirks argues that Parker's appetite for historical verification places him "near, but not within, New England transcendentalism" (*Critical Theology*, p. 136). But he rests the case almost entirely upon a comparsion of Parker with Emerson, whom he seems to take as sufficiently representative of the entire group (ibid., pp. 98, 110, 133, 135-36). Such a criterion would exclude many in the New England movement. For analyses and examples of the intense historical interest of other transcendentalists see A. Robert Caponigri, "Brownson and Emerson: Nature and History," *New England Quarterly*, *18* (1945), 368-90; Frederic H. Hedge, *Conservatism and Reform*, Boston, 1843; James Freeman Clarke, *Ten Great Religions*, 2 vols. Boston, 1883; W. H. Channing, *The Christian Church and Social Reform*, Boston, 1848. Emerson himself had a greater interest in history and practical affairs than is sometimes recognized. Perry Miller, "Jonathan Edwards to Emerson," *New England Quarterly*, *13* (1940), 594-95.

12. Parker, *Works*, *4*, 169-70; *A Discourse on the Transient and Permanent in Christianity . . . May 19, 1841* (Boston, 1841), p. 12.

13. See Parker, *Discourse of Religion*, Bk. I, chaps, 1-3; Bk. II, ch. 1; *Sermons of Theism*, pp. 154-57, 166-70.

14. *Discourse of Religion*, p. 478.

15. Ibid., Bk. II, chaps. 3-5; Bk. III, chap. 3; Bk. IV. For other summaries of Parker's theology see *Works*, *13*, 52-61, 330-37; Chadwick, *Parker*, pp. 192-99; Dirks, *Critical Theology*.

16. *Works*, *4*, 79-81; *Discourse of Religion*, pp. 255-57.

17. Ibid., pp. 383-87.

18. *Sermons of Theism*, p. 85; *Discourse of Religion*, pp. 467-68; see also Dirks, *Critical Theology*, pp. 111-15.

19. *Discourse of Religion,* pp. 470-73.

20. *Works, 13,* 61-62.

21. *Transient and Permanent,* pp. 11-12.

22. Ibid., pp. 16, 18.

23. Frothingham, *Parker,* p. 158; Chadwick, *Parker,* p. 103.

24. Most of the non-Unitarian reaction appeared in the *Courier,* the *Daily Advertiser,* the *Evening Transcript,* the *Recorder* (all of Boston), and the *New England Puritan* (see issues of June-August 1841). Parker's own book of clippings is in the Boston Public Library, but a good portion of the newspaper exchange can be found in an Orthodox booklet called *The South Boston Unitarian Ordination,* Boston, 1841.

25. Samuel Barrett, Cyrus Bartol, and John Sargent of Boston, Joseph Angier of Milton, George Putnam of Roxbury. Ibid., pp. 3-8; *Monthly Miscellany* (June 1841), p. 351.

26. J. H. Fairchild of Phillips Church (Trinitarian Congregational), Thomas Driver of South Baptist Church, and Z. B. C. Dunham of the Fifth Methodist Society. *Unitarian Ordination,* p. 4.

27. Ibid., pp. 3-4.

28. Ibid., pp. 6-7.

29. Ibid., pp. 14-15, 39-40.

30. *Register,* June 12, 26, 1841. The editors at this time were Samuel K. Lothrop and Samuel Barrett, both of whom had been on the Ordaining Council. Parker himself believed the *Transient and Permanent* to be one of his poorest productions, and Ripley agreed. Chadwick, *Parker,* p. 96.

31. *Register,* July 3, 1841.

32. *Monthly Miscellany, 5* (July 1841), pp. 45-47.

33. *Examiner, 31* (1841), 99-109, 111-14.

34. S. E. Brackett, Charles Ellis, William Larned, and Charles L. Thayer. Weiss, *1,* 176-77.

35. Ibid., p. 177; *Monthly Miscellany, 5* (December 1841), pp. 352-53.

36. Frothingham, *Parker,* pp. 158-59.

37. *Examiner, 32* (1842), 388-89, 392-94. Morison's original manuscript, as submitted to the *Examiner,* had added that "we do not feel called upon to cast him out or deny to him the Christian name." The editors, however, deleted this passage, and Morison thereupon published it in the daily papers. Chadwick, *Parker,* p. 127.

38. *Monthly Miscellany, 7* (August 1842), pp. 145-50.

39. See Chadwick, *Parker,* p. 95; Frothingham, *Parker,* pp. 173-75.

40. Mrs. Dall had been especially critical of Parker's use, in the *Discourse of Religion,* of the following lines from Alexander Pope to illustrate his opinion of those who value the sacrament of Communion:

> Behold the child, by Nature's kindly law,
> Pleased with a rattle, tickled with a straw;
> Some livelier plaything gives his youth delight—
> A little louder, but as empty quite.

Parker said he had only meant "that at God's table there was milk for the maidens, meat for the men"; and he professed amazement that anyone should find this insulting. Weiss, *1,* 182. See also ibid., pp. 175-76.

41. Clarke, John Pierpont, J. L. Russell, John Sargent, Shackford, Stetson, Samuel Robbins of Chelsea, and G. A. Briggs of Plymouth. Chadwick, *Parker,* pp. 103-4.

42. Samuel K. Lothrop, *Proceedings of an Ecclesiastical Council in the Case of the Proprietors of Hollis-Street Meeting-House and the Rev. John Pierpont, Their Pastor . . .* Boston, 1841. Eliot, *2,* 188-89.

43. *Dial, 3,* No. 10, 201-21.

44. Chadwick, *Parker,* p. 116; Frothingham, *Parker,* p. 165; Eliot, *2,* 188-89.

45. Pastor at this time of the Pitts Street Chapel of the Benevolent Fraternity of Churches; after 1845 pastor of the Church of the Saviour. Eliot, *2,* 112.

46. This was proposed, but rejected on the ground that it would appear as a victory for Parker: Chadwick, *Parker,* p. 115. A motion for expulsion of Parker received only two affirmative votes: ibid., pp. 173-74.

47. The best account of this meeting is Parker's own, in Weiss, *1,* 188-93. Weiss, however, edited out the names, and a list of these must be pieced together from the Parker biographies by Frothingham (pp. 161-68), Commager (pp. 88-90), and Chadwick (pp. 115-21).

48. *Examiner, 36* (1844), 406-8. Gannett's *Monthly Miscellany* had been discontinued at the end of 1843, and Gannett had become an editor of the *Examiner,* along with the Rev. Alvan Lamson.

49. In Parker, *Works, 4,* 40-57.

50. Chadwick, *Parker,* pp. 141-45; Weiss, *1,* 249-54.

51. A committee of the Association had been unable to persuade Parker to abdicate his right to preach the lecture in his turn. See Weiss, *1,* 251.

52. *Works, 14,* 108-15.

53. *Examiner, 38* (1845), 423.

54. John Sargent's dismissal from the employ of the Benevolent Fraternity for exchanging with Parker provoked a heated exchange between Sargent and his conservative colleague Waterston. This was reproduced with editorial comment in the *Register,* January 18, February 15, March 1, 1845. See also the following pamphlets, all published in Boston in 1845: *Answers to Questions Not Contained in Mr. Parker's Letter . . .* by "One Not of the Association"; *Questions Addressed to Rev. T. Parker and His Friends* (anon.); *An Answer to "Questions Addressed to the Rev. T. Parker and His Friends,"* by "A Friend Indeed"; and John Sargent, *The True Position of Rev. Theodore Parker, Being a Review of Rev. R. C. Waterston's Letter . . .*

55. *Examiner, 38* (1845), 267-71. Gannett did continue to refer to Parker, in a strictly qualified way, as a "Christian believer," and was taken to task by a fellow conservative for so doing. See the *Register,* March 1, 8, 1845; Gannett to George E. Ellis, February 28, 1845. Ellis Papers, Massachusetts Historical Society.

56. "Rights, Claims, and Duties of Opinion," *Examiner, 39* (1845), 82-102. For further support of this position by Ellis and Gannett see the *Examiner, 40* (1846), 77-94, and 459-71; for Dr. Frothingham's position see *Deism or Christianity, Four Discourses . . .* Boston, 1845.

57. Furness, *The Exclusive Principle Considered: Two Sermons on Christian Union and the Truth of the Gospels,* Boston, 1845; W. Ware, *Righteousness before Doctrine: Two Sermons . . .* Boston, 1845; William P. Atkinson, *Remarks on an Article from the "Christian Examiner" Entitled "Mr. Parker and His Views,"* Boston, 1845.

58. For a full discussion of this society as an experiment in church reform see below, Chap. 5.

59. *Monthly Religious Magazine, 2* (1845), 143-44; *Examiner, 42,* 149, 303; *43,* 150; *44,* 474; *48,* 330-31; *52,* 160.

60. Eliot, *3,* 121, 219.

61. Weiss, *1,* 412-13.

62. Gohdes, *Periodicals,* chap. 8; Frothingham, *Parker,* p. 398.

63. *The Twenty-Eighth Report of the American Unitarian Association, with the Addresses at the Anniversary,* Boston, 1853.

64. Chadwick, *Parker,* pp. 267-68.

65. Debates on the Declaration are recorded in the *Register,* June 4, July 16, 1853.

66. The Western Unitarian Conference adopted a similar platform the following year. Wilbur, *History,* p. 463.

67. Other members of the Executive Committee were William R. Alger, Isaiah Banks, George W. Briggs, Albert Fearing, Calvin Lincoln, and Henry A. Miles. Parker, *Works, 14,* 466.

68. These were (1) the negative character of the main Unitarian emphases in the early period, (2) the characteristic placing of intellect above piety, (3) Orthodox prejudices in the community, and (4) the social pressure toward Orthodox conformity. *Twenty-Eighth Report,* pp. 18-21.

69. Ibid., pp. 21-22.

70. Ibid., pp. 22-23.

71. Ibid., pp. 24-29.

72. The second and third resolutions expressed the denominational sense of having "a distinct work" to do, and promised a "new zeal" in the promotion of liberal Christianity. Ibid., p. 30.

73. *Register,* June 4, 1853; *Twenty-Eighth Report,* p. 50. Among those speaking in favor of the *Report,* besides the Executive Committee, were George E. Ellis, E. B. Hall, John H. Morison, Samuel Osgood, and Samuel Hoar. The strongest arguments against it were given by Caleb Stetson, Henry W. Bellows, John Pierpont, and John Sargent. *Register,* May 28, 1853. The opposition of Bellows is of special interest in view of his later emergence as a leader and symbol of Unitarian denominationalism. Letters in the Bellows Papers reveal an ambivalent attitude toward transcendentalism similar to that which he later adopted toward "free religion." Bellows to William Silsbee, December 28, 1841; March 29, 1842; February 11, 1845; Bellows to Orville Dewey, January 10, 1843. Henry W. Bellows Papers, Massachusetts Historical Society. See also Chap: 6, [of *The Transcendentalist Ministers*].

74. *A Friendly Letter . . . Touching Their New Unitarian Creed or General Proclamation of Unitarian Views,* Boston, 1853. References here are to the same in Parker, *Works, 14.*

75. Ibid., pp. 117, 123-26.

76. Ibid., pp. 125, 131.

77. *Register,* October 15, 1853.

78. Neither the *Quarterly Journal* of the Association nor the *Christian Examiner* took notice of the *Friendly Letter,* and Charles W. Wendte searched manuscript minutes of the Executive Committee without finding any mention of the affair. See Parker, *Works, 14,* 466.

79. *Examiner,* 55 (1853), 465-68. For Parker's subsequent relations with the Unitarians see Chap. 6 [in *The Transcendentalist Ministers*].

80. Quoted in Allen, "Historical Sketch," p. 230.

Works Cited

Allen, "Historical Sketch": Joseph H. Allen, "Historical Sketch of the Unitarian Movement since the Reformation," in J. H. Allen and Richard Eddy, *A History of the Unitarians and Universalists in the United States,* American Church History Series (New York, 1894), Vol. *10.*

Brownson, *Convert*: Orestes A. Brownson, *The Convert; or, Leaves from My Experience,* New York, 1857.

Brownson, *Orestes A. Brownson*: Henry F. Brownson, *Orestes A. Brownson's Early Life, Middle Life, Latter Life,* 3 vols. Detroit, 1898-1900.

Brownson, *Works: The Works of Orestes A. Brownson,* collected and arranged by Henry F. Brownson, 20 vols. Detroit, 1882-88.

Cabot, *Memoir*: James E. Cabot, *A Memoir of Ralph Waldo Emerson,* 2 vols. Boston, 1887.

Chadwick, *Parker*: John White Chadwick, *Theodore Parker, Preacher and Reformer,* Boston, 1900.

Commager, *Parker*: Henry Steele Commager, *Theodore Parker,* Boston, Little, Brown, 1936.

Cooke, *Dwight*: George W. Cooke, *John Sullivan Dwight: Brook-Farmer, Editor, and Critic of Music,* Boston, 1898.

Cooke, *Unitarianism*: George Willis Cooke, *Unitarianism in America: A History of Its Origin and Development,* Boston, American Unitarian Association, 1910.

Dirks, *Critical Theology*: John Edward Dirks, *The Critical Theology of Theodore Parker,* New York, Columbia University Press, 1948.

Eliot: Samuel A. Eliot, ed., *Heralds of a Liberal Faith,* 4 vols. Boston, American Unitarian Association, 1910-52.

Emerson, *Letters: The Letters of Ralph Waldo Emerson,* ed. Ralph L. Rusk, 6 vols. New York, Columbia University Press, 1939.

Emerson, *Works: The Complete Works of Ralph Waldo Emerson,* Centenary Edition, 12 vols. Boston, Houghton Mifflin, 1903-04.

Follen, *Works: The Works of Charles Follen, with a Memoir of His Life,* 5 vols. Boston, 1841-42.

Frothingham, *Channing*: Octavius B. Frothingham, *Memoir of William Henry Channing,* Boston, 1886.

Frothingham, *Parker*: Octavius B. Frothingham, *Theodore Parker: A Biography,* Boston, 1874.

Frothingham, *Ripley*: Octavius B. Frothingham, *George Ripley,* Boston, 1899.

Kern, "Transcendentalism": Alexander Kern, "The Rise of Transcendentalism," in Harry Hayden Clark, ed., *Transitions in American Literary History,* Durham, N.C., Duke University Press, 1953.

Miller, *Transcendentalists*: Perry Miller, *The Transcendentalists: An Anthology,* Cambridge, Mass., Harvard University Press, 1950.

NC: Andrews Norton Collection, Harvard University Library.

Newell, "Francis": William Newell, "Memoir of the Rev. Convers Francis, D.D.," *Proceedings of the Massachusetts Historical Society* (March 1865), pp. 233-53.

Parker, *Discourse of Religion*: Theodore Parker, *A Discourse of Matters Pertaining to Religion,* Boston, 1842.

Parker, *Sermons of Theism*: Theodore Parker, *Sermons of Theism, Atheism, and the Popular Theology,* 2d ed. Boston, 1856.

Parker, *Works*: Theodore Parker, Centenary Ed., 15 vols. (titles vary), Boston, American Unitarian Association, 1907-13.

Religious History: The Religious History of New England: King's Chapel Lectures, Cambridge, Harvard University Press, 1917.

Rusk, *Life*: Ralph L. Rusk, *The Life of Ralph Waldo Emerson,* New York, Scribner's, 1949.

Schlesinger: Arthur M. Schlesinger, Jr., *Orestes A. Brownson: A Pilgrim's Progress,* Boston, Little, Brown, 1939.

Schneider, *American Philosophy*: Herbert W. Schneider, *A History of American Philosophy,* New York, Columbia University Press, 1946.

Weiss: John Weiss, *Life and Correspondence of Theodore Parker, Minister of the Twenty-Eighth Congregational Society, Boston,* 2 vols. London, 1863.

Wells: Ronald Vale Wells, *Three Christian Transcendentalists: James Marsh, Caleb Sprague Henry, Frederic Henry Hedge,* New York, Columbia University Press, 1943.

Wilbur, *History*: Earl Morse Wilbur, *A History of Unitarianism,* 2 vols. Cambridge, Mass., Harvard University Press, 1945-52.

Williams, *Divinity School*: George H. Williams, ed., *The Harvard Divinity School: Its Place in Harvard University and in American Culture,* Boston, Beacon Press, 1954.

Charles H. Nichols (essay date 1968)

SOURCE: Nichols, Charles H. "Theodore Parker and the Transcendental Rhetoric: The Liberal Tradition and America's Debate on the Eve of Secession (1832-1861)." *Jahrbuch für Amerikastudien* 13 (1968): 69-83.

[*In the following essay, Nichols credits Parker with establishing a distinctly American rhetorical tradition grounded in Transcendentalist ethics.*]

From its very inception the United States has been an experiment-testing as Abraham Lincoln put it, whether a nation "conceived in liberty, and dedicated to the proposition that all men are created equal . . . can long endure." Whereas the catchwords "opportunity," "freedom" and "justice" created splendid visions of unity, independence and unlimited prosperity in most Americans, the conflict of socio-economic and political interests threatened to negate these hopes as the struggle grew in intensity to explode in the Civil War of 1861-65. The industrial-financial North collided with the agrarian, slaveholding planters of the South. The antebellum years reopened the debate over the real character of our democratic institutions. The leading participants in this debate were aware that their economic prospects, their way of life—indeed that representative government itself was at stake. Perhaps only the more perceptive thinkers of the time—Emerson, Theodore Parker, Wendell Phillips and Abraham Lincoln realized that beyond this struggle lay vital and far-reaching moral issues which must determine the character of American civilization.

It is my purpose here to consider the kind of rhetoric employed by the contestants in the political arena between 1832 and 1861, and to show how Theodore Parker, by seeking a more ethical basis for political rhetoric, created a tradition in our national polemics by which Americans—such as Abraham Lincoln and John F. Kennedy—could fulfill something of the promise of the *Declaration of Independence*. That document itself employed an idealistic rhetoric. This rhetoric—based on the lofty ideal of a transcendental ethic—found its most practical expression in the Unitarian reformer and preacher, Theodore Parker.

By "rhetoric" I mean, of course, speech designed to persuade. Rhetoric

> is rooted in an essential function of language itself, a function that is wholly realistic, and is continually born anew; the use of language as a symbolic means of inducing cooperation in beings that by nature respond to symbols.[1]

Rhetoric is designed to change attitudes and behavior—to stimulate action. Hence it is inescapably bound up with ethics. As Aristotle pointed out, a speaker knows almost instinctively that an audience responds to appeals to virtue, courage, self-control, liberality, gentleness, prudence, and wisdom. Properly considered, rhetoric is effective speech, depending upon skill in the use of evidence, logic, clarity and force, eloquence and conviction. But as Isocrates said the genuine advantage of a speaker is in his moral superiority, since much depends on the quality of the speaker's motives.

In times of crisis, therefore, when urgent, living, momentous questions are to be decided, men have, historically, seized upon three principal forms of rhetorical appeal: persuasion, identification, and mystification.[2] *Persuasion* is essentially the appeal to logical argument. Whether the speaker's approach is deductive or inductive, he seeks by pertinent facts and cogent reasoning, authority and ethical principles to win his audience to his own views. *Identification* is the attempt of the speaker to relate himself favorably to the audience and its interests. "It is not hard," says Socrates, "to praise Athenians among Athenians." Appeals to family, group, patriotism, race, property rights are forms of identification. An orator may also attempt to win his listener's support by appeals to "higher values"—to God, religion, the hope of redemption, the fear of retribution, an association of the policy advocated with the symbolic significance of emblems (like the national flag), dogma and ritual. Such appeals are forms of *mystification,* a kind of magic. The power of identification and mystification lies often in their mobilization of the secret wishes, fears, prejudices, and hatreds of the audience. Sophistry and cogency are often intermingled. "Only those voices from without are effective which can speak in the language of a voice within."[3]

The orators of the 19th century could hardly escape its idealism. Nearly all of them seized upon the influence of the transcendental rhetoric, its identification with "Nature" and intuition and its vague use of mystical sanctions.[4] It must be emphasized, however, that there is a hierarchy of values in argumentation. Persuasion (logical discussion) with its concern for a dialectic which rigorously examines issues in the light of evidence and humane principles, is the most acceptable form of rhetoric. Identification and mystification are often powerful and legitimate techniques of rhetoric: beauty of style, honesty, and eloquence are dependent on them. The very use of metaphor and myth, indeed all figurative language, is freighted with emotional appeals. Yet Iago and Polonius could use language movingly, in spite of despicable motives. The listener must be on his guard, therefore, against those forms of identification and mystification which, though emotionally appealing, support specious reasoning. The purpose of rhetoric is, properly seen, understanding and harmony among men. It has been recognized since ancient times as an indispensable study, together with logic and grammar.

The "Great Debate" in the first half of the 19th century in America produced some of our most distinguished orators. For the slavocracy, men like John C. Calhoun and Alexander Stephens, educated in the law, were resourceful in attack and refutation. Those who spoke for the business interests, Henry Clay and especially Daniel Webster, were equally formidable opponents. The motives of each group were clear. The slave states, subject to the uncertainties of an agricultural economy, dependent on northern capital, northern transportation and slave labor, wished to preserve their livelihood and their way of life. They were well aware that their last, effective defense against their creditors in northern cities was political. Hence they hoped to add to the territory held by the slave power, resist the protective tariff, halt the agitation against slavery (fearing slave rebellion), and recover fugitive slaves. In the Congress of the United States they advocated, and succeeded in bringing about, the Mexican War (which would extend slavery into areas acquired from Mexico), the admission of Missouri as a slave state, the passage of the Fugitive Slave Act (which compelled all American citizens to help catch runaway slaves), and the "gag rule" which forbad the discussion of slavery in the House of Representatives. The northern politicians, on the other hand, wished to restrict slavery to the states where it already obtained, to extend their domestic and foreign market for manufactured goods, to protect local industry, to encourage economic growth by the building of roads and canals, to maintain the Union intact. They were, in many instances, as disturbed by abolitionist agitation as their southern colleagues, since neither their national pride nor their economic interests could endure a break with the South.

John C. Calhoun, the senator from South Carolina, turned after 1828 to the defense of slavery. An austere, somewhat puritanical figure, he combined cogent logic with notions accepted by many of his fellow citizens. He insisted that the federal government enjoyed only those powers delegated to it by the states, that the tyrannical power of the majority must be restrained. As the southern position became more desperate, (with respect to the tariff) Calhoun argued that the acts of the government could properly be vetoed (nullified) by the states. Such a doctrine as nullification grew, of course, out of the widely accepted belief in the "right of revolution" and the "revocable social contract." At the same time Calhoun appealed to the Constitution of the United States which recognized slavery. Calhoun, like Hobbes, found the need for the restraints provided by government in human selfishness. The inflated rhetoric of the demagogue could claim to speak for "the people," but "the people," said Calhoun, is a political fiction. Society is made up of individuals whose interests must be protected by local authorities who understand and respond to their needs. Calhoun's position rested on persuasive reasoning. Yet he was not above appeals to

prejudice and attempts to mystify his audience with visions of a pseudo-aristocratic society. Democracy for him was possible only among equals. And the South's slaveholding society was a workable solution to the natural inferiority of some men. Contrasting the exploitation of industrial labor and the turmoil of northern cities with the "pastoral" setting of the plantation, Calhoun propagated the myth that the states below the Mason-Dixon line constituted a "Greek Democracy."

> . . . It is a great and dangerous error [he wrote] to suppose that all people are equally entitled to liberty. It is a reward to be earned, not a blessing to be gratuitously lavished on all alike;—a reward reserved for the intelligent, the patriotic, the virtuous and deserving;—and not a boon to be bestowed on a people too ignorant, degraded and vicious, to be capable either of appreciating or of enjoying it. Nor is it any disparagement to liberty, that such is, and ought to be the case. On the contrary, its greatest praise,—its proudest distinction is, that an all-wise Providence has reserved it, as the noblest and highest reward for the development of our faculties, moral and intellectual.[5]

Plantation slavery, then, regarded by Jefferson (and even by Calhoun earlier in his career) as an evil, became a gateway to utopia.

> Every plantation is a little community [said Calhoun] with the master at its head, who concentrates in himself the united interests of capital and labor, of which he is the common representative . . . The blessing of this state of things . . . makes that section the balance of the system; the great conservative power, which prevents other portions, less fortunately constituted, from rushing into conflict . . .[6]

In addition to the fact that Calhoun and his numerous followers begged the whole question of the efficiency and morality of the slave system, this argument, replete with fallacies, clouds the issue with mystifying illusions.

Yet this association of the free with "the moral" and "the intelligent," of the plantation society with the arrangements of a divine Providence, the South's feudal, pseudo-aristocracy with the high culture of Periclean Greece became commonplaces of pro-slavery rhetoric in Calhoun's imitators (*e.g.* Fitzhugh, Grayson, Stephens) who were less scrupulous and legalistic than he.

Daniel Webster, the Whig senator and northern spokesman in the sectional struggle, was a political realist. Representing as he did the industrial-financial interest of Massachusetts, he was convinced that politics is the art of the possible. He saw the basis of American society in the idea of "a stake in society." "If the whole people be landlords, then it is a commonwealth." An advocate of Adam Smith's *laissez-faire* economics, Webster sought to mediate the conflicting interests in the body politic. In the Great Debate over slavery and westward expansion Webster turned to the Constitution of the United States for his authority. The social contract, he insisted, is irrevocable. Although opposed to slavery, Webster only resisted its extension into newly acquired territory. It is the function of government, he argued, to protect property—including "property in persons"—*i. e.* slaves. In his most celebrated speech supporting the Missouri Compromise and the Fugitive Slave Law he exclaimed:

> I put it to all the sober and sound minds at the North as a question of morals and a question of conscience. What right have they, in their legislative capacity or any other capacity, to endeavor to get around this Constitution or to embarrass the free exercise of the rights secured by the Constitution to the persons whose slaves escape from them?[7]

Webster's oratory made its strongest appeal to American patriotism—to love of country and the sacredness of the Union. He employed all the standard techniques of identification and mystification. A large, powerful man, he knew how to appeal to an audience by exhortations to prudence and the reconciliation of conflicting interests. His use of the apostrophe, his varied intonations and repeated phrases, his exhilarating celebration of the greatness of America—of its "mainfest destiny" as a world power—were effective rhetorical devices for the audiences of his time. On the suggestion of "peaceable secession" he cried:

> What states are to secede? What is to remain American? What am I to be? An American no longer? Where is the flag of the republic to remain? Where is the eagle still to tower? Or is he to cower, and shrink, and fall to the ground?[8]

In analyzing the political upheaval in which Webster and Calhoun played so prominent a part one is struck by the fact that they—like most of their colleagues in the two political parties—represented specific economic interests. Although they employ some of the traditional phrases of a transcendental rhetoric—"justice," "freedom," "duty," "union," "divine Providence,"—their moral directives apply only within their own sphere of interest. Webster does not speak for mill workers in Lowell, Mass.; Calhoun regards the Negro as unfit for freedom. In spite of the large promises in the "Bill of Rights" and the "Declaration of Independence" their politics is based on invidiuous class distinctions and on expediency. In effect, therefore, "good" policies are those which "work" well for the in-group. The idea of equality is for them a stumbling block. And practically speaking, might is right. Although any reasonable man would interpret universal suffrage, for example, to mean what it says, the great majority of American politicians of a hundred years ago defended laws which restricted the franchise on the basis of color, sex, and property. On the other hand, in searching for an ethic appropriate to the democratic claims of America Theodore Parker insisted:

> There is something in man which scoffs at expediency; which will do right, justice, truth, though hell itself should gape and bid him hold his peace; the morality which anticipates history, loves the right for itself.[9]

"The morality which anticipates history," Parker said, must be enunciated by the intellectual community. For if the politicians were short-sighted and bound by the interests of their constituencies, there was no lack of issues for public debate. The transcendentalists, however, made a contribution to the intellectual life of the United States which has long been underestimated. They insisted on treating man as an end in himself. Their supposed aloofness from social and political issues (as argued, for example, by Arthur Schlesinger, Jr., in *The Age of Jackson*) has been greatly exaggerated. As a group they helped to re-formulate the American democratic ideal, to build visions of the sublime, to make the body politic more responsive to moral issues and to establish the tradition of an intellectual leadership courageous enough to speak unpleasant truths to men in power. "Every actual government is corrupt," wrote Emerson. "Good men must not obey the laws too well."[10] And Thoreau, counselling civil disobedience to unjust laws, exclaimed: "Let your life be a counter-friction to stop the machine!"[11] Emerson, Thoreau, and Parker spoke publicly and repeatedly against the Mexican War and slavery and attacked the compromises of Webster. In short, men of letters, rejecting the rhetoric of both Calhoun and Webster, entered the Great Debate by raising the argument to a new level of consciousness. They saw that a democratic culture must actualize not only the freedom of the individual, but the idea of equality and cooperation; not only the security of property, but the general welfare; not only majority rule and the national honor, but justice to all men. For them this was America's true mission in the world, the enlargement of man's hopes and the civilizing of his group life through education, science, and art.

The transcendental ethic focused on consciousness (intuition) and conscience (the moral sense) in man. In the transcendental scheme there is

> . . . no alloy of expediency, no deference to experience, no crouching behind a fact of human history to hide from ideas of human nature; a scheme of morals which demands that you be you-I, I, balances individualism and socialism on the central point of justice; which puts natural right, natural duty, before all institutions, all laws, all traditions.[12]

The *Declaration of Independence,* as Parker saw it, means (1) each man is endowed with certain inalienable rights and (2) in respect of these rights all men are equal. (3) Government is to protect each man in the entire and actual enjoyment of these rights. These are principles derived not only from human experience but human consciousness of human need. But since the transcendental ethic seeks the "absolute" good—rather than the expedient, the useful or the rewarding, its directives have the quality of exorbitant demands. Thus Thoreau writes,

> If any of them will tell me that to make a man into a sausage would be much worse . . . than to make him into a slave . . . I will accuse him of foolishness, of intellectual incapacity, of making a distinction without a difference.[13]

But understood as exhortations to virtue such a rhetoric has a powerful effect.

Indeed, transcendentalism, as Frothingham pointed out, was not so much a philosophy as a *gospel*. It proclaimed the "opening of the prison to them that were bound" and brought men the good news of liberty and equality in a just society. It was no accident that its rhetoric should be propagated principally by ministers who were accustomed to dealing with the conflict between the sordid facts of life and the mysteries of the soul.

The transcendental rhetoric partakes not only of persuasion but also of identification and mystification. Its lofty idealism tends to identify man with the divine, the eternal, the self-activating power of the human will. The diverse elements of nature and society were for the transcendentalists the means by which men might achieve an ultimate spiritual unity and wholeness. The chief effect of the transcendental rhetoric was to heighten the ordinary American's tendency to regard life with high expectation. It became, in some respects, a "self-fulfilling prophecy." Its faith in the ultimate reality of spirit leads it into the kind of imagery ("clouds," "wind," "stars," "mountain air," "the breath of life") which is visionary and idealistic. The weakness of this transcendental rhetoric is in its tone of irresponsible abandon. Parker warns the transcendentalist against the temptation "to despise the past and its sober teachings," or the "taking of personal and fugitive facts as universal consciousness" and thus

> . . . embrace a cloud for an angel, and miserably perish. It is not for man to transcend his faculties, to be above himself, above reason, conscience, affection, religious trust . . . Madmen in religion are not rare, [nor are] enthusiasts, fanatics.[14]

The transcendental rhetoric was also used by the unscrupulous who made its heady, altruistic expressions cant phrases. Many claimed to be a law unto themselves for selfish and base ends. Although the pietistic philosopher of Königsberg might be entranced by "the starry heavens above and the moral law within," other men could see only their personal need and private interest. The categorical imperative assumed that men are in a moral sense alike, that, in effect, you "should do unto others as you would that others do unto you." But often what nourishes one man gives another dyspepsia. And men have been guilty of grievous crimes in the name of "duty." The ethical problem is made more difficult by the vagueness of language, the gullibility of the public, the complexity of men's motives, and their enormous capacity for self-deception. Clearly as a basis for argument the transcendentalist needed the sobering effect of proved facts and ethical principles based not only on good will and the sense of duty but pragmatically rooted in an understanding of the normality of human differences. Parker's rhetoric attempts this fusion of the ideal and the practical. He states a moral proposition and attempts to prove it by facts.

As a unitarian minister and a transcendentalist, Theodore Parker was seeking an ethical principle beyond expediency and self-interest. As a preacher he formulated a rhetoric of his own, based on firm principle, yet devoted to the day-by-day struggles of ordinary people. He saw that a rhetoric lacking in idealism could only reinforce and maintain the *status quo,* that one based only on intuition was visionary. For him

> The progress of a nation consists in two things: first in the increasing development of the natural faculties of body and spirit—intellectual, moral, affectional, religious . . . and second, in the increasing acquisition of power over the material world, making it yield use and beauty, an increase of material comfort and eloquence. Progress is increase of human welfare for each and for all.[15]

Thus Parker created an ethical idea based not only on human aspiration and religious belief, but on the proved findings of scientific investigation and the realities of our socio-economic and political life. In this effort Parker was true to the Jeffersonian tradition—empirical yet idealistic, forward-looking yet tough-minded. To this end, he embarked upon a three-fold effort: (1) The examination of the grounds of Christian belief and Christian ethics, (2) the systematic study of human relations in American society, (3) the advocacy of moral and social reforms on every level of the body politic.

William Ellery Channing, R. W. Emerson, and Theodore Parker in contemplating the evils of society were dismayed to find them excused or defended in the name of Christianity. Calvinism, asserting the hopeless depravity of man, could defend oppressive laws and the restriction of free speech. The South pointed out that the Bible sanctioned slavery, that "the powers that be are ordained of God." Merchants insisted that God in his inscrutable wisdom had made the rich and the poor. Many, clinging to usages of the past, saw God's all-powerful hand in history and thought it blasphemy for men to interfere with human events. Thus religion became, for the dominant class, an opiate, a mystery, a rationalization of the *status quo*. William Ellery Channing in the "Moral Argument against Calvinism" challenged the Puritan conception of God. God's nature, he insisted, is consistent with reason and with our highest conceptions of good. A capricious God would be an unjust God. Channing was convinced of God's beneficence and of man's capacity for virtue. "An enlightened, disinterested human being, morally strong, and exerting a wide influence by the power of virtue, is the clearest reflection of the divine splendor on earth," he wrote. Ralph Waldo Emerson, the chief spokesman for transcendentalism, insisted that the religious sentiment is an intuition: "It cannot be received at second hand."[16] For him, the will and consciousness of man, inspired by the ideal reality behind all existence, relates him to a beneficent universe. Man is "open to the influx of the all-knowing spirit, which annihilates before its broad noon the little shades and gradations of intelligence . . ."[17] There is "an infinite worthiness in man"—who is himself a center of moral purpose. Hence the past, ritual, convention, Bibles, and saints in abeyance, man is capable of direct revelations from God. Emerson maintained that expediency and conformity prevent men from following the divine spirit within them. But "whoso would be a man, must be a non conformist."[18]

Theodore Parker, influenced by Channing and Emerson and the German idealists, preached his most celebrated sermon in Boston on May 19, 1841. It was *A Discourse of the Transient and Permanent in Christianity.* In this sermon Parker emphasized the fact that "transient things form a great part of what is commonly taught as religion."[19] Form, doctrines, the "idolatry" of the Bible (which men regard as infallible revelation) even the exaggerated glorification of the authority of Christ are the transient doctrines of the faith. The permanent and ever vital significance of Christianity is

> . . . the love of man; the love of God acting without let or hindrance . . . Its watchword is, be perfect as your Father in heaven. The only form it demands is a divine life,—doing the best thing in the best way, from the highest motives; perfect obedience to the great law of God. Its sanction is the voice of God in your heart; the perpetual presence of him who made us and the stars over our head; Christ and the Father abiding within us.[20]

In building his theology Parker turned to German scholars (Strauss, Feuerbach, de Wette, Eichhorn) who had propagated the "higher criticism" of the Bible. His ethics he derived from the New England religious tradition and from Immanuel Kant. Kant begins his consideration of morals by saying: "Es ist überall nichts in der Welt, . . . was ohne Einschränkung für gut könnte gehalten werden, als allein ein *guter Wille*."[21] But he insists that even reason cannot guide the will with certainty in an ethical way. To have moral value, an act must be done out of a sense of duty—rather than inclination, selfishness or even love. An action done from duty derives its moral worth not from the purpose which is to be attained by it, but from the maxim by which it is determined. Hence his categorical imperative: ". . . handle so, als ob die Maxime deiner Handlung durch deinen Willen zum allgemeinen Naturgesetz werden sollte." His practical imperative: "Handle so, daß du die Menschheit . . . jederzeit zugleich als Zweck, niemals bloß als Mittel brauchst."[22]

These ideas led Parker to enunciate certain postulates which would make so lofty an ethical principle possible. Parker's principles are: (1) A belief in the infinite perfection of God whose power and love support—in the last analysis—a just world; (2) the adequacy of man for all his functions (Parker insisted that the religious elements—conscience and the love of justice—were natural to man); (3) absolute and natural religion—a sense of aspiration for a golden age, a reverence for the good, the true and the beautiful. "The religious history of the race is the record of man's continual but unconscious efforts to attain this state."[23]

Such an ethical position did not, of course, necessarily result in a democratic faith. Thomas Carlyle—starting with this noble Kantian idealism and attacking many evils—could employ some of the worst mannerisms of the transcendental rhetoric. In defending "hero-worship," "work," "obedience" and "contemplation" Carlyle rejected popular government and the idea of equality.

Theodore Parker never relinquished his principles. He thought of them increasingly as ideals, as pole stars for the dangerous voyage through life. His practical approach to human experience led him to enlarge his understanding of the nature of man and of the world about him. The discrepancy between the real (the scientifically verifiable fact) and the ideal (the categorical rather than the hypothetical imperative) merely strengthened his will to bring American society closer to the ideal. His study of human history convinced him that this development toward the ethical life was taking place. Parker distinguishes himself from all his contemporaries by the depth of his scholarship and his sensitivity to the weaknesses of the transcendental rhetoric. Even theology, he insisted, must ever renew itself by fresh learning, for the problems of theology are continually changing. In Moses' time the theologian's task was to separate religion from the fetishism of the Canaanites and the polytheism of the Egyptians and connect it with one God. In Jesus' time it was to replace the obsolete ritual and legalism of Moses with the idea of love and forgiveness. In the mid-nineteenth century it was

> To separate religion from whatever is finite—church, book, person—and let it rest on its absolute truth. Is Newton less inspired than Simon Peter? Man must have

a nature sadly anomalous if, unassisted, he is able to accomplish all the triumphs of modern science, and yet cannot discover the plainest and most important principles of religion and morality without a miraculous revelation.[24]

In the great debates over the Mexican War, the Compromise of 1850 and slavery Theodore Parker kept his audience aware of the transcendental ethic, but his appeals were more often to reason and to fact than to the transcendental rhetoric. His consistent call for justice to the poor and the disadvantaged, his very mastery of embarrassing facts, and his uncompromising demand for justice made him many enemies. On questions of conscience he was as unmovable as Martin Luther. His fellow ministers regarded him as a dangerous radical and denied him their pulpits. To be sure, Parker was an image breaker and a revolutionary. He was, at times, vituperative, as when he attacked Daniel Webster.[25] He rejected both political parties as alike in having no moral principle. "A Democrat is a young whig who will legislate for money as soon as he has got it; the whig is an old Democrat who once hurrahed for the majority."[26] In his attack on slavery Parker demonstrated its effect on the moral, intellectual, and economic development of the people of the South. The slave population was kept in ignorance and barbarism. The free population of the slave states, Parker pointed out, produced no distinguished writers or scientists, made no provision for needed social reforms, provided little in the way of education and offered no economic opportunity for men of the working classes.

> In 1840, in the fifteen slave states and territories there were at the various primary schools 201,085 scholars; at the various primary schools of the free states 1,626,028. The State of Ohio alone had 218,609 scholars at her primary schools.[27]

The abundant resources of the South were stagnating under the blight of slavery.

All of Parker's speeches showed a painstaking marshalling of facts and a logical organization. He could attack the Mexican War not only as a moral outrage, but as an inexpedient and wasteful venture.

> If a single regiment of dragoons cost only $ 700 000 a year, which is a good deal less than the actual cost, that is considerably more than the cost of 12 colleges like Harvard University with its schools for theology, law, medicine, its scientific school, observatory and all.[28]

Parker was a zealous man who could rouse an audience to action by strong emotional appeals. When Thomas Sims, a runaway slave, was kidnapped and jailed in Boston, Parker speaking to a large assembly at Faneuil Hall was accused of having incited a riot. On that occasion Parker intoned:

> Out of the iron house of bondage, a man, guilty of no crime but love of liberty, fled to the people of Massachusetts. He came to us a wanderer, and Boston took

him in to an unlawful jail; hungry, and she fed him with a felon's meat; thirsty, she gave him gall and vinegar of a slave to drink; naked, she clothed him with chains . . .[29]

Parker's audience identified themselves with the plight of the imprisoned man and stormed the jail to free Sims. But their sense of moral exhilaration in defying an unjust law was the effect of the transcendental rhetoric: "A man loving liberty" in a land which proclaimed itself the land of the free. The public airing of vital issues seemed to Parker of prime importance in a democratic society. No question seemed to him unrelated to the duties of ethical men. In the clash of conflicting views he expected a just consensus to emerge at last, as the moral sense of the community grew.

> [Parker's] commanding merit as a reformer is this [declared Emerson] that he insisted beyond all men in pulpits . . . that the essence of Christianity is its practical morals; it is there for use, or it is nothing, and if you combine it with sharp trading or private intemperance, or successful fraud, or immoral politics, or unjust wars, or the cheating of the Indians, or the robbery of frontier nations, or leaving your principles at home to follow—. . . in Europe a supple complaisance to tyrants—it is a hypocrisy, and the truth is not in you.[30]

Theodore Parker, much inferior to Emerson as a literary stylist, shines more brightly as a scholar and a reformer. Though critical of the sensationalism of Locke and Hume, Parker was well aware of the service empirical philosophy had done for the world.

> It has stood up for the body, for common sense, protested against spiritual tyranny, against the spiritualism of the middle ages which thought the senses wicked and the material world profane. To sensationalism we are indebted for the great advance of mankind in physical science, in discovery, arts, mechanics, and for many improvements in government.[31]

For Parker the scientists' increased mastery of the world of nature confirmed his faith in human improvability. His own scholarship shows how vigorously he devoted himself to intellectual endeavor. He mastered sixteen foreign languages. A non-resident student at Harvard he largely educated himself. He possessed a library of 20,000 volumes (one of the most extraordinary in New England) and was recognized by his contemporaries as the most learned American of his time.

Parker was widely read not only in theology, literature, and philosophy, but also in history and many branches of natural science. He anticipated the evolutionary ideas of Darwin and Spencer. He carried on an extensive correspondence with learned men all over the world. He made an extended tour of Europe and talked personally to its world-famous scholars whose works he had read. Convinced that the finest scholars of his day were in Germany, he nevertheless complained that they spoke only to one another and did nothing to enlighten the general public. He criticized Emerson for discouraging hard and continuous thought, conscious modes of argument, discipline. "The method of nature," wrote Parker,

> is not ecstasy, but patient attention. Michelangelo and Newton had some genius; Socrates is thought not destitute of philosophical power; but no dauber of canvas, no sportsman with marble, ever worked like Angelo; the two philosophers wrought by their genius, but with an attention, an order, a diligence, a terrible industry and method of thought without which their genius would have ended in nothing but guess work . . . If Newton had never studied, it would be as easy for God to reveal the calculus to his dog, Diamond, as to Newton . . . If all is soul, it takes a man to find it.[32]

It was Parker's view that men of superior culture get it at the cost of the whole community and therefore remain debtors to all mankind.

In his effort to understand human relations in American society, Parker turned more and more to empirical studies. He carried out some of the first thorough-going sociological and economic studies in the United States. (Even in his religious writings he turned constantly to scientific images.) Parker knew the circumstances of the merchant classes, the working classes, the "perishing" classes and the "dangerous" classes. He knew how many waifs, prostitutes and convicts there were in Boston and had a humane program for dealing with them. "The gallows of the barbarian and the gospel of Christianity cannot exist together."[33] He could quote extensive statistics on alcoholism, divorce and insanity. He recognized the corrupting influence of war, slavery and competition on the whole of society. His proposals for rehabilitating criminals and the insane, his plan for government assistance, insurance and public works anticipated later generations of humanitarians: such as Abraham Lincoln, Franklin Roosevelt and John F. Kennedy. Inspired by the potential wealth and resources of the United States Parker was convinced that poverty, crime and war could be abolished. Man, for him, was adequate to all his occasions. Thus the transcendental rhetoric in these sermons became more and more factual, cogent; its moral imperative yet firm; its faith undiminished.

> There are truths enough waiting to be discovered; all the space betwixt us and God is full of ideas waiting for some Columbus to disclose new worlds. [And the scholar] is to represent the higher facts of human consciousness to the people and express them in the speech of the people.[34]

Not an original thinker, Parker translated for tens of thousands what Emerson spoke to hundreds only. He spoke to 3000 people in Boston each week for fifteen years. His influence on the American liberal tradition is unmistakeable. He has been described as "the best

working-plan of an American yet produced."[35] He corresponded with Abraham Lincoln's law partner, William Herndon, who eagerly read the sermons and speeches of Parker and passed them on to Lincoln. One of these speeches was Parker's lecture on *The Effect of Slavery on the American People* which Lincoln read and marked the passage, "Democracy is direct self-government over all the people, for all the people, by all the people." Lincoln later improved upon this expression in "The Gettysburg Address" where he said, "that government of the people, by the people and for the people shall not perish from the earth."

But it was the spirit of Parker's writings which reinforced Lincoln's liberal mind. Herndon wrote of Lincoln,

> No religious views with him seemed to find any favor except of the practical and rationalistic order; and if . . . I was called upon to designate an author whose views most nearly represented Mr. Lincoln's on this subject, I would say that author was Theodore Parker.[36]

From the politically expedient and equivocal moral position he expressed in his First Inaugural Address, Lincoln arrived (through circumstance and conviction) at the ethical position he defended at Gettysburg, in the Emancipation Proclamation, and in the Second Inaugural.

Lincoln's oratory is justly regarded as a permanent literary achievement. He was capable of an extraordinary range of feeling—from laconic humor to tragic grandeur. The simplicity and vigor of his style was built on a personal integrity which was beyond all forms of bombast. In cogency of reasoning Lincoln was the superior of many men better educated than he. In presenting the danger of slavery to all men's freedom his logic rested on an irrefutable principle: the impossibility of freedom for all without equality.

> If A can prove, however conclusively, that he may, of right, enslave B, why may not B snatch the same argument, and prove equally that he may enslave A? You say A is white, B is black. It is *color*, then: the lighter, having the right to enslave the darker? Take care. By this rule, you are to be slave to the first man you meet with a fairer skin than your own. You do not mean *color* exactly? You mean whites are *intellectually* the superiors of the blacks, and therefore have the right to enslave them? Take care again. By this rule, you are to be slave to the first man you meet, with an intellect superior to your own. But, say you, it is a question of *interest*: and if you can make it to your interest, you have the right to enslave another? Very well. And if he can make it his interest, he has the right to enslave you.[37]

Lincoln could establish the basis of his policies with sober judgment and close adherence to fact. On such subjects as the importance of defending the union, the need for the Homestead and Land Grant Acts, and his plan for reconstruction he combined magnanimity and idealism with convincing logic.

> I have never had a feeling, politically [he wrote] that did not spring from the sentiments embodied in *The Declaration of Independence*. That sentiment in the *Declaration of Independence* . . . gave liberty not alone to the people of this country, but hope to all the world, for all future time. It was that which gave promise that in due time the weights would be lifted from the shoulders of all men, and that all should have an equal chance . . . But if this country cannot be saved without giving up that principle, I . . . would rather be assassinated on this spot than surrender it.[38]

The debate over the Union put the American dream to its severest test, but men like Emerson, Thoreau, Parker and Lincoln recalled Americans to those ethical principles of Christianity and democracy by which alone they could hope for its fulfillment in the lives of ordinary men. Theodore Parker's contribution lay in his application of these principles to actual political and socioeconomic facts with an unquestionable probity and an unflagging zeal. Other men carried on the tradition—the Populists, the Progressive Movement, the New Deal. In his book *One Dimensional Man* Herbert Marcuse contends that

> This assimilation of the ideal with reality [in the United States] testifies to the extent to which the ideal has been surpassed. It is brought down from the sublimated realm of the soul or the spirit or the inner man, and translated into operational terms and problems.[39]

Marcuse fears that such modes of protest and transcendence as Parker represented have been digested by the *status quo*. "What has been invalidated is their subversive force, their destructive content—their truth."[40] That the vested interests in America have frequently attempted to adapt aspects of the transcendental rhetoric to their own purposes is true. The important thing to consider, however, is the extent to which American society has, through its fusion of pragmatism and the transcendental ethic, become more just.

John F. Kennedy, a man of our own time, whom we honor in establishing the Institute for American Studies, appeared on the international scene when many men were extremely doubtful of this equalitarian, natural-rights tradition. Having fought a devastating war against fascism and threatened by the totalitarianisms of the left, some saw democracy's best hope in a delaying action, a massive military deterrence to ward off a holocaust. Millions in the world were still hungry and without shelter. Each day presented us with new crises in Berlin, in Laos, in Vietnam, in Cuba, in the Congo. The very nature of industrial society in the United States—its standardization, its vast economic and political power, its forms of commercial indoctrination seemed

to rob the individual of his freedom. John F. Kennedy brought a keen intelligence, an adherence to fact, a prodigious energy to bear on these problems. A new élan, a sense of purpose, a vigorous activity awakened the cynical, the slothful and the hopeless all over the world. Kennedy gave new life to the idealism of Emerson, Lincoln and Parker: The idea of the free individual, the equality of men in their God-given rights, the responsibility of government for the general welfare, the duty of the strong to do justice, America's mission to bring security, hope and peace to men all over the world. But Kennedy's rhetoric was (like that of Parker) rooted in an integrity of character beyond cant: "Peace and freedom do not come cheap, and we are destined—all of us here today—to live out most, if not all of our lives in uncertainty and challenge and peril."[41]

What called his hearers to action and a new faith was, essentially, his recourse to the transcendental ethic:

> To those peoples in the huts and villages of half the globe struggling to break the bonds of mass misery, we pledge our best efforts to help them help themselves, . . . not because the communists may be doing it, not because we seek their votes, *but because it is right*. If a free society cannot help the many who are poor, it cannot save the few who are rich.[42]

His confidence in man's ability to change the world, his encouragement of criticism and dissent, his view that the "hopes of mankind are upon us," his advocacy of common endeavor, unselfishly and courageously promoted, was rooted in a transcendental faith. But it was a faith shorn of mystifying illusion—patient, hardworking and magnanimous even in the midst of controversy. As we launch the John F. Kennedy Institute for research and study with future generations in mind, we might do well to recall the spirit of Theodore Parker and of John F. Kennedy. For the work they initiated has scarcely begun. And the scholar has a most vital role to play.

The human mind is our fundamental resource. The well-being of all mankind is our common goal. Knowledge and faith are our guides. And

> if [in Kennedy's words] a beachhead of co-operation may push back the jungle of suspicion, let both sides [East and West] join in creating a new endeavor, not a new balance of power, but a new world of law, where the strong are just and the weak secure and the peace preserved.[43]

Notes

1. Kenneth Burke, *A Rhetoric of Motives,* New York, 1950, p. 43.

2. *Ibid.*

3. *Ibid.,* p. 39.

4. One of the finest examples of this technique is the often quoted statement of William Jennings Bryan arguing against the gold standard where the economically disadvantaged are identified with Christ: "You shall not press down upon the brow of labor this crown of thorns, you shall not crucify mankind upon a cross of gold," "Cross of Gold Speech," July 8, 1896, in *Great Issues in American History,* ed. Richard Hofstadter, vol. II, *1864-1957,* N. Y., 1959, p. 173.

5. John C. Calhoun, *The Works of . . . , A Disquisition on Government and a Discourse on the Constitution and Government of the United States,* ed. by Richard K. Crallé, vol. I, New York, 1854, pp. 55-56.

6. John C. Calhoun, *The Works of . . . , Speeches . . . delivered in the House of Representatives, and in the Senate of the United States,* ed. by Richard K. Crallé, vol. III, New York, 1853, p. 180.

7. Daniel Webster, "The Constitution and the Union," in *The Writings of Daniel Webster,* vol. X, Boston, 1903, p. 87.

8. *Ibid.,* p. 93.

9. Theodore Parker, "Transcendentalism," in: *The World of Matter and the Spirit of Man,* Boston, American Unitarian Association, 1907, Centenary Edition, vol. VI, p. 16.

10. Emerson, "Politics," *Complete Works,* vol. III, Cambridge, 1883, p. 199.

11. *Thoreau's Writings,* vol. X, Boston and New York, 1900, p. 146.

12. Parker, "Transcendentalism," Centenary Edition, vol. VI, p. 30.

13. Thoreau, "Slavery in Massachusetts," *Thoreau's Writings,* vol. X, Boston and New York, 1900, p. 179.

14. Parker, "Transcendentalism," Centenary Edition, vol. VI, p. 36.

15. Theodore Parker, *The Rights of Man in America,* ed. with preface by F. B. Sanborn, Boston, American Unitarian Association, 1911, Centenary Edition, vol. XIX, p. 433.

16. Emerson, "Divinity School Address," in *Complete Works,* vol. I, Cambridge, 1883, p. 126.

17. *Ibid.,* p. 145.

18. Emerson, "Self-Reliance," *Complete Works,* vol. II, p. 51.

19. Theodore Parker, *Views of Religion,* ed. by F. D. Sanborn, Boston, 1885, p. 294.

20. *Ibid.,* pp. 315-316.

21. Immanuel Kant, "Grundlegung zur Metaphysik der Sitten", *Werke,* ed. by Wilhelm Weischedel, Bd. IV, Darmstadt, 1956, p. 18.

22. *Ibid.,* p. 51, p. 61.

23. *Theodore Parker's Experience as a Minister, with Some Account of His Early Life, and Education for the Ministry,* Boston: Rufus Leighton, Jr., 1859, p. 86.

24. Theodore Parker, *A Discourse of Matters Pertaining to Religion,* ed. with preface by Th. W. Higginson, Boston, American Unitarian Association, 1907, Centenary Edition, vol. III, p. 193.

25. "Slavery, the most hideous snake which southern regions breed, with 15 unequal feet, came crawling north; fold on fold and ring on ring and coil on coil the renowned monster came then avarice, the foulest worm which northern cities gender in their heart, went crawling south . . . At length they met, and twisting their obscene embrace, the twain became one monster hunkerism . . . The dragon wormed its way along, crawled into the church of commerce wherein the minister baptized the beast, 'salvation.' From the Ten Commandments the dragon's breath effaced those which forbid to kill and covet . . ." [Sermon on Daniel Webster]. Henry Steele Commager, ed., *Theodore Parker: An Anthology,* Boston, 1960, p. 243.

26. Theodore Parker, "Nebraska Question," *Additional Speeches,* vol. I, Boston, 1855, pp. 331-335.

27. Henry Steele Commager, ed., *Theodore Parker: An Anthology,* Boston, 1960, p. 235.

28. Theodore Parker, *The Rights of Man in America,* ed. with preface by F. D. Sanborn, Boston American Unitarian Association, 1911, Centenary Edition, vol. XIX, p. 11.

29. Theodore Parker, *Additional Speeches, Addresses and Occasional Sermons,* vol. I, Boston 1855, p. 28.

30. Ralph W. Emerson, "Theodore Parker" [Funeral Address], Address at the Memorial Meeting at the Music Hall, Boston, June 15, 1860, in: Emerson, *Complete Works,* vol. XI, Cambridge, 1883, pp. 265-274.

31. Parker, "Transcendentalism," Centenary Edition, vol. VI, p. 36.

32. Theodore Parker, *The American Scholar,* ed. with notes by George W. Cooke, Boston, American Unitarian Association, 1907, pp. 84-85.

33. Theodore Parker, *Social Classes in a Republic,* ed. with notes by Samuel A. Eliot, Boston, American Unitarian Association, 1909, p. 179.

34. Theodore Parker, *The American Scholar,* ed. with notes by George W. Cooke, Boston, American Unitarian Association, 1907, p. 20.

35. Vernon L. Parrington, *Main Currents in American Thought. An Interpretation of American Literature from the Beginnings to 1920,* vol. II, New York, 1927, p. 414.

36. William H. Herndon & Jesse W. Weik, *Herndon's Life of Lincoln. The History and Personal Recollections of Abraham Lincoln as originally written by William H. Herndon and Jesse W. Weik,* with introduction and notes by Paul M. Angle, New York, 1949 (originally published 1888), p. 359.

37. *The Collected Works of Abraham Lincoln,* ed. by Roy P. Basler, vol. II, *1848-1858,* New Brunswick, N. J., 1953, pp. 222-223.

38. *The Collected Works of Abraham Lincoln,* vol. IV, *1860/61,* p. 240.

39. Herbert Marcuse, *One Dimensional Man. Studies in the Ideology of Advanced Industrial Society,* Boston, 1964, pp. 57-58.

40. *Ibid.,* p. 61.

41. John F. Kennedy, *To Turn the Tide. A Selection of Kennedy's Public Statements . . . through 1961,* ed. by John W. Gardner, New York, 1962, p. 175.

42. *Ibid.,* pp. 7-8.

43. *Ibid.,* p. 9.

Robert C. Albrecht (essay date 1971)

SOURCE: Albrecht, Robert C. "The Abolitionist." In *Theodore Parker,* pp. 91-122. New York: Twayne, 1971.

[*In the following essay, Albrecht studies Parker's writings and beliefs in relation to his activism as an abolitionist.*]

Slavery, which slowly became the central problem for Parker, by 1850 finally absorbed most of his time and interest. In the early 1840's his ostensible concern was slavery in general and in the abstract, but soon his attention was directed wholly to Negro slavery in the Southern states. As he turned to the problems of stopping the expansion of slavery and of destroying the institution, he became more involved with political issues; for he realized that politics was the instrument through which righteousness would have to act. At the same time, he realized that people would have to be convinced of the wrong of slavery and of the justice of abolishing it. Parker therefore assumed two primary tasks: to convince his audiences of the evil of slavery through statistics, exhortation, and pleas for justice; and to persuade politicians to act on the basis of right. The passage in 1850 of the Fugitive Slave Law increased his ire and his activity because he felt that the North was thereby forcibly brought to support slavery. The rendition of slaves—sending them back to their masters—under that law was a touch of hell to Theodore Parker.

Behind all of Parker's actions to eliminate slavery was his belief in Christianity. His absolute religion, dictated not only that all men were created equal and that all men were brothers, but also that this nation was destined by God to become a utopian democracy. With slavery, this achievement was impossible. In his own view, Parker never deserted his position as the spokesman for absolute religion. He turned to antislavery activity to make the nation's conversion to righteousness possible. The publication of two theological works during this decade of most intense antislavery activity demonstrates that he did not wholly neglect theology to work for the abolition of slavery.

Parker's speech during the Anthony Burns affair of 1854 caused his arrest and trial, but the authorities had obviously taken advantage of this opportunity to attack Parker since this speech was no more treasonous or inflammatory than many others he had given. The attack on Parker backfired as it gave him the chance to answer his enemies. When they deprived him of presenting his defense in court, he published it as ***The Trial of Theodore Parker for the Misdemeanor of a Speech in Faneuil Hall against Kidnapping; with the Defence*** (1855). Even during the campaign of 1856 and in the arguments over disunion, Parker insisted that right rather than compromise and justice rather than expediency should prevail. To separate from the South would divorce the North from Negro slavery, but what would such action do for the slaves and for the poor whites? His view encompassed the nation which was the result of God's plan, not the political rearrangements which might result from man's meddling. The nation must be rid of slavery. To this end, Parker gave hundreds of lectures and sought the leader he never found to guide the nation. His actions were required by his religion—sufficient reason for Theodore Parker.

I ATTACKS ON SLAVERY BEFORE 1850

Before 1848 Parker gave only one published sermon and few lectures on slavery, although he did refer to it in his social sermons of the decade. The first sermon on slavery was delivered in January, 1841, the same month in which he delivered the South Boston sermon, ***The Transient and the Permanent in Christianity.*** These two sermons established the two major areas of reform he was to work in—theology and slavery; in them, he set forth the outlines of the arguments he would use;

and, from them, Parker's notoriety sprang. In his *A Sermon of Slavery* he presented the arguments which he employed against that institution for the next twenty years.[1]

Characteristically, he began the sermons with definitions—in this sermon, of slavery, freedom, and man's state. "Now man was made to be free, to govern himself, to be his own master, to have no cause stand between him and God, which shall curtail his birthright of freedom." His argument was based on theological and political concepts of freedom and slavery. He further defined freedom as "a state in which man does, of his own consent, the best things he is capable of doing at that stage of his growth." This definition is a particularly appropriate one for a Transcendentalist who believed in the potential for growth—each man had the possibility of doing what he could with his own capacity for development, though the capacity itself was not a matter of free will. Though the sermon is nominally on bondage rather than on Negro slavery, Parker did not avoid the Negro's situation for long. He rejected arguments that asserted the reasonable conditions of the slaves and those that compared Southern slavery with the wage slavery of the North. And he refused to oppose the slaveholders on the ground that they were not Christians.

In this first sermon about slavery, Parker told one of his best illustrative fables. He imagined a race of men living at the bottom of the sea under a government and a religion which, not surprisingly, include all the abstract principles of American democracy and Protestantism. If one were told that in half of this land slaves were held, he would immediately declare the race hypocritical. Though the parable is obvious, its point was well made Parker showed the relation of the North to the South with regard to slavery. The North bought Southern products, obviously associated with it politically, shared guilt by ignoring the crime, and neglected its duties as brother's keeper. The cause of slavery was "the desire to get gain, comfort, or luxury; to have power over matter, without working or paying the honest price of that gain, comfort, luxury, and power; it is the spirit which would knowingly and of set purpose injure another for the sake of gaining some benefit to yourself." Though Parker had to admit that such chattel or wage slavery also existed in the North, he did not here—or ever—deal at length with that problem.

Southerners charged that wage slavery in the North was at least as bad as Negro slavery in the South, and Parker's definition of the cause of slavery served for both types. But he could not admit that both were equally bad, for the industrial democracy which he anticipated would allow wage slavery though not human bondage. Had he been acutely concerned with converting a Southern audience, he could easily have distinguished between the two types of slavery; but whether or not he could have proved the Northern factory worker to be economically free is another question. Since, in his view, Southern slavery was legal and yet wrong, the law, even the Constitution, had to be changed; for the laws of men had to conform to those of God.

There was another sort of slavery which he touched upon from time to time through the sermon. At one point he called it "internal restrictions" to freedom, at another "soul-slavery." It was caused internally "by some passion or prejudice, superstition or sin." "Body slavery is so bad that the sun might be pardoned if it turned back, refusing to shine on such a sin; on a land contaminated with its stain. But soul-slavery, what shall we say of that?" He can say little more of its horrors. Parker tried to write of abstract slavery which included the slavery of the Negro in the South; but, if the attack on Negro slavery was weak, that on "soul-slavery" was so vague as to be entirely ineffective. Finding greed to be the cause of both and designating the latter as the more heinous weakens his attack on the former.

Though the sermon is important for the development of Parker's personal antislavery effort, it is remarkably weak as a rhetorical accomplishment. From it, one could conclude that slavery exists everywhere in many forms; and, since it is due to the greed of the individual, its elimination is as difficult as that of sin itself. Slavery would be removed when righteousness was attained. The writer is Parker the Transcendentalist rather than Parker the Abolitionist. The sermon belonged in *The Dial,* not on the Abolitionist platform.

A continuation of this course of abstraction and generalization is a speech delivered to the meeting of the American Anti-Slavery Society in celebration of the abolition of slavery by the French in April, 1848.[2] When Parker spoke of equal rights and universal suffrage, he noted that, though liberty and equality are American ideas, they have never been American facts. "America sought liberty only for the whites," he said. "Our fathers thought not of universal suffrage." His approach was again indirect: he did not attack Negro slavery in the United State frontally.

A few weeks later, when he addressed the New England Anti-Slavery Convention,[3] he began with the aim of the Abolitionists—"to remove and destroy the institution of slavery"—and their central ideas—that "all men are created free and equal which is the idea of Christianity, of human nature." However, as Parker pointed out, the thirty-one New Englanders in Congress, only five were even antislavery; since the Republic began, the presidency had been occupied only twelve years by men from the free states; Taylor, a Southerner and a general in the war against Mexico, was to be the nominee of the next Whig convention. Political action could destroy slavery, Parker noted; but the national parties must be convinced they can benefit from abolition. The Abolitionists will finally succeed because they act with the "spirit of the age." Christianity and the rights of man, part of that spirit, will triumph against the practical atheism of their foes. This speech, especially its references to segregation in the Boston schools and its comments on the inclination of Anglo-Saxons to protest only for their own rights foreshadowed the Parker of the 1850's. His concern with political power is characteristic not only of his own work but of that of the New England conscience wing of the antislavery movement.

In the minds of Parker and other New Englanders, as the political power of the New England states, particularly of the New England aristocracy, declined, the power of the South grew. Slavery became more important to the South; the number of slaves increased. The rise of the South, the decline of New England, and the increase in slavery coincided. As these Easterners—consciously or unconsciously—saw it, New England could only regain power by eliminating slavery. The South could then be overcome by the North, and New England could again direct the power of the federal government and the course of the nation. Though most of Parker's addresses rest on this analysis, he did not explicitly connect Abolition with the recovery of power by the New England states. He did, however, believe in the moral superiority of the Abolitionists and in the inevitable elevation of the moral tone of the nation if New England did regain power.

Though Parker spoke at various antislavery meetings before 1848, his first lengthy published statement to the general public is *A Letter to the People of the United States Touching the Matter of Slavery*; and it marks a new phase in his antislavery work. Parker tried in this hundred-page pamphlet, as he did in the **"Levi Blodgett letter of 1840,"** to use a persona effectively. The speaker describes himself as "an obscure man," "one of the undistinguished million," who had "no name, no office, no rank" and is "no aspirant for office or for fame." He speaks because political and religious leaders have kept silent and because to speak is a matter of conscience and duty. Slavery touches him as it does all citizens because the nation supports it through legislation and war; through its extension into the Louisiana territory; through allowing slave markets even in the capital; through permitting no sanctuary for fugitives. He calls upon his fellow citizens because the politicians are busy with other things; the leaders will not admit to the evil. Because men must respond to slavery as human beings, he asks his audience to "decide and act according to Reason and Conscience."[4] With these words the persona is clearly dropped, and it is Parker who speaks.

In giving lengthy statistics on slavery and a history of the institution. Parker again used the devices of *A Ser-*

mon of War (1846). He related the history of slavery to the Declaration of Independence, the Articles of Confederation, the Ordinance of 1787, and the Constitution. Having placed the institution in American history, he described the conditions of the slaves. He introduced the "Idea of Slavery," a phrase which he was to use again and again, often opposing it to the "Idea of Freedom." Much of the pamphlet concerned the effects of slavery on industry, population, education, law, and politics. Retarding industrialization was one of its effects. Only in the North did the invention of machines to replace manpower occur; in the South, no one wished to replace it. Parker assumed a value in industrialization which he did not specify.

Repeatedly, he supplied such statistics as these: "In 1839, the value of all the annual agricultural products of the South, as valued by the last census, was $312,380,151; that of the free $342,007,446." Using such figures, he proved that the population of the North had increased faster than that of the South and that the North had produced more poets, more scholarship, more books, more schools. When he compared New York and Virginia in detail, he blamed all the differences on slavery which necessitated a whole set of laws relating to slaves, their relations among themselves, to their masters, to the law itself. Its effect on politics had been to give the South disproportionate power in the Congress and in the presidency. Beyond all these effects, slavery was a sin—a crime against the Declaration and against humanity:

> When you remember the intelligence of this age, its accumulated stores of Knowledge, Science, Art, and Wealth of Matter and of Mind, its Knowledge of Justice and eternal Right; when you consider that in political Ideas you stand the first people in the language of mankind, now moving towards new and peaceful conquests for the human race; when you reflect on the great doctrines of Universal Right set forth in so many forms amongst you by the senator and the school-boy; when you bring home to your bosoms the Religion whose sacred words are taught in that Bible, laid up in your churches, reverently kept in your courts of justice, carried under the folds of your flag over land and sea— that Bible, by millions multiplied and spread throughout the peopled world in every barbarous and stammering tongue,—and then remember that Slavery is here; that three million men are not by Christian Republican America held in bondage worse than Egyptian, hopeless as hell,—you must take this matter to heart, and confess that American slavery is the greatest, foulest Wrong which man ever did to man; the most hideous and detested Sin a nation has ever committed before the just, all-bounteous god—a Wrong and a Sin wholly without excuse.[5]

In concluding appeals of this sort, Parker always appealed to men's moral conscience in the broadest sense rather to narrower sectarian principles.

In his "Conclusion," addressed to "Fellow-Citizens of America," he spoke first of the effects and cost of slavery. He offered no easy solution. He came back to the state of the civilization of the world, its continual progress, and remarked, "America, the first of the foremost nations to proclaim Equality, and Human Rights inborn with all; the first confessedly to form a State on Nature's Law—America restores Barbarism; will still hold slaves." The nation which he called the "latest Hope of Mankind, the Heir of sixty centuries—the Bridegroom of the virgin West" had slavery, had barbarism. To all this greatness and potential came "the Negro Slave, bought, branded, beat."[6] So he closed—without a plea for action, without a plan for action, without exhortation really, but with a plea for civilized justice. Purity had been violated and must be restored. With astonishing clarity, Parker saw the real nation as the mythic nation. The metaphor *was* the reality. There was no nation but the Bridegroom. Such an image led to the necessity of removing sin, to the duty of perfecting the Hope of Mankind.

Parker's *Letter,* like much of his other work on slavery, reveals what he valued. Civilization, humanity, mankind—these abstractions he often placed on a level with Christianity; for the Christianity he preached as absolute religion includes them as virtues. The nation as the potential fulfillment of the promise of these abstractions had a sacred trust to be true to them. Progress was only a general label for the course of the nation which he conceived in terms of growth—population, wealth, industralization. Since slavery impeded such growth, Parker considered it a sin against Christian morality and against the nation entrusted with the divine mission. The missionary zeal of the Southerners who wished to control the government to preserve slavery, to extend slavery to the West, to the South, to the Caribbean and beyond, clashed directly with that of those who thought, as Parker did, of the mission of the North to extend its values to the West, to the South, perhaps to Canada and to Central America. Slavery interfered with his goal of an industrialized democracy progressing to an ill-defined goal of a millennial state. Slavery was the complete sin; no other was needed. This conviction drove Parker and many other reformers quite conscientiously to turn most of their efforts against it.

The influence of such a publication as the *Letter* is almost impossible to discover. One response it provoked was a letter from a Southerner, J. J. Flourney of Georgia. He had read the *Letter* and advised Parker that he would accomplish little unless he could prove his position with support from the Bible. Parker, who thought this easily done, replied with that support, commenting on and interpreting biblical passages. Flourney would have none of Parker's theology or his interpretation of the Bible. In the fourth letter of the exchange, Parker said that he would prefer an opponent with whom he could reason.[7] He thought Flourney a particularly obtuse man, but the short exchange might have taught Parker something of the nature of the opposition he never saw.

II THE FUGITIVE SLAVE LAW

Parker's attempts to influence others to act against slavery increased sharply about 1850, the year that marked the passage of the Fugitive Slave Bill which carried Parker and other New Englanders into a decade of sustained activity. In Faneuil Hall on March 25, 1850, Parker responded to Webster's famous Seventh of March speech. In the last great debate involving Webster, Clay, and Calhoun, Webster began, "I wish to speak to-day, not as a Massachusetts man, nor as a Northern man, but as an American, and a member of the Senate of the United States." However sweet these words might have sounded to a man of compromise, to Parker and others who would have no conpromise with slavery the speech had no sweetness. That Webster spoke for the nation and against secession did not move Parker, for Webster accused the Abolitionists of having done no good; and, most heinous crime of all, he supported the Fugitive Slave Bill which, he said, merely restated man's duty as previously expressed in the Constitution.

Speaking against the bill which put fugitive slave cases under federal jurisdiction and which reasserted the North's authority and obligation to return fugitive slaves to the South, Parker asked whether freedom or slavery should be extended. He admitted that geography did not limit slavery; it must be limited by law. Parker himself had already hidden fugitives from slavery, and he did not intend to stop: "Does Mr. Webster suppose that such a law could be executed in Boston? that the people of Massachusetts will ever return a single fugitive slave, under such an act as that?" Parker could not believe that such a law could be effective in Massachusetts. In supporting it, Webster must be making "a bid for the Presidency," an act and motive that can only be compared to those of Benedict Arnold. Concluding one of his sharpest attacks to this time, Parker said: "Follow the counsel of Mr. Webster—it [slavery] will end in fire and blood."[8] The hostility of the rhetoric reflects the indignation Parker felt at the prospect of being legally forced to return fugitive slaves. For him, New England had become part of the slave South with the passage of the Fugitive Slave Law.

At a speech two months later before the New England Anti-Slavery Convention, Parker viewed political parties as sources of evil and again compared Webster to Benedict Arnold. He found none of the political leaders and none of the major party factions ready to fight slavery. Despite the conflict between freedom and slavery, despite the rising power of slavery from the time of the

Constitution through the Mexican War, the politicians refused to act against it. He spoke of four political parties—the "Government party," the Whig, the Democrat, and the Free Soil. The first cared only for inaction; the second, for protection and slavery (its Southern wing favored slavery and protection), and the Democrats, almost solely in the tariff. Though the Free Soil party opposed the extension of slavery, it did not regard slavery as a sin. The clergy was also to blame for the continued existence of slavery. In general the "Toryism of America" is responsible for slavery. Parker defines a Tory as "one who prefers the possessions and property of mankind to man himself, to reason and to justice."[9] In opposition to the Tories were those who did not wish slaves returned after jury trial, those who did not wish slavery extended, and those who wanted freedom for all men.

The tone of persecution is evident in these speeches. Parker thought that few agreed with him; the politicians, the press, the clergy, and the merchants did not oppose slavery; but it would be surprising only to discover Parker agreeing with the majority. In social and political issues, as in theological controversies, Parker chose the radical position. Yet he usually lamented the lack of support for his position, even when a substantial minority agreed with him, as it did on the slavery issue.

Though Parker sought a leader for the Abolition forces, the characteristics of the desired leader are not clear. He should discover political ideas, implement these ideas, and administer the institutions which result. Parker asked for genius and admitted that few if any political leaders exhibited that quality. For him the best Presidents had been Washington, Jefferson, and John Adams. The rest had accomplished surprisingly little. More important, to him, were William Ellery Channing, the opening of the Erie Canal, and the railroads of Massachusetts. "Mr. Cunard, in establishing his line of Atlantic steamers, did more for America than any President for five-and-twenty years." In contrast is a typical President such as Taylor: "No prudent man in Boston would hire a cook or a coachman with such inadequate recommendation as General Taylor had to prove his fitness for the place."[10] He was a harmless man and even perhaps a good one, and fortunately he did little harm, said Parker after Taylor's death.

In Parker's view the times called for men of genius, of morality, of conscience; but, instead, there were Taylors in the Presidency. The mass of people in the North and the "humbler clergy" were in the party of freedom; but the slaveholders, the wealthy of the North, and the politicians were in the party of the North; and the politicians were in the party of despotism. Boston had 140,000 people with "intelligence, activity, morality, order, comfort, and general welfare" such as no European city had; yet there was poverty, "unnatural wealth," sin,

and sophistry. The South however, had no virtues."[11] Given this moral and political situation, Parker's judgment was that enforcement of the Fugitive Slave Law should cause the Union to be dissolved by the North. The South, having nothing to lose, would not voluntarily leave the Union.

In a sermon given in November, 1850, Parker expected to disobey the Fugitive Slave Law, and he also anticipated that others would do so. Law by legislature and by statute is not the highest law. Just as men cannot make one and one equal a number other than two, so they cannot say the sun moves around the earth or make the false true or the true false. There are "laws of the human spirit" and justice, that which is "absolutely right." Conscience is the faculty which discovers the rules for moral conduct: "It is the function of conscience to discover to men the moral law of God." Man obeys his conscience because his duty is to keep God's law; therefore, the duty of men is to rescue the fugitive slaves.

Though Parker himself detested violence, he could commit it under certain circumstances: "The man who attacks me to reduce me to slavery, in that moment of attack alienates his right to life, and if I were the fugitive, and could escape in no other way, I would kill him with as little compunction as I would drive a mosquito from my face. It is high time this was said. What grasshoppers we are before the statute of men! What Goliaths against the law of God!"[12] Men disobeyed the laws of God without a quiver but were faithfully and piously subservient to the laws of men. Such a view led to the accusation of treason against Parker.

By the end of 1850, Parker was devoting much time to the Vigilance Committee and to other antislavery activities.[13] New Englanders of Parker's persuasion began to act in earnest after the passage of the hated law, and one of Parker's tasks was helping fugitives such as the Crafts who had come almost two years before to Boston. The light-skinned Ellen had escaped with her husband who had posed as her slave; and both had become members of Parker's congregation. When Hughes (or Hews) a jailer, arrived from Georgia and applied under the Fugitive Slave Law for the papers to have the Crafts seized, they were hidden. The Vigilance Committee was able to force Hughes to run from Boston.

Parker wrote even to President Fillmore about the Craft case, proclaiming his duty to his parishioners. In his letter he admits that he had married the Crafts, and that afterward he had given William Craft a sword and a Bible and had suggested that each had its appropriate use. Parker asked: "When the slave-hunters were here, suppose I had helped the man to escape out of their hands; suppose I had taken the woman to my own house, and sheltered her there till the storm had passed by: should *you* think I did a thing worthy of fine and imprisonment?"[14] Parker virtually told what he had done. He concluded that he and his fellows had to obey the laws of God, even if it meant submitting to the punishments of the law.

Though Parker was unable to bring before the American Unitarian Association this question of duty under the law, he did succeed in bringing the matter to discussion before a meeting of the Boston Ministerial Conference. Almost immediately interfering with the discussion was a statement attributed to Dr. Orville Dewey that he would send his own mother into slavery to preserve the Union. When the discussion finally turned from the Union to the question of obedience to law, Ezra S. Gannett—Parker's mentor when Parker edited the *Scriptural Interpreter* fifteen years earlier—spoke in favor of obeying all laws on the grounds that all law must be obeyed and that a violation of one could lead to violation of all. Furthermore, Gannett argued, without the Fugitive Slave Law and obedience to it, the Union could not be preserved. Parker's answer was that to disobey one law does not lead to the disobedience of all laws; men obey laws because they help men to obey God's laws. He told them that to perform his own duty he wrote his sermons with a pistol in his desk and a sword beside him in case he had to defend the members of his church. He thought non-resistance to be "nonsence."[15] The Boston Ministerial Association could not agree on the duty of ministers under the Fugitive Slave Law. However strongly they might have been impressed by Parker's arguments on their duties under God's laws, they could not escape their belief in the meaning and importance of man's laws. Neither did many of them believe so fervently in their intuition of God's laws.

The response of the Unitarian ministers to his assertions revived in Parker the feelings of persecution and rejection that he had had a decade ago. To Summer, he wrote: "you must remember that I am probably the most unpopular man in the land, certainly the most hated of any one in it." However exaggerated, this distinction which almost pleased him had resulted from his sermons on theology as well as his Abolition work. Some months later he wrote to his old friend, Convers Francis: "Think of me, hated, shunned, hooted at; not thought worthy to be even a member of the Boston Association of Ministers or of the P. B. K. [Phi Beta Kappa]! . . . I have no *child,* and the worst reputation of any minister in all America."[16] Yet Parker gained solace from thinking that he had at least achieved notoriety—for part of his ambition was to have his name known.

By the summer of 1852 Parker was convinced that Franklin Pierce would be elected President in the fall. The Democrats would then work to divide California into two states—one slave, one free. They would also try to take more territory from Mexico, to make slave states

out of New Mexico and Utah, and to annex Cuba—the chief object and the most popular. Most of his estimates of the slave power and of the intentions of Democrats in the 1850's were wrong. But he correctly predicted the coming war. He thought his enemies—they were innumerable—capable of conspiracy and immeasurable evil. Events had occurred which had convinced Parker of the low moral condition of the North; and one of these was the return of Thomas Sims, a slave, to the South.

III 1851-1854—ANTISLAVERY AND THEOLOGY

On February 15, 1851, a fugitive slave named Shadrach who had been taken into custody for return to the South was rescued from the Boston Court House. A short time later, April 3, 1851, another fugitive, Thomas Sims, was taken into custody. Parker was among the first to try to delay Sim's return, though he was able to accomplish little. The Court House where Sims was kept was barracaded and iron chains were put around the building. Friday, the day after the capture, when Sims's case was heard before Commissioner George Ticknor Curtis, Sims was defended by Robert Rantoul, Charles G. Loring, and Samuel E. Sewall, who went before the state supreme court for a writ of habeas corpus which Chief Justice Shaw denied. When the Vigilance Committee held a meeting about the Sims case on the Common on Friday afternoon and in Tremont Temple in the evening, a thousand people attended the evening meeting; and troops patrolled the streets. On Monday, Richard Henry Dana and Rantoul came before Shaw again with petitions, which were again denied. An attempt was even made to have Sims arrested for having stabbed an officer when he was captured; if he were sent to prison for this crime, he could not be returned to Savannah.

When another meeting was held in Tremont Temple on Tuesday, Thomas Wentworth Higginson and others formed a plan to have Sims jump from his third-floor room onto a pile of mattresses below; but, when their intentions were learned, Sim's windows were barred. Thursday morning Charles Summer and Sewall petitioned Judge Peleg Sprague of the United States District Court for a writ of habeas corpus; Thursday evening they were joined by Dana in going before Judge Woodbury on a similar mission. Curtis delivered his opinion on Friday morning; another appeal was made that afternoon; but all petitions failed. About three hundred guards took Sims to the waterfront at dawn to put him on board the *Acorn* for his return to Savannah. Parker had met with others to consider ways of rescuing Sims, but they could find no way. The lawyers had made every reasonable attempt to prevent Sims's return to Georgia and failed, while those who counseled disobedience to the law were able to do nothing. For the cotton Whigs of Boston, the rescue of Shadrach had been avenged.

On the first anniversary of Sims's return to slavery where Parker spoke before the Vigilance Committee at the Melodeon, his subject encompassed what had occurred and what should have been done. Parker rehearsed the facts of the Sims case, though his audience must have known them well, and explained that Sims was kidnapped because some men in Boston—rich and respectable ones—wanted a fugitive returned to slavery from their city. Not the people of rural Massachusetts or the middle-class citizens of Boston but the wealthy were responsible. They led Boston to desert its past and to discard the spirit of the Battle of Lexington and the Revolution. While local government had done nothing, the Committee of Vigilance had saved three or four hundred "citizens of Boston" from being returned to the South. The state should have opposed the desire of the wealthy by passing a law making it a crime to kidnap a man in the fashion permitted by the Fugitive Slave Law.

There is no paradox in Parker's advocating legal means to save the escaped slaves. He was no anarchist; he wanted man's law to reflect God's law; and only when it did not did he disobey it. Additional evidence of his attitude toward the law is that he supported most of the legal efforts to free Sims and later Anthony Burns. On the occasion of the anniversary of Sims's return to the South, when Parker dealt with the causes of the rendition and the remedies that might have existed, he spoke as he hoped an historian would: he presented the facts and judged them with righteousness.[17]

Despite Parker's extensive involvement with the work of the Vigilance Committee against slavery and for the fugitives who came north, no fair account of this period of his life can be made without mentioning that in 1852 he published *Ten Sermons of Religion,* dedicating it to Emerson, and in 1853, *Sermons of Theism, Atheism and the Popular Theology.* Their publication came between the renditions of Sims and Burns, as though there had been some hiatus in his antislavery activity. The misleading coincidence might suggest that he left Abolition to return to theology. In fact, both volumes consist of sermons given over a period of time and, more important, serve as reminders that Parker regarded himself as a theologian whose religion dictated his duty to work for the elimination of slavery. Though it may be convenient to suggest that he forsook one field of endeavor to work in another, as most biographers have done, Parker never changed vocations. These two volumes, particularly the latter, contain the mature theology of Theodore Parker, though it must be added that neither contains new ideas never before presented in his sermons.

In *Sermons of Theism, Atheism and the Popular Theology* Parker attacked two poles of religious thought, atheism and the prevalent popular theology. Those who

called Parker an atheist never read his sermons carefully enough to realize how profoundly he believed in a Deity. Although many orthodox clergymen could not admit it, Theodore Parker was as far from atheism as they themselves were. In the fifty pages devoted to speculative and practical atheism in this volume he proved in spirit and in fact how foreign atheism was to his religion. In brief, Parker did not believe one could be a speculative atheist (one who denies the existence of God); his belief in the religious faculty in every man precluded the possibility. Practical atheism (the denial of moral right, duty and obligation) he detested with all the strength a righteous man could muster.

Against the popular theology Parker marshaled another array of arguments including the truths he had found intuitively and those he had verified through the historical method of biblical criticism. As he had before, he attacked the conceptions of God and man and the relation between them in that theology charging that the popular theology viewed God as "the grimmest object in the universe," man as "a worm" and the relation between them as typified by the notion that God "loves one and rejects nine hundred and ninety-nine out of the thousand." Since he hoped his own absolute religion would displace popular theology, he criticized it more harshly than he did atheism. The popular theology was divorced from history, from reason, from conscience; it drove men from religion and separated science from religion. He thought representatives of popular theology such as Jonathan Edwards had driven more men from religion than the famous atheists. Such theology was a religion of forms, doctrines, and rituals without substance that easily permitted a man to reserve his religion for a short time on Sundays.

Against atheism, popular theology, and Deism (which he would never accept, though his enemies sometimes accused him of accepting its doctrines), Parker set theism, the basis of absolute religion. The keystone is God, who is "not so much a Being, as a Becoming," perfect and infinite. "In nature God is the only cause, the only providence, the only power; the law of nature . . . represents the modes of action of God Himself, His thought made visible. . . ."[18] Neither chance nor evil is possible in Nature. There are no miracles and no providential occurrences, since nature is perfectly ordered. Though God knows all that will happen in history, He does grant man some freedom of will. Deriving his religion from the absolute and ultimate source of all, Parker named it absolute religion. Its thrust was to help all men to virtue in fulfilling God's plan. Parker expected each man to act as he himself did in working toward this end. Absolute religion provided the impetus for man to act for piety and morality and against drunkenness, crime, and slavery. Thus, Parker's theological writings were a justification for his efforts against slavery.

Slavery was an issue which continued to absorb his time. While the issue of organizing the territories of Kansas and Nebraska was being discussed in Congress in 1854, he delivered a sermon, **"The Nebraska Question."** His apparently circuitous approach is his common technique of beginning with the general and the abstract. He opened with "the general course of human conduct in America" and attacked the Spanish for bringing greed and the institutions of theocracy, monarchy, aristocracy and despotocracy ("the dominion of the master over the exploitered [*sic*] slave"). These caused the turn toward materialism which has occurred generally in the country for "Wealth is the great object of American desire. Covetousness is the American passion." Money has been substituted for theocracy, monarchy, and aristocracy; and it has joined forces with despotocracy, as the political parties have stood by and accepted the change. Now the South wanted Nebraska. The South—"I must say it—is the enemy of the North."[19] She must be stopped, even at the price of Union. In Parker's lengthy attack on the South, he included his comparison of Virginia and New York and his catalogue of Southern triumphs. He found his theme and his facts, and he used them at every opportunity, fitting such issues as the Nebraska question into his view and approach.

But Parker seemed to some of his friends to have left religion and theology to work in other fields. When Senator Salmon P. Chase complained of this, Parker justified his own action in a letter to him. His first, and minor, point was that men would not favor slavery because of their prejudice against him; his theological position would not convert them to slavery. But his more important and more rational justification came from his view of the relation of slavery and theology. Parker based his position on his belief in growth principle, for he always opposed that which hindered the development of the individual and mankind.

If mankind were properly developed, the sins of slavery, war, and intemperance would not exist: "I became personally unpopular, *hated* even; but the *special measures* [antislavery] go forward obviously; the *general principle* enters into the public ear, the public mind, and does its work."[20] This concept was the heart of the matter for Parker: he preached a theology which asserted that man would improve as he recognized and accepted true principles. The sins against which he preached had to be removed in the course of development. Therefore, the removal of slavery was an application of his theology. When the idea of political morality became imbedded in the public mind, Parker would then help to organize men in order to achieve the ends dictated by the idea. First came the idea; then the action. This general approach permitted him to say with sincerity that it was slavery he opposed, not slaveholders. Since it was the institution that he attacked and studied, he subscribed to the *Richmond Examiner* and read as many other Southern publications as he could.

Continuing to reach for power and influence, Parker wrote to men in the government whom he thought might listen and be persuasive in the fight against slavery. To Seward he argued that freedom and slavery—North and South—were necessarily hostile to one another. There might be a separation, or freedom or slavery might win. The third alternative seemed most likely, in view of recent and predicted events. If slavery won, the nation would fall to despotism, and the nation "shall have committed the crime against nature, in our Titanic lust of wealth and power."[21] To stop this development, Parker proposed a convention of the Free States in Buffalo on July 4, 1854, "to consider the state of the Union." and to end slavery. A few days later he said in a letter to John P. Hale "If the South will not let it [slavery] down gradually, *we* must let *it down by the run*."[22] The attempt to call a convention failed.

In speaking against slavery in 1854, Parker had these particular aims: to explain how it came to exist and to survive in the United States and to demonstrate why slavery had to be eliminated. He found the source of the North-South conflict in the types of people who settled the regions. Just as the differences between the settlers of North and South America created the differences between the countries of the continents, so the differences between settlers of North and South caused variations between the sections. The motivation of one group was religious and with it came democracy; that of the other was money or escape, and with it appeared oligarchy. Though the first sought theocracy, the people wanted democracy and achieved it; but they had not yet achieved perfection. For example, Negro children were still not allowed in the "common schools" because the Puritans did not reject slavery.

But the group which had settled the South had adopted slavery and had allowed the cruelties perpetrated within the system. The South, settled by those who wanted oligarchy, had been able to control the federal government: "It [the South] debases the legislative and the executive power; the Supreme Court is its venal prostitute. You remember the Inaugural of Mr. Pierce:—'I believe that involuntary servitude is recognised by the Constitution. I believe that it stands like any other admitted right.'[23] To this statement of situation Parker compares what could be: democratic institutions and education can "give an intellectual development to the mass of men such as the world never saw." Men will be able to spend their time "subduing material Nature, and developing human Nature into its higher forms." Though materialism is now excessive, achievements will one day be in the realm of science, letters, and art.

IV THE RENDITION OF ANTHONY BURNS

In the midst of these sermons and analytical addresses came another dark event which had serious consequences for Parker: the rendition of Anthony Burns.

For three years after the return of Sims, no fugitive slave was sent from Boston to the South, though as many as a thousand slaves escaped from their masters every year. Early in 1854 a group of Southerners had come to Massachusetts looking for three slaves and had discovered them in New Bedford; but, by the time they could get official help, the fugitives had disappeared; and the South was more than a little displeased. When Anthony Burns was arrested in Boston on May 24, 1854, he was taken immediately to jail and to a confrontation with his owner, Charles Suttle. Richard Henry Dana, Jr., the first man to learn of the arrest, rushed to help Burns. Though Burns refused his offers of aid, Dana was able to convince Edward G. Loring, the federal slave commissioner, to grant a two-day delay in the hearing.

The Vigilance Committee which met immediately, planned a large evening meeting. Thomas Wentworth Higginson prepared for action and bought a box of axes. That evening he was ready to supply axes to the mob that he expected to rush from the meeting. But those who were speaking at the meeting did not know of the plans of those who intended to storm the Court House. When the signal was given in the meeting, Parker, unaware of the arrangement, tried to calm the mob. Higginson, too impatient to wait for the dilatory mob from the meeting, stormed the Court House with only a few men. They battered down the door; Higginson was cut across the face; James Batchelder, a special policeman, was stabbed; and the would-be rescuers were forced to retreat. As a result of this action, Marshal Freeman wired Washington for instructions; President Pierce replied that the law had to be obeyed.

When Dana tried the various legal maneuvers which had been used in the Sims case, he succeeded in having the hearing delayed until Monday. On Saturday an attempt to gain Burns's release by purchasing him was stopped by District Attorney Hallett, who thought Washington and the South would be enraged if this purchase were allowed to happen, though Suttle had already accepted the $1200 offered him. During the three-day trial there was sufficient confusion in the evidence to warrant the release of Burns (faulty description and other technical errors), but Loring ordered him returned—a decision that did not close the matter in the minds of the people of Boston.

Sentiment had changed since 1851. The United States marshal had to rely upon "a precious set of murderers, thieves, bullies [and] blacklegs," according to Dana. To aid this unsavory group, troops were sent in from Rhode Island and New Hampshire; and over fifteen hundred Boston militia were on duty. As the troops moved Burns from the Court House to the waterfront past fifty thousand people, there was fighting; bricks were thrown at the soldiers; and men were beaten and sabered in return. But Burns was returned. A short time later, Louis Clark, a gambler and pimp who had organized the marshal's guard, hired "a drunken ex-prize fighter named Huxford" to attack Dana. Huxford hit him with an iron bar and left him bleeding and unconscious.[24] President Pierce paid over $14,000 to the mayor for the service of the State militia; the total cost for the rendition of Burns may have been over $100,000.

When Parker spoke in Faneuil Hall on Friday evening, May 26, in the midst of these events, he carefully asserted the right of the people to obey a law other than the slave law. He told his audience they could "put it [such obedience] into execution, just when you see fit." Only by implication did he suggest what they might do: "I love peace. But there is a means, and there is an end; Liberty is the end, and sometimes peace is not the means towards it." Such statements would cause his arrest and subsequent trial, though he did not urge the crowd to leave the hall to rush to the Court House. Later in his address, he even promised the crowd that it would not need to resort to arms to save Burns; he assured them that "if we stand up there resolutely, and declare that this man shall not go out of the city of Boston *without shooting a gun*—then he won't go back."[25]

Aware of the danger of exhorting his excited audience to action and thereafter being accused of treason, Parker in effect advised them to threaten and to show strength. If they did so, Burns would not be returned without battle; and Parker did not expect the guards to fight in order to return Burns to the South. If the city stood resolute, the authorities would retreat. The people almost followed Parker's advice; but the authorities, supported by the President and his power, were not so timid as Parker had supposed. As always, Parker overestimated the strategic plans of the South and underestimated the tactical acuity of the South and that of the federal government as its agent.

In one of Parker's sermons just after the rendition of Burns, *The New Crime Against Humanity,* Parker announced: ". . . there has been a man stolen in this city of our fathers." Though he knew everyone in his audience was familiar with the general facts of the case, he begins with these, admitting that he had played a central part in the affair and frankly estimating the importance of his message: "I know well the responsibility of the place I occupy this morning. To-morrow's sun shall carry my words to all America. They will be read on both sides of the continent. They will cross the ocean." The cause of the rendition under the Fugitive Slave

Law was, to Parker, the battle between slavery and freedom. So strong was the control of the nation by the forces of slavery that, when Parker sent one of the three hundred petitions he had received for the repeal of the law to Eliot, the congressional representative from Boston, Eliot sent it back. Another official ridiculed was Edward G. Loring, slave commissioner, whom Parker pictured as coming to another court where he was asked, "Edward, where is thy brother Anthony?"; and Edward answered, "I know not, am I my brother's keeper, Lord?"[26]

The basis on which Parker continued to oppose the Fugitive Slave Law and to urge its repeal and disobedience to it was justice above law. Man must by will obey God's laws just as the falling leaf obeys natural laws. Parker admitted that there were laws which were not related to morality—voting age, interest, highway laws; but when a statutory law conflicted with justice, a situation discovered by conscience, justice must prevail. If, he said, a convention of murderers made murder legal, men obviously would not accept such a law since it would conflict with justice. The clash between justice and legislative law could occur whenever men did not look to their consciences. In arguing this principle of the supremacy of God's law, Parker did not always mention the Fugitive Slave Law; but this law precipitated the attack.[27] Parker, like most of his fellow Transcendentalists, did not explore the problem of conflicts among the consciences of men since he did not recognize the possibility.

Since Parker could never concentrate on a single problem, the summer of 1854, despite the significant Burns case, marked the occasion of other sermons on general problems such as **"Dangers Which Threaten the Rights of Man in America."** For Parker, the four most serious dangers were those from the "Devotion to Riches"; from the Catholic Church; from the idea that statute law was the highest law; and from slavery, which was based on that atheistic concept. These dangers stood in the way of the establishment of an industrial democracy. America was ruled by men with nothing but money and what it brought—by three hundred thousand slaveholders and their servants, North and South. So attractive was wealth that many Northerners turned from politics, military affairs, and all else to commerce and industry, though in the South the "ablest men almost exclusively attend to politics." Everyone attended to his financial interests. (Parker did not show how the industrial democracy could be built if men did not turn from politics.) The Catholic Church stood in the way because it opposed all that fostered democracy and the natural rights of man; it hated free churches, free press, and free schools; and its allegiance was to Rome. But Parker denied that he wished the Catholic Church excluded; for, if it could defeat Protestantism, "we deserve defeat."[28] The third danger, the prevalence of statute law,

was countermanded by the examples of Christ, Luther, and the Puritans. If obedience to man's law were the highest virtue, what must be said of these "criminals."

The sum of these dangers was slavery. Parker saw three alternatives to resolve the conflict between slavery and freedom: (1) separation into two nations; (2) freedom destroying slavery; (3) slavery overwhelming freedom. He judged severance of the nation to be the most likely result; it would break up because of its large size and the general distaste for strong central government. But commercial interests and politicians benefited too greatly from the union to let it disintegrate soon. In the meantime, slavery would continue to conquer freedom, acquiring Haiti and Cuba, establishing slavery in all states, restoring the slave trade, and taking more territory from Mexico.

These dangers, including slavery itself, could be removed if men would recognize that the rights of man must prevail over the rights of property—and that religion must not be divorced from politics. The seeming simplicity of Parker's view of the national problems and their solutions is in large part a result of his efforts to make these clear to his audience. When reduced to their simplest terms, his analyses are less convincing than they appear in the vigor of his full presentations. Nevertheless, Theodore Parker himself possessed such a compelling sense of duty to right and to justice that he often cut through the complexities of national conditions and institutions in a fashion that less confident men could not.

V PARKER'S "DEFENCE"

Through 1854, a year in which Parker gave many addresses and sermons, he anxiously awaited his own fate in the courts. There had been an attempt to indict him for his part in the Burns affair, though he did not believe it would succeed. In June his enemies failed, but in October a true bill was brought in. In December, Wendell Phillips was arrested; and the trial of both Parker and Phillips was set for March, 1855. Parker feared that the indictment would finally be dismissed and that he would be cheated out of giving the defense which he laboriously produced. When he was denied the opportunity to speak in court, he published his 221-page defense. Parker claimed this defense as his first in fourteen years of being attacked. (In fact, most of his work was a defense of his positions.) He now spoke because the right of free speech was at stake. But first he felt compelled to outline the circumstances leading him to publish his defense: "When Judge Curtis delivered his charge to the Grand-Jury, June 7th, 1854, I made ready for trial, and in three or four days my line of defence was marked out—the fortifications sketched, the place of the batteries determined; I began to collect arms, and was soon ready for his attack."

Like Parker's grandfather at Lexington, he readied his defenses. Yet he was certain that Judges Sprague and Curtis "who have taken such pains to establish slavery in Massachusetts," who sat there "each like a travestied Prometheus, chained up in a silk gown because they had brought to earth fire from the quarter opposite to Heaven," would not allow him publicly to defend himself. They would dismiss the indictment and put the blame on the attorney for drawing a faulty bill. When the trial opened on April 3, his lawyers "rent the indictment into many pieces."

Parker continued his review of the events: on June 7, Curtis charged the grand jury looking into the Burns affair that "obstructing legal process of the United States is to be inquired of and treated by you as a misdemeanor." Judge Curtis instructed the jurors that such obstruction need not consist of violence; that, if a peaceable multitude should stop an officer without violence, this act was such obstruction. Not only were those who actually obstruct or oppose guilty, but those "leagued in the common design" and able to assist and those who "though absent when the offence [the attempted rescue] was committed, did procure, counsel, command, or abet others to commit the offence, are indictable." Moreover, those who advised obstruction were also indictable. Curtis informed the jury that it was not the place of men to decide which laws they would obey and which they would not, that local opinions about the extradition of fugitives were the road to mob rule. The grand jury did not return a true bill.

On October 16, another jury was impaneled. This jury brought in a true bill against Parker charging that he "then and there well knowing the premises, with force and arms did knowingly and wilfully obstruct, resist, and oppose the said Marshal Watson Freeman . . . in serving and attempting to serve and execute the said warrant and legal process . . . to the great damage of the said Watson Freeman, to the great hindrance and obstruction of Justice, to the evil example of all others, in like case offending, against the peace and dignity of the said United States, and contrary to the form of the Statute in such case made and provided." Indictments were returned against Phillips, Higginson, and others. Parker, who was arraigned on November 29 and released on $1500 bail, was to appear in court on March 5 and trial was fixed for April 3. The first motion that the indictment be dismissed was denied. Eventually a motion of *nolle prosequi* was entered, and the indictments were annulled.

In the opening of the defense itself, Parker described it as "more didactic than rhetorical, more like a lecture, less like a speech"; and so it is. He interpreted the charge for the jury: that his trial was a "Political Trial" and that he was charged with no act of self-ambition. He was on trial for his "love of Justice," for his "manly virtue." He presented himself as a minister who had been chiefly concerned with the "Laws of God" in studying "absolute, universal truth, teaching it to men, and applying it to the various departments of life."

Much of his *Defence* consists of his remarks on the situation in America, particularly "the Encroachments of a Power hostile to Democratic Institutions" and its attempts at the "Systematic Corruption of the Judiciary" and of the right of trial by jury. Always he related his own trial to these larger topics: "I am on trial because I hate Slavery, because I love freedom for the black man, and for all the human Race. I am not arraigned because I have violated the statute on which the indictment is framed—no child could think it—but because I am an advocate of Freedom, because my Word, my Thoughts, my Feelings, my Actions, nay, all my life, my very Existence itself, are a protest against Slavery. Despotism cannot happily advance unless I am silenced."

Parker included almost fifty pages on the corruption of the judiciary, beginning with the judges under James I, "the first King of New England." It would be idle to rehearse even a part of this long discourse, and one wonders how Parker expected a jury to react to such a treatise. In addition to supplying historical data, he virtually gave a charge to the jury, explaining to it its function with respect to questions of fact, law, and the application of law to fact. After sixty pages of instructing the jury and telling it what and how it must decide, Parker moved to the general circumstances of his own case which occupy the remaining hundred pages of the defense. He supplied a history of the Fugitive Slave Law and its legal predecessors, its relation to the Constitution, and the cases which had arisen under it in Boston. He even attacked the judge and his family: "This family, though possessing many good qualities, has had a remarkably close and intimate connection with all, or most, of the recent cases of kidnapping [of slaves] in Boston."

Parker asked the jury, contrary to the judge's instructions, to consider the Constitution and the Fugitive Slave Law: "To me, it is very plain that kidnapping a man in Boston and making him a slave, is not the way to form a more perfect Union, establish Justice, insure domestic Tranquility, provide for the Common Defence, promote the General Welfare, or secure the Blessings of Liberty." In his long summary, Parker recounted that he had talked about the slave power and its plans, despotism in England, the corruption of judges, the perversion of trial by jury through the centuries, the course of slavery and slave power in America, and the Curtis family ("When Mr. Webster prostituted himself to the Slave Power this family went out and pimped for him in the streets. . . ."). Parker told the jury that it was deciding whether or not slavery would spread farther. As he closed, he joined patriotism and religion, related

John Hancock and John Q. Adams to Moses and Aaron, and identified himself in the courtroom with his grandfather at Lexington.[29]

The remarkable document which Parker called a "defence" provoked little response. Originally directed at an audience of jurors which could never have followed the elaborate arguments and never have listened alertly to all two hundred pages of it, the defense shares the characteristics of other Parker speeches. From concrete situations and problems, the argument moved toward historical background and abstract principles. Though appropriate to treatises and discussion, such methods are often not effective as arguments. The sections of the *Defence* presenting the specific facts of the trial are the most persuasive. When Parker presented his treatise on judges, jurors, and the judicial system, he provided the "jury" with far more than it needed or could digest. Despite his acumen for political affairs and antislavery work, Parker's scholarly ambitions, ability, and knowledge continually interfered. Seldom could he achieve an appropriate relation between his work and knowledge as scholar and his effort as a politician. Quite capable of arguing theological questions, on the one hand, and the causes of a political situation, on the other, Parker yet had great difficulty in gauging an audience.

In the midst of Parker's consuming antislavery activity, his letters to Convers Francis continued with such information as this: "I got from a foreign catalogue a copy of a rare book; *you* doubtless know it well, but *I* never saw it before, though I have been hunting for it some years: 'Epigrammata Clarissimi Dissertissimique viri Thomae Mori Brittani pleraque ex Graecis versa (Basilaea, apud Joannem Frobenium, Mense Martio, An. MDXVIII)'."[30] Active as he was in public matters, Parker never forgot the scholarly life he wished to pursue; but he could not be both a secluded scholar and an active Abolitionist.

VI 1856-58—POLITICS AND LECTURES

Particularly as the 1856 elections approached, Parker renewed his attempts to influence political leaders. To Governor N. P. Banks he described the dichotomy between slavery and freedom, arguing that the slave party had money, organization, and position; but the freedom group had little of these though it did possess ideas, genius, and "womanly women." He put it to Banks that, as governor, he must want the party of freedom to have political power to carry out ideas: "How shall we do it? that is the question." (Shifts from "you" to "we" are common in Parker's letters.)

The things to consider were "the maximum of the new ideas which the people will accept in the next presidential election" and the minimum which they would accept. The minimum was a man who was so highly principled that the people could put their trust in him and in an appropriate platform for him. Chase had slipped by declaring slavery in the present geographic areas to be untouchable; Sumner, by his slogan "Freedom national and Slavery sectional." Parker could accept no slavery anywhere in the nation. The maximum acceptable to the people was the Declaration—all men are created equal with inalienable rights. The whole people would not yet accept this ideal, but it should be the goal. In the meantime, however, the North wanted the abolition of slavery and, indeed, would accept nothing less. Feigning innocence, Parker asked Banks if John C. Frémont, was a suitable candidate.[31] Though Parker felt he was not, he had to convince others.

Though Parker worked hard to find a suitable Presidential candidate, he had none to suggest. At the same time, he worked for the passage of a personal liberty law and in other ways to defeat and oppose the Fugitive Slave Law. He pressed Sumner to rouse the North, not because Sumner was the best man to do so but because Parker knew few others. War had begun in Kansas and in the Congress. An early stage could, Parker thought, become a Northern victory with a successful candidate in 1856. To be successful, the candidate needed the backing of conscience Whigs, errant Democrats, Northern Know-Nothings, Republicans, and antislavery party men. By the middle of April Parker had given eighty-four lectures in the previous four and a half months—and has done so while preaching weekly sermons, attending meetings, and writing over a thousand letters. Yet he said he had written only necessary notes.

Part of Parker's work in preparation for the election was the preaching of three of his best analyses of the conflict. Two of these, given on the same day, were published as *The Great Battle Between Slavery and Freedom*. The first, **"The Present Aspect of the Anti-Slavery Enterprise,"** is primarily a description of the forces of slavery and freedom. That the antislavery forces were not working for the Negro as much as for the white man was made clear by Parker who also said that, if Anglo-Saxons were enslaved, they would fight for their freedom; but the Negroes were not fighting.[32]

In the second sermon of the day, **"The Present Crisis in American Affairs,"** Parker established his view of the races. The Caucasian had developed farthest and fastest to gain "power over the material world." Of the groups within this most progressive race, the Teutonic led the way. Of them the Anglo-Saxons, "or that portion thereof settled in the Northern States of America, have got the farthest forward in certain important forms of welfare, and now advance the most rapidly in their general progress." Such descriptions of peoples and races can only be made by men who have righteous conceptions of racial and national character. Though Parker realized full well the diverse parties and sentiments of the

North, for example, he often described the section without any recognition of the disagreements within it. In this sermon he characterized the North as antislavery, Christian, and industrial.

Viewing the nation as Parker did—with two opposing socioeconomic systems—it is no wonder he was ready for separation, though he did not then advocate secession or disunion: "I do not propose disunion—at present. I would never leave the black man in bondage, or the whites subject to the slaveholding Oligarchy which rules them." Furthermore, if the nation remained whole and elected an antislavery man as President, federal offices could be filled with antislavery men; Kansas and other new states would be free; slavery could be restricted; a railroad to the Pacific built; and the slave states would be surrounded by free states.[33] While Parker perhaps expected too much of an antislavery President, he did not overestimate the power of political force.

In the last of the three important published sermons of the month, *A New Lesson for the Day,* Parker suggested that the United States was in a "state of incipient civil war." The cases of the Crafts, Shadrach, Sims, Burns, followed by the caning of Sumner by Preston Brooks in the Senate, proved this assertion. To convince his audience, Parker imagined Brooks as the representative of the South, Sumner of the North, so that the blows fell on the members of his audience. In this presentation, Brooks approached Sumner and stole "up behind him as he sits writing, when his arms are pinioned in his heavy chair and his other limbs are under the desk, and on his naked head strikes him with a club loaded with lead, until he falls, stunning and bleeding to the floor, and then continues his blows."[34] Parker felt the impact of this attack both as an Abolitionist and as a personal friend of Sumner. It increased his enmity toward the South as the preserver of sin in the nation and provoked him to work even more vigorously against the section and its evil.

Parker accepted Fremont's nomination, though he was far from being his first choice; and through the summer he believed Fremont could be elected. Yet he was convinced that, if Buchanan were elected, there would be separation. Parker continued to lecture frequently—over one hundred times between October and August, 1856. He feared revolution and expected civil war; and, though he could not go to Kansas, he followed events closely, seeing the fight there as one between slavery and freedom. By October, he saw defeat for Fremont and consequent civil war within four years. He stopped buying books—he had spent fifteen hundred dollars in a year for such purchases—to save money for his wife. When war came, he thought his property would be confiscated and himself hanged. Seldom had he been so pessimistic, as he continued to believe in the coming war between North and South and in an attempt by the

nation to conquer Cuba and then Mexico. Now he was not sure conditions would have been better under Fremont; he doubted both the man and the party, especially the Western Republicans. Though Parker usually had more faith in the potential power of political force than most Transcendentalists had, he occasionally shared their distrust in the efficacy of institutions to improve men.

Despite the defeat of Fremont and Parker's subsequent depression, he would not attend the Disunion Convention that Higginson and others called for January, 1857, on the grounds that the recent election meant four more years of pro-slavery government and an increasing hostility between the North and the South. They believed the present union to be a failure and called the convention "to consider the practicability, probability, and expediency, of a separation."[35] When Parker wrote to Higginson the day before the convention to express his regret that other business would keep him away, he approved the purpose of the meeting though he did not favor separation since he continued to believe it wrong to leave four million poor whites and four million slaves under that government. But Parker had little faith in the force of his argument, for in the last part of the letter he suggested where the line between North and South should be drawn. The land of freedom should be that east of Chesapeake Bay, north of the Potomac and the Ohio, and west of the Mississippi. He thought Virginia and Kentucky might "beg" to stay with the North. Like most other Abolitionists, Parker often misjudged the South.

Rather than sanction disunion, Parker continued to work for Abolition under union. He lectured as often as he could, though he knew the work was ruining his health. He believed in the value of his work, considering the institution of the lecture as church, college, and theater in one. He was certain the lecturing—"six or eight of the most progressive and powerful minds in America have been lecturing fifty or a hundred times in the year"—would influence the people for the better.[36]

To understand the conditions of travel and the labor of lecturing to a man such as Parker, who had also numerous responsibilities at home, one may read his own accounts of such trips:

> I gave up the Anti-Slavery Festival for the lecture, rode fifty-six miles in the cars, leaving Boston at half-past four o'clock, and reaching the end of the railroad at half-past six—drove seven miles in a sleigh, and reached the house of———, who had engaged me to come. It was time to begin; I lectured one hour and three quarters, and returned to the house. Was offered no supper before the lecture, and none after, till the chaise came to the door to take me back again to the railroad station, seven miles off, where I was to pass the night and take the cars at half-past six next morning.

Luckily, I always carry a few little creature-comforts in my wallet. I ate a seed-cake or two, and a fig with lumps of sugar. We reached the tavern at eleven, could get nothing to eat at that hour, and, as it was a temperance house, not a glass of ale, which is a good nightcap. It took three quarters of an hour to thaw out:—went to bed at twelve in a cold room, was called up at five, had what is universal, a tough steak, sour bread, and potatoes swimming in fat. . . .

This experience was not unique, for one may read another account from a letter to Sarah Hunt, written in 1857:

Monday last at seven, George and I walked down to the Lowell Depot, and at eight started for Rouse's Point, two hundred and eighty-seven miles off, sick and only fit to lie on a sofa, and have day-dreams of you, sweet absent ones! and think over again the friendly endearments that are past, but may yet return. A dreadful hard ride ends at nine P. M., and I find myself in the worst tavern (pretending to decency) in the Northern States. Bread which defies eating, crockery which sticks to your hands, fried fish as cold as when drawn from the lake. Rise at half-past four, breakfast (?) at five, off in the cars at half past five, lecture at Malone that night, lie all day on the sofa, ditto at Potsdam next day.

The third day, leave Potsdam at nine, and reach Champlain (if I get there) at half-past eight, spending ten and a half hours in travelling by railroad ninety-three miles! Thence, after lecture, to Rouse's Point, and at half-past five to-morrow morning return to the cars which are to take me home.[37]

These tales of traveling through comfortable and civilized New England could have been told by most of the popular lecturers. Despite the difficulties of this work, Parker lectured to spread his views and to earn money for books and for antislavery work. So dependent was he on this income that the financial crisis of 1857 which caused the cancellation of lectures cut his income in half. Parker had lectured seventy-three times in the season by February, 1858. The previous year he had lectured eighty times "from the Mississippi to the Penobscot" in addition to his temperance and antislavery speeches.

The election of 1856 shows Parker's engrossment in practical politics on a national level. The next few years are punctuated by comments on politics and the Presidency. In 1858 he stated categorically that "Slavery must be put down politically, or else militarily." He asked for a Republican candidate in 1860 other than Fremont or some "Johnny Raw." He must be "a man who can wisely and bravely embody what public opinion there is already. Such a man is one of the forces that *make* public opinion." The President must not be "a fanatic, a dreamer, an enthusiast, but we don't want a coward or a trimmer." A man with these qualities could have been elected in 1856, but Fremont could not

because he could not gain the trust of the people. Even the victory of the Republican candidate would not cause the South to leave the Union because it lacked industry, commerce, schools, and a sufficient population. He explained its threatening attitude in this way:

"Mamma," said a spoiled boy to a mother of ten other and older children, "Mamma, I want a piece of pickled elephant." "No, my dear, he can't have it. Johnny must be a good boy." "No, I won't be a good boy. I don't want to be good. I want a piece of pickled elephant." "But aint he mother's *youngest* boy? When we have some pickled elephant, he shall have the biggest piece!" "Ma'am, I don't want a *piece!* I want a *whole pickled elephant!* I want him *now!* If you don't let me have him now, I'll run right off and catch the measles. I know a boy that's got 'em first rate."[38]

But the South did leave the Union. Parker had underestimated the South in this respect, but he did not miscalculate its political strength and its tenacious fidelity to the institution of slavery. Why the South might want to keep its slaves he did not inquire; but, had he done so, Parker would have explained the reason in terms of the oligarchial greed for power.

There were continuing letters to William Herndon in 1858. In August, Parker wrote that he followed the Illinois campaign with interest and read the speeches—"the noble speeches"—of Abraham Lincoln; and he maintained his opinion that Stephen Douglas was a "mad dog." Though Parker favored neither Horace Greeley nor William Seward, he thought the latter would be the Republican candidate in 1860 to defeat Douglas. He told Herndon the battle was still between slavery and freedom, despotism and democracy. He hoped Lincoln would win, but he has just read the *Tribune* report of the Lincoln-Douglas debate at Ottawa and thinks Douglas had the better of it. Douglas had asked Lincoln the right questions on slavery, and Lincoln had dodged them. To Parker, "That is not the way to fight the battle of freedom." Worse, he said, "Daniel Webster stood on higher anti-slavery ground than Abraham Lincoln now."[39] Though Parker did not then realize it, Lincoln would almost wholly meet his prescription for a Republican candidate in 1860.

By this time, 1858, Parker occasionally could look back on the course of his career. When he had moved to Boston, he had thought of working among "the perishing class"—the lower class. But he discovered that people had "a great horror" of him; that men had no principles, "no correct ideas as a basis of action"; and that the slavery seemed so altogether such a crucial matter that it had to be dealt with first.[40] So Parker had spent his Boston years in setting forth his ideas on the proper relations between God and man and in fighting for Abolition. He was unable to deal with the lower classes, and he could not find men with principles; he could, however, work with a problem which he found significant on both a practical and an idealistic level. Parker must have realized the recurrence of the same difficulties he had as a teacher—being able to reach his pupils.

Notes

1. *Works* (Centenary), XI, 1-20; *Works* (Cobbe), V, 1-16.

2. "The Abolition of Slavery by the French Republic," *Works* (Centenary), XI, 165-75; "Speech at a Meeting of the American Anti-Slavery Society," *Works* (Cobbe), V, 85-92.

3. "The Anti-Slavery Convention," *Works* (Centenary), XI, 176-88; "Speech at Faneuil Hall, Before the New England Anti-Slavery Convention," *Works* (Cobbe), V.

4. *A Letter to the People of the United States Touching The Matter of Slavery* (Boston, 1848), pp. 5-9. Reprinted in *Works* (Centenary), XI, 32-119 and in *Works* (Cobbe), V, 17-84.

5. *A Letter,* pp. 110-11.

6. *A Letter,* pp. 116, 119, 120.

7. Weiss, II, 79-84.

8. *Theodore Parker's Review of Webster* (Boston, 1850), pp. 19, 21, 23, 25. Reprinted in *Works* (Centenary), XI, 218-47 and in *Works* (Cobbe), VI, 212-34.

9. "The Slave Power," *Works* (Centenary), XI, 248-86; "Speech at the New England Anti-Slavery Convention," *Works* (Cobbe), V, 103-33.

10. "A Discourse Occasioned by the Death of the Late President Taylor," *Works* (Cobbe), IV, 184-211.

11. "The Function of Conscience," *Works* (Centenary), XI, 287-315; "The Function and Place of Conscience in Relation to the Laws of Men: A Sermon for the Times," *Works* (Cobbe), V, 134-63.

12. "The State of the Nation," *Works* (Centenary), XII, 92-181; *Works* (Cobbe), IV, 235-65.

13. The Boston Committee of Vigilance was formed to combat the Fugitive Slave Law, according to some sources; but its date of origin is placed at various dates from 1842 to 1850. Theodore Parker was on the Executive Committee in 1850.

14. Frothingham, pp. 409-12.

15. "Speech at the Ministerial Conference in Boston," *Works* (Cobbe), V. To his Shaker friend, Robert White, Parker wrote that he thought too much weight had been put on Christ's words on non-resistance. Since Christ believed the world would

soon end, he could easily council his listeners not to resist evil and to take no thought for the following day. Parker believed violence had its place; he would use force to aid a fugitive, for example. Weiss, I, 392-93.

16. Weiss, II, 112; Frothingham, p. 348.

17. "The Boston Kidnapping," *Works* (Centenary), XI, 316-85; *Works* (Cobbe), V, 172-224.

18. *Works* (Centenary), II, 196, 205. For his definitions of the varieties of atheism, see pp. 60, 87. The work is volume XI of the Cobbe edition.

19. "The Nebraska Question. Some Thoughts on the New Assault Upon Freedom in America," *Works* (Cobbe), V, 245-96.

20. Weiss, II, 226.

21. *Ibid.,* II, 206.

22. Frothingham, p. 445.

23. "The Progress of America," *Works* (Centenary), XII, 196-249; "Some Thoughts on the Progress of America, And the Influence of Her Diverse Institutions," *Works* (Cobbe), VI, 1-43.

24. Samuel Shapiro, "The Rendition of Anthony Burns," *Journal of Negro History,* XLIV (January, 1959), 34-51.

25. *The Liberator,* XXIVI (June 2, 1954).

26. "The New Crime Against Humanity," *Works* (Centenary), XII, 250-332; *Works* (Cobbe), VI, 44-109.

27. "The Law of God and the Statutes of Men," *Works* (Centenary), XIV 137-62; *Works* (Cobbe), V, 225-44.

28. *A Sermon of the Dangers Which Threaten the Rights of Man in America* (Boston, 1854), pp. 19, 24. Reprinted, *Works* (Centenary), XII, 333-96.

29. *The Trial of Theodore Parker, for the "Misdemeanor" of a Speech in Faneuil Hall Against Kidnapping, before the Circuit Court of the United States* (Boston, 1855), pp. v, vii, 171-72, 1-2, 4, 9, 17, 156, 210, 218.

30. Weiss, I, 362.

31. *Ibid.,* II, 207-8.

32. In a letter of November 16, 1857, Parker stated that the Negro "in twenty generations . . . will stand just where [he] is now." He thought the race inferior, as proven by their inability to rise even into the middle class in Massachusetts though they possessed freedom. Frothingham, p. 467.

33. *The Great Battle Between Slavery and Freedom* (Boston, 1856), pp. 41, 76, 88.

34. "A New Lesson for the Day," *Works* (Centenary), XIV, 229-70; *Works* (Cobbe), IV, 279-311.

35. Weiss, II, 191.

36. *Ibid.,* I, 305.

37. *Ibid.,* I, 305.

38. "The Present Aspect of Slavery," *Works* (Centenary), XIV, 271-316; "The Present Aspect of Slavery in America, and the Immediate Duty of the North," *Works* (Cobbe), VI, 287-323, Weiss, II, 230.

39. Weiss, II, 240-41.

40. *Ibid.,* I, 396.

Works Cited

Primary Sources

1. *Bibliographies*

Chadwick, John White. *Theodore Parker: Preacher and Reformer.* Boston and New York: Houghton, Mifflin and Company, 1900, pp. xi-xx. Excellent bibliography of primary source material.

Commager, Henry Steele. *Theodore Parker.* Boston: Little, Brown and Company, 1936, pp. 311-31. A lengthy list of primary and secondary materials in essay form.

Literary History of the United States, ed. by Spiller, Thorp Johnson and Canby. New York: Macmillan Company, 1948, pp. III, 678-80. *Bibliography Supplement,* ed. Richard M. Ludwig (1959).

Wendte, Charles W. *Bibliography and Index to the Works of Theodore Parker.* Boston: Beacon Press, 1910, XV, 11-50. Includes a lengthy list of memorial articles.

2. *Texts*

Parker's complete writings are out of print and unavailable in many libraries. A very few essays and sermons have been reprinted in whole or in part in such works as Perry Miller's *The Transcendentalists* (1950) and Conrad Wright's *Three Prophets of Religious Liberalism* (1961). The list below consists of the collected editions and major works not included in either of those editions. No edition of the letters has been published, but the biographies by Frothingham and Weiss include many.

The Collected Works of Theodore Parker, ed. by Frances P. Cobbe. 14 vols. London: Trübner and Co., 1863-1874. Very uneven and incomplete. No. footnotes, no index, no bibliography. Yet occasionally more reliable than the following edition.

The Works of Theodore Parker. "Centenary Edition." 15 vols. Boston: American Unitarian Association, 1907-1913. Somewhat more satisfactory than the Cobbe edition because some volumes have useful introductions and notes, but it is not a complete collection and the eratic footnoting, changes of titles and numerous other inconsistencies mar the work.

Theodore Parker: An Anthology, ed. by Henry Steele Commager. Boston: Beacon Press, 1960. A very well-organized collection of excerpts from Parker's writings.

West Roxbury Sermons, 1334-1484. Boston: American Unitarian Association, 1902. Collection of early sermons not reprinted elsewhere.

Levi Blodgett Letter. The Previous Question. Boston: Weeks, Jordan, and Co., 1840. (Reprinted in Dirks, pp. 137-159.)

A Critical and Historical Introduction to the Canonical Scriptures of the Old Testament. 2 vols. Boston: Charles C. Little and James Brown, 1843. Parker's primary contribution to scholarship, based on a study in German by Wilhelm M. L. De Wette.

The Trial of Theodore Parker for the Misdemeanor . . . with the Defence. Boston: Pub. for the author, 1855.

3. *Manuscripts*

The important collections of Parker manuscripts are in the Boston Public Library (which also has Parker's library) and the Massachusetts Historical Society; each has over twenty volumes of material. Additional manuscripts are held by the Houghton Library of Harvard University and the American Unitarian Association. Holdings in the libraries include letters, notebooks, journals, sermons, lectures, clippings, scrapbooks and posters. The biographers have taken full advantage of this material. These Boston area libraries hold manuscript collections of other Transcendentalists and Unitarians that contain material relevant to the study of Parker.

Secondary Sources

Aaron, Daniel. *Men of Good Hope.* New York: Oxford University Press, 1951, esp. pp. 21-51. Emphasizes, as no other scholar does, Parker's concept of "industrial democracy" and other aspects of his economic and political philosophy.

Alcott, Louisa M. *Work.* Boston: Roberts Brothers, 1873. Thomas Power, the minister in this novel, is Theodore Parker, whom Miss Alcott knew and admired.

Atkins, Gaius Glenn, and Frederick L. Fagley. *History of American Congregationalism.* Boston and Chicago: The Pilgrim Press, 1942. Chapter nine is a brief account of the Unitarian split from Congregationalism.

Chadwick, John White. *Theodore Parker: Preacher and Reformer.* Boston and New York. Houghton, Mifflin and

Company, 1950. A fine, sympathetic biography that emphasizes Parker's place in the theological battles.

Commager, Henry Steele. "The Dilemma of Theodore Parker," *New England Quarterly,* VI (1933), 257-77. Interpretive description of Parker's dilemma between intuition and experience.

———. "Tempest in a Boston Teacup," *New England Quarterly,* VI (1933), 651-675. A discussion of the Blodgett letter and the controversey over miracles.

———. "Theodore Parker, Intellectual Gourmand," *American Scholar,* III (1934), 257-65. Describes Parker's library and his reading and asserts the primacy of Parker's "journalistic ambitions."

———. *Theodore Parker.* Boston: Little, Brown and Company, 1936. Although this most recent biography is crowded with names and references, it is highly readable. Since the documentation is supplied only chapter by chapter, individual facts and quotations can be traced only with difficulty.

Cooke, George Willis. *Unitarianism in America.* Boston: American Unitarian Association, 1902, Standard history; author sympathetic to the Transcendentalists.

Dicks, John Edward. *The Critical Theology of Theodore Parker.* New York: Columbia University Press, 1948. Excellent study of Parker's theology and its background. The Levi Blodgett letter is reprinted on pp. 137-60.

Emerson, Ralph Waldo. *Works.* Boston: Houghton, Mifflin Company, 1883.

Faust, Clarence H. "The Background of the Unitarian Opposition to Transcendentalism," *Modern Philology,* XXV (1937), 297-324. Indispensable.

Frothingham, O. B. *Recollections and Impressions, 1822-1890.* New York: G. P. Putnam's Sons, 1891. This autobiographical work contains many informed remarks on Parker and remains one of the best accounts of liberal Christianity in the nineteenth century.

———. *Theodore Parker.* Boston: James R. Osgood and Company, 1874. Still the best biography, this is the only source for some of the facts about Parker. Frothingham knew Parker and, here and in other books, has provided much of our information about Parker, his contemporaries and their controversies.

———. *Transcendentalism in New England.* New York: G. P. Putnam's Sons, 1876. The chapter on Parker in this very uneven book contributes little to the understanding of the man.

Goddard, Harold Clarke. *Studies in New England Transcendentalism.* New York: Columbia University Press, 1908. Essential reading for anyone studying Transcendentalism, but the books adds little to the material on Parker in the biographies.

Gohdes, Clarence. *The Periodicals of American Transcendentalism.* Durham, N.C.: Duke University Press, 1931. The best account of Parker's *Massachusetts Quarterly Review* as a periodical of the movement.

Haroutunian, Joseph. *Piety versus Moralism.* New York: Henry Holt and Company, 1932. Excellent analysis of the Unitarian separation from Congregationalism in the chapter "The Unitarian Revolt."

Ladu, Arthur I. "The Political Ideas of Theodore Parker," *Studies in Philology,* XXXVIII (1941), 106-23. Demonstrates that Parker's political ideas are those of most of the other Transcendentalists.

Levy, Leonard W. "Sims' Case: The Fugitive Slave Law in Boston," *Journal of Negro History,* XXXV (1950), 39-74.

Lewis, R. W. B. *The American Adam.* Chicago: University of Chicago Press, 1955. Lewis mitigate the importance of Parker's contribution to theology but emphasizes the view of man Parker held: "every individual was in spirit and in fact a perfectly new man."

Martin, John H. "Theodore Parker" Ph.D. dissertation (University of Chicago, 1953). The most thorough, orderly and detailed presentation of Parker's biography.

Mead, David. *Yankee Eloquence in the Middle West: The Ohio Lyceum 1850-1870.* East Lansing, Mich.: Michigan State College Press, 1951. Account of Parker's lectures in Ohio based on newspaper reports and on Parker's manuscript Lyceum Diary.

Nelson, Truman. *The Passion by the Brook.* Garden City, N.Y.: Doubleday and Company, 1953. Fictional account of Brook Farm, with much attention to Parker.

———. *The Sin of the Prophet.* Boston: Little, Brown and Company, 1952. The author of this fictional account of Parker and Anthony Burns studied Parker for more years and with more care than any other scholar; hence the novel must be considered one of the significant interpretations of Parker.

Newbrough, George F. "Reason and Understanding in the Works of Theodore Parker," *South Atlantic Quarterly,* XLVII (1948), 64-75.

Parrington, Vernon L. *Main Currents in American Thought.* New York: Harcourt, Brace and Company, 1927. In his section on Parker, "Theodore Parker: Transcendental Minister," Parrington describes him as "one of the greatest, if not the last, of the excellent line of Puritan preachers," but the emphasis is on Parker as a political critic.

Persons, Stow. *Free Religion, An American Faith.* New Haven: Yale University Press, 1947. A description and history of the religious movements that were, to a degree, the results of Parker's efforts in theology.

Pochmann, Henry A. *German Culture in America: Philosophical and Literary Influences, 1600-1900.* Madison, Wis.: University of Wisconsin Press, 1957. An excellent short account of Parker's debt to German thought and his contribution to American religion. Pp. 215-22.

Riback, William H. "Theodore Parker of Boston: Social Reformer." *Social Service Review,* XXII (1948), 451-60. The best review of Parker's social efforts. Contains a discussion of the way in which Parker had to work in order to avoid hurting a cause by having his name associated with it.

Shapiro, Samuel. "The Rendition of Anthony Burns," *Journal of Negro History,* XLIV (1959), 34-51. Best account of the series of events.

Smith, H. Shelton. "Was Theodore Parker a Transcendentalist?" *New England Quarterly,* XXIII (1950), 351-64. A reply to Commager's "The Dilemma of Theodore Parker."

Weiss, John. *Life and Correspondence of Theodore Parker.* 2 vols. New York: D. Appleton and Co., 1864. This very lengthy work contains invaluable material for the study of Theodore Parker and his work. Unfortunately, the virtual lack of organization makes it almost impossible to use.

Wellek, Rene. "The Minor Transcendentalists and German Philosophy." *New England Quarterly,* XV (1942), 652-80. Claims that Jacobi and Schleiermacher are more important to the Transcendentalists than Kant and Hegel.

Richard A. Grusin (essay date 1983)

SOURCE: Grusin, Richard A. "Interpretation and Intuition in Theodore Parker." *Bucknell Review* 28, no. 1 (1983): 21-41.

[*In the following essay, Grusin maintains that Parker is an ideal candidate for "revisionist" inclusion in the canon of American literature.*]

By most accounts the study of American literature in the academies is undergoing a radical change. In an essay reviewing three new books in a recent *Sewanee Review,* C. Hugh Holman has bemoaned the fact that "in our day, when, in any conflict between the subjective and objective, subjective is the certain winner, the critic or historian himself has moved to center stage, and his reaction to the work and the usefulness of the work in advancing his cause has usurped the autonomy formerly inherent in the work itself."[1] Writing from the opposing camp, but in the same issue of *Sewanee Review,* Kenneth Dauber has celebrated the fact that "a grand

'decentering,' as it has been called, has been occurring in our culture, a destruction of essentialist or holistic notions of our culture past any possibility of recovering them" (*SR* 88:187). Holman's review cites the "small regard for a canon" among the proponents of the new school of criticism as only one example of their injustices to the received tradition of American literature (*SR* 88:280). Dauber, on the other hand, rejoices that "now that the struggle to establish American literature in the academy has been won, in a period during which interpretation of it has so proliferated as to make its study not merely respectable but a necessary part of any respectable 'English' education, a revisionary tendency has emerged which seems bent on undermining all that has been accomplished" (*SR* 88:184). In spite of the threatening nature of this "revisionary tendency," Dauber does not think that this revisionism is uninterested in the notion of a canon; his essay is in part a redefinition of the criteria that ought to be employed in reconstituting the traditional canon of American literature.

Dauber's essay aims to reduce the sense of a foreign threat that American revisionism has presented to traditionalists like Holman. Dauber argues "the continuity of such revisionism, for all its modishness, with the earliest American sensibility that it seems to reject" (*SR* 88:184). He not only denies that this revisionism threatens the values traditionally attributed to American literature, but in turn accuses those who dismiss "the new thinking" of "an evasion of cultural responsibility. To hold such a position is not to affirm traditional American values but to refuse to reaffirm those values in the face of mounting difficulties" (*SR* 88:186). This new revisionism is not a threat to the canon of American literature because it is not new at all; from the very first the works of American literature have been revisionary ones. Hence, American revisionism does not threaten the American literary community, but instead "give[s] it a linguistic basis capable of withstanding more philosophical attacks" (*SR* 88:188). This "linguistic basis," the relocation of meaning from the objectivity of the autonomous text to the subjectivity of a community of writers and readers, is seen by Dauber as the ground "on which the only continuity now viable may be based" (*SR* 88:190). It is not difficult to see why Holman feels threatened by this revisionism; not only is the critic now on center stage, but he claims that he learned his trade as an understudy to the principal actors in the theater of American literature.

In addition to rewriting traditional interpretations of the particular works of American literature, revisionism threatens to rewrite traditional American literary histories as well: "Accordingly, to begin with the Puritans and a Puritan notion of literature is to narrow from the start the possibilities of American art. It is to begin either too late or too soon" (*SR* 88:190). For Dauber,

"American literature comes into being *as* literature only in the nineteenth century when writers attempt to invent it, without the benefits of what they felt to be a commanding theology or tradition, out of what seemed to them a cultural vacuum" (*SR* 88:190). In particular he singles out the major literary figures in the orbit of Transcendentalism as the first truly American authors—Emerson, Thoreau, Hawthorne, and Melville—because he claims that they were the first to understand that meaning is constituted by the subjective community of writers and readers, and is not objectively inherent in the autonomous literary text. This "decentering" of universal significance from the infinite God of "a commanding theology or tradition" to the multiplicity of finite subjects constitutes for Dauber the quintessential gesture of a revised American literary canon.

Another figure in the Transcendentalist orbit, Theodore Parker, "the man who [in Perry Miller's official academic history] next only to Emerson—and in the world of action even above Emerson—was to give shape and meaning to the Transcendentalist movement in America," would seem to be a prime candidate for revisionary canonization.[2] Parker's most famous (and most controversial) sermon, *A Discourse of the Transient and Permanent in Christianity,* attempts to determine, "without the benefits of . . . a commanding theology or tradition," which elements of Christianity provide it with the continuity of eternal truth, and which elements belong merely to the transient notions of mankind. Parker discusses questions of biblical interpretation and the biblical canon in much the same way that the revisionists discuss their secular counterparts and with much the same effect: Parker's sermon was seen as a threat to the permanent truth of Christianity just as the new revisionism is seen as a threat to the truths of American literature; Parker's sermon was fueled by "new thinking" from abroad just as American revisionism owes much of its polemical force to the Continental criticism of the past couple of decades; Parker saw his sermon not as an attack upon Christianity, but as a defense of its truth on the only grounds on which it could be defended, just as Dauber sees revisionism as establishing the continuity of American literature on its truly legitimate basis. As a look at Parker's sermon will demonstrate, however, the threat that revisionism is seen to pose to American traditionalism is a critical red herring; revisionism ultimately conserves the values maintained by the traditional study of American literature.

The text of Parker's sermon is Luke 21:33, "Heaven and earth shall pass away; but my words shall not pass away." The sermon opens with an amplification of this text, in which Parker at first takes a common-sense approach, questioning the reasonableness of calling Christ's word eternal, for "at first sight, nothing seems more fleeting than a word."[3]

It is an evanescent impulse of the most fickle element. It leaves no track where it went through the air. Yet to this, and this only, did Jesus intrust the truth wherewith he came laden to the earth—truth for the salvation of the world. He took no pains to perpetuate his thoughts; they were poured forth where occasion found him an audience—by the side of the lake, or a well; in a cottage, or the temple; in a fisher's boat, or the synagogue of the Jews. He founds no institution as a monument of his words. He appoints no order of men to preserve his bright and glad relations. He only bids his friends give freely the truth they had freely received. He did not even write his words in a book.

[4:2]

Although words seem the most fleeting way in which to preserve one's ideas, Jesus was not mistaken when he entrusted man's salvation to the spoken word. Those things that appear to be stable, to which men accord a permanent status, like "heaven and earth," are in fact less stable than the evanescent words of Jesus:

In the meantime, the words of great men and mighty, whose name shook whole continents, though graven in metal and stone, though stamped in institutions, and defended by whole tribes of priests and troops of followers—their words have gone to the ground, and the world gives back no echo of their voice. Meanwhile, the great works, also, of old times, castle and tower, and town, their cities and their empires, have perished, and left scarce a mark on the bosom of the earth to show they once have been.

[4:4]

That Parker attributes the permanence of Jesus' words in part to their spoken nature is clear from the paraphrase that sums up his explication of Luke 21:33: "The old heavens and the old earth are indeed passed away, but the Word stands. Nothing shows clearer than this how fleeting is what man calls great, how lasting what God pronounces true" (4:4). The oral quality of "what God pronounces true" helps to distinguish it from the less vocal quality of "what man calls great," as the permanence of Jesus' spoken words is distinguished from the transience of "the words of great men and mighty . . . though graven in metal and stone, though stamped in institutions."[4]

If only "what God pronounces true" is permanent, while "what man calls great" is doomed to perish, then Christianity, as manifested in human history since the time of Christ, must itself be perishable:

Looking at the word of Jesus, at real Christianity, the pure religion he taught, nothing appears more fixed and certain. Its influence widens as light extends; it deepens as the nations grow more wise. But, looking at the history of what men call Christianity, nothing seems more uncertain and perishable. . . . The difference between what is called Christianity by the Unitarians in our times, and that of some ages past, is greater than the difference between Mahomet and the Messiah.

[4:5]

Although "real Christianity" appears to be fixed and certain, and "true religion is always the same thing, in each century and every land, in each man that feels it," man's interpretations of that word have differed so radically that "the Christianity of the pulpit, which is the religion taught, the Christianity of the people, which is the religion that is accepted, and lived out, has never been the same thing in any two centuries or lands, except only in name" (4:5). Parker does not see any immediate prospect of a time when "what men call Christianity" will achieve the permanence of "what God pronounces true," since there is not enough "difference between the nineteenth [century] and some seventeen that have gone before it since Jesus, to warrant the belief that our notion of Christianity shall last for ever" (4:5).

> How do we know there is not a perishing element in what we call Christianity? Jesus tells us *his* word is the word of God, and so shall never pass away. But who tells us that *our* word shall never pass away? that *our notion* of his word shall stand for ever?
>
> [4:5-6]

Because our relation to Jesus' word can only be a second-hand one, can only be "*our notion* of his word," we cannot claim that our interpretation of his word is a true one, that our Christianity is "real Christianity" or our religion "true religion." Because our notion of Christianity is inevitably bound up with institutions, is inevitably written in a book, it cannot achieve the permanence of "the word of Jesus." If Parker's distinction between the permanence of "the pure religion" that Jesus taught and the transience of "the religion that is accepted" by the people is an accurate one, then no interpretation of Jesus' word can ever attain the permanent certainty of "real Christianity" and "what men call Christianity" may not be Christianity at all.

But if we "look at this matter a little more closely," Parker suggests, we can see that "in actual Christianity—that is, in that portion of Christianity which is preached and believed—there seems to have been, ever since the time of its earthly founder, two elements, the one transient, the other permanent" (4:6). Parker here modifies his earlier distinction with a new term, "actual Christianity," which combines the permanence of "real Christianity" with the transience of "the Christianity of the people" and of "the pulpit." The force of this new term carries through the rest of the sermon, although the phrase itself does not get repeated; since we can have only "our notion" of Jesus' word and not the word itself, the problem is to determine how "actual Christianity" can authorize its claims to eternal truth. Too often, Parker says, "transient things form a great part of what is commonly taught as religion. An undue place has often been assigned to forms and doctrines" (4:6). Salvation has been made to depend on the observation

of religious forms. "But they are only the accident of Christianity, not its substance" (4:6). The measure of a form's value, Parker argues (following the logic of Emerson's "Divinity School Address" and his resignation from the Unitarian ministry in 1832), is in its use: "So long as they satisfy or help the pious heart, so long they are good" (4:7). Christian forms, like "actual Christianity," have both their permanent and transient elements. In addition, "the doctrines that have been connected with Christianity, and taught in its name, are quite as changeable as the form" (4:7). Of all the changing doctrines that have gone under the name of Christianity, Parker singles out two "for a more attentive consideration": "the doctrine respecting the origin and authority of the Old and New Testament" (4:12), and those doctrines "which relate to the nature and authority of Christ" (4:17).

The doctrines concerning the origin and authority of Scripture are inextricably entwined with those "which relate to the nature and authority of Christ." To demonstrate this connection Parker first disputes the doctrines regarding the divine inspiration of the Bible, both Old and New Testament. The Old Testament, Parker argues, "was regarded as miraculously inspired, and therefore as infallibly true. It was believed that the Christian religion itself rested thereon, and must stand or fall with the immaculate Hebrew text. He was deemed no small sinner who found mistakes in the manuscripts" (4:13). In fact it was in part a question of manuscript that endangered the notion of an infallibly inspired Old Testament; when the French protestant Capellus demonstrated in 1624 that the Hebrew vowel points were added to the originally consonantal text some time after the original text was written, the notion that every "jot and tittle" of the Old Testament was inspired by God was called into question, particularly because the addition of vowel points constituted an interpretation of the consonantal text which may not have been congruent with what the original, inspired authors had intended.[5] Even further, "modern criticism" has shown that the original authors themselves were not miraculously inspired by God:

> It has shown that here are the most different works thrown together; that their authors, wise as they sometimes were, pious as we feel often their spirit to have been, had only that inspiration which is common to other men equally pious and wise; that they were by no means infallible, but were mistaken in facts or in reasoning—uttered predictions which time has not fulfilled; men who in some measure partook of the darkness and limited notions of their age, and were not always above its mistakes or its corruptions.
>
> [4:15]

Parker's familiarity with the criticism of the Old Testament stems largely from his translation and amplification of De Wette's *Einleitung in das Alte Testament,* which is an almost encyclopaedic account of the way in which the Old Testament has been interpreted throughout history. De Wette was one of the first critics to employ the mythical explanation of certain problematic passages of Scripture: that certain parts of the Bible can best be explained by the fact that biblical authors "in some measure partook of the darkness and limited notions of their age," particularly the tendency to create myths out of unexplained facts. De Wette's introduction was not particularly controversial, either in Germany or in America. But when Strauss extended the mythical interpretation to the entirety of the New Testament in his 1835 *Das Leben Jesu,* the uproar from Germany was heard at least as far away as New England.

If New England Unitarians could accept the implications of an Old Testament written by men who "had only that inspiration which is common to other men equally pious," they had a much more difficult time accepting the same truth about the New Testament. As Parker suggests, "almost every sect that has ever been makes Christianity rest on the personal authority of Jesus" (4:17). And this authority itself rests firmly on "the infallible word of God" represented in the New Testament. Thus, when Parker begins his sermon with the claim that "true religion," "real Christianity," and "what God pronounces true" are, like the words of Jesus, things which "shall not pass away," his auditors would naturally have assumed that he meant that these eternal truths were authorized by the infallible text of the New Testament and its account of the miraculous proofs of Jesus' divinity. Parker, however, adapts Ripley's argument against the necessity of miracles in order to dispute the claim that the truth of Christianity depends on the personal authority of Jesus:

> It is hard to see why the great truths of Christianity rest on the personal authority of Jesus, more than the axioms of geometry rest on the personal authority of Euclid or Archimedes. The authority of Jesus, as of all teachers, one would naturally think, must rest on the truth of his words, and not their truth on his authority.
>
> [4:18]

The personal authority of Jesus, like the infallibly inspired Scripture on which this authority is based, is a transient notion: "These are theological questions, not religious questions. Their connection with Christianity appears accidental" (4:19). "Christianity does not rest on the infallible authority of the New Testament" (4:21). Not just the Bible, but even Jesus appears to be an accident of Christianity. Its true substance is independent of Jesus' life:

> So if it could be proved—as it cannot—in opposition to the greatest amount of historical evidence ever collected on any similar point, that the Gospels were the fabrication of designing and artful men, that Jesus of Nazareth had never lived, still Christianity would stand firm, and fear no evil.
>
> [4:21]

Although Parker does not suggest that "Jesus of Nazareth had never lived," the very idea of a Christianity in which he did not reside was probably more than his contemporaries could handle. Parker's solution, that Christianity "is true, like the axioms of geometry, because it is true, and is to be tried by the oracle God places in the breast" (4:21-22), did not provide his audience with sufficient compensation for the loss of the personal authority of Jesus and of the infallible authority of Scripture. Parker's insistence on the intuitive certainty of religious truths seem to his auditors to found Christianity on an even more tenuous basis than the evanescent words of Jesus. Although the sermon goes on to establish an identity between Jesus' words and the innate intuitive powers on which Parker grounds the truth of Christianity, this identity ultimately demonstrates that an interpretation of "the oracle God places in the breast" can be no more permanent than an interpretation of the oracle that God placed in the world almost two thousand years ago.

In order to persuade his listeners that his account of the intuitive apprehension of religious truths is a true one, Parker reiterates his earlier claim that all doctrinal manifestations of Christianity are inevitably misinterpretations of "real Christianity" because they necessarily partake of the transient notions of their age. Because these notions are so changeable, even if "a Christian teacher of any age, from the sixth to the fourteenth century," was able to discuss questions of theology and religion with us, "his notions of Christianity could not be expressed in our forms, nor could our notions be made intelligible to his ears. The questions of his age, those on which Christianity was thought to depend—questions which perplexed and divided the subtle doctors—are no questions to us" (4:26). This passage is clearly indebted to Strauss for its insistence that human knowledge is contingent upon the presuppositions of each age, presuppositions which change so radically through time that our notions of Christianity could not "be made intelligible" to the ears of a former Christian teacher. Parker does not suggest "that the change is to stop here," "that another age will not smile at our doctrines, disputes, and unchristian quarrels about Christianity. . . . No doubt an age will come in which ours shall be reckoned a period of darkness—like the sixth century—when men groped for the wall, but stumbled and fell, because they trusted a transient notion, not an eternal truth" (4:27-28). Just as we can see the transience of past notions of eternal truth, so a future age will see that our notions of eternal truth are transient, too, and that we "stumbled and fell, because [we] trusted a transient notion, not an eternal truth." Yet the fact that men have trusted transient notions instead of permanent ones does not affect the truth of Jesus' words, since "Christianity itself, that pure religion, which exists eternal in the constitution of the soul and the mind of God, is always the same. The Word that was before

Abraham, in the very beginning, will not change, for that Word is truth. From this Jesus subtracted nothing; to this he added nothing" (4:28). Because Jesus neither added nor subtracted any transient notions to the Word of God, his words are identical to that Word and are thus eternal. Mankind's notions of his Word, however, must inevitably be transient. This point is expressed concisely in another variation of Luke 21:33: "forms and opinions change and perish, but the word of God cannot fail" (4:31). The authority of Christianity's claim to eternal truth has been transferred from the objectified forms and doctrines of "what men call Christianity" to the subjective "word of God," "which exists eternal in the constitution of the soul."

In light of Parker's belief that "an age will come in which ours shall be reckoned a period of darkness," it is not immediately apparent how he can remain convinced that this transference of the eternal truths of Christianity to "the oracle God places in the breast" will not also be reckoned "a transient notion, not an eternal truth." Just as Jesus' words have been misinterpreted throughout the ages, so that "the difference between the Christianity of some sects, and that of Christ himself, is deeper and more vital than that between Jesus and Plato" (4:5), so it seems plausible that "the oracle God places in the breast" would be subject to the same transient misinterpretations. While Parker would certainly accept the weak version of this claim, that his notion of Jesus' word is itself a transient one, he would be less likely to admit the strong version: that the very idea of a subjective, immediate, intuitive apprehension of religious truth is itself the transient product of a dark age which some future age will view with derision. Parker's sermon provides two not entirely compatible explanations of the way in which man's intuitive apprehension of Christian truths could escape the problems of interpretation that the sermon depicts, neither of which is sufficient to authorize the permanence of Parker's distinction between an objective, doctrinal interpretation of Christianity and a subjective, intuitive one.

One defense which Parker's sermon provides depends mainly upon the idea of progress that reappears throughout his sermon. Its basic line of argument is that as time goes on, interpretations of Christianity will gradually eliminate their accidental, transient elements and thus become closer and closer to "real Christianity": "truth will triumph at last and then we shall see the son of God as he is" (4:24). Thus when he compares theories of nature with theories of religion, Parker says that just as "there is but one system of nature as it exists in fact, though many theories of nature, which exist in our imperfect notions of that system, and by which we may approximate and at length reach it," so "there is but one kind of religion, as there is but one kind of love, though the manifestations of this religion" through which "men approximate to the true expressions of this religion" "be

never so diverse" (4:7-8). Parker's account of a progressive approximation to religious truth reappears in an analogy to astronomical truth: "Now, the solar system as it exists in fact is permanent, though the notions of Thales and Ptolemy, of Copernicus and Descartes, about this system, prove transient, imperfect approximations to the true expression" (4:8). The same idea reappears just prior to Parker's account of the transitoriness of doctrines: "It is only gradually that we approach to the true system of nature by observation and reasoning, and work out our philosophy and theology by the toil of the brain" (4:12). Finally, after Parker claims that Christianity would be true even if Jesus had never lived, he explains that if this were in fact the case, we would have suffered the "irreparable loss" of "the example of that character, so beautiful, so divine, that no human genius could have conceived it, as none, after all the progress and refinement of eighteen centuries, seems fully to have comprehended its lustrous life" (4:21).

Although the above passages seem to suggest that a true account of Jesus' word would be one which has freed itself of all transient, accidental notions, they seem equally to suggest that this process would be impossible. If a true account of Jesus' word is the one that is most free from the accidental notions of the age, then Parker's own account would be true only if it had eliminated more of the transient, accidental elements from its own interpretation of Jesus' words than had any previous account. Yet Parker's comparison of true religion with the solar system works finally to belie the possibility of any system of religion ever attaining the permanent status of Jesus' words. For no matter how much of the accidental is eliminated from a theory of the solar system, that theory is of a different order of things than is the solar system which it would explain. Seen in terms of the interpretation of Jesus' words, this analogy suggests that no interpretation of Jesus' words could ever attain its eternal status, since the truth of his words is of a different order which cannot be explained fully by the transient notions of any particular age. Jesus' words are a true account of the "Word that was before Abraham" because "from this Jesus subtracted nothing; to this he added nothing." Our words cannot have the permanent truthfulness of Jesus' words because we must inevitably add something to them in order to make them intelligible to us, just as we must add something to the solar system (if only a new theory) if we are to understand it.

Another defense of the permanence of Parker's truth is implicit in the above account; this defense would deny that the veracity of a doctrinal account of Jesus' words depends on a progressive elimination of the accidental notions of one's time. A true interpretation of Jesus' words would depend not on an objective doctrinal account of Christianity at all, but on a subjective, intuitive apprehension of the truth that is present in even the most accidental, transient doctrine. Although forms and doctrines can serve only as imperfect approximations of Christianity, this does not mean that there can be no true account of Jesus' words. On the contrary, if we "turn away from the disputes of the Catholics and the Protestants, of the Unitarian and the Trinitarian, of old school and new school, and come to the plain words of Jesus of Nazareth, Christianity is a simple thing, very simple" (4:28). It is not to be understood by means of doctrinal disputes, but by the intuitive powers of apprehension:

> It is absolute, pure morality; absolute, pure religion; the love of man; the love of God acting without let or hindrance. The only creed it lays down is the great truth which springs up spontaneous in the holy heart—there is a God. Its watchword is, Be perfect as your Father in heaven. The only form it demands is a divine life; doing the best thing in the best way, from the highest motives; perfect obedience to the great law of God. Its sanction is the voice of God in your heart; the perpetual presence of him who made us and the stars over our head; Christ and the Father abiding within us.

> [4: 28-29]

Although the "perfect obedience to the great law of God" "which springs up spontaneous in the holy heart" does not demand a progressive elimination of the accidental from the forms and doctrines of Christianity, Parker's explication of the "only creed" and "only form" of true Christianity would seem to represent an attempt to express an accident-free interpretation of "absolute, pure morality; absolute, pure religion." His interpretation, however, is sanctioned not by miralces, or by an infallible Scripture, or by the Church: "Its sanction is the voice of God in your heart; the perpetual presence of him who made us and the stars over our head; Christ and the Father abiding within us."

Unlike the earlier progressive account of the interpretation of Jesus' words in which that interpretation which had the fewest transient elements was the closest approximation to the truth, this epistemological account appears to cultivate a proliferation of transient, accidental elements. This distinction between the two accounts can be seen most clearly in Parker's claim that real Christianity "does not demand all men to *think* alike, but to think uprightly, and get as near as possible at truth" (4: 29). The Christianity of sects, however, "would make all men think alike, or smother their convictions in silence" (4:30). Any doctrine, no matter how free of transient, accidental elements, can work as a doctrine only by demanding others to accept its views as truth. "But Christianity gives us the largest liberty of the sons of God; and were all men Christians after the fashion of Jesus, this variety would be a thousand times greater than now: for Christianity is not a system of doctrines, but rather a method of attaining oneness with God" (4: 30). Or more precisely, we might say, a vari-

ety of methods. Because the truth of Christianity depends not on forms and doctrines, but on "the voice of God" "which exists eternal in the constitution of the soul," the result of all men becoming Christians "after the fashion of Jesus" would be a variety "a thousand times greater than now." As the truth of Christianity becomes universally accepted, the number of transient doctrines will not decline, but increase.

Yet Parker's insistence that the truth of his account of Christianity does not demand that men adhere to a "system of doctrines" should not be taken at face value. Although Parker's account does provide a great deal of liberty in respect to traditional forms and doctrines, this liberty is contingent on one's belief in the intuitive apprehension of religious truth. Parker's system can allow for a wide variety of formal and doctrinal manifestations of Christianity because objective forms and doctrines are seen as inconsequential to a true understanding of Jesus' words. It is no accident, however, that Parker employed the accidental language of doctrinal religion to express the necessary beliefs of his system in the passage cited above: "*The only creed* it lays down is the great truth which springs up spontaneous in the holy heart—there is a God. *Its watchword* is, Be perfect as your Father in heaven. . . . *The only form* it demands is a divine life. . . . *Its sanction* is the voice of God in your heart" (emphasis mine). In fact the three essential truths which Parker enjoins in this doctrinal summation—the intuitive apprehension of God, a sense of right and wrong, and a belief in immortality—correspond to the three central tenets of the system of absolute religion on which he was to work for much of his life. Although Parker does not explicitly acknowledge the point, it seems clear that just as our notion of Jesus' eternal words can only be a transient one, and thus untrue, so our notion of the word of God "which exists eternal in the constitution of the soul" must also be transient and untrue. Just as we can have only our notion of Jesus' words, so we can have only our notion of intuitive truth. Thus, it follows from Parker's account of the interpretation of Jesus' words that some day an age will come in which men will deride Parker's belief in the intuitive apprehension of the eternal truths of Christianity as the transient notion of a dark age.

In the end, however, it is precisely its transient, accidental nature that gives this notion the appearance of permanence for Parker. As he suggests, Jesus' words manifest their permanence by the fact that they must be reinterpreted by each age of believers. Although no one interpretation of Christianity could ever attain the eternal status of Jesus' words, just as no system of astronomy could attain the permanent status of the solar system, every interpretation of Christianity contains a permanent element which is the same for all men in all ages. This permanent element is not to be found in objective forms and doctrines, but in a subjective, intuitive apprehension of Jesus' words; forms and doctrines constitute only our accidental notion of the truths of Christianity, while our intuitive apprehension of Jesus' words appears to be immediate and unconditioned by the accidental notions of our age. As Parker's sermon demonstrates, however, our intuitive apprehension of religious truth can only be expressed in the transient language of doctrinal religion; like the forms and doctrines of Christianity, any account of intuition, no matter how "simple" or how generalized, must inevitably partake of the transient notions of one's time. Although this inevitability would seem to undercut the truth of Parker's account of the intuitive apprehension of Jesus' words, this is not the case. On the contrary it is the claim to permanence that calls Parker's intuitive account of Christianity into question, since his sermon has so convincingly demonstrated that no doctrinal account can attain the permanence of Jesus' words. As we shall see, it is ultimately the transient, accidental nature of those intuitive notions that we call permanent that constitutes the truth of Christianity for Parker. This point can most easily be understood if we turn from Parker's sermon to two autobiographical accounts of the origin of his belief in the intuitive apprehension of the truths of Christianity. As these accounts demonstrate, the accidental, conditional nature of this belief does not deny the truth of Parker's account of biblical interpretation, but instead constitutes it.

Although the force of Parker's attempt to ground the permanent truth of Christianity in man's intuitive apprehension of religious truths was to secure that truth as independent of, and unconditioned by, the transient notions of Parker's or any other age, Parker's autobiographical accounts of the development of his belief in the permanence of man's "religious consciousness" demonstrates that intuition itself cannot escape the problems of interpretation that Parker's sermon has depicted. The circumstances surrounding Parker's final illness deprived him of the time and materials to compose a full-fledged autobiography before his death in 1860; he did, however, find the opportunity to write "a long letter, reviewing [his] life and especially [his] connection with" "the members of the Twenty-Eighth Congregational Society of Boston," to whom he had ministered since January 1846 (13: 286-87). This letter was written in March and April of 1859, from the island of Santa Cruz, to which he had sailed in the attempt to recuperate from what was to be his fatal bout with consumption. Among other reasons, this letter is of interest for its account of "the great spiritual trial of [Parker's] life," a trial which culminated in his conversion to Kantianism; this conversion was fueled by Parker's discovery of "certain great primal intuitions of human nature, which depend on no logical process of demonstration, but are rather facts of consciousness given by the instinctive action of human nature itself" (13: 301).

Parker's letter depicts this spiritual trial in a fashion that suggests its affinity with the process of interpretation which he outlines in the *Transient and Permanent.* Parker's dark hour was precipitated by his entrance into "the Theological School at Cambridge, then under the charge of the Unitarians, or 'Liberal Christians'" (13:297). Parker's reading greatly exceeded the bounds prescribed by the Harvard curriculum, as did his theological conclusions; among these conclusions is that which forms the doctrinal core of the *Transient and Permanent*: that neither Scripture, nor Church, nor the miraculous proofs of Jesus' divinity were sufficient to authorize the truth of Christianity, but that this truth could only be authorized by man's instinctive religious consciousness. "In my own consciousness I found it automatic and indispensable; was it really so likewise in the human race?" (13:300). His readings in the philosophy of "the sensational system so ably presented by Locke in his masterly essay, developed into various forms by Hobbes, Berkeley, Hume, Paley and the French Materialists, and modified, but not much mended, by Reid and Stewart, gave little help" to Parker's attempt to "legitimate [his] own religious instincts"; instead, he "found most help in the works of Immanuel Kant, one of the profoundest thinkers in the world, though one of the worst writers, even of Germany; if he did not always furnish conclusions I could rest in, he yet gave me the true method, and put me on the right road" (13: 301).

As both his autobiographical letter and his sermon on the *Transient and Permanent* make clear, Parker has mistaken the existence of an intuitive religious consciousness for his own representation of this consciousness. As he himself explains, although Kant "did not always furnish conclusions" which Parker "could rest in, he yet gave [Parker] the true method, and put [him] on the right road." Unsatisfied with the representation of man's religious consciousness which Kant had provided, Parker simply substituted his own. From this identity between the Kantian fact of an intuitive religious consciousness and his "own religious instincts," Parker derived the three "facts of consciousness" "which exist eternal in the constitution of the soul":[6]

1. The instinctive intuition of the divine, the consciousness that there is a God.

2. The instinctive intuition of the just and right, a consciousness that there is a moral law, independent of our will, which we ought to keep.

3. The instinctive intuition of the immortal, a consciousness that the essential element of man, the principle of individuality, never dies.

Parker is convinced that by positing an identity between these three "facts of consciousne" and the essential truths of Christianity he has found a solution to the hermeneutic problem presented in his sermon, a solution which is attained by grounding Christianity in the universality of man's intuitive religious consciousness. As we have seen, however, the intuitive voice of God is as likely to be misinterpreted as are the eternal words of Jesus. Parker's belief in these three facts of consciousness is anything but unconditioned; as his epistolary autobiography makes clear, his faith in these intuitive truths is due largely to the fact that they helped him through his "spiritual trial" by constituting "a scheme which to the scholar's mind . . . would legitimate what was spontaneously given to all, by the great primal instincts of mankind" (13: 302). Thus it seems obvious that Parker's faith in these three facts of consciousness derives more from the aid they provided him during his personal crisis than from their spontaneous presence in the minds of all men. Parker, however, seems genuinely unable to see that his formulation of these facts provides no more certainty of the permanent truth of Christianity than do the forms and doctrines of the Catholic, or the Unitarian, Church.

An even more pointed instance of Parker's blindness to the accidental nature of his notion of the intuitive apprehension of the truths of Christianity occurs in an autobiographical fragment which he wrote in Rome, just prior to his death. Although this fragment is the most detailed account extant of Parker's childhood, it is of interest not so much for its historical accuracy (Parker in fact apologizes for the inaccuracies resulting from a failing memory and a lack of family records) as for the selection of those details which he remembers as important in the last days of his life. The fragment is primarily a compilation of the botanical, social, and familial circumstances of Parker's early life, so much so that when he finds that he can no longer write, he closes his manuscript with a "*caveat lector*" in which he justifies the inclusion of so many apparently insignificant details:[7]

> The material and human circumstances about a man in his early life have a strong and abiding influence upon all, especially those of a sensitive disposition, who are both easily affected by such externals and rather obstinate in retaining the impression made on them.
>
> [13: 449]

Because one's ideas are so inextricably bound up with the notions of one's age, Parker provides this account of his childhood influences in order to present what may be important clues to his own character. But in spite of the homage that this fragment pays to the important influence of the external "material and human circumstances about a man in his early life," this account of his childhood closes with an inward revelation of which Parker is "sure no event in my life has made so deep and lasting an impression on me" (13:16).

The event Parker depicts is his first awareness of "the voice of God in the soul of man," the intuitive apprehension of the eternal truths of Christianity. It is both a touching and a humorous account. Although it is regularly cited in biographies of Parker, the account is worth quoting in its entirety.

> When a little boy in petticoats in my fourth year, one fine day in spring, my father led me by the hand to a distant part of the farm, but soon sent me home alone. On the way I had to pass a little "pond-hole" then spreading its waters wide; a rhodora in full bloom—a rare flower in my neighborhood, and which grew only in that locality—attracted my attention and drew me to the spot. I saw a little spotted tortoise sunning himself in the shallow water at the root of the flaming shrub. I lifted the stick I had in my hand to strike the harmless reptile; for, though I had never killed any creature, yet I had seen other boys out of sport destroy birds, squirrels, and the like, and I felt a disposition to follow their wicked example. But all at once something checked my little arm, and a voice within me said, clear and loud, "It is wrong!" I held my uplifted stick in wonder at the new emotion—the consciousness of an involuntary but inward check upon my actions, till the tortoise and the rhodora both vanished from my sight. I hastened home and told the tale to my mother, and asked what was it that told me it was wrong? She wiped a tear from her eye with her apron, and taking me in her arms, said, "Some men call it conscience, but I prefer to call it the voice of God in the soul of man. If you listen and obey it, then it will speak clearer, and always guide you right; but if you turn a deaf ear or disobey, then it will fade out little by little, and leave you all in the dark and without a guide. Your life depends on heeding this little voice." She went her way, careful and troubled about many things, but doubtless pondered them in her motherly heart; while I went off to wonder and think it over in my poor, childish way. But I am sure no event in my life has made so deep and lasting an impression on me.
>
> [13:15-16]

That this incident is meant to be revelatory is without question; Parker's account of his first experience of "the voice of God in the soul of man" seems like the Old Testament prelude to the more Christian spiritual crisis of his divinity school days. Interestingly enough, this intensely personal revelation incorporates motifs from the two principal scenes of revelation in the Old Testament: the "flaming shrub" that irresistibly draws Parker to it derives from the bush which burned but did not consume itself when God first revealed himself to Moses; the intervention of the voice of God just as Parker was about "to strike the harmless reptile" parallels God's intervention just as "Abraham stretched forth his hand, and took the knife to slay his son" (Gen. 22:10). Even the most personal, unconditioned revelation from God is already conceived of in the conventional terms of Old Testament revelation. More importantly, however, just as Abraham and Moses did not understand the meaning of God's intervention until it had been explained to them, so the young Parker is confused by this "new emotion—the consciousness of an involuntary but inward check upon [his] actions."

As we have seen, it is Parker's failure to distinguish the fact of an inward, intuitive revelation from his own interpretation of that revelation that prevents him from seeing that the intuitive apprehension of religious truths does not allow him to escape from the hermeneutic circle which he so convincingly outlines in the ***Transient and Permanent.*** In Parker's autobiographical fragment this distinction is evident not only in Parker's need to consult his mother for the explanation of his inward revelation, but also in the response which she gives him. Parker's mother makes it clear that the interpretations which men have given to the fact of intuition have differed radically among different people: "Some men call it conscience, but I prefer to call it the voice of God in the soul of man." One can imagine the way in which Parker's career might have differed if his mother had explained the incident in another way: if she had told him that the voice he had heard was the natural voice of conscience, Parker could have been another Franklin; if she had told him that this voice was only the figment of his actively childish imagination, he could have become a founding father of modern psychology; or if she had told him that it was the voice of the devil which he had heard, and that it was to be resisted at all costs, Parker could have become the sternest of Calvinists. No matter how his mother might have interpreted this voice, the socializing force of this incident seems clear. It is not because the voice he heard was actually that of God, but because it was called the voice of God by his mother that Parker values it as the command of God on whose obedience his life depends, an obedience that led him to the Unitarian ministry. His mother's account was true not because it was free from the accidental notions of her time (as it clearly was not), but because it was the *first* accidental account that Parker received. As Jacques Derrida has pointed out in a discussion of the natural law of pity in Rousseau, the fact that one's obedience to the natural law of God can only become a divine obedience when it has been supplemented by maternal law (both of which laws are represented by "voice") works to prove not the prior, unconditioned nature of "the voice of God in the soul of man," but rather precisely the opposite: that the law of God inscribed in man's heart can only be constituted as prior to the law of man after it has first been understood in the conventional, human terms of maternal law.[8] Although Parker obeys his inner voice even before his mother had explained it to him, this obedience is clearly the product of a prior obedience to the parental voice of authority, not a spontaneous obedience to the eternal voice of God. Parker obeys "the oracle God places in the breast" because his mother told him to.

But to deny the truth of Parker's account of the intuitive apprehension of religious truths because it is not free from the accidental notions of his time is to have missed the point: as Parker's sermon makes clear, because we can have only our notion of the word of God and not the word itself, no doctrine can attain the permanence of real Christianity. "Real Christianity . . . makes us outgrow any form or any system of doctrines we have devised, and approach still closer to the truth" (4:32). But although the "Christianity of sects, of the pulpit, of society is ephemeral—a transitory fly," Parker does not suggest that we can get beyond this ephemerality to the essential form of Christianity; when we outgrow one form, "some new form will take its place, suited to the aspects of the changing times. Each will represent something of the truth, but no one the whole" (4:33). The truth of any doctrine depends on its suitability "to the aspects of the changing time." Transience, not permanence, constitutes a true account of Christianity. This truth, however, is not a permanent one: "Let then the transient pass, fleet as it will, and may God send us some new manifestation of the Christian faith, that shall stir men's hearts as they were never stirred; some new word, which shall teach us what we are, and renew us all in the image of God" (4:34-35). Only Jesus' words can be both permanent and true; our notions of his words can be true, but never permanent. Yet, as Parker made clear early in his sermon, the very permanence of Jesus' words is due to the fact ot their transience, for Jesus "took no pains to perpetuate his thoughts; they were poured forth where occasion found him an audience." The only permanent element of actual Christianity is the transience of any true account of it. Transience is truth; permanence is error.

In light of Parker's account of the interpretation of Jesus' words, it is worthwhile to review Dauber's depiction of the radical revisionism that appears to have beset American literature. Dauber accuses traditional critics of American literature of theologizing the works of the American literary canon into scripture by assuming that these texts were inspired by their authors' meaning in much the same way that nineteenth-century Orthodox critics assumed the verbal inspiration of the Bible. American traditionalists view the critic's job as a priestly one, in which he must interpret the one true meaning of the American literary canon to his flock. These traditionalists mistake their own transient notions of what American literature should mean for its permanently true meaning; in particular the traditionalists believe that the works of American literature are classics whose traditional meaning should be conserved by criticism. For Dauber the fate of American literature depends on its "*un*classic" status: "If American literature is to stand, under the weight of its interpretations, as a special subject after all, it must remain permanently *un*classic" (*SR* 88:185). Rather than represent traditional values which must be conserved by criticism, these texts must permanently deny the very possibility of a literary text containing any fixed values whatsoever. In fact, Dauber argues, the true meaning of American literature is that very fact: that American literature "will remain continuous with us only so long as we do not take continuity for granted" (*SR* 88:197). A literature that denies its continuity with both author and critic is a literature that "must remain permanently *un*-classic." American revisionism is seen as a threat to the traditionalists because it seems to deny them the very foundation on which their American literary canon is based: the inherent greatness of its classic works.

Dauber, however, would merely replace the greatness of the texts with the greatness of the author's gesture toward a meaning and an audience in which he does not believe. The writers of the Transcendentalist epoch are the finest exemplars of this gesturing in Dauber's scheme: "Thoreau leaving the Walden he has elaborated into a complete cosmos because it no longer serves him, Emerson deconstructing Swedenborg and preaching self-reliance alongside the Over-Soul" (*SR* 88:189). In Dauber's view "the finest service to literature which [a critic] can offer" is "to reenact the work he would prefer to study" (*SR* 88:197). Such a reenactment would consist of a gesture similar to those of Emerson and Thoreau: the acknowledgment of "our alienation from the works we explicate" (*SR* 88:197). For Dauber, as for Parker, this alienation is not a permanent one. Just as Parker claims that "it is not so much by the Christ who lived blameless and beautiful eighteen centuries ago that we are saved directly, but by the Christ we form in our hearts and live out in our daily life that we save ourselves" (4:33), so Dauber believes that the only way "to restore something like the original meanings of our literature [is] by re-creating the very conditions of its production" (*SR* 88:185). The fact that the "Christ we form in our hearts and live out in our daily life" is not Christ himself, however, but only our notion of Christ, works ultimately to deny the permanence of our subjective formation of Christ. Likewise the insistence that the discontinuity between the subjectivity of author and critic and the objectivity of the autonomous text constitutes "a history of disruption on which the only continuity now viable may be based" (*SR* 88:190) denies Dauber's claims of their permanence since they, too, are the transient product of critical consensus. We can only have our notion of continuity, not continuity itself.

But as we have seen, to deny the permanence of Dauber's account of revisionism is not necessarily to deny its truth. Just as Parker's account of Christianity was seen to be true by those who heard him speak and were to call themselves Parkerites, so Dauber's account of the academy in peril may be seen to be true by those who would call themselves revisionists. Dauber fails to see that if, as he contends, meaning is truly constituted by the critical "agreement to agree" and not by the fact that critics must agree that a particular meaning is *in* the text, it is very likely that critics will some day soon "agree to agree" that American literature is in need of another revision, one which would perhaps reconstitute

the autonomy of the objective text. In spite of Dauber's protestations to the contrary, the force of his account of revisionism depends on his claim that the works of American literature have been revisionary from the outset, even before this most recent manifestation of American revisionism. In light of Dauber's own account of the discontinuity between subjective critic and objective text, his claim that American literature "must remain permanently *un*classic" if it is to survive in the academies must certainly be false, and this most recent manifestation of American revisionism must ultimately prove itself impermanent.

But what of the threatening aspects of this revisionism? Is the academic study of American literature really undergoing a radical change as both Holman and Dauber contend? Will this change ultimately weaken the academic study of American literature, as Holman fears, or will it, as Dauber hopes, "revive a failing humanities which fails because we grant it too much" (*SR* 88:197)? Although prophecy is at best an uncertain business, perhaps the eventual fate of Parker's account of actual Christianity will provide an augury for the future of the academic study of American literature.

Although Parker was reviled, denounced, and virtually ostracized from the official body of Unitarians until his death, "the Unitarian denomination could be said by the 1890s to have accepted the most extreme Parkerite conclusions about 'the religion of Jesus,'" and Parker had come to be numbered among its revered founders.[9] This is not to say that Parker's account of Christianity did not threaten his Unitarian contemporaries, but that its threatening nature depended more on its denial of the permanence of their doctrinal positions than on any of Parker's doctrines per se. Parker did not threaten the permanent truth of Christianity, only that of his contemporaries' account of Christianity. The situation is much the same with regard to American revisionism. The dispute between revisionism and traditionalism is not a dispute over the value of the academic study of American literature or of the humanities in general. Both Dauber and Holman see themselves (correctly) in the service of American literature; their quarrel, despite its rhetoric, is over the meaning of particular works, not the value of humanistic pursuits. Like Jesus' words, the works of the American (or any other) literary canon resist attempts at permanent interpretations of their meaning. It is this seemingly infinite interpretability that guarantees both the permanence of Jesus' words for a Christian and the permanence of the American literary canon for a critic of American literature. Revisionism threatens traditionalists because it denies the truth of traditional interpretations of particular works of American literature. But this threat is not a threat to the academic study of American literature, as the growing popularity of revisionist readings in traditional journals like the *Sewanee Review* will attest. Although some traditionalists fear that this radical revisionism promises, in Dauber's words, "the end of criticism, the end of literature, and, potentially, the end of culture itself" (*SR* 88:186), this is clearly not the case. The most radical aspect of the revisionism which Dauber celebrates and Holman fears is its radical reaffirmation of the value of the traditional academic study of American literature.

Notes

1. C. Hugh Holman, "Narcissistic Criticism," *Sewanee Review* 88 (1980): 278. Future references to Holman's essay and to Kenneth Dauber's "The Revisionary Company," *Sewanee Review* 88 (1980): 184-97, will be cited in the text as *SR* 88.

2. Perry Miller, *The Transcendentalists: An Anthology* (Cambridge, Mass.: Harvard University Press, 1971), p. 226.

3. Theodore Parker, *Centenary Edition of His Works* (Boston: American Unitarian Association, 1907-1910), 4:2. All future reference to Parker's *Works* are from this edition and will be cited in the text.

4. The primacy of the spoken word over the written, because of its more immediate relation to the truth that it signifies, is a Pauline doctrine which has numbered Father Walter J. Ong among its more recent supporters, and which has been subject to the deconstructive criticism of Jacques Derrida in the past two decades. Father Ong bemoans the fact that modern society privileges vision over voice and yearns for a renewal of the priority of voice. Derrida, on the other hand, argues that this privileging of the spoken word constitutes the ground for what he calls the logocentric epoch of the Western metaphysics of presence, and still dominates even today's more visually oriented world. For further reference see especially Walter J. Ong, S.J., *The Presence of the Word: Some Prolegomena for Cultural and Religious History* (New Haven, Conn.: Yale University Press, 1967) and Jacques Derrida, *Of Grammatology,* trans. Gayatri Chakravorty Spivak (Baltimore, Md.: John Hopkins University Press, 1976).

5. Emil G. Kraeling, *The Old Testament since the Reformation* (New York: Schocken Books, 1969), p. 43.

6. Unsurprisingly, René Wellek has written "that this is a false interpretation of Kant." What Parker takes to be the Kantian road is seen by Wellek as the road to "the intuitive philosophy of Jacobi or Schleiermacher, of the French eclectics, and even of the Scottish commonsense school." René Wellek, "The Minor Transcendentalists and German Philosophy," in *Confrontations: Studies in the Intellectual and Literary Relations Between Germany, England, and the United States during the Nineteenth Century* (Princeton, N.J.: Princeton University Press, 1965), p. 173. In light of Parker's sermon, it seems as if Wellek himself has taken the wrong road. While associating Parker with Schleiermacher and the commonsense school may account for Parker's intuitive certainty, it does not do justice to his interpretive uncertainty, the claim that the word of Jesus can only be understood in terms of our notion of his word.

7. Parker's choice of details is a curious one. His inclusion of several pages of botanical description suggests that his concern with the influence of external, material circumstances on one's character was a genuine one, although the particular relationship between the flora of his childhood environment and the development of his character is not entirely spelled out in his autobiographical fragment.

8. Derrida, *Of Grammatology,* pp. 171-92.

9. William R. Hutchison, *The Transcendentalist Ministers* (New Haven, Conn.: Yale University Press, 1959), p. 201.

Paul E. Teed (essay date June 1995)

SOURCE: Teed, Paul E. "Racial Nationalism and Its Challengers: Theodore Parker, John Rock, and the Antislavery Movement." *Civil War History* 41, no. 2 (June 1995): 142-60.

[*In the following essay, Teed outlines a disagreement between Parker and Dr. John S. Rock, an African-American abolitionist, and analyzes the larger atmosphere of racial tension during the period immediately prior to the American Civil War.*]

On the evening of March 5, 1858, a group of white abolitionists joined members of Boston's small black community at Faneuil Hall to celebrate the eighty-seventh anniversary of the Boston Massacre. Called together by black abolitionist and historian William Cooper Nell, the gathering was intended in part as a protest against the Supreme Court's denial of black citizenship in the Dred Scott decision. Focusing on the role of Crispus Attucks in the origins of the Revolutionary struggle, Nell expected that his impressive list of speakers would commemorate the heroic participation of black Americans in preserving American liberty and thus undermine both the logic and morality of the court's opinion. Instead, however, the meeting became the setting for a dramatic confrontation between two of Boston's most well-known antislavery activists, Dr. John S. Rock and the Reverend Theodore Parker.

John Rock had a score to settle with Theodore Parker, and the issue was race. As a black abolitionist, Rock was incensed over a recent speech at the Massachusetts

State House in which Parker had celebrated the historic courage and industry of the Anglo-Saxon race in eloquent terms while intimating that the inherent absence of bravery in black slaves had prevented them from overthrowing their oppressors. Challenging his white colleague to explain precisely how isolated and repressed slaves could overthrow "twenty millions of intelligent, brave white men," Rock denied any lack of courage in his race and insisted that blacks possessed a fighting spirit that could be seen in the "martyrdom" of Crispus Attucks as well as in the struggle for freedom in Haiti. "The black man is not a coward," he asserted. "If the white man will fight the black man in Africa or in Haiti and the black man does not come off the victor, I am deceived in his prowess." Rock also castigated Parker for his romantic view of Anglo-Saxon character. "The courage of the Anglo-Saxon is best illustrated in his treatment of the negro," he suggested. "A score or two of them pounce upon a poor negro, tie and beat him, and then call him a coward because he submits."[1]

Treated so often with respect and deference by Boston blacks because of his repeated efforts on behalf of the city's fugitive slave population, Parker was surprised by the vehemence of Rock's criticism and struggled to defuse the tension that Rock's speech had created. "My friend Dr. Rock said a great many good things of the African race," he began haltingly. "If I cannot agree with all that he said, I am sorry." Nevertheless, Parker was certain that his own characterization of both Africans and Anglo-Saxons was essentially accurate and set out to review and defend his views. "I have said a hundred times that [the African race] was the most pacific race of men on earth, the least revengeful, the most merciful, the slowest to strike." In comparison with aggressive, liberty-loving Anglo-Saxons "who would rather enslave twenty men and kill twenty more than be a slave himself," Parker asserted with complete confidence that Africans were meek and mild. Without satisfying Rock's demand for an explicit plan, however, Parker was willing to hold out the possibility that blacks would play some role in their own emancipation. "Slavery will not be exterminated with one blow," he predicted, "and I hope the black man will do his part."[2] Not surprisingly, Parker and Rock left the hall that evening without resolving their differences.

While it has received little attention in abolitionist historiography, the Parker-Rock controversy indicates the persistence of racial conflict within the antislavery movement on the eve of the Civil War as well as the ways in which race was linked with violence in debates over the future of the American nation and the shape of a postemancipation society. Widespread belief in the inherent qualities of races, held by those on both sides of the slavery question in the North, became central to an intellectual struggle over the future place of blacks in the social, economic, and political life of the nation in the early 1850s. White antislavery activists who were passionately committed to the idea of black freedom nevertheless found themselves confronted by a rising tide of political and scientific theory that raised serious doubts about the possibility of a multiracial political nation. The intellectual odyssey that led Theodore Parker to a paradoxical acceptance of both abolitionism and Anglo-Saxon racial nationalism (and hence to his conflict with John Rock) is illustrative of this basic tension within the culture of Northern white abolitionism.

Beyond its importance as an indicator of intellectual tensions within white activism, however, the March 5 debate also illustrates the many-sided ideological battle that black leaders waged in the antebellum era. Too often interpreted as a response to Southern proslavery apologetics, black activists and intellectuals in the 1850s often felt compelled to aim their attacks on Anglo-Saxon racialism at their white colleagues in the abolitionist movement. While historians have acknowledged that both the Free-Soil and Republican parties attracted many voters who associated American nationalism with the racial destiny of Anglo-Saxons, they have only begun to examine the ways in which blacks responded to this same romantic racial nationalism among their closest allies in the crusade against slavery. A closer look at the growing opposition of John Rock and several other leading black abolitionists to such views makes it possible to outline the issues and personal dynamics that informed this important ideological struggle.[3] In Rock, at least, the experience of combating white racial stereotypes raised serious doubts about the possibility of interracial cooperation in the long-term movement for black freedom.

As he stood up at Faneuil Hall to deliver his defiant speech in March 1858, John Rock was well aware that Theodore Parker occupied a powerful place in Boston abolitionism. Although he did not join the movement until the mid-1840s, Parker's radical theological assaults on the historicity of the Bible and his biting critiques of Boston's Unitarian social elite had firmly established his intellectual and ideological credentials among radical reformers as early as the late 1830s. Though nominally associated with Unitarianism throughout his ministerial career, Parker was in truth a Transcendentalist who spent much of his public life assailing the "corpse-cold" theology of Harvard Divinity School and preaching to an independent Boston congregation made up of social reformers, abolitionists, religious dissidents, and fugitive slaves. Ostracized by Boston's Unitarian establishment for his religious and social radicalism, Parker had found many supporters among the city's reform community. White abolitionists like William Lloyd Garrison and Wendell Phillips not only found much to admire in Parker's radical religious views, but they also admired the courage and personal sacrifice that marked his confrontations with Boston's religious and social elite. In 1860, Phillips argued that whatever real Christian virtues Boston possessed were "more due to [Parker] than to all the pulpits that vex her Sabbath air."[4]

While white Garrisonians made up Parker's most immediate network of antislavery friends, he also maintained intimate ties with the city's black community as well. After becoming an active abolitionist around 1845, Parker quickly assumed a leading role in the protection of fugitive slaves. Acting as the chairman of the Boston Vigilance Committee after the passage of the Fugitive Slave Act of 1850, Parker worked closely with black leaders such as Leonard Grimes, Louis Hayden, Robert Morris, and William Nell in providing food and shelter for newly arrived fugitives as well as in transporting them out of the city to avoid recapture. Indicative of his stature among the city's two thousand black inhabitants were the numerous invitations he received to speak before all-black audiences at the Adelphic Union Library Association. Accepting whenever his precarious health permitted, Parker offered advice and encouragement on the economic and moral improvement of the black community. While he did not take a formal role in the campaign to integrate Boston's schools in 1855, many of his sermons and addresses from the period indicate his support for William Nell and other black leaders who led that successful effort. In taking on Theodore Parker in 1858, then, John Rock paradoxically assailed a man who most Boston blacks considered a great ally in the white community.[5]

Beyond his ties to both white and black abolitionism in Boston, Parker was also one of the antislavery movement's premier intellectuals in the 1850s. Using his enormous personal library, a reading knowledge of more than twenty languages, and especially his deep immersion in German romantic thought, Parker had developed a reputation as one of New England's most learned and progressive men. His antislavery pamphlets and published addresses, which were packed with historical, economic, moral, and political arguments against slavery, were greeted with praise from Garrisonians and political activists alike. As the editor of the progressive *Massachusetts Quarterly Review,* moreover, Parker published not only his own scholarly attacks on slavery and the "slave power" but also provided space for the views of activists of diverse backgrounds. An enormously popular lyceum speaker, he traversed the North delivering speeches on topics ranging from the evils of slavery to the history of religion. "The subject made no difference, he could talk on anything," wrote Thomas Wentworth Higginson some fifty years after Parker's death. Even famous Europeans paid homage to Parker's abilities as a speaker. "Thackery, on his voyage to this country," remembered Higginson, "declared that the thing in America which he most desired was to hear Theodore Parker talk."[6]

While Parker's intellectual reputation added credibility and luster to the abolitionist movement, his intellectual orientation could not help but raise serious questions in the minds of black activists like John Rock. Despite his personal commitment to the abolition of slavery, Parker subscribed to a racial vision of American nationalism that linked his thought to that of proslavery apologists in uncomfortable ways. Though a belief in the unique political history of Anglo-Saxon peoples had appeared in the rhetoric of many prominent American Revolutionaries, nineteenth-century romantic thinkers had gradually transformed the Anglo-Saxons into a full-fledged racial group with an inherent instinct for freedom and distinctive qualities of aggressiveness and industry. Although inseparable from antislavery principles in Parker's mind, Anglo-Saxonism was most often used to justify the conquest of "less favored races."[7] European political and racial theory were combined with American concepts of national providence and manifest destiny, and many proponents of racial Anglo-Saxonism became supporters of territorial expansionism, the displacement or extermination of Native Americans, and the enslavement of blacks. As a believer in Anglo-Saxonism, then, Parker shared something in common with Southern proslavery apologists like George Fitzhugh and Josiah Nott.

The contradictions inherent in Parker's acceptance of both racial Anglo-Saxonism and abolition can be explained in part by his unique intellectual background. As a Transcendentalist, and a committed disciple of German idealist philosophy, Parker was steeped in the romantic nationalism that emanated from German universities in the early nineteenth century. As early as 1843, for instance, he added the complete works of Johann Gottfried von Herder to his growing library. Among the works contained in those forty-five volumes were Herder's *Outlines of a Philosophy of Human History* and his *Treatise upon the Origin of Language,* both of which developed a theory of nationalism based on the unique characteristics of particular peoples. While Herder maintained the unity of mankind as a single species, he nevertheless celebrated human diversity as evidence of God's creativity and pointed to language as a key to the basic divisions in the human family. "Since men have not continued in one flock, but have dispersed over all the earth and have divided into distinct families, tribes, and nations," he wrote in the *Treatise on Language,* "their languages bear the imprint of their distinct identities."[8] In Herder's philosophy, nations were not the product of political contracts between individuals but rather the expression of cultural, ethnic, religious, and especially linguistic commonalties. As cultural communities with distinct characteristics, he argued, nations represented basic divisions in the human race which commanded a natural and irreversible loyalty from individuals who belonged to them.

Herder's work on language and nationality made a profound impact on Parker's thought in the 1840s and served a vital function in his own growing commitment to a vision of American national distinctiveness. Like Ralph Waldo Emerson, Margaret Fuller, and other intellectuals associated with the New England Transcendentalist movement, Parker's intellectual life revolved in part around the search for a truly American cultural life. As Emerson's essays of the late 1830s had called for the emancipation of American intellectuals from the dead traditions of the European past, Parker's sermons and essays of the following decade called for a literature reflective of the inherent characteristics of Americans. "The permanent literature of America is not national in this sense," he complained in his own essay entitled **"The American Scholar."** "The individuality of the nation is not there, except in the cheap gaudy binding of the book."[9]

While American intellectuals had failed to capture it, Parker was certain that America did possess a unique culture with its own set of individual exemplars. Far more than his colleagues in the Transcendentalist movement, however, he pursued the sources of that uniqueness in political and racial theory. "God makes the family of mankind, but he divides it out into special peoples, and each man is born with his nationality in him," he argued in a sermon on **"Great Men."** "Franklin, the greatest man who ever touched our soil, is most intensely national," he argued. "He could have been born and bred in no other land; that human gold was minted into American coin." Parker argued that the distinctive qualities of a particular nation represented not an accident of climate or environment but, rather, defined its special place in the ongoing drama of providential human history. While Herder often used agricultural metaphors to describe the unified diversity of the human race, Parker preferred more corporeal images. "The hand is one, but it is separated into five fingers, to make it pliant and manifold useful," he suggested. "God makes us diverse in nationality so that we may help each other; . . . the mantel of destiny girdeth us all."[10]

While Herder's political philosophy had pointed out fundamental distinctions between nations, it stopped short of drawing rigid boundaries between peoples. Parker's search for the source of American uniqueness, however, had led him to read widely in the growing science of ethnology, which suggested that national differences might in fact hinge on inherent racial qualities. Most influential on his thought was Johann Friedrich Blumenbach, an eighteenth-century German racial theorist who argued, on the basis of physical comparisons, that the human species was divided into Caucasian, Mongolian, American, Ethiopian, and Malayan races. Parker agreed with Blumenbach's basic classification, but he suspected that human racial variety might actually be much greater than the young science of ethnol-

ogy had yet discovered. "I take Blumenbach's five races as only provisional," he once told his friend David Wasson; "five baskets which will help us hold mankind and help us handle them." Blumenbach's eighteenth-century intellect had shied away from making more than physical comparisons between his racial classes, but, Parker followed nineteenth-century racial theorists like James Prichard in assigning a cultural ranking to racial classifications. "In respect to the power of civilization the African is at the bottom," he wrote in 1857, "the American Indian next."[11]

In ranking the races of the world, Parker followed both European and American intellectual trends in placing Anglo-Saxons at the head of the list. As a vigorous offshoot of what Blumenbach had called the Caucasian race, the Anglo-Saxons appeared to Parker as a distinct racial group whose aggressive spirit and tenacious libertarianism had emerged among the Teutonic peoples of Germany and then moved relentlessly westward while profoundly affecting the politics and culture of Germany, England, and finally the United States. Tracing the history of the race, Parker distinguished a number of qualities that he believed flowed naturally from their character and which defined their place in human history. First, they were expansionist: "The Anglo-Saxon prefers new and wild lands to old and well cultivated territories." Second, they were naturally democratic both in politics and religion: "There is a strong love of freedom; . . . ours is the only tongue which liberty can speak." Third, they were enormously resourceful: "The Anglo-Saxons have eminent practical power to organize things into a mill, or men into a state, and then to administer the organization." Strongly linked in Parker's mind to Yankee virtue, ingenuity, industry, and independence, the Anglo-Saxon race possessed qualities that gave it an advantage over the other races of the world. "It is the richest of all the families of mankind," he argued; "the Anglo-Saxon leads the commerce and the most important manufactures of the world."[12]

In December 1848, Parker formally linked Anglo-Saxon racial destiny with American national character in an article called **"The Political Destination of America,"** which appeared in the *Massachusetts Quarterly Review.* "Every nation has a peculiar character, in which it differs from all others that have been and from all that are to come," he argued. "The most marked characteristic of the American nation is the Anglo-Saxon love of freedom, of man's natural rights; . . . we have a genius for liberty." Parker was certain that in America the racial qualities of Anglo-Saxons had found a natural habitat in which to grow and develop. The availability of land, the absence of a hereditary aristocracy and a tyrannical church had provided fertile ground for the same resourcefulness and independence that had distinguished the history of the race in Europe. The American Revolution and the republican tradition were not so much the products of colonial experience as they were evidence of the Anglo-Saxon love of liberty and organizational talent. The great purpose of the American nation, then, was to perfect the free economic, social, religious, and political institutions that had emerged from the natural proclivities of the people. "The idiosyncrasy of a nation is a sacred gift," he argued. "It is given for some purpose, to be sacredly cherished and patiently enfolded."[13]

While celebrating the nation's racial destiny, however, Parker was certain that America faced serious challenges to the realization of its place in history. In the first place, while he believed that Anglo-Saxons were America's dominant racial group, the presence of other races introduced contradictory impulses to the national character. In the Roman Catholicism of the "Celtic" Irish immigrants who were appearing in greater numbers on the streets of Boston, for instance, Parker detected a distinct lack of any Anglo-Saxon love of liberty. "The Celtic stock," he argued, "never much favored Protestantism or individual liberty in religion and in this respect is widely distinguished from the Teutonic population who have the strongest ethnological instinct for personal freedom." In his 1854 essay on the **"Rights of Man in America,"** he cited the natural willingness of Irish immigrants to submit to an authoritarian church and the political tyranny of the Democratic party as a threat to the integrity of the republic. "The baneful influence of the Church of the dark ages begins to show itself in the press, in the schools and still more in the politics of America," Parker warned. "Catholic votes are in the market; the bishops can dispose of them—politicians will make their bid."[14]

The greatest threat to the historic destiny of Anglo-Saxon America came not from the Irish, however, but emerged instead from the institution of slavery. Since the inherent ideas of the nation were freedom and individual rights, slavery appeared as a gigantic blot on its history and the most important obstacle to its development. Parker's opposition to the Mexican War, for instance, stemmed not from any qualms about the expansion of Anglo-Saxon power but rather because of its proslavery implications. "Before many years, all of this northern continent will doubtless be in the hands of the Anglo-Saxon race," he predicted. "One thing remains to do—to keep it from the blight of slavery."[15] While he acknowledged that slaveholding was itself an outgrowth of a natural Anglo-Saxon "aggressiveness" or lust for conquest, Parker nevertheless referred to the institution as an "accident" of American history that threatened to undermine the nation's more fundamental and progressive libertarian tradition.

Just as the racial characteristics of the Irish had helped Parker explain the presence of tyrannical impulses in American political and religious life, race also provided him with a partial explanation for the continued presence of slavery in a nation committed to liberty. While condemning slaveholders for their moral apostasy, Parker nevertheless concluded that the enslavement of Africans had followed from the inherent characteristics of their race. "The African is the most docile and pliant of all the races of men, none has so little ferocity," he told the Massachusetts Anti-Slavery Convention. "No race is so strong in the affectional instinct which attaches man to man by tender ties, none so easy, indolent, confiding, so little warlike." Had Southerners enslaved four million Anglo-Saxons rather than Africans, Parker often argued, servile insurrection would have put an end to the institution well before the political independence of nation. Lacking the instinct of freedom and naturally opposed to violence, however, blacks fell naturally into a condition of permanent subordination. While Parker avoided blaming blacks for American slavery, he often came very close to blaming them for its longevity. "It is through the absence of [a] desire of natural vengeance that the Africans have been reduced to bondage, and kept in it," he argued.[16]

While Parker's racial nationalism was derived in part from European sources, his view of black character reflected more widely shared American views of the race as essentially childlike, docile, and affectionate. Used commonly in the antebellum South as the intellectual foundation for proslavery paternalism, the black child stereotype was also held by Northern white abolitionists and intellectuals who found the image of the childlike slave a more compelling object of their humanitarianism. A more systematic racial thinker than most Northerners, however, Parker directly confronted the possibility that blacks might find no permanent place in Anglo-Saxon America. While his Garrisonian associations prevented him from considering African colonization as an alternative, Parker suspected that the same inherent qualities that had kept blacks in slavery for three centuries would prevent them from integrating themselves effectively into the social and political life of the nation in the aftermath of emancipation.[17]

Although other white abolitionists clearly shared Parker's doubts about black character, they usually preferred to ascribe the docile and submissive qualities of slaves to the oppressive environment of bondage. "Give [the Negro] his liberty, and as strong a motive to exertion as you have," wrote abolitionist Charles Burleigh, "and see what he can then become."[18] From his own romantic racialist position, however, Parker suspected that environmental forces were powerless to change what the laws of race had decreed. In 1857 he told a friend privately that, while twenty generations might improve the lot of the Irish somewhat, he feared that "the negroes will stand just where they are now; that is if they have not disappeared." Citing the omnipresent poverty of Northern free blacks, he concluded that the race simply lacked the industry to compete effectively with whites.

As much as Parker doubted the capacity of blacks to live with aggressive Anglo-Saxons, however, he remained willing to withhold judgment throughout the 1850s. Final proof of the African's capacity as a citizen, he believed, would come not through abstract racial theory but on the field of battle. Convinced that the sectional conflict would be solved "in the old Anglo-Saxon way—by the sword," Parker saw future civil war as an opportunity for blacks to establish a permanent claim on American citizenship through violence. As a leading advocate of black militancy in the 1850s, then, Parker hoped to encourage the race in redeeming itself in the eyes of Anglo-Saxon Americans and in preparing its members for the realities of freedom. Whites in both sections of the country would never take blacks seriously, he believed, unless they proved their equality through violence. "Why do freemen hold Africans in contempt?" he asked his friend Francis Jackson. "Because the Africans fail to perform the natural duty of freemen in securing their freedom by killing their oppressors."[19]

This position was also enormously satisfying to Parker emotionally since it allowed him to fulfill a parental role in his relationship with blacks both as individuals and as a race. The disappointed husband in a childless marriage, Parker's personal life abounded in relationships that fulfilled his basic desire for parenthood. This was especially true of his contacts with Boston blacks. In 1851, as he helped fugitive slaves William and Ellen Craft to escape their master's agents in Boston, Parker took melodramatic pride in arming William with a Bible and a Bowie knife and in instructing him to defend the freedom of his wife. "I took the Bible, and put it in William's right hand and told him the use of it," he told a parishioner. "I put [the knife] in his right hand and told him if the worst came to the worst to use that to save his wife's liberty, or her life if he could effect it in no other way."[20] To ex-slaves who had survived a hair-raising flight to freedom from Georgia to Massachusetts only two years before, Parker's advice must have seemed rather theatrical.

Nevertheless, Parker took a similar view toward the actions of black abolitionists or fugitive slaves whose actions offered the possibility that blacks might actually possess the same fighting spirit as their oppressors. Upon hearing the news that a group of fugitive slaves had shot and killed a slave-hunter at Christiana, Pennsylvania, in October 1851, for instance, Parker wrote an exuberant letter to the Pennsylvania Anti-Slavery Conference in support of the action. "I am glad that some black men have been found at last, who dared to resist violence with powder and ball," he wrote. "I rejoice that a *negro* has shot a kidnapper . . . black men may now hold up their heads before those haughty Caucasians and say, 'You see that we also can fight!'" In February 1851, when black citizens of Boston forced their

way into the city's Federal Courthouse to rescue the fugitive Shadrach, Parker was surprised but exultant. By putting their own lives in jeopardy to secure the freedom of one man from slavery and oppression, Parker believed that Boston blacks had taken a first step toward claiming the American revolutionary tradition for their own race. "I think it is the noblest deed done in Boston since the destruction of the tea in 1773," he wrote in his journal; "I thank God for it."[21]

As Parker's influence within the abolitionist movement grew steadily during the 1850s, his views on the racial qualities of Anglo-Saxons and Africans engendered numerous responses from Northern black intellectuals and abolitionists. Though many black leaders in the 1850s agreed with his call for violence against slavery and the "slave power," they were profoundly uncomfortable with both the paternalism of his position as well as the racial assumptions that undergirded it. While most black abolitionists avoided direct confrontation with Parker over his racial views and continued to find him a reliable and valued ally in the fight against slavery, they were nevertheless alarmed by the growing popularity of his racial nationalism in antislavery politics. Aware that Anglo-Saxon negrophobia already made up a significant portion of the Free-Soil and Republican movements, black leaders found it hard to swallow such views among their closest allies. John Rock was not alone in simultaneously acknowledging Parker as a "tried and true friend" of the city's black community while condemning the minister's racial views as "a great injustice" to blacks in general.[22]

Perhaps an even greater motivation for countering the racial views of activists like Parker was the need to dampen their intellectual effect on other white abolitionists whose Anglo-Saxonism was usually couched in historical rather than racial terms. Since the origins of immediate abolitionism in the 1830s, white activists like Wendell Phillips, Thomas Wentworth Higginson, and Lydia Maria Child had often argued that slavery and the "slave power" were undermining the progressive Anglo-Saxon tradition of liberty defined by the Declaration of Independence. These abolitionists found emotional satisfaction and intellectual legitimacy in linking their own struggle against slavery to an ancient Anglo-German tradition of libertarian resistance to tyranny. "Saxon pluck has placed our race in the van of modern civilization," Wendell Phillips wrote in 1861. While Phillips, Higginson, and Child seemed oblivious to the "echoes of white superiority" in such rhetoric, black leaders saw them clearly and sensed how easily Anglo-Saxon history slipped into Anglo-Saxon racialism. In a moment of pique in August 1857, Frederick Douglass railed against Garrisonians for talking "of the proud Anglo-Saxon blood, as flippantly as those who profess the inferiority of races."[23] With Parker's almost legendary intellectual reputation added to the racially charged political atmosphere of the 1850s, black abolitionists were rightly concerned that their white antislavery allies were leaning steadily toward a concept of nationalism that permanently excluded blacks.

While paying his respects to Parker's intellectual prowess and praising his personal efforts on behalf of fugitive slaves, Douglass repeatedly assailed the Anglo-Saxon exceptionalism and romantic racial stereotyping that was so prevalent in Parker's abolitionism. Using history as an ally, Douglass repeatedly reminded both white and black audiences that despite their reported tenacity and aggressiveness, the Anglo-Saxons had suffered long periods of oppression and enslavement. "The fathers of our present haughty oppressors in this land . . . were the miserable slaves, the degraded serfs of Norman nobles," he argued. "A profitable comparison might be drawn between the condition of the colored slaves of our land, and the ancient Anglo-Saxon slaves of England." After hearing Parker discourse at length about aggressive Saxons and docile Africans at the 1856 meeting of the New York Anti-Slavery Society, black abolitionist and former slave William Wells Brown responded with an eloquent litany of indignities and horrors endured daily by slaves. Describing the experience of a light-skinned slave who had the words "slave for life" branded on his face for attempting to escape bondage, Brown sarcastically wondered if "he had too much Anglo-Saxon blood in him to be a submissive slave, as Theodore Parker would say."[24]

While Douglass and Brown used the antislavery platform to counter the rising tide of abolitionist Anglo-Saxonism that Parker represented, black New York abolitionist James McCune Smith launched a general scientific and ethnological attack in the first issue of the *Anglo-African Magazine* established in January 1859. Trained in medicine at the University of Glasgow and fluent in several European languages, Smith's article entitled "Civilization" argued that human physical differences were the result of physiological adaptations to divergent environments and thus carried with them no permanent effects. Smith used the work of French and English ethnologists to show that race itself was a vague, relative, and often inappropriate term that obscured the reality of steady human social and physical development. So powerful were environmental forces, Smith argued, they had made Southern blacks more like their oppressors than their ancestors. "The Afric-American race, are not only far superior, in physical symmetry and development, to pure Africans," he maintained, "but actually equal in those respects the white race of the Old Dominion."[25]

As he attacked the notion that blacks possessed permanent qualities derived from their racial origins, Smith also denied that Anglo-Saxons were a race in any meaningful sense. Contrary to Parker's careful distinctions between Anglo-Saxons, Celts, and Slavs, Smith insisted that the origins and history of the Anglo-Saxons were so closely bound up with other groups as to make them indistinguishable. "So far from being a distinct race of mankind, endowed as a race with superior genius," he argued, "this Anglo-Saxon race is an admixture of all the Indo-European races." Turning Parker's racial nationalism entirely on its head, Smith went on to say that the vaunted Anglo-Saxon energy was actually the result of its nonexclusive racial make-up. So willing had Anglo-Saxons been over the centuries to mix with other groups that they had been able to profit from a diversity of experiences and to learn from them in building new and better civilizations. For Smith, it was modern slavery and racial exclusivity that was new to the Anglo-Saxons and that perhaps marked the beginning of the end of their long and glorious history. "The destruction of this caste and slavery will remove the last barrier in the way of our national advancement," he predicted.[26]

Parker's Anglo-Saxon racial nationalism not only provoked direct challenges from black abolitionists like Douglass, Brown, and Smith, but it also led Garrisonian William Nell of Boston to compose a multivolume history of black heroism in the American Revolution. Originally inspired to write his *Coloured Patriots of the Revolution* after reading a short article on the subject by John Greenleaf Whittier, Nell's motivations for writing stemmed from his desire to erase racial stereotypes and to place his race firmly in the vanguard of American republicanism. Working closely with Parker on the Boston Vigilance Committee and appearing many times with him on antislavery platforms in Massachusetts and elsewhere, Nell was well aware that proslavery apologists were not alone in their doubts about black capacity for citizenship. Shortly before the work's appearance in 1855, he told Wendell Phillips that he had "abundant reasons for knowing that it is needed" not the least of which was its instructiveness to "antislavery friends."[27]

Beginning with the "martyrdom" of Crispus Attucks and proceeding though the war of 1812, Nell chronicled the loyalty and service of black Americans in defense of their country, paying close attention to those who had lost their lives in defense of liberty. "Despite the persecutions heaped Olympus high upon them by their fellow countrymen," he argued, "they have ever proved loyal, and ready to worship or die at Freedom's shrine." Nell's tenacious adherence to Garrisonian pacifism separated him from abolitionists like Douglass and Brown, but he nevertheless agreed with his colleagues that the claims of Anglo-Saxon racial nationalists like Parker distorted the past and deprived blacks of a citizenship that they had won through their own heroic efforts. Furthermore, it threatened to invade the antislavery movement at a point when political success seemed more than ever before to be within reach. "I never felt more moved to accomplish any object than now to publish my book," he told Phillips, and expressed his hope that it would be "serviceable in the political campaign now sounding its Battle cry over the country."[28]

Parker responded to the facts of Nell's book much as he had to black militancy in the Christiana riot and the Shadrach rescue. Amidst the general indolence and apathy of the African race, a few heroic individuals and outstanding examples of libertarian aggressiveness pointed the way to a possible future. To the great frustration of black activists like Rock, however, Parker's public racial rhetoric seemed only to increase in its demands for proof that blacks possessed a fighting spirit. On January 29, 1858, Rock attended a meeting of the Massachusetts Anti-Slavery Convention at the State House in Boston where Parker delivered the evening's major address. Despite all of the evidence that Douglass, Brown, and Nell had so carefully assembled, Parker still maintained that blacks were "easy, indolent, and confiding." Perhaps most unbearable to Rock was a story Parker told of a fictitious slave named "John" who refused to strike a master who had brutally disfigured him and broken up his family. "John's story is the story of Africa," Parker argued. "The stroke of an axe would have settled for the matter long ago . . . but the black man would not fight."[29]

In the thirty-three-year-old Dr. John Rock, Parker's romantic racial nationalism found a natural nemesis. Educated as a physician at the American Medical College in Philadelphia, Rock had moved to Boston in 1852 where he became an important figure in the black community as well as a popular lyceum speaker. Though little information remains on the details of his views, Rock's most successful public addresses of the 1850s focused on scientific issues of race. His lecture on "The Unity of the Human Races" was delivered to audiences throughout New England and the Western Reserve in 1855 and was praised in antislavery circles as the product of "superior scholarship and much careful research." By the time of his confrontation with Parker, Rock had perfected his public performances by mixing humor and artistry with intellectual rigor. The lyceum stage was a medium of communication that both men understood quite well.[30]

As he stood on the platform at Faneuil Hall on March 5, however, Rock found anger and sarcasm more reliable than artistry. His vehement response to the State House speech gave vent to both the growing anger and resentment of black activists who saw the fundamental contradictions in Parker's racial attitudes. "White men have no room to taunt us with tamely submitting," he stormed. "If they were black men, they would work wonders; but as white men they can do nothing. O, Consistency thou art a jewel!" Painfully aware of the conditions under which black slaves toiled in the South,

Rock cut through Parker's abstractions about docile Africans to the reality of plantation brutality and the mechanisms of racial repression that maintained the peculiar institution. He made it clear that Parker's expectations for servile insurrection under such conditions were pure fantasy. "His remark[s] call to my mind the day when one shall chase a thousand and two put ten thousand to flight."[31]

After rejecting the hypocrisy of blaming slaves for their own enslavement, Rock exposed the inconsistency in reproaching Northern blacks for failing to succeed in a society that systematically denied them opportunity. Drawing on his own bitter struggle to obtain education and legitimacy in Philadelphia's medical establishment, Rock outlined the enormous social and economic barriers to black success in a white dominated North. While black businesses in Boston were given a good deal of attention in the antislavery press, he argued, they received little patronage from white customers. Indeed, Rock frequently chided not only Theodore Parker, but the entire white abolitionist movement for failing to support economic opportunity for Northern blacks. Like many black abolitionists, Rock employed an expansive definition of freedom that included economic independence as well as political liberty. "How very few colored men are encouraged in their trades or businesses?" he asked. "Who is taking our boys into their shops at a low salary, and given them a chance to rise?"[32]

In Rock, Parker's paternalistic Anglo-Saxonism had also engendered a need to assert a basic pride in his own race. To the largely black audience at Faneuil Hall, Rock inveighed against all those who failed to see the beauty and nobility in black physical features. "If any man does not fancy my color, that is his business," he argued. "I am inclined to think that when the white man was created, nature was pretty well exhausted—but determined to keep up appearances, she pinched up his features and did the best she could under the circumstances." Far from needing to prove themselves worthy of American citizenship, Rock wondered aloud whether Crispus Attucks and other black heroes had been anything but misguided in their efforts on behalf of America. In a dramatic departure from William Nell's historical efforts to integrate blacks into the American republican tradition, Rock equated the republican past with the betrayal of his race. "Our fathers fought nobly for freedom, but they got slavery," he reminded the audience. "The white man benefitted, but the black man was injured."[33]

In responding to the invidious comparisons inherent in Anglo-Saxonism, Rock developed a fierce racial pride and a biting critique of America's republican identity that separated him from the more accommodating views of black activists like William Nell. While Nell used history in attempting to prove his race's commitment to the nation as Parker had defined it, Rock rejected that definition and instead equated the historic extensions of American freedom with the more effective oppression of blacks. Far from proving their libertarian impulses to whites, the black soldiers who had fought in the past for the freedom of white Americans had only fastened the chains more tightly around their own necks. To all those who wondered if blacks would fight in the event of a civil war, Rock made it clear that the answer depended on whether or not white Americans were willing to support a broader concept of liberty. "Will [the black man] fight for this country right or wrong?" asked Rock. "When the time comes, and come it will, the black man will give an intelligent answer."[34] It was Anglo-Saxons, not Africans, who had something to prove.

Met with exclusionist conceptions of American nationalism like those of Parker, it is hardly surprising that Rock moved closer in the late 1850s to the black nationalist movement led by activists like Martin Delany and John Sela Martin. While Rock himself stopped short of advocating actual removal, he nevertheless found Parker's views symptomatic of the enormous obstacles that blacks faced in America. "The position of the colored man today is a trying one," he suggested in 1860, "because the whole country has entered a conspiracy to crush him."[35] Rock advocated black community solidarity and independent racial action in economic and political life as the only means toward eventual equality. Although more conventional thinkers like Nell felt comfortable celebrating Crispus Attucks's contribution to American history, Rock leaned increasingly toward Nat Turner as a symbol of racial power and defiance. While Parker had advocated black militancy as a condition of black citizenship in an Anglo-Saxon nation, Rock saw it as the first step in preserving the independence and integrity of his race in a nation bent on its destruction.

Without accepting the growing black nationalism in Rock's rhetoric, many white abolitionists found his eloquent attack on Parker's black child stereotype extremely convincing. At the Boston Massacre celebration, Wendell Phillips acknowledged the great intellectual weight that Parker's arguments carried but found himself in entire agreement with his black colleague. "It is a hazardous thing to differ with so profound a scholar, so careful a thinker as Theodore Parker," he admitted, "but I cannot accept his argument." Not only had Anglo-Saxons themselves been held as serfs in Europe, he argued, but blacks had proven their ability to fight in Haiti. Phillips appropriately went on to read a prepared statement by another white abolitionist, Thomas Wentworth Higginson, which cited examples of black heroism from several recent fugitive slave rescues and claimed that there were "cowards of all complexions." Though he was careful not to offend a man who had been a valuable ally in the fight

against slavery, Phillips made it clear that his own views on black character were incompatible with Parker's romantic racialism. Won over by Rock's arguments that evening, Phillips sprinkled his speeches over the next several years with references to black heroes like Crispus Attucks and Toussaint L'Ouverture.[36]

Parker's intellectual and emotional commitment to romantic racialism prevented him from abandoning it entirely, but even he found Rock's forceful attack hard to ignore. In speeches directly following the March 5 confrontation, his remarks about the emotional and affectionate qualities of blacks were juxtaposed with hints at the existence of warlike qualities akin to those of Anglo-Saxons. On occasion he even flirted with the notion that the most extreme examples of black docility resulted from the environment of slavery rather than from innate qualities. In July 1858, for instance, he told his congregation at the Boston Music Hall that "slavery degrades the slave, it aims to pervert his nature," and that each slave was forced "to repudiate his own individualism" as a mechanism of survival. If this were the case, he argued, "then no nation has such a dangerous class of proletaries as America, and no carpenter's shop is so littered with inflammable material." While the patience and forbearance of blacks might be greater than that of Anglo-Saxons, he admitted that it might not be unlimited and that an instinct for freedom might eventually produce a servile insurrection like that of Santo Domingo. "Black bondage will yet be red freedom," he predicted; "the South sits on a powder magazine, and then plays with fire."[37]

In an even more dramatic confluence of events, however, the confrontation at the 1858 Boston Massacre celebration took place only one day before Parker's historic meeting with Kansas warrior John Brown at the American House Hotel in Boston. It was at this meeting that Parker and other members of the "Secret Six" conspiracy agreed to raise funds for what became the ill-fated raid on Harpers Ferry, Virginia, in October 1859. With Rock's words of the previous evening ringing in his ears, Parker placed his hopes in Brown's plan to arm and lead a massive slave insurrection from Northern Virginia into the Deep South. Though Parker perceived the plan as a dramatic opportunity for white activists like himself to assist blacks in becoming Americans, the entire enterprise nevertheless hinged on the black fighting spirit described by Rock the previous evening.

Moreover, as his own health began to fail, Parker also saw in Brown's plan a final chance to play a direct role in the destruction of an institution that he had fought at great personal cost for nearly fifteen years. Ironically, however, his hope rested on the willingness and ability of Southern slaves to heed the call to insurrection—a willingness and ability that he had spent so much his own intellectual and emotional energy refuting. Like the nation's call for black soldiers only a few years later, however, Parker's intense desire for Brown's success led to a rapid readjustment of his racial rhetoric. "It is not merely white men who will fight for the liberty of Americans," he suddenly predicted. "The negroes will take their defense into their own hands and slavery will die like a mad dog in a village with only the enemies of the human kind to lament its fate."[38]

In tying the history and destiny of the American nation to the inherent racial qualities of the Anglo-Saxon race, Parker had created a fundamental tension in his abolitionism that called forth a variety of responses from black abolitionists. Dependent though they were on support from the white antislavery community, black leaders like Frederick Douglass, William Wells Brown, James McCune Smith, and William Nell could not ignore the implications of views that made America the sole property of Anglo-Saxons. Whether using history, science, or political theory, these activists argued that African Americans already possessed a legitimate and compelling claim to the privileges and freedoms of a republican nation. For John Rock, however, Parker's use of American freedom as standard with which to *judge* rather than liberate blacks, both slave and free, raised more fundamental doubts about the commitment of white abolitionists to the liberty they professed to support. In order to fight the "great conspiracy to crush" his race, Rock found independent black action the only reliable weapon.

Although their debate over race, violence, and nationalism had focused so directly on the shape of postemancipation America, neither Rock nor Parker lived to experience the hopes and disappointments of the Reconstruction era. Having left the United States in early 1859 in a vain effort to recover from the ravages of tuberculosis, Parker died in Florence, Italy, on April 10, 1860. Though disappointed by the news that John Brown's raid had been a failure, Parker had learned just enough from John Rock to imagine a time when black soldiers could march in uniform through the streets of Boston on their way to a war of liberation. Only a few months before his death he predicted that "one day it will be thought not less heroic for a negro to fight for his personal liberty than for a white man to fight for political independence."[39]

While his reasons were different, John Rock found that same vision equally appealing. Although he spent the Civil War years in Boston building his new career as a lawyer, Rock made good on his promise to give an "intelligent answer" to the issue of black participation in America's latest conflict. In the aftermath of the Emancipation Proclamation, he became a leading recruiter for the 54th Massachusetts Regiment, the 5th Massachusetts Cavalry, and other black units. As an extension of his own racial pride and belief in independent black action, Rock found the image of black liberators enormously satisfying. Although he continued to maintain that his race had nothing to prove to whites, Rock had also learned enough from Theodore Parker to know just how important the battlefield was to both practical and theoretical claims for black citizenship in a racist nation. In part as a result of black participation in the Civil War, moreover, John Rock was able to take part in the symbolic assertion of that citizenship not long before his own death from tuberculosis in 1866. On February 1, 1865, he found himself standing before United States Chief Justice Salmon P. Chase, who admitted him to the Supreme Court Bar. "John Rock was the pall bearer," wrote one Northern newspaper, "the corpse was the Dred Scott decision."[40]

Notes

The author would like to thank R. Kent Newmyer and James B. Stewart for their comments on earlier drafts of this article.

1. *Liberator,* Mar. 12, 1858.

2. Ibid.

3. I have used "racialism" after George Fredrickson's term "romantic racialism" in *Black Image in the White Mind: The Debate over Afro-American Character and Destiny, 1817-1914* (New York: Harper and Row, 1971), 101-2. It denotes a spectrum of racial assumptions based on the romantic idea of inherent racial qualities. Works dealing with other aspects of white racism in the abolitionist movement include Leon Litwack, *North of Slavery: The Negro in the Free States, 1790-1860* (Chicago: Univ. of Chicago Press, 1961); Jane H. Pease and William Pease, *They Who Would Be Free: Blacks' Search for Freedom, 1830-1861* (New York: Atheneum, 1974); and Lawrence Friedman, *Gregarious Saints: Self and Community in American Abolitionism, 1830-1870* (Cambridge: Cambridge Univ. Press, 1982).

4. Wendell Phillips, "Theodore Parker," in *Speeches, Lectures and Letters,* 2d ser. (Boston: Lee and Shepard, 1894), 433. For more details on Parker's background and abolitionism, see Paul E. Teed, "'A Very Excellent Fanatic, A Very Good Infidel and a First-Rate Traitor': Theodore Parker and the Search for Perfection in Antebellum America" (Ph.D. diss., University of Connecticut, 1994).

5. James Oliver Horton and Lois Horton, *Black Bostonians: Family Life and Community Struggle in the Antebellum North* (New York: Holmes and Meier Publishers, 1979), 100.

6. Thomas Wentworth Higginson, *Contemporaries* (Boston: Houghton, Mifflin, 1899), 49-50.

7. Reginald Horsman, *Race and Manifest Destiny: The Origins of American Racial Anglo-Saxonism* (Cambridge: Harvard Univ. Press, 1981).

8. Herder quoted in Elie Kedourie, *Nationalism* (London: Hutchinson and Co., 1966), 63.

9. Theodore Parker, "The American Scholar," in Henry Steele Commager, ed., *Theodore Parker, An Anthology* (Boston: Beacon Press, 1960), 191. On the commitment of the Transcendentalists to the development of an authentic American culture, see Lawrence Buell, *Literary Transcendentalism: Style and Vision in the American Renaissance* (Ithaca: Cornell Univ. Press, 1973); and idem, *New England Literary Culture: From Revolution through Renaissance* (Cambridge: Cambridge Univ. Press, 1986).

10. Theodore Parker, *Lessons from the World of Matter and the World of Men* (Boston: Charles Slack, 1867), 82.

11. Parker to David Wasson, Dec. 12, 1857, Boston, Parker papers, Massachusetts Historical Society, Boston.

12. Horsman, *Race and Manifest Destiny,* 158-86; Theodore Parker, "The Progress of America," in Franklin Sanborn, ed., *The Rights of Man in America* (Boston: American Unitarian Association, 1911), 197-99.

13. Theodore Parker, "The Political Destination of America," *Massachusetts Quarterly Review* 2 (Dec. 1848): 5, 3.

14. Theodore Parker, "The Rights of Man in America," in *Rights of Man,* 355, 357.

15. Parker, "Political Destination," 30.

16. Theodore Parker, *The Present Aspect of Slavery in America* (Boston: William Kent and Co., 1858), 5; Theodore Parker to Francis Jackson, Nov. 24, 1859, Rome, Parker Papers.

17. For Northern images of blacks, see George Fredrickson, *The Black Image in the White Mind: The Debate on Afro-American Character and Destiny, 1817-1914* (New York: Harper and Row, 1971), 97-129; and Ronald Takaki, "The Black Child-Savage in Antebellum America," in Gary Nash and Richard Weiss, eds., *The Great Fear: Race in the Mind of America* (New York: Holt, Rinehart and Winston, 1970).

18. Burleigh quoted in Jane Pease and William Pease, "Antislavery Ambivalence: Immediatism, Expediency, Race," *American Quarterly* 17 (Winter 1965): 685.

19. Theodore Parker to Francis Jackson, Nov. 24, 1859, Rome, Parker Papers.

20. Theodore Parker to Mr. Webster, Dec. 14, 1850, in John Weiss, *Life and Correspondence of Theodore Parker,* 2 vols. (New York: Appleton, 1864), 2:110.

21. Theodore Parker to Pennsylvania Anti-Slavery Conference, in *Liberator,* Oct. 31, 1851; Parker scrapbook on fugitive slave cases, Parker Collection, Boston Public Library.

22. On the growing audience for Parker's views among some white opponents of slavery expansion, see Michael Fellman, "Theodore Parker and the Abolitionist Role in the 1850's," *Journal of American History* 61 (Dec. 1974): 666-84. Rock's statement is in *Liberator,* Mar. 12, 1858.

23. Phillips, "Toussaint," in *Speeches,* 1st ser., 469. For abolitionist uses of Anglo-Saxonism as history, see Daniel McInerney, *The Fortunate Heirs of Freedom: Abolition and Republican Thought* (Lincoln: Univ. of Nebraska Press, 1994), 27-57. Frederick Douglass, "The Significance of Emancipation in the West Indies," in John Blassingame, ed., *The Frederick Douglass Papers,* ser. 1 (New Haven: Yale Univ. Press, 1985), 3:203.

24. Douglass, "Pioneers in a Holy Cause," *Douglass Papers,* 2:73; William Wells Brown, "Speech," in C. Peter Ripley, ed., *The Black Abolitionist Papers* (Chapel Hill: Univ. of North Carolina Press, 1991), 4:341.

25. James M. Smith, "Civilization, Its Dependence on Physical Circumstances," *The Anglo-African Magazine* (1859; reprint, New York: Arno Press, 1968), 7. Biographical information on Smith can be found in Benjamin Quarles, *Black Abolitionists* (New York: Oxford Univ. Press, 1969), 114-15; as well as in Pease and Pease, *They Who Would Be Free,* 49, 241.

26. Smith, "Civilization," 15, 16.

27. William C. Nell to Wendell Phillips, July 8, 1855, in *Black Abolitionist Papers* 4:300. A starting point for analyzing Nell's career as an abolitionist and his stand on a variety of issues is Robert Smith, "William Cooper Nell, Crusading Black Abolitionist," *Journal of Negro History* 55 (July 1970): 182-99.

28. William C. Nell, *Colored Patriots of the American Revolution* (Boston: Robert Walcutt, 1855), 378-79; Nell, to Phillips, July 8, 1855, in *Black Abolitionist Papers* 4:300.

29. Theodore Parker, *The Present Aspect of Slavery in America and the Immediate Duty of the North* (Boston: William Kent, 1858), 5, 7.

30. *Liberator,* Apr. 11, 1856; George A. Levesque, "Boston's Black Brahmin: Dr. John S. Rock," *Civil War History* 26 (Dec. 1980): 326-46.

31. *Liberator,* Mar. 12, 1858.

32. John Rock, "Speech," in *Black Abolitionist Papers* 5:63. For competing views of freedom among white and black abolitionists, see Pease and Pease, *They Who Would Be Free,* 3-16; and Eric Foner, "The Meaning of Freedom in the Age of Emancipation," *Journal of American History* 81 (Sept. 1994): 435-60.

33. *Liberator,* Mar. 12, 1858.

34. Ibid.

35. Rock, "Speech," 61.

36. Ibid. For a detailed look at Phillips's complex racial views, see James B. Stewart, *Wendell Phillips: Liberty's Hero* (Baton Rouge: Louisiana State Univ. Press, 1986), 97-116.

37. Theodore Parker, *The Effect of Slavery on the American People* (Boston, 1858), 5.

38. Ibid.

39. Parker to Francis Jackson, Nov. 24, 1859, Rome, Parker Papers.

40. Quoted in Levesque, "Black Brahmin," 336.

Gary L. Collison (essay date 1997)

SOURCE: Collison, Gary L. "Toward Democratic Vistas: Theodore Parker, Friendship, and Transcendentalism." In *Emersonian Circles: Essays in Honor of Joel Myerson,* edited by Wesley T. Mott and Robert E. Burkholder, pp. 161-80. Rochester, N.Y.: University of Rochester Press, 1997.

[*In the following essay, Collison considers the substantial impact of failed friendships on Parker's increasingly democratic views and greater inclusiveness in his personal life and theoretical perspective.*]

For no one more than Theodore Parker, the Transcendentalist revolution seemed timed precisely right. Parker came of age with the revolution, graduating from the Divinity School in 1836, the year that has been called the *annus mirabilis* of the Transcendental Movement because of the many manifestations of "Newness." Of special importance for the young Parker, 1836 was the year the Transcendental Club came into being. Parker's friend and mentor, Convers Francis, was an original member of the club, and Parker was soon drawn into the circle of these new spirits who seemed able to defy the gravitational pull of earthbound convention and habit and tradition. Emerson, still preaching occasionally when Parker first met him, was the center of the group, and most of the participants in the club—nearly

two dozen—were Unitarian ministers.[1] Among them were Francis, George Ripley, and two of Parker's close friends from the Divinity School, John Sullivan Dwight and Christopher Pearse Cranch. Other students and recent graduates of the school, together with Margaret Fuller, Amos Bronson Alcott, and other Transcendentalists from Emerson's circle of friends, made up an ever-shifting cast.

By the early 1840s, Theodore Parker had begun taking an increasingly large role in the Transcendentalist-led reform movement within Unitarianism. For several years, he had been publishing anonymous articles supporting Transcendentalized Unitarianism, and in 1841, in his famous South Boston Sermon, ***The Transient and Permanent in Christianity,*** he would publicly put the case for jettisoning the theological conservatism that held back mainstream denominational thinking. But as Emerson himself had found out in 1838, the crusading spirit had its hazards. Convers Francis warned bluntly, "He who spits in the wind, spits in his own face."[2] Parker's battle with Unitarian conservatives was to play a large role in shaping his career as a religious and social radical over the next twenty years, as is well known. Less well known is the role played by Parker's personal relationships with other members of the Transcendentalist circle and with minister-friends just outside that circle.[3] Defections of key friends, lukewarm support by nominal Transcendentalists, and the fragmentation of a Transcendentalist-Unitarian group were to result in Parker's deepening sense of isolation and betrayal and help account for the increasing stridency of his tone in the early 1840s. The failure of these critical relationships, almost as much as conservative hostility, would push Parker toward a more democratic voice and themes as well as a wider circle of friends and a broader, more representative American audience.

II

The immediate post-Divinity School days were difficult for the bookish, intellectual young minister. In rural West Roxbury, where Parker was ordained in the Second Church pulpit in 1837, Parker soon found himself fretting under the dull, confining routine of parish work. "I often ask myself what I am doing with my one talent, and can only reply that I deem myself well nigh wasting it," he confided to his journal early in 1838.[4] The practice of endless visiting of the sick and infirm, which Emerson loathed, Parker too found irksome and demoralizing. "Going about and talking little with old women, giving good advice to hypocrites," Parker wearily summarized the experience.

Moreover, Parker's marriage, a source of distress to him in the first years of his ministry, also increased his sense of isolation. As several scholars have noted, Parker's journal of the West Roxbury years is peppered with references—some oblique, some not so oblique—to his painfully unsatisfactory home life.[5] "My life is truly cheerless, loveless, a death were far better," he wrote in his journal in the summer of 1840.[6] It is impossible to judge exactly what the source of the difficulty was (there are vague hints that the root of the problem may have been sexual), but at least part of it was intellectual incompatibility. Lydia Parker strongly disapproved of her husband's intellectual pursuits and controversial stances. Both she and her wealthy aunt, who owned their house and lived with the young couple, pressured him to conform, leaving him feeling agonizingly isolated and alone even in his own house.[7] Clearly Lydia Parker was not the warm companion—certainly not the intellectual companion—that Parker yearned for.

Parker, however, found substantial compensation in his beloved studies, his warm relationships with Divinity School friends, and his participation in the Transcendentalist circle. In those first years of his ministry, his pen was rarely idle and the lamp in his study burned long into the West Roxbury nights. Parker soon was producing not only two new sermons each week for his small congregation but a steady stream of essays, poems, notes, and reviews for the three Unitarian publications, the *Christian Register,* the *Western Messenger,* and the *Christian Examiner,* as well as for other journals. In addition, he buried himself in the study of the history of religion, a labor that would result in his first two books, *The Discourse of Matters Pertaining to Religion* (Boston, 1842), and a two-volume translation of Wilhelm De Wette's *Critical and Historical Introduction to the Old Testament* (Boston, 1843).[8]

From his West Roxbury home, Parker also managed to simulate some of the intense comradeship and daily intellectual exchange of his Divinity Hall years through occasional visits with friends, exchanges by mail, and regular trips into the city. His chief correspondents in the first few years of his ministry were his closest companions from the Divinity School, classmates Samuel Page Andrews, George E. Ellis, and William Silsbee. At the School, Ellis and Silsbee had assisted Parker with the editorial duties of the *Scriptural Interpreter* and helped Parker prepare a report on German theology for the Philanthropic Society, a student discussion group. Though in both cases Parker appears to have been the leader, their shared work reveals companionship and common enthusiasms. Parker's letters from West Roxbury to Andrews, Ellis, and Silsbee were full of gossip and high spirits, and those to Silsbee, in particular, were also full of ideas. Parker was also sharing his developing ideas with his friends Convers Francis and George Ripley and with William Ellery Channing, the elder statesman and guiding spirit of the Unitarian liberal wing.

The Transcendental Club, too, stimulated Parker's thinking. Emerson's 1838 Divinity School Address, which was something of a manifesto for the rising generation of ministers, pushed Parker and the group further toward radicalism. By 1840 the club would be holding meetings to discuss "indications of the new Church," "the inspiration of the Prophet and Bard," "the Doctrine of Reform," and "the organization of a new church" (two meetings).[9] The young Parker found himself in the inner circle of this reform movement and even hosted the first of the two meetings on "the organization of a new church." But by 1840s, Parker's increasingly radical views were encountering regular opposition from older Unitarian ministers. On the second of January, his turn to preach the famous "Great and Thursday" lecture in Boston came around. His subject was "Inspiration," and his Transcendentalist views led Dr. Francis Parkman, the conservative father of Francis Parkman the historian, to complain to Parker of impiety. "I was so grieved," Parker confessed in his journal, "that I left him . . . & went weeping as I went, through the street."[10]

After Parker delivered his famous South Boston Sermon in April of 1841, the criticism, and Parker's sensitivities, increased dramatically. "Sundry of the Brethren have lifted up their heels against me," Parker wrote in his journal near the end of the summer of 1841, listing denominational leaders F. W. P. Greenwood, Nathaniel L. Frothingham, and Ezra Stiles Gannett among his chief public critics.[11] This and similar entries show Parker increasingly preoccupied with, and vulnerable to, his critics. Shortly after delivering the sermon, Parker made the first of several lists of names of ministers who he believed were still willing to exchange pulpits, a sign of fellowship among ministers and an important source of relief from the otherwise endless duty of preparing two fresh sermons each week for his West Roxbury congregation. The first list—the longer of the two—included the names of only twelve ministers. "'Blessed are ye when men shall speak evil of you & separate you from their company,'" Parker reminded himself philosophically, quoting the Bible. "I do not suffer from lack of sympathy, & I am besides able to stand alone."[12]

But the changing dynamics of the Transcendental movement clearly heightened Parker's sense of isolation. In 1838, the storm of criticism over Emerson's Divinity School Address seemed to strengthen the solidarity among the Transcendental group. In 1841, by contrast, the energy that had made the Transcendental Club thrive was diffusing in a dozen directions. The 1840 meetings on reforming the church proved to be the last regular sessions. Emerson, whose Divinity School Address of 1838 had inspired Parker and many other young ministers, increasingly aligned himself with the literary group of Transcendentalists, spurred in part by the necessities of the new *Dial.* Although Emerson welcomed Parker's contributions, his first letters to Parker as editor gently warn against Parker's tendencies toward combativeness and verbose scholarliness.[13] Emerson's literary group, which included Henry Thoreau and Bronson Alcott, was little interested in Unitarian church issues or in joining Parker's battles.

Brook Farm was pulling others, notably George Ripley and Divinity School classmates John Sullivan Dwight and C. P. Cranch, in another direction. Ripley resigned from his pulpit in 1840, at least in part because of hostility toward his Transcendentalist views. Dwight, too, had turned away from the ministry.[14] Ripley, perhaps Parker's closest friend, was almost completely absorbed in directing his communal enterprise at Brook Farm. Parker occasionally saw Cranch and Dwight, but they, too, were soon seeking solace and spirituality in the high ideals and manure-shoveling at Brook Farm.

With Emerson, Ripley, Cranch, and Dwight gone from the ministry by the early 1840s, few members of the Transcendentalist group were available for *ministerial* support. The Transcendentalist ministers remaining— James Freeman Clarke (who had just returned from the West), Frederic Henry Hedge, and Convers Francis— were to prove either too conservative or too timid to join wholeheartedly—or half heartedly—in reform efforts. The *movement* within Unitarianism was no longer like a broad stream of mingled currents flowing in a single direction but was more like a cluster of separate eddies and whirlpools.

Parker's growing sense of isolation within the denomination was further exacerbated by other slights and defections. The additional tensions provided by the widespread criticism of Transcendentalism soon strained Parker's relationships with his Divinity School classmates. By the end of 1839 Parker's correspondence with Samuel Andrews had ended, for all practical purposes.[15] George E. Ellis, another of Parker's closest friends from the Divinity School, grew increasingly chilly toward him. Although Ellis had settled at a church in Charlestown, close enough that he and Parker could have seen each other regularly, they soon drifted apart. Later Ellis would speak at least once in Parker's defense at a meeting of Unitarian ministers, but he had already refused to exchange pulpits, according to Parker's journal note.[16]

Parker's friendship with William Silsbee lasted the longest and was the most substantial. Though Parker's letters to Silsbee were as full of fun as those to Ellis and Andrews, it was Silsbee who inspired Parker's deepest feelings.[17] At the beginning of 1842, Parker wrote revealingly to Silsbee of "a certain communion of Spirit, be the bodies ever so distant." "You do not know how often, nor how ardently I have longed to see you," he added, and then recalled dreaming of seeing Silsbee but being unable to clasp his hand on account of "all the

ado I made . . . and so awoke in great grief and sadness."[18] Parker's dream rather than his hope proved prophetic. Parker's journal for the summer of 1842 records a visit of Silsbee—"the most painful I ever received from any man"—that apparently ended their intimacy.[19] Silsbee did preach once for Parker afterwards, but their close friendship never revived.[20]

The breakdown in his relations with Ellis and Silsbee, together with the fragmenting of the Transcendentalist circle, left Parker increasingly isolated. He had the continued allegiance of his parishioners, led by wealthy merchant George R. Russell and the Shaw family, but his colleagues continued to disappoint him. Parker never got the support he hoped for from Alvan Lamson and Cyrus Bartol, two other young liberal ministers who might have provided the kind of support network Parker sought.[21] Although James Freeman Clarke, William Henry Channing, and Orestes Brownson shared some of Parker's social and religious views, they all had different programs in mind. Clarke was far more conservative theologically than Parker. The prickly Brownson was already openly critical of Parker's positions, and besides, was in the process of making his famous about-face toward "Catholicity without the papacy."[22] And Channing would vacillate. Although he would draft a letter calling for "strenuous and determined action" in the interests of a separate movement within the denomination, before mailing the letter he would open it to add, "this is all too enthusiastic . . . Let us unite with the Unitarians; they may do much."[23]

As is indicated by Parker's declining correspondence of 1841 and 1842, his circle of friends shrank smaller and smaller. Parker's surviving correspondence for 1842 amounts to a mere 30 letters, and although other letters have undoubtedly been lost, Parker seems to have had, at most, only four sustained correspondences through the summer of 1842. Convers Francis and Elizabeth Peabody continued to be his main intellectual correspondents (and Peabody had already expressed misgivings about Parker's conduct). Parker's only other correspondents of note were two women for whom he had begun playing the role of friend and spiritual advisor, Patience Ford and young Caroline Healey [Dall].[24] He still eagerly sought the ear and advice of William Ellery Channing, the "Dr. Channing" mentioned so often in his journal, but Channing's death in the fall of 1842 was to leave Parker even more alone within the denomination.

III

A crisis in Parker's relationship with his old friend and mentor Convers Francis would prove to be Parker's greatest personal trial in the two years following the South Boston Sermon. By the early 1840s, Francis had long been Parker's chief friend, advisor, model, sounding board, and intellectual correspondent. "This week the best things I have got have been in talk with Francis, good man that he is," Parker wrote in his journal on the first of January, 1841.[25] After Parker delivered his South Boston Sermon in April, Francis was wholly sympathetic, appalled by the conservative outcry against Parker. "This in a community boasting of its entire religious freedom!" he wrote in his journal. "And the Unitarians, too, open full-mouthed in the cry, as well as the Orthodox."[26] He told Parker that "it is a great, and good, and pious, and deeply Christian discourse," although he admitted that there were "a few expressions . . . and here and there a sentence, with which perhaps I should not agree."[27]

Through the winter of 1841-1842, the two men regularly exchanged letters and visits. "T. Parker came in to spend the night," Francis wrote in his journal on 11 December 1841. "We had much good talk about matters of learning, & c. In religious things he seems, notwithstanding his reputation of infidelity, more and more pious every time I see him. A mind so affluent in learning and high thought I have never known."[28] Parker's letters to Francis at the end of 1841 and into the early part of 1842 continue to be full of high-spirited good-humor and warm feeling, and Francis's, though more reserved, were almost equally warm.

As criticism of Parker grew and friends like William Silsbee fell away, Francis's importance to Parker increased. By the spring of 1842, Francis would be the only practicing minister left whom Parker felt comfortable confiding to. When Parker needed to vent his anger over his treatment by the other Unitarians, it was to Francis he wrote:

> I do not care a rush—for what men who differ from me *do* or *say,* but it has grieved me a little, I confess it, to see men who think *as I do,* of the historical & mythical matter connected with Xty, who yet take the stand some of them take. It is like opening a drawer, when you expect to find money, & discover that the *Gold* has gone, only the copper is left. This has been my fate very often. I put my finger on a *minister* & "he ain't there." Some body said the ministers were a very selfish set. I fear there is some little truth about it. Some think, & say they are for freedom of thought & all that sort of thing. But it is all *talk, talk, talk.*[29]

Parker's letters to Francis in the late winter continued to be full of high ideas. "What do you think of the *Genesis of our knowledge of God?*" Parker asked Francis and then poured out his own views.[30] "Dr. Francis came here to day—we had a very pleasant talk. He is urbane & bookish & genial & good as ever," Parker began his journal entry in February 1842. But in the same entry Parker noted, almost as a lament, that he had outgrown his mentor. "His words do not stir me as once they did," Parker wrote. "Then I walked long days in the strength of the meat I ate. He solved problems for me. Now I look else-whither."[31]

In the late spring and early summer of 1842, the relationship between the two men became more complicated when Francis was offered the Parkman Professorship in Pulpit Eloquence and Pastoral Care at the Divinity School, a position left vacant by the retirement of Henry Ware, Jr. As the faculty consisted of only two professors, the appointment was critical. The Harvard Divinity School was in an exceedingly fragile condition. Many conservative Unitarian ministers, distrusting both the general freedom of the school and the emphasis on modern biblical scholarship, had been turning away from the school. The Divinity School and its reputation for religious liberalism, if not radicalism, had become something of a liability for Harvard College, a situation that Emerson's Address of 1838 only made worse, and Harvard officials had adopted a policy of ignoring the school as much as possible. As a result of university neglect and Unitarian distrust, funds and student enrollment dwindled precipitously. All of this suggested that the next appointment at the Divinity School would be conservative enough to appease its main critics.[32]

When Francis was offered the Divinity School post, Parker recognized a liberal victory and urged him to accept. This Francis finally did, with much hesitation and expressions of self-doubt about his fitness for the post. Before Francis moved to Cambridge to take up his new duties, Parker wrote several times to offer encouragement and support. "I must rejoice at the thought of your usefulness being so vastly increased, & look forward to the daring hopes you will waken in the minds of young men," Parker wrote. "Would to Heaven you had gone to Cam[bridge]. before I went to the School."[33] But from the time the appointment was first discussed, Parker had doubts about what the appointment would mean to him personally. He and Francis discussed the possible effects of what Frederic Henry Hedge called the "conservative tang" of Cambridge.[34] In May, however, Parker received some assurance that Francis would remain his steadfast ally when Francis sent him a note requesting an exchange of pulpits for the twelfth of June. Although Francis had exchanged pulpits with Parker soon after the South Boston Sermon, nearly a year had passed since then.[35]

In early June, however, Francis discussed the proposed exchange with Harvard professor James Walker, a leading Unitarian figure, who advised against it. With only two days left before the exchange was to take place, Francis left a brief letter at Parker's house asking that the exchange be put off. Citing Walker's recommendation and "the sensitive jealousy" surrounding the school, Francis tried hard to put a good face on the matter, but his arguments were labored. "In the connexion my name stands at Cambridge, I am willing to avoid the apprehended offence, for the sake of the feelings *there* concerned," he explained awkwardly. "I am sure you know that nothing *on my own part,* would induce me to propose any such thing; it is only because, wholly unexpectedly, since we made the arrangement, another party is concerned, whose feelings claim to be regarded."[36]

Undoubtedly Francis's chief concern was for the Divinity School rather than for himself, as Perry Miller would have it in his scathing comment that Francis "fell away when the social hazards became too great."[37] Yet it is also true that strong personal reservations about Parker's recent conduct almost certainly influenced Francis's decision. In his journal he wrote of finding "a great deal to regret in Parker's book [the *Discourse of Matters Pertaining to Religion*], the more so because I love and admire the man so much. The spirit of it *seems* to be bad, derisive, sarcastic, arrogant,—contemptuous of what the wise and good hold sacred."[38] To Francis, Parker's love of combativeness associated him with William Lloyd Garrison, Abner Kneeland, and other strident, indecorous radicals. "Perhaps it is his destiny to become a reformer, and all this sharpness may be necessary to it. But I cannot sympathize with *it*," Francis wrote emphatically.[39] In fact, Francis had just publicly distanced himself from Transcendentalism when his turn came to preach the Thursday lecture. He revealingly titled his sermon **"Afar Off, and Nigh by the Blood of Christ,"** and admitted in his journal that "the sermon, I believe, gave some satisfaction to those who have been disposed to accuse me of the horrible crime of transcendentalism!"

Parker was deeply stung by Francis's apparent capitulation to conservative pressures. Already overwrought by more than two years of slights, rejections, and attacks, he was particularly vulnerable at this moment. Parker had challenged him to provide vocal public support only a few weeks before. "All the *denominational* influence is managed by a dozen conservative m-a-t-e-r-i-a-l-i-s-t-s. Is this *needed*, is it *eternal*. Is conservatism *immanent* in the Unitarians?" Parker brooded out loud.

> . . . If it is not—but only *transient*, its transitions may be *facilitated*. If you & [Caleb] Stetson will "grease the wheels," & get into the traces, I will find half a dozen to push behind, & put shoulders to the wheels. I believe in *leading* & am willing to be led, but not hauled about by the nose, & that by such men as ———& + ∞.[40]

The urgent tone suggests just how wrought up Parker had become and how desperate he was for support.

But neither Caleb Stetson nor Convers Francis had the temperament nor the inclination to "get into the traces." Although associated with the Transcendental Club from its first year, Stetson was never in tune with the more extreme Transcendentalist ideas, and Francis hated controversy and confrontation, in good Unitarian fashion.[41] Emerson himself as well as many other Unitarians shared Francis's distaste for public controversy. But Emerson did not share Francis's fear of "agitating excitement." Emerson and Parker believed it was the minister's duty to shake the listeners from a deadening, mechanical complacency of spirit. This had been the message that Emerson so memorably conveyed in the Divinity School Address of 1838.[42]

Parker enthusiastically endorsed Emerson's notion of the ministerial voice. "Alas for that man who consents to think one thing in his closet and preach another in his pulpit," Parker announced at the end of the South Boston Sermon. ". . . Over his study and over his pulpit might be writ, *Emptiness*; on his canonical robes, on his forehead and right hand, *DECEIT, DECEIT.*"[43] That Parker had in mind not only the conservatives in the denomination but its more cautious liberals is clear from a later comment about Frederic Hedge. Hedge "thinks a minister must have an *official function*— whereby the man is one thing & the minister another—& the minister may say what the *man* knows to be a *lie* & *do* what the *man* abhors," Parker wrote.[44] In an earlier letter to Francis regarding biblical interpretation, Parker had asked urgently, "Is it necessary there should always be this *clerical-view*; & this *laical-view* so different from it. Would not the people be *better, wiser,* & *holier* if they were emancipated from this stupid superstition which now hangs like a millstone about their necks?"[45]

Francis had not agreed. "There always have been . . . and always will be for a season, *esoterics & exoterics,*" Francis replied, "nor am I shocked with this, as indicating hypocrisy or the playing of a game in sacred things, but regard it as one of the natural, perhaps indispensable elements of human culture."[46] Although Francis sympathized with skeptics who saw "the absurdities, improbabilities, puerilities, & bad doctrines" of the Bible, Francis clearly thought it his duty to accommodate, not challenge, many conventional beliefs. "I have something of a conservative element myself," Francis explained to Parker a few months after the South Boston Sermon.[47] "There is a one-sided Radicalism or Reform, as well as one-sided Conservatism," he cautioned. Parker never admitted the point. This was the great divide between the two men. What Francis saw as accommodation and legitimate conservatism Parker saw as hypocrisy. In **"The Pharisees,"** a biting essay Parker wrote for an 1841 issue of *The Dial*, he echoed Dante in describing hypocritical ministers as the worst class of "moral monsters."[48]

At times, Parker had fleetingly recognized how large was the gulf that separated him and Francis on these matters. When the Transcendental Club had discussed "the organization of a new church" at Parker's house in 1840, the division between the radicals and the moderates in the group had been clear.[49] "We had a pretty good talk but only pretty good," Parker had written in his journal afterwards, adding caustically: "it appears that [Frederic Henry] Hedge, Francis, & [Caleb] Stetson are wedded to the past. Now I love the Past but would as soon wed my grandmother whom I love equally well."[50]

IV

"Francis fell back on account of the professorship at Cambridge," Parker noted in his **"Sermon Record Book"** for June 12th, 1842, the day of the cancelled exchange.[51] Then he pasted Francis's letter into his journal and annotated it with angry comments. "Francis is a good man & I love him but this expediency doctrine I don't like," he wrote, recalling how months earlier, when he had defended sending a contribution to the Divinity School, Francis had refused, complaining that the next faculty appointment would be "someone that will call you & me *Infidels* & wont exchange with us."[52] Now Francis's earlier words appeared both hypocritical and ironically prophetic. "The more I think of this affair of Dr. F. the worse it appears, & the more cowardly. That *he* should sneak off in this way!" Parker wrote angrily in his journal after a few days.[53] Three days later Parker wrote, "How he is fallen. False to his idea. *He has no Root in himself.*"[54] Five months later Parker would still be fuming over Francis's behavior. A list of scholarly "questions for Dr. Francis" appeared in his journal with the notation, "Never ask him any questions relating to Phil[osophy] or *Morals* & above all to *Religion* since his shabbiness."[55]

For the remainder of the summer, Parker and Francis continued to correspond, but their relations were greatly strained. "I believe the abolitionists & temperance men are *half* Right when they say '*the Church is a Humbug,*' and the *other half* of the Right is '*the ministers are ditto,*'" Parker wrote bitterly, and pointedly, in late June. "Now I am not to sit down tamely & be driven out of my position by the *opposition* of some & the *neglect* of others whose conduct shows that *they* have no love of freedom, except—for themselves, to sail with the popular wind & tide."[56] Francis, brimming over with doubt about his fitness for the Divinity School post, ignored the thrusts and practically begged Parker to visit. Parker sent encouraging words about the professorship but, nursing his wounded pride, held back from visiting. "Dont *you* know that the charge brought against you . . . [is] that you are *notoriously the companion of suspected & abandoned persons?*" he wrote with sarcasm. "I will not, knowingly, bring on you the censure, (or suspicion) of your brethren."[57] Francis shot back that Parker was making a "chimera" and that his home was always open. After Parker sent a non-committal letter that skirted the issues troubling their relationship, the correspondence lapsed.

Five months later, in early 1843, Parker finally took up his pen to renew the friendship, and over the next three years, Francis was to redeem himself somewhat in Parker's eyes.[58] In the summer of 1843, in the annual address to the alumni of the Divinity School, Francis rebuked the reactionaries in the denomination. "We have had narrowness enough," Francis scolded, according to a summary in the *Christian Register.* "Let every man who feels it to be his duty, speak without fear or favor."[59] Additionally, Francis filled in at Parker's West Roxbury church on a number of Sundays between 1844 and 1846.[60] But though some of the warmth returned to their correspondence, which continued until just before Parker's death, the intensity had gone out of their relationship. Parker never fully forgave his friend. In a sermon delivered before leaving for Europe in the fall of 1843, Parker wrote bitterly of two clergymen who "both failed me,—signally, utterly and with aggravations." A footnote identifies these two as Francis and Lamson.[61] More than fifteen years later, Parker was still smarting from the sting of these defections, especially Francis's. In his 1859 *Experience as a Minister,* written when Parker was nearing the end of his life, he condemned an unnamed minister, "one of the most learned and liberal . . . in New England," who advised him against speaking out.[62] Privately Parker admitted that this man, "so false to the Idea & also to me that I thought he deserved no mention," was his old mentor Convers Francis.[63]

V

The crisis in Parker's private relationships, especially with William Silsbee and Convers Francis, helps explain the bitter, angry tones of Parker's public and private utterances in this period. Parker's letters to and journal entries about Convers Francis also tell us a good deal about Parker's inner turmoil, particularly when his journals are contrasted to the well-known measured calm of Emerson's journals and letters following the Divinity School Address. Emerson, too, had struggled with the *personal* effects of controversy and condemnation. But for Emerson the process of composing his journal was a transforming process. Personal experiences were generalized, philosophized. Emotional responses to criticism "wastes my time" and "puts me into a false position," Emerson wrote, reestablishing equilibrium.[64] The process was clearly a protective, even a healing, strategy.

Parker's journal entries after the South Boston Sermon also differ significantly from Emerson's following the Divinity School Address in regard to the place of friendship. For Emerson, intelligent friendships remained a constant resource. The journals of 1838 and 1839 show him focusing intensely on his circle of close friends, meditating on their importance to him. It is no coincidence that following the Divinity School Address, Emerson composed his essay on friendship.[65] Friendships with Thoreau and Margaret Fuller, among others, clearly helped Emerson maintain his poise by serving as a counterweight to his public life.

By contrast, as Parker's personal struggle deepened, his journal provided principally an outlet for emotion rather than a medium for exploration, self-righting, distancing. When his support group proved so fragile, he had no good strategy for rising above the personal. In both letters and journals his inner self is almost always seen close up, unmediated by reflection, with the jagged edges of his emotions showing in stark relief. Compared to Emerson's entries, Parker's lack ornament, effort for effect, or a sense of an audience—all betraying an unpremeditated, spontaneous monologue. Where Emerson reflected (and deflected), Parker merely cries out. He goes back to the Francis affair numerous times, recording even second-hand and third-hand scraps of gossip about Francis's defense of himself. By turns he is self-pitying, angry, defiant, hurt, and righteous. These emotions spill over directly into the South Boston Sermon, the ***Discourse,*** and other works of this period.

The emotional character of Parker's private writings helps explain the stridency of his public pronouncements (and to some extent the reaction to them). Because he lacked Emerson's ability to transform personal experience, Parker's most intimate emotions are only thinly veiled from view in his public discourse. Though Parker ever denied accusations that he meant to offend anyone, his journal makes it clear that the critics were mostly on the mark when they accused him of attacking them and their sensibilities. His texts sound like his journals. His anger in the polemic sections of the South Boston Sermon, the ***Discourse,*** **"The Pharisees,"** and other writings is raw and immediate.[66]

VI

At the end of 1842, Parker was basically correct in envisioning himself standing friendless and alone in the Unitarian ministry, a Boston Saint Sebastian shot full of arrows. Several of his Divinity School friends shunned him and few voices among the Unitarians supported him even weakly. Dr. Channing had died, drawing from Parker the anguished cry, "Why, oh God, are so many left when such are taken. Why could not I have died in his stead."[67] The Transcendentalist movement within Unitarianism had nearly sputtered out. Parker carefully assembled a small sheaf of letters documenting all the defections and slights of fellow ministers. His list of ministers willing to exchange pulpits with him had dwindled to ten and then to six.[68] Of the remaining names on the list, only Caleb Stetson and James F. Clarke had been connected with the Transcendentalist group. Among the Transcendentalist ministers now missing from Parker's list were three who, sometime in 1842, had declined to exchange pulpits: Convers Francis, Alvan Lamson, and George Putnam.[69] "I have no

fellowship from the other clergy . . .," he lamented. "'They that are younger than I have me in derision . . . [and] turn the cold shoulder.'"[70]

Although by the end of 1842 Parker had good reason for picturing himself as isolated and alone, the picture is also very misleading, if not plain wrong, for several reasons. For one thing, it strongly reflects Parker's own exaggerated, emotionally charged view of himself. At this time in his life he lacked the emotional stability and distance from his experience to give a true reading. Seen through the magnifying glass of Parker's emotions, the slights and hurts loom too large. His own metaphor for his situation—he called himself "a bull whose roaring cant be stopped, but who is tied up in the corner of the Barn-cellar, so that *no body hears him*"—reveals much about his frothing psyche.[71]

More important, Parker misjudged his place in the changing American cultural landscape. If Boston Unitarianism and Boston Whiggery were in a rear-guard action, defending their increasingly threatened elitist position, the American scene—with its burgeoning mass markets, mass production, and mass media—was rife with opportunities for the *new*—for new thought, new forms, new organizations, new voices, and new alliances. One main proof of this was the Lyceum movement. The Lyceum, in Emerson's memorable estimate of it, was the true "panharmonicon," offering a "convertible audience & . . . no stiff conventions that prescribe a method, a style, a limited quotation of books, & an exact respect to certain books, persons, or opinions" (*JMN* 7:265). The Lyceum made Emerson possible. And Emerson helped prepare an audience for a Parker by expanding his range of topics from the time he began his first independent course of lectures in 1835. By the late 1830s, Emerson's annual course of lectures, the cultural highlight of Boston winters, had been introducing genteel and not so genteel Boston and New England audiences to a new, unfettered idealism that was an open, if indirect, challenge to the "famine" of the churches.

Emerson's success was hardly the only proof of a growing heterodox audience and changing cultural climate. In the mid-1830s, Abner Kneeland's atheistic Society of Free Inquirers had proved that there existed an audience impatient with the narrow channel of expression offered by conventional churches.[72] Some advanced Unitarians themselves had succeeded in attracting this new audience. By the time Parker delivered his South Boston Sermon, several new Unitarian churches designed to meet the changing needs of the times had been formed by Transcendentalist ministers. Orestes Brownson's Society for Christian Union and Progress (1836-1843), with its liberal modifications that appealed to the laboring classes, had revealed an appetite for new forms and ideas.[73] James Freeman Clarke, who has been defined as a moderate Transcendentalist, had founded his Church of the Disciples in 1841 to experiment with liberalized ecclesiastical organization.[74] The congregational principle of church organization invited this reformulation. If you wanted to start a new church or reform an old one, you opened the doors with hardly so much as a' "by your leave."

The press, the heterogeneous and rapidly growing urban environment, and the appetite for novelty spurred by the communications and transportation revolutions and by the market economy—all these created the fertile ground on which Parker could find an audience and a new circle of sustaining friendships. By the early summer of 1841 Parker had received an invitation to lecture on the new views of religion. The invitation came from a group of sympathetic Unitarian Boston businessmen who, in America of the 1840s, were no longer firmly attached to local church-communities as they had been in the past.

Although Parker's course of lectures attracted a smaller audience than hoped for, it further advertised his views to a waiting public.[75] By the end of 1842, Parker had been delivering **"Six Plain Sermons for the Times"** in Boston, Salem, and other locations to audiences often numbering in the thousands.[76] The publication of Parker's *Discourse,* which was based on his first lecture series, together with the 1843 publication of Parker's *Critical and Miscellaneous Writings* (which included the South Boston Sermon and a number of Parker's controversial *Dial* pieces) also shows just how much Parkerism had become a marketable commodity. As Elizabeth Peabody had written soon after the South Boston Sermon, "Parker . . . goes on with the rapidity of an Angel—improving and unfolding and making a prodigious impression on people in spite of clerical opposition."[77]

The lesson Parker learned not only from conservatives but from William Silsbee, Convers Francis, and other lukewarm Unitarian ministers with mild Transcendentalist leanings was that old institutions and old habits made reform from within nearly impossible. Institutional inertia and traditional habits were too strong. Diluted by resignations, conservative tendencies, and timidity, the Transcendentalist movement within the denomination failed to spark a thoroughgoing revolution in the 1840s. But the Boston of the 1820s and 1830s, in which the Unitarian elite were a dominant force in a relatively homogeneous society, was rapidly passing, if it had not already passed.[78] Outside Unitarianism, or on its borders, in the new American society of the 1840s, dramatic change was possible. Others who would thrive in this new environment—Wendell Phillips, John Parker Hale, Charles Sumner, Samuel Gridley Howe, and William Lloyd Garrison—were soon to become Parker's close friends and allies. They were men who, like Parker, operated on the margins of established institutions or created new institutions to respond to an increasingly pluralistic, industrialized, and urbanized America.

After returning in 1844 from a year-long trip to Europe to recover both physical and mental health, Parker accepted an invitation from his sophisticated urban audience to become the minister of the independent Twenty-Eighth Congregational Society in the heart of Boston. In his new sermons, he would speak in a more democratic voice, a voice responsive to the sweeping changes being brought about by urbanization and industrialization. That voice was to emerge fully formed, with an almost Whitmanesque sweep, in the great sermons of 1846 on social issues—particularly **"The Perishing Classes," "The Dangerous Classes,"** and **"A Sermon of Merchants."** It was a voice that spoke not simply to Unitarian issues and Unitarian experience but to American experience, a voice that was soon to make Parker one of the best known ministers of the age.

Notes

An earlier version of this paper was presented at the 1992 meeting of the American Literature Association in San Diego. I am grateful to Helen R. Deese and Dean Grodzins for commenting on the draft of this essay. Grodzins also suggested numerous additional sources in the Parker Papers. The author wishes to thank the Massachusetts Historical Society, the Boston Public Library, and the Andover-Harvard Theological Library for granting permission to quote from manuscripts in their collections.

1. Among the Unitarian ministers who are known to have attended at least one meeting are Cyrus Bartol, Henry W. Bellows, Orestes Brownson, William Henry Channing, James Freeman Clarke, Charles Follen, Convers Francis, Frederic Henry Hedge, Samuel J. May, Samuel Osgood, Ephraim Peabody, George Putnam, George Ripley, Chandler Robbins, and Caleb Stetson.

2. Parker, quoting Francis, in Parker to Convers Francis, 14 February 1842, Boston Public Library.

3. There are basically three reasons for this. One is that Parker's own letters and journals have been the main, and sometimes exclusive, source of information about Parker's conflict with Unitarianism. The second is that Parker's first biographer, John Weiss, obscured some aspects of Parker's relationships by deleting, sometimes silently, key portions of letters and journals. And the third is that except for the South Boston Sermon, Parker's writings in this period have not been carefully studied.

4. Quoted in John Weiss, *The Life and Correspondence of Theodore Parker, Minister of the Twenty-*

Eighth Congregational Society, Boston, 2 vols. (New York: D. Appleton, 1864), 1:103.

5. Carol Johnston, "The Journals of Theodore Parker, July-December 1840," Ph.D. dissertation, University of South Carolina, 1980, pp. xiii-xix; Dean Grodzins, "Theodore Parker and Transcendentalism," Ph.D. dissertation, Harvard University, 1993, pp. 151-63.

6. Parker, Ms. Journal "N" (13 July 1838-31 October 1840), Andover-Harvard Theological Library, p. 338.

7. Dean Grodzins, unpublished paper, American Literature Association meeting, 27 May 1992, San Diego, California.

8. By the end of 1842 he would finish the essays and miscellaneous pieces for still another book, *Critical and Miscellaneous Writings* (1843).

9. Joel Myerson, "A Calendar of Transcendental Club Meetings," *American Literature* 44 (May 1972): 205-06.

10. Journal "N," p. 285.

11. Theodore Parker, Ms. Journal "I" (1841-1843), Andover-Harvard Theological Library, p. 101. The entry is undated but the references to public responses to the South Boston Sermon would place it sometime after mid-June. The best summary of the critical response to Parker's sermon is "Theodore Parker and the Confessional Question," chapter 4 of William R. Hutchison, *The Transcendentalist Ministers: Church Reform in the New England Renaissance* (New Haven: Yale University Press, 1959), pp. 98-136. See also Philip F. Gura, "Theodore Parker and the South Boston Ordination: The Textual Tangle of *A Discourse on the Transient and Permanent in Christianity,*" *SAR* 1988: 149-60, and Dean Grodzins, "The Transient and Permanent in Theodore Parker's Christianity, 1832-1841," *The Proceedings of the Unitarian-Universalist Historical Society* 22, part 1 (1990-1991): 1-18.

12. Journal "I," p. 101.

13. Emerson to Parker, 6 April, 11 May 1842, *L* 3:44, 54. Before *The Dial* ended, Emerson wrote that he did not "like to put it in the hands of the Humanity and Reform Men, because they trample on letters & poetry; nor in the hands of the Scholars, for they are dead & dry" (entry for 20 March 1842, *JMN* 8:203). Parker belonged to both of these camps.

14. On Cranch, see F. DeWolfe Miller, *Christopher Pearse Cranch and His Caricatures of New England Transcendentalism* (Cambridge: Harvard University Press, 1951), p. 130-31; Joel Myerson, "Transcendentalism and Unitarianism in 1840: A New Letter by C. P. Cranch," *CLA Journal* 16 (March 1973): 366-68.

15. Andrews did preach at least twice to Parker's congregation in the early 1840s (Dean Grodzins and Joel Myerson, eds., "The Preaching Record of Theodore Parker," *SAR* 1994: 81, 85).

16. Ellis was not on any of Parker's lists of ministers willing to exchange with him. In 1842, he noted Ellis's criticism at a meeting of the Boston Association (Journal "I," p. 256).

17. A month before the South Boston Sermon, four years after leaving Cambridge, Parker tested out his ideas on the knowledge of God in a long letter to Silsbee (Parker to William Silsbee, 23 April 1841, copy, Parker Papers, Massachusetts Historical Society; partially reprinted in Weiss, 1:166-67).

18. Parker to William Silsbee, 1 January 1842, copy, Parker Papers, Massachusetts Historical Society.

19. Entry for 22 December 1842, Journal "I," p. 234.

20. Grodzins and Myerson, eds., "Preaching Record of Theodore Parker," p. 88.

21. For Cyrus Bartol, see William R. Hutchison, "'To Heaven in a Swing': The Transcendentalism of Cyrus Bartol," *Harvard Theological Review* 56 (October 1963): 275-95. West Roxbury's proximity to Brook Farm allowed Parker to continue his intimacy with Ripley and others (see Charles Crowe, *George Ripley: Transcendentalist and Utopian Socialist* [Athens: University of Georgia Press, 1967], pp. 157-58), but Brook Farm was short-lived and the Brook Farmers were in retreat from the Unitarian world Parker still inhabited.

22. Brownson's phrase, quoted in Arthur M. Schlesinger, Jr., *A Pilgrim's Progress: Orestes A. Brownson* (1939; Boston: Little, Brown, 1966), p. 149.

23. The letter was written on 9 June 1842 but not mailed until 12 June (O. B. Frothingham, *Memoir of William Henry Channing* [Boston: Houghton Mifflin, 1886], pp. 173, 176).

24. Parker had recently begun corresponding with Emerson, but their letters were devoted almost entirely to *Dial* business.

25. Journal "I," p. 1.

26. Guy Woodall, ed., "The Journals of Convers Francis, Part Two," *SAR* 1982: 255.

27. Convers Francis to Parker, 30 June 1841, copy, Parker Papers, Massachusetts Historical Society.

28. Woodall, ed., "Journals of Convers Francis," p. 256.

29. Parker to Convers Francis, 14 February 1842, Boston Public Library.

30. Parker to Convers Francis, [5? February 1842], Boston Public Library.

31. Journal "I," p. 157.

32. On the state of the Harvard Divinity School, see Conrad Wright, "The Early Period," in *The Harvard Divinity School: Its Place in Harvard University and American Culture,* ed. George Hunston Williams (Boston: Beacon, 1956), pp. 21-28, and Gary L. Collison, "'A True Toleration': Harvard Divinity School Students and Unitarianism, 1830-1859," in *American Unitarianism, 1805-1865,* ed. Conrad Edick Wright (Boston: Massachusetts Historical Society and Northeastern University Press, 1989), pp. 209-13.

33. Parker to Convers Francis, 3 July 1842, Boston Public Library.

34. Quoted in Ronald Vale Wells, *Three Christian Transcendentalists* (New York: Columbia University Press, 1943), p. 205.

35. The exchange had taken place on 13 June 1841 (Grodzins and Myerson, eds., "Preaching Record of Theodore Parker," p. 81).

36. Convers Francis to Parker, 10 June 1842, Andover-Harvard Theological Library, pasted into Parker's Journal "I," p. 176.

37. Perry Miller, *The Transcendentalists: An Anthology* (Cambridge: Harvard University Press, 1950), p. 63. Although he reprinted a Transcendental-sounding passage from Francis's writings, Miller added almost spitefully that "in the light of his character, this hymn to the inward powers of the soul . . . is not to be taken too seriously."

38. Entry for 25 June 1842, Woodall, ed., "Journals of Convers Francis," p. 256.

39. Entry for 23 July 1842, Woodall, ed., "Journals of Convers Francis," p. 257.

40. Parker to Convers Francis, 5 May 1842, Boston Public Library.

41. Francis, *Christianity as a Purely Internal Principle* (Boston: Leonard C. Bowles, 1836), pp. 14-15. This sermon, originally written in 1831, does argue for the authority of intuitive religious experience and it condemns attachment to ecclesiastical custom, but Francis treats these issues as if they began and ended with the individual. In the second half of the sermon, Francis advances an essentially conservative social-ecclesiastical policy.

42. This challenge, as Mary Kupiec Cayton has recently noted, had "tortured" not only Emerson but many other young clergymen (*Emerson's Emergence: Self and Society in the Transformation of New England, 1800-1845* [Chapel Hill: University of North Carolina Press, 1989], p. 125).

43. Parker, "The Transient and Permanent in Christianity," in Conrad Wright, ed., *Three Prophets of Religious Liberalism: Channing—Emerson—Parker* (Boston: Beacon Press, 1961), p. 149.

44. Parker to Convers Francis, 18 [March 1843], Boston Public Library.

45. Parker to Convers Francis, 9 February 1839, Boston Public Library.

46. Convers Francis to Parker, 6 March 1839, copy, Parker Papers, Massachusetts Historical Society.

47. Convers Francis to Parker, 9 September 1841, copy, Parker Papers, Massachusetts Historical Society.

48. Theodore Parker, [*The Centenary Edition of the Works of Theodore Parker,*] 15 vols. (Boston: American Unitarian Association, 1907-12), 4:103, 123-24.

49. Myerson, "Calendar," p. 206.

50. Entry for 1-2 Sept. [1840], Journal "N," p. 442.

51. Grodzins and Myerson, eds., "Preaching Record of Theodore Parker," p. 87. The note, in pencil, was added at some later point, but perhaps within a few days. Parker also noted that he had secured Frederick A. Whitney as a last minute substitute.

52. Entry for 12 June [1842], Journal "I," p. 176.

53. Entry for 15 June [1842], Journal "I," p. 177. Parker's bitterness toward Francis was undoubtedly intensified by disappointment at the vacillating of William Henry Channing at this time.

54. Entry for 18 June 1842, Journal "I," p. 180.

55. Entry for [October? 1842], Journal "I," p. 210.

56. Parker to Convers Francis, 24 June 1842, Boston Public Library.

57. Parker to Convers Francis, 9 August 1842, Boston Public Library.

58. Parker to Convers Francis, 18 [February 1843], Boston Public Library.

59. *Christian Register,* 29 July 1843.

60. Francis preached for Parker on 13 August 1843, a few months before Parker left for a year in Europe (Grodzins and Myerson, eds., "Preaching Record of Theodore Parker," p. 88). During the

European trip, Francis filled Parker's pulpit an un-known number of times, though this arrangement did not come about without some additional fric-tion. Originally Francis declined taking charge of filling Parker's West Roxbury pulpit, prompting Parker to record their conversation in the journal and to remark angrily, "If Dr. Convers Francis be not a rotten stick—then there is none in the world." Later Parker returned to this entry to add in pencil, "He *did preach* for me part of the time of the absence" (Journal "I," pp. 176, 210). The last time Francis preached for Parker was 11 Janu-ary 1846, shortly before Parker resigned from his West Roxbury pulpit to devote himself to the new 28th Congregational Society ("Sermon Record," p. 54).

61. Parker, "A sermon of my own stewardship," Ser-mon #338, Theodore Parker collection, Andover-Harvard Theological Library.

62. Parker, "Experience as a Minister, with Some Ac-count of His Early Life and Preparation for the Ministry," in Rufus Leighton, ed., *Autobiography, Poems, and Prayers,* vol. 13 of the Centenary Edi-tion of the Works of Theodore Parker, p. 321.

63. Parker to George Ripley, 13 May 1859, Ripley Papers, Massachusetts Historical Society. The lan-guage Parker used to refer to the man's advice were the exact words of Francis (see Parker to Francis, 14 February 1842, Boston Public Library).

64. Shortly after the Divinity School Address, Emer-son had written, "all that befalls me in the way of criticism & extreme blame & praise drawing me out of equilibrium—putting me for a time in false position to people, & disallowing the spontaneous sentiments, wastes my time, bereaves me of thoughts, & shuts me up within poor personal con-siderations" (entry for 8 September 1838, *JMN* 7:65).

65. See Cayton, pp. 207-10.

66. Emerson's anger, as in the Divinity School Ad-dress, is double distilled. At bottom, much of the Address grew out of Emerson's intense dissatis-faction with young Concord minister Barzillai Frost, as Conrad Wright has shown in "Emerson, Barzillai Frost, and the Divinity School Address," in his *The Liberal Christians: Essays on American Unitarian History* (Boston: Unitarian Universalist Association, 1970), pp. 41-61.

67. Entry for 5 October 1842, Journal "I," p. 208.

68. Some time after Parker made up his list of ten in December (but probably within three or four months) he went back to mark four of the names as questionable (22 December 1842, Journal "I," p. 234).

69. For Putnam, see Journal "I," pp. 218, 233. Lam-son had declined to exchange shortly after the South Boston Sermon (Journal "I," p. 101).

70. Parker to Convers Francis, 24 June 1842, Boston Public Library.

71. Parker to Convers Francis, 24 June 1842, Boston Public Library.

72. See Roderick Stuart French, "Liberation from Man and God in Boston: Abner Kneeland's Free-Thought Campaign, 1830-1839," *American Quar-terly* 32 (1980): 202-21; and Robert E. Burkholder, "Emerson, Kneeland, and the Divinity School Ad-dress," *American Literature* 58 (March 1986): 1-14.

73. Brownson had practically been recruited by George Ripley for this work (Ripley to Brownson, 26 March 1834, in Henry F. Brownson, *Orestes A. Brownson's Early Life: From 1803-1844* [Detroit: H. F. Brownson, 1898], pp. 104-06).

74. For Clarke, Brownson, and the Unitarian "Church of the Future" movement, see Chapter 5 of Hutchi-son, *The Transcendentalist Ministers, pp. 137-89.*

75. Attendance was low for what one of the organiz-ers called "peculiar reasons" (William Eddy to Parker, 14 March 1842, copy, Parker Papers, Mas-sachusetts Historical Society).

76. Entry for 25 February 1843, Journal "I," p. [262]; Convers Francis to Frederic Henry Hedge, 24 January 1843, in "The Record of a Friendship: The Letters of Convers Francis to Frederic Henry Hedge in Bangor and Providence, 1835-1850," ed. Guy Woodall, *SAR* 1991: 45.

77. Elizabeth Peabody to John Sullivan Dwight, [10 June 1841], *The Letters of Elizabeth Peabody: American Renaissance Woman,* ed. Bruce Ronda (Middletown, Conn.: Wesleyan University Press, 1984), p. 253.

78. For his part, Parker himself helped create the *sense* of isolation by burying himself in work on the *Discourse* and De Wette and his myriad other projects.

Abbreviations

CW   *The Collected Works of Ralph Waldo Emer-son.* Edited by Alfred R. Ferguson et al. 5 vols. to date. Cambridge: Harvard Univ. Press, 1971-.

ECE   *Emerson Centenary Essays.* Edited by Joel Myerson. Carbondale and Edwardsville: Southern Illinois Univ. Press, 1982.

EL   *The Early Lectures of Ralph Waldo Emerson.* Edited by Stephen E. Whicher, Robert E. Spiller, and Wallace E. Williams. 3 vols. Cambridge: Harvard Univ. Press, 1959-72.

JMN   *The Journals and Miscellaneous Notebooks of Ralph Waldo Emerson.* Edited by William H. Gilman et al. 16 vols. Cambridge: Harvard Univ. Press, 1960-82.

L   *The Letters of Ralph Waldo Emerson.* Vols. 1-6 edited by Ralph L. Rusk; vols. 7-10 edited by Eleanor M. Tilton. New York: Columbia Univ. Press, 1939, 1990-95.

SAR   *Studies in the American Renaissance: An Annual.* Edited by Joel Myerson. Boston: Twayne, 1977-82; Charlottesville: Univ. Press of Virginia, 1983-96.

Sermons   *The Complete Sermons of Ralph Waldo Emerson.* Edited by Albert J. von Frank et al. 4 vols. Columbia: Univ. of Missouri Press, 1989-92.

TN   *The Topical Notebooks of Ralph Waldo Emerson.* 3 vols. Edited by Susan Sutton Smith, Ronald A. Bosco, and Glen M. Johnson. Columbia: Univ. of Missouri Press, 1990-94.

W   *The Complete Works of Ralph Waldo Emerson.* Edited by Edward Waldo Emerson. 12 vols. Centenary Edition. Boston: Houghton Mifflin, 1903-04.

Elizabeth Hurth (essay date 1999)

SOURCE: Hurth, Elizabeth. "From Idealism to Atheism: Theodore Parker and Ludwig Feuerbach." *Journal of Unitarian Universalist History* 26 (1999): 18-46.

[*In the following essay, Hurth describes Parker's approach to the humanist, atheist views of Ludwig Feuerbach as well as the responses of Parker's fellow Universalist and Transcendentalist thinkers.*]

In July 1854, the English author George Eliot published her translation of a book about which she was "entirely without hope." The press, she expected, "will do nothing but abuse or ridicule it"[1] The book was Ludwig Feuerbach's epoch-making *Das Wesen des Christenthums* ("The Essence of Christianity"), which was first published in Germany in June 1841 and quickly earned its author celebrity status. With its anthropologizing of theology, Feuerbach's bestseller struck a raw nerve in theological discourse. Religion, Feuerbach asserted, is a "dream of the human mind." It is a projection of man as a species-being; that is, of man as an expression of "essential" human properties—love, reason and will—that go beyond the boundaries of "individuality."[2] God originates in the mind of man as a "compensation for

the poverty of life" and has no foundation in reality outside and "separate from the existence of man." He is the pure "subjectivity of man," the "expressed self of man" and can no longer be regarded as "objective." Hence the "consciousness of God" is the "self-consciousness of man." But, according to Feuerbach, this fact is ignored in man's attempts to create a separate image of God. Man does not realize that the images he projects out into "objectivity" are only images of his own species-nature. Thus he is alienated from his true self. The "progress of religion" is accordingly linked to the dismantling of this division of God and man: "[W]hat by an earlier religion was regarded as objective, is now recognized as subjective; that is what was formerly contemplated and worshiped as God is now perceived to be something *human*."[3] The metaphysical object of faith was thus eliminated. Man merely objectifies himself in religion.

The author of this projection theory of religion was, as Eliot observed in the preface to *The Essence of Christianity,* an impassioned philosopher who dealt with man's concrete, material reality and downgraded conceptual thought in favor of the "senses, especially sight." Feuerbach had studied theology at Heidelberg University, then transferred to Berlin University, where he came under the influence of Hegel. After publishing a treatise that denied the concept of personal immortality, Feuerbach was denied tenure at the University of Erlangen and forced to lead a life of private study. His prophetic and polemical intentions were addressed to "universal" man and designed to "become the common property of mankind."[4] But when it came to English audiences, Feuerbach's populist aspirations failed. From the outset, both liberal and orthodox camps castigated the book as yet another outcome of the "new Hegelian Atheism."[5] Yet on the whole, the furor Feuerbach caused on his native ground was not met with comparable publicity in England. There, the "lady translator" did not receive any financial reward or public recognition for her skilled work, and was supposed to be just as impious as the German Hegelian "infidel." Eliot, it was suspected, had simply allied herself with the cause of "rank Atheism."[6]

George Eliot was impressed most by Feuerbach's humanitarian morality and confessed, "With the ideas of Feuerbach I everywhere agree."[7] New England readers of Eliot's translation did not. The book attracted negative responses from almost every quarter of religious New England. Reviewing the translation for the orthodox *Bibliotheca Sacra* in 1857, the Congregationalist minister Charles C. Tiffany denounced Feuerbach's book for its attempt to "destroy every religious fabric."[8] In similar terms, Noah Porter, writing for the Congregationalist *New Englander,* connected Feuerbach's atheistic humanism with a "new Infidelity" that played havoc with Christian faith.[9] Robert Turnbull, minister of the Baptist congregation in Hartford, Connecticut, identified Feuerbach's position as a "godless humanism" that "rolls turbidly to the abyss."[10] Unitarian reviewers pronounced the same verdict and reprimanded Feuerbach for his "[a]theistic [n]ihilism."[11]

The hostile reactions Feuerbach elicited in New England were even more pronounced from alleged Unitarian radicals. Curiously, Feuerbach left "New School" Unitarians like George Ripley as concerned as "Old School" representatives like Andrews Norton. While Norton denounced the left-wing Hegelians for their impiety and atheism, Ripley attacked Feuerbach for his materialism and rejected his philosophy as part of an intellectualized system that attacked the "power of spiritual ideas."[12] Ripley's fellow Transcendentalist Amos Bronson Alcott also stopped well short of sympathy for the alleged atheist. Alcott had close personal contact with members of the St. Louis Philosophical Society, which counted Feuerbach as an "auxiliary" or "out of town" member.[13] In 1879, Alcott became the nominal head of the Concord School of Philosophy, where for years Hegelians like William Torrey Harris drew on Feuerbach and other left-wing theologians to contribute to the "progress in Speculative philosophy in Mass[achusetts]."[14] Yet Alcott was not ready to follow Harris and his "German Atheists." "Nothing profound or absolute" was to be expected "from minds . . . if not hostile, at least indifferent to and incapable of idealism: naturalists rather than metaphysicians."[15] A leading member of the younger and supposedly more radical generation of the New School, the Free Religionist Octavius B. Frothingham, also shrank from close association with the German atheist and finally came under the spell of the French historian Ernest Renan's negative verdict on Feuerbach. In 1864, this verdict became more accessible when Frothingham published his translation of Renan's *Studies of Religious History and Criticism.* Renan's work included an essay on the Young Hegelians which transmitted a theological critique of Feuerbach's philosophy of religion that sealed his reputation as a godless, speculative intellectual whose materialism and atheistic humanism rejected religious faith as such.[16]

And yet, as the example of Theodore Parker shows, Feuerbach could be of use. German exiles like Emmanuel V. Scherb had alerted Parker to the extensive influence of Feuerbachian atheism long before Eliot's translation made *The Essence of Christianity* available in English. In December 1852, Parker described in his journal the atheist's "*dreadful scheme*:—a Body without a soul, an Earth without a Heaven, a Universe without a God."[17] Parker's sermons on **Theism, Atheism and the Popular Theology,** first published in 1853, show that he found important challenges and resources in this "scheme." Parker used Feuerbach's antitheological polemics as a welcome weapon to attack the anthropomorphic deity of the "popular theology" of his time.[18] If the church preached a God set up by formal proof, then, Parker judged, atheism was in order. Athe-

ists, Parker emphasized, are often made such by oppressive "ecclesiastical" doctrines, and "[a]ll the way from Greek Epicurus to German Feuerbach, it is the follies taught in the name of God that have driven men to atheism" (4:355, 354).

Parker also put Feuerbach's position to work for his concept of "absolute religion." Parker set this concept over against theological Christianity, arguing that absolute religion is not based on external authority, whether ecclesiastical or biblical, but rather "belongs to man's nature." It is the desire to be in harmony with the "infinitely perfect God . . . immanent in the world of matter and in the world of spirit." In this cornerstone of Parker's religious teaching a theological reorientation showed that turned God into a God "within" (13:330, 331-332, 336). This internalization of the religious consciousness cohered with several aspects of Feuerbach's religious humanism. The rejection of metaphysicalized theology, the elimination of the supernatural, and the emphasis on religious needs and aspirations—these propositions were all quite attractive to a New School prophet who sought to imbed religion in human nature. In terms similar to Feuerbach's critique of religion, Parker argued that religion sprang from natural desires, a "feeling of need, of want" (1:7). But Parker set up strong defenses against a reduction of religion to mere projection. Feuerbach's atheism, George Willis Cooke observed in his comments on Parker's famous sermon, **The Transient and Permanent in Christianity,** "interprets all religious beliefs as subjective in their nature, having no corresponding objective reality; in a word, as the expression of the desires of man" (4:469, n.5). For Parker, this position amounted to "utter irreligion," to the "denial of the actuality of any possible idea of God" (2:88, 4:354). Against this form of atheism, Parker firmly adhered to a basis for religious truth that answered to the reality of a spiritual realm. According to Parker, the "religious consciousness implie[d] its object." This object was not a product of man, but rather, Parker insisted, distinct from and independent of man (1:9).

At this juncture Parker's reception of Feuerbach has a valuable contribution to make. It provides a further demonstration of the commonality between the so-called Old and New School camps of New England Unitarianism. Contrary to cries of godlessness, the New School apostle Parker followed a marked general consensus among New England divines that precluded the interpretation of religion as illusory projection and affirmed instead the objective reference of the religious consciousness. When it came to objective religious belief, Parker, the alleged radical, was indistinguishable from his old-school intellectual peers and at one with the strong phalanx of opposition against the projection theory of religion.[19] On this issue, the whole spectrum of New School disciples, from the Transcendentalists to the Free Religionists, was more conservative than is commonly assumed.

In May 1854, two months before Eliot's translation of *The Essence of Christianity* was published, Parker wrote to the German religious dissenter Johannes Ronge, who had established a church in London: "I am glad to find that you do not follow the lead of Feuerbach or of his coadjutors." Feuerbach was, Parker judged, the "Coryphaeus" of "atheistic men whose creed is . . . 'There is no God, Feuerbach is his prophet, a body but no soul; a here but no hereafter; a world and no God.'" (4:469, n.5). But although Parker explicitly rejected the nihilistic underpinnings of Feuerbach's position as destructive, his own concept of religion was suspected to border on Feuerbachian atheism. In Ripley's view, Parker's "absolute religion" came "dangerously close to an anthropological account of Christianity."[20] Orestes Brownson, the former Transcendentalist converted to Catholicism, went even further, charging that Parker's "theology became simply anthropology" and "reduc[ed] all religion to . . . atheism" (5:152, 153).

This criticism was quite different from the charges of "infidelity" that Parker had to face after preaching his sermon on *The Transient and Permanent in Christianity* (1841). Those who labeled Parker an "infidel" and "unbeliever" read his attack on the "transient" forms of Christianity, and in particular on what he saw as the exaggerated claims of authority for the Bible, as an attack on religion itself (13:324). The charge of infidelity here referred primarily to the denial of an "outward revelation" as "extrinsic, derived and super-induced."[21] New School infidelity entailed faith in an inner revelation, one based on the "voice of God in the soul of man" (13:291). From this "new" revelation, conservative Unitarians charged, issued the Transcendentalists' disbelief in "historical Christianity," their denial of the principle that truth was an index of the evidentiary appeal of facts, in particular of miraculous evidence. "The rejection of all that mass of evidence, which . . . establishes the truth of . . . religion" amounted for Andrews Norton to a "rejection of Christianity, . . . the denial that God revealed himself by Christ."[22]

But for Ripley and above all for Brownson, Parker was guilty of a very different kind of infidelity, one which submerged the "object of worship" and thus evinced its completely "anti-religious" signature (5:151, 153). For Brownson, there was a gulf between Parker's anthropological "scheme of theology" and Christian faith (7:269). This gulf not only pertained, as R. W. Lewis indicated in *The American Adam* (1955), to the opposition between Brownson's supernaturalism and Parker's absolute separation of religion and history.[23] The gulf was deeper and wider than that. Parker's anthropological scheme questioned not only the evidences of histori-

cal Christianity but also the object of faith itself, and thus resulted in an atheistic interpretation of religion that Brownson diagnosed as "pure nullism" and "psychologism" (2:482, 3:40).

In this context, Parker's reception of Feuerbach takes on added value and sheds light on a largely overlooked critique of Transcendentalism, one less concerned with the New School's rejection of historical Christianity and more focused on its threat to religion in general. Parker's reception of Feuerbach also clarifies in a novel way several important aspects of the atheist argument that undergirded the rise of Transcendentalism. Feuerbach's atheism eradicated the objective reference of religion and came to stand for a new anthropocentricity that dissolved the divine in man. This sort of "atheism" however, was reached independently in Transcendentalist thought on the basis of an extreme subjective idealism that Brownson and his conservative intellectual peers identified with the German idealist Johann G. Fichte's philosophy of the self.[24] That transcendental idealism already latently harbored Feuerbach's apotheosis of man becomes evident in the discussions about the "atheistical" tendencies underlying Parker's concept of "absolute religion" (13:324-325). Significantly, a recurrent theme of the charges against Parker was that his idealism became vulnerable to an "ego-theism" and "soul-worship."[25] Anticipating the arguments orthodox critics leveled against Feuerbach, Brownson and the Broad Church men Frederic Henry Hedge and James Freeman Clarke charged that Parker advocated a self-worship that reduced God to a function of the human mind. The transcendental idealist thus seemed prone to an anthropotheistic viewpoint in which man became his own object of thought. In Feuerbach's atheistic humanism the necessary outcome of this anthropotheism came to the fore.

Insofar as Parker, the prophet of "absolute religion," was made a part of the anthropocentric guild, the controversy about his atheistical tendencies is largely consistent with the charges Feuerbach had to face. The discussion, in the 1840s and '50s, of Parker's alleged latent atheism is part of an intellectual dialogue that began much earlier and that culminated, according to the great twentieth-century theologian Karl Barth, in theology becoming a kind of anthropology. For Barth, the Feuerbachian position had haunted the theological scene "ever since Protestantism itself, and especially Luther, emphatically shifted the interest from what God is in himself to what God is for man." Feuerbach's anthropocentric position, Barth maintained, demonstrated poignantly that those who defined religion through "determination[s] of human self-consciousness" were bound to be led to an "apotheosis of man." According to Barth, all schools of thought starting from this perspective suffered from one serious defect: They endorsed a concept of religion and theology based on man's subjective states. Feuerbach's "god is man" appeared to Barth as the conclusion of this theological process of grounding theology in an analysis of human experience—a conclusion which, according to Barth, continued to be "a thorn in the flesh of modern theology."[26]

This conclusion underlay the charge of "atheism" that followed Parker throughout his career as a minister, preacher, and scholar, even though Parker himself utterly rejected this charge. The Feuerbachian conclusion here became a "thorn in the flesh" that troubled in particular the critics of the extreme forms of Transcendentalism. Those who stepped outside the intuitionist approach, like the converted Brownson, acutely sensed that the Transcendentalist elevation of self-reliant man was itself susceptible to the "inversion [of] heaven and earth." And, just as Barth looked back on nineteenth-century liberal theology as having "run right into the arms" of atheistic humanism, so conservative Transcendentalists saw this danger ahead of them. Feuerbach's atheism, as Barth interpreted it, was the natural outcome of a theological trend whose focus on "self-sufficient humanity" marked the Achilles heel of modern theology.[27] Similarly, the critics of Transcendentalism sensed that the extreme idealism of the so-called Parkerites would lead the New School down the path of an anthropotheism that made atheism inevitable. From idealism to atheism seemed but a short step.

I

In the May 1850 issue of the *Christian Examiner*, Samuel Osgood described the theological positions from Friedrich Schleiermacher to David Friedrich Strauss, including the supernaturalist, the rationalist, and the so-called Hegelian. The Hegelian position, Osgood observed, was dominated by the synthesis between philosophy and theology within a "speculative" framework. According to Osgood, the very latest period in "modern ecclesiastical history" witnessed a dissolution of this framework into right and left wings. On the far left end of the spectrum, Osgood located Feuerbach's "utter atheism" which led out of Christian faith entirely and marked for Osgood a culmination in the atheistic speculations by German theorists. Prior to Feuerbach, Osgood observed, atheism had commonly been discussed in an evidentialist context determined by the equation of truth with fact.[28] This equation proceeded on the assumption that "there is . . . [a] mode of establishing religious belief . . . by forming a probable judgement upon facts." A "truth," Andrews Norton declared in his *Discourse on the Latest Form of Infidelity* (1839), is an expression of a "fact." Facts thus understood implied data, miraculous evidences verifying the existence of God. To deny that the essence of Christianity was based on this body of evidence was to follow the lead of atheism.[29] In Feuerbach's approach to the essence of Christianity, a new form of atheism showed that eclipsed the theistic object altogether.

As regards the impact of this atheistic humanism on New England soil, there soon evolved a narrative line that approached Feuerbach's *Essence of Christianity* vis-à-vis the theological threat posed by David Friedrich Strauss's notorious *Life of Jesus* (1835). In this reading, Feuerbach was identified as a "co-laborer" of Strauss, and his theory of the illusory origin of religion was paralleled with the historico-critical question raised by Strauss's dissolution of the Gospel accounts into myths.[30] Similar readings were legion in the literature of the nineteenth century, and not just in New England, as is indicated by the interpretations of Ernest Renan and the English Unitarian James Martineau, both of whom viewed Feuerbach primarily in terms of Strauss's left-wing Hegelianism. Thus Renan insisted that the "criticism of the skies" launched by the "new Hegelian school" under Strauss against "anything transcendental" reached its most powerful expression in Feuerbach.[31] This interpretation, all too prevalent in the criticism of the period, persists in modern criticism. The most recent example of this interpretative model, Mark Y. Hanley's *Beyond a Christian Commonwealth* (1994), establishes a continuity between Strauss's myth criticism and Feuerbach's shift from theology to anthropology. While Strauss read the Gospel stories as "myths" created by the pious imagination of the early church, Feuerbach pushed this demythologization to the point of reducing religion to a projection of human fears and aspirations. According to Hanley, this "antireligious sentiment" fed into a politically-centered ethical rationalism that "could draw fire from its anti-orthodox roots by claiming the mantle of American liberty as its own."[32]

Parker's reading of Feuerbach, by contrast, suggests another line of argument. Parker assigned Feuerbach a special place in the spectrum of atheist positions and associated him with "speculative" rather than politically motivated atheism.[33] Feuerbach's atheism, moreover, was perceived to be far more destructive than the supposed atheism of Strauss. Samuel Osgood, in describing modern ecclesiastical history, observed that compared to Feuerbach, Strauss appeared almost outmoded: "[T]he men on the left have gone so far as to throw Strauss quite into the shade, as a tame conservative."[34] *The Life of Jesus* seemed harmless in comparison to *The Essence of Christianity* and the author of this new atheism was not to be mistaken for another Strauss.

Parker could not agree more. Strauss's *Life of Jesus*, Parker observed in an 1840 review for the *Christian Examiner*, presented an attempt to put Christianity on a more solid basis both historically and dogmatically and thus secured the philosophical truth of Christian faith. Although Strauss set out to uncover the Gospel accounts as "spurious" and "unauthentic," he left the "essence" of Christianity unassailed and granted that there is an objective core underlying religious statements.[35] But Parker later judged that Feuerbach, the "speculative atheist," took Strauss's position a step further, out of historical criticism into materialism and out of Christianity into anthropology. By conceiving God as a function or "dream" of the human mind, a speculative atheist like Feuerbach moved beyond the historical question at issue in Strauss's alleged atheism (2:81). Feuerbach started with the psychological basis of religion and maintained that in religious worship no supernatural object of adoration was involved. For the speculative atheist, Parker observed, "[t]here is no God, all possible ideas thereof lack actuality" (2:152). As Parker acutely realized, this atheism involved much more than a dismantling of historical faith, for the speculative atheist questioned not only the historical truth of Christian dogma but religion "as a whole" (2:99).[36] He classed Feuerbach with the French positivist August Comte in a special atheistic camp completely removed from spiritual religion (14:180-181).

In his sermons on *Theism, Atheism and the Popular Theology*, Parker discusses in detail the "effects" of speculative atheism (2:66ff), which he delineates using Feuerbach's formulas ("There is no God," "A soul without a body"). Over the course of his sermons, Parker mentions prominent thinkers suspected of denying God's existence, such as Epicurus, Celsus, Pietro Pomponatius, and George Sand. What distinguished an atheist like Feuerbach was, according to Parker, his categorical and "absolute denial of any and all forms of God." Feuerbach thus evinced himself as a representative of "real speculative atheism" that denies the "*genus* God, . . . the actuality of all possible ideas of God" (2:62, 64, 65).

In Parker's view, speculative atheism deals a blow to all previous conceptions of God. It rejects the religious concept of God as an independent being and expressly denies spiritual transcendence. On this point, Parker imagines an atheist speaking: "I am a philosopher, . . . I have been up to the sky and there is no heaven. . . . I have been through the universe, and there is no God. God is a whim of men." (2:74). Man, then, does not participate in a divine truth. There is no "faculty" available to man which would enable him to obtain a transcendent perspective on the world. Transcendence presents only an immanent process of human experience. For the "real speculative atheist," Parker observes, there is nothing above and beyond man and, therefore, no "spiritual order." "[T]here are only finite things,—each self-originated, self-sustained, self-directed,—and no more" (2:80, 65).

In the atheistic framework all authority above man was asserted to be a "fancy," a self-conception of human nature itself. In his references to "God," man is not dealing with a transcendent objective reality. For the atheist, writes Parker, "God is not a fact of the universe." All belief in him is an illusion, a "dream." "Man has a no-

tion of God, as of a ghost, or devil; but it is a pure subjective fancy" (2:62, 74). God, then, is nothing but the product of subjective wants—"something which [man] has spun out of his brain." God *is* only in man's fancies, "for there is nothing in the universe to correspond thereto. Man has an idea of God, but the universe has no fact of God" (2:62).

Parker clearly spelled out the consequences of these ideas. The speculative atheist, he observed, torpedoes the meaning of religion itself. He not only denies the "quality of God under all names" but also postulates that religion is essentially self-referential. God is a pseudo-realization, a "mere whimsey of men" (2:62, 88). This theory of religious delusion, Parker judged, ultimately "negat[es] religion as a whole." Religion serves "only the cold, thin atmosphere of fancy" and degenerates into "empty" circular worship (2:82, 83, 99). There cannot be a single being beyond human "essence." Man is self-sufficient, hence all worship is self-worship and the only belief, atheism.

In his rebuttal of speculative atheism, Parker appeals to a "foundation" designed to protect religion from the charge of illusory projection. Parker presents the "foundation of religion . . . [as] deep within" man. Religion in this sense is "natural to man"; it is an "instinct," an impulse of human nature that provides evidence of the existence of God. This evidence appeals to something expressly precluded in the atheist's system, namely an intuitive mode of perception that enables man to apprehend a larger "spiritual providence" (2:80, 85, 86). There are, Parker was convinced, "spiritual faculties" in the soul that make "man turn to God" (2:86). The "evidence of God has been ploughed into nature," he writes; it is "deeply woven into the texture of the human soul" (2:85). Using the terms of Schleiermacher's theology of religious experience, Parker thus established a correspondence between the "essence" of Christianity and the "religious sentiment" that was not to be resolved into a "whim." Religion, Parker averred with Schleiermacher, is not something to be "known" or "made"; rather, it is a feeling of absolute dependence upon God. Religion thus understood yields the "true" idea of God and provides certainty.

From this perspective, the existence of God is a given, founded "on the spontaneous teachings of the religious sentiment" (2:170). The innate religious sentiment makes transcendent reality accessible to man. In his *Discourse of Matters Pertaining to Religion* (1842; 1854), Parker did not offer stringent criteria for identifying this realm "beyond," but he was convinced that it existed. The "substance" of religion is "permanent" in man and validated, Parker explained, by the "connection between the divine and human life" (1:ix; 4:206). Religion, then, is not a dream or human whimsy. There is a spiritual reality of religious truth grounded in enduring facts of consciousness. Religion "can never fail"; it "is ever the same, and its years shall have no end" (1:11, 435).

II

Writing to Theodore Parker in 1852, George Ripley belittled Feuerbach's "atheistical theory" as a speciality of the "confirmed system-lover."[37] In Ripley's view, "the reign of authoritative dogmatic systems ha[d] never been firmly established over the mind of [the American] nation: every exclusive faith . . . called forth a host of dissent."[38] What Feuerbach offered came, according to Ripley, unmistakably from the same "dogmatic" mold. The abstract systematician Feuerbach therefore offered for Ripley "no point of contact with the American mind." He was simply too "crabbed and dogmatic in his atheism."[39]

Parker, however, was ready to enlist the chief "prophet" of atheism into his own cause. Parker sought to dispose of the supernatural foundation of religion by appealing to a "permanent" religious sentiment in man for which Feuerbach's account of the origin of religion offered a helpful springboard. Religion, Parker was convinced, springs from "instinctive desires" and emotional needs. Therefore it "must agree with . . . natural sentiments" and not with doctrinal notions (2:70, 151). Grounded in human spiritual wants, religion is independent of all external authority, the "transient" forms and doctrines of Christianity. The "transient" forms embodied in doctrinal and ecclesiastical worship "hinder . . . religious development" and are incompatible with an internalized religion that "agrees" with "spontaneous intuitions of the true, . . . the holy" (2:151; 13:322).

At this juncture, Feuerbach spoke to Parker in just the antidogmatic tone that served Parker's purposes. For Feuerbach, the predicates attributed to God are derived from man's own nature. Feuerbach in this way presents a religion *of* man and traces its origin and function back to human "wishes of the heart." Religious beliefs stem from innate human needs and care. Religion is therefore located in feeling rather than in thought. The truth of religious facts is constituted not by the application of dogmatic principles but by their correspondence with man's desires and imagination.[40] This experiential approach to religion was particularly congenial to Parker, a disciple of "newness" who attacked Unitarian orthodoxy as emotionally cold and rejected a religion he saw as stifled with abstract creeds and forms. Religion was to Feuerbach what Parker thought it had really been all along, namely a spontaneous affair of the heart. The chief subject of Feuerbach's critique of religion, theological illusion, was irreconcilable with Parker's spiritual philosophy. But what appealed to him was Feuerbach's psychogenetic interest in religion and his attempt to approach religious truth anthropologically. Religion

thus emerged as a gratification of human emotions and had a distinctly involuntary and unconscious signature. On this point, Parker expressly eulogized Feuerbach for "confess[ing] to the natural religious emotions" and for "giv[ing] them sure place in all human affairs" (14:181).

Feuerbach's experiential view of religion also lent itself to Parker's battle against the so-called "popular theology" of Christendom, and its distortion of the religion of the heart. Prior to Feuerbach, Parker's reviews of German studies had distinguished two overriding approaches in the theological domain: the "historico-critical" and the "speculative."[41] Feuerbach's work, however, could be classed with neither approach, for it translated theology into a secular discipline—anthropology. If religion proved to be nothing but wish-fulfillment, then theology was properly concerned only with concrete embodied human consciousness. The study of man thus replaced the study of God. From the perspective of anthropology, theology, the religion of the head, positing God as wholly other, was incompatible with the religion of the heart, which demanded a "human" God. In this opposition, theology appeared as an ill-fated attempt to establish God as a separate being and transform human attributes into metaphysical entities.

This rejection of the false notion of God created by theology was largely consistent with Parker's critique of the popular theology. In his polemics against this theology, Parker presents atheism like that of Feuerbach as a protest against the errors and defects of an oppressive ecclesiastical religion (2:135). In Parker's estimation, "[t]he atheist has abandoned religion because it is painted in such a form that it seems worse than atheism. The Church taught him his denial, and it ought to baptize him, and not blaspheme him" (2:167). For Parker, "atheism" in this context did not signal mere disbelief. It was not simply barren and destructive but rather "taught in the name of philosophy, in the name of man" (2:154). In this way, Feuerbach's atheism could come to pose a legitimitate response to a "tormenting" religion that "revolts the dearest instincts of human nature" (2:154, 163). In a thanks-giving sermon, Parker asserted that the "follies" committed for the sake of religion far outweighed the deficiencies of atheism: "All the attacks made on religion itself by men of science, from Celsus to Feuerbach, have not done so much to bring religion into contempt as a single persecution for witchcraft, or a Bartholomew massacre made in the name of God."[42]

In Parker's sermons on the **"Popular Theology of Christendom,"** there is further evidence that he found in Feuerbach's atheism a useful weapon in his fight against "ecclesiastical" theology. Parker here again plays atheism off against the popular theology; atheism appears as a legitimate reaction to a theology perpetuating the morbidities of Calvinism. "I think," Parker reiterates in provocative terms, "Calvin and Edwards have driven more men from religion than all the speculative 'atheists' have ever done from Pomponatius to Feuerbach" (2:167).

Parker directs his invectives against a repressive theological system centered around an arbitrary and essentially incomprehensible God. This God, forever hidden in a realm of incomprehensible mystery, makes man the "veriest wretch in creation." God's absolute sovereignty abases man to the point of fatalistic dependence. "God exploiters [sic] the human race" (2:150). He is an "angry God, jealous, capricious, selfish, and revengeful," who predestines some of his creatures to salvation and others to damnation (2:159). This "grim" God is for Parker the "worst foe to men," and uses helpless creatures to accomplish his objectives (2:150, 163). Human agency and free will are of no avail. The uncertainty and determinism of human life "makes man a worm: religion a torment to all but ten in a million" (2:188).

In the popular theology's "scheme of the universe" God predetermines everything; he wills not only damnation but also sin itself (2:135). For Parker, this notion of divine omnipotence and providence leads to a paralyzing faith. Man is at the mercy of an "angry," "malignant" God dealing vindictively with him in his arbitrary decrees (2:156). Faith is merely passive, witnessing what God has already done in Christ. Christ's sacrifice—"an atoning sacrifice to appease imaginary wrath"—marks man's remoteness from God, the infinite chasm between man, the "tormented," and God, the "tormentor" (2:154, 188).

At this point in his assault on the "popular theology," Parker calls Feuerbach back to the front line. For Parker, "[a]theism, even annihilation of the soul, would be a relief from such a Deity as that; from such an end" (2:154). Atheism is the lesser of two evils. "[W]hich is the worst," Parker asks rhetorically, "to believe that there is no God who is Mind, Cause, and Providence of this universe . . . ; or to believe there is a God who is almighty, yet omnipotently malignant, who consciously aims the forces of the universe at the wretched head of his own child?" (2:151) Atheism, Parker reiterates, is not just irreligion: "There is much excuse for the speculative atheist in his denial" of the existence of God (2:163). Writing to Johannes Ronge in May 1854, Parker explicity applied this "excuse" to Feuerbach and his disciples. "There are some Germans who accept him as their Coryphaeus. . . . They are much to be pitied—for the superstition of the church, with despotism of the state, has forced their noble natures into this sad conclusion" (4:469, n.5).

In his criticism of Jonathan Edwards's "dark" Calvinism, Parker puts this "conclusion" to use again. Parker castigates Edwards as the hellfire preacher responsible

for the promulgation of a horrifying "scheme of theology" (2:143). His Calvinism, Parker charges, relentlessly justifies God's punishment of man. Even worse, Edwards insists that man's sinful inclination acted as a catalyst of the sinister aspects of God. Edwards's God, Parker observes, traps man. All man wills and does stands under the signs of sin. Sin is inherent in the human condition and therefore inevitable. Man is "prone to wickedness" and so corrupted that he cannot be a correlate of God (2:142). He stands "totally depraved" before the "great jailer and hangman and tormentor of the universe." Edwards's system, Parker judges, thus affirms the cruel "tyrant" of Calvinist theology, the "divine exploiterer of the race" who "has the power to bless men, and prefers to curse them" (2:168, 169).

Parker's anti-Calvinist rationale issues once more in a positive appreciation of atheism. "The atheist is right in denying the existence of an angry and jealous God" (2:164). The repulsive doctrines of depravity, vicarious atonement, and predestination are far more horrifying than the threat of atheism. For Parker, this threat is not merely negative per se. On the contrary, at the heart of atheism is a positive intent: To deny "a portion of the popular Godhead" is to be "constructively an atheist," and in this respect the atheist "has been faithful to himself" (2:62, 152). In similar terms, Parker presents Feuerbach not as an impious heretic or a representative of "*Germanic* atheism," as Parker's audience may have assumed, but as a "faithful" critic of a corrupt religious system (14:180). The atheist Feuerbach, Parker emphasizes in his sermon on **"The Consequences of an Immoral Principle and False Idea of Life"** (1854), is without God, but he is not without religion. Feuerbach "called himself an atheist; and then is not so, in heart, only in head; it is the blood of pious humanity which runs in his nation's vein" (14:180). In fact, it even seemed to Parker that the speculative atheist was "much higher in [his] moral and religious growth" than the popular theologians (2:63).

When it came to the nihilistic consequences of pure speculative atheism, Parker made his opinion unmistakably clear. Speculative atheism, he judged, is "abhorrent" to man's spiritual nature (2:91). "The speculative atheism of Feuerbach analyzes Deity into the blind universe working from no love as motive, with no plan as method, for no purpose as ultimate end" (14:180). And yet, for all that, Parker respected the man behind atheistic philosophy. He perceived Feuerbach as someone who had come not to destroy religion but to rescue it from an inhuman Deity. In this context, atheism appeared as an effective weapon against "selfish" religious despotism (2:159). And here, no matter how nihilistic and destructive sheer atheism appeared to him, Parker had good use for Feuerbach to validate his own rejection of "popular theology." "The 'atheism' of . . . Feuerbach," Parker was convinced, "is higher and better than the theological idea of God, as represented by Jonathan Edwards, the great champion of New England divinity" (2:164).

III

Parker's complex relation to Feuerbach played into the hands of one of Parker's sharpest critics, namely the Catholic convert Orestes Brownson, who was not prepared to accept a rapturous type of transcendentalism marked by an atheistic eclipse of the object of faith. Anticipating the arguments directed against Feuerbach, Brownson described the underlying premises of this atheism in a review (1845) of Parker's *Discourse of Matters Pertaining to Religion.* "Mr. Parker," Brownson observed, defines religion as a "sentiment natural to man, that is, springing from man's nature" (6:12). In this "naturalism," Brownson charged, religion is "inward" to man and "exists in the facts of man's soul." But if there is only a "God *in* the soul" and no God "out of man," then, Brownson concluded, there is no God (6:8, 12, 13). [A]ll a man has to do" is to worship himself and to conform to "his own thoughts, tendencies and impulses." The "existence of God," then, is simply no longer necessary (6:12, 76).

That this form of atheistic soul-worship contributed decisively to Brownson's break with the Transcendentalist movement is evident from his autobiography, *The Convert* (1857), in which he sharply criticizes Parker. Brownson was convinced that the religious element in man had a basis from without. It was something outside of the "me," or the subject, and not the outcome of activity of the human mind. Parker, Brownson believed, made religion "purely subjective," a principle of human nature alone. He thus advocated a religion "which implies no God" (5:153). For Brownson, this atheism did not signal merely a rejection of "supernatural revelation" but rather the denial of an independent object of worship and, consequently, a rejection of religion "in toto" (7:269, 272).

The concept of the religious sentiment in man as the origin and ground of religion made, Brownson asserted, man the "measure" of all things and values (6:13). Religion becomes a predicate of man; it "rests for its authority . . . not on the veracity of God, but on the veracity of man" (6:2). From here, Brownson charged, issued another grand "defect" of Parker's Transcendentalism, namely a "naturalism" or "natural mysticism" that "exhorts" man to "sink [his] personality" in God (6:30, 31, 7:269). Parker thus identified divine and human natures and made man "indistinguishable" from God (6:95). On this point, Brownson saw Parker as just another advocate of Emersonian mystical Transcendentalism. To be sure, there were differences—Parker was not in "command" of his arguments, he did not have the "ease and grace" of Emerson—yet in the final analysis, both "systems" came for Brownson to the same thing: the "autotheism" of transcendental mania (6:30). Parker, Brownson observed, exalts the individual to identity with the divine. He "makes the man who . . . stands in the most immediate relation with absolute truth, beauty, and goodness, a sort of maniac" (6:27).

Brownson's quest for religious certitude expressly precluded such "direct communion" with God. God is "above" man, Brownson reiterated. Moreover, "God is uncreated, independent, infinite; man is created, dependent, finite" (6:48, 49). In religion, Brownson held, the relation between God and man is one between an object and a separate and distinct subject. The object of faith, then,—and this is Brownson's key maxim—must be sought outside man; it "must have . . . [a] foundation . . . [extrinsic] to the human mind" (6:61). For Brownson, the objective intuitionist, the denial of such an extrinsic foundation religion made the "eclipse of faith" inevitable and cleared the way for "intellectual atheists" who incorporate human attributes into a man-made God (2:5; 7:284).

That Parker, a professed critic of utter atheism, had to be counted among this camp was for Brownson not without irony. With his ill-fated attempt to "prove" the existence of God, Parker himself paved the road to atheism (6:71). For Parker, Brownson observed, the consciousness of dependence presupposes the consciousness of a religious element in human nature. The objects are therefore known to exist because "the internal sentiments demand them" (6:14). In other words, "God exists" because man "wants an object to love, reverence, and adore." The religious sentiment "requires" an object of faith; it implies the idea of God (6:12, 13). But this is for Brownson precisely the source of a central "error." To make the "*idea* of God" depend on the "sense of dependence" is to make it a "deduction from the sense of dependence," a "logical inference." But a deduction, Brownson argues, does not establish God as "given" in man's nature. The "sentiment only implies the *necessity* of an object to satisfy it, not that the object exists" (6:68, 77).

For Brownson, the argument from deduction provided a clear entryway into a "religion without God." Parker sought to keep religion in tune with natural sentiments but at the price of creating a God "adapted to man's nature" and this price, Brownson judged, was too high (5:153). By reducing religion to the "sense of dependence and idea of its object" and declaring these to be essential elements of human nature, Parker made the existence of God "quite superfluous" (6:76, 77). Man is lifted up to the position of God until there is only the "godship" of man (6:105). To "account for religion," Brownson observed, you have "no occasion to assume any existence . . . but that of man himself." Such a re-ligion "can dispense with God altogether," for it is merely the "production" of an analysis of human nature (6:72, 77).

What Brownson detects in this "production" is the Feuerbachian view of religion as delusion, and with man as God-maker, creating God in his own image (6:77). He "take[s] up . . . God into [his] own being" and "augment[s] [his] own real being." For Brownson, this "theory, so highly esteemed in Germany, is really nothing but . . . atheism" (6:98). Brownson finds clear traces of it in Parker (6:99), whose God is "what con-forms to man" (6:50). Parker's God is made to meet an "inherent want of man's soul" and "flows naturally into man as man's wants demand" (5:153; 6:47). God no longer exists "*a parte rei*," that is, "distinct from and independent of the subject"; rather, the object of wor-ship turns into a product of man's wants (3:110; 6:13). God is thus dependent on man. He is merely "what [man's] own nature reveals him to be" (6:41).

Against this reduction of religion to "delusion," Brown-son set forth an argument that he trusted would endow all religious beliefs with the "certainty of knowledge." Philosophically, the point of departure can neither be the subject alone nor the object alone but only their "synthesis": *There is no purely subjective, or purely objective knowledge. . . .* [W]e find both the *me* and the *not-me* in the same phenomenon, by the same light, and with equal certainty" (4:356). In this "synthetic philosophy," the reality of the object is given in what Brownson calls "ideal intuition" (1:xviii). This intuition does not deal with an "abstraction" but rather with real, objective being—God himself (2:76).

With this objective intuitionism Brownson strove for a philosophy that bridged the gap between intuition and reason, between subjective and objective evidence. Un-der this heading, Brownson develops an opposition cen-tral to his "refutation of atheism," namely the contrast between "psychologist" and "ontologist" systems.[43] Ac-cording to Brownson, "ontologism" is concerned with the sphere of the object and asserts that "every principle of reason can be obtained by way of logical deduction from the single intuition of . . . Being" (2:479). "Psy-chologism," by contrast, is "restricted to the sphere of the subject" and asserts the "subject as its own object," by assuming that the "soul can think without any real object" (2:482). For Brownson, the outcome of this psychologist road is inevitable. If the philosopher starts with the subject and assumes that the soul can "think without the concurrence of the object" he will, Brown-son insists, end up in "pure nullism" (2:392).

Brownson's rejection of Parker's Transcendental ideal-ism also rests upon the contrast between "ontologism" and "psychologism," and establishes an idealistic de-scent of "egoism" from Fichte's extreme subjective ide-alism to autotheism and atheistic nihilism. Brownson's starting point is the argument that atheism received its preparation at the hands of "egoistic Idealism," a "pure philosophical egoism, which resolves all into the *ego* . . . and its phenomena"—"mere volitions or creations of the ME itself" (1:34; 3:233). In Fichte this "philo-sophical egoism" reached an "absurd" culmination. Fichte, Brownson observes, "asserted the power of the *me* to be his own object, and sought the proof of it in the fact of volition. Hence he fell into the absurdity of representing all ideas as the products of the *me,* and even went so far as to tell his disciples how it is that man makes God" (4:355).

According to Brownson, this pure "autotheism" contin-ued in the "nihilism of the Hegelians" and terminates in "modern" "speculative thought" (2:83, 6:20). Here, too, the view of religion as a delusion, of man as God-maker, stems from a "psychologism" in which man can be his own object. For Brownson, by contrast, the object is al-ways "*le non-moi,*" something that stands "over against" and apart from the subject (2:45, 256). The object is therefore "presented to the soul or given it, not created or furnished by it" (2:44). What Feuerbach offered stood in complete antithesis to this train of thought. In Feuer-bach's discussion of the subject-object relation, the no-tion that a subject "is nothing without an object" con-tains a double relation. It implies, first of all, that man as a subject is recognized on the basis of objects and, secondly, that in knowing an object man knows him-self. Man encounters his own nature in his objects. He projects elements of his own nature out upon objectiv-ity. Consequently, of "[w]hatever kind of object . . . we are at any time conscious of, we are always at the same time conscious of our own nature." With this ar-gument, the circle of Feuerbach's thought was com-plete. The object of any subject is merely "this sub-ject's own, but objective, nature."[44] The ultimate object of man's experience, then, is his species-nature.

The axiom that man is to himself his own object of thought also applies to man's religious consciousness, his knowledge of God. "In the perceptions of the senses," Feuerbach argues, "consciousness of the object is distinguishable from consciousness of self." But in religion this is different. With regard to religious ob-jects, the "consciousness of object and self-consciousness coincide." Applied to man's knowledge of God, this axiom reads: In knowing God, the reli-gious object, man not only knows himself as an indi-vidual but as a "species," an idealized conception of man. Religion, then, is actually no more than man's re-lation to himself. Hence "consciousness of God" is only "self-consciousness." But, as Feuerbach points out, reli-gion is at first only an indirect self-consciousness of man in which this identity is not fully realized. Man is not aware that he is the object of his own worship, and assumes instead that he adores a being outside and above himself. A solution of this indirectness can come only with the insight that man is the true object of religious feeling. For Feuerbach's critics, a clear implication of this was anthropologism: All being and truth were made relative to the human subject.[45]

For Brownson, this "subjective-objectivism, so rife in Germany," opens the door to an atheism in which God is dissolved into a "nullity" (2:257). The alternative view Brownson maintains in the "synthetic philosophy" denies the assumption of "German metaphysics" that the object is only a mode or affection of the subject. Brownson conceives the object "as out of the subject . . . , existing really . . . [and being] intelligible, not *by* us, but *to* us" (3:94-95). The rejection of this premise, Brownson judges, "leads necessarily to the autotheism of Fichte and the Transcendentalists, for whom "the *I* or *Ego* is all that is or exists" (1:222, 223). For Brownson, Parker here was clearly subject to the same charges as "Fichteism" (3:233). Parker's "theoretical errors" are akin to the "root-error" of Fichte: "The absolute ICH, or ego, of Fichte is identical in all men, is the real man, . . . and this 'one man' is the reality, the . . . substance . . . of the whole phenomenal universe" (3:429, 430, 6:47). From here stems Parker's primal error: He "sets himself up as supreme pontiff and god" (7:263). He sinks "the phenomenal man, the *Parkeritas,* which is . . . in reality nothing, and fall[s] back on the impersonal soul, on his real self, and he is universal nature, . . . the omnipotent God, in which sense he assists at the birth of all phenomena, not as spectator only, but as creator" (6:104). To Brownson, the "creator" Parker clearly bore the imprint of Fichte's autotheism. In accordance with Fichte, his "transcendental selfishness" reduced religion to a "worship of [man's] own internal sentiments and affections projected" (5:153).

For Brownson, it was precisely at this point again that Parker fell prey to the projective view of religion asserting man as God-maker. God "is" what is "demanded by an internal want or sentiment, and what answers to that sentiment or want." God has no independent existence; he is "because the internal sentiments . . . are satisfied by [him]" (6:14). In Brownson's view, the philosophical error that underlies this projective view of religion is the subject-object relation characteristic of Feuerbachian "intellectual atheism" which Brownson traces back to Fichteism. In the Transcendentalist vision, Brownson observes, man can be his own object. But God, Brownson reiterates, is "independent"; he is "neither the soul nor its product" (2:455). If man "were his own adequate object, . . . he would be . . . not man, but God" (3:22) This is in Brownson's view precisely the credo of the "supreme pontiff" of Transcendentalism, Parker.

Brownson's interpretation places transcendental idealism and Feuerbachian atheism in parallel and here anticipates Barth's later criticism of nineteenth-century liberal theology. Brownson identifies the philosophical basis of Transcendentalism as "psychologism," and aligns it with the same "autotheism" that Feuerbach was to explicate. This parallelism was already immanent in Parker's conception of the nature of religious experience. In identifying religion with the sense of dependence, Parker opened the door to an anthropological approach in which man could be his own object and was set free in such a way that his "egoistic" dominance submerged the object of faith altogether. The Transcendentalist mind, as a contemporary reviewer observed, "rejoic[es] in the despotism which it can so easily exercise over a world filled with its own creations."[46] In this "despotic" reign, Feuerbach's primary thesis seemed to come true: All affirmations about God built on claims about humanity were only the mind's "own creations"—projected human wishes.

IV

Brownson's turbulant religious pilgrimage to Catholicism and his intellectual wanderings often appeared to his former Transcendentalist comrades as eccentric, if not "unbearable."[47] Yet with regard to his critique of Parker's autotheism, Brownson put forward arguments not uncommon among New School advocates who were also well aware of the atheistical tendencies inherent in idealistic pronouncements. Like Brownson, several New School apostles acutely sensed that Transcendentalist idealism was prone to a form of atheism which questioned not only the evidences of historical Christianity but also the status of the object of worship. An awareness of this type of atheism was particularly prominent among those New School members who believed, as did James Freeman Clarke, in both "an outward witness, coming down through history, and an inner witness of the spirit in our heart." Very wary of the "serious charges" that could be brought against Transcendentalist idealism, Clarke was convinced that its "extreme" version would have to be reformed in order to be maintained at all.[48] A reliance on the "inner witness" alone would, Clarke judged, inevitably eradicate the transcendent object of faith. In similar terms, Frederic Henry Hedge noted that atheism lurked in the background of the transcendental identity with God. From here, Hedge sensed, it was only a small step to replace the object of faith with man become God. In 1840, Hedge identified Emerson and Alcott as "atheists in disguise." Hedge agreed with Clarke that the conclusion of atheism inhered in an "extreme idealism" that drove towards anthropotheism to the point where to "dwell *in God*" was no longer enough; man aspired instead to "*be God*."[49] By 1843, Hedge also counted Parker among those standing on this egotheistic platform and was no longer willing to accord with what was ridiculed as "transcendental selfishness." He felt alienated from those who had incurred the reputation of being fanatic visionaries and sought to avoid the "wild mania of Transcendentalism."[50]

Both Clarke and Hedge launched their attacks against an "ego-theism" that bore a distinct similarity to the position for which Feuerbach was to be denounced. For Clarke, Parker's "Negative Transcendentalism" related the individual directly to absolute Being. But man's partaking in the divine nature amounted to no more than the presumptuous self-confidence of a "shallow naturalism" that left no room for a transcendent God.[51] The similarity of this self-worship to Feuerbach's credo seemed obvious. The "egoistic" pronouncements of Parker's subjective idealism cohered with a primary axiom of the "new" "atheism": "Consciousness of God is self-consciousness." Transcendental idealism, it seemed, already contained the germ of an atheism in which the object of faith "disappeared in the haze of . . . doubt" and the worship of God turned into the worship of self.[52] In Parker's "egotism," the self was, in the manner of Feuerbach, declared to be autonomous in such a way that everything outside man's mind evaporated into an expression of subjective desires.

That Parker actually rejected the Emersonian dream of self-reliance as "extravagant" and "exaggerated," was largely obscured by the recurrent criticism of Parker as an naturalist and autotheist (8:83). To many, Parker was an egotheistic visionary indelibly associated with an extreme individualism and idealism.[53] Of the charter members of the "Transcendental Club," Ripley and his comrades in the Broad Church camp sought to escape this stigma and were anxious to present a basis for religious truth that preserved God as a separate center of consciousness. "We must not," Hedge warned, "confuse the manifest God with the transcendental ground of the manifestation."[54] God was in essence apart from and other than man. The object of religious belief issued from a source outside man's mind. This view provided a bulwark against atheistic soul-worship. It prevented the Feuerbachian eclipse of God and also barred the way to all forms of subjectivism identifying the criteria of religious truth with man's understanding of spiritual wants.

Warnings against the threat of projective religion were numerous in the contemporary responses to the extreme version of Transcendentalism. With remarkable unanimity, reviewers from both Old and New School camps all marked the latent "godless" tendencies of egocentric Transcendentalism and saw in this unmitigated egoism a threat to belief in the existence of God. Like Brownson, Hedge and his conservative brethren judged that the ground for such utter atheism had been prepared by Fichte's "extreme idealism." Transcendental "egotheism" appeared as the outcome of an anthropotheistic

position descending from Fichteism. In this manner, Hedge suspected Fichte of having followed a subjective path to skepticism. For Fichte, Hedge observed, the absolute was conceived as the "I" limited by the "Not-I." Fichte thus arrived at the "altogether too subjective" view that "I am all."[55] The self was bracketed in consciousness as an object of self-reflection. Fichte's egoistic system, Hedge judged, in this way reduced the external world to a mere posit of auto-productive activity—a "projection" Hedge discovered again in the "illusions" of Parker's "extreme idealism."[56] When Feuerbach came on the scene, the attempt to generate atheism out of Fichtean egoism resurfaced with renewed vigor. For Unitarian and orthodox reviewers of *The Essence of Christianity,* Feuerbach merely elaborated what had already become an established fact in the "extreme idealism" perpetuated by Parker. In this respect, the debate about Parker's "Negative Transcendentalism" constituted an overture to the prolonged controversy about Feuerbach's atheistic idealism.

V

For both Unitarian and Congregationalist reviewers, Feuerbach's atheism issued from a pantheistic-idealistic basis. Thus Joseph Henry Allen, grandson of the elder Henry Ware, judged that Feuerbach's position "mark[ed] the easy transition . . . from All-God to No-God." That Feuerbach did not grant any "objective reality at all" to the "Absolute" was, in Allen's view, the source of his error and not without serious consequences: "Metaphysics [took] the sudden plunge from Conservative Orthodoxy to Atheistic Nihilism."[57] In similar terms, the Congregationalist Charles C. Tiffany observed that Feuerbach exemplified the difficulties which beset an "extreme idealist" who fell prey to a "logic" that identified God and man. Man as "subject" was absorbed into divinity and exalted to the position of God.[58]

For Tiffany, the threads of this deification of man, if traced back, led to an "extreme idealism" that issued from Fichte's philosophy of the self. The solipsistic implications of Fichte's system were, Tiffany judged, directly continuous with Feuerbach's "subjectivism." As an "advocate of subjectivism," Feuerbach dissolved everything into egoism. "A spiritual existence without [man], of which [he] may be conscious also" was no longer possible.[59] On this interpretation, which established a line of development from extreme idealism to Feuerbach's atheism, Unitarian and Congregationalist reviewers of *The Essence of Christianity* stood as one. Like Tiffany, the Unitarian reviewer Hasbrouck Davis judged that Feuerbachian atheism came from the same mold as Fichte's idealism because it presented the self as the ground and generator of reality and thus collapsed all being into the dominance of "egoism."[60] In

The Essence of Christianity this "egoism" was taken to its atheistic conclusion. It only remained for Feuerbach to present the divine as the product of subjective human wishes.

Brownson sensed correctly that Parker's concept of religion was vulnerable to a similar anthropologizing of theology. But although Parker agreed with Feuerbach that theistic language referred primarily to subjective experience, he never endorsed Feuerbach's thesis about theological illusion. An analytic demonstration of God's existence was for Parker in vain. God's existence, Parker was convinced, is a statement of belief, and "[t]he belief always precedes the proof" (1:12). It is a certainty, a fact that is neither "self-originated" nor subject-relative (1:5; 6:33,). On this point Parker was closer to the "conservatives" than they themselves were ready to admit. When it came to "dogmatic atheism," Parker was quite sure that he would "appear in the ranks of conservatives in theology."[61] Parker concurred with his Unitarian and Congregationalist brethren that there was an object outside of man that corresponded to the object of religious belief, an object that simply could not be an invention or product of subjective human aspirations (1:10). Religion, Parker was anxious to make clear, had an objective basis in man which precluded its reduction to images of man's own nature.

At this juncture Parker also differed sharply from Emerson's subjectivist concept of God. What Emerson proposed, Parker judged as nothing but "to project God—so to say, out of ourselves."[62] In Parker's concept of religion, by contrast, God serves as a constant reminder of man's dependence and finitude. The God "in the soul of man" does not establish individual divinity, as Emerson asserted, but rather confirms God as "different in kind from both matter and man."[63] "My definition," Parker insisted, "distinguishes God from all other beings; it does not limit Him to the details of my conception" (13:332). The "object and contents" of religion are not "altogether human," as Feuerbach claimed in *The Essence of Christianity.*[64] They also have an anchor outside the self. The God "in the soul of man" is also a God out of man who raises in him the awareness that he is "not conscious of [his] own existence except as a finite existence, that is, as a dependent existence." (6:33). While Feuerbach disparages the argument from consciousness as a delusion of self-objectification and denies that there are any a priori propositions, Parker deduces the existence of God from the nature of religious self-consciousness. For Parker, the primary fact of consciousness is the Schleiermachian a priori assurance of the existence of God, the feeling of being absolutely dependent on God (1:11). "[T]he idea of the infinite, of God on whom I depend, comes at the same time as the logical correlative of a knowledge of myself. So the existence of God is a certainty" (6:33). God is not produced by a thought-process of man; rather, he

is given to consciousness as a constituent element through the feeling of utter dependence.

In this regard, Parker's position, impious though it seemed to many of his contemporaries, cohered again with the conservative front of New England divinity. Parker did not, as Brownson charged, settle for a mere awareness of intuitive facts of consciousness. Intuitive truths, Parker emphasized, were not identical with innate truths. Judgments a priori therefore also had to be legitimated as "facts of observation" (6:32). In bolstering intuitive facts of consciousness by induction, Parker avoided the threat of projective religion. Religious truths, Parker believed, are independent of the self and in this sense are accurate statements free from subjective vagaries and the delusion of self-exteriorization.

In his sermons on *Theism, Atheism and the Popular Theology,* Parker combines the argument from consciousness with a traditional defense strategy that Brownson chose to ignore in his critique of Parker. Drawing on the traditional teleological argument, Parker asserted that the existence of God is evident from the appearance of a spiritual design and purpose in the world. A "conscious power," a "constant mode of operation" underlies all activity "in the world of man" (2:70). Just as material objects have a spiritual agent, so the religious faculty has a "cause" (2:79). What set Feuerbach apart from this framework was, Ripley judged, the "spiritual skepticism" of his "atheistical theory."[65] Parker agreed. To deny, as Feuerbach did, that God has "objective actualness" was to make all human hopes and efforts pointless and leave man to the desolation of an incoherent, "fortuitous" universe, "a jumble of parts with no contexture" (2:70, 74, 95).

The constant refrain of Parker's *Theism* sermons—the atheist's "sad thought, his world without a God; his here, but no hereafter; his body, and no soul"—is the credo of the "prophet" Feuerbach, a credo whose inevitable outcome is a "cruel" and "absurd" atheism that leaves "nought to reverence, to esteem . . . , to love" (2:68, 82, 244). The "prophet" Feuerbach in this respect evinced himself for Parker as a destructive materialist. Feuerbach, Parker observed in his letter to Johannes Ronge, "does a service, but it is purely the destruction of the old and then he roots up the wheat along with the tares" (4:469, n.5).

But Parker was acutely aware of a "far more dangerous" form of atheism (2:122). This threat was not the lapse from idealism to speculative infidelity but the lapse from idealism to "practical atheism." The most destructive form of atheism, Parker judged, did not issue from "undisguised professors" of atheism who were nevertheless "conscientious, just, human, [and] philanthropic," but rather from "disguised practicers" thereof with whom atheism "preponderates in their daily life"

(2:63, 90, 92). For Parker, undisguised, speculative atheism entailed a positive affirmation of the values of human life. The "atheistic Feuerbach," Parker observed, still obeys an "objective restraint." He "bow[s] down before the eternal laws of matter and mind: 'These,' say[s] [he], 'we must keep always come what may'" (14:180). The disguised, practical atheist, however, has no such "restraint" at all. He is a law unto himself, with no duties or obligations to anyone and anything. He takes his stand on his own ego and is his own "mind, cause, providence, lawgiver, and director" (2:94). The only safeguard against such practical atheism was for Parker the belief in a spiritual and immanent God operative in man himself. But for Parker's critics, it was, ironically, in this very safeguard that Feuerbachian atheism left its mark on him—the thorn in the flesh of a theology that reduced all references to God to references about the human self and thus seemed to make the road to a "religion without God" inevitable.

Notes

1. *The George Eliot Letters,* Gordon S. Haight, ed., 7 vols. (New Haven: Yale University Press, 1954-1956), 2:152.

2. Ludwig Feuerbach, *The Essence of Christianity,* trans. George Eliot (1854), reprint, with a foreword by H. Richard Niebuhr (New York: Harper & Row, 1957), xxxix, 2. On Feuerbach's concepts of "species-being" ("Gattungswesen") and "species-nature" ("Gattungsnatur"), see Eugene Kamenka, *The Philosophy of Ludwig Feuerbach* (London: Routledge & Kegan Paul, 1970), 121-122; and Larry Johnston, *Between Transcendence and Nihilism: Species-Ontology in the Philosophy of Ludwig Feuerbach* (New York: Peter Lang, 1995), 107-119.

3. Feuerbach, *The Essence of Christianity,* 12, 13, 31, 196, 203.

4. Ibid., xxxiv, xliii. See also *George Eliot Letters,* 2:140-141.

5. James Martineau, "Contemporary Literature, Theology and Philosophy," *Westminster Review* 6 (1854): 559. See also *George Eliot Letters,* 2:137.

6. *Spectator* 5 (1854): 837; quoted in *George Eliot Letters,* 2:173, n.5. For a discussion of Feuerbach's influence on Eliot, see Basil Willey, *Nineteenth Century Studies: Coleridge to Matthew Arnold,* (London: Chatto & Windus, 1950), 227-236; and Rosemary Ashton, *The German Idea: Four English Writers and the Reception of German Thought* (Cambridge: Cambridge University Press, 1980), 155-165.

7. *George Eliot Letters,* 2:153

8. Charles C. Tiffany, "Feuerbach's Essence of Christianity," *Bibliotheca Sacra* 14 (October 1857): 737. Prior to Eliot's translation, most New Englanders received their first exposure to Feuerbach through intermediate sources. Such indirect contact was provided by Johann B. Stallo, whose *General Principles of the Philosophy of Nature* (1848) identified Feuerbach as a religious philosopher in line with the "physiophilosophy" presented by the German speculative scientist Lorenz Oken. See John Bernhard Stallo, *General Principles of the Philosophy of Nature. With an Outline of Some of its Recent Developments among the Germans, Embracing the Philosophical Systems of Schelling and Hegel, and Oken's System of Nature* (Boston: Wm. Crosby and H. P. Nichols, 1848), 322-323. For a general review of the reception of *The Essence of Christianity* in New England, see Elisabeth Hurth, "When 'Man Makes God': Feuerbachian Atheism in New England," in *ESQ: A Journal of the American Renaissance,* 42 (1996), 255-289.

9. Noah Porter, "The New Infidelity," *New Englander,* 11 (1853): 294.

10. Robert Turnbull, "The Essence and End of Infidelity," (1855), quoted in Charles D. Cashdollar, *The Transformation of Theology, 1830-1890: Positivism and Protestant Thought in Britain and America* (Princeton: Princeton University Press, 1989), 123.

11. Joseph Henry Allen, "Review of Current Literature," *Christian Examiner,* 63 (November 1857): 434.

12. Octavius B. Frothingham, *George Ripley* (Boston: Houghton, Mifflin and Company 1883), 275. On Ripley's criticism of Feuerbach, see Charles Crowe, *George Ripley: Transcendentalist and Utopian Socialist* (Athens, GA: University of Georgia Press, 1967), 249.

13. Loyd D. Easton, *Hegel's First American Followers: The Ohio Hegelians* (Athens: Ohio Univ. Press, 1966) 45. Also see William H. Goetzmann, ed. *The American Hegelians: An Intellectual Episode in the History of Western America* (New York: Knopf, 1973).

14. *The Letters of Ralph Waldo Emerson,* ed. Ralph L. Rusk and Eleanor M. Tilton, 7 vols. to date (New York: Columbia University Press, 1939; 1990-), 4:530-531.

15. *The Letters of Ralph Waldo Emerson,* 5:514; Amos Bronson Alcott, *Concord Days* (Boston: Roberts Brothers, 1872), 145. Also see Henry A. Pochmann, *New England Transcendentalism and St. Louis Hegelianism: Phases in the History of American Idealism* (Philadelphia: Schurz, 1948), 34-53.

16. Ernest Renan, "M. Feuerbach and the New Hegelian School," in *Studies of Religious History and Criticism,* trans. Octavius B. Frothingham (New York: Carleton, 1864), 331-341. On Frothingham's criticism of Feuerbach, see Octavus B. Frothingham, "Imagination in Theology," *Christian Examiner,* 66 (January 1859), 47-78.

17. Theodore Parker, Journal O, 153-154 (December 1, 1852), catalogued as Journal Volume 3, Theodore Parker Papers, bMS101, Andover-Harvard Theological Library. I am grateful to Dean Grodzins for bringing this journal entry to my attention. On Scherb, see Henry A. Pochmann, *German Culture in America: Philosophical and Literary Influences, 1600-1900* (Madison: University of Wisconsin Press, 1957), 172, 199.

18. On Parker's criticism of the "popular theology," see Theodore Parker, *Theism, Atheism and the Popular Theology,* ed. Charles W. Wendte, in the Centenary Edition of *The Works of Theodore Parker,* 15 vols. (Boston: American Unitarian Association, 1907-1913), 2:124-191. Unless otherwise noted, future references to this edition will be cited parenthetically, by volume and page number. The references are from volumes 1: *A Discourse of Matters Pertaining to Religion,* 1856 edition; 2: *Theism, Atheism and the Popular Theology*; 4: *The Transient and Permanent in Christianity*; 6: *The World of Matter and the Spirit of Man*; 8: *The American Scholar*; 13: *Autobiography, Poems and Prayers*; and 14: *Saint Bernard and Other Papers.*

19. Orestes A. Brownson, *The Convert,* in *The Works of Orestes A. Brownson,* ed. Henry F. Brownson, 20 vols. (New York: AMS, 1966), 5:153. Unless otherwise noted, future references to this edition will be cited parenthetically, by volume and page number.

20. Crowe, *Ripley,* 105.

21. Octavius B. Frothingham, *Boston Unitarianism, 1820-1850* (New York: G. P. Putnam, 1890), 169.

22. Andrews Norton, *A Discourse on the Latest Form of Infidelity* (Cambridge: John Owen, 1839), 30. Also see James Freeman Clarke, "R. W. Emerson and the New School," (1838), in *Emerson and Thoreau: The Contemporary Reviews,* ed. Joel Myerson (Cambridge: Cambridge University Press, 1992), 52.

23. See R. W. B. Lewis, *The American Adam* (Chicago: University of Chicago Press, 1955), 184, 188-189.

24. On the forms of exaggerated and extreme idealism, see Hasbrouck Davis, "Feuerbach's Essence of Christianity," *Christian Examiner,* 49 (September 1850): 229 and Tiffany, "Feuerbach's Essence of Christianity," 738. On atheism as the final stage of an extreme idealism set in motion by Fichte's deification of the ego, see René Wellek, *Confrontations: Studies in the Intellectual and Literary Relations between Germany, England and the United States during the Nineteenth Century* (Princeton: Princeton University Press, 1965), 179-180. See also Orestes Brownson, "Charles Elwood Reviewed," *Boston Quarterly Review* (1842), in *Works,* 4:355.

25. Theodore Maynard, *Orestes Brownson. Yankee, Radical, Catholic* (New York: Macmillan, 1943), 90. Also see William Henry Channing, *The Gospel of Today: A Discourse Delivered at the Ordination of T. W. Higginson . . .* (Boston, 1847), 9; quoted in William Hutchison, *The Transcendentalist Ministers: Church Reform in the New England Renaissance* (New Haven: Yale University Press, 1959), 170; and Brownson, *The Convert,* in *Works,* 5:153.

26. Karl Barth, "Introductory Essay," in Feuerbach, *The Essence of Christianity,* xix, xx, xxi, xxiv. For a critique of Barth's historical locating of Feuerbach, see John Glasse, "Barth on Feuerbach," *Harvard Theological Review,* 57 (1964), 89-96.

27. Barth, "Introductory Essay," xxii, xxi, xx.

28. Samuel Osgood, "Modern Ecclesiastical History," *Christian Examiner,* 48 (May 1850), 429.

29. Norton, *A Discourse on the Latest Form of Infidelity,* 22, 53.

30. Davis, "Feuerbach's Essence of Christianity," 224.

31. Renan, *Studies of Religious History and Criticism,* 339.

32. Mark Y. Hanley, *Beyond a Christian Commonwealth: The Protestant Quarrel with the American Republic, 1830-1860* (Chapel Hill: University of North Carolina Press, 1994), 112, 113. For further examples of this trend in scholarship, see Claude Welch, *Protestant Thought in the Nineteenth Century* 2 vols. (New Haven: Yale University Press, 1972, 1985) 1:170-183; Herbert Hovenkamp, *Science and Religion in America. 1800-1860* (Philadelphia: University of Pennsylvania Press, 1978), 59; and Irving Howe, *The American Newness: Culture and Politics in the Age of Emerson* (Cambridge, MA: Harvard University Press, 1986), 10-11.

33. Theodore Parker, "Of Speculative Atheism, Regarded as a Theory of the Universe," in *Works,* 2:62. Also see Moncure Daniel Conway, *Autobiography, Memories and Experiences,* 2 vols. (New York: Cassell and Company, 1904), 2:365.

34. Osgood, "Modern Ecclesiastical History," 429.

35. Theodore Parker, "Strauss's *Life of Jesus*," *Christian Examiner,* 28 (July 1840): 285, 309.

36. Parker, "Strauss's *Life of Jesus*," 310.

37. Frothingham, *Ripley,* 229.

38. George Ripley, ed., *Specimens of Foreign Literature,* 14 vols. (Boston: Hilliard, Gray 1838-1841; Boston: James Munroe, 1842), 1:29, 30.

39. George Ripley, "General Principles . . . by J. B. Stallo," *The Harbinger,* 6 (February 1848): 110, quoted in Pochmann, *German Culture in America,* 619, n. 614; Frothingham, *Ripley,* 229.

40. Feuerbach, *The Essence of Christianity,* 140.

41. Theodore Parker, introduction to *A Critical and Historical Introduction to the Canonical Scriptures of the Old Testament,* from the German of Wilhelm M. L. De Wette (2nd ed; Boston: Little, Brown, 1850), 1:3. Also see Allen, "Review of Current Literature," 437.

42. Theodore Parker, quoted in Octavius B. Frothingham, *Transcendentalism in New England: A History* (1876; reprint, Gloucester: Peter Smith, 1965), 316-317.

43. On Brownson as an objective intuitionist, see Wellek, *Confrontations,* 179. On Brownson's critique of atheism, see his *Essay in Refutation of Atheism,* in *Works,* 2:1-100.

44. Feuerbach, *The Essence of Christianity,* 4, 6.

45. Ibid., 12, 13. See also Tiffany, "Feuerbach's Essence of Christianity," 736.

46. Review of *Essays* (1841), reprinted in Myerson, *Emerson and Thoreau,* 101.

47. George Willis Cooke, *An Historical and Biographical Introduction to Accompany "The Dial" as Reprinted in Numbers for the Rowfant* Club, 2 vols. (Cleveland: Rowfant Club, 1902), 2:73. Also see Pochmann, *German Culture in America,* 108, 234.

48. Clarke, "R. W. Emerson and the New School," 52.

49. Frederic Henry Hedge to Margret Fuller, March 24, 1840, quoted in Bryan F. LeBeau, *Frederic Henry Hedge. Nineteenth Century American Transcendentalist* (Allison Park: Pickwick Publications, 1985), 169; Clarke, "R. W. Emerson and the New School," 53. Also see Joel Myerson, "Frederic Henry Hedge and the Failure of Transcendentalism," *Harvard Library Bulletin,* 23 (1975), 403-404.

50. Frederic Henry Hedge to Convers Francis, February 14, 1843, quoted in LeBeau, *Frederic Henry Hedge,* 169.

51. Quoted in John White Chadwick, *Theodore Parker: Preacher and Reformer* (Boston and New York: Houghton, Mifflin, 1900), 127.

52. Cyrus A. Bartol, "Representative Men" (1850), reprinted in Myerson, *Emerson and Thoreau,* 220.

53. Elizabeth Palmer Peabody, *Reminiscences of Rev. Wm. Ellery Channing, D.D.* (Boston: Roberts Brothers, 1880), 371.

54. Frederic Henry Hedge, *Martin Luther and Other Essays* (Boston: Roberts Brothers, 1888), 289. Also see David Lyttle, *Studies in Religion in Early American Literature: Edwards, Poe, Channing, Emerson, Some Minor Transcendentalists, Hawthorne, and Thoreau* (Lanham: University Press of America, 1983), 94-100.

55. Frederic Henry Hedge, "Coleridge's Literary Character," *Christian Examiner* 14 (1833): 116, 124; *Prose Writers of Germany,* Frederic Henry Hedge, ed. (1847, New York: Francis, 1856), 57. On Transcendentalism as an "outcome" of Fichte's idealism see Joseph Cook, *Transcendentalism, with Preludes on Current Events* (1878), quoted in Pochmann, *German Culture in America,* 243.

56. See LeBeau, *Frederic Henry Hedge,* 19, 45, 170.

57. Allen, "Review of Current Literature," 434, 437.

58. Tiffany, "Feuerbach's Essence of Christianity," 734.

59. Ibid., 737, 738, 739.

60. Davis, "Feuerbach's Essence of Christianity," 229.

61. Theodore Parker, Journal O, 154 (December 1, 1852), Andover-Harvard Theological Library.

62. Theodore Parker to Elizabeth Palmer Peabody, January 8, 1839, Theodore Parker Papers, Massachusetts Historical Society, quoted in Dean Grodzins, "Theodore Parker and Transcendentalism" (Ph.D. dissertation, Harvard University, 1993), 221.

63. Hutchison, *The Transcendentalist Ministers,* 105.

64. Feuerbach, *The Essence of Christianity,* 14.

65. Frothingham, *Ripley,* 229.

FURTHER READING

Bibliographies

Collison, Gary L. "A Calendar of the Letters of Theodore Parker (Part One)." *Studies in the American Renaissance* (1979): 159-229.

Chronological bibliography of Parker's letters written between 1832 and 1855.

————. "A Calendar of the Letters of Theodore Parker (Part Two)." *Studies in the American Renaissance* 128 (1980): 317-408.

Chronological bibliography of Parker's letters written between 1855 and 1860.

Grodzins, Dean and Joel Myerson. "The Preaching Record of Theodore Parker." *Studies in the American Renaissance* (1994): 55-122.

Chronological bibliography of Parker's sermons delivered between 1836 and 1859.

Biographies

Frothingham, Octavius Brooks. *Theodore Parker: A Biography.* New York and London: G. P. Putnam's Sons, 1886, 588 p.

Full-length biography.

Grodzins, Dean. *American Heretic: Theodore Parker and Transcendentalism.* Chapel Hill: University of North Carolina Press, 2002, 631 p.

Full-length biography that includes information on and analysis of the culture and society in which Parker lived and worked.

Criticism

Collins, Robert E. "A Forgotten American." In *Theodore Parker: American Transcendentalist,* pp. 1-46. Metuchen, N.J.: The Scarecrow Press, Inc., 1973.

Illustrates how Parker's Transcendentalist works compare to those of Ralph Waldo Emerson, and argues that Parker should be regarded as a key figure in and influential proponent of American Transcendentalism.

Dirks, John Edward. *Critical Theology of Theodore Parker.* New York: Columbia University Press, 1948, 173 p.

Book-length, scholarly analysis of Parker's theology and philosophy.

Grodzins, Dean. "Theodore Parker and the 28th Congregational Society: The Reform Church and the Spirituality of Reformers in Boston, 1845-1859." In *The Transient and Permanent: The Transcendentalist Movement and its Contexts,* edited by Charles Capper and Conrad E. Wright, pp. 73-117. Boston: Massachusetts Historical Society, 1999.

Offers a portrait of the nature and ideals of the members of Boston's 28th Congregational Society between 1845 and 1859.

Grusin, Richard A. "The Two Theodore Parkers: Interpretation, Intuition, and Maternal Authority." In *Transcendentalist Hermeneutics: Institutional Authority and the Higher Criticism of the Bible,* pp. 115-50. Durham, N.C.: Duke University Press, 1991.

Studies both Parker's autobiographical writings and his theological writings in order to demonstrate that Parker offers a "persistent representation of intuitive truths not as those truths that transcend our institutional experience but as those that are so deeply rooted in the domestic institutions of motherhood, marriage, and family that they no longer seem institutional at all."

Gura, Philip F. "Theodore Parker and the South Boston Ordination: The Textual Tangle of *A Discourse on the Transient & Permanent in Christianity." Studies in the American Renaissance* (1988): 149-78.

Surveys the history and reception of Parker's *Discourse on the Transient and Permanent in Christianity.*

Trimpi, Helen P. "Three of Melville's Confidence Men: William Cullen Bryant, Theodore Parker, and Horace Greeley." *Texas Studies in Literature and Language* 21 (1979): 368-95.

Identifies fictional representations of Parker, William Cullen Bryant, and Horace Greeley in works by Herman Melville.

Additional coverage of Parker's life and career is contained in the following sources published by Thomson Gale: *Dictionary of Literary Biography,* **Vols. 1, 235; and** *Literature Resource Center.*

Christina Rossetti
1830-1894

(Full name, Christina Georgina Rossetti; also wrote under the pseudonym Ellen Alleyn) English poet, short story writer, and prose writer.

The following entry provides critical commentary on Rossetti's works from 1996 to 2005. For further information on Rossetti's life and works, see *NCLC,* Volumes 2 and 50; for discussion of her poem "Goblin Market," see *NCLC,* Volume 66.

INTRODUCTION

Rossetti is ranked among the finest English poets of the nineteenth century. Closely associated with Pre-Raphaelitism—an artistic and literary movement that aspired to recapture the vivid pictorial qualities and sensual aesthetics of Italian religious painting before the year 1500—Rossetti was equally influenced by the religious conservatism and asceticism of the Church of England. Scholars have noted an enduring dialectic between these disparate outlooks in Rossetti's poetry, as well as Rossetti's mastery of a variety of poetic forms.

BIOGRAPHICAL INFORMATION

Rossetti was born in London in 1830, the fourth and youngest child of Gabriele Rossetti, an exiled Italian poet, and Frances Mary (Polidori) Rossetti. Shortly after her birth, Rossetti's father was appointed Professor of Italian at King's College. Educated at home by her mother, a former governess, along with her brothers Dante Gabriel and William Michael, Rossetti studied French, German, and Latin, and was fluent in both English and Italian. She is reputed to have engaged in sonnet-writing competitions with her brothers, and scholars have credited her later command of metrical forms to these early challenges. Rossetti's earliest surviving poem, "To My Mother," was written in 1842 as a birthday present to her mother. Her budding poetic talent is demonstrated in her first volume, *Verses,* a collection privately printed by her maternal grandfather in 1847. At the age of eighteen Rossetti began studying the works of Italian poet Dante Alighieri, who became a major and lasting influence on her poetry, as evidenced by her many allusions to his works in her writing. At this time, Rossetti became engaged to James Collinson, a minor Pre-Raphaelite painter, but two years later refused to marry him when he became a Roman Catholic. In 1862, she fell in love with Charles Bagot Cayley, but again refused to marry because he was an agnostic. Rossetti ultimately chose to remain with her mother, an equally devout Anglican. Far from becoming a recluse, however, Rossetti's social circle contained a number of her brothers' friends, including James Whistler, Algernon Charles Swinburne, F.M. Brown, and Charles Dodgson (Lewis Carroll). She also volunteered for ten years at the Highgate Penitentiary, a home for "fallen women" and unwed mothers, an experience that scholars claim informed a number of her poems, including "Goblin Market" and "The Iniquity of the Fathers Upon the Children." As she grew older, Rossetti's poetic production diminished; a succession of serious illnesses strongly influenced her temperament and outlook on life and she often believed herself to be close to death. Following her recovery from a near-fatal attack of Graves' disease in 1871, Rossetti became increasingly committed to writing religious prose, and religious devotion and mortality are featured prominently in her works. In 1881, her collection *A Pageant, and Other Poems* was published, and her letters reveal that she thought it to be "among the best and most wholesome things I have produced." She underwent surgery for breast cancer in 1892, the same year that *The Face of the Deep: A Devotional Commentary on the Apocalypse* was published. Rossetti's last book, *Verses,* bears the same title as her first unpublished volume and is comprised of previously published devotional poems. It was published in September of 1893; much to her satisfaction, the book sold out in a week. A year later the cancer returned, and Rossetti died December 29, 1894.

MAJOR WORKS

Rossetti's first published poems appeared in the *Athenaeum* when she was eighteen. In 1850, Rossetti contributed seven poems, under the pseudonym of Ellen Alleyn, to *The Germ,* the Pre-Raphaelite Brotherhood journal that Dante Gabriel Rossetti cofounded along with John Everett Millais and William Holman Hunt. Her first collection of poetry, *Goblin Market, and Other Poems* (1862), gained Rossetti immediate recognition as a skilled and original poet. Rossetti demonstrates the influence of Pre-Raphaelitism in this collection in her use of symbolism, allegory, and sensual imagery. The collection's title poem, widely considered one of Rossetti's masterpieces, relates the fate of two sisters, Lizzie and Laura, who respectively resist and succumb to the temptation to buy the luscious fruit peddled by the animal-like goblin merchants of Elfland. The poem, ostensibly written as a simple children's fairy tale, has been variously interpreted as a Christian allegory of sexual sin and redemption, a commentary on capitalism and Victorian market economy, a feminist glorification of "sisterhood," and as a homoerotic exploration of sexual fantasy. This volume and Rossetti's 1866 collection, *The Prince's Progress, and Other Poems,* are regarded as containing some of Rossetti's finest work and established her reputation as an important poet. The title poem of the latter collection recounts a prince's physical, moral, and spiritual journey to meet his bride. This volume also contains "A Royal Princess," in which a princess comes to the realization that her father, the King, is responsible for the hunger and want of the peasants angrily storming the palace gates. She determines that she must attend to their suffering, even at her own peril. In 1874 Rossetti published *Speaking Likenesses,* a collection of prose for children that consists of three linked fantasy stories told to five sisters by their maiden aunt. Rossetti apparently intended the stories to be moral fiction cast in the likeness of Lewis Carroll's *Alice* tales, although hers contain disagreeable characters, purportedly the "speaking likenesses" of the nieces, and some early readers deemed the stories to be violent and disturbing. One poem of apparent importance to Rossetti was "The Lowest Room," which she secretly included in *Goblin Market, The Prince's Progress and Other Poems* (1875), despite Dante Gabriel's previous vetoes to publish the poem in previous collections. In "The Lowest Room," the unmarried speaker, in a discussion with her blissfully married sister, contrasts her dull existence with the exploits she has read about in Homer, revealing her feelings of aimlessness and discontent; she ultimately learns to be "Content to take the lowest place / The place assigned me here." Rossetti's devotional verse explores humanity's relationship with God and the nature of life in the afterworld. It also celebrates Rossetti's decision to deny herself earthly, romantic love for the sake of religious purity, as evidenced in the sonnet sequence "Monna Innominata," which appears in *A Pageant, and Other Poems.* In *Time Flies: A Reading Diary* (1885) Rossetti offers a thought or passage designed to elicit spiritual reflection for each day of the year, and in *The Face of the Deep* she provides a verse-by-verse exegesis of the *Book of Revelation.*

CRITICAL RECEPTION

Although she is remembered by many merely as the ethereal symbol of Pre-Raphaelitism evoked in Dante Gabriel Rossetti's paintings, Rossetti is also credited with producing a unique body of work that transcends the limits of any single movement. Rossetti has been faulted by some critics for alleged indifference to social issues and hailed by others as a covertly feminist author; ultimately, though, her works are widely praised for their simple diction, timeless vision, diversity of stanzaic patterns, and impressive facility in rhyme. The frequency with which the themes of loss, desire, and isolation appear throughout Rossetti's oeuvre has led to a great many biographical interpretations of her works. Numerous scholars have drawn parallels between specific events in Rossetti's life and her work, conjecturing about experiences that may have informed her worldview, while other commentators, such as Joy A. Fehr, argue that alternate interpretations are just as plausible and that such narrow readings prevent a full appreciation of Rossetti's poetic talents. Acknowledging that Rossetti was an ambivalent feminist and held conservative views on many issues, feminist scholars have nevertheless reassessed Rossetti's poetry and prose, claiming that a deeper analysis of her work shows her to be uncommonly radical, particularly in her attempt to understand and critique the deeper realities of religion and literature and to represent them in terms that resonate with the female reader. Much scholarly study and debate of Rossetti's work focuses upon the poet's renunciation of earthly pleasures in the service of religious devotion, as well as on the subtext of her works and the significance of Rossetti's characteristic reticence. Scholars generally regard Rossetti's poetry to be superior to her later nonsecular prose works and observe that much of her most highly regarded verse was inspired by her religious beliefs. Reviewing *Verses,* Theodore Watts-Dunton, critic and friend of Dante Gabriel Rossetti, writes, "In the volume before us, as in all her previously published writings, we see at its best what Christianity is as the motive power of poetry." Similarly, commentator Constance W. Hassett claims, "This, her last book [*Verses*], is a kind of writer's testimonial declaring that though she has published a considerable amount of prose, her commitment, first and last, is to poetry. The reader can be glad of this book in which the best of the poems, now stripped of their prose encumbrances, recover something of the primacy of attention they had for Rossetti when she was writing them."

PRINCIPAL WORKS

Goblin Market, and Other Poems (poetry) 1862

Poems (poetry) 1866

The Prince's Progress, and Other Poems (poetry) 1866

Commonplace, and Other Short Stories (short stories) 1870

Sing-Song: A Nursery Rhyme Book (children's poetry) 1872

Speaking Likenesses (children's prose) 1874

Seek and Find (devotional prose) 1879

Called to Be Saints: The Minor Festivals Devotionally Studied (devotional prose) 1881

A Pageant, and Other Poems (poetry) 1881

Time Flies: A Reading Diary (devotional prose) 1885

The Face of the Deep: A Devotional Commentary on the Apocalypse (devotional prose) 1892

Verses. Reprinted from Called to be Saints, Time Flies, The Face of the Deep (devotional poetry) 1893

New Poems (poetry) 1896

Maude: Prose and Verse (children's stories and poetry) 1897

The Poetical Works of Christina Georgina Rossetti [edited by William Michael Rossetti] (poetry) 1904

The Family Letters of Christina Georgina Rossetti [edited by William Michael Rossetti] (letters) 1908

The Complete Poems of Christina Rossetti: A Variorum Edition. 3 vols. [edited by Rebecca W. Crump] (poetry) 1979-90

The Letters of Christina Rossetti. 4 vols. [edited by Antony H. Harrison] (letters) 1997-2004

CRITICISM

Sharon Smulders (essay date 1996)

SOURCE: Smulders, Sharon. "Fresh Fields of Endeavor: Short Stories and Nursery Rhymes." In *Christina Rossetti Revisited*, pp. 92-122. New York: Twayne, 1996.

[*In the following essay, Smulders surveys the short stories and children's literature Rossetti published between 1870 and 1874.*]

The demand for *Goblin Market, The Prince's Progress, and Other Poems* put the seal on Rossetti's success as a serious poet. She was, however, more than a poet and had, in the years before 1875, expanded her published oeuvre to include prose as well as verse. During these years she also made the unlucky decision to change publishers. Leaving Macmillan in 1870, she approached F. S. Ellis with a manuscript of nursery rhymes illustrated, as she modestly said, with her "own scratches" (Packer, ed., 74) and broached to him the plan for a collection of prose tales. Published later that year, *Commonplace and Other Short Stories* contains most of the fiction she had composed since 1852. While the volume thus realized an ambition heralded in *Maude,* it fared poorly with critics and booksellers. As a result, Rossetti freed Ellis from his obligation to her nursery rhymes

and, in so doing, dispensed with the unwelcome necessity of offending Alice Boyd, whose illustrations, taking the place of the original scratches, had proven unsatisfactory.

When George Routledge and Sons agreed in the following year to publish the rhymes, she had decided on Arthur Hughes as her illustrator. Dated 1872, *Sing-Song: A Nursery Rhyme Book* was released in time for Christmas of 1871. Encouraged by the praise her nursery rhymes received, Rossetti then produced a series of interlinked stories, *Speaking Likenesses,* which she offered to Macmillan in 1874. But when Ruskin, for one, read the tales, he was revolted. "How," he wondered, "could she or Arthur Hughes sink so low after their pretty nursery rhymes?" (Ruskin, 37:155). Nevertheless, insofar as *Speaking Likenesses* succeeds to *Sing-Song* as a work for children and to *Commonplace and Other Short Stories* as a work of fiction, the volume brings to a culmination the experiments in form and genre that Rossetti conducted at the height of her career.

SPEAKING LIKENESSES IN COMMONPLACE AND OTHER SHORT STORIES

Rossetti's reputation as a poet worked to the disadvantage of *Commonplace and Other Short Stories.* Touting the title work among his acquaintance as "very good (in the Miss Austen vein rather)," Gabriel told his sister: "It certainly is not dangerously exciting to the nervous system, but it is far from being dull for all that" (D. G. Rossetti 1965, 2:826). "Of course," he added, "I think your proper business is to write poetry, and not *Commonplaces*" (2:827). Contemporary reviewers made similar criticisms of the volume as a whole. Disappointed to discover "that the authoress of such exquisite verses can indeed write commonplaces," the reader for the *Spectator* observed: "Not that evidence of the same fancy is entirely wanting, but it is chiefly exhibited in the grotesque variety of the wares offered for our acceptance, and which are adapted to such opposite classes of customers, and belong to such different periods of life."[1] The eclecticism that the *Spectator* chose to condemn, however, demonstrates one of Rossetti's strengths as a writer of fiction: her versatility.

In addition to such everyday domestic fare as **"Commonplace"** and the slightly more exotic **"Vanna's Twins,"** *Commonplace and Other Short Stories* includes one brilliantly vivid historical tale (**"The Lost Titian"**), two fairy stories (**"Nick"** and **"Hero: A Metamorphosis"**), and three avowedly polemical pieces (**"A Safe Investment," "Pros and Cons,"** and **"The Waves of this Troublesome World"**). Arranging her prose for publication in much the same way as her poetry, Rossetti opens the volume with a secular novella, **"Commonplace,"** and ends with a devotional narrative, **"The Waves of this Troublesome World."** But despite "individual differences," her tales possess, like the three sisters in the title story, a "strong family likeness."[2] Experimenting with a range of realistic, fantastic, and didactic forms, Rossetti returns time and again to the same motifs—birth and death, loss and gain—that distinguish her verse. Moreover, her stories, whether oriented to secular or religious ends, rely on a symbology informed by an Anglo-Catholic appreciation of the spiritual significance of physical phenomena. "All the world over," says Rossetti in the devotional work **Seek and Find,** "visible things typify things invisible."[3] As a result, her fiction emulates the structure of parable, defined as "a spoken emblem," and uncovers in mere commonplace a resource for "hidden meaning" (**CSS** [**Commonplace and Other Short Stories**], 309-10).

"Commonplace," written in 1870, returns to the preoccupations of **Maude.** But whereas Rossetti's juvenile novella explores alternative forms of feminine fulfillment, **"Commonplace"** focuses on marriage as woman's ordinary lot in life. Finding hidden meaning in the platitudinous phrase and the everyday event, Rossetti examines the romantic illusions and economic realities that shape women's decision to marry. The tale opens as Lucy and Catherine, the eldest of the three Charlmont sisters, attend to the "meat-and-drink responsibilities" of breakfast (**CSS,** 5). Ironically, the youngest sister's frivolous perusal of the *Times* supplement speaks no less to the meat-and-drink affairs of Victorian women:

> Jane read aloud: "'Halbert to Jane'; I wish I were Jane. And here, positively, are two more Janes, and not me. 'Catherine'—that's a death. Lucy, I don't see you anywhere. Catherine was eighty-nine, and much respected. 'Mrs. Anstruther of a son and heir.' I wonder if those are the Anstruthers I met in Scotland: she was very ugly, and short. 'Everilda Stella,'—how can anybody be Everilda?" Then, with a sudden accession of interest, "Why, Lucy, Everilda Stella has actually married your Mr. Hartley!"

> (*CSS,* 6-7)

The notices devoted to births, marriages, and deaths, though ancillary to the reports of men's business in the *Times* proper, constitute the whole of women's business. In this respect the three envied Janes, all recently wed, reveal the youngest Miss Charlmont's dedication to marriage as a career. Catherine's future, on the other hand, is parabolically encoded in fate of the aged and venerable woman whose obituary Jane reads. Not interested in marriage for herself, Catherine looks, at the end of the novella, to a future that lies "further off" (**CSS,** 142). By contrast, Lucy's situation is, as Jane's inability to see her in the *Times* suggests, rather more ambiguous. Having met Alan Hartley at Appletrees House, the home of her father's cousin in London, she has allowed his charm to win her over and, believing herself loved, refused several offers of marriage. Conse-

quently, when Alan marries the "only child and presumptive heiress of George Durham, Esq., of Orpingham Place" (**CSS,** 19), Lucy receives a shock. In effect, her disappointment comes of her childish confidence in the "copy, 'Manners make the Man,'" set her as a girl; Catherine, having also been taught "how in that particular phrase 'Man' includes 'Woman,'" amends the rule to "'Morals make the Man' (including Woman)"; and Jane believes "'Money makes the Man'" (**CSS,** 93). The final maxim, as Jane's circumstances confirm, is not gender inclusive.

Moving the scene from Brompton-on-Sea to London, Rossetti advances the narrative of Jane's career to demonstrate how women's disadvantaged position under patriarchal law undermines the sanctity of marriage. Taking Lucy's place in a second breakfast triptych, Mrs. Tyke observes that Jane has made a conquest of George Durham. Although his daughter Stella's inheritance is thus imperiled, she remains unruffled by her father's courtship of a woman young enough to be her sister. For this reason, however, Jane treats Stella as a rival. The posthumous daughter of William Charlmont, she receives nothing under the terms of her father's will and, hence, is "dependent on her sisters" (**CSS,** 16). Like Margaret's illegitimacy in **"Under the Rose,"** Jane's disinheritance, albeit unintentional, symbolizes the legal exclusion under which the Victorian woman suffers. Unlike Margaret, however, Jane is corrupted by her experience. Courting in George a father to restore her lost patrimony, she transfers her envy of her sisters, as favored daughters, to Stella.[4] Even when Catherine makes Jane her sole heir, she resents the £20,000 that George settles upon his daughter.

Mean-spirited toward Stella, Jane is no more charitable toward her aged suitor, who is merely a means to an end. As she says, "George is Orpingham Place, and Orpingham Place is George" (**CSS,** 95). Although "she would certainly have entered upon Orpingham Place with added zest had it not entailed George" (**CSS,** 104), her love of money outweighs her aversion for the man. "If the pines and the pigs are smitten," she asks, "why shouldn't I marry the pigs and the pines?" (**CSS,** 38). While Jane's objectification of George reveals the crassness of her material ambitions, her jokes at his expense demonstrate her intelligence as well as her scorn. Sending his photograph to Lucy, she facetiously asks, "Don't you see all Orpingham Place in his speaking countenance?" (**CSS,** 60). For her part, Lucy settles on "an arrangement which, in her eyes, showed a symbolic appropriateness" and returns to her sister "Mr. Durham's portrait wrapped in a ten-pound note" (**CSS,** 64). This symbolic gesture suggests, of course, that marriage is but a form of prostitution. Jane, allowing herself to be bought, nonetheless tolerates her husband "as the 'habitation-tax' paid for Orpingham Place" (**CSS,** 141).

The artfulness of Jane's campaign to acquire a wealthy husband, whatever the cost, is epitomized in the event that serves as a prelude to George's proposal: an elaborate three-part charade performed for a party of 200 guests at Appletrees House. While Charlotte Brontë, in a similar episode in *Jane Eyre* (1847), employs the name of a British prison, Bridewell, to associate marriage with captivity, Rossetti's choice of "love-apple" for the "charade word" (*CSS,* 75) exposes romance as pretense, for the grandiloquent "love-apple" is only the commonplace tomato. In each of the charade's three scenes, therefore, Rossetti emphasizes the artificiality of the construct from which the audience must guess the answer. In the first scene, representing *love,* "a file of English-Grecian maidens, singing and carrying garlands, passed across the stage towards a pasteboard temple, presumably their desired goal, although they glanced at their audience, and seemed very independent of Cupid on his pedestal" (*CSS,* 78-79). The maidens' self-conscious awareness of their audience casts doubt on their devotion to love as an ideal. In the second scene, representing *apple,* the stage props—"woolly toy lambs" and a peacock "ingeniously mounted on noiseless wheels" (*CSS,* 80)—draw attention once more to the pasteboard unreality of the action. Having made a real-life choice between Lucy and her "unconscious rival" (*CSS,* 39), Alan Hartley plays the part of Paris. Constrained to choose among three "rival goddesses" (*CSS,* 80), he wavers between Juno and Minerva before passing the prized apple to Venus, played by Jane. Bringing *love* and *apple* together, the third scene grounds the meaning of the charade word in the vulgar context of the marketplace and hence defines love as a commodity on which women trade competitively for economic security. In this act, Stella takes the role of a market girl who, like the little men of **"Goblin Market,"** cries, "'Grapes, melons, peaches, love-apples,' with the most natural inflections" (*CSS,* 82). Her down-to-earth performance is less affecting, however, than Jane's act as a trumped-up goddess. In another charade enacted behind the scenes, Jane crowns her performance as Venus when she accepts George's proposal. Eclipsing Stella on stage and off, she has thereby "attained both her objects" (*CSS,* 84).

That marriage need not be a charade Rossetti suggests by contrasting Jane and George Durham with Sarah and Gawkins Drum. The family likeness between the two couples emerges when Miss Drum, the Charlmont sisters' former teacher, expounds "the Drum-Durham theory": "Our family name of Drum," she tells Lucy, "though less euphonious than that of Durham, is in fact the same" (*CSS,* 90). Nevertheless, the Durhams' marriage is a very different affair from the Drums', for Sarah, having "devoted herself during an ordinary lifetime" to a "bedridden brother" (*CSS,* 69), marries Gawkins when both are in their sixties. Provoking laughter among their acquaintance, their belated marriage so outrages his sister's sense of propriety that she indicts the aged bride and groom as "culprits at the moral bar" (*CSS,* 73). Unconventionality is not immorality, however. Indeed, while the Drums have remained faithful to each other through a lifetime of courtship, Jane refuses to commit herself to George during their short engagement. An incorrigible flirt, she tells Catherine, "Mr. Durham isn't Bluebeard; or, if he is, I had better get a little fun first" (*CSS,* 99). Thus, she attends, upon her return to Brompton-on-Sea, a picnic at which she initially designs to fascinate Mr. Ballantyne, a widowed solicitor, and so dash the marital hopes of Edith Sims. Modifying her plan for amusement, she turns her attention from Ballantyne to a young viscount. Narrated with zest and humor, Jane's activities nevertheless betoken her desperation in the face of her forthcoming marriage.

The picnic is a pivotal event in **"Commonplace,"** for it marks the resumption of Lucy's career as well as the climax of Jane's romantic adventures. But Lucy, far from seeking to conduct a flirtation or initiate a courtship, chooses to take charge of Ballantyne's five-year-old son, who futilely searches for strawberries out of season. While Catherine fails to divert Jane from the viscount, Lucy successfully saves little Frank when he attempts to escape her control and run into danger. In so doing, she wins the admiration of the child's father, who proposes shortly after her birthday in November. Pleased "to find herself not obsolete even at thirty" (*CSS,* 128), she refuses to rush headlong into marriage and declines his offer. Indeed, her rescue of Frank provides a spoken emblem of immature passion restrained by mature conscience.

Through Lucy's experience, Rossetti validates marriage as a vocation based on principle. Having drawn "a false conclusion" from Alan Hartley's superficial charm (*CSS,* 23), Lucy has learnt to appreciate the sincerity of his friend Arthur Tresham, whom she had formerly refused. Accepting an invitation to Appletrees House, she looks forward to renewing his acquaintance. Rossetti ironizes Lucy's newfound happiness, however, by placing her courtship against the mourning of the widowed Mrs. Tyke, born Lucy Charlmont, and by emphasizing Arthur's dullness. Diligent on behalf of London's East End poor as well as Lucy's bereaved kinswoman, Arthur is a moral man and a lackluster lover. Lucy momentarily rues his shortcomings, but "weighing her second love against her first, tears, at once proud and humble, filled her eyes, and 'one cannot have everything' was forgotten in 'I can never give him back half enough'" (*CSS,* 137). Although their courtship and marriage admits "no stereotyped hypocrisies" (*CSS,* 140), Lucy experiences one "romantic moment" before she returns to Brompton-on-Sea to prepare for the wedding: "At the noisy, dirty, crowded railway-station, . . . Arthur terrified Lucy, to her great delight, by standing on the carriage-step, and holding her hand locked fast in his own, an instant after the train had started" (*CSS,* 138). This moment doubles upon Jane's departure from London before her marriage. Having produced a "show of sentiment" for George (*CSS,* 92), Jane "never in her life had experienced a greater relief than . . . when the starting train left him behind on the platform," but soon "it would be too late to leave him behind" (*CSS,* 93). The thought of Paris—the city rather than the Trojan prince—overcomes Jane's feelings of misgiving. Rossetti enhances the significance of these two departures not merely by interposing the death of Dr. Tyke, but by making "London-Bridge Station, with its whirl of traffic," an "emblem of London itself: vast, confused, busy, orderly, more or less dirty" (*CSS,* 33). The site of departures and arrivals, London-Bridge Station is also an emblem of the world in all its tawdry confusion. Consequently, because Lucy's wedding necessitates a return to London, Rossetti ultimately figures marriage as a decision to live *in* rather than *apart* from the world.

While Lucy's marriage to Arthur refuses to "lend itself to any tribute of lies, miscalled white" (*CSS,* 140), Rossetti includes as an epigraph to **"The Lost Titian,"** the second selection in **Commonplace and Other Short Stories,** the enigmatic phrase, "A lie with a circumstance" (*CSS,* 145). Although this tale, richly opulent in the telling, seems the reverse of commonplace, it is a companion piece to the title story. In both, Rossetti addresses the problem of judging from appearances and of distinguishing manners from morals. But turning from the female world of love to the male domain of art, she provides in **"The Lost Titian"** a critique of post-Raphaelite decadence rather than of amatory ideology. In so doing, she offers a rejoinder to Gabriel's short story "Hand and Soul," which she once described as "rich in beauty and power: *that* even my anxious eyes see and admit" (quoted in Bell, 123). Whereas "Hand and Soul," first published in the *Germ,* describes the provenance of a thirteenth-century painting by Chiaro dell' Erma that hangs in Florence's Pitti Gallery, **"The Lost Titian"** relates the disappearance of a sixteenth-century work of Venetian art. And whereas Chiaro dell' Erma's painting incarnates Pre-Raphaelite sincerity in art, the lost Titian symbolizes the loss of moral principle in Victorian as well as Renaissance painting.

For Rossetti, esthetic degradation is a reflex of moral degradation. Drawing perhaps on her understanding the rivalry among her eldest brother, Hunt, and Millais, she opens her post-Raphaelite story as Titian, in company with "his two friends—Gianni the successful, and Giannuccione the universal disappointment" (*CSS,* 146)—completes "the masterpiece of the period; the masterpiece of his life" (*CSS,* 145). Yet Gianni, for all his success, suffers from jealousy and so contrives to rob Titian of his achievement during a game of dice. Wagering all in one desperate gamble, he wins the painting

and loses his friend. When financial insolvency threatens to deprive him of his sordid triumph, Gianni again compromises his integrity by employing art in the service of guile: "Taking coarse pigments, such as, when he pleased, might easily be removed, he daubed over those figures which seemed to live, and that wonderful background, which not Titian himself could reproduce; then, on the blank surface, he painted a dragon, flaming, clawed, preposterous" (*CSS,* 158). Consequently, when Titian arrives with Gianni's other creditors, he seeks his "one unforgotten beauty . . . in vain; only in the forefront sprawled a dragon, flaming, clawed, preposterous; grinned, twinkled, erected his tail, and flouted him" (*CSS,* 159). The dragon's tail, suggestive of phallic power, delivers an insult that Titian, unable to see through Gianni's latest device, fails to appreciate. But although the painting is a lie, it reveals a truth. Just as Chiaro's depiction of a beautiful lady symbolizes his purity of heart, Gianni's preposterous dragon reveals the monstrous perversity of his soul. Furthermore, the dragon's usurpation of beauty, represented in Titian's masterpiece, signifies coarse art's succession to fine art. Thus, insofar as the renovated painting epitomizes the betrayal of art as well as friendship, Rossetti uses the dragon to show the loss of sincerity following the dissolution of the PRB [Pre-Raphaelite Brotherhood].

Ironically, Gianni's revenge redounds against him, for a publican claims the sign of the dragon to settle an outstanding account and the painter fails to redeem it before his death. But even as the Titian is thus twice lost, the story ends with the tantalizing possibility of the painting's recovery:

> Reader, should you chance to discern over wayside inn or metropolitan hotel a dragon pendent, or should you find such an effigy amid the lumber of a broker's shop, whether it be red, green, or piebald, demand it importunately, pay for it liberally, and in the privacy of home scrub it. It *may* be that from behind the dragon will emerge a fair one, fairer than Andromeda, and that to you will appertain the honour of yet further exalting Titian's greatness in the eyes of a world.
>
> (*CSS,* 162-63)

While the final address to the reader is redolent of allegory, an earlier allusion to "an oral tradition of a somewhere extant lost Titian having survived all historical accuracy" (*CSS,* 162) enhances the story's realism. Indeed, because some credulous readers had taken **"The Lost Titian,"** first published in the *Crayon* (1856), to be literally true, Rossetti prefaced **Commonplace and Other Short Stories** with a reminder that her work was "not . . . founded on fact" (*CSS,* [v]). Yet, in fiction, she discovered a means to make a lie serve the circumstance of truth.

Following her historical tale of moral degeneracy with two allegories of spiritual regeneration, Rossetti abandons realist conventions in **"Nick"** and **"Hero: A Meta-**

morphosis." Written in 1853, the first of these companion tales deals with an old man who suffers from envy and discontent, while the second, published in the *Argosy* in 1866, concerns a young maiden who, mistaking the diffidence of her father and her lover for indifference, desires "to become the supreme object of admiration" (*CSS*, 190). Nick's adventures begin when he wishes destruction to farmer Giles's orchard. An outraged fairy, brandishing "her tiny fist . . . in a menacing attitude," responds immediately: "Now listen, you churl, you! henceforward you shall straightway become everything you wish; only mind, you must remain under one form for at least an hour" (*CSS*, 168-69). The vengeful fairy's final "slap in the face" (*CSS*, 169) anticipates the sadism of Rossetti's *Speaking Likenesses* and foreshadows the violence that follows on each of Nick's wishes. When, for example, he becomes a flock of sparrows and begins to devour Giles's cherries, the farmer arms himself and "soon reduce[s] the enemy to one crestfallen biped with broken leg and wing" (*CSS*, 170). After several punishing transformations, Nick finally decides that "if he merely studied his own advantage without trying to annoy other people, perhaps his persecutor might be propitiated" (*CSS*, 176). Consequently, he wishes himself "the rich old man who lived in a handsome house just beyond the turnpike" (*CSS*, 176). In this incarnation, however, he discovers that his miserly wealth makes him the object of envy and spite. Robbed and murdered, he returns to himself just as his assassins toss the first clods of the grave upon his body. Symbolically reborn, devilish old Nick becomes good saint Nick. After making his former victims secret restitution, he "was never again heard to utter a wish" (*CSS*, 179).

"Hero," the feminine complement to "Nick," is likewise a cautionary fairy tale. But when Hero utters her wish, the fairy court is reluctant to burden her with the "perilous preeminence she demanded" (*CSS*, 192). Instead, the Queen Fairy decrees that the girl's "restless spirit" be returned to Man-side in "a heavy blazing diamond" (*CSS*, 195) while her body remains on Elf-side for one year until she understands the magnitude of the gift that she desires. A commodity sold at "the best market of Outerworld" (*CSS*, 196), Hero comes into the possession of Princess Lily, who wears the jewel on her wedding day. But even though "Hero eclipsed the bride, dazzled the bridegroom, distracted the queen-mother, and thrilled the whole assembly" (*CSS*, 197), Lily's husband esteems his wife over the diamond. Experiencing "a shock," Hero then moves into "Lily's pure heart [where] she almost found rest" (*CSS*, 198).

Restlessness returns to Hero when, upon the return of the prince and princess to the public world, they attend the final operatic performance of Melice Rapta. Moving from Lily to Melice, Hero finds herself again eclipsed when the singer's uncle, an avid gardener, turns his at-

tention from his niece to a rare seedling. Reborn in the plant, she is, however, scorned by the woman who takes over Uncle Treeh's estate after his death and who covets, above all else, a picturesque garden ruin. As the object of admiration to one of degraded taste, Hero realizes the ruin of her ambition and feels "a passionate longing for the old lost life, the old beloved love" (*CSS*, 207). At that moment, her spirit returns to her body. Reconciled to herself, she awakens from death to life under the care of Forss, her lover, and Peter, her father. The moral of the story, which Hero, like Laura of "Goblin Market," tells her children, is "that though admiration seems sweet at first, only love is sweet first, and last, and always" (*CSS*, 211).

Apart from **"Vanna's Twins,"** the remaining stories in *Commonplace and Other Short Stories* appeared initially in the *Churchman's Shilling Magazine* in 1867. Although all three take Rossetti's tendency to moral exempla to doctrinal ends, **"A Safe Investment,"** a parable of the apocalypse, and **"Pros and Cons,"** a sermon on pew rents and Christian equality, are of less significance than **"The Waves of this Troublesome World."** Another story of loss and recovery, **"The Waves"** concerns the return of Sarah Hardiman Lane to her childhood home and eventually to her childhood faith. The parable of the lost sheep (Luke 15:4-7) that Mrs. Grey, the curate's wife, assigns Sarah's niece, Jane, as a lesson gives meaning to the widow Lane's experience. As a young woman, Sarah had met and, against her father's will, married a traveling photographer and itinerant Methodist preacher. For Rossetti, Sarah's action represents a grave error. "A wife's paramount duty," she explains in *Letter and Spirit,* "is indeed to her husband, superseding all other human obligations: yet to assume this duty, free-will first stepped in with its liability to err; in this connexion woman has to reap as she has sown, be the crop what it may: while in the filial relation all is safe and flawless."[5] Thus Sarah, having substituted her father for her husband, also substitutes Anglicanism for Methodism. As a dissenter, she rebels against her heavenly as well as her earthly father. Her punishment, wreaked by a truly jealous God, follows in the deaths of the three male relatives she most loves: her father, Henry Hardiman; her son, Henry Lane; and her husband, John Lane. In other words, heaven's trinity cancels Sarah's earthly trinity. The near death of another Henry Hardiman, the nephew whom Sarah dotes on because he is "so like his grandfather" (*CSS*, 328), precipitates her return to Anglicanism.

Dispatching Jane and her brother Henry on an innocuous errand that ends in disaster, Sarah resembles the mother who unwittingly sends her children to their deaths in "Vanna's Twins," which Swinburne, despite his "physical shock" at Rossetti's heartlessness, considered "the sweetest story of them all."[6] But whereas the twins, after fulfilling Vanna's commission to a poor woman with three sick children, get lost in a sudden snowstorm and perish "huddled together in a chalky hollow close to the edge of the cliff" (*CSS*, 236), the Hardiman children find themselves pinned on "a narrow shelf" beneath the cliff as the tide rises inexorably toward them (*CSS*, 323). During their ordeal, Jane prays for the protection of the Good Shepherd. Indeed, even as Rossetti's allusion to "one Holy Innocents' Day" (*CSS*, 228) serves to put the death of Vanna's twins within the context of divine mystery, the miraculous salvation of Sarah's niece and nephew corresponds to the parable of the lost sheep and reveals "its lesson of mercy or warning" (*CSS*, 327). To this lesson, Sarah pays heed and, moved by Jane's plea, accompanies the Hardimans to church to give thanks for the children's restoration. Still torn in her allegiance to her dead father and dead husband, she finds comfort in Mrs. Grey's assurance that John Lane provided her "husband a living lesson of boldness, self-denial, and trampling false shame under foot" (*CSS*, 326). This assurance allows her to respond to the voice of conscience and return to the fold. While Rossetti's emphasis on the Anglican Church as the one true fold is obviously dogmatic, she also suggests that the Church has much to learn from those, like Sarah's husband, who have, as the name "Lane" suggests, chosen other avenues of worship.

Insofar as Sarah's return to the Church follows on her return to celibacy, *Commonplace and Other Short Stories* implicitly rejects marriage as woman's best destiny. Moving from courtship in **"Commonplace"** to widowhood in **"The Waves,"** Rossetti broadens her treatment of feminine experience to reevaluate the situation of the single woman. Making England's cliff-lined shore the scene for liminal subjectivity, she not only sets her opening and closing tales in coastal towns but chooses for the motto of *Commonplace and Other Short Stories* "From sea to sea" (*CSS*, [iii]). Although the waves of this troublesome world threaten to engulf the unwary, the sea also symbolizes the other world and the afterlife. At the end of **"Commonplace"** Catherine looks toward the sea that has claimed her earthly father's life and, awaiting his return, trusts her future to her heavenly father. Similarly, at the end of **"The Waves"** Sarah awaits Christ's second coming. "Thankful that her idol was removed for a season" (*CSS*, 329), she returns to the flawless safety of the filial relation that Catherine, never marrying, has never left. Choosing to remain a widow, she keeps faith not so much with her dead husband as her beloved father(s). In **"The Waves,"** therefore, Rossetti reorients the imperatives of feminine existence from the secular ideal of marriage to the spiritual ideal of self-devotion and brings *Commonplace and Other Short Stories* full circle.

Sing-Song and Full-Grown Femininity

Sing-Song: A Nursery Rhyme Book occupies a position at the center of Rossetti's poetic career. Describing

the volume as "alternating between the merest babyism and a sort of Blakish wisdom and tenderness," Gabriel swore that "no one could have written anything so absolutely right for babies but herself" (D. G. Rossetti 1965, 2:797). *Sing-Song* belongs, however, to a tradition that also includes such undisputed classics as Jane Taylor's "The Star" ("Twinkle, twinkle, little star") and Sarah Josepha Hale's "Mary's Lamb" ("Mary had a little lamb"). In these and other works, Rossetti's female precursors annexed juvenile verse to the prerogatives of feminine lyricism and so pioneered an esthetic of literary maternalism that granted them, as women poets, unparalleled authority.[7] Indeed, as if to acknowledge the expressive freedom she discovered in nursery rhyme, Rossetti opens *Sing-Song*—the only volume of verse not dedicated to her mother—with the delightfully provocative announcement: "RHYMES DEDICATED WITHOUT PERMISSION TO THE BABY WHO SUGGESTED THEM" (*CP The Complete Poems of Christina Rossetti*, 2:19). Although the unnamed muse was, in all likelihood, Charles Cayley's nephew, the cryptic impersonality of the dedication widens the frame of reference from a child to all children. At the same time, the inspirational baby functions as an ideological cipher that not only yields before feminine power in the nursery but reproduces feminine powerlessness outside the nursery. In other words, the construct of the child ironically reconstructs the experience of Victorian wives and mothers who, reading *Sing-Song* to their children, comprised the poet's other audience. Speaking for as well as to nineteenth-century femininity in *Sing-Song,* Rossetti accommodates the childlike simplicity of nursery rhyme to the adult voice of duty and desire, power and passion, doubt and dependence.

Although Rossetti considered herself "deficient in the nice motherly ways which win and ought to win a child's heart" (*FL,* 75), she respected the power that motherhood conferred on women. Polarizing rather than conflating juvenility and femininity, her first four lyrics exploit the dramatic directness of maternal speech to convey women's relationship with children as one of intimacy as well as authority. Furthermore, while the opening quartet includes some of the most babyish of Rossetti's singsongs, it also inscribes an antithetical turn from life to death and, in so doing, encapsulates the total movement of the volume. The first two poems—**"Angels at the foot"** and **"Love me,—I love you"**—depict the mutual joys of mother and child. The second two—**"My baby has a father and a mother"** and **"Our little baby fell asleep"**—reveal their mutual sorrows.[8] Indeed, the initiatory lyric alone hints at Rossetti's breadth of scope in *Sing-Song*: "Angels at the foot, / And Angels at the head, / And like a curly little lamb / My pretty babe in bed" (ll. 1-4). Supernature, represented by the angels, hovers at the outer limits of the child's domain. Nature, suggested by the lamb, constitutes its center.

Reinvoking the resemblance between the child and the lamb several times in the course of *Sing-Song,* Rossetti playfully captures the innocence of youth. In **"Minnie and Mattie"** a "Woolly white lambkin / Frisks all about" (ll. 11-12); in **"Dancing on the hill-tops"** a young girl, Alice, cavorts "with lambkins / In the flowering valleys" (ll. 5-6); in **"A frisky lamb"** the lamb frolics with an equally "frisky child" (l. 2). In **"On the grassy banks,"** moreover, Rossetti widens the analogy inaugurated in **"Angels at the foot"** and makes the flock a metaphor for the family. "Woolly sisters, woolly brothers" (l. 3) gambol under the watchful eyes of "their woolly mothers" (l. 5). Missing from **"On the grassy banks,"** however, is the "patriarchal ram" that, at the end of **"An Old-World Thicket,"** calls and leads the flock "with tinkling bell" (l. 171). Indeed, in *Sing-Song,* the new world of childhood is, as **"On the grassy banks"** suggests, matriarchal.

Making an explicit comparison between babies and lambs in **"Angels at the foot,"** the speaker reveals the vulnerability as well as the innocence of childhood. The poet, on the other hand, ascribes to womanhood a protective power by creating an implicit resemblance between angels and mothers. Rossetti does not, however, subscribe unqualifiedly to the angelic ideal of Victorian femininity. When, for example, the maternal angels that act for the speaker in the opening lyric reappear in **"Three little children,"** their presence marks the mother's radical absence. The mother's death, in other words, brings seraphic womanhood to its logical dénouement. In the interests of balance, therefore, Rossetti broadens her treatment of maternity to include lyrics like **"On the grassy banks"** and **"A white hen sitting."** In these poems she not only puts motherhood into a natural context but elaborates the ideal of heroic femininity that prompted her to lay aside, if only for the sake of argument, her objections to the women's rights movement. Proposing the enfranchisement of married women, she asked Augusta Webster, "Who [are] so apt as Mothers . . . to protect the interests of themselves and of their offspring? I do think if anything ever does sweep away the barrier of sex, and make the female not a giantess or a heroine but at once and full grown a hero and a giant, it is that mighty maternal love which makes little birds and little beasts as well as little women matches for very big adversaries" (quoted in Bell, 112). Defined in terms of love and might, motherhood possesses a power that transcends generic as well as sexual difference.

Assimilating little women to little birds and little beasts, Rossetti aligns maternity to nature. The likeness between human and animal mothers Arthur Hughes cleverly depicts in his design for **"A white hen sitting"**: the hen whose chicks huddle beneath her wing faces a young woman whose daughter stands within her embrace. Implicit in the illustration is the idea of protective or, more properly, heroic motherhood. Giving more explicit form to maternal might in the poem, Rossetti describes the threat posed by three winged adversaries—an owl, a hawk, and a bat—to the hen's newly hatched brood. But just as the orphans of **"Three little children"** are "Safe as safe can be / With guardian Angels" (ll. 9-10), the "chicks beneath their mother's wing / Squat safe as safe can be" (ll. 7-8). By reiterating the phraseology of **"Three little children"** in **"A white hen sitting,"** however, Rossetti ironizes the relationship among angels, women, and animals. Indeed, the resemblance between winged beasts, both protective and predatory, and winged beings strongly suggests the poet's ambivalence toward the conventional ideal of ethereal femininity.

Love as well as might is integral to Rossetti's construction of motherhood in *Sing-Song.* Thus in the second of her lyrics she turns from protective to passionate maternity. Superseding the intercessory angels of the previous poem, her speaker assumes a tone of address that is, at once, more immediate, more intimate, and more intense:

> Love me,—I love you,
> Love me, my baby;
> Sing it high, sing it low,
> Sing it as may be.
>
> Mother's arms under you,
> Her eyes above you;
> Sing it high, sing it low,
> Love me,—I love you.

> (ll. 1-8)

The mother holds the child with her arms, her eyes, and her words. The internal symmetry of the poem's framing lines suggests, moreover, a reciprocity between mother and child. But insofar as the baby's "very limited subjectivity" raises a "justified doubt" about its ability to sing and to feel the desired response, the poem articulates an unrealized ideal.[9] The child's limitations as a reciprocating subject, however, actually maximize the speaker's capacity for pleasure. Dependent, the baby needs its mother's care. Unself-conscious, it cannot reject her love. Thus the mother's relationship with her child, far from being "egalitarian," provides satisfaction because it ratifies her power.[10]

James R. Kincaid's argument that literary and cultural constructions of childhood as "pure nothingness" readily accommodate such strong emotions as adult erotic desire provides further insight into the way Rossetti figures babyhood in *Sing-Song.*[11] Because the baby represents an emptiness more profound than the child, it is infinitely more seductive. In **"Your brother has a falcon,"** then, the baby's nothingness invites the mother's fulfillment:

> Your brother has a falcon,
>   Your sister has a flower;
> But what is left for mannikin,
>   Born within an hour?
>
> I'll nurse you on my knee, my knee,
>   My own little son;
> I'll rock you, rock you, in my arms,
>   My least little one.

(ll. 1-8)

In the first stanza, the contrast between the baby and its siblings establishes the infant's absolute lack. But when the mother poses herself as the object of the child's fulfillment, she reveals her own insufficiency, for her elder son and daughter are, as the falcon and the flower suggest, no longer completely dependent on her. Turning to the infant, she finds the most emotional satisfaction in the least of her children precisely because his total need exceeds her partial want.

As a legitimate object of maternal attention, the baby authorizes the expression of feminine desire. But whereas distance defines sexual desire in the conventional amatory sonnet, nearness characterizes the articulation of maternal desire in Rossetti's nursery rhymes. Indeed, her eroticization of babyhood becomes overtly fleshly in those lyrics which, functioning as infantine blazons, catalog the child's physical charms. In **"My baby has a mottled fist"** the fatness that mottles and creases the child's body makes him "the very thing for kisses" (l. 4). In **"I know a baby, such a baby,"** on the other hand, the knowing mother not only rejoices in the baby's "Round blue eyes and cheeks of pink" (l. 2) but dwells with sensuous languor on "an elbow furrowed with dimples" (l. 3) and "a wrist where creases sink" (l. 4). Having rapturously itemized the baby's attractions in the first stanza, the speaker begins the second by attributing a meaning to the child's crowing: "'Cuddle and love me, cuddle and love me'" (l. 5). The child's imagined response, a projection of the mother's desire, resembles the chiastic refrain of **"Love me,—I love you"** and echoes the ending of **"The dog lies in his kennel"**: "And cuddle and kiss my baby, / And baby kiss me" (ll. 7-8). At the same time, the thrice-repeated "oh" of the lyric's final lines brings the mother's wonder and admiration to a new pitch: "Oh the bald head, and oh the sweet lips, / And oh the sleepy eyes that wink!" (ll. 7-8). The baby's sleepy eyes form a fitting prelude to the volume's two final lullabies, which, with their rocking rhythms and repetitive phrasings, recall the opening cradle songs. But even as these poems return the reader to the beginning of *Sing-Song*, the concluding lines of the last lyric, **"Lie a-bed,"** possess an air of finality: "Never wake:—/ Baby, sleep" (ll. 5-6).

While the faint intimation of mortality in **"Lie a-bed"** has alarmed some twentieth-century critics, it provides an instance of "the ulterior, intenser quality" that nineteenth-century readers such as Sidney Colvin esteemed in *Sing-Song*.[12] Indeed, Colvin describes the volume as "having always a music suited to baby ears, though sometimes a depth of pathos or suggestion far enough transcending baby apprehension" (23). Likewise, another of Rossetti's contemporaries observes that "her devotion to the children" does not deter her "from opening now and then the sluices of pathos and wider meanings, to flood the merry rill of *Sing-Song* for babes."[13] Introducing this note of pathos in the third lyric of the sequence, Rossetti reveals that maternal love, however mighty, cannot safeguard the child from all life's hazards. Thus **"My baby has a father and a mother,"** which one reviewer praised as "not too wise or grave for three years old," develops a contrast between the "Rich little baby" (l. 2) and a "Poor little baby" (l. 5) who, having neither mother nor father, is "Forlorn as may be" (l. 4).[14] Possessing an economic as well as an emotional resonance, the opposition between wealth and poverty distances the threat of parental abandonment to the middle-class child. Nevertheless, the affluent are not immune to the tragedies of life and death in *Sing-Song*.

Whereas poems like **"Love me,—I love you"** figure the relationship between mother and child as private and self-enclosed, Rossetti makes sorrow an emotion to be shared by both parents. In the fourth lyric, therefore, the speaker uses the possessive plural pronoun ("our" rather than "my") to communalize her expression of grief: "Our little baby fell asleep, / And may not wake again / For days and days, and weeks and weeks" (ll. 1-3). As days lengthen into weeks, the mother's ambiguous phrasing ("may not wake") becomes less an expression of uncertainty than a statement of interdicted possibility. But taking comfort from a belief in eternal life, she asserts that her child will "wake again, / And come with his own pretty look, / And kiss Mamma again" (ll. 4-6). Recalling the end of **"The Convent Threshold,"** the anticipated kiss not only provides an assurance of reunion in the hereafter but partakes of the here-and-now intimacy of lyrics like **"Love me,—I love you"** and **"My baby has a mottled fist."**

The consolatory function performed by Rossetti's sing-song dirges acknowledges death as a familiar aspect of life in the Victorian nursery. The high rate of mortality affecting infants and toddlers meant that, in all probability, at least one of the six children born to the average mid-Victorian family would not survive beyond its fifth birthday.[15] In addition to fearing and grieving the loss of a child, a mother had cause for anxiety on her own behalf, for the maternal mortality rate remained steady at 5 per 1,000 live births until the turn of the century. Furthermore, women's chances of hemorrhaging to death or contracting puerperal septicemia, as high after a stillbirth as a live birth, were even higher after a miscarriage.[16] Yet while the number of nineteenth-century poems featuring dead infants and mothers is thus understandable, Rossetti's precursors offered little in the way of comfort for the aggrieved. For example, Jane and Ann Taylor's "The Poor Little Baby," published in *Rhymes for the Nursery* (1806), opens with a macabre description of an infant's interment—"Down, down, in the pit-hole poor baby is gone"—and ends with the child speaker's grim self-admonition: "And let me remember, that I too shall die, / And then in the pit-hole I also must lie."[17] In "The Little Child," on the other hand, a toddler casually remarks, "If my dear mamma were gone, / I should perish soon, and die" (3:38). "The Baby," included in *Original Poems for Infant Minds* (1804-1805), makes a similar point about the child's helplessness: "Without a mother's tender care / The little thing must die" (2:70). While the Taylors' lyrics use the prospect of a mother's demise to frighten children into obedience and gratitude, later poems such as Henry Sharpe Horsley's "The Death of a Mother," which appeared in *The Affectionate Parent's Gift, and the Good Child's Reward* (1828), rely on sentiment to achieve a similar end. By contrast, Rossetti's nursery rhymes possess remarkable restraint. Spare and subtle, they are neither "mawkish" nor "sentimental."[18]

Avoiding the moral tendentiousness of much Victorian verse, Rossetti's singsong elegies provide emotional comfort by presenting death "as one point in a larger pattern, and as a natural event."[19] Furthermore, they provide spiritual comfort by representing nature in accordance with the Tractarian principles of analogy and reserve.[20] The ulterior or sacramental significance of **"Brown and furry,"** for example, resides in the poet's use of nature to impart the mystery of the resurrection: the lowly caterpillar may "Spin and die, / To live again a butterfly" (ll. 9-10). In "Why did baby die," on the other hand, nature supplies a tacit answer to the anguished question of infant mortality:

> Why did baby die,
> Making Father sigh,
> Mother cry?
>
> Flowers, that bloom to die,
> Make no reply
> Of "why?"
> But bow and die.
>
> (ll. 1-7)

"Spring blossoms and youth" are, as Rossetti says in **"What are heavy? sea-sand and sorrow,"** both "frail" (l. 3). Related metonymically rather than sylleptically to youth in **"Why did baby die,"** the unresponsive flowers reveal the natural inevitability of death. The lyric's

position immediately before **"If all were rain and never sun"** suggests, moreover, that joy and sorrow, like rain and sun, are both necessary to life.

By the same token, the consecutive arrangement of **"Hear what the mournful linnets say"** and **"A baby's cradle with no baby in it"** puts the experience of bereavement into a broader consolatory context. In **"Hear what the mournful linnets say,"** Rossetti takes the point of view of the parent birds to condemn the destruction of their eggs by marauding boys. More than an indictment of childish cruelties, the linnets' lament offers a means to understand the paradox of **"A baby's cradle with no baby in it."** The ruined nest, in other words, functions as an analogue for the empty crib. But while the first lyric addresses, albeit obliquely, a mother's sense of impotent rage and despair following the delivery of a stillborn child or the death of an infant, the second redeems the hope that has miscarried: "The sweet soul gathered home to Paradise, / The body waiting here" (ll. 3-4). Similarly, the snowdrop that the speaker of **"Baby lies so fast asleep"** places within the hands of the dead child, now beyond any pain that might "grieve her" (l. 6), represents hope. This hope, inspired by a belief in the resurrection, helps to assuage the mother's pain.

Rossetti's use of nature to express grief and offer religious solace lends her lyrics a succinctness that distinguishes them from contemporary works, such as Jean Ingelow's popular adult sequence, "Poems Written on the Deaths of Three Lovely Children Who Were Taken from Their Parents within a Month of One Another." Rossetti does not, however, make all comfort contingent on the prospect of paradisal reunion. The shortest lyric in *Sing-Song,* for example, delivers the orphaned child to a new mother: "Motherless baby and babyless mother, / Bring them together to love one another" (ll. 1-2). Although Hughes's illustration depicts a woman accepting her foster-child over a tiny grave, Rossetti does not specify, as Alice Meynell does in "Maternity," that the paradox of the babyless mother follows on her child's death. Indeed, in *The Face of the Deep* she argues that single women need not be excluded from the rewards of maternity, for "the childless who make themselves nursing mothers of Christ's little ones are true mothers in Israel" (*FD* [*The Face of the Deep*], 312). In **"Minnie and Mattie,"** therefore, "the nursing hen" (l. 13) is as true a mother to her brood of ducklings as "the mother hen" (l. 17) to her chicks. Amplifying her depiction of true motherhood in **"A motherless soft lambkin,"** Rossetti returns to the parable of the lost sheep used in **"The Waves of this Troublesome World"** to create a spoken emblem for juvenile as well as feminine heroism. Thus the child's rescue of the orphaned beast doubles on Christ's redemption of the lost soul and symbolizes the woman's adoption of an orphaned baby. By mothering the lost lamb, the speaker—child and woman—becomes a full-grown hero.

Refusing to confine her treatment of femininity to maternity, Rossetti seeks to embrace all aspects of the lives of girls and women in *Sing-Song.* Consequently, while pastoral lyrics like **"Minnie and Mattie"** and **"Dancing on the hill-tops"** nostalgically celebrate the freedom of youth, others, such as **"A pocket handkerchief to hem,"** put work before play and so anticipate the emphasis on duty in *Speaking Likenesses.* Using work to distinguish children from adults, Rossetti thus depicts the women in **"Rosy maiden Winifred"** and **"Margaret has a milking-pail"** as dairy-maids. The allusions to the harvest in these lyrics help, moreover, to emphasize the maturity of the maids. Arising early in the morning, Winifred walks through a late summer landscape of ripening grain, while Margaret meets Thomas, who "has a threshing-flail" (l. 3). The produce of the harvest, marital as well as agricultural, Rossetti relates in **"Minnie bakes oaten cakes,"** for Minnie not only makes cakes and ale but awaits her husband, Johnny, as he returns "Home from sea" (l. 4). But although Minnie "glows like a rose" (l. 5) in anticipation of Johnny's arrival, *Sing-Song* generally portrays wifehood as less rewarding to women than is motherhood.

Rossetti's marital singsongs provide a critique of Victorian domestic ideology. Restricted to home, her little wives lack full-grown experience. Thus in **"Wee wee husband"** the wife demands money of her husband to purchase comfits and honey—that is, the sweet desserts of marriage. Because her husband has "no money" (l. 6), however, they must learn to live without even such plain fare as milk, meat, and bread. While this wee parable of marital economics illuminates the frustrations consequent on the wife's financial dependence, **"I have a little husband"** makes the woman's dissatisfaction a function of her emotional dependence:

> I have a little husband
> 　　And he is gone to sea,
> The wind that whistle round his ship
> 　　Fly home to me.
>
> The winds that sigh about me
> 　　Return again to him;
> So I would fly, if only I
> 　　Were light of limb.
>
> 　　　　　　　　　　　　　(ll. 1-8)

The wind aptly suggests the difference between husband and wife as they pursue their separate existences: he whistles briskly while she sighs sadly. Their physical distance becomes, therefore, a measure of their emotional distance.

While the speaker's desire for flight in **"I have a little husband"** may appear childish, it yet reveals a concomitant desire for the freedom and independence of

adulthood. Returning to the motif of flight in **"I caught a little ladybird,"** Rossetti suggests, moreover, that feminine independence would provide greater satisfaction to both husbands and wives. Described as a "little lady wife" (l. 3), the ladybird travels, like the men in **"I have a little husband"** and **"Minnie bakes oaten cakes,"** "far away" (l. 2). Lively and elusive, she is more desirable as a playmate than the lifeless "dolly wife" (l. 7): "She's such a senseless wooden thing / She stares the livelong day; / Her wig of gold is stiff and cold / And cannot change to grey" (ll. 9-12). The dolly wife, forever young and blond, and the lady wife represent two opposing constructs of womanhood. Playing a masculine role, the girlish speaker positions herself as the ladybird's husband, validates her own desire for freedom and experience, and rejects the ideal of childlike femininity as embodied in the unnatural dolly wife.

Divorcing motherhood from wifehood in *Sing-Song,* Rossetti explores the contradictions implicit in Victorian inscriptions of womanhood to relate the totality of adult feminine experience. In so doing, she finds in nursery rhyme a form uniquely adapted to her purposes as a woman poet. Indeed, so thoroughly had she conquered the constraints of simplicity that she judged the volume to include, as she said, "some of my best songs" (*FL,* 94). Willing to explore further the expressive possibilities inherent in children's verse, she moved from nursery rhyme into dramatic spectacle with **"The Months: A Pageant,"** which, occupying a privileged position in her adult canon, appears as the title work in *A Pageant and Other Poems.* Hopeful as to the poem's "success as a drawing-room acting piece" (*FL,* 96), she did not confine her ambitions in the field of juvenile literature to verse. Setting her pen to fiction in *Speaking Likenesses,* she returns once more to the terrain of feminine experience examined in *Sing-Song.*

SPEAKING LIKENESSES: TALES OF FEMININE FORBEARANCE

A devoted daughter, Rossetti dedicates *Speaking Likenesses* "To my dearest mother, in grateful remembrance of the stories with which she used to entertain her children."[21] Although she acknowledged her mother in nearly all of her published works, the dedication to *Speaking Likenesses* serves as an odd introduction to a volume that features, as a narrator, an unamiable maiden aunt rather than a loving mother. Indeed, Aunt refuses to entertain her little listeners in either a hospitable or pleasurable manner. Ridiculing their childishness, she instead relates to them a series of stories in which her "small heroines perpetually encounter 'speaking (literally *speaking*) likenesses' or embodiments or caricatures of themselves" (Packer, ed., 101). But while Aunt, presumably a speaking likeness for her married sister, gives expression to maternal intolerance, she is also the children's secret ally against the parent whose indulgence masks tyranny, for she embodies the grown-up daughter's animus toward a beloved mother. Idealizing mothers in her stories, Aunt marginalizes and silences them. Coveting their power and prestige, she usurps their authority to ratify her own independence as a single woman. Still, while Rossetti thus reveals her ambivalence toward motherhood, she nevertheless makes maternity a potent symbol for feminine creativity.

The tensions that characterize Rossetti's treatment of mothers and daughters in *Speaking Likenesses* derive, in part, from her reliance on a rather unlikely mixture of elements drawn from the fantastic and didactic traditions in juvenile literature.[22] As a moral fiction, *Speaking Likenesses* resembles the tales with which Frances Rossetti had tried—and failed—to amuse her children. But even as the volume follows the pattern of instruction found in Thomas Day's *The History of Sandford and Merton* (1783-89), Maria Edgeworth's *Moral Tales* (1801), and Mary Sherwood's *The Fairchild Family* (1818-47), Rossetti conceived of her work as "a Christmas trifle, would-be in the *Alice* style with an eye to the market" (*FL,* 44). Such blatant imitation worked, however, to the book's disadvantage with reviewers, who noted that it "would have been more original if Alice had never been to 'Wonderland.'"[23] Yet Rossetti could not have been unaware of the criticism she would court in *Speaking Likenesses,* for Colvin had followed his favorable estimate of *Sing-Song* with a complaint about Lewis Carroll's unoriginality in *Through the Looking-Glass* (1871). As the sequel to *Alice's Adventures in Wonderland* (1865), *Through the Looking-Glass* "has," he said, "the misfortune of all sequels—that it is not a commencement" (Colvin, 24).

If the doubly belated *Speaking Likenesses* is not a commencement, it certainly brings Carroll's work to a resounding denouement. Appropriating Carrollian adventure to moral purpose, Rossetti serves up a confection—a Christmas trifle—that derisively mocks the assumptions of didactic and fantastic fiction alike. Opposed to Carroll's "avuncular" ideal of perpetual girlhood, Rossetti creates in Aunt a narrator who, as U. C. Knoepflmacher argues, tells her listeners "stories which relentlessly discourage their potential indulgence in Alice-like fantasies."[24] Unlike Scheherazade in Rossetti's beloved *Arabian Nights,* Aunt declines to "promise first-rate wonders on . . . extremely short notice" (*SL* [*Speaking Likenesses*], 71) and insists on her prerogative "to utilize . . . a brilliant idea twice" (*SL,* 81). Provokingly uninspired as a story-teller, she attempts to impress upon her would-be Alices the moral that concludes the first and longest of her three tales: "how to bear a few trifling disappointments, or how to be obliging and good-humoured under slight annoyances" (*SL,* 49).

Of the stories told in *Speaking Likenesses,* the first is most obviously a mock-*Alice* adventure. The tale opens with Flora, who, exactly six months older than Carroll's heroine in *Through the Looking-Glass,* awakens to her mother's kiss on the morning of her eighth birthday. Describing the little girl's failure to appreciate this sign of maternal favor, Aunt makes the daughter's negligence the object of her first lesson. Speaking "from the sad knowledge of . . . older experience," she somberly tells her auditors, "To every one of you a day will most likely come when sunshine, hope, presents and pleasure will be worth nothing to you in comparison with the unattainable gift of your mother's kiss" (*SL,* 4). After this gloomy prognostication, Aunt returns to her story and recounts Flora's delight upon opening her presents. From her father, she gets a Carrollian "story-book full of pictures" (*SL,* 4). From her mother and her nurse, on the other hand, she receives a writing case and a pin cushion that, housing pen and paper, pin and needle, are emblematic of dual feminine creativity. Unwittingly slighting her mother a second time, the girl is most impressed by the gifts given by her brother and sister: a box of sugar-plums and an expensive doll that, dubbed Flora by Flora, says, "Mamma" (*SL,* 8). In addition to her other gifts, Flora's mother also gives her a party. Crowning her daughter the "queen of the feast," she asks only that the girl and her guests "be very good and happy together" (*SL,* 5). The children are, however, far from either good or happy, for they wrangle over the sugar-plums, find fault with the tea, and fall to fighting at their games. Paradoxically, Flora's punishment for having three times disesteemed her mother's generosity involves reliving experience through the looking glass. In this way the mother's birthday greeting—"I wish you many and many happy returns of the day" (*SL,* 3)—becomes the ungrateful daughter's curse.

Flora's adventures start in earnest when she leaves her tiresome companions, walks from "the sunshine into the shadow" of "the yew alley," and finds "at its furthest end . . . a door with bell and knocker, and 'Ring also' printed in black letters on a brass plate" (*SL,* 16). This marvelous beginning constitutes, as the symbol of the yew tree suggests, a prelude to sorrow. Nevertheless, Flora, having entered a realm in which looking glasses abound, initially finds the experience "quite delightful," for she is able to gratify her vanity by taking "a long look at her little self full length" (*SL,* 21). This intense narcissism leads to bitter self-knowledge when the little girl meets her alter ego. The angry birthday Queen, whose features are "reflected over and over again in five hundred mirrors," magnifies the choler that distorts "Flora's fifty million-fold face" (*SL,* 26). Reflecting the Red Queen and Queen Alice in *Through the Looking-Glass,* Rossetti's queens likewise double upon Carroll's incarnation of fury, the Queen of Hearts, in *Alice's Adventures.* This movement back through Carroll's several queens allows Rossetti, moreover, to recall the rival card players, one of whom is named Flora, in her own **"Queen of Hearts,"** a poem written and published in 1863 before Alice first went to Wonderland. In the 50 million-fold mirrors of *Speaking Likenesses,* Rossetti makes herself not Carroll's imitator but his originator.

Using the looking-glass motif to heighten discordancy, Rossetti reflects other aspects of the world that her heroine has fled. Like Flora's mother, the yew tree chairs and tables "study everybody's convenience" (*SL,* 21), but the Queen's subjects possess an assortment of "exceptional features [that] could not but prove inconvenient":

> One boy bristled with prickly quills like a porcupine, and raised or depressed them at pleasure; but he usually kept them pointed outwards. Another instead of being rounded like most people was facetted at very sharp angles. A third caught in everything he came near, for he was hung round with hooks like fishhooks. One girl exuded a sticky fluid and came off on the fingers; another, rather smaller, was slimy and slipped through the hands.
>
> (*SL,* 28)

These inconvenient children personify all that is vicious and unpleasant: malice, anger, pain, disorder, lubricity. Crudely gendered, the boys are hurtful, and the girls are unctuous. Moreover, the sticky and slimy fluids that the girls exude on hand and finger are, like the boys' phallic quills, angles, and hooks, quite lewdly suggestive. Refusing to romanticize the innocence of the prepubescent eight-year-old, Rossetti establishes a sexual foundation for the three games played subsequently in Flora's dream.

Like Carroll, Rossetti uses games to give form to her heroine's experience. But as if to prove herself more original than Carroll, she rejects cards, croquet, and chess as inadequate to her purpose. Asked to propose the first game, Flora timidly suggests *Les Grâces,* which, roundly abused as "a girl's game" (*SL,* 31), receives little support from the ungracious children. Finally, when she fails to think of something "new," the Queen interposes: "Let her alone;—who's she? It's *my* birthday, and we'll play at Hunt the Pincushion" (*SL,* 32). Since her listeners are unfamiliar with this game, Aunt condescends to outline the rules: "Select the smallest and weakest player (if possible let her be fat: a hump is best of all), chase her round and round the room, overtaking her at short intervals, and sticking pins into her here or there as it happens: repeat, till you choose to catch and swing her; which concludes the game" (*SL,* 33). The children, not surprisingly, make Flora the pin cushion. Whereas Mary Ann Kilner subjectivizes a pin cushion's experience in her moral tale *The Adventures of a Pincushion* (1780), Rossetti's heroine, playing the role of *it* in a children's game, undergoes extreme objectification. Consequently, as Aunt's

shocked listeners observe, Hunt the Pincushion is "a horrid game" (*SL,* 33). In response to her nieces' protests, Aunt argues that she has "seen before now very rough cruel play, if it can be termed play" (*SL,* 33). Insisting that "Nowhere" and "Somewhere" are "not altogether unlike" (*SL,* 36), she collapses rather than maintains the distance between fantasy and reality. Thus, Hunt the Pincushion truly reflects Flora's earlier experience of Blindman's Buff and Hide and Seek.

Rossetti does not limit herself to a caricature of childish faults in *Speaking Likenesses.* Naming the children's second game after Samuel Smiles's *Self-Help* (1859), she extends her parody to the whole of Victorian society:

> The boys were players, the girls were played (if I may be allowed such a phrase): all except the Queen who, being the Queen, looked on, and merely administered a slap or box on the ear now and then to some one coming handy. Hooks, as a Heavy Porter, shone in this sport; and dragged about with him a load of attached captives, all vainly struggling to unhook themselves. Angles, as an Ironer, goffered or fluted several children by sustained pressure. Quills, an Engraver, could do little more than prick and scratch with some permanence of result. Flora falling to the share of Angles had her torn frock pressed and plaited after quite a novel fashion: but this was at any rate preferable to her experience as Pincushion, and she bore it like a philosopher.
>
> (*SL,* 36-37)

In this savage satire of nineteenth-century entrepreneurship, Rossetti creates an "analogy between sexual and social victimization of the female" (Gilbert, 18).[25] The burlesque Queen's monstrous subjects are not simply projections of the id and super ego but reflections of men and women in Victoria's England as well as the boys and girls at Flora's party. By presiding over a game from which she, like Flora's mad double, is ceremonially exempt, Victoria colludes in the subjugation of women. When Rossetti tells her readers to "look at home" (*SL,* 36), she implies, moreover, that the Victorian wife and mother—the queen of domesticity—permits similar chaos to reign. As a result, home is not, as Ruskin posits in "Of Queens' Gardens" (1865), "the place of Peace; the shelter, not only from all injury, but from all terror, doubt, and division" (18: 122).

Further ironizing Flora's eventual return to the safe familiarity of "home precincts" after her experience in the "hall of misery" (*SL,* 47), Rossetti parodies the activity of Victorian homemaking in the children's final game. For this sport, the children leave the maternal confines of the looking-glass parlor. Entering "a spacious playground" (*SL,* 39), they find themselves in the world as so often described in Rossetti's religious lyrics. Indeed, the epigraph to **"A Castle-Builder's World"**—"The line of confusion, and the stones of emptiness" (Isa.

34:11)—aptly modifies the structures that the children erect. Made from bricks of colored glass, their castles resemble nothing so much as Joseph Paxton's monument to Victorian consumerism, the Crystal Palace, which held the Great Exhibition of 1851. Despite the opulence of her surroundings, Flora is horrified to find herself "being built in with the Queen" (*SL,* 42), who, in defiance of proverbial wisdom, begins to hurl bricks as well as abuse at her subjects. The girl escapes, however, when the Queen throws a huge brick at Hooks and shatters the mirrored walls of her castle. Faced with the murderous implications of her own latent rage, Flora severs her attachment to self and thus undergoes an experience akin to that of the soul pierced by the "sharp two-edged sword" of God's word (Rev. 1:16). As Rossetti says, "Life it is, not death, that thus cleaves its way into my heart of hearts" (*FD,* 37). If, she continues, "we [are] afraid of a dividing asunder of our very selves," we should "let fear nerve us to endure it; for more dreadful will be the cutting asunder of the reprobate servant" (*FD,* 37).

Having survived the apocalypse of self, the regenerate Flora returns home, quietly assumes her place among her guests, and whispers an apology to her cousin Anne for having been bad-tempered. Literally as well as figuratively muted, she has learnt how to be an obliging daughter. On the other hand, her older sister, Susan, assumes the role of the absent mother. During the disastrous game of Hide and Seek, she emerges from "her hiding-place" and tries "her best to please everybody" (*SL,* 13). She picks a basket of mulberries, takes Flora and Anne for a walk, and begins to tell a story about a frog who, unwilling to admit his inability to boil a kettle, says, "I can't bear hot water" (*SL,* 15-16). After her "troubled dream" (*SL,* 48), Flora might better appreciate her sister's meaning, but Aunt's listeners do not understand the joke. In Susan's fragmented narrative, they instead hear another possibility for their own diversion.

Asked to relate the frog's adventures, Aunt unobligingly replies, "I was not there to hear Susan tell the story" (*SL,* 49). Finally agreeing "to try" (*SL,* 49), she provides a truly trying narrative, for she tells the story of Edith, who tries but fails to light the kettle for the gypsy tea that her "loving mother had planned [for] a treat" (*SL,* 52). Although Aunt draws exhaustively on folk convention to include a superabundance of talking animals, she minimizes the frog's part in the story. Moreover, unlike the animal helpers of fairy tale, the several beasts that either accompany Edith to the wood or meet her there are unable to assist her in her desire to light the kettle. Making a brief stage appearance in Edith's story, the fabled fox provides a clue to Aunt's intentions. Unable to avail himself of the luscious grapes hanging above the site that Edith's mother has chosen for the family picnic, "he shook his head, turned up his nose, shrugged his shoulders, muttered, 'They must be sour'" (*SL,* 68). Although the fruit also tempts Edith, she is too "wise" to "stand long agape after unattainable grapes" (*SL,* 57). Nevertheless, her effort to light the kettle and prove herself "as wise as her elder brother, sister, and nurse," if not also "her parents" (*SL,* 51), betokens a comparable presumption.

Ironically, while Edith's unhelpful animal helpers—speaking likenesses for Aunt's many bothersome nieces—reify childish incompetence, they also reflect the absent-minded preoccupation of the mother who is deaf to her daughter's demands. Contained within the outer margins of the central story, the conflict between Edith and her doting, albeit inattentive, mother finds form in the little girl's relationship with two other adult female figures—cook and nurse—who perform their mistress's will. At the beginning of Aunt's story, Edith goes into the kitchen and attempts "to talk, whilst cook, with a good-natured red face, made her an occasional random answer, right or wrong as it happened" (*SL,* 53). Indeed, cook's responses answer as little to Edith's questions as the advice she later receives from a pair of pigeons. When the birds, speaking "like two gurgling bottles," tell her to flee the scene of her failure, she says, "I wish you'd advise something sensible, instead of telling me to fly without wings" (*SL,* 63). At the same time, the pigeons' gurgling speech recalls the sound of Edith's voice when she quietly volunteers to light the fire. Distracted, "cook heard nothing beyond the child's voice saying something or other of no consequence" (*SL,* 55).

Cook's negligence notwithstanding, Edith is a pint-sized Prometheus. Surreptitiously taking a box of matches, she covets the maternal knowledge and power that fire represents. Although Rossetti thus uses a standard trope of the cautionary tale, her heroine does not, as in Ann Taylor's "Playing with Fire," suffer horrid disfigurement. Nor is she reduced in one spectacular blaze to a pile of ashes like the disobedient daughter of Heinrich Hoffman's "The Dreadful Story about Harriet and the Matches," included in *The English Struwwelpeter* (1848). Instead, the fire that the girl lights with her last match goes out. At this point, nurse appears, heralding the imminent arrival of Edith's "relations, friends, and other natural enemies" (*SL,* 60). A manifestation of the adversarial mother, nurse tacitly rebukes the ill-prepared girl, for she comes bearing "a box of lucifers in one hand, two fire-wheels in the other, and half-a-dozen newspapers under her arm" (*SL,* 69). Moreover, nurse crowns Edith's disgrace by telling her of the disruption her absence has caused the household. Sent indoors to her mother, the girl finds herself in metaphoric hot water at the end of Aunt's story.

Although Aunt is, like Edith's nurse, an enemy to childhood, she also sympathizes, as a daughter, with her nieces' desire for independence. Thus her next story, which begins on Christmas Eve in a shop tended by the heroine's grandmother, provides a fulfilling pendant to Edith's frustrating adventure. Indeed, Aunt's description of Dame Margaret's shop as the point of origin for the games, gifts, and dolls hitherto mentioned in *Speaking Likenesses* forges an oblique connection between her successive stories. Her heroine, a child of working-class diligence rather than middle-class indulgence, has no leisure to play in this childish vanity fair, however, for unlike Edith and Flora, she does not have a mother. But even though Aunt, at the beginning of her first story, characterizes a mother's death as a daughter's profoundest misfortune, Maggie's orphanhood helps her to succeed insofar as it allows her to overcome her impotence as a daughter and to advance to her mother's place. A miniature version of Dame Margaret, Maggie is, furthermore, a regenerate Red Riding Hood, who, offering to deliver the parcels that the doctor's heedless daughters have left behind in the shop, travels both away from and back toward her grandmother. Setting forth into the darkening day, she abides by her promise "to make great haste" (*SL*, 74) and so succeeds where the folk-tale heroine fails.

Recapitulating the tripartite movement of the volume as a whole, Rossetti triples the wolfish temptations that her heroine must face before she reaches the doctor's house. After an overly hasty beginning that ends with a punitive fall on the ice, Maggie encounters her first temptation to loiter in a group of children, surrounded by barking dogs, who appeal to her desire for play. Recollecting her promise, she hurries away from the sportive children—Flora's erstwhile companions—and next meets a boy with a "wide mouth . . . full of teeth and tusks" (*SL*, 85). This boy, shadowed by "a fat tabby cat, carrying in her mouth a tabby kitten" (*SL*, 84), reifies the hunger that so nearly tempts her to eat the chocolate meant for the doctor's daughters. Indeed, just as the mother cat seems ambivalently poised between devouring and nurturing her offspring, Maggie vacillates between gratifying her hunger and adhering to the purpose of her journey. Conquering her unreasoning appetite, she moves on to find a "tempting group" (*SL*, 88) of sleepers near a fire that attracts a number of birds. Despite her weariness, the girl proceeds with her journey.

Here Aunt interrupts herself to remark that Maggie, if she had stopped to sleep, would have brought the story to "an abrupt end" (*SL*, 87). More than a chilling reminder of the dangers of winter weather, Aunt's comment returns her listeners to the abrupt and unceremonious conclusion of the previous story. In effect, Maggie's tale symbolically redeems and completes Edith's abortive action. Persevering to arrive at the doctor's house "wide awake and on tiptoe with enchanting expectation," Maggie is neither fed nor warmed nor entertained nor given "a glimpse of the Christmas tree" (*SL*, 91).

She accomplishes all her desires on the homeward journey, however. Revisiting the sites of her temptation, she meets a half-frozen wood pigeon, a famished kitten, and an abandoned puppy. While these infantile and commonplace editions of Edith's cockatoo, Persian cat, and Newfoundland dog represent remnants of the girl's desire for warmth, food, and companionship, they have themselves valid claims on the child's attention. Adopting these animals, Maggie becomes, like the speaker of **"A motherless soft lambkin,"** a full-grown hero. Reaching home as the northern lights transform the landscape into a spectacle more brilliant than any illuminated Christmas tree, Maggie receives the necessary creature comforts from her grandmother and, in turn, gives them to her new and needy foster children. In Aunt's final story, therefore, the fruit of feminine forbearance is not, as in so many fairy tales, marriage but motherhood.

Concluding her three stories with the narrative of the daughter's triumph, Aunt responds not merely to her listeners' request for a winter tale but to their growth over the course of three days. Named after the would-be poet of Rossetti's juvenile novella, Maude best exemplifies the progress made by the children under Aunt's tutelage. Compelling her nieces to learn doubly the lesson of feminine forbearance, Rossetti's tasking narrator makes her tales contingent on labor. On the first day, Maude's sulky expression registers her resistance to Aunt's system and provokes a chiding rebuke: "Put away your pout and pull out your needle" (*SL*, 1). Once satisfied that the child has obeyed, Aunt announces, "Now I start my knitting and my story together" (*SL*, 2). By the second day, however, Maude has completed her darning. Ordered to sew for others rather than herself, she expostulates: "But we got through our work yesterday" (*SL*, 50). By way of response, Aunt reproves the girl for her selfishness: "Very well, Maude, as you like: only no help no story. I have too many poor friends ever to get through *my* work. However, as I see thimbles coming out, I conclude you choose story and labour" (*SL*, 50). Since "whoso clothes the poor, weaves for himself (still more obviously weaves for *herself*) a white garment" (*FD*, 138), Aunt's demands on the children serve their spiritual needs. However coercive, her arguments are effective, for Maude complies and, on the third day, makes an effort to be obliging. Although she receives a reprimand for whispering to Jane and for taking a defensive tone in revealing the purport of their murmured conference, she addresses her elder with affection, articulates the children's desire for another story, and utters no complaint when Aunt issues the inevitable order to work.

In *Speaking Likenesses* the relationship between sewing and story-telling serves an esthetic as well as a moral function. Associating industrious and imaginative creativity, manual and oral productivity, textile and textual materiality, Aunt not only insists on feminine cooperation but makes needlework a metonym for narrative. In other words, her stories are yarns. Indeed, just as she and the children sew the breadths of cloth "together, three and three" (*SL,* 50), Rossetti runs her three tales together within a three-part metafictional framework. When the irrepressible Maude asks why Edith hangs her kettle upon a tripod, Aunt's answer illuminates further the rationale for the volume's tripartite design: "Three sticks, Maude, are the fewest that can stand up firmly by themselves; two would tumble down, and four are not wanted" (*SL,* 57). While each tale within Rossetti's "narrative tripod" helps "to prop up the whole" (Knoepflmacher, 323), the frame story features a woman and five girls who work together, three and three, to augment the productivity of the whole. Even as the children's questions and comments form part of the fabric of Aunt's stories, their contributions to her charity basket enlarge the scope of the whole and create a seamless link between domestic and social service.

Engaged in the relief of the poor and the destitute, Rossetti's spinster maidens, old and young, conform to the model of maternity advanced in the last of Aunt's tales. Reversing the order of Catherine's experience in **"Commonplace,"** they succeed to a "motherly position" by emulating "the motherly instinct of self-postponement" (*CSS,* 18). But whereas "postponement means deferment in time" or "personal deference or subordination," Rossetti's ideal of maternal self-postponement paradoxically allows women, single as well as married, to obtain gratification in the here and now as well as the hereafter.[26] Raising maternal self-postponement to an art in storytelling and sewing, *Speaking Likenesses* valorizes feminine creativity over female procreativity and, in this way, establishes the unwed daughter's claim to self-worth.

Notes

1. Review of *Commonplace and Other Short Stories, Spectator,* 29 October 1870, 1292. Even favorable reviews failed to communicate enthusiasm. For example, the contention that Rossetti's "homely fiction" is "more absorbing in its interest than any sensational novel" seems hardly calculated to stimulate a prospective audience (review of *Commonplace and Other Short Stories, Athenaeum* 2223 [4 June 1870]: 734).

2. *Commonplace and Other Short Stories* (London: F. S. Ellis, 1870), 4: hereafter cited in text as *CSS.*

3. *Seek and Find: A Double Series of Short Studies of the Benedicite* (London: Society for Promoting Christian Knowledge, 1879), 309; hereafter cited in text as *SF.*

4. Pamela K. Gilbert provides a more comprehensive discussion of the father's role in "'A Horrid

Game': Woman as Social Entity in Christina Rossetti's Prose," *English* 41 (Spring 1992): 15-16; hereafter cited in text.

5. *Letter and Spirit: Notes on the Commandments* (London: Society for Promoting Christian Knowledge, 1883), 43; hereafter cited in text as *LS.*

6. Algernon Charles Swinburne, *The Swinburne Letters,* 6 vols., ed. Cecil Y. Lang (New Haven: Yale University Press, 1959), 2:116.

7. As a result, children's literature circumvents the contradiction between motherhood and authorship that Margaret Homans describes in *Bearing the Word: Language and Female Experience in Nineteenth-Century Women's Writing* (Chicago: University of Chicago Press, 1986). See especially her discussion of "The Author as Mother: Bearing the Word as Nineteenth-Century Ideology" (153-88).

8. I discuss the importance of the volume's arrangement at greater length in "Sound, Sense, and Structure in Christina Rossetti's *Sing-Song,*" *Children's Literature* 22 (1994): 3-26.

9. Lila Hanft, "The Politics of Maternal Ambivalence in Christina Rossetti's *Sing-Song,*" *Victorian Literature and Culture* 19 (1991): 217.

10. Virginia Sickbert argues for the egalitarianism of the mother-child relationship in "Christina Rossetti and Victorian Children's Poetry: A Maternal Challenge to the Patriarchal Family," *Victorian Poetry* 31 (Winter 1993): 389.

11. James R. Kincaid, *Child-Loving: The Erotic Child and Victorian Culture* (New York: Routledge, 1992), 12.

12. Sidney Colvin, review of *Sing-Song, The Princess and the Goblin, Through the Looking-Glass,* and *More Nonsense, Academy* 3 (15 January 1872): 23; hereafter cited in text. R. Loring Taylor is one modern critic who confesses discomfort with Rossetti's allusions to death (*Sing-Song, Speaking Likenesses, Goblin Market* [New York: Garland Publishing, 1976], xi).

13. Review of *Sing-Song, Nation* 14 (2 May 1872): 295.

14. Review of *Sing-Song, Scribner's Monthly* 3 (1872): 629.

15. The average number of live births for marriages lasting 20 years or longer dropped from 6.16 in the 1860s to 5.8 in the 1870s (Pat Jalland, *Women, Marriage and Politics: 1860-1914* [Oxford: Clarendon, 1986], 175).

16. For a discussion of women's fears in childbirth, see Jalland, 159-85. Also helpful is Patricia

Branca, *Silent Sisterhood: Middle Class Women in the Victorian Home* (London: Croom Helm, 1975), 74-113.

17. Ann and Jane Taylor, *Original Poems for Infant Minds and Rhymes for the Nursery* (New York: Garland Publishing, 1976), 3:19-20; hereafter cited in text.

18. Barbara Garlitz uses these terms in her discussion of "Christina Rossetti's *Sing-Song* and Nineteenth-Century Children's Poetry," *PMLA* 70 (1955): 542.

19. Roderick McGillis, "Simple Surfaces: Christina Rossetti's Work for Children," *The Achievement of Christina Rossetti,* 222.

20. G. B. Tennyson outlines these doctrines in *Victorian Devotional Poetry: The Tractarian Mode* (Cambridge: Harvard University Press, 1981), 44-56; hereafter cited in text.

21. *Speaking Likenesses,* (London: Macmillan, 1874), [v]; hereafter cited in text as *SL.*

22. Wendy R. Katz discusses the relationship between these two traditions in "Muse from Nowhere: Christian Rossetti's Fantasy World in *Speaking Likenesses,*" *Journal of Pre-Raphaelite Studies* 5 (November 1984): 14-35.

23. Review of *Speaking Likenesses, Athenaeum* 2461 (26 December 1874): 877.

24. U. C. Knoepflmacher, "Avenging Alice: Christina Rossetti and Lewis Carroll," *Nineteenth-Century Literature* 41 (December 1986), 310 and 314; hereafter cited in text.

25. Nina Auerbach and U. C. Knoepflmacher make a similar point in their introduction to *Speaking Likenesses* in *Forbidden Journeys: Fairy Tales and Fantasies by Victorian Women Writers* (Chicago: University of Chicago Press, 1992), 320.

26. Kathleen Blake, *Love and the Woman Question in Victorian Literature: The Art of Self-Postponement* (Brighton, England: Harvester Press, 1983), vii; hereafter cited in text. Blake's fine discussion of self-postponement in Rossetti's work does not examine the contradictions in her treatment of motherhood (3-25).

Selected Bibliography

PRIMARY WORKS

POETRY

Verses. London: Privately printed by G. Polidori, 1847.

Goblin Market and Other Poems. Illustrated by D. G. Rossetti. London: Macmillan, 1862.

The Prince's Progress and Other Poems. Illustrated by D. G. Rossetti. London: Macmillan, 1866.

Sing-Song: A Nursery Rhyme Book. Illustrated by Arthur Hughes. London: George Routledge and Sons, 1872.

Goblin Market, The Prince's Progress, and Other Poems. Illustrated by D. G. Rossetti. London: Macmillan, 1875.

A Pageant and Other Poems. London: Macmillan, 1881.

Poems. New and enlarged edition. Illustrated by D. G. Rossetti. London: Macmillan, 1890.

Goblin Market. Illustrated by Laurence Housman. London: Macmillan, 1893.

Verses. Reprinted from *Called to Be Saints, Time Flies,* and *The Face of the Deep.* London: Society for Promoting Christian Knowledge, 1893.

New Poems, Hitherto Unpublished or Uncollected. Edited by William Michael Rossetti. London: Macmillan, 1896.

PROSE FICTION

Commonplace and Other Short Stories. London: F. S. Ellis, 1870.

Speaking Likenesses. Illustrated by Arthur Hughes. London: Macmillan, 1874.

Maude: A Story for Girls. Edited by William Michael Rossetti. London: James Bowden, 1897. Because of copyright restrictions, William had to omit several poems from the English edition of his sister's 1850 tale. R. W. Crump provides the complete text in *Maude: Prose and Verse* (Hamden, Conn.: Archon Books, 1976). [Cited in text as *MPV*]

DEVOTIONAL PROSE

Annus Domini: A Prayer for Each Day of the Year, Founded on a Text of Holy Scripture. Oxford and London: James Parker, 1874.

Seek and Find: A Double Series of Short Studies of the Benedicite. London: Society for Promoting Christian Knowledge, 1879.

Called to Be Saints: The Minor Festivals Devotionally Studied. London: Society for Promoting Christian Knowledge, 1881.

Letter and Spirit: Notes on the Commandments. London: Society for Promoting Christian Knowledge, 1883.

Time Flies: A Reading Diary. London: Society for Promoting Christian Knowledge, 1885. [Cited in text as *TF.*]

The Face of the Deep: A Devotional Commentary on the Apocalypse. London: Society for Promoting Christian Knowledge, 1892. [Cited in text as *FD.*]

COLLECTED WORKS

The Poetical Works of Christina Georgina Rossetti. Edited by William Michael Rossetti. London: Macmillan, 1904. Still useful for memoir and notes. [Cited in text as *PW.*]

Sing-Song; Speaking Likenesses; Goblin Market. Introduction by R. Loring Taylor. New York and London: Garland Publishing, 1976. Brings together facsimile reprints of Rossetti's work for children.

The Complete Poems of Christina Rossetti. A Variorum Edition. 3 vols. Edited by R. W. Crump. Baton Rouge and London: Louisiana State University Press, 1979-90. The standard edition. [When quoting lines from Rossetti's verse, I have used line numbers for citation. Cited in text as *CP.*]

Christina Rossetti: Poems and Prose. An Everyman Edition. Edited by Jan Marsh. London: J. M. Dent; Vermont: Charles E. Tuttle, 1994. A selection featuring several short stories as well as useful explanatory notes.

LETTERS AND ROSSETTIANA

Cline, C. L., ed. *The Owl and the Rossettis: Letters of Charles A. Howell and Dante Gabriel, Christina, and William Michael Rossetti.* University Park: Pennsylvania State University Press, 1978. Contains six letters by Christina Rossetti.

Doughty, Oswald, and John Robert Wahl, eds. *Letters of Dante Gabriel Rossetti.* 4 vols. Oxford: Clarendon Press, 1965-67. Includes many letters and references to his sister.

Fredeman, William E., ed. *The P. R. B. Journal: William Michael Rossetti's Diary of the Pre-Raphaelite Brotherhood, 1849-1853.* Oxford: Clarendon Press, 1975. Provides essential contextual material.

Harrison, Antony H., ed. *The Collected Letters of Christina Rossetti.* 2 vols. Charlottesville: University Press of Virginia, 1997-. Promises to fill the gap in Rossetti scholarship.

Maser, Mary Louise Jarden, and Frederick E. Maser. *Christina Rossetti in the Maser Collection.* Bryn Mawr, Pa.: Bryn Mawr College Library, 1991. Short study of manuscript collection plus 45 letters to friends and acquaintances.

Packer, Lona Mosk, ed. *The Rossetti-Macmillan Letters: Some 133 Unpublished Letters Written to Alexander Macmillan, F. S. Ellis, and Others, by Dante Gabriel, Christina, and William Michael Rossetti.* Berkeley: University of California Press, 1963. Contains 96 letters demonstrating Christina Rossetti's interest in the business of publication.

Peattie, Roger W., ed. *Selected Letters of William Michael Rossetti.* University Park: Pennsylvania State University Press, 1990. Includes letters and references to his sister.

Rossetti, William Michael, ed. *The Family Letters of Christina Georgina Rossetti.* London: Brown, Langham, 1908; reprinted, New York: Haskell House, 1968. Also valuable for notes and appendices. [Cited in text as *FL.*]

———, ed. *Rossetti Papers, 1862-1870.* London: Sands, 1903; reprinted, New York: AMS Press, 1970. Includes several important letters concerning poems for the 1866 volume.

———, ed. *Ruskin: Rossetti: Preraphaelitism. Papers 1854 to 1862.* London: Allen, 1899; reprinted, New York: AMS Press, 1971. Contextual material plus two items by Christina Rossetti.

———. *Some Reminiscences of William Michael Rossetti.* 2 vols. London: Brown, Langham, 1906; reprinted, New York: AMS Press, 1970. William's autobiography, containing many references to his sister.

Troxell, Janet Camp, ed. *Three Rossettis: Unpublished Letters to and from Dante Gabriel, Christina, and William.* Cambridge: Harvard University Press, 1937. Devotes two chapters to Christina Rossetti's correspondence.

SECONDARY WORKS

BOOKS AND PARTS OF BOOKS

Bell, Mackenzie. *Christina Rossetti: A Biographical and Critical Study.* London: Thomas Burleigh, 1898. First full-length study. Indispensable for presentation of generous excerpts from letters and other materials as yet unavailable elsewhere.

Packer, Lona Mosk. *Christina Rossetti.* Berkeley: University of California Press, 1963. Mistakenly discovers a clue to Rossetti's impassioned verse in her unrequited love for a married man. Patient documentation of much previously unpublished material only partially redeems damage done by indefensibility of author's key premise.

Dante Gabriel Rossetti, *Letters of Dante Gabriel Rossetti,* 4 vols., ed. Oswald Doughty and John Robert Wahl (Oxford: Clarendon Press, 1965-67).

John Ruskin, *The Works of John Ruskin,* 39 vols., ed. E. T. Cook and A. Wedderburn (London: George Allen, 1903-12).

Dawn Henwood (essay date spring 1997)

SOURCE: Henwood, Dawn. "Christian Allegory and Subversive Poetics: Christina Rossetti's 'Prince's Progress' Reexamined." *Victorian Poetry* 35, no. 1 (spring 1997): 83-94.

[*In the following essay, Henwood departs from other critics in assessing "Prince's Progress" as a poem that is as subversive and complex as "Goblin Market."*]

Even in recent years, the standard reading of the facts of Christina Rossetti's biography has little deviated in essence from William Michael Rossetti's assessment in the "Memoir" prefixed to his edition of *The Poetical Works of Christina Rossetti*. "Over-scrupulosity," William regrets, "made Christina Rossetti shut up her mind to almost all things save the Bible and the admonitions and ministrations of priests. . . . Her temperament and character, naturally warm and free, became a 'fountain sealed.'"[1] William's image of the instinctive artist pathetically crushed under the weight of her own orthodoxy has had long-lasting appeal for both biographers and critics, who have persistently lamented that Rossetti was not diverted from her self-repressive religious mode long enough to produce more than a handful of poems free from the thematic "transparency"[2] and the doctrinal limitations of most of her verse.

The poem most often recognized as having successfully risen above these charges of narrowness is "Goblin Market," a text that has received so much attention partly because its complexity is widely perceived as an anomalous quality within the Rossetti canon. "The Prince's Progress," another long narrative poem able to share with "Goblin Market" the epithet of "a fairy-tale with overtones,"[3] is commonly relegated to the status of a second-rate, far less interesting, sequel.[4] "The Prince's Progress," however, like its critically acclaimed precursor, reveals complicated depths of ambiguity and paradox regarding the poet's attitude toward the different worlds of experience—sensual, spiritual, and imaginative. Social roles are boldly challenged, spiritual myth is rearranged, and Biblical images are juxtaposed with sensual images and satirical barbs.

The germ of "The Prince's Progress" is contained in the last sixty lines of the poem, the funeral lament for the Bride (ll. 481-540),[5] which Rossetti composed in 1861. When these lines appeared in *Macmillan's Magazine* in 1863, they bore the title "The Fairy Prince Who Arrived Too Late." By bemoaning the faded perfection of the "enchanted princess" whose tardy Prince Charming had failed to arrive in time, the voices of the original lyric fragment would seem to condemn the Fairy Prince outright. When Rossetti completed the rest of the poem four years later, however, she shifted the focus of the work from the dead Princess to the questing Prince. Rather than denouncing the Prince as a negligent character, the new title focuses on the Prince as an active protagonist engaged in a journey through a landscape of pitfalls and temptations. The Prince of the completed poem finds himself no longer in the familiar nursery-tale world of the Sleeping Beauty plot. Instead, the fairy world has merged with and evolved into a spiritual world where, like Bunyan's pilgrim, the Prince must make his own peculiar progress through a series of circumstances and choices.

An early reviewer in the *Athenaeum* was neatly able to summarize the spiritual allegory of The Prince's Progress in the following terms: "'The Prince's Progress,' like the 'Goblin Market' . . . is an allegory, and an allegory, moreover, illustrating a similar idea. In both works the argument is the power of temptation to beguile man from the worthy and earnest work of life. In 'Goblin Market' the temptations are resisted and overcome—in 'The Prince's Progress' they triumph" (*Athenaeum* [June 23, 1866]: 824). This reviewer and many since seem to have overlooked the slipperiness and even subversiveness of both of these allegories, whose "argument" is often convoluted, to say the least. By framing her poem specifically within the tradition of spiritual allegory, Rossetti reminds us that we should be especially sure to enter into our reading with our moral sensibilities alert. But this does not mean that we should prepare ourselves to receive a pat moral tale or even a predictable orthodox allegory. On the contrary, **"The Prince's Progress"** challenges our moral sense and our interpretive faculties by confronting us with ambiguous, even disturbing, situations and characters. Although the Prince is an unsuccessful pilgrim along the road to the celestial city of his Bride, we find that he is not an unsympathetic quester. Neither does his Bride appear as a perfect model of humility and patience. Frustrating our expectations of a straightforward moral narrative, his alleged transgressions are not so easily condemned as outright sins, nor is her supposed sanctity so readily upheld as an exemplary icon.

As the poem opens, a chorus of unidentified voices laments the weeping of the expectant Bride who waits for her late-starting Bridegroom. The Prince, lounging far, far away from her in his "world-end palace" (l. 13), is eventually incited by another disembodied voice, the "true voice of [his] doom" (l. 19), to take up his pilgrim's staff and begin the quest for his unknown mate. Time is short, the voices warn him, and the beauty of his intended is mortal. Their chorus seems to echo the age-old persuasions belonging to the *carpe diem* motif of erotic (or would-be-erotic) poetry:

> Then a hundred sad voices lifted a wail,
> And a hundred glad voices piped on the gale:
> "Time is short, life is short," they took up the tale:
>   "Life is sweet, love is sweet, use today while you may;
> Love is sweet, and tomorrow may fail;
>   Love is sweet, use today."
>
>   (ll. 37-41)

These anonymous voices work an invigorating effect in the Prince, who suddenly rises up with an energetic "flush on his cheek" (l. 44). As he sets out on his journey, he is, the narrator wryly notes, "Strong of limb if of purpose weak" (l. 47).

The narrator's tendency to treat the Prince's character with playful irony does not in any way excuse his failings, but it does invite the reader to indulge in identification with this very human hero. Perhaps "hero" is not even the appropriate title for a figure apparently so unsuited for the appointed task. A solitary route through a devastated wilderness must indeed seem a weary trial to someone who has been prepared for the trek, as far as we know, only by the ambivalent echoes of the voice, or voices, of his doom. There is some pathetic truth to the narrator's gibe that the volcanic landscape of the second leg of his journey constitutes a "Tedious land for a social Prince" (l. 152). Later in the poem, when the Prince is lingering among the maidens who have rescued him from the torrent, the narrative voice presents a more generous, although still gently mocking, view of our pilgrim:

> Had he stayed to weigh and to scan,
> He had been more or less than a man:
> He did what a young man can,
>   Spoke of toil and an arduous way—
> Toil tomorrow, while golden ran
>   The sands of today.

(ll. 355-360)

The Prince's errors are not pardonable but they are certainly understandable. Paradoxically, our quester has indeed fulfilled the message of the mysterious voices, which urged: "Love is sweet, use today." The Prince's digressions have, for the most part, led precisely in the direction traditionally pointed to by the *carpe diem* theme. The Bridegroom, it seems, is only too ready to make the most of today's pleasures at the expense of tomorrow's responsibilities. He falls into luxuriating in the company of a beguiling milkmaid as easily as he falls into "Carolling with the carolling lark" (l. 52). He succumbs even more readily to the soothing touch of the beautiful hands which pull him from the river:

> Oh a moon face in a shadowy place,
> And a light touch and a winsome grace,
> And a thrilling tender voice which says:
>   "Safe from waters that seek the sea—
> Cold waters by rugged ways—
> Safe with me."

(ll. 343-348)

In this stanza, we seem to enter into the Prince's consciousness and share his "Oh" of relief and ecstasy. Not even the narrator, as we have already seen, seems able to blame the Prince too harshly for enjoying the opportunity to rest in such a pleasant harbour. In actuality, the "thrilling tender voice" in his ear and the faceless "kind voices" that "whisper and coo" (l. 332) must remind him of the similarly sweet and disembodied chorus which launched him on his journey so long ago. We are left to guess the source of the voices which surround the Prince at his rescue, just as we must imagine where the voices of his doom are actually coming from at the beginning of the poem. But whether the mysteri-

ous saviors be nymphs, houris, or courtly damsels, here indeed life is sweet and the day is worth the seizing.

One could argue, of course, that the Prince has very obviously mistaken the real message of the voice of his doom. For, while I have cited this chorus as the inspiration for his journey, it is not his only source of instruction. Like Bunyan's Christian or Spenser's Red Cross Knight, Rossetti's Prince undertakes that pilgrimage which every soul must make and he has access, naturally, to all the orienteering tools of the Christian context. As the congregation receiving this sermon or "allegory," we can surely assume that, along with his pilgrim staff, the Bridegroom has at least the proddings of his God-given conscience, even if explicit Biblical guidance has not reached his fairy-tale kingdom. Whether or not he is awake to his spiritual responsibilities, the Prince is indeed sowing the seeds of his actions in moral consequences. "Let him sow," the narrator warns the dilatory pilgrim, "one day he shall reap" (l. 269). The Biblical imagery used here to describe Rossetti's Everyman reminds us that our hero should know better than to interpret the voice of inspiration as the voice of Herrick's narrator in "Gather ye rosebuds while ye may." Anyone, we might say, with a grain of moral sense ought to recognize the voice as capturing something closer to the tone of Jesus' injunction to his disciples wherein he declares: "I must work the works of him that sent me, while it is day; the night cometh when no man can work" (John 9.4).

The Prince, Joan Rees has noted, is a shamefully poor interpreter throughout his journey, misreading not only the floating voices but also the numerous signs of evil that appear on his path.[6] He seems oblivious to the overtly mythical connotations of the apple-tree under which the so-called "milkmaid" (l. 56) with glittering eyes invites him to recline. Neither does he notice the "shining serpent-coils" (l. 94) of her hair which ought to alert him to the "subtle toils" (l. 96) of this Lamia figure. The Prince's decision to honor his royal pledge to his seducer is reinforced by his perception that the road ahead is becoming stormy. He cannot see that the horizon's "fire-cloven edge" (l. 90) portends the beginnings of his own enslavement to infernal snares. This interpretive blindness becomes almost laughable when he seems to mistake the sinister skeleton of an alchemist for a hospitable country host. Not even the eerie light flashing from the mouth of the cave "Like a red-hot eye from a grave" (l. 170), a beacon of warning for the reader, can awaken in him the wariness it should. The Prince stares briefly around the cave, but is still quick to ask for lodgings, adding the ridiculously naive comment that, "In your country the inns seem few, / And scanty the fare" (ll. 191-192).

It is easy to poke fun at the hero's obtuseness without, however, locating a model of interpretive astuteness within the poem. The Prince may be a poor reader, but the Bride hardly even opens her eyes. Most analyses still find her to be the poem's only admirable character, emphasizing her stoic suffering at the hands of a cruelly procrastinating fiancé.[7] Georgina Battiscombe stresses the narrative's biographical parallel with Dante Gabriel Rossetti's protracted courtship of an ailing Lizzie Siddall (p. 116), an argument which has served to buttress feminist readings of the poem as a revelation of the social powerlessness of the single Victorian woman (see, for example, Rosenblum, p. 89). Thus, the pathos generated by the poem has traditionally been seen as emanating from the tragic situation of the innocent, long-enduring Princess.[8] The usual parabolic reading demands, it would seem, a distinct dichotomy of chastity versus dissipation, loyalty versus faithlessness, innocence versus experience. I maintain, however, that such clear-cut thematic divisions of **"The Prince's Progress"** are soon baffled when we turn to examine the poem's development of familiar Biblical tropes.

"The Prince's Progress" is, in fact, a text in which it is surprisingly difficult to gain a critical foothold. Even the poem's basic plot simultaneously invokes and distorts the Biblical myth of Christ's apocalyptical reunion with his cherished Bride, the Church. The description of the Princess' jewel-inlaid valley and her palace "Built all of changing opal stone" (l. 430) clearly aligns the Bride of the poem with the Bride of Revelation, the New Jerusalem. Writes the apostle John:

> And [the angel] carried me away in the spirit to a great and high mountain, and shewed me that great city, the holy Jerusalem, descending out of heaven from God, Having the glory of God: and her light was like unto a stone most precious, even like a jasper stone, clear as crystal.

> (Revelation 21.10-11)

Like the apostle, the Prince is granted his vision of the bridal city from the height of a tall mountain. But, despite his enjoyment of this brief glimpse of prophetic illumination, the Prince's attitude throughout most of the poem is, evidently, extremely removed from that of a holy seer. Rossetti has her Prince play the role of the seeking sinner and, in so doing, effects a radical gender reversal. The Princess appears to embody, on one level, a female representation of Christ, the patient, grieving lover of the pilgrim soul. On another level, however, the Bride's lack of action does not, in fact, enshrine her in as praiseworthy a context as we might first expect. Biblical echoes within the text actually suggest that the apparent self-sacrifice of her retreat from self-fulfillment may contribute toward the formation of just as cowardly and as disloyal a personality as that of the wandering Prince.

We see so little of the Princess in the poem that it is perhaps exaggerative to speak of her as even having a personality. The Bride's shadowiness appears in a somewhat suspicious light when we realize what a pale and static image this maiden evokes as opposed to the Bride of the Bible's Song of Solomon, a fundamental intertext for this poem.[9] The Song of Solomon has often presented an embarrassingly sensual hermeneutical dilemma to the more austere line of theologians, its delightfully erotic language normally accounted for in terms of an allegorical depiction of the love between Christ and his Church. Unlike our pallid Princess, the betrothed virgin of the Song of Solomon actively seeks her beloved, whom she trusts is coming to her. Her speeches, like those of her Bridegroom, give vent to praise of the beloved and magnification of desire, in unmistakably carnal terms. The Biblical maid does not muffle her voice in veils but opens the Song with a passionate declaration of longing: "The song of songs, which is Solomon's. Let him kiss me with the kisses of his mouth: for thy love is better than wine" (Song of Solomon 1.1-2). Her desire for union with her beloved is too strong for her to consider cloistering herself within "one white room" (l. 23) like the Prince's betrothed. Like the Princess situated in her lush green valley "Where fatness laughed, wine, oil, and bread, / Where all fruit trees their sweetness shed" (ll. 422-423), the maiden of the Song is surrounded by fertile garden imagery. However, whereas the Princess' paradisal environment encloses her like a kind of fortress (the Prince must climb a huge mountain in order to gain access), the Biblical Bride beseeches the wind to unleash the beauty of her garden in order to draw her beloved to her: "Awake, O north wind; and come, thou south; blow upon my garden, that the spices thereof may flow out. Let my beloved come into his garden, and eat his pleasant fruits" (Song of Solomon 4.16).

Within this garden, the speaker of the Song declares that she is "the rose of Sharon." Likewise, the Bride of Rossetti's poem is associated with the purity and ephemerality of floral imagery: "By her head lilies and rosebuds grow; / The lilies droop, will the rosebuds blow?" (ll. 25-26). More strongly linked to her than the virginal lily or the romantic rose is, however, the poppy, particularly the white poppy, with its ominous "death-cups drowsy and sweet" (l. 35). The narcotic effect of this flower's seed seems to enshroud the Princess throughout the poem, from the introductory hints about her despairing state to the closing funeral scene, where the white poppy becomes the chosen ceremonial adornment for her corpse.[10]

"Spell-bound" (l. 23) from the outset, the Princess seems destined to have her existence stifled by the forces around her. The poem's first stanza tells us how the waiting Bride "sleepeth, waketh, sleepeth" (l. 4), the repetition implying that she sleepeth more than she waketh. Her one line of direct speech in the poem is hastily suppressed by a chorus of chanting handmaids:

"Sleep, dream and sleep;
Sleep" (they say): "we've muffled the chime,
Better dream than weep."

(ll. 10-12)

The lullaby, like the chant of Tennyson's Lotos-Eaters, seems to have the effect of a sleeping drug. Strangely enough, these supposedly soothing words seem closely akin to the gentle urging of the feminine voices which distract the near-drowned Prince later in the poem, pleading:

"Safe with us, dear lord and friend:
All the sweeter if long deferred
Is rest in the end."

(ll. 352-354)

For the Prince, sleepiness takes the form of yet another temptation which threatens to delay his quest. The "sad, glad voices" (l. 115) which awaken the hero following his day of idle dalliance with the milkmaid reprimand him as a "sluggard" (l. 112): "Be thy bands loosed, O sleeper, long held / In sweet sleep whose end is not sweet" (ll. 117-118). Upon the death of the alchemist, the anonymous chorus again condemns the sleepy Prince. In the same breath, however, it advises the Princess to continue her cocoon-like existence:

"If she watches, go bid her sleep;
Bid her sleep, for the road is steep:
He can sleep who holdeth her cheap,
Sleep and wake and sleep again."

(ll. 265-268)

This ambivalent treatment of the sleep motif within the poem compels us, I think, to ask whether it really is better for the Princess to dream than to weep.[11] The question of the Princess' inactivity becomes a more urgent consideration when we recognize that the Princess' Biblical counterpart boasts of her own constant watchfulness as testimony to the force of her wakeful desire. "I sleep," she declares, "but my heart waketh" (Song of Solomon 5.2). Rossetti's Princess seems to turn a shade more pale, and even a shade culpable, when her comatose retreat from the pain of cognizance is understood as playing against the loving vigilance held up in the scriptural model.

This incongruity is accented by the images representing the Princess' last moments as, like a blighted lily, she droops into her final sleep. "The lamp burns low" (l. 379), the "bodiless cries" (l. 375) chide the tardy Prince, but the image itself suggests that perhaps the warning should also be directed to the slumbering Bride. A wise virgin, we recall from Jesus' parable, comes prepared to the vigil so that, even if she dozes while awaiting the Bridegroom, she will be able to rekindle her lamp upon his arrival (Matthew 25.1-13). In fact, a responsible Christian would not have shut her lamp up within the walls of "one white room." After all, as Jesus admonishes his followers: "No man, when he hath lighted a candle, putteth it in a secret place, neither under a bushel, but on a candlestick, that they which come in may see the light" (Matthew 25.1-13).

The Princess is languishing, we are told, "As a lovely vine without a stay, / As a tree whereof the owner saith, / 'Hew it down today'" (ll. 388-390). Although, at first glance, these similes might enlist our sympathy for the suffering heroine, such Biblical language calls the same heroine to account for her own withered state. No research into scriptural obscurities is necessary to prove this point. The image of Jesus as the true vine is an easily recognizable Christian trope, whose apocalyptic ramifications would have been well known to Rossetti's audience. Jesus' words in the following passage from John's gospel forcibly present the devastating consequences of ignoring the demands of committed spiritual growth. Declares Jesus: "I am the vine, ye are the branches. He that abideth in me, and I in him, the same bringeth forth much fruit; for without me ye can do nothing. If a man abide not in me, he is cast forth as a branch, and is withered; and men gather them, and cast them into the fire; and they are burned" (John 15.5-6).

If the Princess withers as a "vine without a stay," it must be because, by hiding her lamp and abandoning the vigil for a lethean somnolence, she has detached herself from Christ's will, the main stay of every spiritual root. Thus, with the full symbolism of the scriptural vineyard called into play, we must admit that the Bride can be held morally responsible for the barrenness of her own existence and, ultimately, for her own destruction.[12] The image of the diseased tree that the owner orders felled further sabotages the Princess' pretensions to blamelessness. John the Baptist, we recall, urges the people to repentance with the threat of a very similar scenario: "And now also the axe is laid unto the root of the trees: therefore every tree which bringeth not forth good fruit is hewn down and cast into the fire" (Matthew 3.1-10). This strident declamation of divine judgment is strengthened by Jesus' use of the same imagery in his Sermon on the Mount, where he repeats the message that "Every tree that bringeth not forth good fruit is hewn down, and cast into the fire" (Matthew 7.19).

As the belated Prince at last approaches the opal palace, then, we share his doubt, as he wonders: "Rose, will she open the crimson core / Of her heart to him?" (ll. 437-438). Were he alert to the implications brought into play by the images which have finally "stung" (l. 391) him into resolute action, the Prince might change his doubtful musings to Blake's lament of "The Sick Rose." The Princess' retreat into drowsy oblivion has resulted only in stagnation and spiritual desiccation. The "crimson core" of her self has been destroyed, like Blake's rose, by the worm of an inner corruption, primarily the neglect of the Christian responsibility to face the waking world, the failure to cling to the vine and bear fruit even in the face of harsh experience.

The withered, "veriest atomy" (l. 181) of an Alchemist, who feeds his potion with "virgin soil" (l. 227) serves as a sinister pre-figuring of the withered Princess. Like the Princess slumbering through endless days and nights within her room, the Alchemist has sequestered himself within a cave for so long that his eyes can scarcely tolerate the light of day (ll. 185-186). While the gullible Prince believes that the Alchemist's elixir will preserve him from drowning and even from disappointment in his tardy courtship, Joan Rees has pointed out that this is a dubious faith, as the dead brewer may very well have been self-deceived and his cordial may be impotent (pp. 63-64, 70). (When the Prince leaves the dead man, we are left wondering, "were he fool or knave, / Or honest seeker who had not found" [ll. 261-262].) Within the context of the Song of Solomon, the figure of the Bride expecting the divine Bridegroom is, in fact, even closer to the Alchemist since both are awaiting the essence of life eternal. Both characters in Rossetti's poem, it turns out, finish by wasting their lives in the fixed anticipation of a future life.

Thus it seems that both the Prince and the Princess are misguided seekers who represent two different attitudes towards the Christian crux of worldly experience. The mistaken approaches of both of these extreme figures expose some of the paradoxes involved in acting out the heroics of the Christian stance in the midst of a material world of tempting bounty. At the same time, the episode of the Alchemist demonstrates that, as in "Goblin Market," these attitudes are invariably interconnected. The curious Prince, who is too open to invitations of sensual experimentation, is drawn into the Alchemist's lair only to encounter there a grotesque reflection of the attitude of other-worldly retreat embodied in the dying Princess. Both the hero and the heroine of "The Prince's Progress" can be seen as pathetic characters because each, in a peculiar way, is blind to the spiritual demands of life in a material world.

As a fairy tale, the story, one has to agree with Joan Rees, is a failure (p. 68). There is no happy-ever-after here as is posited in "Goblin Market." There is not even an attempt on the narrator's part to provide a concluding moral touchstone to bring the poem's incidents into focus and clasp its disparate pieces together, however loosely. The frustration of nuptial union in "The Prince's Progress" is the more disturbing in light of the unavoidable apocalyptical implications of the plot. In this version of the scriptural story of Christ coming to claim his Church for his own, neither a worthy Bridegroom nor a worthy Bride is to be found. In the shifting symbolic ground of this poem, not only are gendered roles de-stabilized, but a central Christian myth is gravely undermined. Far more than a courtship hangs in the balance of a poem so charged with sacred relevance. When the Prince and Princess fail to fulfill their roles, they fail, in effect, to fulfill Biblical prophecy. Given the poem's inescapable mythical context, its closing funeral lament gives voice, we realize, to the deepest, darkest spiritual despair.

"The Prince's Progress" continues the trend established in "Goblin Market" of probing the subversive potential of conventional imagery. In the later poem, however, the multiplicity of meanings spawned by the interplay of symbolic contexts becomes so confusing that it threatens to plunge the reader into an interpretive aporia and the poem into an atmosphere of indecipherable despair. Rees is right, I think, to detect a "nightmare" quality underlying the surface allegory of traditional readings (p. 68). The Bride's failure to survive her enactment of the hermetically sealed life of the ascetic matches, rather than reverses, the Prince's failure to overcome the fleshly distractions between him and his goal. If Rossetti is calling her static, ethereal Princess to open her senses to the concrete reality of the pilgimage which each Christian must make through the mobile world of experience, all she can offer the Bride upon her awakening is a life of frustrated anguish, where it is only marginally better to weep than to dream.

If the sequel to "Goblin Market" disappoints, it is not, as many have claimed, because it is one-dimensional or monotonous. The poem only disappoints those readers who delight more in answers than in questions. "The Prince's Progress" proves, in the end, to be a disorienting and disturbing text because it provokes so many queries without raising the hope of resolution. Much to our perplexity as literary interpreters, we find that the textual richness of "Goblin Market" is not a freak anomaly within the narrow orthodoxy of the rest of the Rossetti canon. Even the moralizing *Athenaeum* reviewer I quoted at the beginning of this essay had to admit that Rossetti's poetry "is not poetry made easy" (p. 825). If we can allow ourselves to respond to the startling intertextual and inter-image resonances of the text itself, we soon find ourselves discovering in "The Prince's Progress" an equally complex, subversive aberration from the limitations traditionally superimposed on Christina Rossetti's doctrine and art.

Notes

1. William Michael Rossetti, "Memoir," *The Poetical Works of Christina Georgina Rossetti* (1904; London: Macmillan, 1935), p. lxviii.

2. Dolores Rosenblum, *Christina Rossetti: The Poetry of Endurance* (Carbondale: Southern Illinois Univ. Press, 1986), p. 63.

3. Georgina Battiscombe, *Christina Rossetti: A Divided Life* (New York: Holt, 1981), p. 103.

4. Georgina Battiscombe goes so far as to pronounce the poem a definite failure, complaining that "'The Prince's Progress' reads monotonously when compared with 'Goblin Market'" (p. 115).

5. All citations of Rossetti's poetry are taken from *The Complete Poems of Christina Rossetti,* ed. Rebecca W. Crump, 3 vols. (Baton Rouge: Louisiana State Univ. Press, 1979).

6. Joan Rees, "Christina Rossetti: Poet," *CritQ* 26, no. 3 (1984): 62.

7. Antony H. Harrison, *Christina Rossetti in Context* (Chapel Hill: Univ. of North Carolina Press, 1988), p. 115.

8. Such conventional constructions of the Princess' role fail to take into account the more active roles Rossetti gives to some of her most memorable female characters. Lizzie of "Goblin Market" is perhaps the most striking example. Having attempted at first to avoid completely the dangerous sensual world of experience, in the end she ventures into that world in order to perform the heroic healing of her sister. Within the volume *The Prince's Progress and Other Poems,* Rossetti elicits our admiration for the moral courage of "A Royal Princess," who turns her back on her stifling life of sheltered luxury to offer everything she has—even her own life—to the mob of suffering humanity outside her palace door. Like Lizzie, who offers herself as a kind of eucharistic sacrifice to her ailing sister (Sandra M. Gilbert and Susan Gubar, *The Madwoman in the Attic: The Woman Writer and the Nineteenth-Century Literary Imagination* [New Haven: Yale Univ. Press, 1979], p. 566), this princess turns her powerlessness into power. "Fair Margaret" of "Maiden-Song," the poem that directly follows "The Prince's Progress" in the first (1866) edition, also refutes the image of feminine helplessness. Although Margaret sits at home and waits, she does not wait idly. While her vain sisters are out capturing husbands, she sews and sings, and her song becomes her action—a very powerful action that not only leads her sisters home and wins her a royal husband, but also brings all of nature into a sort of divine musical harmony (see Diane D'Amico, "'Fair Margaret' of 'Maiden-Song': Rossetti's Response to the Romantic Nightingale," *VN* 80 [1991]: 8-13).

9. Nilda Jimenez claims that the Song of Solomon was Rossetti's most favored source for direct Biblical quotation in her poetry (Jimenez, *The Bible and the Poetry of Christina Rossetti: A Concordance* [Westport, Connecticut: Greenwood, 1979], p. x). Perhaps Rossetti's most direct comment on the poetic attractions of the book occurs in "'In the day of his Espousals,'" her very melodious encapsulation of the musicality and erotic imagery of "That Song of Songs which is Solomon's." Of Rossetti's many references to the dove-eyed bride of the Song, the most elaborate is the image of the King's Daughter developed in "'She shall be brought unto the King.'" (The title is taken from Psalm 45, one of the wedding Psalms.) As she ascends out of the "dim uttermost depths" of "Dragon's dominion," or earthly experience, this princess-bride sings joyfully and "glows" with an inner vitality ("The King's Daughter is all glorious within"). This bride is not depicted as having been sleeping, but as having been actively engaged with evil and danger. The splendor of her nuptial ascent to the heavenly throne would lose much of its magnificence if we did not see her as emerging from the heart of the "fiery-flying serpent wilderness." Her joy is "joy won," and she has won it in actual battle with the dragons of the sinful world of human experience.

10. The roses that the Prince brings to the funeral bier are, the female voices chide, "too red" (l. 538). So too, it seems, are the red poppies that once budded at the Princess' feet, alongside the white poppies. "Which [flowers] will open the first?" (l. 36) wonders the narrative voice early in the poem— the red poppies traditionally symbolic of consolation, or the white poppies associated with sleep and forgetfulness? (see, for example, *Language of Flowers,* illus. Kate Greenaway [1884], p. 33). The floral funeral wreath, woven of the white petals of oblivion and resting on the virgin Princess' gray head, makes concrete the poem's pervasive sense of premature waste and failed consolation.

11. The ambivalence is, I think, especially puzzling because it is so much more typical of Rossetti to refer to sleep in highly positive, even reverential terms. While the soul sleep that leads to resurrection is usually for Rossetti the greatest of God's blessings, I see no seeds of eternal bliss in this poem. There is no voice here, as there is in "'When My Heart is Vexed, I Will Complain,'" to whisper the assurance, "Peace, peace, I give to My beloved sleep, / Not death but sleep, for love is strong as death." The Song of Song's powerful assertion of transcendence, "love is strong as death," fails the unsuccessful couple of "The Prince's Progress." Consequently, the sleep into which the reclusive bride subsides seems to offer little peace and less hope. Within the larger context of Rossetti's other poetry, the ambiguous treatment of the sleep motif in "The Prince's Progress" is one of the most troubling aspects of this very troubling poem.

12. Rossetti builds more explicitly on the scriptural ideal of the responsible keeper of the vineyard in

"'Yea, I Have a Goodly Heritage,'" which opens with the assertion, "My vineyard is mine I have to keep."

Anna Krugovoy Silver (essay date 1997)

SOURCE: Silver, Anna Krugovoy. "'My Perpetual Fast': The Renunciation of Appetite in Christina Rossetti's *Speaking Likenesses*." *Victorians Institute Journal* 25 (1997): 177-201.

[*In the following essay, Silver focuses on Rossetti's treatment of fasting as a means of achieving moral goodness and spiritual growth in* Speaking Likenesses.]

In the spring of 1874, Christina Rossetti informed her brother Dante Gabriel that she had written "a Christmas trifle, would-be in the *Alice* style with an eye to the market" (*Family Letters* 44).[1] The children's story to which she refers, *Speaking Likenesses,* is a violent and unsentimental tale which gave at least one contemporary reviewer an "uncomfortable feeling" and today remains largely overlooked by scholars interested in Rossetti's canonical "adult" works.[2] Despite its neglect in scholarly criticism, however, *Speaking Likenesses* provides an important contribution to discussions of appetite and the body in Rossetti's work as a whole. In the story Rossetti emphatically praises the renunciation of both food and sexual desire, denouncing gluttony by associating it with sexuality and selfishness. *Speaking Likenesses* portrays appetite and eating as monstrous signifiers of sexual promiscuity, implicitly debasing the body that experiences hunger by figuring both male and female sexual desire as unmitigatedly abusive and predatory.

In much of her poetry and prose, Rossetti posits that fasting, symbolizing a denial of the secular world and the physical body, functions as an aid to the reception of the sacred. Contextualized within Rossetti's devotional writing, *Speaking Likenesses* is a tale of spiritual progress, in the tradition of Bunyan's *Pilgrim's Progress,* in which three children's rejection of gluttony symbolizes their assumption of progressively more moral qualities: the most virtuous of the three steadfastly denies her corporeal desires in the course of the story. While the validation of hunger in *Speaking Likenesses* initially suggests the modern disease anorexia nervosa (which was first officially diagnosed a year before Rossetti's story), an explication of the story alongside Rossetti's devotional prose and poetry reveals that its images of hunger are inextricably rooted in Christian rituals of fasting. The centrality of images of hunger in Rossetti's work situates her within the Anglo-Catholic movement and within the tradition of medieval women saints and mystics, whose spiritual practice often included the control of food intake.

Rossetti divides *Speaking Likenesses* into three stories about a "Land of Nowhere" (338) narrated by a caustic aunt to her nieces.[3] The first story takes place at Flora's eighth birthday party, at which the little girl presides as "queen of the feast" (326).[4] Appetite immediately becomes a locus of discontent as the children quarrel over who gets the biggest sugar-plums, and the narrator wonders "would even finest strawberries and richest cream have been found fault with" (327-28). Flora reveals her own greediness and peevishness, "cross and miserable" because her "sugar-plums [were] almost all gone . . . her chosen tart not a nice one" (330). Frustrated with her playmates, she deserts her own party, crying, "It's my birthday, it's my birthday" (328) and, discovering a door carved in a yew tree, enters an apartment in which animated furniture greets her and strawberries and cream—doubling the strawberries and cream at her own party—serve themselves.

Sitting down, Flora "took up in a spoon one large, very large strawberry with plenty of cream; and was just putting it in her mouth when a voice called out crossly: 'You shan't, they're mine . . . it's my birthday, and everything is mine'" (333). The voice belongs to a "cross grumbling" and "ugly" girl who, "enthroned in an extra high armchair," doubles Flora's position as queen of the feast and personifies her hearty appetite. Flora's impulse immediately to consume a "very large strawberry with plenty of cream" indicates her greediness; however, she is forbidden from eating by the selfish Queen who, along with the other children at the party, "had eaten and stuffed quite greedily; Poor Flora alone had not tasted a morsel" (334). Although the reader feels sorry for Flora, "too honest a little girl to eat strawberries that were not given her" (335), her new self-restraint differentiates her from the other children in the yew tree, whose monstrosity is established by their supernatural consumption of food.

Rossetti employs the trope of gluttony to introduce sexuality into the story. When the children decide to play games, Flora realizes that they are not human: the boys are sharp and angular, covered with hooks and quills, while the girls are sticky and slippery. Rossetti's distaste for sexuality, both male and female, is apparent in the figures of these children. The boys' bodies and names are unmistakably phallic and capable of inflicting pain—Hooks, Quills and Angles—while the two girls, Sticky and Slime, double the simpering girls at Flora's birthday party, one of whom gives Flora a "clinging kiss" (327). More disturbingly though, the girls' names, sticky and slime, allude to female genitalia and to female emissions such as menstrual blood: "One girl exuded a sticky fluid and came off on the fingers; another, rather smaller, was slimy and slipped through the hands" (335). The adjectives that Rossetti uses, "sticky" and "slimy," suggest the repulsive nature of the female sex; Rossetti does not juxtapose a redemptive female eroticism to the masculine brutality of Hooks and Quills.

Sexuality in the story is rendered even more troubling by the rape games that the children play. The first game, Hunt the Pincushion, "is simple and demands only a moderate amount of skill. Select the smallest and weakest player . . . chase her round and round the room, overtaking her at short intervals, and sticking pins into her here or there as it happens" (336). The use of the female pronoun implies that the victim is always female, while "sticking pins into her" associates sexual intercourse with pain and violence. Flora, the victim of the game, is essentially raped: "Quills with every quill erect tilted against her. . . . Hooks who caught and slit her frock" (336). This sexual "deflowering," however, is not merely perpetrated by boys, for Sticky, Slime, and the Queen take part as well. The Queen's presence is particularly noteworthy because her role as Flora's double emphasizes Flora's own participation in the humiliating ordeal. The passage suggests that women somehow buy into their own sexual victimization, perhaps by playing "games" of flirtation and courtship. However, women are not the only victims of those games, for "Angles many times cut his own fingers with his edges" (338). Thus, Hunt the Pincushion is not solely an expression of men's sexual violence toward women; rather, it depicts the viciousness of sexual desire *in general*. The second game, Self Help, is more obviously drawn along gender lines: "The boys were players, the girls were played" (338). Once again, the game involves enacting a symbolic rape, in which "Hooks . . . dragged about with him a load of attached captives, all vainly struggling to unhook themselves" (338).

The final scene in the story underscores the connections that Rossetti draws between food and sexuality. After finishing their games, the children sit down for another feast. This time, Flora refuses to eat while the others gorge on the huge meal: "she was reduced to look hungrily on while the rest of the company feasted, and while successive dainties placed themselves before her and retired untasted" (339). As in **"Goblin Market,"** Rossetti describes the lavish food in detail: "Cold turkey, lobster salad, stewed mushrooms, raspberry tart, cream cheese, a bumper of champagne, a méringue, a strawberry ice" (339). The children who enthusiastically participate in mock-rapes eat just as enthusiastically, "stuffing without limit" (339). Gluttony, therefore, is intimately linked to rampant sexuality. Not surprisingly, the one good girl in the room, Flora, does not "take so much as a fork" (339).

The equation of sexuality and food was so common in Victorian England that Rossetti was undoubtedly aware of it. Helena Michie contends that the Victorian confla-

tion of food and sexuality can be traced in texts as diverse as novels, etiquette books, sex manuals, and pornography, and that the virtuous woman inevitably eats little: "Delicate appetites are linked not only with femininity, but with virginity. The portrait of the appropriately sexed woman, then, emerges as one who eats little and delicately. She is as sickened by meat as by sexual desire" (Michie 16-17). Conduct books and beauty manuals frequently posit a lack of hunger as one of woman's essential characteristics, evidence of her feminine incorporeality and heightened spirituality. In his popular monograph *Beauty: Illustrated Chiefly by an Analysis and Classification of Beauty in Women,* for example, physiognomist Alexander Walker claims that "Women naturally and instinctively affect abstemiousness and delicacy of appetite" (207). While Walker's use of the word "affect" implies artifice, he also assumes that that artifice is both natural and instinctive.

The virtuous, middle-class woman was expected not only to eat small amounts of food, but to eat only those types of food that allayed her emotions and desires. Mrs. Alexander Walker particularly praises milk for its ability to "calm the passions, and to impart a gentleness to the character" (56). Other foods that the Victorians considered appropriate for women were oatmeal, bran, potatoes, and vegetables (Moodie 61, Mrs. Walker 89). On the other hand, "solid and highly seasoned meats, sour and unripe fruit, stimulating articles, alcoholic liquors, and coffee . . . must be carefully avoided" (de L'Isere 543) because of their tendency to stimulate sexual desire in women. According to one doctor, a girl who demonstrated the tendency to engage in erotic thoughts or behaviors (such as masturbation) should be fed milk and vegetables under "strict superintendance," whereas a girl who showed no interest in forming relationships with men should be given "roast meats, feculent substances, and rich soups" to "exaggerate the limits of the appetite" (de L'Isere 554-55).[5] Of all foods, meat is most often cited as pernicious because of its ability to excite desire. Rossetti is probably aware of the popular association of meat with sexual passion when she writes, "Several of the boys seemed to think nothing of a whole turkey at a time" (339).

Most importantly, Rossetti uses food to differentiate Flora from her monstrous self, the Queen. Whereas Flora refuses to eat, the Queen consumes "of sweets alone one quart of strawberry ice, three pine apples, two melons, a score of méringues, and about four dozen sticks of angelica" (339). Just as she does in **"Goblin Market,"** in which Laura eats ravenously while Lizzie abstains, Rossetti creates a double for Flora who represents her appetite and thus her latent sexuality. Because the Queen organizes and supervises Hunt the Pincushion and Self Help, she is the most sexualized child in the enchanted room. Flora also has the potential to become a gluttonous and sexually aggressive Queen, but she renounces the possibility: at the end of the story, when the children build houses out of glass bricks and "to her utter dismay" (340) Flora finds herself walled up with the Queen, she quickly escapes, thereby rejecting her own worst nature. Unlike Laura, who is redeemed at the end of **"Goblin Market"** despite her "fall" into sensual knowledge, the Queen is never redeemed. Gluttony is a sin, pure and simple. Thus, despite images that suggest a radical critique of men's sexual violence against women, the story's conservative ending reifies the conception of female sexuality as a disruptive and threatening force.

Because the second part of the *Speaking Likenesses* trilogy lacks the overt sexual dimension of the first and third parts, it is less compelling within a discussion of Rossetti's conflation of gluttony and lust. However, the story represents an important narrative bridge between the first and third stories. Based on spiritual allegories like *Pilgrim's Progress*, *Speaking Likenesses* revolves around the protagonists' renunciation of self, symbolized by their suppression of appetite. As Nina Auerbach and U. C. Knoepflmacher note, "The stories ascend as the Christian soul does, from Flora's birthday hell to Edith's purgatory . . . to the martyred Maggie's chilly heaven" (319). In the successive stories of the trilogy, Rossetti's heroines are increasingly able to deny their appetites and are, accordingly, increasingly less tormented.

Edith, the second story's subject, has been promised a "gipsy feast" (343) by her mother. Standing in the kitchen with the cook, Edith pesters her with questions about the forthcoming meal, asking, "'What are we to have besides sandwiches and tarts?'" (344) "'Cold fowls, and a syllabub, and champagne, and tea and coffee, and potato-lunns, and tongue, and I can't say what besides'" (344), the servant responds, revealing that the feast will be sizeable. Bored and restless, Edith offers to boil the kettle for tea. Immediately, the narrator undercuts the goodness of her behavior. Not only does Edith demonstrate her own appetite in her eagerness to hasten the meal, but the reader has already learned that she "thought herself by no means such a very little girl, and at any rate as wise as her elder brother, sister, and nurse" (343). Now Edith slips out of the kitchen with the kettle despite the cook's warning that a fire must be lit: "'I can light the fire,' called out Edith after her, *though not very anxious to make herself heard*" (344; emphasis added). By deciding to boil the kettle despite the wishes of the cook, Edith demonstrates the pride of which the narrator accused her. The matches that she carries with her are, appropriately enough, called lucifers.

Once in the woods, Edith is lured from her errand by a grape vine covered with tantalizing fruit: "How she longed for a cluster of those purple grapes which, hanging high above her head, swung to and fro with every breath of wind; now straining a tendril, now displacing a leaf, now dipping towards her but never within reach. Still, as Edith was such a very wise girl, we must not suppose that she would stand long agape after unattainable grapes: nor did she. Her business just then was to boil a kettle, and to this she bent her mind" (345). Edith's decision not to pluck and eat the grapes can be read two ways. Whereas Flora immediately helps herself to strawberries and cream at the enchanted party, Edith suppresses her desire for the grapes and thereby displays a laudable denial of appetite that differentiates her from the other girl. Yet in Rossetti's work, grapes frequently symbolize Christian faith and the wine of the Eucharist, an interpretation underscored in *Speaking Likenesses* by the adverb "agape." Literally, "agape" simply means open-mouthed, but the word assumes metaphorical, sacred meaning as the ancient Christian *agape,* or love feast, a meal related to the Eucharist that was eaten to symbolize fraternal love and charity.[6] Rossetti thus suggests that, because of her unrepentant selfishness and pride, Edith does not demonstrate Christian love and is therefore unprepared to partake of the sacrament. Similarly, in Rossetti's short story **Maude,** the protagonist feels unworthy to receive Communion, saying that "'I will not profane Holy Things. Some day I may be fit again to approach the Holy Altar, but till then I will at least refrain from dishonouring it'" (267). For Rossetti, the Eucharist was a sacrament not to be taken lightly and one that neither Edith nor Maude yet deserves. The dual meaning of the grape scene demonstrates the instability of signs of eating in Rossetti's work: while secular, physical hunger must be repressed, spiritual hunger is virtuous.

Unable to light the fire after carelessly dropping most of her matches, Edith finds herself surrounded by the animals of the wood, creatures who function as more benign versions of the Queen in their role as "speaking likenesses." Just as Edith lazily watched the cook working despite the woman's complaint that "'attendance is just what I should not have liked'" (344), these animals observe and annoy Edith, offering only useless advice. Two hedgehogs sit and watch but do nothing, "why they came and why they stayed never appeared from first to last" (348). The pigeons present the impractical recommendation that she fly away, to which Edith, Alice-like, retorts, "'I wish you'd advise something sensible, instead of telling me to fly without wings'" (348). Edith does not realize that her attempt to boil the kettle is very much like flying without wings: she does not possess the skills necessary to light a fire and has moreover forgotten to fill the kettle with water. The narrator's aside, "Remember, girls, never put an empty kettle on the fire, or you and it will rue the consequences" (348), voices Rossetti's comment on the destructive power of pride. By the time the nurse arrives at the scene and summarily dismisses Edith, she is weeping with frustration.

If the story of Flora in the yew tree is hellish, Edith's adventure is purgatorial in its lack of closure and deferral of pleasure. Undercutting narrative expectation, the luscious meal that Edith anticipates never takes place within the confines of the story, and it is uncertain, by the end, whether Edith will ever enjoy her gipsy feast.[7] Her punishment has already been anticipated by the narrator who, in the preface to the story, prods her nieces to charity sewing with the admonition, "no help no story" (343). Without labor, there is no reward and without self-abnegation, no delight. As far as the story reveals, though, Edith's only punishment for her willfulness is a miserable afternoon in the forest, certainly a less cruel punishment than that accorded to the little glutton, Flora. However, Edith must still learn self-denial, or how to serve others selflessly rather than selfishly. The final figure of the trilogy, Maggie, combines Edith's meritorious repression of appetite with the dutifulness that she lacks.

The third part of the *Speaking Likenesses* trilogy is perhaps the most important for an understanding of Rossetti's moral message. While describing the dolls for sale in Old Dame Margaret's shop at the opening of the tale, the narrator notes, "as they say in the Arabian nights, 'each was more beautiful than the other'" (351). Just as the dolls grow more and more beautiful as they progress, Rossetti's third story is the most beautiful of the three because it delivers her message of Christian redemption.

Dame Margaret, who runs a gift shop full of toys and sweets, is distinguished by her "plain clothes and her plain table" (351). The fact that she always finds money to help out a poor neighbor reinforces the predominant Victorian correspondence of a light diet with a virtuous soul. On Christmas Eve, Margaret's orphan granddaughter Maggie offers to deliver a basket to the doctor's house, and to do so she must travel, like Red Riding Hood, through the woods. As soon as she enters the forest, she encounters a group of playing and dancing children, and though "the thermometer marked half-a-dozen degrees of frost; every pond and puddle far and near was coated with thick sheet ice" (352), the children dance so wildly that their "cheeks were flushed, their hair streamed right out like comets' tails" (354). Rossetti here reintroduces the "monstrous children" (354) that Flora meets in the first tale; now, in winter, their heat makes them all the more hellish, the girl's "pink cotton velvet" (354) party dress grotesquely out of place in a frozen forest. Their excessive heat and flushed cheeks recall the disturbing sexuality with which the children have already been associated. The children are Maggie's first temptation, for she longs to play with them, but remembering her promise to hurry home, she leaves them (and their sexuality) behind.[8] Her first renunciation sets the tone for the rest of the tale.

After leaving the children, Maggie grows hungry and peeks at the tempting chocolate in her basket. Just as she debates whether or not to take a piece, she meets what Auerbach and Knoepflmacher have already identified as the "speaking likeness" of her hunger, a boy whose face "exhibited only one feature, and that was a wide mouth" (355n). His huge mouth makes the boy a trope of walking appetite as Rossetti again emphasizes the connection between gluttony and lust; while the boy snatches at the chocolate in Maggie's basket, he prepares to devour her in a metaphorical rape: "for the two stood all alone together in the forest, and the wide mouth was full of teeth and tusks, and began to grind them" (356). Unlike Flora, however, Maggie stands up for herself, refuses to give him the chocolate, and runs away. She renounces her own appetite and, consequently, the aggressive sexuality symbolized by the Mouth-boy: to abstain from food, Rossetti implies, is to resist one's carnality.

Maggie illustrates Rossetti's belief that one should avoid even looking upon sin. As she writes in her explication of Revelation, *The Face of the Deep,* "Cover and turn away the eye lest it should behold it, stop the ear lest it should admit it; for the blessed pure in heart who shall see God, copy their Lord the Holy one who is of purer eyes than to behold evil" (97). While Flora participates (however unwillingly) in her introduction to sexual knowledge, Maggie demonstrates her moral courage by fleeing the very sight/site of sin. Moreover, when Maggie "spoke so resolutely and seemed altogether so determined" (356), the boy merely slinks off into the wood, indicating that women's renunciation of appetite is empowering, that virtue is stronger than sin.

Maggie's third renunciation, of sleep, leads her to her destination, the doctor's house. Now, however, the world of privilege renounces Maggie, for she is answered at the door only with a brief thank you and left "shut out" of the house (358). Cold and hungry, Maggie turns back towards her home. Clearly, the secular world offers nothing to a poor orphan. Heaven, however, recognizes her goodness, for as she passes the spot of each of her temptations, she receives her rewards: a wood-pigeon, a kitten, and a puppy. And in exchange for being denied a glimpse of the doctor's Christmas tree, "the sky before her flashed with glittering gold, and flushed from horizon to zenith with a rosy glow; for the northern lights came out, and lit up each cloud as if it held lightning, and each hill as if it smouldered ready to burst into a volcano. Every oak-tree seemed turned to coral, and the road itself to a pavement of dusky carnelian" (359).[9] The northern lights represent both a divine Christmas tree and the Star of Bethlehem; in addition, they offer the reader a glimpse of the apocalypse: the images of a volcano about to explode and of lightning hidden in seemingly benign clouds evoke the many instances of lightning and fire in Revelation, including the mountain of fire thrown into the sea (Rev. 8: 8). Moreover, carnelian is the sixth of twelve stones that decorate the walls of the New Jerusalem, towards which Maggie metaphorically travels on that cold winter night.[10] After successfully resisting temptation, Rossetti's heroine receives divine assurance that she will someday be welcomed into the community of the blessed.

Once again, Rossetti places images of consumption at the center of her moral lesson. At Dame Margaret's house, Maggie enjoys a frugal but satisfying meal of tea and toast, the only instance of eating in *Speaking Likenesses* not linked with discord and greed. The story ultimately posits that renunciation of the world's pleasures is the true measure of a Christian and that, by implication, one is not a devout Christian without sacrifice. At the same time, however, Maggie's dinner, with its allusion to the *agape* feast, suggests that the Christian enjoys an alternative and positive spiritual satiety through faith.[11]

Contextualized within nineteenth-century Christian theology, the story's emphasis on hunger becomes more complex. Rossetti was a member of Christ Church in Albany Street, a congregation allied to the Oxford movement through its charismatic preacher, William Dodsworth.[12] As part of a larger effort to reform the Church of England by turning back to the beliefs and rituals of the ancient Church, the Tractarians advocated frequent fasting to humble the flesh and as an aid to prayer. E. B. Pusey, for instance, cites the fasting of the apostles and early Christians to support the restoration of church-sponsored fasting: "Regular and stated Fasts formed a part of the Discipline by which, during almost the whole period since the Christian Church has been founded, all her real sons . . . have subdued the flesh to the spirit, and brought both body and mind into a willing obedience to the Law of God" (109). Isaac Williams, whom Rossetti admired, speaks of "thorough repentance,—daily humbling, daily loving, daily praying, daily fasting, self-judging, self-correcting, self-renouncing, self-hating repentance" as "the jewel of great price" (130). We know that Rossetti fasted for religious reasons from her brother William's description of her "perpetual church-going and communions, her prayers and fasts" (William Rossetti lv).

Rossetti discusses fasting explicitly in her devotional work, including *The Face of the Deep*:

> The balances suggest scarcity short of literal nullity: hunger, but not necessarily starvation. Scarcity imposes frugality, exactness. . . . No waste, latitude, margin; no self-pampering can be tolerated, but only a sustained self-denial: self must be stinted, selfishness starved, to give to him that needeth. And as the poor never cease out of the land and are in various degrees standing representatives of famine, this self-stinting

> seems after all to be the rule and standard of right living; not a desperate, exceptional resource, but a regular, continual, plain duty.
>
> (202)

By advocating fasting as a form of self-denial, Rossetti links eating with selfishness and self-indulgence that must be metaphorically starved by starving the body on a regular, perhaps daily, basis. Although she qualifies the word starvation slightly with the phrase "not *necessarily*," she also implies that, in some cases, starvation is an admirable way to repress desire and vice. Rossetti's language evokes the contours of the thin figure, the body with no "waste" or "margin," the body trimmed down to its most basic and "exact" form. The body thus becomes the vehicle through which the devout express penitence and sympathy for the suffering of the poor.

Flora's greediness, then, is both a sign of her potential sexuality and of a general selfishness that is, in fact, starved out of her in the yew tree. Her refusal to eat differentiates her from the monstrous, super-sexual children at the party: by not eating, she denies her own corporeal desires. Though Edith is less greedy than Flora, she too covets food and is proud and stubborn in its preparation. Only Maggie completely resists her appetite and dutifully follows instructions, sacrificing her own pleasure because she "promised Granny to make haste" (354). Renunciation of self, in Rossetti's theology, is a Christian duty carried out in large part by the renunciation of one's physical appetites. Flora, Edith and Maggie's starvation illustrates the denial of the flesh that Rossetti so often praises in her devotional work; as she claims in *Time Flies: A Reading Diary*, "abstinence from food, stands for all self-mortification" (259).[13]

Rossetti's negative depictions of eating, as well as her advocacy of fasting, indicate the emerging disease anorexia nervosa. Several critics, including Paula Marantz Cohen and Deborah Ann Thompson, have read **"Goblin Market"** within the context of anorexia nervosa, and one can argue evidence of the disease in *Speaking Likenesses* as well. Besides the repression of hunger and sexuality that Rossetti so clearly praises in the story, her technique of doubling indicates anorexia nervosa, a disease characterized by the two extremes of starvation and an obsessive desire to eat.[14] Within an anorexic framework, Flora can be said to represent the refusal to eat whereas the Queen, by devouring huge amounts of food, stands for the desire to binge. Most importantly, like the victims of anorexia nervosa, Rossetti gives moral meaning to abstention. Flora becomes a good girl only when she renounces food.

Although anorexia nervosa was not diagnosed with that name until Sir William Withey Gull labeled it in 1873, there is ample evidence that the disease existed throughout the nineteenth-century. Beauty manuals frequently refer to women fasting in order to reduce their waists to a fashionable slimness: *The Young Lady's Book* alludes to the "dangerous attempt to reduce corpulency by the use of large doses of vinegar" (25) and *The Book of Health and Beauty* cautions women that "eating chalk, drinking vinegar, wearing camphorated charms, and similar destructive means [to lose weight] have been resorted to . . . with no better success" (66). Sometimes, when women's fasting became life-threatening, doctors were called in to treat the behavior. In *A Practical Treatise on the Diseases Peculiar to Women,* Samuel Ashwell describes a female patient's anorexia-like symptoms in a female patient: "Her appetite is capricious, it either fails altogether, or she craves for unwholesome food" (6). Although Ashwell categorizes these symptoms as signs of chlorosis (now diagnosed as iron-deficiency anemia), one can surmise that many girls who were diagnosed as suffering from a variety of illnesses such as chlorosis and hysteria were actually anorexic.

Cohen has even speculated that Rossetti was herself anorexic, citing as evidence her adolescent breakdown, after which she "became withdrawn, overly sensitive, overly polite and exacting in religious matters" (Cohen 10-11). Although Cohen's argument is compelling, she does not sufficiently address Rossetti's deep religiosity, using it as proof of anorexia rather than (as is likely) the other way around; Rossetti fasted *because* of her religious faith. There is no indication in Rossetti's biography that religious fasting negatively affected her health in a manner consistent with the symptoms of anorexia nervosa. Moreover, none of Cohen's arguments prove that Rossetti suffered from anorexia nervosa rather than depression or some other form of mental illness.

Most importantly, the religious impetus behind Rossetti's fasting precludes definitively diagnosing her with anorexia nervosa. Women who wish to deny the secular have historically done so by limiting their food intake because food is one aspect of their lives that they traditionally control (Bynum 191). Rossetti was part of a long line of women who fasted as a means of renouncing worldliness in general and sexuality in particular. Religious fasting and anorexia nervosa are both defined by "self-inflicted starvation in the . . . midst of ample food" and despite a feeling of hunger; nevertheless, they should not be conflated into one pathology (Hilde Bruch, quoted in Bynum 201). Food refusal has many causes: saints who fasted in the Middle Ages, for instance, cannot conclusively be interpreted as anorexic because they fasted for entirely different reasons than anorexic women do today; their behavior was similar but their motivation (and thus the diagnosis) was not. In their comprehensive history of fasting, Walter Vandereycken and Ron Van Deth write that "There is no trace of saints 'dieting' from a fear of becoming fat. . . . Fast-

ing saints were not obsessed by the exterior, outward appearance. By contrast, they strove for an inner, spiritual fusion with Christ's sufferings. It was not a cult of slenderness but a religious-mystical cult that dominated their [lives]" (221). Or, as Caroline Walker Bynum writes, "substituting one's own suffering through illness and starvation for the guilt and destitution of others is not 'symptom'—it is theology" (206). Victims of anorexia nervosa, on the other hand, are obsessively concerned with weight and appearance. Susan Bordo relates anorexia "to the pursuit of an idealized physical weight or shape; it becomes a project in service of 'body' rather than 'soul'" (83).[15] Anorexics, in other words, starve themselves to be thin, not to deny the secular; there is generally no significant religious component to their fasting. Rossetti's fasting, both in her own life and in her writing, is always tied to a larger system of theology: there is no association in *Speaking Likenesses* or "Goblin Market," for instance, between starvation and the quest for a slim figure.

Nevertheless, the boundaries between anorexia nervosa and religious fasting do overlap. Unless we can conceive of a religious tradition wholly isolated from its wider social context, we must assume mutual interaction between theology and secular ideology. Victorian proscriptions about female appetite may have reinforced the value of religious fasting, and some Victorian women may have used religious reasons consciously or subconsciously to justify food refusal because of a disgust with the fat on their bodies. Christina Rossetti could conceivably have been influenced both by her intense religious beliefs and by the larger culture in which she lived. However, her devoutness problematizes any reductive diagnosis of Rossetti as an anorexic.

Rather than diagnosing Rossetti as a victim of anorexia nervosa, one can more productively understand her work within the medieval tradition of fasting saints. Rossetti not only belonged to a religious movement that looked back to the pre-Reformation Church for spiritual guidance, but she studied saints and martyrs on her own, writing two collections of saints' lives, *Called to be Saints* and *Time Flies.* As Bynum contends in *Holy Feast and Holy Fast,* food played a crucial role in the lives of many medieval female saints and mystics. On the one hand, the early and medieval churches emphasized fasting as a way to imitate Christ's sufferings and to mortify the body. On the other hand, Christians actually consumed the body and blood of Christ during communion; food abstinence cannot be understood without simultaneously recognizing that the believer was fed by the body and blood of Christ. Bynum writes that "in the sermon and song, theology and story, of the high Middle Ages . . . the food on the altar was the God who became man; it was bleeding and broken flesh. . . . To eat God, therefore, was to become suffering flesh with his suffering flesh; it was to imitate the cross" (54). This consumption of God was sometimes accompanied, particularly for women, by sensual pleasure, including "visions" of music, sweet smells and delicious tastes in the mouth. Mary of Oignies, for instance, experienced God during communion as the taste of honey (Bynum 59). Not only did "women quite unself-consciously [think] of God as food," but "the biographers who repeated their comments persistently used extended food metaphors to elaborate the significance of women's practices. James repeatedly described Mary's ecstasies as inebriation, as hunger and fullness. . . . Thomas of Cantimpre spoke of Margaret of Ypres as accepting, chewing, and savoring God" (Bynum 116). Food was thus the literal and metaphorical means through which many medieval women experienced and conceptualized religious worship.

Rossetti's avowal of fasting, too, can best be understood within a wider spiritual context, especially considering her belief that she consumed the body and blood of Christ during communion. In *Speaking Likenesses,* for example, Maggie mortifies her body by resisting her desire for chocolate and is subsequently rewarded for her secular self-denial with a satisfying *agape* meal. The text highlights both proper and improper consumption, contrasting gluttony with spiritual communion.

As in **"Goblin Market,"** in which the Eucharistic joining of Lizzie and Laura represents a moment of redemptive consumption, many of Rossetti's devotional poems use images of eating to symbolize the union of God and self. Most frequently, God, often in the person of Christ, is the object of the narrator's hunger or thirst. In "As the sparks fly upwards," for instance, Rossetti asks God to "bid my will go free / Till I too taste thy hidden Sweetness" (6-7).[16] Recalling the tempting grapes of *Speaking Likenesses,* she figures Christ as a "Vine with living Fruit, / The twelvefold fruited Tree of Life" ("I Know you not" 1-2) and yearns to "taste and see how good is God" ("Then they that feared the Lord spake often one to another" 21). Like medieval fasting women, Rossetti conceives of God as food, and like them she considers both fasting and the Eucharist empathic ways of identifying with the pain of Christ's crucifixion. Thus, she writes in **"I know you not"**:

> I thirst for Thee, full fount and flood,
>   My heart calls Thine, as deep to deep:
>   Dost Thou forget Thy sweat and pain,
>   Thy provocation on the cross?
>   Heart pierced for me, vouchsafe to keep
> The purchase of Thy lavished Blood
>
>   (17-22)

Here, Rossetti couples the desire to quench her spiritual thirst at Christ's "full Fount" with a reminder of His torture and death. Her consumption imagery fits well

into the tradition of medieval women who, according to Bynum, "craved . . . not only sweetness, inebriation, joy" but "identification with the suffering of the cross" (119). Within a theological framework, then, Rossetti validates both the pain of hunger and the bliss of satiety.

Rossetti's ultimate wish, as expressed in her poetry, is for a oneness with God, a desire she describes in highly erotic language.[17] She speaks, in "The heart knoweth its own bitterness," of being "full of Christ and Christ of me" (56), on the one hand portraying a fullness that she does not allow her body, and on the other hand depicting an interpenetration between Christ and narrator that is also an image of sexual union and pregnancy. Rossetti's image is curiously reciprocal. Not only does the narrator enter Christ as well as being entered by Him—thus blurring the gender distinction between herself and Christ—but their union satisfies them both. In mutuality with Christ, Rossetti even imagines *becoming* food, as in **"The Offering of the New Law, the One Oblation Once Offered"**:

> Yet, a tree, He feeds my root;
> Yet, a branch, He prunes for fruit;
> Yet, a sheep, these eves and morns,
> He seeks for me among the thorns.
>
> Sacrifice and Offering
> None there is that I can bring;
> None, save what is Thine alone:
> I bring Thee, Lord, but of Thine Own—
>
> Broken Body, Blood Outpoured,
> These I bring, my God, my Lord;
> Wine of Life, and Living Bread,
> With these for me Thy Board is spread.
>
>   (21-36)

The narrator begins as a fruit-bearing branch and as food for the Lamb of God, but by the end of the poem, Rossetti elides the distinction between the speaker and Christ. When the narrator offers her own "Broken Body, Blood Outpoured" in exchange for the Eucharist, she uses images of the crucified body of Christ, rendering it unclear where the narrator ends and God begins. Since the Eucharist consists of God's body and blood, moreover, one must read Rossetti's offering of her own body to Christ as a gift of food.

Rossetti never claims that self-denial comes easily; rather, she emphasizes the pain and loneliness of her spiritual quest, positing satiety in heaven as a reward for her hunger on earth. In *Speaking Likenesses,* Flora's, Edith's and Maggie's lessons in self-denial and starvation are so painful that they amount to torment, and only Maggie is rewarded at the end of the story. Rossetti's poetry is somewhat more hopeful. In **"From House to Home,"** for example, she writes that "Altho' today I fade as doth a leaf, / I languish and grow less . . . Tomorrow I shall put forth buds again / And clothe myself with fruit" (219-224). The narrator's starvation on earth eventually leads to her ripeness in heaven, in which, her roots "nourish[ed]" (222) with Christ's blood, she herself blossoms into food, at once both nourished and nourishment. A similar dynamic of secular hunger and sacred fullness informs **"They Desire a Better Country,"** in which the narrator proclaims that "I would not cast anew the lot once cast, / Or launch a second ship for one that sank, / Or drug with sweets the bitterness I drank, / Or break with feasting my perpetual fast" (5-8). By forsaking the sweetness of earth's pleasures, here figured as "feasting," in order to heed Christ's call to "'Follow me here, rise up, and follow here'" (14), Rossetti hopes to reach the New Jerusalem, with its "golden walls of home" (37-38). Although in this poem Rossetti does not envision the heavenly feasting that succeeds earthly fasting, she assumes that one must sacrifice sensual joy in order to attain heavenly bliss. Fasting, while primarily a metaphor for general self-denial, also signifies the literal refusal of food and appetite that Rossetti praised and practiced throughout her adult life.

Though one cannot entirely differentiate religious and secular fasting in Victorian culture, within Rossetti's work the religious dimensions clearly overwhelm the secular. In the make-believe Land of Nowhere, the abstinence that Rossetti both praises and uses to punish aggressive, hungry little girls draws both on the Victorian ideology of female appetite and, even more importantly, on Rossetti's conception of fasting as a means to approach God. Like Flora, Edith and Maggie, Rossetti struggled with the repression of hunger both in her work and throughout her life. As the aunt in *Speaking Likenesses* wonders, "who knows whether something not altogether unlike it has not ere now taken place in the Land of Somewhere? Look at home, children" (338).

Notes

1. Christina Rossetti, letter to Dante Gabriel Rossetti, 4 May 1874. For the relation between *Speaking Likenesses* and *Alice in Wonderland*, see Knoepflmacher.

2. *Athenaeum* 27 December 1874; quoted in Marsh 425.

3. The original title of *Speaking Likenesses* was *Nowhere*. As Jan Marsh points out, though, the newer title is more appropriate, since "while *Nowhere* invokes imaginary realms *Speaking Likenesses* points a moral lesson" (Marsh 419).

4. All citations to *Speaking Likenesses* refer to the edition in *Forbidden Journeys*, which includes the wonderful illustrations by Arthur Hughes.

5. The fact that certain foods—meat for instance—were denied women illustrates the belief that

woman's sensual nature needed to be repressed by constant vigilance.

6. The word *agape* is a "technical name or proper name for various forms of fraternal meals of a semi-liturgical nature . . . the Christian love feasts had as their specific and basic purpose a practical imitation of Christ's love for men by expressing and fostering fraternal love . . . the agapae were related also to the Eucharist, even when they did not include a Eucharistic banquet" (*New Catholic Encyclopedia* 193). Historically, the *agape* was closely connected to the Eucharist: "the rites were similar and not mutually exclusive" (*NCE* 194). The agape was carefully distinguished from lavish secular banquets by Church fathers: Pliny the Younger specifies that it should include "common and innocent" food (qtd. in *NCE* 194) and, according to Tertulian, "food was eaten in moderation" (*NCE* 194). John Wesley introduced *agape* feasts to London in 1738 and, according to *The Oxford Dictionary of the Christian Church*, "'Love feasts,' as they were called, became an established feature of Methodism until the mid-nineteenth century" (*ODC* 26).

7. Auerbach and Knoepflmacher discuss the ways Edith's tale is a "non-story" in which Rossetti consistently foils reader expectation (321-22).

8. The third part of *Speaking Likenesses* is strongly influenced by Bunyan's *Pilgrim's Progress*, in which Christian is beset by various figures of temptation on his way to the Celestial City. The sleepers whom Flora encounters in the wood, for instance, are clearly based upon Bunyan's sleepers, Simple, Sloth and Presumption, and upon the arbour at the Hill of Difficulty in which Christian falls asleep. In its depiction of hunger, *Speaking Likenesses* draws in particular on the second part of *Pilgrim's Progress*, in which Bunyan carefully distinguishes between sacred food—symbolized by Eucharistic "wine, red as blood" (329)—and worldly food, such as that served by Madam Bubble, who "loveth banqueting, and feasting mainly well" (374). As Gaius explains, "Forbidden fruit will make you sick, but not what our Lord has tolerated" (330). Rossetti's distinctions between the sacred and secular meanings of hunger are surely influenced by her own reading of Bunyan.

9. Auerbach and Knoepflmacher write that Maggie's walk home "may lead to heaven" (322), but they do not examine Rossetti's apocalyptic imagery. Rather, they argue that "Instead of fire at the end, we get cold. . . . *Speaking Likenesses* ends in a perishing arctic world" (322), an argument which ignores Rossetti's explosive fire imagery.

10. See Revelation 21: 20. In *The Face of the Deep*, Rossetti calls the sixth rock "sardius" and then comments: "Sardius, a choice sort of carnelian, is found in rocks. Red it is, the more vividly red the more costly" (509). Rossetti's use of the stone carnelian in *Speaking Likenesses* seems, then, to refer to the New Jerusalem. Flora's return to her grandmother's house after her journey also recollects Christian's arrival at the Celestial City in *Pilgrim's Progress*.

11. Maggie's desire to see a Christmas tree, and her subsequent view of a "divine" Christmas tree, is very much like the experience of the little match girl in Hans Christian Andersen's story of the same title, in which an impoverished child sees a vision of a Christmas tree on New Year's Eve by lighting her bundle of matches. Both stories close with the heroine's reunion with her grandmother. In her biography of Rossetti, Jan Marsh notes that Rossetti was familiar with Andersen, whose stories (though not "The Little Match Girl"), her friend Mary Howitt translated in 1846 as *Wonderful Stories for Children* (Marsh 138). Not only does the Andersen connection provide a source for *Speaking Likenesses*, but the Christianity of Andersen's story, in which the match girl is carried to heaven by the spirit of her grandmother, underscores the Christian message of *Speaking Likenesses*.

12. For discussion of the Oxford Movement see Chadwick, Chapman, and Nockles.

13. In *Time Flies* Rossetti describes a sea-anemone: "The food it assimilates is derived not from the height, but from the depth. It possesses neither eyes nor ears but a multitude of feelers. It . . . gulps all acquisitions into a capacious chasm" (198). The anemone, which does nothing but consume, symbolizes the sensual, worldly Christian who satisfies his or her physical rather than spiritual appetite. Like the anemone, such Christians are blind and deaf to God; they have only "feelers" that bring them sensual pleasure. Here, as in Rossetti's other work, appetite epitomizes sensuality and the temporal life of the body.

14. For overviews of different theories of anorexia nervosa, see Brumberg and MacSween. Most psychologists believe that anorexia nervosa is at least in part a denial of the sexual body.

15. Most psychiatrists and critics (including Bordo) believe that anorexic women have subconscious reasons for their fasting behavior, such as the denial of their sexual selves. However, the immediate reason that anorexic women fast is to get rid of the fat on their bodies.

16. All citations to Rossetti's poetry follow Crump's edition, cited by line number.

17. Many critics have noted that Rossetti uses erotic imagery to discuss religious faith in poems like "A Better Resurrection." Antony Harrison has traced this conflation to the courtly love poetry of Petrarch and Dante, for whom "the secular—especially the erotic—and the religious interpenetrate, often becoming metaphors for each other" (Harrison 54). See also Bristow, Mermin, Rosenblum 80-81, and Shurbutt.

Works Cited

Ashwell, Samuel. *A Practical Treatise on the Diseases of Women*. London: Samuel Highley, 1844.

Auerbach, Nina, and U. C. Knoepflmacher. "A Trio of Antifantasies: *Speaking Likenesses*." *Forbidden Journeys: Fairytales and Fantasies by Victorian Women Writers*. Ed. Nina Auerbach and U. C. Knoepflmacher. Chicago: U of Chicago P, 1992. 317-23.

The Book of Health and Beauty or the Toilette of Rank and Fashion. London: Joseph Thomas, 1837.

Bordo, Susan. "Rereading the Slender Body." *Body/Politics: Women and the Discourses of Science*. Ed. Mary Jacobus, Evelyn Fox Keller, Sally Shuttleworth. New York: Routledge, 1990. 83-112.

Bristow, Joseph. "'No Friend Like a Sister'?: Christina Rossetti's Female Kin." *Victorian Poetry* 33 (1995): 257-81.

Brumberg, Joan Jacobs. *Fasting Girls: The History of Anorexia Nervosa*. New York: Plume, 1989.

Bunyan, John. *The Pilgrim's Progress*. London: Penguin, 1987.

Bynum, Caroline Walker. *Holy Feast and Holy Fast: The Significance of Food to Medieval Women*. Berkeley: U of California P, 1987.

Chadwick, Owen. *The Spirit of the Oxford Movement*. Cambridge: Cambridge UP, 1990.

Chapman, Raymond. *Faith and Revolt: Studies in the Literary Influence of the Oxford Movement*. London: Weidenfeld and Nicholson, 1970.

Cohen, Paula Marantz. "Christina Rossetti's *Goblin Market*: A Paradigm for Nineteenth-Century Anorexia Nervosa." *University of Hartford Studies in Literature* 17 (1985): 1-18.

de L'Isere, Colombat. *A Treatise on the Diseases and Special Hygiene of Females*. Trans. Charles D. Meigs. Philadelphia: Lea and Blanchard, 1845.

Harrison, Antony H. *Christina Rossetti in Context*. Chapel Hill: U of North Carolina P, 1988.

Knoepflmacher, U. C. "Avenging Alice: Christina Rossetti and Lewis Carroll." *Nineteenth Century Literature* 41 (1986): 299-328.

MacSween, Morag. *Anorexic Bodies: A Feminist and Sociological Perspective on Anorexia Nervosa.* London: Routledge, 1993.

Marsh, Jan. *Christina Rossetti: A Writer's Life.* New York: Viking, 1995.

Mermin, Dorothy. "Heroic Sisterhood in 'Goblin Market.'" *Victorian Poetry.* 21 (1983): 107-18.

Michie, Helena. *The Flesh Made Word: Female Figures and Women's Bodies.* New York: Oxford University Press, 1987.

Moodie, John. *A Medical Treatise with Principles and Observations to Preserve Chastity and Morality.* Edinburgh: Stevenson, 1848.

New Catholic Encyclopedia. New York: McGraw-Hill, 1967.

Nockles, Peter. *The Oxford Movement in Context.* Cambridge: Cambridge UP, 1994.

The Oxford Dictionary of the Christian Church. Ed. F. L. Cross. 3rd ed. Ed. E. A. Livingstone. Oxford: Oxford UP, 1997.

Pusey, E. B. "Tract XVIII: Thoughts on the Benefits of the System of Fasting Enjoined by our Church." *The Oxford Movement: Being a Selection from Tracts for the Times.* Ed. William G. Hutchison. London: Walter Scott, n.d. 76-110.

Rosenblum, Dolores. *Christina Rossetti: The Poetry of Endurance.* Carbondale: Southern Illinois UP, 1986.

Rossetti, Christina. *The Complete Poems of Christina Rossetti: A Varorium Edition.* Ed. R. W. Crump. Baton Rouge: Louisiana State UP, 1979.

———. *The Face of the Deep: A Devotional Commentary on the Apocalypse.* London: Society for Promoting Christian Knowledge, 1892.

———. *The Family Letters of Christina Georgina Rossetti.* Ed. William Michael Rossetti. New York: Haskell House, 1968.

———. *Speaking Likenesses. Forbidden Journeys: Fairytales and Fantasies by Victorian Women Writers.* Ed. Nina Auerbach and U. C. Knoepflmacher. Chicago: U of Chicago P, 1992.

———. *Time Flies: A Reading Diary.* London: Society for Promoting Christian Knowledge, 1881.

Rossetti, William. "Memoir." *The Poetical Works of Christina Rossetti.* London: Macmillan, 1928. xlv-lxxi.

Shurbutt, Sylvia Bailey. "Revisionist Mythmaking in Christina Rossetti's 'Goblin Market.' *The Victorian Newsletter* 82 (1992): 40-44.

Stanwood, P. G. "Christina Rossetti's Devotional Prose." *The Achievement of Christina Rossetti.* Ed. David A. Kent. Ithaca: Cornell UP, 1987. 231-247.

Thompson, Deborah Ann. "Anorexia as a Lived Trope: Christina Rossetti's *Goblin Market.*" *Mosaic* 24 (1991): 89-106.

Vandereycken, Walter, and Ron Van Deth. *From Fasting Saints to Anorexic Girls: The History of Self Starvation.* London: Athlone Press, 1994.

Walker, Alexander. *Beauty, Illustrated Chiefly by an Analysis and Classification of Beauty in Women.* 5th edition. Glasgow: n.p., 1892.

Walker, Mrs. Alexander. *Female Beauty as Preserved and Improved by Regimen, Cleanliness and Dress.* London: Thomas Hurst, 1837.

Williams, Isaac. *Sermon XIII. A Course of Sermons on Solemn Subjects: chiefly bearing on repentance and amendment of life.* Ed. E. B. Pusey. Oxford: John Henry Parker, 1847.

The Young Lady's Book. London: Henry G. Bohn, 1859.

Emma Parker (essay date 1998)

SOURCE: Parker, Emma. "A Career of One's Own: Christina Rossetti, Literary Success and Love." *Women's Writing* 5, no. 3 (1998): 305-28.

[*In the following essay, Parker argues that Rossetti's repeated expression of loss and desire in her works reflect the author's angst regarding her thwarted aspirations as a writer.*]

In *A Room of One's Own*, Virginia Woolf states that "a woman must have money and a room of her own if she is to write".[1] As a middle-class woman born into a family of artists and intellectuals, Christina Rossetti enjoyed the space and enough financial support to be able to write. But Rossetti wanted more than to write—she wanted to be read and, what is more, to be read, admired and remembered. In short, she had the room; what she wanted was a reputation, a career of her own which entailed success and celebrity. Feminist literary criticism has done much to reassess the reputation of Christina Rossetti as a limited and minor nineteenth-century lyric voice and to revise the image of her as a conventional Victorian lady poetess. Biographical studies such as those by Jan Marsh and Frances Thomas have also revealed invaluable details about the minutia of her literary life. However, critics and biographers alike still invariably assume that Rossetti's major themes of loss and longing are related to the subject of love, and persist in reading many of her poems as commentaries upon her personal relationships with James Collinson and Charles Cayley, the two men to whom she was engaged. By rereading Rossetti's poetry in conjunction with information about the development of her literary career, I want to propose that a significant degree of her work can be read as a coded comment upon her anxieties about being a poet and a covert statement of her desperate desire for success. This is not to suggest that her poetry can be reduced merely to an expression of authorial angst but rather that it bears witness to anxieties about her work as a writer. It is to suggest, however, that the themes of loss and longing in Rossetti's poetry relate less to men than to fame, less to her love life than her artistic life and, specifically, the progress of her career.

LOVE

The view that love is the subject of many of Christina Rossetti's poems is one shaped by her brother William who, in the "Memoir" included in her posthumously published *Poetical Works* (1904), offers details of Rossetti's relationships with her two suitors and states in a footnote that "Readers of her poems had not failed to see, and to say, that some such affair or affairs must have given rise to several of the compositions".[2] Although feminist critics have challenged the mythical image that William constructed of his sister as a modest, reserved, spontaneous, apolitical poet, the idea that a significant number of her poems are an autobiographical comment on her affairs of the heart has gone largely unquestioned. More than a hundred years after her death, Leighton & Reynolds state in their anthology of Victorian women poets that Rossetti's unhappy relationship with James Collinson gave her "a lifelong topos for her poetry: that of lost love and impending death".[3] Germaine Greer likewise argues that Rossetti's preoccupation with disappointment and betrayal are related to love—not, this time, for either of her suitors but for her brother, Gabriel.[4] Even though Thomas is sceptical of the secret love affair that Lona Mosk Packer invents between Rossetti and William Bell Scott, and even though she ultimately argues that Rossetti rejected men and marriage in order to be able to write, concluding that "Christina was saving herself, not for Prince Charming, but for poetry", she nevertheless indulges in the same romantic speculation for which she criticises Packer: "It is possible", she says, "that one of her priests, Henry Burrows or Charles Gutch, meant more to her than she ever said".[5] The other proposed recipient of Rossetti's passion is yet another man, if one that ignites a different kind of love: God. Regardless of various disagreements, Rossetti's critics seem united in the assumption that her passion is inevitably either sexual or spiritual. Although Antony Harrison stresses Rossetti's commitment to her vocation as a writer and, arguing that emphasis on her lovers is misguided, rejects autobiographical readings of her work, he still accepts that the majority of her works explore the experience of love, even if he demonstrates that Rossetti is critical of romantic love.[6]

It is odd that even feminist critics fail to question the assumption that when a woman writes about love, it must be either the romantic or divine kind. In fact, there is little evidence to support the assumption that Rossetti's poems are about love at all. The object of desire is almost always unstated, as in **"Memory"** (1857, 1865), where she writes, "I nursed it in my bosom while it lived, / I hid it in my heart when it was dead".[7] Furthermore, she herself was anxious that her poems should not be interpreted as "love personals".[8] Significantly, when Rossetti writes about love specifically in relation to a man (apart from her anonymous and generic bridegrooms), it is to dismiss him. As the title suggests, **"No, Thank You, John"** is a categorical rejection of romantic involvement. Unsurprisingly, Gabriel did not like this poem.[9] When Rossetti does write about men she mocks them, as in **"The P. R. B."** (1853) and **"A Sketch"** (1864). The first stanza of **"A Sketch"** reads[10]:

> The blindest buzzard that I know
> Does not wear wings to spread and stir,
> Nor does my special mole wear fur
> And grub among the roots below;
> He sports a tail indeed, but then
> It's to a coat; he's man with men;
> His quill is cut to a pen.

(III, 293)

Moreover, when she wrote love poems they were to her mother. Rossetti lived with her mother all her life and was utterly devoted to her. After once hearing her mother mention that she had never received a valentine, Rossetti sent her one every year thereafter. And as Margaret Reynolds has shown, Victorian women poets used poetry to write love letters to each other: Elizabeth Barrett Browning wrote a poem for Letitia Landon called "L.E.L's Last Question", and Rossetti, taking a line from this, modifies and uses it in her poem **"L.E.L."**.[11] Even those critics who read her poems as autobiographical love lyrics are forced to admit an anomaly between the sentiments expressed in the work and the events in her life. For example, with reference to the sequence of four sonnets **"By Way of Remembrance"**, Thomas writes, "Yet if these sonnets appear to relate to Cayley, some of these later poems do not fit any of the events we know of in Christina's life".[12] In viewing Rossetti as a heartbroken victim, critics and biographers tend to overlook the fact that it was *she* who broke off the engagements.[13] Her aversion to marriage is suggested in poems like **"Wife to Husband"**, in which the wife leaves her husband, albeit through death. Nevertheless, the sense of urgency created through the repetition of "I must" and the absence of any sense of sadness—"not a word for you, / Not a lock or kiss, / Good bye" (I, 55)—suggests that death is a form of escape which is eagerly embraced. In **"From Sunset to Star Rise"** (1865), Rossetti writes, "I live alone, I look to die alone" (I, 191), "I look to" indicative of a hope or intention, and in **Letter and Spirit** (1883) she celebrates the state of being single, all of which casts doubt on her desire to marry. Woolf dismisses the love affairs as "unimportant trifles", as "irrelevant, extraneous, superfluous, unreal" and, with her typically acerbic wit, mocks those who are more interested in Rossetti's personal life than her poetry. Imagining how Rossetti would respond to literary critics, she writes, "all I care for you to know is here. It is a copy of my collected works. It costs four shillings and sixpence. Read that . . . It is poetry that matters".[14] Indeed, it is because poetry matters so much to Rossetti that it becomes the very matter—the subject—of the poems themselves.

Critics assume that Rossetti is writing about love because she self-consciously employs conventionally "feminine" themes and forms (love lyrics, devotional verse and writing for children), which she uses as a mask. Several critics have commented on the motif of masks in Rossetti's poetry but have overlooked the way in which the poems themselves constitute a kind of masquerade.[15] Rossetti employs traditional structures and subjects in a manner that anticipates Luce Irigaray's theory of mimicry:

> One must assume the feminine role deliberately. Which means already to convert a form of subordination into an affirmation, and thus to begin to thwart it . . . To play with mimesis is thus, for a woman, to try to recover the place of her exploitation by discourse, without allowing herself to be reduced to it. It means to resubmit herself—inasmuch as she is on the side of the "perceptible," of "matter"—to "ideas," in particular to ideas about herself, that are elaborated in/by a masculine logic, but so as to make "visible," by an effect of playful repetition, what was supposed to remain invisible.[16]

For Irigaray, excess is the crucial component in such a strategy. As Toril Moi explains, it is to *undo* patriarchal discourse by *overdoing* it.[17] Despite the apparent sparseness and simplicity of individual poems, Rossetti's oeuvre is marked by excesses of various kinds: excessive melancholy, excessive use of repetition, an excessive focus on nature, death, and God. Even her sparseness of style is excessive. However, "excessive" has been mistaken for "obsessive" and thus critics have reduced Rossetti's poems to the very discourse they strive to resist. They have therefore tended to miss the way she struggles to reinvent signification, to wring new meaning out of old forms. By mimicking conventional love lyrics Rossetti uses the subject of love to give expression to her inexpressible ambitions as a poet.

The use of strategies such as mimicry and masquerade was necessitated by Victorian attitudes to women and writing, of which Rossetti was only too aware. When her grandfather privately printed a collection of her poems when she was 16, Rossetti incurred censure and

was warned about the dangers of self-exposure even though the volume was only distributed among friends and family.[18] Such criticism did not abate. According to Ford Maddox Ford, on one occasion "Mr Ruskin shouted at her that her poems were a young lady's work and had much better not be published".[19] Middle-class Victorian ladies were expected to be demure and self-effacing. To openly express ambition was to be guilty of the sin of exhibitionism and the fact that Rossetti gave up playing chess because she liked to win suggests that she knew this.[20] Writing about her desire for public acclaim under the guise of writing about the longing for a lover provided a solution to some of the problems that she faced as a Victorian woman poet. Her approach was necessarily indirect and oblique. Bell has stated that Rossetti never alluded directly to her suffering[21], and **Maude** (1897), her novella about a young female poet who struggles to reconcile the knowledge that her writing is a sin with her religious faith, taught her that it was unacceptable for a woman to write directly and openly about women and writing: despite the story's conventional ending—Maude repents and dies—Rossetti failed to publish it in her lifetime. Given this, it is not improbable that love provides a convenient code for literary success. Bell also notes her "passion for symbolism"[22], but love in Rossetti's poetry, conventionally symbolised by something else (such as a rose), becomes a symbol of success, a metaphor for fame. Love, then, as it appears in many of Rossetti's poems, is self-love and, more specifically, love of self as poet.

SUCCESS

Biographies by Marsh and Thomas have made it clear that Rossetti not only defined herself as a poet but that she was a supremely dedicated and fiercely ambitious writer. She composed her first rhyme when she was less than 6 and wrote her first poem when she was 11. By the age of 12, she was referred to as the poet of the family and she considered writing her vocation rather than a ladylike accomplishment. She thought herself "truly a poetess" and, moreover, "a good one".[23] Rossetti was self-confident as a poet and had a profound faith in her ability as a writer. She wrote regularly and prolifically: by the time she was 16, she had composed 60 poems and she wrote over 1000 more before she died. Clearly, Rossetti was serious about writing. She was also ambitious. Although she claimed to be averse to "display", Rossetti's statements can never be taken at face value. As Thomas remarks, she has an "ability to say one thing whilst appearing to say quite the opposite" and her actions frequently contradict her statements.[24] For example, it is odd that one so averse to display would model for her brother's paintings and make fair copies of her poems in notebooks which could be admired. In 1854, when Rossetti submitted six poems to an editor, she wrote, "I do not blush to confess that

. . . it would afford me some gratification to place my productions before others".[25] So much for Rossetti's meek reserve.

While Rossetti professed that she only wished to please family and friends with her writing, her communication with publishers suggests that she longed for public recognition and acclaim. On the publication of *Goblin Market and Other Poems* (1862), Rossetti wrote to Macmillan saying, "I hope reviews will say something about *G. M.* Even being laughed at is better than being ignored"[26], and when an anonymous parody of **"A Birthday"** was published, she cut it out and pasted it into her *Poems,* showing that she relished being laughed at because she loved being noticed.[27] Her fervent desire for fame is also indicated by an incident that occurred shortly after the publication of *Goblin Market.* When Macmillan accepted more poems for publication, Rossetti complained about the amount she was paid. Jan Marsh admits being puzzled by such behaviour as, she says, Christina was not mercenary, but Marsh overlooks the fact that money signals status.[28] Indeed, it is clear from Marsh's account that this incident has more significance than she herself accords it. As Macmillan paid its authors per page it is likely that what upset Rossetti was not the issue of remuneration but that her poems had been crammed onto one page; that she was not permitted to take up space as a poet. Fundamentally, the incident illustrates her desire to be noticed and to expand her reputation. Later, she always resisted letting anthologists reprint extracts of her work, preferring instead that they include the whole.[29] Rossetti was a woman who refused to be diminished. The voracity of her desire for fame is underlined by another comment to Macmillan. On receiving her six complimentary copies of *Speaking Likenesses,* she wrote back stating, "I only hope that the public appetite will not be satisfied with 6 or 60, but crave 600 or 6000 at least!"[30]

However, Rossetti hankered after fame and fortune alike and to suggest that she did not care about money would be misleading. When her family suffered a financial crisis, she dreamt of being able to rescue them from their impoverished state through her writing. She fantasises that her short story **"Nick"** is "advertised all over the civilised world. The book spreads like wild-fire" and she receives a cheque for £200 and later another for £2000.[31] In 1864, Rossetti informed Macmillan, "Mr. Masson [the editor of *Macmillan's Magazine*] has 2 little things of mine in hand", and adds, "you may think whether I am not happy to attain fame (!) and guineas by means of the Magazine".[32] Direct comments about fame and fortune are always expressed with a combination of eagerness and uneasiness. The bracketed exclamation mark and tortured syntax are telling signs of her recognition of potential impropriety. Elsewhere such statements are qualified with obligatory demure posturing. In 1883 she wrote to Edmund Gosse to thank him

for payment for an article she had written on Dante published in the *Century.* Rossetti begins with a polite protestation that she does not deserve the amount received and offers to return part of the sum, but concludes, "Meanwhile I like my guineas very much".[33]

It is easy, then, to see how the sense of longing in Rossetti's poems relates to her success as a writer rather than her success as a lover, but to understand why loss, in conjunction with the themes of disappointment and betrayal, is such a dominant theme it is necessary to examine the development of her literary career. Details of Rossetti's personal literary history are now well known but it is worth reiterating them here in order to take an overview of the development of her career and to examine particular poems in relation to their moment of production.

In 1847, when she was just 17, Rossetti had two poems published in the *Athenaeum.*[34] Publication in such a prestigious journal was a remarkable achievement, especially for one so young, and marked an audacious start to what promised to be an exceptional writing career. Success had come quickly and easily. However, Rossetti had to wait a further 15 years before her first volume of poetry was accepted for publication and this interval was one characterised by repeated rejection, which inevitably caused disappointment. Between 1851 and 1861, despite being at her creative peak, she published only two poems. The *Athenaeum* refused all subsequent poems Rossetti submitted and she failed to get *Maude* published, all of which left her "discouraged".[35] In 1850 Gabriel included two of his sister's poems in the first edition of *The Germ,* but the magazine set up by the Pre-Raphaelite Brotherhood, which according to William had "next to no circulation", soon collapsed.[36] In 1854 six poems that Rossetti sent to Blackwood's were rejected. In 1856 her short story **"The Lost Titian"** was accepted by *The Crayon* but, as Marsh notes, its circulation was very small and when another short story, **"Nick"**, was published in the *National Magazine* in October 1857, Marsh comments that "[n]o-one seems to have taken much notice".[37] Although things looked bleak for Rossetti at this point, her repeated attempts at publication demonstrate that she avidly sought an audience and her perseverance in the face of repeated rejection and limited success shows staunch determination. **"A Birthday"**, written in 1857 and which begins, "My heart is like a singing bird", suggests that small successes brought enormous happiness (I, 36). Many critics find this brief and sudden burst of joy incongruous.[38] Since 18 November, the date of composition, was not Rossetti's own birthday, it seems likely that the birthday is a metaphor, not for spiritual or emotional rebirth, however, as Marsh suggests[39], but rather for the rebirth of success: the poem was written soon after the appearance of **"Nick"**. In this sense, the line "Because the birthday of my life / Is come, my love is come to me" articulates self-love rather than romantic or spiritual love (I, 37).

However, poems like **"Shut Out"**, written in 1856, and **"At Home"**, written in 1858, are more characteristic of the period and convey the suffering caused by rejection. In **"Shut Out"**, a poem about exclusion and loss, the Edenic garden acts as a metaphor for literary success:

> The door was shut. I looked between
> Its iron bars; and saw it lie,
> My garden, mine, beneath the sky,
> Pied with all flowers bedewed and green:
>
> From bough to bough the song-birds crossed,
> From flower to flower the moths and bees;
> With all its nests and stately trees
> It had been mine, and it was lost.
>
> (I, 56)

"At Home" articulates similar feelings of exclusion as well as sadness at being forgotten. Originally called **"After the Picnic"**, Marsh deems Gabriel's change to the title appropriate as, she says, the poem has nothing to do with picnics.[40] However, awareness of the fact that Rossetti's first exciting success, publication in the *Athenaeum,* was now over 10 years ago and had been followed by a frustratingly long fallow period makes it obvious that, in terms of her poetic career, the picnic was most emphatically over.

A turning point was marked by the year 1861 when *Macmillan's Magazine* published **"Up-Hill"** and then later in the year **"A Birthday"**, which brought Rossetti to public attention. Macmillan offered to print a volume which became *Goblin Market and Other Poems* (1862). Reviews were good but sales were slow—in 1871 Rossetti commented that she was "sorry to see so many Goblins still in the market"[41]—and Marsh states that Rossetti was dismayed that the book did not establish her more securely.[42] Three years after the appearance of *Goblin Market,* Gabriel wrote to Macmillan stating that "You know she *is* a good poet, and some day people will know it".[43] Apparently they still did not know it in 1865, the date of Gabriel's letter. The period following the publication of *Goblin Market* was characterised by illness and a demise in creativity. Rossetti informed Macmillan that her "scribbling faculty" had "come to a long stop".[44] According to Marsh, in 1864 Rossetti was sending out old poems rather than writing new ones and her jealousy of Jean Ingelow, a contemporary poet winning acclaim, led to further insecurity.[45] Poems written in 1864/65 are dominated by wintry imagery. **"From Sunset to Star Rise"** (written in February 1865) begins:

> Go from me, summer friends, and tarry not:
> I am no summer friend, but wintry cold,

> A silly sheep benighted from the fold,
> A sluggard with a thorn-choked garden plot.
>
> (I, 191)

Here, coldness is linked to a demise in creativity through the image of the "thorn-choked garden", and in **"What Would I Give"** (written January 1864), coldness causes silence:

> What would I give for words, if only words would
>   come;
> But now in its misery my spirit has fallen dumb:
> O merry friends, go your way, I have never a word to
>   say.
>
> (I, 142)

Marsh notes the preponderance of winter imagery but does not connect it to Rossetti's progress as a poet. Little was coming to artistic fruition in the form of publication or fame at this point and Rossetti's career seemed to be "frozen", like the heart in her poems. In 1875 she commented that "I for my part am a great believer in the genuine poetic impulse belonging (very often) to the spring and not to the autumn of life".[46] The distaste for winter and longing for summer that is a recurrent motif in many of her poems can thus be understood as an expression of Rossetti's desire to see the fruits of her labour, to see her poetry in print, and to bask in success.

Macmillan offered to do a second volume but progress was slow. At this time Rossetti wrote two poems about brides who die waiting to be united with their bridegrooms, **"A Bird's Eye View"** (written in 1864) and **"The Prince who Arrived too Late"**, which became **"The Prince's Progress"** (finished in 1865). Marsh finds this subject "curious"[47], but the poems are less mysterious if the prince is read as a metaphor for fame. As already stated, sales of *Goblin Market* were disappointing and Rossetti was struggling with her second volume of verse. The orthodox subject of heterosexual romance thus provides a convenient mask for the expression of unorthodox anxieties about her impatient longing for success. Rossetti was anguished by her nonproductivity and when Gabriel further frustrated publication by asking for changes, she was provoked, in her own words, into "six well-defined and several paroxysms of stamping and foaming and hair-uprooting"[48], action indicative of her increasing desperation to see herself in print.

Once the manuscript for her second volume (*The Prince's Progress and Other Poems*) was completed, Rossetti went on a trip to Italy where she became depressed. Oddly, rather than understanding her depression as a result of anguish about a flagging career or anxiety about the reception of the forthcoming volume,

Marsh simply accepts Rossetti's own explanation for her melancholia, which is that looking at the Alps made her sad.[49] Similarly, when Rossetti writes, "Why should I seek and never find / That something which I have not had" in a poem called **"En Route"** that she composed on this trip, Marsh assumes that Rossetti is writing of her disappointment at not having seen a rainbow rather than allusive literary success.[50]

Rossetti had good reason to feel dismay about her poetic career. *The Prince's Progress* received poor reviews and by 1866, the year of its publication, she had been eclipsed by Swinburne, who had become the centre of attention as the new literary voice. Marsh points out that her reputation, that as it was, was damaged when her brother William declared that Swinburne had been influenced by her work and when Swinburne himself made his admiration of Rossetti public knowledge. As Marsh notes, praise from a man who was a notorious bawd and drunkard, who was apt to slide down the banisters of the Rossetti home naked, and who had been declared decadent, depraved and blasphemous, was the kind of praise she did not need. The connection proved damaging.[51] At this point, in 1866, Rossetti stopped making fair copies of her work in notebooks, something she had done for more than 20 years. It must have seemed to her that her success was over before it had ever really begun.

This indeed seemed to be the case when *Commonplace and Other Stories,* published in 1870, was lambasted by critics, so much so that Rossetti felt compelled to release her publishers (F. S. Ellis) from a contract for her next volume of verse, *Sing-Song,* as she feared that poor reviews would adversely affect its reception and sales. *Speaking Likenesses,* published in 1874, did not do well and Rossetti still feared going unnoticed when *A Pageant and Other Poems* was published in 1881. She wrote to Gabriel expressing anxiety about being invisible to reviewers:

> There seems (I am sorry to say) to have been some hobble at the "Saturday Review" office, tho' a copy [of *A Pageant and Other Poems*] was sent in due course: now, I fear, they will not notice me, and at any rate Mr. Gosse is off for a holiday and cannot "do" me. But I am not going to worry myself over this trifle, tho' I should like it to have happened otherwise.[52]

Rossetti's assertion that she is not concerned is clearly contradicted by the rest of the extract. Success, it seems, was still by no means assured. In 1883 Rossetti was included in a biography called *English Poetesses,* but whereas a full chapter was devoted to Elizabeth Barrett Browning, she was mentioned in a general chapter and then only in relation to Gabriel. Even with such a brief mention the editors managed to get factual details about her life and work wrong and Rossetti had to correct the proofs.[53] Neither was this an isolated incident—Amelia

B. Edwards's *A Poetry Book of Modern Poets* (1879) states that Rossetti was born in 1816 instead of 1830. Such mistakes explain why Rossetti had good reason to be concerned about her visibility.[54]

Towards the end of her life, Rossetti published several other books but they contained either prose or religious verse, suggesting that she tried to direct her passion for poetry into piety.[55] Even her most ardent admirers admit that her latter books of prose were not her best work— Bell states that the stories in *Speaking Likenesses* (1874) "cannot be ranked high among its author's books" and describes *Seek and Find* as "not one of Christina Rossetti's great books"[56]—and while the publication of her prose undoubtedly brought pleasure, it most likely produced satisfaction tinged with disappointment because Rossetti defined herself first and foremost as a poet. Despite Thomas's claim that "For now, it cannot be doubted, she was England's foremost woman poet"[57], the report from Lucy (William's wife) in 1889 that she had just met a bookseller who had never heard of *Sing-Song,* suggests that indeed it can.[58] The glory awarded to "England's foremost poet", typified by a request to distribute prizes at a girls' school, was clearly not particularly great and the unflinching "no" with which Rossetti responded to such a request rather undercuts her assertion that "As to literary success, I am fully satisfied with what has befallen me".[59] In 1892 Tennyson died and Rossetti was considered for the Laureateship. She was excited and flattered, and Thomas's view that she would have been "horrified" to have been chosen is spurious[60], but Rossetti was passed over and the post was left vacant until after her death. No Poet Laureate was evidently preferable to a female Poet Laureate. Given this, it is no surprise that Rossetti's poetry expresses sadness, only a surprise that critics and biographers continually attribute her sorrow to disastrous love affairs rather than a disappointing career.

GABRIEL

If Rossetti's bitterness and sadness were caused by a man, it is more likely to have been Gabriel than anyone else. As illustrator, critic, editor and literary agent, Gabriel played a major part in the management of his sister's affairs. He selected poems for publication, often changing their titles, and, like William, he liaised with publishers and dealt with business transactions. Although Rossetti claimed to be happy with and grateful for his help, at times it effectively rendered her a passive participant in her own career. She was strictly excluded from the all-male meetings known as "tobacco parliaments" held in the editor's office at Macmillan's[61], as well as from the meetings of the Pre-Raphaelite Brotherhood at which her work was discussed. The phallocentricity of the P. R. B. is not only underlined by an emphasis on "*Brother*hood" but also by the alternative name by which it jokingly became known to its members: "Penis Rather Better".[62] Gabriel wielded an immense degree of power over his sister and strictly controlled her literary output. A letter to Gabriel shows that poems in *The Prince's Progress* were "re-written to order"[63], and Gabriel not only demanded to check his sister's corrections but also wrote to Macmillan requesting changes before consulting Christina about them.[64] Rossetti resisted such interference where she could, as when she was preparing the second edition of *Goblin Market*—Gabriel wrote to Macmillan requesting a delay to make changes but she wrote to Macmillan instructing them to disregard her brother's suggestions.[65] Such occasions, however, were rare.

The marginalisation that Rossetti experienced in life became inevitable after death. William published two more volumes of her work, one of which was a collection of poems that she had chosen *not* to publish in her lifetime, and even when Rossetti was being lauded it seems she had to share the limelight. William dedicated her *New Poems* (1896) to Swinburne and Bell dedicated his biography to William. While Bell dedicates six pages to reprints of reviews of Rossetti's work towards the end of the book, reviews of his own *Pictures of Travel and Other Poems* occupy a staggering eight pages at the back of the biography. Although Rossetti is ostensibly at the centre of these two books, they also suggest that after death she was used as pawn in a nexus of male literary relations. Ironically, once Rossetti's career was firmly established, it was no longer quite her own.

Furthermore, Gabriel's "support" was invariably less help than hindrance. He offered to supply the woodcuts for *Goblin Market* but repeatedly failed to provide them, and consequently the book's publication was delayed until after Christmas, something which would have undoubtedly caused Rossetti further frustration and inevitably damaged sales. Marsh speculates that Gabriel may have been deliberately holding the book back so that it did not compete with his own *Early Italian Poets,* which was due out at the same time.[66] When Christina was struggling with *The Prince's Progress,* Gabriel gave up on the volume to help Swinburne publish and, despite having distanced himself from the creative project, he jeopardised his sister's contract and good relations with Macmillan when he wrote to them, without her knowledge, requesting an advance on her behalf.[67] He also delayed publication because he was late with the illustrations.[68] Although Rossetti publicly thanked Gabriel for his guidance when she stated, "I would like to acknowledge the general indebtedness of my first and second volume to his suggestive wit and revising hand"[69], it seems likely that the woman who "pulled legs" and "tweaked noses", as Woolf put it, was merely paying lip-service.[70]

That Rossetti had little to thank her brother for became clear when he published his own *Poems* at precisely the same time as her collection of short stories, *Common-*

place and Other Stories (1870). While his volume was a spectacular success, hers was a dismal failure. Throughout his life Gabriel eclipsed Christina in terms of success, even in relation to her own work. When *Goblin Market* came out some reviewers were more impressed with his illustrations than her poems.[71] Despite dutiful acknowledgement of his artistic superiority, certain comments intimate that Rossetti hid resentment of her secondary position. In 1880, following an anonymous review of her work, she wrote to her brother saying, "Don't think me such a goose as to feel keenly mortified at being put below you, the head of house in so many ways".[72] Given that Gabriel's *Poems* was going into its fourth reprint while Rossetti was struggling to find a publisher for *Sing-Song,* it seems unlikely that she "rejoiced", as Marsh states, at her brother's success[73], especially as one reason for the failure of *Commonplace* was that it was published not by Macmillan, "the staunch Mac.", as she called the firm and her friend[74], with whom she had an established relationship, but by F. S. Ellis, whom Gabriel, more concerned with prosperity than posterity, persuaded her to join because they offered better terms. This change proved to be detrimental to Rossetti in both the long and short term because after her defection Macmillan postponed plans for a complete edition of her poems (under discussion in 1870 but not published until 1875, once she had returned to Macmillan), and when the contract with Ellis was broken, Rossetti was left without a publisher for the next 2 years.[75] The lengths to which Gabriel would go for the sake of his own career are well known: in 1869 he had the grave of his wife, Lizzie, exhumed so that he could publish poems he had buried with her.

The notion that what was presented as support was in practice a form of censorship is suggested by Gabriel's displeasure at the treatment of themes such as illegitimacy in his sister's work, but it is epitomised by the long struggle Rossetti waged with him over **"The Lowest Room"**. **"The Lowest Room"** is a poem that protests against the narrowness of women's lives through a debate between two sisters, one of whom dutifully resigns herself to the conventional female role of wife and mother while the other rejects it. The fact that its original title was **"A Fight over the Body of Homer"** indirectly suggests that the struggle between the choices represented in the poem is one that concerns writing. Rossetti wrote it in 1856 but Gabriel criticised its "falsetto muscularity" and decreed it unsuitable for publication in both *Goblin Market* and *The Prince's Progress.*[76] Rossetti disagreed with her brother's decision and resisted, but eventually acquiesced. However, flagrantly denying Gabriel's veto, she eventually published it in *Goblin Market, The Prince's Progress and Other Poems* (1875). The snub is all the more delicious given that having been forbidden to publish it in *Goblin Market* and *The Prince's Progress,* she manages, in her own way, to publish it in both at once. When Gabriel protested, Rossetti apologised and claimed that she had only included it for bulk. However, her perseverance in her efforts to publish this poem for almost 20 years suggests that its inclusion was significantly more important to her than that.

When Gabriel suffered problems with his mental health in 1872 he suffered paranoid delusions and became convinced that people were conspiring to destroy him, but if anyone had a reason to feel that they were the victim of a conspiracy, it was surely Christina Rossetti. Marsh's assertion that Gabriel's insanity was triggered by a bad review produces a further irony given his sister's chequered literary success.[77] If one unfavourable review drove Gabriel into madness, it is difficult to imagine the effect that Christina's struggle for success must have had on her or the extreme strength of mind and degree of dedication needed to continue. Little, if any, attention has been paid to the grief that Gabriel must have caused her, but if the sadness expressed in Rossetti's poetry is her own rather than that of her speakers, it is a sadness that is just as likely to have been caused by him as Collinson or Cayley.

Thomas describes **"Twice"**, written in June 1864, as a poem about the feelings of a woman who has had her declaration of love rejected, and, remarking on its "personal" status, implies that it alludes to her relationship with Charles Cayley[78], but it is equally possible that the poem addresses Gabriel in his role as editor—or indeed any editor—especially if the heart is understood to function as a metaphor for poetry:

> You took my heart in your hand
> With a friendly smile,
> With a critical eye you scanned,
> Then set it down,
> And said: It is still unripe

(I, 125)

The "critical eye" and "scanning" are obvious allusions to literary activity and elsewhere there is a direct reference to writing: "My hope was written on sand". As Rossetti spent several months in Hastings during the winter of 1864-65, the possibility that the reference to sand is literal while "hope" is a metaphor for poetry is not altogether absurd. Poems like **"A pin has a head"**—"a pin has a head, but has no hair; / A clock has a face, but no mouth there" (II, 32)—show that Rossetti delighted in playing with language and exploiting the slippage between the literal and the metaphorical, which is typical of the way that she plays with reader expectations and says one thing while appearing to say another. **"Twice"** thus illustrates that rather than writing to force her feelings under control, as Leighton has argued[79], Rossetti writes to give those feelings (coded) expression.

MAKING A NAME FOR HERSELF

Rossetti's struggle to establish a career of her own was further frustrated by the problems she encountered in getting her name, as well as her poems, into print. The repeated repression of her name, or mistakes concerning her name, meant that Rossetti struggled to make a name for herself literally as well as metaphorically. The poems published in the *Athenaeum* in 1847 were published under her initials instead of her full name, which meant that she effectively remained anonymous. That this concerned her is suggested by the emphasis on names in **"A Pause of Thought"**, written in 1848:

> Sometimes I said: It is an empty name
> I long for; to a name why should I give
> The peace of all the days I have to live?—
> Yet gave it all the same.

(I, 52)

Despite being composed on St Valentine's day, William's view that the poem demonstrated that his sister "aspired ardently after poetic fame" is more convincing than the view that it is about love[80], although William's reading has been rejected by a number of critics including Packer, who states:

> It is doubtful whether the ambition for fame would have disturbed Christina's peace of mind seriously at the age of eighteen. Furthermore, although this kind of ambition characterised Gabriel at an early age, it was, if it existed at all, a recessive feature of Christina's personality.[81]

Similarly, Marsh rejects William's assertion that **"A Pause of Thought"** concerns the progress of his sister's career as too determinate and prefers to see the poem's subject as disappointment and desire, while Greer simply considers it typical of the "despairing" mood of her early work.[82] But resilience and not despair is the keynote of the poem: the speaker says that she will not give up hope, that she continues to watch and wait for that which she desires, that she will not resign or give up, that she is prepared to go on sacrificing her peace to pursue her goal, and even though her efforts appear useless and doomed to failure, she persists. The poem's original title, **"Lines in Memory of Schiller's 'Der Pilgrim'"**, a poem about the quest for artistic excellence, suggests that the unspecified goal is success as a poet.

When Rossetti was published in *The Germ,* she was once more denied the fame she so desired in the very moment that it seemed to be proffered. Concerned that the name "Rossetti" appeared too many times on the title page, Gabriel invented the pseudonym of "Ellen Alleyn" for his sister and published her poems under that name—without obtaining her prior permission. As Bell remarks, "only after he had done this did C[hristina] know anything about it".[83] Gabriel and William remained Rossettis while Christina was sacrificed to obscurity. Although she claimed to like the name, she had little choice but to say so given that she relied on *The Germ* for publication and could not risk alienating her brothers. Her attitude to the name is perhaps better reflected in the fact that she never chose to use it herself. Marsh points out that Rossetti's early reputation rested on the poems published in *The Germ,* but the difficulty of establishing a reputation using a name not one's own is obvious.[84] Rossetti was in print but no one would know the poems were hers. The possibility that Gabriel was not aware that this would be the result is unlikely. He was most particular about his own name, and when Macmillan addressed him as "G. D. Rossetti" rather than "D. G. Rossetti" he responded with a brusque request that the error be rectified, explaining that "variations in one's nomenclature are apt to create confusion".[85]

By 1854 Rossetti was permitted use of her first name when William wrote to the editor of *Fraser's Magazine* asking them to consider some of his sister's poems, requesting that they publish them under the name "Christina G. R.", although they were not accepted.[86] Anxieties about the erosion of selfhood, about autonomy, self-determination and self-possession, are intimated by the title of a poem she wrote in 1856: **"Whatever Happened to Me?"**[87] When **"Maude Clare"** was published in *Once a Week* in 1859, her name appeared in full but was misprinted. The poem was attributed to "Caroline G. Rossetti" rather than "Christina" and, understandably, she was "touchy" about this.[88] The importance of her name in establishing her as a poet is indicated by the comment of an editor who included one of her poems in his poetry anthology called *Nightingale Valley* published in 1859: "But—Who is Christina Rossetti, pray?"[89] In 1860, despite having written over 200 poems, Christina Rossetti was still virtually unknown. Rossetti recognised that her reputation rested on her name and that her name was therefore the currency of her success. In 1870 she wrote to Ellis, "I can readily imagine that if **Commonplace** proves a total failure, *Sing-Song* may dwindle to a very serious risk: and therefore I beg you at once, if you deem the step prudent, to put a stop to all further outlay on the rhymes, until you can judge if my name is marketable".[90] When *Sing-Song* was published by Routledge in 1871 it was a great success. One critic referred to Rossetti as "the poet of female poets", an ambiguous compliment in itself but one which was further undercut by the fact that he too, like others, got her name wrong, referring to her as "Christina Gabriela Rossetti" instead of "Christina Georgina Rossetti".[91] And this was not an isolated incident. When **"When I am dead, my dearest"** was published in a collection called *Flower-Lore,* the poem was also attributed to "Christina Gabriela Rossetti".[92] The slip from "Georgina" to "Gabriela" must have been a particularly painful reminder that her brother had become a more successful poet than herself and was an example of the way in which Rossetti persistently came to be judged secondary.

The importance Rossetti attached to her name is betrayed by the very insistence with which she claimed she did not. She once wrote to Gabriel to tell him that the family name now appeared in some of the London directories and says: "*I,* however individually do not figure in such prominent pages, but consider myself sufficiently represented by the insertion of Mamma. I do not want to notify to all whom it may and whom it may not concern my private and personal habitat".[93] If she was so unconcerned by this it seems odd to mention it at all. Similarly, in a reply to a letter from someone asking for details about her publications, Rossetti writes, "Perhaps it is not worth adding that my name appears amongst the writers of the 'Imperial Dictionary of Universal Biography' to which I contributed some articles on Italian literary men".[94] Of course, stating that it is not worthy of mention provides her with exactly the pretext she requires for mentioning it. Rossetti's preoccupation with her reputation is perhaps best exemplified by an anecdote that Woolf relates about Mrs Virtue Tebbs's tea-party, a gathering at which, "suddenly there uprose from a chair and paced forward into the centre of the room a little woman dressed in black, who announced solemnly, 'I am Christina Rossetti!' and having said so, returned to her chair".[95] Thomas comments that the story is "peculiar, and so unlike Christina that one feels it must have become distorted in the telling"[96], but, recognising its importance, Woolf takes the title of her essay on Rossetti ("I am Christina Rossetti") from this story. With her usual perception, Woolf recognises that the incident is related to Rossetti's status as a poet: "Yes [she seems to say], I am a poet".[97] Certainly the story's significance increases with an awareness of the problems Rossetti encountered in her efforts to make a name for herself.

Rossetti's concern for her name was unusual in a historical moment when many women writers—the Brontës, George Eliot, George Sand—chose to adopt androgynous or male pseudonyms in order to overcome sexual discrimination and get their work published, and is itself a testament to her boldness. It is a cruel irony that one who attached so much importance to her name should have it marginalised so permanently as on her gravestone. Bell points out that by the time Rossetti died there was no room left for her name on the family gravestone in Highgate Cemetery, "so the words about Christina Rossetti are carved on the slanting face of an additional slab placed across its base, and the initials of the persons interred, and the dates of the interments appear on the back of the footstone".[98] While Gabriel's and William's names appear on prominent—vertical—gravestones (one at the head and one at the foot of the family tomb), Christina's lays hidden on a horizontal plaque in the middle. The extract from her own poem **"The Lowest Place"** serves as both an epitaph and an apt description of the position of her name on the grave.

MEMORY

Given the problems Rossetti faced in establishing her career as a poet, it is unsurprising that she had anxieties about being remembered. Such anxieties are evident in her representation of the theme of memory, which receives an astonishing degree of attention in her poems and bespeaks her desire to be remembered as a poet: in Greek myth Mnemosyne (memory) is the mother of the Muses. Rossetti was aware that being forgotten was a common fate for women writers. When asked to contribute to a biographical book called *Eminent Women*, she chose to write about Ann Radcliffe but had to abandon the project because of lack of material.[99] Her poem **"Sappho"** (1846) suggests that Rossetti recognised that the dangers of being written out of literary history were very real, especially for women poets:

> I sigh at day-dawn, and I sigh
> When the dull day is passing by.
> I sigh at evening, and again
> I sigh when night brings sleep to men.
> Oh! it were better far to die
> Than thus for ever mourn and sigh,
> And in death's dreamless sleep to be
> Unconscious that none weep for me;
> Eased from my weight of heaviness,
> Forgetful of forgetfulness,
> Resting from pain and care and sorrow
> Thro' the long night that knows no morrow;
> Living unloved, to die unknown,
> Unwept, untended and alone.

> (III, 81-82)

Marsh remarks that Rossetti would not have been familiar with Sappho's work as Sappho was not widely read at this time, and therefore suggests that what she represented for Rossetti was the woman poet of unhappy love.[100] However, as her own comments suggest, what Sappho also represented was the way that female poets were forgotten. The phrase "forgetful of forgetfulness" is typical of Rossetti's deft use of ambiguity. It can mean either to forget that you have been forgotten or to remember (to forget to forget is to remember). The use of repetition, a defining characteristic of her lyrics both in terms of lexis and structure, verbally enacts a movement into the future, as does the movement from dawn to dusk in the first two lines, which is itself repeated in lines 3 and 4. As the four 'un's in the last two lines demonstrate, both the number and frequency of repetitions increase as the poem progresses. The "long night that knows no morrow" conveys the finality of death but it also suggests fixity or permanence. So, rather than a "juvenile yearning for oblivion"[101], **"Sappho"** can be read as an expression of regret about

oblivion: "to die unknown" is what the poem mourns. In this context, "living unloved" alludes to living without the admiration of the reading public rather than the love of a man.[102] Although it is easy to assume that the desire to be remembered represented in Rossetti's poems is her own personal desire not to be forgotten by her former lovers, one of Gabriel's comments illustrates that Rossetti was aware that her writing was repeatedly being forgotten, remembered and forgotten again. Gabriel once wrote to his mother, "Will you tell her that I am quite ashamed of not being able yet to tell her anything positive about Nick? I am constantly remembering it when [James] Hannay [another writer] is not in the way, and always forgetting it when he is".[103]

Titles of poems such as **"Forget-me Not"** (1844), **"Remember"** (1849), **"Memory"** (part one 1857, part two 1865), **"Unforgotten"** (1855), **"A Bed of Forget-Me-Nots"** (1856) and **"By Way of Remembrance"** (1870) demonstrate that Rossetti's concern with memory spanned her whole career and suggest that she wished to see herself in the future. Her treatment of memory produces a confused temporality that enables her to bring the past into the present and to project herself into the future. The opening line of **"Remember"**— "Remember me when I am gone away" (I, 37)— successfully collapses past, present and future into one another. The speaker speaks in the present about the future in which she will be part of the past but brought into the present by being remembered. Anticipation is cleverly blended with retrospection.

But Rossetti is as much concerned with forgetting as she is with remembering and a significant degree of her poetry pivots on the dialectic between the two. Despite the conclusion in **"Remember"**, which appears to advocate the necessity of forgetting—"better by far you should forget and smile / Than you should remember and be sad"—the sonnet begins with a bold command— "remember me"—which is reiterated throughout. The ostensible movement from self-assertion to self-suppression is counterbalanced if not reversed by a parallel movement from direct statements to the conditional tense and modal verbs ("For *if* the darkness and corruption leave . . . Better by far you *should* forget and smile", emphasis added). Similarly, in **"Song: When I am dead, my dearest"** (1848), the implied indifference to being remembered or forgotten is contradicted by the self-assertion evident in the movement from "thou" to "I":

> When I am dead, my dearest,
> Sing no sad songs for me;
> Plant thou no roses at my head,
> Nor shady cypress tree:
> Be the green grass above me
> With showers and dewdrops wet;
> And if thou wilt, remember,
> And if thou wilt, forget.

I shall not see the shadows,
I shall not feel the rain;
I shall not hear the nightingale
Sing on, as if in pain:
And dreaming through the twilight
That doth not rise nor set,
Haply I may remember,
And haply may forget.

(I, 58)

Here the tension between presence and absence effectively renders the absent present and in doing so the poem problematises the very binary opposites it invokes, illustrating that terms which appear to be mutually exclusive are actually interdependent. As a precondition of remembering, the speaker's forgetting functions as what Barbara DeConcini calls a "losing-in-order-to-find" herself[104] or, alternatively, she can be seen to be engaged in remembering-against-forgetting. Each is only possible in relation to the other and it is precisely this relation that is the central subject of the poem. The binarisms that the poem seems to establish (remembering/forgetting, self/other, life/death) dissolve into a state of in-betweenness, foregrounded by the dreaming (neither an unconscious nor fully conscious state) and the twilight (neither day nor night), in the same way that choice dissolves into chance when "if thou wilt" is superseded by "haply". The final emphasis on chance endorses the sense of uncertainty engendered by the poem as a whole. Like so many of Rossetti's poems, this song is profoundly puzzling despite its apparent simplicity, and deliberately so, not only because such puzzles provide one means of destabilising the discrete categories of binary logic that underpin patriarchal ideology and of privileging feminine possibility over masculine certainty, but also because its teasingly enigmatic character functions as a strategy which makes it difficult to forget. Many of Rossetti's lyrics have, as Isobel Armstrong has noted, a haunting quality.[105] And thus form reflects theme because in the progression from the opening focus on death to the final focus on "the twilight / That doth not rise nor set", what begins as a poem about the speaker's mutability ends as a poem about her permanence.

Rossetti's desperate desire to be remembered partly explains her refusal to support the suffrage campaign. Even though she declined to sign a women's rights petition, she did so only after asserting that "female *M.P.*'s are only right and reasonable. Also I take exceptions at the exclusion of married women from the suffrage"[106], which suggests that she sympathised with the suffrage campaign but did not wish to appear to be seen to support it publicly. The fate of Augusta Webster suggests one reason why this may be. Throughout her life, Rossetti witnessed how overtly feminist writers like Elizabeth Barrett Browning and Augusta Webster incurred censure from the men who dominated literary spheres.

It was the latter who tried, unsuccessfully, to persuade Rossetti to sign a women's rights petition, and when in 1890 Gladstone compiled a list of "distinguished poet-esses", Rossetti noted with regret that the one name that was missing was Webster's.[107] The effectiveness of such a strategy for penalising deviance is evident in the fact that Christina Rossetti is today much more well known than Augusta Webster, a poet who was eminent in her day.

DEATH

Acknowledgement of Rossetti's wish that her work be remembered partly explains her preoccupation with death, which, as **"When I am dead, my dearest"** suggests, is in effect a preoccupation with immortality. For Victorian women enduring a death-in-life existence (a predominant Rossetti theme), death certainly represents an escape or "a desire to move beyond cultural boundaries", as Armstrong has suggested.[108] However, for Rossetti, as a poet, death also has additional significance. Several poems, such as **"Life out of Death"** (date of composition unknown), suggest that Rossetti believed in life after death. Ghosts haunt poems like **"A Chilly Night"** (1856), **"At Home"** (1858), **"The Poor Ghost"** (1863) and **"The Ghost's Petition"** (1864), and many of her female figures seem more alive after death, as in **"After Death"** where the dead woman speaks and seems acutely conscious. In **"Life and Death"** (1863) Rossetti concludes that the best solution to an unhappy life is "To die, then live again" (I, 155). For Rossetti, death is merely a means to an end, and that end is immortality. Such a reading challenges Gilbert & Gubar's contention that Rossetti did not imagine asserting herself beyond the grave.[109] In the context of her poetic career, Rossetti's preoccupation with death is not psychotic but pragmatic. The coolness of tone in poems like **"Remember"** and **"When I am dead, my dearest"** contradicts Rosenblum's description of them as "self-pitying" and Greer's view of them as "despairing".[110] Rather than evidence of self-mortification, Rossetti's discursive obsession with death needs to be understood as a strategy for self-preservation.

As a Christian, Rossetti believed that the meek would inherit the earth and she no doubt hoped for a similar fate as a poet. In **"The Lowest Room"** she concludes, "Yet, sometimes still I lift my heart / To the Archangelic trumpet-burst, / When all deep secrets shall be shown, / And many last be first" (I, 207). As William acknowledges in his "Memoir", little was known about Rossetti until after her death.[111] The obituaries and biographies that followed ensured a rise in her popularity. Sadly, for Rossetti, as for poetic successors like Sylvia Plath, death proved to be an astute career move.

Yet death not only provides Rossetti with a means of articulating her audacious and unspeakable desire for a permanent—and prime—place in literary history, it is also the expedient that enables her to write at all. Sappho's legacy dictated that women poets were supposed to feel suicidal, but Rossetti is not another Sappho and, while she writes obsessively about dying from adolescence onwards, it takes her more than half a century to get round to it: despite almost constant invalidism throughout her life—something which allowed her to write without distraction[112]—she eventually died of cancer aged 64. By writing about the desire to die without actually doing so, Rossetti successfully resists the conventional image of the Victorian woman poet even as she moulds herself in it. Rossetti's obsession with death has been much remarked upon but her obsession with death is actually an obsession with *writing* about death. Writing about a death wish enables her to write on—and on and on and on. In this sense, the preoccupation with death that marks her poetry is less morbid than affirmative. Paradoxically, the treatment of death is symptomatic not of a propensity for self-annihilation but self-assertion. While apparently courting self-destruction, she is actually engaged in self-construction. As Rossetti herself states in **"L.E.L."** (1863), "True life is borne of death" (I, 154). However, unlike Letitia Landon, who supposedly committed suicide in 1838 aged 36, Rossetti creates life out of death—her life as a poet—by writing about dying rather than doing it.

When Bell wrote that "The critic of the far future, of whom we hear so much and think so little, will accord a high place among the great poets of this century to the poet to whom we owe **'Amor Mundi,' 'An Apple Gathering,' 'Maude Clare,' 'The Convent Threshold,'** and **'Maiden-Song'"**, he was right.[113] However, in his belief that poems such as **"When I am dead, my dearest"** are "among the finest love-songs in our language", it is possible that he was wrong, not because they are not fine but because a recognition of Rossetti's ardent desire to establish her career as a poet in conjunction with the difficulties she faced in doing so makes it difficult to read them simply as love songs. The love of which such poems sing, if love at all, is love of that which would have made Rossetti utterly unlovable according to Victorian gender ideology: vanity, conceit, display and ambition. As a woman who wanted fame and fortune, she would have disagreed with Woolf's conclusion to *A Room of One's Own* that it is worthwhile to write "even in poverty and obscurity"[114]: Rossetti spent her life struggling to overcome both and to understand this is to reject the dominant view of her as a poet of renunciation and passive endurance. Ultimately, her poetry points not to affection but affectation. The disappointed and desiring lover was a pose that Rossetti deliberately assumed in order to write about her real passion—her career as a poet.

Notes

1. Virginia Woolf (1977) *A Room of One's Own* (London: Grafton), p. 6. First published 1929.

2. Christina Rossetti (1920) *Poetical Works with Memoir and Notes by William Michael Rossetti* (London: Macmillan), p. li. First published in 1904.

3. Angela Leighton & Margaret Reynolds (eds) (1995) *Victorian Women Poets: An Anthology* (Oxford: Blackwell), p. 353.

4. Germaine Greer (1995) *Slip-Shod Sibyls: Recognition, Rejection and the Woman Poet* (London: Viking), pp. 369-370.

5. Frances Thomas (1994) *Christina Rossetti: A Biography* (London: Virago), p. 382.

6. Antony H. Harrison (1988) *Christina Rossetti in Context* (Chapel Hill and London: University of North Carolina Press), p. 1, pp. 101-102.

7. Christina Rossetti (1979-1990) *The Complete Poems of Christina Rossetti: A Variorum Edition,* 3 vols, ed. R. W. Crump (Baton Rouge and London: Louisiana State University Press), I, p. 147. References hereafter given after quotations in the text.

8. Thomas, *Christina Rossetti,* p. 84.

9. Mackenzie Bell (1898) *Christina Rossetti: A Biographical and Critical Study* (London: Thomas Burleigh), p. 213.

10. Unless otherwise stated, dates of poems are the dates of composition rather than publication.

11. Margaret Reynolds (1996) "'I lived for art, I lived for love': The Woman Poet Sings Sappho's Last Song", in Angela Leighton (ed.) *Victorian Women Poets: A Critical Reader* (Oxford: Blackwell), p. 293.

12. Thomas, *Christina Rossetti,* p. 277.

13. Rossetti broke off both engagements on the grounds of religious differences. The accepted view seems to be that she was betrayed by her suitors who, in becoming a Catholic (Collinson) and expressing religious doubt (Cayley), effectively rejected her, but that decorum dictated they give her the opportunity to end the relationship for the sake of her honour.

14. Virginia Woolf (1932) *The Common Reader,* Second Series (London: Hogarth Press), pp. 240-241.

15. Rosenblum has noted that Rossetti's poetry is littered with masks, veils and shrouds, which simultaneously conceal and reveal. She also observes that disguise, doubleness and duplicity pervade Rossetti's verse. See Dolores Rosenblum (1979) "Christina Rossetti: The Inward Pose", in Sandra Gilbert & Susan Gubar (eds) *Shakespeare's Sisters: Feminist Essays on Women Poets*

(Bloomington and London: Indiana University Press), pp. 82-83. Armstrong likewise provides a useful discussion of the "secretiveness" of Rossetti's poetry. See Isobel Armstrong (1993) *Victorian Poetry: Poetry, Poetics, Politics* (London: Routledge), pp. 344, 352. Harrison points out that Rossetti's Romantic sincerity is a mask and argues that in "Monna Innominata" (date of composition unknown) the unrequited poet-lover is a guise used for experimental purposes. See Harrison, *Christina Rossetti in Context*, pp. 12, 154.

16. Luce Irigaray (1985) *This Sex Which Is Not One*, tr. Catherine Porter (Ithaca: Cornell University Press), p. 76. First published in 1977.

17. Toril Moi (1985) *Sexual/Textual Politics* (London: Methuen), p. 140.

18. Jan Marsh (1994) *Christina Rossetti: A Literary Biography* (London: Pimlico), p. 76.

19. Thomas, *Christina Rossetti*, p. 379.

20. Rossetti, *Poetical Works with Memoir and Notes*, p. lxvi.

21. Bell, *Christina Rossetti*, p. 152.

22. Ibid., p. 305.

23. Rossetti, *Poetical Works with Memoir and Notes*, p. lxix.

24. Thomas, *Christina Rossetti*, p. 190.

25. Marsh, *Christina Rossetti*, p. 156.

26. Ibid., p. 281.

27. Rossetti, *Poetical Works with Memoir and Notes*, p. 481.

28. Marsh, *Christina Rossetti*, p. 295.

29. Lona Mosk Packer (ed.) (1963) *The Rossetti-Macmillan Letters: Some 133 Unpublished Letters Written to Alexander Macmillan, F. S. Ellis, and Others, by Dante Gabriel, Christina, and William Michael Rossetti, 1861-1889* (Berkeley and Los Angeles: University of California Press), p. 154.

30. Ibid., p. 103.

31. Marsh, *Christina Rossetti*, p. 146.

32. Packer, *The Rossetti-Macmillan Letters*, p. 23.

33. Janet Camp Troxell (ed.) (1937) *Three Rossettis: Unpublished Letters to and from Dante Gabriel, Christina, William* (Cambridge: Harvard University Press), pp. 170-175.

34. "Death's Chill Between" on 14 October 1848 and "Heart's Chill Between" on 21 October 1848.

35. Marsh, *Christina Rossetti*, p. 129.

36. Rossetti, *Poetical Works with Memoir and Notes*, p. 481.

37. Marsh, *Christina Rossetti*, p. 200.

38. William declares that he is unable to account for this "outburst of exuberant joy" (p. 481), and Harrison refers to it as a rare exception (p. 98).

39. Marsh, *Christina Rossetti*, p. 205.

40. Ibid., p. 269.

41. Packer, *The Rossetti-Macmillan Letters*, p. 96.

42. Marsh, *Christina Rossetti*, p. 294.

43. Packer, *The Rossetti-Macmillan Letters*, pp. 50-51.

44. Marsh, *Christina Rossetti*, p. 291.

45. Ibid., p. 308.

46. Ibid., p. 470.

47. Ibid., p. 297.

48. Ibid., p. 332.

49. Ibid., p. 335.

50. Ibid., p. 338.

51. Ibid., p. 354.

52. Bell, *Christina Rossetti*, p. 85.

53. Troxell, *Three Rossettis*, p. 170.

54. Bell, *Christina Rossetti*, p. 84.

55. Prose: *Letter and Spirit* (1883), *Time Flies* (1885), *The Face of the Deep* (1892). Poetry: *Verses* (1893).

56. Bell, *Christina Rossetti*, pp. 271, 289.

57. Thomas, *Christina Rossetti*, p. 363.

58. Marsh, *Christina Rossetti*, p. 551.

59. Thomas, *Christina Rossetti*, p. 363.

60. Ibid., p. 356.

61. Marsh, *Christina Rossetti*, p. 268.

62. Thomas, *Christina Rossetti*, p. 84.

63. Troxell, *Three Rossettis*, p. 143.

64. Packer, *The Rossetti-Macmillan Letters*, pp. 50, 54.

65. Ibid., pp. 38-39.

66. Marsh, *Christina Rossetti*, p. 278.

67. Packer, *The Rossetti-Macmillan Letters*, p. 51.

68. Ibid., p. 36.

69. Greer, *Slip-Shod Sibyls,* p. 380.

70. Woolf, *The Common Reader,* p. 243.

71. Packer, *The Rossetti-Macmillan Letters,* p. 7.

72. Angela Leighton (1992) *Victorian Women Poets: Writing Against the Heart* (Hemel Hempstead: Harvester Wheatsheaf), p. 152.

73. Marsh, *Christina Rossetti,* p. 386.

74. Packer, *The Rossetti-Macmillan Letters,* p. 126.

75. Ibid., pp. 84, 72.

76. Thomas, *Christina Rossetti,* p. 134.

77. Marsh, *Christina Rossetti,* p. 401.

78. Thomas, *Christina Rossetti,* p. 244.

79. Leighton, *Victorian Women Poets,* p. 122.

80. Marsh, *Christina Rossetti,* p. 107.

81. Lona Mosk Packer (1963) *Christina Rossetti* (Cambridge: Cambridge University Press), p. 414.

82. Marsh, *Christina Rossetti,* p. 106; Greer, *Slip-Shod Sibyls,* p. 378.

83. Bell, *Christina Rossetti,* pp. 203-204.

84. Marsh, *Christina Rossetti,* p. 107.

85. Packer, *The Rossetti-Macmillan Letters,* p. 49.

86. Troxell, *Three Rossettis,* p. 184.

87. Gabriel changed the title to "Shut Out" when the poem was published in *Goblin Market* in 1862.

88. Marsh, *Christina Rossetti,* p. 247.

89. Ibid., p. 249.

90. Packer, *The Rossetti-Macmillan Letters,* p. 89.

91. Marsh, *Christina Rossetti,* p. 400.

92. Katherine J. Mayberry (1989) *Christina Rossetti and the Poetry of Discovery* (Baton Rouge and London: Louisiana State University Press), p. 14.

93. Bell, *Christina Rossetti,* p. 69.

94. Troxell, *Three Rossettis,* p. 175.

95. Woolf, *The Common Reader,* p. 240.

96. Thomas, *Christina Rossetti,* p. 364.

97. Woolf, *The Common Reader,* pp. 240-241.

98. Bell, *Christina Rossetti,* p. 184.

99. Marsh, *Christina Rossetti,* p. 496.

100. Ibid., p. 66.

101. Ibid., p. 66.

102. Sappho was assumed to be heterosexual at this time.

103. Troxell, *Three Rossettis,* p. 140.

104. Barbara DeConcini (1990) *Narrative Remembering* (Lanham: University Press of America), p. 147.

105. Isobel Armstrong (1987) "Christina Rossetti: Diary of a Feminist Reading", in *Women Reading Women's Writing,* Sue Roe (ed.) (Brighton: Harvester), p. 117.

106. Bell, *Christina Rossetti,* p. 112.

107. Marsh, *Christina Rossetti,* p. 555.

108. Armstrong, *Victorian Poetry,* p. 324.

109. Sandra Gilbert & Susan Gubar (1979) *The Madwoman in the Attic: The Woman Writer and the Nineteenth Century Literary Imagination* (New Haven and London: Yale University Press), p. 575.

110. Rosenblum, in Gilbert & Gubar, *Shakespeare's Sisters,* p. 90 and Greer, *Slip-Shod Sibyls,* p. 361.

111. Rossetti, *Poetical Works with Memoir and Notes,* p. ix.

112. In December 1877, Rossetti told Macmillan, "I am well content with the privileges and immunities which attach to semi-invalidism" (Packer, *The Rossetti-Macmillan Letters,* p. 123).

113. Bell, *Christina Rossetti,* p. 320.

114. Woolf, *A Room of One's Own,* p. 107.

Diane D'Amico (essay date 1999)

SOURCE: D'Amico, Diane. "Rossetti's Response to the Feminine Voice of Woe." In *Christina Rossetti: Faith, Gender, and Time,* pp. 18-42. Baton Rouge: Louisiana State University Press, 1999.

[*In the following essay, D'Amico maintains that Rossetti's Christian faith informs her approach to depicting the tribulations of women in her poetry.*]

The woman poet of the early decades of the nineteenth century was expected to follow the gender ideology of her time. That is, her poetry was to focus on the domestic sphere of home and hearth and to do so with an emphasis on feeling and emotion in sentimental and at times effusive language full of pleasing sound.[1] The careers of Felicia Hemans and Letitia Elizabeth Landon both suggest that if a woman poet met these expectations, she might be both a popular and critical success. Although Hemans is rarely read today, her work had a wide audience throughout the nineteenth century in both Britain and America. William Michael Rossetti edited a collection of her poems in 1873; more important, in the 1840s, when Christina Rossetti was developing her own poetic voice, Hemans was still ranked as "the most generally admired of all English female poets, and deservedly so."[2] Although Landon's verse was less favorably evaluated during the 1840s than it had been when first published, her poetry still had popular appeal. As with Hemans, collections of Landon's poetry were reprinted throughout the nineteenth century.

The melancholy strain of Rossetti's early work clearly belongs to the tradition of woman's poetry characterized by Hemans and Landon. Other scholars have made note of this fact.[3] However, little attention has been given thus far to the significance of Rossetti's faith. A close comparison of Rossetti's early poems with those of these two literary foremothers does suggest that even when beginning her poetic career, Rossetti was not only imitating but also responding to the work of her female predecessors and doing so from the vantage point of her Christian faith. Although Rossetti's early poems often echo their work, suggesting that she felt these women had something to teach her, she also begins to revise and adapt what she learns to suit her purposes, which more often emphasize the religious than the romantic and begin to shift the poetic subject from a woman's heart to her soul. Moreover, while Rossetti was reading the poetry of Hemans and Landon, in a sense listening to the feminine voices of sorrow, she was also listening to voices of preachers and prophets, voices that spoke of the vanity of this life and the need to prepare for the next.

We can begin to examine this process of revision and adaptation by comparing some of Rossetti's early poetic dramatizations of woman's life with Hemans' *Records of Woman,* one of her most successful volumes.[4] *Records of Woman* is a series of monologues and lyric narratives in which individual women drawn from legend and history tell of their suffering for love. Although a few poems in the collection focus on a mother's love, most show a woman suffering as a consequence of love for husband or lover. For example, the first poem in the collection is based on the life of Arabella Stuart, who was imprisoned by King James I for a marriage he found politically dangerous to his reign, and "Costanza," placed midway in the volume, tells of a woman who fled society to live a saintly life, ministering to the sorrow of others, because the man she loved chose the "gauds of pride" over his love for her. The last poem, "The Grave of a Poetess," is written in honor of the eighteenth-century poet Mary Tighe, believed by many to have had a loveless marriage. In general, the message of Hemans' *Records* appears to be that woman's lot is one of suffering caused by love, suggesting therefore that such suffering is the appropriate keynote for the woman poet.

Several of Rossetti's poems of the 1840s, especially the period 1847—1848, strike the same note of suffering, and they recall not only in tone but also in form Hemans' work. Like Hemans, Rossetti borrows from already existing narratives of women's lives and develops monologues in which the character expresses her anguish. Furthermore, even though Rossetti tends to draw her female figures from popular novels rather than history and folktales, she also repeatedly focuses on women who suffer as a consequence of unrequited or ill-fated love. "Eva" (1847) and the two poems entitled "Zara," one written 1847 and one in 1848, are based on Charles Robert Maturin's *Women: Or Pour et Contre,* the plot of which involves a mother and daughter unknowingly falling in love with the same young man. "Isidora" (1847) and "Immalee" (1847) are inspired by Maturin's novel *Melmoth the Wanderer* and refer to the female character who eventually must choose between her soul and her love for Melmoth. "Lady Montrevor" (1848) is based on a character in Maturin's *Wild Irish Boy* whose vanity traps her into marrying a man she does not love. The source of the sonnet "Ellen Middleton" (1848) is Georgina Fullerton's novel of the same name, which tells a tale of married love marred by the wife's guilty secret. "A Hopeless Case," first entitled "Nydia," (1848) is based on a character in Edward Bulwer-Lytton's *Last Days of Pompeii* who suffers from an unrequited love; "Undine" (1848) is based on a popular nineteenth-century folktale by Baron de La Motte Fouque telling of a water spirit betrayed by her mortal husband.

In these Rossettian "records of women," the speakers at times use extravagant language full of cries of longing and self-sacrifice, reminiscent of Hemans' speakers. The two Zara poems are especially Hemans-like in this regard. "Zara" (1847) is a long anguished cry of love, and hate born of love, which ends with a final self-sacrificing statement of forgiveness:

> I forgive thee, dearest, cruel, I forgive thee;—
>   May thy cup of sorrow be poured out for me;
> Though the dregs be bitter yet they shall not grieve me,
>   Knowing that I drink them, O my love, for thee.
>
> (*CP,* 3:112)

In the 1848 version of Zara's monologue, she contemplates suicide because her "false friend" has wearied of her, yet even in her thoughts of suicide she still expresses the hope that the man who betrayed her will be with her after death: "Shall not we twain repose together?" (3:162). Such total devotion to the beloved recalls Hemans' faithful women who continue to love no matter the circumstances: Arabella's husband never rescues her; Juana's husband never awakes from death to love her; Costanza's lover asks forgiveness but only when he is dying; and Properzia Rossi dies because she cannot stop loving the man who has rejected her.

Both Hemans and Rossetti appear to imply that women are doomed to be disappointed because men are less capable than women of loving faithfully. Of course, this negative portrayal of the male is due in part to the source material upon which Hemans and Rossetti draw. For example, the legend associated with the Italian sculptor Properzia Rossi, according to Hemans' note, tells of her dying because the Roman knight she loved was indifferent to both her and her art, and *Women,* a novel to which Rossetti seems to have been especially drawn, depicts the male of the love triangle as easily infatuated and therefore irresponsible. Furthermore, the belief that men were less constant in love was often accepted as more than a literary convention, as Francis Jeffrey's 1829 review of *Records of Woman* indicates. When discussing what he considers the woman poet's strengths and weaknesses, he firmly states that one of women's strengths is "their capacity of noble and devoted attachment, and of the efforts and sacrifices it may require," and he affirms, in that capacity, "they are, beyond all doubt, our [men's] superiors."[5] With such a literary and cultural heritage, it is not surprising that Rossetti's female figures find romantic love disappointing; however, at times their response, in both gesture and speech, to such disappointment is markedly different from that portrayed by Hemans. Whereas the women in Hemans' *Records* do accept what the speaker in her poem "Indian Woman's Death Song" calls "woman's weary lot" (in other words, they do not show anger or resentment directly), Rossetti's female characters do at times act and speak in less conventionally feminine ways. That is, occasionally a Rossetti heroine refuses to weep.

The entire text of **"Undine"** can be read as undercutting the literary convention of the weeping, brokenhearted woman. The poem appears to begin at the moment when the water spirit fully realizes the extent of her husband's betrayal: "She did not answer him again / But walked straight to the door" (*CP,* 3:151). Undine literally turns her back on her husband, and her refusal to "answer him," her silence, can be read as an act of self-respect, if not self-assertion. Moreover, Rossetti's repeated use of the negative effectively points out that Undine is acting contrary to the traditional brokenhearted female: "Her hand nor trembled on the lock, / Nor her foot on the floor," and although her "lips grew white" when she "looked on him once more: . . . the fire / Of her eyes did not fail" (3:152). Contrary to the sentimental portrayal of woman, Rossetti's Undine does not plead or weep. Significantly, Rossetti appears to have imagined this scene in which Undine walks "straight to the door," for there is no exact parallel in Baron de La Motte Fouque's tale.

Perhaps the most striking example in these early poems of the woman who may be brokenhearted but refuses to show it can be found in the sonnet **"Lady Montrevor."**

This poem not only indicates that Rossetti was beginning to find the image of the weeping woman unsatisfactory but also that she was beginning to find her effusive language of lost love equally problematic:

> I do not look for love that is a dream:
>   I only seek for courage to be still;
>   To bear my grief with an unbending will,
> And when I am a-weary not to seem.
> Let the round world roll on; let the sun beam;
>   Let the wind blow, and let the rivers fill
>   The everlasting sea; and on the hill
> The palms almost touch heaven, as children deem.
> And though young Spring and Summer pass away,
>   And Autumn and cold Winter come again;
>   And though my soul, being tired of its pain,
> Pass from the ancient earth; and though my clay
>   Return to dust; my tongue shall not complain:
> No man shall mock me after this my day.

(CP, 3:153)

In this instance, Rossetti seems to have been strongly influenced by her source, for at one point in the novel *Wild Irish Boy,* Lady Montrevor delivers a speech, the sentiment of which this sonnet partially echoes: "I will carry the anguish of a proud heart to the grave: there it is bringing me fast, and not a soul will weep upon my grave, no heart will ache for, no tongue pity me; so much the better; I only asked for admiration, and that I will have till death."[6] Significantly, however, although Rossetti is faithful to her source by indicating that her speaker is motivated by pride (she does not want the world to mock her), Rossetti's version of Lady Montrevor's voice has biblical intonations not characteristic of Maturin's character. The world-weary tones of lines 6-13 with reference to the continual and unchanging movements of the sun, wind, rivers, and sea are reminiscent of the first chapter of Ecclesiastes: "The sun also ariseth, and the sun goeth down. . . . The wind goeth toward the south and turneth about unto the north. . . . All the rivers run into the sea; yet the sea is not full." Until the last line of the sonnet, which is faithful to Rossetti's source, Lady Montrevor sounds as if she has learned the message of the preacher: "Vanity of vanities; all is vanity." This blending of an ill-fated heroine of romance with the message of Ecclesiastes indicates that by the winter of 1848, when Rossetti was still quite young, only seventeen years old, she was clearly beginning to see the image of feminine woe through the lens of her faith. In fact, the cup imagery, which figures so prominently in the concluding lines of **"Zara"** (1847), suggests that perhaps even a year earlier Rossetti was beginning to cast the figure of the broken-hearted woman in biblical terms. Zara's cup of sacrificial love from which she is willing to drink recalls Christ's suffering in the garden of Gethsemane.

"Ellen Middleton," composed during the spring of 1848, offers yet another, and more obvious, example of

Rossetti giving a broken-hearted woman a biblical cadence and idiom. The poem begins with the characteristic mournful tones of the dying woman:

> Raise me; undraw the curtain; that is well.
>   Put up the casement; I would see once more
>   The golden sun-set flooding sea and shore.
>
> (*CP*, 3:158)

In line five, however, this mournful tone suddenly shifts to a more prophetic one:

> The tree of love a bitter fruitage bore,
>   Sweet at the rind but rotten at the core,
>   Pointing to heaven and bringing down to hell.
>
> (3:158)

The imagery of tree and fruit brings to mind the Genesis story of the Fall and the dire consequences of eating the fruit of the tree of the knowledge of good and evil. In these lines, Ellen's voice evokes not so much the image of the dying woman but rather that of a priest delivering a sermon on Chapter 3 of Genesis. The tone of her voice and the warning of love's dangers also bring to mind the voice of Solomon in Prov. 5:5, cautioning the young man against the evil ways of the woman whose "steps take hold on hell." Also echoed is the voice of Isaiah (14:12-15), in a passage read by Christians as telling of the fall of Lucifer from heaven to hell. Finally, the last line of the poem, in which Ellen describes her life as having been one of "hidden" faith and "vain" love, keeps the poem focused as much on the state of her soul as her heart.

At one point in Fullerton's novel, Ellen does compare her case to various passages from Scripture, yet the language of the Bible is not characteristic of her speech, and her death scene and her last words have none of the prophetic power of Rossetti's sonnet. In the novel, she dies as her husband, with whom she has been reconciled, reads the Prayers for the Dying, and her last word is simply "amen." She dies a humble repentant wife; it is Rossetti, not Fullerton, who gives Ellen the intonations of the Bible and thus aligns the dying woman's voice with that of the preacher. Although Rossetti uses her sources, as Hemans does, more for establishing a general situation of distress than for exact details, it is important to give these sources more than a cursory glance, for they offer further evidence that Rossetti's poetic imagination when a young woman was as much drawn to matters of the soul as it was matters of the heart.

Although Fullerton's *Ellen Middleton* is full of melodramatic love scenes, swooning fainting spells, and brain fever brought on by unrequited love, it is also about faith and guilt, especially about the need to confess. As indicated above, the novel focuses on a young woman's guilty secret: in a moment of anger she slapped her eight-year old cousin, who was teasing and tormenting her; the cousin fell down a flight of steps into the water and died before she could be saved. Ellen keeps her part in her cousin's accident a secret. For several years, and through hundreds of pages, she struggles with herself, knowing that to confess is the only way she will find peace, yet fearing she will lose her husband's love if she does. Rossetti's sonnet, with its emphasis on faith and vanity, suggests that she responded to the scenes of religious crisis as much if not more than the love scenes. Similarly, when she read Maturin's *Women,* it is quite possible she found it to be as much about religious belief as about ill-fated love. Loving the weak-willed Charles leads both Eva and Zara to a religious crisis, and Maturin devotes whole chapters to delineating their spiritual struggles. Although unsuccessful in her quest for spiritual peace, Zara tries to keep the image of the crucified savior before her as she attempts to renounce her love for Charles. Ultimately, Eva decides that in loving Charles, she was loving the world too much and that she must renounce him if she is to see God. Maturin's Isidora in *Melmoth the Wanderer* experiences a similar temptation, and although *Melmoth* is full of graphic descriptions of physical and mental suffering, Rossetti's **"Isidora,"** with its focus on the dying woman's struggle to choose "twixt God and man," suggests again that for the young poet the greatest horror was not to lose a man's love but to lose one's soul.

At approximately the same time she was writing most of these poetic portraits of women, Rossetti was writing poems on the vanity of human life. In 1847 she wrote **"Vanity of Vanities,"** a sonnet based, as the title suggests, on Ecclesiastes, and in 1849, **"One Certainty"** and **"A Testimony,"** both echoing the same biblical message. This life and all associated with it must be seen for what it is, ephemeral and therefore of little significance. Rossetti scholars have often noted that an early theme, which came to characterize her mature poetic voice as well, was that of the vanity of earthly things.[7] Yet more attention should be given to how important her echoing of this voice of Ecclesiastes is in regard to her position as a woman poet. In looking closely at how Rossetti uses the Bible, one sees that she does not so much allude to biblical texts as adopt the voice of those texts; thus, her poetic voice takes on tones of authority not characteristic of the woman poet's sphere.

For example, the first stanza of **"A Testimony"** reads:

> I said of laughter: it is vain.
>   Of mirth I said: what profits it?
>   Therefore I found a book, and writ
> Therein how ease and also pain,

How health and sickness, every one
Is vanity beneath the sun.

(CP, 1:77)

The "I" is the author of Ecclesiastes, but in using that first-person pronoun, Rossetti, a woman poet, associates herself with the Preacher. Thus, although in the last stanza, with mention of the "King" who "dwelt in Jerusalem," Rossetti indicates that she has been writing a poetic version of Ecclesiastes, she has in a sense been speaking as if she were "the wisest man on earth" (1:78). In **"One Certainty,"** she quotes Ecclesiastes to establish the voice of the Preacher and then weaves various biblical texts together to convey her own message:

> Vanity of vanities, the Preacher saith,
>   All things are vanity. The eye and ear
>   Cannot be filled with what they see and hear.
> Like early dew, or like the sudden breath
> Of wind, or like the grass that withereth,
>   Is man, tossed to and fro by hope and fear.

(1:72)

In lines 2-3, Rossetti alludes to St. Paul's first epistle to the Corinthians, in which he echoes Isa. 64: "Eye hath not seen, nor ear heard, neither have entered into the heart of man, the things which God hath prepared for them that love him" (1 Cor. 2:9). In line 5, Rossetti's image of withered grass recalls the complaint of Ps. 102:4: "My heart is smitten and withered like grass." Thus, in this sonnet Rossetti has linked her poetic voice with the preacher of Ecclesiastes, the prophet Isaiah, the disciple Paul, and the psalmist David. An especially important mingling of biblical voices occurs in **"Vanity of Vanities,"** where Rossetti borrows from Rev. 8:12 to predict when the weary tones of Ecclesiastes will cease to be repeated: the "sinking heart" will continue to bemoan the vanity of earthly things until "the mighty angel-blast / Is blown, making the sun and moon aghast" (*CP,* 1:153). In these lines, the female poet chooses as her predecessor not only the wise and weary preacher of Ecclesiastes but also the visionary St. John the Divine and, in so doing, links her poetry with his prophecies.

When Rossetti began writing her religious verse, religion was seen as an especially appropriate subject for a woman poet; however, both male and female critics of the time tended to dictate certain limits. Mary Ann Stoddart, for example, in her book on female writers, while claiming a place for women in the religious realm, cautions against self-assertion: "We freely confess that there are departments of religious labour in which it is not meet and proper for a woman to enter, and more extensively than to mere oral instruction perhaps, may the words of the apostle be applied: 'I suffer not a woman to teach, nor to usurp authority over the man,

but to be in silence.'" Stoddart continues, "Anything of an authoritative or a dictatorial manner is peculiarly repulsive in women at any time," because, Stoddart concludes, "the Gospel [inculcated] upon her the duties of modesty, meekness, and humility." Frederick Rowton, in his 1848 anthology of women's poetry, claims that women surpass men in the area of religion, but only in serving as models of faith, hope, and piety: "It has not now to be proved, I imagine, that in simple steadfastness of faith, in gentle calmness of hope and in sweet enthusiasm of piety, woman far surpasses man."[8] Rowton is here discussing Hemans and presenting her as one who "typifies and represents her sex" in her "religious sentiment." Thus, while Rossetti's choice of religious subjects is well within the feminine sphere, and again aligns her with Hemans, who by the end of her career was turning more to religious verse, Rossetti's use of biblical idiom begins to widen that sphere.

The distinction I am making here can perhaps be seen more clearly by comparing Hemans' poem "The Wings of the Dove" with Rossetti's **"Sonnet from the Psalms"** (1847). Both poets borrow from Ps. 55, in which David complains to the Lord: "Fearfulness and trembling are come upon me, and horror hath overwhelmed me. And I said, Oh that I had wings like a dove! for then would I fly away, and be at rest" (Ps. 55:5-6). Hemans begins with a clear echo of verse 6: "Oh! for thy wings, thou dove! / That I too might flee away, and be at rest." However, by the end of the poem, the speaker rejects David's complaint and expresses a willingness to return to woman's lot, with all its tears:

> For even by all the fears
> And thoughts that haunt my dreams—untold, unknown
>   And burning woman's tears,
> Pour'd from my eyes in silence and alone;
>
> *Had* I thy wings, thou dove!
> High 'midst the gorgeous isles of cloud to soar,
>   Soon the strong cords of love
> Would draw me earthwards—homewards—yet once more.[9]

Rossetti's **"Sonnet from the Psalms,"** as the title suggests, weaves together the texts of several psalms (see Pss. 6, 39, 55). After imitating the psalmist's desire for the wings of the dove, Rossetti, unlike Hemans, includes no mention of a returning "earthwards" to home:

> All thro' the livelong night I lay awake
>   Watering my couch with tears of heaviness.
>   None stood beside me in my sore distress;—
> Then cried I to my heart: If thou wilt, break,
> But be thou still; no moaning will I make,
>   Nor ask man's help, nor kneel that he may bless.
>   So I kept silence in my haughtiness,
> Till lo! the fire was kindled, and I spake
> Saying: Oh that I had wings like to a dove,
>   Then would I flee away and be at rest:
> I would not pray for friends, or hope, or love,

> But still the weary throbbing of my breast;
> And, gazing on the changeless heavens above,
> Witness that such a quietness is best.
>
> (*CP*, 3:145)

The speaker rejects all earthly ties of affection, the very center of the feminine sphere; and the "tears of heaviness" with which the sonnet begins are replaced by "quietness," a word that again echoes Ecclesiastes: "Better is an handful with quietness than both the hands full with travail and vexation of spirit" (Eccles. 4:6). Furthermore, while Hemans' speaker reveals that she is a woman, the sex of Rossetti's speaker remains unidentified. However, again as with her other religious poems, her mingling of biblical texts and intonations associates her speaker with Old Testament voices, ones that are associated more with traditional definitions of masculinity than femininity.

One might also compare Rossetti's **"Paradise"** with Hemans' "The Better Land," a poem Rossetti most certainly read. (In 1844, William Michael gave his sister his copy of *The Sacred Harp,* an anthology of religious verse containing "The Better Land" and four other poems by Hemans.) Hemans only briefly employs the idiom of the Bible, and again her use of such language is feminized, so to speak, by her depiction of a mother answering her son's questions about heaven: "Eye hath not seen it, my gentle boy! / Ear hath not heard its deep songs of joy."[10] In Rossetti's **"Paradise,"** on the other hand, the gender of the speaker is not specified. Furthermore, the speaker is not comforting a child but is telling of an actual dream of paradise and hope of seeing the reality itself:

> I hope to see these things again,
> But not as once in dreams by night;
> To see them with my very sight.
>
> (*CP*, 1:222)

Finally, the poem concludes with an expression of hope that conveys an image of the speaker and, by implication, the woman poet as having a role in paradise: "[I hope] To have my part with all the saints, / And with my God" (1:222).

I am not arguing that Rossetti adopted the voice of the preacher, psalmist, and prophet merely to employ a voice of power the patriarchal society denied the woman poet. Certainly, she was not acquiring what William Michael Rossetti described as "truly minute and ready" knowledge of the Bible, merely to use the biblical idiom to empower her own poetic voice.[11] Rather, I am suggesting that her religious faith and the reading and thoughtful study of the Bible, which was an expression of that faith, played a central role in her response to the voices of her literary foremothers, specifically to the voice of the mournful woman who sees life in terms of earthly ties and affections, as so many of Hemans' speakers do, even those who speak of the "better land."

That Rossetti's religious experience played a very significant role in her response to the early nineteenth-century feminine poetic voice can be seen quite clearly when we consider her response to the voice of Letitia Elizabeth Landon. Whereas Hemans was seen as the poetess of home and a model of the "true woman," Landon's verse was seen as the model of feminine melancholy, that is, a melancholy caused by lost love: "No writer certainly has written more of Love and Sorrow than Mrs. Maclean [Landon]. She touches scarcely any other strings."[12] In her preface to *The Venetian Bracelet,* Landon herself described her subjects as "grief, disappointment, the fallen leaf, the faded flower, the broken heart, and the early grave." Rossetti's most recent biographer, Jan Marsh, indicates that when an adolescent Rossetti "devoured" this melancholy poetry.[13] Although Rossetti's response to Hemans is rather indirect, more a question of shifting the feminine perspective from romance to religion and from home to heaven, her response to Landon is more direct and immediate. In other words, at times Rossetti actually appears to be echoing the world-weary voice of L.E.L. so as to critique its earth-bound perspective.

The following poem, simply entitled "Song," provides a characteristic example of Landon's mournful voice:

> Oh never another dream can be
>   Like that early dream of ours,
> When the fairy Hope lay down to sleep,
>   Like a child among the flowers.
>
> But Hope has waken'd since, and wept,
>   Like a rainbow, itself away;
> And the flowers have faded and fallen around—
>   We have none for a wreath to-day.
>
> Now Wisdom wakes in the place of Hope,
>   And our hearts are like winter hours:
> Ah! after-life has been little worth
>   That early dream of ours.[14]

Rossetti's well-known **"Song"** (1849) employs a similar imagery of faded flowers to embody a similar theme of loss:

> Oh roses for the flush of youth,
>   And laurel for the perfect prime;
> But pluck an ivy branch for me
>   Grown old before my time.
>
> Oh violets for the grave of youth,
>   And bay for those dead in their prime;
> Give me the withered leaves I chose
>   Before in the old time.
>
> (*CP*, 1:40)

The tone of this song, however, differs from that of Landon's. In Landon's poem is expressed a dominant note of regret; clearly, the speaker mourns lost hopes and still longs for the "early dream" of youth. In contrast, Rossetti's speaker, "grown old before [her] time," implies she never had that "early dream," and that she wants no pity, for she "chose" the "withered leaves."

The exact nature of this choice is unclear, but it can be clarified by considering the language of flowers, popular in the Victorian period and a language Rossetti often employed.[15] In assigning roses to youth, the speaker gives away love; in associating laurel with the prime of life, she rejects glory. In asking for ivy, a plant associated with fidelity because it is always green, she suggests that she has been faithful to this renunciation of earthly desires. Even on her grave she wants, not violets, a sign of humility, or bay, a sign of honor, especially for the poet, but the memorial of withered leaves. Such leaves are, of course, not part of the language of flowers but within the context of this poem can be read as a symbol of the speaker's renunciation of love and fame, the choice she made in the "old time." Whereas Landon's speaker still longs for earthly rewards, Rossetti's speaker willingly turns away. Behind Rossetti's poem lies a very different set of values and beliefs than that which underlies Landon's mournful song.

Such a difference can be further explored by comparing one of Landon's characteristic songs of death and farewell with what has become one of Rossetti's most famous songs of parting. In Landon's *Vow of the Peacock,* another distressed lady sings a song of farewell, claiming "her heart's best prayers" are all for the beloved who knows little of her passion:

> Farewell! farewell! I would not leave
>   A single trace behind;
> Why should a thought, if me to grieve,
>   Be left upon thy mind?
> I would not have thy memory dwell
>   Upon one thought of pain;
> And sad it must be the farewell
>   Of one who loved in vain.

However, while saying she does not want his memory to dwell upon her, the speaker undercuts that message with the last stanza, which serves to evoke guilt by contrasting her state with his: "Thy course is in the sun . . . For me,—my race is nearly run, / And its goal is the grave."[16] Rossetti's **"Song"** (1848) also bids farewell to the beloved by evoking images of the grave and might easily be likened to the mournful poetic voice of Landon:

> When I am dead, my dearest,
>   Sing no sad songs for me;
> Plant thou no roses at my head,
>   Nor shady cypress tree:
> Be the green grass above me
>   With showers and dewdrops wet;
> And if thou wilt, remember,
>   And if thou wilt, forget.

(*CP,* 1:58)

However, a careful reading of these lines indicates that the speaker is actually rejecting the image of the grave, for that is not her "goal"; rather, it is some world of twilight dreaming:

> I shall not see the shadows,
>   I shall not feel the rain;
> I shall not hear the nightingale
>   Sing on, as if in pain:
> And dreaming through the twilight
>   That doth not rise nor set,
> Haply I may remember,
>   And haply may forget.

(1:58)

There is a playful, even lighthearted quality to the lines that counters the forlorn tones of Landon's broken-hearted woman. Also, it is important to notice that even though Landon's speaker is identified within *Vow of the Peacock* as female, Rossetti's speaker could be either male or female. Scholarship has consistently interpreted the voice as that of a woman, but actually there is no definite sign of gender in the poem. Moreover, Landon's speaker is still very much focused on earthly love and romance, whereas Rossetti's speaker has turned her attention to another world entirely, one of twilight dreaming, a world and a time that can be more thoroughly understood in terms of Rossetti's religious faith.

Throughout her life, Rossetti accepted the doctrine that after death the soul did not enter into its full heavenly reward but had to wait until the Second Coming of Christ, when all would be judged, the living and the dead, and those chosen would then enter into the New Jerusalem. As John Waller has noted in a very significant article on Rossetti, in the Advent season of December 1848 (Rossetti composed **"When I am dead my dearest"** during that month), Rossetti most likely heard several sermons delivered by the vicar of Christ Church, William Dodsworth, on the end of the world and the Second Coming.[17] Such sermons might easily have encouraged Rossetti to wonder about the time between death and resurrection.

Moreover, beginning in the 1840s and continuing throughout the century, considerable debate occurred within the church over the nature of the waiting time after death. The whole subject of eschatology—death, judgment, heaven, and hell—was, as Michael Wheeler points out, a "highly controversial subject in the Victorian age discussed not only in sermons but in general periodicals as well.[18] Indeed, such subjects were possibly topics of discussion within Rossetti's immediate family, especially among the women of her family, who were devout churchgoers. Significantly, at the time of Rossetti's death, her library contained an 1831 copy of John Peers's *The Scripture Doctrine of the State of the Departed Both Before and After the Resurrection,* which was once owned by her maternal grandmother. In this small book, Peers discusses at length the soul's experiences in the "intermediate state," that is, the state between death and resurrection, concluding that this waiting time, though one of "rest," must also be a time of "enjoyment" and not "mere cessation from labour."[19] This state of "rest" may well be akin to Rossetti's world of twilight dreaming, a world that was not at all the static world of rest one unfamiliar with Rossetti's faith might imagine. Indeed, John Henry Newman, a theologian Rossetti much admired even after he became a Roman Catholic, stresses in his sermon on the subject that the spiritual state after death and before the resurrection is not a time of stasis, for it is "full of excellent visions and wonderful revelations."[20]

Rossetti's transcendent view of life, which focused as much on the future as the present, should be considered when assessing her response to the feminine poetic tradition represented by both Hemans and Landon, for such an eschatological perspective clearly plays a major role in her assessment of the woman poet's voice. Although Rossetti was born into a society that expected her to write of love, and the sorrow caused by love, because she was a woman, she was also living at a time when religious debates were an important part of her immediate environment, debates not about woman's heart but about the human soul. In a sense, the warnings of Rossetti's faith regarding the soul were heard more loudly than the warnings of her culture regarding women poets' proper sphere. Her preoccupation with spiritual issues of damnation and redemption may well have diminished any pressure she might have felt to write strictly "female poetry," that is, poetry in which the voice of the weeping woman, a woman still focused on the sorrow of this world, establishes the dominant tone.

That Rossetti's response to Landon was shaped by her interest in eschatology can be seen most clearly in *Maude,* a novella in prose and verse that Rossetti wrote sometime in 1849-1850. *Maude* has often been read autobiographically. The heroine's age, state of health and mind, and, especially, the fact she is a poet have led critics to see Maude as a version of Rossetti during her adolescent years. Certainly, the similarities between Maude and Rossetti do invite an autobiographical reading. However, *Maude* is not a diary entry or a confessional piece but a crafted story.[21] Thus, even though the novella has autobiographical echoes, more attention should be given to ways in which this story is not just a private reflection, revealing Rossetti's inner world, but a public comment. Indeed, *Maude* can be read as Rossetti's attempt at a public response to the feminine melancholy strain of poetry she inherits from her foremothers, especially Landon.

Rossetti did not publish *Maude,* but the finished state of the manuscript suggests she wrote with an audience in mind, and this audience seems to have been primarily female, for the plot involves young Victorian women and the choices life offers them: marriage, the convent, or perhaps the career of a poet of melancholy verse.[22] Mary represents the choice of marriage and seems quite happy in that choice; Magdalen chooses the convent and again is portrayed as content. In contrast, Maude, the poet, struggles with the options offered. She is described by the narrator as "dissatisfied with her circumstances, her friends and herself" (*M* [*Maude*], 49). At times, Rossetti uses Maude's poetry as a device to reveal her heroine's dissatisfaction, and the poetry Maude writes often resembles Landon's weary melancholy strain.

The first poem included is the sonnet that begins, "Yes, I too could face death and never shrink," which Maude appears to write in a spontaneous manner reminiscent of Landon's poet-speakers. Although the speaker asserts her "courage" in claiming that she is willing to face suffering and not commit suicide, nevertheless she appears to long for the grave and to be rather proud of the extent of her suffering: "Thousands taste the full cup; who drains the lees?—" (*M,* 30). That Rossetti wants the reader to see Maude as affected and perhaps indulging in dramatic posturing is suggested by the narrative comment that follows immediately after the last line of the poem: "having done which [having written the sonnet] she yawned, leaned back in her chair, and wondered how she should fill up the time till dinner" (30). At this stage in the story, Maude's suffering appears self-indulgent and exaggerated. As readers, we see that she has a loving mother, friends who care for her, and a poetic talent recognized at least by her immediate circle.

As the story progresses, however, the reader discovers that there is some cause for distress in that Maude accuses herself of hypocrisy. She attends church and yet, as her sonnet beginning "I listen to the holy antheming" reveals, "vanity enters" with her, and her "love / Soars not to Heaven, but grovelleth below" (*M,* 51). Thus, unlike a Landon heroine, who suffers because of ill-fated love, Maude suffers because she feels guilty; her melancholy is religious, not romantic. In an important conversation with Agnes, her calm and well-adjusted cousin who serves as her foil, she states that she feels unable to receive Holy Communion. In his preface to the first published version of the novella, William Michael Rossetti seemed to realize that Maude's refusal to receive Holy Communion was significant, but he nevertheless concluded that "so far as my own views of right and wrong go, I cannot see that the much-reprehended Maude commits a single serious fault from title-page to finis" (reproduced in *M,* 80). Yet one should remember he was not in sympathy with his sister's faith. Rossetti certainly intends the reader to see Maude's refusal to receive Communion as serious, for Agnes' response indicates that Maude's behavior could lead to endangering her soul: "Stop; you cannot mean,—you do not know what you are saying. You will go no more? Only think, if the struggle is so hard now, what it will be when you reject all help" (52). Agnes continues to try to persuade Maude to receive Communion by speaking of her own spiritual struggles: "I was once on the very point of acting as you propose. I was perfectly wretched: harassed and discouraged on all sides. But then it struck me—you won't be angry?—that it was so ungrateful to follow my own fancies, instead of at least endeavouring to do God's Will: and so foolish too; for if our safety is not in obedience, where is it?" (52). Agens realizes that in terms of religious doctrine, Maude's refusal to receive the Eucharist places her soul in danger, for as the catechism states in the Book of Common Prayer, both baptism and the "Supper of the Lord" are "necessary to salvation." That Agnes fears that Maude may well lose her soul is suggested by her pleading, "It is not too late: besides think for one moment what will be the end of this. We must all die; what if you keep to your resolution and do as you have said, and receive the Blessed Sacrament no more?" (53).

Maude's vanity has resulted in much more than pride in her poetic talent. Through Agnes, Rossetti makes it clear that Maude's rejection of the Eucharist is a rejection of Christ as her savior, and that therefore she must turn back to Christ if she is to be saved. After this scene with Agnes, a Christmas carol is heard outside Maude's window reinforcing Agnes' message: "He is our Messenger; beside, / He is our Door, and Path, and Guide" (*M,* 56). This is a carol Rossetti herself wrote, and her insertion of it at this point in the story can be read as Rossetti's response to her troubled heroine. Although Maude hears this carol at this moment, she remains "unpenitent." However, this is the lowest point in her religious crisis, and after this night she does begin to return to her faith. First, we are told she does receive Communion. Furthermore, the poems written before her death indicate a significant change of heart.

Rossetti does resort to the device of a convenient accident leading to Maude's death as a way of bringing closure to the story but does not end the story with a death scene. Rather, she concludes with a description of Agnes choosing to keep three of Maude's poems. That Rossetti leaves the well-adjusted Agnes in charge of Maude's poetry is significant and has been too often overlooked in autobiographical readings of this story. Moreover, when Agnes' selection of poems is read in the order of the supposed dates of composition, the series of three poems suggests that Maude did find spiritual peace before she died.

In this arrangement, which serves to conclude Maude's life story, Rossetti continues to answer and revise the weeping voice of Landon's poetic heroines. **"Sleep let me sleep, for I am sick of care"** is dated ten days after Maude's accident, and it is the most reminiscent of Landon:

> Shut out the light; thicken the heavy air
> With drowsy incense; let a distant stream
> Of music lull me, languid as a dream,
> Soft as the whisper of a Summer sea.
>
> . . . . .
>
> But bring me poppies brimmed with sleepy death,
> And ivy choking what it garlandeth.

> (*M,* 72)

In these lines one hears echoes of Landon's heroines who desire the forgetfulness of death, and even though Rossetti's poem ends with some hint of rebirth in the image of "quickened dust," the graveyard image so characteristic of Landon's work dominates this lament. Nevertheless, the second poem, "evidently composed at a subsequent period" (73), indicates a changed perspective. Although the speaker calls death to come quickly, it is not to bring an end to life and its pain, but to hasten the new life that must follow:

> Birth follows hard on death,
> Life on withering:
> Hasten, we shall come the sooner
> Back to pleasant Spring.

> (*M,* 73)

In this poem, the worries and complaints of the individual voice are gone. Furthermore, there is no suggestion that the speaker does not expect to see the return of spring.

The last poem is especially significant, for it is in this sonnet that we hear the poetic voice of biblical authority, so characteristic of Rossetti but not of either Hemans or Landon. "What is it Jesus saith unto the soul?—" is "dated the morning before [Maude's] death," and thus Rossetti encourages the reader to see the sonnet as representing the last stage in her heroine's earthly struggle. The answer given to the opening lines quotes Jesus' message to his disciples: "Take up the Cross, and come and follow me." Again, as with the first two poems in this series, there is the theme of pain and suffering, but now such pain is placed firmly in a Christian context: "no man may be / Without the Cross, wishing to win the goal" (*M,* 75). The acceptance of suffering is seen as necessary for salvation, yet hope is offered. Those that suffer will be able to bear the trial, for Christ will be there: "He will control the powers of darkness." Moreover, at the end of time, he will release the soul from all suffering and waiting. Then he shall come again to call the faithful soul home:

> He will be with thee, helping, strengthening,
> Until it is enough: for lo, the day
> Cometh when He shall call thee: thou shalt hear
> His Voice That says: "Winter is past, and Spring
> Is come; arise, My Love, and come away."—

> (*M,* 75)

Rossetti's speaker is not lamenting her predicament but comforting the reader by foretelling the Second Coming of Christ. Again, Rossetti's use of the biblical allusion is significant. In the last lines Rossetti's speaker not only echoes the Song of Songs (2:10-11), but she does so in terms of Christian eschatology. The words of the bridegroom calling his beloved to join with him in a springtime of love are to be read as Christ calling the soul to awake and join him in heaven. Thus, *spring,* a word read in the first of these three poems as a mere season associated with youth and gaiety, by the third poem is to be read as symbolic of the resurrection of the body and the final entrance into heaven. In these three poems, Rossetti borrows from Landon but does so ultimately in order to answer her foremother's melancholy lament with tales of rebirth and with echoes of the Song of Songs. Maude, who begins the story echoing one of Landon's weary women, has died thinking not of the forgetfulness of the grave but of the Second Coming of Christ.

That the young Rossetti read Landon in this way, that is, as a poet singing mournfully of lost love without much hope of awakening to a larger spiritual love, is further suggested by her renaming the poem she first entitled **"Spring"** (written in February 1859) as **"L.E.L.,"** the signature Landon most often used when publishing her poems. The poem begins with a speaker, presumably L.E.L., telling that her "heart is breaking for a little love" and therefore she can "feel no spring" even though the season has begun, a characteristic claim of one of Landon's speakers. Indeed, the first four stanzas can be read as depicting a typical Landon mournful woman. However, in stanza five, the speaker wonders if the "saints" and "angels guess the truth." This thought is characteristic of so many of Rossetti's speakers, who look forward to last things more than any of Landon's comparatively earthbound speakers. Rossetti's speaker then quotes saint and angel:

> Yet saith a saint: "Take patience for thy scathe;"
> Yet saith an angel: "Wait, for thou shalt prove
> True best is last, true life is born of death,
> O thou, heart-broken for a little love.
> Then love shall fill thy girth,
> And love make fat thy dearth,
> When new spring builds new heaven and clean new earth."
>
> (*CP,* 1:154-55)

This stanza echoes multiple biblical texts. The most significant, however, is the allusion to Rev. 21:1 ("And I saw a new heaven and a new earth"), for this last line makes clear that the "spring" Rossetti is referring to is that which is to follow Christ's Second Coming, when, in the language of the Song of Songs, the bridegroom would come to call his beloved home.

Rossetti's early poetry, written during the 1840s and 1850s, certainly has mournful strains of what might be considered distinctly feminine suffering, poetic strains that link her to Hemans and Landon. However, there is ample evidence in these poems and her novella *Maude*

that she wants to define for herself a place where she, a woman poet, can speak as preacher and prophet of the vanity of this world and the need to prepare for the next by waiting and watching for the Second Coming.

One might conclude that this transcendent vision would mean that Rossetti's poetry is removed from any socio-historical context; in fact, such a view dominated assessments of Rossetti's poetry for much of this century. She was said not to belong to the Victorian age but rather to the seventeenth century or even to some vague medieval time. On the contrary, as I have indicated above, her preoccupation with eschatology was characteristic of many Victorians who still believed in God. Furthermore, Rossetti's transcendent view actually involved her in very specific nineteenth-century concerns relevant to Victorian women, such as the revival of Anglican religious sisterhoods.

Notes

1. See Stuart Curran, "Romantic Poetry: The Altered I," in *Romanticism and Feminism,* ed. Anne K. Mellor (Bloomington: Indiana University Press, 1988), 185-207; Glennis Stephenson, "Letitia Landon and the Victorian Improvisatrice: The Construction of L.E.L.," *Victorian Poetry* 30 (spring 1992): 1-17; and Angela Leighton, *Victorian Women Poets: Writing Against the Heart* (Charlottesville: University Press of Virginia, 1992).

2. George Bethune, *British Female Poets* (1848; rpr., New York: Books for Libraries, 1972), 188. Regarding the popularity of Hemans' poetry, see Donald H. Reiman, Introduction to *Records of Woman* (1828; rpr., New York: Garland, 1978), v.

3. See, for example, Dolores Rosenblum, *Christina Rossetti: The Poetry of Endurance* (Carbondale, Ill.: Southern Illinois University Press, 1986), 1-20; and Leighton, *Victorian Women Poets,* 118-63.

4. *Dictionary of Literary Biography,* 96:139.

5. Francis Jeffrey, review of Hemans' *Records of Woman, Edinburgh Review* 50 (October 1829): 33.

6. Charles Robert Maturin, *The Wild Irish Boy,* 2 vols. (New York: D. and G. Bruce, 1808), 2:182.

7. For example, see Nilda Jimenez, *The Bible and the Poetry of Christina Rossetti: A Concordance* (Westport, Conn.: Greenwood Press, 1979), x.

8. Mary Ann Stoddart, *Female Writers: Thoughts on Their Proper Sphere and Powers of Usefulness* (London: R. B. Seeley, 1842), 161-62; Frederic Rowton, *The Female Poets of Great Britain* (1848; rpr., Detroit: Wayne State University Press, 1981), 390.

9. Felicia Hemans, "The Wings of the Dove," *The Complete Works of Mrs. Hemans,* ed. Harriet Mary Browne Owen, 2 vols. (New York: D. Appleton, 1852), 1:578.

10. Ibid., 2:262.

11. William Michael Rossetti, ed., *The Poetical Works of Christina Georgina Rossetti* (London: Macmillan, 1904), lxix.

12. Rowton, *The Female Poets,* 425. See also Glennis Stephenson, *Letitia Landon: The Woman Behind L.E.L.* (Manchester: Manchester University Press, 1995).

13. Jan Marsh, *Christina Rossetti: A Writer's Life* (London: Jonathan Cape, 1994), 246.

14. Letitia Elizabeth Landon, *The Poetical Works of Letitia Elizabeth Landon,* ed. F. S. Sypher (Delmar, N.Y.: Scholar's Facsimiles and Reprints, 1990), 329.

15. For an excellent discussion of Rossetti's use of Victorian flower lore, see Gisela Honnighausen, "Emblematic Tendencies in the Works of Christina Rossetti," *Victorian Poetry* 10 (spring 1972): 1-15.

16. The full text of *The Vow of the Peacock* is not included in the 1990 reprint of *Poetical Works* (1873); therefore, I have used *The Poetical Works of Miss Landon* (Philadelphia: E. L. Carey and H. Hart, 1838), 207.

17. John O. Waller, "Christ's Second Coming: Christina Rossetti and the Premillennialist William Dodsworth," *Bulletin of the New York Public Library* 73 (September 1969): 465-82. See also Linda E. Marshall, "What the Dead Are Doing Underground: Hades and Heaven in the Writings of Christina Rossetti," *Victorian Newsletter* 72 (fall 1987): 55-60.

18. Michael Wheeler, *Death and the Future Life in Victorian Literature and Theology* (Cambridge: Cambridge University Press, 1990), xii. See also Geoffrey Rowell, *Hell and the Victorians: A Study of the Nineteenth-Century Theological Controversies Concerning Eternal Punishment and the Future Life* (Oxford: Clarendon Press, 1974).

19. John Peers, *The Scripture Doctrine of the State of the Departed Both Before and After the Resurrection* (London: Hatchard and Son, 1831), 18. For evidence that this book was familiar to Rossetti, see *List of Books Being Relics of the Rossetti Family Purchased from the Executor of the Late Christina G. Rossetti and Now Being Offered for Sale by J. M. Tregaskis,* no. 341 (1896).

20. John Henry Newman, "The Intermediate State," *Parochial and Plain Sermons* (London: Rivingtons, 1870), 3:374.

21. For a recent and insightful analysis of *Maude* that does draw attention to its literary qualities, see Sharon Smulders, *Christina Rossetti Revisited* (New York: Twayne, 1996), 23-32.

22. Rossetti's manuscript of *Maude: Prose and Verse* is held at the Huntington Library, San Marino, California. It has the appearance of a fair copy prepared for publication. I would like to thank David A. Kent for this information.

Abbreviations of Rossetti's Works

AD	*Annus Domini: A Prayer for Each Day of the Year*
CP	*The Complete Poems of Christina Rossetti,* ed. Rebecca W. Crump, 3 vols.
CS	*Called to Be Saints: The Minor Festivals Devotionally Studied*
FD	*The Face of the Deep: A Devotional Commentary on the Apocalypse*
LS	*Letter and Spirit: Notes on the Commandments*
M	*Maude: Prose and Verse,* ed. R. W. Crump
SF	*Seek and Find: A Double Series of Short Studies of the Benedicite*
TF	*Time Flies: A Reading Diary*

Works Cited

Rossetti, Christina. *Annus Domini: A Prayer for Each Day of the Year, Founded on a Text of Holy Scripture.* Oxford: James Parker, 1874.

———. *Called to Be Saints: The Minor Festivals Devotionally Studied.* London: Society for Promoting Christian Knowledge, 1881.

———. *Letter and Spirit: Notes on the Commandments.* London: Society for Promoting Christian Knowledge, 1883.

———. *Maude: Prose and Verse.* Edited by R. W. Crump. Hamden, Conn.: Archon Books, 1976.

———. *Time Flies: A Reading Diary.* London: Society for Promoting Christian Knowledge, 1885.

———. *The Face of the Deep: A Devotional Commentary on the Apocalypse.* London: Society for Promoting Christian Knowledge, 1892.

———. *The Complete Poems of Christina Rossetti.* Edited by Rebecca W. Crump. 3 vols. Baton Rouge: Louisiana State University Press, 1979, 1986, 1990.

Kathy Alexis Psomiades (essay date 1999)

SOURCE: Psomiades, Kathy Alexis. "Whose Body? Christina Rossetti and Aestheticist Femininity." In *Women and British Aestheticism,* edited by Talia Schaffer and Kathy Alexis Psomiades, pp. 101-18. Charlottesville and London: University Press of Virginia, 1999.

[*In the following essay, Psomiades contends that "Christina Rossetti constructs the aestheticist woman*

*poet as drawing authority from her privileged relation-
ship to aestheticism's feminine images . . . , [which]
are part of what makes it possible to imagine aestheticism as a tradition with both masculine and feminine
practitioners."*]

There is perhaps no cannier representation of Christina
Rossetti as aesthete than Max Beerbohm's cartoon in
Rossetti and His Circle (1922). Its caption reads:

> Rossetti, having just had a fresh consignment of stun-
> ning fabrics from that new shop in Regent St., tries
> hard to prevail on his younger sister to accept at any
> rate one of these and have a dress made out of it from
> designs to be furnished by himself.[1]

Brother and sister stand in a paneled room with indecipherable pictures on the walls. The room is full of chairs
draped with swags of material in brilliant colors. In the
center the Rossettis face each other—Gabriel in a black
smocklike garment over trousers, Christina in a black
bonnet, shawl, and gloves and holding an umbrella.
Gabriel frowns and gesticulates, saying, "What *is* the
use, Christina, of having a heart like a singing bird and
a water-shoot and all the rest of it, if you insist on getting yourself up like a pew-opener?" Christina replies,
"Well, Gabriel, I don't know. I'm sure you yourself always dress very quietly."

At first glance this cartoon appears to represent yet another woman writer's refusal to accept aestheticism's
tendency to turn women into beautiful erotic objects.
But as we continue to examine it, a more complex picture emerges. Beerbohm seems to be portraying Christina Rossetti's complicated engagement with aestheticism. In this cartoon Rossetti can be said to have two
bodies—the respectable, black-clad body she presents
to the world, and the imaginary body of the aestheticist
art object. This imaginary body is seen partly as the
product of masculine imagination—Gabriel urges Christina to make this body a reality with his intervention—
and partly as an implication of Rossetti's own poetry:
her poem **"A Birthday"** begins with the lines "My heart
is like a singing bird / Whose nest is in a watered
shoot," and the second stanza describes the use of gorgeous materials in creating a stage for self-display—
"Raise me a dais of silk and down."[2] So the body urged
on Christina by Gabriel in Beerbohm's cartoon is one
she herself has helped to create, and her refusal to occupy it in real life is not the same as the refusal of such
a body *tout court*.

Furthermore, Gabriel attempts to use bolts of cloth to
materialize the aesthetic realm in the everyday world.
Yet here the attempt to aestheticize daily life connotes
participation in commodity culture—the heart like a
singing bird comes from the realm of art, but the fab-
rics come from a new shop in Regent Street. They are
described as "stunning," a word that is both part of the
shopper's common parlance and reminiscent of Dante
Gabriel Rossetti's use of the word "stunner" to describe
women, words, and art objects. So, in an odd way, rather
than refusing aestheticism, Christina Rossetti insists on
an aestheticism more perfect than her brother's, one
that does not traffic so much in the market, one whose
lushly beautiful objects are not for sale.

Finally, the cartoon ties the two Rossettis together, both
by having Christina compare Gabriel's appearance to
her own and by making the poets into black shapes that
face each other. Dressing quietly, the two poets mark
themselves out as producers rather than consumers, as
workers rather than pleasure seekers. By refusing
brightly colored clothing, loose hair, a relaxed posture,
Christina refuses a certain gender dimorphism; her phallic umbrella and Gabriel's feminine smock act to undercut the absolute difference between feminine art object
and masculine artist that Gabriel's gesture seems to
suggest. She thus takes up the dandy's attitude of extreme yet understated self-regulation.

What Beerbohm shows us here, in other words, is an
aestheticism produced by both men and women and
characterized by a particular way of using the feminine
figure. He also provides a critical model of the double
vision necessary for thinking about the work of the
women who produced aestheticism. On the one hand,
this model examines the different relations men and
women might have to aestheticism's feminine images—no one suggests that Dante Gabriel try to look
like the women in his paintings. On the other hand, this
model observes the continuities between the work of
men and women—both poets create aestheticism's feminine images, both have an investment in those images
as the location of their art and artistry, both operate in
the aestheticist tradition.

In this essay I want to follow Beerbohm's lead and
demonstrate how Christina Rossetti constructs the aestheticist woman poet as drawing authority from her
privileged relationship to aestheticism's feminine images. Those images, I want to argue, are part of what
makes it possible to imagine aestheticism as a tradition
with both masculine and feminine practitioners. Many
feminist scholars have seen aestheticism's tendency to
construct and represent aesthetic value in feminine figures as oppressive to women. But to the extent that
these figures value feminine interiority and reveal femininity's artificiality, they may also be enabling for
women. Rather than assuming that aestheticism prescribes a version of femininity as the mute object of
masculine desire, we might shift our focus to what it
means to the men and women who produce culture that
in aestheticism femininity signifies the power of the
aesthetic.[3]

To address this issue is to move toward a new history
of aestheticism, one that takes account of the contribu-

tions made by both men and women. By showing how Rossetti draws on and contributes to the aestheticist trope of Beauty's body—that is, the use of a feminine figure to embody and represent aesthetic experience—I will also show how aestheticism's feminine images invite women's participation in the movement. Ultimately, maintaining our double vision of women's participation in aestheticism means refusing to assume not only that we already know what aestheticism is about but also that we already know what women, or femininity, or women writers are about. In this way we might avoid inscribing in aestheticism the very gender binarisms it works to disrupt.

QUEEN OF PRE-RAPHAELITISM: CHRISTINA ROSSETTI IN THE 1890S

What if we suspend for a moment what we know, and imagine a world in which Christina Rossetti is the inaugurator of British aestheticism? Such a world is not as far from reality as we might think, for if not hailed as the preeminent aestheticist poet of her day, Christina Rossetti was associated with Pre-Raphaelite aestheticism by reviewers as early as the 1860s.[4] Reviewers of *Goblin Market and Other Poems* (1862) and *The Prince's Progress and Other Poems* (1866) noted the illustrations by Dante Gabriel Rossetti and, particularly in America, used the word "Pre-Raphaelite" in relation to the poetry.[5] By the 1880s William Sharp was writing that Rossetti "has, as a poet, a much wider reputation and a much larger circle of readers than even her brother Gabriel, for in England and much more markedly in America, the name of Christina Rossetti is known intimately where perhaps that of the author of the *House of Life* is but a name and nothing more."[6] True, many reviewers do not mention the connection to Pre-Raphaelitism, placing Rossetti instead in the context of devotional poetry or poetry by women. But, as Antony Harrison has pointed out, to those associated with aestheticism in the 1880s and 1890s, Rossetti was an aestheticist poet. Richard Le Gallienne, Arthur Symons, Edmund Gosse, Alice Law, William Sharp, and Oscar Wilde all focused on her formal mastery, compared her work to that of men associated with aestheticism, and described her poetry in language associated with the aestheticist prose of Algernon Charles Swinburne and Walter Pater. Symons noted, "The thought of death has a constant fascination for her, almost such a fascination as it had for Leopardi or Baudelaire."[7] Gosse described "her habitual tone" as "one of melancholy reverie, the pathos of which is strangely intensified by her appreciation of beauty and pleasure."[8] Le Gallienne wrote, "The note of loss and the peculiar sad cadence of the music, even though the songs be of happy things, is the distinctive characteristic of Miss Rossetti's singing. . . . Her songs of love are nearly always of love's loss; of its joy she sings with a passionate throat, but it is joy seen through the mirror of a wild regret."[9] At her death

in 1894, Rossetti was hailed not only as an important woman poet and writer of devotional verse but also as a major aestheticist poet.

Phrases like "Queen of the Pre-Raphaelites" or "High-Priestess of Pre-Raphaelitism" explicitly connect Rossetti's status as cultural producer to aestheticism's use of feminine figures. Both Rossetti's participation in the movement since the days of the *Germ* (the literary magazine of the Pre-Raphaelite Brotherhood) and the presence of imaginary women in Pre-Raphaelite poetry and painting come together in these phrases to make it possible to imagine a woman producing aestheticism. Similarly, aestheticism's association with passionate emotion and sensation, often seen as feminizing male poets and artists, also seems compatible with the participation of a woman poet. Symons wrote of Rossetti, "This motive, passion remembered and repressed, condemned to eternal memory and eternal sorrow, is the motive of much of her finest work."[10] Rossetti's repression of her passion does not erase that passion, any more than her plain clothing erases the idea of the beautiful aestheticist woman in Beerbohm's cartoon. Rather, repression acts further to interiorize and mystify that passion: in this way Rossetti's status as *woman* intensifies, rather than diminishes, her status as *aestheticist poet*. In short, we can see in many reviews of Rossetti's work a sense that she is peculiarly suited to write aestheticist verse *because* she is a woman, a sense that aestheticism's concern with femininity and its turn away from the productive masculine realm on some level invite feminine participation.[11]

Perhaps the most nuanced discussion of the relation between Rossetti's femininity and her aestheticism is Alice Law's eulogistic essay in the *Westminster Review* (1895). In the opening paragraphs of this essay Law asserts the aestheticism of Rossetti's verse—its polished finish, the inseparability of its form and content, its autonomy—by using language and imagery with feminine, as well as aestheticist, connotations: "The absence of all harsher and more rugged qualities, of all topical didacticism, of any rigid philosophical system on which we can lay hold, their seeming artless, yet aesthetic and finished perfection, all these combine to give the poems an air of elevated inaccessibility which renders critical approach difficult."[12] Later, Law employs a metaphor often used to connect femininity and artistry in aestheticist poetry: "Like some magic web, it seems woven of a substance so elusive, intangible, and of such an almost gossamer tenuity as defies handling, and constitutes at once the critic's ecstasy, wonder, and despair" (445). The absence of the harsh, rugged, and rigid and the presence of the elusive and intangible are, of course, characteristic of aestheticist poetry in general. But by showing how these feminine qualities make Rossetti's art resistant to critical consumption and co-optation, Law implies that Rossetti's femininity intensifies her aestheticism, making her poetry even more rigorously autonomous than aestheticist poetry generally is.

Law also uses vocabulary associated with male aestheticist writers like Swinburne, Pater, and Wilde to describe Rossetti's accomplishments:

> But the keynote of much of Miss Rossetti's word-music is its aesthetic mysticism and rich melancholy. It is associated here, as in the works of her brother and the other Pre-Raphaelites, with the deep medieval coloring, and quaint bejewelled setting of an old thirteenth- or fourteenth-century manuscript. . . . Neither dull English skies, nor any sort of Philistine environment, could damp the artistic ardor which burns in such exquisite similes as illuminate her pages. . . . But it is specially in the **Prince's Progress** that Miss Rossetti's subtle and mysterious art finds its most perfect expression. Here we seem to breathe the very atmosphere of old-world charm and mysticism: the stanzas as it were exhale that almost indescribable aesthetic aroma of mingled flowers and herbs—rosemary, thyme, rue, and languorous lilies.
>
> (447-48)

The words "aesthetic," "mysticism," "quaint," "exquisite," "subtle," "mysterious," and "languorous" underline Rossetti's status as a participant in a larger movement and insist on her work being considered along with the writing of her male contemporaries. Furthermore, by providing an occasion for Law to use this language, Rossetti enabled Law's participation in aestheticism as well, as an aestheticist critic.

Yet for Law, Rossetti's central achievement lies in her special relationship to aestheticist figures of femininity. At first Law seems to suggest a fairly straightforward connection between Rossetti's life and her art: Rossetti can convincingly give voice to the figure of the enclosed pining woman because she *is* that woman, because her art is the expression of her life. Yet in her references to aestheticist tradition, and in her use of formulations that simultaneously collapse and reinforce the distinctions between Rossetti and her feminine figures, Law also suggests that Rossetti's life is itself produced by aestheticism, that the links between life and art, real women and imagined women, are as much about femininity as artifice as they are about femininity as authenticity.

In the following passage, for example, Law claims not that Rossetti's poetry is autobiographical but that the aesthetic effects of this poetry depend on the conjunction of traditional tropes of femininity with the idea of a real woman:

> Not only is the atmosphere of her poems old-world, but in all Miss Rossetti's pages we seem to see the medieval heroine herself looking out at us, from an almost cloistered seclusion, with sad patient eyes. We hear the song of her overflowing heart, longing to spend and to be spent for love. There is nothing modern about this singing, unless it be its hopelessness, its troubled emotion and despair. The attitude is throughout that of the old-world heroine—pensive, clinging, *passive*. It is the tearful, uplifted accent of her who, in the silence of barred cell or rush-strewn chamber, weeps and prays for victory to crown the arms of others; of her whose only warfare is with the fears and fightings of her own bursting heart. It is the solitary singing of Shelley's
>
> High born maiden,
> In her palace tower,
> Soothing her love-laden
> Soul in secret hour
> With music sweet as love, that overflows her bower.
>
> The singing conveys all this, I think, and more; and yet, in hearing it, we are constrained to remember that the voice is none other than that of Miss Rossetti herself; that consciously or unconsciously she is her own medieval heroine.
>
> (449)

Law repeatedly conflates and separates the real and the aesthetic in this passage. The enclosed woman of art is distinguished from the real woman of the 1890s, yet the very language of the passage points to the similarities between the heroine and that other hopeless, troubled, despairing creature of suffering sexuality: the New Woman. By using the double entendre "to spend and to be spent," Law makes the desire of the medieval heroine as explicitly sexual (and thus as modern) as the desire of any New Woman. Furthermore, the passage depends on the uncanniness of the vivification of figures of poetic tradition. The heroine looking back at the reader from the page, or the sound of her singing reaching the reader's ears, produces an image not so much of authenticity as of art unexpectedly brought to life. So the poetry simultaneously constructs feminine figures that are recognizably part of a poetic tradition (the singing) and forces the reader to think of Rossetti (the voice) as bringing these figures to life in a new way. The phrase "consciously or unconsciously" introduces the same kind of doubling into the essay that Beerbohm introduced into his cartoon, allowing aesthetic agency to be conceived of as artifice and authenticity at the same moment. If Rossetti is unconsciously her own medieval heroine, the juxtaposition of real woman and feminine figure that occurs in her poetry is a function of her natural femininity. But if she is consciously her own heroine, then that juxtaposition is a function of art and a consciousness of femininity as artifice. By keeping both possibilities constantly in play, Law refuses to pin Rossetti to one model of femininity and poetic production.

Law sees as most typical of Rossetti's genius *The Prince's Progress,* a poem that both separates the feminine body of art from the feminine singer and contrasts masculine and feminine reactions to that body. The poem allows Law to situate Rossetti as aestheticist femininity and as singer and to situate herself as an aestheticist critic with a special relation to femininity. Law prefaces her review with a quotation from the last stanza of the poem, "You should have wept her yesterday," a line spoken by the attendants of a dead princess as a reproach to a prince who arrives too late. Law takes up the positions of both the prince to whom the line is addressed and the princess's attendant who utters it: she should have celebrated Rossetti while she lived, but now her essay can at least rebuke an insufficiently appreciative public. By doing this, Law places Rossetti in the positions of both the dead princess, who must be spoken for, and the attendants who speak for her: "In her lament for the Dead Bride of *The Prince's Progress,* she has, without knowing it, composed her own immortal epitaph" (449). Law places herself and Rossetti in the poem then in such a way as to connect them to and distance them from the aestheticist figure of the dead bride: as a modern woman of the 1890s, Law refuses to identify with the silent suffering object of the gaze, preferring to ally herself with the masculine gazer, but at the same time she and Rossetti are able to speak about femininity because they know it from the inside. If Rossetti is Pre-Raphaelite aestheticism, the full flowering of a tradition based on images of enclosed femininity, then she in turn authorizes Law as an aestheticist critic, who understands aestheticism all the better because of the double vision her femininity allows her.

My point here is simply that comparing Rossetti to a Pre-Raphaelite heroine and to the various feminine figures that people aestheticist verse does not just make her into an art object, on the one hand, or reduce her poetry to the authentic expression of natural emotions, on the other; instead it suggests a connection between aestheticism's uses of femininity and the ability to conceptualize the movement as one in which both men and women write. Aestheticism's tendency to think about the body of woman as mysterious surface always accompanied by some unknowable depth invites accounts of the experience of that body not only from the outside but also from the inside as the proper stuff of poetry. In so doing, it makes women aestheticist poets as imaginable as men. This is not to say that Beauty's body does not put demands on women that men do not experience. It is difficult to imagine Dante Gabriel Rossetti or Swinburne writing, as Christina Rossetti did, "If only my figure would shrink somewhat. For a fat poetess is incongruous, especially when seated by the grave of buried hope."[13] But even in this ironic comment, we can see a gesture of humorous identification and disidentification with the notion of being one's own heroine, one's own body of art.

ONCE SHE WAS FAIR: AESTHETICISM, 1866

The relation between Christina Rossetti's work and Pre-Raphaelite aestheticism has been characterized by scholars in two central ways. First, some of the best feminist criticism of Rossetti's work sees it as criticizing Pre-Raphaelitism's use of feminine images. In particular, Dolores Rosenblum has explored how participating in a movement that revolves around mute, mysterious feminine figures gives the female poet a consciousness divided between "the writer who sees and speaks, and the image/woman who is seen and is mute."[14] Second, some critics, notably Jerome McGann and Antony Harrison, see Rossetti as a recognized participant in Pre-Raphaelite aestheticism.[15] I would like to bring together these approaches in this reading of *The Prince's Progress* to suggest that what is aestheticist about Rossetti's poetry is not merely its turn away from the world in a movement of aesthetic and religious withdrawal but primarily its use of figures of femininity to think through the contradictory nature of art in bourgeois culture. As Law suggests, *The Prince's Progress* makes feminine artistry the logical outcome of aestheticist art. It may not be the "most perfect expression" of Rossetti's "subtle and mysterious art," but it is one of the most aestheticist of her poems.

The Prince's Progress and Other Poems was one of two major volumes of aestheticist poetry published in 1866; the other was Swinburne's *Poems and Ballads* (First Series). Each volume begins with a poem about the incompatibility of masculine heroism and erotic fulfillment: **"The Prince's Progress"** and "Laus Veneris" both explore the gendered and sexualized terrain of the aesthetic and make the sensational experience of a feminine body the central aesthetic moment. By tracing a dangerous but ultimately futile masculine journey to a private space constituted by an erotically charged and ultimately inaccessible feminine body, the poems meditate on the demands of self-enclosed eroticized aestheticist art and its incompatibility with the norms of bourgeois masculinity.

"Laus Veneris" is organized around the public space of a masculine quest, where knights ride and fight and pray, and the private space of femininity, art, and desire, where Venus slumbers in her Horsel.[16] Drawn out of the realm of masculine achievement by Venus's beauty, the poem's speaker unwittingly reveals that the masculine realm that he honors is a place of violence, hypocrisy, and tyranny, whereas the feminine realm of art and sex that he sees as his damnation is the location of the only real beauty and value. In Venus, Swinburne can claim that art is radically incompatible with the praxis of everyday life, based in the very instincts that always threaten to disorder civilization, and experienced, like sex, through the body.[17]

Venus's burning, scented, gorgeous flesh may seem at first to be miles away from the pining, dying body of a virgin princess. Yet Rossetti's poem also marks off two realms: a public masculine space of achievement, and a private feminine space of art and sex. As in "Laus Veneris," the valued space of art is grounded in a feminine body. From its initial association with flowers, gums, and juices, the princess's body brings together the erotic and the aesthetic:

> By her head lilies and rosebuds grow;
> The lilies droop,—will the rosebuds blow?
> The silver slim lilies hang the head low;
>   Their stream is scanty, their sunshine rare;
> Let the sun blaze out, and let the stream flow,
>   They will blossom and wax fair.
>
> Red and white poppies grow at her feet,
> The blood-red wait for sweet summer heat,
> Wrapped in bud-coats hairy and neat;
>   But the white buds swell; one day they will burst,
> Will open their death-cups drowsy and sweet,—
>   Which will open the first?[18]

Here the flowers that surround the princess are so weighted by poetic tradition that it is difficult to tell whether they are literally present or purely metaphorical representations of living and dead sex and virginity. They aestheticize the feminine body as they reduce its meaning to its erotic status.

By contrast, the prince is described surrounded by literal and mundane objects:

> In his world-end palace the strong Prince sat,
> Taking his ease on cushion and mat,
> Close at hand lay his staff and his hat.
>
>   (13-15)

The prince inhabits an oddly domestic world in which objects are used for his body's comfort but have neither aesthetic nor erotic significance. The very language of the passage is offhand and ironic, whereas the language used to describe the princess reverently invokes the elemental forces of nature and is the location of much of the poem's metaphoric energy.

The world of Rossetti's prince, like the world that Swinburne's knight gives up for Venus, is clearly not as valuable as the enclosed realm that contains Beauty's body. If for Swinburne the irony is that the masculine sphere of battle and religion is far more violent and just as sensual as the feminine sphere in which the knight now resides and about which he feels so much guilt, for Rossetti the irony is that the masculine sphere, whose activities are so important and on which the lovely bride waits, is silly and inconsequential. The prince of the poem's title is neither hero nor villain but a jolly incompetent, his quest a series of purposeless tasks that take him far too long. "Strong of limb, if of purpose weak" (47), he sets out only to find himself seduced not by a subtle temptress but by the first passing milkmaid. Finally breaking free, he journeys through a wasteland, arduous chiefly because there is no one to talk to: "Te-

dious land for a social prince" (152). Here he finds himself helping an alchemist make an elixir of life not because he has been enchanted, or because he really needs the elixir, or even because he has a greedy desire for knowledge, but because he is hungry and finds his solitude tedious. When the elixir is made and the magician dies, the prince rests another night before resuming his journey. Forthwith he is rescued from drowning by ladies and stays with them for a while because he cannot think of a polite way to refuse them. The events that in a traditional quest narrative prove the quester's moral fiber here are merely a series of procrastinations and delays. In short, the prince does not progress at all, and, indeed, his lack of progress trivializes masculine activity.

When the prince finally arrives at the princess's palace, he is, of course, too late:

> Day is over, the day that wore.
> What is this that comes through the door,
> The face covered, the feet before?
>   This that coming takes ⸳⸳⸳ reath;
> This Bride not seen, t⸳⸳⸳ n no more
>   Save of the Bri⸳⸳⸳ Death?
>
>   (469-74)

The question "What is this" echoes the "Who is this? and what is here?" that greets Alfred, Lord Tennyson's dead Lady of Shalott as she floats into Camelot. Here is the ideal opportunity for a Lancelot moment, the moment at which the obtuse male lover comes face-to-face with the dead body of the woman who has desired him. But the prince is never allowed the luxury of this moment, not the gazing on the dead face, the musing, or the final interpretive gesture. Instead, he finds himself addressed by the princess's attendants, upbraided for his part in the princess's story, the only story, the poem implies, that really matters:

> You should have wept her yesterday,
>   Wasting upon her bed:
> But wherefore should you weep to-day
>   That she is dead?
> Lo, we who love weep not to-day,
>   But crown her royal head.
> Let be these poppies that we strew,
>   Your roses are too red:
> Let be these poppies, not for you
>   Cut down and spread.
>
>   (531-40)

As an aestheticist poem, then, *The Prince's Progress* makes a strong statement about the dangers of the autonomy aesthetic. The very isolation from the everyday world that keeps the princess pure and poetic threatens to destroy her entirely. The aesthetic and erotic experiences that the princess promises simply cannot compete with the stronger pleasures offered by objects and services of more immediate use—milk, magic, maidens—that can be had by anyone willing to pay for them. The philistine prince is above all else *bored*; like a model bourgeois consumer, he seeks to be amused and entertained.[19] By the time he finally decides he wants direct experience of the princess, there is no princess to be had. The greatest danger that everyday life poses to the aesthetic for Rossetti is not that it will, as in **"Laus Veneris,"** attempt to stamp out the aesthetic realm but that, content with other amusements, it will simply not care enough about the aesthetic even to attempt to stamp it out. In an essay written in 1785 the German writer Karl Philipp Moritz makes a succinct statement about art's value that might serve as a proleptic gloss on Rossetti's poem:

> We do not need the beautiful object in order to be entertained as much as the beautiful object needs us to be recognized. We can easily exist without contemplating beautiful works of art, but they cannot exist as such without our contemplation. The more we can do without them, therefore, the more we contemplate them for their own sake so as to impart to them through our very contemplation, as it were, their true, complete existence.[20]

Beauty, like the princess, dies if left unvalued and unappreciated as easily as it dies if co-opted by the marketplace and seen in purely economic terms.

Despite its statement about autonomy's dangers, what makes *The Prince's Progress* aestheticist is its assertion that the aesthetic realm, attenuated and endangered though it may be, is still the location of all true value in the poem. It makes this assertion through the plot conventions of aestheticist narrative poetry, by producing a narrative that climaxes in the lyric contemplation of the dead or unconscious feminine body of art, a narrative that purports to explain but merely demonstrates the inexplicability of the lyric encounter. Aestheticist poems like Tennyson's "The Lady of Shalott," Dante Gabriel Rossetti's "Jenny," and Swinburne's "Laus Veneris," to name a few, share this structure. In these poems the inadequacy of the narrative as an explanation of feminine mystery marks out a further beyond that signifies art's inviolability even in the most compromising circumstances. *The Prince's Progress* further reorganizes the climactic moment of contemplation to place Beauty's body beyond the reach of heterosexual romance, intimating that a real understanding of Beauty's value is only available to those who have an understanding of femininity from the inside out.

The contemplation and celebration of the body of the dead bride occurs in the poem's final stanzas, which are spoken by the princess's attendants and set off from the rest of the poem by a longer stanza form. Written well before the rest of *The Prince's Progress* as a separate poem titled **"The Fairy Prince Who Arrived Too Late,"** these lines form not only the poem's climax but its origin. (It was Dante Gabriel Rossetti who suggested that Rossetti "turn the dirge into a narrative poem of some length."[21]) These final stanzas depict a process of transformation in which the prince's neglect causes the princess's body to change. Withdrawn from aesthetic, erotic, and economic exchange, valueless in the real world, the body ceases to have the attributes of aestheticist femininity. Yet in their place, new attributes emerge that characterize an even more rigorous aestheticism.

Beauty, sexual exchangeability, and economic value typically come together in aestheticist figures of femininity, whose eroticism acts to manage the complicated relation between art and the market. Here, they appear as qualities gone:

> Is she fair now as she lies?
>   Once she was fair;
> Meet queen for any kingly king,
>   With gold-dust on her hair.
> Now these are poppies in her locks,
>   White poppies she must wear;
> Must wear a veil to shroud her face
>   And the want graven there:
> Or is the hunger fed at length,
>   Cast off the care?

(501-10)

Once beautiful, once admirably suited to sexual exchange, once covered in gold, the princess now wears a veil, or shroud, over her wasted face. Her sexual exchangeability, signified by the veil of virginity, is curtailed by death, as the veil becomes a shroud. The economic value sign of gold is replaced by the poppies that signify her radical unexchangeability. Her face, no longer lovely and thus no longer caught up in the desires of others, is hidden from view: it cannot function any longer as a figure of aesthetic value.

Yet the princess ultimately acts to signify the power of the aesthetic in bourgeois culture, even as she signifies its powerlessness in bourgeois systems of exchange. Because it is "[t]oo late for love, too late for joy," because she will never circulate as a value, the princess's body exists for its own sake. What it looks like is a sign not of the desires of others for it but of its own desires for fulfillment. As the attendants describe the dead princess as she was in life, they locate value in the her interiority, in her regulation of her own passions:

> We never saw her with a smile
>   Or with a frown;
> Her bed seemed never soft to her,
>   Though tossed of down;
> She little heeded what she wore,
>   Kirtle, or wreath, or gown;
> We think her white brows often ached
>   Beneath her crown,

Till silvery hairs showed in her locks
    That used to be so brown.

We never heard her speak in haste:
    Her tones were sweet,
And modulated just so much
    As it was meet:
Her heart sat silent through the noise
    And concourse of the street.
There was no hurry in her hands,
    No hurry in her feet;
There was no bliss drew night to her,
    That she might run to meet.

                    (511-30)

Here the aging, wasting, self-regulating body comes to signify art's tragic isolation, but also its enduring value. Because this value comes from within, from feminine experience, it suggests that women, through their experiences with femininity, might have a special relationship to aestheticist art. No longer a value sign in the world of men, the princess ultimately becomes the sign of the singing maidens' superior artistry. Thus the final lines insist on the women's right to metaphorize the body with white poppies, flowers not usually invoked in poetry, rather than the conventional red roses. If red roses signify feminine beauty as the object of desire, white poppies seem to signify feminine desire unsatisfied, a yearning that ends only in death. The attendants' understanding of the princess makes their metaphors more original and exact than the trite and worn tribute offered by the prince. It is important to recognize that the two sets of flowers, the beautiful body and the pining body, are equally symbolic, equally textual. The pining body is ultimately no more and no less real than the blooming body, no more and no less a surface to be read. What is at issue is who writes and who reads the signs of femininity, who best understands them, and thus who best understands the truths about the aesthetic that they figure.

So in *The Prince's Progress* the princess not only serves as a figure for the aesthetic but also is the occasion for the poem's women singers to produce their own poetry. The singing women must make a double gesture toward the princess of identification and disidentification: they must be enough like her to be able to read the signs of her interior life on her body's surface but enough unlike her to survive. The double gesture of standing inside and outside the body of Beauty is echoed by Dante Gabriel Rossetti's illustrations for *The Prince's Progress and Other Poems,* which, far more than his illustrations for *Goblin Market and Other Poems,* locate Rossetti herself in the realm of art. In the illustration that appears on the title page along with Rossetti's name, the princess sits by a window, waiting, with long hair, full-sleeved robe, full lips, and eyes that gaze out on the landscape below. It seems to suggest that the volume will provide some access to the musing woman's thoughts. In the illustration for the poem's final scene, one woman is distinguished from the collectivity of attendants in the poem. She pushes the prince out the door of the crypt in which the princess lies shrouded in the background. The other maidens have the long, loose hair and full lips of Beauty's body, but the attendant who disposes of the prince turns away from the viewer, her hair hidden in a headdress. As she pushes the prince out the door, she seems to take his place; at the same time, in coming forward to meet him, she takes the place of the bride who would meet him were she alive. Significantly, it is with this figure that Rossetti partly identifies, remarking in a letter to her brother about an early version of this drawing, "Surely the severe female who arrests the Prince somewhat resembles my phiz."[22] By splitting the attendants into beautiful young women and a plainer, more mature figure, Dante Gabriel projects the two bodies the poem locates in the princess onto the serving women, who in the poem remain an undifferentiated collectivity. In the process he makes the severe female into the musing princess's double and opposite. Together, princess and attendant both foster and thwart the reader's desires to see the woman poet as one who is or ought to be a version of the beautiful body of art.

CONCLUSION

What can Christina Rossetti tell us, then, about the relationship between aestheticism's use of feminine figures and the women who made aestheticist art? The answer depends on what we think aestheticism is and what we think women are. If we think that aestheticism is a masculine tradition that turns women into objects and that women authors only write to contradict the demand that women be silent, then what Rossetti tells us is that women aesthetes were participating in an inherently hostile tradition that they could only engage with in the mode of critique. The princess can only die of desire unsatisfied; her women can only weep. I would argue that, while this is by no means an entirely wrong view of aestheticism, it is a very partial one. If, to supplement this partial view, we think of aestheticism as a moment at which the idea of femininity became foundational to the conception of the aesthetic and if we think that women writers emerge in greater and greater numbers in the nineteenth century in part because middle-class femininity was increasingly the location of many different kinds of cultural authority, then we might see these images as connected not only to women's oppression but also to their increasing empowerment.

Aestheticism's concern with feminine images and later with traditionally feminine areas of expertise—dress, decor, gardening—meant that aestheticist and anti-aestheticist women writers alike could claim that their status as "real" women authorized them to speak about "imaginary" women and to give advice about traditionally feminine activities. The figure of the woman as silent art object may seem to have silenced women who would have been poets, but it also incited them to speech. The princess's attendants cannot be silent, cannot let matters rest; they must explain, exhort, interpret, claim the figure of Beauty as not the prince's but their own. If we read aestheticism's beautiful women not as incidental figures but as modes of grounding and representing art itself, then all discussions of aestheticist femininity are of necessity as much about art as about gender ideology. Because these discussions take place through the representation of a specific kind of femininity, they are discussions in which women, as well as men, speak. In short, the work of Rossetti and other women aesthetes allows us to see that arguments about representing and interpreting femininity are always also arguments about representation and interpretation, about art and artistry and their place in bourgeois culture as a whole. That femininity is the ground on which these arguments occur, their guarantee and their alibi, poses difficulties for women but also offers opportunities.

Notes

1. Max Beerbohm, *Rossetti and His Circle* (London: Heinemann, 1922; reprint, New Haven, Conn.: Yale University Press, 1987), 50.

2. Christina Rossetti, *The Complete Poems of Christina Rossetti,* ed. R. W. Crump (Baton Rouge: Louisiana State University Press, 1979-80), 1:36.

3. For more on the relation between femininity and aestheticism, see Kathy Psomiades, *Beauty's Body: Femininity and Representation in British Aestheticism* (Stanford, Calif.: Stanford University Press, 1997).

4. For accounts of Rossetti's reception in the nineteenth century, see Edna Kotin Charles, *Christina Rossetti: Critical Perspectives, 1862-1982* (London and Toronto: Associated University Presses, 1985), 23-67, and Rebecca Crump, *Christina Rossetti: A Reference Guide* (Boston: G. K. Hall, 1976), which lists reviews chronologically.

5. See J. R. Dennet, "Miss Rossetti's Poems," *Nation,* 19 July 1866, 47-48. In *Christina Rossetti in Context* (Chapel Hill: University of North Carolina Press, 1988), Antony Harrison points out that the review of *The Prince's Progress and Other Poems* in the *Athenaeum* (23 June 1866, 824-25) also judges it according to Pre-Raphaelite principles (27).

6. William Sharp, "The Rossetti's," *Fortnightly Review,* 1 March 1886, 427.

7. Arthur Symons, *Studies in Two Literatures* (London: Leonard Smithers, 1897), 142.

8. Edmund Gosse, "Christina Rossetti," *Century Magazine* 46 (June 1893): 215.

9. Richard Le Gallienne, "Review of *Poems,*" *Academy,* 7 February 1891, 132.

10. Symons, 138.

11. Tricia Lootens compellingly argues that fin-de-siècle criticism domesticates and naturalizes Rossetti's poetry. In many of the articles from which I quote, mention is made of Rossetti's narrowness, her technique, the connection between her poetry and her feminine experience. These gestures constitute a misogynistic minimalization of Rossetti's achievement. However, if we look at them in the context of nineteenth-century criticism of aestheticist poetry by men as well as women, we see that accusations of narrowness, of overworking or underworking verse, even of sexual transgression, are made about aestheticist poetry generally. In other words, while these are responses to Rossetti as a woman poet, they are also responses to her as an aestheticist poet, a fact obscured by reading the criticism solely in the context of criticism on other women poets. See Tricia Lootens, *Lost Saints: Silence, Gender, and Victorian Literary Canonization* (Charlottesville: University Press of Virginia, 1996), 158-82.

12. Alice Law, "The Poetry of Christina Rossetti," *Westminster Review* 143 (1895): 444. All further references will be noted parenthetically in the text.

13. William Michael Rossetti, ed., *The Family Letters of Christina Georgina Rossetti* (London: Brown, Langham, 1908), 160.

14. Dolores Rosenblum, *Christina Rossetti: The Poetry of Endurance* (Carbondale: Southern Illinois University Press, 1988), 113. See also "Christina Rossetti: The Inward Pose," in *Shakespeare's Sisters: Feminist Essays on Women Poets,* ed. Sandra Gilbert and Susan Gubar (Bloomington: Indiana University Press, 1979), and "Christina Rossetti's Religious Poetry: Watching, Looking, Keeping Vigil," *Victorian Poetry* 20, no. 1 (spring 1982): 33-49.

15. See Jerome McGann, "Christina Rossetti's Poems: A New Edition and a Revaluation," *Victorian Studies* 23 (1980): 237-54, and "The Religious Poetry of Christina Rossetti," *Critical Inquiry* 10 (1983): 127-44, both reprinted in *The Beauty of Inflections: Literary Investigations in Historical Method and Theory* (Oxford: Clarendon, 1985). See also Harrison.

16. Algernon Charles Swinburne, "Laus Veneris," *The Poems of Algernon Charles Swinburne* (London: Chatto and Windus, 1904).

17. For an extended discussion of both "Laus Veneris" and the relations between Rossetti's and

Swinburne's poetry, see Psomiades, *Beauty's Body*, 60-65, 79-93.

18. Christina Rossetti, *The Prince's Progress*, in Crump, 1: 95-110, ll.25-35. All further citations will be noted parenthetically by line number in the text and are taken from this edition.

19. Rossetti wrote to her brother about the stages of the poem: "1st a prelude and outset; 2nd, an alluring milkmaid; 3rd a trial of barren boredom; 4th the social element again; 5th barren boredom in a more uncompromising form; 6th a wind-up and conclusion" (William Michael Rossetti, ed., *Rossetti Papers* [London: Sands, 1903], 78).

20. "Versuch einer Vereiningung aller schönen Künste und Wissenschaften unter dem Begriff des in sich selbst Vollendeten" (*Schriften zur Ästhetik und Poetick*, ed. Hans Joachim Schrimpf [Tübingen: Max Niemeyer, 1962], 4). Quoted and translated in Martha Woodmansee, *The Author, Art and the Market: Rereading the History of Aesthetics* (New York: Columbia University Press, 1994), 32.

21. William Michael Rossetti, ed., *The Poetical Works of Christina Georgina Rossetti* (London: Macmillan, 1904), 461.

22. William Michael Rossetti, ed., *Rossetti Papers*, 84.

Joy A. Fehr (essay date spring 2000)

SOURCE: Fehr, Joy A. "Christina Rossetti's Nightmares: Fact or Fiction?" *Victorian Newsletter*, no. 97 (spring 2000): 21-6.

[*In the following essay, Fehr disputes other critics' biographical readings of Rossetti's works, focusing on the poem "The Nightmare"—a work that other critics have interpreted as evidence that Rossetti was a victim of incest—to offer an alternate, non-biographical explanation for the author's use of nightmarish, horrific imagery.*]

In 1852 G. H. Lewes published an essay in the *Westminster Review* in which he argued that women were better suited than men to writing novels because the content of novels more closely paralleled their experience (133). He contended that Jane Austen and George Sand were the best female novelists of the time—Austen because she never "transcend[s] her own experience" and Sand because her works are "her confessions. Her biography lies there" (134, 135). Lewes's biographical assumptions regarding women's texts were not unusual among Victorian critics. In fact, according to Allon White, many Victorian critics and reviewers

read nineteenth-century texts "symptomatically"; that is, they believed that by scrutinizing the text carefully for signs of hidden and at times even repressed desires and fears, they could arrive at an understanding of the mind—even the subconscious mind—behind the text. In contrast to what I describe as "autobiographical reading" practices, which develop interpretations of the text based on a knowledge of the life, symptomatic readings move in the opposite direction: symptomatic readers or critics construct a version of the author's life based upon what they regard as "clues" gleaned from the text. White also demonstrates how late nineteenth-century and early twentieth-century male authors resorted to "secrecy, lying, obscurity, impression and withdrawal" to create a gap between art and life and thus frustrate these symptomatic designs (54). These symptomatic critical practices, however, were routinely applied throughout the century to women authors. Most Victorian readers believed that women could write only from personal experience since women were emotional and experiential rather than intelligent and imaginative. Symptomatic reading practices coupled with this belief in women's essential nature placed female authors in an even more tenuous position than their male counterparts. To be successful, women authors, through their work, needed to appear to conform to Victorian ideals of womanhood.

Christina Rossetti's success at negotiating Victorian reading practices and beliefs regarding women is evident in the warm reception her work received throughout her lifetime. Theodore Watts-Dunton, with his review of *Verses* (1893) published shortly after Rossetti's death, summarized public response to Rossetti and her work:

> In the volume before us, as in all her previously published writings, we see at its best what Christianity is as the motive power of poetry. The Christian idea is essentially feminine, and of this feminine quality Christina Rossetti's poetry is full. . . . The history of literature shows no human development so beautiful as the ideal Christian woman of our own day. She is unique indeed. . . . We should search in vain through the entire human record for anything so beautiful as that kind of Christian lady to whom self-abnegation is not only the first of duties, but the first of joys. Yet, no doubt, the Christian idea must needs be more or less flavoured by each personality through which it is expressed. With regard to Christina Rossetti . . . there was in the order of things a sort of ether of universal clarity for all others.
>
> (qtd. in Bell 189-90)

Rossetti's reputation as a saintly woman ensured her continued popularity and literary success. Not until after her death did biographers begin to provide increasingly intrusive readings of her work. In the process, these critics unknowingly perpetuate and reinforce Victorian beliefs and reading practices.

Mackenzie Bell published the first biography of Rossetti, *Christina Rossetti: A Biographical and Critical Study,* in 1898. Throughout the work Bell constantly concerns himself with revealing to whom, or to what event, Rossetti may have been referring in her poetry and prose. Although he did nothing to suggest that Rossetti was less than a respectable Victorian woman, his obsession with identification suggested ways in which future critics could construct far more intrusive readings than his. First, he hinted at a possible method for reading the overt references to silence in Rossetti's poetry:

> Much of her finest work in both verse and prose is the veiled expression of her own individuality. She was deeply religious, and carried her convictions into every detail of life, and her clearly-defined religious opinions gave a special interest to her religious verse. Hers was emphatically a character that it was needful to know personally in order to understand: I doubt if anyone who had not the privilege of knowing her can understand in its fullness, in all its sweetness, in its profundity, and in its fascination, her personality, and the effect of that personality both on her poems and on her prose.
>
> (4)

If Rossetti's "finest work" is the "veiled expression of her own individuality," then perhaps those references to secrets are the clue to understanding that personality. Since to know her is to understand the effect her personality had on her work, then why cannot the reverse be the case? Bell points the way to reading the many silences, secrets, and riddles in her poems and prose as a means of understanding the woman behind the work. Second, Bell provided two possible explanations, besides her religious devotion, for the "veil" in Rossetti's poetry. He claims that the poem **"What?,"** which was written in May 1853 and published in *New Poems,* is one of many in the volume "to depict what her younger brother has called 'an unhappy love-passage' in his sister's life. During 1849, or possibly late 1848, she was sought in marriage by a painter very well-known in her circle. She regarded him with favour. But he was a Roman Catholic, and she determined to decline his suit owing to 'religious considerations'" (30-31). A few pages later, Bell reveals that

> Rossetti received a second offer of marriage—her suitor in this instance, being a man of letters and pre-eminently a scholar. Again she was favourably disposed towards her suitor, and again, actuated by religious scruples, she was constrained to reject his offer, for, in the words of her surviving brother, he was "either not a Christian at all, or else was a Christian of undefined and heterodox views." This incident, which terminated about 1866, was more deeply felt by her than was her first attachment, and it is to this that the touching poem entitled **"Il Rosseggiar dell' Oriente"** relates. This incident, and the other incident of a simi-

lar kind, make clear many allusions in her poetry, particularly the fine lyric called **"Memory."** Both of her suitors pre-deceased her.

> (40-41)

This is all that Bell has to say on the subject of Rossetti's two love affairs and their relationship to her work, but later commentators could not resist the temptation to embellish upon this information by imitating Bell's method.

In her biography of Rossetti, published in 1931, Eleanor Walter Thomas expands upon Bell's brief statements concerning Rossetti's two proposals of marriage. Thomas is certain that Rossetti's failed love affairs resulted in Rossetti's obsession with religion and her passionate love poetry. When she discusses Rossetti's relationship to James Collinson, Rossetti's first suitor, she admits that it is dangerous "to trust imaginative lyrics for biographical facts, [but] some of [Rossetti's] poems of 1848-50 give rise to conjectures as to her state of mind and the causes for it, just as her letters suggest she was not altogether easy with regard to Collinson" (52). Poems Rossetti wrote during the period in which she was engaged to Collinson become fodder for Thomas's suppositions. Thomas is careful to note that "the emotional disturbance of Christina's twentieth year and the months immediately preceding and following were surely not wholly due to a broken love affair"; however, the relationship was certainly partly responsible (53). **"A Pause for Thought,"** written shortly before Rossetti met Collinson, "expresses 'a hope of youth' for the achievement, the fame, which ever seemed to flee away and yet was ever pursued" (52), but by the time the engagement was broken more than two years later, the last section of the **"Three Nuns"** "voices the century-old cry of the soul which sees the fair beauty and the sweetness of the world but turns away from it to find its one true home only when it obeys the command of the Spirit—'Come'" (53). Engagement with the world has turned into renunciation of the world, and the only explanation for this change that Thomas is aware of is Rossetti's broken engagement to Collinson.

Thomas is more certain about the effect Rossetti's second relationship had on her poetry. She contends that Rossetti recorded her relationship with Charles Bagot Cayley in many poems written during the 1860s. Of **"Il Rosseggiar dell' Oriente,"** she argues, "The facts that [Rossetti] did not show anyone the poems [William found them in her desk after her death] and that they were written . . . in Italian suggest that the writer intended them as an unlocking of her heart for herself alone" (72). The first two poems in the series are tentative explorations of love; the third refers to a gift from Cayley, and in the remainder Rossetti "lets herself go and reveals passionate yearning for the presence of her lover [Cayley] and for ever-renewed assurances from him of his love" (73). Even her devotional poems are read in light of Rossetti's relationship with Cayley. **"Despised and Rejected"** indicates Rossetti's difficulty in accepting Christ because she prefers the love of another, while **"I go, Lord, where Thou sendest me"** shows Rossetti's sad resignation yet commitment to her faith (75). **"Cor Mio"** and **"By Way of Remembrance"** strike a note of "self-accusation for having bartered roses for rue in life's mart, and that of praise for a friend silent, and strong, and true, and generous" (75). Thomas contends that these poems indicate Rossetti took comfort in her love for Cayley and her belief in the triumph of love in the hereafter (75). At no point, apparently, in Rossetti's poetic representation of her relationship with Cayley does she blame him for their failure to marry: "If there was error, it was hers" (75). **"Monna Innominata"** is also a chronicle of Rossetti's love affair with Cayley. According to Thomas, "the title and the explanation [Rossetti] prefixed to the series are just such a gesture of concealment for the intimately personal as the title 'Sonnets from the Portuguese'" (75-76). The donna innominata is Rossetti speaking "a dignified and tender utterance of love and of regret at separation from one of high and honored excellence, and yet of loyal faith in love and its immortality" (76) In conflating Rossetti's speaker with Rossetti herself, Thomas continues the symptomatic readings of the Victorian period. Thomas's method is both autobiographic and symptomatic; she uses details of the life to illuminate the poems, and she also uses the poems to provide details of the life.

Lona Mosk Packer, in 1963, moved from autobiographical reading to a form of symptomatic reading that continues to the present. Instead of being satisfied with linking Rossetti's work to known incidents in Rossetti's life, she reads Rossetti's work and then constructs events to fit her thesis. Unlike Victorian symptomatic readers, however, Packer, through her speculations, suggests that Rossetti was less than an ideal Victorian woman. Packer notices that there is a span of approximately twelve years between Rossetti's rejection of Collinson and the beginning of her relationship with Cayley. During this time, she observes, Rossetti wrote much of her "passionate love poetry" (43). The impact of Rossetti's broken engagement to Collinson cannot be the impetus behind this work, she argues, because research has shown that Rossetti was not all that committed to Collinson in the first place. To fill the gap, Packer claims that, during this period, Rossetti was emotionally involved with William Bell Scott, a married man (43). To build a case for their relationship, Packer refers to Scott's meetings with the Rossettis, which Scott mentions briefly in his autobiography—he was a good friend of the Rossetti brothers; to the dates of Scott's trips to London and abroad; to Scott's poetry; and, most important of all, to Rossetti's work written during this period.

Packer builds her case on nothing more than speculation. As a result, critics and biographers were quick to point out the problems with her argument, but that has not discouraged others from symptomatic readings of Rossetti's work.[1] In 1994, Jan Marsh in her biography of Rossetti, *Christina Rossetti: A Literary Life,* suggests that Rossetti was sexually abused by her father when she was twelve or thirteen years old. Through a symptomatic reading of Rossetti's works, Marsh argues that key recurring images in Rossetti's verse and prose hint at "suppressed sexual trauma" (258).

Death, dying, ghosts, monsters, dream/nightmares, and secrets pervade Rossetti's work. Marsh contends that the recurring imagery indicates unconscious disclosure of incest; Rossetti's secrets are secrets that even she does not know (260). Although the victim of abuse represses these memories, according to Marsh, "repetitive intrusions nearly always occur, with an involuntary compulsive tendency towards repetition of some aspects of the trauma. . . . These repetitions include nightmares, hallucinations, unbidden images and obsessive ideas; panic attacks and weeping episodes; or re-enactments of some disguised aspect of the trauma in gesture, movement or artistic production" (262). Other symptoms include "chronic depression . . . guilt, low self-esteem and feelings of powerlessness. Attempts at self-mutilation are common and suicidal feelings are frequent" (261-62). Clearly, Rossetti's work contains nightmares, hallucinations, unbidden images and obsessive ideas, but these indicators cannot be, in themselves, reason enough to diagnose incest.[2]

Marsh understands that she needs more than Gothic imagery to support her contention, so she turns to the details of Rossetti's life for further evidence. Gabriele, Rossetti's father, was a respected professor, "the chair of Italian at Kings College London," for much of Rossetti's childhood (21). His scholarly work, however, became progressively more obscure, even bizarre. Coincidentally, his health began to decline as his colleagues seriously began to question his work. By 1843 his career was over, and he suffered an emotional and physical collapse (35-41). Early in 1844 both Rossetti's older sister and her mother became governesses to replace Professor Rossetti's lost income. Since her brothers were already away at school, Rossetti was left at home, alone for much of the day, to care for her severely depressed invalid father (43). Thus, according to Marsh, the Rossetti family situation provided the catalyst for sexual abuse. A man suddenly bereft of the power and prestige he once enjoyed preys on his vulnerable daughter for emotional and physical comfort (259). Rossetti's own mental breakdown in 1845; her teenage self-mutilation—she ripped her arm with scissors—her drastic personality change; and her guilt-ridden obsession with religion are not, for Marsh, mere coincidences (55-64). She admits, "incest can only be inferred, not proved, for direct evidence is lacking" (260). But, she argues, most cases of incest are extremely difficult to prove and sexual abuse certainly "offers a convincing explanation of the dark and disturbed aspects of [Rossetti's] inner life" (260). Having made the suggestion, however, Marsh invokes the presumed incest to explain segments of Rossetti's life and writing. For example, Rossetti's work with young prostitutes and her concern for the prevention of cruelty to animals are said probably to be the results of her incest experience (520). As well, later works, such as **Sing-Song, Speaking Likenesses,** and **Letter and Spirit,** indicate her use of writing to heal herself psychologically (422-5, 507-8).

Marsh's thesis is well-argued. Unlike Packer, she does not invoke her own inferences to explain every poem Rossetti wrote, but like Packer she reads through the work to the life. Marsh relies heavily on the theories of artistic production advanced by Alice Miller, a psycho-analyst frequently cited by literary critics. For example, D. L. Macdonald refers to Miller's theories in his examination of Byron's sexual abuse, as does Louise de-Salvo in her exploration into how incest affected Virginia Woolf's life and work. Miller argues that some children are more sensitive to suffering than others and that these children often develop into adults who creatively express their early trauma (*Thou* 245, 249-50; *Untouched* 73). Miller's method, however, differs from Marsh's. Miller does not read a text, conclude on the basis of certain image patterns that the author was abused, and then marshal the evidence to argue that abuse *possibly* occurred. Rather, Miller searches for direct evidence of abuse or trauma before asserting that specific childhood events are reenacted in the literary text. In contrast to Marsh, Miller does not identify particular images—for example, ghosts, blood, death, and monsters—and then argue that these configurations are common to incest survivors. Instead, she notes how various themes and techniques convey impressions of suffering. Simply put, if Miller finds no substantiating information, she does not assume that abuse informs the work: circumstantial evidence is not enough.[3] In light of Miller's method, then, Marsh's connection of Rossetti's imagery to incest is problematic in that there is no other corroborating evidence for sexual abuse. Furthermore, Marsh omits a key element of Miller's approach, that of linking the specific nature of the abuse or trauma to the artistic production. Miller analyzes a number of literary works and paintings to demonstrate that, in every instance, the repression is reenacted in ways parallel to the abuse. For example, the paintings of Käthe Kollwitz contain numerous images of death, mothers, and children because her mother was obsessed with her children who had died, and refused to participate in the lives of her surviving children (*Untouched* 19-35). Friedrich Nietzsche's mother's, aunts', and grandmother's fanatical devotion to religion and their rigorous attempts to force Nietzsche into a life of reli-

gious piety resulted in his misogyny and rejection of societal values (*Untouched* 73-133). Franz Kafka's reactions to his parent's neglect can be seen, for example, in Gregor Samsa's "defenselessness, impotence, muteness, and isolation" in "The Metamorphosis," and the "credulity, naïveté, and trust of a child who is the victim of an insane system of child-rearing" in "In the Penal Colony" (*Thou* 281-89). With Miller's work in mind, we should ask how ghosts and death relate to Rossetti's incest. Marsh is unable to explain what aspects of Rossetti's abuse are evident in her imagery patterns because Marsh has no specific information concerning any actual abuse. She can only speculate that the incest was a "form of mutual masturbation" (260).[4]

Even though Marsh's method is suspect, she does point to an intriguing pattern of recurring themes and images. Is there any explanation other than incest for the ghosts, dreams, nightmares, death, dying, and secrets that recur so frequently in Rossetti's work? Since Marsh specifically refers to, among others, **"A Nightmare"** as indicative of Rossetti's abuse, a careful examination of this poem is in order.[5]

Rossetti published a ten-line portion of **"A Nightmare"** in her devotional work **Time Flies** with the title **"A Castle-Builder's World."** After her death, her brother William discovered another fragment of the poem in one of her manuscripts. He published it in his 1896 collection of her poetry with the following explanation: "In my sister's note-book this composition begins on p. 25, and ends on p. 27; the intermediate leaf has been torn out. Mere scrap as it is, I should be sorry to lose it quite" (383). The fragment read:

> I have a friend in ghostland—
>   Early found, ah me how early lost!—
> Blood-red seaweeds drip along that coastland
>   By the strong sea wrenched and tossed.
>   . . . . .
>
> If I wake he rides me like a nightmare:
>   I feel my hair stand up, my body creep:
> Without light I see a blasting sight there,
>   See a secret I must keep.

In an examination of the publication history of the poem, H. B. de Groot remarks, "The fragment has always been a tantalizing mystery for Christina's biographers and critics. Thus T. B. Swann wrote in a book published in 1960: 'Can the destruction of page 26 mean that the poem dealt with an incident in Christina's life so painful that even the record of it on paper was intolerable?'" (48). Packer, naturally, identifies the incident as Rossetti's love for Scott (112). Since Packer wrote her book, the complete poem, including the passage from **Time Flies,** has been discovered in another Rossetti manuscript auctioned at Sotheby's in 1970. In lines 5 to 26 of the complete version, the speaker describes ghostland as a place of "unended twilight," as a "watery misty place" where "indistinguished hazy ghosts abound" (7, 10, 17). Even so Marsh regards the poem as evidence of incest (257-58).

I will provide another explanation for the striking imagery in this poem. Henry Fuseli exhibited his well-known painting, "The Nightmare," at the Royal Academy in London during the spring of 1782. It met with such rave reviews that "engravings of it were published in the same year and quickly spread its fame all over Europe" (Powell 17). The painting became so popular that cartoonists frequently made use of it for personal and political satires, and went on using it for decades afterwards (17). Sigmund Freud had a copy of it hanging in his Vienna apartment although he never referred to it in his published works (15). In England, "over-familiarity with Fuseli's nightmare image through caricatures and prints led to its devaluation in the later nineteenth century—to such popular travesties as the lithograph of 'The Racing Nightmare,' after a painting by A. C. Havell, published in 1891" (94). After the painting's enthusiastic reception, Fuseli painted a number of variants, but the original painting depicts a sleeping woman who is lying on a bed with her head and arms thrown back over the edge in a gesture not only of exhaustion, but also of sexual submission. On her chest sits what art critics refer to as an "incubus." At the other end of the bed, over the woman's feet, a horse rears its head through the drapery. Its nostrils are flaring, its jaw is slightly suspended, and its eyes glow in the darkness. Given her close ties to the Pre-Raphaelite Brotherhood, Rossetti must have been aware of this painting. Not only does the title of her poem suggest an allusion to the painting, but the speaker's description of a ghostly presence that hovers and alternately compels and rides her, causing her "hair [to] stand up, [and her] body [to] creep" (38), is clearly Rossetti's revisioning of Fuseli's "The Nightmare."[6]

Patricia Laurence, who discusses Virginia Woolf's strategies of silence in *The Reading of Silence,* refers to "The Nightmare" as an early example of the way in which women's bodies speak (129). Although she does not elaborate in regard to Fuseli's painting, her reference to the painting is clearly based on eighteenth-century explanations for nightmares. Powell records Samuel Johnson's definition of "nightmare" as "a morbid oppression in the night, resembling the pressure of weight upon the breast" (49-50). Powell also cites a passage from Sir John Floyer, an eighteenth-century physician, who preferred the term "incubus" to "nightmare": "The incubus is an inflation of the membranes of the stomach, which hinders the motion of the diaphragm, lungs, and pulse, with a sense of weight oppressing the breast" (50). Thus, the horse is not the nightmare, but is rather, as Powell points out, an addition to the painting, intended, no doubt, as a visual pun

on the word (59). Fuseli's painting, then, is a visual representation of what the sleeping woman is experiencing physiologically. The incubus on her chest figures the oppressive weight she feels. Both the horse and the phallic incubus are sexual symbols and the woman's expression and posture do suggest ravishment, which adds credence to Susan Wolstenholme's discussion of the painting as an example of the objectification of women (39-43). Nevertheless, the painting also suggests the woman's unspoken mental experience. Laurence contends that Woolf's exploration of the dream state "adds to our cultural definitions of women, fashioning new modes of subjectivity in which we, as readers, are invited 'to consult our own minds'. . . . In portraying the dreaming mind of a woman, Woolf begins to dissolve the boundaries that enforce oppressive hierarchies like that of 'Man Thinking' and defining what woman is" (124).

In her own way, Rossetti, too, is dissolving boundaries. Her speaker paints Fuseli's picture verbally and in doing so voices what is happening in her mind. An oppressive weight, the incubus, is riding her "like a nightmare" (37). Rossetti may or may not have been aware of the sexually charged language she was using, but why must her use of that language imply that she had intimate sexual knowledge? Of course, the speaker in **"A Nightmare"** claims she sees "a secret [she] must keep," but is that secret incest, or is it the secret of the female poet's mind, which draws upon other works of art to construct one of her own? Wolstenholme sees the woman in Fuseli's painting as "object of representation"; Marsh reads Rossetti's poem as a discourse of repressed memory. I contend that neither explanation is adequate. Rossetti's concern is not the sexual female body, but rather the mental processes of the poet. Her poem demonstrates how the creative imagination of the woman artist is impressed by and in turn transforms the aesthetic traditions exemplified in specific works by male artists.

It could be argued that Rossetti's attraction to images such as those found in Fuseli's painting is itself an indication of sexual abuse; perhaps she was attracted to these images precisely because she found them somehow suggestive of her own experience. But in the absence of corroborating evidence, I regard such an argument as being less than persuasive. One could also contend that the examples of symptomatic reading I have referred to are all found in biographies and that biographers are expected to draw connections between the life and the work. I find it disturbing, however, that symptomatic readings, damaging as they are in the biographies, are by no means limited to that field of study. The history of Rossetti scholarship indicates that there is a persistent tendency to read Rossetti autobiographically and symptomatically no matter what theoretical approach may be favored at the time.

Germaine Greer provides one of the more recent examples of this type of criticism.[7] In *Slip-Shod Sibyls: Recognition, Rejection and the Woman Poet* (1995), Greer claims that the secret to Rossetti's poetry is not her relationships with Collinson or Cayley, not her love for William Bell Scott, not her experience of sexual abuse, but is, instead, the unfulfilled love she felt for her brother Gabriel. As with the biographers I have discussed, Greer's theory is founded on nothing other than her symptomatic reading of Rossetti's poetry. Even more amazing is Greer's tendency to confuse the persona with the person. For example, she states, "One of the recurrent aspects of the love that racks so many of Rossetti's personae is that it dare not speak its name . . . it seems to me rather that she chose a male persona in order to utter the truth about her own complex feelings about sexual passion and about her brother" (370). Clearly, Greer assumes that the speaking voice of the poetry and Rossetti are one and the same.

Bell, Thomas, Packer, Marsh, and Greer, in one way or another, all share the Victorian assumption that Rossetti must have experienced some form of sexual intimacy in order to write, convincingly, poetry of passion and longing. Their arguments also imply that women, Rossetti in particular, lack the imaginative capacity to express what they have not experienced.[8] Bell et al. seem not even to take seriously the possibility that a woman with literary ability might study other works of art or previous literary traditions and then draw upon that aesthetic in the service of her own art. Critics such as these perpetuate Victorian assumptions about women, for example, that they are experiential and emotional rather than imaginative and intelligent. No critic that I am aware of has suggested that Fuseli was sexually abused or frustrated; why, then, is it necessary to assume this regarding Rossetti?

I suggest that readers who are interested in the way a writer's life intersects with her work explore the personae that writer constructs. In doing so, though, we must ensure that we do not fall into the same trap that Greer does in assuming that the persona is the person. Persona criticism, as theorized by Cheryl Walker, connects an author to her work through a persona that is informed by a number of "cultural and literary" voices which may or may not include the author's life and may even contradict what we know about her ("Persona Criticism" 114). Although it may be entertaining to speculate about the personal life of the author, I believe such speculations are rarely of any use to the literary critic. They contribute neither to our understanding of specific texts, nor to our understanding of women authors in general. Indeed, the assumptions involved in symptomatic speculations often serve to reinforce patriarchal values rather than to resist them. I encourage future readers to examine Rossetti's work, not as a record of her life, but as a record of the culture in which she lived and worked. Doing so will open up new perspectives not only on Rossetti's work, but also on the work of other women writers who were struggling with the same constraints to speech as she was.

Notes

1. Georgina Battiscombe in *Christina Rossetti* (1965) was one of the first critics to discuss the difficulties with Packer's Rossetti-Scott hypothesis. She also examined Packer's methodology at length in her own biography of Rossetti published in 1981.

2. Recently the concept of repressed memory has been seriously questioned. Some psychologists are arguing that this type of repression is so rare as to be practically non-existent. See Gorman, Loftus and Ketcham, and Showalter.

3. Only once, as indicated by my research, does Miller seem to deviate from this method. When she discusses Samuel Beckett in *Thou Shalt Not Be Aware,* she discounts his description of his happy childhood because his work so powerfully demonstrates abuse. She does, however, base her claim on the evidence that Beckett's mother daily "forced [him] to examine his conscience because [she] hoped this would bring about a religious awakening" (249). Although Beckett does not realize his mother's actions were abusive, Miller demonstrates that his experience revealed itself as abuse in Beckett's work (249-50).

4. Marsh also refers to Denise J. Gelinas's article "Persisting Negative Effects of Incest." Much of this essay describes the typical family relational pattern that allows incest to occur. Briefly, the mother, who was also abused as a child, abdicates her parental responsibilities. Consequently, her oldest daughter is forced to fill the vacated role and become mother to the other children and wife to the husband, her father. According to Marsh's own account of Rossetti's childhood, this familial pattern does not describe Rossetti's situation.

5. In an article that appeared in 1996, Marsh again discusses "A Nightmare." She makes no mention of Rossetti's possible sexual abuse, but instead argues that the "unseen incubus" in the poem is a common Romantic image and thus an indication of Romantic influence in Rossetti's work (27). She does not refer to Fuseli's painting.

6. I am indebted to Patricia Srebrnik for bringing Fuseli's painting to my attention.

7. For other late twentieth-century examples of symptomatic critical reading see Shaw and Schad.

8. In her examination of the hysterical narrative and its relationship to recovered memory syndrome,

Elaine Showalter briefly discusses Marsh's allegation of Rossetti's sexual abuse and concludes, "Apparently some feminist literary critics still find it hard to accept that women can have cruel fantasies or visions, even though they live outwardly pious lives" (90).

Works Cited

Battiscombe, Georgina. *Christina Rossetti.* Bibliographical Series of Supplements to "British Book News" on Writers and Their Work. London: Longmans, 1965.

———. *Christina Rossetti: A Divided Life.* New York: Henry Holt, 1981.

Bell, Mackenzie. *Christina Rossetti: A Biographical and Critical Study.* London: Hurst & Blackett, 1898.

de Groot, H. B. "Christina Rossetti's 'A Nightmare': A Fragment Completed." *Review of English Studies* 24.93 (1973): 48-52.

deSalvo, Louise. *Virginia Woolf: The Impact of Childhood Sexual Abuse on Her Life and Work.* Boston: Beacon, 1989.

Gelinas, Denise J. "The Persisting Negative Effects of Incest." *Psychiatry* 46 (1983): 312-32.

Gorman, Christine. "Memory on Trial." *Time* 17 April 1995: 40-41.

Greer, Germaine. *Slip-Shod Sibyls: Recognition, Rejection and the Woman Poet.* London: Viking, 1995.

Laurence, Patricia Ondek. *The Reading of Silence: Virginia Woolf in the English Tradition.* Stanford: Stanford UP, 1991.

Lewes, G. H. "The Lady Novelists." *Westminster Review* 58 (1852): 131-36.

Loftus, Dr. Elizabeth, and Katherine Ketcham. *The Myth of Repressed Memory: False Memories and Allegations of Sexual Abuse.* New York: St. Martin's, 1994.

Macdonald, D. L. "Childhood Abuse as Romantic Reality: The Case of Byron." *Literature and Psychology* 30. 1-2 (1994): 24-47.

Marsh, Jan. *Christina Rossetti: A Literary Biography.* London: Jonathan Cape, 1994.

———. "The Spider's Shadow: Christina Rossetti and the Dark Double Within." *Beauty and the Beast.* Eds. Peter Liebregts and Wim Tiggs. DQR Studies in Literature 19. Atlanta: Rodopi, 1996. 21-30.

Miller, Alice. *The Untouched Key: Tracing Childhood Trauma in Creativity and Destructiveness.* Trans. Hildegarde and Hunter Hannum. New York: Doubleday, 1990.

———. *Thou Shalt Not Be Aware: Society's Betrayal of the Child.* Trans. Hildegarde and Hunter Hannum. New York: Farrar, 1984.

Packer, Lona Mosk. *Christina Rossetti.* Berkeley: U of California P, 1963.

Powell, Nicolas. *Fuseli: The Nightmare.* Art in Context. New York: Viking, 1972.

Rossetti, William., ed. *New Poems by Christina Rossetti.* London: Macmillan, 1896.

Schad, John. *Victorians in Theory: From Derrida to Browning.* Manchester: Manchester UP, 1999.

Shaw, W. David. "Poet of Mystery: The Art of Christina Rossetti." *The Achievement of Christina Rossetti.* Ed. David A. Kent. Ithaca: Cornell UP, 1987. 23-56.

Showalter, Elaine. *Hystories: Hysterical Epidemics and Modern Media.* Paperback edition. New York: Columbia UP, 1997.

Thomas, Eleanor Walter. *Christina Georgina Rossetti.* New York: Columbia UP, 1931.

Walker, Cheryl. "Persona Criticism and the Death of the Author." *Contesting the Subject: Essays in the Postmodern Theory and Practice of Biography and Biographical Criticism.* Ed. William H. Epstein. The Theory and Practice of Biography and Biographical Criticism Vol. 1. West Lafayette: Purdue UP, 1991. 109-21.

White, Allon. *The Uses of Obscurity: The Fiction of Early Modernism.* London: Routledge, 1981.

Wolstenholme, Susan. *Gothic Revisions: Writing Women as Readers.* SUNY Series in Feminist Criticism and Theory. Albany: SUNY P, 1993.

Barbara Garlick (essay date 2002)

SOURCE: Garlick, Barbara. "Defacing the Self: Christina Rossetti's *The Face of the Deep* as Absolution." In *Tradition and the Poetics of Self in Nineteenth-Century Women's Poetry,* edited by Barbara Garlick, pp. 155-75. Amsterdam and New York: Rodopi, 2002.

[*In the following essay, Garlick interprets* The Face of the Deep *as both a biblical exegesis and Rossetti's reflection on her own spiritual journey.*]

Christina Rossetti's last prose work, ***The Face of the Deep: A Devotional Commentary on the Apocalypse,*** was published by the London Society for Promoting Christian Knowledge in 1892, two years before her death.[1] It appears to be, certainly from the title page, a fairly standard piece of late-nineteenth-century biblical commentary on a text by which many women writers in particular were both influenced and excited in the period, that is, The Revelation of St John the Divine.[2] However, Rossetti's text is more personal than any standard biblical commentary in its expression of a valedictory mood which relates intimately to and retrospectively illuminates the concerns in her earlier poetry. ***The Face of the Deep*** is not simply exegetical; rather it represents a spiritual journey towards a private absolution. If the definition of apocalypse is an unveiling, or an uncovering, then in this last prose work Rossetti participates in the same process of disclosure as the text by which she is inspired; she becomes a further voice in that series of ventriloquial voices represented by Revelation, which Paul Ricoeur describes as "the original nucleus of the traditional idea of revelation":

> The prophet presents himself as not speaking in his own name, but in the name of another, in the name of Yahweh. So here the idea of revelation appears as identified with the idea of a double author of speech and writing. Revelation is the speech of another behind the speech of the prophet.[3]

Moreover Rossetti's disclosure in ***The Face of the Deep*** is of the profane rather than of the divine self.

Biblical commentary in the nineteenth century, building on the previous century's more empirical view of the Bible as a fallible and human record,[4] gradually strengthened and made more diverse the challenge to traditional exegesis; it became more secular, it questioned sources, it moved into the academy. Certain key moments are familiar: Strauss's *Life of Jesus* (1835; George Eliot's English translation published 1846); *Essays and Reviews* (1860); Matthew Arnold's *Literature and Dogma* (1873); the Revised Version of the King James Bible (1881/85); Farrar's *History of Interpretation* (1886). What all these moments signified moreover was not simply a diversity of approaches, but also that a more direct conduit was now possible between modern writer/commentator and ancient text; centuries of dogma could be set aside in favour of a more personal reading of the Scriptures. That this also valorized women's engagement with the sacred texts was a not always welcome by-product, with Elizabeth Cady Stanton's *The Woman's Bible* (1895/98) being the predictable end-result.[5]

Rossetti's devotional writings, however, like the majority produced by women in the period, are neither revolutionary nor even missionary. Instead they have a consciously domestic air about them; they appear to offer prayers, a reading diary, biblical explanation, and devotional thoughts on the Commandments or on the Benedicite for the already devout. Her work may be seen as part of a strong tradition of women interpreting the scriptures and writing devotional essays (as well as poems), such as Charlotte M. Yonge's articles in the 1850s and 1860s in her *Monthly Packet* in the form of dialogues on the Catechism and the Commandments. While these were aimed at a conservative, domestic and necessarily feminized market, they also provide an antidote to Ruskin's Pauline injunction that women should not engage in theology,[6] a viewpoint which has been as narrowly interpreted by some modern critics. Joel Westerholm, for instance, reads Ruskin's injunction as indicative of a general suspicion of women's devotional writings, even while admitting that "The historical data on Victorian acceptance of a woman's writing devotional prose is not definitive".[7] Despite this reservation Westerholm still appears to be applying Ruskin's narrow view of theology—as a discipline to be taught by means of a classical education—to a more general area of religious witness.

The Face of the Deep is Rossetti's only "commentary" on a biblical text, and while there is evidence in it of wide theological knowledge, with frequent cross-references to other biblical books, and regular comparisons between the Authorised and the Revised Versions in order to tease out some linguistic nicety, the commentary has the appearance of a rambling, almost free-associational, meditation on one person's engagement with Revelation. At times it casuistically plays with ideas prompted by a particular verse or image; it includes her own devotional poems to elaborate on or justify a point; and it frequently expresses a messianic fervour as she moves into prayer rather than commentary. Her readers occupy an ambiguous position, however. In a text which slips almost randomly between the contemplative and the hortatory, the reader is at one and the same time equal partner and audience. As the equal partner on her spiritual journey, the reader is included in generalized statement and rhetorical question as the pronouns, "I", "we", "one", jostle awkwardly. Periodically Rossetti remembers and defers to an implied audience: "But my reader (if I have one) may object" (342).

It is also in this final prose work that we see Rossetti reaching obsessively toward her own truths about the self, its insistent dominance over her thought and actions, and the problematic relation of the self to its most obvious physical manifestation, the face. In seeing "this burdensome body" (185) as the physical focus for her metaphysical quest, she also gestures towards a possible transcendent moment, a stepping through the mirror to confront the beatific vision,[8] not through mystical union in the afterlife, but through language—her own text: "Created loveliness and lustre can be defaced by sin only. Every faithfully good creature abides in its degree as a mirror of God" (187). In order to see face to face, even dimly, the beatific vision of God, Rossetti must first reconcile the other face within the mirror, the exterior self, with the demands and the equivocations of the inner self. The mirror therefore is the medium through which she interrogates the "degree" of her spirituality and the worldly self which threatens it.

The title, *The Face of the Deep,* is ambiguously rich: it points in multiple interpretive directions within the work itself and beyond to both the secular and the devotional poetry. The Book of Job is present throughout the work, not only in Rossetti's early exhortation in the Prefatory Note on the value of patience handed down to her from her mother, to whom the work is dedicated—"this dear person once pointed out to me Patience as our lesson in the Book of Revelations [*sic*]" (7)[9]—but also through specific reference and, most importantly, by providing the title: "The waters are hid as with a stone, and the face of the deep is frozen" (Job 38.30).

The deep is, firstly, Christ: "Christ is our fountain-head and our abyss; we begin from Him, we end in Him." The deep is also likened to the sea, "We . . . pour and empty ourselves and our treasures into Him, yet we enrich Him not . . . 'All the rivers run into the sea; yet the sea is not full'; . . . full it is, yet not filled, and it moans as with a craving unappeasable" (29). More specifically the deep is the face of Christ, of which she exhibits an almost eidetic awareness both here and, more directly, in her devotional poetry from the fifties onwards. In a short, late poem **"The Descent from the Cross"** (1881) Rossetti articulates clearly her mature acceptance of the dubious relation between exterior image and interior depth, a recognition which is at the heart of *The Face of the Deep*:

> Is this the Face that thrills with awe
> Seraphs who veil their face above?
> Is this the Face without a flaw,
> The Face that is the Face of Love?
> Yea, this defaced, a lifeless clod,
> Hath all creation's love sufficed,
> Hath satisfied the love of God,
> This Face the Face of Jesus Christ.
>
> (II, 153-54)[10]

That strength needed to see "face to face" (1 Corinthians 13.12),[11] to look up, is apparently not possible in the early poems, and it is only towards the end of Rossetti's life that the future tense which predominates in the earlier devotional poetry has become present knowledge, as in her own hymn sung at her funeral service:

> Lord, grant us grace to mount by steps of grace
> From grace to grace nearer, my God, to Thee;
> Not tarrying for to-morrow,
> Lest we lie down in sorrow
> And never see
> Unveiled Thy Face.
>
> (II, 204)

The deep is also Christianity, for "a religion without depth is not Christ's religion. The necessity of depth is set forth in the Parable of the Sower" (37). Through Rossetti's present task moreover the text, Revelation, metonymically and paradoxically becomes the deep as she specifies her own position with regard to Christ: "what I write professes to be a surface study of an unfathomable depth: if it incites any to dive deeper than I attain to, it will so far have accomplished a worthy work" (365).

The ambivalence of revelation, which is both light and dark at the same time, is paralleled both by knowledge and by death in the same passage which glosses Revelation 8.10-11:

> And the third angel sounded, and there fell a great star from heaven, burning as it were a lamp, and it fell upon the third part of the rivers, and upon the fountains of waters;
>
> And the name of the star is called Wormwood: and the third part of the waters became wormwood; and many men died of the waters, because they were made bitter.

Rossetti's gloss is, in part:

> For in the text we behold light introducing men to the darkness of death; an emblem of unsanctified knowledge and its tendency. The star is a genuine illuminator: so may the knowledge be genuine knowledge; yet not being mixed with faith in them that hold it, it becomes to them perilous or even deadly.
>
> (252)

Knowledge, for Rossetti, is here purveyed either through speech, "a noble gift entailing a vast responsibility" (253), or, in her case and more importantly, through writing. As she prays for renewal, "O Longsuffering Lord Jesus, curse not our blessings which we have slighted, but renew them to us" (253), she invokes again that centuries-old convention of the writer, the rather disingenuous claim to unworthiness which reappears throughout the work. For Rossetti, however, this is not simply a literary convention. Writing is seen as both the source of her particular sin and as possessing a potentially redemptive power which it is necessary to exploit, in order to mitigate God's wrath at the exercise of her talent; the text itself becomes its own justification. Writing implies interpretation, but "Interpretation is the gift of some, thought of all" (404); interpretation, then, is a problematic gift which may invoke another abyss, that of false doctrine:

> The bottomless pit preaches a sermon. It has a lid: which keep shut, and the pit's bottomlessness remains neutral. But lift the lid, and none can calculate the volume of deathly outcome from a fathomless abyss, or the depth of a fall into it. . . . But if I lift any lid of evil, I have no power to shut off the dire escape from myself or from others: death and defilement I may let loose, but I cannot recapture.
>
> (258)

The antidote to the imminent danger of false prophecy is only indicated in the final pages:

Interpretation may err and darken knowledge . . . Prayer is the safeguard of interpretation, and without interpretation is still profitable. We seem to bring something of our own to interpretation, and if puffed up may destroy ourselves. . . . Interpretation is safe and seemly for some. Prayer is safe and seemly for all.

(549)

The text closes with the separate italicized sentence, *"If I have been overbold in attempting such a work as this, I beg pardon"* (551). Here the redemptive power of the word and the literary convention merge as Rossetti ends with the flourish of two short poems, **"For Each"** and **"For All"**, on the theme of **"My harvest is done"** (551-52).

The progression through a right understanding of vocation, then, arrives at the most alarming of those deeps, that of the self, which is the deep to which the verse from Job seems best to apply. In a work that at least on the surface appears to offer comfort as well as interpreted scripture to the devout reader, the emphasis on selfhood, and particularly on the relation between the self and God—on how the self can remain integrated and yet submit to God—is disconcerting. It is no accident that Rossetti absolves herself of the appearance of self-absorption and pride by invoking the other religious poet to whom she is often compared, "holy George Herbert", quoting from *The Temple* the poem **"Miserie"**, "My God, I mean myself" (226). She follows this quotation with a sentence which both justifies and asserts her emphasis on the self, "God grant us a like self-knowledge and humility" (226). It is only through a searing self-knowledge that she can hope to attain a suitable Christian humility.

In a gloss on Exodus 3.14 which asserts the unsearchability of God, "I am that I am",[12] Rossetti makes clear that the self in all its manifestations is central to her commentary:

[M]an's inherent feeling of personality seems in some sort to attest and correspond to this revelation: I who am myself cannot but be myself. I am what God has constituted me: so that however I may have modified myself yet do I remain that same I . . . Who I was I am, who I am I am, who I am I must be for ever and ever.

I the sinner of to-day am the sinner of all the yesterdays of my life. I may loathe myself or be amazed at myself, but I cannot unself myself for ever and ever.

(47)

Here what appears to be mere egocentricity, an assertion of the primacy of self, can also be seen as a rather masochistic recognition of original sin which intensifies later in the work:

From what do I need deliverance: from punishment? Yes, and from very much besides punishment. If I were saved from the punishment outside me, how save me from the punishment within; from the fire, but how from the worm? Rescued from all else, how rescue me from myself. . . . What I do, I will to do: what I leave undone, I will to leave undone. Who then is it that betrayeth me: Lord, is it I?—It is I.

(78-79)

And again, "Temptations are what I have to overcome, and at the root of every possible temptation I have to overcome myself" (519). The possibility of sin therefore is programmed into the self, and it is incumbent upon the self to overcome its presence and its power.

Up to this point, and indeed throughout *The Face of the Deep,* it is, of course, possible to consider the work and these apparently personal strictures as having a more generalized admonitory purpose, but the personal note is insistent, as it is in her earlier prose work *Time Flies: A Reading Diary,* where the days which have personal meaning for Rossetti, such as birthdays and anniversaries, are made the subject of a more apposite, even intimate, entry.[13] As we learn in her gloss on 14.8 concerning the city of Babylon (the Whore of Babylon):

Temptation, by a common instinct, seems to be personified as feminine: let us thence derive courage; the symbol itself insinuating that as woman is weaker than man, so temptation is never so strong as the individual assailed. . . . We daughters of Eve may beyond her sons be kept humble by that common voice which makes temptation feminine.

(357)

And, in an echo of Ruskin again, "Woman is a mighty power for good or evil. She constrains though she cannot compel" (358). Her attitude to woman's original sin and the reiteration of this misogyny throughout Revelation is at the very least equivocal, however.[14] Like Milton, Rossetti appears to be more poetically inspired in her descriptions of the profane world, which, following Revelation, is gendered female:

For Satan is the showman of her goodly show: he who can himself appear as an angel of light understands how to inflate her scale, tint her mists and bubbles with prismatic colours, hide her thorns under roses and her worms under silk. He can paint her face, and tire her head, and set her on a wall and at a window, as the goal of a vain race, and the prize of a vain victory. . . . so has she her men singers and women singers, her brazen wind instruments and her hollow drums.

(357)

Rossetti is able to envisage a future woman-centred world, however: "Society may be personified as a human figure whose right hand is man, whose left woman. . . . Rules admit of and are proved by exceptions. There are left-handed people, and there may arise a left-handed society!" (410). Her ambivalence about prevailing truisms regarding woman's frailties is further suggested in two late comments on curiosity:

These two instances [Eve and Lot's wife] suggest Curiosity as a feminine weak point inviting temptation, and doubly likely to facilitate a fall when to indulge it woman affects independence. Thus we see Eve assume the initiative with Adam, and Lot's wife take her own way behind her husband's back.

(520)

While not endorsing the actions of Eve and Lot's wife, Rossetti nevertheless is able to accept that there is a positive aspect to the feminine weakness of curiosity, that is, independent action. She extends this positive aspect furthermore by neatly justifying her own text, her present task, and her position as a woman writer through arguing that "To study the Apocalypse out of idle curiosity would turn it, so far as the student's self were concerned, into a branch of the Tree of the Knowledge of Good and Evil" (531). Nevertheless her recognition of the source of responsibility which is in the self is repeatedly emphasized in the text, although the strongly gendered nature of her concern appears to vacillate.

The relation between the self and its most immediate external sign, the face, coalesces in the title of *The Face of the Deep.* Rossetti not only obsessively pursues her anatomizing of the self as she moves through her commentary on Revelation, she also chooses to make explicit the connection between the self and its outward sign:

> I pursuing my own evil from point to point find that it leads me not outward amid a host of foes laid against me, but inward within myself: it is not mine enemy that doeth me this dishonour, neither is it mine adversary that magnifieth himself against me: it is I, it is not another, not primarily any other; it is I who undo, defile, deface myself.

(489)

The pun is surely intentional, given the strong emphasis on visuality and the visual within the text: for example, a discussion of innocence allows her to theorize whiteness, implicitly alluding to Ruskin's "innocent eye" and the truer principles of the pathetic (72-73, 99),[15] and in a long gloss on 1.13-16 she takes the opportunity to probe the relation between colour and light (39).

Recognizing and accommodating the narcissistic self is one of the major concerns in the text: "every sin, fleshly or spiritual, is a sin of idolatry, inasmuch as it is the preference of some object tangible or intangible to God All Good: indeed further reflection recognizes sin as simply the preference of *self* to God" (397). *The Face of the Deep* is thus the culmination of the journey begun in the early poetry.

One of the most intriguing aspects of the early poems is the way in which the poet looks at the self as if in a mirror, whereby the poetic self is both voyeur and protagonist. This specularity is characterized not by embarrassment or by a reluctance to confront the self, but by a keen scepticism and developing self-knowledge which can take account of both libidinal and spiritual desire. The clarity of Rossetti's growing self-awareness—and indeed of her perceptions of others—is seen indirectly in the dramatic dialogues of many poems, as, for example, in **"The Lowest Room"** where the older sister reluctantly acknowledges the emptiness of her asceticism contrasted with the richer world of domesticity lived by her fairer sister. Rossetti's percipience emerges more directly in the Preface to and indeed the title of the sonnet sequence **"Monna Innominata",** and her subsequent dismantling of the love sonnet convention, "there's a problem for your art!" (Sonnet 7). More lightheartedly her two cynical poems about the PRB [Pre-Raphaelite Brotherhood],[16] her amusement at the parody of her poem **"A Birthday"**,[17] and the small poem she sent to William Bell Scott on the publication of his book of poems, an event which took place very soon after the death of her brother,[18] also illustrate her ability to see through pretension—her own and that of others.

Self-knowledge for Rossetti is inexorably linked to the problematic relation between outward appearance and inner turmoil. The five lines which she added to the beginning of **"Mirrors of Life and Death"** on its second publication in 1881 (first published in the *Athenaeum* in 1877) illustrate her developing ability to resolve what she saw as an atavistic paradox:

> The mystery of Life, the mystery
> Of Death, I see
> Darkly as in a glass;
> Their shadows pass,
> And talk with me.

(II, 75)

Here presence and absence are both shadows and both necessary.[19] However, it is the figure of "the sinner double-faced" of the poem **"By the Waters of Babylon B.C. 570"** (June 1864) which orchestrates the many disturbing dualisms directing the thematic energies of the poems of the first two collections, *Goblin Market* (1862) and *The Prince's Progress* (1866), and those poems written up to the mid-sixties but not published until later. The dissociation of self from the shadow or mirror image and of self from other is rarely accepted easily in these poems. In **"A Royal Princess"**, for instance, the mirror image serves to emphasize rather than resolve alienation, figured in the protagonist's distance from the people starving beyond the royal palace with whom she must unite herself to achieve fulfilment even though in death:

> All my walls are lost in mirrors, whereupon I trace
> Self to right hand, self to left hand, self in every place,
> Self-same solitary figure, self-same seeking face.

(I, 149)

The double location in **"A Royal Princess"**—within and beyond the palace walls—provides a spatial figure for Rossetti's repeated trope of the divided self. For Rossetti this self-division is geographically and literally embodied in Italy and England, the countries of her dual heritage. The words on her father's tombstone, for instance, reflect the emphasis in the family on their difference: the first epitaph reads in part "for he shall return no more, nor see his native country" (Jeremiah 22.10), and the second, from Hebrews 11.16, reads "But now they desire a better country, that is, an heavenly". Both geographical and spiritual alienation can only be resolved in the afterlife for Rossetti. That double country leads to the recognition of southern passion and northern reserve in **"Enrica, 1865"**, which is reflected through the face in the emphasis on pure blondeness and light, and in the dubious value of dark hair and hazel eyes, a contrast which had been prefigured in the 1856 poem **"Look on this Picture and on This"**. The dark and the light selves are most terrifyingly evoked in the double face of day and night of **"The World"**, a poem which recalls the many luxuriant descriptions of the Whore of Babylon in *The Face of the Deep*:

> By day she woos me, soft, exceeding fair:
>   But all night as the moon so changeth she;
>   Loathsome and foul with hideous leprosy
> And subtle serpents gliding in her hair.
> By day she woos me to the outer air,
>   Ripe fruits, sweet flowers, and full satiety:
>   But thro' the night, a beast she grins at me,
> A very monster void of love and prayer.
> By day she stands a lie: by night she stands
>   In all the naked horror of the truth
> With pushing horns and clawed and clutching hands.
> Is this a friend indeed; that I should sell
>   My soul to her, give her my life and youth,
> Will my feet, cloven too, take hold on hell?
>
> (I, 76-77)

The face is the visible sign of Rossetti's alienated poetic self; it may be veiled, shrouded, masked, turned to the wall, as, for example, in **"The Convent Threshold"**, **"After Death"**, **"Rest"**, **"The Prince's Progress"**, **"Winter, My Secret"**, **"L.E.L."**, **"Dead before Death"**. It may be downcast, averted or showing the pallor of blighted sexuality as in **"The Iniquity of the Fathers upon the Children"**, **"Light Love"**, **"Goblin Market"**, **"A Portrait"**. False or bold faces are those which look up: Laura of **"Goblin Market"** has a second chance through her second self, her sister Lizzie, but for Jessie Cameron the result of looking up, of being "a careless, fearless girl" (I, 116) is death by drowning.

In Rossetti's devotional poems of this period the face masked or shrouded is shown to be basic to religious consciousness, and the words of Ecclesiastes, the preacher, resonate like a refrain: "vanity of vanities"

becomes an incantation against the seduction of worldly pleasures and the lure of the mirror image. William Rossetti's categorizing of 449 of the poems in the 1904 edition as devotional diverts the reader's attention from Rossetti's complex intermingling of the sacred and profane, seen clearly in **"The World"** quoted earlier. In many of these "devotional" poems Rossetti's Teresa-like and eager acceptance of the love of Christ as bridegroom and her use of the language of profane love, conventionally associated with female religious hysteria, represent yet another deliberate and self-conscious playing out of a drama in which she can legitimately look up face to face with her sacred groom in the final scene. As the physical transmutes through metaphor into the spiritual, the face too becomes steadfast through devotion. Here again though there is anomaly: in that fine and complex poem **"From House to Home"** we move through the ecstacy within the vision:

> Each face looked one way like a moon new-lit,
>   Each face looked one way towards its Sun of Love;
> Drank love and bathed in love and mirrored it
>   And knew no end thereof
>
> (I, 82)

to a post-visionary state not of rejoicing but of a muted triumph only, a precise example of the self engaged in a highly conscious and secular drama:

> Therefore in patience I possess my soul;
>   Yea, therefore as a flint I set my face,
> To pluck down, to build up again the whole—
>   But in a distant place.
>
> (I, 88)

The engagement of the self in this drama, the playing-out of an intercessionary desire—both the desire for intercession and the desire to intercede—focuses in *The Face of the Deep* on that right positioning of the face, whereby the face becomes the metaphor or image of what has been accomplished in a life:

> My page in the Book of Works is to me awful: the contents are my own, the record is not my own. It is my life's record without oversights, without false entries or suppressions: any good set down accurately as good; all evil, unless erased by Divine Compassion, set down accurately as evil. Nothing whatever is there except what I have genuinely endeavoured, compassed, done, been: I meant it all, though I meant not to meet it again face to face. It is as if all along one had walked in a world of invisible photographic cameras charged with instantaneous plates.
>
> (*Face* 473)

In this startling simile Rossetti envisages the mirror self as inescapable, as having had a separate existence through the power of the independent photographic representation. Such a troubling concern recalls Rossetti's role as PRB model and her recognition of the anonymity of that role. Just as biographies seal "as in a magic tank", as Virginia Woolf said in her essay on the centenary of Rossetti's birth, fittingly entitled "I am Christina Rossetti",[20] so do paintings, photographs, drawings depict and fix the sitter in a pose or mood which may have little to do with the model as individual. From the mid-nineteenth century onwards, beginning with the paintings and drawings by her brother and his circle, and culminating in the apparently definitive pronouncements by her brother William, the prolific family archivist, and the influential Edmund Gosse, there have been attempts to define the complexities of the woman and the poet by confining Rossetti to a visual moment,[21] wherein the face is frozen or emblematized. The face thus becomes yet another commodity, item or object where the woman is sign and the signified is masculine creativity[22] or, more generally, a patriarchal worldview. William Rossetti in his "Memoir" which prefaces the 1904 collected edition of the poems, for instance, lists 45 portraits/representations of Rossetti, and elsewhere gives a similar list of representations of Dante Gabriel's wife, Elizabeth Siddall. William states specifically that certain portraits of Christina—and he numbers them—"would afford to any one who sees them a very exact knowledge of what she was like from the age of seventeen onwards" (lxiii, lxiv). This disingenuous leap on William's part between exterior image and interior self—"what she was like"—tellingly endorses Rossetti's recognition of the dangers implicit in reliance on that exterior face and her bitter understanding of the power of the visual seen in her reference to the "invisible photographic cameras charged with instantaneous plates".

We are now used to thinking of the Pre-Raphaelite goddess either as the Elizabeth Siddall figure, or as the later type epitomized by Jane Morris with her luxuriant hair, sensuous lips, strong muscular neck and body and soulful eyes. If we look at the earliest Pre-Raphaelite paintings and drawings though, we find that another very different type predominates: this type has a slight figure and a narrow, straightnosed face, usually dark, and with a clearly defined profile and a serious rather than a sensuous expression. It is Rossetti's face in a variety of guises, both devotional and worldly.[23] While it is not known exactly how many of these paintings and drawings she actually sat for, it is clear that, for a while at least, she represented the type of female beauty preferred by the Brotherhood. The type appears as Queen Elizabeth of Hungary in James Collinson's painting (it is accepted that Rossetti was the model here), as Mary in the first drawing for Millais's "Christ in the House of his Parents" (1850)—and in the final painting possibly as the young Christ himself—and in his "Garden Scene with Girl Cutting a Rose" (1849).

Perhaps the strangest of these depictions is Millais's "St Agnes of Intercession" which was intended for the fifth issue of *The Germ* (which never appeared) to illustrate "a plaintive story by Dante Gabriel Rossetti about a dying girl having her portrait painted by her lover".[24] The two most important representations of her by her brother are "The Girlhood of Mary Virgin", of which Holman Hunt said "Miss Christina was exactly the pure and docile-hearted damsel that her brother portrayed God's Virgin pre-elect to be",[25] and "Ecce ancilla domini" or "The Annunciation". The face or type also appears in many of Dante Gabriel's early Dante paintings and drawings as both Dante and Beatrice, where it becomes exaggeratedly Italianate. Rossetti was also one of Holman Hunt's chosen sitters for "The Light of the World", because he admired "her gravity and sweetness of expression".[26]

While the Rossetti face is represented in predominantly pure and/or sanctified guises, there are also those depictions in which the erotic or the worldly enters more insistently, such as Millais's "Two Lovers: The Woman's Dress Caught by the Thorns of a Rose Bush" (1848), an illustration intended (but not used) for a poem by Thomas Woolner in the first issue of *The Germ*; or Dante Gabriel's "Hesterna Rosa", yesterday's rose. In both drawing and painting the symbolism is overt, the world corrupts and innocence is jeopardized, a drama played out in Rossetti's poem **"The World"** and throughout ***The Face of the Deep.***

Rossetti's mirror image, then, which is in part supplied by these two-dimensional portrayals of her, has itself been through many permutations. She is both the innocent and the worldly, the saintly and the fallen. As if to drive home the point, her own poems are furnished with illustrations which support the worldly rather than the innocent, thereby highlighting the potentiality for a symbolic or allegorical reading. Her brother's illustrations to **"Goblin Market"**, for instance, which emphasize the voluptuous sensuality of Laura and Lizzie, encourage the diversity of readings which the poem has received since its publication.[27]

Portraits of Rossetti as Christina Rossetti—in both drawings and photographs—also present a studied style and persona, which are in part a reflection of the roles she played for the PRB, and in part the development of the poetic role she chose. She is the acolyte, taking "the lowest place" at her mother's knee; eventually she is the sybil of equal power, standing behind the formidably serious maternal figure. My term here is not original: Edmund Gosse recalls that "I have seen her sitting alone in the midst of a noisy drawing-room, like a pillar of cloud, a Sibyl whom no one had the audacity to approach". Alone she is at first the shy innocent and later the forbiddingly melancholy woman with, as Gosse says, the "weary-looking, bistred, Italian eyes".[28] To a large extent the long exposures of nineteenth-century photography demanded an unsmiling pose, but it is nevertheless striking how the photographic poses are reproduced in the drawings: contemplative hooded eyes look downwards or beyond the viewer, the dress is plain, the hair severely parted in a style reminiscent of her mother's.[29] As her reputation matured the sybilline qualities in these representations increasingly underwrite her chosen role of Christina Rossetti, the devout, reclusive writer of hymns, light verse and devotional prose.

Her death, her funeral and her memorial, similarly served the image rather than the poet, by this time an image which was fixed into the narrow frame of the saint. Her funeral was held in Christ Church, Woburn Square, the church where she had worshipped for the last ten or so years of her life and from which her mother was buried. The incumbent, the Reverend Nash, visited Rossetti regularly during her last illness and used her poems set to music in his services. Two of these were sung during her own funeral service. *The Times* obituary stated that "The earnest religious convictions of the deceased poetess were ever translated into daily thought and action, and her life may well be described as saintly in character" (1 January 1895). Lines from one of her hymns sung at the funeral service likewise appear to support *The Times*:

> Lord bring us to that morrow
> Which makes an end of sorrow,
> Where all saints are
> On holyday.

(II, 204)

William Rossetti records that after her death a subscription was taken up for a suitable memorial to her (lix), which consisted of a reredos designed by Burne-Jones, who had been influenced by PRB ideals and who became an associate of Dante Gabriel Rossetti after their meeting in 1856. It was painted by Thomas Rooke, Burne-Jones's pupil and studio assistant. The reredos depicts Christ with the four Gospel evangelists who are recording his words as he consecrates the bread and wine of the Eucharist.[30]

Even in death, it seems, Rossetti the poet was eclipsed by the dominance of the visual sign. That cloying Pre-Raphaelite obsession with particular types of beauty appears in the painting in the familiar faces which had characterized the group's work from the beginning: Christ has the narrow, straight-nosed, contemplative look of the young Rossetti, with markedly feminine bare arms crossed at his breast; Mark and John both have a similarly feminized, but sensuous, look of the later Siddall and Morris figures. The seductive identification with her portrayed roles in which Rossetti indulges in her early poem on St Elizabeth of Hungary, written approximately two years after she had posed for Collinson's painting,[31] has, as we have seen, developed

by the time of *The Face of the Deep* into a clearsighted view of the double face of the mirror, a recognition that the mirror image can never be anything other than an illusion, narcissism is only ever two-dimensional. The memorial painting moreover is doubly ironic: not only does it perpetuate the obsessive power of the exterior image, its subject matter in retrospect is egregiously inappropriate, for it was precisely the Eucharist which provided the greatest agony and stumbling block to the eponymous protagonist of Rossetti's early novella *Maude*. The reredos was doubtless considered a worthy memorial with its emphasis on the chosen and on the recording of the gospels, but in context we can see how this constraining mythicization of Rossetti serves to remove the woman from her work and the emotional diversity reflected in it. In the process moreover it diminishes, however unintentionally, her own position as a female interpreter of scripture, and it colludes with that process of sanctification of the woman who throughout her work indicates how little worthy she feels herself to be of such sanctification.

Rossetti's spiritual journey proceeds not towards sanctification, but towards the incarnation of the face within the mirror[32] to achieve, rather than the limiting dualism to which women are so often confined, that three-dimensional singularity in which there is multitudinousness, of which she speaks in *The Face of the Deep* and which recalls Gosse's description of her as "a pillar of cloud". She says, "A cloud as a cloud is one, while as raindrops it is a multitude" (15). If there is a certain presumption in anticipating by means of her last work the beatific vision normally only allowed to the blessed in heaven, Rossetti nevertheless justifies her textual impertinence by her emphasis on the necessity of the face-to-face confrontation with the self. This confrontation, which mimics that of the beatific vision, is the prerequisite for her own spiritual redemption. The text has enabled her to break through that Dantean forest of obscurity she sees as **"An Old-World Thicket"** (1881), in which "Each sore defeat of my defeated life / Faced and outfaced me in that bitter hour" (II, 125). Working with the male discourse of Revelation paradoxically allows Rossetti in this last work to speak the diversity of self without narcissism and to play out that drama she began in the early poems to its end.

Notes

1. References to *The Face of the Deep* are to page numbers and are placed in parentheses within the text.

2. Northrop Frye calls Revelation "our grammar of apocalyptic imagery", which in part explains its attraction for these writers (*Anatomy of Criticism*, Princeton, NJ, 1957, 141). See, e.g., of the best known, Elizabeth Barrett Browning in *Aurora Leigh*, Charlotte Brontë's *Juvenilia, Jane Eyre*,

and *Villette,* in particular, and Emily Brontë's poems and *Wuthering Heights.*

3. "Toward a Hermeneutic of the Idea of Revelation", in *Essays on Biblical Interpretation,* ed. and intro. Lewis S. Mudge, Philadelphia, 1980, 75.

4. Stephen Prickett also associates this move with a recognition of the "poetic sublimity" of biblical texts, in keeping with Longinus's classical notions of the aesthetic qualities of the Scriptures (*Words and* The Word: *Language, Poetics and Biblical Interpretation,* Cambridge, 1986, 38ff). Cf. also Jowett's essay in *Essays and Reviews* (1860) where the interest is also in the Bible as literature.

5. Elizabeth Cady Stanton was one of the early leaders of the American women's movement, a co-organizer of the 1848 Seneca Falls Convention and longtime associate of Susan B. Anthony. *The Woman's Bible,* published in two parts in 1895 and 1898 was a series of commentaries "on those sections of Scripture which particularly bore on woman's status" (Mary D. Pellauer, *Toward a Tradition of Feminist Theology: The Religious Social Thought of Elizabeth Cady Stanton, Susan B. Anthony, and Anna Howard Shaw,* Brooklyn, 1991, 46). *The Woman's Bible* attempted to redress what Stanton and her collaborators described as "the indictment served on her [woman] in Paradise", considering that the Pentateuch emanated "from the most obscene minds of a barbarous age" (qtd Pellauer, 47).

6. John Ruskin, "Of Queens' Gardens", *Sesame and Lilies* (1865), London, n.d., 127.

7. Joel Westerholm, "'I Magnify Mine Office': Christina Rossetti's Authoritative Voice in her Devotional Prose", *Victorian Newsletter,* LXXXIV (Fall 1993), 12. See also Robert M. Kachur, "Repositioning the Female Christian Reader: Christina Rossetti as Tractarian Hermeneut in *The Face of the Deep*", *Victorian Poetry,* XXXV/2 (Summer 1997), 193-214, for a more nuanced discussion of this issue.

8. See Antony Harrison, *Christina Rossetti in Context,* Chapel Hill, NC, 1988, particularly chapter 3, for an extended discussion of the relation between Rossetti's poetry and Tractarian ideology and aesthetic theory. The concept of the beatific vision had been a subject of dispute for centuries from Aquinas onwards; it is now a standard part of Catholic teaching.

9. It is interesting—and not surprising—to note the pervasive internalizing of patience as a dominant female virtue in the nineteenth century. See, e.g., an early and somewhat bizarre example in Mary Shelley's *Matilda*: "*A little patience and all will be over*" (201). These are Matilda's encouraging words to Woodville in the suicide pact she has set up! Kachur, however, asserts "Rossetti did not succeed in finding Patience in the book of Revelation . . . what she did find was one last opportunity to speak out against the status quo in the church" ("Repositioning", 211).

10. Quotations from the poems are taken from *The Complete Poems of Christina Rossetti: A Variorum Edition,* ed. R. W. Crump, 3 vols, Baton Rouge, LA, 1979-90. References are to volume and page numbers.

11. Dolores Rosenblum deals at some length with the gaze and the subsequent reification of the face in Rossetti's poetry in *Christina Rossetti: The Poetry of Endurance,* Carbondale/Edwardsville, IL, 1986, chapter 3. Inevitably some of my examples will be the same as Rosenblum's, but I wish to go beyond the conclusions of her fine study and show how that specular concern with the face both determines and reflects the dualisms which structure the poetry and through which Rossetti pushes towards the singularity of the self seen in *The Face of the Deep.*

12. This recalls both the title of Virginia Woolf's essay "I am Christina Rossetti", and Rossetti's letter to her brother Dante Gabriel of 13 March 1865 on the imminent publication of the collection *The Prince's Progress*: "*The Prince* shall keep your modification of stanza 2, as regards the main point: though 'I am I' is so strong within me that I again may modify details" (*Three Rossettis: Unpublished Letters to and from Dante Gabriel, Christina, and William,* ed. Janet Camp Troxell, Cambridge, MA, 1939, 142). See also "The Thread of Life", "Thus am I mine own prison . . . I am not what I have nor what I do; / But what I was I am, I am even I" (II, 122, lines 15, 28-29).

13. The entry for Dante Gabriel's birthday, for instance, 12 May, emphasizes the inescapably profane basis of human beauty: "So human love rises and responds to human beauty, excellence, endearment. Yet that to which it rises is not a light-giver, but a shadow-caster: is not God, but man" (*Time Flies: A Reading Diary,* London, 1885, 91).

14. A biographical reading of this aspect could take one of the final lines in this gloss as the motivation for her emphasis on the self throughout the work: "Taking physical corruption as the foul image of sin, we see how it consists not with stability, permanence; but dissolves, disintegrates its prey" (358). This after some years of various illnesses and an imminent operation for cancer of the left breast and shoulder.

15. "The whole technical power of painting depends on our recovery of what may be called the *inno-*

cence of the eye: that is to say, of a sort of child-ish perception of these flat stains of colour, merely as such, without consciousness of what they signify, as a blind man would see them if suddenly gifted with sight" (John Ruskin, *The Elements of Drawing and the Elements of Perspective* [1857], London, 1907, 3-4n). See also, "And the whole difference between a man of genius and other men, it has been said a thousand times, and most truly, is that the first remains in great part a child, seeing with the large eyes of children, in perpetual wonder, not conscious of much knowledge,—conscious, rather, of infinite ignorance, and yet infinite power" (*The Stones of Venice. Vol. III. The Fall* [1853], London, 1907, chapter 2, para. 28, 48). Like Rossetti, Ruskin links right seeing with moral virtue and emphasizes the relation between visual elements and states of mind or passions: "the men who feel strongly, think strongly, and see truly (first order of poets) . . . The greatness of a poet depends upon the two faculties, acuteness of feeling, and command of it. A poet is great, first in proportion to the strength of his passion, and then, that strength being granted, in proportion to his government of it" (*Modern Painters III. Of Many Things* [1856], chapter 12. para. 9, 168; para. 14, 173). See also the whole of chapter 12, "Of the Pathetic Fallacy", and his further comments on Dante and Scott in chapter 16, 283-96). On Ruskin and whiteness, see, e.g., "pure white . . . the sign of the most intense sunbeams . . . it is only the white light, the perfect unmodified group of rays, which will bring out local colour perfectly" (*Modern Painters I. Of General Principles* [1843], London, 1903, Pt 2, Sect. 2, chapter 2, 152, 159). See also his experiments with the white sheet of paper in "Of Turnerian Light" (*Modern Painters IV. Of Mountain Beauty* [1856], London, 1910, chapter 3, 35-38).

16. "So luscious fruit must fall when over-ripe" ("The P. R. B. 2"). William Rossetti, in his notes on these poems, recognizes the "joke", but refutes Rossetti's references to his own part in the failure of the Brotherhood (*The Poetical Works of Christina Georgina Rossetti,* ed. with memoir and notes by William Michael Rossetti, London, 1904, 491).

17. W. M. Rossetti, *Poetical Works,* 481.

18. William Bell Scott, *Autobiographical Notes of the Life of William Bell Scott,* ed. W. Minto, 2 vols (1892), New York, 1970, II, 314.

19. The interesting combination here of biblical (1 Corinthians 13.12) and Shakespearean (*Richard III,* 1.2) reference reinforces Rossetti's struggle with the conflicting demands of the sacred and the secular worlds.

20. "I am Christina Rossetti", in *The Common Reader: Second Series,* London, 1932, 237.

21. W. M. Rossetti, "Memoir", *Poetical Works, passim*; see also Edmund Gosse, *Critical Kit-Kats,* London, 1896, 157.

22. For an extended discussion of this issue see Griselda Pollock, "Woman as Sign in Pre-Raphaelite Literature: The Representation of Elizabeth Siddall", in *Vision and Difference: Femininity, Feminism and Histories of Art,* London, 1988, 91-114.

23. These paintings are discussed more fully in my essay "The Frozen Fountain: Christina Rossetti, the Virgin Model, and Youthful Pre-Raphaelitism", in *Virginal Sexuality and Textuality in Victorian Literature,* ed. Lloyd Davis, New York, 1993, 110-14, which also contains reproductions of many of them.

24. Geoffroy Millais, *Sir John Everett Millais,* London, 1979, 59.

25. W. Holman Hunt, *Pre-Raphaelitism and the Pre-Raphaelite Brotherhood,* 2 vols, London, 1905, I, 154.

26. Diana Holman-Hunt, *My Grandfather, His Wives and Lovers,* London, 1969, 89.

27. Edmund Gosse, e.g., says that "Goblin Market" "is one of the very few purely fantastic poems of recent times which have really kept up the old tradition of humoresque literature . . . I confess that while I dimly perceive the underlying theme to be a didactic one . . . I cannot follow the parable through all its delicious episodes" (149). Compare this with the review in the *Victoria Magazine,* "When Miss Rossetti wings her way to fairyland, she writes charmingly" (XV [June 1870]). Lorraine Kooistra convincingly demonstrates that the poem was read in a number of different ways from its publication until the twentieth century, when it became more closely associated with a juvenile readership ("Modern Markets for *Goblin Market*", *Victorian Poetry,* XXXII/3-4 [Autumn-Winter]), 249-77). This has, of course, changed again in recent years with a diverse range of feminist readings.

28. Gosse, 158.

29. Rossetti's asceticism in dress is parodied by Max Beerbohm in his book of caricatures, *Rossetti and His Circle,* intro. John Hall, new edn, New Haven, CT, 1987, 12.

30. After a chequered career, the reredos, when last sighted, was housed in the vicarage of All Saints' Church, Margaret Street, London W.1.

31. "When if ever life is sweet, / Save in heart in all a child, / A fair virgin undefiled, / Knelt she at her Saviour's feet . . . Fair she was as any rose, / But more pale than lilies white: / Her eyes full of deep repose / Seemed to see beyond our sight" (III, 202).

32. Cf. Luce Irigaray, "Le miroir devrait assister et non réduire mon incarnation" ("Femmes Divines", *Critique,* 454 [March 1985], 301). Lacanian theories of the mirror stage of psychological development and Irigaray's critique of them are clearly implicit in my reading of *The Face of the Deep.*

Diane D'Amico (essay date spring 2003)

SOURCE: D'Amico, Diane. "Christina Rossetti's Last Poem: 'Sleeping at Last' or 'Heaven Overarches?'" *Victorian Newsletter,* no. 103 (spring 2003): 10-16.

[*In the following essay, D'Amico reviews the biographical and historical reasons that William Michael Rossetti—and many critics and biographers after him—regarded "Sleeping At Last" as his sister's last poem, rather than the poem "Heaven Overarches," even though the latter can be more precisely dated as being written c. 1893 than the former.*]

In 1896, two years after Christina Rossetti's death, her brother William Michael Rossetti published **New Poems,** a collection of his sister's previously unpublished or uncollected poems. Included in this collection are two that he identified as the very last his sister wrote: **"Sleeping at Last"** and **"Heaven Overarches."** The titles are William Michael's; Christina had left both untitled. After each poem, appears the date "circa 1893." **"Heaven Overarches"** concludes the section William titles "devotional poems" and **"Sleeping at Last"** concludes the section he titles "general poems." Importantly, in his editorial note to **"Sleeping at Last,"** William also describes it as a "fitting close" to his sister's "poetic performance." Although Dorothy Stuart in 1930 and Margaret Sawtell in 1955 ignore this brotherly preference for **"Sleeping at Last"** and use **"Heaven Overarches"** to conclude their biographies of Rossetti, on the whole, Rossetti scholarship has followed William Michael's judgment. For example, in 1963, Lona Mosk Packer concludes her biography of Rossetti by quoting in full **"Sleeping at Last,"** as does Georgina Battiscombe in 1981, and Kathleen Jones in 1991.[1] Other critics as well echo William in their descriptions of this poem. Jerome McGann, for example, refers to the lyric as Rossetti's "famous culminant lyric" (135), and Dolores Rosenblum describes **"Sleeping at Last"** as the poet's own "valediction" (211). Furthermore, despite Stuart's and Sawtell's efforts to draw attention to

"Heaven Overarches," this other last poem has received little if any critical attention. Obviously, William Michael's opinion has had considerable influence on Rossetti scholarship. Yet thus far no close analysis of his preference for **"Sleeping at Last"** has been done. The purpose of this essay is to offer such an analysis by considering the context in which Rossetti's brother first read these two poems. Such contextualizing suggests that William Michael's judgment was influenced by his own sympathetic and yet troubled response to a beloved sister's breast cancer and a less than sympathetic response to her religious faith. Furthermore, recognizing the role Rossetti's illness and faith played in William Michael's preference for **"Sleeping at Last"** over **"Heaven Overarches"** not only sheds light on those scholarly readings that have followed his, but also suggests new possibilities for future interpretation.

Although William Michael places the approximate date of c. 1893 after both **"Sleeping at Last"** and **"Heaven Overarches,"** in the editorial notes to *New Poems* he clearly indicates that he thinks **"Sleeping at Last"** should be read as the later of the two. Concerning this lyric of a sleeper lying in her grave he writes:

> I regard these verses (the title again is mine) as being the very last that Christina ever wrote; probably late in 1893, or it may be early in 1894. They form a very fitting close to her poetic performance, the longing for rest (even as distinguished from actual bliss in heaven) being most marked throughout the whole course of her writings. I found the lines after her death, and had the gratification of presenting them, along with the childish script of her very first verse **"To my Mother,"** to the MS. Department of the British Museum.
>
> (*New Poems* 388)

This preference for regarding **"Sleeping at Last"** as the final poem is also revealed in his note to **"Heaven Overarches"**: "I found these verses [**"Heaven Overarches"**] rather roughly written in a little memorandum-book. Their date must, I think, be as late as 1893; except 'Sleeping at Last' they appear to be about the last lines produced by my sister" (*New Poems* 392). William's reason, or at least part of his reason, for this dating of **"Sleeping at Last"** is indicated in the note, dated 13/2/95, that he wrote, on the back of the manuscript. However, again his wording indicates that he is in part guessing: "I found these verses at Christina's house in a millboard case containing some recent memoranda, et.—nothing of old date—the verse must *I think* [emphasis mine] be the last Christina ever wrote—perhaps late in 1893, or early 1894."

Unfortunately, William Michael does not record what else was in the millboard case that held the manuscript of **"Sleeping at Last,"** and so we cannot consider all the evidence that he may have used to date the poem. We have available only the text of the poem itself and this manuscript. Both offer only hints as to date. First, the fact that **"Sleeping at Last"** is a roundel may indicate that it was written sometime after the publication in 1883 of Algernon Swinburne's *Century of Roundels.* Swinburne dedicated this volume to Rossetti, and she herself began writing roundels following Swinburne's particular variation on the form not long after this date. *Time Flies,* published in 1885, contains several, and numerous roundels are among the poems included in Rossetti's *Face of the Deep,* published in 1892. Second, the fact that the manuscript is a fair copy written in a steady hand provides something of an end date as to composition. Evidence indicates that Rossetti's handwriting seriously deteriorated during the last months of her life. Margaret Sandars describes Rossetti's letter of 15 September 1894 to Frederick Shields as "shaky and rather illegible" (266); similarly, Jan Marsh describes a letter to Edmund McClure dated October 1894 as a "scrawl" (565). Thus the very precise penmanship of the **"Sleeping at Last"** manuscript places the composition of the poem at some point before the early autumn months of 1894. However, neither the roundel form nor the handwriting confirms William Michael's more precise date of "late in 1893, or early 1894."

Similarly, it is now impossible to consider all the clues William Michael used to date **"Heaven Overarches"**; however, the extant evidence in this case does actually date the poem as being one of the early 1890s. The manuscript of **"Heaven Overarches,"** now held in the Princeton Library collection, is on a small sheet of paper that appears to have been taken out of the little memorandum book that William mentions.[2] On one side of this sheet is a mixture of brief notes, three of which contain dates: 27 October 1891, 23 November 1891, and 28 December 1891. On the other side, appear the lines that William Michael later titled **"Heaven Overarches."** They are in pencil with minor revisions in ink and appear on the right side of the page. On the left-hand side is a list of journal titles and book titles. Among these are the following: "Edinburgh Review—Poems" and "Verses SPCK." A review of Rossetti's volume *Poems: New and Enlarged Edition* did appear in the October 1893 issue of the *Edinburgh Review,* and Rossetti's volume *Verses* was published by the Society for Promoting Christian Knowledge in September of 1893. Such surrounding bits of evidence suggest that William Michael's labeling of **"Heaven Overarches"** as c. 1893 and therefore one of the very last his sister wrote is perfectly reasonable. Yet, the reason that he would date it as most definitely before **"Sleeping at Last"** is not immediately clear, especially since the manuscript of **"Sleeping at Last"** offers none of the obvious references to dates found in the **"Heaven Overarches"** manuscript. When we focus more closely on the fact that William found **"Sleeping at Last"** not long after his sister's death (in his diary he gives the date 13 February 1895), possible reasons for his being disposed

to see the poem as the very last she wrote become apparent.[3] First, although both **"Sleeping at Last"** and **"Heaven Overarches"** draw the reader to thoughts of the afterlife, **"Sleeping at Last"** speaks directly of a woman who has recently died:

> Sleeping at last, the troubles and the tumult over,
> Sleeping at last, the struggle and horror past,
> Cold & white out of sight of friend & of lover
> Sleeping at last.
>
> No more a tired heart downcast or overcast,
> No more pangs that wring or shifting fears that hover,
> Sleeping at last in a dreamless sleep locked fast.
>
> Fast asleep. Singing birds in their leafy cover
> Cannot wake her, nor shake her the gusty blast.
> Under the purple thyme & the purple clover
> Sleeping at last.

(Crump 3:340)

In reading this poem only five weeks after his sister's death, William likely read the "she" of the poem as Christina herself. Furthermore, while the apocalyptic image in **"Heaven Overarches"** of the night that "wrecks you and me" alludes to human suffering, **"Sleeping at Last"** makes daily human suffering a major focus. Thus, quite possibly William saw in the lines speaking of "the struggle and horror," and "shifting fears" something of the physical and mental suffering that his sister had endured during the long process of her dying.

As her death certificate indicates Rossetti died on the 29th December 1894 of "scirrhus of the breast." ("Cardiac failure" is also recorded but appears after "scirrhus" as if a secondary cause.) Significantly, beneath "scirrhus of the breast" is written "2 ½ years operation 25, May 1892." Exactly when Rossetti knew of the cancer is not clear. However, William indicates in his diary entry for 26 May 1892 that she "had had ever since 29 December [1891] some idea of what was in prospect for her." Looking closely at William's response to this surgery reveals how much he perceived his sister's surgery and her slow dying as a "horror."

In his published memoirs, William Michael describes this operation as being of a "very severe kind" and a "truly formidable one" without elaborating (*Poetical Works* lix; *Some Reminiscences* 530). Only in a more private form, a letter to his wife Lucy, written just three days before this operation, does he reveal any details:

> For some little while past, say 2 months, she [Christina] has been conscious at times of a certain sensation in the left breast: it has never once amounted to what she would call pain: and a double lump can be felt. She spoke to Stewart [Dr. William Edward Stewart], who has as yet treated the case with medicines, and she referred to cancer: he did not definitely say that such it

is, but she understands him to imply it. She is now told that severe pain may shortly be expected unless an operation is performed: so on Wednesday it is to be perfomed. I presume the breast, or some large part of it, will be removed. The operator will be Lawson—whom Christina has already seen. . . . Of course she contemplates immediate death as a possibility.

(Selected Letters 555)

In another letter to Lucy he indicates that the operation will take place in Christina's home at 2:30 in the afternoon and that the anesthesia used will be ether. He will be present in the house, although not in the room, at the time of the surgery (*Selected Letters* 556). In this letter he simply mentions "that shocking stage" when referring to the surgery itself. William consistently seems to avoid offering any details of Rossetti's surgery. In fact at times, he appears quite intentionally to avoid mentioning it. Even in letters to friends, whether male or female, he avoids even a vague mention to either breast cancer or this surgery. In a letter to Alice Boyd, dated 17 September 1894, he writes as follows: "It is too true that she [Christina] is exceedingly ill—in fact she is undoubtedly dying, owning to a malady of the heart and other grave matters" (*Selected Letters* 574). In a letter dated 29 December 1894 to Theodore Watts-Dunton informing him of Christina's death, he again stresses the heart ailment: "Her illness was functional malady of the heart, with dropsy in left arm and hand: there was another matter, painful to dwell upon, which I leave in the background" (*Letters* 575).[4]

Clearly, William was deeply troubled by the nature of this other matter. He was, of course, not unusual in his reluctance to speak of breast cancer. Such reluctance lingered well into the twentieth century. Stanley Weintraub in *The Four Rossettis,* published in 1978, appears to be the first biographer to use the word "mastectomy" when trying to decipher William's vague phrases regarding the operation (262). Previous to Weintraub, scholars were far more comfortable simply echoing William's "formidable" operation. For example, Dorothy Stuart refers only to a "formidable operation" (159). Even Georgina Battiscombe in 1981 uses the same phrasing; no mention is made of the possible amputation of the breast (202). Only in the 1990s did Rossetti's biographers begin to state directly that Rossetti underwent a mastectomy, apparently basing that claim on William's letter to Lucy in which he mentions his assumption that the breast will be removed: Frances Thomas uses the word "mastectomy" in her 1992 biography (368), as does Jan Marsh in 1994 (563). Thus far, however, no biographer has offered much information on what this type of surgery meant in 1892. William's comment to his wife that Christina recognized that "immediate death" might result certainly reminds us that surgery in the late nineteenth century was not what it is today.

Although William's diary suggests that he was kept regularly informed by his sister's doctors regarding her health, he offers very few details of this surgery. In fact, the day after her surgery, 26 May 1892, he records the event in very vague terms: "A dreadful complication in Christina's condition came to a crisis yesterday." Importantly, however, in 1881 Dr. George Lawson, Rossetti's surgeon, delivered a paper before the Medical Society of London titled "On the Evil Results which Follow Partial Operations in Cases of Cancer of the Breast." This paper provides some information on the type of operation Rossetti most likely underwent and thus provides us with a sense of what William Michael might have known. In this paper, Lawson recommends not only removal of the breast but the tissue under the arm as well: "If a patient has a scirrhus of the breast, and it is decided that an operation shall be performed for its removal, the whole breast should be excised, and if there be enlarged glands in the axilla, these also should be taken away" (350). He argues that to remove just the tumor is "worse than useless," for such a limited procedure "stimulates the growth of the cancer and hastens the progress of the disease, instead of retarding it" (350). Although Lawson argues strongly for this radical surgery, he indicates that "a pause" of only 5-8 years in the disease's progress might be expected (351). Based on this paper, it seems quite likely that Rossetti agreed to the surgery not expecting a complete cure, but perhaps hoping for several more years of life. And as William's letter to Lucy suggests, Rossetti must have hoped to avoid severe pain. On the subject of pain, Lawson writes, "in some cases the cancer does not return in the same locality, but years subsequently there is a recurrence in some internal organ, and without suffering the patient dies . . . (350-51). Unfortunately, for Rossetti the operation brought neither the five to eight years of life nor a painless death.

Not quite a year later, on 3 March 1893, William Michael records in his diary: "seems only too certain cancer recurring." While at first it seems Rossetti experienced what she herself referred to as "trifling pain" (*Family Letters* 199), that was not the case by mid 1894. William's diary entry for 24 July 1894 reads: "Called on Christina, whose state is now one of considerable suffering, and I fear rapidly becoming critical." About three weeks later on August 15th he describes a dire situation that seems to distress him greatly: "Went to see Christina. She is now in bed, and I greatly fear will not rise again. Spoke to Stewart, who gives a very gloomy and alarming account of her condition. I don't care to enter in the details." At times the pain is controlled by drugs, for William occasionally records as he does for August 23 that Christina is "comparatively free from pain." And in *Reminiscences,* he mentions that during the last stages of the disease, "opiates, more especially solfanel, were freely administered" (2: 531). These "opiates,' however, seem not to have been administered at first or perhaps not in sufficient amounts to control the pain during the autumn months. On 15 September 1894, William writes, "I regret to say that her pain continues on the increase." And on October 6th he writes: "Saw Christina. She confesses now, but only if she is asked about it, to pain that must be called severe, especially in the left shoulder."

A letter William received from one of the Torrington street neighbors strongly suggests that the pain was indeed severe. At the very end of October, Charlotte Stopes wrote to William to complain about "distressing screams" she heard coming from Rossetti's drawing room: "Since my return (to 31 T Sq) on the 17th of Sept. I have been perfectly unable to work, from the distressing screams that sound clear from her drawing room to mine, especially at the hours I have hitherto devoted to writing, between 8 & 11 p. m." (Stopes). A second letter from Stopes, one dated November 4th, indicates that during the last week there had been "no long-continued fits of hysterical screaming" (Stopes). Exactly what occasioned the screams is now impossible to know for certain. As Jan Marsh suggests, it seems most likely that the cries were caused by physical pain, and that their cessation may indicate that William asked Dr. Stewart to increase the dosage of the opiates. However, Marsh also considers the possibility that mental distress played a role as well (566). Several weeks later on December 17th, William Michael describes his sister as "gloomy and distressed." Of course, this "gloom" may have been at least in part a side effect of the drugs being administered. In any case, clearly as William watched his sister die, he was witness to considerable suffering both physical and mental. Indeed, he has moments when he cannot imagine how she continues to live. On 15 November 1894, he writes in his diary: "Her condition of weakness and prostration is so extreme, and her voice so near to extinction, that I hardly understand how it could be possible for her to live more than a day or two."

Throughout Rossetti's illness from the surgery to her last days, William Michael was involved. As indicated above he was in the house when the surgery was performed: he regularly followed his sister's recovery from that surgery: and later when it was clear she was indeed dying, he faithfully visited her every other day for months before her death. Clearly being a witness to such suffering disturbed him deeply. In fact, his diary note for the day of her death is suggestive of his relief that she was no longer in pain: "My noble, admirable Christina passed away about 7:20 a. m. on Saturday (29). Far better so than that she should continue any longer in suffering of mind or of body." He then describes her actual death: "She gave one sigh, and so, in perfect peace, *at last* left us for ever [emphasis mine]." In a letter to Theodore Watts-Dunton, he writes similarly of the peace of her last moments: "My dear good

Christina died this morning—most peacefully at the last" (*Selected Letters* 575). Years later when William Michael describes first viewing his sister as she lay dead, he reveals his relief that the suffering did not, in a sense, show itself: "Her appearance as she lay lifeless was not so very greatly changed as the long duration and severe nature of her malady might have led one to dread" (*Some Reminiscences* 2: 533). He seems to have found some comfort in her calm appearance in death.

Significantly, **"Sleeping at Last"** is a poem in which the idea of death is comforting for the speaker, that is, for the one who now imagines the dead woman lying at peace in her grave. Appropriately, the key phrase of this roundel is strongly reminiscent of a lullaby. In fact, **"Sleeping at Last"** was used by Anna Montague as the title of a slumber song published in 1878. Certain lines of Rossetti's poem might easily be read as the expression of a parent relieved that a sick child is finally sleeping peacefully: "Singing birds in their leafy cover / Cannot wake her, nor shake her the gusty blast." The tone of **"Sleeping at Last"** is appropriate to one who has recently watched over a loved one's long illness.

William was not actually present at the moment of death, but apparently based his description of his sister's last hours on what was told him by Harriet Read, Rossetti's nurse-companion. Read records her own description of Christina's last day in a letter to Mrs. Hake: "[B]ut I would not wish her back. Poor darling she is at last with her dear Lord and all whom she loved so well, although she said several times in her illness she loved every body and was so fond of her god child Miss Ursula and wishes her well. I am sorry to say she was obliged to be fastened down the same night she died in the morning" (Read). Since Harriet Read told Rose Hake, a family friend, of the need to restrain Christina, it seems likely she conveyed this information to William Michael as well. The fact his diary makes no mention of this fastening down is not surprising since the diary was to be something of a public document: he published sections of it as an appendix to *The Family Letters of Christina Rossetti*. The image of his sister having to be tied to the bed the night before her death is not an image he wants to offer the public. Rather it is the image depicted in **"Sleeping at Last,"** an image of a woman whose suffering has now ended. William Michael's diary entry recording Rossetti's death offers further insight into why he favored **"Sleeping at Last"** over **"Heaven Overarches,"** for it reveals something of his questions regarding the Christian belief in an afterlife. While Harriet Read speaks of Christina being with "her dear Lord," William sees her death more in terms of loss: she "left us for ever." Although William did not consider himself to be an atheist, he saw "theism" as an "unfathomable mystery" (*Selected Letters* 235). More specially, Christianity was not a religion he could at all embrace. He wrote to Mackenzie Bell not long after her death of these matters: "Deeply as I have always reverenced her [Christina's] attitude of soul on religious matters, I don't in the least share her form of belief—not partaking of the Christian faith at all" (*Selected Letters* 578). Not surprisingly, the doctrine of hell was particularly problematic. In *Reminiscences* he writes of hell as "not a wholly comforting prospect," deciding that in comparison to such a possibility the "quiet expectation of extinction" is to be favored (534). Even the joyful side of Christian cosmology, a heaven where all the redeemed would be reunited with those loved on earth, was not something he could easily imagine. While he was willing to entertain the idea of "ghosts" in some form, he considered that the possibility of "personal immortality" was "exceedingly slender" (*Selected Letters* 443).

William's view that the "longing for rest" rather than the "bliss in heaven" characterized his sister's poetic performance is most likely due in part to his own doubts regarding such "bliss." Although Rossetti does indeed have numerous poems that speak of the rest to be found after death, poems of the "bliss" of heaven are also numerous. An entire section of her last collection *Verses,* a collection of devotional poems, is devoted to telling of such bliss: New Jerusalem and its Citizens. Significantly, when Christina wanted to dedicate *Verses* to her brother, he declined her offer because he did not "share the same beliefs in full" (*Family Letters* 193).

Considering that William was in a sense not fully responsive to his sister's devotional poetry, it is not at all surprising he favored **"Sleeping at Last"** over **"Heaven Overarches."** Unlike the speaker of **"Sleeping at Last,"** the speaker of this other last poem directly calls the reader to remember Christ's promise of resurrection of the body and entrance of the redeemed into heaven:

> Heaven overarches earth and sea,
>   Earth-sadness and sea-bitterness;
> Heaven overarches you and me:
> A little while, and we shall be
> (Please God) where there is no more sea
>   Or barren wilderness.
>
> Heaven overarches you and me
>   And all earth's gardens and her graves:
> Look up with me, until we see
> The day break and the shadows flee
> What tho' tonight wrecks you and me,
>   If so tomorrow saves?

(Crump 3: 339)

The first stanza calls to mind the Chosen People of God trusting in His promises. The overarching heaven recalls the rainbow of God's promise after the flood (Genesis 9:13), and the landscape of bitter sea and barren wilderness echoes Exodus 15:22-25. (Moses while leading his people through the wilderness first finds only the "bitter waters" to drink until God indicates that he must throw a tree into the waters to make them sweet.) Moreover, the second stanza serves to point to the promise of the New Testament. The fourth line of this stanza is taken directly from Song of Solomon 2:17: "Until the day break, and the shadows flee away, turn my beloved, and be thou like a roe or a young hart upon the mountain of Bether." The Song of Solomon is traditionally read by many Christians in terms of their belief in the Second Coming of Christ, and thus one can read "day break" as the day of that Second Coming, the day when the sorrows, "shadows," of this world would pass away.

Although William Michael respected his sister's faith, this call to hope in salvation would not have evoked a sympathetic response from him. William's agnosticism also well might have influenced how he interpreted the mental anguish Christina exhibited towards the end of her life. Although he allows for the effects of "opiates," as a possible explanation, he places more emphasis on her religion and what he appears to see as its failure to comfort (*Reminiscences* 2:532). In his 1904 memoir, he creates a disturbing image of the weeks before her death: "the terrors of her religion compassed her about, to the over clouding of its radiance" (*Poetical Works* lix). In *Reminiscences,* he again writes of her "troubles of soul," and he blames the clergyman Charles Gutch for increasing her fears, describing him as "foolish and unfeeling" (2:534). David Kent has convincingly challenged this view of Rossetti's death as one clouded by despair in his recent article "Christina Rossetti's Dying," reminding us that William's own agnosticism and anticlerical views might have "blinkered" his eyes (94). If William in some way blamed either the clergy or Rossetti's Christian faith for some of the distress he saw as she lay dying, all the more reason for him to, in a sense, resist **"Heaven Overarches."**

Although William Michael was certain both that **"Sleeping at Last"** was his sister's last poem and a fitting one to be used to bring closure to her "poetic performance," there is a slight sign that he feared that in giving it such prominence he might be misrepresenting her religious faith. In a collection of Rossetti's poems for Macmillan's *Golden Treasury Series,* a collection published in 1904, he includes a brief section titled "The Aspiration after Rest." Not surprisingly he places **"Sleeping at Last"** in this section. But importantly, he includes the following note: "As a subsidiary to the Devotional Poems come these few pieces in which an aspiration for rest after the turmoil of this mundane life is more marked than the yearning for heavenly bliss. As to these cognate topics, it may be remarked in general that Christina's poems contemplate (in accordance with a dominant form of Christian belief) 'an intermediate state' of perfect rest and inchoate beatific vision before the day of judgement and the resurrection of the body and sanctification in heaven" (ix). Clearly although he found **"Sleeping at Last"** to be a more appropriate closing poem for his sister than **"Heaven Overarches,"** he did not want to create the impression that Christina did not believe in the resurrection from the dead.

Indeed, if one reads **"Sleeping at Last"** within a Christian framework, one sees inferred a divine presence that brings such sleep. For example, the comforting text Wisdom 3:1 comes to mind: "The souls of the righteous are in the hand of God and there shall no torment touch them." And the tone of weariness is especially reminiscent of certain of the Psalms. For example, the "struggle & horror" of line three echoes slightly Psalm 55:5 in which the psalmist expresses his fear of death: "Fearfulness and trembling are come upon me and horror hath overwhelmed me." The "tired heart downcast or overcast" is a descriptive phrase that might be applied to the voice heard in several of the psalms. For example Psalm 42:5 speaks of the troubled soul: "Why art thou cast down, O my soul? and why art thou disquieted within me?" Most significantly, however, the key word "sleep" brings to mind Psalm 127:2: "He giveth his beloved sleep." This biblical text recurs in Christian hymns and poetry. For example, Elizabeth Barrett Browning, a poet Rossetti much admired, uses it as both an epigraph and a refrain in her poem "The Sleep." Rossetti herself had used this biblical text in an earlier poem **"When my heart is vexed I will complain,"** published in 1875. In this poem the line from Psalm 127 is spoken by Jesus:

> Peace, peace: I give to my beloved sleep,
> Not death but sleep, for love is strong as death:
> Take patience; sweet thy sleep shall be,
> Yea, thou shalt wake in Paradise with Me.
>
> (Crump 1: 228)

One might argue, therefore, that although resurrection is not mentioned in **"Sleeping at Last,"** it is implied if the poem is read with a Christian context in mind. Furthermore if one reads this poem in the context of other Rossetti poems that focus on the waiting time before resurrection, one might not imagine this sleeping person as entirely without some awareness of the spiritual realm. Elsewhere in Rossetti's poetry on death, she reveals that she was able to represent in one poem two spaces for the dead: the grave with the body lying at rest beneath the earth, and a place above the stars in a twilight world of paradise where the soul might be singing. For example, in **"Better So"** the person who has died is described as "fast asleep" with a "heart at rest," and yet the speaker states, "angels sing around thy singing soul" (Crump 3:283). In **"Let them rejoice in their beds,"** Rossetti depicts the dead both "underneath the daisies" and "far above the stars" (Crump 2:286).

William's editorial decision, however, to place **"Sleeping at Last"** in the general section of Rossetti's poems rather than devotional while understandable, since no direct mention is made of a Christian heaven, tends to discourage any reading that might see the grave as merely a part of a larger spiritual landscape. Thus far critics have tended to follow his primarily secular reading of the poem by arguing that the poem is one about the sorrows of this life and a desire to escape those sorrows. Moreover, critics have also tended to employ the biographical approach suggested by William's linking of the poem with Rossetti's last days. For example, Margaret Sandars suggests that the poem reveals that Rossetti herself as she neared death was "utterly weary" (268). Eleanor Thomas offers a similar reading, seeing in the poem Rossetti's "longing for a culmination which would end not only months of utter weariness and recurrent pain but also years of ill health, of mental conflict, of conscious separation from loved ones" (117). Similarly, the three biographers who use the poem as closure, Lona Mosk Packer, Georgina Battiscombe, and Kathleeen Jones, also interpret **"Sleeping at Last"** as an expression of Rossetti's own longing for the rest of death after a painful life. Jones, for example, argues that by the end of Rossetti's life the "external existence of religious ritual, conformity and submission" had "won" and that **"Sleeping at Last"** is proof that when dying Rossetti viewed death "not as a triumph but as a release" (232-233). As these readings suggest, there is a tendency to read the poem not simply as a fitting close to her months of painful dying but as fitting close to the whole life. Furthermore, the whole life is read as William read her death; in other words, the implication is made that Rossetti's faith somehow failed her.

No critic, as far as I know, has yet even entertained the idea that in **"Sleeping at Last"** Rossetti is writing about someone else. Yet the speaker of **"Sleeping at Last"** need not be seen to be writing about her own death. There is a slight tone of detachment that suggests a distance between speaker and the "cold & white" corpse, as if the poem is to be read at the graveside. Indeed, Rossetti's lyric is reminiscent of Shakespeare's "Fear no more the feat of the sun," the song from the grave scene in *Cymbeline*. If William's supposition that the poem might be as late as 1894 is correct, then something of Rossetti's awareness of her own approaching death certainly may be reflected in the subject and tone of the poem. However, it is quite possible that someone else's death actually provided the occasion for writing the poem. For example, William's wife Lucy died in April of 1894 after a long period of illness. Perhaps Lucy was in Rossetti's thoughts as she composed this poem of the sleeper "out of sight of friend & of lover."

Despite the need to consider both **"Sleeping at Last"** and **"Heaven Overarches"** for more than the autobiographical impulse, quite likely the use of these lyrics as closing poems for Rossetti's life and/or poetic work will continue. This seems especially likely in the case of **"Sleeping at Last."** When a selection of Rossetti poems is included in an anthology of British poetry **"Sleeping at Last"** often appears as the final poem. Such is the case in the most recent edition of the *Norton Anthology of English Literature, Victorian Anthology* edited by Dorothy Mermin and Herbert Tucker, published in 2002, and *The Longman Anthology of British Literature,* published in 2003. On the other hand, **"Heaven Overarches"** is not even included in these anthologies. Clearly, William Michael's preference for **"Sleeping at Last"** as the poem to bring closure to his sister's "poetic performance" still influences contemporary scholarship. Perhaps as more attention is drawn to Rossetti's religious poetry, **"Heaven Overarches"** will begin to appear in the privileged position of last poem.

In either case, whether **"Sleeping at Last"** or **"Heaven Overarches"** is seen as Rossetti's valediction, we need to keep in mind William Michael's role in dating these poems, especially in terms of **"Sleeping at Last."** Second, if we are going to continue to read either poem biographically, we should use the evidence we do have to place the poems more precisely in terms of the life. For example, if we are connecting these poems to Rossetti's last illness, we should be more specific about that illness and the treatment she had undergone. Although William Michael was vague on this point, there is no need for scholars to follow his reticence. Furthermore, recognizing the ways in which both brotherly grief and religious doubt influenced William's response to these last poems should serve as a caution. For whether we use **"Sleeping at Last"** or **"Heaven Overarches"** as closure for Rossetti's life or work, the choice we make will reflect our purposes and perceptions. For example, if we wish to stress a world-weariness heard in many of Rossetti's poems, then **"Sleeping at Last"** with its image of the sleep of death might seem more appropriate than **"Heaven Overarches"** with its call to look beyond gardens and graves. However, if we wish to depict Rossetti as an important religious poet for the Victorian Age, then **"Heaven Overarches"** might appear to be the better choice. In either case, the poem we select may function more as our last statement to Rossetti than her last statement to us.

Notes

1. The most recent biographies of Rossetti do not mention either "Sleeping at Last" or "Heaven Overarches," although the convention of concluding with a poem is still followed. Frances Thomas chooses "My harvest is done, its promise is ended" to conclude her 1992 biography *Christina Rossetti,* as does Jan Marsh to conclude *Christina Rossetti: a Writer's Life* published in 1994.

2. R. W. Crump also lists a "fair copy" of "Heaven Overarches" as being held in the Bodelian Library collection. However, Steven Tomlinson of the Bodelian Library has informed me that there is no record of this fair copy ever having been a part of the Bodelian collection. Unfortunately, I have been unable to locate its whereabouts and have therefore been unable to examine it.

3. All quotations from William Michael Rossetti's diary are taken from the manuscript now held in The University of British Columbia Library in the Angeli-Dennis Collection.

4. The dropsy William refers to in this letter may have been the result of the breast surgery. Lymphodema, a swelling of the arm and hand, sometimes results after a radical mastectomy.

Works Cited

Battiscombe, Georgina. *Christina Rossetti: A Divided Life.* London: Constable, 1981.

Crump, R. W., ed. *The Complete Poems of Christina Rossetti.* 3 vols. Baton Rouge: Louisiana State UP, 1979-1990.

Jones, Kathleen. *Learning Not to Be First: The Life of Christina Rossetti.* Gloucestershire: The Windrush Press, 1991.

Kent. David A. "Christina Rossetti's Dying." *The Journal of Pre-Raphaelite Studies* 5 (Fall 1996): 83-97.

Lawson, George. "On the Evil Results which Follow Partial Operations in Cases of Cancer of the Breast." *Proceedings of The Medical Society of London.* Eds. Thomas Gilbart-Smith and Edmund Owen. London, 1881. 349-353.

Marsh, Jan. *Christina Rossetti: A Literary Biography.* London: Jonathan Cape, 1994.

McGann, Jerome. "The Religious Poetry of Christina Rossetti." *Critical Inquiry* 10 (1983): 127-144.

Packer, Lona Mosk. *Christina Rossetti.* Berkeley: U of California P, 1963.

Read, Harriet. Letter to Mrs. M. R. D. Hake. 4 January 1895. Additional MSS 49470 f198. British Lib., London.

Rosenblum, Dolores. *Christina Rossetti: The Poetry of Endurance.* Carbondale: Southern Illinois UP, 1986.

Rossetti, Christina. *The Family Letters of Christina Georgina Rossetti.* Ed. William Michael Rossetti. 1908. New York: Haskell House, 1968.

———. "Sleeping at Last." Additional MSS 34813, folio 42-41v. British Lib., London.

———. "Heaven Overarches." Box 1, folder 8. Rossetti Collection of Janet Camp Troxell. Princeton University Library, Princeton.

Rossetti, William Michael. "The Diaries of William Michael Rossetti." Angeli-Dennis Collection. University of British Columbia, Vancouver.

———. ed. *New Poems, Hitherto Unpublished or Uncollected.* London: Macmillan, 1896.

———. ed. *Poems of Christina Rossetti.* London: Macmillan, 1904.

———. ed. *The Poetical Works of Christina Georgina Rossetti with a Memoir and Notes by William Michael Rossetti.* London: Macmillan, 1904.

———. *Selected Letters of William Michael Rossetti.* Ed. Roger W. Peattie. University Park: Pennsylvania State UP, 1990.

———. *Some Reminiscences.* 2 vols. 1906. New York: AMS Press, 1970.

Sawtell, Margaret. *Christina Rossetti: Her Life and Religion.* London: A. R. Mowbray, 1955.

Sandars, Mary. *Christina Rossetti.* London: Hutchinson, 1930.

Stopes, Charlotte. Letter to William Michael Rossetti. 31 October 1894. Angeli-Dennis Collection. University of British Columbia Library, Vancouver.

———. Letter to William Michael Rossetti. 4 November 1894. Angeli-Dennis Collection. University of British Columbia Library, Vancouver.

Stuart, Dorothy Margaret. *Christina Rossetti.* London: Macmillan, 1930.

Thomas, Eleanor. *Christina Georgina Rossetti.* New York: Columbia UP, 1931.

Thomas, Frances. *Christina Rossetti.* Hanley Swan, Worcester: Self-Help Publishing Association, 1992.

Weintraub, Stanley. *The Four Rossettis: A Victorian Biography.* London: W. H. Allen, 1978.

Debra Cumberland (essay date 2004)

SOURCE: Cumberland, Debra. "Ritual and Performance in Christina Rossetti's 'Goblin Market.'" In *Things of the Spirit: Women Writers Constructing Spirituality,* edited by Kristina K. Groover, pp. 108-27. Notre Dame, Ind.: University of Notre Dame Press, 2004.

[*In the following essay, Cumberland delineates Rossetti's exploration of "the role of Christian ritual as a means of empowerment to women" in "Goblin Market."*]

Christina Rossetti's poem **"Goblin Market,"** composed in 1859 and published in her 1862 volume, **Goblin Market and Other Poems,** has received more critical response than any of her other works. The poem recounts the tale of two young sisters, apparently living alone, who are tempted by evil goblin merchant men. Laura gives in, nearly dies as a result, and is saved by her sister Lizzie. William Michael Rossetti claimed that his sister did not mean anything profound by the poem,[1] while the critic Mrs. Charles Eliot Norton referred to **"Goblin Market"** as "one of the works which are said to defy criticism."[2] Despite these assertions, critics have discussed **"Goblin Market"** as (among other things) a diatribe against capitalism, a celebration of lesbian love, an early analysis of anorexia nervosa, and a "commentary on the shaping of Christina Rossetti within the Victorian literary marketplace."[3] The richness of the poem, however, accommodates yet another interpretation, one that emphasizes the performative nature of **"Goblin Market"**: a poem intended to be felt and enacted as an embodiment of the construction of a faith rather than to transcribe a straightforward religious message.

The study of Laura and Lizzie's religious performances—in other words, the enactment of their faith—is important to understand women's religious sensibility in nineteenth-century England. Despite prohibitions against engaging in theological debate (described by John Ruskin as the "dangerous science for women"), women nonetheless often looked to transform biblical exegesis by reappropriating sacred imagery. Lizzie's enactment of Christ's passion and her Eucharistic offering of herself to Laura is experienced primarily through her physical being rather than through language. Her faith is acted out and interpreted through the body, much in the manner of mystics such as Julian of Norwich, who depicted Christ as a nurturing mother, "in whome we be endlesly borne."[4] Mysticism appealed to women such as Rossetti since it offered an alternative vocabulary that needed no interpretation from a higher authority. **"Goblin Market"** thus explores the role of Christian ritual as a means of empowerment to women. The religious performances in the poem become the catalyst for creative and personal autonomy.

By rejecting the patriarchal, commercial values of the goblins with their gold-plated dishes, Rossetti instead reclaims the power of sacred myth and ritual for Laura and Lizzie, and hence for all women, when they take on the ancient roles themselves and retell the stories on their own terms. When the sisters gather later in life to recount their experiences to their little ones, their husbands are mentioned but not seen, and the sisters do not mention God; instead of asking their little girls to look to Christ for help, they ask them to look to each other, for "there is no friend like a sister."[5] God-given power is found in a narrative celebrating women's outwardly directed sacred powers, much as Christ's passion would be narrated and performed within the Christian Church.

Ritual is an important aspect of **"Goblin Market,"** for it is through ritual that Laura and Lizzie gain power and understanding of themselves and learn to interpret their world. According to Mircea Eliade, "Rituals are symbols in actual reality; they function to make concrete and experiential the mythic values of a society, and they can therefore provide clues to the mythic values themselves. Hence rituals *act,* they perform, modulate, transform. . . . [S]ymbolic items and places in rituals are transformations of the ordinary into the extraordinary."[6] As Eliade implies, there is a strong connection between performance, theater, and ritual, meaning that ultimately every religious worship service and ritualistic action has performative dimensions. This is especially clear in the context of medieval mysticism, where the performance of one's religion was often a means of gaining power and authenticity for women.[7] The term *performance,* of course, covers a wide range of meanings and activities, including dance, music, sport, and work, all of which have their own rituals. As Richard Schechner and Willa Appel suggest, performance offers "transformation of being and/or consciousness" whereby the performers and the spectators are often transformed, either "permanently, as in initiation rites, or temporarily as in aesthetic theatre."[8] When an audience weeps through a play, or a family participates in a community ritual, they are, for a brief moment, transported into another reality and subtly shaped and changed through their leap of faith into another realm and time. By telling family stories that have been handed down through the generations and participating in community ceremonies, we gain strength and insight through connectedness with each other and through our attempt to recapture (as Eliade notes) a past sacred moment in the present.

Barred from participating in theological discourse, women needed to seek out other means of interpreting Scripture.[9] Thus Christina Rossetti presents her readership with a narrative that embodies and reenacts Christ's passion rather than engaging in discussion and analysis. In short, she chooses to embody faith. As a result, Rossetti not only reclaims Christian ritual for women through Lizzie's own reenactment of Christ's sufferings but potentially offers the same transformative experience for her audience. John Keble, Victorian sermon writer and author of the popular *The Christian Year,* also believed in the sacramental power of poetry, whereby words could enact a change within the reader, much as God's word enacts change.[10] Readers therefore have the opportunity to share Laura and Lizzie's experience of the sacred through the body—auditory and oral (the experience of reading aloud/listening) as well as emotional (the transformative potential of reading as incantatory a piece as **"Goblin Market"**).

As Jan Marsh notes, **"Goblin Market"** "demands that it be read aloud," for "half the pleasure of the verse is lost if read silently."[11] D. M. R. Bentley hypothesizes that **"Goblin Market"** was written to be read aloud to

an audience of fallen women and Anglican Sisters at the St. Mary Magdalene Home for Fallen Women at Highgate Hill, where Christina Rossetti worked as an associate sister before the publication of ***Goblin Market and Other Poems*** in 1862.[12] The performative power of the piece also was evident to Rossetti's contemporaries. Alexander Macmillan, Rossetti's publisher, read the poem out loud to his wife and family to see if they liked it as much as he did. Macmillan wrote to Dante Gabriel Rossetti that he had read it to a "number of people belonging to a small working-man's society here [Cambridge.] They seemed at first to wonder whether I was making fun of them; by degrees they got still as death, and when I finished there was a tremendous burst of applause. I wish Miss Rossetti could have heard it."[13] Christina also refers to a reading in a letter to her brother Dante Gabriel: "Have you heard about the Goblin Market reading? It comes off tomorrow at the Queen's Concert Rooms," to which, she notes, "Mama and Maria intend to go."[14] These stories indicate that Rossetti's work relies heavily upon a communal, ritualistic understanding of performance and the reading act as a shared experience, much as the hearing of the spoken word of God in a church service would have the effect of transforming the listener/reader. As a result, her work often defies logical analysis, since it relies largely upon a more emotional and embodied understanding of faith. Critics looking for linear, rational plots have, as a result, often been confused.

In 1881, when Rossetti published ***A Pageant and Other Poems,*** featuring **"The Months: A Pageant,"** as a drawing room piece, some critics responded by seeking rational explanations for the plot. D. M. Stuart notes in her biography, *Christina Rossetti,* that ***The Pageant*** was "written at the request of Maria Francesca's sisterhood."[15] **"The Months: A Pageant"** was performed at the Albert Hall "and elsewhere," though Stuart notes that "the only defect is one of monotony" and states with relief that no other plays sprang from her pen, since ***The Pageant*** reads as if the "characters come on and announce themselves like the tyrants and patriarchs of a medieval drama."[16] Rossetti's dramatic sensibilities lay in the direction of the medieval: the miracle play, for instance, with which **"The Months: A Pageant"** has dramatic affinities. In fact, the same complaint Stuart wields against *The Pageant* is often heard in regard to **"Goblin Market"**: that there is no logical explanation for why things happen. Rossetti's interest was not really in creating a plot-oriented narrative but in dramatically re-creating key aspects of Christianity: temptation, Eucharist, redemption. She attempted to make the experience as vivid to her readers as if they were experiencing it for themselves firsthand by creating a mythic landscape strong in ritualistic, performative language.

Much of Rossetti's poetry is, in fact, set up as opposing characters having a conversation. This conversational colloquy lies at the heart of the meditative exercise. Many of her poems, such as **"The Hour and the Ghost,"** **"Christian and Jew: A Dialogue,"** and **"The Three Enemies,"** are written in dialogue form. As Louis Martz notes, the meditative poem is "a work that creates an interior drama of the mind; this dramatic action is usually . . . created by some form of self-address, in which the mind grasps firmly a problem or situation deliberately evoked by the memory, brings it forward toward the full light of consciousness, and concludes with a moment of illumination, where the speaker's self has, for a time, found an answer to its conflicts."[17] As Martz explains, the poetry of meditation was given form in the spiritual exercises of St. Ignatius and was adopted by British poets Southwell, Donne, Crashaw, and Herbert, all of whom Rossetti read as a young woman and copied into her own verse-books.[18]

This meditative mode of poetry for Rossetti has a powerful, dramatic, and transformative capacity, for meditation has the ability to re-create spiritual events within the self and thus transform the self. Martz explains that "meditation . . . brings together the senses, the emotions, and the intellectual faculty of man: brings them together in a moment of dramatic, creative experience."[19] Rossetti's most meditative poems reenact Christ's passion as if she were a participant. As a result, they have the capacity through the dramatic reenactment within the poem to inscribe the passion and Christ's suffering onto the reader's own psyche, most notably through questions in the poem that demand answers. In **"Behold the Man!"** Rossetti asks, in recreating the crucifixion, "Can Christ hang on the cross, and we not look?"—demanding that the reader too place him- or herself dramatically and imaginatively back at the moment of Christ's suffering. In **"The Descent from the Cross,"** Rossetti likewise asks the reader to re-envision Christ's moment of death: "Is this the Face without a flaw, / The Face that is the Face of Love?" (3-4). Rossetti's imposition of the sacred experience, written from an "if I were there" perspective, effectively inscribes the experience upon the reader's heart and mind.

"Goblin Market" borrows from these performative qualities inherent in the meditative mode, both in its dramatic reenactment of sacred events and in its transformative qualities. Part of the transformative power of **"Goblin Market"** springs from its free-form rhythm and structure, so expressive of an individual self. No less a critic than John Ruskin was unnerved by the absence of order in Rossetti's verse. Rossetti was fond of a more free-form verse, while Ruskin favored a tidier line. He objected to the irregular metrical freedom in Christina's verse and to its distinctive musicality. When Dante Gabriel sent **"Goblin Market"** to Ruskin for his opinion, Ruskin responded,

> I sate up till late last night reading poems. They are full of beauty and power. But no publisher—I am deeply grieved to know this—would take them, so full are they of quaintnesses and offenses. Irregular measure (introduced to my great regret in its chief willfulness by Coleridge) is the calamity of modern poetry. The *Iliad*, the *Divina Commedia*, the *Aeniad*, the whole of Spenser, Milton, Keats, are written without taking a single license or violating the commonplace for metre: your sister should exercise herself in the severest commonplace of metre until she can write as the public like.[20]

Ruskin here associates regularity and conformity with order, control, and economic success (writing as the public liked and expected), while Rossetti, in practicing an irregular rhythmic style, chose a path celebrating an independence of spirit that valorized the feminine, the rhythmic, and the sensual. Ruskin's criticism thus sets up the essential dilemma enacted in **"Goblin Market"**: the commercial values of the spirit, embodied in the goblins, as opposed to Lizzie, who follows the path she finds the least corrupting, no matter what the lure.

Rossetti's independent spirit, captured both in her form and in her celebration of female spirituality, intrigued, baffled, and occasionally alarmed reviewers. Most reviews were complimentary, with the most unequivocal praise coming from Mrs. Charles Eliot Norton. Norton praised Rossetti as a "mystic" in her 1863 review of **"Goblin Market,"** citing Rossetti's ability to link the everyday world with the supernatural, rendering a "vivid and wonderful power" akin to "The Rime of the Ancient Mariner."[21] Other reviews, more guarded, were in keeping with the *Saturday Review*'s anonymous critic, who maintained that "**Goblin Market**" was a "story of too flimsy and insubstantial character to justify or to bear the elaborate detail with which it is worked out."[22] This "flimsy character," however, is a part of its ritualistic element, for the point of the poem is not the character of Laura and Lizzie but their enactment of a faith, the "mysticism" that Mrs. Norton praised. As in "The Rime of the Ancient Mariner," to which Norton compared **"Goblin Market,"** the characters reenact a sacred event and capture its meaning through ritualistic storytelling at the end of the poem.

The ritualism of **"Goblin Market"** is first expressed through the incantatory sound of its language and the manner in which it is performed. Lizzie's enactment and embodiment of Christ, as she offers herself Eucharistically to Laura, valorizes the feminine, performative dimension of mysticism over the goblins' rational, corrupt materialism. Rossetti accomplishes this first through an exploration of the spoken word. As in church ritual, such as a priest/minister's performance of a communion, marriage, or baptism, Rossetti is interested in drawing attention not so much to what is *said* as to what is *reenacted* as a result of what is being said: in other words, the performative element of language. She draws attention to sound in terms of how people speak and how people react to what is spoken. For instance, the goblins "sound like doves," only the sound is deceptive. However, when Laura and Lizzie leave their safe home and head out to do their errands, Laura is fooled by the goblins' cries and refuses to listen to Lizzie's warnings.

Laura's capacity for temptation says as much about her spirituality as it does about the goblins' deceptive nature. Rossetti herself notes in her spiritual tract **Letter and Spirit** that one of the first injunctions in the commandments is to "Hear O Israel; The Lord our God is one Lord."[23] As Rossetti comments, Eve's problem is that by being, through birth, "gracious and accessible, she lends an ear to all petitions from all petitioners."[24] Laura is unable to discriminate and interpret accurately what she hears. Like Eve, she lacks the capacity for proper interpretation through these senses, and this leads to her transgression.

Attentive critical interpretation is especially important in **"Goblin Market"** because the seductive rhythmic quality of the verse is intentionally calculated to confuse both Laura and Lizzie, as well as the reader.[25] **"Goblin Market"** begins by confronting the issue of interpretation as performance. How does an audience interpret and understand what it sees and hears? How do we accurately name and understand what we are presented with in the world around us, whether on a stage, on a page, or within our own home? Rossetti casts her audience in the same situation as the two girls: the audience must listen to the long, lush, musical rendering of twenty-nine recited orchard fruits, "All ripe together / In summer weather" (15-16), and decide how to interpret what they hear. As Rossetti's poems, such as **"The Descent from the Cross,"** place the reader at the moment of crucifixion, so here Rossetti places the reader at the moment of temptation and seduces them alongside Laura and Lizzie. Part of **"Goblin Market"** thus becomes a reclaiming and cleansing of the senses in order to force the reader to be aware and hear, see, and accurately learn how to interpret the sacred.

The incantatory quality of Rossetti's verse obscures that the girls—and the poem's readers—are outside a normal understanding of space and time. Her lush language seduces, causing Laura (and by implication the poem's readers) to believe that it is possible for pears, plump greengages, apples, oranges, and "plump unpecked cherries" to be "all ripe together in summer weather." The mythic quality of the world in **"Goblin Market"** is further elaborated by Lizzie's urgent question, "Who knows upon what soil they fed their hungry, thirsty roots?" (44-45). By heightening the mystery of origins, the poem leads the reader to realize that the world of **"Goblin Market"** belongs to the mysterious, the unnatural—even the mythic. This collapse of the ordinary rules of time is another example of how sound seduces in **"Goblin Market,"** enticing Laura to forget that contemplating the origins of things—the soil upon which the goblins feed—is key to understanding spiritual truths.

Not initially seeing the fruit, Laura and Lizzie first hear the fruit described by the goblins: "Morning and evening / Maids heard the goblins cry / Come buy our orchard fruits, / Come buy / Come buy" (1-4). The warm, open vowel sounds, the long litany of repeated fruit, urge the reader to linger alongside Laura and feast over the words: "Apples and quinces, / Lemons and oranges, / Plump unpecked cherries" (5-7). The doubleness of the sounds makes it difficult to distinguish one fruit from another, just as it becomes increasingly difficult for Laura to distinguish right from wrong. As the goblins insinuate, the fruits are "Sweet to tongue and sound to eye" (30). They sound good, they taste good, but their fundamental nature is, in fact, anything but good.

Laura is transformed as she *listens* to the goblins; crouching in the rushes, she hears them, "pricking up her golden head" (41). Transformation is the effect that hearing the word of Christ is supposed to have upon the listener, of course, as is easily noted in much Christian ritual, where the singing of hymns or the spoken and written word of God transforms the errant soul and leads him or her back to the fold. Laura's transformation is not of this nature, for only Christ can truly transform. Lizzie's "veiled . . . blushes" (35) indicate that she is attracted by the goblins' seductive, musical cry, but Laura responds in a manner more appropriate to answering the call of Christ: she bows her head in prayer-like submission. Laura, however, submits to the goblins, not to God. The goblins seduce her through their proper ritualistic props, imitative of Christian ritual: one goblin "weaves a crown" (99), and one "heaved the golden weight of dish and fruit" (102-3), in parody of communion. While Laura lingers, Lizzie, knowing that their "offers should not charm us," responds by thrusting "a dimpled finger / In each ear, shut eyes and ran" (67-68), blocking herself off from the goblins' sensory assault that is slowly transforming her sister.

In setting up this dichotomy between the girls and the goblins (the pure love of Christ as opposed to the feast the goblins offer), Rossetti contrasts the rational and commercial world of the goblins, lugging their dishes and their plates, with the prerational, feminine world that she celebrates. The Oxford Movement, with its burgeoning interest in ritual, mysticism, and the medieval, valorized mysticism for its feminine qualities. John Keble's Tract 89, "On the Mysticism Attributed to the Early Fathers of the Church," celebrates the mystical and irrational, as opposed to the "common sense and practical utility" that Keble calls "the very idols of this age," an age he describes as full of "hurry and business."[26] The Oxford Movement's celebration of more feminine, mystical elements in Christianity alarmed some, such as Charles Kingsley, who found the movement effeminate and as a result called for a more "muscular Christianity." By contrast, the Oxford Movement did in fact find a place for women in the Anglican sisterhoods, which, despite their limitations, fostered feminine communities, female friendships, and women's right to choose—although the choices were still limited. Rossetti herself valorized the role of the contemplative above the role of the wife, for "Her maker is her Husband, endowing her with a name better than of sons and of daughters."[27] Rossetti contrasts a female meditative approach to spirituality with the goblins' crass commercialization of Christian ritual with their shrill cries of "come buy, come buy" and their appropriation of Christian symbols (dishes and plates) for commercial uses.

Rossetti makes this distinction clear by her emphasis upon the goblins as "merchant men" (474) and by their commodification of Laura's body.[28] Laura gives in to the goblins after they "clipped a golden lock" (126) from her head in exchange for the money that she does not have. She eagerly sucks "their fruit globes fair or red: / Sweeter than honey from the rock, / Stronger than man-rejoicing wine, / Clearer than water flowed that juice: / She never tasted such before" (128-32). However, as with Eve's new-found knowledge when she tastes the fruit, Laura finds that her knowledge comes with a price. The next day, heading to the bank, Laura discovers that although she listens, she cannot catch "the customary cry," with its "iterated jingle / Of sugar-baited words" (230-34). Lizzie, however, can hear the goblins' fruit-call, but she "dare not look" (243). When Laura realizes that she can no longer hear the cry of the goblin fruit merchants, she turns "cold as stone" and fears that she has "gone deaf and blind" (259). The goblins' seduction has rendered her powerless by cutting her off from the sensory world. Laura peers through the "dimness, nought discerning" (262), and loses the capacity to perform her daily household tasks: "She no more swept the house, / Tended the fowls or cows, / Fetched honey, kneaded cakes of wheat / Brought water from the brook: / But sat down listless in the chimney-nook / And would not eat" (293-98). She grows gray, her tree of life "withering at the root," and becomes incapable of performing her domestic tasks with Lizzie. Her seduction has stripped her of her creative, interpretative self, leaving her as good as dead to her world.

Laura's illness is significant, for the housework that Laura and Lizzie perform is celebrated through Rossetti's heightened language as a sacred and consecrated act, performed in a particular manner, and part of the rhythmic pattern of the sisters' lives.[29] The tasks are part of the ordinary makeup of their lives as well as an act ordering and consecrating their household. The domestic rituals of milking, kneading, fetching water, and airing out the house sustain, purify, and structure their world and serve to reflect the quality of that natural order. They do not stay out past twilight, a time significant in that it separates night from day, or the world of the goblins from the world of the girls. As they sleep, they are depicted not simply as two sisters curled up for rest but as images that conjoin purity and power: "two blossoms on one stem, / Like two flakes of new-fall'n snow, / Like two wands of ivory / Tipped with gold for awful kings" (188-91). Nature guards and smiles upon them benevolently, the wind sings a lullaby, the moon and stars gaze down at them, and owls and bats flap discreetly so that they sleep peacefully.

The contrast Rossetti draws between the girls and the goblins reflects the two modes of being Eliade identifies in the world: those of the sacred and the profane. The girls' world, belonging to the domestic, harmonious with nature, wholly distinct and other from that of the goblins, evokes the divine, the sacred, while the goblins' world, associated with the secular world of the commercial, evokes the profane. The sacred, however, exists not only within the domestic space inhabited by Laura and Lizzie, but also within the sisters themselves: the sacred is housed within them. Laura dwindles because her "fire" has been burned away by her contaminating encounter with the goblins. As Rossetti writes, "But when the moon waxed bright / Her hair grew thin and gray; / She dwindled, as the fair full moon doth turn / To swift decay and burn / Her fire away" (276-80). Rossetti uses "fire" elsewhere in her writings to refer to Christ as a "fire of love," emblematic of the mystic's passion for union with the divine. Laura's inability to think and feel has plunged her into a "dark night of the soul"; she loses her ability to hear and see ("gone deaf and blind" [259]) and, as a result, her ability to perform her household rituals, effectively cutting her off from the sacred. Her symbolic loss of virginity at the hands of the goblins also reflects the religious notion of virginity as a key to the contemplative life, an inner "spiritual state," as Elizabeth Petroff notes, "that makes visions possible"[30] in the contemplative's union with the divine. Thus the goblins not only lull Laura in through their false, melodic cries but gain their ultimate control over her by making her incapable of hearing and interpreting.

Unlike the sisters, Jeanie dwindled and died through an encounter with the goblin men. She died because she, like Laura, read the wrong meaning into the goblins and thus "took their gifts both choice and many" (159). As a result, she "who should have been a bride; / But who for joys brides hope to have / Fell sick and died" (313-15). The key word for Rossetti here may be *gift*. Unlike the goblin merchants, Lizzie offers herself to her sister with the right attitude, freely and out of love, with no expectation in return. Her fruit therefore heals instead of harms. The goblin fruit only serves to commodify and corrupt human and divine relationships.[31] Its transformative powers lead to a slow withering away, as opposed to the fruit of Christ, which has the power to transform and heal.

The erotic element in Laura and Lizzie's relationship is further evidence of their spirituality, much like the sublimated erotic relationship between the worshipper and the divine, a longing for the Godhead that often manifested itself in highly sexualized language and imagery. One example would be of St. John the Divine, who described his communion with God as laying "his head on his lover's breast," the lover being Christ, just as Laura and Lizzie lie "cheek to cheek and breast to breast / Locked together in one nest" (197-98). The sisters' differentiation springs from how they interpret the world, for physically they are practically identical.[32] Some critics, such as Germaine Greer, interpret this "doubleness" as suggesting a lesbian identity.[33] Rossetti quotes extensively from the erotic, mystical Bride/ Bridegroom imagery of the Song of Songs in all of her devotional texts, and *Letter and Spirit* uses similar language in its description of the mystic seeking divine love: "Her spiritual eyes behold the king in his beauty; wherefore, she forgets, by comparison, her own people and her father's house. . . . She loves Him with all her heart and soul and mind and strength; she is jealous that she cannot love him more; her desire to love Him outruns her possibility, yet by outrunning it enlarges it."[34] The sublimated eroticism in this passage is similar to the relationship that Laura and Lizzie have to each other, where their personalities are so fused that they are described as "locked together in one nest."

The fruit listed at the beginning of the poem is an emblem of erotic love as well as sin and hence also has this double quality, which becomes differentiated through interpretation. Temptation through fruit, of course, recalls Eve and sin, but the apple can also be connected to Christ, as in the Song of Songs, which in its most traditional interpretation (certainly common in the nineteenth century) was an allegory of the church's longing for God. In the Song of Songs, the lover sits beneath the shade of the apple tree, which is compared to Christ. The anonymous eighteenth-century hymn, called "Jesus Christ the Apple Tree," arranged by Elizabeth Poston, depicts Christ in similar language: "The tree of life my soul hath seen / Laden with fruit and always green. / . . . / The trees of nature fruitless be / compared with Christ the apple tree." Christ here is connected to the apple, which brings life and health, not sin. As the hymn reads, the fruit of the apple tree pro-

vides restoration, as opposed to the goblins' fruit, which causes Jeanie to die and Laura to waste away, for "This fruit doth make my soul to thrive / It keeps my dying faith alive."[35] Laura, while hungering for more, grows thin and wastes away, but Lizzie, who does not "open her mouth lest the goblins should cram a mouthful in," thrives. The key difference between the two, however, is not that Laura ate and ate till she could eat no more and that Lizzie kept her lips shut but that they have different interpretations of what the fruit signifies. The fruit thus is the fruit of sin as well as the fruit of Christ. The apple and the rest of the fruits are neither good nor evil but both, because each element in the poem has the capacity to be both. Laura's capacity for misinterpretation (her inability to read accurately the signs of grace in the natural world, as the Tractarians remind us) can be mimicked by the audience, calling attention to the precarious, unstable quality of salvation. The story could, and often does, turn out quite differently, depending upon the power of interpretation that the reader/ audience brings to the experience.

Like Laura and Lizzie, the reader must also learn to accurately interpret the goblins. Just as the fruit symbolizes both the fruit of sin and the fruit of Christ, Laura and Lizzie learn that the goblins may sound like "doves" (77) as well as sounding "shrill" (89). The goblins in fact are constantly shifting; they do not seem to have a stable identity. When they spy Lizzie, the goblins come toward her, "Flying, running, leaping, / Puffing and blowing / Chuckling, clapping, crowing, / Clucking and gobbling, / Mopping and mowing, / Full of airs and graces, / Pulling wry faces, / Demure grimaces, / Catlike and Rat-like / Ratel and wombat-like / Snail-paced in a hurry" (331-44). Many of these descriptions are contradictory, and many involve both masculine and feminine characteristics. "Demure" certainly sounds stereotypically feminine, as does "pulling airs and graces." Others, particularly the words connected to animals, such as "rats" and "wombats," remind us of the Pre-Raphaelite Brotherhood, the circle of artists surrounding Christina Rossetti and her brothers, Dante Gabriel and William Michael Rossetti. Wombats were, of course, Dante Gabriel Rossetti's favorite animal; the entire menagerie might be found at his home, Cheyne Walk, another speculation that critics cite to compare the goblins to the Pre-Raphaelite Brotherhood.[36]

Who or what the goblins represent is not as important as their means of wielding power over the two girls through the use of masks. Rossetti clearly indicates that the goblins are intentionally altering their features for an intended effect: "pulling wry faces" and "demure grimaces" and moving "catlike" and "ratlike" in an attempt to simulate a foreign identity. Ronald Grimes defines masking broadly enough to include any "body transforming device concerned with the head area . . . for masking is the making of a second face, often used for concealing identity and wielding power."[37] The goblins wield such power over Laura. The use of masks, Grimes notes, increases the power of performance; the goblins' myriad facial expressions and gestures can be interpreted as springing from the desire to conceal identity and wield control by appearing as something Other. This Otherness lends them the element of mystery, of seduction, perhaps even of the transcendent. Lizzie, through her ability to accurately read the goblins as evil ("We must not look at goblin men / We must not buy their fruits" [42-43]), gains power over the goblins through this ability to identify and name them, which in turn gives her the strength to resist their assault.

Lizzie's ability to accurately read the goblins' true nature grants her God-like powers: an ability to transform herself and the world around her. Salvation in **"Goblin Market"** comes through Lizzie's reenactment of Christian ritual: taking on and performing the role of Christ.[38] Such a reenactment of Christian ritual, described by Eliade, seeks a "reactualization of the same mythical events," and with "each reactualization" humanity "has the opportunity to transfigure" human existence in the present.[39] While Lizzie does not literally nail herself to a cross, her gesture is equivalent in female terms: she leaves herself vulnerable by placing her body in danger at the goblins' hands. She allows herself to be assaulted in order to take back the restorative fruit. The goblins "[k]icked and knocked her" (428), "mauled and mocked her" (429), "scratched her" (427), and "pinched her black as ink" (427) as they turn to violence in an attempt to make her eat. However, Lizzie's affliction (an attempted rape rather than Laura's seduction), willingly undergone for another, is depicted as the source of her strength, for as she crosses the bank, on her pilgrimage, she sees and hears in a new way: "for the first time in her life / [She] began to listen and look" (328-29), Rossetti writes.

Lizzie's heightened awareness and performance as Christ transform her physical being and move her into the realm of the sacred. She is no longer described in relation to her sister, in terms of twos, "like two blossoms" (188) or "two flakes of new-fall'n snow" (189), but in language linking her to Christ. She is "white and gold" (408), the colors of purity; like a lily (409), a flower linking her to Easter and Christ; and "like a rock" (410), the phrase Christ used to describe Simon Peter, as the rock upon whom he would build his church. Lizzie is also described as a "beacon left alone / In a hoary roaring sea" (412-13), another link to Christ, who is described as the light of the world. Lizzie recognizes her power, for she, even under the goblins' assault, "Would not open lip from lip / Lest they should cram a mouthful in: / But laughed in heart to feel the drip / Of juice that syrupped all her face" (431-34). Lizzie's sacrificial gesture is one not of passivity but of choice; her silence is not powerlessness but strength.

As **"Goblin Market"** makes clear, Lizzie's new-found strength overwhelms the goblins; defeated by her resistance, they vanish: "Some writhed into the ground, / Some dived into the brook / With ring and ripple, / Some scudded on the gale without a sound, / Some vanished in the distance" (442-46). Lizzie's defeat of the goblins has caused some critics to compare **"Goblin Market"** to fairy tales,[40] where, after the heroine performs her task, the harsh conditions she endured mysteriously vanish, and happiness is restored, usually through the betrothal of the prince and the princess. Rossetti, however, revises this form by emphasizing that the strength Lizzie gains through self-knowledge leads to spiritual enlightenment. The trials both sisters endure are similar to the tasks enacted in the Bible as a part of a trial or test of spirituality, a honing of the will and the mind: Christ's sojourn in the wilderness for forty days and forty nights, Abraham's trial on Mt. Moriah with his son Isaac. Lizzie's task is to bridge the two worlds of the sacred and profane and offer, like Christ, nothing less than herself. What she brings to the world is her knowledge. Lizzie also offers herself to Laura in an echo of Christ's words: "She cried 'Laura,' up the garden, / 'Did you miss me? / Come and kiss me. / Never mind my bruises, / Hug me, kiss me, suck my juices / Squeezed from goblin fruit for you'" (464-69). Lizzie's ritual reenactment of the Eucharist in this scene is not simply a proffering of the body and blood of Christ but an offering of herself as the Eucharistic food, gained through her strength, self-sacrifice, and love.[41]

Lizzie's offering of her body as a Eucharistic feast is in the medieval tradition; C. W. Bynum has observed the medieval association of Christ's body with female bodies, both giving nourishment.[42] The Eucharist is, of course, as Grimes notes, the most sacred and ritualistic of gestures in the Christian tradition. Christians who "eat the ritual body and drink the symbolic blood ingest power which resides in the elements as a result of the primal sacrifice and the subsequent priestly consecration of the elements."[43] In return for the power consumed, devotees are to make their lives a "living sacrifice," as Lizzie does with Laura. Laura recognizes the quality of this ritualistic sacrifice, for when she hears Lizzie's words, she starts "from her chair, / Flung her arms up in the air, / Clutched her hair: / "Lizzie, Lizzie, have you tasted / for my sake the fruit forbidden?" (475-79). This exchange between Laura and Lizzie contrasts with the goblins' feast, which brings death instead of life. In *The Face of the Deep,* Rossetti speaks of the word of God as a nourishing substance, telling of a young woman who, when dying, "fed on the Word of Life, being evidently fed with food convenient for her."[44] Elsewhere, she asks that all might receive "the sincere milk of thy word"[45] and pleads, "O Christ our God, remember Thy strong and weak ones, great and small, men and women for good. Remember the nursing Fathers and nursing Mothers of Holy Church."[46] Rossetti thus looks to Christ's maternal behavior for an understanding of the sacred.

As Elizabeth Petroff notes, "[T]he process of visions taught women not to sacrifice their desire but to transform it" so that their ultimate desire would be directed toward a divine union.[47] Rossetti contrasts this pure, healthy eroticism, celebrated through Lizzie's offering of herself, to the carnal knowledge gleaned at the hands of the goblins. Communion is celebrated as a gift; we receive Christ's offering and, in return, freely offer up our own lives. Laura, at Lizzie's bidding, "kissed and kissed and kissed her with a hungry mouth" (492) until "Swift fire spread through her veins, knocked at her heart, / Met the fire smouldering there" (507-8), and she falls down at last, "Pleasure past and anguish past" (522), her sister's gift curing her. The passionate ecstasy Laura experiences in **"Goblin Market"** is evoked elsewhere in Rossetti's spiritual writings, where she speaks of consuming the body and the blood of Christ as part of a loving relationship leading to divine union. As Rossetti asks in one prayer, "[G]ive us grace, I implore Thee, to discern Thee spiritually in the most Blessed Sacrament of Thy Body and Blood; to receive Thee into souls prostrate in adoration, to entertain Thee with our utmost love."[48] Christ's sacrifice is thus reenacted in **"Goblin Market"** through Lizzie and Laura's loving relationship.

Christ's sacrifice is also understood through enactment of his suffering and physical pain. Lizzie's illness likewise attests to Rossetti's emphasis upon affliction as a process toward spiritual growth. Public displays of such suffering become one means of validating and authorizing spiritual experience. Lizzie's and Laura's afflictions gain meaning and authenticity because the girls witness them and interpret their meaning for each other. Rossetti understood the significance of suffering and public witness and instructed her readers to suffer, in her spiritual tract *Time Flies*. Referring to Christ, Rossetti wrote: "His natural and His spiritual life began one with privation, the other with suffering. Let us not be too eager to lie soft and warm, or too chary of undergoing pain."[49] Suffering and the desire to suffer properly for God were connected with the saint's spiritual journey and path to saintly power. Victorian sermon writers such as Thomas Keble also referred to the necessity of affliction along the path to spiritual growth: "[C]omprehending as one may almost say the dying words of the Savior, the not merely benefit, but the absolute *necessity* of affliction in some shape or other, to wean our hearts from worldly affections, and to turn them to God, is most energetically set forth."[50] That growth, however, comes at great physical and mental cost. In Laura's case, she must suffer a near-death experience to understand her sister's sacrifice; in Lizzie's, her spiritual power is validated through her abuse at the hands of the goblins, which gives her the authority and power to heal her sister. In so doing, Lizzie embodies the Victorian feminized Christ, who was often depicted as a compassionate healer, the "great physician," "characterized by 'feminine' attributes of compassion, pity and sympathy."[51]

Such an emphasis upon affliction, suffering, and abuse as steps toward spiritual growth reveals a seemingly contradictory flight into the body, as well as a desire to escape traditional expressions of female sexuality without shame, a plight apparent to Christina Rossetti through her work as an associate sister at Highgate Hill. By "performing" as Christ, women are able to evade the fate of heterosexual sex and motherhood. While Laura and Lizzie do have children in **"Goblin Market,"** they seem to appear minus any fathers, which recalls the invisible father of the Incarnation and the Immaculate Conception. Salvation occurs through the intimate relationship with another woman, rather than a man, and a communal sense of shared experience, not through any doctrine or representative of the institutional church.

At the end of the poem, Laura and Lizzie function, it seems, much like an Anglican sisterhood. The Anglican sisterhoods also celebrated women's shared experience and women's narratives. Rossetti's work as a volunteer at the St. Mary Magdalene Penitentiary in Highgate Hill, a home for fallen women, gave her "access to a uniquely feminocentric view of women's sexuality and simultaneously opened her eyes to its problematic position in Victorian culture."[52] The women joining Anglican sisterhoods were engaging in a radical act, for they chose to "reject the law of the father" by choosing a heavenly bridegroom rather than an earthly one and by living in a community of women forgoing marriage and childbirth. Christina Rossetti's own sister, Maria, was a member of an Anglican sisterhood, and Rossetti throughout much of her life lived in a household composed of women: her mother, her sister (until she moved into the Anglican convent), and her aunts.

Sisterhoods were also deviant in terms that **"Goblin Market"** celebrates: through their rejection of the patriarchy and their celebration of empowering female narratives. Stories of female martyrs could give women a sense of potential in their own lives and a sense of their own autonomy. Like the sisterhoods, Laura and Lizzie create their own community. When Laura and Lizzie's girls' "little hands" (560) are joined together, to form a circle at the end of the story, their handholding becomes a ritualistic celebration of female power in community. The creation of a circle forms sacred space and conjoined power. In forming the circle, and telling the story, time once again takes on the mythic proportions experienced in what Rossetti calls that "long gone" time. The insights gained when touched by what Richard Schechner calls the "Transcendent Other" must now be applied to "real time." Laura alludes to this, for when "little hands" are joined together at the end, in preparation for her story, she speaks of herself and her sister Lizzie and cautions the little ones to look to them, their mothers, and to each other for salvation—she makes no mention of any heavenly father or the patriarchal church.

The offering of salvation in **"Goblin Market"** occurs through the two women and their loving relationship, evoked through their capacity to inscribe meaning on their lives through their ritualistic narrative powers and reenactment of Christian ritual. Storytelling in **"Goblin Market,"** taking place at the domestic hearth, becomes a way to reinterpret God and spirituality in terms of a female epistemology that defines the divine in domestic terms, the creation of an intentional community, and the dedication and fostering of women's spiritual development. The gift Lizzie significantly gives to Laura through her Christ-like gesture is not simply the gift of life but the gift of language as well.

Notes

1. William Michael Rossetti, ed., *Poetical Works of Christina Georgina Rossetti, with Memoir and Notes* (London: Macmillan, 1906), 459.

2. Mrs. Charles Eliot Norton, "'The Angel in the House' and 'The Goblin Market,'" *Macmillan's Magazine*, September 1863, 401.

3. For an outline of criticism on "Goblin Market," consult Jane Addison, "Christina Rossetti Studies, 1974-1991: A Checklist and Synthesis," *Bulletin of Bibliography* 2 (March 1995): 73-93. For an analysis of "Goblin Market" within the context of the Victorian literary marketplace, see Alison Chapman's "The Afterlife of Poetry: 'Goblin Market,'" in *The Afterlife of Christina Rossetti* (New York: St. Martin's Press, 2000), 131-56.

4. Julian of Norwich, *A Book of Showings: Long Text,* ed. Edmund Colledge and James Walsh (Toronto: Pontifical Institute of Medieval Studies, 1978), 580. My understanding of the term *mysticism* is derived from Evelyn Underhill's definition of it as "the expression of the innate tendency of the human spirit towards complete harmony with the transcendental order" that "dominates [one's] life and, in the experience called 'mystic union,' attains its end" (xxi). For a detailed analysis of mysticism, see Underhill's *Mysticism: The Preeminent Study in the Nature and Development of Spiritual Consciousness* (New York: Doubleday, 1990).

5. Christina G. Rossetti, "Goblin Market," in *The Complete Poems of Christina Rossetti,* 3 vols., ed. R. W. Crump (Baton Rouge: Louisiana State University Press, 1979-90), 562. Subsequent line numbers will be cited parenthetically in the text.

6. Mircea Eliade, *Myths Rites, Symbols: A Mircea Eliade Reader,* ed. Wendell C. Beane and William G. Doty (New York: Harper and Row, 1975), 1:164.

7. See Caroline Walker Bynum's classic study *Jesus as Mother: Studies in the Spirituality of the High Middle Ages* (Berkeley: University of California Press, 1982) for a discussion of medieval women's embodiment of their faith. Bynum explores how women's efforts to imitate Christ involved becoming the crucified, fusing with the body on the cross, rather than simply patterning themselves after him.

8. Richard Schechner and Willa Appel, *By Means of Performance: Intercultural Studies of Theatre and Ritual* (New York: Cambridge University Press, 1990), 4. For an introduction to performance theory, see Richard Schechner, *Essays on Performance Theory, 1970-1976* (New York: Drama Book Specialists, 1977).

9. See Joel Westerholm, "'I Magnify Mine Office': Christina Rossetti's Authoritative Voice in Her Devotional Prose," *Victorian Newsletter* 84 (1992): 11-17.

10. John Keble, "Tract No. 89: On the Mysticism Attributed to the Early Church Fathers," in *The Evangelical and Oxford Movements,* ed. Elisabeth Jay (New York: Cambridge University Press, 1983), 149.

11. Jan Marsh, *Christina Rossetti: A Writer's Life* (New York: Viking, 1994), 235.

12. D. M. R. Bentley, "The Metricious and the Meritorious in 'Goblin Market': A Conjecture and Analysis," in *The Achievement of Christina Rossetti,* ed. David Kent (Ithaca, N.Y.: Cornell University Press, 1987), 58.

13. Dante Gabriel Rossetti, Christina Rossetti, and William Michael Rossetti, *The Rossetti-Macmillan Letters: Some 133 Unpublished Letters Written to Alexander Macmillan, F. S. Ellis, and Others, by Dante Gabriel, Christina, and William Michael Rossetti, 1861-1869,* ed. Lona Mosk Packer (Berkeley: University of California Press, 1963), 7.

14. Christina Rossetti, *The Letters of Christina Rossetti,* vol. 1, *1843-1873,* ed. Antony Harrison (Charlottesville: University Press of Virginia, 1997), 294.

15. D. M. Stuart, *Christina Rossetti* (London: Macmillan, 1930), 109.

16. Ibid., 109.

17. Louis L. Martz, *The Poetry of Meditation: A Study in English Religious Literature of the Seventeenth-*

Century (1954; rev. ed., New Haven, Conn.: Yale University Press, 1962), 330.

18. Marsh, *Christina Rossetti,* 46.

19. Martz, *The Poetry of Meditation,* 1.

20. William Michael Rossetti, ed., *Ruskin: Rossetti: Pre-Raphaelitism. Papers 1854 to 1862* (New York: Dodd, Mead, 1899), 258-59.

21. Norton, "The Angel in the House," 404.

22. "Review of *Goblin Market and Other Poems,*" *Saturday Review,* May 24, 1862, 595-96.

23. Christina Rossetti, *Letter and Spirit* (London: Society for Promoting Christian Knowledge, 1883), 7.

24. Ibid., 17.

25. Mary Arseneau, "Incarnation and Interpretation: Christina Rossetti, the Oxford Movement, and 'Goblin Market,'" *Victorian Poetry* 31 (Spring 1993): 79-93, also discusses Rossetti's emphasis upon interpretation as a moral act. Katherine J. Mayberry notes the importance of a "moral interpretive system" to "Goblin Market" in *Christina Rossetti and the Poetry of Discovery* (Baton Rouge: Louisiana State University Press, 1989). Chapman's "The Afterlife of Poetry" explores the poem as a "paradigm for reading its own reception history" and ends with a "consideration of Jeanie as a figure for reading and the reading effect" (131).

26. Keble, "Tract No. 89," 133.

27. Rossetti, *Letter and Spirit,* 91-92.

28. For a Marxist discussion of "Goblin Market," see Terrence Holt, "'Men Sell Not Such in Any Town': Exchange in 'Goblin Market,'" *Victorian Poetry* 28 (Spring 1990): 51-67. Also see Elizabeth Campbell, "Of Mothers and Merchants: Female Economics in Christina Rossetti's 'Goblin Market,'" *Victorian Studies* 33 (Spring 1990): 393-410, for an argument exploring the commodification of women in the marketplace.

29. See Kathryn Allen Rabuzzi's *The Sacred and the Feminine: Toward a Theology of Housework* (New York: Seabury Press, 1982) for a discussion of housework as a sacred, ritualistic activity.

30. Elizabeth Alvida Petroff, *Medieval Women's Visionary Literature* (New York: Oxford University Press, 1986), 34.

31. See Richard Menke's article "The Political Economy of Fruit" for a discussion on imperialism and "Goblin Market" in *The Culture of Christina Rossetti: Female Poetics and Victorian Con-*

texts, ed. Mary Arseneau, Antony H. Harrison, and Lorraine Janzen Kooistra (Athens: Ohio University Press, 1999), 105-35.

32. A large number of critics have written on sisterhood in "Goblin Market." Among them are Helena Michie, "'There Is No Friend Like a Sister': Sisterhood as Sexual Difference," *ELH* 56 (Summer 1989): 401-21, as well as Dorothy Mermin, "Heroic Sisterhood in 'Goblin Market,'" *Victorian Poetry* 21 (Spring 1983): 107-18, and Janet Calligani Casey, "The Potential of Sisterhood: Christina Rossetti's 'Goblin Market,'" *Victorian Poetry* 29 (1991): 63-78. An earlier study of sisterhood is Winston Weathers's "Christina Rossetti: The Sisterhood of Self," *Victorian Poetry* 3 (Spring 1965): 81-89.

33. Germaine Greer, introduction to *Goblin Market,* by Christina Rossetti (New York: Stonehill, 1975), xxxv.

34. Rossetti, *Letter and Spirit,* 91-92.

35. See Sir David Willcocks and John Rutter, eds., *100 Carols for Choirs* (New York: Oxford University Press, 1988), 330.

36. For a discussion of visual representations of the goblins, see Lorraine Janzen Kooistra, "The Representation of Violence/The Violence of Representation: Housman's Illustrations to Rossetti's 'Goblin Market,'" *English Studies in Canada* 19 (September 1993): 305-28.

37. Ronald Grimes, *Beginnings in Ritual Studies* (Washington, D.C.: University Press of America, 1982), 76.

38. Lizzie's role as a female savior is discussed by Marian Shalkhauser, "The Feminine Christ," *Victorian Newsletter* 10 (Autumn 1956): 19-20, among others.

39. Mircea Eliade, *The Sacred and the Profane: The Nature of Religion,* trans. Willard R. Trask (New York: Harper and Row, 1959), 106-7.

40. See Maureen Duffy, *The Erotic World of Faery* (London: Hodder and Stoughton, 1972), for a discussion of "Goblin Market" in relation to fairytales.

41. See Lynda Palazzo, *Christina Rossetti's Feminist Theology* (New York: Palgrave Press, 2002), for a discussion of Lizzie's spiritual authority as representative of both Christ and wisdom figures.

42. See Caroline Walker Bynum, *Holy Feast and Holy Fast: The Religious Significance of Food to Medieval Women* (Berkeley: University of California Press, 1987), for an exploration of food and food-related practices in the piety of medieval women.

43. Grimes, *Beginnings in Ritual Studies,* 41.

44. Christina Rossetti, *The Face of the Deep: A Devotional Commentary on the Apocalypse* (London: Society for Promoting Christina Knowledge, 1892), 534.

45. Christina Rossetti, *Annus Domini: A Prayer for Each Day of the Year, Founded on a Text of Holy Scripture* (Oxford, England: James Parker, 1874), 7.

46. Rossetti, *The Face of the Deep,* 434-35.

47. Petroff, *Medieval Women's Visionary Literature,* 18.

48. Rossetti, *Annus Domini,* 133.

49. Christina Rossetti, *Time Flies: A Reading Diary* (London: Society for Promoting Christian Knowledge, 1885), 1.

50. Keble's sermon is given as an appendix ("A Sermon of Thomas Keble's") in Isaac Williams, B.D., *The Autobiography of Isaac Williams,* ed. Sir George Prevost (London: Longmans, Green, 1892), 182.

51. Catherine Judd, *Bedside Seductions: Nursing and the Victorian Imagination* (New York: St. Martin's Press, 1998), 161.

52. Mary Carpenter, "'Eat Me, Drink Me, Love Me': The Consumable Female Body in Christina Rossetti's 'Goblin Market,'" *Victorian Poetry* 29 (Winter 1991): 417.

Noelle Bowles (essay date 2005)

SOURCE: Bowles, Noelle. "A Chink in the Armour: Christina Rossetti's 'The Prince's Progress,' 'A Royal Princess,' and Victorian Medievalism." *Women's Writing* 12, no. 1 (2005): 115-26.

[*In the following essay, Bowles interprets "The Prince's Progress" and "A Royal Princess" as Rossetti's condemnation of women's oppression within a patriarchal social paradigm.*]

Grendel, the mute and inhuman monster of Saxon legend, ravages the people of Hrothgar's hall, and through his eyes we see Beowulf as something less than truly heroic in John Gardner's *Grendel* (1971). Angela Carter's "The Company of Wolves" offers us a Little Red Riding Hood who "is nobody's meat"[1], a heroine who embraces the carnal knowledge of the carnivore. Twentieth-century revisions reveal monster and victim alike casting aside their traditional roles, finding articulation and agency under authors who rework myths,

legends, and fairytales to expose and undermine the cultural assumptions and expectations that both define and confine us.[2] We may, in fact, even prefer the revision to the original tale. Although literature and film of the twentieth and twenty-first centuries call attention to oppressive cultural codes embedded in "harmless" fictions of fairies, knights, and damsels, nineteenth-century writers like Christina Rossetti were first aware of how revision might shift our perception of gender and social convention. Composed within 11 days of each other[3], **"The Prince's Progress"** and **"A Royal Princess"**, more than any of her other works, revise and subvert the cultural framework of Victorian neo-feudalism and its authoritarian, patriarchal philosophy.

Victorian medievalism covers a broad spectrum of interest and representation, encompassing architecture, religious politics, social philosophy, art, and literature, and the perspectives from which Victorians approached medievalism are nearly as varied as the forms themselves. The socialist Utopia of William Morris's *News from Nowhere* (1890) or the aesthetic poetry of Charles Algernon Swinburne, for example, differ significantly from the ideology expressed by socially conservative writers such as Thomas Carlyle or Alfred Lord Tennyson[4], and I do not mean to suggest that Christina Rossetti's poems stand counter to the whole of medievalism. Rather, the poems challenge medieval paradigms that idealise hierarchical social systems.

It is, therefore, useful to examine briefly those philosophies against which Rossetti positions her reforming revisions. The class strata of kings and knights down to peasants and slaves are, Carlyle argues in *Past and Present* (1847), ones that bring comfort, not oppression. And it is Carlyle's imagery and language to which Rossetti at least partially responds in **"A Royal Princess"**. Borrowing the model of master/slave from Sir Walter Scott's *Ivanhoe* (1819), Carlyle proclaims that:

> Gurth's brass collar did not gall him: Cedric *deserved* to be his Master. The pigs were Cedric's, but Gurth too would get his parings of them. Gurth had the inexpressible satisfaction of feeling himself related indissolubly, though in a rude brass-collar way, to his fellow mortals in this Earth. He had superiors, inferiors, equals.[5]

Release from authoritarian structures was not, according to Carlyle, what even the most radical movements of the day truly sought as their goal. Benjamin Disraeli takes up a similar logic in his novel *Sybil: Or the Two Nations* (1845) and asserts that, "as the power of the Crown has diminished, the privileges of the People have disappeared; till at length the scepter has become a pageant, and its subject has degraded again into a serf".[6]

The medieval social ideal is realised fully in the Camelot of Alfred Lord Tennyson's *Idylls of the King* that, according to Prince Albert:

Quite rekindle the feelings with which the legends of King Arthur must have inspired the chivalry of old, whilst the graceful form in which they are presented blend those feelings with the softer tone of the present age.[7]

The world Prince Albert and many other Victorians so admire is one to which Tennyson makes a few revisions of his own. His "chivalry of old" edits out Arthur's incestuous liaison with his half-sister and his subsequent Herod-like slaughter of the male infants who might be his heir. Moreover, Tennyson demonises Vivien[8], making her the "evil genius of the Round Table"[9], while in Malory's *Morte D'Arthur* Merlin is a kind of medieval stalker who "would let [Vivien] have no rest, but always he would be with her".[10] In Tennyson's version Arthur is "[t]he blameless King"[11] and Guinevere is "the sinful Queen"[12] who "hast spoilt the purpose of"[13] Arthur's life and from whose contagious immorality the world must be protected.

The chivalric ideal was pervasive enough in Victorian society for Dinah Mulock Craik to caution women from seeking a place on a pedestal, a place where they may be simultaneously raised and deserted. In *A Woman's Thoughts about Women* (1857), she warns that:

The age of chivalry, with all its benefits and harmfulness, is gone by, for us women. We cannot now have men for our knights-errant, expending blood and life for our sake, while we have nothing to do but sit idle on balconies, and drop flowers on half-dead victors at the tilt and tourney. Nor, on the other hand, are we dressed-up dolls, pretty playthings, to be fought and scrambled for—petted and caressed, or flung out the window, as our several lords and masters may please. Life is much more equally divided between us and them. We are neither goddesses nor slaves; they are neither heroes nor semi-demons.[14]

Craik's admonition that women not consider themselves heroines of medieval romance indicates that chivalric codes of social conduct were prevalent enough to be a disturbing influence upon the expectations and behaviours of Victorian women.

Elizabeth Barrett Browning's heroine Aurora Leigh derides the penchant for all things medieval when she sets forth her artistic aims and says, "[poets'] sole work is to represent the age, / Their age, not Charlemagne's", and she adds that to "Cry out for togas and the picturesque, / Is fatal,—foolish too" (Book 5, ll. 209-210).[15] Unlike Barrett Browning's protagonist, Christina Rossetti saw the problem of the past rather differently and recognised that she might more effectively undermine medievalism's allure if she couched her objections in an identical framework. For, while coloured by the fairy-tale fantastic, Rossetti's poems reject the idealisation of servitude and subservience, whether for serf or princess, and force the reader to reconsider the prescription of present social limits endorsed by an unthinking acceptance of a quasi-fictional past.

The seeds of Rossetti's revisionist insight can be found as early as 1850 in **"The Three Nuns"**, whose first segment begins as an anti-fairy tale:

Shadow, shadow on the wall
Spread thy shelter over me;
Wrap me in a heavy pall,
With the dark that none may see.[16]

The speaker of these first lines, a nun who was formerly "full of vanity and care" (l. 25), reverses the incantation of *Snow White*'s evil queen and wishes, not to see herself, but to be hidden from view, her own as well as others'. Rossetti here rejects the invidious gaze of the tale's original antagonist and replaces feminine competition with a desire to escape from the "intruding eyes" (l. 30) of those who see, not what she is, but what they wish to project upon her. **"In an Artist's Studio"** (1856) builds upon masculine misperceptions and reveals Dante Gabriel Rossetti's apparent inability to reconcile his fantasy of his fiancée with the reality of her existence, painting her, according to Christina, "Not as she is, but was when hope shone bright; / Not as she is, but as she fills his dream" (ll. 13-14). Gabriel uses Elizabeth Siddal's image for all aspects of womanhood—queen, peasant, saint, and angel—but that the artist "feeds upon [Siddal's] face" (l. 9) suggests a vampiric quality of male fantasy that casts the woman in any role that suits the artist's whim. The artist of the poem is blind to the toll his changing fancy exacts from the model. Elizabeth Siddal is a creature that "fills his dream", not a woman who experiences suffering or even true existence aside from her life on his canvas. Rossetti's critique of women's subjection and objectification is further developed in her most famous work **"Goblin Market"** (1859) and although not specifically medieval, the poem does embrace a fairy-tale "neverwhen" setting in which Rossetti proves that damsels, traditional objects of quests, can indeed rescue each other without masculine intervention.

"The Prince's Progress", though following the fairy-tale motif in its obverse retelling of *Sleeping Beauty*, ventures into medievalism in its depiction of the prince's trials and feats. In Rossetti's poem, the princess bride, rather than being rescued from a deathlike trance by a kiss from her betrothed, is depressed into sleep, spirals into a coma and finally into death by the prince's wandering sexual interest and his sloth-like "progress" toward her tower. The title of the piece is, in fact, a joke, for it is the prince's lack of progress that dooms his beloved. The poem has received relatively little critical attention and "very few full readings".[17] Such attention as it has attracted focuses principally on the poem as a spiritual parable.[18] And while the poem certainly does function as a religious allegory, the prince's indifference to the fate of his beloved and vapid self-interest present an awkward resolution if his quest is, indeed, spiritual.

An alternative possibility is that the poem intends, at least in part, to critique the century's burgeoning interest in and admiration for a chivalric past. Rossetti is careful always to maintain an ironic distance between the trials of her hedonistic prince and the efforts of Tennysonian heroes. The princess who serves as the reward for the prince's quest has little part in the poem. She is not a damsel distressed by an evil knight, tyrannical father, or other foe; she is merely a type—the woman who waits. Jan Marsh states that the poem "spoke of the confinement of womanhood, condemned to inaction and emotional atrophy unless 'woken' by marriage".[19] Indeed, the princess is confined to inaction, told by her servants that it is "better to dream than weep" (l. 12). Modern readers may be frustrated by the bride's willingness to slip into a dream, and her passive embrace of sleep and death makes us wonder if she can "do nothing to save herself".[20] Yet if we read the poem as a negative critique of the roles women were forced to play, the princess's passivity becomes pitiable rather than reprehensible. That such a reading was probably Rossetti's purpose is borne out by Craik's observation that:

> The difference between a man's vocation and a woman's seems naturally to be this—one is abroad, the other at home: one external, the other internal: one active, the other passive. He has to go out and seek out his path; hers usually lies close under her feet.[21]

Thus we see that Rossetti's objections were not uncommon, nor is such a reading forced upon the text by twenty-first century sensibilities. In "The Problem of the Damsel and the Knight", Dorothy Mermin examines the thematic and rhetorical strategies of Elizabeth Barrett Browning and Christina Rossetti, and remarks that "the surface of their poetry—diction, subject matter and (at least apparently) tone—did not contradict what Victorian women were expected to say".[22] Certainly in its representation of the princess and her seclusion within the tower, the work does conform to social expectations, but it does not necessarily condone them. Indeed, **"The Prince's Progress"** appears to caution women who may be tempted to put their lives on hold for the advent of a husband. Unlike the sleeping princess in Tennyson's "The Day Dream", who is so thrilled by the other-worldly sexuality of the fairy prince who wakes her that she says, "I'd sleep another hundred years, / O love, for such another kiss"[23], Rossetti's poem indicates that the man real women wait for may not be worth the suffering and self-abnegation.

"The Prince's Progress" also resonates with another of Tennyson's works, "The Lady of Shalott" (1832), for both pieces present confined and socially constrained women, who through opposite actions meet the same unenviable fate. The death of Tennyson's virginal weaver is, like the princess bride's, due to unrequited love, but unlike Rossetti's woman, Tennyson's Lady acts upon her desire for male companionship. As with Rossetti's bride, the Lady of Shalott remains within a single domestic setting and, as the title indicates, her identity is linked to the place she inhabits, "the island of Shalott"[24]; she has no linguistic connection or identity other than that of her domestic sphere. Indeed, her confinement is nearly total, for she may not even look directly upon the outside world, viewing it instead through mirrors, understanding that "A curse is on her if she stay / To look down to Camelot" (ll. 40-41). Her domestic spinning is both literal and figurative; it is women's work that bears witness to the cycle of life: she sees weddings, funerals, and lovers coming together, but her own existence is confined to the margins. She is, in fact, so marginal that when she violates the curse and looks upon the passing figure of Lancelot with desire, she must inscribe her name on the boat that will bear her corpse to Camelot because no one will know her otherwise. That she names the boat after herself is not a positive act, for she becomes a drifting vessel— loose physically and morally. Like the Victorian ideal of the domestic angel, she remains pure only so long as she remains oblivious to any urge to join in the doings of the world outside her own feminine sphere. While Rossetti's princess waits and wilts within her isolation, Tennyson's Lady moves out of her socially prescribed, feminine domain of weaving and away from the source of her identity, transgressing on the male world of action. In leaving her loom, she abandons domesticity for desire and violates the accepted and expected behaviour of her sex. What Rossetti's **"The Prince's Progress"** reveals is that, within the medieval paradigm, the woman cannot win. If she waits in domestic tranquillity, taking no action on her own behalf, she may languish and die upon a man's inconstant whim, but if she violates the circumscribed domestic sphere with her own agency, she faces a similar, though perhaps more public, demise.

The poem is also an indictment of the chivalric ideal embraced by Victorian society, for the piece gives a less than glamorous account of the many trials the prince faces in his "progress" toward his beloved. This particular prince is easily diverted from his course, not by the sort of rousing quests of Tennyson's *Idylls of the King,* but by the insipid succubus of a milkmaid. At this point in the tale he has "journeyed at least a mile" (l. 59) when he must stop and beg refreshment. Taking a sip from her pail, he is beguiled and wonders:

> Was it milk now, was it cream?
> Was she maid, or an evil dream?
> Her eyes began to glitter and gleam;
> He would have gone, but he stayed instead;
>
> (ll. 67-70)

We are led to understand that he tarries with her, not so much because of the kiss she demands as a reward for the sip of milk, but because rather nasty weather is approaching (ll. 85-90). His perils, such as they are, are of his own making, and we come to see that his delays are self-inflicted. He does not want to rescue his bride because he is far too interested in indulging his own fancies.

The "peril-less" journey on which the hero embarks is a deliberate inversion of the hero's quest, and Rossetti affords the prince none of the pomp and pageant present in works like the *Idylls*. In February 1865—during the poem's re-editing and expansion—Rossetti wrote of taking a "holiday from all attempt at **'[The Prince's] Progress'**" and expressed her trepidation at Gabriel's suggestion that she include a tournament as one of the prince's distractions:

> How shall I express my sentiments about the terrible tournament? Not a phrase to be relied on, not a correct knowledge on the subject, not the faintest impulse of inspiration, incites me to the tilt: and looming before me in horrible bugbeardom stand TWO of Tennyson's *Idylls*. Moreover, the Alchemist, according to convention, took the place of the lists: remember this in my favour, please. You see, were you next to propose my writing a classic epic in quantitative hexameters or in the hendecasyllables which might almost trip up Tennyson, what could I do?[25]

The "tilt" for which Rossetti lacks inspiration is both the tournament her brother proposed for **"The Prince's Progress"** and her awareness of her incursion into the medieval constructions of Tennyson. Her words her "hint at a sense of rivalry which she was careful to deny; as a mere woman, she did not aspire to compete with epic works by the classical authors or current laureate".[26] What Rossetti does, in the guise of modesty, is refuse to participate in the glorification of men in armour with their lances on full display.

The prince's encounter with the Alchemist is to serve as his real trial, and while the scene is grimly amusing—the Alchemist dies with his finger in the pot, inadvertently adding the final crucial ingredient to the Elixir of Life he has spent a lifetime trying to make—the danger of obsession is the lesson the prince exactly fails to learn from the experience. The prince's obsession is self-indulgence. Though he suspects that his stay with the Alchemist may not be in his bride's best interest, he convinces himself that "she may forgive" (l. 222), partly because he will bring her the Elixir of Life and partly, we suspect, because he imagines himself irresistibly charming. But she is no more than a goal, a bride to be "won and worn" (l. 53) like a ring or other prize.

"A Royal Princess"

"A Royal Princess" makes bolder objections to the problem of the damsel on the pedestal (or in the tower) and unites oppression of gender and class, for the poem exposes the class system upon which medievalism relies. There cannot, after all, be kings and knights without peasants and serfs. Confined within the gilded palace and subject to her father's will, the princess narrator considers her shallow and stunted existence and, overhearing palace gossip, comes to realise that the lower classes suffer great privations under her father's tyrannical rule. As her father's men prepare to put down the peasant rebellion, the princess decides to toss her wealth down to the needy. The poem ends with her decision to act, but we do not witness her confrontation with the crowd or her reception by the masses. To enact the envisioned solidarity of women and workers was perhaps too radical a step for Rossetti to take.

Although we see no outcome of the princess's stated purpose, either positive or otherwise, Rossetti does reveal the circumscription of women's lives in the complaints of her protagonist. Early in the poem the narrator sees herself as a "poor dove that must not coo— eagle that must not soar" (l. 6). She spends her time with mirrors that reflect only the superficial exterior:

> All my walls are lost in mirrors, whereupon I trace
> Self to right hand, self to left hand, self in every place,
> Self-same solitary figure, self-same seeking face.
>
> (ll. 10-12)

In her existence of mere reflection her life resembles the isolation of the Lady of Shalott, whose mirrored experiences are "Shadows of the world" (l. 48), similarly removed and shallow. The restrictions on both women carry sexual implications: the "curse" (l. 116) comes upon the Lady when she looks upon Lancelot, and the princess's curse, although not as severe, is manifested in the ways her social rank and paternal ambition block her physical connection with others. She cannot find what she seeks because her father has taken control of all the men who might be her equal. The "vassal counts and princes" (l. 23) are "each of these my courteous servant, none of these my mate" (l. 27). The paternal control and her subsequent frustration at being unable to do more than passively acquiesce to it speaks to the condition of middle-class women of the nineteenth century who, though not royalty, were confined by the same sort of familial and social domination and restriction.

This poem openly criticises the roles medieval maidens and Victorian women were supposed to occupy in the name of chivalry. The princess acknowledges, as proponents of medievalism do not, that the feudal system benefits only those who hold the power. The princess's father dominates everyone's fate, and he is no beneficent Arthur. He thinks of his estate and people as "so many head of cattle, head of horses, head of men; / These for slaughter, these for labour, with the how and when" (ll. 29-30). The juxtaposition of men and cattle recalls Carlyle's use of Scott's *Ivanhoe* with a difference, for in Rossetti's poem men are counted last among the lord's property and thought equally fit for labour or slaughter. The princess thinks of her golden chains of jewellery and states, "I could have / wept / To think of some in galling chains whether they waked or / slept" (ll. 50-53). The chains of these serfs do gall, unlike those imagined by Carlyle in his defence of social hierarchy, and unlike the rule of Tennyson's Arthur, whose reign is dedicated to "redressing human wrongs".[27]

"A Royal Princess" was the poem Rossetti "chose to donate to a fund-raising anthology in support of textile workers who were suffering the effects of a trade embargo against the Southern slave crop, cotton"[28], and we must speculate about the reception factory workers might have given to a poem that urges the rejection of a tyrannical overlord and a repressive social system. One peasant cries out in a voice reminiscent of the French Revolution: "'Sit and roast there with your meat, sit and bake with your bread, / You who sat to see us starve,' one shrieking woman said, / 'Sit on your throne and roast with your crown upon your head'" (ll. 94-96). The poem certainly offers a strong indictment of aristocratic indifference.

Rossetti was well aware of the poem's radical aspects, for "when Gabriel objected, violently, to **'The Lowest Room'** on the grounds that it was infected with the 'falsetto masculinity' of Barrett Browning's work"[29], she noted that he ought also to object to **"A Royal Princess"**, which she felt was even more feminist in its stance than **"The Lowest Room"**.[30] In the end, the narrator rejects the passive position to which she is expected to adhere, and, forsaking family and social position (as well as, possibly, her life), goes out to the rioting mob with her jewels, the value of which she hopes may feed the hungry. The act is not, however, as completely altruistic as it first appears—woman donates money to the deserving poor—for her real desire is for self-expression and revelation, those things which paternal feudalism has denied her. Her last action and admitted "goal" (l. 105) within the poem is "once to speak before the world" (l. 106). The princess seeks to voice the objections of those marginalised by authoritarian social structures. In writing the poem, Rossetti also "speaks before the world" of women's secondary position in the ideal of conservative medievalism.

Both poems delineate the problems inherent in using paternalistic feudal models as a path to social stability in both the fictionalised past and the political present. Glorifying a highly mythologised past required Victorians to ignore the abuses of hard and violent times in favour of the rigid social order that seemed to promise security. Although participating in feudalism in their setting, Rossetti's **"The Prince's Progress"** and **"A Royal Princess"** tear the veil of nostalgia from the nineteenth-century fascination with medievalism and insist that readers confront the darker aspects of this cultural fantasy.

As readers of **"The Prince's Progress"**, our sympathy is not engaged with the do-nothing prince and his self-inflated drama of not especially taxing obstacles. There is no just reward for the princess's patient waiting—unless we are to think that death is better than marriage to this princely dolt—nor does the prince appear to experience any growth of character. Neither the prince nor the princess are characters that readers would wish to emulate in behaviour or circumstance. **"A Royal Princess"** further impedes reader desire for the life of a pampered princess. Although Marjorie Stone maintains that "the princess herself remains too idealized for the poem to be successful as either a dramatic monologue or a political poem"[31], the poem does succeed as a condemnation of repressive authoritarian government and the military pomp that, typically, supports it. Here, there is no glory, no tournaments or chivalry. We are told of battles, but they are fought off the page, and their result is not peace but only further conquests. The king leads "long-descended valiant lords whom the vulture knows, / on whose track the vulture swoops, when they ride in state" (ll. 24-25); Rossetti's poems remind us that carrion, not a courtly pageant, is the harvest of masculine, martial pursuits and that women confined to towers pass into death or despair. If readers are enchanted by the glamour of medievalism and blindly accept its sociopolitical tenets, Christina Rossetti suggests they will be happy never after.

Notes

1. John Gardner (1971) *Grendel* (New York: Alfred A. Knopf). Angela Carter (1979) "The Company of Wolves", *The Bloody Chamber* (London: Penguin), p. 118.

2. In fiction see Emma Donoghue (1997) *Kissing the Witch: Old Tales in New Skins* (New York: HarperCollins), a collection of revised tales; and Anne Claffey, Linda Kavanagh & Sue Russell (Eds) (1985) *Rapunzel's Revenge* (Dublin: Attic Press), an anthology of revised tales from various authors. Examples in recent films include Jerry Zucker's *First Knight* (1997), which significantly reimagines Guinevere's role and motives in the Arthurian cycle; and Peter Jackson's *Lord of the Rings: The Fellowship of the Ring* (2001), wherein the original trophy figure of Arwen is recast as a heroine capable of outrunning and subduing the ring wraiths.

3. Jan Marsh (1995) *Christina Rossetti: A Writer's Life* (New York: Viking Press), p. 275 informs us that "The Prince Who Arrived Too Late" (the original title for "The Prince's Progress") and "A Royal Princess" were written in October 1860. Rossetti changed the title to "The Prince's Progress" when she revised and expanded the poem for publication in *The Prince's Progress and Other Poems*, which was printed in 1865.

4. It is important to note that Tennyson's poetry became more conservative over time. The fragment poem "Sir Lancelot and Queen Guinevere" (1830), for example, follows a more Romantic tradition and does not condemn the knight's love for the queen but merely represents its existence. "The Lady of Shalott" (1832) is similarly free of the moralising that marks the later *Idylls of the King,* which Tennyson wrote and revised from 1842 until 1888.

5. Thomas Carlyle (1847) *Past and Present* (New York: Wiley & Putnam), p. 212; emphasis in original.

6. Benjamin Disraeli (1995) *Sybil: Or the Two Nations* (New York: Penguin), p. 497.

7. Alfred Lord Tennyson (1981, 1987) *The Letters,* ed. Cecil Lang & Edgar F. Shannon, 2 vols (Cambridge, MA: Harvard University Press), II, p. 257.

8. Tennyson appeared to be well aware of how disagreeable women readers found Vivien's representation. Apparently seeking to distance real-life women from the vile sorceress, one reader and friend of the poet, Caroline Fox, asked him "whether or not Vivien might be the old Brittany fairy who wiled Merlin into her net, and not an actual woman. 'But no,' he said; 'it is full of distinct personality, though I never expect women to like it'" (*Letters,* ed. Lang & Shannon, II, p. 267).

9. Hallam Tennyson notes his father's opinion of Vivien in Christopher Ricks (1987) *The Poems of Tennyson,* 3 vols (Berkeley: University of California Press), III, p. 393.

10. Sir Thomas Malory (1993) *Le Morte D'Arthur* (New York: Random House), Book 4.1., p. 88.

11. Alfred Lord Tennyson (1961) "Geraint and Enid", *Idylls of the King* (New York: Signet Classic), p. 101. Arthur's blamelessness is mentioned on numerous occasions throughout the *Idylls.* Tennyson clearly envisioned him as a medieval Adam, who falls through no fault or sin of his own. In 1859 he indicated to his publisher that he wanted the original title page of the *Idylls* to read: "Idyls of the King / By Alfred Lord Tennyson D.C.L. / Poet Laureate / "God had not made since Adam was, / the man more perfect than Arthur." / Brut ab Arthur. / "Flos regum Arthurus," / Joseph of Exeter" (*Letters,* ed. Lang & Shannon, II, p. 232).

12. Ibid., "Guinevere", p. 231.

13. Ibid., p. 235.

14. Dinah Mulock Craik (1993) On Sisterhoods; A Woman's Thoughts about Women, in *Maude/Christina Rossetti and On Sisterhoods; A Woman's Thoughts about Women/Dinah Mulock Craik,* ed. Elaine Showalter (New York: New York University Press), p. 78.

15. Elizabeth Barrett Browning (1996) *Aurora Leigh,* ed. Margaret Reynolds (New York: W.W. Norton), Book 5, ll. 203-204 and 209-210. *Aurora Leigh* was first published in 1856.

16. Christina Georgina Rossetti (1979) "The Three Nuns", in *Maude/Christina Rossetti and On Sisterhoods; A Woman's Thoughts about Women/ Dinah Mulock Craik,* ed. Elaine Showalter (New York: New York University Press), ll. 1-4. (Subsequent line references from this edition will follow in parentheses in the body of the article.) All other Rossetti poems are taken from *The Complete Poems of Christina Rossetti: a Variorum Edition,* ed. R. W. Crump, 3 vols (Baton Rouge: Louisiana State University Press, 1979-1990).

17. Mary Arseneau (1994) "Pilgrimage and Postponement: Christina Rossetti's 'The Prince's Progress'", *Victorian Poetry,* 32, pp. 279-299 (p. 295).

18. See Mary Arseneau, "Pilgrimage and Postponement" and also Linda Peterson (1994) "Restoring the Book: The Typological Hermeneutics of Christina Rossetti and the PRB", *Victorian Poetry,* 32, pp. 209-227.

19. Marsh, *Christina Rossetti,* p. 275.

20. Ibid., p. 325.

21. Craik, *A Woman's Thoughts,* p. 69.

22. Dorothy Mermin (1996) "The Problem of the Damsel and the Knight", in *Victorian Women Poets: A Critical Reader,* ed. Angela Leighton (Oxford: Blackwell), pp. 211-212.

23. Alfred Lord Tennyson (1884) "The Day Dream", *The Complete Works* (New York: Hurst), l. 73.

24. Alfred Lord Tennyson (1971) "The Lady of Shalott", *Tennyson's Poetry,* ed. Robert W. Hill, Jr. (New York: W.W. Norton), l. 9. (Subsequent line references from this edition will follow in parentheses in the body of the article.)

25. William Michael Rossetti (1970) *Rossetti Papers: 1862-1870* (New York: AMS Press), p. 77.

26. Marsh, *Christina Rossetti,* p. 324.

27. Tennyson, "Guinevere", *Idylls of the King,* p. 235.

28. Marsh, *Christina Rossetti,* p. 276.

29. Ibid., p. 184.

30. Ibid., p. 328.

31. Marjorie Stone (1994) "Sisters in Art: Christina Rossetti and Elizabeth Barrett Browning", *Victorian Poetry*, 32, pp. 339-364 (p. 354).

Constance W. Hassett (essay date 2005)

SOURCE: Hassett, Constance W. "Rossetti's Finale: *The Face of the Deep* (1892) and *Verses* (1893)." In *Christina Rossetti: The Patience of Style*, pp. 198-237. Charlottesville and London: University of Virginia Press, 2005.

[*In the following essay, Hassett examines Rossetti's final collections of poetry, noting the author's thoughtful and controlled approach to topics about which she felt passionate, such as religious beliefs and the beauty of poetry.*]

In her admiring essay occasioned by the centenary of Christina Rossetti's birth, Virginia Woolf greets the poet with cordial intimacy, "O Christina Rossetti . . . I know many of your poems by heart," and casts a cold eye on the buying public's stinginess, noting that "Her annual income from her poetry was for many years about ten pounds." Without delaying over Woolf's resentment on Rossetti's behalf or her well-known hunch about the happy effect on women writers of "five hundred a year" and "rooms of our own," we might confirm that sales figures were not a source of pleasure to Rossetti until late in life. Although her poetry was always well received, she never enjoyed anything like the demand for successive editions that met Gabriel's *Poems* of 1870 nor was she ever to report such jubilant news as that of his letter to their Aunt Charlotte Polidori: "I dare say you have heard . . . of the commercial success of the book. [That the] first thousand sold in little more than a week is not amiss for poetry. The second edition is now out, and I have already received £300 for my share of the profits. Of course it will not go on like this for ever, but perhaps a quiet steady sale may be hoped to go on. I am now about to republish my book of the *Early Italian Poets,* as perhaps a new edition may profit by the luck of the other book" (*LDGR* [*Letters of Dante Gabriel Rossetti,*], 2:880). Aunt Charlotte must have been delighted, since she had often been asked, early in Gabriel's career, for loans she cheerfully gave. Christina's triumph would come at age sixty-three, only a year before her death, when she had the satisfaction of seeing the first edition of *Verses* sold out in a week. The Society for Promoting Christian Knowledge had brought out the book in September 1893 and "by Christmas" her friend Mrs. Garnett loyally complained that "there was no meeting the demand for 'Verses': at one considerable shop she tried at she heard that twenty or thirty applications had had to be negatived for the moment" (*L* [*The Letters of Christina Rossetti,*], 4:364). By January a deeply gratified Christina would tell William of seeing a *"4th thousand"* copy "which looks grand" (*L,* 4:367).[1]

In her letters, Rossetti usually refers to *Verses* as "my reprint" since, as indicated by her subtitle, *Reprinted from Called to be Saints, Time Flies, The Face of the Deep,* the poems had first appeared in her volumes of religious prose (*L,* 4:316, 340); there they attracted the attention of those Anglican worshipers whom Lynda Palazzo, in her recent study of Rossetti's theology, graciously admires for seeking devotional guidance on the "journey into spiritual understanding." As a collection, however, *Verses* reached the broader audience who had already made **"Up-hill,"** with its wry cautioning of "wayfarers" about the inn they "cannot miss," a nearly universal favorite (*CP,* [*The Complete Poems of Christina Rossetti: A Variorum Edition*], 1:66). These readers knew that Rossetti's first two books each included a section of "Devotional Pieces," announced as such in the table of contents and marked by an interior title page, and they valued what they found there. Arthur Symons, for example, admired **"Advent"** from *Goblin Market* for "startling us perhaps by its profound and unthought-of naturalness"; others singled out **"Good Friday"** from *The Prince's Progress* and **"Who Shall Deliver Me?"** from the collected edition of 1875. The division of these first books "into two distinct sections" had been a suggestion of Gabriel's, who early in his own career had been writing what he called "Songs of the Art Catholic." When William and Gabriel were bringing out *The Germ,* their short-lived literary magazine of 1850, they had eagerly included among the "pure" lyrics—such as Christina's **"Song"** ("Oh roses for the flush of youth") and **"Dream-Land"**—her explicitly religious **"A Testimony,"** replete with borrowings from Psalm 39 and Ecclesiastes, as well as **"Sweet Death."** The latter, a traditional meditation on petal-fall, opens in a churchyard and takes up the refrain of George Herbert's "Virtue," gravely modifying his lament that all things "must die":

> The sweetest blossoms die.
> And so it was that, going day by day
> Unto the Church to praise and pray,
> And crossing the green churchyard thoughtfully,
> I saw how on the graves the flowers
> Shed their fresh leaves in showers,
> And how their perfume rose up to the sky
> Before it passed away.
>
> The youngest blossoms die.
> They die and fall and nourish the rich earth
> From which they lately had their birth;
> Sweet life, but sweeter death that passeth by
> And is as though it had not been:—
> All colours turn to green.

(*CP,* 1:74)

"Thoughtfully" accepting the evidence of spring's easeful passing into the all-green of summer, the churchgoer imagines death as a change that allows its devastation to be pleasantly effaced, passing "as though it had not been." Rossetti's inference is, of course, too wishful and subsumes too readily the actual terror of individual death, but she redeems her poem by coming to a subtle close. Her seasonal metaphor turns typological and remembers Ruth amid Boaz' autumn fields:

> Why should we shrink from our full harvest? why
> > Prefer to glean with Ruth?

> > > (*CP,* 1:75)

The final question, spread across the line break, puts delicate emphasis on the word "prefer." Ruth herself, as we know, did *not* prefer to glean but managed to raise her status (another meaning of "prefer" is to promote in rank) to that of Boaz's handmaiden (Ruth 2:9). Rossetti's question, by displacing and faintly punning on its verb, gently wonders at the mysteriousness of human inclination. This final deftness is probably what earned **"Sweet Death"** its place in the *Germ*.[2]

Many years later, when once again writing of a churchyard, Rossetti again elides what terrifies—the "full harvest" of death—only this time it is because she knows all too well how cruel a death can be and how anxiously a mourner shrinks from posing questions about the soul's status in the afterlife. **"Birchington Churchyard"** is separated from **"Sweet Death"** by Rossetti's three decades of experience as a poet and by the culminating agony of Dante Gabriel Rossetti's death on Easter Sunday, April 9, 1882. Christina and their mother, Frances, were with Gabriel throughout the final weeks and the very last minutes of his life. As she would soon write to George Hake, the "amiable" companion to Gabriel after his suicide attempt a decade earlier, her brother was buried in the churchyard of the seaside town where they had hoped he would recuperate (*L,* 1:432). It is a subdued letter that purports to give "a few particulars of poor dear Gabriel's last days" but is, in fact, solicitous of Gabriel's reputation and aims at preventing blame; she does not want Hake to believe that Gabriel's reliance on chloral had killed him: "The immediate cause of death arose from blood-poisoning induced not by an extraneous cause but by an internal derangement. The last moments appeared to pass (and [I] am assured did really so pass) quite free from pain, nor was there the slightest struggle" (*L,* 3:36, 37). Having performed this tender work, she has one further task: she must make the location of his grave a thing too natural to question. To her it was an added and unintelligible grief that Gabriel refused to be buried at Highgate Cemetery with their father and his wife Elizabeth Siddal. Christina could not have known that Hake was the very person Gabriel had apprised of his aversion to the cemetery in a letter instructing that he "not on any account be bur-

ied at Highgate" (*LDGR,* 3:1437), and she probably knew nothing of the now-legendary exhumation that Gabriel's friends had undertaken to retrieve his poems from Siddal's coffin. So she covers over the strange fact of his solitary grave with a description of the prospect from the Birchington churchyard and assures Hake that friends and family had gathered at the last: "The country about Birchington is not very pretty, but the Churchyard where he is buried—not a cemetery; but a small quiet Churchyard—lies high, and commands a fair exposure of land and sea with sunsets over the sea. Two days before Gabriel died William joined us, and we and nurse and three dear friends and Dr. Harris of Birchington were gathered round the bed at the moment of death. Mr Marshall had seen him in the morning, having passed the night on the spot" (*L,* 3:37). Brief and restrained, Christina's remarks are a model of mourner's denial (Gabriel probably did not "really" die "quite free from pain") and decorous irrelevance (Hake does not care where John Marshall spent the night). She substitutes what is acceptably thinkable for what cannot be said about this especially unhappy dying.[3]

Within a few days of this letter, Christina's elegy for Gabriel, **"Birchington Churchyard,"** would appear in the *Athenaeum*. It too takes up the landscape and manages to be both poignantly lovely and austerely uncomforted. This churchyard poem intimates the consolation that is wanted but which, given all she knows of Gabriel's troubled agnosticism, she is far too honest to profess. She had long been distressed that her much-loved brother tended, as McGann puts it, to regard "the whole of Christian history" as "a poetic construction" rather than the grounds for spiritual trust. And so she begins her poem with the muted sound of the "low-voiced" sea and the sterility of the chalky shore, perfect correlatives for the flattened, dull ache of grief:

> A lowly hill which overlooks a flat,
> > Half sea, half country side;
> > A flat-shored sea of low-voiced creeping tide
> Over a chalky weedy mat.

> > > (*CP,* 2:167)

The dignified laboriousness in the stanza's movement—an effect of the long vowels, the hyphen-bonded accents ("A flát-shóred séa of lów-vóiced créeping tíde"), and the constraining of verbs as participles)—mimes the slowness of the tide and the lowness of emotion. Together the sea and the poetic line cross inevitably "over" their boundaries, while the word "creeping" recalls Tennyson's thought about the feeling of ghostliness that sends a mourner to "creep / At earliest morning" around a loved friend's door (*AT,* 352). The "weedy mat" is a reminder, too, that the Victorians wrapped themselves in mourning "weeds." Attention then moves to the churchyard itself:

> A hill of hillocks, flowery and kept green
>   Round Crosses raised for hope,
>   With many-tinted sunsets where the slope
> Faces the lingering western sheen.

The scene is both religious and domestic. The word "hillocks" is almost affectionately diminutive while the sign of human tendance is preserved in the phrase "kept green." The sacred aura of the place is subtly enhanced by the "many-tinted sunsets" and the "sheen" on the ocean. Set amid moving lights, the crosses "raised" in hope and the hillside that "faces" into the light are touchingly more animated than the earthbound dead who neither see nor feel the sun. Sadly, then, the focus shifts from the near to the distant prospect, from the grave site to eternity. But grief is severe and Rossetti is so vastly experienced in the ways of poetic restraint that she manages to say no more about hope than she actually feels—and what she feels is inconsolable loss:

> A lowly hope, a height that is but low,
>   While Time sets solemnly,
>   While the tide rises of Eternity,
> Silent and neither swift nor slow.

The low voice of the opening stanza's incoming sea is refigured as a "silent" tide, and the attendant abstractions Time and Eternity resist any attempt at allegorically intoned comfort. An assertion of belief or claim about "sweeter death" would bring no solace; the exultation that forms the lovely close to a poem in the previous year's *Pageant* volume, Paul's jubilant words to the Corinthians, would be jarring and false: "He bids me sing: O death, where is thy sting? / And sing: O grave, where is thy victory?" (*CP*, 2:123). The mourner at Birchington cannot imagine gaining emotional access to any such sentiment. A mourner's sense of loss, as Stephen Booth vehemently explains, is "altogether immune to invasion by comforting conclusions based on consideration of such 'facts' as the inevitability of mortality, the painfulness of life, the immortality of the soul, and the reunion of body and soul at the Last Judgment." Booth cites precisely the "facts" implied by Rossetti's raised churchyard crosses, and her poem shows that, despite the religious convictions represented by such symbols, there is no acceptance of the terrible fact of Gabriel's death. His passing brings a mood and a pain that will be assuaged only slowly and imperceptibly; and so instead of hope, **"Birchington Churchyard"** aspires toward calm. The poem's beauty is a temporary relief from numbness; it brings sorrow into words and momentarily fills the vacuity of inarticulate pain. It surmounts muteness to speak of eternity's tide as a silently relentless motion that takes no cognizance of human death and grief.[4]

"Tune Me, O Lord": Invocation, Lamentation, and Consolation

The bleakness of the final image of **"Birchington Churchyard"** releases Rossetti from the burden of articulating a sentiment she does not feel and maybe also from enacting the one she does. It shows, at the same time, the contours of a difficulty that is paradigmatic for her as a writer. There is a sense in which the struggle enacted in the poem's final lines corresponds fairly precisely to the challenge every poet faces in the late stages of a career, viz., the depletions of one sort or another that weaken the desire to write. An author's gradual fall into silence was once described as writing less and less until one stops altogether, and this seems to be the pattern Rossetti herself feared. She once told Macmillan, in a famous misstatement, that "the fire has died out, it seems"; this was in 1874 when a collected edition and much new work was yet to come (*L*, 2:7). In the 1880s, however, such discouraged comments became more adamant, as when she told Swinburne in 1884 that "dumbness is not my *choice*" (*L*, 3:231) and Frances Kingsley in 1885 that *Time Flies* "exhausted my last scrap" (*L*, 3:284). Viewing Rossetti's work in retrospect, we know better than to take these as serious forecasts, and yet the evidence of the publication history suggests she was losing the "patience and desire" to write (*CP*, 2:181). After its appearance in the *Athenaeum*, **"Birchington Churchyard"** would be included among the handful of new pieces in the reissued *Pageant* volume (1888) when it was not at all clear that there would ever be another collection of new poems. But for all this, the poems do come—sometimes with worries attached.

In the dozen years it takes her to assemble the devotional poems that eventually become the *Verses* of 1893, Rossetti's attention often turns, not surprisingly, to the worldlessness she dreads, the specter she calls "utterless desire," "voicelessness," "breath that fails" (*CP*, 2:250, 185, 204). The imagined muteness that was once an unfailing stimulus—variously recast as the hushed eavesdropping in **"At Home,"** the lonely withdrawal in **"L.E.L.,"** and the resolve at Lake Como to include song among the "host of things" taken "on trust" (2:147)—now looms as a debilitating threat. The silence that once defined a perimeter, its negotiation a source of enlivening aesthetic tension, now constitutes an all too literal barrier portending the loss of imaginative power. When the late poems assess the waning of spiritual stamina, they often ask, as Rossetti's friend Mary Howitt put it, "to be delivered from *Self*," and in the same words to be blessed with an infusion of aesthetic energy. Since at some level a poet's invocations are all the same, a means to the elevation that is the poem's inception, it is literally the case that the substance of Rossetti's devotional pleading is to recover the ability to write devotional poems. The Lord of Apostrophe is both the Christian's and the poet's deity, and metaphors for spiritual union are musical. "Tuning of my breast," as Herbert puts it, will "make the music better" and Rossetti prays accordingly:

Tune me, O Lord, unto one harmony
   With Thee, one full responsive vibrant chord;
Unto thy praise all love and melody,
   Tune me, O Lord.

(CP, 2:255)

With an access of melody and spiritual trust, poetic song becomes a "hopeful quiet psalm" and the singer tells of searching her "heart-field" for a gift of thanksgiving (*CP,* 2:184). There she finds the "sun-courting heliotrope," a flower that brings the memory of Apollo's sponsorship of poets delicately into alignment with the reverent Christian pun on *sun* and *Son.* Once tuned, the "responsive chord" yields as many tonalities as the vocal cords permit; and the formed breath of the late poems ranges in pitch from a "lonely beseeching cry" to a rapturous "shout" (*CP,* 2:208, 211). Sometimes the prospect of death's imminent silence prompts a kind of spiritual hedonism, and Rossetti imagines an imperative to sing while she can:

Thou who must fall silent in a while,
   Chant thy sweetest, gladdest, best, at once;
Sun thyself today, keep peace and smile;
     By love upward send
Orisons,
     Accounting love thy lot and love thine end.

(CP, 2:269)

The urgency of the exhortation to chant "at once" is felt in the velocity of the phrasing "thy sweetest, gladdest, best," as each of the final *st*'s arrives more quickly than the last. The third line makes "sun" sound like a verb meaning "rise towards the sun" and activates the "horizon" and more exactly the "risen" in "orison." As if to revel in this achieved sense of sun/Son-blessed exhilaration, "orisons" is awarded the unshaded splendor of a line to itself. The acoustic flamboyance of this stanza is a reminder, albeit an unusual one, that a good Rossetti poem is never too far from an awareness that it might not have come into existence. One of the strangest versions of this same hint takes the form of a tormented complaint about shortness of breath:

Good Lord, today
I scarce find breath to say:
   Scourge, but receive me.
For stripes are hard to bear, but worse
Thy intolerable curse;
   So do not leave me.

(CP, 2:222)

By alluding to scourging, this prayer holds up the model of the Savior's exemplary docility (Mark 10:34). But in professing a near inability "to say" what is required and by distancing the plea for pain as an indirect citation, the speaker nearly refuses to accept affliction. This ambivalence about the fearsome signs of divine attention are the poem's strength; there is no pretense that suffering is anything less than an ordeal. But there is also the suggestion that suffering might be something more, something attractive. The cascading syllables of the "intolerable curse" are braked and slowed to an abject final whisper of the kind made to a lover, "So do not leave me." Not only does Rossetti suggest that a connection with the divine has the vividness of physical pain, she pushes that idea toward the erotic and welcomes inflicted "stripes" with a submission that borders on masochism. **"Good Lord, today"** is a double poem—completely conventional and utterly perverse—and its speaker does, in fact, "find breath" to confront the central issue of Christian spirituality, the peril of relying on an unseen god.[5]

For Rossetti, the beliefs that some cherish and others scorn as the conventionally "secure pieties" are not always *felt* to be secure. The chief tenets of her religion remain uncontested, of course, and she refuses to entertain doubt about spiritual realities—as she says in a letter, "I have not *played* at Xtianity, & therefore I cannot play at unbelief" (*L,* 2:167)—but hopefulness often pales against the glare of what she calls the "instinctive dread of death" (*FD,* [*The Face of the Deep*], 63). Confidence in the ultimate value of the life she is committed to is a crucially unstable emotion. Because Rossetti is neither a docile nor an opiated believer, her devotional poems confront all that confounds her ways of making sense of life, helping her, as an earlier poem says, to "fix upon the lack" and to contend with what she now calls "the fume and the fret" of life's seeming pointlessness (*CP,* 2:140, 292). One of her most distinctive modes, therefore, is lamentation, as she lodges complaint after complaint against the temporal process whereby all good things "decrease" (*CP,* 2:181). One poem mourns the cosmos itself:

A moon impoverished amid stars curtailed,
   A sun of its exuberant lustre shorn,
   A transient morning that is scarcely morn,
A lingering night in double dimness veiled—
Our hands are slackened and our strength has failed:
   We born to darkness, wherefore were we born?

(CP, 2:252)

The scene at first resembles the paled landscape of **"Dream-Land"** in the *Goblin Market* volume, and even **"Birchington Churchyard"** with its verblessness and many participles, but the tone and culminating challenge are new. The extremity of the question approaches defiance; though the "hands" are said to have "slackened," one at least takes up the pen in protest. In other poems, when Rossetti turns, as so often in her career, to the image of the sea, it is with a forceful new severity. Gone are the "flower-like" anemones, the "argus-eyed" sea creatures, and the "pebbly strand" (*CP,* 1:19; 2:145); the darkening waves have become the "very embodiment of unrest" (*P* [*Selected Prose of Christina Ros-*

setti], 230), no longer teeming with life forms but "lifting" cadaverlike hands:

> The sea laments with unappeasable
>   Hankering wail of loss,
>   Lifting its hands on high and passing by
>   Out of the lovely light:
> No foambow any more may crest that swell
>   Of clamorous waves which toss;
>   Lifting its hands on high it passes by
>   From light into the night.
> Peace, peace, thou sea! God's wisdom worketh well,
>   Assigns it crown or cross:
>   Lift we all hands on high, and passing by
>   Attest: God doeth right.

(CP, 2:268)

These waves that wave their "hands" as if drowning are startlingly surreal and at the same time precisely biblical. Rossetti takes the image, along with her title, from Habakkuk, where the prophet questions the Lord's "wrath against the sea" and grieves that "the overflowing of the water passed by: the deep uttered his voice, and lifted up his hands on high" (Hab. 3:8, 10). To amplify the "wail of loss" that needs appeasing, Rossetti creates a high degree of acoustic tension and, because this poem is moving in the prophetically affirmative direction, works audibly toward formal resolution. The first quatrain seems unrhymed, and not until the second do the echoes of the end words emerge; but even here the term "unappeasable" finds only an idiosyncratic match in "swell." In committing what Fried wittily designates one of "rhyme's sins," Rossetti's "mannered, quaint, contrived" pairing virtually puns with the word's "unappeasable" need for a rhyme partner and manages, at the same time, to intensify the reader's own hankering for a perfect chime. Finally, when the third quatrain complements the second with a full set of exact matches, the satisfaction of hearing the words themselves work "well" encourages acceptance of the thought that "God's wisdom worketh well." With the final line's solemn command, "Attest: God doeth right," the language itself sounds biblically and acoustically "right," an echo of Herbert's technique when he ends "Denial" with the phrase "and mend my rhyme." If the poem succeeds, it is because of the skill that brings the prophet's text into Rossetti's own and then, by subduing strange rhymes, mimes the bringing of restless emotions to order.[6]

The closing assertiveness of **"Was Thy Wrath against the Sea?"** is somewhat atypical in Rossetti's poetry. Keenly aware of what she elsewhere calls "renewed incompleteness," the recurrent anxiety that belies the confidence of this poem's exhortation, Rossetti tends to complain more softly and to be more ambiguous in her assurances (*FD*, 524). One sighing, weary poem asks about the slow coming of time's end using a nearly petulant phrasing, "Will it never," as if restless about minor annoyances:

> Oh knell of a passing time,
> Will it never cease to chime?
> Oh stir of the tedious sea,
> Will it never cease to be?
> Yea, when night and when day,
> Moon and sun, pass away.

(CP, 2:274)

Though the questions elicit an answering "Yea," it comes with the tautological information that time will end when the cosmic signs of time end. Vague in content, the answer is also mysterious in origin: the poem is either a lyric whose speaker has grown tired of her own discontent or a dialogue with an unidentified (possibly divine) tutor. The ambiguity raises the question of genre—is there one voice or two? It is important for the poem's effect that the reader remains of two minds about what is happening and slightly agitated. This unsettling formal mystery precludes naive assumptions about access to the greater eschatological mystery—even when the next stanza begins with a seemingly confident "surely":

> Surely the sun burns low,
> The moon makes ready to go,
> Broad ocean ripples to waste,
> Time is running in haste,
> Night is numbered, and day
> Numbered to pass away.

In retrospect, the "surely" seems to have been concessive, guardedly coaxing, and lacking the force to sustain its meaning through to the end of the sentence. The only sure numbering that goes on—since there is no knowable total of days past or future—is the poem's own play with metrical number. And it gives shape, not to temporality per se, but to human impatience. This covertly self-allegorizing poem examines its own ways of facing uncertainty and all but promises that Rossetti will "never cease to chime." Rhymed and "numbered" language (she repeats this punning hint) is her devotional tool, and throughout the *Verses* she plays repeatedly with the long and short of duration to achieve the paradoxical serenity of aesthetically molded unrest. A pentameter sonnet, for example, opens with the thought that "Time lengthening, in the lengthening seemeth long" (*CP*, 2:275). Acoustically, the line drags out its own length with falling rhythm, softly thickening *th* sounds, and the unelided syllables of "lengthening" while repetition takes the thought back to the beginning of the line and arrests its momentum. Such artistic handling disciplines even as it voices its complaint.

But lamentation is not the only, or even the dominant, mood of the late poems. Some are cheering and almost colloquially heartening; instead of mourning humanity's "deathstruck" condition or bearing witness to divine wisdom, they suggest ways one might "take comfort" in this life (*CP*, 2:182, 297). Neither blithe nor carefree, they offer consolation by admitting the prevalence of discouragement and showing a kindly regard for the "heart disheartened thro' and thro'" (*CP,* 2:190). There is respect for the rigors of despondency and sheer miserableness that strain the "patience" she once called "a tedious, indomitable grace" (*FD,* 68). The poems charm by their understatement and by their refusal to blunder into abrasive imperatives about joy. Rossetti may or may not remember Dr. Johnson's insistence that "The only end of writing is to enable the readers better to enjoy life or better to endure it," but certainly she knows Paul's advice to Timothy. Imprisoned and bound in chains, the apostle exhorts his follower to partake in "the afflictions of the gospel" and to "endure hardness" (2 Tim. 1:8; 2:3). Rossetti borrows this last phrase to introduce a spring poem, or rather a poem that glimpses spring from the perspective of winter. Noting the wind's "keenness," she offers more than a Pauline exhortation to endure the season's bone-chilling cold; she envisions coming sprays of snowlike blossoms:

> A cold wind stirs the blackthorn
>   To burgeon and to blow,
> Besprinkling half-green hedges
>   With flakes and sprays of snow.
>
> Thro' coldness and thro' keenness,
>   Dear hearts, take comfort so:
> Somewhere or other doubtless
>   These make the blackthorn blow.

(*CP,* 2:297)

The secret of this poem is that it takes delight in what it proposes enduring. There is physical pleasure in the alliterated first sentence as the lips shape the *b*'s of "burgeon," "blow," "besprinkling" and then open for the continuants of "flakes," "sprays," "snow." The sound is not mimetic in any strict sense, but the shift in mouth's articulation, from obstructed to free-flowing air mimes the emergence the words describe. An attentive weather-watcher, the speaker plainly enjoys detecting the earliest hint of flakes that are not made of snow. Convincing in its modest precision ("half-green hedges" are still half-brown) the speaker's joy becomes all the more cogent with the second stanza's gentle diffidence. The word "doubtless" makes the poem. Instead of insisting absolutely on a burgeoning not yet in evidence, the speaker offers a plausible claim that "somewhere or other" the season breaks into bloom, which might, of course mean "unpredictably later in life" or even "after life," while the cajoling "doubtless" half-admits to doubts about the coming change. The point is not pressed, and even the dourest of the "dear hearts" would agree that the suggested connection between cold and bloom is not improbable and that it might be, in the words of another poem, "possible, or probable, or true" (*CP,* 2:102). To gauge the effect of the poem's mild unassertiveness, one need only turn to the vigorous expostulation in a passage from *Seek and Find* (1879): "Win-

ter even while we shrink from it abounds in hope; or ever its short days are at the coldest they lengthen and wax more sunny. Winter is the threshold of spring, and Spring resuscitates and reawakens the world. Winter which nips can also brace" (*P,* 227). The seasonal analogy is meant as an aid to reflection, for it is literally true that days lengthen for five or six weeks before the temperature bottoms out; at London's latitude, February 1 is often colder than December 21 when days start lengthening. Nonetheless, in overlooking the disproportion between allegedly abounding hope and midwinter's imperceptible increases in daylight, the passage seems nearly facile. The supposition that winter is bracing offers nothing but its own briskness to invigorate a chilled reader. The poem, however, by its honest admission of the bitterness of bitter weather and its accuracy about the black-thorn yet-to-bloom succeeds in communicating its sense of vernal expectation.[7]

This sensible good-heartedness, this wish to console reliably and without falsification, moves Rossetti to celebrate even fleeting occasions for hope, admitting that they are temporary and perhaps only a brief remission of the sorrows that "overhang" us (*CP,* 2:324). Among the strengths of these late devotional poems is their emphasis on the mood in flux, or more accurately, the sensation of rebound from some pain or frustration that will come again:

> One woe is past. Come what come will
>   Thus much is ended and made fast:
> Two woes may overhang us still;
>   One woe is past.
>
> As flowers when winter puffs its last
> Wake in the vale, trail up the hill,
>   Nor wait for skies to overcast;
>
> So meek souls rally from the chill
>   Of pain and fear and poisonous blast,
> To lift their heads: come good, come ill,
>   One woe is past.

(*CP,* 2:324)

The poem makes a delicate effort to contain suffering, to distinguish and tally up discrete episodes, not always to take the long view because, both perversely and wisely, we don't want to face unremitting woe. In the interval, the afflicted might become as beautifully reckless as first blooms in a chilly spring. Newly volitional with three brisk verbs, these flowers "wake," "trail" after the light, and refuse to "wait" for what another poem calls the "fattening rain" (*CP,* 1:31). The focused quality of Rossetti's attention to germination, infinitesimal growth, and the not-so-random spread of seed and root makes this brief observation compelling. Just as these flowers "rally" from winter's "blast," the verb suggestive of resilient loyalists and soldiers, so will the meekly woebegone. The very shape of the poem, a roundel with a prescribed rentrement, encourages a rally by its own example, confining "woe" to the framing stanzas while the springtime image flourishes in the interval. There is even an exemplary staunchness in the phrase "One woe is past." It not only resists false hope by refusing to evolve semantically into the "one" that is once-and-for-all or somehow climactic, it also fends off dread; for as many readers will recognize, the phrase denies knowledge of the prediction it echoes, the warning of "two more woes hereafter" (Rev. 9:12). With its extraordinarily subdued use of the carpe diem motif, this roundel remains "unsnared" by improbable optimism, "unscared" of future pain, and affirms, by its own austerity, the value of even small recoveries (*CP,* 2:182).

Occasionally Rossetti's spring poems find winter's lingering chill less oppressive: the "poisonous blast" goes unmentioned, and the emphasis is on the cheering botanical fact that flowers detect the slightest gradations of temperature and can be said to "know" the new season is arriving. Ordinary violets and daisies, because they are "unaccounted rare," become the speaker's personal emblems:

> As violets so be I recluse and sweet,
>> Cheerful as daisies unaccounted rare,
> Still sunward-gazing from a lowly seat,
>> Still sweetening wintry air.
>
> While half-awakened Spring lags incomplete,
>> While lofty forest-trees tower bleak and bare,
> Daisies and violets own remotest heat
>> And bloom and make them fair.
>
> (*CP,* 2:257)

The final image is unexpectedly but delicately sensuous: were these flowers fully personified, the reader would be close to or even inside their bodies, feeling a temperature change along the skin. Because this tactile intimacy is a response to "remotest heat," touching occurs without touch and perfectly symbolizes a spirituality the poem need not actually mention. Rossetti has other images for the hopefulness that persists despite (and in part *because of*) all that is numbing, frightful, or dire. Alone in "a chill blank world," a desolate sky watcher discerns a faint lessening of the gloom. The change detected is "No more than a paler shade of darkness as yet," but it is enough; the coming of light has unmistakably begun and straining attention is rewarded (*CP,* 2:210). A favorite figure is the half-moon, which shows

> a face of plaintive sweetness
> Ready and poised to wax or wane;
> A fire of pale desire in incompleteness.
>
> (*CP,* 2:273)

Hope and vulnerability are here mingled in a glowing state of readiness, and dissatisfaction is a suspenseful sweetness too aesthetically appealing to be desolating.

What might feel, in actuality, like mere instability or gloomy anticipation of recurrent loss is tactfully re-imagined as a kind of "poised" luminosity.

The watchfulness that underlies so many of Rossetti's images, the empathetic heeding of what evolves, whether it be the emergent day or season or lunar phase, might be taken as a figure for Rossetti's own relation to her art. A contemporary poet-critic reminds us that "absolute attention" must be paid at every moment of "the poem's process" because in the finest instances tones modulate, the end is not foreseen from the beginning, and the poem provokes or yields unlooked-for results. Patience, in other words, with the poem's own mobility is the means to surprising grace. Rossetti often begins with a devotional commonplace and then carefully, almost courteously, allows it to become unfamiliar. In one instance, an easy contradiction tells us that joy is not really joy:

> Joy is but sorrow,
>> While we know
> It ends tomorrow:—
>> Even so!
> Joy with lifted veil
> Shows a face as pale
> As the fair changing moon so fair and frail.
>
> (*CP,* 2:302)

The austere paradox is familiar, but the buoyant affirmative is unexpected and fixes the proposition so vehemently that one is curious about what else can possibly be added. What comes next seems to portend a stereotypical unveiling; but instead of the "loathsome and foul" hag who is the traditional symbol of deception (*CP,* 1:77), a delicately fair face is revealed. In this scenario, ephemeral joy is not a woman to be excoriated like the "false" temptress in **"Amor Mundi,"** but one who is to be seen as truly lovely and almost excused for her fragility (*CP,* 1:216). The next stanza, as one sees even before reading it, has an identical, manifestly predictive, shape. Given the symmetrical assertion in the first line, "Pain is but pleasure," and the glimpsed exclamation mark, expectation is set for a stanza like the first and a reiterated pattern of contradiction, endorsement, image. But because this is a Rossetti poem, one half-expects something unexpected:

> Pain is but pleasure,
>> If we know
> It heaps up treasure:—
>> Even so!
> Turn, transfigured Pain,
> Sweetheart, turn again,
> For fair thou art as moonrise after rain.

With the unforeseen figure of address, "Pain" is startlingly greeted as if she were a paramour. Like Rossetti's other lovers who "turn with yearning eyes" (*CP,*

1:63), this "Sweetheart" is asked to "turn" her face to the speaker so her beauty may be celebrated. The success or failure of the poem rests on the conviction with which pain's loveliness is conveyed, and the last phrase manages this with a pristine and almost anticlimactic image. The evocative phrase "after rain" comes, as Rossetti tells us in **Seek and Find,** from the book of Samuel, where it describes new grass "springing out of the earth by clear shining after rain" (2 Sam. 23:4; *P,* 236). In adapting this botanical observation to the radiance of moonrise, Rossetti turns it synesthetic and gives light itself a soft, misty texture. The association with rinsed freshness turns pain into a tenderly intimate cleansing. All this is subtly corroborated by an evolving sound pattern; the poem unobtrusively reweaves the vowels and consonants of "pain" through "fair" "turn" "again" "moonrise" until they become "rain," whose very sound is an affirmation that "pain" may turn into something else.[8]

Perhaps the least expected turn in a devotional poem is to humor; and yet, because an unremitting struggle with ephemerality and depletion can leave the poet *as poet* feeling "unrefreshed from foregone weariness," Rossetti is not unwilling to parody her own mode of lamentation (*CP,* 2:139). In a solemn bit of spoofery, one of the sonnets from the **Time Flies** volume (1885) takes covert aim at *aesthetic* tiredness:

> No thing is great on this side of the grave,
> Nor any thing of any stable worth:
> Whatso is born from earth returns to earth:
> No thing we grasp proves half the thing we crave.
>
>> (*CP,* 2:325)

This could almost be mistaken for straightforward Rossettian ruefulness. Phrased as negatively as her favorite borrowing from Ecclesiastes, "And there is nothing new under the sun" (*CP,* 1:72; Eccl. 1:8), and reliant on the term "half," which is her watermark—as in "Half content, half un-content" (*CP,* 2:98) and "glories half unveiled" (*CP,* 2:143)—it seems characteristic and serious. The reader detects, however, such oddities as the expansion of "nothing" to "no thing," the truncation of "whatsoever" to "whatso," and the feebleness of the second line's twice-generalizing "any." As the poem continues, the increasing glibness of rapid-fire generalizations climaxes in the eighth line's egregious cliché:

> The tidal wave shrinks to the ebbing wave:
> Laughter is folly, madness lurks in mirth:
> Mankind sets off a-dying from the birth:
> Life is a losing game, with what to save?
>
>> (*CP,* 2:326)

With this question, the joke is sprung; at the sonnet's turn, the next phrase, "Thus I," retroactively exposes the octave as a self-citation and a mild satire on the speaker's whiningly intoned *contemptus mundi*. What follows are three lines of alliterative high jinks at the expense of her own bias towards gloom:

> Thus I sat mourning like a mournful owl,
> And like a doleful dragon made ado,
>   Companion of all monsters of the dark.

Though the owl and dragon are genuinely scriptural (Mic. 1:8), Rossetti is responsible for the irreverent plethora of *m*'s and *d*'s. With only a tercet left and monsters to dispatch, Rossetti signals the speaker's epiphany with a quick exclamation and brings on the dawn:

> When lo! the light cast off its nightly cowl,
> And up to heaven flashed a carolling lark,
> And all creation sang its hymn anew.

The ascending skylark is an obvious makeshift, but it suffices. Rossetti has shared her fun, and after the archaically clunky, doleful "ado" we gladly allow her the bird's carol. It accomplishes the needed transition to the natural canticle that turns the speaker's gloom into exultation or at least a sense that the singing, which has gotten labored and predictable, will now be done *for* her.

The reader's sense of making allowances for this ending is instructive, a reminder that the representation of gained or recovered spiritual happiness is no guarantee of a successful poem. It is an undeniable truth that Rossetti's efforts at saintly rapture are routinely disappointing. For persuasive gladness, none supersedes **"A Birthday,"** so admired by Virginia Woolf, or passes the litmus text of its final lines' exuberance: "the birthday of my life / Is come, my love is come to me" (*CP,* 1:37). **The Face of the Deep** includes one auspicious attempt at imagining eternal bliss, a sonnet beginning with an image of ignited joy and a perfectly worded, nearly palindromic characterization of the fullness of heavenly desire:

> The joy of Saints, like incense turned to fire
> In golden censers, soars acceptable;
> And high their heavenly hallelujahs swell
> Desirous still with still-fulfilled desire.
>
>> (*CP,* 2:289)

All the meanings of "still" ("ever yet" unsatisfied, "calm" with ecstasy) and the contradictions of desire (to be desire, desire must not be fulfilled) are at work to enrich the lines that follow. Rossetti does not, unfortunately, maintain the force of her "incense" simile or the pleasing idea that human joy is inherently a form of homage. Instead she falls to narrating—"Sweet thrill the harpstrings of the heavenly quire"—and to inventorying the props, costumes, and details of the paradisal milieu:

All robed in white and all with palm in hand,
   Crowns too they have of gold and thrones of gold;
     The street is golden which their feet have trod,
Or on a sea of glass and fire they stand:
   And none of them is young, and none is old,
     Except as perfect by the Will of God.

There are enough poems in this mode to turn readers away from the religious verse and lend prima facie support to Stevenson's claim that Rossetti's late work adds "little of significance to her achievement." The difficulty with **"The joy of Saints"** is, in part, its dependence on what McGann faults as a "portentous but obscure" idiom that leaves readers unable to find "any human or worlded equivalents" for its textual conventions. Even those who know the biblical code and might ordinarily find comfort in its familiar images and phrasings detect the problem, viz., that Rossetti is impatient with her poem. Instead of moving with the poem's emotion (the joy that "soars" and "swells"), she moves through a static list, relying on grammatical parataxis to accumulate robe *and* palm, crown *and* throne, glass *and* fire, young *and* old in a hurried substitute for empathy; such compounding does not, in the end, communicate the sweet joy it purports to tell of.[9]

It might be taken as a general rule that when a Rossetti poem seems merely rote or dull, the formal culprit is a discernible forcing of its momentum. **"Whitsun Eve"** is an especially instructive example of a poem that comes to ruin despite an especially promising beginning. The speaker is one of Rossetti's beguilingly timid souls, one of "the small who fear" or worry that they are "failing now" (*CP*, 2:333; 2:224-25), but who occasionally become resentful (a sign of their smallness) and familiarly accusatory. In this instance, the opening words belong to the Lord (Rev. 3:14), and the speaker, in a mildly emboldened bit of back talk, impugns divinely professed love with an "if/why" question:

"As many as I love."—Ah, Lord, Who lovest all,
   If thus it is with Thee why sit remote above,
Beholding from afar, stumbling and marred and small,
   So many Thou dost love?

               (*CP*, 2:233)

The poetic rules of encounter prescribe two ways to resolve such a challenge: either the Lord has the last, winning word (in both the endearing and the triumphant sense of that term) or the speaker is moved to recant, prompted by a recollection of the appalling sacrifice made by the God who "died for us" (*CP*, 2:321). Here, however, the speaker crumples instantly, castigates the stumblers "Whom sin and sorrow make their worn reluctant thrall," and proceeds to amplify their unworthiness in three additional lines:

Who fain would flee away but lack the wings of
   dove;
Who long for love and rest; who look to Thee, and
   call
   To Thee for rest and love.

               (*CP*, 2:233)

Somewhere between the stanzas an understanding takes shape that does not make it into the poem. Without it, these guilty admissions on behalf of "so many" seem authorially preconceived. Rossetti *knows* too precisely how she wants this exchange to end and hasn't the patience to discover the speaker's motive for getting there. There is no turn, nothing comparable to the move from paradox to assurance to image in "Joy is but sorrow" or the apostrophic shift that greets "sweetheart Pain." There is nothing unexpected in the poem's own process: what had begun so vigorously, with bold language and a rhythmically witty "stumbling" into the sudden cascade of "stumbling and marred and small" becomes utterly programmed. The syntax goes so slack that phrase boundaries recur exactly at midverse while simple coordination ("sin and sorrow," "love and rest," "look . . . and call," "rest and love") ekes out the dully unmodified iambic rhythm. A possible reason for the flatness of the second stanza is that the poem itself is a "reluctant thrall" to the scriptural source of its opening line and the appended gloss in *The Face of the Deep*. In the text of Rev. 3:19, the expression of divine love is coupled with a warning to the backsliding Christians of Laodicea, "As many as I love, I rebuke and chasten: be zealous therefore, and repent." Rossetti's prose meditation on the passage accepts the injunction to "repent" and provides a remorseful collective echo: "We know that Thou lovest us all, we all being liable to chastening" (*FD*, 141). Then comes her poem and its quietly brazen chiding of the Lord with a portion of his own utterance: "'As many as I love'—Ah, Lord, Who lovest all / If thus it is with Thee why sit remote above?" Unfortunately, the biblical context has already made the response to this question so apparent—the Lord is present (not "remote") in the sufferings that chastise sinners—that it short-circuits the poetic process. At their best, Rossetti's poems are acts of sustained self-surprise; they find out where they are going only when they get there, or, to put it another way, "the clarity" they "arrive at is unforeseeable." The true devotional poem grapples with its truth and refuses to be aesthetically "overburdened by foreseen" endings (*CP*, 2:140). It has texture.[10]

BRAZENNESS: *THE FACE OF THE DEEP* AND THE EMANCIPATION OF POETRY

Critics have speculated on what prompted Rossetti to undertake a prose study of Revelation and to amass 552 pages of citation, prayerful meditation, and "little bits of verse" as a commentary on the most daunting book in the scriptural canon (*L*, 3:346). The impetus, as biographers suggest, might well have been the death of her mother, Frances, the lifelong companion whom Christina did not hesitate to describe as "so dear a saint" (*CGRFL* [*The Family Letters of Christina Georgina Rossetti,*], 232). In a black-bordered letter to a family friend, the unhappy daughter candidly admits that she has "been grieved before but never so desolate as now" (*L*, 3:309). It is not hard to imagine a sorrowful Rossetti turning to the prophecy that describes, in Carolyn Bynum's words, "how time and individual experience are permeated with the eternal" and committing herself to a study of humankind's apocalyptic destiny. Formally, Rossetti's title, *The Face of the Deep: A Devotional Commentary on the Apocalypse,* suggests the influence of Isaac Williams, a contributor to the *Tracts for the Times* and, more germanely, the first author in a series entitled *Devotional Commentary on the Gospel Narrative*. Rossetti respected Williams's devotional poetry and made illustrations in her personal copy of *The Altar* (1849). Her departures from Williams's mode of commentary suggest, however, a distinctive hermeneutic ambition. Palazzo points out that Rossetti's combination of prayers, litanies, and scriptural parallels "to a certain extent replace the quotations from the Church Fathers, which abound in Williams's work," and Robert M. Kachur finds her intending to demonstrate "how she and other 'unlearned' women" might assume the traditionally male privilege of scriptural exegesis. The aim of her commentary, in his view, is "to critique the patriarchal restrictions on women's writing practices within the church itself" and to influence the thinking of Anglican clergymen. This clarification of the gendered division of commentators' labor is helpful, since Rossetti may indeed have felt antagonized by clerical objections to women's interpretive efforts, but as a general explanation it probably loses sight of a deeper concern.[11]

Rossetti's motive for writing, as every page of the book shows, is revulsion from the "taint of cruelty" that suffuses the sacred text and the terror that, as Northrop Frye tells us, "is inseparable" from apocalypse (*FD*, 458). It is not the Anglican male exegete but John of Patmos who stands as Rossetti's adversarial muse and against whose fearsome narrative she raises her protest. When presented with Revelation's image of a vengeful Christ wielding a sickle, Rossetti explains that he comes not to mow but to reap and that "the reaper embraces and draws to his bosom that good grain which he cuts down" (*FD*, 364). Confronted with the horrific punishment of the great whore—"these shall hate the whore, and shall make her desolate and naked, and shall eat her flesh, and burn her with fire" (Rev. 17:16)—Rossetti decries such brutal loathing of evil and makes an eloquent plea against the sin of hating sinners (*FD*, 408). Throughout *The Face of the Deep,* Rossetti sets herself to do the nearly impossible, to meditate as a believer on John's warnings and threats while somehow softening his account of "doom, the Judgment, the opened Books, the lake of fire"; she is to admit the uncertainty of "fi-

nal perseverance," to remember Christ's words on "the resurrection of damnation," and yet to master the anxiety these instill (*FD*, 15, 75, 100). Her aim as she works her way through John's repetitive text is to achieve, over and over, the equilibrium she identifies as holy fear "without terror" and trust "without misgiving" (*FD*, 10).[12]

When describing Rossetti's method in *The Face of the Deep* it is easiest to begin with what she does not do. First and foremost, her patience with received doctrine prevents her from rejecting passages as "unrecoverable" in the manner of such later writers as theologian Mary Daly or professing such nonstandard beliefs as, say, universal amnesty at the Last Judgment. Her orthodoxy is certified by the title-page motto, "Published under the Direction of the Tract Committee," which means, practically speaking, that an editorial board of Anglican priests vetted the manuscript. Their approval, Lorraine Kooistra assures us, was "no easy matter." Second, despite occasionally mentioning a "commentator" she has "turned to" (*FD*, 195), Rossetti gives no information about John's overall structure, omitting to point out, for example, that the epistolary opening is followed by a series of visions associated with two heavenly books, the one opened (Rev. 6:1), the other ingested (Rev. 10:10). Nor does she offer even a cursory narrative outline: there is nothing comparable to the sketch she once provided for *The Divine Comedy* or her efficient hint that the *Vita nuova* is "composed of alternate prose and verse" in which the reader finds "an elaborate continuous exposition of [Dante's] love for Beatrice, interspersed with ever-renewed tribute of praise from his lowliness to her loftiness" (*P*, 188-89). It would have been appropriate to say that Revelation is insistently repetitive and that, as Bernard McGinn explains, many sections of John's vision reiterate "the same basic message of present persecution, imminent destruction of the wicked and reward of the just." Perhaps such information is obviated by what Rossetti takes to be the likemindedness of a readership that belongs to her "beloved Anglican Church" (*FD*, 540). Orthodox believers hardly needed to be told the book's contents or reminded of the recent debates about its transmission and the challenge, by Ernest Renan and others, to the identity of John himself. To them the apocalyptic visionary was none other than the Galilean son of Zebedee, the Savior's "beloved Disciple," the author of three New Testament epistles and the Gospel According to John (*FD*, 11). Rossetti assumes, moreover, that her readers have no interest in the kind of speculation she dismisses in her earlier book, *Letter and Spirit,* as irrelevant fretting over "the precise architecture of Noah's Ark," "the astronomy of Joshua's miracle," and "the botany of Jonah's gourd" (*P*, 283). Her tone is less amused in *Face of the Deep* but her attitude is the same: "curious investigation" is an impediment to "meditation" (*FD*, 334, 409).[13]

Rossetti's broadest statement about her project comes more than mid-way into the book where, in an allusion to her title, she offers a modest, perhaps even a baffled, admission of inexpertness. Because the obscure wording of Rev. 15:15 creates some uncertainty about the speaker, she pauses to explain her hesitation and her procedure:

> But I take this opportunity of calling attention to my ignorance of, sometimes, a very critical point in the text on which I venture to meditate; and if in consequence I misrepresent the person of the speaker or the word spoken, I ask pardon for my involuntary error. Only should I have readers, let me remind them that what I write professes to be a *surface* study of an unfathomable depth: if it incites any to dive deeper than I attain to, it will so far have accomplished a worthy work. My suggestions do not necessarily amount to beliefs; they may be no more than tentative thoughts compatible with acknowledged ignorance.
>
> (*FD,* 365)

This is a genuinely humble disclaimer, but one that also permits her, as Colleen Hobbs succinctly puts it, to reserve "her right to observe the obvious." There are knots in the text that Rossetti—untrained in Greek—cannot pretend to unsnarl and so she needs to invoke some version of the modesty topos if she is to continue her study. Similarly, her professed conviction that Revelation announces a "divine mystery" to all, but explains it to none, releases her from the expectation that she "expound prophecy" (*FD,* 401, 195). She avoids, for example, a historical reading of the millennium and spurns chiliastic expectations that stem from the promise that the faithful will have "power over the nations" (Rev. 2:26); she writes bluntly that "this power appears to be punitive, destructive," and that a Christian's proper concern is with "overcoming himself" and not his neighbor (*FD,* 83). Her approach to the violence of John's prophecy is to read it as a warning to become "harmless as doves"; the book, she contends, "shows us destruction lest we destroy ourselves" (*FD,* 195, 15).[14]

In practice, Rossetti's habit is to take "disjointed portions" of the text, a few verses at a time, and to work through them "piece by piece" (*FD,* 174). "Words," she says, are the "wards" of apocalyptic mystery, and she allows individual terms to direct her to related passages throughout Scripture (*FD,* 103). Wholeheartedly accepting what Frank Kermode describes as commentators' typical assumption, i.e., that "the Bible is its own interpreter," she develops her meditations by exploring textual correspondences. Her hunt for glosses is not strictly exegetical and never philological or even aesthetic. She is not tempted by "wormwood" at Rev. 8:11—which she might have traced back to the Psalms or Jeremiah—a fascinating word used by George Herbert in "Repentance" and by Rossetti herself in the purgation scene of **"Goblin Market,"**

> Her lips began to scorch,
> That juice was wormwood to her tongue,
> She loathed the feast.
>
> (*CP,* 1:24; 493-95)

Instead she pursues simple and generic terms which, because they occur in a wide range of contexts, permit her to liberate the meaning she seeks. She has designs on these words and wants them to help her mute this hectoring Apocalypse. Needless to say, a purposefully segmenting method permits her to lift passages discretely out of context and strip them of their original reference. Her appropriation of Job's aphorism on the inevitability of suffering, "Yet man is born unto trouble, as the sparks fly upward" (Job 5:7), provides a signal example of what can be gained by careful selection and realignment. Rossetti modifies the tenor, making the "sparks" a simile for aspiration toward the divine: "sparks fly upward scaling heaven by fire" (*FD,* 460). Incorporated into her sonnet on "the bottomless pit" at Rev. 20:3, Job's canonical image allows her to express a hope that for those who have set their faces "upward," the threatened "abyss / Is as mere nothing":

> So sparks fly upward scaling heaven by fire,
> Still mount and still attain not, yet draw nigher
> While they have being to their fountain flame.
> To saints who mount, the bottomless abyss
> Is as mere nothing: they have set their face
> Onward and upward toward that blessed place
> Where man rejoices with his God. . . .
>
> (*FD,* 460; *CP,* 2:182)

While neither expounding nor disclaiming a doctrine of hell, Rossetti takes biblical fire as "a figure" for meditation and manages, by orthodox means, to soften the threat of damnation (*FD,* 460).[15]

The single most striking aspect of *The Face of the Deep* is that, like the *Vita nuova,* it is a formal hybrid. In an extraordinary feat of devotion and presumption, Rossetti gives her poems a place within the larger verbal structure of commentary and canonical text; the 403 verses of John's 22 chapters share space with 210 lyrics by Rossetti. The brazenness of aligning prophecy and her own poetry, of suggesting an affinity between John's divine prompting and her own aesthetic inspiration, is protectively obscured by the modest diligence of her prose. A brief example from Rev. 3 will show how she cites a verse, then isolates a single clause and works through her sequence of text-prose-poem.

> 11. Behold, I come quickly: hold that fast which thou hast, that no man take thy crown.

> "Behold, I come quickly."—But some man would answer Lord, sayest Thou that Thou comest quickly Who all these eighteen hundred years hast not come? Well may we pray that we may interpret.

> Christ's blessed words are truth, sending forth wisdom by unnumbered channels. For He uses many seasons and modes of coming, besides and before that final

coming when every eye shall see Him. To some exalted souls He has come ere now in vision and special revelation. To all His brethren down to the poorest and hungriest He comes, or is ready to come, in the Blessed Sacrament of His Body and Blood. To every man who loves Him and keeps His words He comes beyond the world's comprehension and makes His abode with him (*see* St. John xiv. 22, 23).[16] To His beloved He comes in their death whereby they go to Him. In any or in all of these ways we believe and are sure that He kept faith with His faithful Philadelphians.

On the other hand not the creature of time but only the Lord of time and eternity can pronounce on what is or is not *quickly* brought to pass. At eighteen we think a year long, at eighty we think it short: what terminable duration would seem long to us, what such duration would not seem short, if we had already passed out of time into eternity? Wherefore He alone Who saith "quickly" can define quickly.

O Gracious Lord Christ, Who lovest Thine elect with an everlasting love, keep us, I pray Thee, peaceful and trustful in our due ignorance until the day break and the shadows flee away.

Oh knell of a passing time,
Will it never cease to chime?
Oh stir of the tedious sea,
Will it never cease to be?
Yea, when night and when day,
Moon and sun pass away.
Surely the sun burns low,
The moon makes ready to go,
Broad ocean ripples to waste,
Time is running in haste,
Night is numbered, and day
Numbered to pass away.

(FD, 120-21)

Rossetti's method is to fend off the literalist's complaint about "all these eighteen hundred years" with a literalism of her own. First she glosses the word "come," carefully tracing its uses as these vary in application from external to inward manifestation: Christ comes in vision, in the sacrament, in life and at death to those who love him. She corroborates the verb's semantic richness with an allusion to Christ's own use of it at the Last Supper (John 14:23). Her sentence "He comes beyond the world's comprehension" tactfully conflates an uncomprehending apostle's question with Christ's answer so that readers who consult the gospel—and Rossetti's directive to "*see* St. John" virtually inscribes such readerly activity—will find an inference about the vice of skepticism. For the word "quickly," she provides a rather charming reminder of an eighteen-year-old's or an eighty-year-old's eager misperception of time. It is perhaps relevant to recall that as a young woman, Rossetti's own sense of time's dragging oppressiveness found expression in lines that would appear in *The Germ.* **"A Pause of Thought,"** dated February 14, 1848, is impatiently unresigned to the need for patience:

And hope deferred made my heart sick in truth:
But years must pass before a hope of youth
    Is resigned utterly.

(CP, 1:51)

And while still in her teens she wrote a **"Song"** lamenting the desynchronizing effect of an obscure grief that leaves the singer "old before my time" (*CP,* 1:40). Now, four decades later, youth's misunderstanding of duration provides an analogy for all humanity's time-bound restiveness and its possible abatement. So she prays for trust and adds her poem. To resume her meditation, she isolates the next scriptural clause, "hold that fast which thou hast," then adds more commentary and another poem.

"Oh knell of a passing time" was discussed above, and it is interesting to see how its import differs in its two published contexts. To the reader who comes upon it latterly in Rossetti's collection of poems, the discomfort recorded seems endemic to the human condition, for as James Merrill brilliantly says of poets' abstractions, "when we say 'Time' we mean ourselves." In *Verses,* as time's wearing depredations are lamented, the uncertain origin of the responding "yea" and "Surely" keeps the poem properly open to the tension between exhaustion and the assurance that exhaustion will end. On its prior appearance in *The Face of the Deep,* however, it is precisely this openness that is foreclosed by the glossing commentary. The temporal-eternal polarity established in Rossetti's meditation instructs the reader to fault human restlessness as a failure of trust while the included prayer fends off any sense of ambiguity in the poem's structure: the reiterated question, "Will it never cease?" is pre-interpreted as an expression of "our due ignorance" and the answering "Yea" becomes the Lord's graciously corrective reply. From the divine perspective "time *is* running in haste" and the firm "yea . . . surely" refutes humanly subjective misunderstanding. Such an overdetermined interpretation is welcome to some readers but a problem for those who prefer a poetry that acknowledges without rebuking humankind's temporal discontent. Eventually—and fortunately—when the poems have accomplished their devotional purpose in *The Face of the Deep,* Rossetti liberates them from her prose, entrusting them to readers who develop weak or strong readings according to their own lights. As we shall see, Rossetti arranges the *Verses* in a way that celebrates her medium and the richness of poems *as* poems.[17]

The Face of the Deep is both a focused and a sprawling project. Rossetti's narrowing of attention to individual verses opens the text to the play of solemnly quirky associations and enables her to decant various worries about contemporary culture. Like many a writer before and after her, she is alarmed about what her contemporaries read. Wordsworth set a famous example in the "Preface" to *Lyrical Ballads* by complaining that "frantic novels," "extravagant stories in verse," and newspaper reports of "extraordinary" incidents have a blunting effect on the "discriminating powers of the mind." Rossetti suspects that the danger extends to the soul as well and suggests that "it becomes a matter of conscience what poems and novels to read, and how much of the current news of the day" (*FD*, 76). While she never mounts a coherently historical—and certainly not a political—interpretation of John's vision, she does comment on what she takes to be "ominous" signs of the times (*FD*, 243). Apocalyptic commentary, as Steven Goldsmith observes in *Unbuilding Jerusalem*, virtually requires the author to complain in more or less "cranky" and antithetical fashion "about the degenerate state" of contemporary affairs.[18]

In keeping, then, with her chosen genre, Rossetti offers scattered remarks on what she vaguely calls modern "women's self-assertion" (*FD*, 409). The utter conventionality of her notion of gender relations has been a cause of regret and resentment as well as protectively sympathetic interpretation by recent critics. Sharon Smulders explains that "for Rossetti, enfranchisement and equality were spiritual rather than temporal objectives," and she virtually assures women who are "subordinate on earth" that they will "profit from the reversal prefigured" in Luke 14:10, i.e., those who sit in "the lowest room" will be summoned to "go up higher." Smulders concludes that "Rossetti's conservatism is curiously revolutionary," though her use of "curiously" admits to the strain in her argument. Diane D'Amico's ampler account begins with the "public stand" Rossetti takes in 1889 when she allows her name to appear among the signatories to "An Appeal against Female Suffrage," published in the journal *Nineteenth Century*. Once again, the Rossettian distinction between social and spiritual subordination, or, in D'Amico's words, the belief that women will be equal with men in "a time and place beyond the world of exile," is said to mitigate what otherwise seems to be a "reactionary" view of women's rights. Such analyses may be thought to concede as much as they contest, and in any case, even the staunchest appreciation of what Hobbs chooses to call Rossetti's "startling revision of gender roles" can do little to make certain of her pronouncements palatable. Rossetti exasperates with the invidiousness of her comparison crediting men with "keener, tougher, more work-worthy gifts" than women and the sourness of her explanation that curiosity is "a feminine weak point inviting temptation, and doubly likely to facilitate a fall when to indulge it woman affects independence" (*FD*, 76, 520). We are left to conclude that a great poet need not be a particularly adventurous social thinker and perhaps ruefully concede that she cannot or need not prefigure us. At the same time, however, Rossetti confronts the reality of biblical misogyny and gamely attempts to take the sting out of the lesson that "we women may

elicit" from religious tradition (*FD*, 416). Faced with the legacy of Eve's "lapse," Jezebel's prophetic "pretensions," and the apocalyptic prostitute's "transcendent wickedness," Rossetti still manages to find scrupulously precise biblical authority for women's positive role in the world (*FD*, 310, 76, 416). "Woman" may often figure as the temptress, but this does not presume her to be incapable of good; for "in the Bible," Rossetti explains as she makes a typical move from image to word, "the word *tempt* (or its derivatives) is used in a good or in an evil sense, according to the agent or to the object aimed at" (*FD*, 358).[19]

As a conservative, practicing Anglican, Rossetti is wary of secularism in all its forms, whether manifested as the declining and "chilled" observance of the Sabbath, the degrading of charitable giving to a mere "investment," or the latter-day fascination with mesmerism, hypnotism, and that spiritualism "which is not spirituality" (*FD*, 243, 337). Regarding this last, Rossetti tactfully allows it to go unmentioned that in the 1860s her two brothers attempted to retrieve what F. D. Maurice, in his *Lectures on the Apocalypse*, scorns as "mock messages from the departed." At the time, she responded to Gabriel's report on a seance with typically firm resistance: "To me the whole subject is awful and mysterious: though, in spite of my hopeless inability to conceive a clue to the source of sundry manifestations, I still hope simple imposture may be the missing key:—I hope it, at least, so far as the hope is not uncharitable" (*L*, 1:209). The strongest disapproval in *The Face of the Deep* is aimed, not surprisingly, at the indifference of fellow Christians "who stand callous amidst the fears, torments, miseries of others" (*FD*, 418). Parenthetically, we might mention Rossetti's own efforts, in later years, for the relief of indigent women; the famous letter to Swinburne in which she describes herself as "an escaped Governess" is, in fact, an appeal on behalf of an applicant for a pension from the Governesses Benevolent Institution (*L*, 3:231). Rossetti knows, as Auden will later say, that everyone "turns away / Quite leisurely" from another's "disaster," and so she specifically praises those activists who "all but enter within the vortex of evil" to do "rescue work" (*FD*, 418). Activism has its limits, however, and as a woman true to her class, Rossetti cringes whenever political agitation goes beyond peaceful petitioning or the organizing of relief aid. When commenting on the "recent troubles in Ireland" and the "strikes and unions" in England, she condemns the "terrorism resorted to" as a rehearsal "on a minor scale" of the last days' disruptions (*FD*, 349). We might note that in the nineteenth century, the word "terrorism" alludes to the French Revolution, as in "the terrorism of the Jacobins" (*OED*), but it comes to be used for all forms of intimidation, from the "boycotting" practiced during the Irish land agitation of 1880s (*FD*, 349) to the London Dock Strike of 1889, which, while signally important in the history of collective bargaining, involved violence between strikers and strike-breakers. Given this history, Rossetti's use of the word "minor" (rehearsal "on a minor scale") may be significant, for it shows that she is not heavily invested in reactionary class-antagonism or inclined to rant about growing social chaos. It is indicative of her true concern that none of the poems in *Face of the Deep* deal topically with the social evils she mentions. Sensing perhaps that her prose strays too far into mere opinion and finding herself beyond the range of her reticent lyric voice, she closes off such passages without a culminating or strictly relevant poem.[20]

Another look at the text-prose-poem alignments shows that while the times may be distressing, the text of Revelation is, to her, the truly frightening phenomenon. Her piecemeal method aims to localize and her commentary to master the anxiety triggered by "these appalling revelations" (*FD,* 335). Over and again, her glosses work to minimize apocalyptic threats so that her poems can then replace harrowing fear with subtler feelings. It is worth remembering that even a high degree of literary sophistication is not incompatible with dread of the "second death" foretold so insistently in Revelation. Confronted with lurid calls to repent and frequent warnings of damnation, Rossetti is on the alert to extract every bit of consolation and scrap of a hint, however implausible, concerning the extent of divine mercy. Thus she responds to an utterly formulaic adoration passage in which all creation is said to praise God—"every creature which is in heaven, and on the earth, and under the earth, and such as are in the sea" (Rev. 5:13)—as if it were a factual report on the "absolute unanimity amongst all creatures" (*FD,* 189). Since the vision presents all "in company" with each other, she strains for the inference that none are pre-destined to damnation:

> whoever conscientiously and unflinchingly puts and keeps himself in harmony with this text, must find that for practical purposes even predestination itself is shorn of difficulties and terrors. For here we behold things transitory in company with things permanent uplifting praises; the former utilizing for praise the only time they have; the latter for identical praise anticipating the eternity which awaits them. This is to take our Master at His word when He said: "Take therefore no thought for the morrow: for the morrow shall take thought for the things of itself."
>
> (*FD,* 190)

Drawing her last phrase from the Sermon on the Mount (Matt. 6:34), Rossetti attempts to bring together the warnings of the fiery visionary with the reassurances of his loving master. As modern Bible scholars concede, such alignment is the signal challenge John's text poses: his "harsh and demanding" warnings that evildoers will be "condemned to eternal torment" has a far different impact from the exhortation by Jesus to love one's enemies and his own practice of healing and forgiving.

After wending her way through the ensuing glosses on Rev. 5:13, Rossetti returns to the thought of "absolute unanimity" among the praise-giving creatures and imagines a chant that includes all creation. Her poem's elegant redundancy as it hymns their hymn is itself a form of joyous excess in a poem about "measureless" joy:

> Voices from above and from beneath,
> > Voices of creation near and far,
> Voices out of life and out of death,
> > Out of measureless space,
> > Sun, moon, star,
> > In oneness of contentment offering praise.
> Heaven and earth and sea jubilant,
> > Jubilant all things that dwell therein;
> Filled to fullest overflow they chant,
> > Still roll onward, swell,
> > Still begin,
> > Never flagging praise interminable.
>
> (*FD,* 191; *CP,* 2:269)

There is excess, too, in the repetition of "jubilant" and in the happy proliferation of negatives, "Never flagging" and "interminable." There is pleasure in the contraction of the stanzas to three-syllable lines that isolate the "Sun, moon, star" amid cosmic/poetic space and constrain the unstoppable song so that the reader may *feel* it "still begin." In each stanza the short verse gauges the following pentameter's expansion so that it manifests something of the "unflagging" pulsation of the praise it praises. In celebrating creation's rolling, swelling "chant," Rossetti frees herself to acknowledge the harmonious "overflow" of feelings into language. The final stanza, as noted earlier, instructs the reader to eschew apocalyptic fear and participate "today" in the cosmic orison:

> Thou who must fall silent in a while,
> > Chant thy sweetest, gladdest, best, at once;
> Sun thyself today, keep peace and smile;
> > By love upward send
> > Orisons,
> > Accounting love thy lot and love thine end.

The tranquil joy of this "accounting" is, of course, a hard thing to hold on to; seventeen more chapters of Revelation will strain and severely test the ability to "keep peace and smile." It has been said that "Knowledge is a continual process of knowing, Love of loving," and the same should be said of spiritual hope. Eric Griffiths puts the matter precisely when he remarks that the "calm" such a poem achieves "is not something possessed once and for all, but will have to be worked towards again, patience being an incessant rehearsal of itself."[21]

At the opening of the seventh seal, in one of Revelation's typically cataclysmic visions, a third of earth's trees and grass are burnt up; a third of the sea becomes blood, its creatures die and ships sink; a third of all rivers and fountains are made bitterly poisonous to men. Finally, there is mayhem in the sky: "And the fourth angel sounded, and the third part of the sun was smitten, and the third part of the moon, and the third part of the stars; so as the third part of them was darkened, and the day shone not for a third part of it, and the night likewise" (Rev. 8:12). In an attempt to mitigate the ferocity of this cosmos-smashing chapter, Rossetti focuses on the *limited* extent of the sky's damage! With Pauline hints about divine "long-suffering" and urgings to "redeem the time," she assesses the devastation, finds "*two*-thirds left," and takes heart (Col. 1:11; Eph. 5:16; *FD,* 254-55). Accusing herself of having "long dwelt on the threat" and "too long overlooked the promise," she resolves to remain hopeful until absolutely all "brightness is diminished" (*FD,* 254-55). Even as a mathematical allegory, this resolve to ignore partial annihilation is absurd; but as a step in the meditation process it moves far enough away from John's text to allow access to legitimately devotional feelings. In a telling passage cited later in the book, the psalmist admits to quailing dread of God's wrath and pleads, "while I suffer thy terrors I am distracted" (Ps. 88:15; *FD,* 485). This emotional logic is the key to Rossetti's handling of the present passage; extreme fear of the Lord must and does give way to the calmer vigilance of true spirituality. The meditation culminates with the sonnet noted earlier, the beautifully sad lament at the dimming of the sun's "exuberant lustre" and the pallor of a "morning that is scarcely morn" (*CP,* 2:252). The strength of the poem is that its grief is prelude to a "softly protesting" reminder that "light" will shine "full" in the New Jerusalem.

Though the poems in *The Face of the Deep* work resourcefully to contain Revelation's horrifying implications, John's text still enmeshes them in its nightmarish scenarios. In obvious and not-so-obvious ways, the generic mixing has some regrettable consequences. The famous difficulty of the canonical material creates a predisposition to regard the poems as virtual prose and to focus on their contribution, however evasive, to the prophecy's abstractable meaning. As discussed earlier with the example of "**Whitsun Eve**" (*CP,* 2:233), John's hectoring text sometimes completely overdetermines the direction a poem takes and damages it at the moment of its inception. More typically, the harm occurs at the reading stage when the conjoined Scripture and commentary have a tendency to dispel valuable ambiguities of the kind found in "**Oh knell of a passing time**" and to overwhelm subtle tonalities (*CP,* 2:274). In context, the fine small courage of "One woe is past," the "meek" rebound after a "blast" of "pain and fear," is almost ludicrously incommensurate with the visitation of Apollyon's locust horde, which is the woe Revelation 9:12 actually enumerates (*FD,* 265).

And there came out of the smoke locusts upon the earth: and unto them was given power, as the scorpions of the earth have power. And it was commanded them that they should not hurt the grass of the earth, neither any green thing, neither any tree; but only those men which have not the seal of God in their foreheads. And to them it was given that they should not kill them, but that they should be tormented five months: and their torment was as the torment of a scorpion, when he striketh a man. And in those days shall men seek death, and shall not find it; and shall desire to die, and death shall flee from them.

(Rev. 9:3-6)

The idea of a torment so agonizing that its victims yearn for death absolutely precludes stratagems for endurance and Rossetti's poem cannot effectively absorb or displace such ominous cruelty. Comparable damage is inflicted on many of the poems, though it would be a heart-wearying task to spell out the enfeebled readings thus produced. Attention might be called, however, to the way the prose *as prose* casts a lingering pall that prevents full engagement with the medium of poetry per se. The reader who is immersed in John's cryptic formulations and Rossetti's densely packed glosses is repeatedly disconcerted by syntactical strangeness and the nearly physical strain of the book's glaring and frequent disjunctions. Anyone committed to penetrating this challenging text-and-commentary is induced to forget what some readers, distracted by topicality, are already too likely to forget, viz., that poetry does not accomplish its ends by the same means as prose. Its primary concern is not to arrange an argument but to order the flow of emotions as these are felt in the timing of syllables and verses, the pacing of rhymes, and the overall momentum of stanzas. Palpably and irreparably, the congested ongoingness of *The Face of the Deep* makes an onerous imposition on the rhythms of Rossetti's lyrics. James Merrill, author of the epic trilogy *The Changing Light at Sandover,* once described prose as "a mildly nightmarish medium, to which *there is no end . . .* and only at rare and irregular intervals affording that least pause in flight." What Merrill means with his pun is that the pause is poetry's essential feature; ranging from the "least" possible hesitation between paired stresses to the stretch across line breaks. The "pause" is Merrill's metonym for tempo, for the momentum of the poem as a whole including the pace of individual lines and the gradual or sudden halt that confers closure. It is precisely the reader's sensitivity to poetry's emphatic or faint or nearly subliminal pausing that is numbed by the demands of John's long and Rossetti's even longer prose discourse. With the publication of *Verses,* the poems escape the commentary's "nightmarish medium."[22]

In the final pages of *The Face of the Deep,* Rossetti insists that the full meaning of Revelation still eludes her and that, once again, her "understanding breaks down"

(*FD,* 547). At the same time, however, it is clear that her "anxious ignorance" has dissipated and that the book's terrors are no longer a persecution (*FD,* 342). Never expecting to decipher the vision's "occult unfulfilled signification" but only to find the "consolatoriness" hidden there, her commentary comes to a calmly prayerful close (*FD,* 309, 237). She has succeeded in finding each and every "loophole of hope" the sacred text allows (*FD,* 260). A little over a year later, and while the commentary is well on its way to multiple reprintings, Rossetti brings out the collected *Verses* of 1893. This, her last book, is a kind of writer's testimonial declaring that though she has published a considerable amount of prose, her commitment, first and last, is to poetry. The reader can be glad of this book in which the best of the poems, now stripped of their prose encumbrances, recover something of the primacy of attention they had for Rossetti when she was writing them. Absorption in the aesthetic, which poets have variously described as absolute, exhilarating, passionate, "the pure case of the human attempt to find in consciousness freedom from consciousness," is what enabled her to endure her long immersion in Revelation. Now that her poems are free to *be* poems, Rossetti clusters them in thematic groups that call attention to their differences *as* poems and to the virtuosity prompted by successive new formal ideas. A profession of faith in her art, the volume asks us to understand that for her the writing of these poems is every bit as dignified and spiritual as the themes they take up.[23]

A brief look at one pair will indicate what is gained when poem adjoins poem. The first, **"Our Mothers, lovely women pitiful,"** originally appears in the comment on the infamous Mother of Harlots at Revelation 17:4-5. Temporarily overwhelmed by the depiction of sin's own "filthiness," Rossetti mounts a startlingly uncharacteristic diatribe complete with a reference to the blood-sucking horseleech's daughters (Prov. 31:10) and verses from Proverbs warning "woman against herself" (*FD,* 400). Unfortunately, this vigorous pastiche allows Rossetti insufficient maneuverability to separate the allegorical Mother and her evil scriptural daughters from women in general. Alarmed at the possibility Palazzo acknowledges, i.e., that Rossetti "seems to be reiterating the very victimisation and blatant misogyny which angers modern feminist theologians," one welcomes as a general proposition Antony Harrison's view that a Rossettian lapse into patriarchal vilification entails an implicit rejection of its misogyny. Citing an example from her *Goblin Market* volume, Harrison finds Rossetti using such material to condemn "materialism, hedonism, and false amatory ideologies" while at the same time displaying traditionally "degraded constructions of woman's nature" and exposing them as crude stereotypes. In this particular section of *The Face of the Deep* Rossetti most certainly balks at the ugliness of what she assembles and, without even attempting a

transitional comment, inserts her sonnet **"Our Mothers, lovely women pitiful"** (*FD,* 401). An elegy to the mothers and sisters whose gracious lives provide an "unforgotten memory" of what can be "learned in life's sufficient school," this lyric counterexample contests, if only obliquely, the tendency of biblical authors to disparage women (*CP,* 2:292). In *Verses,* of course, the Great Whore is nowhere in sight and hostile portrayals of women are not an immediate concern; there the sonnet is followed by another, better elegy, **"Safe where I cannot lie yet."** In *The Face of the Deep,* this second poem accompanies Revelation 6:7, the opening of the fourth seal (the signal that beckons Death on a pale horse), and a grisly apostrophe hailing "corruption" and "the worm" as "my father . . . my mother, and my sister" (Job 17:14). Such kinship prompts Rossetti to express a humble "trust that some we love rest safely in Paradise," and her poem immediately takes up the word "safe" (*FD,* 205). Though its lovely little quintains are meant to dispel the ghastliness of the biblical material, the attempt, needless to say, is not altogether successful.[24]

Once these poems are moved to *Verses,* not only do they shed their onerous expository burdens, they become linked expressions of affection for the cherished dead. The tenderness of the sonnet becomes visible as it imagines humanly flawed saints encouraging their faltering kinswoman: "Hope as we hoped, despite our slips and scathe, / Fearful in joy and confident in dule" (*CP,* 2:292). The slight oddity of their diction, which owes something to Arthurian romance and medieval balladry, serves to locate their kindly exhortation in a verbal realm suggestive (on the analogy between earlier and higher) of heavenly origin. The following elegy, which is spoken from earth, reciprocates this warm regard, but in an utterly different style. With all the spareness of bereavement, it longingly remembers the loved dead:

> Safe where I cannot lie yet,
>   Safe where I hope to lie too,
> Safe from the fume and the fret;
>   You, and you,
> Whom I never forget.
>
> (*CP,* 2:292)

The magical intimacy of these lines is achieved without a single particularizing detail, not even the previous poem's kinship terms. Instead there are the well-paced pronouns suggesting that the speaker need only shift her remembering glance to signal the loved addressee. The comma does it all; separating the words "you, and you," it allows the merest pause for turning the head or the mind's eye from one "you" to another. The second stanza builds a protective list of sensations manqué, as in **"Dream-Land,"** only now they portend both safety and the return of sentience (*CP,* 1:27). Lilting and alliterated, the stanza glides along until slowed by paired stresses at the word "wait":

Safe from the frost and the snow,
    Safe from the storm and the sun,
Safe where the séeds wáit to grow
    One by one
And to come back in blow.

The thought must "wait," as do the seeds, for the completion deferred until the absolutely last word and the emblematic blooming in eternity. The vowel sounds of "seeds wait to grow" shift from a high frontal to low back as the thought goes underground, while the running-on of the line mimes the pushing growth it describes. This time the unhesitating pace of "one by one" (without comma) conveys the sense of proliferation: each and every one, one after another after another. The final line adds a further little acoustic surprise as the word "back" recedes to the back of the mouth and then brings the "b" forward to shape the awaited "blow." By its gently solemn playfulness, the lyric corroborates the speaker's affection for the preceding sonnet's "unforgotten" women. Together the two poems dramatize the reach of love's reminiscence.[25]

Rossetti knows a great deal about loss and frailty and the plain fact that life is often unrewarding. When the irritable English poet Philip Larkin grumbled to his twentieth-century interviewer that "it is very much easier to imagine happiness than to experience it," he quoted Rossetti to illustrate his own discontent, "Life, and the world, and mine own self, are changed / For a dream's sake," testifying to the resonance of **"Mirage"** and to the impact of its ever-so-mild verb "changed" (*CP,* 1:56). Rossetti takes bitter disappointment as her topic without being embittered and tells of silent hopelessness in an evocative language that lodges itself permanently in the reader's memory. The poem was written at one of Rossetti's creative peaks, between the completion and publication of **"Goblin Market,"** but it has something like the blended honesty and understatement that characterize the best work of her later years. In each of her books, Rossetti writes poignantly of comfortless isolation, imperfect affections, and the affliction that in her early devotional poems goes by the name of weariness. Over the years, she repeatedly summons the courage that is only fitfully adequate to the "gnawing pain" of accumulating sorrows; **"Parting after parting"** has taught her that patience is not indomitable and consolation only sporadic and fleeting (*CP,* 2:277). Nonetheless, Rossetti knows that poetry recovers the intensity that helps one live and, as McClatchy so beautifully says, that it "raises the pitch and status" of the human cry. Her protracted involvement with John of Patmos's eschatological prophecy, whatever its elusive meanings, plainly stimulates her own tendency to imagine life viewed-from-the-end. His fierce vision of all creation as deathstruck draws her out of whatever dark silence tempts her, and she rallies like the heliotropic flowers in her spring roundel. She is stirred to lament spiritual dullness as the cruelly inflicted "stripes" of divine abandonment and to protest wasting tedium with

the matching restlessness of her poem's formal agitation. In a broad range of voices and attitudes she wails clamorously with a "wail of loss," beckons pain with the tenderest of love songs, and makes mock of dolefulness. One of her favorite biblical passages, the protesting verse "Thou hast asked a hard thing," might be taken as her motto, not as a feeble complaint but as a clear-sighted statement of fact and a way of bracing for the effort life requires (2 Kings 2). Faced again and again with the reality of hard things, she responds with a supple resilience that locates the precise moment of courageous rebound from woe, that scrounges for cheer in sensations of "remotest heat," and that finds exhilaration in winter's "keenness." All the while, and with a wonderful tenaciousness, she refuses to give up on the chance of joy and allows gladness to ripple through her poems with speeding rhythm and flamboyant language. Most important, she has the true artist's talent for self-forgetfulness amid a paradoxically liberating absorption in the individual poem. *Verses* attests by its scrupulous and exquisite variations on lyric form that the hard things *are* hard and that art gives repeated and time-resistant access to a necessary harmony, courage, and clarity. Rossetti's last book is a crucial endorsement of poetry as a way of life.[26]

Notes

1. Virginia Woolf, "I Am Christina Rossetti," [in *The Second Common Reader* (New York: Harcourt, 1932),] 263, 262. For "five hundred a year," see the conclusion to *A Room of One's Own* (1929; Harmondsworth, UK: Penguin, 1945). According to [Diane D'Amico, in *Christina Rossetti: Faith, Gender and Time* (Baton Rouge: Louisinia State Univ. Press, 1999),] Rossetti's *Verses* (1893) continued to be published into the twentieth century and "by 1912, twenty-one thousand copies . . . had been printed" (148).

2. Lynda Palazzo, *Christina Rossetti's Feminist Theology* (New York: Palgrave, 2002), 94. Arthur Symons's 1887 review of "Miss Rossetti's Poetry" is excerpted in Edna Kotin Charles, *Christina Rossetti: Critical Perspectives, 1862-1982* (London: Associated University Presses, 1985), 41; see Charles for others' comments on "Good Friday" (63) and "Who Shall Deliver Me?" (29). For Gabriel Rossetti's "Songs of the Art Catholic," see *Dante Gabriel Rossetti: His Family Letters,* ed. William Michael Rossetti (London, 1895), 113. The religious poems in *The Germ* include William Michael Rossetti's "Jesus Wept" as well as, among Dante Gabriel Rossetti's sonnets for pictures, "A Virgin and Child, by Hans Memmeling" and "A Marriage of St. Katharine, by the same"; see *The Germ: The Literary Magazine of the Pre-Raphaelites,* pref. Andrea Rose (Oxford: Ashmolean Museum, 1984), 179, 180. For "Virtue," see *George Herbert,* ed. Louis L. Martz (Oxford:

Oxford Univ. Press, 1994), 73. David A. Kent, "'By thought, word, and deed': George Herbert and Christina Rossetti," in [*The Achievement of Christina Rossetti*, ed. David A. Kent (Ithaca, N.Y.: Cornell Univ. Press, 1987),] notes that Rossetti owned "William Pickering's edition of Herbert's complete writings (the first such edition)," the first volume of which is signed and "dated December 5, 1848, her eighteenth birthday" (255). In her fourteenth year, Rossetti had written "Charity," which, as indicated by Maria Rossetti's manuscript note, was also "imitated from that beautiful little poem 'Virtue' by George Herbert" (*CP*, 3:101, 399).

3. The facts of Gabriel Rossetti's death are as follows: After what William Michael Rossetti describes as "an attack of partial paralysis" on December 11, 1881, Gabriel moved to Birchington-on-Sea and was joined by Frances and Christina in early March; he died there on Easter Sunday April 9 and was buried April 14, 1882, in Birchington Churchyard (*CGRFL*, 103, 223); see the diary that Christina kept for her mother at this time (*CGRFL*, 222-26), her letters from Birchington (*L*, 3:15-35), and also Jan Marsh, *Dante Gabriel Rossetti: Painter and Poet* (London: Weidenfeld, 1999), 525-27.

4. For Gabriel's "prohibition of burial at Highgate where Lizzie was buried," see [Oswald Doughty, *A Victorian Romantic: Dante Gabriel Rossetti* (London: Muller, 1949),] 583, 669, and [Jan Marsh, *Christina Rossetti: A Writer's Life* (New York: Viking, 1995),] 494. The painlessness of Gabriel's death is emphasized in Christina's diary entry for April 9, 1882: "The instant cause of death assigned by Dr. Harris was that the uraemic poison touched the brain, and he afterwards assured us that there was no pain" (*CGRFL*, 225); for the implausibility of such an assurance, see Sherwin B. Nuland, *How We Die: Reflections on Life's Final Chapter* (New York: Knopf, 1994), 140-43. On Gabriel's a-religious views, see [Jerome McGann, *Dante Gabriel Rossetti and the Game that Must Be Lost* (New Haven, Conn.: Yale Univ. Press, 2000),] 91; see Marsh, *Christina Rossetti*, for the view that "To Christina . . . it was grievous that Gabriel died unbelieving" (494). [Stephen Booth, *Precious Nonsense: The Gettysburg Address, Ben Jenson's Epitaphs on His Children and Tuelfth Night* (Berkeley: Univ. of California Press, 1998],] 90.

5. Mary Howitt, who in 1854 had been almost the first to publish Rossetti's work, reacts in 1879 to one of the recent lyrics as if it were uttering "a cry out of my own heart—to be delivered from *Self*. It was the whole cry of an earnest soul embodied in a few words; a wonderful little outburst of prayer" (*L*, 1:79 n. 7). Howitt does not give the title, though possibly, as an extraordinarily busy author, editor, and translator (of Hans Christian Andersen, among others), she may have been struck by "Who Shall Deliver Me?" with its lament about life's "turmoil, tedium, gad-about" (*CP*, 1:227). For "Tuning of my breast," see "The Temper," *George Herbert*, 44. "Orisons" is the only noun Rossetti ever allows to appropriate a full line (*CP*, 2:269). In the *Pageant* volume, "What's in a Name?" notes the brevity of the word "spring" and suggests, in a single verse, that the actual season may "Superabound" (*CP*, 2:110). See pp. 127 and 129 (chapter 3 of [*Christina Rossetti: The Patience of Style*]) for discussion of "Gratuitous" in "My God, wilt Thou accept and will not we" (*CP*, 2:210) and "Everywhere!" in the nursery rhyme "Wrens and robins in the hedge" (*CP*, 2:24).

6. For "secure pieties," see [Robert Hass, *Twentieth-Century Pleasures: Prose on Poetry* (New York: Ecco, 1984,] 20. [Debra Fried, "Rhyme Puns," in *On Puns: The Foundation of Letters*, ed. Jonathan Culler (Oxford: Blackwell, 1988,] 83.

7. For Dr. Johnson, see [Christopher Ricks, *The Force of Poetry* (1984; Oxford: Clarendon, 2001),] 278.

8. For "absolute . . . process," see Hass, *Twentieth Century Pleasures*, 16.

9. Woolf, "I Am Christina Rossetti," 265. [Lionel Stevenson, *The Pre-Raphaelite Poets* (New York: Norton, 1974),] *The Pre-Raphaelite Poets*, 117. McGann, in Kent, *Achievement of Christina Rossetti*, 8.

10. For "clarity . . . unforeseeable," see *Recitative: Prose by James Merrill*, ed. J. D. McClatchy (San Francisco: North Point Press, 1986), 8.

11. Carolyn Walker Bynum, *Last Things: Death and the Apocalypse in the Middle Ages*, ed. Carolyn Walker Bynum and Paul Freedmen (Philadelphia: Univ. of Pennsylvania Press, 2000), 4. Kent and Stanwood summarize biographers' estimates (ranging from two and a half to seven years) for how long Rossetti worked on *The Face of the Deep*, published in 1892 (*P*, 331). Little is known of the book's composition except that within a few months of Frances Rossetti's death on April 8, 1886, Christina mentions in a letter to Theodore Watts that she has begun "reading and thinking over part of the New Testament, writing down what I can as I go along. I work at prose and help myself forward with little bits of verse" (*L*, 3:346). She provides no information about her project's evolution, the order of her poems' composition, or the process of fitting them to the prose text, i.e., whether the poems were already available to be

gathered into the commentary or written specifically for individual glosses or both. For Rossetti's illustration in Isaac Williams's *The Altar,* see the page reproduced in Mary F. Sandars, *The Life of Christina Rossetti* (London: Hutchinson, 1906), 211. Palazzo, *Christina Rossetti's Feminist Theology,* 122. Robert M. Kachur, "Repositioning the Female Christian Reader: Christina Rossetti as Tractarian Hermeneut in *The Face of the Deep,*" *Victorian Poetry* 35, no. 2 (1997): 205, 207.

12. Northrop Frye, *Words with Power: Being a Second Study of "The Bible and Literature"* (New York: Viking, 1990), 113. For a thoroughgoing account of John's admonitions, see Adela Yarbro Collins, "The Book of Revelation," in *The Origins of Apocalypticism,* ed. John J. Collins, vol. 1 of *The Encyclopedia of Apocalypticism,* ed. Bernard McGinn and Stephen J. Stein, 3 vols. (New York: Continuum, 1998); John's threats and promises were meant, in Collins's view, to encourage the Christian religious minority "to avoid compromise with the corrupt and idolatrous culture of the hellenized and romanized cities of Asia Minor, no matter what the cost" and may have contributed "to the survival of a Christian perspective that could not simply take its place as one ancient cult among many" (412).

13. For discussion of Daly's *Gyn-Ecology: The Metaethics of Radical Feminism,* see Palazzo, *Christina Rossetti's Feminist Theology,* 131. [Lorraine Janzen Kooistra, *Christina Rossetti and Illustration: A Publishing History* (Athens: Ohio Univ. Press, 2002),] 144. Bernard McGinn, "Revelation" in *The Literary Guide to the Bible,* ed. Robert Alter and Frank Kermode (Cambridge: Harvard Univ. Press, 1987), 525; McGinn provides a brief "history of the ways in which Revelation has been read," along with a reminder that current scholarship does not identify the author of Revelation as the gospel writer or the disciple but as "an itinerant Christian prophet of Asia Minor who wrote in the last decade of the first century" (527-40, 524).

14. Colleen Hobbs, "A View from 'The Lowest Place': Christina Rossetti's Devotional Prose," *Victorian Poetry* 32, nos. 3-4 (1994): 416. Hobbs finds analogues for Rossetti's disclaimer in the writings of fourteenth-century women mystics and cites Elizabeth Alvilda Petroff, *Medieval Women's Visionary Literature* (New York: Oxford Univ. Press, 1986), for the observation, "Women writers assert that they have not studied how to express themselves; they are ignorant of rhetoric; they have not read any of their ideas in books" (Petroff, 27, qtd. in Hobbs, 426). Regarding expectations about the millennium, Adela Yarbro Collins, "Book of Revelation," summarizes the divergent views, noting

that "the official eschatological teaching of the major denominations . . . is rooted in Augustine . . . and does not include an earthly reign of Christ between the second coming and the final state," but fundamentalist teaching regards Revelation as a literal forecast of the end times when resurrected martyrs will reign with Christ on earth (411).

15. Frank Kermode, "The Canon," in Alter and Kermode, *Literary Guide to the Bible,* 605.

16. Rossetti's parenthesis directs the reader to John's narrative of the Passover supper and Jude's quizzing of Jesus about his promise to manifest himself to those who keep his commandments: "Judas saith unto him, not Iscariot, Lord, how is it that thou wilt manifest thyself unto us, and not unto the world? Jesus answered and said unto him, If a man love me, he will keep my words: and my Father will love him, and we will come unto him, and make our abode with him" (John 14:22-23).

17. Merrill, *Recitative,* 102.

18. Wordsworth, "Preface to *Lyrical Ballads*" (1800), in [*Lyrical Ballads and Other Poems, 1797-1800,* ed. James Butler and Karen Green (Ithaca, N.Y.: Cornell Univ. Press, 1992),] 746-47. On "cranky apocalypses," see Steven Goldsmith, *Unbuilding Jerusalem: Apocalypse and Romantic Representation* (Ithaca, N.Y.: Cornell Univ. Press, 1993), 4; Goldsmith objects to any "aesthetic" or other version of apocalypse that "makes obsolete and thus displaces the need for political apocalypse" (7).

19. Sharon Smulders, "Women's Enfranchisement in Christina Rossetti's Poetry," *Texas Studies in Literature and Language* 34, no. 4 (1992): 578, 583. D'Amico, *Christina Rossetti,* 130, 138, 134. Hobbs, "A View from 'The Lowest Place,'" 411. In commenting on the word "tempt," Rossetti surely has in mind the divine injunction to sacrifice Isaac: "And it came to pass after these things, that God did tempt Abraham" (Gen. 22:1).

20. Frederick Denison Maurice, *Lectures on the Apocalypse* (London: Macmillan, 1885), 314.

21. For "harsh . . . torment," see Adela Yarbro Collins, "Book of Revelation," 412. For "Knowledge . . . loving," see McGann, *Dante Gabriel Rossetti and the Game,* 37. [Eric Griffiths, "The Disappointment of Christina G. Rossetti," *Essays in Criticism* 47, no. 2 (1997),] 126.

22. Merrill, *Recitative,* xiii.

23. For "pure . . . consciousness," see Hass, *Twentieth Century Pleasures,* 169.

24. Palazzo, *Christina Rossetti's Feminist Theology,* 127. Antony H. Harrison, *Victorian Poets and the*

Politics of Culture: Discourse and Ideology (Charlottesville: Univ. Press of Virginia, 1998), 129.

25. For Rossetti's other uses of "scathe," see the discussion of "L.E.L." on p. 84 of [*Christina Rossetti: The Patience of Style*]. For "dule," see the ballad "Edward, Edward," in which Edward's mother suspects that he grieves "Sum other dule" besides the loss of his horse [Thomas Percy, ed., *Reliques of Ancient English Poetry*, 3 vols. (Edinburgh, 1858),] 1:46).

26. Larkin, *Required Writing: Miscellaneous Pieces 1955-1982* (New York: Farrar, 1982), 56. See J. D. McClatchy's introduction to Merrill, *Recitative*, viii.

Abbreviations

References to the works listed below are made within the text. Typically, these references include, in addition to the abbreviated title, the volume number (if any) and page number from which the specific quotation or reference is drawn. For longer poems or for those discussed extensively in the text, the full page range for the poem is given at first citation only, followed by line numbers for specific quotations; subsequent citations to the poem include line numbers only. For the sonnet sequences, such as *Monna Innominata* and *Later Life*, only the title abbreviation and the number of the sonnet or division are included, although in some instances line numbers are cited as well.

AT	Alfred Tennyson, *Tennyson: A Selected Edition*, ed. Christopher Ricks. London: Longman, 1989.
EBB	Elizabeth Barrett Browning, *The Poetical Works of Elizabeth Barrett Browning*, with intro. by Ruth M. Adams. Boston: Houghton Mifflin, 1974.
C	*Petrarch: The Canzoniere; or, Rerum vulgarium fragmenta*, trans. Mark Musa. Bloomington: Indiana Univ. Press, 1996.
CGRFL	*The Family Letters of Christina Georgina Rossetti*, ed. William Michael Rossetti. London: Brown, 1908.
CP	Christina Rossetti, *The Complete Poems of Christina Rossetti: A Variorum Edition*, ed. Rebecca W. Crump, 3 vols. Baton Rouge: Louisiana State Univ. Press, 1979-90.
FD	Christina G. Rossetti, *The Face of the Deep: A Devotional Commentary on the Apocalypse*. London: Society for Promoting Christian Knowledge, 1892.
Hemans	*Felicia Hemans: Selected Poems, Letters, Reception Materials*, ed. Susan J. Wolfson. Princeton, N.J.: Princeton Univ. Press, 2000.

HL	*The House of Life*, in *The Pre-Raphaelites and Their Circle*, ed. Cecil Y. Lang, 2nd ed. Chicago: Univ. of Chicago Press, 1975, 79-129.
Keats	John Keats, *Complete Poems and Selected Letters of John Keats*, with intro. by Edward Hirsch. New York: Modern Library, 2001.
Landon	*Letitia Elizabeth Landon: Selected Writings*, ed. Jerome McGann and Daniel Riess. Peterborough, Ontario: Broadview, 1997.
L	*The Letters of Christina Rossetti*, ed. Antony H. Harrison, 4 vols. Charlottesville: Univ. Press of Virginia, 1997-2004.
LL	*Later Life*, in *The Complete Poems of Christina Rossetti: A Variorum Edition*, ed. Rebecca W. Crump, vol. 2. Baton Rouge: Louisiana State Univ. Press, 1986, 138-50.
LDGR	*Letters of Dante Gabriel Rossetti*, ed. Oswald Doughty and John Robert Wahl, 4 vols. Oxford: Clarendon, 1965-67.
MI	*Monna Innominata*, in *The Complete Poems of Christina Rossetti: A Variorum Edition*, ed. Rebecca W. Crump, vol. 2. Baton Rouge: Louisiana State Univ. Press, 1986, 86-93.
NRNT	*Nursery Rhymes and Nursery Tales of England*, ed. James Orchard Halliwell, 5th ed. London, 1855.
P	Christina Rossetti, *Selected Prose of Christina Rossetti*, ed. David S. Kent and P. G. Stanwood. New York: St. Martin's, 1998.
PW	Christina Rossetti, *Christina Georgina Rossetti: The Poetical Works*, ed. William Michael Rossetti. 1906; New York: Olms, 1970.
PWH	*The Poetical Works of Mrs. Felicia Hemans*, ed. William Michael Rossetti. Boston, 1856.
SP	*Sonnets from the Portuguese*, in *A Variorum Edition of Elizabeth Barrett Browning's "Sonnets from the Portuguese,"* ed. Miroslava Wein Dow. Troy, N. Y.: Whitston, 1980.

FURTHER READING

Biographies

Jones, Kathleen. *Learning Not To Be First: The Life of Christina Rossetti*. Gloucestershire, England: The Windrush Press, 1991, 252 p.

Full-length biography of Rossetti that focuses on the sense of wanting that permeates the author's life and works.

Marsh, Jan. *Christina Rossetti: A Literary Biography.* London: Jonathan Cape, 1994, 634 p.

> Biography of Rossetti organized chronologically around the composition and publication of her works.

Criticism

Chapman, Alison. *The Afterlife of Christina Rossetti.* Basingstoke, England and New York: Macmillan—St. Martin's Press, 2000, 213 p.

> "[A]ttempts to forge a link between uncanny literary subjectivities and a new mode of critical reading that refuses to recuperate the personal and the author's personage as a stable monolithic presence" with various interpretations of Rossetti's works.

Easley, Alexis. "Christina Rossetti and the Problem of Literary Fame." In *First-Person Anonymous: Women Writers and Victorian Print Media, 1830-70,* pp. 153-76. Aldershot, England: Ashgate, 2004.

> Offers a detailed, scholarly analysis of Rossetti's approach to women's issues, particularly to the social dilemma faced by women writers.

Harrison, Anthony H. *Christina Rossetti in Context.* Chapel Hill and London: University of North Carolina Press, 1988, 231 p.

> Interprets social, moral, and religious commentary in Rossetti's works within the context of the society and culture in which she lived.

Kent, David A., ed. *The Achievement of Christina Rossetti.* Ithaca, N.Y.: Cornell University Press, 1987, 367 p.

> Collection of scholarly essays offering a variety of interpretations of Rossetti's works and their significance in the literary canon.

Linley, Margaret. "Dying to Be a Poetess: The Conundrum of Christina Rossetti." In *The Culture of Christina Rossetti: Female Poetics and Victorian Contexts,* edited by Mary Arseneau, Antony H. Harrison, and Lorraine Janzen Kooistra, pp. 285-314. Athens: Ohio University Press, 1999.

> Examines the manner in which Rossetti rejects the traditional cultural classification of the poetess in *Maude.*

Lysack, Krista. "The Economics of Ecstasy in Christina Rossetti's 'Monna Innominata.'" *Victorian Poetry* 36, no. 4 (winter 1998): 399-416.

> Illustrates how Rossetti adapts the Petrarchan poetic tradition and uses physical imagery to comment upon the suppression of women's pursuit of sexual, spiritual, and professional fulfillment.

Winters, Sarah Fiona. "Christina Rossetti's Poetic Vocation." *Women's Writing* 12, no. 2 (2005): 291-307.

> Views the influence of Christianity on Rossetti's works, asserting that the author takes advantage of her faith to increase the acceptance of her writing in the male-dominated literary society.

Additional coverage of Rossetti's life and career is contained in the following sources published by Thomson Gale: *Authors and Artists for Young Adults,* Vol. 51; *Beacham's Guide to Literature for Young Adults,* Vol. 4; *British Writers,* Vol. 5; *Children's Literature Review,* Vol. 115; *Dictionary of Literary Biography,* Vols. 35, 163, 240; *DISCovering Authors; DISCovering Authors: British; DISCovering Authors: Canadian; DISCovering Authors Modules: Most-studied Authors* and *Poets; DISCovering Authors 3.0; Exploring Poetry; Feminism in Literature: A Gale Critical Companion; Literature and Its Times Supplement; Literature Resource Center; Major Authors and Illustrators for Children and Young Adults,* Eds. 1, 2; *Nineteenth-Century Literature Criticism,* Vols. 2, 50, 66; *Poetry Criticism,* Vol. 7; *Poetry for Students,* Vols. 10, 14; *Reference Guide to English Literature,* Ed. 2; *Something about the Author,* Vol. 20; *Twayne's English Authors; World Literature Criticism;* **and** *Writers for Children.*

How to Use This Index

The main references

> **Calvino, Italo**
> 1923-1985 .... CLC 5, 8, 11, 22, 33, 39,
> 73; SSC 3, 48

list all author entries in the following Thomson Gale Literary Criticism series:

AAL = *Asian American Literature*
BG = *The Beat Generation: A Gale Critical Companion*
BLC = *Black Literature Criticism*
BLCS = *Black Literature Criticism Supplement*
CLC = *Contemporary Literary Criticism*
CLR = *Children's Literature Review*
CMLC = *Classical and Medieval Literature Criticism*
DC = *Drama Criticism*
FL = *Feminism in Literature: A Gale Critical Companion*
GL = *Gothic Literature: A Gale Critical Companion*
HLC = *Hispanic Literature Criticism*
HLCS = *Hispanic Literature Criticism Supplement*
HR = *Harlem Renaissance: A Gale Critical Companion*
LC = *Literature Criticism from 1400 to 1800*
NCLC = *Nineteenth-Century Literature Criticism*
NNAL = *Native North American Literature*
PC = *Poetry Criticism*
SSC = *Short Story Criticism*
TCLC = *Twentieth-Century Literary Criticism*
WLC = *World Literature Criticism, 1500 to the Present*
WLCS = *World Literature Criticism Supplement*

The cross-references

> See also CA 85-88, 116; CANR 23, 61;
> DAM NOV; DLB 196; EW 13; MTCW 1, 2;
> RGSF 2; RGWL 2; SFW 4; SSFS 12

list all author entries in the following Thomson Gale biographical and literary sources:

AAYA = *Authors & Artists for Young Adults*
AFAW = *African American Writers*
AFW = *African Writers*
AITN = *Authors in the News*
AMW = *American Writers*
AMWR = *American Writers Retrospective Supplement*
AMWS = *American Writers Supplement*
ANW = *American Nature Writers*
AW = *Ancient Writers*
BEST = *Bestsellers*
BPFB = *Beacham's Encyclopedia of Popular Fiction: Biography and Resources*
BRW = *British Writers*
BRWS = *British Writers Supplement*
BW = *Black Writers*
BYA = *Beacham's Guide to Literature for Young Adults*
CA = *Contemporary Authors*
CAAS = *Contemporary Authors Autobiography Series*
CABS = *Contemporary Authors Bibliographical Series*
CAD = *Contemporary American Dramatists*
CANR = *Contemporary Authors New Revision Series*
CAP = *Contemporary Authors Permanent Series*
CBD = *Contemporary British Dramatists*
CCA = *Contemporary Canadian Authors*
CD = *Contemporary Dramatists*
CDALB = *Concise Dictionary of American Literary Biography*

CDALBS = *Concise Dictionary of American Literary Biography Supplement*
CDBLB = *Concise Dictionary of British Literary Biography*
CMW = *St. James Guide to Crime & Mystery Writers*
CN = *Contemporary Novelists*
CP = *Contemporary Poets*
CPW = *Contemporary Popular Writers*
CSW = *Contemporary Southern Writers*
CWD = *Contemporary Women Dramatists*
CWP = *Contemporary Women Poets*
CWRI = *St. James Guide to Children's Writers*
CWW = *Contemporary World Writers*
DA = *DISCovering Authors*
DA3 = *DISCovering Authors 3.0*
DAB = *DISCovering Authors: British Edition*
DAC = *DISCovering Authors: Canadian Edition*
DAM = *DISCovering Authors: Modules*
   DRAM: *Dramatists Module;* **MST:** *Most-studied Authors Module;*
   MULT: *Multicultural Authors Module;* **NOV:** *Novelists Module;*
   POET: *Poets Module;* **POP:** *Popular Fiction and Genre Authors Module*
DFS = *Drama for Students*
DLB = *Dictionary of Literary Biography*
DLBD = *Dictionary of Literary Biography Documentary Series*
DLBY = *Dictionary of Literary Biography Yearbook*
DNFS = *Literature of Developing Nations for Students*
EFS = *Epics for Students*
EXPN = *Exploring Novels*
EXPP = *Exploring Poetry*
EXPS = *Exploring Short Stories*
EW = *European Writers*
FANT = *St. James Guide to Fantasy Writers*
FW = *Feminist Writers*
GFL = *Guide to French Literature,* Beginnings to 1789, 1798 to the Present
GLL = *Gay and Lesbian Literature*
HGG = *St. James Guide to Horror, Ghost & Gothic Writers*
HW = *Hispanic Writers*
IDFW = *International Dictionary of Films and Filmmakers: Writers and Production Artists*
IDTP = *International Dictionary of Theatre: Playwrights*
LAIT = *Literature and Its Times*
LAW = *Latin American Writers*
JRDA = *Junior DISCovering Authors*
MAICYA = *Major Authors and Illustrators for Children and Young Adults*
MAICYAS = *Major Authors and Illustrators for Children and Young Adults Supplement*
MAWW = *Modern American Women Writers*
MJW = *Modern Japanese Writers*
MTCW = *Major 20th-Century Writers*
NCFS = *Nonfiction Classics for Students*
NFS = *Novels for Students*
PAB = *Poets: American and British*
PFS = *Poetry for Students*
RGAL = *Reference Guide to American Literature*
RGEL = *Reference Guide to English Literature*
RGSF = *Reference Guide to Short Fiction*
RGWL = *Reference Guide to World Literature*
RHW = *Twentieth-Century Romance and Historical Writers*
SAAS = *Something about the Author Autobiography Series*
SATA = *Something about the Author*
SFW = *St. James Guide to Science Fiction Writers*
SSFS = *Short Stories for Students*
TCWW = *Twentieth-Century Western Writers*
WLIT = *World Literature and Its Times*
WP = *World Poets*
YABC = *Yesterday's Authors of Books for Children*
YAW = *St. James Guide to Young Adult Writers*

Literary Criticism Series
Cumulative Author Index

Aleshkovsky, Yuz .... **CLC 44**
See Aleshkovsky, Joseph
See also DLB 317

Alexander, Lloyd 1924-2007 .... **CLC 35**
See also AAYA 1, 27; BPFB 1; BYA 5, 6,
7, 9, 10, 11; CA 1-4R; CANR 1, 24, 38,
55, 113; CLR 1, 5, 48; CWRI 5; DLB 52;
FANT; JRDA; MAICYA 1, 2; MAICYAS
1; MTCW 1; SAAS 19; SATA 3, 49, 81,
129, 135; SUFW; TUS; WYA; YAW

Alexander, Lloyd Chudley
See Alexander, Lloyd

Alexander, Meena 1951- .... **CLC 121**
See also CA 115; CANR 38, 70, 146; CP 5,
6, 7; CWP; DLB 323; FW

Alexander, Samuel 1859-1938 .... **TCLC 77**

Alexeiev, Konstantin
See Stanislavsky, Constantin

Alexeyev, Constantin Sergeivich
See Stanislavsky, Constantin

Alexeyev, Konstantin Sergeyevich
See Stanislavsky, Constantin

Alexie, Sherman 1966- .... **CLC 96, 154;**
NNAL; PC 53
See also AAYA 28; BYA 15; CA 138;
CANR 65, 95, 133; CN 7; DA3; DAM
MULT; DLB 175, 206, 278; LATS 1:2;
MTCW 2; MTFW 2005; NFS 17; SSFS
18

al-Farabi 870(?)-950 .... **CMLC 58**
See also DLB 115

Alfau, Felipe 1902-1999 .... **CLC 66**
See also CA 137

Alfieri, Vittorio 1749-1803 .... **NCLC 101**
See also EW 4; RGWL 2, 3; WLIT 7

Alfonso X 1221-1284 .... **CMLC 78**

Alfred, Jean Gaston
See Ponge, Francis

Alger, Horatio, Jr. 1832-1899 .... **NCLC 8, 83**
See also CLR 87; DLB 42; LAIT 2; RGAL
4; SATA 16; TUS

Al-Ghazali, Muhammad ibn Muhammad
1058-1111 .... **CMLC 50**
See also DLB 115

Algren, Nelson 1909-1981 ..... **CLC 4, 10, 33;**
SSC 33
See also AMWS 9; BPFB 1; CA 13-16R;
CAAS 103; CANR 20, 61; CDALB 1941-
1968; CN 1, 2; DLB 9; DLBY 1981,
1982, 2000; EWL 3; MAL 5; MTCW 1,
2; MTFW 2005; RGAL 4; RGSF 2

al-Hariri, al-Qasim ibn 'Ali Abu
Muhammad al-Basri
1054-1122 .... **CMLC 63**
See also RGWL 3

Ali, Ahmed 1908-1998 .... **CLC 69**
See also CA 25-28R; CANR 15, 34; CN 1,
2, 3, 4, 5; DLB 323; EWL 3

Ali, Tariq 1943- .... **CLC 173**
See also CA 25-28R; CANR 10, 99, 161

Alighieri, Dante
See Dante
See also WLIT 7

al-Kindi, Abu Yusuf Ya'qub ibn Ishaq c.
801-c. 873 .... **CMLC 80**

Allan, John B.
See Westlake, Donald E.

Allan, Sidney
See Hartmann, Sadakichi

Allan, Sydney
See Hartmann, Sadakichi

Allard, Janet .... **CLC 59**

Allen, Edward 1948- .... **CLC 59**

Allen, Fred 1894-1956 .... **TCLC 87**

Allen, Paula Gunn 1939- .... **CLC 84, 202;**
NNAL
See also AMWS 4; CA 143; CAAE 112;
CANR 63, 130; CWP; DA3; DAM
MULT; DLB 175; FW; MTCW 2; MTFW
2005; RGAL 4; TCWW 2

Allen, Roland
See Ayckbourn, Alan

Allen, Sarah A.
See Hopkins, Pauline Elizabeth

Allen, Sidney H.
See Hartmann, Sadakichi

Allen, Woody 1935- .... **CLC 16, 52, 195**
See also AAYA 10, 51; AMWS 15; CA 33-
36R; CANR 27, 38, 63, 128; DAM POP;
DLB 44; MTCW 1; SSFS 21

Allende, Isabel 1942- ... **CLC 39, 57, 97, 170;**
HLC 1; SSC 65; WLCS
See also AAYA 18, 70; CA 130; CAAE 125;
CANR 51, 74, 129; CDWLB 3; CLR 99;
CWW 2; DA3; DAM MULT, NOV; DLB
145; DNFS 1; EWL 3; FL 1:5; FW; HW
1, 2; INT CA-130; LAIT 5; LAWS 1;
LMFS 2; MTCW 1, 2; MTFW 2005;
NCFS 1; NFS 6, 18; RGSF 2; RGWL 3;
SATA 163; SSFS 11, 16; WLIT 1

Alleyn, Ellen
See Rossetti, Christina

Alleyne, Carla D. .... **CLC 65**

Allingham, Margery (Louise)
1904-1966 .... **CLC 19**
See also CA 5-8R; CAAS 25-28R; CANR
4, 58; CMW 4; DLB 77; MSW; MTCW
1, 2

Allingham, William 1824-1889 ...... **NCLC 25**
See also DLB 35; RGEL 2

Allison, Dorothy E. 1949- .... **CLC 78, 153**
See also AAYA 53; CA 140; CANR 66, 107;
CN 7; CSW; DA3; FW; MTCW 2; MTFW
2005; NFS 11; RGAL 4

Alloula, Malek .... **CLC 65**

Allston, Washington 1779-1843 .... **NCLC 2**
See also DLB 1, 235

Almedingen, E. M. .... **CLC 12**
See Almedingen, Martha Edith von
See also SATA 3

Almedingen, Martha Edith von 1898-1971
See Almedingen, E. M.
See also CA 1-4R; CANR 1

Almodovar, Pedro 1949(?)- .... **CLC 114, 229;**
HLCS 1
See also CA 133; CANR 72, 151; HW 2

Almqvist, Carl Jonas Love
1793-1866 .... **NCLC 42**

al-Mutanabbi, Ahmad ibn al-Husayn Abu
al-Tayyib al-Jufi al-Kindi
915-965 .... **CMLC 66**
See Mutanabbi, Al-
See also RGWL 3

Alonso, Damaso 1898-1990 .... **CLC 14**
See also CA 131; CAAE 110; CAAS 130;
CANR 72; DLB 108; EWL 3; HW 1, 2

Alov
See Gogol, Nikolai (Vasilyevich)

al'Sadaawi, Nawal
See El Saadawi, Nawal
See also FW

al-Shaykh, Hanan 1945- .... **CLC 218**
See Shaykh, al- Hanan
See also CA 135; CANR 111; WLIT 6

Al Siddik
See Rolfe, Frederick (William Serafino Aus-
tin Lewis Mary)
See also GLL 1; RGEL 2

Alta 1942- .... **CLC 19**
See also CA 57-60

Alter, Robert B. 1935- .... **CLC 34**
See also CA 49-52; CANR 1, 47, 100, 160

Alter, Robert Bernard
See Alter, Robert B.

Alther, Lisa 1944- .... **CLC 7, 41**
See also BPFB 1; CA 65-68; 30; CANR 12,
30, 51; CN 4, 5, 6, 7; CSW; GLL 2;
MTCW 1

Althusser, L.
See Althusser, Louis

Althusser, Louis 1918-1990 .... **CLC 106**
See also CA 131; CAAS 132; CANR 102;
DLB 242

Altman, Robert 1925-2006 .... **CLC 16, 116**
See also CA 73-76; CAAS 254; CANR 43

Alurista .... **HLCS 1; PC 34**
See Urista (Heredia), Alberto (Baltazar)
See also CA 45-48R; DLB 82; LLW

Alvarez, A. 1929- .... **CLC 5, 13**
See also CA 1-4R; CANR 3, 33, 63, 101,
134; CN 3, 4, 5, 6; CP 1, 2, 3, 4, 5, 6, 7;
DLB 14, 40; MTFW 2005

Alvarez, Alejandro Rodriguez 1903-1965
See Casona, Alejandro
See also CA 131; CAAS 93-96; HW 1

Alvarez, Julia 1950- .... **CLC 93; HLCS 1**
See also AAYA 25; AMWS 7; CA 147;
CANR 69, 101, 133; DA3; DLB 282;
LATS 1:2; LLW; MTCW 2; MTFW 2005;
NFS 5, 9; SATA 129; WLIT 1

Alvaro, Corrado 1896-1956 .... **TCLC 60**
See also CA 163; DLB 264; EWL 3

Amado, Jorge 1912-2001 ... **CLC 13, 40, 106,**
232; HLC 1
See also CA 77-80; CAAS 201; CANR 35,
74, 135; CWW 2; DAM MULT, NOV;
DLB 113, 307; EWL 3; HW 2; LAW;
LAWS 1; MTCW 1, 2; MTFW 2005;
RGWL 2, 3; TWA; WLIT 1

Ambler, Eric 1909-1998 .... **CLC 4, 6, 9**
See also BRWS 4; CA 9-12R; CAAS 171;
CANR 7, 38, 74; CMW 4; CN 1, 2, 3, 4,
5, 6; DLB 77; MSW; MTCW 1, 2; TEA

Ambrose, Stephen E. 1936-2002 .... **CLC 145**
See also AAYA 44; CA 1-4R; CANR 209;
CANR 3, 43, 57, 83, 105; MTFW 2005;
NCFS 2; SATA 40, 138

Amichai, Yehuda 1924-2000 .. **CLC 9, 22, 57,**
116; PC 38
See also CA 85-88; CAAS 189; CANR 46,
60, 99, 132; CWW 2; EWL 3; MTCW 1,
2; MTFW 2005; PFS 24; RGHL; WLIT 6

Amichai, Yehudah
See Amichai, Yehuda

Amiel, Henri Frederic 1821-1881 .... **NCLC 4**
See also DLB 217

Amis, Kingsley 1922-1995 . **CLC 1, 2, 3, 5, 8,**
13, 40, 44, 129
See also AITN 2; BPFB 1; BRWS 2; CA
9-12R; CAAS 150; CANR 8, 28, 54; CD-
BLB 1945-1960; CN 1, 2, 3, 4, 5, 6; CP
1, 2, 3, 4; DA; DA3; DAB; DAC; DAM
MST, NOV; DLB 15, 27, 100, 139, 326;
DLBY 1996; EWL 3; HGG; INT
CANR-8; MTCW 1, 2; MTFW 2005;
RGEL 2; RGSF 2; SFW 4

Amis, Martin 1949- ... **CLC 4, 9, 38, 62, 101,**
213
See also BEST 90:3; BRWS 4; CA 65-68;
CANR 8, 27, 54, 73, 95, 132; CN 5, 6, 7;
DA3; DLB 14, 194; EWL 3; INT CANR-
27; MTCW 2; MTFW 2005

Ammianus Marcellinus c. 330-c.
395 .... **CMLC 60**
See also AW 2; DLB 211

Ammons, A.R. 1926-2001 .. **CLC 2, 3, 5, 8, 9,**
25, 57, 108; PC 16
See also AITN 1; AMWS 7; CA 9-12R;
CAAS 193; CANR 6, 36, 51, 73, 107,
156; CP 1, 2, 3, 4, 5, 6, 7; CSW; DAM
POET; DLB 5, 165; EWL 3; MAL 5;
MTCW 1, 2; PFS 19; RGAL 4; TCLE 1:1

Apuleius, (Lucius Madaurensis) c. 125-c.
164 .... **CMLC 1, 84**
See also AW 2; CDWLB 1; DLB 211;
RGWL 2, 3; SUFW; WLIT 8

Aquin, Hubert 1929-1977 .... **CLC 15**
See also CA 105; DLB 53; EWL 3

Aquinas, Thomas 1224(?)-1274 ..... **CMLC 33**
See also DLB 115; EW 1; TWA

Aragon, Louis 1897-1982 .... **CLC 3, 22;
TCLC 123**
See also CA 69-72; CAAS 108; CANR 28,
71; DAM NOV, POET; DLB 72, 258; EW
11; EWL 3; GFL 1789 to the Present;
GLL 2; LMFS 2; MTCW 1, 2; RGWL 2,
3

Arany, Janos 1817-1882 .... **NCLC 34**

Aranyos, Kakay 1847-1910
See Mikszath, Kalman

Aratus of Soli c. 315B.C.-c.
240B.C. .... **CMLC 64**
See also DLB 176

Arbuthnot, John 1667-1735 .... **LC 1**
See also DLB 101

Archer, Herbert Winslow
See Mencken, H(enry) L(ouis)

Archer, Jeffrey 1940- .... **CLC 28**
See also AAYA 16; BEST 89:3; BPFB 1;
CA 77-80; CANR 22, 52, 95, 136; CPW;
DA3; DAM POP; INT CANR-22; MTFW
2005

Archer, Jeffrey Howard
See Archer, Jeffrey

Archer, Jules 1915- .... **CLC 12**
See also CA 9-12R; CANR 6, 69; SAAS 5;
SATA 4, 85

Archer, Lee
See Ellison, Harlan

Archilochus c. 7th cent. B.C.- .... **CMLC 44**
See also DLB 176

Arden, John 1930- .... **CLC 6, 13, 15**
See also BRWS 2; CA 13-16R; 4; CANR
31, 65, 67, 124; CBD; CD 5, 6; DAM
DRAM; DFS 9; DLB 13, 245; EWL 3;
MTCW 1

Arenas, Reinaldo 1943-1990 .. **CLC 41; HLC
1; TCLC 191**
See also CA 128; CAAE 124; CAAS 133;
CANR 73, 106; DAM MULT; DLB 145;
EWL 3; GLL 2; HW 1; LAW; LAWS 1;
MTCW 2; MTFW 2005; RGSF 2; RGWL
3; WLIT 1

Arendt, Hannah 1906-1975 .... **CLC 66, 98**
See also CA 17-20R; CAAS 61-64; CANR
26, 60; DLB 242; MTCW 1, 2

Aretino, Pietro 1492-1556 .... **LC 12**
See also RGWL 2, 3

Arghezi, Tudor .... **CLC 80**
See Theodorescu, Ion N.
See also CA 167; CDWLB 4; DLB 220;
EWL 3

Arguedas, Jose Maria 1911-1969 .... **CLC 10,
18; HLCS 1; TCLC 147**
See also CA 89-92; CANR 73; DLB 113;
EWL 3; HW 1; LAW; RGWL 2, 3; WLIT
1

Argueta, Manlio 1936- .... **CLC 31**
See also CA 131; CANR 73; CWW 2; DLB
145; EWL 3; HW 1; RGWL 3

Arias, Ron 1941- .... **HLC 1**
See also CA 131; CANR 81, 136; DAM
MULT; DLB 82; HW 1, 2; MTCW 2;
MTFW 2005

Ariosto, Lodovico
See Ariosto, Ludovico
See also WLIT 7

Ariosto, Ludovico 1474-1533 ... **LC 6, 87; PC
42**
See Ariosto, Lodovico
See also EW 2; RGWL 2, 3

Aristides
See Epstein, Joseph

Aristophanes 450B.C.-385B.C. .... **CMLC 4,
51; DC 2; WLCS**
See also AW 1; CDWLB 1; DA; DA3;
DAB; DAC; DAM DRAM, MST; DFS
10; DLB 176; LMFS 1; RGWL 2, 3;
TWA; WLIT 8

Aristotle 384B.C.-322B.C. .... **CMLC 31;
WLCS**
See also AW 1; CDWLB 1; DA; DA3;
DAB; DAC; DAM MST; DLB 176;
RGWL 2, 3; TWA; WLIT 8

Arlt, Roberto (Godofredo Christophersen)
1900-1942 .... **HLC 1; TCLC 29**
See also CA 131; CAAE 123; CANR 67;
DAM MULT; DLB 305; EWL 3; HW 1,
2; IDTP; LAW

Armah, Ayi Kwei 1939- . **BLC 1; CLC 5, 33,
136**
See also AFW; BRWS 10; BW 1; CA 61-
64; CANR 21, 64; CDWLB 3; CN 1, 2,
3, 4, 5, 6, 7; DAM MULT, POET; DLB
117; EWL 3; MTCW 1; WLIT 2

Armatrading, Joan 1950- .... **CLC 17**
See also CA 186; CAAE 114

Armin, Robert 1568(?)-1615(?) .... **LC 120**

Armitage, Frank
See Carpenter, John (Howard)

Armstrong, Jeannette (C.) 1948- .... **NNAL**
See also CA 149; CCA 1; CN 6, 7; DAC;
DLB 334; SATA 102

Arnette, Robert
See Silverberg, Robert

**Arnim, Achim von (Ludwig Joachim von
Arnim)** 1781-1831 .. **NCLC 5, 159; SSC
29**
See also DLB 90

Arnim, Bettina von 1785-1859 ...... **NCLC 38,
123**
See also DLB 90; RGWL 2, 3

Arnold, Matthew 1822-1888 ..... **NCLC 6, 29,
89, 126; PC 5; WLC 1**
See also BRW 5; CDBLB 1832-1890; DA;
DAB; DAC; DAM MST, POET; DLB 32,
57; EXPP; PAB; PFS 2; TEA; WP

Arnold, Thomas 1795-1842 .... **NCLC 18**
See also DLB 55

Arnow, Harriette (Louisa) Simpson
1908-1986 .... **CLC 2, 7, 18**
See also BPFB 1; CA 9-12R; CAAS 118;
CANR 14; CN 2, 3, 4; DLB 6; FW;
MTCW 1, 2; RHW; SATA 42; SATA-Obit
47

Arouet, Francois-Marie
See Voltaire

Arp, Hans
See Arp, Jean

Arp, Jean 1887-1966 .... **CLC 5; TCLC 115**
See also CA 81-84; CAAS 25-28R; CANR
42, 77; EW 10

Arrabal
See Arrabal, Fernando

Arrabal (Teran), Fernando
See Arrabal, Fernando
See also CWW 2

Arrabal, Fernando 1932- ... **CLC 2, 9, 18, 58**
See Arrabal (Teran), Fernando
See also CA 9-12R; CANR 15; DLB 321;
EWL 3; LMFS 2

Arreola, Juan Jose 1918-2001 .... **CLC 147;
HLC 1; SSC 38**
See also CA 131; CAAE 113; CAAS 200;
CANR 81; CWW 2; DAM MULT; DLB
113; DNFS 2; EWL 3; HW 1, 2; LAW;
RGSF 2

Arrian c. 89(?)-c. 155(?) .... **CMLC 43**
See also DLB 176

Arrick, Fran .... **CLC 30**
See Gaberman, Judie Angell
See also BYA 6

Arrley, Richmond
See Delany, Samuel R., Jr.

Artaud, Antonin (Marie Joseph)
1896-1948 .... **DC 14; TCLC 3, 36**
See also CA 149; CAAE 104; DA3; DAM
DRAM; DFS 22; DLB 258, 321; EW 11;
EWL 3; GFL 1789 to the Present; MTCW
2; MTFW 2005; RGWL 2, 3

Arthur, Ruth M(abel) 1905-1979 ..... **CLC 12**
See also CA 9-12R; CAAS 85-88; CANR
4; CWRI 5; SATA 7, 26

Artsybashev, Mikhail (Petrovich)
1878-1927 .... **TCLC 31**
See also CA 170; DLB 295

Arundel, Honor (Morfydd)
1919-1973 .... **CLC 17**
See also CA 21-22; CAAS 41-44R; CAP 2;
CLR 35; CWRI 5; SATA 4; SATA-Obit
24

Arzner, Dorothy 1900-1979 .... **CLC 98**

Asch, Sholem 1880-1957 .... **TCLC 3**
See also CAAE 105; DLB 333; EWL 3;
GLL 2; RGHL

Ascham, Roger 1516(?)-1568 .... **LC 101**
See also DLB 236

Ash, Shalom
See Asch, Sholem

Ashbery, John 1927- ... **CLC 2, 3, 4, 6, 9, 13,
15, 25, 41, 77, 125, 221; PC 26**
See Berry, Jonas
See also AMWS 3; CA 5-8R; CANR 9, 37,
66, 102, 132; CP 1, 2, 3, 4, 5, 6, 7; DA3;
DAM POET; DLB 5, 165; DLBY 1981;
EWL 3; INT CANR-9; MAL 5; MTCW
1, 2; MTFW 2005; PAB; PFS 11; RGAL
4; TCLE 1:1; WP

Ashdown, Clifford
See Freeman, R(ichard) Austin

Ashe, Gordon
See Creasey, John

Ashton-Warner, Sylvia (Constance)
1908-1984 .... **CLC 19**
See also CA 69-72; CAAS 112; CANR 29;
CN 1, 2, 3; MTCW 1, 2

Asimov, Isaac 1920-1992 ..... **CLC 1, 3, 9, 19,
26, 76, 92**
See also AAYA 13; BEST 90:2; BPFB 1;
BYA 4, 6, 7, 9; CA 1-4R; CAAS 137;
CANR 2, 19, 36, 60, 125; CLR 12, 79;
CMW 4; CN 1, 2, 3, 4, 5; CPW; DA3;
DAM POP; DLB 8; DLBY 1992; INT
CANR-19; JRDA; LAIT 5; LMFS 2;
MAICYA 1; MAL 5; MTCW 1, 2;
MTFW 2005; RGAL 4; SATA 1, 26, 74;
SCFW 1, 2; SFW 4; SSFS 17; TUS; YAW

Askew, Anne 1521(?)-1546 .... **LC 81**
See also DLB 136

Assis, Joaquim Maria Machado de
See Machado de Assis, Joaquim Maria

Astell, Mary 1666-1731 .... **LC 68**
See also DLB 252, 336; FW

Astley, Thea (Beatrice May)
1925-2004 .... **CLC 41**
See also CA 65-68; CAAS 229; CANR 11,
43, 78; CN 1, 2, 3, 4, 5, 6, 7; DLB 289;
EWL 3

Astley, William 1855-1911
See Warung, Price

Aston, James
See White, T(erence) H(anbury)

Asturias, Miguel Angel 1899-1974 .... **CLC 3,
8, 13; HLC 1; TCLC 184**
See also CA 25-28; CAAS 49-52; CANR
32; CAP 2; CDWLB 3; DA3; DAM
MULT, NOV; DLB 113, 290, 329; EWL
3; HW 1; LAW; LMFS 2; MTCW 1, 2;
RGWL 2, 3; WLIT 1

EW 12; EWL 3; FL 1:5; FW; GFL 1789
to the Present; LMFS 2; MTCW 1, 2;
MTFW 2005; RGSF 2; RGWL 2, 3; TWA

Beauvoir, Simone Lucie Ernestine Marie
   Bertrand de
   See Beauvoir, Simone de

Becker, Carl (Lotus) 1873-1945 ..... **TCLC 63**
   See also CA 157; DLB 17

Becker, Jurek 1937-1997 .... **CLC 7, 19**
   See also CA 85-88; CAAS 157; CANR 60,
   117; CWW 2; DLB 75, 299; EWL 3;
   RGHL

Becker, Walter 1950- .... **CLC 26**

Becket, Thomas a 1118(?)-1170 .... **CMLC 83**

Beckett, Samuel 1906-1989 ... **CLC 1, 2, 3, 4,
   6, 9, 10, 11, 14, 18, 29, 57, 59, 83; DC
   22; SSC 16, 74; TCLC 145; WLC 1**
   See also BRWC 2; BRWR 1; BRWS 1; CA
   5-8R; CAAS 130; CANR 33, 61; CBD;
   CDBLB 1945-1960; CN 1, 2, 3, 4; CP 1,
   2, 3, 4; DA; DA3; DAB; DAC; DAM
   DRAM, MST, NOV; DFS 2, 7, 18; DLB
   13, 15, 233, 319, 321, 329; DLBY 1990;
   EWL 3; GFL 1789 to the Present; LATS
   1:2; LMFS 2; MTCW 1, 2; MTFW 2005;
   RGSF 2; RGWL 2, 3; SSFS 15; TEA;
   WLIT 4

Beckford, William 1760-1844 .... **NCLC 16**
   See also BRW 3; DLB 39, 213; GL 2; HGG;
   LMFS 1; SUFW

Beckham, Barry (Earl) 1944- .... **BLC 1**
   See also BW 1; CA 29-32R; CANR 26, 62;
   CN 1, 2, 3, 4, 5, 6; DAM MULT; DLB 33

Beckman, Gunnel 1910- .... **CLC 26**
   See also CA 33-36R; CANR 15, 114; CLR
   25; MAICYA 1, 2; SAAS 9; SATA 6

Becque, Henri 1837-1899 .... **DC 21; NCLC 3**
   See also DLB 192; GFL 1789 to the Present

Becquer, Gustavo Adolfo
   1836-1870 .... **HLCS 1; NCLC 106**
   See also DAM MULT

Beddoes, Thomas Lovell 1803-1849 .. **DC 15;
   NCLC 3, 154**
   See also BRWS 11; DLB 96

Bede c. 673-735 .... **CMLC 20**
   See also DLB 146; TEA

Bedford, Denton R. 1907-(?) .... **NNAL**

Bedford, Donald F.
   See Fearing, Kenneth (Flexner)

Beecher, Catharine Esther
   1800-1878 .... **NCLC 30**
   See also DLB 1, 243

Beecher, John 1904-1980 .... **CLC 6**
   See also AITN 1; CA 5-8R; CAAS 105;
   CANR 8; CP 1, 2, 3

Beer, Johann 1655-1700 .... **LC 5**
   See also DLB 168

Beer, Patricia 1924- .... **CLC 58**
   See also CA 61-64; CAAS 183; CANR 13,
   46; CP 1, 2, 3, 4, 5, 6; CWP; DLB 40;
   FW

Beerbohm, Max
   See Beerbohm, (Henry) Max(imilian)

Beerbohm, (Henry) Max(imilian)
   1872-1956 .... **TCLC 1, 24**
   See also BRWS 2; CA 154; CAAE 104;
   CANR 79; DLB 34, 100; FANT; MTCW
   2

Beer-Hofmann, Richard
   1866-1945 .... **TCLC 60**
   See also CA 160; DLB 81

Beg, Shemus
   See Stephens, James

Begiebing, Robert J(ohn) 1946- .... **CLC 70**
   See also CA 122; CANR 40, 88

Begley, Louis 1933- .... **CLC 197**
   See also CA 140; CANR 98; DLB 299;
   RGHL; TCLE 1:1

Behan, Brendan (Francis)
   1923-1964 .... **CLC 1, 8, 11, 15, 79**
   See also BRWS 2; CA 73-76; CANR 33,
   121; CBD; CDBLB 1945-1960; DAM
   DRAM; DFS 7; DLB 13, 233; EWL 3;
   MTCW 1, 2

Behn, Aphra 1640(?)-1689 .. **DC 4; LC 1, 30,
   42, 135; PC 13; WLC 1**
   See also BRWS 3; DA; DA3; DAB; DAC;
   DAM DRAM, MST, NOV, POET; DFS
   16, 24; DLB 39, 80, 131; FW; TEA;
   WLIT 3

Behrman, S(amuel) N(athaniel)
   1893-1973 .... **CLC 40**
   See also CA 13-16; CAAS 45-48; CAD;
   CAP 1; DLB 7, 44; IDFW 3; MAL 5;
   RGAL 4

Bekederemo, J. P. Clark
   See Clark Bekederemo, J.P.
   See also CD 6

Belasco, David 1853-1931 .... **TCLC 3**
   See also CA 168; CAAE 104; DLB 7; MAL
   5; RGAL 4

Belcheva, Elisaveta Lyubomirova
   1893-1991 .... **CLC 10**
   See Bagryana, Elisaveta

Beldone, Phil "Cheech"
   See Ellison, Harlan

Beleno
   See Azuela, Mariano

Belinski, Vissarion Grigoryevich
   1811-1848 .... **NCLC 5**
   See also DLB 198

Belitt, Ben 1911- .... **CLC 22**
   See also CA 13-16R; 4; CANR 7, 77; CP 1,
   2, 3, 4, 5, 6; DLB 5

Belknap, Jeremy 1744-1798 .... **LC 115**
   See also DLB 30, 37

Bell, Gertrude (Margaret Lowthian)
   1868-1926 .... **TCLC 67**
   See also CA 167; CANR 110; DLB 174

Bell, J. Freeman
   See Zangwill, Israel

Bell, James Madison 1826-1902 .... **BLC 1;
   TCLC 43**
   See also BW 1; CA 124; CAAE 122; DAM
   MULT; DLB 50

Bell, Madison Smartt 1957- ..... **CLC 41, 102,
   223**
   See also AMWS 10; BPFB 1; CA 183; 111,
   183; CANR 28, 54, 73, 134; CN 5, 6, 7;
   CSW; DLB 218, 278; MTCW 2; MTFW
   2005

Bell, Marvin (Hartley) 1937- .... **CLC 8, 31**
   See also CA 21-24R; 14; CANR 59, 102;
   CP 1, 2, 3, 4, 5, 6, 7; DAM POET; DLB
   5; MAL 5; MTCW 1; PFS 25

Bell, W. L. D.
   See Mencken, H(enry) L(ouis)

Bellamy, Atwood C.
   See Mencken, H(enry) L(ouis)

Bellamy, Edward 1850-1898 ..... **NCLC 4, 86,
   147**
   See also DLB 12; NFS 15; RGAL 4; SFW
   4

Belli, Gioconda 1948- .... **HLCS 1**
   See also CA 152; CANR 143; CWW 2;
   DLB 290; EWL 3; RGWL 3

Bellin, Edward J.
   See Kuttner, Henry

Bello, Andres 1781-1865 .... **NCLC 131**
   See also LAW

**Belloc, (Joseph) Hilaire (Pierre Sebastien
   Rene Swanton)** 1870-1953 .... **PC 24;
   TCLC 7, 18**
   See also CA 152; CAAE 106; CLR 102;
   CWRI 5; DAM POET; DLB 19, 100, 141,
   174; EWL 3; MTCW 2; MTFW 2005;
   SATA 112; WCH; YABC 1

Belloc, Joseph Peter Rene Hilaire
   See Belloc, (Joseph) Hilaire (Pierre Sebastien Rene Swanton)

Belloc, Joseph Pierre Hilaire
   See Belloc, (Joseph) Hilaire (Pierre Sebastien Rene Swanton)

Belloc, M. A.
   See Lowndes, Marie Adelaide (Belloc)

Belloc-Lowndes, Mrs.
   See Lowndes, Marie Adelaide (Belloc)

Bellow, Saul 1915-2005 ...... **CLC 1, 2, 3, 6, 8,
   10, 13, 15, 25, 33, 34, 63, 79, 190, 200;
   SSC 14, 101; WLC 1**
   See also AITN 2; AMW; AMWC 2; AMWR
   2; BEST 89:3; BPFB 1; CA 5-8R; CAAS
   238; CABS 1; CANR 29, 53, 95, 132;
   CDALB 1941-1968; CN 1, 2, 3, 4, 5, 6,
   7; DA; DA3; DAB; DAC; DAM MST,
   NOV, POP; DLB 2, 28, 299, 329; DLBD
   3; DLBY 1982; EWL 3; MAL 5; MTCW
   1, 2; MTFW 2005; NFS 4, 14; RGAL 4;
   RGHL; RGSF 2; SSFS 12, 22; TUS

Belser, Reimond Karel Maria de 1929-
   See Ruyslinck, Ward
   See also CA 152

Bely, Andrey .... **PC 11; TCLC 7**
   See Bugayev, Boris Nikolayevich
   See also DLB 295; EW 9; EWL 3

Belyi, Andrei
   See Bugayev, Boris Nikolayevich
   See also RGWL 2, 3

Bembo, Pietro 1470-1547 .... **LC 79**
   See also RGWL 2, 3

Benary, Margot
   See Benary-Isbert, Margot

Benary-Isbert, Margot 1889-1979 .... **CLC 12**
   See also CA 5-8R; CAAS 89-92; CANR 4,
   72; CLR 12; MAICYA 1, 2; SATA 2;
   SATA-Obit 21

Benavente (y Martinez), Jacinto
   1866-1954 .... **DC 26; HLCS 1; TCLC 3**
   See also CA 131; CAAE 106; CANR 81;
   DAM DRAM, MULT; DLB 329; EWL 3;
   GLL 2; HW 1, 2; MTCW 1, 2

Benchley, Peter 1940-2006 .... **CLC 4, 8**
   See also AAYA 14; AITN 2; BPFB 1; CA
   17-20R; CAAS 248; CANR 12, 35, 66,
   115; CPW; DAM NOV, POP; HGG;
   MTCW 1, 2; MTFW 2005; SATA 3, 89,
   164

Benchley, Peter Bradford
   See Benchley, Peter

Benchley, Robert (Charles)
   1889-1945 .... **TCLC 1, 55**
   See also CA 153; CAAE 105; DLB 11;
   MAL 5; RGAL 4

Benda, Julien 1867-1956 .... **TCLC 60**
   See also CA 154; CAAE 120; GFL 1789 to
   the Present

Benedict, Ruth 1887-1948 .... **TCLC 60**
   See also CA 158; CANR 146; DLB 246

Benedict, Ruth Fulton
   See Benedict, Ruth

Benedikt, Michael 1935- .... **CLC 4, 14**
   See also CA 13-16R; CANR 7; CP 1, 2, 3,
   4, 5, 6, 7; DLB 5

Benet, Juan 1927-1993 .... **CLC 28**
   See also CA 143; EWL 3

Benet, Stephen Vincent 1898-1943 ..... **PC 64;
   SSC 10, 86; TCLC 7**
   See also AMWS 11; CA 152; CAAE 104;
   DA3; DAM POET; DLB 4, 48, 102, 249,
   284; DLBY 1997; EWL 3; HGG; MAL 5;
   MTCW 2; MTFW 2005; RGAL 4; RGSF
   2; SSFS 22; SUFW; WP; YABC 1

Benet, William Rose 1886-1950 ..... **TCLC 28**
   See also CA 152; CAAE 118; DAM POET;
   DLB 45; RGAL 4

Benford, Gregory 1941- .... **CLC 52**
  See also BPFB 1; CA 175; 69-72, 175; 27;
  CANR 12, 24, 49, 95, 134; CN 7; CSW;
  DLBY 1982; MTFW 2005; SCFW 2;
  SFW 4
Benford, Gregory Albert
  See Benford, Gregory
Bengtsson, Frans (Gunnar)
  1894-1954 .... **TCLC 48**
  See also CA 170; EWL 3
Benjamin, David
  See Slavitt, David R(ytman)
Benjamin, Lois
  See Gould, Lois
Benjamin, Walter 1892-1940 .... **TCLC 39**
  See also CA 164; DLB 242; EW 11; EWL
  3
Ben Jelloun, Tahar 1944-
  See Jelloun, Tahar ben
  See also CA 135; CWW 2; EWL 3; RGWL
  3; WLIT 2
Benn, Gottfried 1886-1956 .. **PC 35; TCLC 3**
  See also CA 153; CAAE 106; DLB 56;
  EWL 3; RGWL 2, 3
Bennett, Alan 1934- .... **CLC 45, 77**
  See also BRWS 8; CA 103; CANR 35, 55,
  106, 157; CBD; CD 5, 6; DAB; DAM
  MST; DLB 310; MTCW 1, 2; MTFW
  2005
Bennett, (Enoch) Arnold
  1867-1931 .... **TCLC 5, 20**
  See also BRW 6; CA 155; CAAE 106; CD-
  BLB 1890-1914; DLB 10, 34, 98, 135;
  EWL 3; MTCW 2
Bennett, Elizabeth
  See Mitchell, Margaret (Munnerlyn)
Bennett, George Harold 1930-
  See Bennett, Hal
  See also BW 1; CA 97-100; CANR 87
Bennett, Gwendolyn B. 1902-1981 .... **HR 1:2**
  See also BW 1; CA 125; DLB 51; WP
Bennett, Hal .... **CLC 5**
  See Bennett, George Harold
  See also CA 13; DLB 33
Bennett, Jay 1912- .... **CLC 35**
  See also AAYA 10, 73; CA 69-72; CANR
  11, 42, 79; JRDA; SAAS 4; SATA 41, 87;
  SATA-Brief 27; WYA; YAW
Bennett, Louise 1919-2006 .. **BLC 1; CLC 28**
  See also BW 2, 3; CA 151; CAAS 252; CD-
  WLB 3; CP 1, 2, 3, 4, 5, 6, 7; DAM
  MULT; DLB 117; EWL 3
Bennett, Louise Simone
  See Bennett, Louise
Bennett-Coverley, Louise
  See Bennett, Louise
Benoit de Sainte-Maure fl. 12th cent.
  - .... **CMLC 90**
Benson, A. C. 1862-1925 .... **TCLC 123**
  See also DLB 98
Benson, E(dward) F(rederic)
  1867-1940 .... **TCLC 27**
  See also CA 157; CAAE 114; DLB 135,
  153; HGG; SUFW 1
Benson, Jackson J. 1930- .... **CLC 34**
  See also CA 25-28R; DLB 111
Benson, Sally 1900-1972 .... **CLC 17**
  See also CA 19-20; CAAS 37-40R; CAP 1;
  SATA 1, 35; SATA-Obit 27
Benson, Stella 1892-1933 .... **TCLC 17**
  See also CA 154, 155; CAAE 117; DLB
  36, 162; FANT; TEA
Bentham, Jeremy 1748-1832 .... **NCLC 38**
  See also DLB 107, 158, 252
Bentley, E(dmund) C(lerihew)
  1875-1956 .... **TCLC 12**
  See also CA 232; CAAE 108; DLB 70;
  MSW

Bentley, Eric 1916- .... **CLC 24**
  See also CA 5-8R; CAD; CANR 6, 67;
  CBD; CD 5, 6; INT CANR-6
Bentley, Eric Russell
  See Bentley, Eric
ben Uzair, Salem
  See Horne, Richard Henry Hengist
Beolco, Angelo 1496-1542 .... **LC 139**
Beranger, Pierre Jean de
  1780-1857 .... **NCLC 34**
Berdyaev, Nicolas
  See Berdyaev, Nikolai (Aleksandrovich)
Berdyaev, Nikolai (Aleksandrovich)
  1874-1948 .... **TCLC 67**
  See also CA 157; CAAE 120
Berdyayev, Nikolai (Aleksandrovich)
  See Berdyaev, Nikolai (Aleksandrovich)
Berendt, John 1939- .... **CLC 86**
  See also CA 146; CANR 75, 83, 151
Berendt, John Lawrence
  See Berendt, John
Beresford, J(ohn) D(avys)
  1873-1947 .... **TCLC 81**
  See also CA 155; CAAE 112; DLB 162,
  178, 197; SFW 4; SUFW 1
Bergelson, David (Rafailovich)
  1884-1952 .... **TCLC 81**
  See Bergelson, Dovid
  See also CA 220; DLB 333
Bergelson, Dovid
  See Bergelson, David (Rafailovich)
  See also EWL 3
Berger, Colonel
  See Malraux, (Georges-)Andre
Berger, John 1926- .... **CLC 2, 19**
  See also BRWS 4; CA 81-84; CANR 51,
  78, 117, 163; CN 1, 2, 3, 4, 5, 6, 7; DLB
  14, 207, 319, 326
Berger, John Peter
  See Berger, John
Berger, Melvin H. 1927- .... **CLC 12**
  See also CA 5-8R; CANR 4, 142; CLR 32;
  SAAS 2; SATA 5, 88, 158; SATA-Essay
  124
Berger, Thomas 1924- .... **CLC 3, 5, 8, 11, 18,
  38**
  See also BPFB 1; CA 1-4R; CANR 5, 28,
  51, 128; CN 1, 2, 3, 4, 5, 6, 7; DAM
  NOV; DLB 2; DLBY 1980; EWL 3;
  FANT; INT CANR-28; MAL 5; MTCW
  1, 2; MTFW 2005; RHW; TCLE 1:1;
  TCWW 1, 2
Bergman, (Ernst) Ingmar 1918- ...... **CLC 16,
  72, 210**
  See also AAYA 61; CA 81-84; CANR 33,
  70; CWW 2; DLB 257; MTCW 2; MTFW
  2005
Bergson, Henri(-Louis) 1859-1941 . **TCLC 32**
  See also CA 164; DLB 329; EW 8; EWL 3;
  GFL 1789 to the Present
Bergstein, Eleanor 1938- .... **CLC 4**
  See also CA 53-56; CANR 5
Berkeley, George 1685-1753 .... **LC 65**
  See also DLB 31, 101, 252
Berkoff, Steven 1937- .... **CLC 56**
  See also CA 104; CANR 72; CBD; CD 5, 6
Berlin, Isaiah 1909-1997 .... **TCLC 105**
  See also CA 85-88; CAAS 162
Bermant, Chaim (Icyk) 1929-1998 ... **CLC 40**
  See also CA 57-60; CANR 6, 31, 57, 105;
  CN 2, 3, 4, 5, 6
Bern, Victoria
  See Fisher, M(ary) F(rances) K(ennedy)
Bernanos, (Paul Louis) Georges
  1888-1948 .... **TCLC 3**
  See also CA 130; CAAE 104; CANR 94;
  DLB 72; EWL 3; GFL 1789 to the
  Present; RGWL 2, 3

Bernard, April 1956- .... **CLC 59**
  See also CA 131; CANR 144
Bernard, Mary Ann
  See Soderbergh, Steven
Bernard of Clairvaux 1090-1153 .. **CMLC 71**
  See also DLB 208
Bernard Silvestris fl. c. 1130-fl. c.
  1160 .... **CMLC 87**
  See also DLB 208
Berne, Victoria
  See Fisher, M(ary) F(rances) K(ennedy)
Bernhard, Thomas 1931-1989 ..... **CLC 3, 32,
  61; DC 14; TCLC 165**
  See also CA 85-88; CAAS 127; CANR 32,
  57; CDWLB 2; DLB 85, 124; EWL 3;
  MTCW 1; RGHL; RGWL 2, 3
Bernhardt, Sarah (Henriette Rosine)
  1844-1923 .... **TCLC 75**
  See also CA 157
Bernstein, Charles 1950- .... **CLC 142,**
  See also CA 129; 24; CANR 90; CP 4, 5, 6,
  7; DLB 169
Bernstein, Ingrid
  See Kirsch, Sarah
Beroul fl. c. 12th cent. - .... **CMLC 75**
Berriault, Gina 1926-1999 .... **CLC 54, 109;
  SSC 30**
  See also CA 129; CAAE 116; CAAS 185;
  CANR 66; DLB 130; SSFS 7,11
Berrigan, Daniel 1921- .... **CLC 4**
  See also CA 187; 33-36R, 187; 1; CANR
  11, 43, 78; CP 1, 2, 3, 4, 5, 6, 7; DLB 5
Berrigan, Edmund Joseph Michael, Jr.
  1934-1983
  See Berrigan, Ted
  See also CA 61-64; CAAS 110; CANR 14,
  102
Berrigan, Ted .... **CLC 37**
  See Berrigan, Edmund Joseph Michael, Jr.
  See also CP 1, 2, 3; DLB 5, 169; WP
Berry, Charles Edward Anderson 1931-
  See Berry, Chuck
  See also CA 115
Berry, Chuck .... **CLC 17**
  See Berry, Charles Edward Anderson
Berry, Jonas
  See Ashbery, John
  See also GLL 1
Berry, Wendell 1934- .... **CLC 4, 6, 8, 27, 46;
  PC 28**
  See also AITN 1; AMWS 10; ANW; CA
  73-76; CANR 50, 73, 101, 132; CP 1,
  2, 3, 4, 5, 6, 7; CSW; DAM POET; DLB 5,
  6, 234, 275; MTCW 2; MTFW 2005;
  TCLE 1:1
Berryman, John 1914-1972 ... **CLC 1, 2, 3, 4,
  6, 8, 10, 13, 25, 62; PC 64**
  See also AMW; CA 13-16; CAAS 33-36R;
  CABS 2; CANR 35; CAP 1; CDALB
  1941-1968; CP 1; DAM POET; DLB 48;
  EWL 3; MAL 5; MTCW 1, 2; MTFW
  2005; PAB; RGAL 4; WP
Bertolucci, Bernardo 1940- ...... **CLC 16, 157**
  See also CA 106; CANR 125
Berton, Pierre (Francis de Marigny)
  1920-2004 .... **CLC 104**
  See also CA 1-4R; CAAS 233; CANR 2,
  56, 144; CPW; DLB 68; SATA 99; SATA-
  Obit 158
Bertrand, Aloysius 1807-1841 .... **NCLC 31**
  See Bertrand, Louis oAloysiusc
Bertrand, Louis oAloysiusc
  See Bertrand, Aloysius
  See also DLB 217
Bertran de Born c. 1140-1215 .... **CMLC 5**
Besant, Annie (Wood) 1847-1933 ..... **TCLC 9**
  See also CA 185; CAAE 105

Bessie, Alvah 1904-1985 .... **CLC 23**
See also CA 5-8R; CAAS 116; CANR 2,
80; DLB 26

Bestuzhev, Aleksandr Aleksandrovich
1797-1837 .... **NCLC 131**
See also DLB 198

Bethlen, T. D.
See Silverberg, Robert

Beti, Mongo .... **BLC 1; CLC 27**
See Biyidi, Alexandre
See also AFW; CANR 79; DAM MULT;
EWL 3; WLIT 2

Betjeman, John 1906-1984 ...... **CLC 2, 6, 10,
34, 43; PC 75**
See also BRW 7; CA 9-12R; CAAS 112;
CANR 33, 56; CDBLB 1945-1960; CP 1,
2, 3; DA3; DAB; DAM MST, POET;
DLB 20; DLBY 1984; EWL 3; MTCW 1,
2

Bettelheim, Bruno 1903-1990 .... **CLC 79;
TCLC 143**
See also CA 81-84; CAAS 131; CANR 23,
61; DA3; MTCW 1, 2; RGHL

Betti, Ugo 1892-1953 .... **TCLC 5**
See also CA 155; CAAE 104; EWL 3;
RGWL 2, 3

Betts, Doris (Waugh) 1932- ..... **CLC 3, 6, 28;
SSC 45**
See also CA 13-16R; CANR 9, 66, 77; CN
6, 7; CSW; DLB 218; DLBY 1982; INT
CANR-9; RGAL 4

Bevan, Alistair
See Roberts, Keith (John Kingston)

Bey, Pilaff
See Douglas, (George) Norman

Bialik, Chaim Nachman
1873-1934 .... **TCLC 25**
See Bialik, Hayyim Nahman
See also CA 170; EWL 3

Bialik, Hayyim Nahman
See Bialik, Chaim Nachman
See also WLIT 6

Bickerstaff, Isaac
See Swift, Jonathan

Bidart, Frank 1939- .... **CLC 33**
See also AMWS 15; CA 140; CANR 106;
CP 5, 6, 7

Bienek, Horst 1930- .... **CLC 7, 11**
See also CA 73-76; DLB 75

Bierce, Ambrose (Gwinett)
1842-1914(?) ..... **SSC 9, 72; TCLC 1, 7,
44; WLC 1**
See also AAYA 55; AMW; BYA 11; CA
139; CAAE 104; CANR 78; CDALB
1865-1917; DA; DA3; DAC; DAM MST;
DLB 11, 12, 23, 71, 74, 186; EWL 3;
EXPS; HGG; LAIT 2; MAL 5; RGAL 4;
RGSF 2; SSFS 9; SUFW 1

Biggers, Earl Derr 1884-1933 .... **TCLC 65**
See also CA 153; CAAE 108; DLB 306

Billiken, Bud
See Motley, Willard (Francis)

Billings, Josh
See Shaw, Henry Wheeler

Billington, (Lady) Rachel (Mary)
1942- .... **CLC 43**
See also AITN 2; CA 33-36R; CANR 44;
CN 4, 5, 6, 7

Binchy, Maeve 1940- .... **CLC 153**
See also BEST 90:1; BPFB 1; CA 134;
CAAE 127; CANR 50, 96, 134; CN 5, 6,
7; CPW; DA3; DAM POP; DLB 319; INT
CA-134; MTCW 2; MTFW 2005; RHW

Binyon, T(imothy) J(ohn)
1936-2004 .... **CLC 34**
See also CA 111; CAAS 232; CANR 28,
140

Bion 335B.C.-245B.C. .... **CMLC 39**

Bioy Casares, Adolfo 1914-1999 ... **CLC 4, 8,
13, 88; HLC 1; SSC 17, 102**
See Casares, Adolfo Bioy; Miranda, Javier;
Sacastru, Martin
See also CA 29-32R; CAAS 177; CANR
19, 43, 66; CWW 2; DAM MULT; DLB
113; EWL 3; HW 1, 2; LAW; MTCW 1,
2; MTFW 2005

Birch, Allison .... **CLC 65**

Bird, Cordwainer
See Ellison, Harlan

Bird, Robert Montgomery
1806-1854 .... **NCLC 1**
See also DLB 202; RGAL 4

Birkerts, Sven 1951- .... **CLC 116**
See also CA 176; 133, 176; 29; CAAE 128;
CANR 151; INT CA-133

Birney, (Alfred) Earle 1904-1995 .. **CLC 1, 4,
6, 11; PC 52**
See also CA 1-4R; CANR 5, 20; CN 1, 2,
3, 4; CP 1, 2, 3, 4, 5, 6; DAC; DAM MST;
POET; DLB 88; MTCW 1; PFS 8; RGEL
2

Biruni, al 973-1048(?) .... **CMLC 28**

Bishop, Elizabeth 1911-1979 ..... **CLC 1, 4, 9,
13, 15, 32; PC 3, 34; TCLC 121**
See also AMWR 2; AMWS 1; CA 5-8R;
CAAS 89-92; CABS 2; CANR 26, 61,
108; CDALB 1968-1988; CP 1, 2, 3; DA;
DA3; DAC; DAM MST; DLB 5,
169; EWL 3; GLL 2; MAL 5; MBL;
MTCW 1, 2; PAB; PFS 6, 12; RGAL 4;
SATA-Obit 24; TUS; WP

Bishop, John 1935- .... **CLC 10**
See also CA 105

Bishop, John Peale 1892-1944 ..... **TCLC 103**
See also CA 155; CAAE 107; DLB 4, 9,
45; MAL 5; RGAL 4

Bissett, Bill 1939- .... **CLC 18; PC 14**
See also CA 69-72; 19; CANR 15; CCA 1;
CP 1, 2, 3, 4, 5, 6, 7; DLB 53; MTCW 1

Bissoondath, Neil (Devindra)
1955- .... **CLC 120**
See also CA 136; CANR 123; CN 6, 7;
DAC

Bitov, Andrei (Georgievich) 1937- ... **CLC 57**
See also CA 142; DLB 302

Biyidi, Alexandre 1932-
See Beti, Mongo
See also BW 1, 3; CA 124; CAAE 114;
CANR 81; DA3; MTCW 1, 2

Bjarme, Brynjolf
See Ibsen, Henrik (Johan)

Bjoernson, Bjoernstjerne (Martinius)
1832-1910 .... **TCLC 7, 37**
See also CAAE 104

Black, Benjamin
See Banville, John

Black, Robert
See Holdstock, Robert

Blackburn, Paul 1926-1971 .... **CLC 9, 43**
See also BG 1:2; CA 81-84; CAAS 33-36R;
CANR 34; CP 1; DLB 16; DLBY 1981

Black Elk 1863-1950 .... **NNAL; TCLC 33**
See also CA 144; DAM MULT; MTCW 2;
MTFW 2005; WP

Black Hawk 1767-1838 .... **NNAL**

Black Hobart
See Sanders, (James) Ed(ward)

Blacklin, Malcolm
See Chambers, Aidan

Blackmore, R(ichard) D(oddridge)
1825-1900 .... **TCLC 27**
See also CAAE 120; DLB 18; RGEL 2

Blackmur, R(ichard) P(almer)
1904-1965 .... **CLC 2, 24**
See also AMWS 2; CA 11-12; CAAS 25-
28R; CANR 71; CAP 1; DLB 63; EWL
3; MAL 5

Black Tarantula
See Acker, Kathy

Blackwood, Algernon (Henry)
1869-1951 .... **TCLC 5**
See also CA 150; CAAE 105; DLB 153,
156, 178; HGG; SUFW 1

Blackwood, Caroline (Maureen)
1931-1996 .... **CLC 6, 9, 100**
See also BRWS 9; CA 85-88; CAAS 151;
CANR 32, 61, 65; CN 3, 4, 5, 6; DLB 14,
207; HGG; MTCW 1

Blade, Alexander
See Hamilton, Edmond; Silverberg, Robert

Blaga, Lucian 1895-1961 .... **CLC 75**
See also CA 157; DLB 220; EWL 3

Blair, Eric (Arthur) 1903-1950 .... **TCLC 123**
See Orwell, George
See also CA 132; CAAE 104; DA; DA3;
DAB; DAC; DAM MST, NOV; MTCW
1, 2; MTFW 2005; SATA 29

Blair, Hugh 1718-1800 .... **NCLC 75**

Blais, Marie-Claire 1939- .... **CLC 2, 4, 6, 13,
22**
See also CA 21-24R; 4; CANR 38, 75, 93;
CWW 2; DAC; DAM MST; DLB 53;
EWL 3; FW; MTCW 1, 2; MTFW 2005;
TWA

Blaise, Clark 1940- .... **CLC 29**
See also AITN 2; CA 231; 53-56, 231; 3;
CANR 5, 66, 106; CN 4, 5, 6, 7; DLB 53;
RGSF 2

Blake, Fairley
See De Voto, Bernard (Augustine)

Blake, Nicholas
See Day Lewis, C(ecil)
See also DLB 77; MSW

Blake, Sterling
See Benford, Gregory

Blake, William 1757-1827 . **NCLC 13, 37, 57,
127, 173; PC 12, 63; WLC 1**
See also AAYA 47; BRW 3; BRWR 1; CD-
BLB 1789-1832; CLR 52; DA; DA3;
DAB; DAC; DAM MST, POET; DLB 93,
163; EXPP; LATS 1:1; LMFS 1; MAI-
CYA 1, 2; PAB; PFS 2, 12, 24; SATA 30;
TEA; WCH; WLIT 3; WP

Blanchot, Maurice 1907-2003 .... **CLC 135**
See also CA 144; CAAE 117; CAAS 213;
CANR 138; DLB 72, 296; EWL 3

Blasco Ibanez, Vicente 1867-1928 . **TCLC 12**
See Ibanez, Vicente Blasco
See also BPFB 1; CA 131; CAAE 110;
CANR 81; DA3; DAM NOV; EW 8;
EWL 3; HW 1, 2; MTCW 1

Blatty, William Peter 1928- .... **CLC 2**
See also CA 5-8R; CANR 9, 124; DAM
POP; HGG

Bleeck, Oliver
See Thomas, Ross (Elmore)

Blessing, Lee (Knowlton) 1949- .... **CLC 54**
See also CA 236; CAD; CD 5, 6; DFS 23

Blight, Rose
See Greer, Germaine

Blish, James (Benjamin) 1921-1975 . **CLC 14**
See also BPFB 1; CA 1-4R; CAAS 57-60;
CANR 3; CN 2; DLB 8; MTCW 1; SATA
66; SCFW 1, 2; SFW 4

Bliss, Frederick
See Card, Orson Scott

Bliss, Gillian
See Paton Walsh, Jill

Bliss, Reginald
See Wells, H(erbert) G(eorge)

Blixen, Karen (Christentze Dinesen)
1885-1962
See Dinesen, Isak
See also CA 25-28; CANR 22, 50; CAP 2;
DA3; DLB 214; LMFS 1; MTCW 1, 2;
SATA 44; SSFS 20

Bourdieu, Pierre 1930-2002 .... **CLC 198**
See also CA 130; CAAS 204

Bourget, Paul (Charles Joseph)
1852-1935 .... **TCLC 12**
See also CA 196; CAAE 107; DLB 123;
GFL 1789 to the Present

Bourjaily, Vance (Nye) 1922- .... **CLC 8, 62**
See also CA 1-4R; 1; CANR 2, 72; CN 1,
2, 3, 4, 5, 6, 7; DLB 2, 143; MAL 5

Bourne, Randolph S(illiman)
1886-1918 .... **TCLC 16**
See also AMW; CA 155; CAAE 117; DLB
63; MAL 5

Bova, Ben 1932- .... **CLC 45**
See also AAYA 16; CA 5-8R; 18; CANR
11, 56, 94, 111, 157; CLR 3, 96; DLBY
1981; INT CANR-11; MAICYA 1, 2;
MTCW 1; SATA 6, 68, 133; SFW 4

Bova, Benjamin William
See Bova, Ben

Bowen, Elizabeth (Dorothea Cole)
1899-1973 . **CLC 1, 3, 6, 11, 15, 22, 118;
SSC 3, 28, 66; TCLC 148**
See also BRWS 2; CA 17-18; CAAS 41-
44R; CANR 35, 105; CAP 2; CDBLB
1945-1960; CN 1; DA3; DAM NOV;
DLB 15, 162; EWL 3; EXPS; FW; HGG;
MTCW 1, 2; MTFW 2005; NFS 13;
RGSF 2; SSFS 5, 22; SUFW 1; TEA;
WLIT 4

Bowering, George 1935- .... **CLC 15, 47**
See also CA 21-24R; 16; CANR 10; CN 7;
CP 1, 2, 3, 4, 5, 6, 7; DLB 53

Bowering, Marilyn R(uthe) 1949- .... **CLC 32**
See also CA 101; CANR 49; CP 4, 5, 6, 7;
CWP; DLB 334

Bowers, Edgar 1924-2000 .... **CLC 9**
See also CA 5-8R; CAAS 188; CANR 24;
CP 1, 2, 3, 4, 5, 6, 7; CSW; DLB 5

Bowers, Mrs. J. Milton 1842-1914
See Bierce, Ambrose (Gwinett)

Bowie, David .... **CLC 17**
See Jones, David Robert

Bowles, Jane (Sydney) 1917-1973 ..... **CLC 3,
68**
See Bowles, Jane Auer
See also CA 19-20; CAAS 41-44R; CAP 2;
CN 1; MAL 5

Bowles, Jane Auer
See Bowles, Jane (Sydney)
See also EWL 3

Bowles, Paul 1910-1999 ..... **CLC 1, 2, 19, 53;
SSC 3, 98**
See also AMWS 4; CA 1-4R; 1; CAAS 186;
CANR 1, 19, 50, 75; CN 1, 2, 3, 4, 5, 6;
DA3; DLB 5, 6, 218; EWL 3; MAL 5;
MTCW 1, 2; MTFW 2005; RGAL 4;
SSFS 17

Bowles, William Lisle 1762-1850 . **NCLC 103**
See also DLB 93

Box, Edgar
See Vidal, Gore
See also GLL 1

Boyd, James 1888-1944 .... **TCLC 115**
See also CA 186; DLB 9; DLBD 16; RGAL
4; RHW

Boyd, Nancy
See Millay, Edna St. Vincent
See also GLL 1

Boyd, Thomas (Alexander)
1898-1935 .... **TCLC 111**
See also CA 183; CAAE 111; DLB 9;
DLBD 16, 316

Boyd, William (Andrew Murray)
1952- .... **CLC 28, 53, 70**
See also CA 120; CAAE 114; CANR 51,
71, 131; CN 4, 5, 6, 7; DLB 231

Boyesen, Hjalmar Hjorth
1848-1895 .... **NCLC 135**
See also DLB 12, 71; DLBD 13; RGAL 4

Boyle, Kay 1902-1992 .... **CLC 1, 5, 19, 58,
121; SSC 5, 102**
See also CA 13-16R; 1; CAAS 140; CANR
29, 61, 110; CN 1, 2, 3, 4, 5; CP 1, 2, 3,
4, 5; DLB 4, 9, 48, 86; DLBY 1993; EWL
3; MAL 5; MTCW 1, 2; MTFW 2005;
RGAL 4; RGSF 2; SSFS 10, 13, 14

Boyle, Mark
See Kienzle, William X.

Boyle, Patrick 1905-1982 .... **CLC 19**
See also CA 127

Boyle, T. C.
See Boyle, T. Coraghessan
See also AMWS 8

Boyle, T. Coraghessan 1948- ..... **CLC 36, 55,
90; SSC 16**
See Boyle, T. C.
See also AAYA 47; BEST 90:4; BPFB 1;
CA 120; CANR 44, 76, 89, 132; CN 6, 7;
CPW; DA3; DAM POP; DLB 218, 278;
DLBY 1986; EWL 3; MAL 5; MTCW 2;
MTFW 2005; SSFS 13, 19

Boz
See Dickens, Charles (John Huffam)

Brackenridge, Hugh Henry
1748-1816 .... **NCLC 7**
See also DLB 11, 37; RGAL 4

Bradbury, Edward P.
See Moorcock, Michael
See also MTCW 2

Bradbury, Malcolm (Stanley)
1932-2000 .... **CLC 32, 61**
See also CA 1-4R; CANR 1, 33, 91, 98,
137; CN 1, 2, 3, 4, 5, 6, 7; CP 1; DA3;
DAM NOV; DLB 14, 207; EWL 3;
MTCW 1, 2; MTFW 2005

Bradbury, Ray 1920- ... **CLC 1, 3, 10, 15, 42,
98, 235; SSC 29, 53; WLC 1**
See also AAYA 15; AITN 1, 2; AMWS 4;
BPFB 1; BYA 4, 5, 11; CA 1-4R; CANR
2, 30, 75, 125; CDALB 1968-1988; CN
1, 2, 3, 4, 5, 6, 7; CPW; DA; DA3; DAB;
DAC; DAM MST, NOV, POP; DLB 2, 8;
EXPN; EXPS; HGG; LAIT 3, 5; LATS
1:2; LMFS 2; MAL 5; MTCW 1, 2;
MTFW 2005; NFS 1, 22; RGAL 4; RGSF
2; SATA 11, 64, 123; SCFW 1, 2; SFW 4;
SSFS 1, 20; SUFW 1, 2; TUS; YAW

Braddon, Mary Elizabeth
1837-1915 .... **TCLC 111**
See also BRWS 8; CA 179; CAAE 108;
CMW 4; DLB 18, 70, 156; HGG

Bradfield, Scott 1955- .... **SSC 65**
See also CA 147; CANR 90; HGG; SUFW
2

Bradfield, Scott Michael
See Bradfield, Scott

Bradford, Gamaliel 1863-1932 .... **TCLC 36**
See also CA 160; DLB 17

Bradford, William 1590-1657 .... **LC 64**
See also DLB 24, 30; RGAL 4

Bradley, David (Henry), Jr. 1950- .... **BLC 1;
CLC 23, 118**
See also BW 1, 3; CA 104; CANR 26, 81;
CN 4, 5, 6, 7; DAM MULT; DLB 33

Bradley, John Ed 1958- .... **CLC 55**
See also CA 139; CANR 99; CN 6, 7; CSW

Bradley, John Edmund, Jr.
See Bradley, John Ed

Bradley, Marion Zimmer
1930-1999 .... **CLC 30**
See Chapman, Lee; Dexter, John; Gardner,
Miriam; Ives, Morgan; Rivers, Elfrida
See also AAYA 40; BPFB 1; CA 57-60; 10;
CAAS 185; CANR 7, 31, 51, 75, 107;
CPW; DA3; DAM POP; DLB 8; FANT;

FW; MTCW 1, 2; MTFW 2005; SATA 90,
139; SATA-Obit 116; SFW 4; SUFW 2;
YAW

Bradshaw, John 1933- .... **CLC 70**
See also CA 138; CANR 61

Bradstreet, Anne 1612(?)-1672 .... **LC 4, 30,
130; PC 10**
See also AMWS 1; CDALB 1640-1865;
DA; DA3; DAC; DAM MST, POET; DLB
24; EXPP; FW; PFS 6; RGAL 4; TUS;
WP

Brady, Joan 1939- .... **CLC 86**
See also CA 141

Bragg, Melvyn 1939- .... **CLC 10**
See also BEST 89:3; CA 57-60; CANR 10,
48, 89, 158; CN 1, 2, 3, 4, 5, 6, 7; DLB
14, 271; RHW

Brahe, Tycho 1546-1601 .... **LC 45**
See also DLB 300

Braine, John (Gerard) 1922-1986 . **CLC 1, 3,
41**
See also CA 1-4R; CAAS 120; CANR 1,
33; CDBLB 1945-1960; CN 1, 2, 3, 4;
DLB 15; DLBY 1986; EWL 3; MTCW 1

Braithwaite, William Stanley (Beaumont)
1878-1962 .... **BLC 1; HR 1:2; PC 52**
See also BW 1; CA 125; DAM MULT; DLB
50, 54; MAL 5

Bramah, Ernest 1868-1942 .... **TCLC 72**
See also CA 156; CMW 4; DLB 70; FANT

Brammer, Billy Lee
See Brammer, William

Brammer, William 1929-1978 .... **CLC 31**
See also CA 235; CAAS 77-80

Brancati, Vitaliano 1907-1954 .... **TCLC 12**
See also CAAE 109; DLB 264; EWL 3

Brancato, Robin F(idler) 1936- .... **CLC 35**
See also AAYA 9, 68; BYA 6; CA 69-72;
CANR 11, 45; CLR 32; JRDA; MAICYA
2; MAICYAS 1; SAAS 9; SATA 97;
WYA; YAW

Brand, Dionne 1953- .... **CLC 192**
See also BW 2; CA 143; CANR 143; CWP;
DLB 334

Brand, Max
See Faust, Frederick (Schiller)
See also BPFB 1; TCWW 1, 2

Brand, Millen 1906-1980 .... **CLC 7**
See also CA 21-24R; CAAS 97-100; CANR
72

Branden, Barbara .... **CLC 44**
See also CA 148

Brandes, Georg (Morris Cohen)
1842-1927 .... **TCLC 10**
See also CA 189; CAAE 105; DLB 300

Brandys, Kazimierz 1916-2000 .... **CLC 62**
See also CA 239; EWL 3

Branley, Franklyn M(ansfield)
1915-2002 .... **CLC 21**
See also CA 33-36R; CAAS 207; CANR
14, 39; CLR 13; MAICYA 1, 2; SAAS
16; SATA 4, 68, 136

Brant, Beth (E.) 1941- .... **NNAL**
See also CA 144; FW

Brant, Sebastian 1457-1521 .... **LC 112**
See also DLB 179; RGWL 2, 3

Brathwaite, Edward Kamau
1930- .... **BLCS; CLC 11; PC 56**
See also BRWS 12; BW 2, 3; CA 25-28R;
CANR 11, 26, 47, 107; CDWLB 3; CP 1,
2, 3, 4, 5, 6, 7; DAM POET; DLB 125;
EWL 3

Brathwaite, Kamau
See Brathwaite, Edward Kamau

Cabell, James Branch 1879-1958 .... **TCLC 6**
See also CA 152; CAAE 105; DLB 9, 78;
FANT; MAL 5; MTCW 2; RGAL 4;
SUFW 1

Cabeza de Vaca, Alvar Nunez
1490-1557(?) .... **LC 61**

Cable, George Washington
1844-1925 .... **SSC 4; TCLC 4**
See also CA 155; CAAE 104; DLB 12, 74;
DLBD 13; RGAL 4; TUS

Cabral de Melo Neto, Joao
1920-1999 .... **CLC 76**
See Melo Neto, Joao Cabral de
See also CA 151; DAM MULT; DLB 307;
LAW; LAWS 1

Cabrera Infante, G. 1929-2005 ... **CLC 5, 25,
45, 120; HLC 1; SSC 39**
See also CA 85-88; CAAS 236; CANR 29,
65, 110; CDWLB 3; CWW 2; DA3; DAM
MULT; DLB 113; EWL 3; HW 1, 2;
LAW; LAWS 1; MTCW 1, 2; MTFW
2005; RGSF 2; WLIT 1

Cabrera Infante, Guillermo
See Cabrera Infante, G.

Cade, Toni
See Bambara, Toni Cade

Cadmus and Harmonia
See Buchan, John

Caedmon fl. 658-680 .... **CMLC 7**
See also DLB 146

Caeiro, Alberto
See Pessoa, Fernando (Antonio Nogueira)

Caesar, Julius .... **CMLC 47**
See Julius Caesar
See also AW 1; RGWL 2, 3; WLIT 8

Cage, John (Milton), (Jr.)
1912-1992 .... **CLC 41; PC 58**
See also CA 13-16R; CAAS 169; CANR 9,
78; DLB 193; INT CANR-9; TCLE 1:1

Cahan, Abraham 1860-1951 .... **TCLC 71**
See also CA 154; CAAE 108; DLB 9, 25,
28; MAL 5; RGAL 4

Cain, G.
See Cabrera Infante, G.

Cain, Guillermo
See Cabrera Infante, G.

Cain, James M(allahan) 1892-1977 .. **CLC 3,
11, 28**
See also AITN 1; BPFB 1; CA 17-20R;
CAAS 73-76; CANR 8, 34, 61; CMW 4;
CN 1, 2; DLB 226; EWL 3; MAL 5;
MSW; MTCW 1; RGAL 4

Caine, Hall 1853-1931 .... **TCLC 97**
See also RHW

Caine, Mark
See Raphael, Frederic (Michael)

Calasso, Roberto 1941- .... **CLC 81**
See also CA 143; CANR 89

Calderon de la Barca, Pedro
1600-1681 . **DC 3; HLCS 1; LC 23, 136**
See also DFS 23; EW 2; RGWL 2, 3; TWA

Caldwell, Erskine 1903-1987 ... **CLC 1, 8, 14,
50, 60; SSC 19; TCLC 117**
See also AITN 1; AMW; BPFB 1; CA 1-4R;
1; CAAS 121; CANR 2, 33; CN 1, 2, 3,
4; DA3; DAM NOV; DLB 9, 86; EWL 3;
MAL 5; MTCW 1, 2; MTFW 2005;
RGAL 4; RGSF 2; TUS

Caldwell, (Janet Miriam) Taylor (Holland)
1900-1985 .... **CLC 2, 28, 39**
See also BPFB 1; CA 5-8R; CAAS 116;
CANR 5; DA3; DAM NOV, POP; DLBD
17; MTCW 2; RHW

Calhoun, John Caldwell
1782-1850 .... **NCLC 15**
See also DLB 3, 248

Calisher, Hortense 1911- ..... **CLC 2, 4, 8, 38,
134; SSC 15**
See also CA 1-4R; CANR 1, 22, 117; CN
1, 2, 3, 4, 5, 6, 7; DA3; DAM NOV; DLB
2, 218; INT CANR-22; MAL 5; MTCW
1, 2; MTFW 2005; RGAL 4; RGSF 2

Callaghan, Morley Edward
1903-1990 ..... **CLC 3, 14, 41, 65; TCLC
145**
See also CA 9-12R; CAAS 132; CANR 33,
73; CN 1, 2, 3, 4; DAC; DAM MST; DLB
68; EWL 3; MTCW 1, 2; MTFW 2005;
RGEL 2; RGSF 2; SSFS 19

Callimachus c. 305B.C.-c.
240B.C. .... **CMLC 18**
See also AW 1; DLB 176; RGWL 2, 3

Calvin, Jean
See Calvin, John
See also DLB 327; GFL Beginnings to 1789

Calvin, John 1509-1564 .... **LC 37**
See Calvin, Jean

Calvino, Italo 1923-1985 .... **CLC 5, 8, 11, 22,
33, 39, 73; SSC 3, 48; TCLC 183**
See also AAYA 58; CA 85-88; CAAS 116;
CANR 23, 61, 132; DAM NOV; DLB
196; EW 13; EWL 3; MTCW 1, 2; MTFW
2005; RGHL; RGSF 2; RGWL 2, 3; SFW
4; SSFS 12; WLIT 7

Camara Laye
See Laye, Camara
See also EWL 3

Camden, William 1551-1623 .... **LC 77**
See also DLB 172

Cameron, Carey 1952- .... **CLC 59**
See also CA 135

Cameron, Peter 1959- .... **CLC 44**
See also AMWS 12; CA 125; CANR 50,
117; DLB 234; GLL 2

Camoens, Luis Vaz de 1524(?)-1580
See Camoes, Luis de
See also EW 2

Camoes, Luis de 1524(?)-1580 . **HLCS 1; LC
62; PC 31**
See Camoens, Luis Vaz de
See also DLB 287; RGWL 2, 3

Campana, Dino 1885-1932 .... **TCLC 20**
See also CA 246; CAAE 117; DLB 114;
EWL 3

Campanella, Tommaso 1568-1639 .... **LC 32**
See also RGWL 2, 3

Campbell, John W(ood, Jr.)
1910-1971 .... **CLC 32**
See also CA 21-22; CAAS 29-32R; CANR
34; CAP 2; DLB 8; MTCW 1; SCFW 1,
2; SFW 4

Campbell, Joseph 1904-1987 .... **CLC 69;
TCLC 140**
See also AAYA 3, 66; BEST 89:2; CA 1-4R;
CAAS 124; CANR 3, 28, 61, 107; DA3;
MTCW 1, 2

Campbell, Maria 1940- .... **CLC 85; NNAL**
See also CA 102; CANR 54; CCA 1; DAC

Campbell, (John) Ramsey 1946- ..... **CLC 42;
SSC 19**
See also AAYA 51; CA 228; 57-60, 228;
CANR 7, 102; DLB 261; HGG; INT
CANR-7; SUFW 1, 2

Campbell, (Ignatius) Roy (Dunnachie)
1901-1957 .... **TCLC 5**
See also AFW; CA 155; CAAE 104; DLB
20, 225; EWL 3; MTCW 2; RGEL 2

Campbell, Thomas 1777-1844 .... **NCLC 19**
See also DLB 93, 144; RGEL 2

Campbell, Wilfred .... **TCLC 9**
See Campbell, William

Campbell, William 1858(?)-1918
See Campbell, Wilfred
See also CAAE 106; DLB 92

Campbell, William Edward March
1893-1954
See March, William
See also CAAE 108

Campion, Jane 1954- .... **CLC 95, 229**
See also AAYA 33; CA 138; CANR 87

Campion, Thomas 1567-1620 .... **LC 78**
See also CDBLB Before 1660; DAM POET;
DLB 58, 172; RGEL 2

Camus, Albert 1913-1960 ...... **CLC 1, 2, 4, 9,
11, 14, 32, 63, 69, 124; DC 2; SSC 9,
76; WLC 1**
See also AAYA 36; AFW; BPFB 1; CA 89-
92; CANR 131; DA; DA3; DAB; DAC;
DAM DRAM, MST, NOV; DLB 72, 321,
329; EW 13; EWL 3; EXPN; EXPS; GFL
1789 to the Present; LATS 1:2; LMFS 2;
MTCW 1, 2; MTFW 2005; NFS 6, 16;
RGHL; RGSF 2; RGWL 2, 3; SSFS 4;
TWA

Canby, Vincent 1924-2000 .... **CLC 13**
See also CA 81-84; CAAS 191

Cancale
See Desnos, Robert

Canetti, Elias 1905-1994 .. **CLC 3, 14, 25, 75,
86; TCLC 157**
See also CA 21-24R; CAAS 146; CANR
23, 61, 79; CDWLB 2; CWW 2; DA3;
DLB 85, 124, 329; EW 12; EWL 3;
MTCW 1, 2; MTFW 2005; RGWL 2, 3;
TWA

Canfield, Dorothea F.
See Fisher, Dorothy (Frances) Canfield

Canfield, Dorothea Frances
See Fisher, Dorothy (Frances) Canfield

Canfield, Dorothy
See Fisher, Dorothy (Frances) Canfield

Canin, Ethan 1960- .... **CLC 55; SSC 70**
See also CA 135; CAAE 131; DLB 335;
MAL 5

Cankar, Ivan 1876-1918 .... **TCLC 105**
See also CDWLB 4; DLB 147; EWL 3

Cannon, Curt
See Hunter, Evan

Cao, Lan 1961- .... **CLC 109**
See also CA 165

Cape, Judith
See Page, P(atricia) K(athleen)
See also CCA 1

Capek, Karel 1890-1938 .... **DC 1; SSC 36;
TCLC 6, 37; WLC 1**
See also CA 140; CAAE 104; CDWLB 4;
DA; DA3; DAB; DAC; DAM DRAM,
MST, NOV; DFS 7, 11; DLB 215; EW
10; EWL 3; MTCW 2; MTFW 2005;
RGSF 2; RGWL 2, 3; SCFW 1, 2; SFW 4

Capella, Martianus fl. 4th cent. - .. **CMLC 84**

Capote, Truman 1924-1984 . **CLC 1, 3, 8, 13,
19, 34, 38, 58; SSC 2, 47, 93; TCLC
164; WLC 1**
See also AAYA 61; AMWS 3; BPFB 1; CA
5-8R; CAAS 113; CANR 18, 62; CDALB
1941-1968; CN 1, 2, 3; CPW; DA; DA3;
DAB; DAC; DAM MST, NOV, POP;
DLB 2, 185, 227; DLBY 1980, 1984;
EWL 3; EXPS; GLL 1; LAIT 3; MAL 5;
MTCW 1, 2; MTFW 2005; NCFS 2;
RGAL 4; RGSF 2; SATA 91; SSFS 2;
TUS

Capra, Frank 1897-1991 .... **CLC 16**
See also AAYA 52; CA 61-64; CAAS 135

Caputo, Philip 1941- .... **CLC 32**
See also AAYA 60; CA 73-76; CANR 40,
135; YAW

Caragiale, Ion Luca 1852-1912 ...... **TCLC 76**
See also CA 157

Castle, Robert
See Hamilton, Edmond

Castro (Ruz), Fidel 1926(?)- .... **HLC 1**
See also CA 129; CAAE 110; CANR 81;
DAM MULT; HW 2

Castro, Guillen de 1569-1631 .... **LC 19**

Castro, Rosalia de 1837-1885 ... **NCLC 3, 78;
PC 4**
See also DAM MULT

Cather, Willa (Sibert) 1873-1947 . **SSC 2, 50;
TCLC 1, 11, 31, 99, 132, 152; WLC 1**
See also AAYA 24; AMW; AMWC 1;
AMWR 1; BPFB 1; CA 128; CAAE 104;
CDALB 1865-1917; CLR 98; DA; DA3;
DAB; DAC; DAM MST, NOV; DLB 9,
54, 78, 256; DLBD 1; EWL 3; EXPN;
EXPS; FL 1:5; LAIT 3; LATS 1:1; MAL
5; MBL; MTCW 1, 2; MTFW 2005; NFS
2, 19; RGAL 4; RGSF 2; RHW; SATA
30; SSFS 2, 7, 16; TCWW 1, 2; TUS

Catherine II
See Catherine the Great
See also DLB 150

Catherine the Great 1729-1796 .... **LC 69**
See Catherine II

Cato, Marcus Porcius
234B.C.-149B.C. .... **CMLC 21**
See Cato the Elder

Cato, Marcus Porcius, the Elder
See Cato, Marcus Porcius

Cato the Elder
See Cato, Marcus Porcius
See also DLB 211

Catton, (Charles) Bruce 1899-1978 . **CLC 35**
See also AITN 1; CA 5-8R; CAAS 81-84;
CANR 7, 74; DLB 17; MTCW 2; MTFW
2005; SATA 2; SATA-Obit 24

Catullus c. 84B.C.-54B.C. .... **CMLC 18**
See also AW 2; CDWLB 1; DLB 211;
RGWL 2, 3; WLIT 8

Cauldwell, Frank
See King, Francis (Henry)

Caunitz, William J. 1933-1996 .... **CLC 34**
See also BEST 89:3; CA 130; CAAE 125;
CAAS 152; CANR 73; INT CA-130

Causley, Charles (Stanley)
1917-2003 .... **CLC 7**
See also CA 9-12R; CAAS 223; CANR 5,
35, 94; CLR 30; CP 1, 2, 3, 4, 5; CWRI
5; DLB 27; MTCW 1; SATA 3, 66; SATA-
Obit 149

Caute, (John) David 1936- .... **CLC 29**
See also CA 1-4R; 4; CANR 1, 33, 64, 120;
CBD; CD 5, 6; CN 1, 2, 3, 4, 5, 6, 7;
DAM NOV; DLB 14, 231

Cavafy, C(onstantine) P(eter) .... **PC 36;
TCLC 2, 7**
See Kavafis, Konstantinos Petrou
See also CA 148; DA3; DAM POET; EW
8; EWL 3; MTCW 2; PFS 19; RGWL 2,
3; WP

Cavalcanti, Guido c. 1250-c.
1300 .... **CMLC 54**
See also RGWL 2, 3; WLIT 7

Cavallo, Evelyn
See Spark, Muriel

Cavanna, Betty .... **CLC 12**
See Harrison, Elizabeth (Allen) Cavanna
See also JRDA; MAICYA 1; SAAS 4;
SATA 1, 30

Cavendish, Margaret Lucas
1623-1673 .... **LC 30, 132**
See also DLB 131, 252, 281; RGEL 2

Caxton, William 1421(?)-1491(?) .... **LC 17**
See also DLB 170

Cayer, D. M.
See Duffy, Maureen (Patricia)

Cayrol, Jean 1911-2005 .... **CLC 11**
See also CA 89-92; CAAS 236; DLB 83;
EWL 3

Cela (y Trulock), Camilo Jose
See Cela, Camilo Jose
See also CWW 2

Cela, Camilo Jose 1916-2002 .... **CLC 4, 13,
59, 122; HLC 1; SSC 71**
See Cela (y Trulock), Camilo Jose
See also BEST 90:2; CA 21-24R; 10; CAAS
206; CANR 21, 32, 76, 139; DAM MULT;
DLB 322; DLBY 1989; EW 13; EWL 3;
HW 1; MTCW 1, 2; MTFW 2005; RGSF
2; RGWL 2, 3

Celan, Paul .... **CLC 10, 19, 53, 82; PC 10**
See Antschel, Paul
See also CDWLB 2; DLB 69; EWL 3;
RGHL; RGWL 2, 3

Celine, Louis-Ferdinand .. **CLC 1, 3, 4, 7, 9,
15, 47, 124**
See Destouches, Louis-Ferdinand
See also DLB 72; EW 11; EWL 3; GFL
1789 to the Present; RGWL 2, 3

Cellini, Benvenuto 1500-1571 .... **LC 7**
See also WLIT 7

Cendrars, Blaise .... **CLC 18, 106**
See Sauser-Hall, Frederic
See also DLB 258; EWL 3; GFL 1789 to
the Present; RGWL 2, 3; WP

Centlivre, Susanna 1669(?)-1723 .... **DC 25;
LC 65**
See also DLB 84; RGEL 2

Cernuda (y Bidon), Luis
1902-1963 .... **CLC 54; PC 62**
See also CA 131; CAAS 89-92; DAM
POET; DLB 134; EWL 3; GLL 1; HW 1;
RGWL 2, 3

Cervantes, Lorna Dee 1954- ..... **HLCS 1; PC
35**
See also CA 131; CANR 80; CP 7; CWP;
DLB 82; EXPP; HW 1; LLW

Cervantes (Saavedra), Miguel de
1547-1616 .... **HLCS; LC 6, 23, 93; SSC
12; WLC 1**
See also AAYA 56; BYA 1, 14; DA; DAB;
DAC; DAM MST, NOV; EW 2; LAIT 1;
LATS 1:1; LMFS 1; NFS 8; RGSF 2;
RGWL 2, 3; TWA

Cesaire, Aime 1913- ..... **BLC 1; CLC 19, 32,
112; DC 22; PC 25**
See also BW 2, 3; CA 65-68; CANR 24,
43, 81; CWW 2; DA3; DAM MULT,
POET; DLB 321; EWL 3; GFL 1789 to
the Present; MTCW 1, 2; MTFW 2005;
WP

Chabon, Michael 1963- ... **CLC 55, 149; SSC
59**
See also AAYA 45; AMWS 11; CA 139;
CANR 57, 96, 127, 138; DLB 278; MAL
5; MTFW 2005; NFS 25; SATA 145

Chabrol, Claude 1930- .... **CLC 16**
See also CA 110

Chairil Anwar
See Anwar, Chairil
See also EWL 3

Challans, Mary 1905-1983
See Renault, Mary
See also CA 81-84; CAAS 111; CANR 74;
DA3; MTCW 2; MTFW 2005; SATA 23;
SATA-Obit 36; TEA

Challis, George
See Faust, Frederick (Schiller)

Chambers, Aidan 1934- .... **CLC 35**
See also AAYA 27; CA 25-28R; CANR 12,
31, 58, 116; JRDA; MAICYA 1, 2; SAAS
12; SATA 1, 69, 108, 171; WYA; YAW

Chambers, James 1948-
See Cliff, Jimmy
See also CAAE 124

Chambers, Jessie
See Lawrence, D(avid) H(erbert Richards)
See also GLL 1

Chambers, Robert W(illiam)
1865-1933 .... **SSC 92; TCLC 41**
See also CA 165; DLB 202; HGG; SATA
107; SUFW 1

Chambers, (David) Whittaker
1901-1961 .... **TCLC 129**
See also CAAS 89-92; DLB 303

Chamisso, Adelbert von
1781-1838 .... **NCLC 82**
See also DLB 90; RGWL 2, 3; SUFW 1

Chance, James T.
See Carpenter, John (Howard)

Chance, John T.
See Carpenter, John (Howard)

Chandler, Raymond (Thornton)
1888-1959 .... **SSC 23; TCLC 1, 7, 179**
See also AAYA 25; AMWC 2; AMWS 4;
BPFB 1; CA 129; CAAE 104; CANR 60,
107; CDALB 1929-1941; CMW 4; DA3;
DLB 226, 253; DLBD 6; EWL 3; MAL
5; MSW; MTCW 1, 2; MTFW 2005; NFS
17; RGAL 4; TUS

Chang, Diana 1934- .... **AAL**
See also CA 228; CWP; DLB 312; EXPP

Chang, Eileen 1921-1995 .... **AAL; SSC 28;
TCLC 184**
See Chang Ai-Ling; Zhang Ailing
See also CA 166

Chang, Jung 1952- .... **CLC 71**
See also CA 142

Chang Ai-Ling
See Chang, Eileen
See also EWL 3

Channing, William Ellery
1780-1842 .... **NCLC 17**
See also DLB 1, 59, 235; RGAL 4

Chao, Patricia 1955- .... **CLC 119**
See also CA 163; CANR 155

Chaplin, Charles Spencer
1889-1977 .... **CLC 16**
See Chaplin, Charlie
See also CA 81-84; CAAS 73-76

Chaplin, Charlie
See Chaplin, Charles Spencer
See also AAYA 61; DLB 44

Chapman, George 1559(?)-1634 . **DC 19; LC
22, 116**
See also BRW 1; DAM DRAM; DLB 62,
121; LMFS 1; RGEL 2

Chapman, Graham 1941-1989 .... **CLC 21**
See Monty Python
See also CA 116; CAAS 129; CANR 35, 95

Chapman, John Jay 1862-1933 .... **TCLC 7**
See also AMWS 14; CA 191; CAAE 104

Chapman, Lee
See Bradley, Marion Zimmer
See also GLL 1

Chapman, Walker
See Silverberg, Robert

Chappell, Fred (Davis) 1936- .... **CLC 40, 78,
162**
See also CA 198; 5-8R, 198; 4; CANR 8,
33, 67, 110; CN 6; CP 6, 7; CSW; DLB
6, 105; HGG

Char, Rene(-Emile) 1907-1988 .... **CLC 9, 11,
14, 55; PC 56**
See also CA 13-16R; CAAS 124; CANR
32; DAM POET; DLB 258; EWL 3; GFL
1789 to the Present; MTCW 1, 2; RGWL
2, 3

Charby, Jay
See Ellison, Harlan

Chardin, Pierre Teilhard de
See Teilhard de Chardin, (Marie Joseph)
Pierre

Chariton fl. 1st cent. (?)- .... **CMLC 49**

Christine de Pisan
See Christine de Pizan
See also FW

Christine de Pizan 1365(?)-1431(?) ...... **LC 9, 130; PC 68**
See Christine de Pisan; de Pizan, Christine
See also DLB 208; FL 1:1; RGWL 2, 3

Chuang-Tzu c. 369B.C.-c. 286B.C. .... **CMLC 57**

Chubb, Elmer
See Masters, Edgar Lee

Chulkov, Mikhail Dmitrievich 1743-1792 .... **LC 2**
See also DLB 150

Churchill, Caryl 1938- .... **CLC 31, 55, 157; DC 5**
See Churchill, Chick
See also BRWS 4; CA 102; CANR 22, 46, 108; CBD; CD 6; CWD; DFS 12, 16; DLB 13, 310; EWL 3; FW; MTCW 1; RGEL 2

Churchill, Charles 1731-1764 .... **LC 3**
See also DLB 109; RGEL 2

Churchill, Chick
See Churchill, Caryl
See also CD 5

Churchill, Sir Winston (Leonard Spencer) 1874-1965 .... **TCLC 113**
See also BRW 6; CA 97-100; CDBLB 1890-1914; DA3; DLB 100, 329; DLBD 16; LAIT 4; MTCW 1, 2

Chute, Carolyn 1947- .... **CLC 39**
See also CA 123; CANR 135; CN 7

Ciardi, John (Anthony) 1916-1986 . **CLC 10, 40, 44, 129; PC 69**
See also CA 5-8R; 2; CAAS 118; CANR 5, 33; CLR 19; CP 1, 2, 3, 4; CWRI 5; DAM POET; DLB 5; DLBY 1986; INT CANR-5; MAICYA 1, 2; MAL 5; MTCW 1, 2; MTFW 2005; RGAL 4; SAAS 26; SATA 1, 65; SATA-Obit 46

Cibber, Colley 1671-1757 .... **LC 66**
See also DLB 84; RGEL 2

Cicero, Marcus Tullius 106B.C.-43B.C. .... **CMLC 3, 81**
See also AW 1; CDWLB 1; DLB 211; RGWL 2, 3; WLIT 8

Cimino, Michael 1943- .... **CLC 16**
See also CA 105

Cioran, E(mil) M. 1911-1995 .... **CLC 64**
See also CA 25-28R; CAAS 149; CANR 91; DLB 220; EWL 3

Cisneros, Sandra 1954- .... **CLC 69, 118, 193; HLC 1; PC 52; SSC 32, 72**
See also AAYA 9, 53; AMWS 7; CA 131; CANR 64, 118; CLR 123; CN 7; CWP; DA3; DAM MULT; DLB 122, 152; EWL 3; EXPN; FL 1:5; FW; HW 1, 2; LAIT 5; LATS 1:2; LLW; MAICYA 2; MAL 5; MTCW 2; MTFW 2005; NFS 2; PFS 19; RGAL 4; RGSF 2; SSFS 3, 13; WLIT 1; YAW

Cixous, Helene 1937- .... **CLC 92**
See also CA 126; CANR 55, 123; CWW 2; DLB 83, 242; EWL 3; FL 1:5; FW; GLL 2; MTCW 1, 2; MTFW 2005; TWA

Clair, Rene .... **CLC 20**
See Chomette, Rene Lucien

Clampitt, Amy 1920-1994 .... **CLC 32; PC 19**
See also AMWS 9; CA 110; CAAS 146; CANR 29, 79; CP 4, 5; DLB 105; MAL 5

Clancy, Thomas L., Jr. 1947-
See Clancy, Tom
See also CA 131; CAAE 125; CANR 62, 105; DA3; INT CA-131; MTCW 1, 2; MTFW 2005

Clancy, Tom .... **CLC 45, 112**
See Clancy, Thomas L., Jr.
See also AAYA 9, 51; BEST 89:1, 90:1; BPFB 1; BYA 10, 11; CANR 132; CMW 4; CPW; DAM NOV, POP; DLB 227

Clare, John 1793-1864 .. **NCLC 9, 86; PC 23**
See also BRWS 11; DAB; DAM POET; DLB 55, 96; RGEL 2

Clarin
See Alas (y Urena), Leopoldo (Enrique Garcia)

Clark, Al C.
See Goines, Donald

Clark, Brian (Robert)
See Clark, (Robert) Brian
See also CD 6

Clark, (Robert) Brian 1932- .... **CLC 29**
See Clark, Brian (Robert)
See also CA 41-44R; CANR 67; CBD; CD 5

Clark, Curt
See Westlake, Donald E.

Clark, Eleanor 1913-1996 .... **CLC 5, 19**
See also CA 9-12R; CAAS 151; CANR 41; CN 1, 2, 3, 4, 5, 6; DLB 6

Clark, J. P.
See Clark Bekederemo, J.P.
See also CDWLB 3; DLB 117

Clark, John Pepper
See Clark Bekederemo, J.P.
See also AFW; CD 5; CP 1, 2, 3, 4, 5, 6, 7; RGEL 2

Clark, Kenneth (Mackenzie) 1903-1983 .... **TCLC 147**
See also CA 93-96; CAAS 109; CANR 36; MTCW 1, 2; MTFW 2005

Clark, M. R.
See Clark, Mavis Thorpe

Clark, Mavis Thorpe 1909-1999 ...... **CLC 12**
See also CA 57-60; CANR 8, 37, 107; CLR 30; CWRI 5; MAICYA 1, 2; SAAS 5; SATA 8, 74

Clark, Walter Van Tilburg 1909-1971 .... **CLC 28**
See also CA 9-12R; CAAS 33-36R; CANR 63, 113; CN 1; DLB 9, 206; LAIT 2; MAL 5; RGAL 4; SATA 8; TCWW 1, 2

Clark Bekederemo, J.P. 1935- . **BLC 1; CLC 38; DC 5**
See Bekederemo, J. P. Clark; Clark, J. P.; Clark, John Pepper
See also BW 1; CA 65-68; CANR 16, 72; DAM DRAM, MULT; DFS 13; EWL 3; MTCW 2; MTFW 2005

Clarke, Arthur C. 1917- .... **CLC 1, 4, 13, 18, 35, 136; SSC 3**
See also AAYA 4, 33; BPFB 1; BYA 13; CA 1-4R; CANR 2, 28, 55, 74, 130; CLR 119; CN 1, 2, 3, 4, 5, 6, 7; CPW; DA3; DAM POP; DLB 261; JRDA; LAIT 5; MAICYA 1, 2; MTCW 1, 2; MTFW 2005; SATA 13, 70, 115; SCFW 1, 2; SFW 4; SSFS 4, 18; TCLE 1:1; YAW

Clarke, Austin 1896-1974 .... **CLC 6, 9**
See also CA 29-32; CAAS 49-52; CAP 2; CP 1, 2; DAM POET; DLB 10, 20; EWL 3; RGEL 2

Clarke, Austin C. 1934- . **BLC 1; CLC 8, 53; SSC 45**
See also BW 1; CA 25-28R; 16; CANR 14, 32, 68, 140; CN 1, 2, 3, 4, 5, 6, 7; DAC; DAM MULT; DLB 53, 125; DNFS 2; MTCW 2; MTFW 2005; RGSF 2

Clarke, Gillian 1937- .... **CLC 61**
See also CA 106; CP 3, 4, 5, 6, 7; CWP; DLB 40

Clarke, Marcus (Andrew Hislop) 1846-1881 .... **NCLC 19; SSC 94**
See also DLB 230; RGEL 2; RGSF 2

Clarke, Shirley 1925-1997 .... **CLC 16**
See also CA 189

Clash, The
See Headon, (Nicky) Topper; Jones, Mick; Simonon, Paul; Strummer, Joe

Claudel, Paul (Louis Charles Marie) 1868-1955 .... **TCLC 2, 10**
See also CA 165; CAAE 104; DLB 192, 258, 321; EW 8; EWL 3; GFL 1789 to the Present; RGWL 2, 3; TWA

Claudian 370(?)-404(?) .... **CMLC 46**
See also RGWL 2, 3

Claudius, Matthias 1740-1815 .... **NCLC 75**
See also DLB 97

Clavell, James 1925-1994 .... **CLC 6, 25, 87**
See also BPFB 1; CA 25-28R; CAAS 146; CANR 26, 48; CN 5; CPW; DA3; DAM NOV, POP; MTCW 1, 2; MTFW 2005; NFS 10; RHW

Clayman, Gregory .... **CLC 65**

Cleaver, (Leroy) Eldridge 1935-1998 .... **BLC 1; CLC 30, 119**
See also BW 1, 3; CA 21-24R; CAAS 167; CANR 16, 75; DA3; DAM MULT; MTCW 2; YAW

Cleese, John (Marwood) 1939- .... **CLC 21**
See Monty Python
See also CA 116; CAAE 112; CANR 35; MTCW 1

Cleishbotham, Jebediah
See Scott, Sir Walter

Cleland, John 1710-1789 .... **LC 2, 48**
See also DLB 39; RGEL 2

Clemens, Samuel Langhorne 1835-1910
See Twain, Mark
See also CA 135; CAAE 104; CDALB 1865-1917; DA; DA3; DAB; DAC; DAM MST, NOV; DLB 12, 23, 64, 74, 186, 189; JRDA; LMFS 1; MAICYA 1, 2; NCFS 4; NFS 20; SATA 100; YABC 2

Clement of Alexandria 150(?)-215(?) .... **CMLC 41**

Cleophil
See Congreve, William

Clerihew, E.
See Bentley, E(dmund) C(lerihew)

Clerk, N. W.
See Lewis, C.S.

Cleveland, John 1613-1658 .... **LC 106**
See also DLB 126; RGEL 2

Cliff, Jimmy .... **CLC 21**
See Chambers, James
See also CA 193

Cliff, Michelle 1946- .... **BLCS; CLC 120**
See also BW 2; CA 116; CANR 39, 72; CD-WLB 3; DLB 157; FW; GLL 2

Clifford, Lady Anne 1590-1676 .... **LC 76**
See also DLB 151

Clifton, Lucille 1936- ... **BLC 1; CLC 19, 66, 162; PC 17**
See also AFAW 2; BW 2, 3; CA 49-52; CANR 2, 24, 42, 76, 97, 138; CLR 5; CP 2, 3, 4, 5, 6, 7; CSW; CWP; CWRI 5; DA3; DAM MULT, POET; DLB 5, 41; EXPP; MAICYA 1, 2; MTCW 1, 2; MTFW 2005; PFS 1, 14; SATA 20, 69, 128; WP

Clinton, Dirk
See Silverberg, Robert

Clough, Arthur Hugh 1819-1861 .. **NCLC 27, 163**
See also BRW 5; DLB 32; RGEL 2

Clutha, Janet Paterson Frame 1924-2004
See Frame, Janet
See also CA 1-4R; CAAS 224; CANR 2, 36, 76, 135; MTCW 1, 2; SATA 119

Clyne, Terence
See Blatty, William Peter

Connor, Ralph .... **TCLC 31**
See Gordon, Charles William
See also DLB 92; TCWW 1, 2

Conrad, Joseph 1857-1924 ..... **SSC 9, 67, 69, 71; TCLC 1, 6, 13, 25, 43, 57; WLC 2**
See also AAYA 26; BPFB 1; BRW 6; BRWC 1; BRWR 2; BYA 2; CA 131; CAAE 104; CANR 60; CDBLB 1890-1914; DA; DA3; DAB; DAC; DAM MST, NOV; DLB 10, 34, 98, 156; EWL 3; EXPN; EXPS; LAIT 2; LATS 1:1; LMFS 1; MTCW 1, 2; MTFW 2005; NFS 2, 16; RGEL 2; RGSF 2; SATA 27; SSFS 1, 12; TEA; WLIT 4

Conrad, Robert Arnold
See Hart, Moss

Conroy, Pat 1945- .... **CLC 30, 74**
See also AAYA 8, 52; AITN 1; BPFB 1; CA 85-88; CANR 24, 53, 129; CN 7; CPW; CSW; DA3; DAM NOV, POP; DLB 6; LAIT 5; MAL 5; MTCW 1, 2; MTFW 2005

Constant (de Rebecque), (Henri) Benjamin 1767-1830 .... **NCLC 6, 182**
See also DLB 119; EW 4; GFL 1789 to the Present

Conway, Jill K(er) 1934- .... **CLC 152**
See also CA 130; CANR 94

Conybeare, Charles Augustus
See Eliot, T(homas) S(tearns)

Cook, Michael 1933-1994 .... **CLC 58**
See also CA 93-96; CANR 68; DLB 53

Cook, Robin 1940- .... **CLC 14**
See also AAYA 32; BEST 90:2; BPFB 1; CA 111; CAAE 108; CANR 41, 90, 109; CPW; DA3; DAM POP; HGG; INT CA-111

Cook, Roy
See Silverberg, Robert

Cooke, Elizabeth 1948- .... **CLC 55**
See also CA 129

Cooke, John Esten 1830-1886 .... **NCLC 5**
See also DLB 3, 248; RGAL 4

Cooke, John Estes
See Baum, L(yman) Frank

Cooke, M. E.
See Creasey, John

Cooke, Margaret
See Creasey, John

Cooke, Rose Terry 1827-1892 ...... **NCLC 110**
See also DLB 12, 74

Cook-Lynn, Elizabeth 1930- .... **CLC 93; NNAL**
See also CA 133; DAM MULT; DLB 175

Cooney, Ray .... **CLC 62**
See also CBD

Cooper, Anthony Ashley 1671-1713 .. **LC 107**
See also DLB 101, 336

Cooper, Dennis 1953- .... **CLC 203**
See also CA 133; CANR 72, 86; GLL 1; HGG

Cooper, Douglas 1960- .... **CLC 86**

Cooper, Henry St. John
See Creasey, John

Cooper, J. California (?)- .... **CLC 56**
See also AAYA 12; BW 1; CA 125; CANR 55; DAM MULT; DLB 212

Cooper, James Fenimore 1789-1851 .... **NCLC 1, 27, 54**
See also AAYA 22; AMW; BPFB 1; CDALB 1640-1865; CLR 105; DA3; DLB 3, 183, 250, 254; LAIT 1; NFS 25; RGAL 4; SATA 19; TUS; WCH

Cooper, Susan Fenimore 1813-1894 .... **NCLC 129**
See also ANW; DLB 239, 254

Coover, Robert 1932- .. **CLC 3, 7, 15, 32, 46, 87, 161; SSC 15, 101**
See also AMWS 5; BPFB 1; CA 45-48; CANR 3, 37, 58, 115; CN 1, 2, 3, 4, 5, 6, 7; DAM NOV; DLB 2, 227; DLBY 1981; EWL 3; MAL 5; MTCW 1, 2; MTFW 2005; RGAL 4; RGSF 2

Copeland, Stewart (Armstrong) 1952- .... **CLC 26**

Copernicus, Nicolaus 1473-1543 .... **LC 45**

Coppard, A(lfred) E(dgar) 1878-1957 .... **SSC 21; TCLC 5**
See also BRWS 8; CA 167; CAAE 114; DLB 162; EWL 3; HGG; RGEL 2; RGSF 2; SUFW 1; YABC 1

Coppee, Francois 1842-1908 .... **TCLC 25**
See also CA 170; DLB 217

Coppola, Francis Ford 1939- ... **CLC 16, 126**
See also AAYA 39; CA 77-80; CANR 40, 78; DLB 44

Copway, George 1818-1869 .... **NNAL**
See also DAM MULT; DLB 175, 183

Corbiere, Tristan 1845-1875 .... **NCLC 43**
See also DLB 217; GFL 1789 to the Present

Corcoran, Barbara (Asenath) 1911- .... **CLC 17**
See also AAYA 14; CA 191; 21-24R, 191; 2; CANR 11, 28, 48; CLR 50; DLB 52; JRDA; MAICYA 2; MAICYAS 1; RHW; SAAS 20; SATA 3, 77; SATA-Essay 125

Cordelier, Maurice
See Giraudoux, Jean(-Hippolyte)

Corelli, Marie .... **TCLC 51**
See Mackay, Mary
See also DLB 34, 156; RGEL 2; SUFW 1

Corinna c. 225B.C.-c. 305B.C. ...... **CMLC 72**

Corman, Cid .... **CLC 9**
See Corman, Sidney
See also CA 2; CP 1, 2, 3, 4, 5, 6, 7; DLB 5, 193

Corman, Sidney 1924-2004
See Corman, Cid
See also CA 85-88; CAAS 225; CANR 44; DAM POET

Cormier, Robert 1925-2000 .... **CLC 12, 30**
See also AAYA 3, 19; BYA 1, 2, 6, 8, 9; CA 1-4R; CANR 5, 23, 76, 93; CDALB 1968-1988; CLR 12, 55; DA; DAB; DAC; DAM MST, NOV; DLB 52; EXPN; INT CANR-23; JRDA; LAIT 5; MAICYA 1, 2; MTCW 1, 2; MTFW 2005; NFS 2, 18; SATA 10, 45, 83; SATA-Obit 122; WYA; YAW

Corn, Alfred (DeWitt III) 1943- .... **CLC 33**
See also CA 179; 179; 25; CANR 44; CP 3, 4, 5, 6, 7; CSW; DLB 120, 282; DLBY 1980

Corneille, Pierre 1606-1684 .. **DC 21; LC 28, 135**
See also DAB; DAM MST; DFS 21; DLB 268; EW 3; GFL Beginnings to 1789; RGWL 2, 3; TWA

Cornwell, David
See le Carre, John

Cornwell, Patricia 1956- .... **CLC 155**
See also AAYA 16, 56; BPFB 1; CA 134; CANR 53, 131; CMW 4; CPW; CSW; DAM POP; DLB 306; MSW; MTCW 2; MTFW 2005

Cornwell, Patricia Daniels
See Cornwell, Patricia

Corso, Gregory 1930-2001 .... **CLC 1, 11; PC 33**
See also AMWS 12; BG 1:2; CA 5-8R; CAAS 193; CANR 41, 76, 132; CP 1, 2, 3, 4, 5, 6, 7; DA3; DLB 5, 16, 237; LMFS 2; MAL 5; MTCW 1, 2; MTFW 2005; WP

Cortazar, Julio 1914-1984 ... **CLC 2, 3, 5, 10, 13, 15, 33, 34, 92; HLC 1; SSC 7, 76**
See also BPFB 1; CA 21-24R; CANR 12, 32, 81; CDWLB 3; DA3; DAM MULT, NOV; DLB 113; EWL 3; EXPS; HW 1, 2; LAW; MTCW 1, 2; MTFW 2005; RGSF 2; RGWL 2, 3; SSFS 3, 20; TWA; WLIT 1

Cortes, Hernan 1485-1547 .... **LC 31**

Corvinus, Jakob
See Raabe, Wilhelm (Karl)

Corwin, Cecil
See Kornbluth, C(yril) M.

Cosic, Dobrica 1921- .... **CLC 14**
See also CA 138; CAAE 122; CDWLB 4; CWW 2; DLB 181; EWL 3

Costain, Thomas B(ertram) 1885-1965 .... **CLC 30**
See also BYA 3; CA 5-8R; CAAS 25-28R; DLB 9; RHW

Costantini, Humberto 1924(?)-1987 . **CLC 49**
See also CA 131; CAAS 122; EWL 3; HW 1

Costello, Elvis 1954- .... **CLC 21**
See also CA 204

Costenoble, Philostene
See Ghelderode, Michel de

Cotes, Cecil V.
See Duncan, Sara Jeannette

Cotter, Joseph Seamon Sr. 1861-1949 .... **BLC 1; TCLC 28**
See also BW 1; CA 124; DAM MULT; DLB 50

Couch, Arthur Thomas Quiller
See Quiller-Couch, Sir Arthur (Thomas)

Coulton, James
See Hansen, Joseph

Couperus, Louis (Marie Anne) 1863-1923 .... **TCLC 15**
See also CAAE 115; EWL 3; RGWL 2, 3

Coupland, Douglas 1961- .... **CLC 85, 133**
See also AAYA 34; CA 142; CANR 57, 90, 130; CCA 1; CN 7; CPW; DAC; DAM POP; DLB 334

Court, Wesli
See Turco, Lewis (Putnam)

Courtenay, Bryce 1933- .... **CLC 59**
See also CA 138; CPW

Courtney, Robert
See Ellison, Harlan

Cousteau, Jacques-Yves 1910-1997 .. **CLC 30**
See also CA 65-68; CAAS 159; CANR 15, 67; MTCW 1; SATA 38, 98

Coventry, Francis 1725-1754 .... **LC 46**

Coverdale, Miles c. 1487-1569 .... **LC 77**
See also DLB 167

Cowan, Peter (Walkinshaw) 1914-2002 .... **SSC 28**
See also CA 21-24R; CANR 9, 25, 50, 83; CN 1, 2, 3, 4, 5, 6, 7; DLB 260; RGSF 2

Coward, Noel (Peirce) 1899-1973 . **CLC 1, 9, 29, 51**
See also AITN 1; BRWS 2; CA 17-18; CAAS 41-44R; CANR 35, 132; CAP 2; CBD; CDBLB 1914-1945; DA3; DAM DRAM; DFS 3, 6; DLB 10, 245; EWL 3; IDFW 3, 4; MTCW 1, 2; MTFW 2005; RGEL 2; TEA

Cowley, Abraham 1618-1667 .... **LC 43**
See also BRW 2; DLB 131, 151; PAB; RGEL 2

Cowley, Malcolm 1898-1989 .... **CLC 39**
See also AMWS 2; CA 5-8R; CAAS 128; CANR 3, 55; CP 1, 2, 3, 4; DLB 4, 48; DLBY 1981, 1989; EWL 3; MAL 5; MTCW 1, 2; MTFW 2005

Cumberland, Richard
1732-1811 .... **NCLC 167**
See also DLB 89; RGEL 2

Cummings, Bruce F(rederick) 1889-1919
See Barbellion, W. N. P.
See also CAAE 123

Cummings, E(dward) E(stlin)
1894-1962 .. **CLC 1, 3, 8, 12, 15, 68; PC 5; TCLC 137; WLC 2**
See also AAYA 41; AMW; CA 73-76; CANR 31; CDALB 1929-1941; DA; DA3; DAB; DAC; DAM MST, POET, DLB 4, 48; EWL 3; EXPP; MAL 5; MTCW 1, 2; MTFW 2005; PAB; PFS 1, 3, 12, 13, 19; RGAL 4; TUS; WP

Cummins, Maria Susanna
1827-1866 .... **NCLC 139**
See also DLB 42; YABC 1

Cunha, Euclides (Rodrigues Pimenta) da
1866-1909 .... **TCLC 24**
See also CA 219; CAAE 123; DLB 307; LAW; WLIT 1

Cunningham, E. V.
See Fast, Howard

Cunningham, J(ames) V(incent)
1911-1985 .... **CLC 3, 31**
See also CA 1-4R; CAAS 115; CANR 1, 72; CP 1, 2, 3, 4; DLB 5

Cunningham, Julia (Woolfolk)
1916- .... **CLC 12**
See also CA 9-12R; CANR 4, 19, 36; CWRI 5; JRDA; MAICYA 1, 2; SAAS 2; SATA 1, 26, 132

Cunningham, Michael 1952- .... **CLC 34**
See also AMWS 15; CA 136; CANR 96, 160; CN 7; DLB 292; GLL 2; MTFW 2005; NFS 23

Cunninghame Graham, R. B.
See Cunninghame Graham, Robert (Gallnigad) Bontine

Cunninghame Graham, Robert (Gallnigad) Bontine 1852-1936 .... **TCLC 19**
See Graham, R(obert) B(ontine) Cunninghame
See also CA 184; CAAE 119

Curnow, (Thomas) Allen (Monro)
1911-2001 .... **PC 48**
See also CA 69-72; CAAS 202; CANR 48, 99; CP 1, 2, 3, 4, 5, 6, 7; EWL 3; RGEL 2

Currie, Ellen 19(?)- .... **CLC 44**

Curtin, Philip
See Lowndes, Marie Adelaide (Belloc)

Curtin, Phillip
See Lowndes, Marie Adelaide (Belloc)

Curtis, Price
See Ellison, Harlan

Cusanus, Nicolaus 1401-1464 .... **LC 80**
See Nicholas of Cusa

Cutrate, Joe
See Spiegelman, Art

Cynewulf c. 770- .... **CMLC 23**
See also DLB 146; RGEL 2

Cyrano de Bergerac, Savinien de
1619-1655 .... **LC 65**
See also DLB 268; GFL Beginnings to 1789; RGWL 2, 3

Cyril of Alexandria c. 375-c. 430 . **CMLC 59**

Czaczkes, Shmuel Yosef Halevi
See Agnon, S(hmuel) Y(osef Halevi)

Dabrowska, Maria (Szumska)
1889-1965 .... **CLC 15**
See also CA 106; CDWLB 4; DLB 215; EWL 3

Dabydeen, David 1955- .... **CLC 34**
See also BW 1; CA 125; CANR 56, 92; CN 6, 7; CP 5, 6, 7

Dacey, Philip 1939- .... **CLC 51**
See also CA 231; 37-40R, 231; 17; CANR 14, 32, 64; CP 4, 5, 6, 7; DLB 105

Dacre, Charlotte c. 1772-1825(?) . **NCLC 151**

Dafydd ap Gwilym c. 1320-c. 1380 ..... **PC 56**

Dagerman, Stig (Halvard)
1923-1954 .... **TCLC 17**
See also CA 155; CAAE 117; DLB 259; EWL 3

D'Aguiar, Fred 1960- .... **CLC 145**
See also CA 148; CANR 83, 101; CN 7; CP 5, 6, 7; DLB 157; EWL 3

Dahl, Roald 1916-1990 ...... **CLC 1, 6, 18, 79; TCLC 173**
See also AAYA 15; BPFB 1; BRWS 4; BYA 5; CA 1-4R; CAAS 133; CANR 6, 32, 37, 62; CLR 1, 7, 41, 111; CN 1, 2, 3, 4; CPW; DA3; DAB; DAC; DAM MST, NOV, POP; DLB 139, 255; HGG; JRDA; MAICYA 1, 2; MTCW 1, 2; MTFW 2005; RGSF 2; SATA 1, 26, 73; SATA-Obit 65; SSFS 4; TEA; YAW

Dahlberg, Edward 1900-1977 .. **CLC 1, 7, 14**
See also CA 9-12R; CAAS 69-72; CANR 31, 62; CN 1, 2; DLB 48; MAL 5; MTCW 1; RGAL 4

Daitch, Susan 1954- .... **CLC 103**
See also CA 161

Dale, Colin .... **TCLC 18**
See Lawrence, T(homas) E(dward)

Dale, George E.
See Asimov, Isaac

d'Alembert, Jean Le Rond
1717-1783 .... **LC 126**

Dalton, Roque 1935-1975(?) ..... **HLCS 1; PC 36**
See also CA 176; DLB 283; HW 2

Daly, Elizabeth 1878-1967 .... **CLC 52**
See also CA 23-24; CAAS 25-28R; CANR 60; CAP 2; CMW 4

Daly, Mary 1928- .... **CLC 173**
See also CA 25-28R; CANR 30, 62; FW; GLL 1; MTCW 1

Daly, Maureen 1921-2006 .... **CLC 17**
See also AAYA 5, 58; BYA 6; CAAS 253; CANR 37, 83, 108; CLR 96; JRDA; MAICYA 1, 2; SAAS 1; SATA 2, 129; SATA-Obit 176; WYA; YAW

Damas, Leon-Gontran 1912-1978 .... **CLC 84**
See also BW 1; CA 125; CAAS 73-76; EWL 3

Dana, Richard Henry Sr.
1787-1879 .... **NCLC 53**

Daniel, Samuel 1562(?)-1619 .... **LC 24**
See also DLB 62; RGEL 2

Daniels, Brett
See Adler, Renata

Dannay, Frederic 1905-1982 .... **CLC 11**
See Queen, Ellery
See also CA 1-4R; CAAS 107; CANR 1, 39; CMW 4; DAM POP; DLB 137; MTCW 1

D'Annunzio, Gabriele 1863-1938 ... **TCLC 6, 40**
See also CA 155; CAAE 104; EW 8; EWL 3; RGWL 2, 3; TWA; WLIT 7

Danois, N. le
See Gourmont, Remy(-Marie-Charles) de

Dante 1265-1321 .... **CMLC 3, 18, 39, 70; PC 21; WLCS**
See Alighieri, Dante
See also DA; DA3; DAB; DAC; DAM MST, POET; EFS 1; EW 1; LAIT 1; RGWL 2, 3; TWA; WP

d'Antibes, Germain
See Simenon, Georges (Jacques Christian)

Danticat, Edwidge 1969- . **CLC 94, 139, 228; SSC 100**
See also AAYA 29; CA 192; 152, 192; CANR 73, 129; CN 7; DNFS 1; EXPS; LATS 1:2; MTCW 2; MTFW 2005; SSFS 1; YAW

Danvers, Dennis 1947- .... **CLC 70**

Danziger, Paula 1944-2004 .... **CLC 21**
See also AAYA 4, 36; BYA 6, 7, 14; CA 115; CAAE 112; CAAS 229; CANR 37, 132; CLR 20; JRDA; MAICYA 1, 2; MTFW 2005; SATA 36, 63, 102, 149; SATA-Brief 30; SATA-Obit 155; WYA; YAW

Da Ponte, Lorenzo 1749-1838 .... **NCLC 50**

d'Aragona, Tullia 1510(?)-1556 .... **LC 121**

Dario, Ruben 1867-1916 .... **HLC 1; PC 15; TCLC 4**
See also CA 131; CANR 81; DAM MULT; DLB 290; EWL 3; HW 1, 2; LAW; MTCW 1, 2; MTFW 2005; RGWL 2, 3

Darley, George 1795-1846 .... **NCLC 2**
See also DLB 96; RGEL 2

Darrow, Clarence (Seward)
1857-1938 .... **TCLC 81**
See also CA 164; DLB 303

Darwin, Charles 1809-1882 .... **NCLC 57**
See also BRWS 7; DLB 57, 166; LATS 1:1; RGEL 2; TEA; WLIT 4

Darwin, Erasmus 1731-1802 .... **NCLC 106**
See also DLB 93; RGEL 2

Daryush, Elizabeth 1887-1977 ...... **CLC 6, 19**
See also CA 49-52; CANR 3, 81; DLB 20

Das, Kamala 1934- .... **CLC 191; PC 43**
See also CA 101; CANR 27, 59; CP 1, 2, 3, 4, 5, 6, 7; CWP; DLB 323; FW

Dasgupta, Surendranath
1887-1952 .... **TCLC 81**
See also CA 157

Dashwood, Edmee Elizabeth Monica de la Pasture 1890-1943
See Delafield, E. M.
See also CA 154; CAAE 119

da Silva, Antonio Jose
1705-1739 .... **NCLC 114**

Daudet, (Louis Marie) Alphonse
1840-1897 .... **NCLC 1**
See also DLB 123; GFL 1789 to the Present; RGSF 2

Daudet, Alphonse Marie Leon
1867-1942 .... **SSC 94**
See also CA 217

d'Aulnoy, Marie-Catherine c.
1650-1705 .... **LC 100**

Daumal, Rene 1908-1944 .... **TCLC 14**
See also CA 247; CAAE 114; EWL 3

Davenant, William 1606-1668 .... **LC 13**
See also DLB 58, 126; RGEL 2

Davenport, Guy (Mattison, Jr.)
1927-2005 .... **CLC 6, 14, 38; SSC 16**
See also CA 33-36R; CAAS 235; CANR 23, 73; CN 3, 4, 5, 6; CSW; DLB 130

David, Robert
See Nezval, Vitezslav

Davidson, Avram (James) 1923-1993
See Queen, Ellery
See also CA 101; CAAS 171; CANR 26; DLB 8; FANT; SFW 4; SUFW 1, 2

Davidson, Donald (Grady)
1893-1968 .... **CLC 2, 13, 19**
See also CA 5-8R; CAAS 25-28R; CANR 4, 84; DLB 45

Davidson, Hugh
See Hamilton, Edmond

Davidson, John 1857-1909 .... **TCLC 24**
See also CA 217; CAAE 118; DLB 19; RGEL 2

Deleuze, Gilles 1925-1995 .... **TCLC 116**
    See also DLB 296
Delgado, Abelardo (Lalo) B(arrientos)
    1930-2004 .... **HLC 1**
    See also CA 131; 15; CAAS 230; CANR
    90; DAM MST, MULT; DLB 82; HW 1,
    2
Delibes, Miguel .... **CLC 8, 18**
    See Delibes Setien, Miguel
    See also DLB 322; EWL 3
Delibes Setien, Miguel 1920-
    See Delibes, Miguel
    See also CA 45-48; CANR 1, 32; CWW 2;
    HW 1; MTCW 1
DeLillo, Don 1936- ..... **CLC 8, 10, 13, 27, 39,**
    54, 76, 143, 210, 213
    See also AMWC 2; AMWS 6; BEST 89:1;
    BPFB 1; CA 81-84; CANR 21, 76, 92,
    133; CN 3, 4, 5, 6, 7; CPW; DA3; DAM
    NOV, POP; DLB 6, 173; EWL 3; MAL 5;
    MTCW 1, 2; MTFW 2005; RGAL 4; TUS
de Lisser, H. G.
    See De Lisser, H(erbert) G(eorge)
    See also DLB 117
De Lisser, H(erbert) G(eorge)
    1878-1944 .... **TCLC 12**
    See de Lisser, H. G.
    See also BW 2; CA 152; CAAE 109
Deloire, Pierre
    See Peguy, Charles (Pierre)
Deloney, Thomas 1543(?)-1600 .... **LC 41**
    See also DLB 167; RGEL 2
Deloria, Ella (Cara) 1889-1971(?) ..... **NNAL**
    See also CA 152; DAM MULT; DLB 175
Deloria, Vine, Jr. 1933-2005 .... **CLC 21, 122;**
    NNAL
    See also CA 53-56; CAAS 245; CANR 5,
    20, 48, 98; DAM MULT; DLB 175;
    MTCW 1; SATA 21; SATA-Obit 171
Deloria, Vine Victor, Jr.
    See Deloria, Vine, Jr.
del Valle-Inclan, Ramon (Maria)
    See Valle-Inclan, Ramon (Maria) del
    See also DLB 322
Del Vecchio, John M(ichael) 1947- .. **CLC 29**
    See also CA 110; DLBD 9
de Man, Paul (Adolph Michel)
    1919-1983 .... **CLC 55**
    See also CA 128; CAAS 111; CANR 61;
    DLB 67; MTCW 1, 2
DeMarinis, Rick 1934- .... **CLC 54**
    See also CA 184; 57-60; 184; 24; CANR 9,
    25, 50, 160; DLB 218; TCWW 2
de Maupassant, (Henri Rene Albert) Guy
    See Maupassant, (Henri Rene Albert) Guy
    de
Dembry, R. Emmet
    See Murfree, Mary Noailles
Demby, William 1922- .... **BLC 1; CLC 53**
    See also BW 1, 3; CA 81-84; CANR 81;
    DAM MULT; DLB 33
de Menton, Francisco
    See Chin, Frank (Chew, Jr.)
Demetrius of Phalerum c.
    307B.C.- .... **CMLC 34**
Demijohn, Thom
    See Disch, Thomas M.
De Mille, James 1833-1880 .... **NCLC 123**
    See also DLB 99, 251
Deming, Richard 1915-1983
    See Queen, Ellery
    See also CA 9-12R; CANR 3, 94; SATA 24
Democritus c. 460B.C.-c. 370B.C. . **CMLC 47**
de Montaigne, Michel (Eyquem)
    See Montaigne, Michel (Eyquem) de
de Montherlant, Henry (Milon)
    See Montherlant, Henry (Milon) de

Demosthenes 384B.C.-322B.C. ...... **CMLC 13**
    See also AW 1; DLB 176; RGWL 2, 3;
    WLIT 8
de Musset, (Louis Charles) Alfred
    See Musset, Alfred de
de Natale, Francine
    See Malzberg, Barry N(athaniel)
de Navarre, Marguerite 1492-1549 ... **LC 61;**
    SSC 85
    See Marguerite d'Angouleme; Marguerite
    de Navarre
    See also DLB 327
Denby, Edwin (Orr) 1903-1983 .... **CLC 48**
    See also CA 138; CAAS 110; CP 1
de Nerval, Gerard
    See Nerval, Gerard de
Denham, John 1615-1669 .... **LC 73**
    See also DLB 58, 126; RGEL 2
Denis, Julio
    See Cortazar, Julio
Denmark, Harrison
    See Zelazny, Roger
Dennis, John 1658-1734 .... **LC 11**
    See also DLB 101; RGEL 2
Dennis, Nigel (Forbes) 1912-1989 ...... **CLC 8**
    See also CA 25-28R; CAAS 129; CN 1, 2,
    3, 4; DLB 13, 15, 233; EWL 3; MTCW 1
Dent, Lester 1904-1959 .... **TCLC 72**
    See also CA 161; CAAE 112; CMW 4;
    DLB 306; SFW 4
De Palma, Brian 1940- .... **CLC 20**
    See also CA 109
De Palma, Brian Russell
    See De Palma, Brian
de Pizan, Christine
    See Christine de Pizan
    See also FL 1:1
De Quincey, Thomas 1785-1859 ..... **NCLC 4,**
    87
    See also BRW 4; CDBLB 1789-1832; DLB
    110, 144; RGEL 2
Deren, Eleanora 1908(?)-1961
    See Deren, Maya
    See also CA 192; CAAS 111
Deren, Maya .... **CLC 16, 102**
    See Deren, Eleanora
Derleth, August (William)
    1909-1971 .... **CLC 31**
    See also BPFB 1; BYA 9, 10; CA 1-4R;
    CAAS 29-32R; CANR 4; CMW 4; CN 1;
    DLB 9; DLBD 17; HGG; SATA 5; SUFW
    1
Der Nister 1884-1950 .... **TCLC 56**
    See Nister, Der
de Routisie, Albert
    See Aragon, Louis
Derrida, Jacques 1930-2004 ...... **CLC 24, 87,**
    225
    See also CA 127; CAAE 124; CAAS 232;
    CANR 76, 98, 133; DLB 242; EWL 3;
    LMFS 2; MTCW 2; TWA
Derry Down Derry
    See Lear, Edward
Dersonnes, Jacques
    See Simenon, Georges (Jacques Christian)
Der Stricker c. 1190-c. 1250 .... **CMLC 75**
    See also DLB 138
Desai, Anita 1937- .... **CLC 19, 37, 97, 175**
    See also BRWS 5; CA 81-84; CANR 33,
    53, 95, 133; CN 1, 2, 3, 4, 5, 6, 7; CWRI
    5; DA3; DAB; DAM NOV; DLB 271,
    323; DNFS 2; EWL 3; FW; MTCW 1, 2;
    MTFW 2005; SATA 63, 126
Desai, Kiran 1971- .... **CLC 119**
    See also BYA 16; CA 171; CANR 127
de Saint-Luc, Jean
    See Glassco, John
de Saint Roman, Arnaud
    See Aragon, Louis

Desbordes-Valmore, Marceline
    1786-1859 .... **NCLC 97**
    See also DLB 217
Descartes, Rene 1596-1650 .... **LC 20, 35**
    See also DLB 268; EW 3; GFL Beginnings
    to 1789
Deschamps, Eustache 1340(?)-1404 .. **LC 103**
    See also DLB 208
De Sica, Vittorio 1901(?)-1974 .... **CLC 20**
    See also CAAS 117
Desnos, Robert 1900-1945 .... **TCLC 22**
    See also CA 151; CAAE 121; CANR 107;
    DLB 258; EWL 3; LMFS 2
Destouches, Louis-Ferdinand
    1894-1961 .... **CLC 9, 15**
    See Celine, Louis-Ferdinand
    See also CA 85-88; CANR 28; MTCW 1
de Tolignac, Gaston
    See Griffith, D(avid Lewelyn) W(ark)
Deutsch, Babette 1895-1982 .... **CLC 18**
    See also BYA 3; CA 1-4R; CAAS 108;
    CANR 4, 79; CP 1, 2, 3; DLB 45; SATA
    1; SATA-Obit 33
Devenant, William 1606-1649 .... **LC 13**
Devkota, Laxmiprasad 1909-1959 . **TCLC 23**
    See also CAAE 123
De Voto, Bernard (Augustine)
    1897-1955 .... **TCLC 29**
    See also CA 160; CAAE 113; DLB 9, 256;
    MAL 5; TCWW 1, 2
De Vries, Peter 1910-1993 ..... **CLC 1, 2, 3, 7,**
    10, 28, 46
    See also CA 17-20R; CAAS 142; CANR
    41; CN 1, 2, 3, 4, 5; DAM NOV; DLB 6;
    DLBY 1982; MAL 5; MTCW 1, 2;
    MTFW 2005
Dewey, John 1859-1952 .... **TCLC 95**
    See also CA 170; CAAE 114; CANR 144;
    DLB 246, 270; RGAL 4
Dexter, John
    See Bradley, Marion Zimmer
    See also GLL 1
Dexter, Martin
    See Faust, Frederick (Schiller)
Dexter, Pete 1943- .... **CLC 34, 55**
    See also BEST 89:2; CA 131; CAAE 127;
    CANR 129; CPW; DAM POP; INT CA-
    131; MAL 5; MTCW 1; MTFW 2005
Diamano, Silmang
    See Senghor, Leopold Sedar
Diamant, Anita 1951- .... **CLC 239**
    See also CA 145; CANR 126
Diamond, Neil 1941- .... **CLC 30**
    See also CA 108
Diaz del Castillo, Bernal c.
    1496-1584 .... **HLCS 1; LC 31**
    See also DLB 318; LAW
di Bassetto, Corno
    See Shaw, George Bernard
Dick, Philip K. 1928-1982 ... **CLC 10, 30, 72;**
    SSC 57
    See also AAYA 24; BPFB 1; BYA 11; CA
    49-52; CAAS 106; CANR 2, 16, 132; CN
    2, 3; CPW; DA3; DAM NOV, POP; DLB
    8; MTCW 1, 2; MTFW 2005; NFS 5;
    SCFW 1, 2; SFW 4
Dick, Philip Kindred
    See Dick, Philip K.
Dickens, Charles (John Huffam)
    1812-1870 .... **NCLC 3, 8, 18, 26, 37, 50,**
    86, 105, 113, 161; SSC 17, 49, 88; WLC
    2
    See also AAYA 23; BRW 5; BRWC 1, 2;
    BYA 1, 2, 3, 13, 14; CDBLB 1832-1890;
    CLR 95; CMW 4; DA; DA3; DAB; DAC;
    DAM MST, NOV; DLB 21, 55, 70, 159,
    166; EXPN; GL 2; HGG; JRDA; LAIT 1,

2; LATS 1:1; LMFS 1; MAICYA 1, 2;
NFS 4, 5, 10, 14, 20, 25; RGEL 2; RGSF
2; SATA 15; SUFW 1; TEA; WCH; WLIT
4; WYA

Dickey, James (Lafayette)
1923-1997 .... **CLC 1, 2, 4, 7, 10, 15, 47,
109; PC 40; TCLC 151**
See also AAYA 50; AITN 1, 2; AMWS 4;
BPFB 1; CA 9-12R; CAAS 156; CABS
2; CANR 10, 48, 61, 105; CDALB 1968-
1988; CP 1, 2, 3, 4, 5, 6; CPW; CSW;
DA3; DAM NOV, POET, POP; DLB 5,
193; DLBD 7; DLBY 1982, 1993, 1996,
1997, 1998; EWL 3; INT CANR-10;
MAL 5; MTCW 1, 2; NFS 9; PFS 6, 11;
RGAL 4; TUS

Dickey, William 1928-1994 .... **CLC 3, 28**
See also CA 9-12R; CAAS 145; CANR 24,
79; CP 1, 2, 3, 4; DLB 5

Dickinson, Charles 1951- .... **CLC 49**
See also CA 128; CANR 141

Dickinson, Emily (Elizabeth)
1830-1886 ..... **NCLC 21, 77, 171; PC 1;
WLC 2**
See also AAYA 22; AMW; AMWR 1;
CDALB 1865-1917; DA; DA3; DAB;
DAC; DAM MST, POET; DLB 1, 243;
EXPP; FL 1:3; MBL; PAB; PFS 1, 2, 3,
4, 5, 6, 8, 10, 11, 13, 16; RGAL 4; SATA
29; TUS; WP; WYA

Dickinson, Mrs. Herbert Ward
See Phelps, Elizabeth Stuart

Dickinson, Peter (Malcolm de Brissac)
1927- .... **CLC 12, 35**
See also AAYA 9, 49; BYA 5; CA 41-44R;
CANR 31, 58, 88, 134; CLR 29; CMW 4;
DLB 87, 161, 276; JRDA; MAICYA 1, 2;
SATA 5, 62, 95, 150; SFW 4; WYA; YAW

Dickson, Carr
See Carr, John Dickson

Dickson, Carter
See Carr, John Dickson

Diderot, Denis 1713-1784 .... **LC 26, 126**
See also DLB 313; EW 4; GFL Beginnings
to 1789; LMFS 1; RGWL 2, 3

Didion, Joan 1934- . **CLC 1, 3, 8, 14, 32, 129**
See also AITN 1; AMWS 4; CA 5-8R;
CANR 14, 52, 76, 125; CDALB 1968-
1988; CN 2, 3, 4, 5, 6, 7; DA3; DAM
NOV; DLB 2, 173, 185; DLBY 1981,
1986; EWL 3; MAL 5; MBL; MTCW 1,
2; MTFW 2005; NFS 3; RGAL 4; TCLE
1:1; TCWW 2; TUS

di Donato, Pietro 1911-1992 .... **TCLC 159**
See also CA 101; CAAS 136; DLB 9

Dietrich, Robert
See Hunt, E. Howard

Difusa, Pati
See Almodovar, Pedro

Dillard, Annie 1945- ...... **CLC 9, 60, 115, 216**
See also AAYA 6, 43; AMWS 6; ANW; CA
49-52; CANR 3, 43, 62, 90, 125; DA3;
DAM NOV; DLB 275, 278; DLBY 1980;
LAIT 4, 5; MAL 5; MTCW 1, 2; MTFW
2005; NCFS 1; RGAL 4; SATA 10, 140;
TCLE 1:1; TUS

Dillard, R(ichard) H(enry) W(ilde)
1937- .... **CLC 5**
See also CA 21-24R; 7; CANR 10; CP 2, 3,
4, 5, 6, 7; CSW; DLB 5, 244

Dillon, Eilis 1920-1994 .... **CLC 17**
See also CA 182; 9-12R, 182; 3; CAAS
147; CANR 4, 38, 78; CLR 26; MAICYA
1, 2; MAICYAS 1; SATA 2, 74; SATA-
Essay 105; SATA-Obit 83; YAW

Dimont, Penelope
See Mortimer, Penelope (Ruth)

Dinesen, Isak ..... **CLC 10, 29, 95; SSC 7, 75**
See Blixen, Karen (Christentze Dinesen)
See also EW 10; EWL 3; EXPS; FW; GL
2; HGG; LAIT 3; MTCW 1; NCFS 2;
NFS 9; RGSF 2; RGWL 2, 3; SSFS 3, 6,
13; WLIT 2

Ding Ling .... **CLC 68**
See Chiang, Pin-chin
See also DLB 328; RGWL 3

Diodorus Siculus c. 90B.C.-c.
31B.C. .... **CMLC 88**

Diphusa, Patty
See Almodovar, Pedro

Disch, Thomas M. 1940- .... **CLC 7, 36**
See Disch, Tom
See also AAYA 17; BPFB 1; CA 21-24R; 4;
CANR 17, 36, 54, 89; CLR 18; CP 5, 6,
7; DA3; DLB 8; HGG; MAICYA 1, 2;
MTCW 1, 2; MTFW 2005; SAAS 15;
SATA 92; SCFW 1, 2; SFW 4; SUFW 2

Disch, Tom
See Disch, Thomas M.
See also DLB 282

d'Isly, Georges
See Simenon, Georges (Jacques Christian)

Disraeli, Benjamin 1804-1881 ... **NCLC 2, 39,
79**
See also BRW 4; DLB 21, 55; RGEL 2

Ditcum, Steve
See Crumb, R.

Dixon, Paige
See Corcoran, Barbara (Asenath)

Dixon, Stephen 1936- .... **CLC 52; SSC 16**
See also AMWS 12; CA 89-92; CANR 17,
40, 54, 91; CN 4, 5, 6, 7; DLB 130; MAL
5

Dixon, Thomas, Jr. 1864-1946 ..... **TCLC 163**
See also RHW

Djebar, Assia 1936- .... **CLC 182**
See also CA 188; EWL 3; RGWL 3; WLIT
2

Doak, Annie
See Dillard, Annie

Dobell, Sydney Thompson
1824-1874 .... **NCLC 43**
See also DLB 32; RGEL 2

Doblin, Alfred .... **TCLC 13**
See Doeblin, Alfred
See also CDWLB 2; EWL 3; RGWL 2, 3

Dobroliubov, Nikolai Aleksandrovich
See Dobrolyubov, Nikolai Alexandrovich
See also DLB 277

Dobrolyubov, Nikolai Alexandrovich
1836-1861 .... **NCLC 5**
See Dobroliubov, Nikolai Aleksandrovich

Dobson, Austin 1840-1921 .... **TCLC 79**
See also DLB 35, 144

Dobyns, Stephen 1941- .... **CLC 37, 233**
See also AMWS 13; CA 45-48; CANR 2,
18, 99; CMW 4; CP 4, 5, 6, 7; PFS 23

Doctorow, Edgar Laurence
See Doctorow, E.L.

Doctorow, E.L. 1931- . **CLC 6, 11, 15, 18, 37,
44, 65, 113, 214**
See also CA 22; AITN 2; AMWS 4;
BEST 89:3; BPFB 1; CA 45-48; CANR
2, 33, 51, 76, 97, 133; CDALB 1968-
1988; CN 3, 4, 5, 6, 7; CPW; DA3; DAM
NOV, POP; DLB 2, 28, 173; DLBY 1980;
EWL 3; LAIT 3; MAL 5; MTCW 1, 2;
MTFW 2005; NFS 6; RGAL 4; RGHL;
RHW; TCLE 1:1; TCWW 1, 2; TUS

Dodgson, Charles L(utwidge) 1832-1898
See Carroll, Lewis
See also CLR 2; DA; DA3; DAB; DAC;
DAM MST, NOV, POET; MAICYA 1, 2;
SATA 100; YABC 2

Dodsley, Robert 1703-1764 .... **LC 97**
See also DLB 95; RGEL 2

Dodson, Owen (Vincent) 1914-1983 .. **BLC 1;
CLC 79**
See also BW 1; CA 65-68; CAAS 110;
CANR 24; DAM MULT; DLB 76

Doeblin, Alfred 1878-1957 .... **TCLC 13**
See Doblin, Alfred
See also CA 141; CAAE 110; DLB 66

Doerr, Harriet 1910-2002 .... **CLC 34**
See also CA 122; CAAE 117; CAAS 213;
CANR 47; INT CA-122; LATS 1:2

Domecq, H(onorio Bustos)
See Bioy Casares, Adolfo

Domecq, H(onorio) Bustos
See Bioy Casares, Adolfo; Borges, Jorge
Luis

Domini, Rey
See Lorde, Audre
See also GLL 1

Dominique
See Proust, (Valentin-Louis-George-Eugene)
Marcel

Don, A
See Stephen, Sir Leslie

Donaldson, Stephen R(eeder)
1947- .... **CLC 46, 138**
See also AAYA 36; BPFB 1; CA 89-92;
CANR 13, 55, 99; CPW; DAM POP;
FANT; INT CANR-13; SATA 121; SFW
4; SUFW 1, 2

Donleavy, J(ames) P(atrick) 1926- .... **CLC 1,
4, 6, 10, 45**
See also AITN 2; BPFB 1; CA 9-12R;
CANR 24, 49, 62, 80, 124; CBD; CD 5,
6; CN 1, 2, 3, 4, 5, 6, 7; DLB 6, 173; INT
CANR-24; MAL 5; MTCW 1, 2; MTFW
2005; RGAL 4

Donnadieu, Marguerite
See Duras, Marguerite

Donne, John 1572-1631 ... **LC 10, 24, 91; PC
1, 43; WLC 2**
See also AAYA 67; BRW 1; BRWC 1;
BRWR 2; CDBLB Before 1660; DA;
DAB; DAC; DAM MST, POET; DLB
121, 151; EXPP; PAB; PFS 2, 11; RGEL
3; TEA; WLIT 3; WP

Donnell, David 1939(?)- .... **CLC 34**
See also CA 197

Donoghue, Denis 1928- .... **CLC 209**
See also CA 17-20R; CANR 16, 102

Donoghue, Emma 1969- .... **CLC 239**
See also CA 155; CANR 103, 152; DLB
267; GLL 2; SATA 101

Donoghue, P.S.
See Hunt, E. Howard

Donoso (Yanez), Jose 1924-1996 ... **CLC 4, 8,
11, 32, 99; HLC 1; SSC 34; TCLC 133**
See also CA 81-84; CAAS 155; CANR 32,
73; CDWLB 3; CWW 2; DAM MULT;
DLB 113; EWL 3; HW 1, 2; LAW; LAWS
1; MTCW 1, 2; MTFW 2005; RGSF 2;
WLIT 1

Donovan, John 1928-1992 .... **CLC 35**
See also AAYA 20; CA 97-100; CAAS 137;
CLR 3; MAICYA 1, 2; SATA 72; SATA-
Brief 29; YAW

Don Roberto
See Cunninghame Graham, Robert
(Gallnigad) Bontine

Doolittle, Hilda 1886-1961 . **CLC 3, 8, 14, 31,
34, 73; PC 5; WLC 3**
See H. D.
See also AAYA 66; AMWS 1; CA 97-100;
CANR 35, 131; DA; DAC; DAM MST,
POET; DLB 4, 45; EWL 3; FW; GLL 1;
LMFS 2; MAL 5; MBL; MTCW 1, 2;
MTFW 2005; PFS 6; RGAL 4

Doppo, Kunikida .... **TCLC 99**
See Kunikida Doppo

Erskine, John 1879-1951 .... **TCLC 84**
See also CA 159; CAAE 112; DLB 9, 102;
FANT

Erwin, Will
See Eisner, Will

Eschenbach, Wolfram von
See von Eschenbach, Wolfram
See also RGWL 3

Eseki, Bruno
See Mphahlele, Ezekiel

Esenin, S.A.
See Esenin, Sergei
See also EWL 3

Esenin, Sergei 1895-1925 .... **TCLC 4**
See Esenin, S.A.
See also CAAE 104; RGWL 2, 3

Esenin, Sergei Aleksandrovich
See Esenin, Sergei

Eshleman, Clayton 1935- .... **CLC 7**
See also CA 212; 33-36R, 212; 6; CANR
93; CP 1, 2, 3, 4, 5, 6, 7; DLB 5

Espada, Martin 1957- .... **PC 74**
See also CA 159; CANR 80; CP 7; EXPP;
LLW; MAL 5; PFS 13, 16

Espriella, Don Manuel Alvarez
See Southey, Robert

Espriu, Salvador 1913-1985 .... **CLC 9**
See also CA 154; CAAS 115; DLB 134;
EWL 3

Espronceda, Jose de 1808-1842 ..... **NCLC 39**

Esquivel, Laura 1950(?)- ... **CLC 141; HLCS
1**
See also AAYA 29; CA 143; CANR 68, 113,
161; DA3; DNFS 2; LAIT 3; LMFS 2;
MTCW 2; MTFW 2005; NFS 5; WLIT 1

Esse, James
See Stephens, James

Esterbrook, Tom
See Hubbard, L. Ron

Estleman, Loren D. 1952- .... **CLC 48**
See also AAYA 27; CA 85-88; CANR 27,
74, 139; CMW 4; CPW; DA3; DAM
NOV, POP; DLB 226; INT CANR-27;
MTCW 1, 2; MTFW 2005; TCWW 1, 2

Etherege, Sir George 1636-1692 . **DC 23; LC
78**
See also BRW 2; DAM DRAM; DLB 80;
PAB; RGEL 2

Euclid 306B.C.-283B.C. .... **CMLC 25**

Eugenides, Jeffrey 1960(?)- .... **CLC 81, 212**
See also AAYA 51; CA 144; CANR 120;
MTFW 2005; NFS 24

Euripides c. 484B.C.-406B.C. .... **CMLC 23,
51; DC 4; WLCS**
See also AW 1; CDWLB 1; DA; DA3;
DAB; DAC; DAM DRAM, MST; DFS 1,
4, 6; DLB 176; LAIT 1; LMFS 1; RGWL
2, 3; WLIT 8

Evan, Evin
See Faust, Frederick (Schiller)

Evans, Caradoc 1878-1945 ... **SSC 43; TCLC
85**
See also DLB 162

Evans, Evan
See Faust, Frederick (Schiller)

Evans, Marian
See Eliot, George

Evans, Mary Ann
See Eliot, George
See also NFS 20

Evarts, Esther
See Benson, Sally

Everett, Percival
See Everett, Percival L.
See also CSW

Everett, Percival L. 1956- .... **CLC 57**
See Everett, Percival
See also BW 2; CA 129; CANR 94, 134;
CN 7; MTFW 2005

Everson, R(onald) G(ilmour)
1903-1992 .... **CLC 27**
See also CA 17-20R; CP 1, 2, 3, 4; DLB 88

Everson, William (Oliver)
1912-1994 .... **CLC 1, 5, 14**
See Antoninus, Brother
See also BG 1:2; CA 9-12R; CAAS 145;
CANR 20; CP 2, 3, 4, 5; DLB 5, 16, 212;
MTCW 1

Evtushenko, Evgenii Aleksandrovich
See Yevtushenko, Yevgeny (Alexandrovich)
See also CWW 2; RGWL 2, 3

Ewart, Gavin (Buchanan)
1916-1995 .... **CLC 13, 46**
See also BRWS 7; CA 89-92; CAAS 150;
CANR 17, 46; CP 1, 2, 3, 4, 5, 6; DLB
40; MTCW 1

Ewers, Hanns Heinz 1871-1943 ..... **TCLC 12**
See also CA 149; CAAE 109

Ewing, Frederick R.
See Sturgeon, Theodore (Hamilton)

Exley, Frederick (Earl) 1929-1992 .... **CLC 6,
11**
See also AITN 2; BPFB 1; CA 81-84;
CAAS 138; CANR 117; DLB 143; DLBY
1981

Eynhardt, Guillermo
See Quiroga, Horacio (Sylvestre)

Ezekiel, Nissim (Moses) 1924-2004 .. **CLC 61**
See also CA 61-64; CAAS 223; CP 1, 2, 3,
4, 5, 6, 7; DLB 323; EWL 3

Ezekiel, Tish O'Dowd 1943- .... **CLC 34**
See also CA 129

Fadeev, Aleksandr Aleksandrovich
See Bulgya, Alexander Alexandrovich
See also DLB 272

Fadeev, Alexandr Alexandrovich
See Bulgya, Alexander Alexandrovich
See also EWL 3

Fadeyev, A.
See Bulgya, Alexander Alexandrovich

Fadeyev, Alexander .... **TCLC 53**
See Bulgya, Alexander Alexandrovich

Fagen, Donald 1948- .... **CLC 26**

Fainzil'berg, Il'ia Arnol'dovich
See Fainzilberg, Ilya Arnoldovich

Fainzilberg, Ilya Arnoldovich
1897-1937 .... **TCLC 21**
See Il'f, Il'ia
See also CA 165; CAAE 120; EWL 3

Fair, Ronald L. 1932- .... **CLC 18**
See also BW 1; CA 69-72; CANR 25; DLB
33

Fairbairn, Roger
See Carr, John Dickson

Fairbairns, Zoe (Ann) 1948- .... **CLC 32**
See also CA 103; CANR 21, 85; CN 4, 5,
6, 7

Fairfield, Flora
See Alcott, Louisa May

Fairman, Paul W. 1916-1977
See Queen, Ellery
See also CAAS 114; SFW 4

Falco, Gian
See Papini, Giovanni

Falconer, James
See Kirkup, James

Falconer, Kenneth
See Kornbluth, C(yril) M.

Falkland, Samuel
See Heijermans, Herman

Fallaci, Oriana 1930-2006 .... **CLC 11, 110**
See also CA 77-80; CAAS 253; CANR 15,
58, 134; FW; MTCW 1

Faludi, Susan 1959- .... **CLC 140**
See also CA 138; CANR 126; FW; MTCW
2; MTFW 2005; NCFS 3

Faludy, George 1913- .... **CLC 42**
See also CA 21-24R

Faludy, Gyoergy
See Faludy, George

Fanon, Frantz 1925-1961 ... **BLC 2; CLC 74;
TCLC 188**
See also BW 1; CA 116; CAAS 89-92;
DAM MULT; DLB 296; LMFS 2; WLIT
2

Fanshawe, Ann 1625-1680 .... **LC 11**

Fante, John (Thomas) 1911-1983 .... **CLC 60;
SSC 65**
See also AMWS 11; CA 69-72; CAAS 109;
CANR 23, 104; DLB 130; DLBY 1983

Far, Sui Sin .... **SSC 62**
See Eaton, Edith Maude
See also SSFS 4

Farah, Nuruddin 1945- ...... **BLC 2; CLC 53,
137**
See also AFW; BW 2, 3; CA 106; CANR
81, 148; CDWLB 3; CN 4, 5, 6, 7; DAM
MULT; DLB 125; EWL 3; WLIT 2

Fargue, Leon-Paul 1876(?)-1947 .... **TCLC 11**
See also CAAE 109; CANR 107; DLB 258;
EWL 3

Farigoule, Louis
See Romains, Jules

Farina, Richard 1936(?)-1966 .... **CLC 9**
See also CA 81-84; CAAS 25-28R

Farley, Walter (Lorimer)
1915-1989 .... **CLC 17**
See also AAYA 58; BYA 14; CA 17-20R;
CANR 8, 29, 84; DLB 22; JRDA; MAI-
CYA 1, 2; SATA 2, 43, 132; YAW

Farmer, Philip Jose 1918- .... **CLC 1, 19**
See also AAYA 28; BPFB 1; CA 1-4R;
CANR 4, 35, 111; DLB 8; MTCW 1;
SATA 93; SCFW 1, 2; SFW 4

Farquhar, George 1677-1707 .... **LC 21**
See also BRW 2; DAM DRAM; DLB 84;
RGEL 2

Farrell, J(ames) G(ordon)
1935-1979 .... **CLC 6**
See also CA 73-76; CAAS 89-92; CANR
36; CN 1, 2; DLB 14, 271, 326; MTCW
1; RGEL 2; RHW; WLIT 4

Farrell, James T(homas) 1904-1979 . **CLC 1,
4, 8, 11, 66; SSC 28**
See also AMW; BPFB 1; CA 5-8R; CAAS
89-92; CANR 9, 61; CN 1, 2; DLB 4, 9,
86; DLBD 2; EWL 3; MAL 5; MTCW 1,
2; MTFW 2005; RGAL 4

Farrell, Warren (Thomas) 1943- ...... **CLC 70**
See also CA 146; CANR 120

Farren, Richard J.
See Betjeman, John

Farren, Richard M.
See Betjeman, John

Fassbinder, Rainer Werner
1946-1982 .... **CLC 20**
See also CA 93-96; CAAS 106; CANR 31

Fast, Howard 1914-2003 .... **CLC 23, 131**
See also AAYA 16; BPFB 1; CA 181; 1-4R,
181; 18; CAAS 214; CANR 1, 33, 54, 75,
98, 140; CMW 4; CN 1, 2, 3, 4, 5, 6, 7;
CPW; DAM NOV; DLB 9; INT CANR-
33; LATS 1:1; MAL 5; MTCW 2; MTFW
2005; RHW; SATA 7; SATA-Essay 107;
TCWW 1, 2; YAW

Faulcon, Robert
See Holdstock, Robert

Faulkner, William (Cuthbert)
1897-1962 .... **CLC 1, 3, 6, 8, 9, 11, 14,
18, 28, 52, 68; SSC 1, 35, 42, 92, 97;
TCLC 141; WLC 2**
See also AAYA 7; AMW; AMWR 1; BPFB
1; BYA 5, 15; CA 81-84; CANR 33;
CDALB 1929-1941; DA; DA3; DAB;
DAC; DAM MST, NOV; DLB 9, 11, 44,
102, 316, 330; DLBD 2; DLBY 1986,
1997; EWL 3; EXPN; EXPS; GL 2; LAIT

2; LATS 1:1; LMFS 2; MAL 5; MTCW 1, 2; MTFW 2005; NFS 4, 8, 13, 24; RGAL 4; RGSF 2; SSFS 2, 5, 6, 12; TUS

Fauset, Jessie Redmon
1882(?)-1961 .. **BLC 2; CLC 19, 54; HR 1:2**
See also AFAW 2; BW 1; CA 109; CANR 83; DAM MULT; DLB 51; FW; LMFS 2; MAL 5; MBL

Faust, Frederick (Schiller)
1892-1944 .... **TCLC 49**
See Brand, Max; Dawson, Peter; Frederick, John
See also CA 152; CAAE 108; CANR 143; DAM POP; DLB 256; TUS

Faust, Irvin 1924- .... **CLC 8**
See also CA 33-36R; CANR 28, 67; CN 1, 2, 3, 4, 5, 6, 7; DLB 2, 28, 218, 278; DLBY 1980

Fawkes, Guy
See Benchley, Robert (Charles)

Fearing, Kenneth (Flexner)
1902-1961 .... **CLC 51**
See also CA 93-96; CANR 59; CMW 4; DLB 9; MAL 5; RGAL 4

Fecamps, Elise
See Creasey, John

Federman, Raymond 1928- .... **CLC 6, 47**
See also CA 208; 17-20R, 208; 8; CANR 10, 43, 83, 108; CN 3, 4, 5, 6; DLBY 1980

Federspiel, J.F. 1931-2007 .... **CLC 42**
See also CA 146; CAAS 257

Federspiel, Juerg F.
See Federspiel, J.F.

Federspiel, Jurg F.
See Federspiel, J.F.

Feiffer, Jules 1929- .... **CLC 2, 8, 64**
See also AAYA 3, 62; CA 17-20R; CAD; CANR 30, 59, 129, 161; CD 5, 6; DAM DRAM; DLB 7, 44; INT CANR-30; MTCW 1; SATA 8, 61, 111, 157

Feiffer, Jules Ralph
See Feiffer, Jules

Feige, Hermann Albert Otto Maximilian
See Traven, B.

Feinberg, David B. 1956-1994 .... **CLC 59**
See also CA 135; CAAS 147

Feinstein, Elaine 1930- .... **CLC 36**
See also CA 69-72; 1; CANR 31, 68, 121, 162; CN 3, 4, 5, 6, 7; CP 2, 3, 4, 5, 6, 7; CWP; DLB 14, 40; MTCW 1

Feke, Gilbert David .... **CLC 65**

Feldman, Irving (Mordecai) 1928- ..... **CLC 7**
See also CA 1-4R; CANR 1; CP 1, 2, 3, 4, 5, 6, 7; DLB 169; TCLE 1:1

Felix-Tchicaya, Gerald
See Tchicaya, Gerald Felix

Fellini, Federico 1920-1993 .... **CLC 16, 85**
See also CA 65-68; CAAS 143; CANR 33

Felltham, Owen 1602(?)-1668 .... **LC 92**
See also DLB 126, 151

Felsen, Henry Gregor 1916-1995 ..... **CLC 17**
See also CA 1-4R; CAAS 180; CANR 1; SAAS 2; SATA 1

Felski, Rita .... **CLC 65**

Fenelon, Francois de Pons de Salignac de la Mothe- 1651-1715 .... **LC 134**
See also DLB 268; EW 3; GFL Beginnings to 1789

Fenno, Jack
See Calisher, Hortense

Fenollosa, Ernest (Francisco)
1853-1908 .... **TCLC 91**

Fenton, James 1949- .... **CLC 32, 209**
See also CA 102; CANR 108, 160; CP 2, 3, 4, 5, 6, 7; DLB 40; PFS 11

Fenton, James Martin
See Fenton, James

Ferber, Edna 1887-1968 .... **CLC 18, 93**
See also AITN 1; CA 5-8R; CAAS 25-28R; CANR 68, 105; DLB 9, 28, 86, 266; MAL 5; MTCW 1, 2; MTFW 2005; RGAL 4; RHW; SATA 7; TCWW 1, 2

Ferdowsi, Abu'l Qasem
940-1020(?) .... **CMLC 43**
See Firdawsi, Abu al-Qasim
See also RGWL 2, 3

Ferguson, Helen
See Kavan, Anna

Ferguson, Niall 1964- .... **CLC 134**
See also CA 190; CANR 154

Ferguson, Samuel 1810-1886 .... **NCLC 33**
See also DLB 32; RGEL 2

Fergusson, Robert 1750-1774 .... **LC 29**
See also DLB 109; RGEL 2

Ferling, Lawrence
See Ferlinghetti, Lawrence

Ferlinghetti, Lawrence 1919(?)- .... **CLC 2, 6, 10, 27, 111; PC 1**
See also AAYA 74; BG 1:2; CA 5-8R; CAD; CANR 3, 41, 73, 125; CDALB 1941-1968; CP 1, 2, 3, 4, 5, 6, 7; DA3; DAM POET; DLB 5, 16; MAL 5; MTCW 1, 2; MTFW 2005; RGAL 4; WP

Ferlinghetti, Lawrence Monsanto
See Ferlinghetti, Lawrence

Fern, Fanny
See Parton, Sara Payson Willis

Fernandez, Vicente Garcia Huidobro
See Huidobro Fernandez, Vicente Garcia

Fernandez-Armesto, Felipe .... **CLC 70**
See Fernandez-Armesto, Felipe Fermin Ricardo
See also CANR 153

Fernandez-Armesto, Felipe Fermin Ricardo
1950-
See Fernandez-Armesto, Felipe
See also CA 142; CANR 93

Fernandez de Lizardi, Jose Joaquin
See Lizardi, Jose Joaquin Fernandez de

Ferre, Rosario 1938- ...... **CLC 139; HLCS 1; SSC 36**
See also CA 131; CANR 55, 81, 134; CWW 2; DLB 145; EWL 3; HW 1, 2; LAWS 1; MTCW 2; MTFW 2005; WLIT 1

Ferrer, Gabriel (Francisco Victor) Miro
See Miro (Ferrer), Gabriel (Francisco Victor)

Ferrier, Susan (Edmonstone)
1782-1854 .... **NCLC 8**
See also DLB 116; RGEL 2

Ferrigno, Robert 1948(?)- .... **CLC 65**
See also CA 140; CANR 125, 161

Ferron, Jacques 1921-1985 .... **CLC 94**
See also CA 129; CAAE 117; CCA 1; DAC; DLB 60; EWL 3

Feuchtwanger, Lion 1884-1958 .... **TCLC 3**
See also CA 187; CAAE 104; DLB 66; EWL 3; RGHL

Feuerbach, Ludwig 1804-1872 ..... **NCLC 139**
See also DLB 133

Feuillet, Octave 1821-1890 .... **NCLC 45**
See also DLB 192

Feydeau, Georges (Leon Jules Marie)
1862-1921 .... **TCLC 22**
See also CA 152; CAAE 113; CANR 84; DAM DRAM; DLB 192; EWL 3; GFL 1789 to the Present; RGWL 2, 3

Fichte, Johann Gottlieb
1762-1814 .... **NCLC 62**
See also DLB 90

Ficino, Marsilio 1433-1499 .... **LC 12**
See also LMFS 1

Fiedeler, Hans
See Doeblin, Alfred

Fiedler, Leslie A(aron) 1917-2003 ..... **CLC 4, 13, 24**
See also AMWS 13; CA 9-12R; CAAS 212; CANR 7, 63; CN 1, 2, 3, 4, 5, 6; DLB 28, 67; EWL 3; MAL 5; MTCW 1, 2; RGAL 4; TUS

Field, Andrew 1938- .... **CLC 44**
See also CA 97-100; CANR 25

Field, Eugene 1850-1895 .... **NCLC 3**
See also DLB 23, 42, 140; DLBD 13; MAICYA 1, 2; RGAL 4; SATA 16

Field, Gans T.
See Wellman, Manly Wade

Field, Michael 1915-1971 .... **TCLC 43**
See also CAAS 29-32R

Fielding, Helen 1958- .... **CLC 146, 217**
See also AAYA 65; CA 172; CANR 127; DLB 231; MTFW 2005

Fielding, Henry 1707-1754 .... **LC 1, 46, 85; WLC 2**
See also BRW 3; BRWR 1; CDBLB 1660-1789; DA; DA3; DAB; DAC; DAM DRAM, MST, NOV; DLB 39, 84, 101; NFS 18; RGEL 2; TEA; WLIT 3

Fielding, Sarah 1710-1768 .... **LC 1, 44**
See also DLB 39; RGEL 2; TEA

Fields, W. C. 1880-1946 .... **TCLC 80**
See also DLB 44

Fierstein, Harvey (Forbes) 1954- ..... **CLC 33**
See also CA 129; CAAE 123; CAD; CD 5, 6; CPW; DA3; DAM DRAM, POP; DFS 6; DLB 266; GLL; MAL 5

Figes, Eva 1932- .... **CLC 31**
See also CA 53-56; CANR 4, 44, 83; CN 2, 3, 4, 5, 6, 7; DLB 14, 271; FW; RGHL

Filippo, Eduardo de
See de Filippo, Eduardo

Finch, Anne 1661-1720 ..... **LC 3, 137; PC 21**
See also BRWS 9; DLB 95

Finch, Robert (Duer Claydon)
1900-1995 .... **CLC 18**
See also CA 57-60; CANR 9, 24, 49; CP 1, 2, 3, 4, 5, 6; DLB 88

Findley, Timothy (Irving Frederick)
1930-2002 .... **CLC 27, 102**
See also CA 25-28R; CAAS 206; CANR 12, 42, 69, 109; CCA 1; CN 4, 5, 6, 7; DAC; DAM MST; DLB 53; FANT; RHW

Fink, William
See Mencken, H(enry) L(ouis)

Firbank, Louis 1942-
See Reed, Lou
See also CAAE 117

Firbank, (Arthur Annesley) Ronald
1886-1926 .... **TCLC 1**
See also BRWS 2; CA 177; CAAE 104; DLB 36; EWL 3; RGEL 2

Firdawsi, Abu al-Qasim
See Ferdowsi, Abu'l Qasem
See also WLIT 6

Fish, Stanley
See Fish, Stanley Eugene

Fish, Stanley E.
See Fish, Stanley Eugene

Fish, Stanley Eugene 1938- .... **CLC 142**
See also CA 132; CAAE 112; CANR 90; DLB 67

Fisher, Dorothy (Frances) Canfield
1879-1958 .... **TCLC 87**
See also CA 136; CAAE 114; CANR 80; CLR 71; CWRI 5; DLB 9, 102, 284; MAICYA 1, 2; MAL 5; YABC 1

Fisher, M(ary) F(rances) K(ennedy)
1908-1992 .... **CLC 76, 87**
See also CA 77-80; CAAS 138; CANR 44; MTCW 2

Fisher, Roy 1930- .... **CLC 25**
See also CA 81-84; 10; CANR 16; CP 1, 2, 3, 4, 5, 6, 7; DLB 40

Fisher, Rudolph 1897-1934 . **BLC 2; HR 1:2; SSC 25; TCLC 11**
See also BW 1, 3; CA 124; CAAE 107; CANR 80; DAM MULT; DLB 51, 102

Fisher, Vardis (Alvero) 1895-1968 .... **CLC 7; TCLC 140**
See also CA 5-8R; CAAS 25-28R; CANR 68; DLB 9, 206; MAL 5; RGAL 4; TCWW 1, 2

Fiske, Tarleton
See Bloch, Robert (Albert)

Fitch, Clarke
See Sinclair, Upton

Fitch, John IV
See Cormier, Robert

Fitzgerald, Captain Hugh
See Baum, L(yman) Frank

FitzGerald, Edward 1809-1883 ...... **NCLC 9, 153**
See also BRW 4; DLB 32; RGEL 2

Fitzgerald, F(rancis) Scott (Key) 1896-1940 ... **SSC 6, 31, 75; TCLC 1, 6, 14, 28, 55, 157; WLC 2**
See also AAYA 24; AITN 1; AMW; AMWC 2; AMWR 1; BPFB 1; CA 123; CAAE 110; CDALB 1917-1929; DA; DA3; DAB; DAC; DAM MST, NOV; DLB 4, 9, 86, 219, 273; DLBD 1, 15, 16; DLBY 1981, 1996; EWL 3; EXPN; EXPS; LAIT 3; MAL 5; MTCW 1, 2; MTFW 2005; NFS 2, 19, 20; RGAL 4; RGSF 2; SSFS 4, 15, 21; TUS

Fitzgerald, Penelope 1916-2000 . **CLC 19, 51, 61, 143**
See also BRWS 5; CA 85-88; 10; CAAS 190; CANR 56, 86, 131; CN 3, 4, 5, 6, 7; DLB 14, 194, 326; EWL 3; MTCW 2; MTFW 2005

Fitzgerald, Robert (Stuart) 1910-1985 .... **CLC 39**
See also CA 1-4R; CAAS 114; CANR 1; CP 1, 2, 3, 4; DLBY 1980; MAL 5

FitzGerald, Robert D(avid) 1902-1987 .... **CLC 19**
See also CA 17-20R; CP 1, 2, 3, 4; DLB 260; RGEL 2

Fitzgerald, Zelda (Sayre) 1900-1948 .... **TCLC 52**
See also AMWS 9; CA 126; CAAE 117; DLBY 1984

Flanagan, Thomas (James Bonner) 1923-2002 .... **CLC 25, 52**
See also CA 108; CAAS 206; CANR 55; CN 3, 4, 5, 6, 7; DLBY 1980; INT CA-108; MTCW 1; RHW; TCLE 1:1

Flaubert, Gustave 1821-1880 .... **NCLC 2, 10, 19, 62, 66, 135, 179, 185; SSC 11, 60; WLC 2**
See also DA; DA3; DAB; DAC; DAM MST, NOV; DLB 119, 301; EW 7; EXPS; GFL 1789 to the Present; LAIT 2; LMFS 1; NFS 14; RGSF 2; RGWL 2, 3; SSFS 6; TWA

Flavius Josephus
See Josephus, Flavius

Flecker, Herman Elroy
See Flecker, (Herman) James Elroy

Flecker, (Herman) James Elroy 1884-1915 .... **TCLC 43**
See also CA 150; CAAE 109; DLB 10, 19; RGEL 2

Fleming, Ian 1908-1964 .... **CLC 3, 30**
See also AAYA 26; BPFB 1; CA 5-8R; CANR 59; CDBLB 1945-1960; CMW 4; CPW; DA3; DAM POP; DLB 87, 201; MSW; MTCW 1, 2; MTFW 2005; RGEL 2; SATA 9; TEA; YAW

Fleming, Ian Lancaster
See Fleming, Ian

Fleming, Thomas 1927- .... **CLC 37**
See also CA 5-8R; CANR 10, 102, 155; INT CANR-10; SATA 8

Fleming, Thomas James
See Fleming, Thomas

Fletcher, John 1579-1625 .... **DC 6; LC 33**
See also BRW 2; CDBLB Before 1660; DLB 58; RGEL 2; TEA

Fletcher, John Gould 1886-1950 .... **TCLC 35**
See also CA 167; CAAE 107; DLB 4, 45; LMFS 2; MAL 5; RGAL 4

Fleur, Paul
See Pohl, Frederik

Flieg, Helmut
See Heym, Stefan

Flooglebuckle, Al
See Spiegelman, Art

Flora, Fletcher 1914-1969
See Queen, Ellery
See also CA 1-4R; CANR 3, 85

Flying Officer X
See Bates, H(erbert) E(rnest)

Fo, Dario 1926- .... **CLC 32, 109, 227; DC 10**
See also CA 128; CAAE 116; CANR 68, 114, 134; CWW 2; DA3; DAM DRAM; DFS 23; DLB 330; DLBY 1997; EWL 3; MTCW 1, 2; MTFW 2005; WLIT 7

Foden, Giles 1967- .... **CLC 231**
See also CA 240; DLB 267; NFS 15

Fogarty, Jonathan Titulescu Esq.
See Farrell, James T(homas)

Follett, Ken 1949- .... **CLC 18**
See also AAYA 6, 50; BEST 89:4; BPFB 1; CA 81-84; CANR 13, 33, 54, 102, 156; CMW 4; CPW; DA3; DAM NOV, POP; DLB 87; DLBY 1981; INT CANR-33; MTCW 1

Follett, Kenneth Martin
See Follett, Ken

Fondane, Benjamin 1898-1944 ..... **TCLC 159**

Fontane, Theodor 1819-1898 . **NCLC 26, 163**
See also CDWLB 2; DLB 129; EW 6; RGWL 2, 3; TWA

Fonte, Moderata 1555-1592 .... **LC 118**

Fontenelle, Bernard Le Bovier de 1657-1757 .... **LC 140**
See also DLB 268, 313; GFL Beginnings to 1789

Fontenot, Chester .... **CLC 65**

Fonvizin, Denis Ivanovich 1744(?)-1792 .... **LC 81**
See also DLB 150; RGWL 2, 3

Foote, Horton 1916- .... **CLC 51, 91**
See also CA 73-76; CAD; CANR 34, 51, 110; CD 5, 6; CSW; DA3; DAM DRAM; DFS 20; DLB 26, 266; EWL 3; INT CANR-34; MTFW 2005

Foote, Mary Hallock 1847-1938 .. **TCLC 108**
See also DLB 186, 188, 202, 221; TCWW 2

Foote, Samuel 1721-1777 .... **LC 106**
See also DLB 89; RGEL 2

Foote, Shelby 1916-2005 .... **CLC 75, 224**
See also AAYA 40; CA 5-8R; CAAS 240; CANR 3, 45, 74, 131; CN 1, 2, 3, 4, 5, 6, 7; CPW; CSW; DA3; DAM NOV, POP; DLB 2, 17; MAL 5; MTCW 2; MTFW 2005; RHW

Forbes, Cosmo
See Lewton, Val

Forbes, Esther 1891-1967 .... **CLC 12**
See also AAYA 17; BYA 2; CA 13-14; CAAS 25-28R; CAP 1; CLR 27; DLB 22; JRDA; MAICYA 1, 2; RHW; SATA 2, 100; YAW

Forche, Carolyn 1950- .. **CLC 25, 83, 86; PC 10**
See also CA 117; CAAE 109; CANR 50, 74, 138; CP 4, 5, 6, 7; CWP; DA3; DAM POET; DLB 5, 193; INT CA-117; MAL 5; MTCW 2; MTFW 2005; PFS 18; RGAL 4

Forche, Carolyn Louise
See Forche, Carolyn

Ford, Elbur
See Hibbert, Eleanor Alice Burford

Ford, Ford Madox 1873-1939 ... **TCLC 1, 15, 39, 57, 172**
See Chaucer, Daniel
See also BRW 6; CA 132; CAAE 104; CANR 74; CDBLB 1914-1945; DA3; DAM NOV; DLB 34, 98, 162; EWL 3; MTCW 1, 2; RGEL 2; TEA

Ford, Henry 1863-1947 .... **TCLC 73**
See also CA 148; CAAE 115

Ford, Jack
See Ford, John

Ford, John 1586-1639 .... **DC 8; LC 68**
See also BRW 2; CDBLB Before 1660; DA3; DAM DRAM; DFS 7; DLB 58; IDTP; RGEL 2

Ford, John 1895-1973 .... **CLC 16**
See also AAYA 75; CA 187; CAAS 45-48

Ford, Richard 1944- .... **CLC 46, 99, 205**
See also AMWS 5; CA 69-72; CANR 11, 47, 86, 128; CN 5, 6, 7; CSW; DLB 227; EWL 3; MAL 5; MTCW 2; MTFW 2005; NFS 25; RGAL 4; RGSF 2

Ford, Webster
See Masters, Edgar Lee

Foreman, Richard 1937- .... **CLC 50**
See also CA 65-68; CAD; CANR 32, 63, 143; CD 5, 6

Forester, C(ecil) S(cott) 1899-1966 . **CLC 35; TCLC 152**
See also CA 73-76; CAAS 25-28R; CANR 83; DLB 191; RGEL 2; RHW; SATA 13

Forez
See Mauriac, François (Charles)

Forman, James
See Forman, James D(ouglas)

Forman, James D(ouglas) 1932- .... **CLC 21**
See also AAYA 17; CA 9-12R; CANR 4, 19, 42; JRDA; MAICYA 1, 2; SATA 8, 70; YAW

Forman, Milos 1932- .... **CLC 164**
See also AAYA 63; CA 109

Fornes, Maria Irene 1930- .... **CLC 39, 61, 187; DC 10; HLCS 1**
See also CA 25-28R; CAD; CANR 28, 81; CD 5, 6; CWD; DLB 7; HW 1, 2; INT CANR-28; LLW; MAL 5; MTCW 1; RGAL 4

Forrest, Leon (Richard) 1937-1997 .... **BLCS; CLC 4**
See also AFAW 2; BW 2; CA 89-92; 7; CAAS 162; CANR 25, 52, 87; CN 4, 5, 6; DLB 33

Forster, E(dward) M(organ) 1879-1970 ...... **CLC 1, 2, 3, 4, 9, 10, 13, 15, 22, 45, 77; SSC 27, 96; TCLC 125; WLC 2**
See also AAYA 2, 37; BRW 6; BRWR 2; BYA 12; CA 13-14; CAAS 25-28R; CANR 45; CAP 1; CDBLB 1914-1945; DA; DA3; DAB; DAC; DAM MST, NOV; DLB 34, 98, 162, 178, 195; DLBD 10; EWL 3; EXPN; LAIT 3; LMFS 1; MTCW 1, 2; MTFW 2005; NCFS 1; NFS 3, 10, 11; RGEL 2; RGSF 2; SATA 57; SUFW 1; TEA; WLIT 4

Forster, John 1812-1876 .... **NCLC 11**
See also DLB 144, 184

Gertler, T. .... **CLC 34**
See also CA 121; CAAE 116

Gertsen, Aleksandr Ivanovich
See Herzen, Aleksandr Ivanovich

Ghalib .... **NCLC 39, 78**
See Ghalib, Asadullah Khan

Ghalib, Asadullah Khan 1797-1869
See Ghalib
See also DAM POET; RGWL 2, 3

Ghelderode, Michel de 1898-1962 ..... **CLC 6, 11; DC 15; TCLC 187**
See also CA 85-88; CANR 40, 77; DAM DRAM; DLB 321; EW 11; EWL 3; TWA

Ghiselin, Brewster 1903-2001 .... **CLC 23**
See also CA 13-16R; 10; CANR 13; CP 1, 2, 3, 4, 5, 6, 7

Ghose, Aurabinda 1872-1950 .... **TCLC 63**
See Ghose, Aurobindo
See also CA 163

Ghose, Aurobindo
See Ghose, Aurabinda
See also EWL 3

Ghose, Zulfikar 1935- .... **CLC 42, 200**
See also CA 65-68; CANR 67; CN 1, 2, 3, 4, 5, 6, 7; CP 1, 2, 3, 4, 5, 6, 7; DLB 323; EWL 3

Ghosh, Amitav 1956- .... **CLC 44, 153**
See also CA 147; CANR 80, 158; CN 6, 7; DLB 323; WWE 1

Giacosa, Giuseppe 1847-1906 .... **TCLC 7**
See also CAAE 104

Gibb, Lee
See Waterhouse, Keith (Spencer)

Gibbon, Edward 1737-1794 .... **LC 97**
See also BRW 3; DLB 104, 336; RGEL 2

Gibbon, Lewis Grassic .... **TCLC 4**
See Mitchell, James Leslie
See also RGEL 2

Gibbons, Kaye 1960- .... **CLC 50, 88, 145**
See also AAYA 34; AMWS 10; CA 151; CANR 75, 127; CN 7; CSW; DA3; DAM POP; DLB 292; MTCW 2; MTFW 2005; NFS 3; RGAL 4; SATA 117

Gibran, Kahlil 1883-1931 . **PC 9; TCLC 1, 9**
See also CA 150; CAAE 104; DA3; DAM POET, POP; EWL 3; MTCW 2; WLIT 6

Gibran, Khalil
See Gibran, Kahlil

Gibson, Mel 1956- .... **CLC 215**

Gibson, William 1914- .... **CLC 23**
See also CA 9-12R; CAD; CANR 9, 42, 75, 125; CD 5, 6; DA; DAB; DAC; DAM DRAM, MST; DFS 2; DLB 7; LAIT 2; MAL 5; MTCW 2; MTFW 2005; SATA 66; YAW

Gibson, William 1948- .... **CLC 39, 63, 186, 192; SSC 52**
See also AAYA 12, 59; AMWS 16; BPFB 2; CA 133; CAAE 126; CANR 52, 90, 106; CN 6, 7; CPW; DA3; DAM POP; DLB 251; MTCW 2; MTFW 2005; SCFW 2; SFW 4

Gibson, William Ford
See Gibson, William

Gide, Andre (Paul Guillaume) 1869-1951 ...... **SSC 13; TCLC 5, 12, 36, 177; WLC 3**
See also CA 124; CAAE 104; DA; DA3; DAB; DAC; DAM MST, NOV; DLB 65, 321, 330; EW 8; EWL 3; GFL 1789 to the Present; MTCW 1, 2; MTFW 2005; NFS 21; RGSF 2; RGWL 2, 3; TWA

Gifford, Barry (Colby) 1946- .... **CLC 34**
See also CA 65-68; CANR 9, 30, 40, 90

Gilbert, Frank
See De Voto, Bernard (Augustine)

Gilbert, W(illiam) S(chwenck) 1836-1911 .... **TCLC 3**
See also CA 173; CAAE 104; DAM DRAM, POET; RGEL 2; SATA 36

Gilbert of Poitiers c. 1085-1154 .... **CMLC 85**

Gilbreth, Frank B(unker), Jr. 1911-2001 .... **CLC 17**
See also CA 9-12R; SATA 2

Gilchrist, Ellen (Louise) 1935- .. **CLC 34, 48, 143; SSC 14, 63**
See also BPFB 2; CA 116; CAAE 113; CANR 41, 61, 104; CN 4, 5, 6, 7; CPW; CSW; DAM POP; DLB 130; EWL 3; EXPS; MTCW 1, 2; MTFW 2005; RGAL 4; RGSF 2; SSFS 9

Giles, Molly 1942- .... **CLC 39**
See also CA 126; CANR 98

Gill, Eric .... **TCLC 85**
See Gill, (Arthur) Eric (Rowton Peter Joseph)

Gill, (Arthur) Eric (Rowton Peter Joseph) 1882-1940
See Gill, Eric
See also CAAE 120; DLB 98

Gill, Patrick
See Creasey, John

Gillette, Douglas .... **CLC 70**

Gilliam, Terry 1940- .... **CLC 21, 141**
See Monty Python
See also AAYA 19, 59; CA 113; CAAE 108; CANR 35; INT CA-113

Gilliam, Terry Vance
See Gilliam, Terry

Gillian, Jerry
See Gilliam, Terry

Gilliatt, Penelope (Ann Douglass) 1932-1993 .... **CLC 2, 10, 13, 53**
See also AITN 2; CA 13-16R; CAAS 141; CANR 49; CN 1, 2, 3, 4, 5; DLB 14

Gilligan, Carol 1936- .... **CLC 208**
See also CA 142; CANR 121; FW

Gilman, Charlotte (Anna) Perkins (Stetson) 1860-1935 ...... **SSC 13, 62; TCLC 9, 37, 117**
See also AAYA 75; AMWS 11; BYA 11; CA 150; CAAE 106; DLB 221; EXPS; FL 1:5; FW; HGG; LAIT 2; MBL; MTCW 2; MTFW 2005; RGAL 4; RGSF 2; SFW 4; SSFS 1, 18

Gilmour, David 1946- .... **CLC 35**

Gilpin, William 1724-1804 .... **NCLC 30**

Gilray, J. D.
See Mencken, H(enry) L(ouis)

Gilroy, Frank D(aniel) 1925- .... **CLC 2**
See also CA 81-84; CAD; CANR 32, 64, 86; CD 5, 6; DFS 17; DLB 7

Gilstrap, John 1957(?)- .... **CLC 99**
See also AAYA 67; CA 160; CANR 101

Ginsberg, Allen 1926-1997 .... **CLC 1, 2, 3, 4, 6, 13, 36, 69, 109; PC 4, 47; TCLC 120; WLC 3**
See also AAYA 33; AITN 1; AMWC 1; AMWS 2; BG 1:2; CA 1-4R; CAAS 157; CANR 2, 41, 63, 95; CDALB 1941-1968; CP 1, 2, 3, 4, 5, 6; DA; DA3; DAB; DAC; DAM MST, POET; DLB 5, 16, 169, 237; EWL 3; GLL 1; LMFS 2; MAL 5; MTCW 1, 2; MTFW 2005; PAB; PFS 5; RGAL 4; TUS; WP

Ginzburg, Eugenia .... **CLC 59**
See Ginzburg, Evgeniia

Ginzburg, Evgeniia 1904-1977
See Ginzburg, Eugenia
See also DLB 302

Ginzburg, Natalia 1916-1991 .... **CLC 5, 11, 54, 70; SSC 65; TCLC 156**
See also CA 85-88; CAAS 135; CANR 33; DFS 14; DLB 177; EW 13; EWL 3; MTCW 1, 2; MTFW 2005; RGHL; RGWL 2, 3

Giono, Jean 1895-1970 .... **CLC 4, 11; TCLC 124**
See also CA 45-48; CAAS 29-32R; CANR 2, 35; DLB 72, 321; EWL 3; GFL 1789 to the Present; MTCW 1; RGWL 2, 3

Giovanni, Nikki 1943- ...... **BLC 2; CLC 2, 4, 19, 64, 117; PC 19; WLCS**
See also AAYA 22; AITN 1; BW 2, 3; CA 29-32R; 6; CANR 18, 41, 60, 91, 130; CDALBS; CLR 6, 73; CP 2, 3, 4, 5, 6, 7; CSW; CWP; CWRI 5; DA; DA3; DAB; DAC; DAM MST, MULT, POET; DLB 5, 41; EWL 3; EXPP; INT CANR-18; MAICYA 1, 2; MAL 5; MTCW 1, 2; MTFW 2005; PFS 17; RGAL 4; SATA 24, 107; TUS; YAW

Giovene, Andrea 1904-1998 .... **CLC 7**
See also CA 85-88

Gippius, Zinaida (Nikolaevna) 1869-1945
See Hippius, Zinaida (Nikolaevna)
See also CA 212; CAAE 106

Giraudoux, Jean(-Hippolyte) 1882-1944 .... **TCLC 2, 7**
See also CA 196; CAAE 104; DAM DRAM; DLB 65, 321; EW 9; EWL 3; GFL 1789 to the Present; RGWL 2, 3; TWA

Gironella, Jose Maria (Pous) 1917-2003 .... **CLC 11**
See also CA 101; CAAS 212; EWL 3; RGWL 2, 3

Gissing, George (Robert) 1857-1903 .... **SSC 37; TCLC 3, 24, 47**
See also BRW 5; CA 167; CAAE 105; DLB 18, 135, 184; RGEL 2; TEA

Gitlin, Todd 1943- .... **CLC 201**
See also CA 29-32R; CANR 25, 50, 88

Giurlani, Aldo
See Palazzeschi, Aldo

Gladkov, Fedor Vasil'evich
See Gladkov, Fyodor (Vasilyevich)
See also DLB 272

Gladkov, Fyodor (Vasilyevich) 1883-1958 .... **TCLC 27**
See Gladkov, Fedor Vasil'evich
See also CA 170; EWL 3

Glancy, Diane 1941- .... **CLC 210; NNAL**
See also CA 225; 136, 225; 24; CANR 87, 162; DLB 175

Glanville, Brian (Lester) 1931- .... **CLC 6**
See also CA 5-8R; 9; CANR 3, 70; CN 1, 2, 3, 4, 5, 6, 7; DLB 15, 139; SATA 42

Glasgow, Ellen (Anderson Gholson) 1873-1945 .... **SSC 34; TCLC 2, 7**
See also AMW; CA 164; CAAE 104; DLB 9, 12; MAL 5; MBL; MTCW 2; MTFW 2005; RGAL 4; RHW; SSFS 9; TUS

Glaspell, Susan 1882(?)-1948 ..... **DC 10; SSC 41; TCLC 55, 175**
See also AMWS 3; CA 154; CAAE 110; DFS 8, 18, 24; DLB 7, 9, 78, 228; MBL; RGAL 4; SSFS 3; TCWW 2; TUS; YABC 2

Glassco, John 1909-1981 .... **CLC 9**
See also CA 13-16R; CAAS 102; CANR 15; CN 1, 2; CP 1, 2, 3; DLB 68

Glasscock, Amnesia
See Steinbeck, John (Ernst)

Glasser, Ronald J. 1940(?)- .... **CLC 37**
See also CA 209

Glassman, Joyce
See Johnson, Joyce

Gleick, James (W.) 1954- .... **CLC 147**
See also CA 137; CAAE 131; CANR 97; INT CA-137

Glendinning, Victoria 1937- .... **CLC 50**
See also CA 127; CAAE 120; CANR 59, 89; DLB 155

Gosse, Edmund (William)
1849-1928 .... **TCLC 28**
See also CAAE 117; DLB 57, 144, 184;
RGEL 2

Gotlieb, Phyllis (Fay Bloom) 1926- .. **CLC 18**
See also CA 13-16R; CANR 7, 135; CN 7;
CP 1, 2, 3, 4; DLB 88, 251; SFW 4

Gottesman, S. D.
See Kornbluth, C(yril) M.; Pohl, Frederik

Gottfried von Strassburg fl. c.
1170-1215 .... **CMLC 10**
See also CDWLB 2; DLB 138; EW 1;
RGWL 2, 3

Gotthelf, Jeremias 1797-1854 .... **NCLC 117**
See also DLB 133; RGWL 2, 3

Gottschalk, Laura Riding
See Jackson, Laura (Riding)

Gould, Lois 1932(?)-2002 .... **CLC 4, 10**
See also CA 77-80; CAAS 208; CANR 29;
MTCW 1

Gould, Stephen Jay 1941-2002 .... **CLC 163**
See also AAYA 26; BEST 90:2; CA 77-80;
CAAS 205; CANR 10, 27, 56, 75, 125;
CPW; INT CANR-27; MTCW 1, 2;
MTFW 2005

Gourmont, Remy(-Marie-Charles) de
1858-1915 .... **TCLC 17**
See also CA 150; CAAE 109; GFL 1789 to
the Present; MTCW 2

Gournay, Marie le Jars de
See de Gournay, Marie le Jars

Govier, Katherine 1948- .... **CLC 51**
See also CA 101; CANR 18, 40, 128; CCA
1

Gower, John c. 1330-1408 .... **LC 76; PC 59**
See also BRW 1; DLB 146; RGEL 2

Goyen, (Charles) William
1915-1983 .... **CLC 5, 8, 14, 40**
See also AITN 2; CA 5-8R; CAAS 110;
CANR 6, 71; CN 1, 2, 3; DLB 2, 218;
DLBY 1983; EWL 3; INT CANR-6; MAL
5

Goytisolo, Juan 1931- .... **CLC 5, 10, 23, 133;
HLC 1**
See also CA 85-88; CANR 32, 61, 131;
CWW 2; DAM MULT; DLB 322; EWL
3; GLL 2; HW 1, 2; MTCW 1, 2; MTFW
2005

Gozzano, Guido 1883-1916 .... **PC 10**
See also CA 154; DLB 114; EWL 3

Gozzi, (Conte) Carlo 1720-1806 .... **NCLC 23**

Grabbe, Christian Dietrich
1801-1836 .... **NCLC 2**
See also DLB 133; RGWL 2, 3

Grace, Patricia Frances 1937- .... **CLC 56**
See also CA 176; CANR 118; CN 4, 5, 6,
7; EWL 3; RGSF 2

Gracian y Morales, Baltasar
1601-1658 .... **LC 15**

Gracq, Julien .... **CLC 11, 48**
See Poirier, Louis
See also CWW 2; DLB 83; GFL 1789 to
the Present

Grade, Chaim 1910-1982 .... **CLC 10**
See also CA 93-96; CAAS 107; DLB 333;
EWL 3; RGHL

Grade, Khayim
See Grade, Chaim

Graduate of Oxford, A
See Ruskin, John

Grafton, Garth
See Duncan, Sara Jeannette

Grafton, Sue 1940- .... **CLC 163**
See also AAYA 11, 49; BEST 90:3; CA 108;
CANR 31, 55, 111, 134; CMW 4; CPW;
CSW; DA3; DAM POP; DLB 226; FW;
MSW; MTFW 2005

Graham, John
See Phillips, David Graham

Graham, Jorie 1950- .... **CLC 48, 118; PC 59**
See also AAYA 67; CA 111; CANR 63, 118;
CP 4, 5, 6, 7; CWP; DLB 120; EWL 3;
MTFW 2005; PFS 10, 17; TCLE 1:1

Graham, R(obert) B(ontine) Cunninghame
See Cunninghame Graham, Robert
(Gallnigad) Bontine
See also DLB 98, 135, 174; RGEL 2; RGSF
2

Graham, Robert
See Haldeman, Joe

Graham, Tom
See Lewis, (Harry) Sinclair

Graham, W(illiam) S(ydney)
1918-1986 .... **CLC 29**
See also BRWS 7; CA 73-76; CAAS 118;
CP 1, 2, 3, 4; DLB 20; RGEL 2

Graham, Winston (Mawdsley)
1910-2003 .... **CLC 23**
See also CA 49-52; CAAS 218; CANR 2,
22, 45, 66; CMW 4; CN 1, 2, 3, 4, 5, 6,
7; DLB 77; RHW

Grahame, Kenneth 1859-1932 ...... **TCLC 64,
136**
See also BYA 5; CA 136; CAAE 108;
CANR 80; CLR 5; CWRI 5; DA3; DAB;
DLB 34, 141, 178; FANT; MAICYA 1, 2;
MTCW 2; NFS 20; RGEL 2; SATA 100;
TEA; WCH; YABC 1

Granger, Darius John
See Marlowe, Stephen

Granin, Daniil 1918- .... **CLC 59**
See also DLB 302

Granovsky, Timofei Nikolaevich
1813-1855 .... **NCLC 75**
See also DLB 198

Grant, Skeeter
See Spiegelman, Art

Granville-Barker, Harley
1877-1946 .... **TCLC 2**
See Barker, Harley Granville
See also CA 204; CAAE 104; DAM
DRAM; RGEL 2

Granzotto, Gianni
See Granzotto, Giovanni Battista

Granzotto, Giovanni Battista
1914-1985 .... **CLC 70**
See also CA 166

Grasemann, Ruth Barbara
See Rendell, Ruth

Grass, Guenter
See Grass, Gunter
See also CWW 2; DLB 330; RGHL

Grass, Gunter 1927- .. **CLC 1, 2, 4, 6, 11, 15,
22, 32, 49, 88, 207; WLC 3**
See Grass, Guenter
See also BPFB 2; CA 13-16R; CANR 20,
75, 93, 133; CDWLB 2; DA; DA3; DAB;
DAC; DAM MST, NOV; DLB 75, 124;
EW 13; EWL 3; MTCW 1, 2; MTFW
2005; RGWL 2, 3; TWA

Grass, Gunter Wilhelm
See Grass, Gunter

Gratton, Thomas
See Hulme, T(homas) E(rnest)

Grau, Shirley Ann 1929- .... **CLC 4, 9, 146;
SSC 15**
See also CA 89-92; CANR 22, 69; CN 1, 2,
3, 4, 5, 6, 7; CSW; DLB 2, 218; INT CA-
89-92; CANR-22; MTCW 1

Gravel, Fern
See Hall, James Norman

Graver, Elizabeth 1964- .... **CLC 70**
See also CA 135; CANR 71, 129

Graves, Richard Perceval
1895-1985 .... **CLC 44**
See also CA 65-68; CANR 9, 26, 51

Graves, Robert 1895-1985 ... **CLC 1, 2, 6, 11,
39, 44, 45; PC 6**
See also BPFB 2; BRW 7; BYA 4; CA 5-8R;
CAAS 117; CANR 5, 36; CDBLB 1914-
1945; CN 1, 2, 3; CP 1, 2, 3, 4; DA3;
DAB; DAC; DAM MST, POET; DLB 20,
100, 191; DLBD 18; DLBY 1985; EWL
3; LATS 1:1; MTCW 1, 2; MTFW 2005;
NCFS 2; NFS 21; RGEL 2; RHW; SATA
45; TEA

Graves, Valerie
See Bradley, Marion Zimmer

Gray, Alasdair 1934- .... **CLC 41**
See also BRWS 9; CA 126; CANR 47, 69,
106, 140; CN 4, 5, 6, 7; DLB 194, 261,
319; HGG; INT CA-126; MTCW 1, 2;
MTFW 2005; RGSF 2; SUFW 2

Gray, Amlin 1946- .... **CLC 29**
See also CA 138

Gray, Francine du Plessix 1930- ..... **CLC 22,
153**
See also BEST 90:3; CA 61-64; 2; CANR
11, 33, 75, 81; DAM NOV; INT CANR-
11; MTCW 1, 2; MTFW 2005

Gray, John (Henry) 1866-1934 ...... **TCLC 19**
See also CA 162; CAAE 119; RGEL 2

Gray, John Lee
See Jakes, John

Gray, Simon (James Holliday)
1936- .... **CLC 9, 14, 36**
See also AITN 1; CA 21-24R; 3; CANR 32,
69; CBD; CD 5, 6; CN 1, 2, 3; DLB 13;
EWL 3; MTCW 1; RGEL 2

Gray, Spalding 1941-2004 .... **CLC 49, 112;
DC 7**
See also AAYA 62; CA 128; CAAS 225;
CAD; CANR 74, 138; CD 5, 6; CPW;
DAM POP; MTCW 2; MTFW 2005

Gray, Thomas 1716-1771 .... **LC 4, 40; PC 2;
WLC 3**
See also BRW 3; CDBLB 1660-1789; DA;
DA3; DAB; DAC; DAM MST; DLB 109;
EXPP; PAB; PFS 9; RGEL 2; TEA; WP

Grayson, David
See Baker, Ray Stannard

Grayson, Richard (A.) 1951- .... **CLC 38**
See also CA 210; 85-88, 210; CANR 14,
31, 57; DLB 234

Greeley, Andrew M. 1928- .... **CLC 28**
See also BPFB 2; CA 5-8R; 7; CANR 7,
43, 69, 104, 136; CMW 4; CPW; DA3;
DAM POP; MTCW 1, 2; MTFW 2005

Green, Anna Katharine
1846-1935 .... **TCLC 63**
See also CA 159; CAAE 112; CMW 4;
DLB 202, 221; MSW

Green, Brian
See Card, Orson Scott

Green, Hannah
See Greenberg, Joanne (Goldenberg)

Green, Hannah 1927(?)-1996 .... **CLC 3**
See also CA 73-76; CANR 59, 93; NFS 10

Green, Henry .... **CLC 2, 13, 97**
See Yorke, Henry Vincent
See also BRWS 2; CA 175; DLB 15; EWL
3; RGEL 2

Green, Julian .... **CLC 3, 11, 77**
See Green, Julien (Hartridge)
See also EWL 3; GFL 1789 to the Present;
MTCW 2

Green, Julien (Hartridge) 1900-1998
See Green, Julian
See also CA 21-24R; CAAS 169; CANR
33, 87; CWW 2; DLB 4, 72; MTCW 1, 2;
MTFW 2005

Green, Paul (Eliot) 1894-1981 .... **CLC 25**
See also AITN 1; CA 5-8R; CAAS 103;
CAD; CANR 3; DAM DRAM; DLB 7, 9,
249; DLBY 1981; MAL 5; RGAL 4

Hall, Donald 1928- ... **CLC 1, 13, 37, 59, 151, 240; PC 70**
See also AAYA 63; CA 5-8R; 7; CANR 2, 44, 64, 106, 133; CP 1, 2, 3, 4, 5, 6, 7; DAM POET; DLB 5; MAL 5; MTCW 2; MTFW 2005; RGAL 4; SATA 23, 97

Hall, Donald Andrew, Jr.
See Hall, Donald

Hall, Frederic Sauser
See Sauser-Hall, Frederic

Hall, James
See Kuttner, Henry

Hall, James Norman 1887-1951 ..... **TCLC 23**
See also CA 173; CAAE 123; LAIT 1; RHW 1; SATA 21

Hall, Joseph 1574-1656 .... **LC 91**
See also DLB 121, 151; RGEL 2

Hall, Marguerite Radclyffe
See Hall, Radclyffe

Hall, Radclyffe 1880-1943 .... **TCLC 12**
See also BRWS 6; CA 150; CAAE 110; CANR 83; DLB 191; MTCW 2; MTFW 2005; RGEL 2; RHW

Hall, Rodney 1935- .... **CLC 51**
See also CA 109; CANR 69; CN 6, 7; CP 1, 2, 3, 4, 5, 6, 7; DLB 289

Hallam, Arthur Henry
1811-1833 .... **NCLC 110**
See also DLB 32

Halldor Laxness .... **CLC 25**
See Gudjonsson, Halldor Kiljan
See also DLB 293; EW 12; EWL 3; RGWL 2, 3

Halleck, Fitz-Greene 1790-1867 .... **NCLC 47**
See also DLB 3, 250; RGAL 4

Halliday, Michael
See Creasey, John

Halpern, Daniel 1945- .... **CLC 14**
See also CA 33-36R; CANR 93; CP 3, 4, 5, 6, 7

Hamburger, Michael 1924-2007 ... **CLC 5, 14**
See also CA 196; 5-8R, 196; 4; CANR 2, 47; CP 1, 2, 3, 4, 5, 6, 7; DLB 27

Hamburger, Michael Peter Leopold
See Hamburger, Michael

Hamill, Pete 1935- .... **CLC 10**
See also CA 25-28R; CANR 18, 71, 127

Hamilton, Alexander
1755(?)-1804 .... **NCLC 49**
See also DLB 37

Hamilton, Clive
See Lewis, C.S.

Hamilton, Edmond 1904-1977 .... **CLC 1**
See also CA 1-4R; CANR 3, 84; DLB 8; SATA 118; SFW 4

Hamilton, Elizabeth 1758-1816 ... **NCLC 153**
See also DLB 116, 158

Hamilton, Eugene (Jacob) Lee
See Lee-Hamilton, Eugene (Jacob)

Hamilton, Franklin
See Silverberg, Robert

Hamilton, Gail
See Corcoran, Barbara (Asenath)

Hamilton, (Robert) Ian 1938-2001 . **CLC 191**
See also CA 106; CAAS 203; CANR 41, 67; CP 1, 2, 3, 4, 5, 6, 7; DLB 40, 155

Hamilton, Jane 1957- .... **CLC 179**
See also CA 147; CANR 85, 128; CN 7; MTFW 2005

Hamilton, Mollie
See Kaye, M.M.

Hamilton, (Anthony Walter) Patrick
1904-1962 .... **CLC 51**
See also CA 176; CAAS 113; DLB 10, 191

Hamilton, Virginia 1936-2002 .... **CLC 26**
See also AAYA 2, 21; BW 2, 3; BYA 1, 2, 8; CA 25-28R; CAAS 206; CANR 20, 37, 73, 126; CLR 1, 11, 40; DAM MULT; DLB 33, 52; DLBY 2001; INT CANR-

20; JRDA; LAIT 5; MAICYA 1, 2; MAI-CYAS 1; MTCW 1, 2; MTFW 2005; SATA 4, 56, 79, 123; SATA-Obit 132; WYA; YAW

Hammett, (Samuel) Dashiell
1894-1961 .... **CLC 3, 5, 10, 19, 47; SSC 17; TCLC 187**
See also AAYA 59; AITN 1; AMWS 4; BPFB 2; CA 81-84; CANR 42; CDALB 1929-1941; CMW 4; DA3; DLB 226, 280; DLBD 6; DLBY 1996; EWL 3; LAIT 3; MAL 5; MSW; MTCW 1, 2; MTFW 2005; NFS 21; RGAL 4; RGSF 2; TUS

Hammon, Jupiter 1720(?)-1800(?) .... **BLC 2; NCLC 5; PC 16**
See also DAM MULT, POET; DLB 31, 50

Hammond, Keith
See Kuttner, Henry

Hamner, Earl (Henry), Jr. 1923- ...... **CLC 12**
See also AITN 2; CA 73-76; DLB 6

Hampton, Christopher 1946- .... **CLC 4**
See also CA 25-28R; CD 5, 6; DLB 13; MTCW 1

Hampton, Christopher James
See Hampton, Christopher

Hamsun, Knut .... **TCLC 2, 14, 49, 151**
See Pedersen, Knut
See also DLB 297, 330; EW 8; EWL 3; RGWL 2, 3

Handke, Peter 1942- .... **CLC 5, 8, 10, 15, 38, 134; DC 17**
See also CA 77-80; CANR 33, 75, 104, 133; CWW 2; DAM DRAM, NOV; DLB 85, 124; EWL 3; MTCW 1, 2; MTFW 2005; TWA

Handy, W(illiam) C(hristopher)
1873-1958 .... **TCLC 97**
See also BW 3; CA 167; CAAE 121

Hanley, James 1901-1985 ..... **CLC 3, 5, 8, 13**
See also CA 73-76; CAAS 117; CANR 36; CBD; CN 1, 2, 3; DLB 191; EWL 3; MTCW 1; RGEL 2

Hannah, Barry 1942- .. **CLC 23, 38, 90; SSC 94**
See also BPFB 2; CA 110; CAAE 108; CANR 43, 68, 113; CN 4, 5, 6, 7; CSW; DLB 6, 234; INT CA-110; MTCW 1; RGSF 2

Hannon, Ezra
See Hunter, Evan

Hansberry, Lorraine (Vivian)
1930-1965 ... **BLC 2; CLC 17, 62; DC 2**
See also AAYA 25; AFAW 1, 2; AMWS 4; BW 1, 3; CA 109; CAAS 25-28R; CABS 3; CAD; CANR 58; CDALB 1941-1968; CWD; DA; DA3; DAB; DAC; DAM DRAM, MST, MULT; DFS 2; DLB 7, 38; EWL 3; FL 1:6; FW; LAIT 4; MAL 5; MTCW 1, 2; MTFW 2005; RGAL 4; TUS

Hansen, Joseph 1923-2004 .... **CLC 38**
See Brock, Rose; Colton, James
See also BPFB 2; CA 29-32R; 17; CAAS 233; CANR 16, 44, 66, 125; CMW 4; DLB 226; GLL 1; INT CANR-16

Hansen, Karen V. 1955- .... **CLC 65**
See also CA 149; CANR 102

Hansen, Martin A(lfred)
1909-1955 .... **TCLC 32**
See also CA 167; DLB 214; EWL 3

Hanson, Kenneth O(stlin) 1922- .... **CLC 13**
See also CA 53-56; CANR 7; CP 1, 2, 3, 4, 5

Hardwick, Elizabeth 1916- .... **CLC 13**
See also AMWS 3; CA 5-8R; CANR 3, 32, 70, 100, 139; CN 4, 5, 6; CSW; DA3; DAM NOV; DLB 6; MBL; MTCW 1, 2; MTFW 2005; TCLE 1:1

Hardy, Thomas 1840-1928 .... **PC 8; SSC 2, 60; TCLC 4, 10, 18, 32, 48, 53, 72, 143, 153; WLC 3**
See also AAYA 69; BRW 6; BRWC 1, 2; BRWR 1; CA 123; CAAE 104; CDBLB 1890-1914; DA; DA3; DAB; DAC; DAM MST, NOV, POET; DLB 18, 19, 135, 284; EWL 3; EXPN; EXPP; LAIT 2; MTCW 1, 2; MTFW 2005; NFS 3, 11, 15, 19; PFS 3, 4, 18; RGEL 2; RGSF 2; TEA; WLIT 4

Hare, David 1947- . **CLC 29, 58, 136; DC 26**
See also BRWS 4; CA 97-100; CANR 39, 91; CBD; CD 5, 6; DFS 4, 7, 16; DLB 13, 310; MTCW 1; TEA

Harewood, John
See Van Druten, John (William)

Harford, Henry
See Hudson, W(illiam) H(enry)

Hargrave, Leonie
See Disch, Thomas M.

Hariri, Al- al-Qasim ibn 'Ali Abu Muhammad al-Basri
See al-Hariri, al-Qasim ibn 'Ali Abu Muhammad al-Basri

Harjo, Joy 1951- ..... **CLC 83; NNAL; PC 27**
See also AMWS 12; CA 114; CANR 35, 67, 91, 129; CP 6, 7; CWP; DAM MULT; DLB 120, 175; EWL 3; MTCW 2; MTFW 2005; PFS 15; RGAL 4

Harlan, Louis R(udolph) 1922- .... **CLC 34**
See also CA 21-24R; CANR 25, 55, 80

Harling, Robert 1951(?)- .... **CLC 53**
See also CA 147

Harmon, William (Ruth) 1938- .... **CLC 38**
See also CA 33-36R; CANR 14, 32, 35; SATA 65

Harper, F. E. W.
See Harper, Frances Ellen Watkins

Harper, Frances E. W.
See Harper, Frances Ellen Watkins

Harper, Frances E. Watkins
See Harper, Frances Ellen Watkins

Harper, Frances Ellen
See Harper, Frances Ellen Watkins

Harper, Frances Ellen Watkins
1825-1911 ..... **BLC 2; PC 21; TCLC 14**
See also AFAW 1, 2; BW 1, 3; CA 125; CAAE 111; CANR 79; DAM MULT, POET; DLB 50, 221; MBL; RGAL 4

Harper, Michael S(teven) 1938- .... **CLC 7, 22**
See also AFAW 2; BW 1; CA 224; 33-36R, 224; CANR 24, 108; CP 2, 3, 4, 5, 6, 7; DLB 41; RGAL 4; TCLE 1:1

Harper, Mrs. F. E. W.
See Harper, Frances Ellen Watkins

Harpur, Charles 1813-1868 .... **NCLC 114**
See also DLB 230; RGEL 2

Harris, Christie
See Harris, Christie (Lucy) Irwin

Harris, Christie (Lucy) Irwin
1907-2002 .... **CLC 12**
See also CA 5-8R; CANR 6, 83; CLR 47; DLB 88; JRDA; MAICYA 1, 2; SAAS 10; SATA 6, 74; SATA-Essay 116

Harris, Frank 1856-1931 .... **TCLC 24**
See also CA 150; CAAE 109; CANR 80; DLB 156, 197; RGEL 2

Harris, George Washington
1814-1869 .... **NCLC 23, 165**
See also DLB 3, 11, 248; RGAL 4

Harris, Joel Chandler 1848-1908 ..... **SSC 19; TCLC 2**
See also CA 137; CAAE 104; CANR 80; CLR 49; DLB 11, 23, 42, 78, 91; LAIT 2; MAICYA 1, 2; RGSF 2; SATA 100; WCH; YABC 1

Harris, John (Wyndham Parkes Lucas) Beynon 1903-1969
See Wyndham, John
See also CA 102; CAAS 89-92; CANR 84; SATA 118; SFW 4

Harris, MacDonald .... **CLC 9**
See Heiney, Donald (William)

Harris, Mark 1922-2007 .... **CLC 19**
See also CA 5-8R; 3; CANR 2, 55, 83; CN 1, 2, 3, 4, 5, 6, 7; DLB 2; DLBY 1980

Harris, Norman .... **CLC 65**

Harris, (Theodore) Wilson 1921- .... **CLC 25, 159**
See also BRWS 5; BW 2, 3; CA 65-68; 16; CANR 11, 27, 69, 114; CDWLB 3; CN 1, 2, 3, 4, 5, 6, 7; CP 1, 2, 3, 4, 5, 6, 7; DLB 117; EWL 3; MTCW 1; RGEL 2

Harrison, Barbara Grizzuti 1934-2002 .... **CLC 144**
See also CA 77-80; CAAS 205; CANR 15, 48; INT CANR-15

Harrison, Elizabeth (Allen) Cavanna 1909-2001
See Cavanna, Betty
See also CA 9-12R; CAAS 200; CANR 6, 27, 85, 104, 121; MAICYA 2; SATA 142; YAW

Harrison, Harry (Max) 1925- .... **CLC 42**
See also CA 1-4R; CANR 5, 21, 84; DLB 8; SATA 4; SCFW 2; SFW 4

Harrison, James
See Harrison, Jim

Harrison, James Thomas
See Harrison, Jim

Harrison, Jim 1937- .... **CLC 6, 14, 33, 66, 143; SSC 19**
See also AMWS 8; CA 13-16R; CANR 8, 51, 79, 142; CN 5, 6; CP 1, 2, 3, 4, 5, 6; DLBY 1982; INT CANR-8; RGAL 4; TCWW 2; TUS

Harrison, Kathryn 1961- .... **CLC 70, 151**
See also CA 144; CANR 68, 122

Harrison, Tony 1937- .... **CLC 43, 129**
See also BRWS 5; CA 65-68; CANR 44, 98; CBD; CD 5, 6; CP 2, 3, 4, 5, 6, 7; DLB 40, 245; MTCW 1; RGEL 2

Harriss, Will(ard Irvin) 1922- .... **CLC 34**
See also CA 111

Hart, Ellis
See Ellison, Harlan

Hart, Josephine 1942(?)- .... **CLC 70**
See also CA 138; CANR 70, 149; CPW; DAM POP

Hart, Moss 1904-1961 .... **CLC 66**
See also CA 109; CAAS 89-92; CANR 84; DAM DRAM; DFS 1; DLB 7, 266; RGAL 4

Harte, (Francis) Bret(t) 1836(?)-1902 ... **SSC 8, 59; TCLC 1, 25; WLC 3**
See also AMWS 2; CA 140; CAAE 104; CANR 80; CDALB 1865-1917; DA; DA3; DAC; DAM MST; DLB 12, 64, 74, 79, 186; EXPS; LAIT 2; RGAL 4; RGSF 2; SATA 26; SSFS 3; TUS

Hartley, L(eslie) P(oles) 1895-1972 ... **CLC 2, 22**
See also BRWS 7; CA 45-48; CAAS 37-40R; CANR 33; CN 1; DLB 15, 139; EWL 3; HGG; MTCW 1, 2; MTFW 2005; RGEL 2; RGSF 2; SUFW 1

Hartman, Geoffrey H. 1929- .... **CLC 27**
See also CA 125; CAAE 117; CANR 79; DLB 67

Hartmann, Sadakichi 1869-1944 ... **TCLC 73**
See also CA 157; DLB 54

Hartmann von Aue c. 1170-c. 1210 .... **CMLC 15**
See also CDWLB 2; DLB 138; RGWL 2, 3

Hartog, Jan de
See de Hartog, Jan

Haruf, Kent 1943- .... **CLC 34**
See also AAYA 44; CA 149; CANR 91, 131

Harvey, Caroline
See Trollope, Joanna

Harvey, Gabriel 1550(?)-1631 .... **LC 88**
See also DLB 167, 213, 281

Harwood, Ronald 1934- .... **CLC 32**
See also CA 1-4R; CANR 4, 55, 150; CBD; CD 5, 6; DAM DRAM, MST; DLB 13

Hasegawa Tatsunosuke
See Futabatei, Shimei

Hasek, Jaroslav (Matej Frantisek) 1883-1923 .... **SSC 69; TCLC 4**
See also CA 129; CAAE 104; CDWLB 4; DLB 215; EW 9; EWL 3; MTCW 1, 2; RGSF 2; RGWL 2, 3

Hass, Robert 1941- ... **CLC 18, 39, 99; PC 16**
See also AMWS 6; CA 111; CANR 30, 50, 71; CP 3, 4, 5, 6, 7; DLB 105, 206; EWL 3; MAL 5; MTFW 2005; RGAL 4; SATA 94; TCLE 1:1

Hastings, Hudson
See Kuttner, Henry

Hastings, Selina .... **CLC 44**
See also CA 257

Hastings, Selina Shirley
See Hastings, Selina

Hathorne, John 1641-1717 .... **LC 38**

Hatteras, Amelia
See Mencken, H(enry) L(ouis)

Hatteras, Owen .... **TCLC 18**
See Mencken, H(enry) L(ouis); Nathan, George Jean

Hauff, Wilhelm 1802-1827 .... **NCLC 185**
See also DLB 90; SUFW 1

Hauptmann, Gerhart (Johann Robert) 1862-1946 .... **SSC 37; TCLC 4**
See also CA 153; CAAE 104; CDWLB 2; DAM DRAM; DLB 66, 118, 330; EW 8; EWL 3; RGSF 2; RGWL 2, 3; TWA

Havel, Vaclav 1936- ..... **CLC 25, 58, 65, 123; DC 6**
See also CA 104; CANR 36, 63, 124; CD-WLB 4; CWW 2; DA3; DAM DRAM; DFS 10; DLB 232; EWL 3; LMFS 2; MTCW 1, 2; MTFW 2005; RGWL 3

Haviaras, Stratis .... **CLC 33**
See Chaviaras, Strates

Hawes, Stephen 1475(?)-1529(?) .... **LC 17**
See also DLB 132; RGEL 2

Hawkes, John 1925-1998 .. **CLC 1, 2, 3, 4, 7, 9, 14, 15, 27, 49**
See also BPFB 2; CA 1-4R; CAAS 167; CANR 2, 47, 64; CN 1, 2, 3, 4, 5, 6; DLB 2, 7, 227; DLBY 1980, 1998; EWL 3; MAL 5; MTCW 1, 2; MTFW 2005; RGAL 4

Hawking, S. W.
See Hawking, Stephen W.

Hawking, Stephen W. 1942- ..... **CLC 63, 105**
See also AAYA 13; BEST 89:1; CA 129; CAAE 126; CANR 48, 115; CPW; DA3; MTCW 2; MTFW 2005

Hawkins, Anthony Hope
See Hope, Anthony

Hawthorne, Julian 1846-1934 .... **TCLC 25**
See also CA 165; HGG

Hawthorne, Nathaniel 1804-1864 ... **NCLC 2, 10, 17, 23, 39, 79, 95, 158, 171; SSC 3, 29, 39, 89; WLC 3**
See also AAYA 18; AMW; AMWC 1; AMWR 1; BPFB 2; BYA 3; CDALB 1640-1865; CLR 103; DA; DA3; DAB; DAC; DAM MST, NOV; DLB 1, 74, 183, 223, 269; EXPN; EXPS; GL 2; HGG; LAIT 1; NFS 1, 20; RGAL 4; RGSF 2; SSFS 1, 7, 11, 15; SUFW 1; TUS; WCH; YABC 2

Hawthorne, Sophia Peabody 1809-1871 .... **NCLC 150**
See also DLB 183, 239

Haxton, Josephine Ayres 1921-
See Douglas, Ellen
See also CA 115; CANR 41, 83

Hayaseca y Eizaguirre, Jorge
See Echegaray (y Eizaguirre), Jose (Maria Waldo)

Hayashi, Fumiko 1904-1951 .... **TCLC 27**
See Hayashi Fumiko
See also CA 161

Hayashi Fumiko
See Hayashi, Fumiko
See also DLB 180; EWL 3

Haycraft, Anna 1932-2005
See Ellis, Alice Thomas
See also CA 122; CAAS 237; CANR 90, 141; MTCW 2; MTFW 2005

Hayden, Robert E(arl) 1913-1980 ..... **BLC 2; CLC 5, 9, 14, 37; PC 6**
See also AFAW 1, 2; AMWS 2; BW 1, 3; CA 69-72; CAAS 97-100; CABS 2; CANR 24, 75, 82; CDALB 1941-1968; CP 1, 2, 3; DA; DAC; DAM MST, MULT, POET; DLB 5, 76; EWL 3; EXPP; MAL 5; MTCW 1, 2; PFS 1; RGAL 4; SATA 19; SATA-Obit 26; WP

Haydon, Benjamin Robert 1786-1846 .... **NCLC 146**
See also DLB 110

Hayek, F(riedrich) A(ugust von) 1899-1992 .... **TCLC 109**
See also CA 93-96; CAAS 137; CANR 20; MTCW 1, 2

Hayford, J(oseph) E(phraim) Casely
See Casely-Hayford, J(oseph) E(phraim)

Hayman, Ronald 1932- .... **CLC 44**
See also CA 25-28R; CANR 18, 50, 88; CD 5, 6; DLB 155

Hayne, Paul Hamilton 1830-1886 . **NCLC 94**
See also DLB 3, 64, 79, 248; RGAL 4

Hays, Mary 1760-1843 .... **NCLC 114**
See also DLB 142, 158; RGEL 2

Haywood, Eliza (Fowler) 1693(?)-1756 .... **LC 1, 44**
See also BRWS 12; DLB 39; RGEL 2

Hazlitt, William 1778-1830 ...... **NCLC 29, 82**
See also BRW 4; DLB 110, 158; RGEL 2; TEA

Hazzard, Shirley 1931- .... **CLC 18, 218**
See also CA 9-12R; CANR 4, 70, 127; CN 1, 2, 3, 4, 5, 6, 7; DLB 289; DLBY 1982; MTCW 1

Head, Bessie 1937-1986 ...... **BLC 2; CLC 25, 67; SSC 52**
See also AFW; BW 2, 3; CA 29-32R; CAAS 119; CANR 25, 82; CDWLB 3; CN 1, 2, 3, 4; DA3; DAM MULT; DLB 117, 225; EWL 3; EXPS; FL 1:6; FW; MTCW 1, 2; MTFW 2005; RGSF 2; SSFS 5, 13; WLIT 2; WWE 1

Headon, (Nicky) Topper 1956(?)- ..... **CLC 30**

Heaney, Seamus 1939- . **CLC 5, 7, 14, 25, 37, 74, 91, 171, 225; PC 18; WLCS**
See also AAYA 61; BRWR 1; BRWS 2; CA 85-88; CANR 25, 48, 75, 91, 128; CD-BLB 1960 to Present; CP 1, 2, 3, 4, 5, 6, 7; DA3; DAB; DAM POET; DLB 40, 330; DLBY 1995; EWL 3; EXPP; MTCW 1, 2; MTFW 2005; PAB; PFS 2, 5, 8, 17; RGEL 2; TEA; WLIT 4

Hearn, (Patricio) Lafcadio (Tessima Carlos) 1850-1904 .... **TCLC 9**
See also CA 166; CAAE 105; DLB 12, 78, 189; HGG; MAL 5; RGAL 4

Horgan, Paul (George Vincent
    O'Shaughnessy) 1903-1995 .. **CLC 9, 53**
    See also BPFB 2; CA 13-16R; CAAS 147;
    CANR 9, 35; CN 1, 2, 3, 4, 5; DAM
    NOV; DLB 102, 212; DLBY 1985; INT
    CANR-9; MTCW 1, 2; MTFW 2005;
    SATA 13; SATA-Obit 84; TCWW 1, 2

Horkheimer, Max 1895-1973 .... **TCLC 132**
    See also CA 216; CAAS 41-44R; DLB 296

Horn, Peter
    See Kuttner, Henry

Horne, Frank (Smith) 1899-1974 ...... **HR 1:2**
    See also BW 1; CA 125; CAAS 53-56; DLB
    51; WP

Horne, Richard Henry Hengist
    1802(?)-1884 .... **NCLC 127**
    See also DLB 32; SATA 29

Hornem, Horace Esq.
    See Byron, George Gordon (Noel)

Horney, Karen (Clementine Theodore
    Danielsen) 1885-1952 .... **TCLC 71**
    See also CA 165; CAAE 114; DLB 246;
    FW

Hornung, E(rnest) W(illiam)
    1866-1921 .... **TCLC 59**
    See also CA 160; CAAE 108; CMW 4;
    DLB 70

Horovitz, Israel (Arthur) 1939- .... **CLC 56**
    See also CA 33-36R; CAD; CANR 46, 59;
    CD 5, 6; DAM DRAM; DLB 7; MAL 5

Horton, George Moses
    1797(?)-1883(?) .... **NCLC 87**
    See also DLB 50

Horvath, odon von 1901-1938
    See von Horvath, Odon
    See also EWL 3

Horvath, Oedoen von -1938
    See von Horvath, Odon

Horwitz, Julius 1920-1986 .... **CLC 14**
    See also CA 9-12R; CAAS 119; CANR 12

Horwitz, Ronald
    See Harwood, Ronald

Hospital, Janette Turner 1942- .... **CLC 42,
    145**
    See also CA 108; CANR 48; CN 5, 6, 7;
    DLB 325; DLBY 2002; RGSF 2

Hostos, E. M. de
    See Hostos (y Bonilla), Eugenio Maria de

Hostos, Eugenio M. de
    See Hostos (y Bonilla), Eugenio Maria de

Hostos, Eugenio Maria
    See Hostos (y Bonilla), Eugenio Maria de

Hostos (y Bonilla), Eugenio Maria de
    1839-1903 .... **TCLC 24**
    See also CA 131; CAAE 123; HW 1

Houdini
    See Lovecraft, H. P.

Houellebecq, Michel 1958- .... **CLC 179**
    See also CA 185; CANR 140; MTFW 2005

Hougan, Carolyn 1943-2007 .... **CLC 34**
    See also CA 139; CAAS 257

Household, Geoffrey (Edward West)
    1900-1988 .... **CLC 11**
    See also CA 77-80; CAAS 126; CANR 58;
    CMW 4; CN 1, 2, 3, 4; DLB 87; SATA
    14; SATA-Obit 59

Housman, A(lfred) E(dward)
    1859-1936 .... **PC 2, 43; TCLC 1, 10;
    WLCS**
    See also AAYA 66; BRW 6; CA 125; CAAE
    104; DA; DA3; DAB; DAC; DAM MST,
    POET; DLB 19, 284; EWL 3; EXPP;
    MTCW 1, 2; MTFW 2005; PAB; PFS 4,
    7; RGEL 2; TEA; WP

Housman, Laurence 1865-1959 .... **TCLC 7**
    See also CA 155; CAAE 106; DLB 10;
    FANT; RGEL 2; SATA 25

Houston, Jeanne Wakatsuki 1934- .... **AAL**
    See also AAYA 49; CA 232; 103, 232; 16;
    CANR 29, 123; LAIT 4; SATA 78, 168;
    SATA-Essay 168

Howard, Elizabeth Jane 1923- ..... **CLC 7, 29**
    See also BRWS 11; CA 5-8R; CANR 8, 62,
    146; CN 1, 2, 3, 4, 5, 6, 7

Howard, Maureen 1930- .... **CLC 5, 14, 46,
    151**
    See also CA 53-56; CANR 31, 75, 140; CN
    4, 5, 6, 7; DLBY 1983; INT CANR-31;
    MTCW 1, 2; MTFW 2005

Howard, Richard 1929- .... **CLC 7, 10, 47**
    See also AITN 1; CA 85-88; CANR 25, 80,
    154; CP 1, 2, 3, 4, 5, 6, 7; DLB 5; INT
    CANR-25; MAL 5

Howard, Robert E 1906-1936 .... **TCLC 8**
    See also BPFB 2; BYA 5; CA 157; CAAE
    105; CANR 155; FANT; SUFW 1;
    TCWW 1, 2

Howard, Robert Ervin
    See Howard, Robert E

Howard, Warren F.
    See Pohl, Frederik

Howe, Fanny (Quincy) 1940- .... **CLC 47**
    See also CA 187; 117, 187; 27; CANR 70,
    116; CP 6, 7; CWP; SATA-Brief 52

Howe, Irving 1920-1993 .... **CLC 85**
    See also AMWS 6; CA 9-12R; CAAS 141;
    CANR 21, 50; DLB 67; EWL 3; MAL 5;
    MTCW 1, 2; MTFW 2005

Howe, Julia Ward 1819-1910 .... **TCLC 21**
    See also CA 191; CAAE 117; DLB 1, 189,
    235; FW

Howe, Susan 1937- .... **CLC 72, 152; PC 54**
    See also AMWS 4; CA 160; CP 5, 6, 7;
    CWP; DLB 120; FW; RGAL 4

Howe, Tina 1937- .... **CLC 48**
    See also CA 109; CAD; CANR 125; CD 5,
    6; CWD

Howell, James 1594(?)-1666 .... **LC 13**
    See also DLB 151

Howells, W. D.
    See Howells, William Dean

Howells, William D.
    See Howells, William Dean

Howells, William Dean 1837-1920 ... **SSC 36;
    TCLC 7, 17, 41**
    See also AMW; CA 134; CAAE 104;
    CDALB 1865-1917; DLB 12, 64, 74, 79,
    189; LMFS 1; MAL 5; MTCW 2; RGAL
    4; TUS

Howes, Barbara 1914-1996 .... **CLC 15**
    See also CA 9-12R; 3; CAAS 151; CANR
    53; CP 1, 2, 3, 4, 5, 6; SATA 5; TCLE 1:1

Hrabal, Bohumil 1914-1997 ...... **CLC 13, 67;
    TCLC 155**
    See also CA 106; 12; CAAS 156; CANR
    57; CWW 2; DLB 232; EWL 3; RGSF 2

Hrabanus Maurus 776(?)-856 .... **CMLC 78**
    See also DLB 148

Hrotsvit of Gandersheim c. 935-c.
    1000 .... **CMLC 29**
    See also DLB 148

Hsi, Chu 1130-1200 .... **CMLC 42**

Hsun, Lu
    See Lu Hsun

Hubbard, L. Ron 1911-1986 .... **CLC 43**
    See also AAYA 64; CA 77-80; CAAS 118;
    CANR 52; CPW; DA3; DAM POP;
    FANT; MTCW 2; MTFW 2005; SFW 4

Hubbard, Lafayette Ronald
    See Hubbard, L. Ron

Huch, Ricarda (Octavia)
    1864-1947 .... **TCLC 13**
    See also CA 189; CAAE 111; DLB 66;
    EWL 3

Huddle, David 1942- .... **CLC 49**
    See also CA 57-60; 20; CANR 89; DLB
    130

Hudson, Jeffrey
    See Crichton, Michael

Hudson, W(illiam) H(enry)
    1841-1922 .... **TCLC 29**
    See also CA 190; CAAE 115; DLB 98, 153,
    174; RGEL 2; SATA 35

Hueffer, Ford Madox
    See Ford, Ford Madox

Hughart, Barry 1934- .... **CLC 39**
    See also CA 137; FANT; SFW 4; SUFW 2

Hughes, Colin
    See Creasey, John

Hughes, David (John) 1930-2005 ..... **CLC 48**
    See also CA 129; CAAE 116; CAAS 238;
    CN 4, 5, 6, 7; DLB 14

Hughes, Edward James
    See Hughes, Ted
    See also DA3; DAM MST, POET

Hughes, (James Mercer) Langston
    1902-1967 ...... **BLC 2; CLC 1, 5, 10, 15,
    35, 44, 108; DC 3; HR 1:2; PC 1, 53;
    SSC 6, 90; WLC 3**
    See also AAYA 12; AFAW 1, 2; AMWR 1;
    AMWS 1; BW 1, 3; CA 1-4R; CAAS 25-
    28R; CANR 1, 34, 82; CDALB 1929-
    1941; CLR 17; DA; DA3; DAB; DAC;
    DAM DRAM, MST, MULT, POET; DFS
    6, 18; DLB 4, 7, 48, 51, 86, 228, 315;
    EWL 3; EXPP; EXPS; JRDA; LAIT 3;
    LMFS 2; MAICYA 1, 2; MAL 5; MTCW
    1, 2; MTFW 2005; NFS 21; PAB; PFS 1,
    3, 6, 10, 15; RGAL 4; RGSF 2; SATA 4,
    33; SSFS 4, 7; TUS; WCH; WP; YAW

Hughes, Richard (Arthur Warren)
    1900-1976 .... **CLC 1, 11**
    See also CA 5-8R; CAAS 65-68; CANR 4;
    CN 1, 2; DAM NOV; DLB 15, 161; EWL
    3; MTCW 1; RGEL 2; SATA 8; SATA-
    Obit 25

Hughes, Ted 1930-1998 . **CLC 2, 4, 9, 14, 37,
    119; PC 7**
    See Hughes, Edward James
    See also BRWC 2; BRWR 2; BRWS 1; CA
    1-4R; CAAS 171; CANR 1, 33, 66, 108;
    CLR 3; CP 1, 2, 3, 4, 5, 6; DAB; DAC;
    DLB 40, 161; EWL 3; EXPP; MAICYA
    1, 2; MTCW 1, 2; MTFW 2005; PAB;
    PFS 4, 19; RGEL 2; SATA 49; SATA-
    Brief 27; SATA-Obit 107; TEA; YAW

Hugo, Richard
    See Huch, Ricarda (Octavia)

Hugo, Richard F(ranklin)
    1923-1982 .... **CLC 6, 18, 32; PC 68**
    See also AMWS 6; CA 49-52; CAAS 108;
    CANR 3; CP 1, 2, 3; DAM POET; DLB
    5, 206; EWL 3; MAL 5; PFS 17; RGAL 4

Hugo, Victor (Marie) 1802-1885 .... **NCLC 3,
    10, 21, 161; PC 17; WLC 3**
    See also AAYA 28; DA; DA3; DAB; DAC;
    DAM DRAM, MST, NOV, POET; DLB
    119, 192, 217; EFS 2; EW 6; EXPN; GFL
    1789 to the Present; LAIT 1, 2; NFS 5,
    20; RGWL 2, 3; SATA 47; TWA

Huidobro, Vicente
    See Huidobro Fernandez, Vicente Garcia
    See also DLB 283; EWL 3; LAW

Huidobro Fernandez, Vicente Garcia
    1893-1948 .... **TCLC 31**
    See Huidobro, Vicente
    See also CA 131; HW 1

Hulme, Keri 1947- .... **CLC 39, 130**
    See also CA 125; CANR 69; CN 4, 5, 6, 7;
    CP 6, 7; CWP; DLB 326; EWL 3; FW;
    INT CA-125; NFS 24

Kendall, Henry 1839-1882 .... **NCLC 12**
See also DLB 230

Keneally, Thomas 1935- .... **CLC 5, 8, 10, 14, 19, 27, 43, 117**
See also BRWS 4; CA 85-88; CANR 10, 50, 74, 130; CN 1, 2, 3, 4, 5, 6, 7; CPW; DA3; DAM NOV; DLB 289, 299, 326; EWL 3; MTCW 1, 2; MTFW 2005; NFS 17; RGEL 2; RGHL; RHW

Kennedy, A(lison) L(ouise) 1965- ... **CLC 188**
See also CA 213; 168, 213; CANR 108; CD 5, 6; CN 6, 7; DLB 271; RGSF 2

Kennedy, Adrienne (Lita) 1931- .... **BLC 2; CLC 66; DC 5**
See also AFAW 2; BW 2, 3; CA 103; 20; CABS 3; CAD; CANR 26, 53, 82; CD 5, 6; DAM MULT; DFS 9; DLB 38; FW; MAL 5

Kennedy, John Pendleton 1795-1870 .... **NCLC 2**
See also DLB 3, 248, 254; RGAL 4

Kennedy, Joseph Charles 1929-
See Kennedy, X. J.
See also CA 201; 1-4R, 201; CANR 4, 30, 40; CWRI 5; MAICYA 2; MAICYAS 1; SATA 14, 86, 130; SATA-Essay 130

Kennedy, William 1928- .. **CLC 6, 28, 34, 53, 239**
See also AAYA 1, 73; AMWS 7; BPFB 2; CA 85-88; CANR 14, 31, 76, 134; CN 4, 5, 6, 7; DA3; DAM NOV; DLB 143; DLBY 1985; EWL 3; INT CANR-31; MAL 5; MTCW 1, 2; MTFW 2005; SATA 57

Kennedy, X. J. .... **CLC 8, 42**
See Kennedy, Joseph Charles
See also AMWS 15; CA 9; CLR 27; CP 1, 2, 3, 4, 5, 6, 7; DLB 5; SAAS 22

Kenny, Maurice (Francis) 1929- ..... **CLC 87; NNAL**
See also CA 144; 22; CANR 143; DAM MULT; DLB 175

Kent, Kelvin
See Kuttner, Henry

Kenton, Maxwell
See Southern, Terry

Kenyon, Jane 1947-1995 .... **PC 57**
See also AAYA 63; AMWS 7; CA 118; CAAS 148; CANR 44, 69; CP 6, 7; CWP; DLB 120; PFS 9, 17; RGAL 4

Kenyon, Robert O.
See Kuttner, Henry

Kepler, Johannes 1571-1630 .... **LC 45**

Ker, Jill
See Conway, Jill K(er)

Kerkow, H. C.
See Lewton, Val

Kerouac, Jack 1922-1969 ...... **CLC 1, 2, 3, 5, 14, 29, 61; TCLC 117; WLC**
See Kerouac, Jean-Louis Lebris de
See also AAYA 25; AMWC 1; AMWS 3; BG 3; BPFB 2; CDALB 1941-1968; CP 1; CPW; DLB 2, 16, 237; DLBD 3; DLBY 1995; EWL 3; GLL 1; LATS 1:2; LMFS 2; MAL 5; NFS 8; RGAL 4; TUS; WP

Kerouac, Jean-Louis Lebris de 1922-1969
See Kerouac, Jack
See also AITN 1; CA 5-8R; CAAS 25-28R; CANR 26, 54, 95; DA; DA3; DAB; DAC; DAM MST, NOV, POET, POP; MTCW 1, 2; MTFW 2005

Kerr, (Bridget) Jean (Collins) 1923(?)-2003 .... **CLC 22**
See also CA 5-8R; CAAS 212; CANR 7; INT CANR-7

Kerr, M. E. .... **CLC 12, 35**
See Meaker, Marijane
See also AAYA 2, 23; BYA 1, 7, 8; CLR 29; SAAS 1; WYA

Kerr, Robert .... **CLC 55**

Kerrigan, (Thomas) Anthony 1918- .. **CLC 4, 6**
See also CA 49-52; 11; CANR 4

Kerry, Lois
See Duncan, Lois

Kesey, Ken 1935-2001 .... **CLC 1, 3, 6, 11, 46, 64, 184; WLC 3**
See also AAYA 25; BG 1:3; BPFB 2; CA 1-4R; CAAS 204; CANR 22, 38, 66, 124; CDALB 1968-1988; CN 1, 2, 3, 4, 5, 6, 7; CPW; DA; DA3; DAB; DAC; DAM MST, NOV, POP; DLB 2, 16, 206; EWL 3; EXPN; LAIT 4; MAL 5; MTCW 1, 2; MTFW 2005; NFS 2; RGAL 4; SATA 66; SATA-Obit 131; TUS; YAW

Kesselring, Joseph (Otto) 1902-1967 .... **CLC 45**
See also CA 150; DAM DRAM, MST; DFS 20

Kessler, Jascha (Frederick) 1929- ...... **CLC 4**
See also CA 17-20R; CANR 8, 48, 111; CP 1

Kettelkamp, Larry (Dale) 1933- .... **CLC 12**
See also CA 29-32R; CANR 16; SAAS 3; SATA 2

Key, Ellen (Karolina Sofia) 1849-1926 .... **TCLC 65**
See also DLB 259

Keyber, Conny
See Fielding, Henry

Keyes, Daniel 1927- .... **CLC 80**
See also AAYA 23; BYA 11; CA 181; 17-20R, 181; CANR 10, 26, 54, 74; DA; DA3; DAC; DAM MST, NOV; EXPN; LAIT 4; MTCW 2; MTFW 2005; NFS 2; SATA 37; SFW 4

Keynes, John Maynard 1883-1946 .... **TCLC 64**
See also CA 162, 163; CAAE 114; DLBD 10; MTCW 2; MTFW 2005

Khanshendel, Chiron
See Rose, Wendy

Khayyam, Omar 1048-1131 ... **CMLC 11; PC 8**
See Omar Khayyam
See also DA3; DAM POET; WLIT 6

Kherdian, David 1931- .... **CLC 6, 9**
See also AAYA 42; CA 192; 21-24R, 192; 2; CANR 39, 78; CLR 24; JRDA; LAIT 3; MAICYA 1, 2; SATA 16, 74; SATA-Essay 125

Khlebnikov, Velimir .... **TCLC 20**
See Khlebnikov, Viktor Vladimirovich
See also DLB 295; EW 10; EWL 3; RGWL 2, 3

Khlebnikov, Viktor Vladimirovich 1885-1922
See Khlebnikov, Velimir
See also CA 217; CAAE 117

Khodasevich, V.F.
See Khodasevich, Vladislav

Khodasevich, Vladislav 1886-1939 .... **TCLC 15**
See also CAAE 115; DLB 317; EWL 3

Khodasevich, Vladislav Felitsianovich
See Khodasevich, Vladislav

Kielland, Alexander Lange 1849-1906 .... **TCLC 5**
See also CAAE 104

Kiely, Benedict 1919-2007 . **CLC 23, 43; SSC 58**
See also CA 1-4R; CAAS 257; CANR 2, 84; CN 1, 2, 3, 4, 5, 6, 7; DLB 15, 319; TCLE 1:1

Kienzle, William X. 1928-2001 .... **CLC 25**
See also CA 93-96; 1; CAAS 203; CANR 9, 31, 59, 111; CMW 4; DA3; DAM POP; INT CANR-31; MSW; MTCW 1, 2; MTFW 2005

Kierkegaard, Soren 1813-1855 ..... **NCLC 34, 78, 125**
See also DLB 300; EW 6; LMFS 2; RGWL 3; TWA

Kieslowski, Krzysztof 1941-1996 .... **CLC 120**
See also CA 147; CAAS 151

Killens, John Oliver 1916-1987 .... **CLC 10**
See also BW 2; CA 77-80; 2; CAAS 123; CANR 26; CN 1, 2, 3, 4; DLB 33; EWL 3

Killigrew, Anne 1660-1685 .... **LC 4, 73**
See also DLB 131

Killigrew, Thomas 1612-1683 .... **LC 57**
See also DLB 58; RGEL 2

Kim
See Simenon, Georges (Jacques Christian)

Kincaid, Jamaica 1949- ...... **BLC 2; CLC 43, 68, 137, 234; SSC 72**
See also AAYA 13, 56; AFAW 2; AMWS 7; BRWS 7; BW 2, 3; CA 125; CANR 47, 59, 95, 133; CDALBS; CDWLB 3; CLR 63; CN 4, 5, 6, 7; DA3; DAM MULT, NOV; DLB 157, 227; DNFS 1; EWL 3; EXPS; FW; LATS 1:2; LMFS 2; MAL 5; MTCW 2; MTFW 2005; NCFS 1; NFS 3; SSFS 5, 7; TUS; WWE 1; YAW

King, Francis (Henry) 1923- .... **CLC 8, 53, 145**
See also CA 1-4R; CANR 1, 33, 86; CN 1, 2, 3, 4, 5, 6, 7; DAM NOV; DLB 15, 139; MTCW 1

King, Kennedy
See Brown, George Douglas

King, Martin Luther, Jr. 1929-1968 . **BLC 2; CLC 83; WLCS**
See also BW 2, 3; CA 25-28; CANR 27, 44; CAP 2; DA; DA3; DAB; DAC; DAM MST, MULT; LAIT 5; LATS 1:2; MTCW 1, 2; MTFW 2005; SATA 14

King, Stephen 1947- .... **CLC 12, 26, 37, 61, 113, 228; SSC 17, 55**
See also AAYA 1, 17; AMWS 5; BEST 90:1; BPFB 2; CA 61-64; CANR 1, 30, 52, 76, 119, 134; CN 7; CPW; DA3; DAM NOV, POP; DLB 143; DLBY 1980; HGG; JRDA; LAIT 5; MTCW 1, 2; MTFW 2005; RGAL 4; SATA 9, 55, 161; SUFW 1, 2; WYAS 1; YAW

King, Stephen Edwin
See King, Stephen

King, Steve
See King, Stephen

King, Thomas 1943- .... **CLC 89, 171; NNAL**
See also CA 144; CANR 95; CCA 1; CN 6, 7; DAC; DAM MULT; DLB 175, 334; SATA 96

Kingman, Lee .... **CLC 17**
See Natti, (Mary) Lee
See also CWRI 5; SAAS 3; SATA 1, 67

Kingsley, Charles 1819-1875 .... **NCLC 35**
See also CLR 77; DLB 21, 32, 163, 178, 190; FANT; MAICYA 2; MAICYAS 1; RGEL 2; WCH; YABC 2

Kingsley, Henry 1830-1876 .... **NCLC 107**
See also DLB 21, 230; RGEL 2

Kingsley, Sidney 1906-1995 .... **CLC 44**
See also CA 85-88; CAAS 147; CAD; DFS 14, 19; DLB 7; MAL 5; RGAL 4

Kingsolver, Barbara 1955- .... **CLC 55, 81, 130, 216**
See also AAYA 15; AMWS 7; CA 134; CAAE 129; CANR 60, 96, 133; CDALBS; CN 7; CPW; CSW; DA3; DAM POP; DLB 206; INT CA-134; LAIT 5; MTCW 2; MTFW 2005; NFS 5, 10, 12, 24; RGAL 4; TCLE 1:1

Kops, Bernard 1926- .... **CLC 4**
See also CA 5-8R; CANR 84, 159; CBD;
CN 1, 2, 3, 4, 5, 6, 7; CP 1, 2, 3, 4, 5, 6,
7; DLB 13; RGHL

Kornbluth, C(yril) M. 1923-1958 .... **TCLC 8**
See also CA 160; CAAE 105; DLB 8;
SCFW 1, 2; SFW 4

Korolenko, V.G.
See Korolenko, Vladimir G.

Korolenko, Vladimir
See Korolenko, Vladimir G.

Korolenko, Vladimir G.
1853-1921 .... **TCLC 22**
See also CAAE 121; DLB 277

Korolenko, Vladimir Galaktionovich
See Korolenko, Vladimir G.

Korzybski, Alfred (Habdank Skarbek)
1879-1950 .... **TCLC 61**
See also CA 160; CAAE 123

Kosinski, Jerzy 1933-1991 ..... **CLC 1, 2, 3, 6,**
10, 15, 53, 70
See also AMWS 7; BPFB 2; CA 17-20R;
CAAS 134; CANR 9, 46; CN 1, 2, 3, 4;
DA3; DAM NOV; DLB 2, 299; DLBY
1982; EWL 3; HGG; MAL 5; MTCW 1,
2; MTFW 2005; NFS 12; RGAL 4;
RGHL; TUS

Kostelanetz, Richard (Cory) 1940- .. **CLC 28**
See also CA 13-16R; 8; CANR 38, 77; CN
4, 5, 6; CP 2, 3, 4, 5, 6, 7

Kostrowitzki, Wilhelm Apollinaris de
1880-1918
See Apollinaire, Guillaume
See also CAAE 104

Kotlowitz, Robert 1924- .... **CLC 4**
See also CA 33-36R; CANR 36

Kotzebue, August (Friedrich Ferdinand) von
1761-1819 .... **NCLC 25**
See also DLB 94

Kotzwinkle, William 1938- ..... **CLC 5, 14, 35**
See also BPFB 2; CA 45-48; CANR 3, 44,
84, 129; CLR 6; CN 7; DLB 173; FANT;
MAICYA 1, 2; SATA 24, 70, 146; SFW
4; SUFW 2; YAW

Kowna, Stancy
See Szymborska, Wislawa

Kozol, Jonathan 1936- .... **CLC 17**
See also AAYA 46; CA 61-64; CANR 16,
45, 96; MTFW 2005

Kozoll, Michael 1940(?)- .... **CLC 35**

Kramer, Kathryn 19(?)- .... **CLC 34**

Kramer, Larry 1935- .... **CLC 42; DC 8**
See also CA 126; CAAE 124; CANR 60,
132; DAM POP; DLB 249; GLL 1

Krasicki, Ignacy 1735-1801 .... **NCLC 8**

Krasinski, Zygmunt 1812-1859 .... **NCLC 4**
See also RGWL 2, 3

Kraus, Karl 1874-1936 .... **TCLC 5**
See also CA 216; CAAE 104; DLB 118;
EWL 3

Kreve (Mickevicius), Vincas
1882-1954 .... **TCLC 27**
See also CA 170; DLB 220; EWL 3

Kristeva, Julia 1941- .... **CLC 77, 140**
See also CA 154; CANR 99; DLB 242;
EWL 3; FW; LMFS 2

Kristofferson, Kris 1936- .... **CLC 26**
See also CA 104

Krizanc, John 1956- .... **CLC 57**
See also CA 187

Krleza, Miroslav 1893-1981 .... **CLC 8, 114**
See also CA 97-100; CAAS 105; CANR
50; CDWLB 4; DLB 147; EW 11; RGWL
2, 3

Kroetsch, Robert (Paul) 1927- .... **CLC 5, 23,**
57, 132
See also CA 17-20R; CANR 8, 38; CCA 1;
CN 2, 3, 4, 5, 6, 7; CP 6, 7; DAC; DAM
POET; DLB 53; MTCW 1

Kroetz, Franz
See Kroetz, Franz Xaver

Kroetz, Franz Xaver 1946- .... **CLC 41**
See also CA 130; CANR 142; CWW 2;
EWL 3

Kroker, Arthur (W.) 1945- .... **CLC 77**
See also CA 161

Kroniuk, Lisa
See Berton, Pierre (Francis de Marigny)

Kropotkin, Peter (Aleksieevich)
1842-1921 .... **TCLC 36**
See Kropotkin, Petr Alekseevich
See also CA 219; CAAE 119

Kropotkin, Petr Alekseevich
See Kropotkin, Peter (Aleksieevich)
See also DLB 277

Krotkov, Yuri 1917-1981 .... **CLC 19**
See also CA 102

Krumb
See Crumb, R.

Krumgold, Joseph (Quincy)
1908-1980 .... **CLC 12**
See also BYA 1, 2; CA 9-12R; CAAS 101;
CANR 7; MAICYA 1, 2; SATA 1, 48;
SATA-Obit 23; YAW

Krumwitz
See Crumb, R.

Krutch, Joseph Wood 1893-1970 ..... **CLC 24**
See also ANW; CA 1-4R; CAAS 25-28R;
CANR 4; DLB 63, 206, 275

Krutzch, Gus
See Eliot, T(homas) S(tearns)

Krylov, Ivan Andreevich
1768(?)-1844 .... **NCLC 1**
See also DLB 150

Kubin, Alfred (Leopold Isidor)
1877-1959 .... **TCLC 23**
See also CA 149; CAAE 112; CANR 104;
DLB 81

Kubrick, Stanley 1928-1999 .... **CLC 16;**
TCLC 112
See also AAYA 30; CA 81-84; CAAS 177;
CANR 33; DLB 26

Kumin, Maxine 1925- .... **CLC 5, 13, 28, 164;**
PC 15
See also AITN 2; AMWS 4; ANW; CA
1-4R; 8; CANR 1, 21, 69, 115, 140; CP 2,
3, 4, 5, 6, 7; CWP; DA3; DAM POET;
DLB 5; EWL 3; EXPP; MTCW 1, 2;
MTFW 2005; PAB; PFS 18; SATA 12

Kundera, Milan 1929- . **CLC 4, 9, 19, 32, 68,**
115, 135, 234; SSC 24
See also AAYA 2, 62; BPFB 2; CA 85-88;
CANR 19, 52, 74, 144; CDWLB 4; CWW
2; DA3; DAM NOV; DLB 232; EW 13;
EWL 3; MTCW 1, 2; MTFW 2005; NFS
18; RGSF 2; RGWL 3; SSFS 10

Kunene, Mazisi 1930-2006 .... **CLC 85**
See also BW 1, 3; CA 125; CAAS 252;
CANR 81; CP 1, 6, 7; DLB 117

Kunene, Mazisi Raymond
See Kunene, Mazisi

Kunene, Mazisi Raymond Fakazi Mngoni
See Kunene, Mazisi

Kung, Hans .... **CLC 130**
See Kung, Hans

Kung, Hans 1928-
See Kung, Hans
See also CA 53-56; CANR 66, 134; MTCW
1, 2; MTFW 2005

Kunikida Doppo 1869(?)-1908
See Doppo, Kunikida
See also DLB 180; EWL 3

Kunitz, Stanley 1905-2006 ..... **CLC 6, 11, 14,**
148; PC 19
See also AMWS 3; CA 41-44R; CAAS 250;
CANR 26, 57, 98; CP 1, 2, 3, 4, 5, 6, 7;
DA3; DLB 48; INT CANR-26; MAL 5;
MTCW 1, 2; MTFW 2005; PFS 11;
RGAL 4

Kunitz, Stanley Jasspon
See Kunitz, Stanley

Kunze, Reiner 1933- .... **CLC 10**
See also CA 93-96; CWW 2; DLB 75; EWL
3

Kuprin, Aleksander Ivanovich
1870-1938 .... **TCLC 5**
See Kuprin, Aleksandr Ivanovich; Kuprin,
Alexandr Ivanovich
See also CA 182; CAAE 104

Kuprin, Aleksandr Ivanovich
See Kuprin, Aleksander Ivanovich
See also DLB 295

Kuprin, Alexandr Ivanovich
See Kuprin, Aleksander Ivanovich
See also EWL 3

Kureishi, Hanif 1954- .. **CLC 64, 135; DC 26**
See also BRWS 11; CA 139; CANR 113;
CBD; CD 5, 6; CN 6, 7; DLB 194, 245;
GLL 2; IDFW 4; WLIT 4; WWE 1

Kurosawa, Akira 1910-1998 ..... **CLC 16, 119**
See also AAYA 11, 64; CA 101; CAAS 170;
CANR 46; DAM MULT

Kushner, Tony 1956- .... **CLC 81, 203; DC 10**
See also AAYA 61; AMWS 9; CA 144;
CAD; CANR 74, 130; CD 5, 6; DA3;
DAM DRAM; DFS 5; DLB 228; EWL 3;
GLL 1; LAIT 5; MAL 5; MTCW 2;
MTFW 2005; RGAL 4; RGHL; SATA 160

Kuttner, Henry 1915-1958 .... **TCLC 10**
See also CA 157; CAAE 107; DLB 8;
FANT; SCFW 1, 2; SFW 4

Kutty, Madhavi
See Das, Kamala

Kuzma, Greg 1944- .... **CLC 7**
See also CA 33-36R; CANR 70

Kuzmin, Mikhail (Alekseevich)
1872(?)-1936 .... **TCLC 40**
See also CA 170; DLB 295; EWL 3

Kyd, Thomas 1558-1594 .. **DC 3; LC 22, 125**
See also BRW 1; DAM DRAM; DFS 21;
DLB 62; IDTP; LMFS 1; RGEL 2; TEA;
WLIT 3

Kyprianos, Iossif
See Samarakis, Antonis

L. S.
See Stephen, Sir Leslie

Labe, Louise 1521-1566 .... **LC 120**
See also DLB 327

Labrunie, Gerard
See Nerval, Gerard de

La Bruyere, Jean de 1645-1696 .... **LC 17**
See also DLB 268; EW 3; GFL Beginnings
to 1789

LaBute, Neil 1963- .... **CLC 225**
See also CA 240

Lacan, Jacques (Marie Emile)
1901-1981 .... **CLC 75**
See also CA 121; CAAS 104; DLB 296;
EWL 3; TWA

Laclos, Pierre-Ambroise Francois
1741-1803 .... **NCLC 4, 87**
See also DLB 313; EW 4; GFL Beginnings
to 1789; RGWL 2, 3

Lacolere, Francois
See Aragon, Louis

La Colere, Francois
See Aragon, Louis

La Deshabilleuse
See Simenon, Georges (Jacques Christian)

Lady Gregory
See Gregory, Lady Isabella Augusta (Persse)

Lady of Quality, A
See Bagnold, Enid

La Fayette, Marie-(Madelaine Pioche de la
Vergne) 1634-1693 .... **LC 2**
See Lafayette, Marie-Madeleine
See also GFL Beginnings to 1789; RGWL
2, 3

Levin, Ira 1929- .... **CLC 3, 6**
　　See also CA 21-24R; CANR 17, 44, 74,
　　139; CMW 4; CN 1, 2, 3, 4, 5, 6, 7; CPW;
　　DA3; DAM POP; HGG; MTCW 1, 2;
　　MTFW 2005; SATA 66; SFW 4

Levin, Meyer 1905-1981 .... **CLC 7**
　　See also AITN 1; CA 9-12R; CAAS 104;
　　CANR 15; CN 1, 2, 3; DAM POP; DLB
　　9, 28; DLBY 1981; MAL 5; RGHL; SATA
　　21; SATA-Obit 27

Levine, Albert Norman
　　See Levine, Norman
　　See also CN 7

Levine, Norman 1923-2005 .... **CLC 54**
　　See Levine, Albert Norman
　　See also CA 73-76; 23; CAAS 240; CANR
　　14, 70; CN 1, 2, 3, 4, 5, 6; CP 1; DLB 88

Levine, Norman Albert
　　See Levine, Norman

Levine, Philip 1928- .. **CLC 2, 4, 5, 9, 14, 33,**
　　118; PC 22
　　See also AMWS 5; CA 9-12R; CANR 9,
　　37, 52, 116, 156; CP 1, 2, 3, 4, 5, 6, 7;
　　DAM POET; DLB 5; EWL 3; MAL 5;
　　PFS 8

Levinson, Deirdre 1931- .... **CLC 49**
　　See also CA 73-76; CANR 70

Levi-Strauss, Claude 1908- .... **CLC 38**
　　See also CA 1-4R; CANR 6, 32, 57; DLB
　　242; EWL 3; GFL 1789 to the Present;
　　MTCW 1, 2; TWA

Levitin, Sonia (Wolff) 1934- .... **CLC 17**
　　See also AAYA 13, 48; CA 29-32R; CANR
　　14, 32, 79; CLR 53; JRDA; MAICYA 1,
　　2; SAAS 2; SATA 4, 68, 119, 131; SATA-
　　Essay 131; YAW

Levon, O. U.
　　See Kesey, Ken

Levy, Amy 1861-1889 .... **NCLC 59**
　　See also DLB 156, 240

Lewes, George Henry 1817-1878 ... **NCLC 25**
　　See also DLB 55, 144

Lewis, Alun 1915-1944 .... **SSC 40; TCLC 3**
　　See also BRW 7; CA 188; CAAE 104; DLB
　　20, 162; PAB; RGEL 2

Lewis, C. Day
　　See Day Lewis, C(ecil)
　　See also CN 1

Lewis, Cecil Day
　　See Day Lewis, C(ecil)

Lewis, Clive Staples
　　See Lewis, C.S.

Lewis, C.S. 1898-1963 ... **CLC 1, 3, 6, 14, 27,**
　　124; WLC 4
　　See also AAYA 3, 39; BPFB 2; BRWS 3;
　　BYA 15, 16; CA 81-84; CANR 33, 71,
　　132; CDBLB 1945-1960; CLR 3, 27, 109;
　　CWRI 5; DA; DA3; DAB; DAC; DAM
　　MST, NOV, POP; DLB 15, 100, 160, 255;
　　EWL 3; FANT; JRDA; LMFS 2; MAI-
　　CYA 1, 2; MTCW 1, 2; MTFW 2005;
　　NFS 24; RGEL 2; SATA 13, 100; SCFW
　　1, 2; SFW 4; SUFW 1; TEA; WCH;
　　WYA; YAW

Lewis, Janet 1899-1998 .... **CLC 41**
　　See Winters, Janet Lewis
　　See also CA 9-12R; CAAS 172; CANR 29,
　　63; CAP 1; CN 1, 2, 3, 4, 5, 6; DLBY
　　1987; RHW; TCWW 2

Lewis, Matthew Gregory
　　1775-1818 .... **NCLC 11, 62**
　　See also DLB 39, 158, 178; GL 3; HGG;
　　LMFS 1; RGEL 2; SUFW

Lewis, (Harry) Sinclair 1885-1951 . **TCLC 4,**
　　13, 23, 39; WLC 4
　　See also AMW; AMWC 1; BPFB 2; CA
　　133; CAAE 104; CANR 132; CDALB
　　1917-1929; DA; DA3; DAB; DAC; DAM

MST, NOV; DLB 9, 102, 284, 331; DLBD
1; EWL 3; LAIT 3; MAL 5; MTCW 1, 2;
MTFW 2005; NFS 15, 19, 22; RGAL 4;
TUS

Lewis, (Percy) Wyndham
　　1884(?)-1957 .. **SSC 34; TCLC 2, 9, 104**
　　See also BRW 7; CA 157; CAAE 104; DLB
　　15; EWL 3; FANT; MTCW 2; MTFW
　　2005; RGEL 2

Lewisohn, Ludwig 1883-1955 .... **TCLC 19**
　　See also CA 203; CAAE 107; DLB 4, 9,
　　28, 102; MAL 5

Lewton, Val 1904-1951 .... **TCLC 76**
　　See also CA 199; IDFW 3, 4

Leyner, Mark 1956- .... **CLC 92**
　　See also CA 110; CANR 28, 53; DA3; DLB
　　292; MTCW 2; MTFW 2005

Lezama Lima, Jose 1910-1976 .... **CLC 4, 10,**
　　101; HLCS 2
　　See also CA 77-80; CANR 71; DAM
　　MULT; DLB 113, 283; EWL 3; HW 1, 2;
　　LAW; RGWL 2, 3

L'Heureux, John (Clarke) 1934- ...... **CLC 52**
　　See also CA 13-16R; CANR 23, 45, 88; CP
　　1, 2, 3, 4; DLB 244

Li Ch'ing-chao 1081(?)-1141(?) .... **CMLC 71**

Liddell, C. H.
　　See Kuttner, Henry

Lie, Jonas (Lauritz Idemil)
　　1833-1908(?) .... **TCLC 5**
　　See also CAAE 115

Lieber, Joel 1937-1971 .... **CLC 6**
　　See also CA 73-76; CAAS 29-32R

Lieber, Stanley Martin
　　See Lee, Stan

Lieberman, Laurence (James)
　　1935- .... **CLC 4, 36**
　　See also CA 17-20R; CANR 8, 36, 89; CP
　　1, 2, 3, 4, 5, 6, 7

Lieh Tzu fl. 7th cent. B.C.-5th cent.
　　B.C. .... **CMLC 27**

Lieksman, Anders
　　See Haavikko, Paavo Juhani

Lifton, Robert Jay 1926- .... **CLC 67**
　　See also CA 17-20R; CANR 27, 78, 161;
　　INT CANR-27; SATA 66

Lightfoot, Gordon 1938- .... **CLC 26**
　　See also CA 242; CAAE 109

Lightfoot, Gordon Meredith
　　See Lightfoot, Gordon

Lightman, Alan P(aige) 1948- .... **CLC 81**
　　See also CA 141; CANR 63, 105, 138;
　　MTFW 2005

Ligotti, Thomas (Robert) 1953- ...... **CLC 44;**
　　SSC 16
　　See also CA 123; CANR 49, 135; HGG;
　　SUFW 2

Li Ho 791-817 .... **PC 13**

Li Ju-chen c. 1763-c. 1830 .... **NCLC 137**

Lilar, Francoise
　　See Mallet-Joris, Francoise

Liliencron, Detlev
　　See Liliencron, Detlev von

Liliencron, Detlev von 1844-1909 .. **TCLC 18**
　　See also CAAE 117

Liliencron, Friedrich Adolf Axel Detlev von
　　See Liliencron, Detlev von

Liliencron, Friedrich Detlev von
　　See Liliencron, Detlev von

Lille, Alain de
　　See Alain de Lille

Lillo, George 1691-1739 .... **LC 131**
　　See also DLB 84; RGEL 2

Lilly, William 1602-1681 .... **LC 27**

Lima, Jose Lezama
　　See Lezama Lima, Jose

Lima Barreto, Afonso Henrique de
　　1881-1922 .... **TCLC 23**
　　See Lima Barreto, Afonso Henriques de
　　See also CA 181; CAAE 117; LAW

Lima Barreto, Afonso Henriques de
　　See Lima Barreto, Afonso Henrique de
　　See also DLB 307

Limonov, Eduard
　　See Limonov, Edward
　　See also DLB 317

Limonov, Edward 1944- .... **CLC 67**
　　See Limonov, Eduard
　　See also CA 137

Lin, Frank
　　See Atherton, Gertrude (Franklin Horn)

Lin, Yutang 1895-1976 .... **TCLC 149**
　　See also CA 45-48; CAAS 65-68; CANR 2;
　　RGAL 4

Lincoln, Abraham 1809-1865 .... **NCLC 18**
　　See also LAIT 2

Lind, Jakov 1927-2007 ... **CLC 1, 2, 4, 27, 82**
　　See Landwirth, Heinz
　　See also CA 4; CAAS 257; DLB 299; EWL
　　3; RGHL

Lindbergh, Anne Morrow
　　1906-2001 .... **CLC 82**
　　See also BPFB 2; CA 17-20R; CAAS 193;
　　CANR 16, 73; DAM NOV; MTCW 1, 2;
　　MTFW 2005; SATA 33; SATA-Obit 125;
　　TUS

Lindsay, David 1878(?)-1945 .... **TCLC 15**
　　See also CA 187; CAAE 113; DLB 255;
　　FANT; SFW 4; SUFW 1

Lindsay, (Nicholas) Vachel
　　1879-1931 .... **PC 23; TCLC 17; WLC 4**
　　See also AMWS 1; CA 135; CAAE 114;
　　CANR 79; CDALB 1865-1917; DA;
　　DA3; DAC; DAM MST, POET; DLB 54;
　　EWL 3; EXPP; MAL 5; RGAL 4; SATA
　　40; WP

Linke-Poot
　　See Doeblin, Alfred

Linney, Romulus 1930- .... **CLC 51**
　　See also CA 1-4R; CAD; CANR 40, 44,
　　79; CD 5, 6; CSW; RGAL 4

Linton, Eliza Lynn 1822-1898 .... **NCLC 41**
　　See also DLB 18

Li Po 701-763 .... **CMLC 2, 86; PC 29**
　　See also PFS 20; WP

Lipsius, Justus 1547-1606 .... **LC 16**

Lipsyte, Robert 1938- .... **CLC 21**
　　See also AAYA 7, 45; CA 17-20R; CANR
　　8, 57, 146; CLR 23, 76; DA; DAC; DAM
　　MST, NOV; JRDA; LAIT 5; MAICYA 1,
　　2; SATA 5, 68, 113, 161; WYA; YAW

Lipsyte, Robert Michael
　　See Lipsyte, Robert

Lish, Gordon 1934- .... **CLC 45; SSC 18**
　　See also CA 117; CAAE 113; CANR 79,
　　151; DLB 130; INT CA-117

Lish, Gordon Jay
　　See Lish, Gordon

Lispector, Clarice 1925(?)-1977 .... **CLC 43;**
　　HLCS 2; SSC 34, 96
　　See also CA 139; CAAS 116; CANR 71;
　　CDWLB 3; DLB 113, 307; DNFS 1; EWL
　　3; FW; HW 2; LAW; RGSF 2; RGWL 2,
　　3; WLIT 1

Littell, Robert 1935(?)- .... **CLC 42**
　　See also CA 112; CAAE 109; CANR 64,
　　115, 162; CMW 4

Little, Malcolm 1925-1965
　　See Malcolm X
　　See also BW 1, 3; CA 125; CAAS 111;
　　CANR 82; DA; DA3; DAB; DAC; DAM
　　MST, MULT; MTCW 1, 2; MTFW 2005

Littlewit, Humphrey Gent.
　　See Lovecraft, H. P.

Lowell, Robert (Traill Spence, Jr.)
1917-1977 .... **CLC 1, 2, 3, 4, 5, 8, 9, 11, 15, 37, 124; PC 3; WLC 4**
See also AMW; AMWC 2; AMWR 2; CA 9-12R; CAAS 73-76; CABS 2; CAD; CANR 26, 60; CDALBS; CP 1, 2; DA; DA3; DAB; DAC; DAM MST, NOV; DLB 5, 169; EWL 3; MAL 5; MTCW 1, 2; MTFW 2005; PAB; PFS 6, 7; RGAL 4; WP

Lowenthal, Michael (Francis)
1969- .... **CLC 119**
See also CA 150; CANR 115

Lowndes, Marie Adelaide (Belloc)
1868-1947 .... **TCLC 12**
See also CAAE 107; CMW 4; DLB 70; RHW

Lowry, (Clarence) Malcolm
1909-1957 .... **SSC 31; TCLC 6, 40**
See also BPFB 2; BRWS 3; CA 131; CAAE 105; CANR 62, 105; CDBLB 1945-1960; DLB 15; EWL 3; MTCW 1, 2; MTFW 2005; RGEL 2

Lowry, Mina Gertrude 1882-1966
See Loy, Mina
See also CA 113

Lowry, Sam
See Soderbergh, Steven

Loxsmith, John
See Brunner, John (Kilian Houston)

Loy, Mina .... **CLC 28; PC 16**
See Lowry, Mina Gertrude
See also DAM POET; DLB 4, 54; PFS 20

Loyson-Bridet
See Schwob, Marcel (Mayer Andre)

Lucan 39-65 .... **CMLC 33**
See also AW 2; DLB 211; EFS 2; RGWL 2, 3

Lucas, Craig 1951- .... **CLC 64**
See also CA 137; CAD; CANR 71, 109, 142; CD 5, 6; GLL 2; MTFW 2005

Lucas, E(dward) V(errall)
1868-1938 .... **TCLC 73**
See also CA 176; DLB 98, 149, 153; SATA 20

Lucas, George 1944- .... **CLC 16**
See also AAYA 1, 23; CA 77-80; CANR 30; SATA 56

Lucas, Hans
See Godard, Jean-Luc

Lucas, Victoria
See Plath, Sylvia

Lucian c. 125-c. 180 .... **CMLC 32**
See also AW 2; DLB 176; RGWL 2, 3

Lucilius c. 180B.C.-102B.C. .... **CMLC 82**
See also DLB 211

Lucretius c. 94B.C.-c. 49B.C. .... **CMLC 48**
See also AW 2; CDWLB 1; DLB 211; EFS 2; RGWL 2, 3; WLIT 8

Ludlam, Charles 1943-1987 .... **CLC 46, 50**
See also CA 85-88; CAAS 122; CAD; CANR 72, 86; DLB 266

Ludlum, Robert 1927-2001 .... **CLC 22, 43**
See also AAYA 10, 59; BEST 89:1, 90:3; BPFB 2; CA 33-36R; CAAS 195; CANR 25, 41, 68, 105, 131; CMW 4; CPW; DA3; DAM NOV, POP; DLBY 1982; MSW; MTCW 1, 2; MTFW 2005

Ludwig, Ken 1950- .... **CLC 60**
See also CA 195; CAD; CD 6

Ludwig, Otto 1813-1865 .... **NCLC 4**
See also DLB 129

Lugones, Leopoldo 1874-1938 .... **HLCS 2; TCLC 15**
See also CA 131; CAAE 116; CANR 104; DLB 283; EWL 3; HW 1; LAW

Lu Hsun .... **SSC 20; TCLC 3**
See Shu-Jen, Chou
See also EWL 3

Lukacs, George .... **CLC 24**
See Lukacs, Gyorgy (Szegeny von)

Lukacs, Gyorgy (Szegeny von) 1885-1971
See Lukacs, George
See also CA 101; CAAS 29-32R; CANR 62; CDWLB 4; DLB 215, 242; EW 10; EWL 3; MTCW 1, 2

Luke, Peter (Ambrose Cyprian)
1919-1995 .... **CLC 38**
See also CA 81-84; CAAS 147; CANR 72; CBD; CD 5, 6; DLB 13

Lunar, Dennis
See Mungo, Raymond

Lurie, Alison 1926- ..... **CLC 4, 5, 18, 39, 175**
See also BPFB 2; CA 1-4R; CANR 2, 17, 50, 88; CN 1, 2, 3, 4, 5, 6, 7; DLB 2; MAL 5; MTCW 1; NFS 24; SATA 46, 112; TCLE 1:1

Lustig, Arnost 1926- .... **CLC 56**
See also AAYA 3; CA 69-72; CANR 47, 102; CWW 2; DLB 232, 299; EWL 3; RGHL; SATA 56

Luther, Martin 1483-1546 .... **LC 9, 37**
See also CDWLB 2; DLB 179; EW 2; RGWL 2, 3

Luxemburg, Rosa 1870(?)-1919 ..... **TCLC 63**
See also CAAE 118

Luzi, Mario (Egidio Vincenzo)
1914-2005 .... **CLC 13**
See also CA 61-64; CAAS 128; CANR 9, 70; CWW 2; DLB 128; EWL 3

L'vov, Arkady .... **CLC 59**

Lydgate, John c. 1370-1450(?) .... **LC 81**
See also BRW 1; DLB 146; RGEL 2

Lyly, John 1554(?)-1606 .... **DC 7; LC 41**
See also BRW 1; DAM DRAM; DLB 62, 167; RGEL 2

L'Ymagier
See Gourmont, Remy(-Marie-Charles) de

Lynch, B. Suarez
See Borges, Jorge Luis

Lynch, David 1946- .... **CLC 66, 162**
See also AAYA 55; CA 129; CAAE 124; CANR 111

Lynch, David Keith
See Lynch, David

Lynch, James
See Andreyev, Leonid (Nikolaevich)

Lyndsay, Sir David 1485-1555 .... **LC 20**
See also RGEL 2

Lynn, Kenneth S(chuyler)
1923-2001 .... **CLC 50**
See also CA 1-4R; CAAS 196; CANR 3, 27, 65

Lynx
See West, Rebecca

Lyons, Marcus
See Blish, James (Benjamin)

Lyotard, Jean-Francois
1924-1998 .... **TCLC 103**
See also DLB 242; EWL 3

Lyre, Pinchbeck
See Sassoon, Siegfried (Lorraine)

Lytle, Andrew (Nelson) 1902-1995 ... **CLC 22**
See also CA 9-12R; CAAS 150; CANR 70; CN 1, 2, 3, 4, 5, 6; CSW; DLB 6; DLBY 1995; RGAL 4; RHW

Lyttelton, George 1709-1773 .... **LC 10**
See also RGEL 2

Lytton of Knebworth, Baron
See Bulwer-Lytton, Edward (George Earle Lytton)

Maas, Peter 1929-2001 .... **CLC 29**
See also CA 93-96; CAAS 201; INT CA-93-96; MTCW 2; MTFW 2005

Mac A'Ghobhainn, Iain
See Smith, Iain Crichton

Macaulay, Catherine 1731-1791 .... **LC 64**
See also DLB 104, 336

Macaulay, (Emilie) Rose
1881(?)-1958 .... **TCLC 7, 44**
See also CAAE 104; DLB 36; EWL 3; RGEL 2; RHW

Macaulay, Thomas Babington
1800-1859 .... **NCLC 42**
See also BRW 4; CDBLB 1832-1890; DLB 32, 55; RGEL 2

MacBeth, George (Mann)
1932-1992 .... **CLC 2, 5, 9**
See also CA 25-28R; CAAS 136; CANR 61, 66; CP 1, 2, 3, 4, 5; DLB 40; MTCW 1; PFS 8; SATA 4; SATA-Obit 70

MacCaig, Norman (Alexander)
1910-1996 .... **CLC 36**
See also BRWS 6; CA 9-12R; CANR 3, 34; CP 1, 2, 3, 4, 5, 6; DAB; DAM POET; DLB 27; EWL 3; RGEL 2

MacCarthy, Sir (Charles Otto) Desmond
1877-1952 .... **TCLC 36**
See also CA 167

MacDiarmid, Hugh .... **CLC 2, 4, 11, 19, 63; PC 9**
See Grieve, C(hristopher) M(urray)
See also BRWS 12; CDBLB 1945-1960; CP 1, 2; DLB 20; EWL 3; RGEL 2

MacDonald, Anson
See Heinlein, Robert A.

Macdonald, Cynthia 1928- .... **CLC 13, 19**
See also CA 49-52; CANR 4, 44, 146; DLB 105

MacDonald, George 1824-1905 .... **TCLC 9, 113**
See also AAYA 57; BYA 5; CA 137; CAAE 106; CANR 80; CLR 67; DLB 18, 163, 178; FANT; MAICYA 1, 2; RGEL 2; SATA 33, 100; SFW 4; SUFW; WCH

Macdonald, John
See Millar, Kenneth

MacDonald, John D. 1916-1986 .. **CLC 3, 27, 44**
See also BPFB 2; CA 1-4R; CAAS 121; CANR 1, 19, 60; CMW 4; CPW; DAM NOV, POP; DLB 8, 306; DLBY 1986; MSW; MTCW 1, 2; MTFW 2005; SFW 4

Macdonald, John Ross
See Millar, Kenneth

Macdonald, Ross ..... **CLC 1, 2, 3, 14, 34, 41**
See Millar, Kenneth
See also AMWS 4; BPFB 2; CN 1, 2, 3; DLBD 6; MAL 5; MSW; RGAL 4

MacDougal, John
See Blish, James (Benjamin)

MacDougal, John
See Blish, James (Benjamin)

MacDowell, John
See Parks, Tim(othy Harold)

MacEwen, Gwendolyn (Margaret)
1941-1987 .... **CLC 13, 55**
See also CA 9-12R; CAAS 124; CANR 7, 22; CP 1, 2, 3, 4; DLB 53, 251; SATA 50; SATA-Obit 55

Macha, Karel Hynek 1810-1846 .... **NCLC 46**

Machado (y Ruiz), Antonio
1875-1939 .... **TCLC 3**
See also CA 174; CAAE 104; DLB 108; EW 9; EWL 3; HW 2; PFS 23; RGWL 2, 3

Machado de Assis, Joaquim Maria
1839-1908 .... **BLC 2; HLCS 2; SSC 24; TCLC 10**
See also CA 153; CAAE 107; CANR 91; DLB 307; LAW; RGSF 2; RGWL 2, 3; TWA; WLIT 1

Machaut, Guillaume de c.
1300-1377 .... **CMLC 64**
See also DLB 208

Malherbe, Francois de 1555-1628 .... **LC 5**
 See also DLB 327; GFL Beginnings to 1789
Mallarme, Stephane 1842-1898 ...... **NCLC 4,
 41; PC 4**
 See also DAM POET; DLB 217; EW 7;
 GFL 1789 to the Present; LMFS 2; RGWL
 2, 3; TWA
Mallet-Joris, Francoise 1930- .... **CLC 11**
 See also CA 65-68; CANR 17; CWW 2;
 DLB 83; EWL 3; GFL 1789 to the Present
Malley, Ern
 See McAuley, James Phillip
Mallon, Thomas 1951- .... **CLC 172**
 See also CA 110; CANR 29, 57, 92
Mallowan, Agatha Christie
 See Christie, Agatha (Mary Clarissa)
Maloff, Saul 1922- .... **CLC 5**
 See also CA 33-36R
Malone, Louis
 See MacNeice, (Frederick) Louis
Malone, Michael (Christopher)
 1942- .... **CLC 43**
 See also CA 77-80; CANR 14, 32, 57, 114
Malory, Sir Thomas 1410(?)-1471(?) . **LC 11,
 88; WLCS**
 See also BRW 1; BRWR 2; CDBLB Before
 1660; DA; DAB; DAC; DAM MST; DLB
 146; EFS 2; RGEL 2; SATA 59; SATA-
 Brief 33; TEA; WLIT 3
Malouf, David 1934- .... **CLC 28, 86**
 See also BRWS 12; CA 124; CANR 50, 76;
 CN 3, 4, 5, 6, 7; CP 1, 3, 4, 5, 6, 7; DLB
 289; EWL 3; MTCW 2; MTFW 2005;
 SSFS 24
Malouf, George Joseph David
 See Malouf, David
Malraux, (Georges-)Andre
 1901-1976 .... **CLC 1, 4, 9, 13, 15, 57**
 See also BPFB 2; CA 21-22; CAAS 69-72;
 CANR 34, 58; CAP 2; DA3; DAM NOV;
 DLB 72; EW 12; EWL 3; GFL 1789 to
 the Present; MTCW 1, 2; MTFW 2005;
 RGWL 2, 3; TWA
Malthus, Thomas Robert
 1766-1834 .... **NCLC 145**
 See also DLB 107, 158; RGEL 2
Malzberg, Barry N(athaniel) 1939- ... **CLC 7**
 See also CA 61-64; 4; CANR 16; CMW 4;
 DLB 8; SFW 4
Mamet, David 1947- .. **CLC 9, 15, 34, 46, 91,
 166; DC 4, 24**
 See also AAYA 3, 60; AMWS 14; CA 81-
 84; CABS 3; CAD; CANR 15, 41, 67, 72,
 129; CD 5, 6; DA3; DAM DRAM; DFS
 2, 3, 6, 12, 15; DLB 7; EWL 3; IDFW 4;
 MAL 5; MTCW 1, 2; MTFW 2005;
 RGAL 4
Mamet, David Alan
 See Mamet, David
Mamoulian, Rouben (Zachary)
 1897-1987 .... **CLC 16**
 See also CA 25-28R; CAAS 124; CANR 85
Mandelshtam, Osip
 See Mandelstam, Osip (Emilievich)
 See also EW 10; EWL 3; RGWL 2, 3
Mandelstam, Osip (Emilievich)
 1891(?)-1943(?) .... **PC 14; TCLC 2, 6**
 See Mandelshtam, Osip
 See also CA 150; CAAE 104; MTCW 2;
 TWA
Mander, (Mary) Jane 1877-1949 ... **TCLC 31**
 See also CA 162; RGEL 2
Mandeville, Bernard 1670-1733 .... **LC 82**
 See also DLB 101
Mandeville, Sir John fl. 1350- ...... **CMLC 19**
 See also DLB 146
Mandiargues, Andre Pieyre de .... **CLC 41**
 See Pieyre de Mandiargues, Andre
 See also DLB 83

Mandrake, Ethel Belle
 See Thurman, Wallace (Henry)
Mangan, James Clarence
 1803-1849 .... **NCLC 27**
 See also RGEL 2
Maniere, J.-E.
 See Giraudoux, Jean(-Hippolyte)
Mankiewicz, Herman (Jacob)
 1897-1953 .... **TCLC 85**
 See also CA 169; CAAE 120; DLB 26;
 IDFW 3, 4
Manley, (Mary) Delariviere
 1672(?)-1724 .... **LC 1, 42**
 See also DLB 39, 80; RGEL 2
Mann, Abel
 See Creasey, John
Mann, Emily 1952- .... **DC 7**
 See also CA 130; CAD; CANR 55; CD 5,
 6; CWD; DLB 266
Mann, (Luiz) Heinrich 1871-1950 ... **TCLC 9**
 See also CA 164, 181; CAAE 106; DLB
 66, 118; EW 8; EWL 3; RGWL 2, 3
Mann, (Paul) Thomas 1875-1955 . **SSC 5, 80,
 82; TCLC 2, 8, 14, 21, 35, 44, 60, 168;
 WLC 4**
 See also BPFB 2; CA 128; CAAE 104;
 CANR 133; CDWLB 2; DA; DA3; DAB;
 DAC; DAM MST, NOV; DLB 66, 331;
 EW 9; EWL 3; GLL 1; LATS 1:1; LMFS
 1; MTCW 1, 2; MTFW 2005; NFS 17;
 RGSF 2; RGWL 2, 3; SSFS 4, 9; TWA
Mannheim, Karl 1893-1947 .... **TCLC 65**
 See also CA 204
Manning, David
 See Faust, Frederick (Schiller)
Manning, Frederic 1882-1935 .... **TCLC 25**
 See also CA 216; CAAE 124; DLB 260
Manning, Olivia 1915-1980 .... **CLC 5, 19**
 See also CA 5-8R; CAAS 101; CANR 29;
 CN 1, 2; EWL 3; FW; MTCW 1; RGEL 2
Mannyng, Robert c. 1264-c.
 1340 .... **CMLC 83**
 See also DLB 146
Mano, D. Keith 1942- .... **CLC 2, 10**
 See also CA 25-28R; 6; CANR 26, 57; DLB
 6
Mansfield, Katherine .... **SSC 9, 23, 38, 81;
 TCLC 2, 8, 39, 164; WLC 4**
 See Beauchamp, Kathleen Mansfield
 See also BPFB 2; BRW 7; DAB; DLB 162;
 EWL 3; EXPS; FW; GLL 1; RGEL 2;
 RGSF 2; SSFS 2, 8, 10, 11; WWE 1
Manso, Peter 1940- .... **CLC 39**
 See also CA 29-32R; CANR 44, 156
Mantecon, Juan Jimenez
 See Jimenez (Mantecon), Juan Ramon
Mantel, Hilary 1952- .... **CLC 144**
 See also CA 125; CANR 54, 101, 161; CN
 5, 6, 7; DLB 271; RHW
Mantel, Hilary Mary
 See Mantel, Hilary
Manton, Peter
 See Creasey, John
Man Without a Spleen, A
 See Chekhov, Anton (Pavlovich)
Manzano, Juan Francisco
 1797(?)-1854 .... **NCLC 155**
Manzoni, Alessandro 1785-1873 ... **NCLC 29,
 98**
 See also EW 5; RGWL 2, 3; TWA; WLIT 7
Map, Walter 1140-1209 .... **CMLC 32**
Mapu, Abraham (ben Jekutiel)
 1808-1867 .... **NCLC 18**
Mara, Sally
 See Queneau, Raymond
Maracle, Lee 1950- .... **NNAL**
 See also CA 149
Marat, Jean Paul 1743-1793 .... **LC 10**

Marcel, Gabriel Honore 1889-1973 . **CLC 15**
 See also CA 102; CAAS 45-48; EWL 3;
 MTCW 1, 2
March, William .... **TCLC 96**
 See Campbell, William Edward March
 See also CA 216; DLB 9, 86, 316; MAL 5
Marchbanks, Samuel
 See Davies, Robertson
 See also CCA 1
Marchi, Giacomo
 See Bassani, Giorgio
Marcus Aurelius
 See Aurelius, Marcus
 See also AW 2
Marguerite
 See de Navarre, Marguerite
Marguerite d'Angouleme
 See de Navarre, Marguerite
 See also GFL Beginnings to 1789
Marguerite de Navarre
 See de Navarre, Marguerite
 See also RGWL 2, 3
Margulies, Donald 1954- .... **CLC 76**
 See also AAYA 57; CA 200; CD 6; DFS 13;
 DLB 228
Marias, Javier 1951- .... **CLC 239**
 See also CA 167; CANR 109, 139; DLB
 322; HW 2; MTFW 2005
Marie de France c. 12th cent. - ..... **CMLC 8;
 PC 22**
 See also DLB 208; FW; RGWL 2, 3
Marie de l'Incarnation 1599-1672 ...... **LC 10**
Marier, Captain Victor
 See Griffith, D(avid Lewelyn) W(ark)
Mariner, Scott
 See Pohl, Frederik
Marinetti, Filippo Tommaso
 1876-1944 .... **TCLC 10**
 See also CAAE 107; DLB 114, 264; EW 9;
 EWL 3; WLIT 7
Marivaux, Pierre Carlet de Chamblain de
 1688-1763 .... **DC 7; LC 4, 123**
 See also DLB 314; GFL Beginnings to
 1789; RGWL 2, 3; TWA
Markandaya, Kamala .... **CLC 8, 38**
 See Taylor, Kamala
 See also BYA 13; CN 1, 2, 3, 4, 5, 6, 7;
 DLB 323; EWL 3
Markfield, Wallace (Arthur)
 1926-2002 .... **CLC 8**
 See also CA 69-72; 3; CAAS 208; CN 1, 2,
 3, 4, 5, 6, 7; DLB 2, 28; DLBY 2002
Markham, Edwin 1852-1940 .... **TCLC 47**
 See also CA 160; DLB 54, 186; MAL 5;
 RGAL 4
Markham, Robert
 See Amis, Kingsley
Marks, J.
 See Highwater, Jamake (Mamake)
Marks-Highwater, J.
 See Highwater, Jamake (Mamake)
Markson, David M. 1927- .... **CLC 67**
 See also CA 49-52; CANR 1, 91, 158; CN
 5, 6
Markson, David Merrill
 See Markson, David M.
Marlatt, Daphne (Buckle) 1942- .... **CLC 168**
 See also CA 25-28R; CANR 17, 39; CN 6,
 7; CP 4, 5, 6, 7; CWP; DLB 60; FW
Marley, Bob .... **CLC 17**
 See Marley, Robert Nesta
Marley, Robert Nesta 1945-1981
 See Marley, Bob
 See also CA 107; CAAS 103

Mattheson, Rodney
See Creasey, John

Matthews, (James) Brander
1852-1929 .... **TCLC 95**
See also CA 181; DLB 71, 78; DLBD 13

Matthews, Greg 1949- .... **CLC 45**
See also CA 135

Matthews, William (Procter III)
1942-1997 .... **CLC 40**
See also AMWS 9; CA 29-32R; 18; CAAS
162; CANR 12, 57; CP 2, 3, 4, 5, 6; DLB
5

Matthias, John (Edward) 1941- .... **CLC 9**
See also CA 33-36R; CANR 56; CP 4, 5, 6,
7

Matthiessen, F(rancis) O(tto)
1902-1950 .... **TCLC 100**
See also CA 185; DLB 63; MAL 5

Matthiessen, Peter 1927- ... **CLC 5, 7, 11, 32,
64**
See also AAYA 6, 40; AMWS 5; ANW;
BEST 90:4; BPFB 2; CA 9-12R; CANR
21, 50, 73, 100, 138; CN 1, 2, 3, 4, 5, 6,
7; DA3; DAM NOV; DLB 6, 173, 275;
MAL 5; MTCW 1, 2; MTFW 2005; SATA
27

Maturin, Charles Robert
1780(?)-1824 .... **NCLC 6, 169**
See also BRWS 8; DLB 178; GL 3; HGG;
LMFS 1; RGEL 2; SUFW

Matute (Ausejo), Ana Maria 1925- .. **CLC 11**
See also CA 89-92; CANR 129; CWW 2;
DLB 322; EWL 3; MTCW 1; RGSF 2

Maugham, W. S.
See Maugham, W(illiam) Somerset

Maugham, W(illiam) Somerset
1874-1965 .. **CLC 1, 11, 15, 67, 93; SSC
8, 94; WLC 4**
See also AAYA 55; BPFB 2; BRW 6; CA
5-8R; CAAS 25-28R; CANR 40, 127;
CDBLB 1914-1945; CMW 4; DA; DA3;
DAB; DAC; DAM DRAM, MST, NOV;
DFS 22; DLB 10, 36, 77, 100, 162, 195;
EWL 3; LAIT 3; MTCW 1, 2; MTFW
2005; RGEL 2; RGSF 2; SATA
54; SSFS 17

Maugham, William Somerset
See Maugham, W(illiam) Somerset

Maupassant, (Henri Rene Albert) Guy de
1850-1893 . **NCLC 1, 42, 83; SSC 1, 64;
WLC 4**
See also BYA 14; DA; DA3; DAB; DAC;
DAM MST; DLB 123; EW 7; EXPS; GFL
1789 to the Present; LAIT 2; LMFS 1;
RGSF 2; RGWL 2, 3; SSFS 4, 21; SUFW;
TWA

Maupin, Armistead 1944- .... **CLC 95**
See also CA 130; CAAE 125; CANR 58,
101; CPW; DA3; DAM POP; DLB 278;
GLL 1; INT CA-130; MTCW 2; MTFW
2005

Maupin, Armistead Jones, Jr.
See Maupin, Armistead

Maurhut, Richard
See Traven, B.

Mauriac, Claude 1914-1996 .... **CLC 9**
See also CA 89-92; CAAS 152; CWW 2;
DLB 83; EWL 3; GFL 1789 to the Present

Mauriac, Francois (Charles)
1885-1970 .... **CLC 4, 9, 56; SSC 24**
See also CA 25-28; CAP 2; DLB 65, 331;
EW 10; EWL 3; GFL 1789 to the Present;
MTCW 1, 2; MTFW 2005; RGWL 2, 3;
TWA

Mavor, Osborne Henry 1888-1951
See Bridie, James
See also CAAE 104

Maxwell, Glyn 1962- .... **CLC 238**
See also CA 154; CANR 88; CP 6, 7; PFS
23

Maxwell, William (Keepers, Jr.)
1908-2000 .... **CLC 19**
See also AMWS 8; CA 93-96; CAAS 189;
CANR 54, 95; CN 1, 2, 3, 4, 5, 6, 7; DLB
218, 278; DLBY 1980; INT CA-93-96;
MAL 5; SATA-Obit 128

May, Elaine 1932- .... **CLC 16**
See also CA 142; CAAE 124; CAD; CWD;
DLB 44

Mayakovski, Vladimir (Vladimirovich)
1893-1930 .... **TCLC 4, 18**
See Maiakovskii, Vladimir; Mayakovsky,
Vladimir
See also CA 158; CAAE 104; EWL 3;
MTCW 2; MTFW 2005; SFW 4; TWA

Mayakovsky, Vladimir
See Mayakovski, Vladimir (Vladimirovich)
See also EW 11; WP

Mayhew, Henry 1812-1887 .... **NCLC 31**
See also DLB 18, 55, 190

Mayle, Peter 1939(?)- .... **CLC 89**
See also CA 139; CANR 64, 109

Maynard, Joyce 1953- .... **CLC 23**
See also CA 129; CAAE 111; CANR 64

Mayne, William (James Carter)
1928- .... **CLC 12**
See also AAYA 20; CA 9-12R; CANR 37,
80, 100; CLR 25, 123; FANT; JRDA;
MAICYA 1, 2; MAICYAS 1; SAAS 11;
SATA 6, 68, 122; SUFW 2; YAW

Mayo, Jim
See L'Amour, Louis

Maysles, Albert 1926- .... **CLC 16**
See also CA 29-32R

Maysles, David 1932-1987 .... **CLC 16**
See also CA 191

Mazer, Norma Fox 1931- .... **CLC 26**
See also AAYA 5, 36; BYA 1, 8; CA 69-72;
CANR 12, 32, 66, 129; CLR 23; JRDA;
MAICYA 1, 2; SAAS 1; SATA 24, 67,
105, 168; WYA; YAW

Mazzini, Guiseppe 1805-1872 .... **NCLC 34**

McAlmon, Robert (Menzies)
1895-1956 .... **TCLC 97**
See also CA 168; CAAE 107; DLB 4, 45;
DLBD 15; GLL 1

McAuley, James Phillip 1917-1976 .. **CLC 45**
See also CA 97-100; CP 1, 2; DLB 260;
RGEL 2

McBain, Ed
See Hunter, Evan
See also MSW

McBrien, William (Augustine)
1930- .... **CLC 44**
See also CA 107; CANR 90

McCabe, Patrick 1955- .... **CLC 133**
See also BRWS 9; CA 130; CANR 50, 90;
CN 6, 7; DLB 194

McCaffrey, Anne 1926- .... **CLC 17**
See also AAYA 6, 34; AITN 2; BEST 89:2;
BPFB 2; BYA 5; CA 227; 25-28R, 227;
CANR 15, 35, 55, 96; CLR 49; CPW;
DA3; DAM NOV, POP; DLB 8; JRDA;
MAICYA 1, 2; MTCW 1, 2; MTFW 2005;
SAAS 11; SATA 8, 70, 116, 152; SATA-
Essay 152; SFW 4; SUFW 2; WYA; YAW

McCaffrey, Anne Inez
See McCaffrey, Anne

McCall, Nathan 1955(?)- .... **CLC 86**
See also AAYA 59; BW 3; CA 146; CANR
88

McCann, Arthur
See Campbell, John W(ood, Jr.)

McCann, Edson
See Pohl, Frederik

McCarthy, Charles, Jr.
See McCarthy, Cormac

McCarthy, Cormac 1933- .... **CLC 4, 57, 101,
204**
See also AAYA 41; AMWS 8; BPFB 2; CA
13-16R; CANR 10, 42, 69, 101, 161; CN
6, 7; CPW; CSW; DA3; DAM POP; DLB
6, 143, 256; EWL 3; LATS 1:2; MAL 5;
MTCW 2; MTFW 2005; TCLE 1:2;
TCWW 2

McCarthy, Mary (Therese)
1912-1989 .. **CLC 1, 3, 5, 14, 24, 39, 59;
SSC 24**
See also AMW; BPFB 2; CA 5-8R; CAAS
129; CANR 16, 50, 64; CN 1, 2, 3, 4;
DA3; DLB 2; DLBY 1981; EWL 3; FW;
INT CANR-16; MAL 5; MBL; MTCW 1,
2; MTFW 2005; RGAL 4; TUS

McCartney, James Paul
See McCartney, Paul

McCartney, Paul 1942- .... **CLC 12, 35**
See also CA 146; CANR 111

McCauley, Stephen (D.) 1955- .... **CLC 50**
See also CA 141

McClaren, Peter .... **CLC 70**

McClure, Michael (Thomas) 1932- ... **CLC 6,
10**
See also BG 1:3; CA 21-24R; CAD; CANR
17, 46, 77, 131; CD 5, 6; CP 1, 2, 3, 4, 5,
6, 7; DLB 16; WP

McCorkle, Jill (Collins) 1958- .... **CLC 51**
See also CA 121; CANR 113; CSW; DLB
234; DLBY 1987; SSFS 24

McCourt, Frank 1930- .... **CLC 109**
See also AAYA 61; AMWS 12; CA 157;
CANR 97, 138; MTFW 2005; NCFS 1

McCourt, James 1941- .... **CLC 5**
See also CA 57-60; CANR 98, 152

McCourt, Malachy 1931- .... **CLC 119**
See also SATA 126

McCoy, Horace (Stanley)
1897-1955 .... **TCLC 28**
See also AMWS 13; CA 155; CAAE 108;
CMW 4; DLB 9

McCrae, John 1872-1918 .... **TCLC 12**
See also CAAE 109; DLB 92; PFS 5

McCreigh, James
See Pohl, Frederik

McCullers, (Lula) Carson (Smith)
1917-1967 .... **CLC 1, 4, 10, 12, 48, 100;
SSC 9, 24, 99; TCLC 155; WLC 4**
See also AAYA 21; AMW; AMWC 2; BPFB
2; CA 5-8R; CAAS 25-28R; CABS 1, 3;
CANR 18, 132; CDALB 1941-1968; CN
DA3; DAB; DAC; DAM MST, NOV;
DFS 5, 18; DLB 2, 7, 173, 228; EWL 3;
EXPS; FW; GLL 1; LAIT 3, 4; MAL 5;
MBL; MTCW 1, 2; MTFW 2005; NFS 6,
13; RGAL 4; RGSF 2; SATA 27; SSFS 5;
TUS; YAW

McCulloch, John Tyler
See Burroughs, Edgar Rice

McCullough, Colleen 1937- ...... **CLC 27, 107**
See also AAYA 36; BPFB 2; CA 81-84;
CANR 17, 46, 67, 98, 139; CPW; DA3;
DAM NOV, POP; MTCW 1, 2; MTFW
2005; RHW

McCunn, Ruthanne Lum 1946- .... **AAL**
See also CA 119; CANR 43, 96; DLB 312;
LAIT 2; SATA 63

McDermott, Alice 1953- .... **CLC 90**
See also CA 109; CANR 40, 90, 126; CN
7; DLB 292; MTFW 2005; NFS 23

McElroy, Joseph 1930- .... **CLC 5, 47**
See also CA 17-20R; CANR 149; CN 3, 4,
5, 6, 7

McElroy, Joseph Prince
See McElroy, Joseph

Mendelsohn, Jane 1965- .... **CLC 99**
See also CA 154; CANR 94

Mendoza, Inigo Lopez de
See Santillana, Inigo Lopez de Mendoza, Marques de

Menton, Francisco de
See Chin, Frank (Chew, Jr.)

Mercer, David 1928-1980 .... **CLC 5**
See also CA 9-12R; CAAS 102; CANR 23; CBD; DAM DRAM; DLB 13, 310; MTCW 1; RGEL 2

Merchant, Paul
See Ellison, Harlan

Meredith, George 1828-1909 .. **PC 60; TCLC 17, 43**
See also CA 153; CAAE 117; CANR 80; CDBLB 1832-1890; DAM POET; DLB 18, 35, 57, 159; RGEL 2; TEA

Meredith, William 1919-2007 ...... **CLC 4, 13, 22, 55; PC 28**
See also CA 9-12R; 14; CANR 6, 40, 129; CP 1, 2, 3, 4, 5, 6, 7; DAM POET; DLB 5; MAL 5

Meredith, William Morris
See Meredith, William

Merezhkovsky, Dmitrii Sergeevich
See Merezhkovsky, Dmitry Sergeyevich
See also DLB 295

Merezhkovsky, Dmitry Sergeevich
See Merezhkovsky, Dmitry Sergeyevich
See also EWL 3

Merezhkovsky, Dmitry Sergeyevich 1865-1941 .... **TCLC 29**
See Merezhkovsky, Dmitrii Sergeevich; Merezhkovsky, Dmitry Sergeevich
See also CA 169

Merimee, Prosper 1803-1870 ... **NCLC 6, 65; SSC 7, 77**
See also DLB 119, 192; EW 6; EXPS; GFL 1789 to the Present; RGSF 2; RGWL 2, 3; SSFS 8; SUFW

Merkin, Daphne 1954- .... **CLC 44**
See also CA 123

Merleau-Ponty, Maurice 1908-1961 .... **TCLC 156**
See also CA 114; CAAS 89-92; DLB 296; GFL 1789 to the Present

Merlin, Arthur
See Blish, James (Benjamin)

Mernissi, Fatima 1940- .... **CLC 171**
See also CA 152; FW

Merrill, James 1926-1995 ...... **CLC 2, 3, 6, 8, 13, 18, 34, 91; PC 28; TCLC 173**
See also AMWS 3; CA 13-16R; CAAS 147; CANR 10, 49, 63, 108; CP 1, 2, 3, 4; DA3; DAM POET; DLB 5, 165; DLBY 1985; EWL 3; INT CANR-10; MAL 5; MTCW 1, 2; MTFW 2005; PAB; PFS 23; RGAL 4

Merrill, James Ingram
See Merrill, James

Merriman, Alex
See Silverberg, Robert

Merriman, Brian 1747-1805 .... **NCLC 70**

Merritt, E. B.
See Waddington, Miriam

Merton, Thomas (James) 1915-1968 . **CLC 1, 3, 11, 34, 83; PC 10**
See also AAYA 61; AMWS 8; CA 5-8R; CAAS 25-28R; CANR 22, 53, 111, 131; DA3; DLB 48; DLBY 1981; MAL 5; MTCW 1, 2; MTFW 2005

Merwin, W.S. 1927- ..... **CLC 1, 2, 3, 5, 8, 13, 18, 45, 88; PC 45**
See also AMWS 3; CA 13-16R; CANR 15, 51, 112, 140; CP 1, 2, 3, 4, 5, 6, 7; DA3; DAM POET; DLB 5; EWL 3; INT CANR-15; MAL 5; MTCW 1, 2; MTFW 2005; PAB; PFS 5, 15; RGAL 4

Metastasio, Pietro 1698-1782 .... **LC 115**
See also RGWL 2, 3

Metcalf, John 1938- .... **CLC 37; SSC 43**
See also CA 113; CN 4, 5, 6, 7; DLB 60; RGSF 2; TWA

Metcalf, Suzanne
See Baum, L(yman) Frank

Mew, Charlotte (Mary) 1870-1928 .. **TCLC 8**
See also CA 189; CAAE 105; DLB 19, 135; RGEL 2

Mewshaw, Michael 1943- .... **CLC 9**
See also CA 53-56; CANR 7, 47, 147; DLBY 1980

Meyer, Conrad Ferdinand 1825-1898 .... **NCLC 81; SSC 30**
See also DLB 129; EW; RGWL 2, 3

Meyer, Gustav 1868-1932
See Meyrink, Gustav
See also CA 190; CAAE 117

Meyer, June
See Jordan, June

Meyer, Lynn
See Slavitt, David R(ytman)

Meyers, Jeffrey 1939- .... **CLC 39**
See also CA 186; 73-76, 186; CANR 54, 102, 159; DLB 111

Meynell, Alice (Christina Gertrude Thompson) 1847-1922 .... **TCLC 6**
See also CA 177; CAAE 104; DLB 19, 98; RGEL 2

Meyrink, Gustav .... **TCLC 21**
See Meyer, Gustav
See also DLB 81; EWL 3

Michaels, Leonard 1933-2003 ..... **CLC 6, 25; SSC 16**
See also AMWS 16; CA 61-64; CAAS 216; CANR 21, 62, 119; CN 3, 45, 6, 7; DLB 130; MTCW 1; TCLE 1:2

Michaux, Henri 1899-1984 .... **CLC 8, 19**
See also CA 85-88; CAAS 114; DLB 258; EWL 3; GFL 1789 to the Present; RGWL 2, 3

Micheaux, Oscar (Devereaux) 1884-1951 .... **TCLC 76**
See also BW 3; CA 174; DLB 50; TCWW 2

Michelangelo 1475-1564 .... **LC 12**
See also AAYA 43

Michelet, Jules 1798-1874 .... **NCLC 31**
See also EW 5; GFL 1789 to the Present

Michels, Robert 1876-1936 .... **TCLC 88**
See also CA 212

Michener, James A. 1907(?)-1997 . **CLC 1, 5, 11, 29, 60, 109**
See also AAYA 27; AITN 1; BEST 90:1; BPFB 2; CA 5-8R; CAAS 161; CANR 21, 45, 68; CN 1, 2, 3, 4, 5, 6; CPW; DA3; DAM NOV, POP; DLB 6; MAL 5; MTCW 1, 2; MTFW 2005; RHW; TCWW 1, 2

Mickiewicz, Adam 1798-1855 . **NCLC 3, 101; PC 38**
See also EW 5; RGWL 2, 3

Middleton, (John) Christopher 1926- .... **CLC 13**
See also CA 13-16R; CANR 29, 54, 117; CP 1, 2, 3, 4, 5, 6, 7; DLB 40

Middleton, Richard (Barham) 1882-1911 .... **TCLC 56**
See also CA 187; DLB 156; HGG

Middleton, Stanley 1919- .... **CLC 7, 38**
See also CA 25-28R; 23; CANR 21, 46, 81, 157; CN 1, 2, 3, 4, 5, 6, 7; DLB 14, 326

Middleton, Thomas 1580-1627 ...... **DC 5; LC 33, 123**
See also BRW 2; DAM DRAM, MST; DFS 18, 22; DLB 58; RGEL 2

Mieville, China 1972(?)- .... **CLC 235**
See also AAYA 52; CA 196; CANR 138; MTFW 2005

Migueis, Jose Rodrigues 1901-1980 . **CLC 10**
See also DLB 287

Mikszath, Kalman 1847-1910 .... **TCLC 31**
See also CA 170

Miles, Jack .... **CLC 100**
See also CA 200

Miles, John Russiano
See Miles, Jack

Miles, Josephine (Louise) 1911-1985 .... **CLC 1, 2, 14, 34, 39**
See also CA 1-4R; CAAS 116; CANR 2, 55; CP 1, 2, 3, 4; DAM POET; DLB 48; MAL 5; TCLE 1:2

Militant
See Sandburg, Carl (August)

Mill, Harriet (Hardy) Taylor 1807-1858 .... **NCLC 102**
See also FW

Mill, John Stuart 1806-1873 ... **NCLC 11, 58, 179**
See also CDBLB 1832-1890; DLB 55, 190, 262; FW 1; RGEL 2; TEA

Millar, Kenneth 1915-1983 .... **CLC 14**
See Macdonald, Ross
See also CA 9-12R; CAAS 110; CANR 16, 63, 107; CMW 4; CPW; DAM POP; DLB 2, 226; DLBD 6; DLBY 1983; MTCW 1, 2; MTFW 2005

Millay, E. Vincent
See Millay, Edna St. Vincent

Millay, Edna St. Vincent 1892-1950 ..... **PC 6, 61; TCLC 4, 49, 169; WLCS**
See Boyd, Nancy
See also AMW; CA 130; CAAE 104; CDALB 1917-1929; DA; DA3; DAB; DAC; DAM MST, POET; DLB 45, 249; EWL 3; EXPP; FL 1:6; MAL 5; MBL; MTCW 1, 2; MTFW 2005; PAB; PFS 3, 17; RGAL 4; TUS; WP

Miller, Arthur 1915-2005 ..... **CLC 1, 2, 6, 10, 15, 26, 47, 78, 179; DC 1; WLC 4**
See also AAYA 15; AITN 1; AMW; AMWC 1; CA 1-4R; CAAS 236; CABS 3; CAD; CANR 2, 30, 54, 76, 132; CD 5, 6; CDALB 1941-1968; DA; DA3; DAB; DAC; DAM DRAM, MST; DFS 1, 3, 8; DLB 7, 266; EWL 3; LAIT 1, 4; LATS 1:2; MAL 5; MTCW 1, 2; MTFW 2005; RGAL 4; RGHL; TUS; WYAS 1

Miller, Henry (Valentine) 1891-1980 .... **CLC 1, 2, 4, 9, 14, 43, 84; WLC 4**
See also AMW; BPFB 2; CA 9-12R; CAAS 97-100; CANR 33, 64; CDALB 1929-1941; CN 1, 2; DA; DA3; DAB; DAC; DAM MST, NOV; DLB 4, 9; DLBY 1980; EWL 3; MAL 5; MTCW 1, 2; MTFW 2005; RGAL 4; TUS

Miller, Hugh 1802-1856 .... **NCLC 143**
See also DLB 190

Miller, Jason 1939(?)-2001 .... **CLC 2**
See also AITN 1; CA 73-76; CAAS 197; CAD; CANR 130; DFS 12; DLB 7

Miller, Sue 1943- .... **CLC 44**
See also AMWS 12; BEST 90:3; CA 139; CANR 59, 91, 128; DA3; DAM POP; DLB 143

Miller, Walter M(ichael, Jr.) 1923-1996 .... **CLC 4, 30**
See also BPFB 2; CA 85-88; CANR 108; DLB 8; SCFW 1, 2; SFW 4

Millett, Kate 1934- .... **CLC 67**
See also AITN 1; CA 73-76; CANR 32, 53, 76, 110; DA3; DLB 246; FW; GLL 1; MTCW 1, 2; MTFW 2005

6, 7; CPW; DA; DA3; DAB; DAC; DAM MST, MULT, NOV, POP; DLB 6, 33, 143, 331; DLBY 1981; EWL 3; EXPN; FL 1:6; FW; GL 3; LAIT 2, 4; LATS 1:2; LMFS 2; MAL 5; MBL; MTCW 1, 2; MTFW 2005; NFS 1, 6, 8, 14; RGAL 4; RHW; SATA 57, 144; SSFS 5; TCLE 1:2; TUS; YAW

Morrison, Van 1945- .... **CLC 21**
See also CA 168; CAAE 116

Morrissy, Mary 1957- .... **CLC 99**
See also CA 205; DLB 267

Mortimer, John 1923- .... **CLC 28, 43**
See also CA 13-16R; CANR 21, 69, 109; CBD; CD 5, 6; CDBLB 1960 to Present; CMW 4; CN 5, 6, 7; CPW; DA3; DAM DRAM, POP; DLB 13, 245, 271; INT CANR-21; MSW; MTCW 1, 2; MTFW 2005; RGEL 2

Mortimer, Penelope (Ruth)
1918-1999 .... **CLC 5**
See also CA 57-60; CAAS 187; CANR 45, 88; CN 1, 2, 3, 4, 5, 6

Mortimer, Sir John
See Mortimer, John

Morton, Anthony
See Creasey, John

Morton, Thomas 1579(?)-1647(?) .... **LC 72**
See also DLB 24; RGEL 2

Mosca, Gaetano 1858-1941 .... **TCLC 75**

Moses, Daniel David 1952- .... **NNAL**
See also CA 186; CANR 160; DLB 334

Mosher, Howard Frank 1943- .... **CLC 62**
See also CA 139; CANR 65, 115

Mosley, Nicholas 1923- .... **CLC 43, 70**
See also CA 69-72; CANR 41, 60, 108, 158; CN 1, 2, 3, 4, 5, 6, 7; DLB 14, 207

Mosley, Walter 1952- .... **BLCS; CLC 97, 184**
See also AAYA 57; AMWS 13; BPFB 2; BW 2; CA 142; CANR 57, 92, 136; CMW 4; CN 7; CPW; DA3; DAM MULT, POP; DLB 306; MSW; MTCW 2; MTFW 2005

Moss, Howard 1922-1987 . **CLC 7, 14, 45, 50**
See also CA 1-4R; CAAS 123; CANR 1, 44; CP 1, 2, 3, 4; DAM POET; DLB 5

Mossgiel, Rab
See Burns, Robert

Motion, Andrew 1952- .... **CLC 47**
See also BRWS 7; CA 146; CANR 90, 142; CP 4, 5, 6, 7; DLB 40; MTFW 2005

Motion, Andrew Peter
See Motion, Andrew

Motley, Willard (Francis)
1909-1965 .... **CLC 18**
See also BW 1; CA 117; CAAS 106; CANR 88; DLB 76, 143

Motoori, Norinaga 1730-1801 .... **NCLC 45**

Mott, Michael (Charles Alston)
1930- .... **CLC 15, 34**
See also CA 5-8R; 7; CANR 7, 29

Mountain Wolf Woman 1884-1960 . **CLC 92; NNAL**
See also CA 144; CANR 90

Moure, Erin 1955- .... **CLC 88**
See also CA 113; CP 5, 6, 7; CWP; DLB 60

Mourning Dove 1885(?)-1936 .... **NNAL**
See also CA 144; CANR 90; DAM MULT; DLB 175, 221

Mowat, Farley 1921- .... **CLC 26**
See also AAYA 1, 50; BYA 2; CA 1-4R; CANR 4, 24, 42, 68, 108; CLR 20; CPW; DAC; DAM MST; DLB 68; INT CANR-24; JRDA; MAICYA 1, 2; MTCW 1, 2; MTFW 2005; SATA 3, 55; YAW

Mowatt, Anna Cora 1819-1870 ..... **NCLC 74**
See also RGAL 4

Moyers, Bill 1934- .... **CLC 74**
See also AITN 2; CA 61-64; CANR 31, 52, 148

Mphahlele, Es'kia
See Mphahlele, Ezekiel
See also AFW; CDWLB 3; CN 4, 5, 6; DLB 125, 225; RGSF 2; SSFS 11

Mphahlele, Ezekiel 1919- ... **BLC 3; CLC 25, 133**
See Mphahlele, Es'kia
See also BW 2, 3; CA 81-84; CANR 26, 76; CN 1, 2, 3; DA3; DAM MULT; EWL 3; MTCW 2; MTFW 2005; SATA 119

Mqhayi, S(amuel) E(dward) K(rune Loliwe)
1875-1945 .... **BLC 3; TCLC 25**
See also CA 153; CANR 87; DAM MULT

Mrozek, Slawomir 1930- .... **CLC 3, 13**
See also CA 13-16R; 10; CANR 29; CD-WLB 4; CWW 2; DLB 232; EWL 3; MTCW 1

Mrs. Belloc-Lowndes
See Lowndes, Marie Adelaide (Belloc)

Mrs. Fairstar
See Horne, Richard Henry Hengist

M'Taggart, John M'Taggart Ellis
See McTaggart, John McTaggart Ellis

Mtwa, Percy (?)- .... **CLC 47**
See also CD 6

Mueller, Lisel 1924- .... **CLC 13, 51; PC 33**
See also CA 93-96; CP 6, 7; DLB 105; PFS 9, 13

Muggeridge, Malcolm (Thomas)
1903-1990 .... **TCLC 120**
See also AITN 1; CA 101; CANR 33, 63; MTCW 1, 2

Muhammad 570-632 .... **WLCS**
See also DA; DAB; DAC; DAM MST; DLB 311

Muir, Edwin 1887-1959 . **PC 49; TCLC 2, 87**
See Moore, Edward
See also BRWS 6; CA 193; CAAE 104; DLB 20, 100, 191; EWL 3; RGEL 2

Muir, John 1838-1914 .... **TCLC 28**
See also AMWS 9; ANW; CA 165; DLB 186, 275

Mujica Lainez, Manuel 1910-1984 ... **CLC 31**
See Lainez, Manuel Mujica
See also CA 81-84; CAAS 112; CANR 32; EWL 3; HW 1

Mukherjee, Bharati 1940- ..... **AAL; CLC 53, 115, 235; SSC 38**
See also AAYA 46; BEST 89:2; CA 232; 107, 232; CANR 45, 72, 128; CN 5, 6, 7; DAM NOV; DLB 60, 218, 323; DNFS 1, 2; EWL 3; FW; MAL 5; MTCW 1, 2; MTFW 2005; RGAL 4; RGSF 2; SSFS 7, 24; TUS; WWE 1

Muldoon, Paul 1951- .... **CLC 32, 72, 166**
See also BRWS 4; CA 129; CAAE 113; CANR 52, 91; CP 2, 3, 4, 5, 6, 7; DAM POET; DLB 40; INT CA-129; PFS 7, 22; TCLE 1:2

Mulisch, Harry (Kurt Victor)
1927- .... **CLC 42**
See also CA 9-12R; CANR 6, 26, 56, 110; CWW 2; DLB 299; EWL 3

Mull, Martin 1943- .... **CLC 17**
See also CA 105

Muller, Wilhelm .... **NCLC 73**

Mulock, Dinah Maria
See Craik, Dinah Maria (Mulock)
See also RGEL 2

Multatuli 1820-1881 .... **NCLC 165**
See also RGWL 2, 3

Munday, Anthony 1560-1633 .... **LC 87**
See also DLB 62, 172; RGEL 2

Munford, Robert 1737(?)-1783 .... **LC 5**
See also DLB 31

Mungo, Raymond 1946- .... **CLC 72**
See also CA 49-52; CANR 2

Munro, Alice 1931- .... **CLC 6, 10, 19, 50, 95, 222; SSC 3, 95; WLCS**
See also AITN 2; BPFB 2; CA 33-36R; CANR 33, 53, 75, 114; CCA 1; CN 1, 2, 3, 4, 5, 6, 7; DA3; DAC; DAM MST, NOV; DLB 53; EWL 3; MTCW 1, 2; MTFW 2005; RGEL 2; RGSF 2; SATA 29; SSFS 5, 13, 19; TCLE 1:2; WWE 1

Munro, H(ector) H(ugh) 1870-1916
See Saki
See also AAYA 56; CA 130; CAAE 104; CANR 104; CDBLB 1890-1914; DA; DA3; DAB; DAC; DAM MST, NOV; DLB 34, 162; EXPS; MTCW 1, 2; MTFW 2005; RGEL 2; SSFS 15

Murakami, Haruki 1949- .... **CLC 150**
See Murakami Haruki
See also CA 165; CANR 102, 146; MJW; RGWL 3; SFW 4; SSFS 23

Murakami Haruki
See Murakami, Haruki
See also CWW 2; DLB 182; EWL 3

Murasaki, Lady
See Murasaki Shikibu

Murasaki Shikibu 978(?)-1026(?) .. **CMLC 1, 79**
See also EFS 2; LATS 1:1; RGWL 2, 3

Murdoch, Iris 1919-1999 .. **CLC 1, 2, 3, 4, 6, 8, 11, 15, 22, 31, 51; TCLC 171**
See also BRWS 1; CA 13-16R; CAAS 179; CANR 8, 43, 68, 103, 142; CBD; CD-BLB 1960 to Present; CN 1, 2, 3, 4, 5, 6; CWD; DA3; DAB; DAC; DAM MST, NOV; DLB 14, 194, 233, 326; EWL 3; INT CANR-8; MTCW 1, 2; MTFW 2005; NFS 18; RGEL 2; TCLE 1:2; TEA; WLIT 4

Murfree, Mary Noailles 1850-1922 .. **SSC 22; TCLC 135**
See also CA 176; CAAE 122; DLB 12, 74; RGAL 4

Murglie
See Murnau, F.W.

Murnau, Friedrich Wilhelm
See Murnau, F.W.

Murnau, F.W. 1888-1931 .... **TCLC 53**
See also CAAE 112

Murphy, Richard 1927- .... **CLC 41**
See also BRWS 5; CA 29-32R; CP 1, 2, 3, 4, 5, 6, 7; DLB 40; EWL 3

Murphy, Sylvia 1937- .... **CLC 34**
See also CA 121

Murphy, Thomas (Bernard) 1935- ... **CLC 51**
See Murphy, Tom
See also CA 101

Murphy, Tom
See Murphy, Thomas (Bernard)
See also DLB 310

Murray, Albert 1916- .... **CLC 73**
See also BW 2; CA 49-52; CANR 26, 52, 78, 160; CN 7; CSW; DLB 38; MTFW 2005

Murray, Albert L.
See Murray, Albert

Murray, James Augustus Henry
1837-1915 .... **TCLC 117**

Murray, Judith Sargent
1751-1820 .... **NCLC 63**
See also DLB 37, 200

Murray, Les(lie Allan) 1938- .... **CLC 40**
See also BRWS 7; CA 21-24R; CANR 11, 27, 56, 103; CP 1, 2, 3, 4, 5, 6, 7; DAM POET; DLB 289; DLBY 2001; EWL 3; RGEL 2

Murry, J. Middleton
See Murry, John Middleton

Paine, Thomas 1737-1809 .... **NCLC 62**
See also AMWS 1; CDALB 1640-1865; DLB 31, 43, 73, 158; LAIT 1; RGAL 4; RGEL 2; TUS

Pakenham, Antonia
See Fraser, Antonia

Palamas, Costis
See Palamas, Kostes

Palamas, Kostes 1859-1943 .... **TCLC 5**
See Palamas, Kostis
See also CA 190; CAAE 105; RGWL 2, 3

Palamas, Kostis
See Palamas, Kostes
See also EWL 3

Palazzeschi, Aldo 1885-1974 .... **CLC 11**
See also CA 89-92; CAAS 53-56; DLB 114, 264; EWL 3

Pales Matos, Luis 1898-1959 .... **HLCS 2**
See Pales Matos, Luis
See also DLB 290; HW 1; LAW

Paley, Grace 1922- .. **CLC 4, 6, 37, 140; SSC 8**
See also AMWS 6; CA 25-28R; CANR 13, 46, 74, 118; CN 2, 3, 4, 5, 6, 7; CPW; DA3; DAM POP; DLB 28, 218; EWL 3; EXPS; FW; INT CANR-13; MAL 5; MBL; MTCW 1, 2; MTFW 2005; RGAL 4; RGSF 2; SSFS 3, 20

Palin, Michael (Edward) 1943- .... **CLC 21**
See Monty Python
See also CA 107; CANR 35, 109; SATA 67

Palliser, Charles 1947- .... **CLC 65**
See also CA 136; CANR 76; CN 5, 6, 7

Palma, Ricardo 1833-1919 .... **TCLC 29**
See also CA 168; LAW

Pamuk, Orhan 1952- .... **CLC 185**
See also CA 142; CANR 75, 127; CWW 2; WLIT 6

Pancake, Breece Dexter 1952-1979
See Pancake, Breece D'J
See also CA 123; CAAS 109

Pancake, Breece D'J .... **CLC 29; SSC 61**
See Pancake, Breece Dexter
See also DLB 130

Panchenko, Nikolai .... **CLC 59**

Pankhurst, Emmeline (Goulden) 1858-1928 .... **TCLC 100**
See also CAAE 116; FW

Panko, Rudy
See Gogol, Nikolai (Vasilyevich)

Papadiamantis, Alexandros 1851-1911 .... **TCLC 29**
See also CA 168; EWL 3

Papadiamantopoulos, Johannes 1856-1910
See Moreas, Jean
See also CA 242; CAAE 117

Papini, Giovanni 1881-1956 .... **TCLC 22**
See also CA 180; CAAE 121; DLB 264

Paracelsus 1493-1541 .... **LC 14**
See also DLB 179

Parasol, Peter
See Stevens, Wallace

Pardo Bazan, Emilia 1851-1921 .... **SSC 30; TCLC 189**
See also EWL 3; FW; RGSF 2; RGWL 2, 3

Pareto, Vilfredo 1848-1923 .... **TCLC 69**
See also CA 175

Paretsky, Sara 1947- .... **CLC 135**
See also AAYA 30; BEST 90:3; CA 129; CAAE 125; CANR 59, 95; CMW 4; CPW; DA3; DAM POP; DLB 306; INT CA-129; MSW; RGAL 4

Parfenie, Maria
See Codrescu, Andrei

Parini, Jay (Lee) 1948- .... **CLC 54, 133**
See also CA 229; 97-100, 229; 16; CANR 32, 87

Park, Jordan
See Kornbluth, C(yril) M.; Pohl, Frederik

Park, Robert E(zra) 1864-1944 ..... **TCLC 73**
See also CA 165; CAAE 122

Parker, Bert
See Ellison, Harlan

Parker, Dorothy (Rothschild) 1893-1967 . **CLC 15, 68; PC 28; SSC 2, 101; TCLC 143**
See also AMWS 9; CA 19-20; CAAS 25-28R; CAP 2; DA3; DAM POET; DLB 11, 45, 86; EXPP; FW; MAL 5; MBL; MTCW 1, 2; MTFW 2005; PFS 18; RGAL 4; RGSF 2; TUS

Parker, Robert B. 1932- .... **CLC 27**
See also AAYA 28; BEST 89:4; BPFB 3; CA 49-52; CANR 1, 26, 52, 89, 128; CMW 4; CPW; DAM NOV, POP; DLB 306; INT CANR-26; MSW; MTCW 1; MTFW 2005

Parker, Robert Brown
See Parker, Robert B.

Parker, Theodore 1810-1860 .... **NCLC 186**
See also DLB 1, 235

Parkin, Frank 1940- .... **CLC 43**
See also CA 147

Parkman, Francis, Jr. 1823-1893 .. **NCLC 12**
See also AMWS 2; DLB 1, 30, 183, 186, 235; RGAL 4

Parks, Gordon 1912-2006 .... **BLC 3; CLC 1, 16**
See also AAYA 36; AITN 2; BW 2, 3; CA 41-44R; CAAS 249; CANR 26, 66, 145; DA3; DAM MULT; DLB 33; MTCW 2; MTFW 2005; SATA 8, 108; SATA-Obit 175

Parks, Suzan-Lori 1964(?)- .... **DC 23**
See also AAYA 55; CA 201; CAD; CD 5, 6; CWD; DFS 22; RGAL 4

Parks, Tim(othy Harold) 1954- ...... **CLC 147**
See also CA 131; CAAE 126; CANR 77, 144; CN 7; DLB 231; INT CA-131

Parmenides c. 515B.C.-c. 450B.C. .... **CMLC 22**
See also DLB 176

Parnell, Thomas 1679-1718 .... **LC 3**
See also DLB 95; RGEL 2

Parr, Catherine c. 1513(?)-1548 .... **LC 86**
See also DLB 136

Parra, Nicanor 1914- ... **CLC 2, 102; HLC 2; PC 39**
See also CA 85-88; CANR 32; CWW 2; DAM MULT; DLB 283; EWL 3; HW 1; LAW; MTCW 1

Parra Sanojo, Ana Teresa de la 1890-1936 .... **HLCS 2**
See de la Parra, (Ana) Teresa (Sonojo)
See also LAW

Parrish, Mary Frances
See Fisher, M(ary) F(rances) K(ennedy)

Parshchikov, Aleksei 1954- .... **CLC 59**
See Parshchikov, Aleksei Maksimovich

Parshchikov, Aleksei Maksimovich
See Parshchikov, Aleksei
See also DLB 285

Parson, Professor
See Coleridge, Samuel Taylor

Parson Lot
See Kingsley, Charles

Parton, Sara Payson Willis 1811-1872 .... **NCLC 86**
See also DLB 43, 74, 239

Partridge, Anthony
See Oppenheim, E(dward) Phillips

Pascal, Blaise 1623-1662 .... **LC 35**
See also DLB 268; EW 3; GFL Beginnings to 1789; RGWL 2, 3; TWA

Pascoli, Giovanni 1855-1912 .... **TCLC 45**
See also CA 170; EW 7; EWL 3

Pasolini, Pier Paolo 1922-1975 .. **CLC 20, 37, 106; PC 17**
See also CA 93-96; CAAS 61-64; CANR 63; DLB 128, 177; EWL 3; MTCW 1; RGWL 2, 3

Pasquini
See Silone, Ignazio

Pastan, Linda (Olenik) 1932- .... **CLC 27**
See also CA 61-64; CANR 18, 40, 61, 113; CP 3, 4, 5, 6, 7; CSW; CWP; DAM POET; DLB 5; PFS 8, 25

Pasternak, Boris 1890-1960 ... **CLC 7, 10, 18, 63; PC 6; SSC 31; TCLC 188; WLC 4**
See also BPFB 3; CA 127; CAAS 116; DA; DA3; DAB; DAC; DAM MST, NOV, POET; DLB 302, 331; EW 10; MTCW 1, 2; MTFW 2005; RGSF 2; RGWL 2, 3; TWA; WP

Patchen, Kenneth 1911-1972 .... **CLC 1, 2, 18**
See also BG 1:3; CA 1-4R; CAAS 33-36R; CANR 3, 35; CN 1; CP 1; DAM POET; DLB 16, 48; EWL 3; MAL 5; MTCW 1; RGAL 4

Pater, Walter (Horatio) 1839-1894 . **NCLC 7, 90, 159**
See also BRW 5; CDBLB 1832-1890; DLB 57, 156; RGEL 2; TEA

Paterson, A(ndrew) B(arton) 1864-1941 .... **TCLC 32**
See also CA 155; DLB 230; RGEL 2; SATA 97

Paterson, Banjo
See Paterson, A(ndrew) B(arton)

Paterson, Katherine 1932- .... **CLC 12, 30**
See also AAYA 1, 31; BYA 1, 2, 7; CA 21-24R; CANR 28, 59, 111; CLR 7, 50; CWRI 5; DLB 52; JRDA; LAIT 4; MAICYA 1, 2; MAICYAS 1; MTCW 1; SATA 13, 53, 92, 133; WYA; YAW

Paterson, Katherine Womeldorf
See Paterson, Katherine

Patmore, Coventry Kersey Dighton 1823-1896 .... **NCLC 9; PC 59**
See also DLB 35, 98; RGEL 2; TEA

Paton, Alan 1903-1988 ..... **CLC 4, 10, 25, 55, 106; TCLC 165; WLC 4**
See also AAYA 26; AFW; BPFB 3; BRWS 2; BYA 1; CA 13-16; CAAS 125; CANR 22; CAP 1; CN 1, 2, 3, 4; DA; DA3; DAB; DAC; DAM MST, NOV; DLB 225; DLBD 17; EWL 3; EXPN; LAIT 4; MTCW 1, 2; MTFW 2005; NFS 3, 12; RGEL 2; SATA 11; SATA-Obit 56; TWA; WLIT 2; WWE 1

Paton Walsh, Gillian
See Paton Walsh, Jill
See also AAYA 47; BYA 1, 8

Paton Walsh, Jill 1937- .... **CLC 35**
See Paton Walsh, Gillian; Walsh, Jill Paton
See also AAYA 11; CANR 38, 83, 158; CLR 2, 65; DLB 161; JRDA; MAICYA 1, 2; SAAS 3; SATA 4, 72, 109; YAW

Patsauq, Markoosie 1942- .... **NNAL**
See also CA 101; CLR 23; CWRI 5; DAM MULT

Patterson, (Horace) Orlando (Lloyd) 1940- .... **BLCS**
See also BW 1; CA 65-68; CANR 27, 84; CN 1, 2, 3, 4, 5, 6

Patton, George S(mith), Jr. 1885-1945 .... **TCLC 79**
See also CA 189

Paulding, James Kirke 1778-1860 ... **NCLC 2**
See also DLB 3, 59, 74, 250; RGAL 4

Paulin, Thomas Neilson
See Paulin, Tom

Paulin, Tom 1949- .... **CLC 37, 177**
See also CA 128; CAAE 123; CANR 98; CP 3, 4, 5, 6, 7; DLB 40

Pausanias c. 1st cent. - .... **CMLC 36**

Plomer, William Charles Franklin
1903-1973 .... **CLC 4, 8**
See also AFW; BRWS 11; CA 21-22; CANR
34; CAP 2; CN 1; CP 1, 2; DLB 20, 162,
191, 225; EWL 3; MTCW 1; RGEL 2;
RGSF 2; SATA 24

Plotinus 204-270 .... **CMLC 46**
See also CDWLB 1; DLB 176

Plowman, Piers
See Kavanagh, Patrick (Joseph)

Plum, J.
See Wodehouse, P(elham) G(renville)

Plumly, Stanley (Ross) 1939- .... **CLC 33**
See also CA 110; CAAE 108; CANR 97;
CP 3, 4, 5, 6, 7; DLB 5, 193; INT CA-
110

Plumpe, Friedrich Wilhelm
See Murnau, F.W.

Plutarch c. 46-c. 120 .... **CMLC 60**
See also AW 2; CDWLB 1; DLB 176;
RGWL 2, 3; TWA; WLIT 8

Po Chu-i 772-846 .... **CMLC 24**

Podhoretz, Norman 1930- .... **CLC 189**
See also AMWS 8; CA 9-12R; CANR 7,
78, 135

Poe, Edgar Allan 1809-1849 ..... **NCLC 1, 16,
55, 78, 94, 97, 117; PC 1, 54; SSC 1,
22, 34, 35, 54, 88; WLC 4**
See also AAYA 14; AMW; AMWC 1;
AMWR 2; BPFB 5, 11; CDALB
1640-1865; CMW 4; DA; DA3; DAB;
DAC; DAM MST, POET; DLB 3, 59, 73,
74, 248, 254; EXPP; EXPS; GL 3; HGG;
LAIT 2; LATS 1:1; LMFS 1; MSW; PAB;
PFS 1, 3, 9; RGAL 4; RGSF 2; SATA 23;
SCFW 1, 2; SFW 4; SSFS 2, 4, 7, 8, 16;
SUFW; TUS; WP; WYA

Poet of Titchfield Street, The
See Pound, Ezra (Weston Loomis)

Poggio Bracciolini, Gian Francesco
1380-1459 .... **LC 125**

Pohl, Frederik 1919- .... **CLC 18; SSC 25**
See also AAYA 24; CA 188; 61-64, 188; 1;
CANR 11, 37, 81, 140; CN 1, 2, 3, 4, 5,
6; DLB 8; INT CANR-11; MTCW 1, 2;
MTFW 2005; SATA 24; SCFW 1, 2; SFW
4

Poirier, Louis 1910-
See Gracq, Julien
See also CA 126; CAAE 122; CANR 141

Poitier, Sidney 1927- .... **CLC 26**
See also AAYA 60; BW 1; CA 117; CANR
94

Pokagon, Simon 1830-1899 .... **NNAL**
See also DAM MULT

Polanski, Roman 1933- .... **CLC 16, 178**
See also CA 77-80

Poliakoff, Stephen 1952- .... **CLC 38**
See also CA 106; CANR 116; CBD; CD 5,
6; DLB 13

Police, The
See Copeland, Stewart (Armstrong); Sum-
mers, Andy

Polidori, John William
1795-1821 .... **NCLC 51; SSC 97**
See also DLB 116; HGG

Poliziano, Angelo 1454-1494 .... **LC 120**
See also WLIT 7

Pollitt, Katha 1949- .... **CLC 28, 122**
See also CA 122; CAAE 120; CANR 66,
108; MTCW 1, 2; MTFW 2005

Pollock, (Mary) Sharon 1936- .... **CLC 50**
See also CA 141; CANR 132; CD 5; CWD;
DAC; DAM DRAM, MST; DFS 3; DLB
60; FW

Pollock, Sharon 1936- .... **DC 20**
See also CD 6

Polo, Marco 1254-1324 .... **CMLC 15**
See also WLIT 7

Polonsky, Abraham (Lincoln)
1910-1999 .... **CLC 92**
See also CA 104; CAAS 187; DLB 26; INT
CA-104

Polybius c. 200B.C.-c. 118B.C. ...... **CMLC 17**
See also AW 1; DLB 176; RGWL 2, 3

Pomerance, Bernard 1940- .... **CLC 13**
See also CA 101; CAD; CANR 49, 134;
CD 5, 6; DAM DRAM; DFS 9; LAIT 2

Ponge, Francis 1899-1988 .... **CLC 6, 18**
See also CA 85-88; CAAS 187; CANR 40,
86; DAM POET; DLBY 2002; EWL 3;
GFL 1789 to the Present; RGWL 2, 3

Poniatowska, Elena 1932- . **CLC 140; HLC 2**
See also CA 101; CANR 32, 66, 107, 156;
CDWLB 3; CWW 2; DAM MULT; DLB
113; EWL 3; HW 1, 2; LAWS 1; WLIT 1

Pontoppidan, Henrik 1857-1943 .... **TCLC 29**
See also CA 170; DLB 300, 331

Ponty, Maurice Merleau
See Merleau-Ponty, Maurice

Poole, Josephine .... **CLC 17**
See Helyar, Jane Penelope Josephine
See also SAAS 2; SATA 5

Popa, Vasko 1922-1991 . **CLC 19; TCLC 167**
See also CA 148; CAAE 112; CDWLB 4;
DLB 181; EWL 3; RGWL 2, 3

Pope, Alexander 1688-1744 ...... **LC 3, 58, 60,
64; PC 26; WLC 5**
See also BRW 3; BRWC 1; BRWR 1; CD-
BLB 1660-1789; DA; DA3; DAB; DAC;
DAM MST, POET; DLB 95, 101, 213;
EXPP; PAB; PFS 12; RGEL 2; WLIT 3;
WP

Popov, Evgenii Anatol'evich
See Popov, Yevgeny
See also DLB 285

Popov, Yevgeny .... **CLC 59**
See Popov, Evgenii Anatol'evich

Poquelin, Jean-Baptiste
See Moliere

Porete, Marguerite (?)-1310 .... **CMLC 73**
See also DLB 208

Porphyry c. 233-c. 305 .... **CMLC 71**

Porter, Connie (Rose) 1959(?)- .... **CLC 70**
See also AAYA 65; BW 2, 3; CA 142;
CANR 90, 109; SATA 81, 129

Porter, Gene(va Grace) Stratton .. **TCLC 21**
See Stratton-Porter, Gene(va Grace)
See also BPFB 3; CAAE 112; CWRI 5;
RHW

Porter, Katherine Anne 1890-1980 ... **CLC 1,
3, 7, 10, 13, 15, 27, 101; SSC 4, 31, 43**
See also AAYA 42; AITN 2; AMW; BPFB
3; CA 1-4R; CAAS 101; CANR 1, 65;
CDALBS; CN 1, 2; DA; DA3; DAB;
DAC; DAM MST, NOV; DLB 4, 9, 102;
DLBD 12; DLBY 1980; EWL 3; EXPS;
LAIT 3; MAL 5; MBL; MTCW 1, 2;
MTFW 2005; NFS 14; RGAL 4; RGSF 2;
SATA 39; SATA-Obit 23; SSFS 1, 8, 11,
16, 23; TCWW 2; TUS

Porter, Peter (Neville Frederick)
1929- .... **CLC 5, 13, 33**
See also CA 85-88; CP 1, 2, 3, 4, 5, 6, 7;
DLB 40, 289; WWE 1

Porter, William Sydney 1862-1910
See Henry, O.
See also CA 131; CAAE 104; CDALB
1865-1917; DA; DA3; DAB; DAC; DAM
MST; DLB 12, 78, 79; MTCW 1, 2;
MTFW 2005; TUS; YABC 2

Portillo (y Pacheco), Jose Lopez
See Lopez Portillo (y Pacheco), Jose

Portillo Trambley, Estela 1927-1998 .. **HLC 2**
See Trambley, Estela Portillo
See also CANR 32; DAM MULT; DLB
209; HW 1

Posey, Alexander (Lawrence)
1873-1908 .... **NNAL**
See also CA 144; CANR 80; DAM MULT;
DLB 175

Posse, Abel .... **CLC 70**
See also CA 252

Post, Melville Davisson
1869-1930 .... **TCLC 39**
See also CA 202; CAAE 110; CMW 4

Potok, Chaim 1929-2002 ... **CLC 2, 7, 14, 26,
112**
See also AAYA 15, 50; AITN 1, 2; BPFB 3;
BYA 1; CA 17-20R; CAAS 208; CANR
19, 35, 64, 98; CLR 92; CN 4, 5, 6; DA3;
DAM NOV; DLB 28, 152; EXPN; INT
CANR-19; LAIT 4; MTCW 1, 2; MTFW
2005; NFS 4; RGHL; SATA 33, 106;
SATA-Obit 134; TUS; YAW

Potok, Herbert Harold -2002
See Potok, Chaim

Potok, Herman Harold
See Potok, Chaim

Potter, Dennis (Christopher George)
1935-1994 .... **CLC 58, 86, 123**
See also BRWS 10; CA 107; CAAS 145;
CANR 33, 61; CBD; DLB 233; MTCW 1

Pound, Ezra (Weston Loomis)
1885-1972 .. **CLC 1, 2, 3, 4, 5, 7, 10, 13,
18, 34, 48, 50, 112; PC 4; WLC 5**
See also AAYA 47; AMW; AMWR 1; CA
5-8R; CAAS 37-40R; CANR 40; CDALB
1917-1929; CP 1; DA; DA3; DAB; DAC;
DAM MST, POET; DLB 4, 45, 63; DLBD
15; EFS 2; EWL 3; EXPP; LMFS 2; MAL
5; MTCW 1, 2; MTFW 2005; PAB; PFS
2, 8, 16; RGAL 4; TUS; WP

Povod, Reinaldo 1959-1994 .... **CLC 44**
See also CA 136; CAAS 146; CANR 83

Powell, Adam Clayton, Jr.
1908-1972 .... **BLC 3; CLC 89**
See also BW 1, 3; CA 102; CAAS 33-36R;
CANR 86; DAM MULT

Powell, Anthony 1905-2000 ... **CLC 1, 3, 7, 9,
10, 31**
See also BRW 7; CA 1-4R; CAAS 189;
CANR 1, 32, 62, 107; CDBLB 1945-
1960; CN 1, 2, 3, 4, 5, 6; DLB 15; EWL
3; MTCW 1, 2; MTFW 2005; RGEL 2;
TEA

Powell, Dawn 1896(?)-1965 .... **CLC 66**
See also CA 5-8R; CANR 121; DLBY 1997

Powell, Padgett 1952- .... **CLC 34**
See also CA 126; CANR 63, 101; CSW;
DLB 234; DLBY 01

Powell, (Oval) Talmage 1920-2000
See Queen, Ellery
See also CA 5-8R; CANR 2, 80

Power, Susan 1961- .... **CLC 91**
See also BYA 14; CA 160; CANR 135; NFS
11

Powers, J(ames) F(arl) 1917-1999 ..... **CLC 1,
4, 8, 57; SSC 4**
See also CA 1-4R; CAAS 181; CANR 2,
61; CN 1, 2, 3, 4, 5, 6; DLB 130; MTCW
1; RGAL 4; RGSF 2

Powers, John J(ames) 1945-
See Powers, John R.
See also CA 69-72

Powers, John R. .... **CLC 66**
See Powers, John J(ames)

Powers, Richard 1957- .... **CLC 93**
See also AMWS 9; BPFB 3; CA 148;
CANR 80; CN 6, 7; MTFW 2005; TCLE
1:2

Powers, Richard S.
See Powers, Richard

Pownall, David 1938- .... **CLC 10**
See also CA 89-92, 180; 18; CANR 49, 101;
CBD; CD 5, 6; CN 4, 5, 6, 7; DLB 14

Powys, John Cowper 1872-1963 ... **CLC 7, 9, 15, 46, 125**
See also CA 85-88; CANR 106; DLB 15, 255; EWL 3; FANT; MTCW 1, 2; MTFW 2005; RGEL 2; SUFW

Powys, T(heodore) F(rancis)
1875-1953 .... **TCLC 9**
See also BRWS 8; CA 189; CAAE 106; DLB 36, 162; EWL 3; FANT; RGEL 2; SUFW

Pozzo, Modesta
See Fonte, Moderata

Prado (Calvo), Pedro 1886-1952 ... **TCLC 75**
See also CA 131; DLB 283; HW 1; LAW

Prager, Emily 1952- .... **CLC 56**
See also CA 204

Pratchett, Terry 1948- .... **CLC 197**
See also AAYA 19, 54; BPFB 3; CA 143; CANR 87, 126; CLR 64; CN 6, 7; CPW; CWRI 5; FANT; MTFW 2005; SATA 82, 139; SFW 4; SUFW 2

Pratolini, Vasco 1913-1991 .... **TCLC 124**
See also CA 211; DLB 177; EWL 3; RGWL 2, 3

Pratt, E(dwin) J(ohn) 1883(?)-1964 . **CLC 19**
See also CA 141; CAAS 93-96; CANR 77; DAC; DAM POET; DLB 92; EWL 3; RGEL 2; TWA

Premchand .... **TCLC 21**
See Srivastava, Dhanpat Rai
See also EWL 3

Prescott, William Hickling
1796-1859 .... **NCLC 163**
See also DLB 1, 30, 59, 235

Preseren, France 1800-1849 .... **NCLC 127**
See also CDWLB 4; DLB 147

Preussler, Otfried 1923- .... **CLC 17**
See also CA 77-80; SATA 24

Prevert, Jacques (Henri Marie)
1900-1977 .... **CLC 15**
See also CA 77-80; CAAS 69-72; CANR 29, 61; DLB 258; EWL 3; GFL 1789 to the Present; IDFW 3, 4; MTCW 1; RGWL 2, 3; SATA-Obit 30

Prevost, (Antoine Francois)
1697-1763 .... **LC 1**
See also DLB 314; EW 4; GFL Beginnings to 1789; RGWL 2, 3

Price, Reynolds 1933- .. **CLC 3, 6, 13, 43, 50, 63, 212; SSC 22**
See also AMWS 6; CA 1-4R; CANR 1, 37, 57, 87, 128; CN 1, 2, 3, 4, 5, 6, 7; CSW; DAM NOV; DLB 2, 218, 278; EWL 3; INT CANR-37; MAL 5; MTFW 2005; NFS 18

Price, Richard 1949- .... **CLC 6, 12**
See also CA 49-52; CANR 3, 147; CN 7; DLBY 1981

Prichard, Katharine Susannah
1883-1969 .... **CLC 46**
See also CA 11-12; CANR 33; CAP 1; DLB 260; MTCW 1; RGEL 2; RGSF 2; SATA 66

Priestley, J(ohn) B(oynton)
1894-1984 .... **CLC 2, 5, 9, 34**
See also BRW 7; CA 9-12R; CAAS 113; CANR 33; CDBLB 1914-1945; CN 1, 2, 3; DA3; DAM DRAM, NOV; DLB 10, 34, 77, 100, 139; DLBY 1984; EWL 3; MTCW 1, 2; MTFW 2005; RGEL 2; SFW 4

Prince 1958- .... **CLC 35**
See also CA 213

Prince, F(rank) T(empleton)
1912-2003 .... **CLC 22**
See also CA 101; CAAS 219; CANR 43, 79; CP 1, 2, 3, 4, 5, 6, 7; DLB 20

Prince Kropotkin
See Kropotkin, Peter (Aleksieevich)

Prior, Matthew 1664-1721 .... **LC 4**
See also DLB 95; RGEL 2

Prishvin, Mikhail 1873-1954 .... **TCLC 75**
See Prishvin, Mikhail Mikhailovich

Prishvin, Mikhail Mikhailovich
See Prishvin, Mikhail
See also DLB 272; EWL 3

Pritchard, William H(arrison)
1932- .... **CLC 34**
See also CA 65-68; CANR 23, 95; DLB 111

Pritchett, V(ictor) S(awdon)
1900-1997 ... **CLC 5, 13, 15, 41; SSC 14**
See also BPFB 3; BRWS 3; CA 61-64; CAAS 157; CANR 31, 63; CN 1, 2, 3, 4, 5, 6; DA3; DAM NOV; DLB 15, 139; EWL 3; MTCW 1, 2; MTFW 2005; RGEL 2; RGSF 2; TEA

Private 19022
See Manning, Frederic

Probst, Mark 1925- .... **CLC 59**
See also CA 130

Procaccino, Michael
See Cristofer, Michael

Proclus c. 412-c. 485 .... **CMLC 81**

Prokosch, Frederic 1908-1989 ...... **CLC 4, 48**
See also CA 73-76; CAAS 128; CANR 82; CN 1, 2, 3, 4; CP 1, 2, 3, 4; DLB 48; MTCW 2

Propertius, Sextus c. 50B.C.-c. 16B.C. .... **CMLC 32**
See also AW 2; CDWLB 1; DLB 211; RGWL 2, 3; WLIT 8

Prophet, The
See Dreiser, Theodore

Prose, Francine 1947- .... **CLC 45, 231**
See also AMWS 16; CA 112; CAAE 109; CANR 46, 95, 132; DLB 234; MTFW 2005; SATA 101, 149

Protagoras c. 490B.C.-420B.C. ...... **CMLC 85**
See also DLB 176

Proudhon
See Cunha, Euclides (Rodrigues Pimenta) da

Proulx, Annie
See Proulx, E. Annie

Proulx, E. Annie 1935- .... **CLC 81, 158**
See also AMWS 7; BPFB 3; CA 145; CANR 65, 110; CN 6, 7; CPW 1; DA3; DAM POP; DLB 335; MAL 5; MTCW 2; MTFW 2005; SSFS 18, 23

Proulx, Edna Annie
See Proulx, E. Annie

Proust, (Valentin-Louis-George-Eugene) Marcel 1871-1922 ..... **SSC 75; TCLC 7, 13, 33; WLC 5**
See also AAYA 58; BPFB 3; CA 120; CAAE 104; CANR 110; DA; DA3; DAB; DAC; DAM MST, NOV; DLB 65; EW 8; EWL 3; GFL 1789 to the Present; MTCW 1, 2; MTFW 2005; RGWL 2, 3; TWA

Prowler, Harley
See Masters, Edgar Lee

Prudentius, Aurelius Clemens 348-c. 405 .... **CMLC 78**
See also EW 1; RGWL 2, 3

Prudhomme, Rene Francois Armand
1839-1907
See Sully Prudhomme, Rene-Francois-Armand
See also CA 170

Prus, Boleslaw 1845-1912 .... **TCLC 48**
See also RGWL 2, 3

Pryor, Aaron Richard
See Pryor, Richard

Pryor, Richard 1940-2005 .... **CLC 26**
See also CA 152; CAAE 122; CAAS 246

Pryor, Richard Franklin Lenox Thomas
See Pryor, Richard

Przybyszewski, Stanislaw
1868-1927 .... **TCLC 36**
See also CA 160; DLB 66; EWL 3

Pseudo-Dionysius the Areopagite fl. c. 5th cent. - .... **CMLC 89**
See also DLB 115

Pteleon
See Grieve, C(hristopher) M(urray)
See also DAM POET

Puckett, Lute
See Masters, Edgar Lee

Puig, Manuel 1932-1990 .... **CLC 3, 5, 10, 28, 65, 133; HLC 2**
See also BPFB 3; CA 45-48; CANR 2, 32, 63; CDWLB 3; DA3; DAM MULT; DLB 113; DNFS 1; EWL 3; GLL 1; HW 1, 2; LAW; MTCW 1, 2; MTFW 2005; RGWL 2, 3; TWA; WLIT 1

Pulitzer, Joseph 1847-1911 .... **TCLC 76**
See also CAAE 114; DLB 23

Purchas, Samuel 1577(?)-1626 .... **LC 70**
See also DLB 151

Purdy, A(lfred) W(ellington)
1918-2000 .... **CLC 3, 6, 14, 50**
See also CA 81-84; 17; CAAS 189; CANR 42, 66; CP 1, 2, 3, 4, 5, 6, 7; DAC; DAM MST, POET; DLB 88; PFS 5; RGEL 2

Purdy, James (Amos) 1923- .... **CLC 2, 4, 10, 28, 52**
See also AMWS 7; CA 33-36R; 1; CANR 19, 51, 132; CN 1, 2, 3, 4, 5, 6, 7; DLB 2, 218; EWL 3; INT CANR-19; MAL 5; MTCW 1; RGAL 4

Pure, Simon
See Swinnerton, Frank Arthur

Pushkin, Aleksandr Sergeevich
See Pushkin, Alexander (Sergeyevich)
See also DLB 205

Pushkin, Alexander (Sergeyevich)
1799-1837 .... **NCLC 3, 27, 83; PC 10; SSC 27, 55, 99; WLC 5**
See Pushkin, Aleksandr Sergeevich
See also DA; DA3; DAB; DAC; DAM DRAM, MST, POET; EW 5; EXPS; RGSF 2; RGWL 2, 3; SATA 61; SSFS 9; TWA

P'u Sung-ling 1640-1715 .... **LC 49; SSC 31**

Putnam, Arthur Lee
See Alger, Horatio, Jr.

Puttenham, George 1529(?)-1590 ...... **LC 116**
See also DLB 281

Puzo, Mario 1920-1999 .... **CLC 1, 2, 6, 36, 107**
See also BPFB 3; CA 65-68; CAAS 185; CANR 4, 42, 65, 99, 131; CN 1, 2, 3, 4, 5, 6; CPW; DA3; DAM NOV, POP; DLB 6; MTCW 1, 2; MTFW 2005; NFS 16; RGAL 4

Pygge, Edward
See Barnes, Julian

Pyle, Ernest Taylor 1900-1945
See Pyle, Ernie
See also CA 160; CAAE 115

Pyle, Ernie .... **TCLC 75**
See Pyle, Ernest Taylor
See also DLB 29; MTCW 2

Pyle, Howard 1853-1911 .... **TCLC 81**
See also AAYA 57; BYA 2, 4; CA 137; CAAE 109; CLR 22, 117; DLB 42, 188; DLBD 13; LAIT 1; MAICYA 1, 2; SATA 16, 100; WCH; YAW

Pym, Barbara (Mary Crampton)
1913-1980 .... **CLC 13, 19, 37, 111**
See also BPFB 3; BRWS 2; CA 13-14; CAAS 97-100; CANR 13, 34; CAP 1; DLB 14, 207; DLBY 1987; EWL 3; MTCW 1, 2; MTFW 2005; RGEL 2; TEA

Raphael, Frederic (Michael) 1931- ... **CLC 2, 14**
See also CA 1-4R; CANR 1, 86; CN 1, 2, 3, 4, 5, 6, 7; DLB 14, 319; TCLE 1:2
Raphael, Lev 1954- .... **CLC 232**
See also CA 134; CANR 72, 145; GLL 1
Ratcliffe, James P.
See Mencken, H(enry) L(ouis)
Rathbone, Julian 1935- .... **CLC 41**
See also CA 101; CANR 34, 73, 152
Rattigan, Terence (Mervyn)
1911-1977 .... **CLC 7; DC 18**
See also BRWS 7; CA 85-88; CAAS 73-76; CBD; CDBLB 1945-1960; DAM DRAM; DFS 8; DLB 13; IDFW 3, 4; MTCW 1, 2; MTFW 2005; RGEL 2
Ratushinskaya, Irina 1954- .... **CLC 54**
See also CA 129; CANR 68; CWW 2
Raven, Simon (Arthur Noel)
1927-2001 .... **CLC 14**
See also CA 81-84; CAAS 197; CANR 86; CN 1, 2, 3, 4, 5, 6; DLB 271
Ravenna, Michael
See Welty, Eudora
Rawley, Callman 1903-2004
See Rakosi, Carl
See also CA 21-24R; CAAS 228; CANR 12, 32, 91
Rawlings, Marjorie Kinnan
1896-1953 .... **TCLC 4**
See also AAYA 20; AMWS 10; ANW; BPFB 3; BYA 3; CA 137; CAAE 104; CANR 74; CLR 63; DLB 9, 22, 102; DLBD 17; JRDA; MAICYA 1, 2; MAL 5; MTCW 2; MTFW 2005; RGAL 4; SATA 100; WCH; YABC 1; YAW
Ray, Satyajit 1921-1992 .... **CLC 16, 76**
See also CA 114; CAAS 137; DAM MULT
Read, Herbert Edward 1893-1968 ..... **CLC 4**
See also BRW 6; CA 85-88; CAAS 25-28R; DLB 20, 149; EWL 3; PAB; RGEL 2
Read, Piers Paul 1941- .... **CLC 4, 10, 25**
See also CA 21-24R; CANR 38, 86, 150; CN 2, 3, 4, 5, 6, 7; DLB 14; SATA 21
Reade, Charles 1814-1884 .... **NCLC 2, 74**
See also DLB 21; RGEL 2
Reade, Hamish
See Gray, Simon (James Holliday)
Reading, Peter 1946- .... **CLC 47**
See also BRWS 8; CA 103; CANR 46, 96; CP 5, 6, 7; DLB 40
Reaney, James 1926- .... **CLC 13**
See also CA 41-44R; 15; CANR 42; CD 5, 6; CP 1, 2, 3, 4, 5, 6, 7; DAC; DAM MST; DLB 68; RGEL 2; SATA 43
Rebreanu, Liviu 1885-1944 .... **TCLC 28**
See also CA 165; DLB 220; EWL 3
Rechy, John 1934- ..... **CLC 1, 7, 14, 18, 107; HLC 2**
See also CA 195; 5-8R, 195; 4; CANR 6, 32, 64, 152; CN 1, 2, 3, 4, 5, 6, 7; DAM MULT; DLB 122, 278; DLBY 1982; HW 1, 2; INT CANR-6; LLW; MAL 5; RGAL 4
Rechy, John Francisco
See Rechy, John
Redcam, Tom 1870-1933 .... **TCLC 25**
Reddin, Keith 1956- .... **CLC 67**
See also CAD; CD 6
Redgrove, Peter (William)
1932-2003 .... **CLC 6, 41**
See also BRWS 6; CA 1-4R; CAAS 217; CANR 3, 39, 77; CP 1, 2, 3, 4, 5, 6, 7; DLB 40; TCLE 1:2
Redmon, Anne .... **CLC 22**
See Nightingale, Anne Redmon
See also DLBY 1986
Reed, Eliot
See Ambler, Eric

Reed, Ishmael 1938- ..... **BLC 3; CLC 2, 3, 5, 6, 13, 32, 60, 174; PC 68**
See also AFAW 1, 2; AMWS 10; BPFB 3; BW 2, 3; CA 21-24R; CANR 25, 48, 74, 128; CN 1, 2, 3, 4, 5, 6, 7; CP 1, 2, 3, 4, 5, 6, 7; CSW; DA3; DAM MULT; DLB 2, 5, 33, 169, 227; DLBD 8; EWL 3; LMFS 2; MAL 5; MSW; MTCW 1, 2; MTFW 2005; PFS 6; RGAL 4; TCWW 2
Reed, John (Silas) 1887-1920 .... **TCLC 9**
See also CA 195; CAAE 106; MAL 5; TUS
Reed, Lou .... **CLC 21**
See Firbank, Louis
Reese, Lizette Woodworth
1856-1935 .... **PC 29; TCLC 181**
See also CA 180; DLB 54
Reeve, Clara 1729-1807 .... **NCLC 19**
See also DLB 39; RGEL 2
Reich, Wilhelm 1897-1957 .... **TCLC 57**
See also CA 199
Reid, Christopher (John) 1949- .... **CLC 33**
See also CA 140; CANR 89; CP 4, 5, 6, 7; DLB 40; EWL 3
Reid, Desmond
See Moorcock, Michael
Reid Banks, Lynne 1929-
See Banks, Lynne Reid
See also AAYA 49; CA 1-4R; CANR 6, 22, 38, 87; CLR 24; CN 1, 2, 3, 7; JRDA; MAICYA 1, 2; SATA 22, 75, 111, 165; YAW
Reilly, William K.
See Creasey, John
Reiner, Max
See Caldwell, (Janet Miriam) Taylor (Holland)
Reis, Ricardo
See Pessoa, Fernando (Antonio Nogueira)
Reizenstein, Elmer Leopold
See Rice, Elmer (Leopold)
See also EWL 3
Remarque, Erich Maria 1898-1970 . **CLC 21**
See also AAYA 27; BPFB 3; CA 77-80; CAAS 29-32R; CDWLB 2; DA; DA3; DAB; DAC; DAM MST, NOV; DLB 56; EWL 3; EXPN; LAIT 3; MTCW 1, 2; MTFW 2005; NFS 4; RGHL; RGWL 2, 3
Remington, Frederic S(ackrider)
1861-1909 .... **TCLC 89**
See also CA 169; CAAE 108; DLB 12, 186, 188; SATA 41; TCWW 2
Remizov, A.
See Remizov, Aleksei (Mikhailovich)
Remizov, A. M.
See Remizov, Aleksei (Mikhailovich)
Remizov, Aleksei (Mikhailovich)
1877-1957 .... **TCLC 27**
See Remizov, Alexey Mikhaylovich
See also CA 133; CAAE 125; DLB 295
Remizov, Alexey Mikhaylovich
See Remizov, Aleksei (Mikhailovich)
See also EWL 3
Renan, Joseph Ernest 1823-1892 . **NCLC 26, 145**
See also GFL 1789 to the Present
Renard, Jules(-Pierre) 1864-1910 .. **TCLC 17**
See also CA 202; CAAE 117; GFL 1789 to the Present
Renart, Jean fl. 13th cent. - .... **CMLC 83**
Renault, Mary .... **CLC 3, 11, 17**
See Challans, Mary
See also BPFB 3; BYA 2; CN 1, 2, 3; DLBY 1983; EWL 3; GLL 1; LAIT 1; RGEL 2; RHW

Rendell, Ruth 1930- .... **CLC 28, 48**
See Vine, Barbara
See also BPFB 3; BRWS 9; CA 109; CANR 32, 52, 74, 127, 162; CN 5, 6, 7; CPW; DAM POP; DLB 87, 276; INT CANR-32; MSW; MTCW 1, 2; MTFW 2005
Rendell, Ruth Barbara
See Rendell, Ruth
Renoir, Jean 1894-1979 .... **CLC 20**
See also CA 129; CAAS 85-88
Rensie, Willis
See Eisner, Will
Resnais, Alain 1922- .... **CLC 16**
Revard, Carter 1931- .... **NNAL**
See also CA 144; CANR 81, 153; PFS 5
Reverdy, Pierre 1889-1960 .... **CLC 53**
See also CA 97-100; CAAS 89-92; DLB 258; EWL 3; GFL 1789 to the Present
Rexroth, Kenneth 1905-1982 .... **CLC 1, 2, 6, 11, 22, 49, 112; PC 20**
See also BG 1:3; CA 5-8R; CAAS 107; CANR 14, 34, 63; CDALB 1941-1968; CP 1, 2, 3; DAM POET; DLB 16, 48, 165, 212; DLBY 1982; EWL 3; INT CANR-14; MAL 5; MTCW 1, 2; MTFW 2005; RGAL 4
Reyes, Alfonso 1889-1959 .... **HLCS 2; TCLC 33**
See also CA 131; EWL 3; HW 1; LAW
Reyes y Basoalto, Ricardo Eliecer Neftali
See Neruda, Pablo
Reymont, Wladyslaw (Stanislaw)
1868(?)-1925 .... **TCLC 5**
See also CA CAAE 104; DLB 332; EWL 3
Reynolds, John Hamilton
1794-1852 .... **NCLC 146**
See also DLB 96
Reynolds, Jonathan 1942- .... **CLC 6, 38**
See also CA 65-68; CANR 28
Reynolds, Joshua 1723-1792 .... **LC 15**
See also DLB 104
Reynolds, Michael S(hane)
1937-2000 .... **CLC 44**
See also CA 65-68; CAAS 189; CANR 9, 89, 97
Reznikoff, Charles 1894-1976 .... **CLC 9**
See also AMWS 14; CA 33-36; CAAS 61-64; CAP 2; CP 1, 2; DLB 28, 45; RGHL; WP
Rezzori, Gregor von
See Rezzori d'Arezzo, Gregor von
Rezzori d'Arezzo, Gregor von
1914-1998 .... **CLC 25**
See also CA 136; CAAE 122; CAAS 167
Rhine, Richard
See Silverstein, Alvin; Silverstein, Virginia B(arbara Opshelor)
Rhodes, Eugene Manlove
1869-1934 .... **TCLC 53**
See also CA 198; DLB 256; TCWW 1, 2
R'hoone, Lord
See Balzac, Honore de
Rhys, Jean 1890-1979 .... **CLC 2, 4, 6, 14, 19, 51, 124; SSC 21, 76**
See also BRWS 2; CA 25-28R; CAAS 85-88; CANR 35, 62; CDBLB 1945-1960; CDWLB 3; CN 1, 2; DA3; DAM NOV; DLB 36, 117, 162; DNFS 2; EWL 3; LATS 1:1; MTCW 1, 2; MTFW 2005; NFS 19; RGEL 2; RGSF 2; RHW; TEA; WWE 1
Ribeiro, Darcy 1922-1997 .... **CLC 34**
See also CA 33-36R; CAAS 156; EWL 3
Ribeiro, Joao Ubaldo (Osorio Pimentel)
1941- .... **CLC 10, 67**
See also CA 81-84; CWW 2; EWL 3
Ribman, Ronald (Burt) 1932- .... **CLC 7**
See also CA 21-24R; CAD; CANR 46, 80; CD 5, 6

Robinson, Edwin Arlington
1869-1935 .... **PC 1, 35; TCLC 5, 101**
See also AAYA 72; AMW; CA 133; CAAE
104; CDALB 1865-1917; DA; DAC;
DAM MST, POET; DLB 54; EWL 3;
EXPP; MAL 5; MTCW 1, 2; MTFW
2005; PAB; PFS 4; RGAL 4; WP

Robinson, Henry Crabb
1775-1867 .... **NCLC 15**
See also DLB 107

Robinson, Jill 1936- .... **CLC 10**
See also CA 102; CANR 120; INT CA-102

Robinson, Kim Stanley 1952- .... **CLC 34**
See also AAYA 26; CA 126; CANR 113,
139; CN 6, 7; MTFW 2005; SATA 109;
SCFW 2; SFW 4

Robinson, Lloyd
See Silverberg, Robert

Robinson, Marilynne 1944- ...... **CLC 25, 180**
See also AAYA 69; CA 116; CANR 80, 140;
CN 4, 5, 6, 7; DLB 206; MTFW 2005;
NFS 24

Robinson, Mary 1758-1800 .... **NCLC 142**
See also DLB 158; FW

Robinson, Smokey .... **CLC 21**
See Robinson, William, Jr.

Robinson, William, Jr. 1940-
See Robinson, Smokey
See also CAAE 116

Robison, Mary 1949- .... **CLC 42, 98**
See also CAAE 113; CANR 87;
CN 4, 5, 6, 7; DLB 130; INT CA-116;
RGSF 2

Roches, Catherine des 1542-1587 ...... **LC 117**
See also DLB 327

Rochester
See Wilmot, John
See also RGEL 2

Rod, Edouard 1857-1910 .... **TCLC 52**

Roddenberry, Eugene Wesley 1921-1991
See Roddenberry, Gene
See also CA 110; CAAS 135; CANR 37;
SATA 45; SATA-Obit 69

Roddenberry, Gene .... **CLC 17**
See Roddenberry, Eugene Wesley
See also AAYA 5; SATA-Obit 69

Rodgers, Mary 1931- .... **CLC 12**
See also BYA 5; CA 49-52; CANR 8, 55,
90; CLR 20; CWRI 5; INT CANR-8;
JRDA; MAICYA 1, 2; SATA 8, 130

Rodgers, W(illiam) R(obert)
1909-1969 .... **CLC 7**
See also CA 85-88; DLB 20; RGEL 2

Rodman, Eric
See Silverberg, Robert

Rodman, Howard 1920(?)-1985 .... **CLC 65**
See also CAAS 118

Rodman, Maia
See Wojciechowska, Maia (Teresa)

Rodo, Jose Enrique 1871(?)-1917 .... **HLCS 2**
See also CA 178; EWL 3; HW 2; LAW

Rodolph, Utto
See Ouologuem, Yambo

Rodriguez, Claudio 1934-1999 .... **CLC 10**
See also CA 188; DLB 134

Rodriguez, Richard 1944- .... **CLC 155; HLC 2**
See also AMWS 14; CA 110; CANR 66,
116; DAM MULT; DLB 82, 256; HW 1,
2; LAIT 5; LLW; MTFW 2005; NCFS 3;
WLIT 1

Roelvaag, O(le) E(dvart) 1876-1931
See Rolvaag, O(le) E(dvart)
See also AAYA 75; CA 171; CAAE 117

Roethke, Theodore (Huebner)
1908-1963 .... **CLC 1, 3, 8, 11, 19, 46,
101; PC 15**
See also AMW; CA 81-84; CABS 2;
CDALB 1941-1968; DA3; DAM POET;
DLB 5, 206; EWL 3; EXPP; MAL 5;
MTCW 1, 2; PAB; PFS 3; RGAL 4; WP

Rogers, Carl R(ansom)
1902-1987 .... **TCLC 125**
See also CA 1-4R; CAAS 121; CANR 1,
18; MTCW 1

Rogers, Samuel 1763-1855 .... **NCLC 69**
See also DLB 93; RGEL 2

Rogers, Thomas Hunton 1927-2007 . **CLC 57**
See also CA 89-92; CANR 163; INT CA-
89-92

Rogers, Will(iam Penn Adair)
1879-1935 .... **NNAL; TCLC 8, 71**
See also CA 144; CAAE 105; DA3; DAM
MULT; DLB 11; MTCW 2

Rogin, Gilbert 1929- .... **CLC 18**
See also CA 65-68; CANR 15

Rohan, Koda
See Koda Shigeyuki

Rohlfs, Anna Katharine Green
See Green, Anna Katharine

Rohmer, Eric .... **CLC 16**
See Scherer, Jean-Marie Maurice

Rohmer, Sax .... **TCLC 28**
See Ward, Arthur Henry Sarsfield
See also DLB 70; MSW; SUFW

Roiphe, Anne 1935- .... **CLC 3, 9**
See also CA 89-92; CANR 45, 73, 138;
DLBY 1980; INT CA-89-92

Roiphe, Anne Richardson
See Roiphe, Anne

Rojas, Fernando de 1475-1541 ... **HLCS 1, 2;
LC 23**
See also DLB 286; RGWL 2, 3

Rojas, Gonzalo 1917- .... **HLCS 2**
See also CA 178; HW 2; LAWS 1

Roland (de la Platiere), Marie-Jeanne
1754-1793 .... **LC 98**
See also DLB 314

**Rolfe, Frederick (William Serafino Austin
Lewis Mary)** 1860-1913 .... **TCLC 12**
See Al Siddik
See also CA 210; CAAE 107; DLB 34, 156;
RGEL 2

Rolland, Romain 1866-1944 .... **TCLC 23**
See also CA 197; CAAE 118; DLB 65, 284,
332; EWL 3; GFL 1789 to the Present;
RGWL 2, 3

Rolle, Richard c. 1300-c. 1349 ...... **CMLC 21**
See also DLB 146; LMFS 1; RGEL 2

Rolvaag, O(le) E(dvart) .... **TCLC 17**
See Roelvaag, O(le) E(dvart)
See also DLB 9, 212; MAL 5; NFS 5;
RGAL 4

Romain Arnaud, Saint
See Aragon, Louis

Romains, Jules 1885-1972 .... **CLC 7**
See also CA 85-88; CANR 34; DLB 65,
321; EWL 3; GFL 1789 to the Present;
MTCW 1

Romero, Jose Ruben 1890-1952 .... **TCLC 14**
See also CA 131; CAAE 114; EWL 3; HW
1; LAW

Ronsard, Pierre de 1524-1585 . **LC 6, 54; PC
11**
See also DLB 327; EW 2; GFL Beginnings
to 1789; RGWL 2, 3; TWA

Rooke, Leon 1934- .... **CLC 25, 34**
See also CA 25-28R; CANR 23, 53; CCA
1; CPW; DAM POP

Roosevelt, Franklin Delano
1882-1945 .... **TCLC 93**
See also CA 173; CAAE 116; LAIT 3

Roosevelt, Theodore 1858-1919 ..... **TCLC 69**
See also CA 170; CAAE 115; DLB 47, 186,
275

Roper, William 1498-1578 .... **LC 10**

Roquelaure, A. N.
See Rice, Anne

Rosa, Joao Guimaraes 1908-1967 ... **CLC 23;
HLCS 1**
See Guimaraes Rosa, Joao
See also CAAS 89-92; DLB 113, 307; EWL
3; WLIT 1

Rose, Wendy 1948- . **CLC 85; NNAL; PC 13**
See also CA 53-56; CANR 5, 51; CWP;
DAM MULT; DLB 175; PFS 13; RGAL
4; SATA 12

Rosen, R. D.
See Rosen, Richard (Dean)

Rosen, Richard (Dean) 1949- .... **CLC 39**
See also CA 77-80; CANR 62, 120; CMW
4; INT CANR-30

Rosenberg, Isaac 1890-1918 .... **TCLC 12**
See also BRW 6; CA 188; CAAE 107; DLB
20, 216; EWL 3; PAB; RGEL 2

Rosenblatt, Joe .... **CLC 15**
See Rosenblatt, Joseph
See also CP 3, 4, 5, 6, 7

Rosenblatt, Joseph 1933-
See Rosenblatt, Joe
See also CA 89-92; CP 1, 2; INT CA-89-92

Rosenfeld, Samuel
See Tzara, Tristan

Rosenstock, Sami
See Tzara, Tristan

Rosenstock, Samuel
See Tzara, Tristan

Rosenthal, M(acha) L(ouis)
1917-1996 .... **CLC 28**
See also CA 1-4R; 6; CAAS 152; CANR 4,
51; CP 1, 2, 3, 4, 5, 6; DLB 5; SATA 59

Ross, Barnaby
See Dannay, Frederic; Lee, Manfred B.

Ross, Bernard L.
See Follett, Ken

Ross, J. H.
See Lawrence, T(homas) E(dward)

Ross, John Hume
See Lawrence, T(homas) E(dward)

Ross, Martin 1862-1915
See Martin, Violet Florence
See also DLB 135; GLL 2; RGEL 2; RGSF
2

Ross, (James) Sinclair 1908-1996 ... **CLC 13;
SSC 24**
See also CA 73-76; CANR 81; CN 1, 2, 3,
4, 5, 6; DAC; DAM MST; DLB 88;
RGEL 2; RGSF 2; TCWW 1, 2

Rossetti, Christina 1830-1894 ... **NCLC 2, 50,
66, 186; PC 7; WLC 5**
See also AAYA 51; BRW 5; BYA 4; CLR
115; DA; DA3; DAB; DAC; DAM MST,
POET; DLB 35, 163, 240; EXPP; FL 1:3;
LATS 1:1; MAICYA 1, 2; PFS 10, 14;
RGEL 2; SATA 20; TEA; WCH

Rossetti, Christina Georgina
See Rossetti, Christina

Rossetti, Dante Gabriel 1828-1882 . **NCLC 4,
77; PC 44; WLC 5**
See also AAYA 51; BRW 5; CDBLB 1832-
1890; DA; DAB; DAC; DAM MST,
POET; DLB 35; EXPP; RGEL 2; TEA

Rossi, Cristina Peri
See Peri Rossi, Cristina

Rossi, Jean-Baptiste 1931-2003
See Japrisot, Sebastien
See also CA 201; CAAS 215

Saba, Umberto 1883-1957 .... **TCLC 33**
See also CA 144; CANR 79; DLB 114;
EWL 3; RGWL 2, 3

Sabatini, Rafael 1875-1950 .... **TCLC 47**
See also BPFB 3; CA 162; RHW

Sabato, Ernesto 1911- ... **CLC 10, 23; HLC 2**
See also CA 97-100; CANR 32, 65; CD-
WLB 3; CWW 2; DAM MULT; DLB 145;
EWL 3; HW 1, 2; LAW; MTCW 1, 2;
MTFW 2005

Sa-Carneiro, Mario de 1890-1916 . **TCLC 83**
See also DLB 287; EWL 3

Sacastru, Martin
See Bioy Casares, Adolfo
See also CWW 2

Sacher-Masoch, Leopold von
1836(?)-1895 .... **NCLC 31**

Sachs, Hans 1494-1576 .... **LC 95**
See also CDWLB 2; DLB 179; RGWL 2, 3

Sachs, Marilyn 1927- .... **CLC 35**
See also AAYA 2; BYA 6; CA 17-20R;
CANR 13, 47, 150; CLR 2; JRDA; MAI-
CYA 1, 2; SAAS 2; SATA 3, 68, 164;
SATA-Essay 110; WYA; YAW

Sachs, Marilyn Stickle
See Sachs, Marilyn

Sachs, Nelly 1891-1970 .. **CLC 14, 98; PC 78**
See also CA 17-18; CAAS 25-28R; CANR
87; CAP 2; DLB 332; EWL 3; MTCW 2;
MTFW 2005; PFS 20; RGHL; RGWL 2,
3

Sackler, Howard (Oliver)
1929-1982 .... **CLC 14**
See also CA 61-64; CAAS 108; CAD;
CANR 30; DFS 15; DLB 7

Sacks, Oliver 1933- .... **CLC 67, 202**
See also CA 53-56; CANR 28, 50, 76, 146;
CPW; DA3; INT CANR-28; MTCW 1, 2;
MTFW 2005

Sacks, Oliver Wolf
See Sacks, Oliver

Sackville, Thomas 1536-1608 .... **LC 98**
See also DAM DRAM; DLB 62, 132;
RGEL 2

Sadakichi
See Hartmann, Sadakichi

Sa'dawi, Nawal al-
See El Saadawi, Nawal
See also CWW 2

Sade, Donatien Alphonse Francois
1740-1814 .... **NCLC 3, 47**
See also DLB 314; EW 4; GFL Beginnings
to 1789; RGWL 2, 3

Sade, Marquis de
See Sade, Donatien Alphonse Francois

Sadoff, Ira 1945- .... **CLC 9**
See also CA 53-56; CANR 5, 21, 109; DLB
120

Saetone
See Camus, Albert

Safire, William 1929- .... **CLC 10**
See also CA 17-20R; CANR 31, 54, 91, 148

Sagan, Carl 1934-1996 .... **CLC 30, 112**
See also AAYA 2, 62; CA 25-28R; CAAS
155; CANR 11, 36, 74; CPW; DA3;
MTCW 1, 2; MTFW 2005; SATA 58;
SATA-Obit 94

Sagan, Francoise .... **CLC 3, 6, 9, 17, 36**
See Quoirez, Francoise
See also CWW 2; DLB 83; EWL 3; GFL
1789 to the Present; MTCW 2

Sahgal, Nayantara (Pandit) 1927- .... **CLC 41**
See also CA 9-12R; CANR 11, 88; CN 1,
2, 3, 4, 5, 6, 7; DLB 323

Said, Edward W. 1935-2003 .... **CLC 123**
See also CA 21-24R; CAAS 220; CANR
45, 74, 107, 131; DLB 67; MTCW 2;
MTFW 2005

Saint, H(arry) F. 1941- .... **CLC 50**
See also CA 127

St. Aubin de Teran, Lisa 1953-
See Teran, Lisa St. Aubin de
See also CA 126; CAAE 118; CN 6, 7; INT
CA-126

Saint Birgitta of Sweden c.
1303-1373 .... **CMLC 24**

Sainte-Beuve, Charles Augustin
1804-1869 .... **NCLC 5**
See also DLB 217; EW 6; GFL 1789 to the
Present

Saint-Exupery, Antoine de
1900-1944 .... **TCLC 2, 56, 169; WLC**
See also AAYA 63; BPFB 3; BYA 3; CA
132; CAAE 108; CLR 10; DA3; DAM
NOV; DLB 72; EW 12; EWL 3; GFL
1789 to the Present; LAIT 3; MAICYA 1,
2; MTCW 1, 2; MTFW 2005; RGWL 2,
3; SATA 20; TWA

**Saint-Exupery, Antoine Jean Baptiste Marie
Roger de**
See Saint-Exupery, Antoine de

St. John, David
See Hunt, E. Howard

St. John, J. Hector
See Crevecoeur, Michel Guillaume Jean de

Saint-John Perse
See Leger, (Marie-Rene Auguste) Alexis
Saint-Leger
See also EW 10; EWL 3; GFL 1789 to the
Present; RGWL 2

Saintsbury, George (Edward Bateman)
1845-1933 .... **TCLC 31**
See also CA 160; DLB 57, 149

Sait Faik .... **TCLC 23**
See Abasiyanik, Sait Faik

Saki .... **SSC 12; TCLC 3; WLC 5**
See Munro, H(ector) H(ugh)
See also BRWS 6; BYA 11; LAIT 2; RGEL
2; SSFS 1; SUFW

Sala, George Augustus 1828-1895 . **NCLC 46**

Saladin 1138-1193 .... **CMLC 38**

Salama, Hannu 1936- .... **CLC 18**
See also CA 244; EWL 3

Salamanca, J(ack) R(ichard) 1922- .. **CLC 4,
15**
See also CA 193; 25-28R, 193

Salas, Floyd Francis 1931- .... **HLC 2**
See also CA 119; 27; CANR 44, 75, 93;
DAM MULT; DLB 82; HW 1, 2; MTCW
2; MTFW 2005

Sale, J. Kirkpatrick
See Sale, Kirkpatrick

Sale, John Kirkpatrick
See Sale, Kirkpatrick

Sale, Kirkpatrick 1937- .... **CLC 68**
See also CA 13-16R; CANR 10, 147

Salinas, Luis Omar 1937- ... **CLC 90; HLC 2**
See also AMWS 13; CA 131; CANR 81,
153; DAM MULT; DLB 82; HW 1, 2

Salinas (y Serrano), Pedro
1891(?)-1951 .... **TCLC 17**
See also CAAE 117; DLB 134; EWL 3

Salinger, J.D. 1919- . **CLC 1, 3, 8, 12, 55, 56,
138; SSC 2, 28, 65; WLC 5**
See also AAYA 2, 36; AMW; AMWC 1;
BPFB 3; CA 5-8R; CANR 39, 129;
CDALB 1941-1968; CLR 18; CN 1, 2, 3,
4, 5, 6, 7; CPW 1; DA; DA3; DAB; DAC;
DAM MST, NOV, POP; DLB 2, 102, 173;
EWL 3; EXPN; LAIT 4; MAICYA 1, 2;
MAL 5; MTCW 1, 2; MTFW 2005; NFS
1; RGAL 4; RGSF 2; SATA 67; SSFS 17;
TUS; WYA; YAW

Salisbury, John
See Caute, (John) David

Sallust c. 86B.C.-35B.C. .... **CMLC 68**
See also AW 2; CDWLB 1; DLB 211;
RGWL 2, 3

Salter, James 1925- .. **CLC 7, 52, 59; SSC 58**
See also AMWS 9; CA 73-76; CANR 107,
160; DLB 130

Saltus, Edgar (Everton) 1855-1921 . **TCLC 8**
See also CAAE 105; DLB 202; RGAL 4

Saltykov, Mikhail Evgrafovich
1826-1889 .... **NCLC 16**
See also DLB 238:

Saltykov-Shchedrin, N.
See Saltykov, Mikhail Evgrafovich

Samarakis, Andonis
See Samarakis, Antonis
See also EWL 3

Samarakis, Antonis 1919-2003 .... **CLC 5**
See Samarakis, Andonis
See also CA 25-28R; 16; CAAS 224; CANR
36

Sanchez, Florencio 1875-1910 .... **TCLC 37**
See also CA 153; DLB 305; EWL 3; HW 1;
LAW

Sanchez, Luis Rafael 1936- .... **CLC 23**
See also CA 128; DLB 305; EWL 3; HW 1;
WLIT 1

Sanchez, Sonia 1934- .... **BLC 3; CLC 5, 116,
215; PC 9**
See also BW 2, 3; CA 33-36R; CANR 24,
49, 74, 115; CLR 18; CP 2, 3, 4, 5, 6, 7;
CSW; CWP; DA3; DAM MULT; DLB 41;
DLBD 8; EWL 3; MAICYA 1, 2; MAL 5;
MTCW 1, 2; MTFW 2005; SATA 22, 136;
WP

Sancho, Ignatius 1729-1780 .... **LC 84**

Sand, George 1804-1876 ..... **NCLC 2, 42, 57,
174; WLC 5**
See also DA; DA3; DAB; DAC; DAM
MST, NOV; DLB 119, 192; EW 6; FL 1:3;
FW; GFL 1789 to the Present; RGWL 2,
3; TWA

Sandburg, Carl (August) 1878-1967 . **CLC 1,
4, 10, 15, 35; PC 2, 41; WLC 5**
See also AAYA 24; AMW; BYA 1, 3; CA
5-8R; CAAS 25-28R; CANR 35; CDALB
1865-1917; CLR 67; DA; DA3; DAB;
DAC; DAM MST, POET; DLB 17, 54,
284; EWL 3; EXPP; LAIT 2; MAICYA 1,
2; MAL 5; MTCW 1, 2; MTFW 2005;
PAB; PFS 3, 6, 12; RGAL 4; SATA 8;
TUS; WCH; WP; WYA

Sandburg, Charles
See Sandburg, Carl (August)

Sandburg, Charles A.
See Sandburg, Carl (August)

Sanders, (James) Ed(ward) 1939- .... **CLC 53**
See Sanders, Edward
See also BG 1:3; CA 13-16R; 21; CANR
13, 44, 78; CP 1, 2, 3, 4, 5, 6, 7; DAM
POET; DLB 16, 244

Sanders, Edward
See Sanders, (James) Ed(ward)
See also DLB 244

Sanders, Lawrence 1920-1998 .... **CLC 41**
See also BEST 89:4; BPFB 3; CA 81-84;
CAAS 165; CANR 33, 62; CMW 4;
CPW; DA3; DAM POP; MTCW 1

Sanders, Noah
See Blount, Roy (Alton), Jr.

Sanders, Winston P.
See Anderson, Poul

Sandoz, Mari(e Susette) 1900-1966 .. **CLC 28**
See also CA 1-4R; CAAS 25-28R; CANR
17, 64; DLB 9, 212; LAIT 2; MTCW 1,
2; SATA 5; TCWW 1, 2

Sandys, George 1578-1644 .... **LC 80**
See also DLB 24, 121

Saner, Reg(inald Anthony) 1931- .... **CLC 9**
See also CA 65-68; CP 3, 4, 5, 6, 7

Shepard, James R.
See Shepard, Jim

Shepard, Jim 1956- .... **CLC 36**
See also AAYA 73; CA 137; CANR 59, 104, 160; SATA 90, 164

Shepard, Lucius 1947- .... **CLC 34**
See also CA 141; CAAE 128; CANR 81, 124; HGG; SCFW 2; SFW 4; SUFW 2

Shepard, Sam 1943- .... **CLC 4, 6, 17, 34, 41, 44, 169; DC 5**
See also AAYA 1, 58; AMWS 3; CA 69-72; CABS 3; CAD; CANR 22, 120, 140; CD 5, 6; DA3; DAM DRAM; DFS 3, 6, 7, 14; DLB 7, 212; EWL 3; IDFW 3, 4; MAL 5; MTCW 1, 2; MTFW 2005; RGAL 4

Shepherd, Jean (Parker)
1921-1999 .... **TCLC 177**
See also AAYA 69; AITN 2; CA 77-80; CAAS 187

Shepherd, Michael
See Ludlum, Robert

Sherburne, Zoa (Lillian Morin)
1912-1995 .... **CLC 30**
See also AAYA 13; CA 1-4R; CAAS 176; CANR 3, 37; MAICYA 1, 2; SAAS 18; SATA 3; YAW

Sheridan, Frances 1724-1766 .... **LC 7**
See also DLB 39, 84

Sheridan, Richard Brinsley
1751-1816 . **DC 1; NCLC 5, 91; WLC 5**
See also BRW 3; CDBLB 1660-1789; DA; DAB; DAC; DAM DRAM, MST; DFS 15; DLB 89; WLIT 3

Sherman, Jonathan Marc 1968- .... **CLC 55**
See also CA 230

Sherman, Martin 1941(?)- .... **CLC 19**
See also CA 123; CAAE 116; CAD; CANR 86; CD 5, 6; DFS 20; DLB 228; GLL 1; IDTP; RGHL

Sherwin, Judith Johnson
See Johnson, Judith (Emlyn)
See also CANR 85; CP 2, 3, 4, 5; CWP

Sherwood, Frances 1940- .... **CLC 81**
See also CA 220; 146, 220; CANR 158

Sherwood, Robert E(mmet)
1896-1955 .... **TCLC 3**
See also CA 153; CAAE 104; CANR 86; DAM DRAM; DFS 11, 15, 17; DLB 7, 26, 249; IDFW 3, 4; MAL 5; RGAL 4

Shestov, Lev 1866-1938 .... **TCLC 56**

Shevchenko, Taras 1814-1861 .... **NCLC 54**

Shiel, M(atthew) P(hipps)
1865-1947 .... **TCLC 8**
See Holmes, Gordon
See also CA 160; CAAE 106; DLB 153; HGG; MTCW 2; MTFW 2005; SCFW 1, 2; SFW 4; SUFW

Shields, Carol 1935-2003 .. **CLC 91, 113, 193**
See also AMWS 7; CA 81-84; CAAS 218; CANR 51, 74, 98, 133; CCA 1; CN 6, 7; CPW; DA3; DAC; DLB 334; MTCW 2; MTFW 2005; NFS 23

Shields, David 1956- .... **CLC 97**
See also CA 124; CANR 48, 99, 112, 157

Shields, David Jonathan
See Shields, David

Shiga, Naoya 1883-1971 .... **CLC 33; SSC 23; TCLC 172**
See Shiga Naoya
See also CA 101; CAAS 33-36R; MJW; RGWL 3

Shiga Naoya
See Shiga, Naoya
See also DLB 180; EWL 3; RGWL 3

Shilts, Randy 1951-1994 .... **CLC 85**
See also AAYA 19; CA 127; CAAE 115; CAAS 144; CANR 45; DA3; GLL 1; INT CA-127; MTCW 2; MTFW 2005

Shimazaki, Haruki 1872-1943
See Shimazaki Toson
See also CA 134; CAAE 105; CANR 84; RGWL 3

Shimazaki Toson .... **TCLC 5**
See Shimazaki, Haruki
See also DLB 180; EWL 3

Shirley, James 1596-1666 .... **DC 25; LC 96**
See also DLB 58; RGEL 2

Shirley Hastings, Selina
See Hastings, Selina

Sholokhov, Mikhail (Aleksandrovich)
1905-1984 .... **CLC 7, 15**
See also CA 101; CAAS 112; DLB 272, 332; EWL 3; MTCW 1, 2; MTFW 2005; RGWL 2, 3; SATA-Obit 36

Sholom Aleichem 1859-1916 .... **SSC 33; TCLC 1, 35**
See Rabinovitch, Sholem
See also DLB 333; TWA

Shone, Patric
See Hanley, James

Showalter, Elaine 1941- .... **CLC 169**
See also CA 57-60; CANR 58, 106; DLB 67; FW; GLL 2

Shreve, Susan
See Shreve, Susan Richards

Shreve, Susan Richards 1939- .... **CLC 23**
See also CA 49-52; 5; CANR 5, 38, 69, 100, 159; MAICYA 1, 2; SATA 46, 95, 152; SATA-Brief 41

Shue, Larry 1946-1985 .... **CLC 52**
See also CA 145; CAAS 117; DAM DRAM; DFS 7

Shu-Jen, Chou 1881-1936
See Lu Hsun
See also CAAE 104

Shulman, Alix Kates 1932- .... **CLC 2, 10**
See also CA 29-32R; CANR 43; FW; SATA 7

Shuster, Joe 1914-1992 .... **CLC 21**
See also AAYA 50

Shute, Nevil .... **CLC 30**
See Norway, Nevil Shute
See also BPFB 3; DLB 255; NFS 9; RHW; SFW 4

Shuttle, Penelope (Diane) 1947- .... **CLC 7**
See also CA 93-96; CANR 39, 84, 92, 108; CP 3, 4, 5, 6, 7; CWP; DLB 14, 40

Shvarts, Elena 1948- .... **PC 50**
See also CA 147

Sidhwa, Bapsi 1939-
See Sidhwa, Bapsy (N.)
See also CN 6, 7; DLB 323

Sidhwa, Bapsy (N.) 1938- .... **CLC 168**
See Sidhwa, Bapsi
See also CA 108; CANR 25, 57; FW

Sidney, Mary 1561-1621 .... **LC 19, 39**
See Sidney Herbert, Mary

Sidney, Sir Philip 1554-1586 .... **LC 19, 39, 131; PC 32**
See also BRW 1; BRWR 2; CDBLB Before 1660; DA; DA3; DAB; DAC; DAM MST, POET; DLB 167; EXPP; PAB; RGEL 2; TEA; WP

Sidney Herbert, Mary
See Sidney, Mary
See also DLB 167

Siegel, Jerome 1914-1996 .... **CLC 21**
See Siegel, Jerry
See also CA 169; CAAE 116; CAAS 151

Siegel, Jerry
See Siegel, Jerome
See also AAYA 50

Sienkiewicz, Henryk (Adam Alexander Pius)
1846-1916 .... **TCLC 3**
See also CA 134; CAAE 104; CANR 84; DLB 332; EWL 3; RGSF 2; RGWL 2, 3

Sierra, Gregorio Martinez
See Martinez Sierra, Gregorio

Sierra, Maria de la O'LeJarraga Martinez
See Martinez Sierra, Maria

Sigal, Clancy 1926- .... **CLC 7**
See also CA 1-4R; CANR 85; CN 1, 2, 3, 4, 5, 6, 7

Siger of Brabant 1240(?)-1284(?) . **CMLC 69**
See also DLB 115

Sigourney, Lydia H.
See Sigourney, Lydia Howard (Huntley)
See also DLB 73, 183

Sigourney, Lydia Howard (Huntley)
1791-1865 .... **NCLC 21, 87**
See Sigourney, Lydia H.; Sigourney, Lydia Huntley
See also DLB 1

Sigourney, Lydia Huntley
See Sigourney, Lydia Howard (Huntley)
See also DLB 42, 239, 243

Siguenza y Gongora, Carlos de
1645-1700 .... **HLCS 2; LC 8**
See also LAW

Sigurjonsson, Johann
See Sigurjonsson, Johann

Sigurjonsson, Johann 1880-1919 ... **TCLC 27**
See also CA 170; DLB 293; EWL 3

Sikelianos, Angelos 1884-1951 .... **PC 29; TCLC 39**
See also EWL 3; RGWL 2, 3

Silkin, Jon 1930-1997 .... **CLC 2, 6, 43**
See also CA 5-8R; 5; CANR 89; CP 1, 2, 3, 4, 5, 6; DLB 27

Silko, Leslie 1948- ...... **CLC 23, 74, 114, 211; NNAL; SSC 37, 66; WLCS**
See also AAYA 14; AMWS 4; ANW; BYA 12; CA 122; CAAE 115; CANR 45, 65, 118; CN 4, 5, 6, 7; CP 4, 5, 6, 7; CPW 1; CWP; DA; DA3; DAC; DAM MST, MULT, POP; DLB 143, 175, 256, 275; EWL 3; EXPP; EXPS; LAIT 4; MAL 5; MTCW 2; MTFW 2005; NFS 4; PFS 9, 16; RGAL 4; RGSF 2; SSFS 4, 8, 10, 11; TCWW 1, 2

Sillanpaa, Frans Eemil 1888-1964 ... **CLC 19**
See also CA 129; CAAS 93-96; DLB 332; EWL 3; MTCW 1

Sillitoe, Alan 1928- .. **CLC 1, 3, 6, 10, 19, 57, 148**
See also AITN 1; BRWS 5; CA 191; 9-12R, 191; 2; CANR 8, 26, 55, 139; CDBLB 1960 to Present; CN 1, 2, 3, 4, 5, 6; CP 1, 2, 3, 4, 5; DLB 14, 139; EWL 3; MTCW 1, 2; MTFW 2005; RGEL 2; RGSF 2; SATA 61

Silone, Ignazio 1900-1978 .... **CLC 4**
See also CA 25-28; CAAS 81-84; CANR 34; CAP 2; DLB 264; EW 12; EWL 3; MTCW 1; RGSF 2; RGWL 2, 3

Silone, Ignazione
See Silone, Ignazio

Silver, Joan Micklin 1935- .... **CLC 20**
See also CA 121; CAAE 114; INT CA-121

Silver, Nicholas
See Faust, Frederick (Schiller)

Silverberg, Robert 1935- .... **CLC 7, 140**
See also AAYA 24; BPFB 3; BYA 7, 9; CA 186; 1-4R, 186; 3; CANR 1, 20, 36, 85, 140; CLR 59; CN 6, 7; CPW; DAM POP; DLB 8; INT CANR-20; MAICYA 1, 2; MTCW 1, 2; MTFW 2005; SATA 13, 91; SATA-Essay 104; SCFW 1, 2; SFW 4; SUFW 2

Silverstein, Alvin 1933- .... **CLC 17**
See also CA 49-52; CANR 2; CLR 25; JRDA; MAICYA 1, 2; SATA 8, 69, 124

Starbuck, George (Edwin)
1931-1996 .... **CLC 53**
See also CA 21-24R; CAAS 153; CANR 23; CP 1, 2, 3, 4, 5, 6; DAM POET

Stark, Richard
See Westlake, Donald E.

Statius c. 45-c. 96 .... **CMLC 91**
See also AW 2; DLB 211

Staunton, Schuyler
See Baum, L(yman) Frank

Stead, Christina (Ellen) 1902-1983 ... **CLC 2, 5, 8, 32, 80**
See also BRWS 4; CA 13-16R; CAAS 109; CANR 33, 40; CN 1, 2, 3; DLB 260; EWL 3; FW; MTCW 1, 2; MTFW 2005; RGEL 2; RGSF 2; WWE 1

Stead, William Thomas
1849-1912 .... **TCLC 48**
See also CA 167

Stebnitsky, M.
See Leskov, Nikolai (Semyonovich)

Steele, Richard 1672-1729 .... **LC 18**
See also BRW 3; CDBLB 1660-1789; DLB 84, 101; RGEL 2; WLIT 3

Steele, Timothy (Reid) 1948- .... **CLC 45**
See also CA 93-96; CANR 16, 50, 92; CP 5, 6, 7; DLB 120, 282

Steffens, (Joseph) Lincoln
1866-1936 .... **TCLC 20**
See also CA 198; CAAE 117; DLB 303; MAL 5

Stegner, Wallace (Earle) 1909-1993 .. **CLC 9, 49, 81; SSC 27**
See also AITN 1; AMWS 4; ANW; BEST 90:3; BPFB 3; CA 1-4R; 9; CAAS 141; CANR 1, 21, 46; CN 1, 2, 3, 4, 5; DAM NOV; DLB 9, 206, 275; DLBY 1993; EWL 3; MAL 5; MTCW 1, 2; MTFW 2005; RGAL 4; TCWW 1, 2; TUS

Stein, Gertrude 1874-1946 .... **DC 19; PC 18; SSC 42; TCLC 1, 6, 28, 48; WLC 5**
See also AAYA 64; AMW; AMWC 2; CA 132; CAAE 104; CANR 108; CDALB 1917-1929; DA; DA3; DAB; DAC; DAM MST, NOV, POET; DLB 4, 54, 86, 228; DLBD 15; EWL 3; EXPS; FL 1:6; GLL 1; MAL 5; MBL; MTCW 1, 2; MTFW 2005; NCFS 4; RGAL 4; RGSF 2; SSFS 5; TUS; WP

Steinbeck, John (Ernst) 1902-1968 ... **CLC 1, 5, 9, 13, 21, 34, 45, 75, 124; SSC 11, 37, 77; TCLC 135; WLC 5**
See also AAYA 12; AMW; BPFB 3; BYA 2, 3, 13; CA 1-4R; CAAS 25-28R; CANR 1, 35; CDALB 1929-1941; DA; DA3; DAB; DAC; DAM DRAM, MST, NOV; DLB 7, 9, 212, 275, 309, 332; DLBD 2; EWL 3; EXPS; LAIT 3; MAL 5; MTCW 1, 2; MTFW 2005; NFS 1, 5, 7, 17, 19; RGAL 4; RGSF 2; RHW; SATA 9; SSFS 3, 6, 22; TCWW 1, 2; TUS; WYA; YAW

Steinem, Gloria 1934- .... **CLC 63**
See also CA 53-56; CANR 28, 51, 139; DLB 246; FL 1:1; FW; MTCW 1, 2; MTFW 2005

Steiner, George 1929- .... **CLC 24, 221**
See also CA 73-76; CANR 31, 67, 108; DAM NOV; DLB 67, 299; EWL 3; MTCW 1, 2; MTFW 2005; RGHL; SATA 62

Steiner, K. Leslie
See Delany, Samuel R., Jr.

Steiner, Rudolf 1861-1925 .... **TCLC 13**
See also CAAE 107

Stendhal 1783-1842 .... **NCLC 23, 46, 178; SSC 27; WLC 5**
See also DA; DA3; DAB; DAC; DAM MST, NOV; DLB 119; EW 5; GFL 1789 to the Present; RGWL 2, 3; TWA

Stephen, Adeline Virginia
See Woolf, (Adeline) Virginia

Stephen, Sir Leslie 1832-1904 .... **TCLC 23**
See also BRW 5; CAAE 123; DLB 57, 144, 190

Stephen, Sir Leslie
See Stephen, Sir Leslie

Stephen, Virginia
See Woolf, (Adeline) Virginia

Stephens, James 1882(?)-1950 .... **SSC 50; TCLC 4**
See also CA 192; CAAE 104; DLB 19, 153, 162; EWL 3; FANT; RGEL 2; SUFW

Stephens, Reed
See Donaldson, Stephen R(eeder)

Stephenson, Neal 1959- .... **CLC 220**
See also AAYA 38; CA 122; CANR 88, 138; CN 7; MTFW 2005; SFW 4

Steptoe, Lydia
See Barnes, Djuna
See also GLL 1

Sterchi, Beat 1949- .... **CLC 65**
See also CA 203

Sterling, Brett
See Bradbury, Ray; Hamilton, Edmond

Sterling, Bruce 1954- .... **CLC 72**
See also CA 119; CANR 44, 135; CN 7; MTFW 2005; SCFW 2; SFW 4

Sterling, George 1869-1926 .... **TCLC 20**
See also CA 165; CAAE 117; DLB 54

Stern, Gerald 1925- .... **CLC 40, 100**
See also AMWS 9; CA 81-84; CANR 28, 94; CP 3, 4, 5, 6, 7; DLB 105; RGAL 4

Stern, Richard (Gustave) 1928- ... **CLC 4, 39**
See also CA 1-4R; CANR 1, 25, 52, 120; CN 1, 2, 3, 4, 5, 6, 7; DLB 218; DLBY 1987; INT CANR-25

Sternberg, Josef von 1894-1969 .... **CLC 20**
See also CA 81-84

Sterne, Laurence 1713-1768 .... **LC 2, 48; WLC 5**
See also BRW 3; BRWC 1; CDBLB 1660-1789; DA; DAB; DAC; DAM MST, NOV; DLB 39; RGEL 2; TEA

Sternheim, (William Adolf) Carl
1878-1942 .... **TCLC 8**
See also CA 193; CAAE 105; DLB 56, 118; EWL 3; IDTP; RGWL 2, 3

Stevens, Margaret Dean
See Aldrich, Bess Streeter

Stevens, Mark 1951- .... **CLC 34**
See also CA 122

Stevens, Wallace 1879-1955 . **PC 6; TCLC 3, 12, 45; WLC 5**
See also AMW; AMWR 1; CA 124; CAAE 104; CDALB 1929-1941; DA; DA3; DAB; DAC; DAM MST, POET; DLB 54; EWL 3; EXPP; MAL 5; MTCW 1, 2; PAB; PFS 13, 16; RGAL 4; TUS; WP

Stevenson, Anne (Katharine) 1933- .. **CLC 7, 33**
See also BRWS 6; CA 17-20R; 9; CANR 9, 33, 123; CP 3, 4, 5, 6, 7; CWP; DLB 40; MTCW 1; RHW

Stevenson, Robert Louis (Balfour)
1850-1894 ...... **NCLC 5, 14, 63; SSC 11, 51; WLC 5**
See also AAYA 24; BPFB 3; BRW 5; BRWC 1; BRWR 1; BYA 1, 2, 4, 13; CDBLB 1890-1914; CLR 10, 11, 107; DA; DA3; DAB; DAC; DAM MST, NOV; DLB 18, 57, 141, 156, 174; DLBD 13; GL 3; HGG; JRDA; LAIT 1, 3; MAICYA 1, 2; NFS 11, 20; RGEL 2; RGSF 2; SATA 100; SUFW; TEA; WCH; WLIT 4; WYA; YABC 2; YAW

Stewart, J(ohn) I(nnes) M(ackintosh)
1906-1994 .... **CLC 7, 14, 32**
See Innes, Michael
See also CA 85-88; 3; CAAS 147; CANR 47; CMW 4; CN 1, 2, 3, 4, 5; MTCW 1, 2

Stewart, Mary (Florence Elinor)
1916- .... **CLC 7, 35, 117**
See also AAYA 29, 73; BPFB 3; CA 1-4R; CANR 1, 59, 130; CMW 4; CPW; DAB; FANT; RHW; SATA 12; YAW

Stewart, Mary Rainbow
See Stewart, Mary (Florence Elinor)

Stifle, June
See Campbell, Maria

Stifter, Adalbert 1805-1868 .. **NCLC 41; SSC 28**
See also CDWLB 2; DLB 133; RGSF 2; RGWL 2, 3

Still, James 1906-2001 .... **CLC 49**
See also CA 65-68; 17; CAAS 195; CANR 10, 26; CSW; DLB 9; DLBY 01; SATA 29; SATA-Obit 127

Sting 1951-
See Sumner, Gordon Matthew
See also CA 167

Stirling, Arthur
See Sinclair, Upton

Stitt, Milan 1941- .... **CLC 29**
See also CA 69-72

Stockton, Francis Richard 1834-1902
See Stockton, Frank R.
See also AAYA 68; CA 137; CAAE 108; MAICYA 1, 2; SATA 44; SFW 4

Stockton, Frank R. .... **TCLC 47**
See Stockton, Francis Richard
See also BYA 4, 13; DLB 42, 74; DLBD 13; EXPS; SATA-Brief 32; SSFS 3; SUFW; WCH

Stoddard, Charles
See Kuttner, Henry

Stoker, Abraham 1847-1912
See Stoker, Bram
See also CA 150; CAAE 105; DA; DA3; DAC; DAM MST, NOV; HGG; MTFW 2005; SATA 29

Stoker, Bram . **SSC 62; TCLC 8, 144; WLC 6**
See Stoker, Abraham
See also AAYA 23; BPFB 3; BRWS 3; BYA 5; CDBLB 1890-1914; DAB; DLB 304; GL 3; LATS 1:1; NFS 18; RGEL 2; SUFW; TEA; WLIT 4

Stolz, Mary 1920-2006 .... **CLC 12**
See also AAYA 8, 73; AITN 1; CA 5-8R; CAAS 255; CANR 13, 41, 112; JRDA; MAICYA 1, 2; SAAS 3; SATA 10, 71, 133; YAW

Stolz, Mary Slattery
See Stolz, Mary

Stone, Irving 1903-1989 .... **CLC 7**
See also AITN 1; BPFB 3; CA 1-4R; 3; CAAS 129; CANR 1, 23; CN 1, 2, 3, 4; CPW; DA3; DAM POP; INT CANR-23; MTCW 1, 2; MTFW 2005; RHW; SATA 3; SATA-Obit 64

Stone, Oliver 1946- .... **CLC 73**
See also AAYA 15, 64; CA 110; CANR 55, 125

Stone, Oliver William
See Stone, Oliver

Stone, Robert 1937- .... **CLC 5, 23, 42, 175**
See also AMWS 5; BPFB 3; CA 85-88; CANR 23, 66, 95; CN 4, 5, 6, 7; DLB 152; EWL 3; INT CANR-23; MAL 5; MTCW 1; MTFW 2005

Stone, Ruth 1915- .... **PC 53**
See also CA 45-48; CANR 2, 91; CP 5, 6, 7; CSW; DLB 105; PFS 19

Sutcliff, Rosemary 1920-1992 .... **CLC 26**
See also AAYA 10; BYA 1, 4; CA 5-8R; CAAS 139; CANR 37; CLR 1, 37; CPW; DAB; DAC; DAM MST, POP; JRDA; LATS 1:1; MAICYA 1, 2; MAICYAS 1; RHW; SATA 6, 44, 78; SATA-Obit 73; WYA; YAW

Sutro, Alfred 1863-1933 .... **TCLC 6**
See also CA 185; CAAE 105; DLB 10; RGEL 2

Sutton, Henry
See Slavitt, David R(ytman)

Suzuki, D. T.
See Suzuki, Daisetz Teitaro

Suzuki, Daisetz T.
See Suzuki, Daisetz Teitaro

Suzuki, Daisetz Teitaro
1870-1966 .... **TCLC 109**
See also CA 121; CAAS 111; MTCW 1, 2; MTFW 2005

Suzuki, Teitaro
See Suzuki, Daisetz Teitaro

Svevo, Italo .... **SSC 25; TCLC 2, 35**
See Schmitz, Aron Hector
See also DLB 264; EW 8; EWL 3; RGWL 2, 3; WLIT 7

Swados, Elizabeth 1951- .... **CLC 12**
See also CA 97-100; CANR 49, 163; INT CA-97-100

Swados, Elizabeth A.
See Swados, Elizabeth

Swados, Harvey 1920-1972 .... **CLC 5**
See also CA 5-8R; CAAS 37-40R; CANR 6; CN 1; DLB 2, 335; MAL 5

Swados, Liz
See Swados, Elizabeth

Swan, Gladys 1934- .... **CLC 69**
See also CA 101; CANR 17, 39; TCLE 1:2

Swanson, Logan
See Matheson, Richard (Burton)

Swarthout, Glendon (Fred)
1918-1992 .... **CLC 35**
See also AAYA 55; CA 1-4R; CAAS 139; CANR 1, 47; CN 1, 2, 3, 4, 5; LAIT 5; SATA 26; TCWW 1, 2; YAW

Swedenborg, Emanuel 1688-1772 ..... **LC 105**

Sweet, Sarah C.
See Jewett, (Theodora) Sarah Orne

Swenson, May 1919-1989 ...... **CLC 4, 14, 61, 106; PC 14**
See also AMWS 4; CA 5-8R; CAAS 130; CANR 36, 61, 131; CP 1, 2, 3, 4; DA; DAB; DAC; DAM MST, POET; DLB 5; EXPP; GLL 2; MAL 5; MTCW 1, 2; MTFW 2005; PFS 16; SATA 15; WP

Swift, Augustus
See Lovecraft, H. P.

Swift, Graham 1949- .... **CLC 41, 88, 233**
See also BRWC 2; BRWS 5; CA 122; CAAE 117; CANR 46, 71, 128; CN 4, 5, 6, 7; DLB 194, 326; MTCW 2; MTFW 2005; NFS 18; RGSF 2

Swift, Jonathan 1667-1745 ..... **LC 1, 42, 101; PC 9; WLC 6**
See also AAYA 41; BRW 3; BRWC 1; BRWR 1; BYA 5, 14; CDBLB 1660-1789; CLR 53; DA; DA3; DAB; DAC; DAM MST, NOV, POET; DLB 39, 95, 101; EXPN; LAIT 1; NFS 6; RGEL 2; SATA 19; TEA; WCH; WLIT 3

Swinburne, Algernon Charles
1837-1909 ... **PC 24; TCLC 8, 36; WLC 6**
See also BRW 5; CA 140; CAAE 105; CDBLB 1832-1890; DA; DA3; DAB; DAC; DAM MST, POET; DLB 35, 57; PAB; RGEL 2; TEA

Swinfen, Ann .... **CLC 34**
See also CA 202

Swinnerton, Frank (Arthur)
1884-1982 .... **CLC 31**
See also CA 202; CAAS 108; CN 1, 2, 3; DLB 34

Swinnerton, Frank Arthur
1884-1982 .... **CLC 31**
See also CAAS 108; DLB 34

Swithen, John
See King, Stephen

Sylvia
See Ashton-Warner, Sylvia (Constance)

Symmes, Robert Edward
See Duncan, Robert

Symonds, John Addington
1840-1893 .... **NCLC 34**
See also DLB 57, 144

Symons, Arthur 1865-1945 .... **TCLC 11**
See also CA 189; CAAE 107; DLB 19, 57, 149; RGEL 2

Symons, Julian (Gustave)
1912-1994 .... **CLC 2, 14, 32**
See also CA 49-52; 3; CAAS 147; CANR 3, 33, 59; CMW 4; CN 1, 2, 3, 4, 5; CP 1, 3, 4; DLB 87, 155; DLBY 1992; MSW; MTCW 1

Synge, (Edmund) J(ohn) M(illington)
1871-1909 .... **DC 2; TCLC 6, 37**
See also BRW 6; BRWR 1; CA 141; CAAE 104; CDBLB 1890-1914; DAM DRAM; DFS 18; DLB 10, 19; EWL 3; RGEL 2; TEA; WLIT 4

Syruc, J.
See Milosz, Czeslaw

Szirtes, George 1948- .... **CLC 46; PC 51**
See also CA 109; CANR 27, 61, 117; CP 4, 5, 6, 7

Szymborska, Wislawa 1923- ... **CLC 99, 190; PC 44**
See also CA 154; CANR 91, 133; CDWLB 4; CWP; CWW 2; DA3; DLB 232, 332; DLBY 1996; EWL 3; MTCW 2; MTFW 2005; PFS 15; RGHL; RGWL 3

T. O., Nik
See Annensky, Innokenty (Fyodorovich)

Tabori, George 1914- .... **CLC 19**
See also CA 49-52; CANR 4, 69; CBD; CD 5, 6; DLB 245; RGHL

Tacitus c. 55-c. 117 .... **CMLC 56**
See also AW 2; CDWLB 1; DLB 211; RGWL 2, 3; WLIT 8

Tagore, Rabindranath 1861-1941 .... **PC 8; SSC 48; TCLC 3, 53**
See also CA 120; CAAE 104; DA3; DAM DRAM, POET; DLB 323, 332; EWL 3; MTCW 1, 2; MTFW 2005; PFS 18; RGEL 2; RGSF 2; RGWL 2, 3; TWA

Taine, Hippolyte Adolphe
1828-1893 .... **NCLC 15**
See also EW 7; GFL 1789 to the Present

Talayesva, Don C. 1890-(?) .... **NNAL**

Talese, Gay 1932- .... **CLC 37, 232**
See also AITN 1; CA 1-4R; CANR 9, 58, 137; DLB 185; INT CANR-9; MTCW 1, 2; MTFW 2005

Tallent, Elizabeth 1954- .... **CLC 45**
See also CA 117; CANR 72; DLB 130

Tallmountain, Mary 1918-1997 .... **NNAL**
See also CA 146; CAAS 161; DLB 193

Tally, Ted 1952- .... **CLC 42**
See also CA 124; CAAE 120; CAD; CANR 125; CD 5, 6; INT CA-124

Talvik, Heiti 1904-1947 .... **TCLC 87**
See also EWL 3

Tamayo y Baus, Manuel
1829-1898 .... **NCLC 1**

Tammsaare, A(nton) H(ansen)
1878-1940 .... **TCLC 27**
See also CA 164; CDWLB 4; DLB 220; EWL 3

Tam'si, Tchicaya U
See Tchicaya, Gerald Felix

Tan, Amy 1952- ...... **AAL; CLC 59, 120, 151**
See also AAYA 9, 48; AMWS 10; BEST 89:3; BPFB 3; CA 136; CANR 54, 105, 132; CDALBS; CN 6, 7; CPW 1; DA3; DAM MULT, NOV, POP; DLB 173, 312; EXPN; FL 1:6; FW; LAIT 3, 5; MAL 5; MTCW 2; MTFW 2005; NFS 1, 13, 16; RGAL 4; SATA 75; SSFS 9; YAW

Tandem, Carl Felix
See Spitteler, Carl

Tandem, Felix
See Spitteler, Carl

Tanizaki, Jun'ichiro 1886-1965 ... **CLC 8, 14, 28; SSC 21**
See Tanizaki Jun'ichiro
See also CA 93-96; CAAS 25-28R; MJW; MTCW 2; MTFW 2005; RGSF 2; RGWL 2

Tanizaki Jun'ichiro
See Tanizaki, Jun'ichiro
See also DLB 180; EWL 3

Tannen, Deborah 1945- .... **CLC 206**
See also CA 118; CANR 95

Tannen, Deborah Frances
See Tannen, Deborah

Tanner, William
See Amis, Kingsley

Tante, Dilly
See Kunitz, Stanley

Tao Lao
See Storni, Alfonsina

Tapahonso, Luci 1953- .... **NNAL; PC 65**
See also CA 145; CANR 72, 127; DLB 175

Tarantino, Quentin (Jerome)
1963- .... **CLC 125, 230**
See also AAYA 58; CA 171; CANR 125

Tarassoff, Lev
See Troyat, Henri

Tarbell, Ida M(inerva) 1857-1944 . **TCLC 40**
See also CA 181; CAAE 122; DLB 47

Tardieu d'Esclavelles, Louise-Florence-Petronille
See Epinay, Louise d'

Tarkington, (Newton) Booth
1869-1946 .... **TCLC 9**
See also BPFB 3; BYA 3; CA 143; CAAE 110; CWRI 5; DLB 9, 102; MAL 5; MTCW 2; RGAL 4; SATA 17

Tarkovskii, Andrei Arsen'evich
See Tarkovsky, Andrei (Arsenyevich)

Tarkovsky, Andrei (Arsenyevich)
1932-1986 .... **CLC 75**
See also CA 127

Tartt, Donna 1964(?)- .... **CLC 76**
See also AAYA 56; CA 142; CANR 135; MTFW 2005

Tasso, Torquato 1544-1595 .... **LC 5, 94**
See also EFS 2; EW 2; RGWL 2, 3; WLIT 7

Tate, (John Orley) Allen 1899-1979 .. **CLC 2, 4, 6, 9, 11, 14, 24; PC 50**
See also AMW; CA 5-8R; CAAS 85-88; CANR 32, 108; CN 1, 2; CP 1, 2; DLB 4, 45, 63; DLBD 17; EWL 3; MAL 5; MTCW 1, 2; MTFW 2005; RGAL 4; RHW

Tate, Ellalice
See Hibbert, Eleanor Alice Burford

Tate, James (Vincent) 1943- ..... **CLC 2, 6, 25**
See also CA 21-24R; CANR 29, 57, 114; CP 1, 2, 3, 4, 5, 6, 7; DLB 5, 169; EWL 3; PFS 10, 15; RGAL 4; WP

Tate, Nahum 1652(?)-1715 .... **LC 109**
See also DLB 80; RGEL 2

Tauler, Johannes c. 1300-1361 ...... **CMLC 37**
See also DLB 179; LMFS 1

Thomas, Ross (Elmore) 1926-1995 .. **CLC 39**
See also CA 33-36R; CAAS 150; CANR
22, 63; CMW 4

Thompson, Francis (Joseph)
1859-1907 .... **TCLC 4**
See also BRW 5; CA 189; CAAE 104; CD-
BLB 1890-1914; DLB 19; RGEL 2; TEA

Thompson, Francis Clegg
See Mencken, H(enry) L(ouis)

Thompson, Hunter S. 1937(?)-2005 .. **CLC 9,**
17, 40, 104, 229
See also AAYA 45; BEST 89:1; BPFB 3;
CA 17-20R; CAAS 236; CANR 23, 46,
74, 77, 111, 133; CPW; CSW; DA3; DAM
POP; DLB 185; MTCW 1, 2; MTFW
2005; TUS

Thompson, James Myers
See Thompson, Jim (Myers)

Thompson, Jim (Myers)
1906-1977(?) .... **CLC 69**
See also BPFB 3; CA 140; CMW 4; CPW;
DLB 226; MSW

Thompson, Judith (Clare Francesca)
1954- .... **CLC 39**
See also CA 143; CD 5, 6; CWD; DFS 22;
DLB 334

Thomson, James 1700-1748 .... **LC 16, 29, 40**
See also BRWS 3; DAM POET; DLB 95;
RGEL 2

Thomson, James 1834-1882 .... **NCLC 18**
See also DAM POET; DLB 35; RGEL 2

Thoreau, Henry David 1817-1862 .. **NCLC 7,**
21, 61, 138; PC 30; WLC 6
See also AAYA 42; AMW; ANW; BYA 3;
CDALB 1640-1865; DA; DA3; DAB;
DAC; DAM MST; DLB 1, 183, 223, 270,
298; LAIT 2; LMFS 1; NCFS 3; RGAL
4; TUS

Thorndike, E. L.
See Thorndike, Edward L(ee)

Thorndike, Edward L(ee)
1874-1949 .... **TCLC 107**
See also CAAE 121

Thornton, Hall
See Silverberg, Robert

Thorpe, Adam 1956- .... **CLC 176**
See also CA 129; CANR 92, 160; DLB 231

Thorpe, Thomas Bangs
1815-1878 .... **NCLC 183**
See also DLB 3, 11, 248; RGAL 4

Thubron, Colin 1939- .... **CLC 163**
See also CA 25-28R; CANR 12, 29, 59, 95;
CN 5, 6, 7; DLB 204, 231

Thubron, Colin Gerald Dryden
See Thubron, Colin

Thucydides c. 455B.C.-c. 395B.C. . . **CMLC 17**
See also AW 1; DLB 176; RGWL 2, 3;
WLIT 8

Thumboo, Edwin Nadason 1933- .... **PC 30**
See also CA 194; CP 1

Thurber, James (Grover)
1894-1961 .. **CLC 5, 11, 25, 125; SSC 1,**
47
See also AAYA 56; AMWS 1; BPFB 3;
BYA 5; CA 73-76; CANR 17, 39; CDALB
1929-1941; CWRI 5; DA; DA3; DAB;
DAC; DAM DRAM, MST, NOV; DLB 4,
11, 22, 102; EWL 3; EXPS; FANT; LAIT
3; MAICYA 1, 2; MAL 5; MTCW 1, 2;
MTFW 2005; RGAL 4; RGSF 2; SATA
13; SSFS 1, 10, 19; SUFW; TUS

Thurman, Wallace (Henry)
1902-1934 ..... **BLC 3; HR 1:3; TCLC 6**
See also BW 1, 3; CA 124; CAAE 104;
CANR 81; DAM MULT; DLB 51

Tibullus c. 54B.C.-c. 18B.C. .... **CMLC 36**
See also AW 2; DLB 211; RGWL 2, 3;
WLIT 8

Ticheburn, Cheviot
See Ainsworth, William Harrison

Tieck, (Johann) Ludwig
1773-1853 ..... **NCLC 5, 46; SSC 31, 100**
See also CDWLB 2; DLB 90; EW 5; IDTP;
RGSF 2; RGWL 2, 3; SUFW

Tiger, Derry
See Ellison, Harlan

Tilghman, Christopher 1946- .... **CLC 65**
See also CA 159; CANR 135, 151; CSW;
DLB 244

Tillich, Paul (Johannes)
1886-1965 .... **CLC 131**
See also CA 5-8R; CAAS 25-28R; CANR
33; MTCW 1, 2

Tillinghast, Richard (Williford)
1940- .... **CLC 29**
See also CA 29-32R; 23; CANR 26, 51, 96;
CP 2, 3, 4, 5, 6, 7; CSW

Tillman, Lynne (?)- .... **CLC 231**
See also CA 173; CANR 144

Timrod, Henry 1828-1867 .... **NCLC 25**
See also DLB 3, 248; RGAL 4

Tindall, Gillian (Elizabeth) 1938- ...... **CLC 7**
See also CA 21-24R; CANR 11, 65, 107;
CN 1, 2, 3, 4, 5, 6, 7

Tiptree, James, Jr. .... **CLC 48, 50**
See Sheldon, Alice Hastings Bradley
See also DLB 8; SCFW 1, 2; SFW 4

Tirone Smith, Mary-Ann 1944- .... **CLC 39**
See also CA 136; CAAE 118; CANR 113;
SATA 143

Tirso de Molina 1580(?)-1648 .... **DC 13;**
HLCS 2; LC 73
See also RGWL 2, 3

Titmarsh, Michael Angelo
See Thackeray, William Makepeace

Tocqueville, Alexis (Charles Henri Maurice
Clerel Comte) de 1805-1859 .. **NCLC 7,**
63
See also EW 6; GFL 1789 to the Present;
TWA

Toer, Pramoedya Ananta
1925-2006 .... **CLC 186**
See also CA 197; CAAS 251; RGWL 3

Toffler, Alvin 1928- .... **CLC 168**
See also CA 13-16R; CANR 15, 46, 67;
CPW; DAM POP; MTCW 1, 2

Toibin, Colm 1955- .... **CLC 162**
See also CA 142; CANR 81, 149; CN 7;
DLB 271

Tolkien, John Ronald Reuel
See Tolkien, J.R.R

Tolkien, J.R.R 1892-1973 ...... **CLC 1, 2, 3, 8,**
12, 38; TCLC 137; WLC 6
See also AAYA 10; AITN 1; BPFB 3;
BRWC 2; BRWS 2; CA 17-18; CAAS 45-
48; CANR 36, 134; CAP 2; CDBLB
1914-1945; CLR 56; CN 1; CPW 1;
CWRI 5; DA; DA3; DAB; DAC; DAM
MST, NOV, POP; DLB 15, 160, 255; EFS
2; EWL 3; FANT; JRDA; LAIT 1; LATS
1:2; LMFS 2; MAICYA 1, 2; MTCW 1,
2; MTFW 2005; NFS 8; RGEL 2; SATA
2, 32, 100; SATA-Obit 24; SFW 4; SUFW;
TEA; WCH; WYA; YAW

Toller, Ernst 1893-1939 .... **TCLC 10**
See also CA 186; CAAE 107; DLB 124;
EWL 3; RGWL 2, 3

Tolson, M. B.
See Tolson, Melvin B(eaunorus)

Tolson, Melvin B(eaunorus)
1898(?)-1966 .... **BLC 3; CLC 36, 105**
See also AFAW 1, 2; BW 1, 3; CA 124;
CAAS 89-92; CANR 80; DAM MULT,
POET; DLB 48, 76; MAL 5; RGAL 4

Tolstoi, Aleksei Nikolaevich
See Tolstoy, Alexey Nikolaevich

Tolstoi, Lev
See Tolstoy, Leo (Nikolaevich)
See also RGSF 2; RGWL 2, 3

Tolstoy, Aleksei Nikolaevich
See Tolstoy, Alexey Nikolaevich
See also DLB 272

Tolstoy, Alexey Nikolaevich
1882-1945 .... **TCLC 18**
See Tolstoy, Aleksei Nikolaevich
See also CA 158; CAAE 107; EWL 3; SFW
4

Tolstoy, Leo (Nikolaevich)
1828-1910 . **SSC 9, 30, 45, 54; TCLC 4,**
11, 17, 28, 44, 79, 173; WLC 6
See Tolstoi, Lev
See also AAYA 56; CA 123; CAAE 104;
DA; DA3; DAB; DAC; DAM MST, NOV;
DLB 238; EFS 2; EW 7; EXPS; IDTP;
LAIT 2; LATS 1:1; LMFS 1; NFS 10;
SATA 26; SSFS 5; TWA

Tolstoy, Count Leo
See Tolstoy, Leo (Nikolaevich)

Tomalin, Claire 1933- .... **CLC 166**
See also CA 89-92; CANR 52, 88; DLB
155

Tomasi di Lampedusa, Giuseppe 1896-1957
See Lampedusa, Giuseppe (Tomasi) di
See also CAAE 111; DLB 177; EWL 3;
WLIT 7

Tomlin, Lily 1939(?)-
See Tomlin, Mary Jean
See also CAAE 117

Tomlin, Mary Jean .... **CLC 17**
See Tomlin, Lily

Tomline, F. Latour
See Gilbert, W(illiam) S(chwenck)

Tomlinson, (Alfred) Charles 1927- .... **CLC 2,**
4, 6, 13, 45; PC 17
See also CA 5-8R; CANR 33; CP 1, 2, 3, 4,
5, 6, 7; DAM POET; DLB 40; TCLE 1:2

Tomlinson, H(enry) M(ajor)
1873-1958 .... **TCLC 71**
See also CA 161; CAAE 118; DLB 36, 100,
195

Tonna, Charlotte Elizabeth
1790-1846 .... **NCLC 135**
See also DLB 163

Tonson, Jacob fl. 1655(?)-1736 .... **LC 86**
See also DLB 170

Toole, John Kennedy 1937-1969 ..... **CLC 19,**
64
See also BPFB 3; CA 104; DLBY 1981;
MTCW 2; MTFW 2005

Toomer, Eugene
See Toomer, Jean

Toomer, Eugene Pinchback
See Toomer, Jean

Toomer, Jean 1894-1967 .. **BLC 3; CLC 1, 4,**
13, 22; HR 1:3; PC 7; SSC 1, 45;
TCLC 172; WLCS
See also AFAW 1, 2; AMWS 3, 9; BW 1;
CA 85-88; CDALB 1917-1929; DA3;
DAM MULT; DLB 45, 51; EWL 3; EXPP;
EXPS; LMFS 2; MAL 5; MTCW 1, 2;
MTFW 2005; NFS 11; RGAL 4; RGSF 2;
SSFS 5

Toomer, Nathan Jean
See Toomer, Jean

Toomer, Nathan Pinchback
See Toomer, Jean

Torley, Luke
See Blish, James (Benjamin)

Tornimparte, Alessandra
See Ginzburg, Natalia

Torre, Raoul della
See Mencken, H(enry) L(ouis)

Torrence, Ridgely 1874-1950 .... **TCLC 97**
See also DLB 54, 249; MAL 5

Turner, Frederick 1943- .... **CLC 48**
See also CA 227; 73-76, 227; 10; CANR 12, 30, 56; DLB 40, 282

Turton, James
See Crace, Jim

Tutu, Desmond M(pilo) 1931- .. **BLC 3; CLC 80**
See also BW 1, 3; CA 125; CANR 67, 81; DAM MULT

Tutuola, Amos 1920-1997 ..... **BLC 3; CLC 5, 14, 29; TCLC 188**
See also AFW; BW 2, 3; CA 9-12R; CAAS 159; CANR 27, 66; CDWLB 3; CN 1, 2, 3, 4, 5, 6; DA3; DAM MULT; DLB 125; DNFS 2; EWL 3; MTCW 1, 2; MTFW 2005; RGEL 2; WLIT 2

Twain, Mark .... **SSC 6, 26, 34, 87; TCLC 6, 12, 19, 36, 48, 59, 161, 185; WLC 6**
See Clemens, Samuel Langhorne
See also AAYA 20; AMW; AMWC 1; BPFB 3; BYA 2, 3, 11, 14; CLR 58, 60, 66; DLB 11; EXPN; EXPS; FANT; LAIT 2; MAL 5; NCFS 4; NFS 1, 6; RGAL 4; RGSF 2; SFW 4; SSFS 1, 7, 16, 21; SUFW; TUS; WCH; WYA; YAW

Tyler, Anne 1941- . **CLC 7, 11, 18, 28, 44, 59, 103, 205**
See also AAYA 18, 60; AMWS 4; BEST 89:1; BPFB 3; BYA 12; CA 9-12R; CANR 11, 33, 53, 109, 132; CDALBS; CN 1, 2, 3, 4, 5, 6, 7; CPW; CSW; DAM NOV, POP; DLB 6, 143; DLBY 1982; EWL 3; EXPN; LATS 1:2; MAL 5; MBL; MTCW 1, 2; MTFW 2005; NFS 2, 7, 10; RGAL 4; SATA 7, 90, 173; SSFS 17; TCLE 1:2; TUS; YAW

Tyler, Royall 1757-1826 .... **NCLC 3**
See also DLB 37; RGAL 4

Tynan, Katharine 1861-1931 .... **TCLC 3**
See also CA 167; CAAE 104; DLB 153, 240; FW

Tyndale, William c. 1484-1536 .... **LC 103**
See also DLB 132

Tyutchev, Fyodor 1803-1873 .... **NCLC 34**

Tzara, Tristan 1896-1963 .... **CLC 47; PC 27; TCLC 168**
See also CA 153; CAAS 89-92; DAM POET; EWL 3; MTCW 2

Uchida, Yoshiko 1921-1992 .... **AAL**
See also AAYA 16; BYA 2, 3; CA 13-16R; CAAS 139; CANR 6, 22, 47, 61; CDALBS; CLR 6, 56; CWRI 5; DLB 312; JRDA; MAICYA 1, 2; MTCW 1, 2; MTFW 2005; SAAS 1; SATA 1, 53; SATA-Obit 72

Udall, Nicholas 1504-1556 .... **LC 84**
See also DLB 62; RGEL 2

Ueda Akinari 1734-1809 .... **NCLC 131**

Uhry, Alfred 1936- .... **CLC 55**
See also CA 133; CAAE 127; CAD; CANR 112; CD 5, 6; CSW; DA3; DAM DRAM, POP; DFS 11, 15; INT CA-133; MTFW 2005

Ulf, Haerved
See Strindberg, (Johan) August

Ulf, Harved
See Strindberg, (Johan) August

Ulibarri, Sabine R(eyes) 1919-2003 .... **CLC 83; HLCS 2**
See also CA 131; CAAS 214; CANR 81; DAM MULT; DLB 82; HW 1, 2; RGSF 2

Unamuno (y Jugo), Miguel de 1864-1936 .. **HLC 2; SSC 11, 69; TCLC 2, 9, 148**
See also CA 131; CAAE 104; CANR 81; DAM MULT, NOV; DLB 108, 322; EW 8; EWL 3; HW 1, 2; MTCW 1, 2; MTFW 2005; RGSF 2; RGWL 2, 3; SSFS 20; TWA

Uncle Shelby
See Silverstein, Shel

Undercliffe, Errol
See Campbell, (John) Ramsey

Underwood, Miles
See Glassco, John

Undset, Sigrid 1882-1949 .. **TCLC 3; WLC 6**
See also CA 129; CAAE 104; DA; DA3; DAB; DAC; DAM MST, NOV; DLB 293, 332; EW 9; EWL 3; FW; MTCW 1, 2; MTFW 2005; RGWL 2, 3

Ungaretti, Giuseppe 1888-1970 ... **CLC 7, 11, 15; PC 57**
See also CA 19-20; CAAS 25-28R; CAP 2; DLB 114; EW 10; EWL 3; PFS 20; RGWL 2, 3; WLIT 7

Unger, Douglas 1952- .... **CLC 34**
See also CA 130; CANR 94, 155

Unsworth, Barry (Forster) 1930- .... **CLC 76, 127**
See also BRWS 7; CA 25-28R; CANR 30, 54, 125; CN 6, 7; DLB 194, 326

Updike, John 1932- . **CLC 1, 2, 3, 5, 7, 9, 13, 15, 23, 34, 43, 70, 139, 214; SSC 13, 27; WLC 6**
See also AAYA 36; AMW; AMWC 1; AMWR 1; BPFB 3; BYA 12; CA 1-4R; CABS 1; CANR 4, 33, 51, 94, 133; CDALB 1968-1988; CN 1, 2, 3, 4, 5, 6, 7; CP 1, 2, 3, 4, 5, 6, 7; CPW 1; DA; DA3; DAB; DAC; DAM MST, NOV, POET, POP; DLB 2, 5, 143, 218, 227; DLBD 3; DLBY 1980, 1982, 1997; EWL 3; EXPP; HGG; MAL 5; MTCW 1, 2; MTFW 2005; NFS 12, 24; RGAL 4; RGSF 2; SSFS 3, 19; TUS

Updike, John Hoyer
See Updike, John

Upshaw, Margaret Mitchell
See Mitchell, Margaret (Munnerlyn)

Upton, Mark
See Sanders, Lawrence

Upward, Allen 1863-1926 .... **TCLC 85**
See also CA 187; CAAE 117; DLB 36

Urdang, Constance (Henriette) 1922-1996 .... **CLC 47**
See also CA 21-24R; CANR 9, 24; CP 1, 2, 3, 4, 5, 6; CWP

Urfe, Honore d' 1567(?)-1625 .... **LC 132**
See also DLB 268; GFL Beginnings to 1789; RGWL 2, 3

Uriel, Henry
See Faust, Frederick (Schiller)

Uris, Leon 1924-2003 .... **CLC 7, 32**
See also AITN 1, 2; BEST 89:2; BPFB 3; CA 1-4R; CAAS 217; CANR 1, 40, 65, 123; CN 1, 2, 3, 4, 5, 6; CPW 1; DA3; DAM NOV, POP; MTCW 1, 2; MTFW 2005; RGHL; SATA 49; SATA-Obit 146

Urista (Heredia), Alberto (Baltazar) 1947- .... **HLCS 1**
See Alurista
See also CA 182; CANR 2, 32; HW 1

Urmuz
See Codrescu, Andrei

Urquhart, Guy
See McAlmon, Robert (Menzies)

Urquhart, Jane 1949- .... **CLC 90**
See also CA 113; CANR 32, 68, 116, 157; CCA 1; DAC; DLB 334

Usigli, Rodolfo 1905-1979 .... **HLCS 1**
See also CA 131; DLB 305; EWL 3; HW 1; LAW

Usk, Thomas (?)-1388 .... **CMLC 76**
See also DLB 146

Ustinov, Peter (Alexander) 1921-2004 .... **CLC 1**
See also AITN 1; CA 13-16R; CAAS 225; CANR 25, 51; CBD; CD 5, 6; DLB 13; MTCW 2

U Tam'si, Gerald Felix Tchicaya
See Tchicaya, Gerald Felix

U Tam'si, Tchicaya
See Tchicaya, Gerald Felix

Vachss, Andrew 1942- .... **CLC 106**
See also CA 214; 118, 214; CANR 44, 95, 153; CMW 4

Vachss, Andrew H.
See Vachss, Andrew

Vachss, Andrew Henry
See Vachss, Andrew

Vaculik, Ludvik 1926- .... **CLC 7**
See also CA 53-56; CANR 72; CWW 2; DLB 232; EWL 3

Vaihinger, Hans 1852-1933 .... **TCLC 71**
See also CA 166; CAAE 116

Valdez, Luis (Miguel) 1940- ..... **CLC 84; DC 10; HLC 2**
See also CA 101; CAD; CANR 32, 81; CD 5, 6; DAM MULT; DFS 5; DLB 122; EWL 3; HW 1; LAIT 4; LLW

Valenzuela, Luisa 1938- .... **CLC 31, 104; HLCS 2; SSC 14, 82**
See also CA 101; CANR 32, 65, 123; CD-WLB 3; CWW 2; DAM MULT; DLB 113; EWL 3; FW; HW 1, 2; LAW; RGSF 2; RGWL 3

Valera y Alcala-Galiano, Juan 1824-1905 .... **TCLC 10**
See also CAAE 106

Valerius Maximus fl. 20- .... **CMLC 64**
See also DLB 211

Valery, (Ambroise) Paul (Toussaint Jules) 1871-1945 .... **PC 9; TCLC 4, 15**
See also CA 122; CAAE 104; DA3; DAM POET; DLB 258; EW 8; EWL 3; GFL 1789 to the Present; MTCW 1, 2; MTFW 2005; RGWL 2, 3; TWA

Valle-Inclan, Ramon (Maria) del 1866-1936 .... **HLC 2; TCLC 5**
See del Valle-Inclan, Ramon (Maria)
See also CA 153; CAAE 106; CANR 80; DAM MULT; DLB 134; EW 8; EWL 3; HW 2; RGSF 2; RGWL 2, 3

Vallejo, Antonio Buero
See Buero Vallejo, Antonio

Vallejo, Cesar (Abraham) 1892-1938 .... **HLC 2; TCLC 3, 56**
See also CA 153; CAAE 105; DAM MULT; DLB 290; EWL 3; HW 1; LAW; RGWL 2, 3

Valles, Jules 1832-1885 .... **NCLC 71**
See also DLB 123; GFL 1789 to the Present

Vallette, Marguerite Eymery 1860-1953 .... **TCLC 67**
See Rachilde
See also CA 182; DLB 123, 192

Valle Y Pena, Ramon del
See Valle-Inclan, Ramon (Maria) del

Van Ash, Cay 1918-1994 .... **CLC 34**
See also CA 220

Vanbrugh, Sir John 1664-1726 .... **LC 21**
See also BRW 2; DAM DRAM; DLB 80; IDTP; RGEL 2

Van Campen, Karl
See Campbell, John W(ood, Jr.)

Vance, Gerald
See Silverberg, Robert

Vance, Jack 1916-
See Queen, Ellery; Vance, John Holbrook
See also CA 29-32R; CANR 17, 65, 154; CMW 4; MTCW 1

Villiers de l'Isle Adam, Jean Marie Mathias Philippe Auguste 1838-1889 ... NCLC 3; SSC 14
See also DLB 123, 192; GFL 1789 to the Present; RGSF 2

Villon, Francois 1431-1463(?) . LC 62; PC 13
See also DLB 208; EW 2; RGWL 2, 3; TWA

Vine, Barbara .... CLC 50
See Rendell, Ruth
See also BEST 90:4

Vinge, Joan (Carol) D(ennison) 1948- .... CLC 30; SSC 24
See also AAYA 32; BPFB 3; CA 93-96; CANR 72; SATA 36, 113; SFW 4; YAW

Viola, Herman J(oseph) 1938- .... CLC 70
See also CA 61-64; CANR 8, 23, 48, 91; SATA 126

Violis, G.
See Simenon, Georges (Jacques Christian)

Viramontes, Helena Maria 1954- .... HLCS 2
See also CA 159; DLB 122; HW 2; LLW

Virgil
See Vergil
See also CDWLB 1; DLB 211; LAIT 1; RGWL 2, 3; WLIT 8; WP

Visconti, Luchino 1906-1976 .... CLC 16
See also CA 81-84; CAAS 65-68; CANR 39

Vitry, Jacques de
See Jacques de Vitry

Vittorini, Elio 1908-1966 .... CLC 6, 9, 14
See also CA 133; CAAS 25-28R; DLB 264; EW 12; EWL 3; RGWL 2, 3

Vivekananda, Swami 1863-1902 .... TCLC 88

Vizenor, Gerald Robert 1934- .... CLC 103; NNAL
See also CA 205; 13-16R, 205; 22; CANR 5, 21, 44, 67; DAM MULT; DLB 175, 227; MTCW 2; MTFW 2005; TCWW 2

Vizinczey, Stephen 1933- .... CLC 40
See also CA 128; CCA 1; INT CA-128

Vliet, R(ussell) G(ordon) 1929-1984 .... CLC 22
See also CA 37-40R; CAAS 112; CANR 18; CP 2, 3

Vogau, Boris Andreyevich 1894-1938
See Pilnyak, Boris
See also CA 218; CAAE 123

Vogel, Paula A. 1951- .... CLC 76; DC 19
See also CA 108; CAD; CANR 119, 140; CD 5, 6; CWD; DFS 14; MTFW 2005; RGAL 4

Voigt, Cynthia 1942- .... CLC 30
See also AAYA 3, 30; BYA 1, 3, 6, 7, 8; CA 106; CANR 18, 37, 40, 94, 145; CLR 13, 48; INT CANR-18; JRDA; LAIT 5; MAICYA 1, 2; MAICYAS 1; MTFW 2005; SATA 48, 79, 116, 160; SATA-Brief 33; WYA; YAW

Voigt, Ellen Bryant 1943- .... CLC 54
See also CA 69-72; CANR 11, 29, 55, 115; CP 5, 6, 7; CSW; CWP; DLB 120; PFS 23

Voinovich, Vladimir 1932- .. CLC 10, 49, 147
See also CA 81-84; 12; CANR 33, 67, 150; CWW 2; DLB 302; MTCW 1

Voinovich, Vladimir Nikolaevich
See Voinovich, Vladimir

Vollmann, William T. 1959- ...... CLC 89, 227
See also CA 134; CANR 67, 116; CN 7; CPW; DA3; DAM NOV, POP; MTCW 2; MTFW 2005

Voloshinov, V. N.
See Bakhtin, Mikhail Mikhailovich

Voltaire 1694-1778 . LC 14, 79, 110; SSC 12; WLC 6
See also BYA 13; DA; DA3; DAB; DAC; DAM DRAM, MST; DLB 314; EW 4; GFL Beginnings to 1789; LATS 1:1; LMFS 1; NFS 7; RGWL 2, 3; TWA

von Aschendrof, Baron Ignatz
See Ford, Ford Madox

von Chamisso, Adelbert
See Chamisso, Adelbert von

von Daeniken, Erich 1935- .... CLC 30
See also AITN 1; CA 37-40R; CANR 17, 44

von Daniken, Erich
See von Daeniken, Erich

von Eschenbach, Wolfram c. 1170-c. 1220 .... CMLC 5
See Eschenbach, Wolfram von
See also CDWLB 2; DLB 138; EW 1; RGWL 2

von Hartmann, Eduard 1842-1906 .... TCLC 96

von Hayek, Friedrich August
See Hayek, F(riedrich) A(ugust von)

von Heidenstam, (Carl Gustaf) Verner
See Heidenstam, (Carl Gustaf) Verner von

von Heyse, Paul (Johann Ludwig)
See Heyse, Paul (Johann Ludwig von)

von Hofmannsthal, Hugo
See Hofmannsthal, Hugo von

von Horvath, Odon
See von Horvath, Odon

von Horvath, Odon
See von Horvath, Odon

von Horvath, Odon 1901-1938 .... TCLC 45
See von Horvath, Oedoen
See also CA 194; CAAE 118; DLB 85, 124; RGWL 2, 3

von Horvath, Oedoen
See von Horvath, Odon
See also CA 184

von Kleist, Heinrich
See Kleist, Heinrich von

Vonnegut, Kurt, Jr.
See Vonnegut, Kurt

Vonnegut, Kurt 1922-2007 .... CLC 1, 2, 3, 4, 5, 8, 12, 22, 40, 60, 111, 212; SSC 8; WLC 6
See also AAYA 6, 44; AITN 1; AMWS 2; BEST 90:4; BPFB 3; BYA 3, 14; CA 1-4R; CANR 1, 25, 49, 75, 92; CDALB 1968-1988; CN 1, 2, 3, 4, 5, 6, 7; CPW 1; DA; DA3; DAB; DAC; DAM MST, NOV, POP; DLB 2, 8, 152; DLBD 3; DLBY 1980; EWL 3; EXPN; EXPS; LAIT 4; LMFS 2; MAL 5; MTCW 1, 2; MTFW 2005; NFS 3; RGAL 4; SCFW; SFW 4; SSFS 5; TUS; YAW

Von Rachen, Kurt
See Hubbard, L. Ron

von Sternberg, Josef
See Sternberg, Josef von

Vorster, Gordon 1924- .... CLC 34
See also CA 133

Vosce, Trudie
See Ozick, Cynthia

Voznesensky, Andrei (Andreievich) 1933- .... CLC 1, 15, 57
See Voznesensky, Andrey
See also CA 89-92; CANR 37; CWW 2; DAM POET; MTCW 1

Voznesensky, Andrey
See Voznesensky, Andrei (Andreievich)
See also EWL 3

Wace, Robert c. 1100-c. 1175 .... CMLC 55
See also DLB 146

Waddington, Miriam 1917-2004 .... CLC 28
See also CA 21-24R; CAAS 225; CANR 12, 30; CCA 1; CP 1, 2, 3, 4, 5, 6, 7; DLB 68

Wagman, Fredrica 1937- .... CLC 7
See also CA 97-100; INT CA-97-100

Wagner, Linda W.
See Wagner-Martin, Linda (C.)

Wagner, Linda Welshimer
See Wagner-Martin, Linda (C.)

Wagner, Richard 1813-1883 ..... NCLC 9, 119
See also DLB 129; EW 6

Wagner-Martin, Linda (C.) 1936- .... CLC 50
See also CA 159; CANR 135

Wagoner, David (Russell) 1926- .... CLC 3, 5, 15; PC 33
See also AMWS 9; CA 1-4R; 3; CANR 2, 71; CN 1, 2, 3, 4, 5, 6, 7; CP 1, 2, 3, 4, 5, 6, 7; DLB 5, 256; SATA 14; TCWW 1, 2

Wah, Fred(erick James) 1939- .... CLC 44
See also CA 141; CAAE 107; CP 1, 6, 7; DLB 60

Wahloo, Per 1926-1975 .... CLC 7
See also BPFB 3; CA 61-64; CANR 73; CMW 4; MSW

Wahloo, Peter
See Wahloo, Per

Wain, John (Barrington) 1925-1994 . CLC 2, 11, 15, 46
See also CA 5-8R; 4; CAAS 145; CANR 23, 54; CDBLB 1960 to Present; CN 1, 2, 3, 4, 5; CP 1, 2, 3, 4, 5; DLB 15, 27, 139, 155; EWL 3; MTCW 1, 2; MTFW 2005

Wajda, Andrzej 1926- .... CLC 16, 219
See also CA 102

Wakefield, Dan 1932- .... CLC 7
See also CA 211; 21-24R, 211; 7; CN 4, 5, 6, 7

Wakefield, Herbert Russell 1888-1965 .... TCLC 120
See also CA 5-8R; CANR 77; HGG; SUFW

Wakoski, Diane 1937- ...... CLC 2, 4, 7, 9, 11, 40; PC 15
See also CA 216; 13-16R, 216; 1; CANR 9, 60, 106; CP 1, 2, 3, 4, 5, 6, 7; CWP; DAM POET; DLB 5; INT CANR-9; MAL 5; MTCW 2; MTFW 2005

Wakoski-Sherbell, Diane
See Wakoski, Diane

Walcott, Derek 1930- .... BLC 3; CLC 2, 4, 9, 14, 25, 42, 67, 76, 160; DC 7; PC 46
See also BW 2; CA 89-92; CANR 26, 47, 75, 80, 130; CBD; CD 5, 6; CDWLB 3; CP 1, 2, 3, 4, 5, 6, 7; DA3; DAB; DAC; DAM MST, MULT, POET; DLB 117, 332; DLBY 1981; DNFS 1; EFS 1; EWL 3; LMFS 2; MTCW 1, 2; MTFW 2005; PFS 6; RGEL 2; TWA; WWE 1

Waldman, Anne (Lesley) 1945- .... CLC 7
See also BG 1:3; CA 37-40R; 17; CANR 34, 69, 116; CP 1, 2, 3, 4, 5, 6, 7; CWP; DLB 16

Waldo, E. Hunter
See Sturgeon, Theodore (Hamilton)

Waldo, Edward Hamilton
See Sturgeon, Theodore (Hamilton)

Walker, Alice 1944- ...... BLC 3; CLC 5, 6, 9, 19, 27, 46, 58, 103, 167; PC 30; SSC 5; WLCS
See also AAYA 3, 33; AFAW 1, 2; AMWS 3; BEST 89:4; BPFB 3; BW 2, 3; CA 37-40R; CANR 9, 27, 49, 66, 82, 131; CDALB 1968-1988; CN 4, 5, 6, 7; CPW; CSW; DA; DA3; DAB; DAC; DAM MST, MULT, NOV, POET, POP; DLB 6, 33, 143; EWL 3; EXPN; EXPS; FL 1:6; FW; INT CANR-27; LAIT 3; MAL 5; MBL; MTCW 1, 2; MTFW 2005; NFS 5; RGAL 4; RGSF 2; SATA 31; SSFS 2, 11; TUS; YAW

Walker, Alice Malsenior
See Walker, Alice

Walker, David Harry 1911-1992 ...... **CLC 14**
See also CA 1-4R; CAAS 137; CANR 1;
CN 1, 2; CWRI 5; SATA 8; SATA-Obit
71

Walker, Edward Joseph 1934-2004
See Walker, Ted
See also CA 21-24R; CAAS 226; CANR
12, 28, 53

Walker, George F(rederick) 1947- .. **CLC 44, 61**
See also CA 103; CANR 21, 43, 59; CD 5,
6; DAB; DAC; DAM MST; DLB 60

Walker, Joseph A. 1935-2003 .... **CLC 19**
See also BW 1, 3; CA 89-92; CAD; CANR
26, 143; CD 5, 6; DAM DRAM, MST;
DFS 12; DLB 38

Walker, Margaret 1915-1998 .. **BLC; CLC 1, 6; PC 20; TCLC 129**
See also AFAW 1, 2; BW 2, 3; CA 73-76;
CAAS 172; CANR 26, 54, 76, 136; CN
1, 2, 3, 4, 5, 6; CP 1, 2, 3, 4, 5, 6; CSW;
DAM MULT; DLB 76, 152; EXPP; FW;
MAL 5; MTCW 1, 2; MTFW 2005;
RGAL 4; RHW

Walker, Ted .... **CLC 13**
See Walker, Edward Joseph
See also CP 1, 2, 3, 4, 5, 6, 7; DLB 40

Wallace, David Foster 1962- ... **CLC 50, 114; SSC 68**
See also AAYA 50; AMWS 10; CA 132;
CANR 59, 133; CN 7; DA3; MTCW 2;
MTFW 2005

Wallace, Dexter
See Masters, Edgar Lee

Wallace, (Richard Horatio) Edgar
1875-1932 .... **TCLC 57**
See also CA 218; CAAE 115; CMW 4;
DLB 70; MSW; RGEL 2

Wallace, Irving 1916-1990 .... **CLC 7, 13**
See also AITN 1; BPFB 3; CA 1-4R; 1;
CAAS 132; CANR 1, 27; CPW; DAM
NOV, POP; INT CANR-27; MTCW 1, 2

Wallant, Edward Lewis 1926-1962 .. **CLC 5, 10**
See also CA 1-4R; CANR 22; DLB 2, 28,
143, 299; EWL 3; MAL 5; MTCW 1, 2;
RGAL 4; RGHL

Wallas, Graham 1858-1932 .... **TCLC 91**

Waller, Edmund 1606-1687 .... **LC 86; PC 72**
See also BRW 2; DAM POET; DLB 126;
PAB; RGEL 2

Walley, Byron
See Card, Orson Scott

Walpole, Horace 1717-1797 .... **LC 2, 49**
See also BRW 3; DLB 39, 104, 213; GL 3;
HGG; LMFS 1; RGEL 2; SUFW 1; TEA

Walpole, Hugh (Seymour)
1884-1941 .... **TCLC 5**
See also CA 165; CAAE 104; DLB 34;
HGG; MTCW 2; RGEL 2; RHW

Walrond, Eric (Derwent) 1898-1966 . **HR 1:3**
See also BW 1; CA 125; DLB 51

Walser, Martin 1927- .... **CLC 27, 183**
See also CA 57-60; CANR 8, 46, 145;
CWW 2; DLB 75, 124; EWL 3

Walser, Robert 1878-1956 ..... **SSC 20; TCLC 18**
See also CA 165; CAAE 118; CANR 100;
DLB 66; EWL 3

Walsh, Gillian Paton
See Paton Walsh, Jill

Walsh, Jill Paton .... **CLC 35**
See Paton Walsh, Jill
See also CLR 2, 65; WYA

Walter, Villiam Christian
See Andersen, Hans Christian

Walters, Anna L(ee) 1946- .... **NNAL**
See also CA 73-76

Walther von der Vogelweide c.
1170-1228 .... **CMLC 56**

Walton, Izaak 1593-1683 .... **LC 72**
See also BRW 2; CDBLB Before 1660;
DLB 151, 213; RGEL 2

Walzer, Michael (Laban) 1935- ..... **CLC 238**
See also CA 37-40R; CANR 15, 48, 127

Wambaugh, Joseph (Aloysius), Jr.
1937- .... **CLC 3, 18**
See also AITN 1; BEST 89:3; BPFB 3; CA
33-36R; CANR 42, 65, 115; CMW 4;
CPW 1; DA3; DAM NOV, POP; DLB 6;
DLBY 1983; MSW; MTCW 1, 2

Wang Wei 699(?)-761(?) .... **PC 18**
See also TWA

Warburton, William 1698-1779 .... **LC 97**
See also DLB 104

Ward, Arthur Henry Sarsfield 1883-1959
See Rohmer, Sax
See also CA 173; CAAE 108; CMW 4;
HGG

Ward, Douglas Turner 1930- .... **CLC 19**
See also BW 1; CA 81-84; CAD; CANR
27; CD 5, 6; DLB 7, 38

Ward, E. D.
See Lucas, E(dward) V(errall)

Ward, Mrs. Humphry 1851-1920
See Ward, Mary Augusta
See also RGEL 2

Ward, Mary Augusta 1851-1920 ... **TCLC 55**
See Ward, Mrs. Humphry
See also DLB 18

Ward, Nathaniel 1578(?)-1652 .... **LC 114**
See also DLB 24

Ward, Peter
See Faust, Frederick (Schiller)

Warhol, Andy 1928(?)-1987 .... **CLC 20**
See also AAYA 12; BEST 89:4; CA 89-92;
CAAS 121; CANR 34

Warner, Francis (Robert Le Plastrier)
1937- .... **CLC 14**
See also CA 53-56; CANR 11; CP 1, 2, 3, 4

Warner, Marina 1946- .... **CLC 59, 231**
See also CA 65-68; CANR 21, 55, 118; CN
5, 6, 7; DLB 194; MTFW 2005

Warner, Rex (Ernest) 1905-1986 ...... **CLC 45**
See also CA 89-92; CAAS 119; CN 1, 2, 3,
4; CP 1, 2, 3, 4; DLB 15; RGEL 2; RHW

Warner, Susan (Bogert)
1819-1885 .... **NCLC 31, 146**
See also DLB 3, 42, 239, 250, 254

Warner, Sylvia (Constance) Ashton
See Ashton-Warner, Sylvia (Constance)

Warner, Sylvia Townsend
1893-1978 .. **CLC 7, 19; SSC 23; TCLC 131**
See also BRWS 7; CA 61-64; CAAS 77-80;
CANR 16, 60, 104; CN 1, 2; DLB 34,
139; EWL 3; FANT; FW; MTCW 1, 2;
RGEL 2; RGSF 2; RHW

Warren, Mercy Otis 1728-1814 ..... **NCLC 13**
See also DLB 31, 200; RGAL 4; TUS

Warren, Robert Penn 1905-1989 .. **CLC 1, 4, 6, 8, 10, 13, 18, 39, 53, 59; PC 37; SSC 4, 58; WLC 6**
See also AITN 1; AMW; AMWC 2; BPFB
3; BYA 1; CA 13-16R; CAAS 129; CANR
10, 47; CDALB 1968-1988; CN 1, 2, 3,
4; CP 1, 2, 3, 4; DA; DA3; DAB; DAC;
DAM MST, NOV, POET; DLB 2, 48, 152,
320; DLBY 1980, 1989; EWL 3; INT
CANR-10; MAL 5; MTCW 1, 2; MTFW
2005; NFS 13; RGAL 4; RGSF 2; RHW;
SATA 46; SATA-Obit 63; SSFS 8; TUS

Warrigal, Jack
See Furphy, Joseph

Warshofsky, Isaac
See Singer, Isaac Bashevis

Warton, Joseph 1722-1800 ... **LC 128; NCLC 118**
See also DLB 104, 109; RGEL 2

Warton, Thomas 1728-1790 .... **LC 15, 82**
See also DAM POET; DLB 104, 109, 336;
RGEL 2

Waruk, Kona
See Harris, (Theodore) Wilson

Warung, Price .... **TCLC 45**
See Astley, William
See also DLB 230; RGEL 2

Warwick, Jarvis
See Garner, Hugh
See also CCA 1

Washington, Alex
See Harris, Mark

Washington, Booker T(aliaferro)
1856-1915 .... **BLC 3; TCLC 10**
See also BW 1; CA 125; CAAE 114; DA3;
DAM MULT; LAIT 2; RGAL 4; SATA
28

Washington, George 1732-1799 .... **LC 25**
See also DLB 31

Wassermann, (Karl) Jakob
1873-1934 .... **TCLC 6**
See also CA 163; CAAE 104; DLB 66;
EWL 3

Wasserstein, Wendy 1950-2006 . **CLC 32, 59, 90, 183; DC 4**
See also AAYA 73; AMWS 15; CA 129;
CAAE 121; CAAS 247; CABS 3; CAD;
CANR 53, 75, 128; CD 5, 6; CWD; DA3;
DAM DRAM; DFS 5, 17; DLB 228;
EWL 3; FW; INT CA-129; MAL 5;
MTCW 2; MTFW 2005; SATA 94; SATA-
Obit 174

Waterhouse, Keith (Spencer) 1929- . **CLC 47**
See also CA 5-8R; CANR 38, 67, 109;
CBD; CD 6; CN 1, 2, 3, 4, 5, 6, 7; DLB
13, 15; MTCW 1, 2; MTFW 2005

Waters, Frank (Joseph) 1902-1995 .. **CLC 88**
See also CA 5-8R; 13; CAAS 149; CANR
3, 18, 63, 121; DLB 212; DLBY 1986;
RGAL 4; TCWW 1, 2

Waters, Mary C. .... **CLC 70**

Waters, Roger 1944- .... **CLC 35**

Watkins, Frances Ellen
See Harper, Frances Ellen Watkins

Watkins, Gerrold
See Malzberg, Barry N(athaniel)

Watkins, Gloria Jean
See hooks, bell

Watkins, Paul 1964- .... **CLC 55**
See also CA 132; CANR 62, 98

Watkins, Vernon Phillips
1906-1967 .... **CLC 43**
See also CA 9-10; CAAS 25-28R; CAP 1;
DLB 20; EWL 3; RGEL 2

Watson, Irving S.
See Mencken, H(enry) L(ouis)

Watson, John H.
See Farmer, Philip Jose

Watson, Richard F.
See Silverberg, Robert

Watts, Ephraim
See Horne, Richard Henry Hengist

Watts, Isaac 1674-1748 .... **LC 98**
See also DLB 95; RGEL 2; SATA 52

Waugh, Auberon (Alexander)
1939-2001 .... **CLC 7**
See also CA 45-48; CAAS 192; CANR 6,
22, 92; CN 1, 2, 3; DLB 14, 194

West, Nathanael 1903-1940 .. SSC 16; TCLC
  1, 14, 44
    See also AMW; AMWR 2; BPFB 3; CA
      125; CAAE 104; CDALB 1929-1941;
      DA3; DLB 4, 9, 28; EWL 3; MAL 5;
      MTCW 1, 2; MTFW 2005; NFS 16;
      RGAL 4; TUS
West, Owen
    See Koontz, Dean R.
West, Paul 1930- .... CLC 7, 14, 96, 226
    See also CA 13-16R; 7; CANR 22, 53, 76,
      89, 136; CN 1, 2, 3, 4, 5, 6, 7; DLB 14;
      INT CANR-22; MTCW 2; MTFW 2005
West, Rebecca 1892-1983 ... CLC 7, 9, 31, 50
    See also BPFB 3; BRWS 3; CA 5-8R;
      CAAS 109; CANR 19; CN 1, 2, 3; DLB
      36; DLBY 1983; EWL 3; FW; MTCW 1,
      2; MTFW 2005; NCFS 4; RGEL 2; TEA
Westall, Robert (Atkinson)
  1929-1993 .... CLC 17
    See also AAYA 12; BYA 2, 6, 7, 8, 9, 15;
      CA 69-72; CAAS 141; CANR 18, 68;
      CLR 13; FANT; JRDA; MAICYA 1, 2;
      MAICYAS 1; SAAS 23, 69;
      SATA-Obit 75; WYA; YAW
Westermarck, Edward 1862-1939 . TCLC 87
Westlake, Donald E. 1933- .... CLC 7, 33
    See also BPFB 3; CA 17-20R; 13; CANR
      16, 44, 65, 94, 137; CMW 4; CPW; DAM
      POP; INT CANR-16; MSW; MTCW 2;
      MTFW 2005
Westlake, Donald Edwin
    See Westlake, Donald E.
Westmacott, Mary
    See Christie, Agatha (Mary Clarissa)
Weston, Allen
    See Norton, Andre
Wetcheek, J. L.
    See Feuchtwanger, Lion
Wetering, Janwillem van de
    See van de Wetering, Janwillem
Wetherald, Agnes Ethelwyn
  1857-1940 .... TCLC 81
    See also CA 202; DLB 99
Wetherell, Elizabeth
    See Warner, Susan (Bogert)
Whale, James 1889-1957 .... TCLC 63
    See also AAYA 75
Whalen, Philip (Glenn) 1923-2002 .... CLC 6,
  29
    See also BG 1:3; CA 9-12R; CAAS 209;
      CANR 5, 39; CP 1, 2, 3, 4, 5, 6, 7; DLB
      16; WP
Wharton, Edith (Newbold Jones)
  1862-1937 ... SSC 6, 84; TCLC 3, 9, 27,
  53, 129, 149; WLC 6
    See also AAYA 25; AMW; AMWC 2;
      AMWR 1; BPFB 3; CA 132; CAAE 104;
      CDALB 1865-1917; DA; DA3; DAB;
      DAC; DAM MST, NOV; DLB 4, 9, 12,
      78, 189; DLBD 13; EWL 3; EXPS; FL
      1:6; GL 3; HGG; LAIT 2, 3; LATS 1:1;
      MAL 5; MBL; MTCW 1, 2; MTFW 2005;
      NFS 5, 11, 15, 20; RGAL 4; RGSF 2;
      RHW; SSFS 6, 7; SUFW; TUS
Wharton, James
    See Mencken, H(enry) L(ouis)
Wharton, William (a pseudonym)
  1925- .... CLC 18, 37
    See also CA 93-96; CN 4, 5, 6, 7; DLBY
      1980; INT CA-93-96
Wheatley (Peters), Phillis
  1753(?)-1784 ... BLC 3; LC 3, 50; PC 3;
  WLC 6
    See also AFAW 1, 2; CDALB 1640-1865;
      DA; DA3; DAC; DAM MST, MULT,
      POET; DLB 31, 50; EXPP; FL 1:1; PFS
      13; RGAL 4

Wheelock, John Hall 1886-1978 .... CLC 14
    See also CA 13-16R; CAAS 77-80; CANR
      14; CP 1, 2; DLB 45; MAL 5
Whim-Wham
    See Curnow, (Thomas) Allen (Monro)
Whisp, Kennilworthy
    See Rowling, J.K.
Whitaker, Rod 1931-2005
    See Trevanian
    See also CA 29-32R; CAAS 246; CANR
      45, 153; CMW 4
White, Babington
    See Braddon, Mary Elizabeth
White, E. B. 1899-1985 .... CLC 10, 34, 39
    See also AAYA 62; AITN 2; AMWS 1; CA
      13-16R; CAAS 116; CANR 16, 37;
      CDALBS; CLR 1, 21, 107; CPW; DA3;
      DAM POP; DLB 11, 22; EWL 3; FANT;
      MAICYA 1, 2; MAL 5; MTCW 1, 2;
      MTFW 2005; NCFS 5; RGAL 4; SATA 2,
      29, 100; SATA-Obit 44; TUS
White, Edmund 1940- .... CLC 27, 110
    See also AAYA 7; CA 45-48; CANR 3, 19,
      36, 62, 107, 133; CN 5, 6, 7; DA3; DAM
      POP; DLB 227; MTCW 1, 2; MTFW
      2005
White, Elwyn Brooks
    See White, E. B.
White, Hayden V. 1928- .... CLC 148
    See also CA 128; CANR 135; DLB 246
White, Patrick (Victor Martindale)
  1912-1990 ...... CLC 3, 4, 5, 7, 9, 18, 65,
  69; SSC 39; TCLC 176
    See also BRWS 1; CA 81-84; CAAS 132;
      CANR 43; CN 1, 2, 3, 4; DLB 260, 332;
      EWL 3; MTCW 1; RGEL 2; RGSF 2;
      RHW; TWA; WWE 1
White, Phyllis Dorothy James 1920-
    See James, P. D.
    See also CA 21-24R; CANR 17, 43, 65,
      112; CMW 4; CN 7; CPW; DA3; DAM
      POP; MTCW 1, 2; MTFW 2005; TEA
White, T(erence) H(anbury)
  1906-1964 .... CLC 30
    See also AAYA 22; BPFB 3; BYA 4, 5; CA
      73-76; CANR 37; DLB 160; FANT;
      JRDA; LAIT 1; MAICYA 1, 2; RGEL 2;
      SATA 12; SUFW 1; YAW
White, Terence de Vere 1912-1994 ... CLC 49
    See also CA 49-52; CAAS 145; CANR 3
White, Walter
    See White, Walter F(rancis)
White, Walter F(rancis) 1893-1955 ... BLC 3;
  HR 1:3; TCLC 15
    See also BW 1; CA 124; CAAE 115; DAM
      MULT; DLB 51
White, William Hale 1831-1913
    See Rutherford, Mark
    See also CA 189; CAAE 121
Whitehead, Alfred North
  1861-1947 .... TCLC 97
    See also CA 165; CAAE 117; DLB 100,
      262
Whitehead, Colson 1970- .... CLC 232
    See also CA 202; CANR 162
Whitehead, E(dward) A(nthony)
  1933- .... CLC 5
    See Whitehead, Ted
    See also CA 65-68; CANR 58, 118; CBD;
      CD 5; DLB 310
Whitehead, Ted
    See Whitehead, E(dward) A(nthony)
    See also CD 6
Whiteman, Roberta J. Hill 1947- ...... NNAL
    See also CA 146
Whitemore, Hugh (John) 1936- .... CLC 37
    See also CA 132; CANR 77; CBD; CD 5,
      6; INT CA-132

Whitman, Sarah Helen (Power)
  1803-1878 .... NCLC 19
    See also DLB 1, 243
Whitman, Walt(er) 1819-1892 .. NCLC 4, 31,
  81; PC 3; WLC 6
    See also AAYA 42; AMW; AMWR 1;
      CDALB 1640-1865; DA; DA3; DAB;
      DAC; DAM MST, POET; DLB 3, 64,
      224, 250; EXPP; LAIT 2; LMFS 1; PAB;
      PFS 2, 3, 13, 22; RGAL 4; SATA 20;
      TUS; WP; WYAS 1
Whitney, Isabella fl. 1565-fl. 1575 ..... LC 130
    See also DLB 136
Whitney, Phyllis A(yame) 1903- .... CLC 42
    See also AAYA 36; AITN 2; BEST 90:3;
      CA 1-4R; CANR 3, 25, 38, 60; CLR 59;
      CMW 4; CPW; DA3; DAM POP; JRDA;
      MAICYA 1, 2; MTCW 2; RHW; SATA 1,
      30; YAW
Whittemore, (Edward) Reed, Jr.
  1919- .... CLC 4
    See also CA 219; 9-12R, 219; 8; CANR 4,
      119; CP 1, 2, 3, 4, 5, 6, 7; DLB 5; MAL
      5
Whittier, John Greenleaf
  1807-1892 .... NCLC 8, 59
    See also AMWS 1; DLB 1, 243; RGAL 4
Whittlebot, Hernia
    See Coward, Noel (Peirce)
Wicker, Thomas Grey 1926-
    See Wicker, Tom
    See also CA 65-68; CANR 21, 46, 141
Wicker, Tom .... CLC 7
    See Wicker, Thomas Grey
Wideman, John Edgar 1941- ... BLC 3; CLC
  5, 34, 36, 67, 122; SSC 62
    See also AFAW 1, 2; AMWS 10; BPFB 4;
      BW 2, 3; CA 85-88; CANR 14, 42, 67,
      109, 140; CN 4, 5, 6, 7; DAM MULT;
      DLB 33, 143; MAL 5; MTCW 2; MTFW
      2005; RGAL 4; RGSF 2; SSFS 6, 12, 24;
      TCLE 1:2
Wiebe, Rudy 1934- .... CLC 6, 11, 14, 138
    See also CA 37-40R; CANR 42, 67, 123;
      CN 1, 2, 3, 4, 5, 6, 7; DAC; DAM MST;
      DLB 60; RHW; SATA 156
Wiebe, Rudy Henry
    See Wiebe, Rudy
Wieland, Christoph Martin
  1733-1813 .... NCLC 17, 177
    See also DLB 97; EW 4; LMFS 1; RGWL
      2, 3
Wiene, Robert 1881-1938 .... TCLC 56
Wieners, John 1934- .... CLC 7
    See also BG 1:3; CA 13-16R; CP 1, 2, 3, 4,
      5, 6, 7; DLB 16; WP
Wiesel, Elie 1928- ...... CLC 3, 5, 11, 37, 165;
  WLCS
    See also AAYA 7, 54; AITN 1; CA 5-8R; 4;
      CANR 8, 40, 65, 125; CDALBS; CWW
      2; DA; DA3; DAB; DAC; DAM MST,
      NOV; DLB 83, 299; DLBY 1987; EWL
      3; INT CANR-8; LAIT 4; MTCW 1, 2;
      MTFW 2005; NCFS 4; NFS 4; RGHL;
      RGWL 3; SATA 56; YAW
Wiesel, Eliezer
    See Wiesel, Elie
Wiggins, Marianne 1947- .... CLC 57
    See also AAYA 70; BEST 89:3; CA 130;
      CANR 60, 139; CN 7; DLB 335
Wigglesworth, Michael 1631-1705 .... LC 106
    See also DLB 24; RGAL 4
Wiggs, Susan .... CLC 70
    See also CA 201
Wight, James Alfred 1916-1995
    See Herriot, James
    See also CA 77-80; SATA 55; SATA-Brief
      44

Wilbur, Richard 1921- .. **CLC 3, 6, 9, 14, 53, 110; PC 51**
See also AAYA 72; AMWS 3; CA 1-4R; CABS 2; CANR 2, 29, 76, 93, 139; CDALBS; CP 1, 2, 3, 4, 5, 6, 7; DA; DAB; DAC; DAM MST, POET; DLB 5, 169; EWL 3; EXPP; INT CANR-29; MAL 5; MTCW 1, 2; MTFW 2005; PAB; PFS 11, 12, 16; RGAL 4; SATA 9, 108; WP

Wilbur, Richard Purdy
See Wilbur, Richard

Wild, Peter 1940- .... **CLC 14**
See also CA 37-40R; CP 1, 2, 3, 4, 5, 6, 7; DLB 5

Wilde, Oscar (Fingal O'Flahertie Wills)
1854(?)-1900 .... **DC 17; SSC 11, 77; TCLC 1, 8, 23, 41, 175; WLC 6**
See also AAYA 49; BRW 5; BRWC 1, 2; BRWR 2; BYA 15; CA 119; CAAE 104; CANR 112; CDBLB 1890-1914; CLR 114; DA; DA3; DAB; DAC; DAM DRAM, MST, NOV; DFS 4, 8, 9, 21; DLB 10, 19, 34, 57, 141, 156, 190; EXPS; FANT; GL 3; LATS 1:1; NFS 20; RGEL 2; RGSF 2; SATA 24; SSFS 7; SUFW; TEA; WCH; WLIT 4

Wilder, Billy .... **CLC 20**
See Wilder, Samuel
See also AAYA 66; DLB 26

Wilder, Samuel 1906-2002
See Wilder, Billy
See also CA 89-92; CAAS 205

Wilder, Stephen
See Marlowe, Stephen

Wilder, Thornton (Niven)
1897-1975 .. **CLC 1, 5, 6, 10, 15, 35, 82; DC 1, 24; WLC 6**
See also AAYA 29; AITN 2; AMW; CA 13-16R; CAAS 61-64; CAD; CANR 40, 132; CDALBS; CN 1, 2; DA; DA3; DAB; DAC; DAM DRAM, MST, NOV; DFS 1, 4, 16; DLB 4, 7, 9, 228; DLBY 1997; EWL 3; LAIT 3; MAL 5; MTCW 1, 2; MTFW 2005; NFS 24; RGAL 4; RHW; WYAS 1

Wilding, Michael 1942- ...... **CLC 73; SSC 50**
See also CA 104; CANR 24, 49, 106; CN 4, 5, 6, 7; DLB 325; RGSF 2

Wiley, Richard 1944- .... **CLC 44**
See also CA 129; CAAE 121; CANR 71

Wilhelm, Kate .... **CLC 7**
See Wilhelm, Katie
See also AAYA 20; BYA 16; CA 5; DLB 8; INT CANR-17; SCFW 2

Wilhelm, Katie 1928-
See Wilhelm, Kate
See also CA 37-40R; CANR 17, 36, 60, 94; MTCW 1; SFW 4

Wilkins, Mary
See Freeman, Mary E(leanor) Wilkins

Willard, Nancy 1936- .... **CLC 7, 37**
See also BYA 5; CA 89-92; CANR 10, 39, 68, 107, 152; CLR 5; CP 2, 3, 4, 5; CWP; CWRI 5; DLB 5, 52; FANT; MAICYA 1, 2; MTCW 1; SATA 37, 71, 127; SATA-Brief 30; SUFW 2; TCLE 1:2

William of Malmesbury c. 1090B.C.-c. 1140B.C. .... **CMLC 57**

William of Moerbeke c. 1215-c. 1286 .... **CMLC 91**

William of Ockham 1290-1349 ..... **CMLC 32**

Williams, Ben Ames 1889-1953 ..... **TCLC 89**
See also CA 183; DLB 102

Williams, Charles
See Collier, James Lincoln

Williams, Charles (Walter Stansby)
1886-1945 .... **TCLC 1, 11**
See also BRWS 9; CA 163; CAAE 104; DLB 100, 153, 255; FANT; RGEL 2; SUFW 1

Williams, C.K. 1936- .... **CLC 33, 56, 148**
See also CA 37-40R; 26; CANR 57, 106; CP 1, 2, 3, 4, 5, 6, 7; DAM POET; DLB 5; MAL 5

Williams, Ella Gwendolen Rees
See Rhys, Jean

Williams, (George) Emlyn
1905-1987 .... **CLC 15**
See also CA 104; CAAS 123; CANR 36; DAM DRAM; DLB 10, 77; IDTP; MTCW 1

Williams, Hank 1923-1953 .... **TCLC 81**
See Williams, Hiram King

Williams, Helen Maria
1761-1827 .... **NCLC 135**
See also DLB 158

Williams, Hiram Hank
See Williams, Hank

Williams, Hiram King
See Williams, Hank
See also CA 188

Williams, Hugo (Mordaunt) 1942- ... **CLC 42**
See also CA 17-20R; CANR 45, 119; CP 1, 2, 3, 4, 5, 6, 7; DLB 40

Williams, J. Walker
See Wodehouse, P(elham) G(renville)

Williams, John A(lfred) 1925- . **BLC 3; CLC 5, 13**
See also AFAW 2; BW 2, 3; CA 195; 53-56, 195; 3; CANR 6, 26, 51, 118; CN 1, 2, 3, 4, 5, 6, 7; CSW; DAM MULT; DLB 2, 33; EWL 3; INT CANR-6; MAL 5; RGAL 4; SFW 4

Williams, Jonathan (Chamberlain)
1929- .... **CLC 13**
See also CA 9-12R; 12; CANR 8, 108; CP 1, 2, 3, 4, 5, 6, 7; DLB 5

Williams, Joy 1944- .... **CLC 31**
See also CA 41-44R; CANR 22, 48, 97; DLB 335

Williams, Norman 1952- .... **CLC 39**
See also CA 118

Williams, Roger 1603(?)-1683 .... **LC 129**
See also DLB 24

Williams, Sherley Anne 1944-1999 ... **BLC 3; CLC 89**
See also AFAW 2; BW 2, 3; CA 73-76; CAAS 185; CANR 25, 82; DAM MULT, POET; DLB 41; INT CANR-25; SATA 78; SATA-Obit 116

Williams, Shirley
See Williams, Sherley Anne

Williams, Tennessee 1911-1983 . **CLC 1, 2, 5, 7, 8, 11, 15, 19, 30, 39, 45, 71, 111; DC 4; SSC 81; WLC 6**
See also AAYA 31; AITN 1, 2; AMW; AMWC 1; CA 5-8R; CAAS 108; CABS 3; CAD; CANR 31, 132; CDALB 1941-1968; CN 1, 2, 3; DA; DA3; DAB; DAC; DAM DRAM, MST; DFS 17; DLB 7; DLBD 4; DLBY 1983; EWL 3; GLL 1; LAIT 4; LATS 1:2; MAL 5; MTCW 1, 2; MTFW 2005; RGAL 4; TUS

Williams, Thomas (Alonzo)
1926-1990 .... **CLC 14**
See also CA 1-4R; CAAS 132; CANR 2

Williams, William C.
See Williams, William Carlos

Williams, William Carlos
1883-1963 .... **CLC 1, 2, 5, 9, 13, 22, 42, 67; PC 7; SSC 31; WLC 6**
See also AAYA 46; AMW; AMWR 1; CA 89-92; CANR 34; CDALB 1917-1929; DA; DA3; DAB; DAC; DAM MST, POET; DLB 4, 16, 54, 86; EWL 3; EXPP; MAL 5; MTCW 1, 2; MTFW 2005; NCFS 4; PAB; PFS 1, 6, 11; RGAL 4; RGSF 2; TUS; WP

Williamson, David (Keith) 1942- ..... **CLC 56**
See also CA 103; CANR 41; CD 5, 6; DLB 289

Williamson, Ellen Douglas 1905-1984
See Douglas, Ellen
See also CA 17-20R; CAAS 114; CANR 39

Williamson, Jack .... **CLC 29**
See Williamson, John Stewart
See also CA 8; DLB 8; SCFW 1, 2

Williamson, John Stewart 1908-2006
See Williamson, Jack
See also CA 17-20R; CAAS 255; CANR 23, 70, 153; SFW 4

Willie, Frederick
See Lovecraft, H. P.

Willingham, Calder (Baynard, Jr.)
1922-1995 .... **CLC 5, 51**
See also CA 5-8R; CAAS 147; CANR 3; CN 1, 2, 3, 4, 5; CSW; DLB 2, 44; IDFW 3, 4; MTCW 1

Willis, Charles
See Clarke, Arthur C.

Willy
See Colette, (Sidonie-Gabrielle)

Willy, Colette
See Colette, (Sidonie-Gabrielle)
See also GLL 1

Wilmot, John 1647-1680 .... **LC 75; PC 66**
See Rochester
See also BRW 2; DLB 131; PAB

Wilson, A.N. 1950- .... **CLC 33**
See also BRWS 6; CA 122; CAAE 112; CANR 156; CN 4, 5, 6, 7; DLB 14, 155, 194; MTCW 2

Wilson, Andrew Norman
See Wilson, A.N.

Wilson, Angus (Frank Johnstone)
1913-1991 . **CLC 2, 3, 5, 25, 34; SSC 21**
See also BRWS 1; CA 5-8R; CAAS 134; CANR 21; CN 1, 2, 3, 4; DLB 15, 139, 155; EWL 3; MTCW 1, 2; MTFW 2005; RGEL 2; RGSF 2

Wilson, August 1945-2005 .. **BLC 3; CLC 39, 50, 63, 118, 222; DC 2; WLCS**
See also AAYA 16; AFAW 2; AMWS 8; BW 2, 3; CA 122; CAAE 115; CAAS 244; CAD; CANR 42, 54, 76, 128; CD 5, 6; DA; DA3; DAB; DAC; DAM DRAM, MST, MULT; DFS 3, 7, 15, 17, 24; DLB 228; EWL 3; LAIT 4; LATS 1:2; MAL 5; MTCW 1, 2; MTFW 2005; RGAL 4

Wilson, Brian 1942- .... **CLC 12**

Wilson, Colin (Henry) 1931- .... **CLC 3, 14**
See also CA 1-4R; 5; CANR 1, 22, 33, 77; CMW 4; CN 1, 2, 3, 4, 5, 6; DLB 14, 194; HGG; MTCW 1; SFW 4

Wilson, Dirk
See Pohl, Frederik

Wilson, Edmund 1895-1972 .. **CLC 1, 2, 3, 8, 24**
See also AMW; CA 1-4R; CAAS 37-40R; CANR 1, 46, 110; CN 1; DLB 63; EWL 3; MAL 5; MTCW 1, 2; MTFW 2005; RGAL 4; TUS

Wilson, Ethel Davis (Bryant)
1888(?)-1980 .... **CLC 13**
See also CA 102; CN 1, 2; DAC; DAM POET; DLB 68; MTCW 1; RGEL 2

Wilson, Harriet
See Wilson, Harriet E. Adams
See also DLB 239

Wilson, Harriet E.
See Wilson, Harriet E. Adams
See also DLB 243

Wouk, Herman 1915- .... **CLC 1, 9, 38**
See also BPFB 2, 3; CA 5-8R; CANR 6, 33, 67, 146; CDALBS; CN 1, 2, 3, 4, 5, 6; CPW; DA3; DAM NOV, POP; DLBY 1982; INT CANR-6; LAIT 4; MAL 5; MTCW 1, 2; MTFW 2005; NFS 7; TUS

Wright, Charles 1935- ... **CLC 6, 13, 28, 119, 146**
See also AMWS 5; CA 29-32R; 7; CANR 23, 36, 62, 88, 135; CP 3, 4, 5, 6, 7; DLB 165; DLBY 1982; EWL 3; MTCW 1, 2; MTFW 2005; PFS 10

Wright, Charles Stevenson 1932- ..... **BLC 3; CLC 49**
See also BW 1; CA 9-12R; CANR 26; CN 1, 2, 3, 4, 5, 6, 7; DAM MULT, POET; DLB 33

Wright, Frances 1795-1852 .... **NCLC 74**
See also DLB 73

Wright, Frank Lloyd 1867-1959 .... **TCLC 95**
See also AAYA 33; CA 174

Wright, Harold Bell 1872-1944 .... **TCLC 183**
See also BPFB 3; CAAE 110; DLB 9; TCWW 2

Wright, Jack R.
See Harris, Mark

Wright, James (Arlington)
1927-1980 .... **CLC 3, 5, 10, 28; PC 36**
See also AITN 2; AMWS 3; CA 49-52; CAAS 97-100; CANR 4, 34, 64; CDALBS; CP 1, 2; DAM POET; DLB 5, 169; EWL 3; EXPP; MAL 5; MTCW 1, 2; MTFW 2005; PFS 7, 8; RGAL 4; TUS; WP

Wright, Judith 1915-2000 ... **CLC 11, 53; PC 14**
See also CA 13-16R; CAAS 188; CANR 31, 76, 93; CP 1, 2, 3, 4, 5, 6, 7; CWP; DLB 260; EWL 3; MTCW 1, 2; MTFW 2005; PFS 8; RGEL 2; SATA 14; SATA-Obit 121

Wright, L(aurali) R. 1939- .... **CLC 44**
See also CA 138; CMW 4

Wright, Richard (Nathaniel)
1908-1960 ... **BLC 3; CLC 1, 3, 4, 9, 14, 21, 48, 74; SSC 2; TCLC 136, 180; WLC 6**
See also AAYA 5, 42; AFAW 1, 2; AMW; BPFB 3; BW 1; BYA 2; CA 108; CANR 64; CDALB 1929-1941; DA; DA3; DAB; DAC; DAM MST, MULT, NOV; DLB 76, 102; DLBD 2; EWL 3; EXPN; LAIT 3, 4; MAL 5; MTCW 1, 2; MTFW 2005; NCFS 1; NFS 1, 7; RGAL 4; RGSF 2; SSFS 3, 9, 15, 20; TUS; YAW

Wright, Richard B(ruce) 1937- .... **CLC 6**
See also CA 85-88; CANR 120; DLB 53

Wright, Rick 1945- .... **CLC 35**

Wright, Rowland
See Wells, Carolyn

Wright, Stephen 1946- .... **CLC 33**
See also CA 237

Wright, Willard Huntington 1888-1939
See Van Dine, S. S.
See also CA 189; CAAE 115; CMW 4; DLBD 16

Wright, William 1930- .... **CLC 44**
See also CA 53-56; CANR 7, 23, 154

Wroth, Lady Mary 1587-1653(?) .... **LC 30, 139; PC 38**
See also DLB 121

Wu Ch'eng-en 1500(?)-1582(?) .... **LC 7**

Wu Ching-tzu 1701-1754 .... **LC 2**

Wulfstan c. 10th cent. -1023 .... **CMLC 59**

Wurlitzer, Rudolph 1938(?)- .... **CLC 2, 4, 15**
See also CA 85-88; CN 4, 5, 6, 7; DLB 173

Wyatt, Sir Thomas c. 1503-1542 . **LC 70; PC 27**
See also BRW 1; DLB 132; EXPP; PFS 25; RGEL 2; TEA

Wycherley, William 1640-1716 .... **LC 8, 21, 102, 136**
See also BRW 2; CDBLB 1660-1789; DAM DRAM; DLB 80; RGEL 2

Wyclif, John c. 1330-1384 .... **CMLC 70**
See also DLB 146

Wylie, Elinor (Morton Hoyt)
1885-1928 .... **PC 23; TCLC 8**
See also AMWS 1; CA 162; CAAE 105; DLB 9, 45; EXPP; MAL 5; RGAL 4

Wylie, Philip (Gordon) 1902-1971 ... **CLC 43**
See also CA 21-22; CAAS 33-36R; CAP 2; CN 1; DLB 9; SFW 4

Wyndham, John .... **CLC 19**
See Harris, John (Wyndham Parkes Lucas) Beynon
See also DLB 255; SCFW 1, 2

Wyss, Johann David Von
1743-1818 .... **NCLC 10**
See also CLR 92; JRDA; MAICYA 1, 2; SATA 29; SATA-Brief 27

Xenophon c. 430B.C.-c. 354B.C. ... **CMLC 17**
See also AW 1; DLB 176; RGWL 2, 3; WLIT 8

Xingjian, Gao 1940-
See Gao Xingjian
See also CA 193; DFS 21; DLB 330; RGWL 3

Yakamochi 718-785 .... **CMLC 45; PC 48**

Yakumo Koizumi
See Hearn, (Patricio) Lafcadio (Tessima Carlos)

Yamada, Mitsuye (May) 1923- .... **PC 44**
See also CA 77-80

Yamamoto, Hisaye 1921- .... **AAL; SSC 34**
See also CA 214; DAM MULT; DLB 312; LAIT 4; SSFS 14

Yamauchi, Wakako 1924- .... **AAL**
See also CA 214; DLB 312

Yanez, Jose Donoso
See Donoso (Yanez), Jose

Yanovsky, Basile S.
See Yanovsky, V(assily) S(emenovich)

Yanovsky, V(assily) S(emenovich)
1906-1989 .... **CLC 2, 18**
See also CA 97-100; CAAS 129

Yates, Richard 1926-1992 .... **CLC 7, 8, 23**
See also AMWS 11; CA 5-8R; CAAS 139; CANR 10, 43; CN 1, 2, 3, 4, 5; DLB 2, 234; DLBY 1981, 1992; INT CANR-10; SSFS 24

Yau, John 1950- .... **PC 61**
See also CA 154; CANR 89; CP 4, 5, 6, 7; DLB 234, 312

Yearsley, Ann 1753-1806 .... **NCLC 174**
See also DLB 109

Yeats, W. B.
See Yeats, William Butler

Yeats, William Butler 1865-1939 . **PC 20, 51; TCLC 1, 11, 18, 31, 93, 116; WLC 6**
See also AAYA 48; BRW 6; BRWR 1; CA 127; CAAE 104; CANR 45; CDBLB 1890-1914; DA; DA3; DAB; DAC; DAM DRAM, MST, POET; DLB 10, 19, 98, 156, 332; EWL 3; EXPP; MTCW 1, 2; MTFW 2005; NCFS 3; PAB; PFS 1, 2, 5, 7, 13, 15; RGEL 2; TEA; WLIT 4; WP

Yehoshua, A.B. 1936- .... **CLC 13, 31**
See also CA 33-36R; CANR 43, 90, 145; CWW 2; EWL 3; RGHL; RGSF 2; RGWL 3; WLIT 6

Yehoshua, Abraham B.
See Yehoshua, A.B.

Yellow Bird
See Ridge, John Rollin

Yep, Laurence 1948- .... **CLC 35**
See also AAYA 5, 31; BYA 7; CA 49-52; CANR 1, 46, 92, 161; CLR 3, 17, 54; DLB 52, 312; FANT; JRDA; MAICYA 1, 2; MAICYAS 1; SATA 7, 69, 123, 176; WYA; YAW

Yep, Laurence Michael
See Yep, Laurence

Yerby, Frank G(arvin) 1916-1991 ..... **BLC 3; CLC 1, 7, 22**
See also BPFB 3; BW 1, 3; CA 9-12R; CAAS 136; CANR 16, 52; CN 1, 2, 3, 4, 5; DAM MULT; DLB 76; INT CANR-16; MTCW 1; RGAL 4; RHW

Yesenin, Sergei Aleksandrovich
See Esenin, Sergei

Yevtushenko, Yevgeny (Alexandrovich)
1933- ...... **CLC 1, 3, 13, 26, 51, 126; PC 40**
See Evtushenko, Evgenii Aleksandrovich
See also CA 81-84; CANR 33, 54; DAM POET; EWL 3; MTCW 1; RGHL

Yezierska, Anzia 1885(?)-1970 .... **CLC 46**
See also CA 126; CAAS 89-92; DLB 28, 221; FW; MTCW 1; RGAL 4; SSFS 15

Yglesias, Helen 1915- .... **CLC 7, 22**
See also CA 37-40R; 20; CANR 15, 65, 95; CN 4, 5, 6, 7; INT CANR-15; MTCW 1

Yokomitsu, Riichi 1898-1947 .... **TCLC 47**
See also CA 170; EWL 3

Yonge, Charlotte (Mary)
1823-1901 .... **TCLC 48**
See also CA 163; CAAE 109; DLB 18, 163; RGEL 2; SATA 17; WCH

York, Jeremy
See Creasey, John

York, Simon
See Heinlein, Robert A.

Yorke, Henry Vincent 1905-1974 ..... **CLC 13**
See Green, Henry
See also CA 85-88; CAAS 49-52

Yosano, Akiko 1878-1942 ... **PC 11; TCLC 59**
See also CA 161; EWL 3; RGWL 3

Yoshimoto, Banana .... **CLC 84**
See Yoshimoto, Mahoko
See also AAYA 50; NFS 7

Yoshimoto, Mahoko 1964-
See Yoshimoto, Banana
See also CA 144; CANR 98, 160; SSFS 16

Young, Al(bert James) 1939- ... **BLC 3; CLC 19**
See also BW 2, 3; CA 29-32R; CANR 26, 65, 109; CN 2, 3, 4, 5, 6, 7; CP 1, 2, 3, 4, 5, 6, 7; DAM MULT; DLB 33

Young, Andrew (John) 1885-1971 ...... **CLC 5**
See also CA 5-8R; CANR 7, 29; CP 1; RGEL 2

Young, Collier
See Bloch, Robert (Albert)

Young, Edward 1683-1765 .... **LC 3, 40**
See also DLB 95; RGEL 2

Young, Marguerite (Vivian)
1909-1995 .... **CLC 82**
See also CA 13-16; CAAS 150; CAP 1; CN 1, 2, 3, 4, 5, 6

Young, Neil 1945- .... **CLC 17**
See also CA 110; CCA 1

Young Bear, Ray A. 1950- ... **CLC 94; NNAL**
See also CA 146; DAM MULT; DLB 175; MAL 5

Yourcenar, Marguerite 1903-1987 ... **CLC 19, 38, 50, 87**
See also BPFB 3; CA 69-72; CANR 23, 60, 93; DAM NOV; DLB 72; DLBY 1988; EW 12; EWL 3; GFL 1789 to the Present; GLL 1; MTCW 1, 2; MTFW 2005; RGWL 2, 3

Yuan, Chu 340(?)B.C.-278(?)B.C. . **CMLC 36**

Literary Criticism Series
Cumulative Topic Index

This index lists all topic entries in Thomson Gale's *Children's Literature Review* (CLR), *Classical and Medieval Literature Criticism* (CMLC), *Contemporary Literary Criticism* (CLC), *Drama Criticism* (DC), *Literature Criticism from 1400 to 1800* (LC), *Nineteenth-Century Literature Criticism* (NCLC), *Short Story Criticism* (SSC), and *Twentieth-Century Literary Criticism* (TCLC). The index also lists topic entries in the Gale Critical Companion Collection, which includes the following publications: *The Beat Generation* (BG), *Feminism in Literature* (FL), *Gothic Literature* (GL), and *Harlem Renaissance* (HR).

Topic Index

Topic Index

NCLC Cumulative Nationality Index

NCLC-186 Title Index

Title Index

ISBN-13: 978-0-7876-9857-7
ISBN-10: 0-7876-9857-1